Data Center Virtu
Fundamentals

Gustavo Alessandro Andrade Santana, CCIE No. 8806

Cisco Press

800 East 96th Street

Indianapolis, IN 46240

Data Center Virtualization Fundamentals

Copyright © 2014 Cisco Systems, Inc.

Published by:
Cisco Press
800 East 96th Street
Indianapolis, IN 46240 USA

All rights reserved. No part of this book may be reproduced or transmitted in any form or by any means, electronic or mechanical, including photocopying, recording, or by any information storage and retrieval system, without written permission from the publisher, except for the inclusion of brief quotations in a review.

Library of Congress Control Number: 2013940880

Printed in the United States of America

Second Printing, September 2013

ISBN-13: 978-1-58714-324-3

ISBN-10: 1-58714-324-0

Warning and Disclaimer

This book is designed to provide information about data center technologies. Every effort has been made to make this book as complete and as accurate as possible, but no warranty or fitness is implied.

The information is provided on an "as is" basis. The author, Cisco Press, and Cisco Systems, Inc., shall have neither liability nor responsibility to any person or entity with respect to any loss or damages arising from the information contained in this book or from the use of the discs or programs that may accompany it.

The opinions expressed in this book belong to the author and are not necessarily those of Cisco Systems, Inc.

Trademark Acknowledgments

All terms mentioned in this book that are known to be trademarks or service marks have been appropriately capitalized. Cisco Press or Cisco Systems, Inc. cannot attest to the accuracy of this information. Use of a term in this book should not be regarded as affecting the validity of any trademark or service mark.

Corporate and Government Sales

The publisher offers excellent discounts on this book when ordered in quantity for bulk purchases or special sales, which may include electronic versions and/or custom covers and content particular to your business, training goals, marketing focus, and branding interests . For more information, please contact: **U.S. Corporate and Government Sales** 1-800-382-3419 corpsales@pearsontechgroup.com

For sales outside of the U.S. please contact: **International Sales** international@pearsoned.com

Feedback Information

At Cisco Press, our goal is to create in-depth technical books of the highest quality and value. Each book is crafted with care and precision, undergoing rigorous development that involves the unique expertise of members from the professional technical community.

Readers' feedback is a natural continuation of this process. If you have any comments regarding how we could improve the quality of this book, or otherwise alter it to better suit your needs, you can contact us through e-mail at feedback@ciscopress.com. Please make sure to include the book title and ISBN in your message.

We greatly appreciate your assistance.

Publisher: Paul Boger	**Business Operation Manager, Cisco Press:** Jan Cornelssen
Associate Publisher: Dave Dusthimer	**Executive Editor:** Mary Beth Ray
Development Editor: Eleanor C. Bru	**Managing Editor:** Sandra Schroeder
Copy Editor: John Edwards	**Project Editor:** Seth Kerney
Technical Editors: Maurilio Gorito, Krishna Arji	
Editorial Assistant: Vanessa Evans	**Proofreader:** Sheri Cain
Cover Designer: Mark Shirar	**Indexer:** Larry Sweazy
Composition: Jake McFarland	

Americas Headquarters
Cisco Systems, Inc.
San Jose, CA

Asia Pacific Headquarters
Cisco Systems (USA) Pte. Ltd.
Singapore

Europe Headquarters
Cisco Systems International BV
Amsterdam, The Netherlands

Cisco has more than 200 offices worldwide. Addresses, phone numbers, and fax numbers are listed on the Cisco Website at www.cisco.com/go/offices.

CCDE, CCENT, Cisco Eos, Cisco HealthPresence, the Cisco logo, Cisco Lumin, Cisco Nexus, Cisco StadiumVision, Cisco TelePresence, Cisco WebEx, DCE, and Welcome to the Human Network are trademarks; Changing the Way We Work, Live, Play, and Learn and Cisco Store are service marks; and Access Registrar, Aironet, AsyncOS, Bringing the Meeting To You, Catalyst, CCDA, CCDP, CCIE, CCIP, CCNA, CCNP, CCSP, CCVP, Cisco, the Cisco Certified Internetwork Expert logo, Cisco IOS, Cisco Press, Cisco Systems, Cisco Systems Capital, the Cisco Systems logo, Cisco Unity, Collaboration Without Limitation, EtherFast, EtherSwitch, Event Center, Fast Step, Follow Me Browsing, FormShare, GigaDrive, HomeLink, Internet Quotient, IOS, iPhone, iQuick Study, IronPort, the IronPort logo, LightStream, Linksys, MediaTone, MeetingPlace, MeetingPlace Chime Sound, MGX, Networkers, Networking Academy, Network Registrar, PCNow, PIX, PowerPanels, ProConnect, ScriptShare, SenderBase, SMARTnet, Spectrum Expert, StackWise, The Fastest Way to Increase Your Internet Quotient, TransPath, WebEx, and the WebEx logo are registered trademarks of Cisco Systems, Inc. and/or its affiliates in the United States and certain other countries.

All other trademarks mentioned in this document or website are the property of their respective owners. The use of the word partner does not imply a partnership relationship between Cisco and any other company. (0812R)

About the Author

Gustavo A. A. Santana, CCIE No. 8806, is a Cisco Technical Solutions Architect working in enterprise and service provider data center projects that require a greater integration among multiple technology areas such as networking, application optimization, storage, and servers.

With more than 15 years of experience in the data center industry, Gustavo has led and coordinated a team of specialized Cisco engineers in Brazil. A true believer of education as a technology catalyst, he has also dedicated himself to the technical development of many IT professionals from customer, partner, and strategic alliance organizations.

In addition to holding two CCIE certifications (Routing & Switching and Storage Networking), Gustavo is also a VMware Certified Professional (VCP) and an SNIA Certified Storage Networking Expert (SCSN-E). A frequent speaker at Cisco and data center industry events, he holds a degree in computer engineering from Instituto Tecnológico de Aeronáutica (ITA-Brazil) and an MBA in strategic IT management from Fundação Getúlio Vargas (FGV-Brazil).

Gustavo maintains a personal blog in which he discusses topics related to data center virtualization technologies at http://gustavoaasantana.net.

About the Technical Reviewers

Maurilio Gorito, CCIE, is the certification manager at Riverbed Technology Institute, leading Riverbed Technology's Certification Program. Previously, he managed the Cisco CCIE Routing and Switching certification program, and he is a triple Cisco Certified Internetwork Expert (CCIE). Maurilio has 25 years of experience in the IT field and more than 20 years of combined experience in education, testing, and assessment. Maurilio has written a book, written articles, and reviewed several technical books for Cisco Press. Maurilio holds bachelor's degrees in education, pedagogy, and mathematics from Centro Universitario Geraldo Di Biasi, Brazil. Maurilio is currently serving on the board of directors at Performance Testing Council (PTC).

Krishna Arji is a senior manager at Cisco. In this role, he is responsible for the development of technology that enables the delivery of Cisco services. Krishna has held various positions in the Cisco Services Technology Group at Cisco. His current assignment is to enable delivery for the Cisco BYOD service offerings. In the past, he played a key role in evaluating and developing technologies required for the delivery of cloud planning, design, and implementation services. Under his leadership, his team developed several technologies to perform routing, switching, data center, security, and WLAN assessments of customers' infrastructures. His areas of expertise include networking, software design and development, and data center technologies such as virtualization. Krishna holds a bachelor's degree in electronics and communications engineering, and he has a master's degree in enterprise software technologies. He is currently enrolled in an MBA program at Haas School of Business, University of California, Berkeley. He has a patent pending with USPTO for Automated Assessments of Storage Area Networks (Serial No. 13/115, 141).

Dedications

This book is dedicated to my wife and true love, Carlene, whose sacrifice and unconditional support were crucial to this endeavor, and to my lovely daughter, Carolina, whose one-year-old curiosity constantly inspired me to go one step further.

I also dedicate this book to my parents, Honorio and Cleia, who have taught me that one can only learn by being fearless and humble.

Finally, this book is also dedicated to every person who has devoted efforts to the rewarding experience of teaching someone.

Acknowledgments

The process of creating a book can be aptly defined as a "sponsored solitude." Certainly, the uncountable lonely writing hours would be fruitless without the support of an entire network of relatives, friends, and professionals who are acknowledged here.

First, I would like to thank my sister Raquel and brother André for the family support during this book writing.

I would also like to express my gratitude to my friend and trusted advisor Alexandre M. S. P. Moraes, who has shared invaluable opinions and insights since the very early stages of this book.

Many thanks to Andrey Lee for the wonderful illustrations in Chapters 1 and 17.

Sincere thanks to Paulo Quinta, Fernanda Spinardi, and Marcelo Ehalt for helping me coordinate my professional life and this writing.

My thanks to the technical reviewers Maurilio Gorito and Krishna Arji for their active contributions and focus to make this work more effective for its targeted readership.

A personal thanks to the Brazilian data center tiger team, which has always served as my favorite "think tank" for best practices and the exchange of experiences.

I would also like to thank two very talented instructors from Firefly: Dan Murray and Fabricio Grimaldi.

I am also very grateful to the people who have contributed with the equipment used in this publication: Shane Hudson and Bilal El-Ayi (from GoldLabs), Ohad Richberg (and his amazing CPOC Israel team), François Tallet and Mark Allen (from the Cisco Enterprise Core Business Unit), and Hugo Marques.

Thanks to all the Pearson production team, especially Ellie Bru and Seth Kerney, who helped me to create the final version of this book.

A special thank-you goes to Mary Beth Ray and Anand Sundaram for supporting the idea of a data center book with a different approach.

Contents at a Glance

Foreword   xxiii

Introduction   xxv

Part I   **What Is Virtualization?**

Chapter 1   Virtualization History and Definitions   1

Part II   **Virtualization in Network Technologies**

Chapter 2   Data Center Network Evolution   25

Chapter 3   The Humble Beginnings of Network Virtualization   45

Chapter 4   An Army of One: ACE Virtual Contexts   109

Chapter 5   Instant Switches: Virtual Device Contexts   183

Chapter 6   Fooling Spanning Tree   231

Chapter 7   Virtualized Chassis with Fabric Extenders   287

Chapter 8   A Tale of Two Data Centers   319

Part III   **Virtualization in Storage Technologies**

Chapter 9   Storage Evolution   387

Chapter 10   Islands in the SAN   409

Chapter 11   Secret Identities   453

Chapter 12   One Cable to Unite Us All   493

Part IV   **Virtualization in Server Technologies**

Chapter 13   Server Evolution   559

Chapter 14   Changing Personalities   581

Chapter 15   Transcending the Rack   657

Chapter 16   Moving Targets   735

Part V   **End-to-End Virtualization**

Chapter 17   The Virtual Data Center and Cloud Computing   785

Part VI: Appendixes

Appendix A   Cisco Data Center Portfolio   809

Appendix B   IOS, NX-OS, and Application Control Software Command-Line Interface Basics   847

Index   873

Contents

Foreword xxiii
Introduction xxv

Part I **What Is Virtualization?**

Chapter 1 **Virtualization History and Definitions** 1

Data Center Essential Definitions 2
   Data Center Evolution 3
   Operational Areas and Data Center Architecture 5

The Origins of Data Center Virtualization 8
   Virtual Memory 8
   Mainframe Virtualization 10
   Hot Standby Router Protocol 11
   Defining Virtualization 12
   Data Center Virtualization Timeline 12

Classifying Virtualization Technologies 14
   A Virtualization Taxonomy 15
   Virtualization Scalability 17
   Technology Areas 18
   Classification Examples 21

Summary 22
Further Reading 22

Part II **Virtualization in Network Technologies**

Chapter 2 **Data Center Network Evolution** 25

Ethernet Protocol: Then and Now 26
   Ethernet Media 27
   Coaxial Cable 27
   Twisted-Pair 28
   Optical Fiber 30
   Direct-Attach Twinaxial Cables 32
   Ethernet Data Rate Timeline 33

Data Center Network Topologies 34
   Data Center Network Layers 35
   Design Factors for Data Center Networks 36
   Physical Network Layout Considerations 39
   The ANSI/TIA-942 Standard 40

Network Virtualization Benefits   42
   Network Logical Partitioning   42
   Network Simplification and Traffic Load Balancing   43
   Management Consolidation and Cabling Optimization   44
   Network Extension   44
Summary   44
Further Reading   44

Chapter 3 The Humble Beginnings of Network Virtualization   45
Network Partitioning   47
Concepts from the Bridging World   47
Defining VLANs   49
   VLAN Trunks   52
Two Common Misconceptions About VLANs   56
   Misconception Number 1: A VLAN Must Be Associated to an IP Subnet   56
   Misconception Number 2: Layer 3 VLANs   58
Spanning Tree Protocol and VLANs   61
   Spanning Tree Protocol at Work   63
   Port States   70
   Spanning Tree Protocol Enhancements   72
   Spanning Tree Instances   74
Private VLANs   78
VLAN Specifics   83
   Native VLAN   84
   Reserved VLANs IDs   84
   Resource Sharing   85
   Control and Management Plane   85
Concepts from the Routing World   87
Overlapping Addresses in a Data Center   87
Defining and Configuring VRFs   90
VRFs and Routing Protocols   92
VRFs and the Management Plane   98
   VRF-Awareness   100
VRF Resource Allocation Control   101
Use Case: Data Center Network Segmentation   103
Summary   105
Further Reading   107

Chapter 4   An Army of One: ACE Virtual Contexts   109

    Application Networking Services   111

    The Use of Load Balancers   111

        Load-Balancing Concepts   115

        Layer 4 Switching Versus Layer 7 Switching   120

        Connection Management   122

        Address Translation and Load Balancing   124

        Server NAT   124

        Dual NAT   125

        Port Redirection   126

        Transparent Mode   126

        Other Load-Balancing Applications   127

        Firewall Load Balancing   127

        Reverse Proxy Load Balancing   128

        Offloading Servers   130

        SSL Offload   130

        TCP Offload   133

        HTTP Compression   134

    Load Balancer Proliferation in the Data Center   135

        Load Balancer Performance   135

        Security Policies   136

        Suboptimal Traffic   137

        Application Environment Independency   138

    ACE Virtual Contexts   139

        Application Control Engine Physical Connections   141

        Connecting an ACE Appliance   141

        Connecting an ACE Module   144

        Creating and Allocating Resources to Virtual Contexts   145

        Integrating ACE Virtual Contexts to the Data Center Network   156

        Routed Design   156

        Bridged Design   158

        One-Armed Design   160

        Managing and Configuring ACE Virtual Contexts   162

        Allowing Management Traffic to a Virtual Context   162

        Allowing Load Balancing Traffic Through a Virtual Context   163

        Controlling Management Access to Virtual Contexts   171

ACE Virtual Context Additional Characteristics   176
Sharing VLANs Among Contexts   *177*
Virtual Context Fault Tolerance   *177*
Use Case: Multitenant Data Center   179
Summary   181
Further Reading   182

Chapter 5   Instant Switches: Virtual Device Contexts   183

Extending Device Virtualization   184
Why Use VDCs?   187
VDCs in Detail   188
Creating and Configuring VDCs   190
   VDC Names and CLI Prompts   198
   Virtualization Nesting   199
Allocating Resources to VDCs   202
Using Resource Templates   211
Managing VDCs   214
   VDC Operations   214
   Processes Failures and VDCs   216
   VDC Out-of-Band Management   217
   Role-Based Access Control and VDCs   222
Global Resources   225
Use Case: Data Center Security Zones   225
Summary   227
Further Reading   229

Chapter 6   Fooling Spanning Tree   231

Spanning Tree Protocol and Link Utilization   232
Link Aggregation   234
   Server Connectivity and NIC Teaming   238
Cross-Switch PortChannels   240
Virtual PortChannels   241
   Virtual PortChannel Definitions   242
   Configuring Virtual PortChannels   247
   Step 1: Defining the Domain   *248*
   Step 2: Establishing Peer Keepalive Connectivity   *248*
   Step 3: Creating the Peer Link   *250*

　　　　　　　　Step 4: Creating the Virtual PortChannel 252
　　　　　　　　Spanning Tree Protocol and Virtual PortChannels 254
　　　　　　　　Peer Link Failure and Orphan Ports 258
　　　　　　　　First-Hop Routing Protocols and Virtual PortChannels 259
　　　　　　Layer 2 Multipathing and vPC+ 265
　　　　　　　　FabricPath Data Plane 266
　　　　　　　　FabricPath Control Plane 269
　　　　　　　　FabricPath and Spanning Tree Protocol 272
　　　　　　　　Virtual PortChannel Plus 276
　　　　　　Use Case: Evolution of Network PODs 281
　　　　　　Summary 285
　　　　　　Further Reading 286

Chapter 7　Virtualized Chassis with Fabric Extenders　287
　　　　　　Server Access Models 288
　　　　　　Understanding Fabric Extenders 291
　　　　　　　　Fabric Extender Options 295
　　　　　　　　Connecting a Fabric Extender to a Parent Switch 296
　　　　　　　　Fabric Extended Interfaces and Spanning Tree Protocol 299
　　　　　　　　Fabric Interfaces Redundancy 301
　　　　　　Fabric Extender Topologies 305
　　　　　　　　Straight-Through Topologies 305
　　　　　　　　Dual-Homed Topologies 309
　　　　　　Use Case: Mixed Access Data Center 315
　　　　　　Summary 317
　　　　　　Further Reading 318

Chapter 8　A Tale of Two Data Centers　319
　　　　　　A Brief History of Distributed Data Centers 321
　　　　　　The Cold Age (Mid-1970s to 1980s) 321
　　　　　　The Hot Age (1990s to Mid-2000s) 322
　　　　　　The Active-Active Age (Mid-2000s to Today) 324
　　　　　　The Case for Layer 2 Extensions 324
　　　　　　　　Challenges of Layer 2 Extensions 325
　　　　　　Ethernet Extensions over Optical Connections 327
　　　　　　　　Virtual PortChannels 328
　　　　　　　　FabricPath 330

Ethernet Extensions over MPLS   332
   MPLS Basic Concepts   333
   Ethernet over MPLS   338
   Virtual Private LAN Service   342
Ethernet Extensions over IP   352
   MPLS over GRE   352
   Overlay Transport Virtualization   354
   OTV Terminology   357
   OTV Basic Configuration   359
   OTV Loop Avoidance and Multihoming   365
   Migration to OTV   366
   OTV Site Designs   373
VLAN Identifiers and Layer 2 Extensions   377
Internal Routing in Connected Data Centers   380
Use Case: Active-Active Greenfield Data Centers   382
Summary   384
Further Reading   386

Part III   Virtualization in Storage Technologies

Chapter 9   Storage Evolution   387

Data Center Storage Devices   387
   Hard Disk Drives   388
   Disk Arrays   389
   Tape Drives and Libraries   390
Accessing Data in Rest   391
   Block-Based Access   392
   Small Computer Systems Interface   392
   Mainframe Storage Access   396
   Advanced Technology Attachment   397
   File Access   397
   Network File System   398
   Common Internet File System   398
   Record Access   398
Storage Virtualization   399
   Virtualizing Storage Devices   402
   Virtualizing LUNs   404

>   Virtualizing File Systems   406
>   Virtualizing SANs   407
>   Summary   408
>   Further Reading   408

Chapter 10   Islands in the SAN   409
>   Some Fibre Channel Definitions   410
>   Fibre Channel Layers   411
>   Fibre Channel Topologies and Port Types   412
>   Fibre Channel Addressing   413
>   Frames, Sequences, and Exchanges   415
>   Flow Control   417
>   Classes of Service   420
>   Fabric Processes   420
>   Fabric Initialization   422
>   Fabric Shortest Path First   424
>   Register State Change Notification   426
>   Fibre Channel Logins   427
>   Zoning   429
>   Defining and Exploring VSANs   430
>   SAN Islands   430
>   VSAN Creation   432
>   VSAN Trunking   434
>   Zoning and VSANs   439
>   FSPF and VSANs   442
>   VSAN Scoping   445
>   Use Case: SAN Consolidation   447
>   Summary   450
>   Further Reading   451

Chapter 11   Secret Identities   453
>   Fibre Channel over IP   454
>   FCIP High Availability   460
>   Use Case: SAN Extension with Traffic Engineering   462
>   Inter-VSAN Routing   464
>   IVR Infrastructure   465
>   IVR Zoning   467
>   Use Case: Transit VSAN   472

N_Port Virtualization   473
   Configuring N_Port Virtualization   476
   NPV Traffic Management   482
   Deploying Port WWN Virtualization on NPV   486
   Use Case: Blade Server Hosting Data Center   488
Summary   490
Further Reading   491

Chapter 12 One Cable to Unite Us All   493
The Case for Data Center Networking Convergence   495
Data Center Bridging   497
   Priority-Based Flow Control   498
   Enhanced Transmission Selection   500
   Data Center Bridging eXchange Protocol   501
   Congestion Notification   503
Introducing Fibre Channel over Ethernet   504
   FCoE Elements   505
   FCoE Initialization Protocol   507
Deploying Unified Server Access   509
   Configuring Unified Server Access on Single-Context Switches   510
   Configuring Unified Server Access with Storage VDCs   519
Configuring Multihop FCoE   523
   Configuring Virtual Fibre Channel PortChannels   528
   FCoE N_Port Virtualization   532
Unified Fabric Designs   535
   Server Access Layer Unified Designs   536
   FCoE and Virtual PortChannels   538
   FCoE and Blade Servers   540
   Beyond the Access Layer   542
   Converged Access Model   542
   Converged Aggregation Model   543
FCoE and SAN Extension   545
Use Case: LAN and SAN Management Separation   546
Summary   556
Further Reading   557

Part IV   **Virtualization in Server Technologies**

Chapter 13   **Server Evolution   559**

    Server Architectures   560

        Mainframes   560

        RISC Servers   561

        x86 Servers   562

    x86 Hardware Evolution   562

        CPU Evolution   564

        Memory Evolution   566

        Expansion Bus Evolution   569

        Physical Format Evolution   571

    Introducing x86 Server Virtualization   572

        Virtualization Unleashed   574

    Unified Computing   578

    Summary   580

    Further Reading   580

Chapter 14   **Changing Personalities   581**

    Server Provisioning Challenges   583

        Server Domain Operations   584

        Infrastructure Domain Operations   585

    Unified Computing and Service Profiles   586

    Building Service Profiles   588

        Identifying a Service Profile   594

        Storage Definitions   595

        Network Definitions   599

        Virtual Interface Placement   602

        Server Boot Order   604

        Maintenance Policy   606

        Server Assignment   606

        Operational Policies   608

        Configuration   608

        External IPMI Management Configuration   609

        Management IP Address   610

        Additional Policies   611

Associating a Service Profile to a Server   612
Installing an Operating System   620
Verifying Stateless Computing   625
Using Policies   626
BIOS Setting Policies   627
Firmware Policies   633
Industrializing Server Provisioning   637
Cloning   638
Pools   639
Service Profile Templates   640
Server Pools   649
Use Case: Seasonal Workloads   653
Summary   655
Further Reading   656

Chapter 15   Transcending the Rack   657
Introduction to Virtual Networking   658
Virtual Switch Challenges   660
Cisco Nexus 1000V Architecture   661
Nexus 1000V Communication Modes   663
Port Profiles and Dynamic Interface Provisioning   664
Deploying Nexus 1000V   666
External Connectivity and Link Aggregation   684
NX-OS Features in the Virtual World   688
MAC Address Table   691
Access Lists   692
Online Migrations and Nexus 1000V   693
Virtual Extensible Local Area Networks   697
Introducing Virtual Machine Fabric Extender   705
Deploying VM-FEX   707
Enabling Dynamic vNICs on a UCS Service Profile   707
Preparing VMware vSphere Host to Deploy VM-FEX   709
Using the UCS Manager VMware Integration Wizard   711
Migrating Virtual Machines to VM-FEX   716
Online Migrations and VM-FEX   720
VM-FEX High-Performance Mode   723

Use Case: Data Center Merging   731
Summary   733
Further Reading   734

Chapter 16   **Moving Targets**   735
Virtual Network Services Definitions   736
Virtual Network Services Data Path   738
vPath-Enabled Virtual Network Services   740
   Cisco Virtual Security Gateway: Compute Virtual Firewall   742
   Installing Virtual Security Gateway   743
   Creating Security Policies   745
   Sending Data Traffic to VSG   747
   Virtual Machine Attributes and Virtual Zones   751
   Cisco ASA 1000V: Edge Virtual Firewall   754
   Installing ASA 1000V   755
   Sending Data Traffic to ASA 1000V   758
   Configuring Security Policies on ASA 1000V   761
   Application Acceleration   763
   WAN Acceleration and Online Migration   769
Routing in the Virtual World   771
Site Selection and Server Virtualization   775
   Route Health Injection   775
   Global Server Load Balancing   777
   Location/ID Separation Protocol   779
Use Case: Virtual Data Center   781
Summary   783
Further Reading   784

Part V   **End-to-End Virtualization**

Chapter 17   **The Virtual Data Center and Cloud Computing**   785
The Virtual Data Center   786
Automation and Standardization   789
What Is Cloud Computing?   793
Cloud Implementation Example   797
Journey to the Cloud   799
Networking in the Clouds   800

Software-Defined Networks   800
OpenStack   801
Network Overlays   802
Cisco Open Network Environment   804
Before We Go...   805
Summary   806
Further Reading   807

Part VI: Appendixes

Appendix A   Cisco Data Center Portfolio   809
Cisco Application Control Engine   809
Cisco Adaptive Security Appliances 5585-X   811
Cisco ASA 1000V Cloud Firewall   812
Cisco Catalyst 6500 Series Switches   813
Cisco Cloud Portal   816
Cisco Intelligent Automation Solutions   817
Automation Software Components   817
Cisco Intelligent Automation for Cloud Solution   819
Cisco Intelligent Automation for SAP   820
Cisco MDS 9000 Series Multilayer Switches   820
Cisco Prime Network Analysis Module   823
Cisco Nexus Data Center Switches   823
Cisco Nexus 1000V Series Switches   824
Nexus 1010 and 1100 Virtual Services Appliances   824
Cisco Nexus 2000 Series Fabric Extenders   825
Cisco Nexus 3000 Series Switches   827
Cisco Nexus 4000 Series Switches   828
Cisco Nexus 5000 and 5500 Series Switches   829
Cisco Nexus 6000 Series Switches   831
Cisco Nexus 7000 Series Switches   832
Cisco Unified Computing System   835
Cisco 6100 and 6200 Series Fabric Interconnects   836
Cisco UCS 5100 Series Blade Server Chassis   836
Cisco UCS 2100 and 2200 Series Fabric Extenders   837
Cisco UCS B-Series Blade Servers   837
Cisco UCS C-Series Rack Servers   838

Cisco UCS Virtual Interface Cards   839
Unified Management Solutions   840
Cisco Application Network Manager   840
Cisco Prime Data Center Network Manager   841
Cisco UCS Manager and UCS Central   842
Virtual Network Management Center   843
Virtual Security Gateway   843
Virtualization Techniques Mapping   844
Further Reading   844

Appendix B   IOS, NX-OS, and Application Control Software Command-Line Interface Basics   847

IOS Command-Line Interface Basics   847
Command Modes   848
Getting Context-Sensitive Help   850
Abbreviating Commands and Using Shortcuts   854
Managing Configuration Files   855
Using Debug Commands   858
NX-OS Command-Line Interface   859
NX-OS Access   860
NX-OS Modularity   861
NX-OS and Running Configuration Files   863
NX-OS Command-Line Interface Optimizations   866
Configuration Version Management, Batches, and Scripts   866
Application Control Software Command-Line Interface   870

Index   873

Icons Used in This Book

Command Syntax Conventions

The conventions used to present command syntax in this book are the same conventions used in the IOS Command Reference. The Command Reference describes these conventions as follows:

- Boldface indicates commands and keywords that are entered literally, as shown. In actual configuration examples and output (not general command syntax), boldface indicates commands that are manually input by the user (such as a **show** command).
- Italics indicate arguments for which you supply actual values.
- Vertical bars (|) separate alternative, mutually exclusive elements.
- Square brackets [ ] indicate optional elements.
- Braces { } indicate a required choice.
- Braces within brackets [{ }] indicate a required choice within an optional element.
- Introduction

Foreword

With the rapid growth of the Internet economy and the explosion of information technology, the data center is playing a pivotal role and is one of the most exciting fields in the world of IT today. The trend continues with both virtualization and cloud computing fueling growth and making data center solutions more efficient and scalable. More specifically, organizations using virtualization technologies are seeing greater returns and more viability to deal with the growing demands of the economy.

Data center virtualization is an evolutionary process that was started several years ago within mainframe computer rooms, and it has dramatically intensified in the last few years. Its proposed freedom from physical boundaries has produced benefits in each technology area, and much more importantly, from an architectural perspective.

However, due to these environments' increasing complexity, a data center professional must possess a challenging breadth of knowledge in several different areas, such as networking, storage, servers, operating systems, application, and security.

Data Center Virtualization Fundamentals is a comprehensive book that introduces virtualization technologies in data center environments, encompassing all these knowledge areas. It does not take a product-based approach as many others do, but an architectural one, offering theoretical concepts, illustrative configurations, and real-world designs for each virtualization technique. The book provides a first step for students and professionals who want to understand the state of data center technologies today. And in my opinion, virtualization technologies are the best way to achieve this feat because one must be aware of the physical challenges of data center environments before learning such techniques.

There is a lot of misconception when talking about virtualization, and people immediately think of it in the context of virtual servers. However, virtualization is not restricted to a single technology area in the data center. This book intends to make an account of the main data center virtualization technologies, revealing their impact and applicability to these environments as a whole. It encourages readers to escape their technical comfort-zone and learn how each decision may impact other data center teams. A strong knowledge of the theoretical basis of the data center is necessary to walk amidst clouds, and this is exactly what this book brings.

Author Gustavo A. A. Santana is a seasoned expert with years of experience, and has done a superb job putting this material together. He has demonstrated his skills and command of the technology, using a unique approach in translating the most complex and highly technical information into simple, easy-to-understand material. Readers will definitely appreciate this book.

Finally, this book is an essential reference and will be valuable asset for potential candidates pursuing their Cisco Data Center certifications. I am confident that in reading this book, individuals will inevitably gain extensive knowledge and hands-on experience during their certification preparations. If you're looking for a truly comprehensive guide to virtualization, this is the one!

Yusuf Bhaiji
Senior Manager, Expert Certifications (CCIE, CCDE, CCAr)
Learning@Cisco

"If you can't explain it simply, you don't understand it well enough."
—Albert Einstein

Introduction

"I am very interested in learning data center technologies. How should I start?"

Since I first heard this question, I have seen many IT professionals become overwhelmed with the vertigo-inducing development of new data center technologies. From my perspective, their frustration was mainly caused by attempting to understand this subject without being properly introduced to the most fundamental concepts and definitions related to these complex environments. And that opinion has always formed the basis of my advice to them.

However, as the years passed, I observed how my answer to this question was becoming more elaborate. Understandably, an increasingly diverse background was being required from these professionals, mainly because data center technologies were repeatedly consolidating different areas of knowledge such as networking, storage, application, servers, cabling, and several others. And much to my chagrin, I had to admit that the job of creating an effective introduction to these technologies was getting even harder to "crack."

After developing many learning road maps and customized trainings, I decided to challenge myself in writing a book that would address cutting-edge data center technologies and the core concepts they were based upon. From the start, the mammoth level of minutiae made me realize how close I was to a task such as writing a Beatles biography. And that exact thought inspired me to follow the steps of the best publications about the band: I had to use a *unifying theme*, something that could provide a firm backbone to a progressive presentation of these technologies. It was fairly easy for me to conclude that virtualization was this theme.

Nowadays, virtualization is deeply rooted in data center installations through technologies such as virtual memory, virtual gateways, VLANs, VRFs, virtual contexts, VDCs, vPCs, VNTag, VPLS, OTV, virtual LUNs, VSANs, IVR, NPV, FCoE, virtual machines, service profiles, virtual networking, virtual network services, and many others. All these successful techniques share a common characteristic: They were created to provide *resource optimization*. And for that reason, their examination opens up the chance to address the following:

- Traditional data center deployments and their limitations

- The benefits of each virtualization technology and their behavior

- The changes these technologies provide in data center designs and architectures

As the book cover suggests, virtualization has also modified the human aspects within data center environments. Relieved from the "chains of reality," technical teams have been able to simplify operational tasks and accelerate the adoption of new IT models such as cloud computing. With such a central theme, it was just a question of defining *how* to approach it.

Goals and Methods

This book provides a gradual introduction to innovative data center technologies through a systematic examination of the main infrastructure virtualization techniques. And as an intentional outcome, the book also introduces fundamental concepts and definitions that are required from any professional who is involved with modern data center designs.

Because it is primarily focused on the three main data center infrastructure areas (networking, storage, and server), the book is not based on a single product nor it is written as a configuration guide. Instead, it leverages the broad Cisco Data Center portfolio (and other solutions from the Cisco ecosystem of partners and alliances) to analyze the behavior of each virtualization technique and to offer an architectural perspective of the virtualized data center.

Besides providing an technical account of the evolution of these areas, the book will address each virtualization technology through a flow of topics that involves

- A virtualization classification system (explained in the first chapter), which quickly informs the reader about the main characteristics of the specific technology

- A technology primer that immerses the reader in the physical challenges this virtualization technology overcomes

- A detailed analysis of the technique, including its characteristics, possibilities, scalability, results, and consequences

- A real-world use case scenario that demonstrates the examined technology "in action."

I sincerely believe that design and deployment must be complementary processes. Therefore, *Data Center Virtualization Fundamentals* contains actual configuration examples that were exclusively created to illustrate each virtualization technology and its applicability to data center designs. Nonetheless, I have also included unusual topologies to specifically reinforce concepts explored throughout the book.

Who Should Read This Book

This book was written with a wide audience in mind. Because it provides an in-depth examination of data center virtualization technologies (from conceptualization to implementation), the book will satisfy beginners and experienced IT professionals alike.

In essence, its target audience comprises the following:

- Individuals with basic networking and operating system knowledge who are interested in modern data center design, deployment, and infrastructure optimization techniques

- Candidates for the Cisco Data Center certifications, including CCNA Data Center, CCNP Data Center, and CCIE Data Center

- Professionals that are specialized in a single data center technology area but also intend to acquire a broader architectural knowledge to accelerate their career development

How This Book Is Organized

With the explosion of information brought by the Internet, education in the twenty-first century must always present alternatives to the random accumulation of unstructured data. Therefore, I have intentionally applied constructivist learning theory principles (such as systematic analysis and concept synthesis) to distribute the content throughout the book. Although each chapter can be read out of sequence, their arrangement was designed to provide a logical progression of explanations that brings a more rewarding learning experience for the reader.

In times where blog posts and tweets provide "snacks" of information (do not get me wrong; there are nutritious knowledge bites out there), this book intends to serve a complete "meal," where order and harmonization between chapters matter.

Chapters 1 through 17 and the appendixes cover the following topics:

- **Chapter 1, "Virtualization History and Definitions":** This introductory chapter presents a historical account of virtualization in data center environments and, through some illustrative examples, provides a unified definition of virtualization in this context. It also proposes a classification system (which is called "virtualization taxonomy") that will be used throughout the book to quickly introduce a new virtualization technology for the reader.

- **Chapter 2, "Data Center Network Evolution":** Using the evolution of the Ethernet protocol as a canvas, this chapter addresses the main aspects and factors that govern traditional data center network topologies. It also discusses the general benefits that virtualization can offer to these networks.

- **Chapter 3, "The Humble Beginnings of Network Virtualization":** Focused on the explanation of virtual local-area networks (VLAN) and Virtual Routing and Forwarding (VRF), this chapter provides a deep analysis of these well-established structures as virtualization techniques, illustrating the book approach and revealing important concepts that are hidden behind common knowledge.

- **Chapter 4, "An Army of One: ACE Virtual Contexts":** This chapter discusses the importance of network services in data centers, concentrating on server load balancers. It presents virtual contexts as important tools that can increase flexibility and optimize hardware resources as these application environments scale.

- **Chapter 5, "Instant Switches: Virtual Device Contexts":** The innovative characteristics of virtual device contexts (VDC) are detailed in this chapter, which also shows their applicability in challenging data center network scenarios.

- **Chapter 6, "Fooling Spanning Tree":** This chapter demonstrates how virtualization techniques such as EtherChannel and virtual PortChannel (vPC) have adapted the limitation of Spanning Tree Protocol (STP) to the strict requirements of data center networks. It also introduces FabricPath, a Layer 2 multipathing technology that has provided the most secure path toward the replacement of STP in these environments.

- **Chapter 7, "Virtualized Chassis with Fabric Extenders":** Fabric Extenders (FEX) constitute a virtualization technique that provides cabling optimization and network management consolidation in the data center network access layer. This chapter fully explores the many flavors of this technology.

- **Chapter 8, "A Tale of Two Data Centers":** The classic problem of extending Layer 2 domains between geographically distinct data center sites is discussed throughout this chapter. It builds on concepts developed in previous chapters to offer a hands-on examination of the many different virtualization technologies that can solve this challenge.

- **Chapter 9, "Storage Evolution":** This chapter explores the main concepts related to storage and storage access technologies that are used in data centers today. It also provides an account of how virtualization is deeply ingrained in the interpretation of stored data.

- **Chapter 10, "Islands in the SAN":** Virtual storage-area networks (VSAN) can overcome Fibre Channel fabric challenges in a simple and elegant way. This chapter presents the necessary protocol concepts to understand how they can be applied in real-world scenarios.

- **Chapter 11, "Secret Identities":** This chapter presents three virtualization techniques whose dissimulation tactics benefits data protection, environment isolation, and scalability in storage-area networks.

- **Chapter 12, "One Cable to Unite Us All":** Binding concepts from network and storage virtualization, this chapter fully examines the details and benefits from the I/O consolidation brought about by Data Center Bridging (DCB) and Fibre Channel over Ethernet (FCoE).

- **Chapter 13, "Server Evolution":** This chapter introduces the main concepts related to modern server architectures. It also presents server virtualization and describes how it has changed the operational landscape of data centers in the beginning of the twenty-first century. The chapter also deals with the definition of unified computing and explains how its innovative architecture principles can drastically simplify server environments.

- **Chapter 14, "Changing Personalities":** Although server virtualization has helped to streamline server workloads within a data center, "bare metal" server provisioning and management are still considered massive challenges in these environments. This chapter demonstrates how service profiles can bring several server virtualization benefits to these scenarios.

- **Chapter 15, "Transcending the Rack":** Demonstrating how the technologies explored in this book are extremely intertwined, this chapter shows how server virtualization has also revolutionized networking. It presents the virtual networking concepts through the analysis of VMware vSwitches, Nexus 1000V, and Virtual Machine Fabric Extender (VM-FEX).

- **Chapter 16, "Moving Targets":** The way that virtual machines can migrate between different hosts and locations has also changed the way network services are deployed. This chapter explores the unique characteristics of services provided by solutions such as virtual firewalls (Virtual Security Gateway [VSG] and ASA 1000V), virtual accelerators (virtual Wide Area Application Services [vWAAS]), and virtual routers (CSR 1000V). It also presents site selection as a special network service and illustrates some solutions that can optimize client session routing to roaming virtual machines.

- **Chapter 17, "The Virtual Data Center and Cloud Computing":** This chapter consolidates concepts explained throughout the book to discuss how 1+1 can be more than 2. It discusses how the deployment of multiple virtualization technologies has created a perfect storm for "cloud computing" momentum and how this IT delivery model is influencing the evolution of data center networks.

- **Appendix A, "Cisco Data Center Portfolio":** To preserve the book's focus on virtualization concepts and feature behavior, this appendix contains the description of all Cisco Data Center products that actually deploy these technologies.

- **Appendix B, "IOS, NX-OS, and Application Control Software Command-Line Interface Basics":** If you are not used to the command-line interface characteristics from the different network operating systems used in this book, this appendix will introduce you to their most typical characteristics and definitions.

Chapter 1

Virtualization History and Definitions

"Half the work that is done in the world is to make things appear what they are not." (E. R. Beadle)

Putting it bluntly, virtualization is deception.

Even if we refuse to believe it, fabrication, faking, and feigning are just as much a part of our lives as creation and originality. In truth, entire arts and sciences are solely dedicated to the manipulation of perception.

Nevertheless, with the dissemination of personal computing, the overloaded term *virtualization* has escaped the technical jargon to invade common language, popular culture, and philosophy. Since the early days of the Internet boom in the 1990s, it has become a complete cliché (or simply lazy writing) to name any web-related activity as "virtual." However, the concept of *emulated realities* still fascinates our technology-savvy society through the influence of Philip K. Dick's science fiction books, Jean Baudrillard's postmodern studies, and recent movies such as "The Matrix" and "Inception."

According to the Oxford English Dictionary, in the context of computing, *virtual* means "not physically existing as such but made by software to appear to do so." Therefore, in the same context, it can be said that a virtual element is a particular abstraction of such an element.

Abstraction, or the process of considering something independently of its associations or attributes, is naturally present in Information Technology (IT). Actually, many areas of computer science are built upon *layers* of abstraction.

Computer data itself is an abstract entity, because it can represent *anything*, from house appliances to human lives. For computer systems, symbols and representations are the raw material for their routine operations, but as users, we have to add an extra layer of abstraction to correctly interpret the meaning of such data.

But if the concept of abstraction is so mundane in IT, what explains the increasing fascination with virtualization in recent years? The trend is even more hard-core in data centers, where virtualization is deeply ingrained in the development strategy of these environments since the mid-2000s. And the infatuation continues to grow: in a survey conducted by International Data Corporation (IDC), where almost 40 percent of chief information officers (CIO) have picked virtualization as their top priority for 2012.

Accordingly, these facilities have been assaulted with virtual servers, virtual networks, virtual storage, virtual appliances, and other "V-technologies" that promise relief from the cuffs of reality. Broadly speaking, these technologies are designed to provide the following benefits for data center environments:

- Cost reduction and higher asset utilization
- Greater stability and higher availability
- Simplification of operational processes

Considering that operational aspects represent the great majority of expenses in data centers, virtualization technologies are supposed to work as a magic sleight of hand, offering a shortcut to these benefits without requiring a complete retrofit of systems and processes.

However, some questions might arise from these statements:

- Can all these technologies really bring these benefits?
- What is a virtual device? Is it almost a device? Is it better?
- Are all virtualization technologies alike?

This book intends to answer these questions through the analysis of a group of technologies collectively known as *data center virtualization*. Its main objective is to explain how and why these technologies have been instrumental in the last great architectural shifts in the development of these environments.

Data Center Essential Definitions

A *data center* is a special facility conceived to house, manage, and support computing resources that are considered critical for one or more organizations. A particularly complex structure, a typical data center encompasses special building structures, power backup structures, cooling systems, special-purpose rooms (entrance and telecommunications, for example), equipment cabinets, structured cabling, network devices, storage systems, servers, mainframes, application software, physical security systems, monitoring centers, and many other support systems. All these resources and their interaction are (locally or remotely) managed by specialized personnel.

Figure 1-1 depicts a data center physical view and some of its main components.

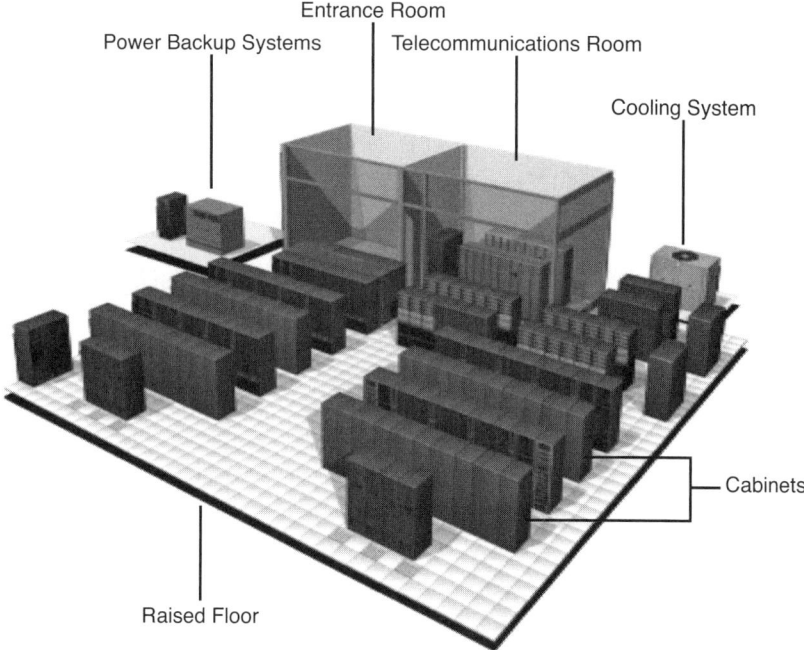

Figure 1-1 *Data Center*

While Figure 1-1 portrays a single *data center computer room*, real-world modular data centers can contain several of these rooms spread across different floors or buildings. Besides size, data centers can also vary in their infrastructure robustness, depending on how critical their supported systems are.

With business strongly relying on IT to increase profits, data centers have surely stepped into the spotlight during the last decade. For organizations, it is expected that all its components work harmonically to guarantee an adequate service-level agreement (SLA) to business applications, such as Business Intelligence (BI), Customer Relationship Management (CRM), Data Warehouse (DW), e-commerce, Enterprise Resource Planning (ERP), Supply Chain Management (SCM), and many others.

Not all data centers are company owned. In fact, the operational complexity of these environments has also motivated multiple corporations to host their systems in specialized service provider data centers.

Data Center Evolution

Data centers have seen greatly changed characteristics and purposes throughout the last six decades, mirroring the transformations that computer systems have undergone over the same period. Nevertheless, it is important to observe that this evolution has occurred with varying pace among different industries and regions of the world.

The graph depicted in Figure 1-2 will be used as a visual aid to a high-level analysis of the evolution of data centers.

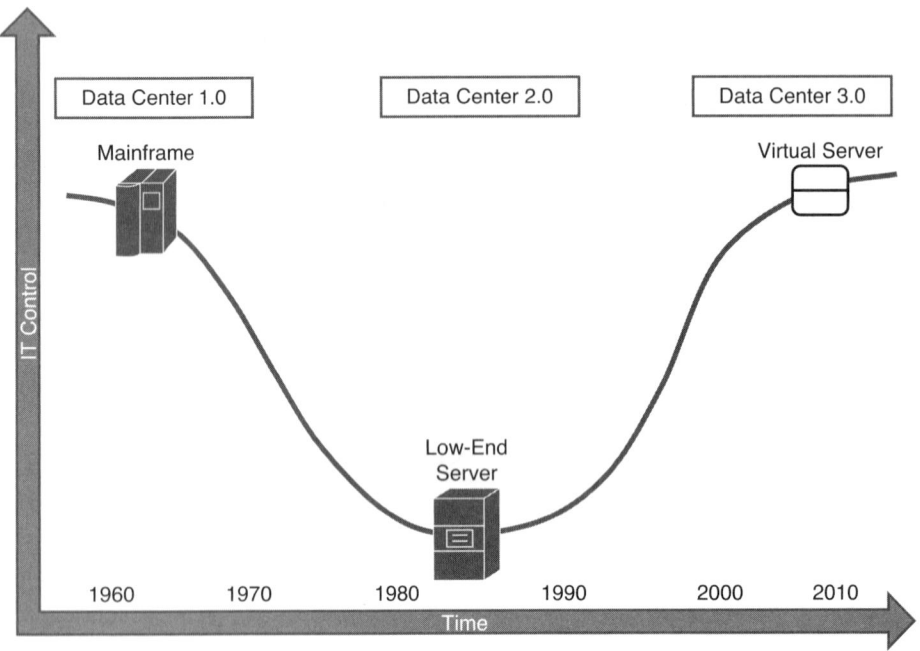

Figure 1-2 *Data Center Evolution Phases*

You can consider the *Data Center 1.0* phase name an "artistic license" because these facilities were simply known as *computer rooms* then. Large and special installations, these rooms supported mainframe systems since the 1950s and, consequently, were usually designed by IBM and other manufacturers to better accommodate their central processing units (CPU) and peripherals (storage devices, terminals, printers, among others).

Based on a monolithic software architecture, these centralized systems allowed a tighter control from an IT perspective and, with that, a higher resource utilization.

The *Data Center 2.0* phase began to take shape as the client-server application model increased its adoption in the 1980s. Leveraging the popularity of personal computers (PC), application environments started a migration from mainframes to smaller "server" platforms that were accessed through client applications installed on PCs.

With low costs of computer hardware and the scarce bandwidth of wide-area network (WAN) links, servers in this phase were commonly deployed closer to the clients and, consequently, away from the centralized IT management. Therefore, this phase was first characterized with a multitude of low-end servers accommodated into distributed, and sometimes improvised, data centers.

With the Internet boom in the 1990s, computer power was once again compelled to be concentrated into *Internet data centers*, which were sometimes adapted from deactivated mainframe computer rooms. The development of internetworking and web-based applications generated a perfect storm that further increased server centralization into properly designed data centers.

In the name of performance predictability and software modularization, the client-server model evolved to include *application tiers*, where each tier embodied dedicated servers that were deployed to execute specific functions. The best-known example of a tiered application architecture is the three-tier, which includes presentation, application (or business logic), and database servers.

Tip Three-tier applications will be further detailed in Chapter 4, "An Army of One: ACE Virtual Contexts."

The *Data Center 3.0* phase shares its origins with the exposed limitations of these facilities. Around the turn of the century, data centers were continuously approaching space and power saturation, while expansions and new facilities were the obvious expensive solutions.

Paradoxically, IT departments were discovering that data center resources had a disconcertingly low utilization. As an illustration, a 2005 Cisco IT study pointed out that servers and network equipment were being used at 20 percent of their capacity on average. *Application silos*, with their discrete set of network, server, and storage resources, were considered the root cause for this situation.

This phase is better characterized with a series of data center transformation projects that intended to improve resource utilization and increase operational simplicity. Most of these initiatives consisted of infrastructure consolidation projects, which standardized and reduced the number of components, processes, and even facilities in a corporation.

In parallel, projects based on cutting-edge virtualization technologies were also started up. In summary, their objectives were

- The isolation of environments in a consolidated structure
- The aggregation of discrete resources into a shared pool
- The simplification of operational procedures, preferably with the enablement of automation technologies

Operational Areas and Data Center Architecture

In several technical publications, the human factor is often overlooked in favor of the analysis of pure technical aspects. Although this might be an understandable approach, it can hide a series of explanations to the question: "Why did technology A replace technology B over time?"

In my opinion, the study of extremely complex environments such as data centers cannot afford neglecting "an IT component called Homo sapiens." Consequently, in this book, you will see multiple mentions of the influence of human resources on data center designs and deployments. Even if they are sometimes questionable, these decisions certainly uncover some very interesting liaisons between theory and reality.

Data center operational personnel are classically divided into highly specialized technology support teams such as server, storage, network, application, cabling, facilities, and so on. And with the growth of a data center, these teams can be further separated, to the point where the company's chief executive officer (CEO) might be the only person with authority over two different teams.

Figure 1-3 depicts a real data center organizational structure that illustrates the aforementioned situation.

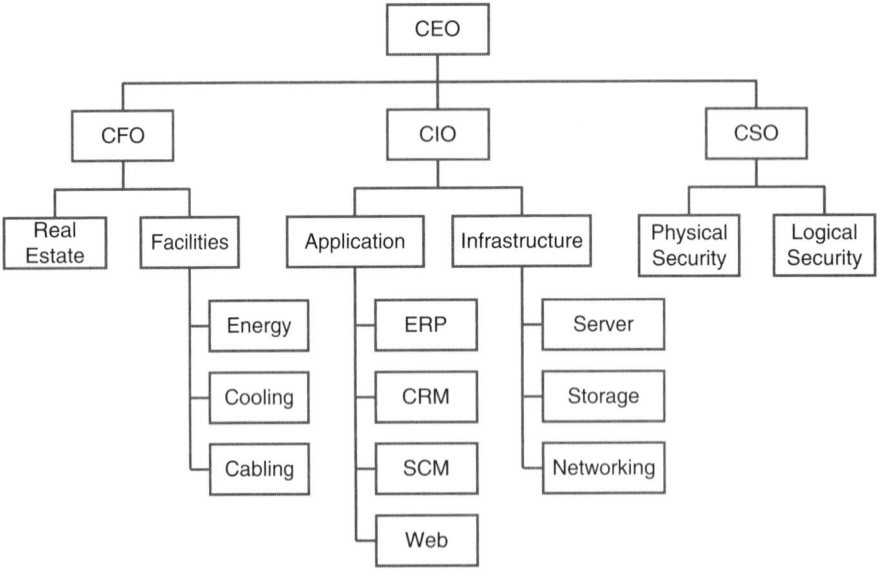

Figure 1-3 *Data Center Organization*

Note These structures can vary widely according to the organization's individual characteristics and the idiosyncrasies of each industry.

In Figure 1-3, you can see how data center technologies can be distributed among distinct decision domains, represented by a CIO, a chief financial officer (CFO), and a chief security officer (CSO).

However, data center solutions do not work as independently as the figure might suggest. Actually, they can be extremely interdependent. For example,

- The number of servers per cabinet depends on the power distribution design.
- A network design must be based on the knowledge of how many servers will the installed in each rack and how many interfaces they have.
- The network devices' physical position in the data center influences the structure's cabling project.
- Cabling can be laid out under the raised floor.
- The raised floor can have a direct influence over the cooling system, which is usually the highest contributor to the power system.

In the "everything is connected" condition of data centers, isolated decisions from one team can be potentially detrimental to the facility as a whole. Hence, an end-to-end vision is highly recommended in coordinating how a data center can evolve.

Data center architecture is the set of directives that drive all the designs within a data center facility. If a data center were a city, you can picture a data center architect as the city planner, coordinating the construction of corporate buildings (servers) according to the nearby street capacity (network) and the number of public parking spaces (storage). This same professional must also be able to handle the differences between "neighborhoods," exemplified by mainframe and low-end servers.

A data center architecture should have a clear vision of the technology's future evolution to avoid the entire facility being held "hostage" to bad decisions made years ago. Consequently, it must be acutely aware of the different technology life cycles. Although the duration of each cycle varies considerably depending on multiple factors such as industry and geography, I will present average technology life cycles that I have observed during my career:

- **Building:** 10 to 15 years
- **Cabling:** 7 to 10 years.
- **Network:** 3 to 5 years.
- **Storage:** 1 to 2 years.
- **Server:** 6 to 18 months.

Even if few people envy this job, I believe that a data center architect is a critical position for the IT strategy of any organization. And considering that some data center projects can cost billions of dollars, this professional can be the main bridge between the organization's business objectives and its IT budget.

The understanding of the relationship between data center technologies also influences the development of converged solutions. As a consequence, some corporations have adapted their data center support diagram to cover these growing "gray" areas of knowledge.

The Origins of Data Center Virtualization

One of the main objectives of this book is to properly characterize the technologies that are part of the so-called data center virtualization trend. Illustrating the hype we are living in, during my initial research, I have come across assorted virtualization definitions that can only be applied to a single solution. For example:

> "Virtualization lets you run multiple virtual machines on a single physical machine, with each virtual machine sharing the resources of that one physical computer across multiple environments."

> "Virtualization provides a physical-to-logical storage device abstraction. It presents a simple, consistent representation of a complex infrastructure to entities that consume resources."

> "The term *network virtualization* refers to the creation of logical isolated network partitions overlaid on top of a common physical infrastructure. Each partition is logically isolated from the others, and must behave and appear as a fully dedicated network to provide privacy, security, and an independent set of policies, service levels, and even routing decisions."

Although a little disappointing at first, it was easy to realize that virtualization **must** be placed in a context to make any sense from a technical perspective. By itself, the term *virtualization* is a generic umbrella term that can include anything from social networks to simulated realities.

Besides, the term *true virtualization* always seemed like an oxymoron to me.

In an effort to propose a unified definition for data center virtualization technologies, I decided to analyze their affinities first. As a direct result of these observations, allow me to present some historical virtual technologies that will better illustrate such common aspects, which are still present in modern virtualization solutions.

Virtual Memory

Storage can be defined as the capacity to retain data used for computing for some interval of time. Since its infancy, computers deploy at least two levels of storage:

- **Primary storage (or main memory)**, which can be directly accessed by the CPU and is usually volatile.
- **Secondary storage (or auxiliary memory)**, which demands an additional system to transfer data to the primary storage and is usually nonvolatile. By definition, it is larger, cheaper, and slower than primary storage.

In 1950s, the main memory was deployed through magnetic cores, while the auxiliary memory was based on magnetic rotating drums. Then, programmers really struggled to write code whose data would not surpass the main memory size. In some cases, they had to include a custom strategy to transfer data to the auxiliary memory to free the main memory for more data from their programs.

In 1959, the Atlas Team at the University of Manchester implemented an automatic mechanism that relieved programmers from these storage allocation annoyances. As with any great idea, *virtual memory* is based on a simple concept: to use the auxiliary memory as an extension of the main memory.

Figure 1-4 illustrates this virtualization technology.

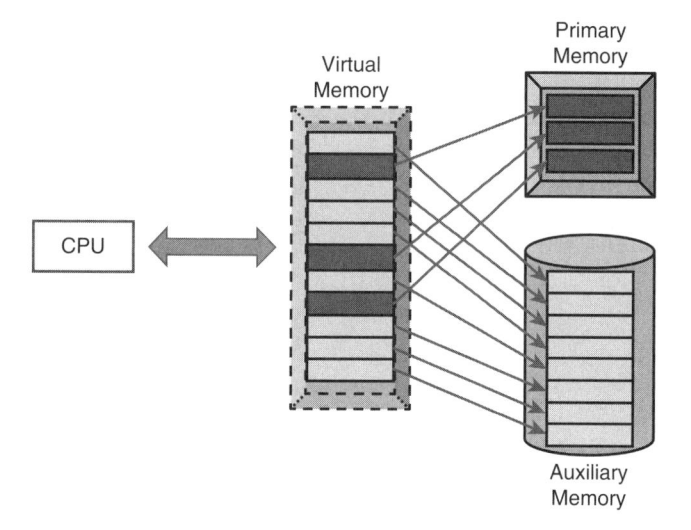

Figure 1-4 *Virtual Memory*

Using virtual memory, a computer's CPU can directly access a virtual memory address unbeknownst to its location at the main or auxiliary memory. In this technology, a virtualization mechanism is necessary to perform the following actions:

1. Translate virtual memory addresses into main or auxiliary memory locations.
2. Transfer data between both storage devices.
3. Choose which data would be ideally positioned in the faster main memory.

With this arrangement, an emulated main memory is presented to the CPU, providing the benefit of expansion and increasing code reusability.

Virtual memory is an important component of most current computer operating systems, such as Microsoft Windows and Linux. Their most-used virtual memory method is called *paging*, in which homogenous blocks of data called *pages* are retrieved from the auxiliary memory, allowing a noncontiguous storage of data. The principles of virtual memory were also applied in the creation of the "cache memory."

Tip Computer storage and memory technologies will be respectively discussed in more detail in Chapter 9, "Storage Evolution," and Chapter 13, "Server Evolution."

Mainframe Virtualization

IBM officially released mainframe virtualization solutions in 1972 along with its new generation of processors (System/370). This concept was based on the emulation of the mainframe architecture, allowing an operating system to be transparently run over a *virtual machine (VM)*.

Figure 1-5 further illustrates the basic concepts of this virtualization technology.

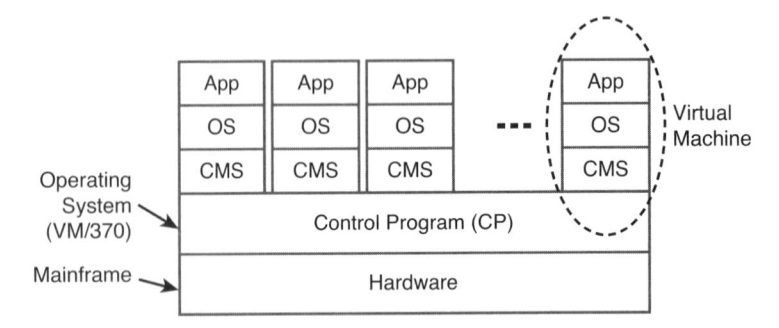

Figure 1-5 *Mainframe Virtualization*

As the figure shows, the VM/370 operating system contained a software component called *Control Program (CP)*, which can also be called a **hypervisor**. This piece of software was responsible for the creation of the VMs, resource sharing, device management, virtual storage management, and other traditional operating system tasks. In this environment, each mainframe user could interact with a *Conversational Monitor System (CMS)* as his own dedicated processor emulation.

For IBM, virtual machines provided a solution to the operating system migration problems that their customers were facing whenever a new processor was released. After all, using this virtualization, a single mainframe could simultaneously host different versions of operating systems (including yet another CP instance!).

The efforts behind the creation of mainframe virtualization were actually initiated eight years earlier, as an alternative to the *time-sharing* technologies, which were also intended to divide the expensive resources of a mainframe among different users. In summation, time sharing offered an equal slice of time of the mainframe resources to each user through the halting of a user job, saving the user state in memory, and loading of another user state.

Time-sharing mechanisms can be considered a "prehistoric" virtualization technology because each user had the illusion he was in complete control of the computer. However, contrary to virtual machines, all users were sharing the same operating system, without an unequal proper resource allocation and under the same failure domain.

Both concepts are really important to the current state of computer systems. While time sharing is used as the basis of multitasking operating systems, virtual machines have become the flagship technology for the Data Center 3.0 phase.

Hot Standby Router Protocol

In the TCP/IP networking architecture, a host commonly uses a router interface as its default gateway to forward packets to another IP subnet. Although several routers can be deployed in a local-area network (LAN), the great majority of TCP/IP stacks only allow one default gateway definition per host.

The described situation unveils an inherent single point of failure in the architecture, where traffic can be interrupted if the router that contains the defined gateway IP address from the host fails.

In 1998, Cisco created a solution to overcome this limitation called *Hot Standby Router Protocol (HSRP)*, which is portrayed in Figure 1-6.

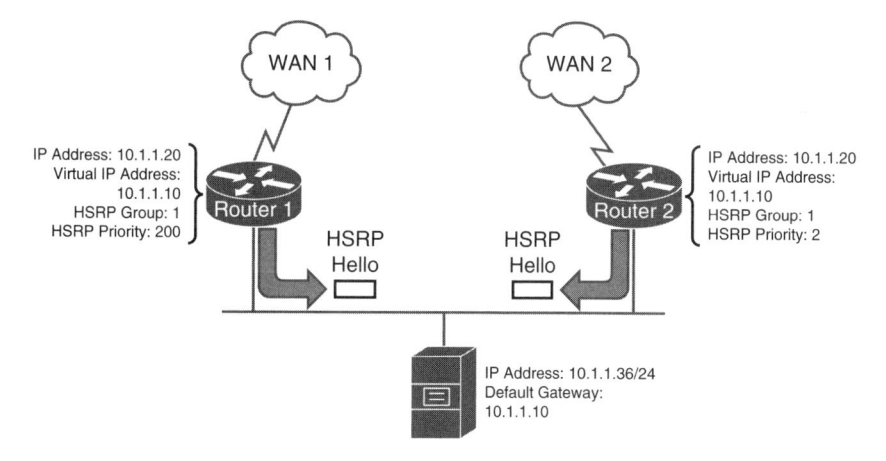

Figure 1-6 *Hot Standby Router Protocol*

As shown in the figure, HSRP provides default gateway redundancy through the following process:

- Both routers send HSRP Hello messages to state parameters such as a configured virtual IP address, HSRP group, and priority.
- Through these packets, they discover and decide which should emulate the virtual IP address (and a derived virtual MAC address) for the local hosts. The interface with the higher priority is always elected as the active interface.
- If the active interface fails, its absence is noticed by other HSRP routers, and a new router will emulate the same virtual IP. A router can also decrease the priority from the active interface if its WAN interface fails.

In 1998, HSRP was ratified in the informational Request for Comments (RFC) 2281 from the Internet Engineering Task Force (IETF). Although it has inspired the creation of other similar protocols such as Virtual Router Redundancy Protocol (VRRP) and Gateway Load

Balancing Protocol (GLBP), HSRP is still widely deployed in data center and campus networks in two versions: HSRP v1 and v2.

Defining Virtualization

From the virtualization technologies presented in the previous section (virtual memory, mainframe virtualization, and HSRP), you can observe the following similarities:

- **Emulation:** In all examples, a preexisting resource was emulated (main memory, mainframe, and default gateway IP address, respectively).

- **Transparency:** Without exception, the consumers of the IT resource (CPU, mainframe users, and TCP/IP hosts, respectively) cannot make a distinction between the emulated resources and their physical counterparts.

- **Benefit:** These examples bring some benefit when compared to a physical IT resource (memory expansion, resource optimization, and high availability, respectively).

Consequently, using data center infrastructure technologies as context, this book will employ the following definition:

> "Virtualization is the transparent emulation of an IT resource producing to its consumers benefits that were unavailable in its physical form."

As you will observe during the remaining chapters of this book, emulation can essentially be offered in two different flavors:

- **Simulation:** The act of pretending to have a characteristic that something does not.

- **Dissimulation:** The act of concealing a real attribute from the knowledge of others.

On the flip side, transparency can vary widely among these technologies, from the change of a single address to the building of an entire new logical structure. Similarly, their benefits have a very diverse range, sometimes even including collateral advantages that were not originally planned.

Data Center Virtualization Timeline

With a definition in hand, it is easier to aggregate data center infrastructure technologies under the same umbrella group. Hence, the following timeline of implementations represents the evolution of this group through a sequence of milestones that had an influence on the status quo of modern data centers:

- **1957:** Time sharing (University of Stanford).

- **1962:** Virtual memory (University of Manchester).

- **1972:** Virtual machine (IBM).

- **1984:** Virtual LocalArea Networks (Bellcore).
- **1987:** Redundant Array of Independent Disks (University of California, Berkeley).
- **1994:** EtherChannel (Kalpana).
- **1996:** Virtual Routing and Forwarding (Cisco), logical unit number (Shugart Associates).
- **1997:** Virtual Tape Library (IBM), LAN Emulation over Asynchronous Transfer Mode (Bay Networks and Madge Networks).
- **1998:** Hot Standby Router Protocol (Cisco).
- **1999:** x86 Virtualization (VMware).
- **2001:** Storage Virtualization (DataCore) and VMware ESX (VMware).
- **2003:** Firewall Virtual Contexts (Cisco), Virtual SAN (Cisco), XEN (University of Cambridge), and vMotion (VMware).
- **2004:** Microsoft Virtual Server (Microsoft).
- **2005:** MetroCluster (NetApp), SAN Volume Controller (IBM), and Invista (EMC).
- **2006:** Server Load Balancer Virtual Context (Cisco), N_Port Identifier Virtualization (Emulex, IBM, McData), Elastic Compute Cloud (Amazon).
- **2007:** Virtual Switching System (Cisco), KVM (open source).
- **2008:** Fibre Channel over Ethernet (Cisco, Emulex, QLogic), Virtual Device Context (Cisco), Hyper-V (Microsoft)
- **2009:** vSphere Virtual Infrastructure (VMware), Virtual PortChannel (Cisco), Fabric Extender (Cisco), Unified Computing System (UCS) service profile, Distributed Virtual Switch (VMware).
- **2010:** Overlay Transport Virtualization (Cisco), Virtual Machine Fabric Extender (Cisco), VPLEX (EMC), Open vSwitch (open source), FabricPath (Cisco), vCloud Director (VMware), OpenStack (Rackspace and NASA).
- **2011:** Virtual Network Data Path (Cisco), Virtual eXtensible Local Area Network (VMware, Cisco, Red Hat, Citrix, and others), OpenFlow (Open Networking Foundation), Cisco Intelligent Automation for Cloud (Cisco).
- **2012:** ASA 1000V (Cisco), vCloud Suite (VMware), Cisco OpenStack Edition (Cisco), and Cisco Open Network Environment (Cisco).

Note This timeline is not an exhaustive list of data center virtualization technologies. It simply illustrates the development of infrastructure virtualization over time and the technologies that are significantly related to the book content.

Classifying Virtualization Technologies

Whereas a formal definition helps to understand the similarities between technologies, the analysis of a single technology demands the observation of their distinctions. With that intention, this book proposes a *classification system* designed to assist in the analysis of the various virtualization technologies.

In ancient Greek, *taxonomy* literally means "a method of arrangement." Generically speaking, a taxonomy provides a high-level vision of the variance and relationships within a group of elements.

Undoubtedly the best-known taxonomy is the biological, which defines hierarchical groups of living organisms based on scientifically observed features. In modern biological taxonomies, each hierarchical group is given a rank, such as (from most general to most specific) domain, kingdom, phylum, class, order, family, genus, and species.

Because each group is split into subgroups until a species is fully characterized, biological taxonomies can be graphically represented in the form of a tree. Figure 1-7 exemplifies the biological taxonomy through a small subset of the currently accepted "Tree of Life."

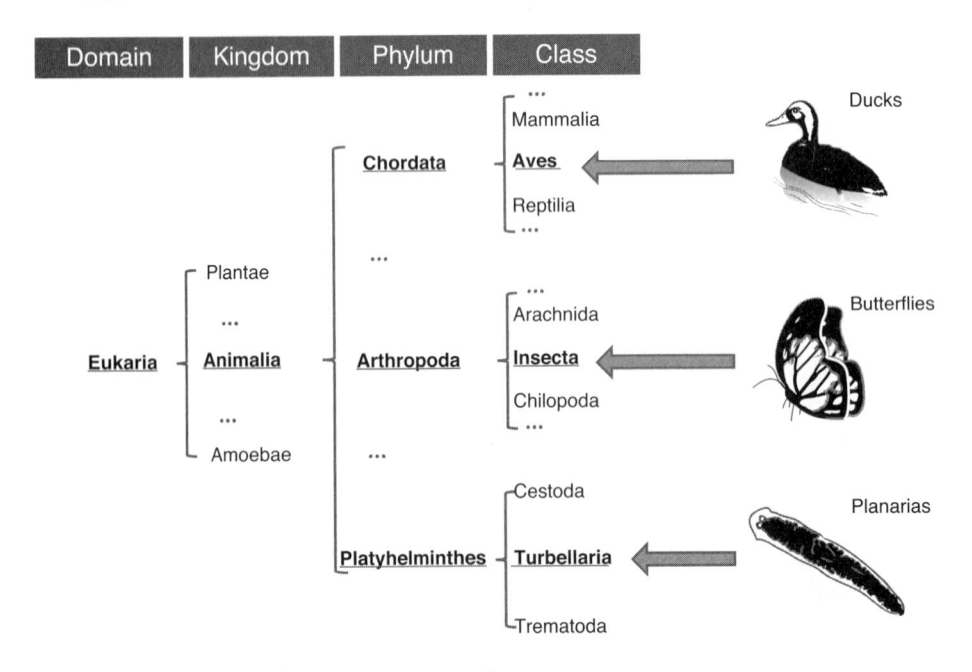

Figure 1-7 *Biological Taxonomy Example*

For the sake of simplicity, Figure 1-7 only depicts four levels (domain, kingdom, phylum, and class). From the Eukarya domain (multicellular organisms) and the Animalia kingdom (animals), three phyla are represented:

- **Chordata:** Aggregates animals with a pharyngeal slit, dorsal nerve cord, notochord, and postanal tail at some point of their life. Subgroups include Mammalia, Aves, and Reptilia classes.

- **Arthropoda:** Includes invertebrate animals with an external skeleton, a segmented body, and jointed appendages. Insecta, Arachnida, and Chilopoda classes are part of this phylum.

- **Platyhelminthes:** Bilateral unsegmented soft-bodied animals without body cavities. They are also divided into several subtypes, which are represented in the figure by Cestoda, Turbellaria, and Trematoda classes.

Additionally, Figure 1-7 exemplifies animals that are part of three classes from distinct phyla (ducks, butterflies, and planarias).

Beyond the typification defined by a taxonomy, species can be further characterized with additional information such as geographic distribution, size, identification, life cycle, and even trivia facts. This model of characterization mirrors the one I will apply to the group of data center virtualization technologies studied in this book.

Henceforth, each virtualization "species" will be characterized with the following peculiarities:

- Emulation
- Type and subtype
- Scalability
- Technology area and subarea
- Advantages

At this point, I believe you are already aware of the meanings of *emulation* (which IT resource is being generated by the virtualization) and *advantages* (the benefits of the virtualization). Therefore, in the next sections will discuss the remaining characterization features.

A Virtualization Taxonomy

Although virtualization technologies are infinitely inferior in variety when compared to the biosphere, our classification system can also benefit from hierarchical levels. The first level will be simply called *type* and will relate to the ratio between the number of physical and logical elements in a virtualization technology.

Figure 1-8 graphically symbolizes the three types of virtualization technologies.

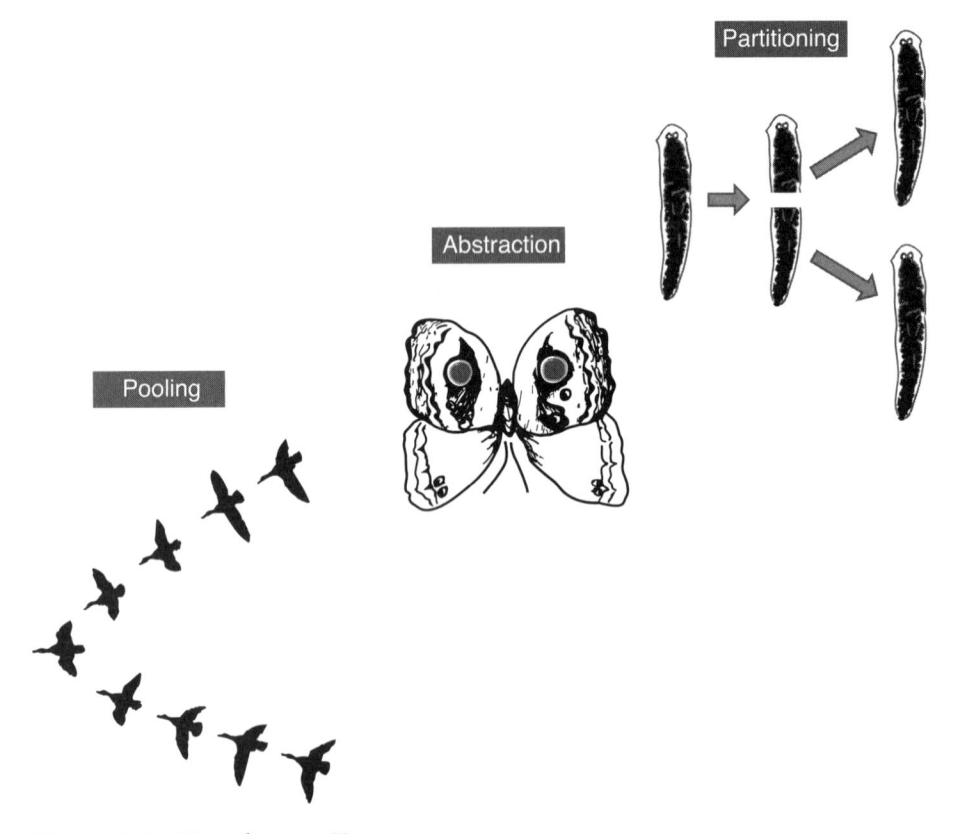

Figure 1-8 *Virtualization Types*

In *pooling* virtualization technologies, several physical elements work simultaneously to form a single logical entity that shares characteristics with the original entities. As shown in Figure 1-8, an analogy in the animal world would be a flock of ducks, which boosts the efficiency and range of a single element, flying together in a more aerodynamic "V" formation (a letter that, by coincidence, is also present in the naming of most virtualization techniques).

Pooling techniques can be further divided into two subtypes:

- **Homogeneous:** Where all elements in the resource pool are comprised of similar elements.

- **Heterogeneous:** Where the pool comprises different physical elements that can deploy some kind of hierarchy. In this case, the virtual entity must possess similarity with at least one of the pooled physical resources.

From the examples explained in the earlier section, "The Origins of Data Center Virtualization," virtual memory can be categorized as a pooling virtualization technology with a heterogeneous subtype (because the virtual memory is comprised of two different storage devices: main and auxiliary memory).

By definition, in *abstraction* virtualization technologies, the emulation does not increase or decrease the number of physical elements to create a logical entity. In these techniques, one physical resource creates a single virtual element to offer different characteristics to interacting devices or users. Figure 1-8 illustrates these technologies with the mimicry used by the *Caligo mennon* (owl butterfly), which is used as a defense mechanism against predators.

Regarding all virtualization technologies analyzed in the book, I have observed two abstraction subtypes:

- **Address remapping:** Where only addresses or identifiers are changed, while the logical device shares the nature with the physical entity.
- **Structural:** Where a virtual element that does not share the format of the device is deploying its virtualization. For example: Two routers can create a virtual back-to-back connection through a tunnel.

According this taxonomy, HSRP deploys an abstraction virtualization with the address remapping subtype.

Note Although several router interfaces can be part of the same HSRP group, under common conditions, only one can be active in a single IP. However, this taxonomy considers GLBP (which deploys load balancing between multiple gateways) as a pooling virtualization technique.

Finally, *partitioning* virtualization technologies are characterized by independent logical partitions that emulate the characteristics of the physical resource. Although a little gross, Figure 1-8 illustrates a mirrored behavior in the animal kingdom through the Planaria segmentation, which creates perfect living copies from the original specimen.

This book taxonomy divides partitioning technologies into two subtypes:

- **Resource allocation:** Where assets from the physical resource can be reserved for each virtual partition.
- **No resource allocation:** Where no resource control is deployed for each created partition.

From what was discussed in the earlier section, "Mainframe Virtualization," IBM virtual machines certainly fit into this partitioning virtualization type, within the resource allocation subtype.

Virtualization Scalability

One of the great risks related to a virtualization technology is the fact that its emulation can be **blindly** accepted. Constantly, I have seen engineers who were so confident in a virtualization technology that they have completely forgotten to include its limitations in the designs.

To avoid disastrous situations (or at least sad disillusionments), I highly recommend that you always be aware of the *scalability* of each virtualization technology, such as

- Maximum number of devices that can be pooled together
- Maximum number of address remappings per device
- Maximum number of partitions

Technology Areas

As one animal species can be located in a single geographic region, a virtualization technique can also be placed in a "technology area." These metaphysical locations were briefly mentioned in the earlier section "Operational Areas and Data Center Architecture."

During the last three decades, data center infrastructure virtualization solutions have being attached to three basic areas: *server*, *storage*, and *networking*. "Locating" a virtualization technology in one of these areas further specifies the operational teams that will probably have a direct interaction with it.

Figure 1-9 illustrates the technology location of the virtualization technologies discussed in this book.

Just like living species are not aware of imaginary country borders, Figure 1-9 portrays a large number of technologies that belong to more than one technology area. This recent trend mirrors the technological consolidation that has been happening in data centers, with the objective of operational simplification and resource optimization.

Note Although *application virtualization* technologies (such as Java Virtual Machine [JVM] and SAP Netweaver Landscape Virtualization Management [LVM]) could also provide another area in our classification system, they are beyond the scope of this book. As Figure 1-9 demonstrates, this publication's focus is directed toward infrastructure virtualization techniques.

This classification system goes one step further, with the definition of *subareas* within each technology area. Therefore, the subarea will pinpoint exactly "where" the virtualization is being performed among the most usual components of a single technology area. For example, storage virtualization can be performed at the

- **Storage device:** Symbolizes the location of data at rest.
- **Host:** Represents the computer system that is effectively retrieving and saving the data.
- **Interconnect:** Encompasses the network or medium between the host and the storage device.

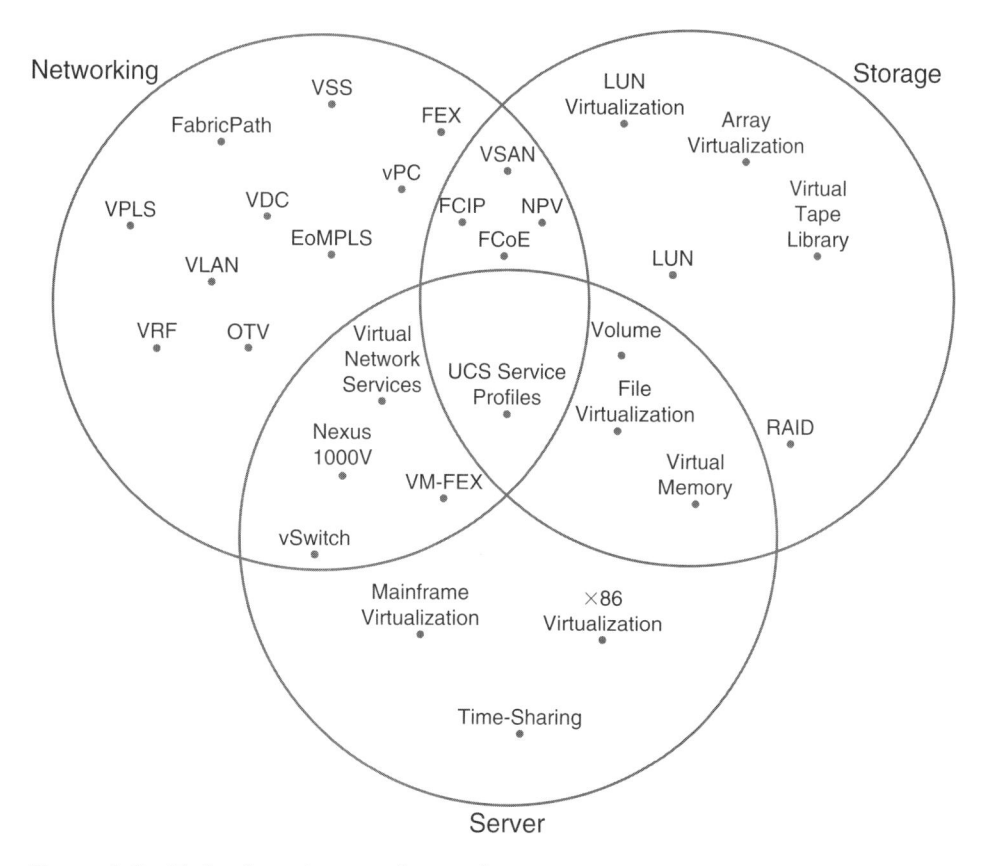

Figure 1-9 *Technology Areas and Virtualization Technologies*

In server technologies, virtualization will definitely occur inside a computer system. Nevertheless, there are multiple components that can effectively deploy virtualization within these devices:

- **Hardware:** Does not depend on the installation of any operating system to provide the virtualization.
- **Operating system:** The software layer that directly controls the server hardware and consequently provides the virtualization feature.
- **Application:** The virtualization is performed by a standard application that runs over the server operating system.

Tip Server virtualization will discussed in more detail in Chapter 13.

In general, network virtualization is performed on network devices (although in this book you will learn noteworthy exceptions to this statement). Nevertheless, these virtualization techniques can be distributed among *network planes*, which represent different functional components from network devices.

A network virtualization technology can aggregate, create, or segment one (or more) of the following planes:

- **Data plane:** Handles the traffic that is traversing two or more interfaces of a network device (transit packets). Responsible for the majority of data influx on these devices, it is also known as forwarding plane.

- **Control plane:** Processes traffic directed to the networking device itself and originated from other devices. It is exemplified with control packets from routing protocols and controls the behavior of the data plane.

- **Management plane:** Runs components meant for device management purposes, such as the command-line interface (CLI) and Simple Network Management Protocol (SNMP). This plane usually interacts with third-party software and is able to modify the behavior of both control and data planes.

Figure 1-10 portrays the areas and subareas used for the classification of the virtualization technologies contained in this book.

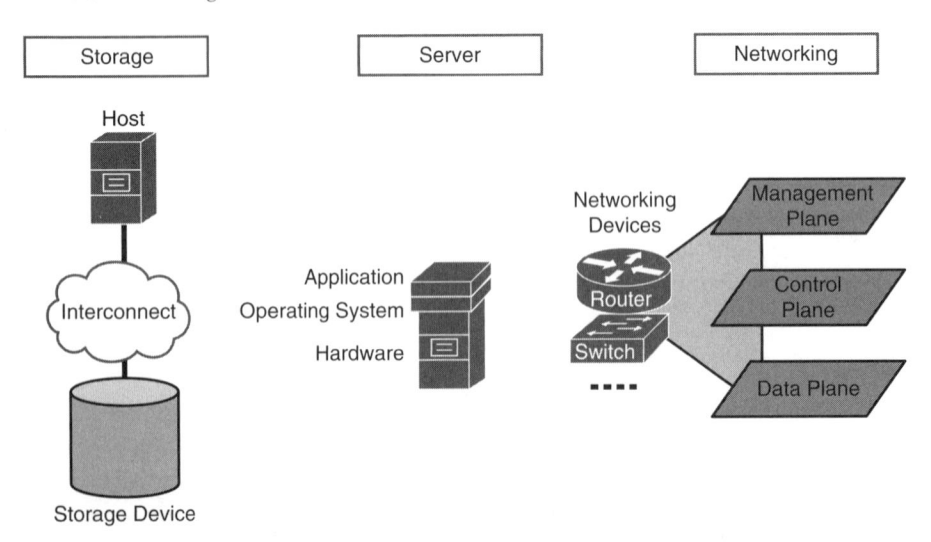

Figure 1-10 *Data Center Virtualization Technologies Areas and Subareas*

Note This publication will only use the networking planes to establish the subareas to *storage networking* technologies because they clearly correspond to interconnect subareas from a storage perspective. Additionally, for the sake of simplicity, Unified Computing System (UCS) service profiles will be classified as server virtualization technologies.

Classification Examples

Allow me to demonstrate how this classification system (from now on simply referred to as *virtualization taxonomy*) actually works. In Table 1-1, I will use it to classify the technologies described in the earlier section "The Origins of Data Center Virtualization."

Table 1-1 *Virtualization Technologies Classified According to the Virtualization Taxonomy*

Characteristic	Virtual Memory	Mainframe Virtualization	HSRP
Emulation	Main memory	Mainframe	Router interface IP address
Type	Pooling	Partitioning	Abstraction
Subtype	Heterogeneous	Resource allocation	Address remapping
Scalability	Implementation dependent[1]	Hardware availability and software version dependent	255 groups, one active router, and one standby router per group[2]
Technology area	Storage and server	Server	Networking
Subarea	Host (storage) hardware or operating system (server)	Operating system	Data plane
Advantages	Memory expansion and code reusability	Resource optimization and software compatibility	Default gateway high availability

[1] The Atlas Computer's virtual memory was originally comprised of 16,000 words of main memory and 96,000 words of auxiliary storage.

[2] These values refer to HSRP version 1.

Obviously, this classification system is not the only way to categorize virtualization technologies. It was primarily designed to support this book, providing a quick visualization of a technology before it is analyzed in a chapter.

However, in defense of this specific system, let me point out a fact: Since Swedish botanist Carl Linneaeus has proposed the first scientific classification approach to animals and plants in 1735, the biological taxonomy field has been the source of endless discussions and constant revisions. Therefore, much like the living forms they classify, taxonomies can evolve incrementally. Hopefully, the one presented in this book can represent one small step toward a better understanding of IT evolution. Or at least an amusing mutation....

Summary

In this chapter, you learned the following:

- Abstraction is an integral component of any computer system.

- A data center is the infrastructure that supports critical computing systems from one or more corporations.

- Data centers originated from mainframe computer rooms and have grown in importance since the Internet boom in the 1990s.

- Virtualization technologies have assisted data center infrastructure modernization since the mid-2000s.

- Data center personnel are traditionally divided into teams that support distinct technology areas. However, data center designs should usually be coordinated through a consistent data center architecture strategy.

- Data center virtualization technologies have existed since the 1950s with virtual memory and time-sharing techniques.

- In the context of data center infrastructure technologies, virtualization can be defined as the transparent emulation of an IT resource producing to its consumers benefits that were unavailable in its physical form.

- Inspired by the biological taxonomy, this book proposes a classification method that can be applied to understand virtualization techniques. This taxonomy includes the following characteristics: emulation, type, subtype, scalability, technology area, sub-area, and advantages.

Further Reading

Arregoces, Mauricio and Portolani, Maurizio. *Data Center Fundamentals.* Cisco Press, 2003.

Baudrillard, Jean. *Simulacra and Simulation.* University of Michigan Press, 1995.

Virtualization Tops CIO Priorities in 2012, www.informationweek.com/storage/virtualization/virtualization-tops-cio-priorities-in-20/232400150

Cisco on Cisco Data Center Case Study: How Cisco IT Achieves Consolidation and Standardization in the Data Center, www.cisco.com/web/about/ciscoitatwork/downloads/ciscoitatwork/pdf/Cisco_IT_Case_Study_Service_Oriented_Data_Center.pdf

Virtualization Basics, www.vmware.com/virtualization/what-is-virtualization.html

Networked Storage Virtualization, www.emc.com/collateral/software/white-papers/h1533-networked-storage-virtualization-ldv.pdf

Network Virtualization - Access Control Design Guide, www.cisco.com/en/US/docs/solutions/Enterprise/Network_Virtualization/AccContr.html

Denning, Dr. Peter J. *Before Memory Was Virtual*. George Mason University, 1996, http://cs.gmu.edu/cne/pjd/PUBS/bvm.pdf

Cisco Hot Standby Router Protocol, www.ietf.org/rfc/rfc2281.txt

Yoon, Carol K. *Naming Nature: The Clash Between Instinct and Science*. W.W. Norton & Company, 2009.

Chapter 2

Data Center Network Evolution

"Invisible threads are the strongest ties." (Friedrich Nietzsche)

This chapter will address the development of the Ethernet protocol, the most important factors you should consider when designing a data center Ethernet network, and how virtualization can help overcome significant implementation limitations in these structures. It contains the following topics:

- Ethernet Protocol: Then and Now
- Data Center Network Topologies
- Network Virtualization Benefits

The primary objective of a data center network is transporting server data to clients and to other servers. And considering that data centers are evidently built to provide data services, networking can accurately define how effective these installations really are.

To match the growth and reliability that are expected from data center environments today, a network must embody the following attributes:

- **Availability:** Is sufficiently robust to quickly recover from failures, or at least mask their effects to the users and connected devices.
- **Scalability:** Expands as proportionally (and easily) as the data center itself.
- **Flexibility:** Supports design and deployment changes without adverse outcomes.
- **Efficiency:** Is capable of deploying its maximum available resources.
- **Predictability:** Displays an expected behavior, even during and after a failure.

Because of its simplicity, low cost, and extensibility, Ethernet is the most popular data-link protocol today. Actually, it is not an exaggeration to affirm that every active device in a data center computer room has at least one Ethernet port. And clearly indicating how quickly this protocol has evolved, these Ethernet interfaces range from 10 Mbps to 100 Gbps.

In tandem with Internet Protocol (IP), Ethernet forms the basis of data center networking. Furthermore, both protocols practically defined how topologies and best practices were deployed during the last three decades. Their limitations also spurred innovation, which was materialized on network virtualization technologies. And over the years, these techniques have helped data center networks to pursue their necessary attributes.

This chapter will focus on the main requirements and designs that have shaped the evolution of data center networking, as well as the main motivations for network virtualization in these environments.

Ethernet Protocol: Then and Now

Named after the *luminiferous aether*, an omnipresent substance that was once believed to be the medium for the propagation of light, Ethernet was conceived in the Xerox Palo Alto Research Center (PARC) in 1973.

Created by Robert Metcalfe and Dave Boggs, Ethernet has escaped the research laboratories to reach the world in 1980, when it was first commercialized with the blessing of Digital Equipment Company (DEC), Intel, and of course, Xerox. Then, the protocol was defined as a networking technology that allowed up to 1024 stations connected to a shielded coaxial cable to communicate with each other using a shared data rate of 10 Mbps.

In its originally published specifications, Ethernet's main goals were simplicity, low cost, compatibility, addressing flexibility, fairness, progress, high speed, low delay, stability, maintainability, and a layered architecture. This last goal is arguably the biggest contributor to the longevity of Ethernet. The protocol's systemic organization, broken into a *data link layer* and a *physical layer*, has segregated the medium-dependent aspects of the coaxial cable from the frame-related operations. Consequently, Ethernet was free to adopt new cabling and transmission speeds while using the very same Layer 2 characteristics, such as frame format with variable size, carrier sense multiple access collision detect (CSMA/CD) link control, best-effort delivery, and error-detection mechanisms.

In 1983, the Institute of Electrical and Electronics Engineers (IEEE) ratified Ethernet in the IEEE 802.3 standard. Using the second version of the DIX (acronym representing the association between DEC, Intel, and Xerox) standard as its basis, IEEE has since this occasion stewarded the protocol data rate development from 10 Mbps (Ethernet) to 100 Mbps (Fast Ethernet) to 1 Gbps (Gigabit Ethernet) to 10 Gbps (10 Gigabit Ethernet) to 40 Gbps (40 Gigabit Ethernet) and to 100 Gbps (100 Gigabit Ethernet).

To characterize each physical layer option, IEEE has created a naming system based on three values: a number representing the transmission speed in Mbps, BASE denoting that baseband transmission is used, and one or two letters designating the used media. In that manner, 10BASE-T represents Ethernet baseband transmission in 10 Mbps using twisted-pair cables.

Note Besides its speed scaling, much has also been done to optimize Ethernet throughput from a frame exchange perspective. In particular, the introduction of Ethernet switches and full-duplex communications in the 1990s has transformed Ethernet networks from collision-ridden structures into high-performance environments.

Ethernet Media

During its 40 years of continuing development, Ethernet frames have being transmitted over a varied range of media, including wireless technologies and even barbed wire. Server networking, however, has always relied on standard cabled technologies that varied among coaxial, twisted-pair, optical fiber, and recently, direct-attach twinaxial cables.

Historic relics or cutting-edge standards, a closer examination of these physical layer technologies certainly helps explain some of the underlying trends of data center networking.

Coaxial Cable

The first Ethernet standardized medium, coaxial cables transmitted electrical signals using a copper core that is separated from a conducting metallic shield through an insulating layer. The composition is further protected by an outer plastic jacket.

Two different Ethernet physical layer implementations were based on coaxial cables:

- **10BASE5 (or Thicknet):** Originally ratified in the IEEE 802.3 standard, it could reach up to 500 meters. To insert new nodes, this cable relied on "vampire taps" which simultaneously pierced spikes to the core and shield, providing an Attachment Unit Interface (AUI) connection to the node.

- **10GBASE2 (or Thinnet):** Specified in the IEEE 802.3a standard, it could reach up to 185 meters. New stations could be disruptively added to the media through the use of BNC (Bayonet Neil-Concelman) T-connectors.

Figure 2-1 illustrates the internal structure of a coaxial cable and some physical components from 10GBASE5 and 10GBASE2.

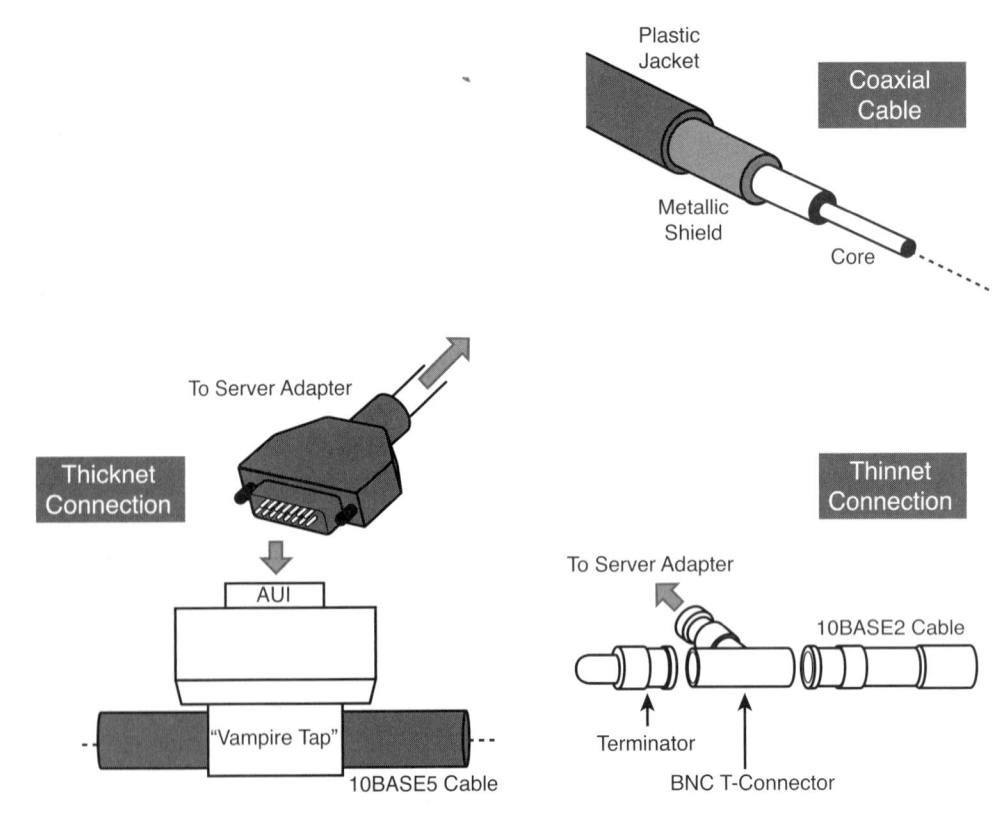

Figure 2-1 *Coaxial Cabling and Ethernet Components*

In both standards, resistors (terminators) were required at each end of the cable to avoid signal reflection and loss of communication. Because of these operational difficulties and the widespread adoption of twisted-pair in the 1990s, coaxial cables are considered an obsolete option for Ethernet networks. Nonetheless, they still can be found in radio equipment, cable television distribution systems, and nightmares of experienced network engineers.

Twisted-Pair

An extremely popular Ethernet medium option for both in-campus and data center networks, twisted-pair originated from telephony wiring systems (in fact, its patent is authored by the telephone father himself, Graham Bell).

A twisted-pair cable system is an assembly of several conductor pairs, each one forming a single circuit. The wires on a pair are twisted together to reduce electromagnetic interference (EMI) from external sources, including *crosstalk* interference from adjacent pairs.

Twisted-pair cables can be found in two variations:

- **Shielded twisted-pair (STP):** Individual pairs (or a collection of them) are shielded to prevent electromagnetic interference. This cable is recommended for connections with longer length or higher speed.

- **Unshielded twisted-pair (UTP):** This does not use shielded protection for each pair and is used for shorter-length or slower connections because of its lower cost.

A twisted-pair cable system usually employs eight-wire Registered Jack 45 (RJ-45) connectors for Ethernet ports on switches and servers. Figure 2-2 depicts both basic types of twisted-pair cables and the RJ-45 connector.

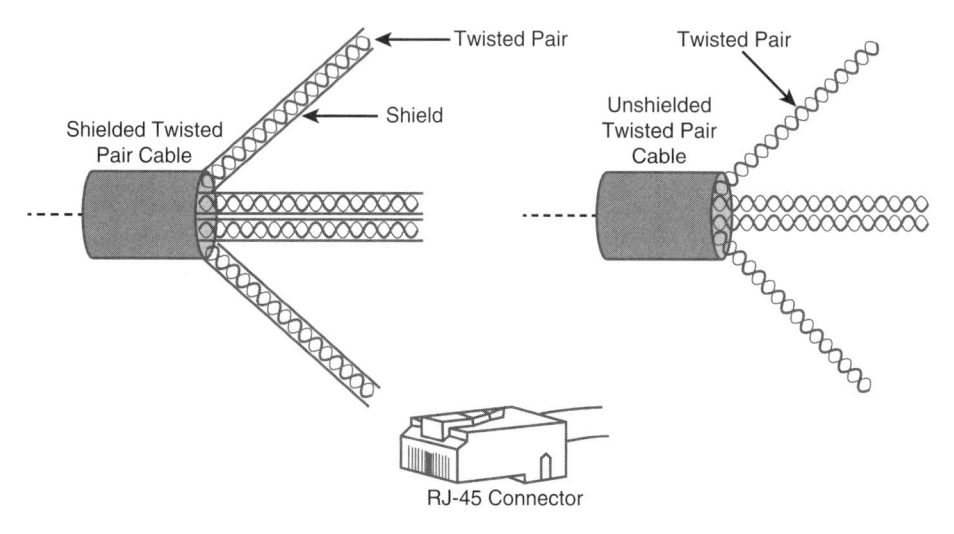

Figure 2-2 *Twisted-Pair Types and RJ-45 Connector*

The American National Standards Institute and Telecommunications Industry Association ANSI/TIA-568 family of standards specifies Ethernet twisted-pair cabling. Besides providing general structured cabling guidelines, these standards also define categories of twisted-pair cable systems, with different levels of performance and vulnerability to interference.

Table 2-1 details the ANSI/TIA-568 twisted-pair categories and their supported Ethernet physical layer standards.

Table 2-1 *ANSI/TIA-568 Twisted-Pair Categories*

Name	Type	Ethernet Physical Layer[1]
Category 3	UTP	10BASE-T and 10BASE-T4
Category 5	UTP	100BASE-TX and 1000BASE-T

Name	Type	Ethernet Physical Layer[1]
Category 5e	UTP	100BASE-TX and 1000BASE-T, 10GBASE-T (55m)
Category 6	UTP	10GBASE-T (55m)
Category 6	STP	10GBASE-T
Category 6a	UTP or STP	10GBASE-T
Category 7	STP	10GBASE-T

[1] Maximum distance is 100m, unless otherwise noted.

Optical Fiber

Optical fiber is a silica- or plastic-based medium that can carry information through the transmission of light. It consists of a core and a cladding surrounding it, with their refractive index discrepancy provoking light reflection back to the core whenever it reaches the cladding. Hence, when light enters an optical fiber cable, it is confined to the core and conducted down the fiber through the internal reflection between the boundaries of the core and the cladding.

The mainstream types of optical fibers manufactured and marketed today are

- **Multimode fiber (MMF):** Designed for shorter distances, this cabling allows multiple modes of light propagating through the fiber. This type of fiber has a core diameter of 50 or 62.5 microns and a cladding diameter of 125 microns.

- **Single-mode fiber (SMF):** Designed for longer distances, this cabling only allows one mode of light to propagate through the fiber. It has a core diameter between 8 and 10.5 microns and a cladding diameter of 125 microns. It permits lower light dispersion than MMF and, for that reason, has a higher cost.

Figure 2-3 graphically illustrates how differently light propagates in multimode and single-mode fibers.

IEEE cites the International Organization for Standardization and International Eletrotechnical Comission ISO/IEC 11801 fiber-optic specification as a reference for Ethernet optical cabling. This standard classifies multimode fibers into four types (OM1, OM2, OM3, and OM4), depending on their signaling rate per distance (modal bandwidth). OM3 and OM4 are the most used multimode fiber cabling in data centers today because they allow longer distances within the same data rate.

ISO/IEC 11801 and 24702 categorizes single-mode fibers into two types (OS1 and OS2), with decreasing attenuation per distance and, consequently, better performance.

The characteristics of Ethernet transmission over optical fiber vary according to the physical layer standard, as Table 2-2 demonstrates.

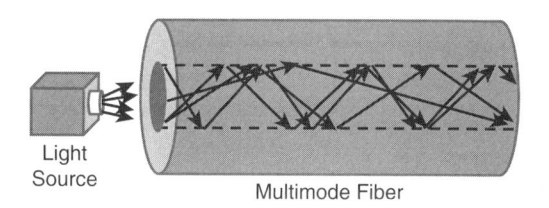

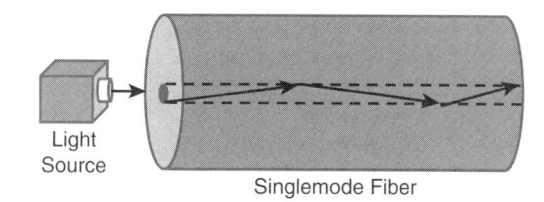

Figure 2-3 *Light Propagation Comparison*

Table 2-2 *Ethernet over Fiber Standards*

Data Rate	Type	Physical Layer	Maximum Distance[1]
10 Mbps	MMF	10BASE-F	2000m
100 Mbps	MMF	100BASE-FX	2000m
1 Gbps	MMF	1000BASE-SX	550m
		1000BASE-LX	550m
1 Gbps	SMF	1000BASE-LX	5km
		1000BASE-EX	40km
		1000BASE-ZX	70km
10 Gbps	MMF	10GBASE-SR	400m
		10GBASE-LX4	300m
		10GBASE-LRM	220m
10 Gbps	SMF	10GBASE-LR	10km
		10GBASE-ER	40km
		10GBASE-ZR	80km
		10GBASE-LX4	10km
40 Gbps	MMF	40GBASE-SR4	125m
40 Gbps	SMF	40GBASE-LR4	10km
100 Gbps	MMF	100GBASE-SR10	125m
100 Gbps	SMF	100GBASE-LR4	10km
		100GBASE-ER4	40km

[1] Considering OM4 multimode fibers and OS2 single-mode fibers.

A fiber cable system is comprised of one or more pairs of optical fibers, and each Ethernet device uses separate fibers for signal transmission or reception. All Ethernet physical layers employ a single pair of fiber, except for 40GBASE-SR4 and 100GBASE-SR4, which respectively use four and ten pairs of multimode fibers.

For Ethernet, the distances each fiber type reach suggest that multimode fibers are generally used to connect devices within the same data center computer room, whereas single-mode fibers are usually deployed to connect distinct computer rooms or even data centers sites.

Direct-Attach Twinaxial Cables

Also referred to as *twinax*, a direct-attach twinaxial cable is very similar to coaxial cable, except for one additional copper conductor core. Both twinax cores are protected by an insulator layer and another metallic conductor surrounding the core pair. Analogous to twisted-pair cables, both cores are twirled together to diminish interference effects from outside sources.

Originally created by IBM for shorter-distance connections, twinax cables offer a cost-effective way to interconnect Ethernet devices within racks and across adjacent racks. These cables are usually accommodated into the transceiver housing of a switch or server.

Direct-attach 10 Gigabit Ethernet twinax cables have Enhanced Small Form Factor Pluggable (SFP+) compatible connectors while 40 Gigabit Ethernet twinax cables deploy Enhanced Quad Small Form Factor Pluggable (QSFP+) connectors. On both data rates, twinax cables are available in the following types:

- **Active:** Have components in the SFP+ or QSFP+ housing to improve the signal quality. Usually covers 7 and 10 meters.
- **Passive:** Have straight conduction between devices and are available in 1, 3, and 5 meters.

Twinax cables have achieved high popularity in data centers because of their high benefit/cost ratio. Table 2-3 details these benefits through the comparison of some 10 Gigabit Ethernet transmission characteristics on other media.

Table 2-3 *10 Gigabit Ethernet Characteristics*

Technology	Maximum Distance (m)	Power[1] (W)	Latency (Microseconds)
Twinax Passive	5	0.1	0.1
Twinax Active	10	0.5	0.1
10GBASE-T	100	2.5[2] to 6.5	1.5[2] to 2.5
10GBASE-SR	400	1	0.1

[1] Each side

[2] Short-reach mode (up to 30 meters)

As an additional advantage, twinax cables present a much lower bit error rate (1 error in 10E18 bits transmitted) than the IEEE requirements for 10 Gigabit Ethernet connections (1 error in 10E12 bits transmitted).

Note Although the 2004 IEEE 802.3ak standard was the first to introduce 10 Gigabit Ethernet in twinax cables (10GBASE-CX4), this superseded solution was based on Infiniband twinax cables. The twinax cables currently used in 10 Gigabit Ethernet are standardized by the Small Form Format committee standards SFF-8431 and 8461.

Ethernet Data Rate Timeline

Since its inception, Ethernet development has been heavily based on standards as an effort to maintain absolute compatibility among different vendors. This goal is another major factor that explains the protocol's ubiquity and dominance over other proprietary architectures such as Token Ring.

Although the Ethernet standardization process has its fair share of politics, the study of its timeline remains a good way to assess the networking industry trends over the last three decades. With that intention, Figure 2-4 exhibits the Ethernet data rate in Mbps development on different media (coaxial, twisted-pair, fiber, and twinax) according to the year of its standard publication.

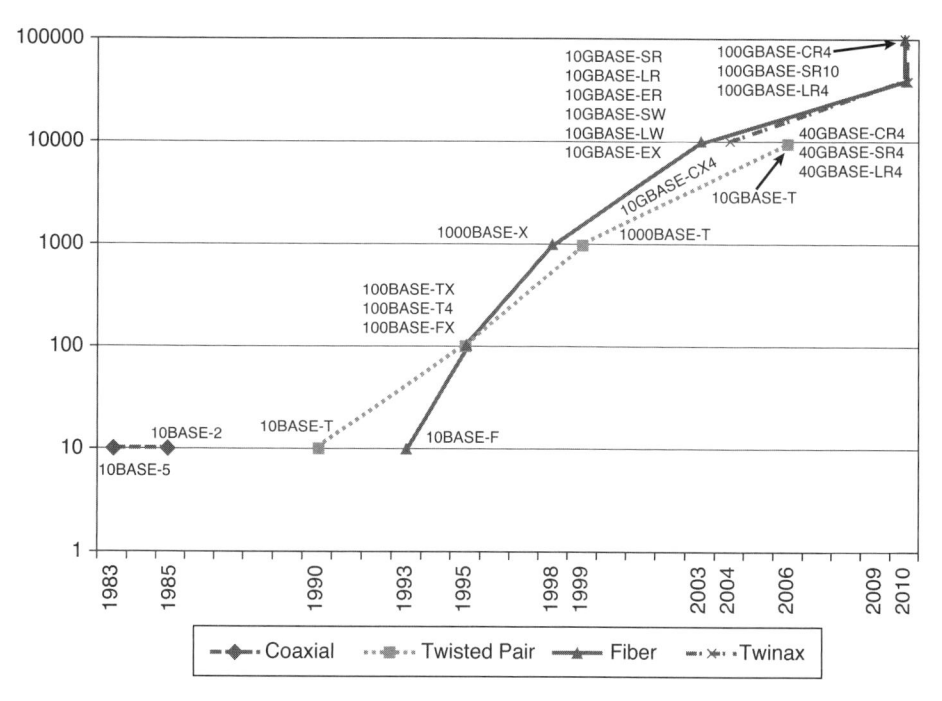

Figure 2-4 *Ethernet Standards Data Rate and Cabling Technologies*

The following trends can be observed from Figure 2-4:

- Twisted-pair roughly increased ten times its data rate every five years. That pace, however, did not continue in speeds higher than 10 Gbps.
- Optical fiber had a slightly faster development, being the first media to support data rates higher than 100 Mbps. It also presented the highest longevity among all media.
- Twinax cables have risen as a viable Ethernet option for 10-Gbps connections.

Because of the higher cost of optical transceivers, fiber is typically employed on links between switches, where higher speeds are required the earliest. High-volume connections, such as server access, depend on lower costs to justify an upgrade to faster data rates. For that reason, twisted-pair and direct-attach twinax cables have been the most popular choices for these connections.

Data Center Network Topologies

Broadly speaking, data center networks can be considered a specialized evolution from campus networks. In fact, until the late 1990s, it was not uncommon to find companies whose servers were connected to the same network structure that provided connectivity to local end users.

As an illustration, Figure 2-5 portrays a network design transition that I have personally witnessed with several customers.

As depicted on the left side of Figure 2-5, this company followed a traditional three-layer campus design structure (core-distribution-access) in the late 1990s, with its internal servers directly connected to the campus core. Then, the connection of critical servers on these switches made sense, because they are usually highly available devices and are centrally positioned in the campus network.

Nevertheless, with the continuing proliferation of servers and their increasing importance to the company business, its network designed had to evolve accordingly. The right side of Figure 2-5 represents the state of the customer network at the early 2010s. In this design, a separate three-layer network structure was created to provide connectivity to the company servers. And although both structures might be using similar network devices (Ethernet switches), their arrangement and configuration must satisfy different requirements.

More than a "spot-the-difference" game, the distinctions between desktop and server connectivity can be summarized as follows:

- **Failure impact:** A failure in a campus switch means that some users will not be able to access their applications. A failure in a data center switch can signify that all users, including remote users, cannot access their applications.

- **Host connectivity:** An average user desktop has only one connection to a campus access, while each server on a data center network usually has a minimum of two Ethernet connections.
- **Traffic direction:** Statistically, the majority of the campus traffic is directed toward servers that are reachable through the uplinks in the access and distribution layers. The same statement cannot be made in data center networks because traffic between servers is a significant proportion.

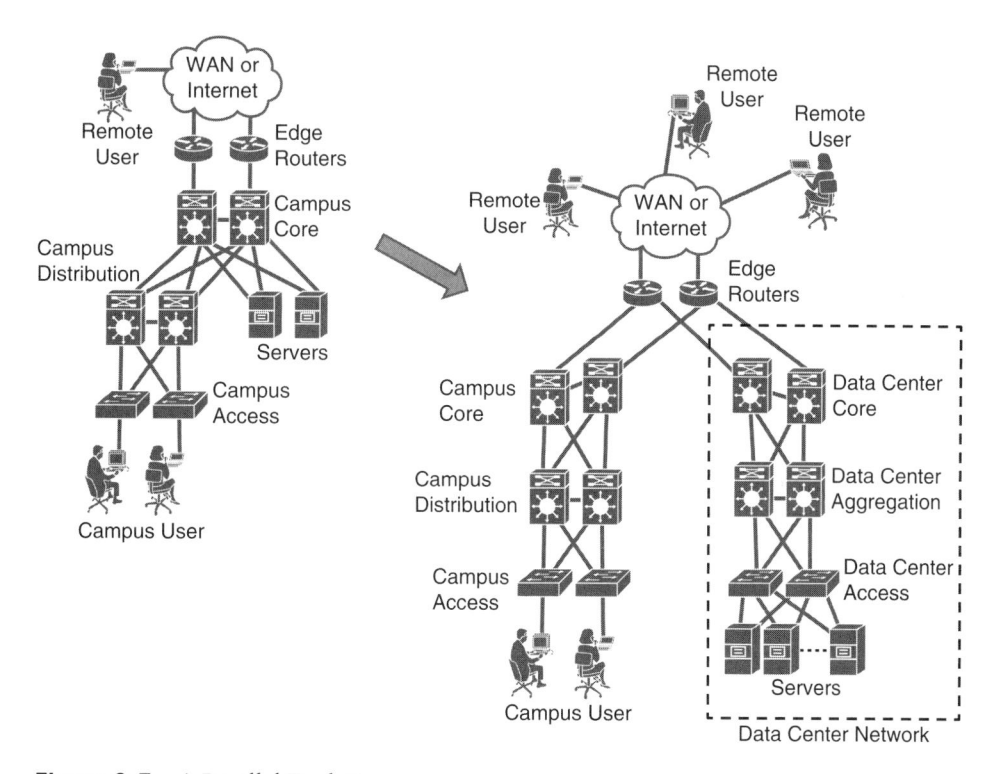

Figure 2-5 *A Parallel Evolution*

Data Center Network Layers

The core-aggregation-access layered data center architecture concentrates years of integration experience, originated from the first Internet service providers (ISP). And because this layered approach improves network modularity, flexibility, and resilience, it has been successfully adopted in multiple data center implementations.

In this architecture, each switch layer is planned to offer different networking functionalities for distinct traffic profiles. For example, the *core layer* provides forwarding power to the data center ingress and egress traffic. Using specialized routing features, core switches provide a highly scalable, flexible, and resilient structure that can offer connectivity between *multiple pairs of aggregation switches* (aggregation blocks) in highly populated data centers.

The *aggregation layer* is originally designed to be the "meeting point" for server IP subnets, usually being their default gateway and forwarding server-to-server traffic between *multiple pairs of access switches*. Consequently, aggregation switches are also considered the sweet spot for the insertion of stateful network services, such as firewalls and server load balancers.

> **Note** A *stateful* network device takes forwarding decisions based on the state of established network connections defined by protocols such as TCP (Transmission Control Protocol). In opposition, *stateless* devices process a frame or packet based solely on the information contained in this information unit.

The *access layer* encompasses Ethernet switches that must be physically attached to servers. Because this layer possesses the highest number of ports, its configuration usually aims for simplicity to improve management. For that reason, access switches are usually focused on the communication between servers that are on the same IP subnet. This design decision facilitates the exchange of **any type of traffic** (unicast, multicast, or broadcast) between servers.

Obviously, the core-aggregation-access model does not apply to every single data center network on our planet. Instead, it provides a general guidance that can be adapted to specific environment requisites. For example, small data centers might consider collapsing core and aggregation switches into a single layer, or even use the campus core switches to connect a few aggregation blocks.

Alternatively, very large data center networks from service providers can deploy routing solely in the core switches to allow all IP subnets to be present on every server rack, regardless of the aggregation block they belong to.

Design Factors for Data Center Networks

When designing a data center network, a network professional must take into account factors that might not be directly related to his area of specialization. For example, a design must take into account the *growth rate* of the data center (expressed as the number of servers, switch ports, customers, or any other metric) to avoid a network topology from becoming a bottleneck for the environment expansion.

Application bandwidth demand is also an important aspect for data center network designs. Commonly, network professionals use the *oversubscription* concept to translate such demand into more relatable units (for example, ports or switch modules). In communications systems in which multiple elements share a common resource, oversubscription refers to the ratio of allocated resources per user compared to the maximum value each user can potentially consume.

In data center networking, oversubscription basically refers to how much bandwidth switches at each layer can effectively offer to downstream devices. For example, if an access layer switch has 32 10 Gigabit Ethernet server ports and eight uplink 10 Gigabit Ethernet interfaces, it deploys a 4:1 oversubscription ratio for upstream server traffic.

Through testing and fine-tuning, it is possible to discover the oversubscription ratios supported in each application environment and define the optimal network design that will serve the application's present and future needs.

Business-related decisions also affect design aspects of a data center network, such as *failure domain sizing*. Therefore, if an organization simply cannot afford to lose multiple application environments at the same time, the number of servers per IP subnet, access switch, or aggregation switches will not be solely defined by technical aspects.

Application resilience is one of the factors that most affects network designs in data centers because it demands perfect harmony between application and network availability mechanisms. For example:

- Server-redundant Ethernet interfaces should be connected to different access switches and avoid traffic "black holes" (where an active server connection is connected to an isolated network device).

- The network must be able to react faster to a connection failure when compared to the application server.

Finally, a data center network designer should be aware of situations where all the factors should be prioritized, because benefiting one aspect will be potentially detrimental to another. One classic example of this situation is the connection topology between aggregation and access layers.

Figure 2-6 portrays four redundant design options that can be deployed with conventional Ethernet switches.

Tip The dashed lines crossing the aggregation switches represent the demarcation between routed (Layer 3) and switched (Layer 2) interfaces on these devices.

The options in Figure 2-6 can be divided into looped and loop-free topologies, depending on their reliance on a mechanism such as *Spanning Tree Protocol (STP)* to avoid loss of connectivity caused by Ethernet loops.

The *looped triangle topology* is arguably the most widely deployed in data centers today, because of its deterministic characteristics and flexibility. In this design, access-to-aggregation oversubscription remains constant in the case of an uplink or aggregation switch failure. However, STP does not allow all deployed uplinks to be used.

In comparison, the *looped square topology* increases the access layer switch density because each access switch demands only one connection to the aggregation layer (such a situation can be achieved forcing STP to block the link between both access switches).

38 Data Center Virtualization Fundamentals

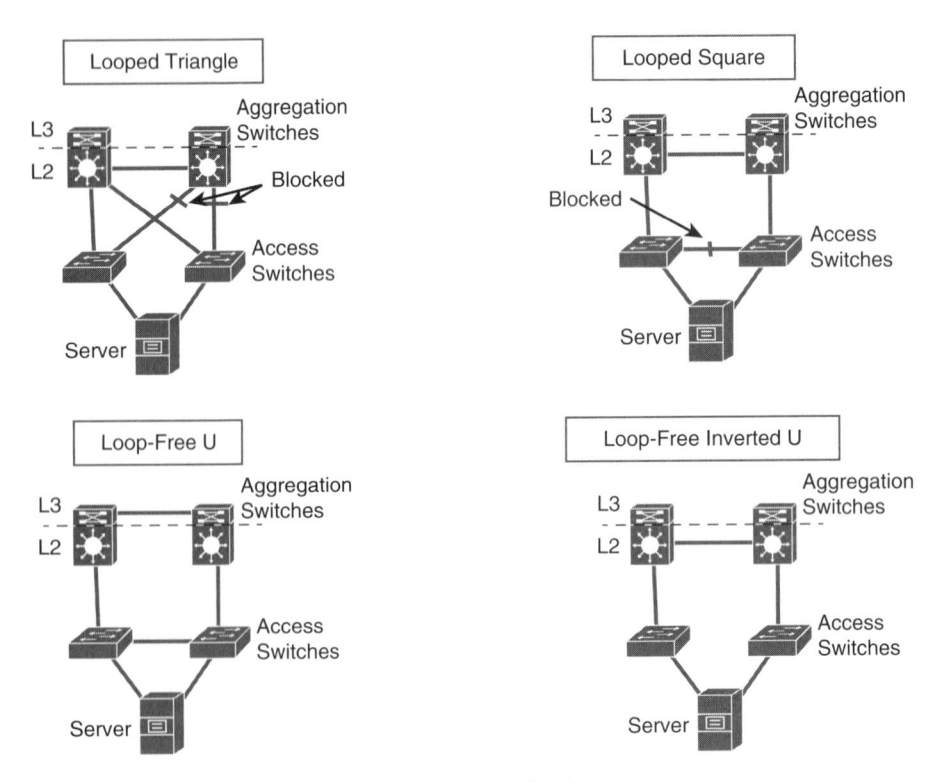

Figure 2-6 *Access-Aggregation Connection Options*

A potential drawback for this design is the fact that the traffic oversubscription to the aggregation layer doubles if an aggregation switch or uplink fails.

In a *loop-free U topology*, there are no blocked paths simply because a loop cannot be formed, but STP is still recommended to counterfeit connection mistakes. As with the looped square topology, this design allows a higher number of access switches per aggregation pair and an optimized use of uplinks. Nonetheless, loop-free U topologies only allow one pair of access switches per Layer 2 domain (or else, a loop can be formed between multiple access pairs). In addition, a failure in any of the switch connections will stop all Layer 2 communication (including hello messages from First Hop Redundancy Protocols) between aggregation switches.

Besides sharing all advantages from U topologies, a *loop-free inverted U topology* allows more than one pair of access switches on a single Layer 2 domain. However, uplink or aggregation failures are tricky for networks based on this topology because they can "black-hole" the server traffic.

It is up to the network designer to carefully weigh the most important factors in a data center network project before deciding in favor of a certain topology. Not an easy task, I might add.

Note I will discuss Spanning Tree Protocol and its extensions in detail in Chapter 3, "The Humble Beginnings of Network Virtualization," and Chapter 6, "Fooling Spanning Tree." As you will learn in these chapters, some network virtualization technologies are specifically designed to deliver benefits from multiple design choices without facing their shortcomings.

Physical Network Layout Considerations

Picking the right logical topology does not conclude a data center network design. The physical placement of network devices and servers surely influences the outcomes achieved with these structures. As an illustration, Figure 2-7 exhibits two popular data center physical access designs for rack-mountable servers.

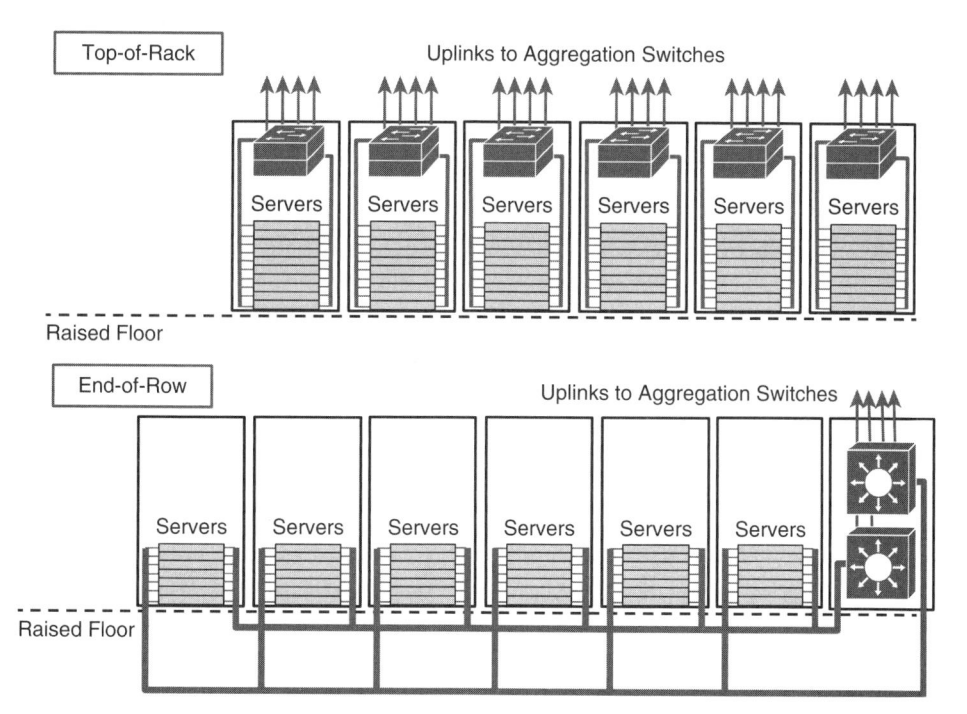

Figure 2-7 *Server Connection Models*

The *Top-of-Rack (ToR)* and *End-of-Row (EoR)* designs represent how access switches and servers are connected to each other. And both of them have a direct impact over a major part of the entire data center cabling system.

ToR designs are based on intra-rack cabling between servers and smaller switches, which can be installed on the same racks as the servers. While these designs reduce the amount of cabling and optimize the space used by network equipment, they offer the network team the challenge to manage a higher number of devices (two per server rack, as shown in Figure 2-7).

On the other hand, EoR designs are based on inter-rack cabling between servers and high-density switches installed on the same row as the server racks. Comparatively, EoR designs reduce the number of network devices and optimize port utilization on the network devices. But EoR flexibility taxes data centers with a great quantity of *horizontal cabling* running under the raised floor or on aerial trays.

If you are asking, "Which one is better?" the right answer is a vague "It depends." In truth, the best design choice leans on the number of servers per rack, the data rate for the connections, the budget, and the operational complexity.

Note I will discuss ToR and EoR designs (and their variations) in much more detail in Chapter 7, "Virtualized Chassis with Fabric Extenders." Additionally, the chapter will present a virtualization technology that permits customers to gain the benefits from both designs.

The ANSI/TIA-942 Standard

Published in 2005 by the Telecommunications Industry Association's TR-42 Engineering Committee, the EIA/TIA-942 Telecommunications Infrastructure Standard for Data Centers offers very useful guidelines for the design and installation of a data center.

Targeting flexibility, scalability, reliability, and space management on a data center project, the standard defines a tiered reliability classification for data centers, and states important environmental considerations.

In particular, ANSI/TIA-942-2005 also offers best practices on cabling infrastructure and space layout. On these subjects, the standard defines the following major spaces and structured cabling elements:

- **Computer room:** An architectural space whose primary function is to accommodate data processing equipment.
- **Entrance room:** Used as an interface between the data center structured cabling system and the external-building cabling (service provider or customer-owned). It should be located outside the computer room to avoid physical security breaches.
- **Main Distribution Area (MDA):** Located inside the computer room, it is the central point of the structured cabling. Core network devices are often located in this space because of its flexibility to reach other points in the data center.
- **Horizontal Distribution Area (HDA):** It is the distribution point for cabling that extends from active equipment. It is also located inside the computer room. A small data center might not require an HDA, as the entire computer room might be able to be supported from the MDA.

- **Equipment Distribution Area (EDA):** It is the space allocated for active equipment, including computer systems and telecommunications devices. In an EDA, horizontal cabling from an HDA is typically terminated with patch panels, and server racks are organized to form alternate hot and cold aisles for better cooling control.

- **Zone Distribution Area (ZDA):** Optional interconnection point located between the HDA and the EDA to allow reconfiguration and flexibility.

- **Cross-connect:** It is a facility that enables the termination of cable elements through a connection scheme between cabling runs, subsystems, patch cords, or jumpers that attach to connecting hardware on each end.

- **Backbone cabling:** Provides connections between the MDA, HDA, and entrance room in the data center structured cabling system. It is expected to serve the needs of the data center occupants for one or several planning phases, accommodating growth and changes in service requirements without the installation of additional cabling.

ANSI/TIA-942-2005 recommends the use of a hierarchical star topology for the backbone cabling, using cross-connects between different areas (nonstar configurations can be permitted, but without connections between HDAs). The standard also advocates locating the MDA closer the data center geometrical center of a site to minimize cabling distances.

A star topology is also suggested for the horizontal cabling; however, the presence of cross-connects in this case is not mandatory. On both backbone and horizontal cablings, the maximum suggested distances are 90 meters for twisted-pair and 300 meters for fiber.

Figure 2-8 illustrates how the standard defines a typical data center layout.

Figure 2-8 also depicts possible placements for the switches from a conventional three-layer network architecture. As you can visualize, both core and End-of-Row aggregation switches can be positioned in the MDA, to leverage its access to all other data center areas. End-of-Row access switches are commonly positioned on an HDA while horizontal cabling is laid out to its corresponding EDA. Ethernet horizontal cabling for an EoR EDA can be based on twisted-pair or optical fiber (of course, depending on the intended server access data rate, power resources, and budget).

Alternatively, Top-of-Rack aggregation switches can be positioned at the HDA because the access switches will occupy server racks on the EDA. In these designs, both backbone and horizontal cabling (between HDA and EDA) ideally employ optical cabling in order to future-proof cabling investments, while intra-rack cabling can be adapted more quickly to server environments with heterogeneous connectivity characteristics.

This content, from the ANSI/TIA-942-2005 Standard, Telecommunications Infrastructure Standard for Data Centers, is reproduced under written permission from Telecommunications Industry Association (www.tiaonline.org). All standards are subject to revision, and parties to agreements based on any Standard are encouraged to investigate the possibility of applying the most recent editions of the standards published by them.

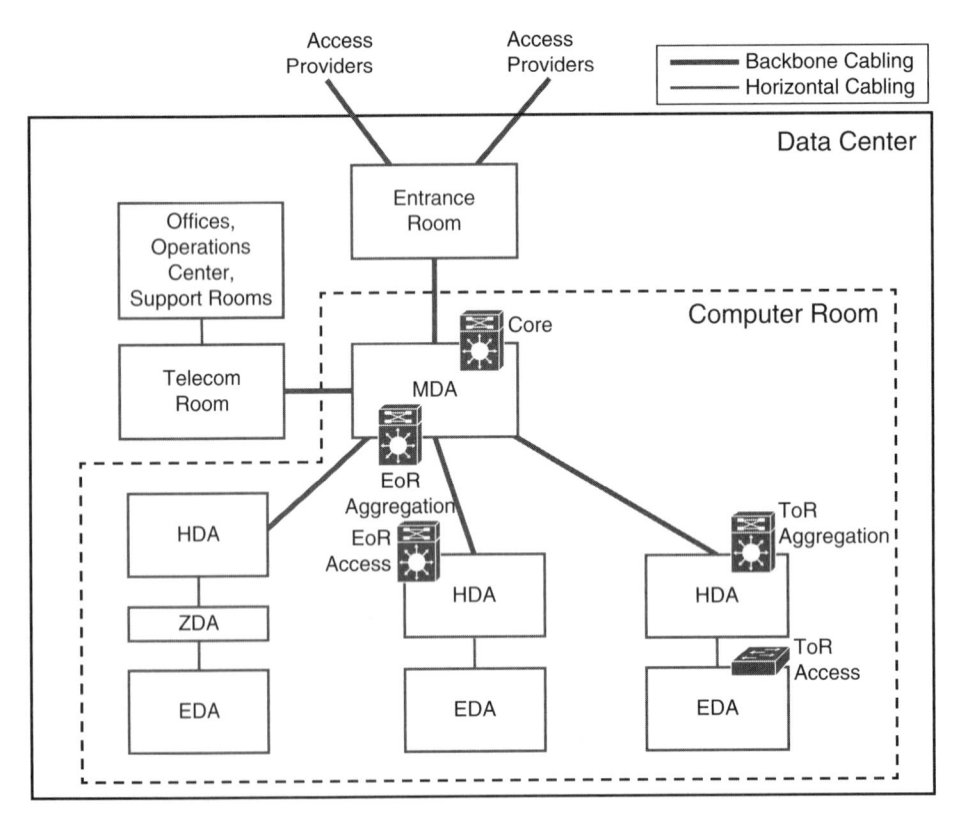

Figure 2-8 *Data Center Typical Topology and Ethernet Device Positioning*

Network Virtualization Benefits

As briefly mentioned in this chapter, network virtualization technologies can aggregate the benefits of two conflicting designs, while minimizing their disadvantages. And in the remaining chapters of Part II, "Virtualization in Network Technologies," you will be introduced to some features and techniques that solve different problems with subtle operational adaptations.

Network Logical Partitioning

Consolidation is a definitive trend in data center networking. Considering that the objective of any network is improving connectivity, it is only common sense that multiple physical networks would result in a high-cost and difficult-to-manage communication infrastructure.

With a consolidated data center network, resources such as ports and forwarding capacity can have its use maximized. However, there are strong motivations in favor of network partitioning, such as the implementation of distinct security zones and multitenancy.

Virtualization can bring both concepts together through the introduction of logical partitioning technologies, as illustrated in Figure 2-9.

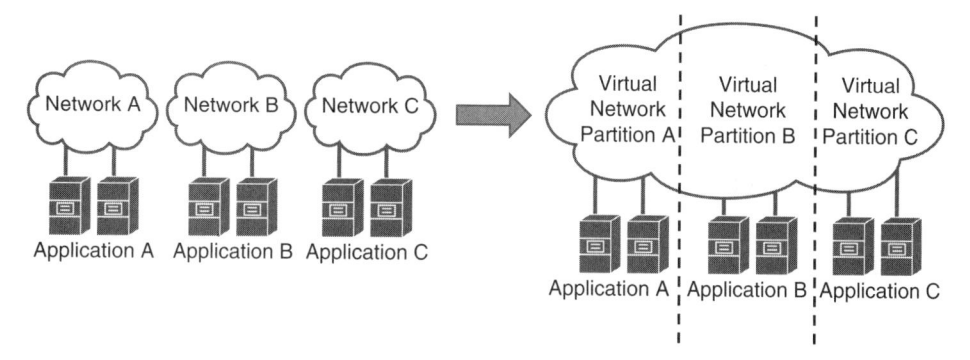

Figure 2-9 *Network Partitioning*

In Figure 2-9, three different physical networks are consolidated into a single infrastructure and segmented into virtual partitions.

Data center network resources can employ different technologies to deploy virtual partitions with different characteristics. The following chapters will deal with these special virtualization techniques:

- Chapter 3 will discuss virtual local-area networks (VLAN) and Virtual Routing and Forwarding (VRF) instances.
- Chapter 4 will examine virtual contexts for server load balancers.
- Chapter 5 will study virtual device contexts (VDC) for data center switches.

Network Simplification and Traffic Load Balancing

Spanning Tree Protocol (STP) is a network standard that was created to avoid loops in Ethernet networks. However, it is based on port blocking to dismount these looped structures, resulting in network resources that cannot be used and a fairly challenging implementation planning.

Network virtualization introduces the possibility of transforming physical connections and devices into simpler logical entities, both improving resource utilization and reducing design complexities. These techniques include

- EtherChannel
- Virtual PortChannel (vPC)
- Layer 2 multipathing with FabricPath

These virtualization technologies will be detailed in Chapter 6.

Management Consolidation and Cabling Optimization

Fabric Extenders are network devices that depend on a parent switch to work. However, they work as a remote linecard of a virtual distributed chassis that can leverage advantages from both End-of-Row and Top-of-Rack access physical designs.

The virtualization deployed by Fabric Extenders will be discussed in Chapter 7.

Network Extension

Network virtualization can also be used to connect Layer 2 networks over Multiprotocol Lable Switching (MPLS) or IP networks. Forfeiting the deployment of expensive physical fiber connections, virtualization technologies such as Ethernet over MPLS (EoMPLS), Virtual Private LAN Service (VPLS), and Overlay Transport Virtualization (OTV) emulate Ethernet networking components to enable server clustering and workload migration between data center sites.

These emulation technologies, as well as other aspects of Layer 2 extensions, will be detailed in Chapter 8, "A Tale of Two Data Centers."

Summary

In this chapter, you learned the following:

- Although data center Ethernet networks can be considered an evolution from campus networks, they diverge on several characteristics such as end-host connections, availability, and traffic patterns.
- The generic data center network model is comprised of three layers (core, aggregation, and access). Each layer has different design options, with varying advantages and drawbacks.
- ANSI/TIA-942-2005 provides guidelines for space layout and cabling infrastructure for modern data centers.
- Network virtualization techniques can help network partitioning, resource optimization, management consolidation, and network extension.

Further Reading

Moreno, Victor. Reddy, Kumar. *Network Virtualization*. Cisco Press, 2006.

IEEE Standards Association, 445 Hoes Lane, Piscataway, NJ 08854-4141 USA

http://standards.ieee.org

Telecommunications Industry Association (TIA), 1320 N. Courthouse Road, Suite 200, Arlington, VA 22201 USA

www.tiaonline.org

Chapter 3

The Humble Beginnings of Network Virtualization

"The creation of a thousand forests is in one acorn." (Ralph Waldo Emerson)

This chapter will address two very popular network virtualization techniques: virtual local-area networks (VLAN) and Virtual Routing and Forwarding (VRF). It will cover the following topics:

- Network Partitioning
- Concepts from the Bridging World
- Defining VLANs
- Two Common Misconceptions About VLANs
- Spanning Tree Protocol and VLANs
- Private VLANs
- VLAN Specifics
- Concepts from the Routing World
- Overlapping Addresses in a Data Center
- Defining VRFs
- VRFs and Routing Protocols
- VRFs and the Management Plane
- VRF Resource Allocation Control
- Use Case: Data Center Network Segmentation

Table 3-1 explains how VLANs and VRFs fit into the virtualization taxonomy described in Chapter 1, "Virtualization History and Definitions."

Table 3-1 *VLAN and VRF Virtualization Classification*

Virtualization Characteristics	VLAN	VRF
Emulation	Ethernet local-area network	Router
Type	Partitioning	Partitioning
Subtype	No resource allocation control	Some resource allocation control (maximum routes)
Scalability	Hardware dependent[1]	Hardware dependent[1]
Technology Area	Networking	Networking
Subarea	Data plane[2]	Data and control plane
Advantages	Path isolation, broadcast control, traffic manipulation	Path isolation, traffic manipulation, IP address space independence

[1] Refer to Appendix A, "Cisco Data Center Portfolio" for more details and the Cisco online documentation for updated information.

[2] As section "Spanning Tree Protocol and VLANs" will explain, a VLAN can also deploy control plane virtualization when implemented with some versions of Spanning Tree Protocol, such as PVST+, RPVST+, and MST.

The evolution of networking technologies is an incremental process. But as the Icarus of Greek myth would agree, problems arise whenever a new technology concept is deployed. And it does not matter if this concept is a shared network or wings made of feathers and wax.

Since its inception in the 1970s, the development of Ethernet was especially focused on the scalability of two parameters: *data speed* and *number of connected devices*. Meanwhile, in the 1990s, the Internet Protocol (IP) was adapted to spread itself globally in the waves created by the Internet boom.

To react to known scalability problems and unexpected forwarding behaviors, network designers recurred to *partitioning* as a way to break the problem into controllable subdomains. And motivated by budget constraints, network virtualization technologies were developed to avoid unnecessary expenses in additional networking devices.

VLANs and VRFs are arguably the most known virtualization techniques among network designers. They are heavily used in campus and data center networks, and their adequate deployment is usually crucial to the success of a network project.

VLANs were created to group together network devices and hosts that communicate directly with each other. Nowadays, VLANs continue to perform the same role, but with several enhancements and variations.

VRFs were created as part of Multiprotocol Label Switching (MPLS) to provide routing and path isolation to Virtual Private Networks (VPN). However, the simplicity and flexibility of a VRF inspired advanced designs and implementations that are very beneficial to data centers.

This chapter presents these virtualization techniques, their concepts, relationships with Layer 2 and Layer 3 protocols, limitations, and sample designs for modern data centers.

Network Partitioning

Networks were created to allow free exchange of traffic among hosts. Contrary to the hierarchical relationship between the mainframe and its terminals, all the hosts connected to a network are usually independent entities that follow defined rules of behavior and protocols. With that principle, Ethernet and IP networks aimed to provide connectivity services, leaving the definition of master-slave relationships to application designers.

Such communication democracy has advantages, but also, lots of opportunities to achieve chaos. A bigger number of connected devices can expose scalability limitations and force different hosts to share undesired behavior.

Therefore, *network partitioning* is a design concept that IT architects deploy whenever they face challenges such as

   Traffic isolation for groups of hosts

   Distinct security areas

   Different device groups with overlapping IP addresses

   Different path behavior

   Shared failure domains

Different partitioning techniques can be used depending on how the hosts communicate. As you will learn in the next sections, switched Ethernet networks use VLANs for this purpose.

Concepts from the Bridging World

To save you a longer visit to the "museum of networking," allow me to quickly present some definitions and devices that belong to the origins of Ethernet networks. Although these concepts are often overlooked today, they are extremely useful to understand why VLANs were developed in the first place:

- **Segment:** It relates to the original Ethernet bus that used coaxial cables as shared communication media. In a segment, all transmitted frames are received by all connected devices. Ethernet hubs also constitute a segment and were introduced as a replacement for the error-prone coaxial buses. A segment also defines a *collision domain* because the shared media allows that a frame can be erroneously transmitted while another frame is still being transported on the segment.

- **Bridge:** A device created to allow the communication between multiple Ethernet segments without the formation of one big collision domain. A bridge transports

Ethernet frames from one segment to another if its destination MAC address was not detected on this segment. A bridge also defines a *broadcast domain* because it must forward broadcast frames to all bridged segments.

- **Switch:** An evolution of the concept of bridges. Its forwarding process is hardware based, and usually has more ports than a bridge. A switch also defines a broadcast domain.

> **Note** As you will verify in this chapter, network manufacturers easily blur the lines that separate theoretical definitions. However, for the sake of simplicity, I will use the bridge and switch definitions from Cisco Learning Network material.

Figure 3-1 clarifies further the distinct behavior of hubs and switches.

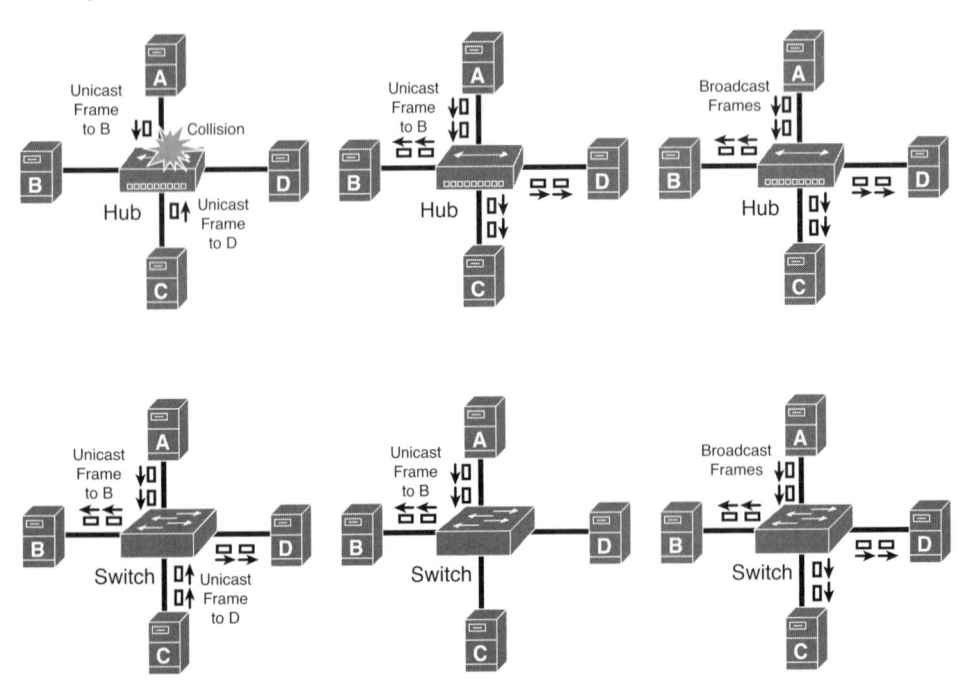

Figure 3-1 *Compared Behavior of Hubs and Switches*

In legacy segment-based networks, the number of connected hosts raised the probability of collisions, up to the point where communication was not possible. Bridges and switches were introduced to break these networks in smaller segments and to isolate these communication errors in more limited collision domains.

Nevertheless, even within a switched Ethernet network, an undesired amount of broadcast frames could be achieved with a great quantity of connected hosts, with similar communication problems. Therefore, *routers* have been deployed to connect hosts from different broadcast domains. Because, by definition, these devices do not forward Ethernet broadcast traffic, they allowed local-area networks (LAN) to efficiently connect a much bigger number of hosts.

At this point of evolution, each Ethernet switch could only deploy a single broadcast domain, and additional devices should be acquired if more domains were desired in a LAN. Thus, to avoid low utilization of network resources and permit the segregation of hosts in the same switch, *virtual local-area networks (VLAN)* were created.

Defining VLANs

A VLAN can be defined as a broadcast domain in a single Ethernet switch or shared among connected switches. Whenever a switch interface that belongs to a VLAN receives a broadcast Ethernet frame (destination MAC address is ffff.ffff.ffff), the device must forward this frame to all other ports that are defined in the same VLAN.

Figure 3-2 illustrates this behavior in a switch that has three VLANs.

Within each VLAN, a switch emulates an Ethernet bridge, forwarding Ethernet frames based on their destination MAC address. And because they still belong to a physical switch, each port of a VLAN defines a collision domain.

Because broadcast and flooding are responsible for some problems in Layer 2 networks, they are unjustly treated as undesirable frames. However, you should not overlook how essential they are in IP over Ethernet networks.

For example, broadcast communication is the principle behind *Address Resolution Protocol (ARP)*. ARP allows Ethernet hosts to learn MAC addresses from hosts connected to the same broadcast domain.

Figures 3-3 and 3-4 depict the use of ARP broadcast request and unicast response within a VLAN.

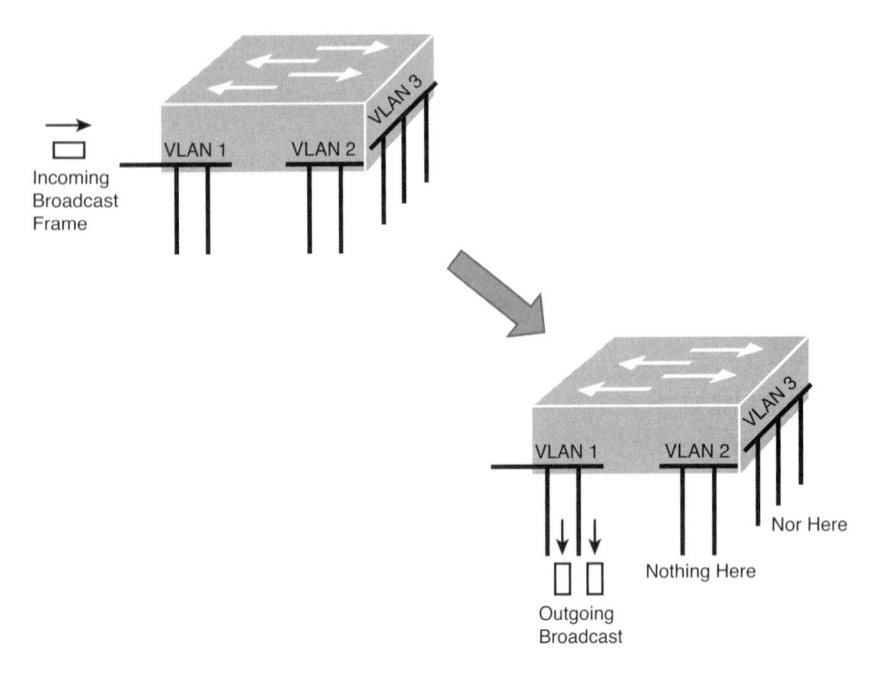

Figure 3-2 *Broadcast Behavior in a VLAN-Enabled Switch*

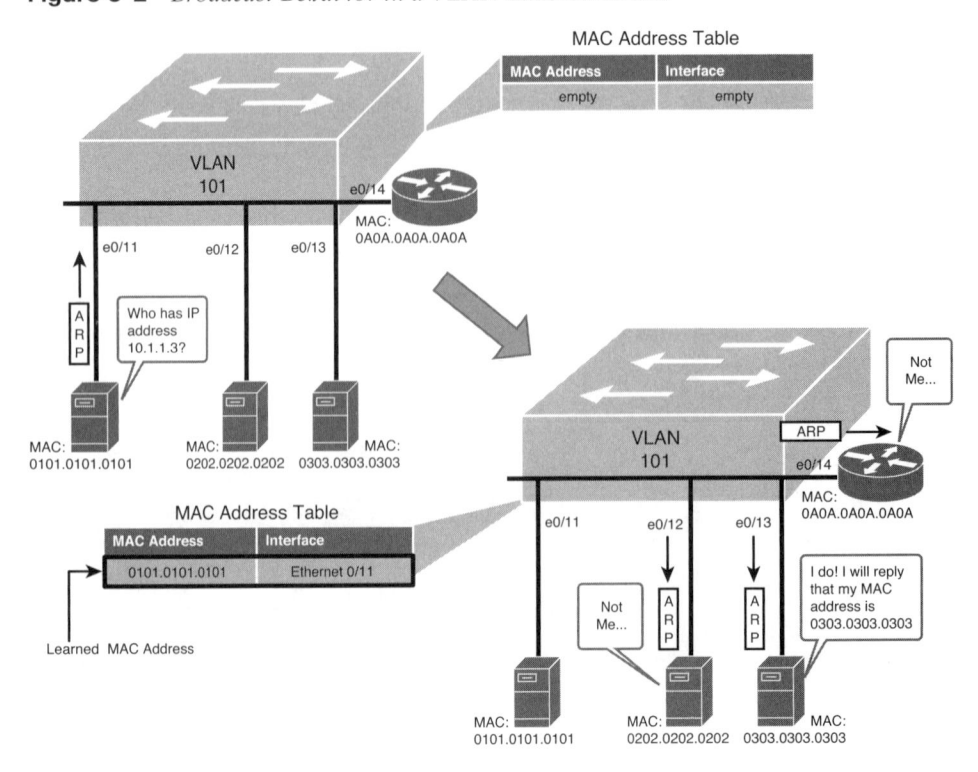

Figure 3-3 *ARP Request*

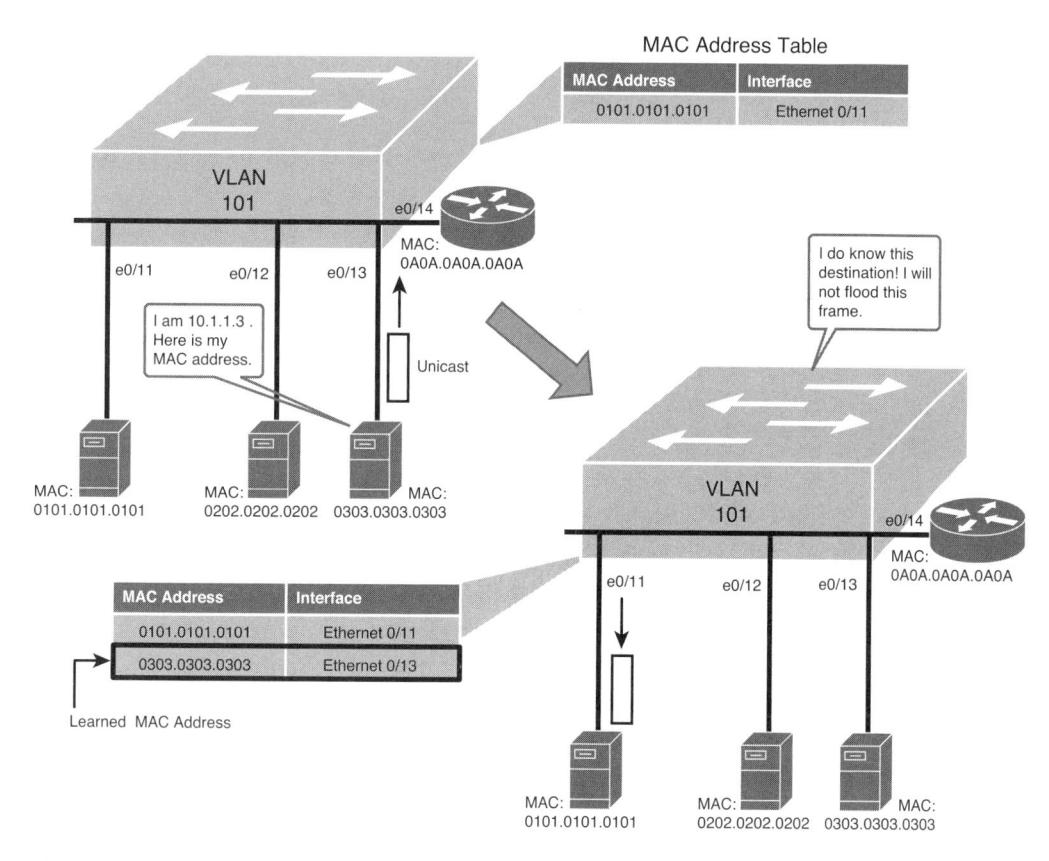

Figure 3-4 *ARP Response*

Figures 3-3 and 3-4 also portray the transparent MAC learning process in a switch, where entries are inserted in the MAC address table every time an unknown MAC address is detected as the source of an Ethernet frame (or a known MAC address is detected on a different interface). A new entry is maintained during a defined *aging time* interval (which is 300 seconds, by default, on Cisco switches) and is automatically deleted if other packets are not sent (and the timer is not restarted).

Other protocols, such as *Dynamic Host Configuration Protocol (DHCP)* and *Bootstrap Protocol (BOOTP)*, also rely on broadcast frames to function properly.

Similarly, flooding is a necessary behavior to allow a unicast frame to reach its destination host when a switch is not aware of the latter's MAC address. Whenever a MAC address table entry is aged and automatically deleted, a switch will always flood frames destined to this MAC address to assure that they will reach the "forgotten" host.

Caution Although they are required in the great majority of data center networks, excessive broadcast and flooding traffic can drastically reduce their performance. Based on my personal experience, I strongly advise you to dedicate special attention to broadcast- or flooding-based server load balance techniques. Even if they seem easy to deploy, their lack of scalability can be a very effective way to put a network out of service.

Because of its behavior, a VLAN is usually deployed to allow direct IP communication among a group of hosts, be they servers, routers, desktops, or any other Ethernet device. There are several methods to assign a frame to a VLAN:

Source interface

Source MAC address

Source IP address

Application (defined by TCP or UDP destination port)

By far, the most common VLAN assignment method is based on source interface. As a result, an *access port* can be defined as an interface whose transmitted and received frames belong to a single VLAN.

The creation of a VLAN and the configuration of an access port in the NX-OS network operating system, which is available on the entire Cisco Data Center switching portfolio, is detailed in Example 3-1.

Example 3-1 *VLAN Creation and Interface VLAN Assignment*

```
! Creating VLAN 101
N7K-Switch1(config)# vlan 101
N7K-Switch1(config-vlan)# name VLAN-Example
! Including port 11 from module 3 in VLAN 101
N7K-Switch1(config-vlan)# interface Ethernet 3/11
N7K-Switch1(config-if)# switchport
N7K-Switch1(config-if)# switchport mode access
N7K-Switch1(config-if)# switchport access vlan 101
! Enabling the interface
N7K-Switch1(config-if)# no shutdown
```

In Example 3-1, VLAN 101 was created with a name "VLAN-Example." Afterward, an Ethernet interface (port 11 from module 3) was configured as a Layer 2 (bridged) interface, an access port, included in VLAN 101, and finally enabled.

VLAN Trunks

A VLAN can be extended over multiple switches. But imagine if you could only use access ports to connect these VLANs over a pair of switches. In this scenario, you would need as many connections as the number of VLANs defined on the devices. And it is not very difficult to notice that this design can be extremely cumbersome when you are deploying a high number of VLANs.

VLAN trunks were created to transport multiple VLANs over a single Ethernet interface. In a trunk, two devices can recognize which VLAN each frame belongs to.

As an example, Figure 3-5 presents two VLAN trunks between three different switches.

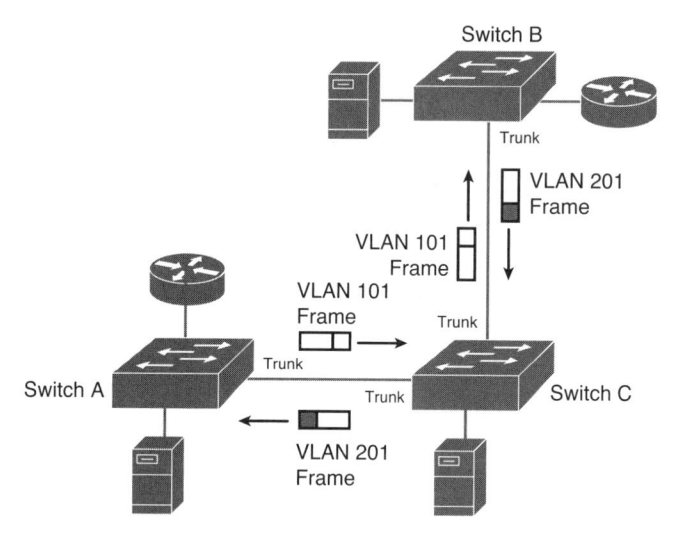

Figure 3-5 *VLAN Trunking Example*

In Figure 3-5, each pair of switches has only one Ethernet connection between them. In a trunk, each frame has a *tag* that contains a VLAN identifier. Therefore, it is possible for the receiving switch to recognize the VLAN a frame belongs to.

IEEE 802.1Q is the standard for this tag. Figure 3-6 details its structure and describes how a tagged frame is derived from a standard Ethernet frame.

The IEEE 802.1Q tag has four main fields:

- **Tag Protocol Identifier (TPI):** Set to the hexadecimal value of 8100. It assumes the function of the type/length field to identify the frame as an IEEE 802.1Q–tagged frame.

- **Priority Code Point (PCP):** Refers to the standard IEEE 802.1p. The field indicates a frame classification that can be used for the prioritization of traffic (classes of service 0 to 7).

- **Canonical Format Indicator (CFI):** Used for compatibility between Ethernet and legacy Layer 2 protocols such as Token Ring. It is always set to 0 for Ethernet switches.

- **VLAN Identifier (VLAN ID):** Represents the VLAN to which the frame belongs. Because the VLAN ID field has 12 bits, the IEEE tag theoretically allows the communication of 4096 VLANs.

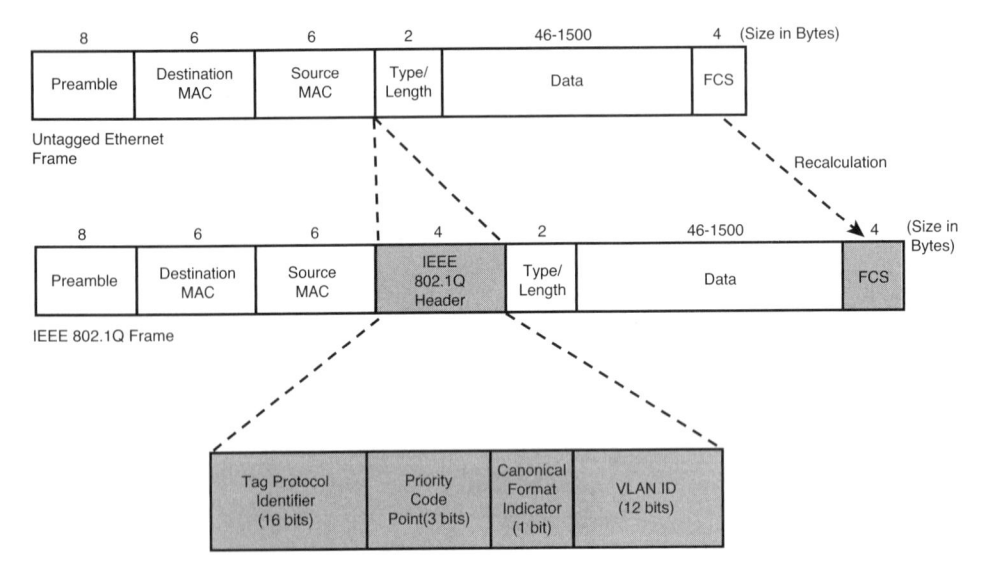

Figure 3-6 *IEEE 802.1Q VLAN Tagging*

Note There is a distinction between the range of VLAN IDs a switch can support and the maximum number of *active VLANs* that are supported simultaneously. However, even if a switch only supports a smaller number of active VLANs (64, for example), to avoid compatibility problems, it must be able to use any VLAN ID from the 0–4095 range.

It is common to refer to other devices that implement VLAN tagging as *VLAN-aware devices*. As an example, a VLAN-aware router can route IP packets between hosts located in different VLANs through a single Ethernet connection. This design, also known as "router-on-a-stick," is represented in Figure 3-7.

Hence, instead of multiple interfaces, it is possible for a router to dedicate one single interface, connected to a switch trunk port, to route IP packets between VLANs. In Figure 3-7, the router has one subinterface (GigabitEthernet 0/0.101) in VLAN 101 and another (GigabitEthernet 0/0.201) in VLAN 201. Each router subinterface has an IP address that can be configured as the default gateway on the servers connected in each VLAN.

Tip You can observe that Server 2 has two interfaces, each one connected to a different VLAN. With a VLAN-aware network interface card (NIC), this server could also deploy VLAN tagging and connect to both VLANs through a trunk port.

```
Router#show running-config interface GigabitEthernet 0/0.101
[output suppressed]
interface GigabitEthernet0/0.101
 encapsulation dot1Q 101
 ip address 10.1.1.100 255.255.255.0
end

Router#show running-config interface GigabitEthernet 0/0.201
[output suppressed]
interface GigabitEthernet0/0.201
 encapsulation dot1Q 201
 ip address 10.2.2.200 255.255.255.0
end
```

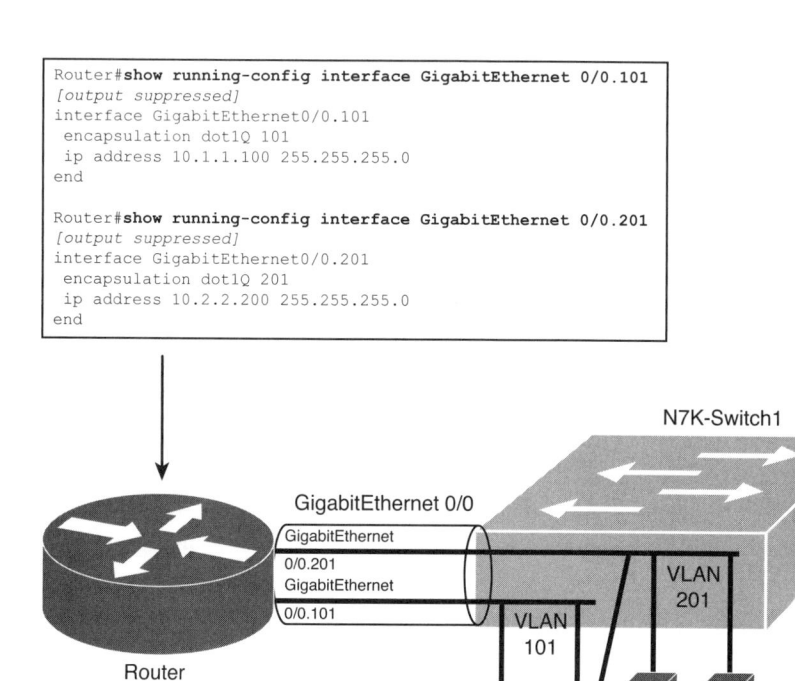

Figure 3-7 *"Router-on-a-Stick" Design for Inter-VLAN Communication*

Example 3-2 details the interface configuration of an NX-OS switch connected to the router in Figure 3-7.

Example 3-2 *Trunk Interface Configuration*

```
! Creating the VLANs 101 and 201 in the switch
N7K-Switch1(config)# vlan 101, 201
! Creating a Trunk Interface that only contains VLANs 101 and 201
N7K-Switch1(config-vlan)# interface ethernet 1/11
N7K-Switch1(config-if)# switchport
N7K-Switch1(config-if)# switchport mode trunk
N7K-Switch1(config-if)# switchport trunk allowed vlan 101,201
N7K-Switch1(config-if)# no shutdown
```

In Example 3-2, VLANs 101 and 201 were created and then allowed to use the Ethernet trunk interface 11 in module 1. If you want to indistinctively allow all VLANs to use this trunk, you can use the **switchport trunk allowed vlan all** command instead.

> **Tip** It is not required to define the interface trunk encapsulation method in NX-OS switches, because they no longer deploy the prestandard trunk protocol ISL (Inter-Switch Link). Other differences with IOS-based switches are further explored in Appendix B, "IOS, NX-OS, and ACE Control Software Command-Line Interface Basics."

Two Common Misconceptions About VLANs

At the time of this writing, VLANs have almost 30 years of existence. Consequently, it became quite usual for network administrators to assume that some common practices were the only way to deploy VLANs.

However, common sense can be a dangerous trap (especially if basic concepts are not taken into account). My objective in the following sections is to discuss two VLAN "dogmas" that many times introduce unnecessary confusion in data center network designs.

Misconception Number 1: A VLAN Must Be Associated to an IP Subnet

This is a common oversight from network rookies, and it is fairly easy to understand why. Because a VLAN defines a broadcast domain, it is intuitive that hosts connected to this VLAN will discover each other using broadcast-based mechanisms such as ARP (as shown in the earlier section "Defining VLANs"). In this way, common sense dictates that each VLAN should be associated to an IP subnet.

Although this one-to-one relationship between VLANs and subnets can be a good fit for simple campus and data center networks, it is not the only option. As a counterpoint to this affinity, it is technically possible for two subnets to share the same VLAN, as shown in Figure 3-8.

In Figure 3-8, direct IP communication occurs among hosts that belong to each IP subnet. Nevertheless, because they share the same VLAN, every host receives all broadcast and flooded frames from both subnets.

Even if this is not a typical design, it can be helpful if it is difficult to change a device IP address or to deploy more VLANs in an application environment, such as in a service provider–managed network.

On the other hand, the scenario where two VLANs share an IP subnet is much more frequent in data centers. If you are asking what is the real advantage of transforming two broadcast domains into one, Figure 3-9 is the key for that answer.

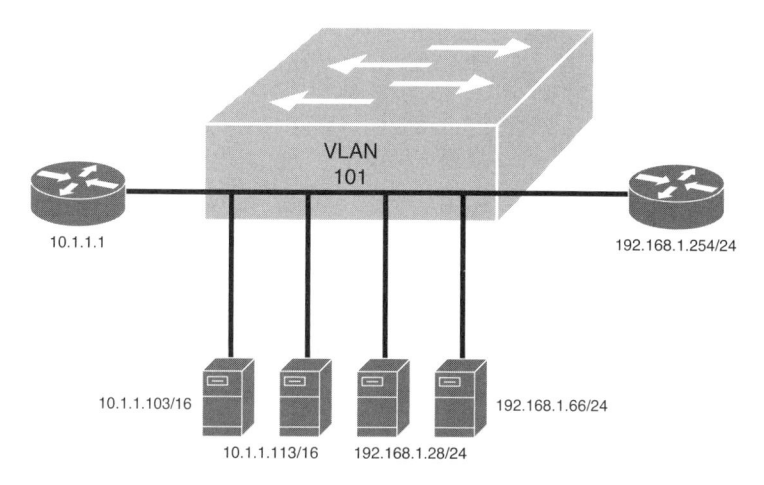

Figure 3-8 *Two IP Subnets Sharing a VLAN*

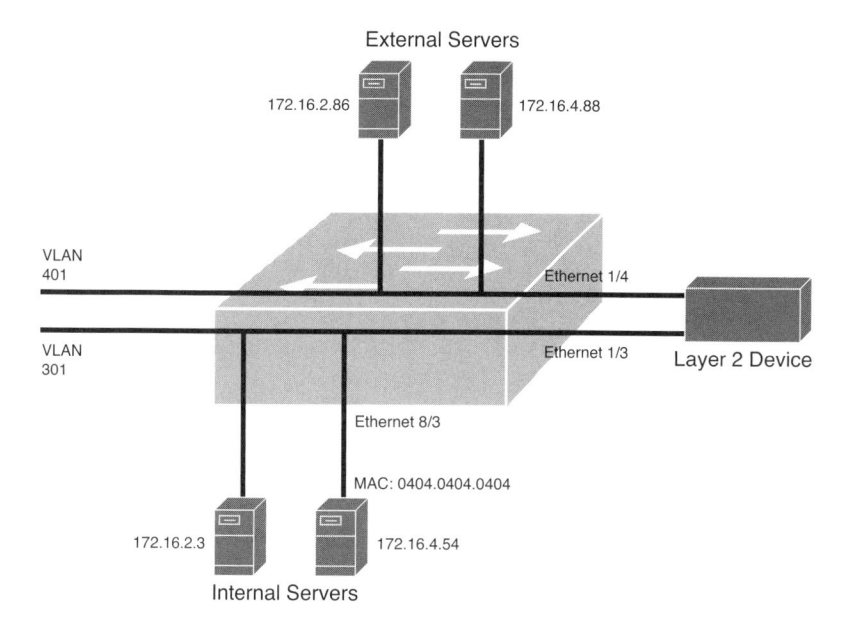

Figure 3-9 *Two VLANs Sharing a Subnet*

Using a real-world scenario example: Suppose that you want to position a Layer 2 device to deploy a special operation on traffic between two groups of hosts that belong to the same subnet (for example, internal and external servers). If these groups are configured as distinct VLANs, the Layer 2 device can be used to *bridge* both VLANs in a single broadcast domain. Therefore, traffic between both VLANs is forced to traverse the Layer 2 device, because it is the only bridging path available.

In Figure 3-9, Ethernet communication happens normally among hosts from both VLANs with one exception: Each MAC address appears twice in the switch MAC address table, once in each VLAN. For example, MAC 0404.0404.0404 exists in VLAN 301 in interface Ethernet 8/3 and in VLAN 401 in the interface connected to the Layer 2 device (Ethernet 1/4).

This design can be extremely useful if you want to deploy operations such as traffic analysis, acceleration, content security, and load balancing in a Layer 2 server environment. In fact, you will see it applied thoroughly in Chapter 4, "An Army of One: ACE Virtual Contexts."

Please notice one important achievement from this scenario: If originally all the hosts belonged to the same VLAN (301, for example), the Layer 2 device deployment would only require logical configurations to work properly. In this case, two configurations are needed: VLAN 401 creation and its assignment to the external server interfaces.

As a result, VLANs also bring the advantage of traffic manipulation without the deployment of additional switches or recabling.

Misconception Number 2: Layer 3 VLANs

In my opinion, the marketing pitch of *Layer 3 switches* caused this conceptual error in the minds of lots of network designers. To understand why that happened, allow me to define these devices first.

An evolution from the "router-on-a-stick" design (explained in the earlier section "VLAN Trunks"), a Layer 3 switch is network equipment that can implement hardware-based Layer 2 switching *and Layer 3 forwarding*. Cisco Layer 3 switches can deploy routing through one logical interface called *Switch Virtual Interface (SVI)*, represented in Figure 3-10.

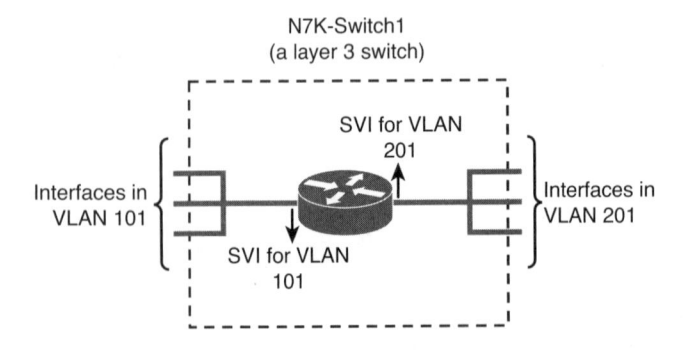

Figure 3-10 *Layer 3 Switches and Switch Virtual Interfaces*

An SVI is a virtual interface that can be used to route IP packets from its associated VLAN. Just like an interface on a router, you can assign an IP address to an SVI and use it as the default gateway for the servers that belong to the VLAN.

> **Note** You can also assign an IP address to each interface in a Layer 3 switch (which is called a *routed port*), exactly like you would do in a router. However, there are several advantages in using SVIs instead of routed ports, as I will illustrate in the remaining sections of this chapter.

Example 3-3 shows the SVI configuration in the Nexus 7000 switch depicted in Figure 3-10. This example also hints at the main cause of the misconception described in this section.

Example 3-3 *Switch Virtual Interface Configuration*

```
N7K-Switch1(config)# vlan 101,201
! Enabling the creation of SVIs
N7K-Switch1(config-vlan)# feature interface-vlan
! Creating SVI for VLAN 101
N7K-Switch1(config)# interface vlan 101
N7K-Switch1(config-if)# ip address 10.1.1.1/24
N7K-Switch1(config-if)# no shutdown
! Creating SVI for VLAN 201
N7K-Switch1(config-if)# interface vlan 201
N7K-Switch1(config-if)# ip address 10.2.1.3/24
N7K-Switch1(config-if)# no shutdown
```

> **Tip** Because NX-OS is a modular operating system, some features (such as SVI) must be enabled before its use through the **feature** command. Refer to Appendix B for more details.

In Example 3-3, two SVIs (for VLANs 101 and 201) were created using the **interface vlan** command. However, both VLANs continue to behave exactly in the same way as before. The only difference is that the switch can now provide IP routing to the hosts connected to these VLANs, without the need of an external router. Unfortunately, there was a time when this simple condition was sold as a marketing feature called "Layer 3 VLAN," and because of it, lots of confusion followed.

> **Note** By default in Nexus switches, all created SVIs receive the same MAC address (a special one called *switch MAC address*). Although such behavior assures address uniqueness in each VLAN, you should be aware that it might cause some connectivity problems when two or more VLANs are merged into a single broadcast domain. Nonetheless, if required, it is quite possible to change this assigned SVI MAC address with the **mac** interface configuration command.

Nevertheless, SVIs are an extremely useful feature in data centers and campus networks. Besides its configuration simplicity, an SVI can also react to specific VLAN situations. For example, a feature called *autostate* can define the operational state of an SVI in a Cisco Layer 3 switch.

By default, an SVI will only show as "up" if two conditions happen simultaneously:

- Its associated VLAN exists.
- There is at least one active (access or trunk) port in this VLAN.

Example 3-4 demonstrates autostate for a new VLAN created in the same switch.

Example 3-4 *Autostate Feature for VLAN 501 SVI*

```
! Creating SVI for VLAN 501
N7K-Switch1(config)# interface vlan 501
N7K-Switch1(config-if)# ip address 192.168.5.1/24
N7K-Switch1(config-if)# no shutdown
! SVI is down because VLAN 501 does not exist yet
N7K-Switch1(config-if)# show interface vlan 501 brief

Interface  Secondary VLAN(Type)      Status Reason
--------------------------------------------------------------
Vlan501    --                        down   VLAN does not exist
N7K-Switch1(config-if)# exit
! Creating VLAN 501
N7K-Switch1(config)# vlan 501
N7K-Switch1(config-vlan)# show interface vlan 501 brief


--------------------------------------------------------------
Interface  Secondary VLAN(Type)      Status Reason
--------------------------------------------------------------
Vlan501    --                        down   VLAN is down
! Including an Interface to VLAN 501
N7K-Switch1(config-vlan)# interface Ethernet 3/11
N7K-Switch1(config-if)# switchport
N7K-Switch1(config-if)# switchport mode access
N7K-Switch1(config-if)# switchport access vlan 501
```

```
N7K-Switch1(config-if)# no shutdown
! Verifying SVI state
N7K-Switch1(config-if)# show interface vlan 501 brief

-------------------------------------------------------------------
Interface  Secondary VLAN(Type)          Status  Reason
-------------------------------------------------------------------
Vlan501    --                            up      --
```

Note You can exclude an interface from the autostate computation set through the **switchport autostate exclude** Nexus 7000 command. If you configure this command in Ethernet 3/11 from Example 3-4, VLAN 501 would go to the "down" status again.

Spanning Tree Protocol and VLANs

Any connectivity media is susceptible to failures, be they human-related or not (actually I know an organization whose main network problem was caused by rats). Therefore, it is only natural that network designers would want to define redundant paths in critical networks.

However, in classical Ethernet networks, if two or more paths between two hosts are active at the same time, an unfortunate effect known as *loop* can happen.

As an example, Figure 3-11 details how a loop can be formed in an Ethernet switched network that receives a single broadcast frame.

The switch's behavior for broadcast frames ("*always forward a broadcast frame to every Ethernet interface except the one that received it*") basically provokes the loop. In a few microseconds, as Steps 2, 3, and 4 happen continuously, the loop can consume all available bandwidth, and no other traffic is able to use the network.

Note An Ethernet frame with an unknown destination MAC address can also cause a loop in such topology. In this scenario, the switches could flood the frame indefinitely with similar results.

Unlike IP packets, Ethernet frames do not have a *Time-to-Live (TTL)* header field, which would be decreased each time it traversed a switch. Because of that characteristic, a broadcast or flooded Ethernet frame can be forwarded indefinitely within a loop, until a manual intervention is performed.

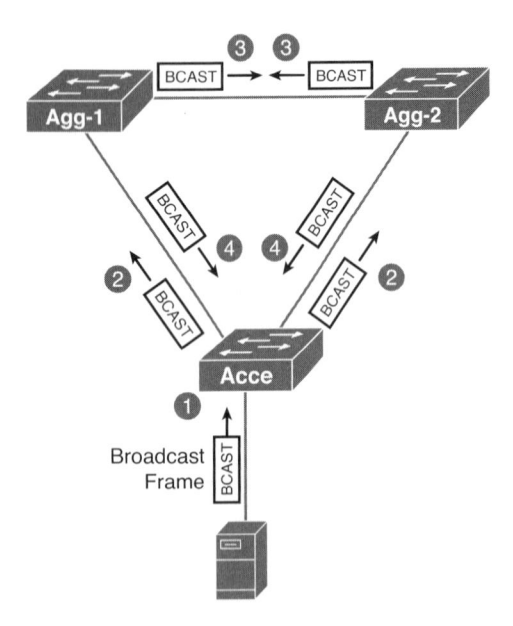

Figure 3-11 *Broadcast Loop in an Ethernet Network*

To prevent loops, and still remain available in the case of a connection failure, an Ethernet network can deploy one of the versions of the *Spanning Tree Protocol (STP)*. Created in the 1980s by Radia Pearlman (also known as the "mother of the Internet"), STP detects loops in a bridged network and blocks traffic in chosen ports to form a loopless logical topology defined by *spanning tree*. In 1990, this protocol was ratified in the IEEE 802.1D standard.

Figure 3-12 depicts the objective of STP in a fully meshed Ethernet network (where there are multiple opportunities for loop formation).

By definition, a spanning tree topology does not allow the formation of loops because

There is a *root bridge* (or switch) from which the active paths will be formed.

The other switches can only have one active connection toward the root.

Hence, if all switches deploy the same STP version, they will communicate with each other to form such a topology. This process is called *convergence*, and it lasts until all switches agree on a single stable spanning tree. Afterward, if an active connection fails or if there is a change in the topology, a new spanning tree must be calculated and a *reconvergence* happens.

Ethernet switches usually have STP enabled by default. And that might be the reason why not enough network engineers bother to understand this protocol (at least until a problem occurs). Experienced network architects know that a good Ethernet design must always plan the expected STP behavior. If no concern is given to this important protocol, a network can be vulnerable to suboptimal spanning trees and outages.

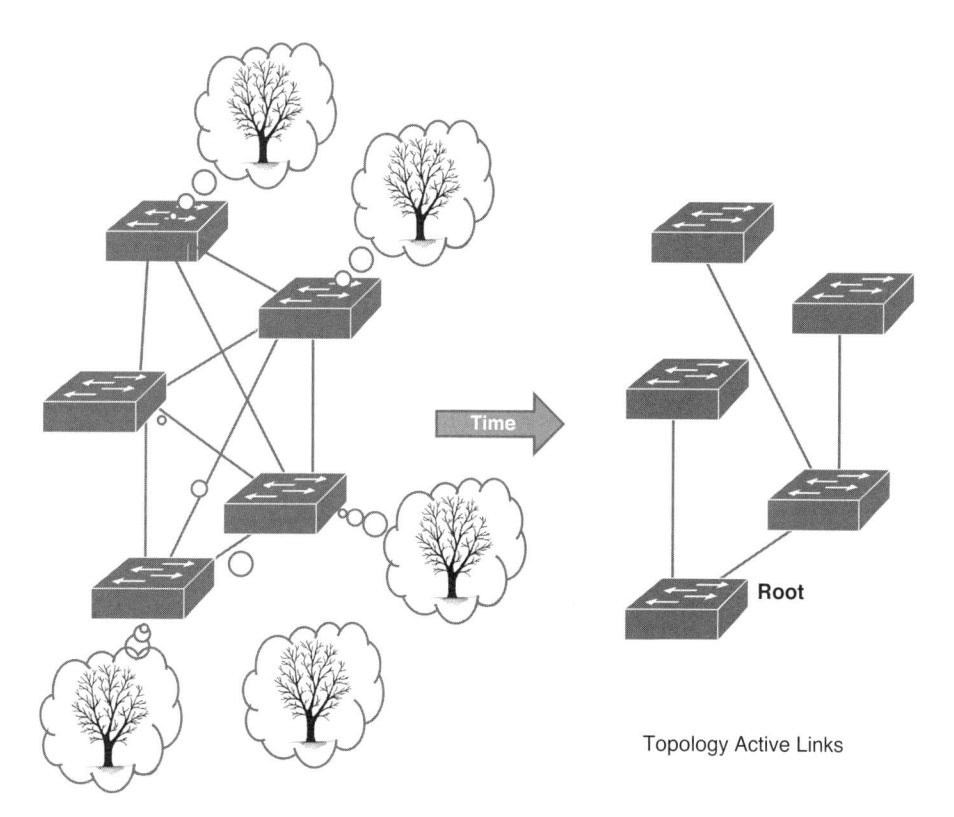

Figure 3-12 *Spanning Tree Protocol in Action*

Spanning Tree Protocol is already the subject of several technical books. And in my opinion, its variations, implementation details, and intricacies really deserve the attention. However, this chapter will only explore basic concepts and mechanisms from this protocol and, mainly, its relation to VLANs.

You can also find more information about Spanning Tree Protocols in Chapter 6, "Fooling Spanning Tree," and Chapter 8, "A Tale of Two Data Centers." These chapters will describe the risks and challenges modern data centers face when dealing with STP, as well as virtualization techniques that can lessen these risks and help solve these challenges.

Spanning Tree Protocol at Work

First, as in classical Greek drama, you will meet the characters from a theater play called "Spanning Tree Formation." And by characters, I mean STP identifiers and parameters that must be present in standard Ethernet switches.

Each STP switch has a *bridge ID* that is defined by the concatenation of the following parameters (from most to least significant) for NX-OS switches:

- **Bridge Priority** (4 bits): Defines a value, which is a multiple of 4096 (from 0 to 61440). The default Bridge Priority is 32768.

- **Extended System ID** (12 bits): It is used to distinguish different bridge IDs in distinct *STP instances* present in the same switch. This identifier was defined in the IEEE 802.1t standard.

> **Note** Yes, a switch can have more than one STP instance! I will explain this concept further in the section "Spanning Tree Instances," later in this chapter.

- **Switch MAC Address** (6 bytes): A MAC address that represents the switch in all STP instances. It is usually generated by the switch supervisor or derived from the switch chassis.

Path cost is another identifier that influences how a spanning tree topology is calculated. On STP, the path with the lowest total cost to the root is considered the best one. And, to differentiate Ethernet connections with different speeds, IEEE defined the values shown in Table 3-2.

Table 3-2 *Default Path Cost for Switches*

Bandwidth	Short-Path Cost Method	Long-Path Cost Method
10 Mbps	100	2,000,000
100 Mbps	19	200,000
1 Gbps	4	20,000
10 Gbps	2	2000
40 Gbps	1	500
100 Gbps	1	200

As you can see, there are two methods for cost value assignment:

- **Short:** These were defined in the original version of Spanning Tree and cannot differentiate speeds that are higher than 20 Gbps.

- **Long:** These were created to solve the limitation from the short method. They were defined in the standard IEEE 802.1t and can be calculated if you divide 20 Tbps by the connection bandwidth (in bits per second).

> **Tip** In STP implementations, Nexus switches use short-path cost as their default method.

Additionally, each switch interface owns an identifier called *port ID*, which is mapped to the interface naming order (Ethernet 1/1, Ethernet 1/2, and so on). Port ID is formed by the concatenation of the following parameters (from most to least significant):

- **Port Priority** (6 bits): This is a user-configurable parameter among the values of 0, 32, 64, 96, 128 (default), 160, 192, or 224.

- **Port Index** (10 bits): This is assigned according to the interface order in a switch. As an example, a Nexus 5000 switch uses 129 for interface Ethernet 1/1, 130 for Ethernet 1/2, and 131 for Ethernet 1/3.

All these identifiers are inserted into *bridge protocol data unit (BPDU)* frames. BPDUs are sent to connected switches every 2 seconds, if the switch is using the default value for the STP *Hello timer*. A sample BPDU is represented in Figure 3-13.

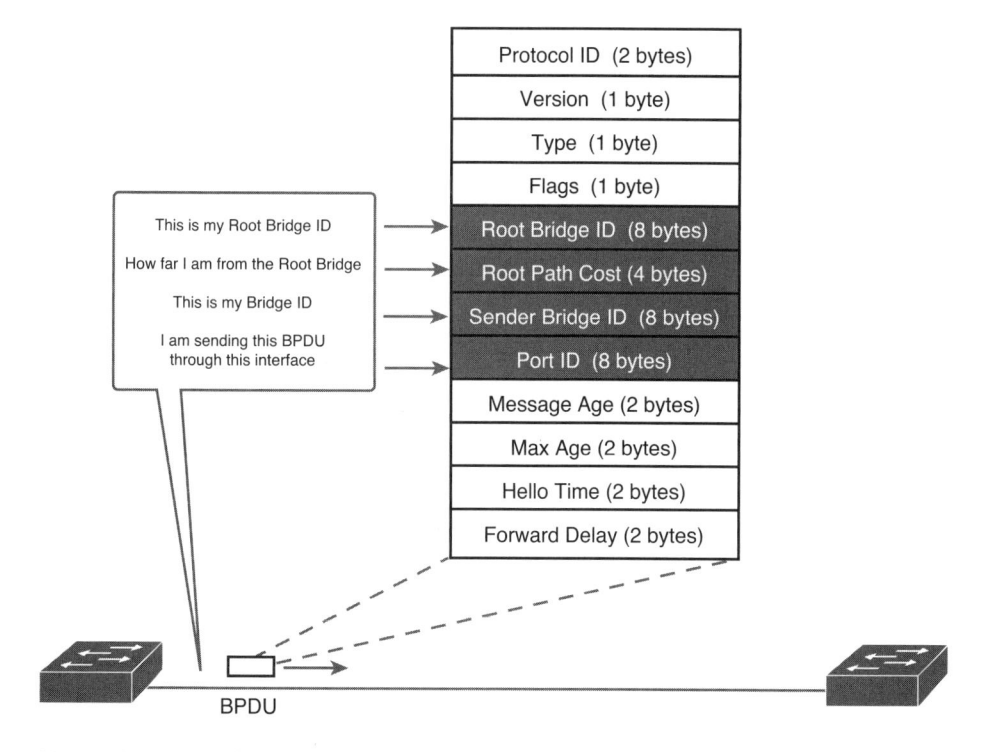

Figure 3-13 *Bridge Protocol Data Unit*

Note BPDU frames are sent with MAC address 0180.c200.0000 as the destination and a unique port MAC address as the source.

An STP switch must always compare BPDUs, be they received from other switches or generated by itself. Therefore, in different situations, a switch will select the "best" BPDU according to the following decision sequence (also known, informally, as the "BPDU death match"):

Lowest root bridge ID

Lowest path cost to root bridge

Lowest sender bridge ID

Lowest port ID

> **Tip** From now on, I will refer to a BPDU as *superior* when it contains a lower root bridge ID, a lower path cost, a lower bridge ID, or a lower port ID, when compared to an "inferior" BPDU.

With these definitions, it is time to know how the characters from our theater play interact with each other.

There are three clear phases that define Spanning Tree Protocol convergence, as Radia Pearlman described in her lovely *Algorhyme* poem:

I think that I shall never see

A graph more lovely than a tree.

A tree whose crucial property

Is loop-free connectivity.

A tree that must be sure to span

So packets can reach every LAN.

First, the root must be selected.

By ID, it is elected.

Least-cost paths from root are traced.

In the tree, these paths are placed.

A mesh is made by folks like me,

Then bridges find a spanning tree.

(*"An Algorithm for Distributed Computation of a Spanning Tree in an Extended LAN"* ©1985 Association for Computing Machinery, Inc. Reprinted by permission.)

The first convergence phase is called **Root Selection** (*"First, the root must be selected"*). Its objective is to choose one switch (or bridge) from which the spanning tree will grow.

When a switch is turned on, because it is not aware of any other Ethernet device, it considers itself (in a very lonely statement) as the root of a single switch network. After it starts to exchange BPDUs with other connected switches, it is expected that the switch with the lowest bridge ID is elected as the root of the network spanning tree.

> **Note** As a prize for its undeniable victory, the root switch has the right to have all its ports active in the future topology.

As an illustration for the STP convergence process, I will use three connected Gigabit Ethernet switches:

- Switch A (bridge ID 32768.1.aaaa.aaaa.aaaa) using interfaces Ethernet 1/1 and 1/4
- Switch B (bridge ID 32768.1.bbbb.bbbb.bbbb) using interfaces Ethernet 1/2 and 1/5
- Switch C (bridge ID 32768.1.cccc.cccc.cccc) using interfaces Ethernet 1/3 and 1/6

Figure 3-14 deals with the Root Selection phase for this network.

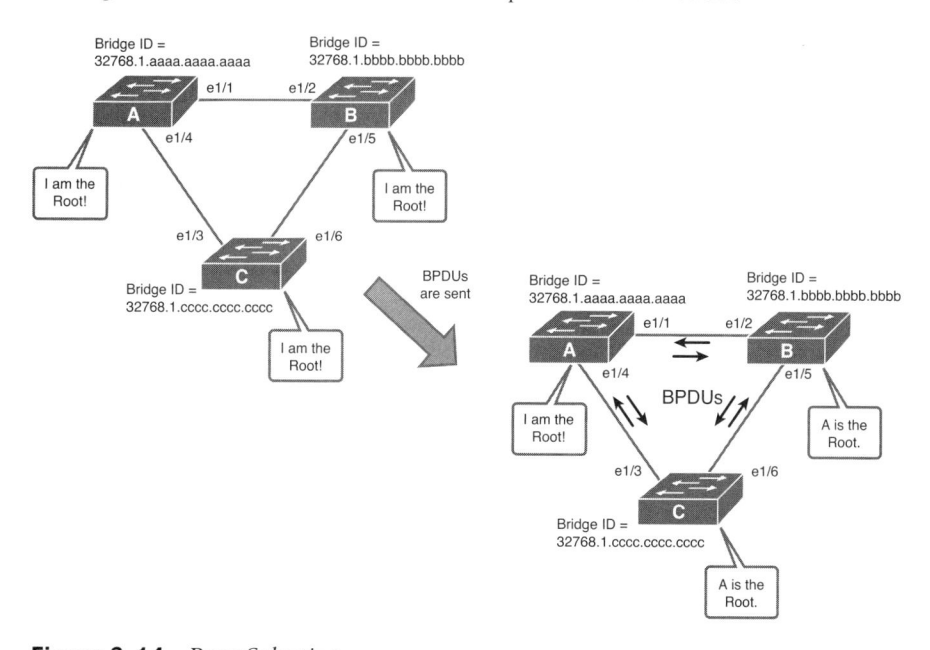

Figure 3-14 *Root Selection*

When switches A, B, and C start to exchange BPDUs, they discover that other switches are present in the network. In Figure 3-14, switches B and C learn that switch A has the lowest bridge ID for the entire network, and both of them recognize switch A as the root. After this common agreement, all switches from this network start to transmit BPDUs with the root bridge ID set to 32768.1.aaaa.aaaa.aaaa.

A phase called **Root Port Selection** (*"Least-cost paths from root are traced"*) begins immediately after the root is selected. In this phase, every nonroot switch in the network must choose a single interface that is "closer" to the root switch. This interface is called *root port*, and it is defined by the interface that receives the superior BPDU based on the "BPDU death match" decision process.

Figure 3-15 shows how the Root Port Selection phase happens in the same three-switch topology.

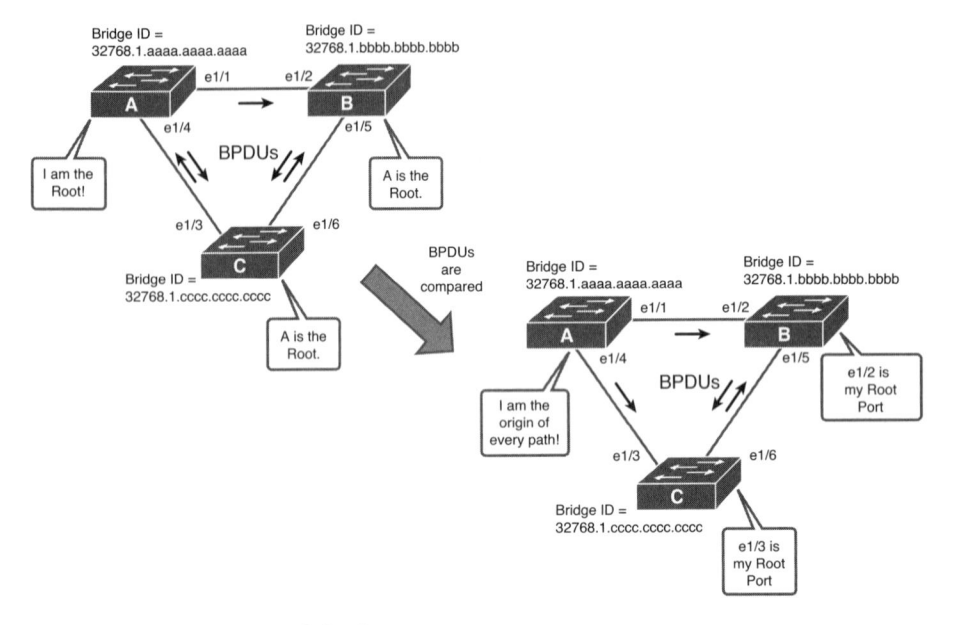

Figure 3-15 *Root Port Selection*

In Figure 3-15, switches B and C compare the received BPDUs to choose a single interface "closer" to the root. Using the short method for path cost, switch B elects interface Ethernet 1/2 (path cost is 4 because it uses a Gigabit Ethernet connection) and switch C elects interface Ethernet 1/3 (path cost is also 4).

Tip Interface Ethernet 1/5 on switch B was not selected as a root port because it has a cost of 8 to the root. The same happens to interface Ethernet 1/6 on switch C.

The last phase is called **Designated Ports Selection** (*"In the tree, these paths are placed"*). In STP, when several bridges are connected to the same segment, only one non-root interface must be allowed to transmit and receive Ethernet frames. This special interface is called the *designated port*, and all the other ports in the segment must be forbidden to receive and transmit Ethernet frames, and therefore, are defined in STP as *blocked*.

> **Tip** Switched Ethernet networks do not possess segments that are shared by more than two devices. Therefore, in modern networks, you can expect one of the following situations in each switch connection: a root port connected to a designated port, or a designated port connected to a blocked port.

Figure 3-16 represents the Designated Ports Election phase in the sample three-switch topology.

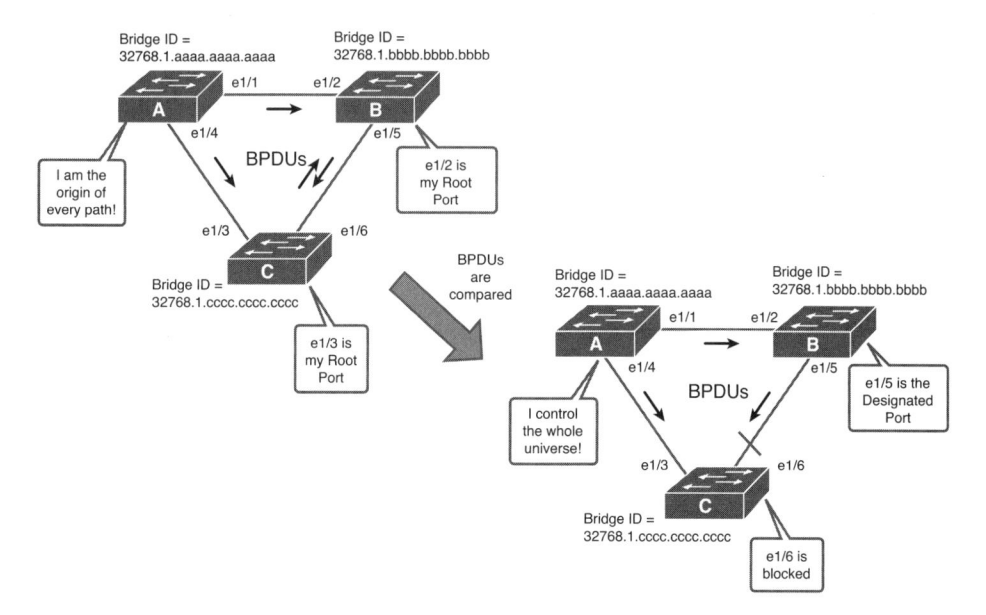

Figure 3-16 *Designated Port Selection*

In this figure, all nonroot switches must decide which ports will be blocked in each segment. Because segments A-B and A-C have root ports, only segment B-C must block an interface. Which port will be designated for this segment will be chosen through the same "BPDU death match" process between switches B and C. In the scenario:

Both switches have the same root bridge ID (32678.1.aaaa.aaaa.aaaa).

Both switches have the same path cost to the root (4).

Switch B has a lower bridge ID (32678.1.bbbb.bbbb.bbbb) than switch C (32678.1.cccc.ccccc.cccc). The tie is broken.

Interface Ethernet 1/5 on switch B is the designated port for segment B-C. As a result, switch C recognizes the superior BPDU switch B is sending, stops sending its inferior BPDU, and politely blocks port Ethernet 1/6.

And, at the end of our play, *"the bridges find a spanning tree."*

Port States

To avoid loops during the formation of the spanning tree, standard root and designated ports are not immediately allowed to forward data frames. Actually, these ports are forced to spend some time in intermediary states.

Figure 3-17 depicts the transition process for the five port states originally defined for STP.

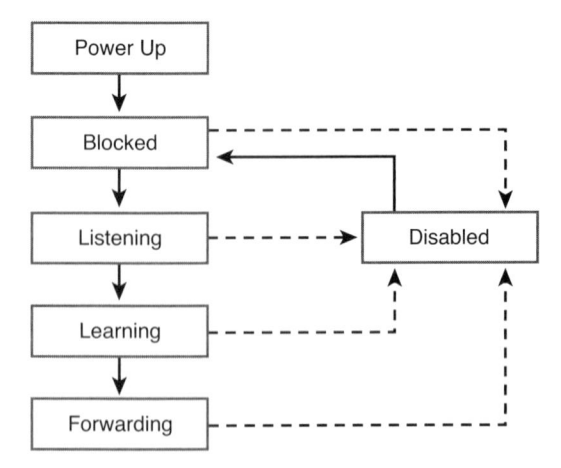

Figure 3-17 *Spanning Tree Port State Transition Process*

Each STP port state can be defined by some distinctive characteristics:

- **Disabled:** The interface is not operational. It can be reached from any other state with the **shutdown** command (dashed arrows in the figure). In this state, the interface does not receive or forward any traffic.

- **Blocked:** The port does not send Ethernet frames and does not learn any MAC addresses. It does process BPDUs sent by connected devices. If STP determines that a blocked port must forward traffic (root or designated port), it will spend the time defined by the Max Age timer (20 seconds by default) and transition to the next state (listening).

- **Listening:** The interface does not send any Ethernet traffic and does not learn any MAC addresses, but it can send BPDUs. The port remains at this state, and if it still deserves to have a transition from the blocked state, it will go to the next state in the time defined in the Forward Delay timer (15 seconds by default).

- **Learning:** In this state, the port can populate the switch MAC address table with detected source addresses. After an interval also defined by the Forward Delay timer, the port transitions to the next state.

- **Forwarding:** Now the interface can transmit and receive Ethernet frames. Root and designated ports remain in this state.

During the convergence processes illustrated in Figures 3-14, 3-15, and 3-16, almost all interfaces transitioned from disabled to forwarding state (passing through the blocked, listening, and learning intermediary states). Only interface Ethernet 1/6 transitioned from the disabled state and remained in the blocked state.

A spanning tree should remain stable until a topology change happens. A connection failure, new connected switch, or change in a STP parameter (Bridge Priority, for example) can provoke such change.

As an example, I will use Figure 3-18 to illustrate how STP builds a new spanning tree around a link failure.

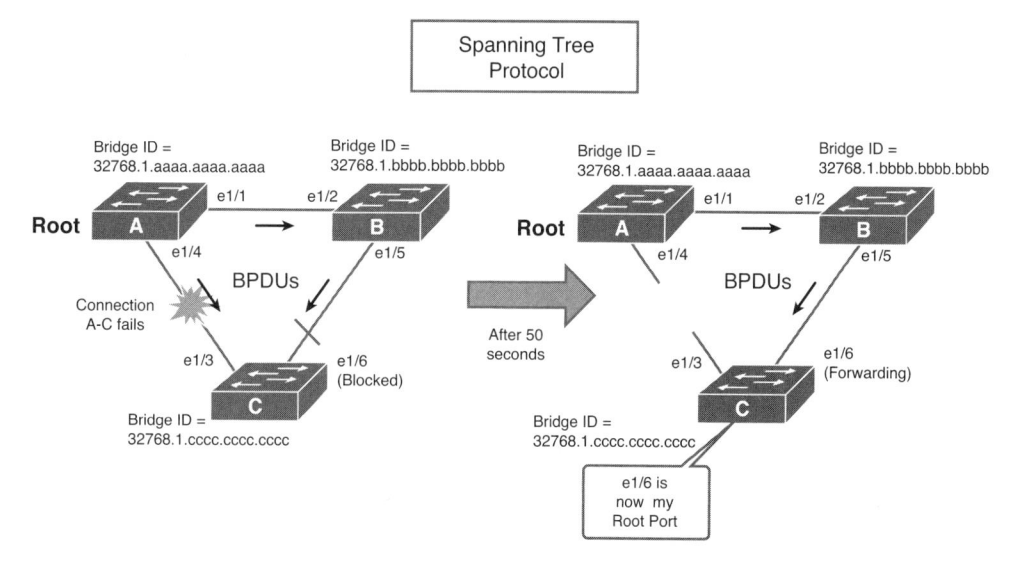

Figure 3-18 *Spanning Tree Behavior with Link Failure*

In Figure 3-18, switch C detects the topology change because the failure happened in one of its interfaces. This failure can be detected in two ways: through signal loss at the physical level or through missing BPDU information for 20 seconds (which the default value for the Max Age timer).

If this failure is detected through signal loss, and with default STP timer values, the following behavior is expected in the topology:

> Switch C immediately invalidates the stored BPDU in Ethernet 1/3 and, therefore, loses its root information.
>
> Switch C declares itself as a new root and starts to send inferior BPDUs to switch B. However, switch C will also receive superior BPDUs from switch B.

After 20 seconds (Max Age timer), switch C decides that Ethernet 1/6 must become its new root port.

Interface Ethernet 1/6 on switch C transitions from the blocked to forwarding state in 30 seconds (15 seconds in listening state plus 15 seconds in learning).

Therefore, as a reaction to a link failure, interface Ethernet 1/6 on switch C will become active after 50 seconds!

Caution Deliberate changes in STP timer values can cause network instabilities, CPU peaks, and application outages.

Spanning Tree Protocol Enhancements

As you have learned, a topology change in the spanning tree can represent almost one minute without traffic in an Ethernet network. Knowing that this behavior is unbearable for most modern applications (after all, it is sufficient to destroy all TCP-established connections that use this network), Cisco and other switch manufacturers began to work on proprietary STP enhancements. Afterward, these collected efforts were amalgamated in an evolution of STP called *Rapid Spanning Tree Protocol (RSTP)*.

Note RSTP was ratified in standard IEEE 802.1w and incorporated to IEEE 802.1D in 2004.

RSTP convergence executes all the phases described in the earlier section "Spanning Tree Protocol at Work" and even uses the same identifiers from legacy STP. However, RSTP deploys a series of enhancements and *rapid transition mechanisms* that allow a much faster convergence when compared to STP.

RSTP switch interfaces can have different behaviors. Actually, the protocol classifies Ethernet ports in different three types:

- **Edge-ports:** Interfaces connected to end stations or servers that cannot create bridging loops in the network. Therefore, they will not generate topology changes when the link fails or activates. An edge-port can skip the listening and learning states and transition directly to the forwarding state. This port should not receive any BPDUs.

Note Older network professionals might recognize this concept as the Cisco-proprietary STP enhancement called *PortFast*.

- **Point-to-Point:** Ports that connect two switches and are configured in full-duplex. They can deploy RSTP rapid transitions.

- **Shared:** Interfaces that connect more than two switches or are configured in half-duplex. They operate in legacy STP, and because of that, cannot deploy RSTP rapid transitions.

Furthermore, RSTP deploys a complete distinction between a port role and a port state. *Port role* refers to the stable function of a port in an active topology. Two new roles were created to replace the blocked port function from legacy STP: *backup* and *alternate*.

In summary, RSTP has five port roles. They are as follows:

- **Root:** Provides the lowest-cost path to the root switch (similar to STP).
- **Designated:** A nonroot port that is allowed to transmit and receive traffic in a segment (similar to STP).
- **Backup:** Blocked ports that receive a superior BPDU from another port on the *same switch*.
- **Alternate:** Blocked ports that receive a superior BPDU from *another switch* in the same segment. An alternate port can replace the root port in case the last one fails.
- **Disabled:** Does not participate in the spanning tree process.

The condition of a switch interface, according to its capacity to receive and transmit frames, defines its *port state*. RSTP port states are very similar to STP states with one exception: In RSTP, the disabled, blocking, and listening states were merged into a single state called *discarding*.

Instead of uniquely relying on timers for its transition decisions, RSTP enhancements include fast-transition negotiation mechanisms such as sync operations, BPDU handling, and MAC address table flushing with topology changes.

The complete description for these mechanisms is beyond the scope of this book; nevertheless, you can see RSTP in action in Figure 3-19.

In Figure 3-19, all the switches now deploy Rapid Spanning Tree Protocol. Before the link failure, they have formed a spanning tree topology where switch A is the root (after all, it has the lowest bridge ID) and links A-B and A-C are active.

When the connection between switches A and C fails, because interface Ethernet 1/6 on switch C is an alternate port, it will *almost immediately* become the root port. This happens because RSTP switches can store and process not only the "best" received BPDU but also information about other path alternatives that can be used quickly in the case of a topology change.

Tip Again, more experienced network specialists will recognize this behavior as a pre-RSTP Cisco-proprietary feature called *UplinkFast*.

74 Data Center Virtualization Fundamentals

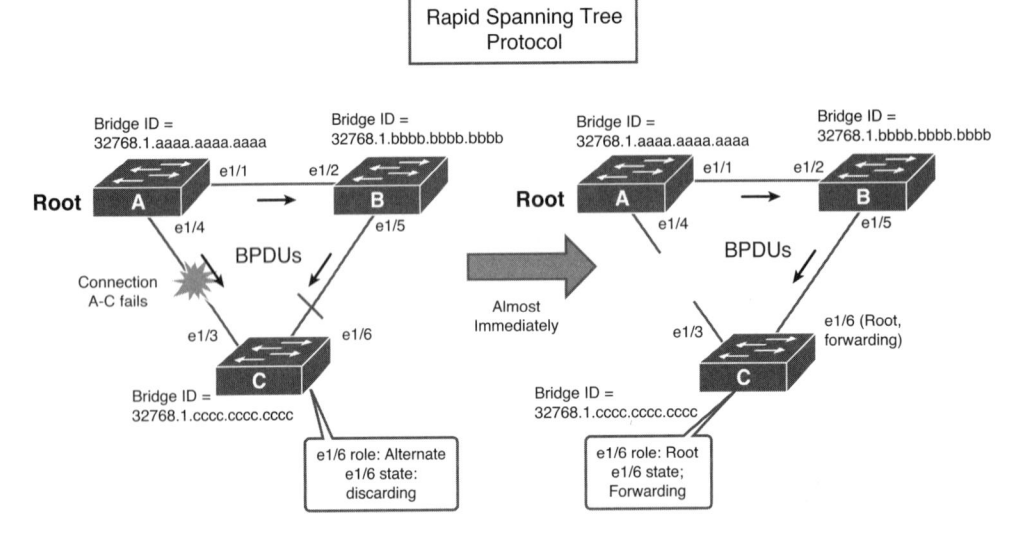

Figure 3-19 *Rapid Spanning Tree Behavior with Link Failure*

Spanning Tree Instances

When VLANs started to become popular, Cisco developed a special way to implement STP in its switches. Increasing the independence on these network partitions, by default, each VLAN owned a completely distinct spanning tree instance. This deployment method was called Per VLAN Spanning Tree (PVST), and its IEEE 802.1Q–compatible version, *Per VLAN Spanning Tree Plus (PVST+)*.

Later, after the creation of RSTP, Cisco developed *Rapid Per VLAN Spanning Tree Plus (Rapid PVST+)*, where each VLAN possesses a distinct RSTP instance.

In Rapid PVST+, the VLAN ID is part of the BPDUs, and the receiving switch is capable of differentiating BPDUs that belong to different RSTP instances. The VLAN ID is also copied to the Extended System identifier in the bridge ID, allowing each switch to have a complete distinct bridge ID per VLAN.

As an illustration, Figure 3-20 represents our familiar triad of switches deploying different RSTP instances for VLANs 11 and 21.

In Figure 3-20, the spanning tree instances for each VLAN have different root switches. This was achieved through a change in the Bridge Priority in switches A and B for VLANs 11 and 21, respectively. More specifically, I have used the following global configuration commands:

- **spanning-tree vlan 11 priority 4096** in switch A
- **spanning-tree vlan 21 priority 4096** in switch B

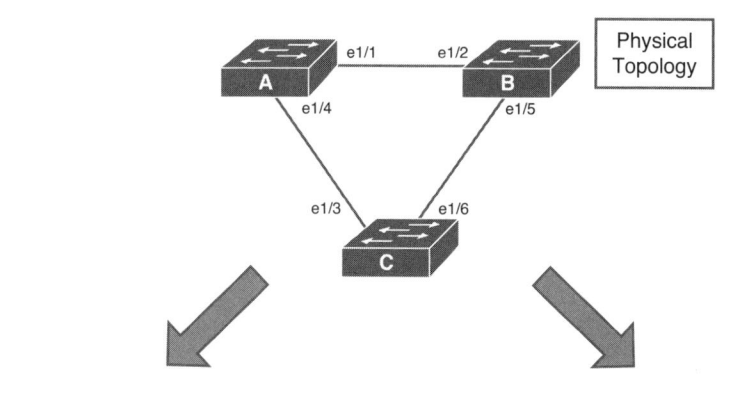

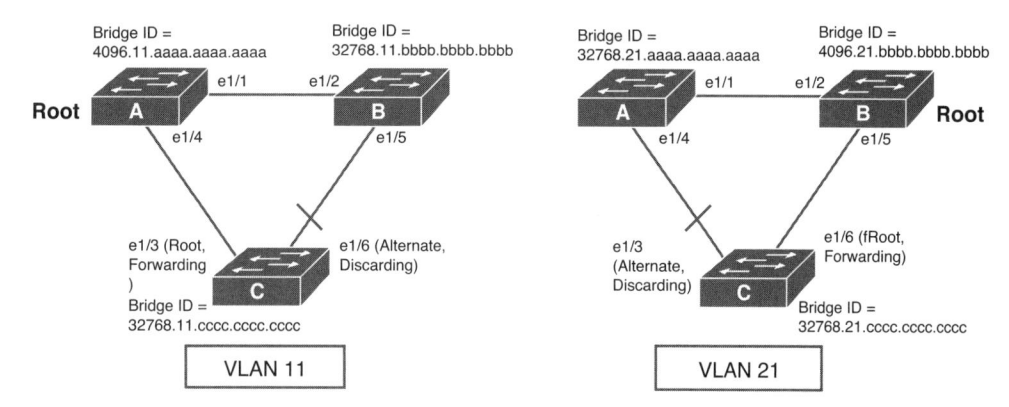

Figure 3-20 *Spanning Tree Instances in Two Different VLANs*

In that way, you can influence in the spanning tree formation on each VLAN. This virtualization technique can offer the following advantages over networks that deploy a single instance of STP (or RSTP) for all VLANs:

Traffic from and to switch C can be statically load balanced (per VLAN) between both links.

A failure in segment A-C only affects the VLANs that are active in this segment.

A failure in switch A only affects VLANs that have this device as its root bridge.

Note If a network deploys a single STP instance for all VLANs, this instance is usually called *Common Spanning Tree (CST)*.

Although they are flexible and very easy to configure, PVST+ and Rapid PVST+ are Cisco-proprietary implementations. To help customers who need interoperability between devices from different manufacturers, a protocol called *Multiple Spanning Tree (MST)* was created to bring similar functionalities to non-Cisco switches. MST allows the deployment of several spanning tree instances and the mapping of multiple VLANs in a single instance.

> **Note** MST was ratified in standard IEEE 802.1s and incorporated to IEEE 802.1Q in 2005.

Figure 3-21 illustrates a scenario with two MST instances.

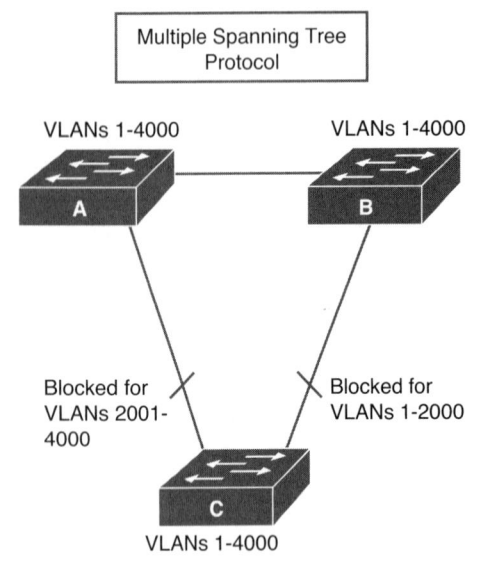

Figure 3-21 *Multiple Spanning Tree Instances*

> **Note** At the time of this writing, Nexus switches only support Multiple Spanning Tree Protocol or Rapid PVST+.

MST switches that share the same configuration parameters belong to the same MST *region*. This configuration includes

- **Name for the region:** A 32-byte alphanumerical string
- **Revision number:** Two bytes that represent a configuration change version for the entire region
- **VLAN-to-instance mapping:** A table that associates a group of VLANs to a spanning tree instance

The first two configuration parameters, and a hash of the VLAN-to-instance table, are included in the BPDUs sent by MST switches. Example 3-5 details the configuration of a single switch in an MST region.

Example 3-5 *Multiple Spanning Tree Region Configuration*

```
! Changing from Rapid PVST+ to MST
N7K-Switch1(config)# spanning-tree mst configuration
! Configuring the MST Region
N7K-Switch1(config-mst)# name DC-Region
N7K-Switch1(config-mst)# revision 1
N7K-Switch1(config-mst)# instance 0 vlan 1
N7K-Switch1(config-mst)# instance 1 vlan 2-2000
N7K-Switch1(config-mst)# instance 2 vlan 2001-4000
```

In Example 3-5, I have changed the switch configuration from Rapid PVST+ to MST; created a region ("DC-Region"), a revision (1); and three MST instances (instance 0 for VLAN 1, instance 1 for VLANs 2 to 2000, and instance 2 for VLANs 2001 to 4000).

With such a configuration, a switch is capable of identifying whether a BPDU belongs to a switch from the same region or from a *neighbor* from a different region. If a port receives a legacy STP BPDU or an MST BPDU from a different region, it is considered to be at the *boundary of the region*.

According to the IEEE 802.1s standard, an MST switch must be able to implement at least two types of spanning tree instances:

- **One Internal Spanning Tree (IST) instance:** This is instance 0. This is the instance responsible for carrying the information from all the other instances and for interoperating to the Common Spanning Tree from legacy STP switches (see Figure 3-22).

- **One or more Multiple Spanning Tree (MST) instances:** These are RSTP instances within a region. MST switches do not send individual BPDUs for each instance, but simply include instance records in the IST-generated BPDUs.

It is up to the network designer to define which deployment is better for his Nexus-based network: Rapid PVST+ or MST.

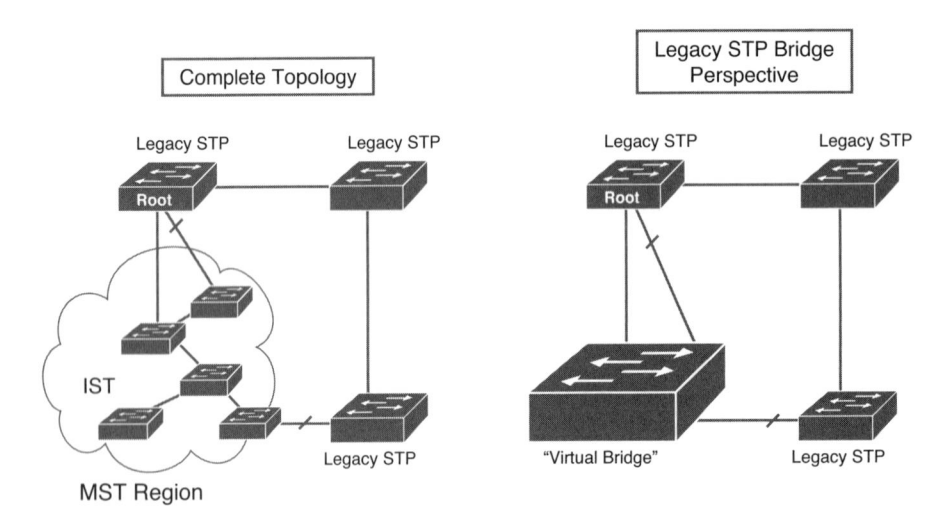

Figure 3-22 *Interoperability Between MST and STP Switches*

As an example, Table 3-3 exhibits a short comparison of both technologies to illustrate their main differences (as implemented in the Nexus 7000 platform at the time of this writing).

Table 3-3 *Rapid PVST+ and MST Comparison for Nexus 7000*

Characteristics	RPVST+	MST
Spanning tree failure domain	One VLAN	Multiple VLANs
Maximum instances*	4000	64
Number of ports	16,000	90,000
Troubleshooting	Per VLAN	Per MST instance
Interoperability with non-Cisco switches	No	Yes

* Per VDC (for more details, see Chapter 5, "Instant Switches: Virtual Device Contexts")

Note Interestingly, with the implementation of spanning tree instances, VLANs can also achieve virtualization in the control plane. However, you should notice that, in general, all STP instances in a switch share the same software processes.

Private VLANs

In data center networks, the main reason for VLAN deployment is the segregation of traffic in distinct environments. More specifically, when two servers are in different

VLANs, they are not expected to communicate directly with each other without the presence of another network element such as a router or a firewall.

Standard IEEE 802.1Q defines 12 bits to identify a VLAN ID, and potentially, 4096 VLANs can be deployed in a contiguous Ethernet network. However, for some data centers, this number is considered small when compared to the quantity of required environments.

Private VLAN is yet another Cisco switch feature that allows complete traffic isolation, but with a difference: It permits the segregation of environments that belong to the same VLAN. When a customer is deploying private VLANs, he can create three types of interfaces within a single VLAN:

- **Promiscuous ports:** Can exchange Ethernet frames with all the ports in a private VLAN
- **Isolated ports:** Communicate only with promiscuous ports in a private VLAN
- **Community ports:** Only communicate with other ports in the same community and the promiscuous ports

Figure 3-23 depicts the behavior of each type of port within a private VLAN.

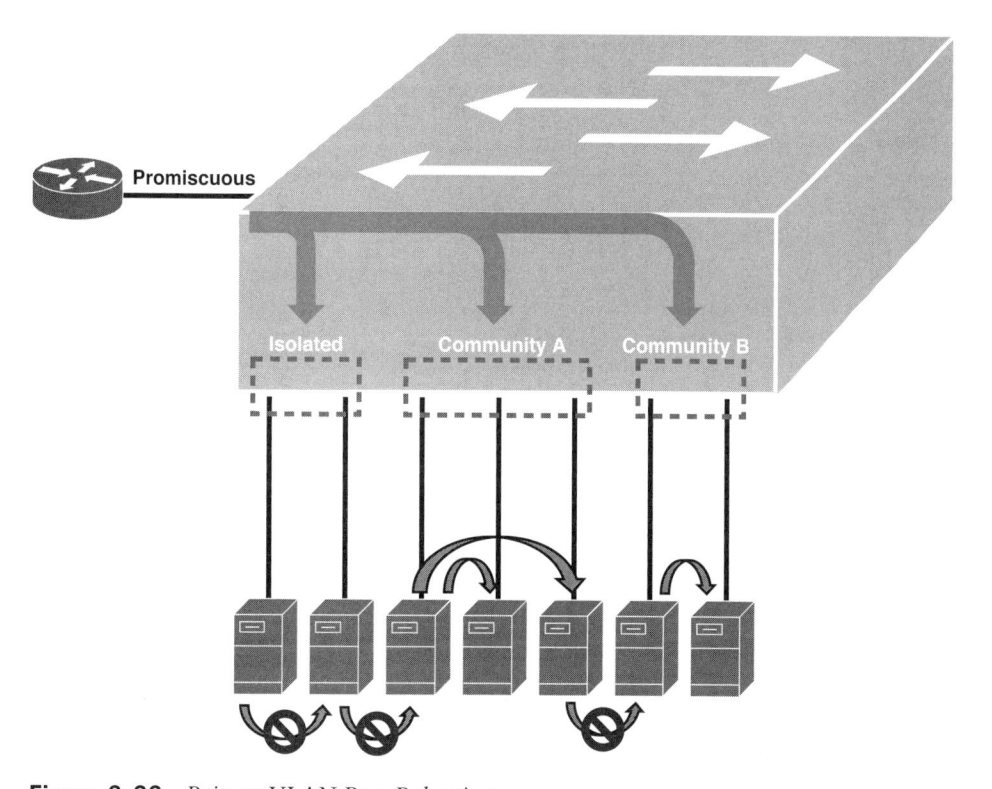

Figure 3-23 *Private VLAN Port Behavior*

In summary, private VLANs

- Define broadcast subdomains within a VLAN
- Provide additional security at the Layer 2 level
- Expand the scalability of environments that do not need to interact directly inside an Ethernet network

The configuration of private VLANs requires the creation of a *primary VLAN* that contains the promiscuous ports, and *secondary VLANs*, which include the isolated or the community ports. The association between the primary VLAN and one or more secondary VLANs defines a private VLAN.

> **Note** In Nexus switches, you can configure only one isolated secondary VLAN per primary VLAN.

Example 3-6 details how private VLANs are configured in an NX-OS switch. In this example, VLAN 50 is the primary VLAN, VLAN 60 is the isolated VLAN, and VLAN 70 is the community VLAN. If this private VLAN is spread over multiple switches, all these devices must abide to this primary-to-secondary VLAN association.

Also, in Example 3-6, you can verify how two access interfaces can be assigned to the isolated and community VLANs.

Example 3-6 *Private VLAN Configuration*

```
! Enabling the Private VLAN Feature in NX-OS
Switch1(config)# feature private-vlan
Switch1(config)# vlan 50
! Configuring VLAN 50 as the primary VLAN and Associating it to the secondary VLANs
Switch1(config-vlan)# private-vlan primary
Switch1(config-vlan)# private-vlan association 60,70
! Configuring VLAN 60 as an isolated secondary VLAN
Switch1(config-vlan)# vlan 60
Switch1(config-vlan)# private-vlan isolated
! Configuring VLAN 70 as a community secondary VLAN
Switch1(config-vlan)# vlan 70
Switch1(config-vlan)# private-vlan community
! Configuring Interface Ethernet 1/11 as an Isolated Port in VLAN 60
Switch1(config-vlan)# interface ethernet 1/11
Switch1(config-if)# switchport
Switch1(config-if)# switchport mode private-vlan host
Switch1(config-if)# switchport private-vlan host-association 50 60
Switch1(config-if)# no shutdown
! Configuring Interface Ethernet 1/12 as a Community Port
Switch1(config-if)# interface ethernet 1/12
```

```
Switch1(config-if)# switchport
Switch1(config-if)# switchport mode private-vlan host
Switch1(config-if)# switchport private-vlan host-association 50 70
Switch1(config-if)# no shutdown
```

Tip If more interfaces have the same configuration as Ethernet 1/12, they will belong to the same community (VLAN 70).

Example 3-7 illustrates the configuration of a *promiscuous access interface* (Ethernet 1/2) and a standard IEEE 802.1Q trunk to another switch (Ethernet 1/1).

Example 3-7 *Private VLAN Access Promiscuous Ports Configuration*

```
! Configuring an Access Promiscuous Port
Switch1(config)# interface ethernet 1/2
Switch1(config-if)# switchport
Switch1(config-if)# switchport mode private-vlan promiscuous
Switch1(config-if)# switchport private-vlan mapping 50 60,70
Switch1(config-if)# no shutdown
! Configuring a standard trunk to another switch
Switch1(config)# interface Ethernet 1/1
Switch1(config-if)# switchport
Switch1(config-if)# switchport mode trunk
Switch1(config-if)# switchport trunk allowed vlan all
Switch1(config-if)# no shutdown
```

Trunks naturally abide to the private VLAN behavior in networks with multiple switches. When a trunk transmits a frame originated from an isolated or community access port, it tags the frame with the corresponding secondary VLAN ID. On the other hand, when the same trunk transmits a frame originated from a promiscuous port, it tags the frame with the primary VLAN ID. Therefore, the switch on the other side of the trunk is always aware of the port type (promiscuous, isolated, or community) that originally received the frame.

Figure 3-24 exhibits a trunk transporting frames from a primary VLAN (50) and an isolated VLAN (60).

82 Data Center Virtualization Fundamentals

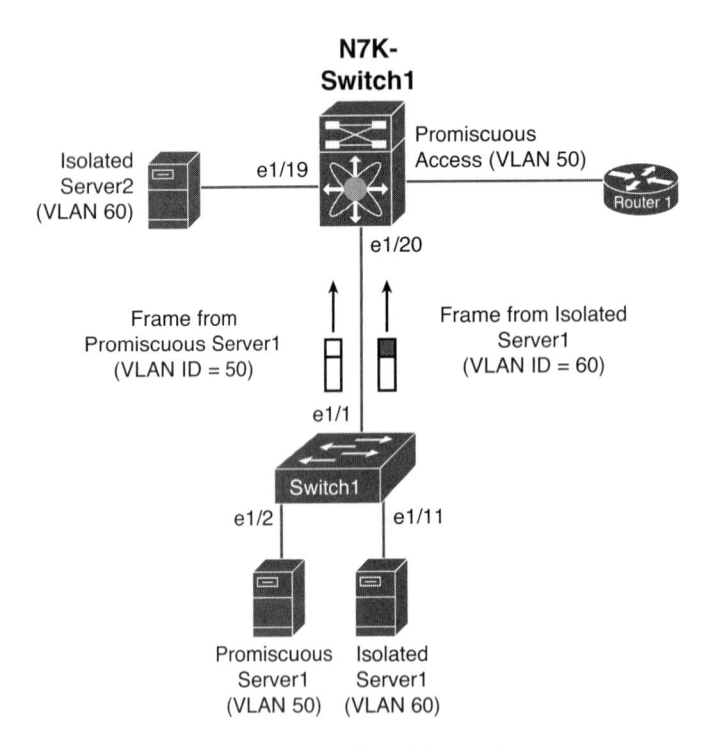

Figure 3-24 *Private VLAN Trunk Example*

You can recognize, in Figure 3-24, that Router1 is deployed as a "router-on-a-stick." This router exists to connect the members of the private VLAN to other subnets.

As I have explained in the earlier section "Two Common Misconceptions About VLANs," an SVI can elegantly replace Router1. Nevertheless, to correctly configure an SVI in a private VLAN, it is necessary to declare the primary-to-secondary association in the SVI.

Example 3-8 presents the corresponding configuration of an SVI for N7K-Switch1 from Figure 3-24.

Example 3-8 *SVI Configuration for Private VLANs in N7K-Switch1*

```
! Enabling Private VLANs and SVIs in NX-OS
N7K-Switch1(config)# feature private-vlan
N7K-Switch1(config)# feature interface-vlan
! Configuring the same Private VLAN association from Switch1
N7K-Switch1(config)# vlan 50
N7K-Switch1(config-vlan)# private-vlan primary
N7K-Switch1(config-vlan)# private-vlan association 60,70
N7K-Switch1(config-vlan)# vlan 60
N7K-Switch1(config-vlan)# private-vlan isolated
N7K-Switch1(config-vlan)# vlan 70
```

```
N7K-Switch1(config-vlan)# private-vlan community
! Configuring the trunk to Switch1 (nothing special in this trunk)
N7K-Switch1(config-vlan)# interface Ethernet 1/20
N7K-Switch1(config-if)# switchport
N7K-Switch1(config-if)# switchport mode trunk
N7K-Switch1(config-if)# switchport trunk allowed vlan all
N7K-Switch1(config-if)# no shutdown
! Creating the SVI for the Private VLAN
N7K-Switch1(config-if)# interface vlan 50
N7K-Switch1(config-if)# ip address 10.0.50.1/24
! This is necessary to allow the communication between the secondary VLANs and the SVI
N7K-Switch1(config-if)# private-vlan mapping 60,70
```

Tip If you want to allow the traffic between isolated ports (or members of different communities), you can enable the SVI to proxy the ARP requests within the private VLAN through the interface command **ip local-proxy-arp**. Be aware that, without any type of control, this configuration invalidates the private VLAN isolation properties.

You can picture a private VLAN use case in a data center network where all the servers belong to the same subnet (10.0.50.0/24, for example). This data center has security policies that do not allow any communication between web servers, because they belong to different departments. Therefore, these servers can be connected to isolated ports, just as Isolated Server1 and Isolated Server2 are in Figure 3-24.

These web servers need to access an application server that is shared among all the departments. Hence, this server can be connected to a promiscuous port. In Figure 3-24, Promiscuous Server1 represents this application server.

Additionally, this application server must access a group of database servers. Because the database servers must also exchange frames among themselves, they can be connected to a community VLAN, such as VLAN 70.

Finally, an SVI associated with the promiscuous VLAN can be used as the default gateway for all servers. If this interface is configured similarly to the one described on Example 3-8, all the servers in the private VLAN would be able to exchange IP packets with other subnets.

VLAN Specifics

VLANs are a great way to isolate traffic in an Ethernet network. However, as with every other virtualization technique, VLANs have special characteristics and points of attention. The ones this section explores are native VLANs, reserved VLANs, resource sharing, and management plane.

Native VLAN

Overlooked by some network administrators, the native VLAN can cause serious security and availability problems.

A native VLAN can be defined as the VLAN that receives and transmits *untagged* Ethernet frames in a trunk. Therefore, in misconfigured IEEE 802.1Q interfaces, unwanted communication between hosts from different VLANs can happen.

Figure 3-25 exhibits an undesired native VLAN communication scenario.

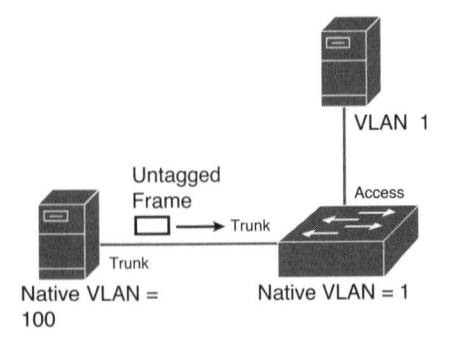

Figure 3-25 *Native VLAN Mismatch*

In Figure 3-25, frames from VLAN 100 are unwillingly sent to VLAN 1 in the switch. As a consequence, the server in VLAN 100 can be vulnerable to Layer 2 attacks and unnecessary traffic (flooding and broadcast) that can be happening in VLAN 1.

To avoid this situation, it is highly recommended that data center switches tag every VLAN, including the native VLAN, in their trunks. Nexus switches use the **vlan dot1Q tag native** command to deploy such a configuration.

Another best practice, for the data center and campus, is to never use VLAN 1, because it is the default native VLAN in Cisco switches.

Note It is not possible to delete VLAN 1.

Reserved VLANs IDs

Although IEEE 802.1Q defines 4096 available VLANs IDs (because the header field has 12 bits), some of them are not meant to be used for user data traffic. This standard dictates that VLAN 0 must be used for user priority data (IEEE 802.1p) and that VLAN 4095 is reserved for future use.

Other VLANs IDs cannot be used for implementation reasons such as legacy, multicast, or management traffic. For example, the following VLAN ranges are reserved:

Nexus 7000: VLANs 3968 to 4094

Nexus 5000: VLANs 3968 to 4094

Catalyst 6500: VLANs 1002 to 1005

Note Some NX-OS switches allow you to change the range of reserved VLANs to another contiguous 128-VLAN range. Refer to the Cisco online documentation for more details.

Resource Sharing

VLANs share an important resource inside a single switch: the MAC address table.

When one VLAN is using an excessive number of MAC addresses (if it is suffering an attack, for example), it can starve the MAC table and cause unnecessary flooding on other VLANs.

Without any resource control mechanisms in the switch MAC table, it is recommended that network administrators correctly size the switches according to the expected total number of MAC addresses.

A feature called *port security*, which limits the number of learned MAC addresses in each access port, can help to avoid excessive learning of MAC addresses on an access port. However, special attention must be given to interfaces connected to virtualized servers, because they can potentially learn hundreds of MAC addresses on a single interface.

Control and Management Plane

As I have discussed in the earlier section "Spanning Tree Instances," VLANs implement control plane virtualization in switches that deploy distinct STP instances. However, VLANs do not possess a clear separation in the management plane, because VLAN-enabled switches do not emulate a separate management environment (command-line interface, Simple Network Management Protocol [SNMP] agents, and so on) per VLAN.

However, Nexus switches offer an interesting feature to limit the administrative actions that can be executed in a group of VLANs. This feature is called *VLAN scope*.

Example 3-9 explains how a VLAN scope can be associated to a switch administrator account.

Example 3-9 *VLAN Scope Configuration*

```
N7K-Switch1# show running-config | begin "role name VLAN1xx" next 3
role name VLAN1xx
! Permitting every command to users associated to this role
```

```
    rule 1 permit read-write
! Changing the default policy for users associated to this role
    vlan policy deny
        permit vlan 100-199
N7K-Switch1# show running-config | include "username User1"
! Creating a user that belongs to this role
username User1 password [output suppressed]   role VLAN1xx
```

A role defines the operations that user accounts are allowed to execute in a switch. In Example 3-9, the VLAN1xx role allows any type of configuration, but not on every VLAN. The **vlan policy deny** command allows only explicitly declared VLANs to be configured by users that belong to this role. In the example, VLANs 100 to 199 were allowed to be controlled by users that belong to this role.

Example 3-10 shows a simple user login I used to test this configuration.

Example 3-10 *Login Test to Check VLAN Commands*

```
login as: User1
User Access Verification
Using keyboard-interactive authentication.
Password:
Cisco Nexus Operating System (NX-OS) Software
[Output suppressed]
! User1 Can View the Running Configuration File
N7K-Switch1# show running-config
[Output suppressed]
! User1 Can View All VLANs
N7K-Switch1# show vlan brief

VLAN Name                          Status    Ports
---- -------------------------     --------- -------------------------------
1    default                       active    Eth1/11, Eth1/12, Eth1/13
                                             Eth1/14, Eth1/15, Eth1/16
                                             Eth1/17, Eth1/18, Eth1/19
                                             Eth1/20
100  VLAN0100                      active    Eth1/19
200  VLAN0200                      active    Eth1/19
! But it cannot configure any VLAN outside the scope
N7K-Switch1# configure terminal
Enter configuration commands, one per line.  End with CNTL/Z.
N7K-Switch1(config)# vlan 199
N7K-Switch1(config-vlan)# vlan 201
% VLAN permission denied
```

Because User1 belongs to VLAN1xx, he cannot configure any VLAN outside the defined range (VLAN 100 to 199).

Concepts from the Routing World

The parallel evolution of Ethernet and IP positioned *routing* as the traditional way traffic leaves the confinement of broadcast domains. Through routing, it is possible to control how a subnet can communicate with the external world.

In data center networks, two classes of devices generally perform IP routing:

- **Layer 3 switches:** Used for routing between internal IP subnets

- **Edge routers:** Connect data centers to external networks such as the Internet, a corporate wide-area network (WAN), or to other data centers

These devices deploy a control plane element that defines how they direct a received IP packet based on its destination address. Such an element is known as a *Routing Information Base (RIB)* or simply, a *routing table*.

Routing tables can be controlled through manual configuration (static routes) or through routing protocols such as

> Open Shortest Path First (OSPF)
>
> Enhanced Interior Gateway Routing Protocol (EIGRP)
>
> Routing Information Protocol (RIP)
>
> Intermediate System–to–Intermediate System (IS-IS)
>
> Border Gateway Protocol (BGP)

The data plane element that effectively receives, stores, analyzes and forwards IP packets is called the *Forwarding Information Base (FIB)*. A Layer 3 device takes the information from the RIB to derive its FIB and use it directly on its hardware.

Overlapping Addresses in a Data Center

Usually, in privately controlled data centers, the local administration designs and controls the IP subnet allocation. But how do you manage traffic that requires a different behavior from the routing tables? Life is easier with examples, so allow me present you with one.

Imagine that you are the network administrator of a corporate data center (since you are reading this book, chances are you are one indeed). One Friday morning, your boss enters your office to announce that a team of consultants will arrive next week along with their equipment, which includes preconfigured servers and a router that the consulting company rented from a service provider. It was negotiated (during a meeting you were not invited to) that your organization will provide connectivity services for that company's hardware.

Figure 3-26 represents this scenario.

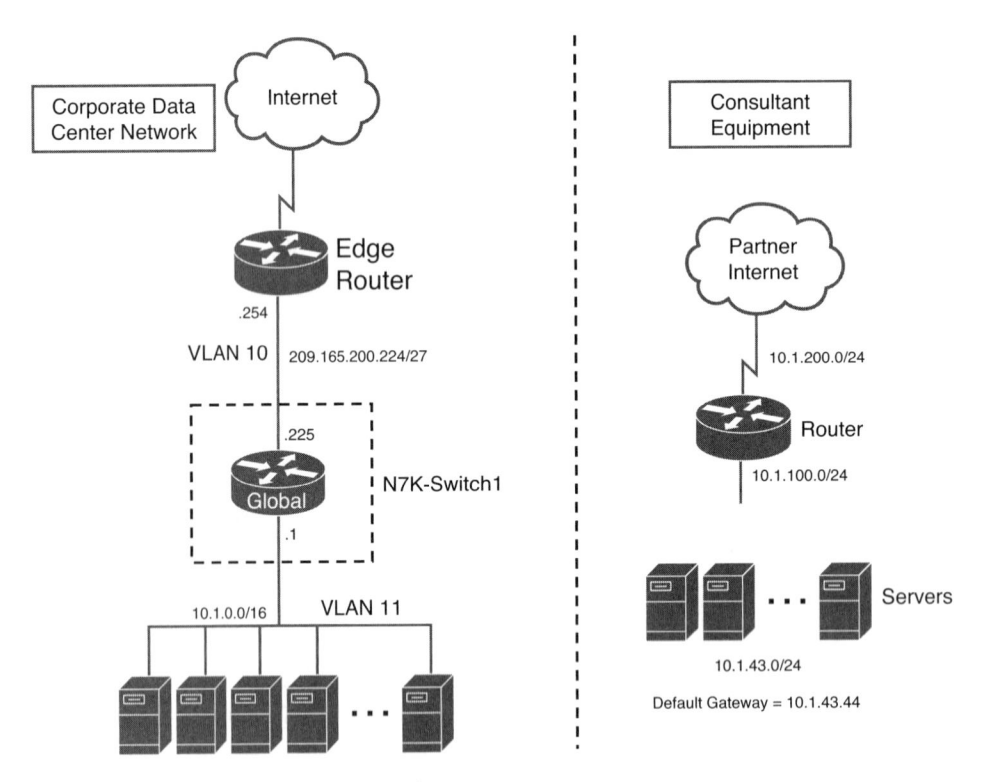

Figure 3-26 *Overlapping Networks*

After your boss leaves your office (and wishes you a good weekend), you start to analyze some documents and designs sent by the consulting company. With some anxiety, you perceive that its application servers use an address on subnet 10.1.42.0/24 which unfortunately overlaps with your company server subnet (10.1.0.0/16).

Example 3-11 exhibits the routing table from your organization's sole Layer 3 switch (a redundant device will only be acquired the next fiscal year).

Example 3-11 *Company Layer 3 Switch Routing Table*

```
N7K-Switch# show ip route
IP Route Table for VRF "default"
'*' denotes best ucast next-hop
'**' denotes best mcast next-hop
'[x/y]' denotes [preference/metric]

0.0.0.0/0, ubest/mbest: 1/0
    *via 209.165.200.254, [1/0], 00:02:38, static
10.1.0.0/16, ubest/mbest: 1/0, attached
    *via 10.1.0.1, Vlan112, [0/0], 00:03:51, direct
[output suppressed]
```

> **Note** This scenario has only one switch for the sake of simplicity, not for the lack of budget.

Another overlap happens in the service provider router Ethernet interface (it belongs to subnet 10.1.100.0/24). The consulting company agreement explicitly says that you cannot ask for changes on its addresses, because that customization is impossible for its traveling set of servers and router.

A solution seems easy enough: Create two VLANs (2000 and 2001, for example) and deploy an exclusive router between them. Unfortunately, your organization ran out of spare routers (you've already checked with three different people).

Now your virtualization superpowers are needed! How do you use the company data center infrastructure to accommodate these devices? The main challenges at the top of your head are as follows:

   You cannot insert the company's equipment in existent VLANs for security reasons and because you can run into duplicate IP addresses.

   You cannot create an SVI with an address that belongs to another interface in the switch.

From the back of your mind, you remember someone mumbling about an MPLS-originated technology called *Virtual Routing and Forwarding (VRF)*. And by the way, your organizations Cisco Layer 3 switch supports it!

In five minutes, you create the VRF "CONSULTANTS" shown in Figure 3-27 and go home early.

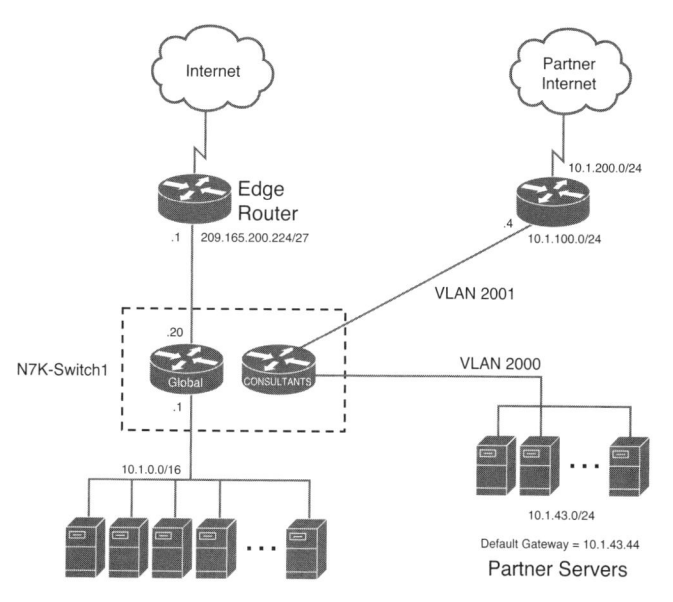

Figure 3-27 *Solution for Overlapping Address Challenge*

Defining and Configuring VRFs

A VRF is a routing instance that can coexist with several others in the same routing equipment. A VRF is associated to the following elements:

- An IP routing table
- A derived forwarding table
- A set of interfaces
- Optional routing protocols and peers that exchange routing information with the VRF

If an interface does not belong to a defined VRF, it belongs to the *global routing table*, which is the default routing instance for Cisco routers and Layer 3 switches.

VRFs were created to allow the deployment of MPLS Layer 3 Virtual Private Networks (VPN). In that context, each VRF represents a portion of a service provider router that is responsible for VPN customer routes. For campus and data center networks, the concept of *VRF-lite* is used to allow the creation of independent routing instances that do not deploy MPLS.

Note I am a firm believer that diet yogurt is still yogurt. Therefore, this book will refer to VRF-lite simply as VRF.

Just as VLANs deploy additional bridged networks without the acquisition of new hardware, VRFs allow the creation of virtual routing elements that can be logically provisioned within existing equipment. However, adversely from VLANs, it can be said that a VRF natively virtualizes both data and control planes because they provide the partitioning of forwarding and routing tables within a networking device.

Example 3-12 details the NX-OS configuration of the VRF depicted in Figure 3-27.

Note Although Layer 3 NX-OS devices can also implement IPv6, for the sake of simplicity, the VRF configurations in this chapter will only explore IPv4 configurations.

Example 3-12 *VRF CONSULTANTS Creation*

```
N7K-Switch# show running-config vlan 2000-2001
[output suppressed]
vlan 2000
  name CONSULTANT-SERVERS
vlan 2001
  name CONSULTANT-NETWORK
N7K-Switch# show running-config vrf CONSULTANTS
```

```
[output suppressed]
! Creating the VRF and its default route
vrf context CONSULTANTS
  ip route 0.0.0.0/0 10.1.100.4
! Including SVI 2000 in the VRF
interface Vlan2000
  vrf member CONSULTANTS
  ip address 10.1.43.44/24
! Including SVI 2001 in the VRF
interface Vlan2001
  vrf member CONSULTANTS
  ip address 10.1.100.1/24
```

Caution With the **vrf member** interface command, all previous Layer 3 information (IP address, for example) is erased.

Example 3-13 details the routing table for the created VRF.

Example 3-13 *VRF CONSULTANTS Routing Table*

```
N7K-Switch# show ip route vrf CONSULTANTS
[output suppressed]
0.0.0.0/0, ubest/mbest: 1/0
    *via 10.1.100.4, [1/0], 00:11:32, static
10.1.43.0/24, ubest/mbest: 1/0, attached
    *via 10.1.43.44, Vlan2000, [0/0], 00:08:41, direct
10.1.43.44/32, ubest/mbest: 1/0, attached
    *via 10.1.43.44, Vlan2000, [0/0], 00:08:41, local
10.1.100.0/24, ubest/mbest: 1/0, attached
    *via 10.1.100.1, Vlan2001, [0/0], 00:11:32, direct
10.1.100.1/32, ubest/mbest: 1/0, attached
    *via 10.1.100.1, Vlan2001, [0/0], 00:11:32, local
```

As you can see, VRF CONSULTANTS has a completely distinct routing table from the Layer 3 switch. And more importantly, it was created without the need for additional hardware.

Note By default, two VRFs created in the same physical device are not allowed to share a route to the same IP network (for example, one defined by the same VLAN). However, in more complex MPLS VPN designs, it is possible to deploy such scenario through a feature called *route leaking*.

VRFs and Routing Protocols

A VRF has components that belong to the control and data plane (RIB and FIB, respectively). And since its inception in MPLS VPNs, a VRF can import and export routes from routing peers, which are unaware of this virtualization technique.

To demonstrate that VRFs (from a single physical device) can have distinct routing characteristics, I deployed two different routing protocols in a set of VRFs configured in two Nexus 7000 switches.

Figure 3-28 depicts how the routing protocols are configured. In this scenario, VRF-A1 and VRF-A2 exchange routers through OSPF, while VRF-B1 and VRF-B2 use EIGRP for the same purpose.

> **Note** At the time of this writing, Layer 3 Nexus switches support static routes and the following routing protocols: OSPFv2, OSPFv3, EIGRP, IS-IS, and RIPv2.

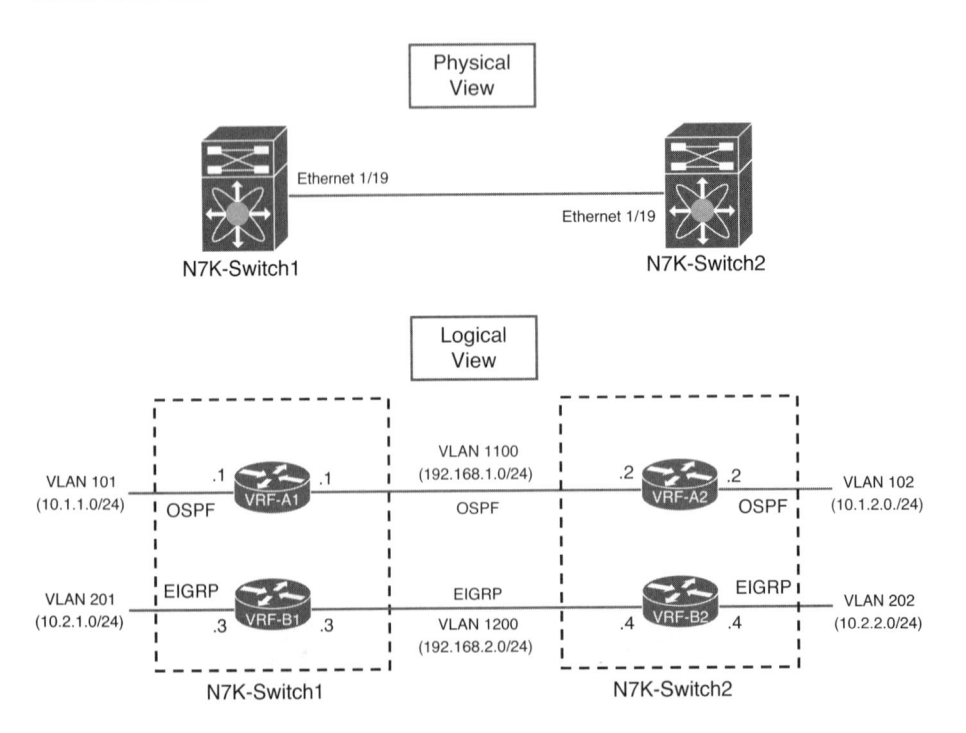

Figure 3-28 *EIGRP and OSPFv2 VRFs in Two Nexus 7000s*

In this section, you will be able to analyze the corresponding configuration for each VRF. First, it is necessary to prepare the basic Layer 2 and 3 connectivity on both switches. Examples 3-14 and 3-15 detail this configuration for each Layer 3 switch.

Example 3-14 *VLAN and Physical Connection Configuration for N7K-Switch1*

```
! Creating the VLANs
N7K-Switch1(config)# vlan 101, 201, 1100, 1200
! Configuring the single trunk to N7K-Switch2
N7K-Switch1(config-vlan)# interface ethernet 1/19
N7K-Switch1(config-if)# switchport
N7K-Switch1(config-if)# switchport mode trunk
! By default all VLANs are allowed in the trunk
N7K-Switch1(config-if)# no shutdown
! Enabling SVI Creation
N7K-Switch1(config)# feature interface-vlan
```

Example 3-15 *VLAN and Physical Connection Configuration for N7K-Switch2*

```
! Creating the VLANs
N7K-Switch2(config)# vlan 102, 202, 1100, 1200
N7K-Switch2(config-vlan)# exit
! Configuring the single trunk to N7K-Switch1
N7K-Switch2(config)# interface ethernet 1/19
N7K-Switch2(config-if)# switchport
N7K-Switch2(config-if)# switchport mode trunk
! All VLANs are allowed in the trunk by default
N7K-Switch2(config-if)# no shutdown
! Enabling SVI Creation
N7K-Switch2(config)# feature interface-vlan
```

There are two common VLANs between both switches: VLAN 1100 and VLAN 1200. Because they are used for Layer 3 communication between other subnets, they can also be called *transit VLANs*. And because an SVI cannot belong to more than one VRF at the same time, the transit VLANs also provide isolated paths for VRFs in the same device (VRF-A1 and VRF-B1, for example).

Example 3-16 describes the OSPF configuration for VRF-A1 in N7K-Switch1, and Example 3-17 does the same for VRF-A2 in N7K-Switch2.

Example 3-16 *OSPF Configuration in VRF-A1 in N7K-Switch1*

```
N7K-Switch1# show running-config ospf
[output suppressed]
! Enabling OSPF in NX-OS
feature ospf

! Creating the OSPF process A12
router ospf A12
```

```
[output suppressed]
N7K-Switch1# show running-config vrf VRF-A1
[output suppressed]
! Creating VRF-A1
vrf context VRF-A1

interface Vlan101
  vrf member VRF-A1
  ip address 10.1.1.1/24
! Adding this interface to the OSPF process
  ip router ospf A12 area 0.0.0.0

interface Vlan1100
  vrf member VRF-A1
  ip address 192.168.1.1/24
! Adding this interface to the OSPF process
  ip router ospf A12 area 0.0.0.0
```

Example 3-17 *OSPF Configuration in VRF-A2 in N7K-Switch1*

```
N7K-Switch2# show running-config ospf
[output suppressed]
! Enabling OSPF in NX-OS
feature ospf

! Creating OSPF process A21
router ospf A21

[output suppressed]
N7K-Switch2# show running-config vrf VRF-A2
[output suppressed]
! Creating VRF-A2
vrf context VRF-A2

interface Vlan102
  vrf member VRF-A2
  ip address 10.1.2.3/24
! Adding this interface to the OSPF process
  ip router ospf A21 area 0.0.0.0

interface Vlan1100
  vrf member VRF-A2
```

```
  ip address 192.168.1.3/24
! Adding this interface to the OSPF process
  ip router ospf A21 area 0.0.0.0
```

In Examples 3-16 and 3-17, I have dedicated a single OSPF process for each VRF (process A12 for VRF-A1 and process A21 for VRF-A2). In OSPF, these names only represent the process names that are not exchanged or validated in the routing protocol communication between both devices.

Note The creation and assignment of distinct routing protocol processes for different VRFs in the same device is a popular Layer 3 virtualization approach. Even considering that it provides better failure isolation in VRF environments, I recommend that you always observe how many routing protocol processes your device supports to avoid future scalability problems.

The resulting OSPF neighborhood information and routing table for VRF-A1 and VRF-A2 are respectively represented in Examples 3-18 and 3-19.

Example 3-18 *VRF-A1 OSPF Neighbor Information and Routing Table*

```
N7K-Switch1# show ip ospf neighbors vrf VRF-A1
 OSPF Process ID A12 VRF VRF-A1
 Total number of neighbors: 1
 Neighbor ID    Pri State      Up Time  Address        Interface
 10.1.2.3         1 FULL/BDR   00:32:06 192.168.1.3    Vlan1100

N7K-Switch1# show ip route vrf VRF-A1
[output suppressed]
! VRF-A2 sent this route
10.1.2.0/24, ubest/mbest: 1/0
    *via 192.168.1.3, Vlan1100, [110/80], 00:26:37, ospf-A12, intra
[output suppressed]
```

Example 3-19 *VRF-A2 OSPF Neighbor Information and Routing Table*

```
N7K-Switch2# show ip ospf neighbors vrf VRF-A2
 OSPF Process ID A21 VRF VRF-A2
 Total number of neighbors: 1
 Neighbor ID    Pri State        Up Time  Address        Interface
 10.1.1.1         1 FULL/DR      01:28:17 192.168.1.1    Vlan1100
```

```
N7K-Switch2# show ip route vrf VRF-A2
[output suppressed]
! VRF-A1 sent this route
10.1.1.0/24, ubest/mbest: 1/0
    *via 192.168.1.1, Vlan1100, [110/80], 01:23:53, ospf-A21, intra
[output suppressed]
```

Similarly, Examples 3-20 and 3-21 depict an EIGRP configuration between VRF-B1 (in N7K-Switch1) and VRF-B2 (in N7K-Switch2).

Example 3-20 *EIGRP Configuration for VRF-B1*

```
N7K-Switch1# show running-config eigrp
[output suppressed]
! Enabling EIGRP in NX-OS
feature eigrp

[output suppressed]
N7K-Switch1# show running-config vrf VRF-B1
[output suppressed]
! Creating VRF-B1
vrf context VRF-B1

router eigrp B12
! Configuring EIGRP instance for VRF-B1
  vrf VRF-B1
! Defining EIGRP Autonomous System 200 for process B12
    autonomous-system 200

interface Vlan201
  vrf member VRF-B1
  ip address 10.2.1.2/24
! Adding Interface VLAN 201 to EIGRP process B12
  ip router eigrp B12

interface Vlan1200
  vrf member VRF-B1
  ip address 192.168.2.2/24
! Adding Interface VLAN 201 to EIGRP process B12
  ip router eigrp B12
```

Example 3-21 *EIGRP Configuration for VRF-B2*

```
N7K-Switch2# show running-config eigrp
[output suppressed]
! Enabling EIGRP in NX-OS
feature eigrp

[output suppressed]
N7K-Switch2# show running-config vrf VRF-B2

[output suppressed]
! Creating VRF-B2
vrf context VRF-B2

router eigrp B21
! Configuring EIGRP instance for VRF-B2
  vrf VRF-B2
! Defining EIGRP Autonomous System 200 for process B21
    autonomous-system 200

interface Vlan202
  vrf member VRF-B2
  ip address 10.2.2.4/24
! Adding Interface VLAN 201 to EIGRP process B21
  ip router eigrp B21

interface Vlan1200
  vrf member VRF-B2
  ip address 192.168.2.4/24
! Adding Interface VLAN 201 to EIGRP process B21
  ip router eigrp B21
```

As you can see, the depicted EIGRP configuration for VRFs is a bit more complex than for OSPF. You should observe two important details in Examples 3-20 and 3-21:

> I have created an exclusive routing protocol *instance* inside the EIGRP process for the VRF that will use the routing protocol in each switch.
>
> The communicating EIGRP processes must have the same autonomous system to exchange internal routes.

Note The creation of routing protocol instances for distinct VRFs, which run together within the same process, is another popular Layer 3 virtualization approach. Although this method allows better scalability, it is important to notice that a routing protocol process failure can affect all its instances.

With these configurations, VRF-B1 and VRF-B2 start to exchange EIGRP internal routes, as you can verify in the switch outputs illustrated in Examples 3-22 and 3-23.

Example 3-22 *VRF-B1 Neighbor Information and Routing Table*

```
N7K-Switch1# show ip eigrp neighbors vrf VRF-B1
IP-EIGRP neighbors for process 200 VRF VRF-B1
H    Address        Interface      Hold  Uptime   SRTT  RTO   Q    Seq
                                   (sec)          (ms)        Cnt  Num
0    192.168.2.4    Vlan1200       13    00:37:55  1    200   0    3

N7K-Switch1# show ip route vrf VRF-B1
[output suppressed]
! VRF-B2 sent this route
10.2.2.0/24, ubest/mbest: 1/0
    *via 192.168.2.4, Vlan1200, [90/3072], 00:38:21, eigrp-B12, internal
[output suppressed]
```

Example 3-23 *VRF-B2 Neighbor Information and Routing Table*

```
N7K-Switch2# show ip eigrp neighbors vrf VRF-B2
IP-EIGRP neighbors for process 200 VRF VRF-B2
H    Address        Interface      Hold  Uptime   SRTT  RTO   Q    Seq
                                   (sec)          (ms)        Cnt  Num
0    192.168.2.2    Vlan1200       12    00:41:22  1276  5000  0    4

N7K-Switch2# show ip route vrf VRF-B2
[output suppressed]
! VRF-B1 sent this route
10.2.1.0/24, ubest/mbest: 1/0
    *via 192.168.2.2, Vlan1200, [90/3072], 00:41:09, eigrp-B21, internal
[output suppressed]
```

As expected from a control plane virtualization technology, VRFs defined in the same Layer 3 device can deploy completely different routing tables and independently exchange routes through distinct routing protocols.

VRFs and the Management Plane

From the management plane point of view, VRFs are not independent entities. A management session (such as Telnet, SSH, or SNMP), targeted to a VRF interface, will provide the same results as a management session directed to an interface that belongs to the global routing table.

Nevertheless, in Nexus switches, it is possible to limit the access from administrators to a group of VRFs. As with VLANs, user roles can restrict commands for administrators that manage a switch.

This feature is called *VRF scope*, and to demonstrate it, I will use the VRFs created in the earlier section "VRFs and Routing Protocols" and exhibited in Figure 3-28.

Example 3-24 exposes the "VRF-Ax" role configuration, whose scope is restricted to VRF-A1. It also shows the configuration of a user account ("User2") that belongs to this role.

Example 3-24 *Scope Configuration in Switch 1*

```
N7K-Switch1# show running-config | begin "role name VRF-Ax" next 3
role name VRF-Ax
  rule 1 permit read-write
! Only the permitted VRFs will be accessible to users that belong to this role
  vrf policy deny
    permit vrf VRF-A1

N7K-Switch1# show running-config | include "username User2"
username User2 password [output suppressed]  role VRF-Ax
```

In Example 3-25, you can observe User2 performing a Telnet session directed to an interface that belongs to VRF-B1 (address 192.168.2.2) and executing several VRF-related commands.

Example 3-25 *User2 Login and Tentative of VRF Access*

```
! Telnet session to VRF-B1 from VRF-B2
N7K-Switch2# telnet 192.168.2.2 vrf VRF-B2
[output suppressed]
login: User2
Password:
[output suppressed]
! Accessing the same CLI environment as if User2 was connected to the console
N7K-Switch1# show vrf
VRF-Name                        VRF-ID State  Reason
VRF-A1                               4 Up     --
```

```
VRF-B1                                  5 Up      --
default                                 1 Up      --
management                              2 Up      --
N7K-Switch1# configure terminal
Enter configuration commands, one per line.  End with CNTL/Z.
! Accessing VRF-A1 Configuration
N7K-Switch1(config)# vrf context VRF-A1
N7K-Switch1(config-vrf)# exit
! Trying to change the default context for CLI output to VRF-B1
N7K-Switch1# routing-context vrf VRF-B1
% VRF permission denied
```

As Example 3-26 illustrated, although User2 did not have configuration rights over VRF-B1, it was perfectly possible for him to have a Telnet session to an IP that belongs to VRF-B1. This happened because all the VRFs (and global routing table) share the same management plane in the switch.

After he gets the privileged mode prompt (N7K-Switch1#), he can visualize all VRFs including the *default* (global routing table) and the *management* (where the management interfaces are statically assigned) VRFs. However, User2 is not allowed to configure parameters or change the default context for show commands to a VRF that is different from VRF-A1.

VRF-Awareness

Whenever a service configuration can specify which VRF it will use in its operation, this service is defined as a *VRF-aware* feature. Here are some examples of VRF-aware capabilities in Layer 3 NX-OS devices:

- Authentication, Authorization, and Accounting (AAA)
- Domain Name Service (DNS)
- NetFlow
- Network Time Protocol (NTP)
- Ping
- Traceroute
- Secure Shell (SSH)
- Simple Network Management Protocol (SNMP)
- Syslog
- TFTP

Usually, when you are configuring one of these services, an IP address (or name) is needed to define the target for such function. When using VRFs, you should also define the VRF that should be used.

Tip VRF-aware features can be recognized through the complementary commands **use-vrf** or **vrf**.

Example 3-26 exhibits a sample configuration for a group of VRF-aware features, such as DNS, SNMP, Syslog, NetFlow, RADIUS, and Ping.

Example 3-26 *VRF-Aware Configuration Examples*

```
N7K-Switch1# show running-config | include use-vrf
! Defining a DNS server reachable through VRF-A1
ip name-server 10.10.10.10 use-vrf VRF-A1
! Defining a SNMP server reachable through VRF-A1
snmp-server host 20.20.20.20 use-vrf VRF-A1
! Defining a Syslot server reachable through VRF-A1
logging server 30.30.30.30 5 use-vrf VRF-A1
! Issuing an ICMP Echo through VRF-A1
N7K-Switch1# ping 192.168.1.3 vrf VRF-A1
PING 192.168.1.3 (192.168.1.3): 56 data bytes
64 bytes from 192.168.1.3: icmp_seq=0 ttl=254 time=1.232 ms
[output suppressed]
```

As you can see, all these features were configured using addresses reachable through VRF-A1. Another Syslog or DNS server could be independently added in VRF-B1.

Note The *management VRF*, which owns the Management interface on Nexus switches (mgmt0), natively requires the use of VRF-aware features. If you want to use this interface in an out-of-band network for management purposes, you must include the management VRF in each management feature operation.

VRF Resource Allocation Control

VRFs can control how much of the physical resources a single virtual instance can use. More specifically, through the **maximum routes** command, it is possible to limit the number of routes a VRF can use in its routing table.

Example 3-27 explains how this configuration can be done in VRF-B1 from Figure 3-28.

Example 3-27 *Maximum Routes Configuration*

```
N7K-L2-Switch1# show running-config vrf VRF-B1
[output suppressed]
```

```
! Defining the maximum number of routes in VRF-B1
vrf context VRF-B1
  address-family ipv4 unicast
    maximum routes 12
[output suppressed]
```

Although it is possible to limit the number of prefixes received by one routing protocol (BGP, for example), the maximum routes value for VRF-B1 relates to the total of routes, independently of how they were generated.

Example 3-28 shows the result of a test. On N7K-Switch2, I have sequentially created three loopback interfaces:

Loopback0 (address 172.16.0.1/24)

Loopback1 (address 172.16.1.1/24)

Loopback2 (address 172.16.2.1/24)

After their inclusion in the EIGRP process B21, N7K-Switch1 informed that it cannot include a route in the VRF-B1 routing table.

Example 3-28 *What Happens When the Limit Is Reached*

```
N7K-L2-Switch1# show ip route vrf VRF-B1 detail
%URIB-4-ROUTELIMIT_EXCEEDED: Number of routes (12) reached or exceeds configured
limit (12); dropped (1)
[output suppressed]
0.0.0.0/32, ubest/mbest: 1/0
    *via Null0, [220/0], 05:08:00, broadcast, discard
127.0.0.0/8, ubest/mbest: 1/0
    *via Null0, [220/0], 05:08:00, broadcast, discard
255.255.255.255/32, ubest/mbest: 1/0
    *via sup-eth1, [0/0], 05:07:40, broadcast
10.2.1.0/24, ubest/mbest: 1/0, attached
    *via 10.2.1.3, Vlan201, [0/0], 00:19:21, direct
[output suppressed]
```

Tip Because it provides full routing visualization, always use the **show ip route detail** command for maximum routes purposes.

In modern Layer 3 switches and routers, forwarding is implemented through application-specific integrated circuits (ASIC). It is expected that these devices deploy a finite number of routes, hence the *maximum routes* resource control feature avoids the situation where a single VRF (or a group of them) can starve other VRFs configured on the same physical equipment.

Use Case: Data Center Network Segmentation

After you solved the consultant addressing problem (described in the earlier section "Overlapping Addresses in a Data Center"), your boss seems very impressed by your virtualization abilities. The consultant company is gone and instead of simple compliment, he decides you should get yet another challenge.

He explains that the organization business is expanding and, for that reason, more server environments will be added in the data center. More specifically, two new definitive environments will be required:

- Internet servers that, from now on, will be hosted in your data center
- Servers from outsourced companies

And here comes the twist: You should not buy more networking equipment (routers or switches) because the budget this year was already spent. Besides, unbeknownst to you, your boss has personally checked that there are enough ports for these two new environments in the installed routers and switches in the data center.

Without much choice, you accept the challenge. The boundary conditions are

- There will be three distinct environments (Internet, corporate, and partner).
- These environments can support overlapping IP addresses (even if this situation does not occur today, the network must be prepared for it).
- Only the switches deploy IEEE 802.1Q trunking. Other devices (servers, firewalls, and routers) are not VLAN-aware.

Some companies have security policies that do not allow the sharing of a network device for two or more application environments. Luckily, as you have checked, your company permits the use of network virtualization techniques.

Now, you are sure that these conditions allow you to use VLANs and VRFs to build network partitions. The logical topology you design is represented in Figure 3-29.

Note Although data center networks must always consider device high availability, I will only depict one edge router and one Layer 3 switch to describe the concepts explained in this chapter. Redundant topologies will be further explored in detail in Chapter 6, "Fooling Spanning Tree."

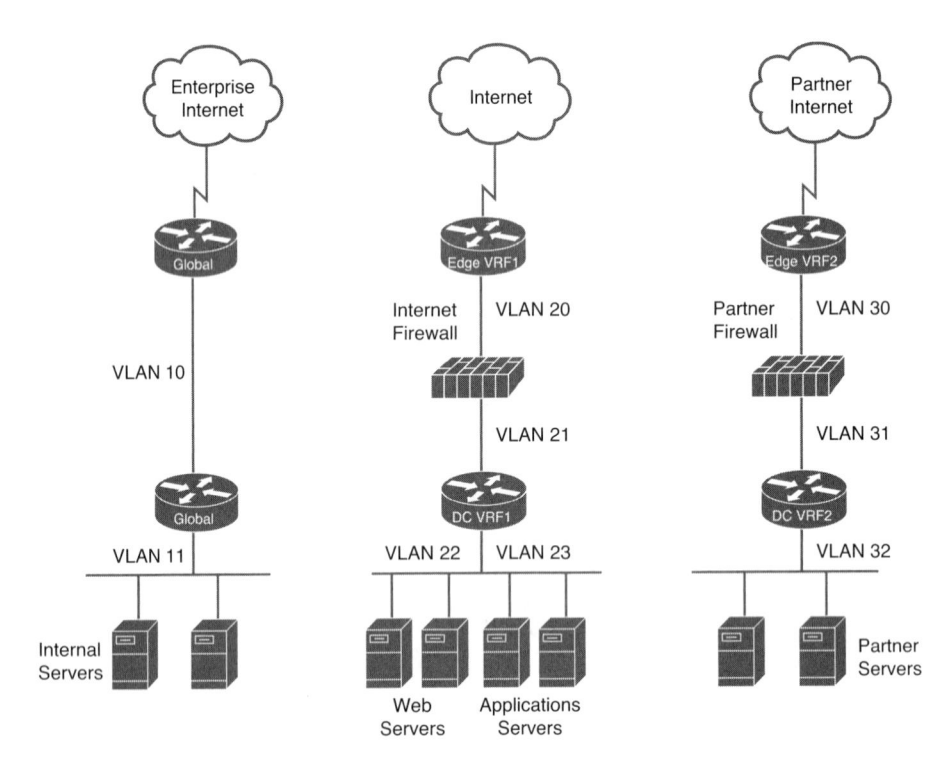

Figure 3-29 *Logical Topology for the Data Center Network Segmentation Challenge*

In your design, the global routing tables from the edge router and the Layer 3 switch will continue to be used in the corporate environment. However, you deploy two VRFs on each one of these devices: an Internet VRF and a partner VRF. These VRFs connect the servers, firewalls, and external networks through distinct VLANs under your control. The VRFs on the edge router encompass physical interfaces, while the VRFs on the switch use SVIs.

From the logical topology, you derived the physical one depicted in Figure 3-30.

When your project is implemented, you win a prize vacation from your company and your success awakens your colleagues' envy.

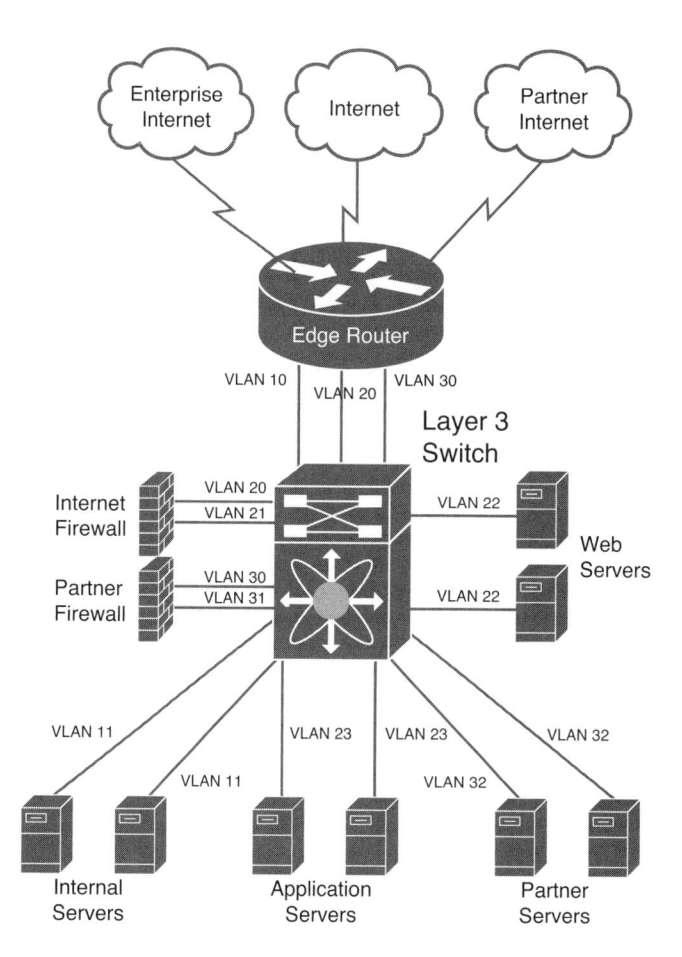

Figure 3-30 *Physical Topology for the Data Center Network Segmentation Challenge*

Summary

This chapter examined, in detail, two popular virtualization techniques that provide network partitioning: VLANs and VRFs.

More precisely, the following concepts were covered:

- VLANs are Ethernet broadcast domains.
- VLANs enable traffic manipulation without physical recabling or additional switches.

- A Layer 3 switch can deploy a VLAN-associated SVI to provide routing services in this VLAN.
- Spanning Tree Protocol (and its variations) guarantees loopless topologies and path availability in Ethernet switched networks.
- Rapid PVST+ and MST provide independent spanning tree instances per VLAN (or group of VLANs).
- Private VLANs can implement broadcast subdomains within a VLAN, thus improving the partitioning scalability of a single Ethernet network.
- VRFs are routing instances that can have different behaviors from one device's global routing table.
- Routing protocols can be independently deployed by VRFs in the same physical devices.
- In Nexus switches, it is possible to limit administrative actions to a group of VLANs and VRFs.
- VRF resource control can be deployed through the limitation of routes per instance.
- Through VLANs and VRFs, you can easily build network virtual partitions.

Figure 3-31 summarizes how VLANs and VRFs can be logically represented.

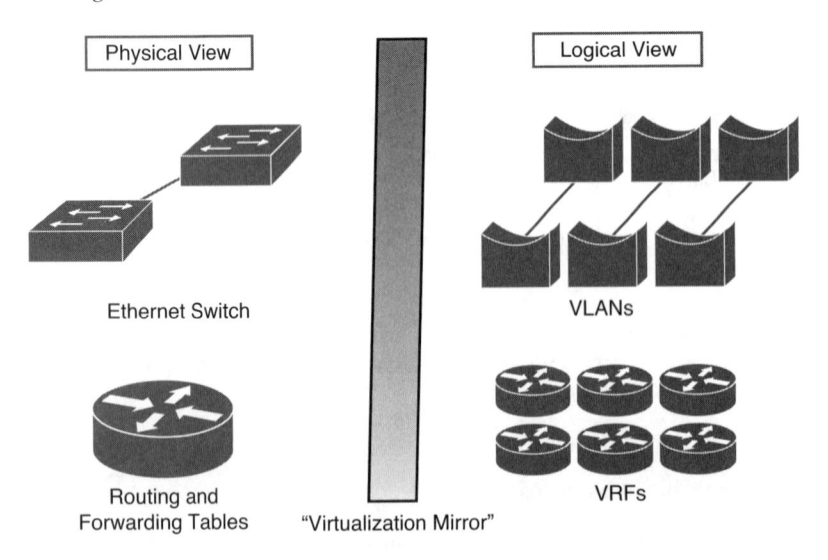

Figure 3-31 *Through the Virtualization Mirror*

Further Reading

Clark, Kennedy and Hamilton, Kevin. *Cisco LAN Switching*. Cisco Press, 1999.

Pepelnjak, Ivan and Guichard, Jim. *MPLS and VPN Architectures*. Cisco Press, 2000.

Doyle, Jeff and Carrol, Jennifer. *Routing TCP/IP Volume 1 (2nd Edition)*. Cisco Press, 2005.

Perlman, Radia. *Interconnections: Bridges, Routers, Switches, and Internetworking Protocols (2nd Edition)*. Addison-Wesley Professional, 1999.

Perlman, Radia (1985). *"An Algorithm for Distributed Computation of a Spanning Tree in an Extended LAN"*. ACM SOGCOMM Computer Communication Review: http://dx.doi.org/10.1145/318951.319004.

Chapter 4

An Army of One: ACE Virtual Contexts

"All warfare is based on deception. Hence, when we are able to attack, we must seem unable; when using our forces, we must appear inactive; when we are near, we must make the enemy believe we are far away; when far away, we must make him believe we are near." (Sun-Tzu)

This chapter will explore the importance of application networking, load-balancing fundamental concepts, and the benefits of Cisco Application Control Engine (ACE) virtual contexts. It will cover the following topics:

- Application Networking Services
- The Use of Load Balancers
- Load-Balancing Concepts
- Load Balancer Proliferation in the Data Center
- ACE Virtual Contexts
- Use Case: Multitenant Data Center

Table 4-1 details how ACE virtual contexts are classified according to the virtualization taxonomy described in Chapter 1, "Virtualization History and Definitions."

Table 4-1 *ACE Virtual Context Virtualization Classification*

Virtualization Characteristics	ACE Virtual Contexts
Emulation	Load balancer
Type	Partitioning
Subtype	Resource allocation control

Virtualization Characteristics	ACE Virtual Contexts
Scalability	20 contexts (ACE 4710) and 250 contexts (ACE Module for Catalyst 6500)
Technology Area	Networking
Subarea	Management, control, and data plane virtualization
Advantages	Consolidation of devices, higher resource utilization, and dynamic load-balancing deployment

As business and IT develop more strict relationships inside each corporation, networks are evolving away from the perception of a mere amount of "data pipes." Nowadays, a network is considered an infrastructure element that helps to increase business results and the speed of growth of a company.

And more than plain connectivity, a network device is capable of granting services that save capital and operational investments. Network services are a set of repetitive operations that application servers or client devices would normally deploy, but because of these services characteristics, can be implemented by specialized network equipment.

Dedicated devices that run network services are very common in data centers today. The services they provide range from load balancing to high availability, offload, security, and monitoring. They also bring simplicity to the data center operations, avoiding multiple software configurations on servers and client devices.

However, the increasing adoption of these devices presents two challenges for data center architects:

- How do you isolate these devices according to the company policies?
- How do you correctly size these devices?

These challenges have a direct impact on the hardware budget and resource utilization. After all, the acquisition of additional devices can easily represent more wasted hardware capacity.

Cisco created *virtual contexts* to propose a smart solution to these challenges. This type of virtualization allows the creation of abstract instances of network equipment inside a single physical device. But, differently from virtual local-area networks (VLANs) and Virtual Routing and Forwarding (VRF), a virtual context supports enhanced resource allocation control and management isolation.

This chapter explores virtualization on one specific network service: application load balancing. My objective is to explain the main reasons for this service adoption, show the load balancer deployment challenges, and describe how virtualization brings several advantages for data center architects and administrators.

Application Networking Services

In the IT architecture context, a *service* is defined as a functionality that can be reused in different situations and for different purposes. Examples of services for application environments are security, monitoring, acceleration, offload, and so on.

A service can be provided by different systems in a company infrastructure. In the classic client-server architecture, three elements can provide services for applications: the client devices, the servers, or the network.

One must admire the daunting task of service deployment in client devices. In this case, a service has to be installed and controlled in every device that accesses this application, independently of model and quantity. While some specific applications might work fine within this service model (distributed file sharing and some philanthropic distributed computing projects come to mind), it does not fit the majority of enterprise and Internet applications, where there is little or no control over each client device.

Although application servers are generally centralized in data centers, service deployment on these equipments can present challenges too. A service would have to be deployed for different hardware and operational systems, meaning higher operational costs. And more: Sometimes the administration team does not even have control of the server in the data center, such as in cases of outsourced hosting facilities.

Therefore, the network seems like a good place to deploy services because it encompasses the application traffic at all times. Standardized and repetitive services such as compression or encryption can be inserted transparently to client-server applications by network devices.

A great variety of application networking devices were created since client-server applications became popular in the 1980s. These devices include security firewalls, intrusion prevention systems (IPS), accelerators, performance monitor tools, and the object of this chapter: the load balancer.

The Use of Load Balancers

Dedicated network load balancers have been heavily used since the Internet explosion in the second half of the 1990s. They were created to scale the performance of websites, and their use has increased in data centers as they incorporate new features and functions.

They were originally created to improve the server load-balancing solution that Domain Name System (DNS) servers provide. As explained in Figure 4-1, a DNS server can respond to each client name request with a different IP address chosen from a configured ordered list of possible servers that provide the same application.

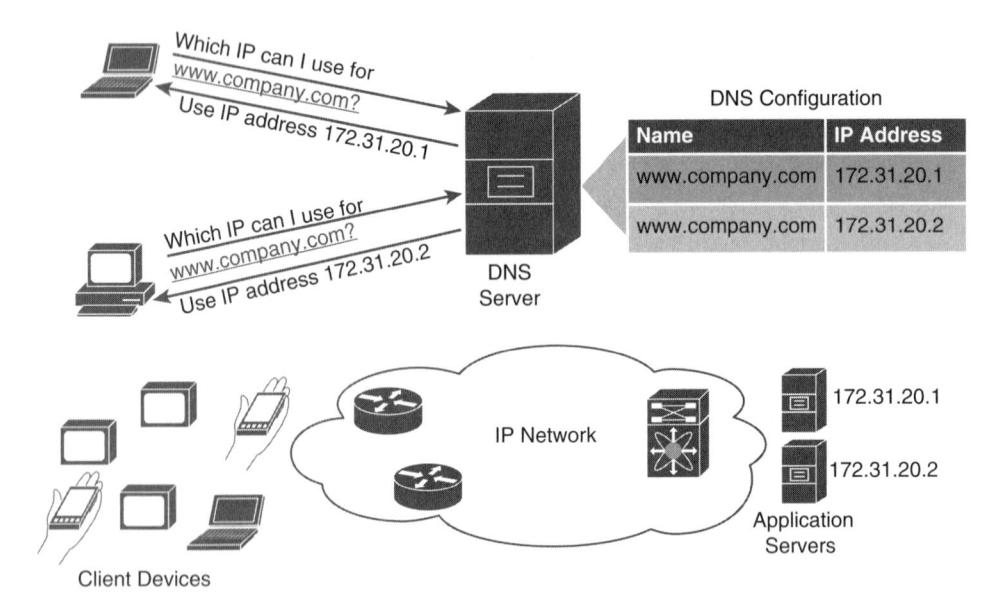

Figure 4-1 *DNS Server Load Balancing*

Although DNS load balancing can be easily deployed (if you have configuration access to DNS records, of course) it presents challenges such as

- The DNS servers are not aware of the application state in the balanced servers. Consequently, clients will receive the IP address of a failed server.

- The load-balancing service DNS servers can provide does not take into account any load information from the balanced servers. Therefore, it can overload them and seriously menace the application performance and availability.

- A DNS request does not specify which type of traffic the client will use afterward or the type of device (tablet, phone, or desktop) the client is. Hence, the choice of the best server cannot be defined by these parameters.

A complete load-balancing paradigm was made available with the creation of hardware-based load balancers. They can be defined as a network device with forwarding decisions that are based on Layers 4 to 7 parameters from the OSI model. These parameters include

- TCP destination port
- UDP destination port
- HTTP URL
- HTTP session cookie
- Strings recognized in the connection data

As new features were incorporated to these devices, they were called, during each "marketing campaign," by names such as Layer 7 switches, content switches, and application delivery controllers. For the sake of simplicity, this book will use the well-known generic name *load balancer* to represent this class of devices.

> **Note** Some network devices (such as routers and switches) also present software-based load-balancing capabilities, sharing resources with other functions. This chapter refers to hardware-based devices, which were optimally designed for load balancing and related activities.

Although it is possible to deploy load balancers as traffic engineering tools (as you will see further in this chapter), the main use for this equipment still remains the original one: application scaling. A load balancer allows the simple insertion of more application servers to process more client requests, as shown in Figure 4-2.

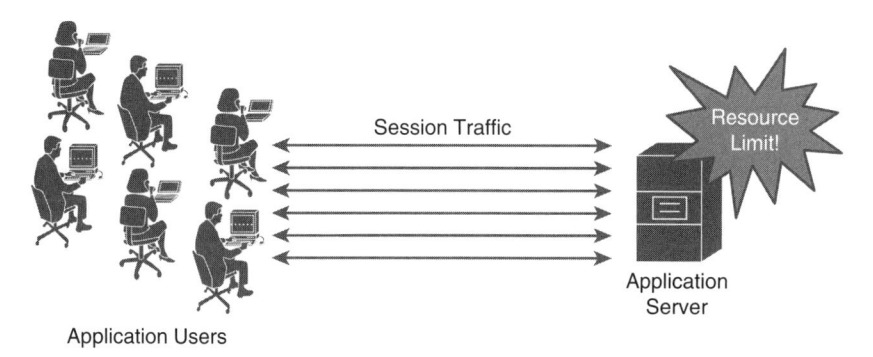

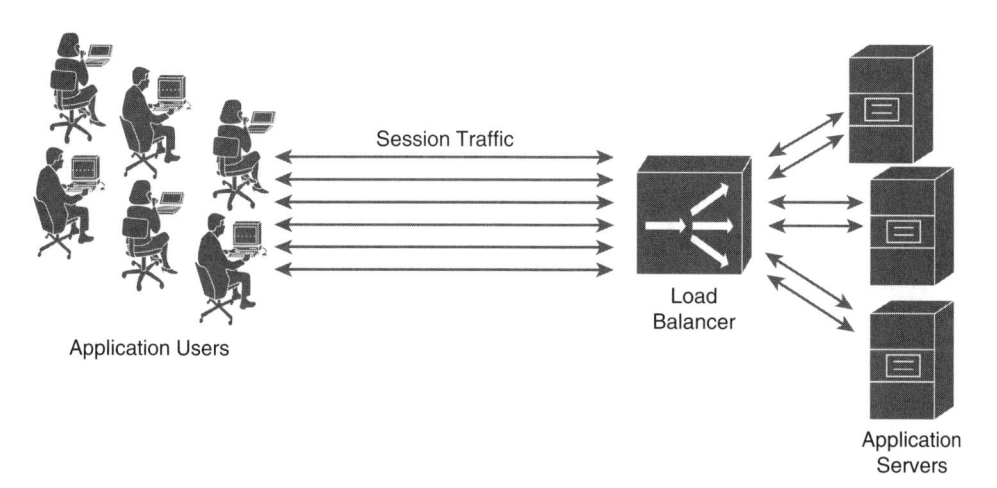

Figure 4-2 *Scale-Out of an Application*

A load balancer deployment has some advantages over server-based software solutions that perform the same function, such as

- A load balancer configuration does not depend on the operational system or application software installed on the servers. Software-based load-balancing solutions generally do.

- Software solutions must be configured and managed in every server that will be load-balanced, and the number of administrative operations generally is proportional to the number of balanced servers.

- A software-based load-balancing solution shares server resources with the main application running on these servers. Therefore, it can affect the overall application performance for the users. A load balancer generally has specialized hardware and predictable performance values.

These dedicated pieces of equipment can also offer high availability for an application that was not originally conceived to have fault tolerance. It is rather easy for a load balancer to forward the application users to another server in the case of a system failure.

Load balancers link the concepts of application availability and network availability. Hence, they can produce active network information (such as an IP address or a route), but only if an application is working properly. This concept connection is extremely important for topics such as disaster recovery and business continuity.

Also, as a centralized solution, a load balancer has access to aggregated information of user access (simultaneous users or hits per day, for example) that is difficult to obtain if server logs are analyzed individually.

A metaphor that helps summarize the function a load balancer involves the traffic control process in an airport:

- An airplane landing in a city will wait for instructions from the airport's traffic control tower. The control tower decides which runway this aircraft should use depending on its characteristics (airplane size, for example) and whether the runway is being occupied by another landing. In this scenario, the aircraft, the control tower, and the runways respectively represent user traffic, the load balancer, and the servers.

- The control tower will follow a predefined method to balance, among the airport runways, flights that are arriving at the airport.

- If a runway is in maintenance, the control tower will not proceed with a landing on this structure. This reflects the load-balance knowledge of the application health on each server.

- If this airplane is carrying an authority (such as the president of a country), the control tower can authorize its landing on a special runway. In the load balancer world, this could be called "content switching" or a balance decision based on connection data.

Load-Balancing Concepts

Whereas a great variety of load-balancing devices exist in the market (and even inside Cisco), every load balancer deployment has common elements and definitions.

Figure 4-3 presents the main configuration elements on a load balancer in a server environment.

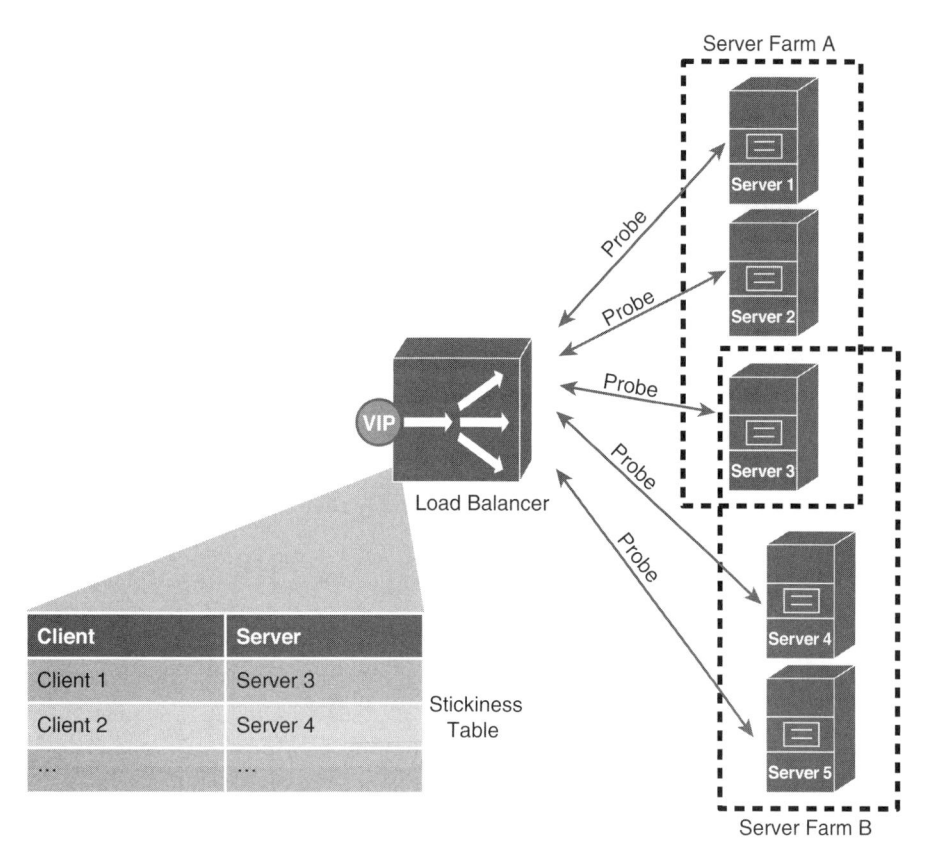

Figure 4-3 *Server Load Balancer Configuration Elements*

When you configure a load balancer, you must define the following elements:

- **Real servers,** which represent the addresses from servers that will receive the sessions from the load balancer.
- **A server farm**, which is a set of real servers that share the same application. A real server can belong to multiple server farms, as Server 3 does in Figure 4-3.

> **Note** Conceptually speaking, a server farm is not a server cluster. A cluster is defined as a set of servers with an additional layer of software that allows some kind of centralized administration and internal information sharing between its members. In contrast, a server farm simply characterizes a group of servers that have the same application, be they part of a cluster or not.

- **Probes,** which are synthetic requests the load balancer creates to check whether an application is available on a real server. They can be simple as an Internet Control Message Protocol (ICMP) echo request or as sophisticated as a Hypertext Transfer Protocol (HTTP) GET operation bundled with a database query.
- **The virtual IP,** or simply VIP, which is an internal address the load balancer uses to receive client connections. This IP address is usually provided by the DNS servers that are responsible for the application IP address advertisement to the clients.

> **Note** A VIP can be considered a pooling virtualization technique because it abstracts the group of real servers as a single virtual server for the application users.

- **The stickiness table,** which is an optional element that can store client information during its first access. The load balancer can use this information to always forward the client subsequent connections to the first selected server, thus maintaining session states inside the same server. Examples of stored client information are source IP address, HTTP cookies, and special strings.
- **A predictor,** which is the configured method of user traffic distribution among the real servers in a server farm. A wide variety of algorithms are available today for these devices, and Figure 4-4 illustrates how some of them work. In this figure, the arrows represent new client connections (or connections whose clients are not part of the stickiness table yet).

Figure 4-4 depicts the following predictors:

- **Round-robin:** With this predictor, the load balancer forwards a new user connection to the next available server in an ordered list created for the server farm. It goes back to the first real server in the list when the last one is served.
- **Least-connections:** In this case, the load balancer directs the new connection to the server with the lowest number of existing connections in the server farm. This method is generally deployed with a slow-start algorithm that avoids overload on servers that were recently added to a server farm.
- **Hashing:** When a new connection arrives, the load balancer will perform a hashing operation on a predefined parameter such as IP address, HTTP cookie, or Uniform Resource Locator (URL). The range of hashing results will be distributed among the servers in such a way that another connection with the same parameter will always reach the same server.

- **Least-loaded:** With this method, the load balancer is able to measure the current utilization (or load) of the real servers. This algorithm usually deploys a Simple Network Management Protocol (SNMP) GET request and allows the load balancer to define the next server based on how many CPU cycles and how much memory a server is using, for example.

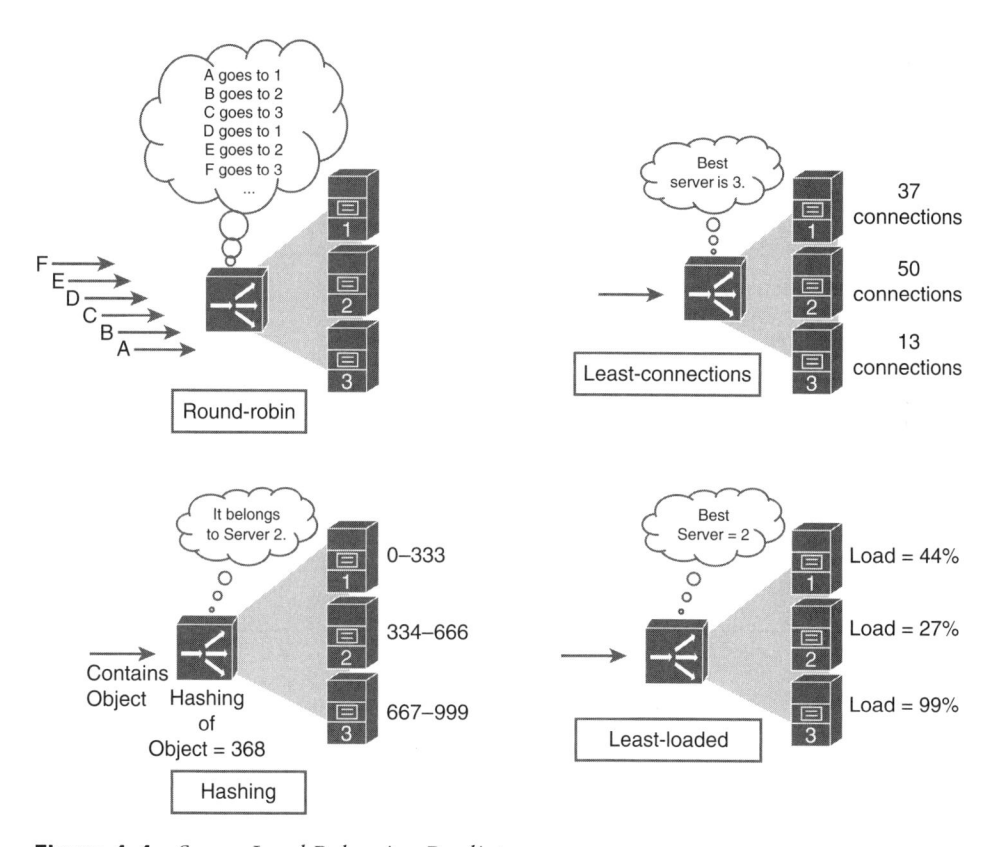

Figure 4-4 *Server Load-Balancing Predictors*

The choice of the best algorithm depends entirely on the application traffic characteristics. In real implementations, it is common to test different predictors (on real traffic) to evaluate which algorithm can achieve expected results. It is not unusual to perform some configuration fine-tuning until an optimal situation is reached.

Table 4-2 enlists possible application traffic profiles and corresponding suggestions for the first choice of predictor during these initial tests.

Table 4-2 *Best Practices for First Predictor Choice*

Application Traffic Characteristics	Predictor Suggestion
If the application has one of the following characteristics: ■ Homogeneous user connections (in duration and data exchange) ■ Unknown behavior	Round-robin
If the application has one of the following characteristics: ■ Heterogeneous user connections (in duration and data exchange) ■ Known maximum connections inflection point on server (see Figure 4-5)	Least-connections
If the application has one of the following characteristics: ■ Single-server selection for a user since the first connection ■ Cache or firewall load balancing ■ IP addresses, accessed URLs, or cookies that are "well-spread" among clients	Hashing
If the application has one of the following characteristics: ■ Server has SNMP agent ■ Management Information Base (MIB) variable value can be used to define the load of a server	Least-loaded

The load balancing fine-tuning includes the assignment of weights and connections limitations for the real servers in a server farm.

When *weights* are assigned to the real servers, the load balancer will use these values to define the proportion of connections each server will receive. For example: The round-robin predictor sends double the connections for a server if its weight is two times bigger than the other servers in a server farm. Similarly, for the least-connections predictor, the weight determines the percentage of current connections that are distributed to each server. This percentage can be calculated by the following formula:
Server-assigned weight / Sum of all weights

Note Weights usually do not have any effect on predictors such as least-loaded or hashing.

The *limitation of connections* on a real server can be used to avoid undesirable server response time caused by excessive simultaneous connections. Figure 4-5 describes the typical behavior of an application server according to the number of simultaneous connections it is processing.

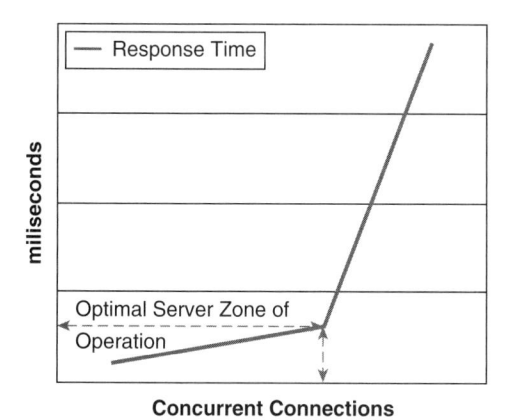

Figure 4-5 *Server Response Time Behavior*

The inflection point position, shown in Figure 4-5, varies wildly depending on a number of factors such as server hardware (CPU, memory, and storage access), software (operating system and application version), and other parameters. However, if this value is empirically known, the load balancer can be configured to limit the number of simultaneous connections a server maintains before its response time becomes unacceptable. If that real server reaches its maximum number of configured connections, the load balancer will consider it as a nonoperational server until it lowers its value below another parameter called *minimum connections*.

However, the difficulty in measuring this inflection point value led to the creation of yet another type of predictor: *server response time*. With this algorithm, a load balancer can send new user connections to the server with the lowest average response time in a server farm.

It seems rather clever to base the health measurement of a server on its main performance metric, but it is really important to define exactly what time interval is being measured. Usually a load balancer considers server response time as the time interval between

- A SYN sent to a server and a SYN/ACK received by the load balancer (Layer 4 response-time)
- An HTTP GET to a server and its response (Layer 7 response time)
- The establishment (three-way handshake for TCP) and explicit termination of a connection (end-to-end connection response time)

Note The response time predictor behavior can be usually modified through the use of weights assigned to real servers.

The choice of the best response time measurement depends on the type of switching operation the load balancer is configured to perform. These operations will be further discussed in the next section.

Layer 4 Switching Versus Layer 7 Switching

When a load balancer receives a new connection on a VIP, it selects a server farm based on client connection parameters. If this forwarding decision takes into consideration parameters such as IP addresses, IP protocols, or TCP/UDP ports, the load balancer is performing *Layer 4 switching*.

Note Although it is not a technically accurate definition, a load balancer usually treats UDP datagrams exchanged between two hosts as a "connection." It does that by reserving memory space for this UDP communication as it would do for TCP connections. This book uses this simplification.

Figure 4-6 details how a load balancer performs Layer 4 switching in a TCP connection that uses port 80.

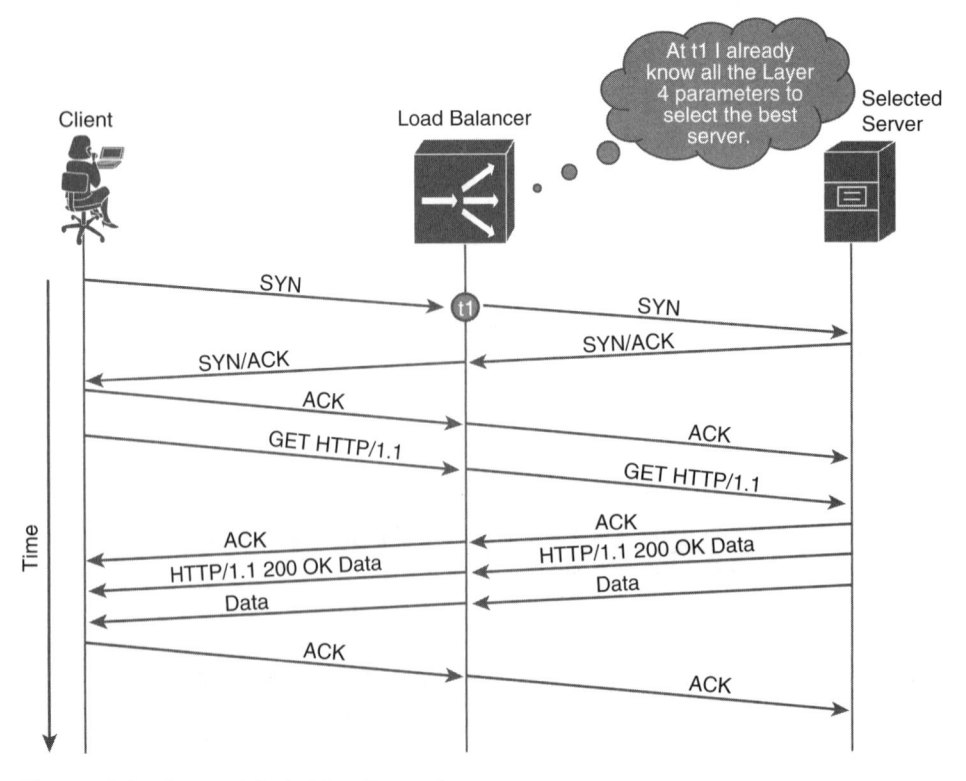

Figure 4-6 *Layer 4 Switching Example*

When a load balancer is performing Layer 4 switching, all the information it needs to select the best server for a new connection is contained in the TCP SYN (or UDP first datagram). The load balancer does not treat differently connections that have different parameters in the connection data payload (content).

Adversely, Layer 7 switching happens when the load balancer forwards a connection to a server using information obtained from the upper layers (5, 6, or 7) of the OSI model. Figure 4-7 depicts how a load balancer with a Layer 7 switching configuration treats the same TCP connection.

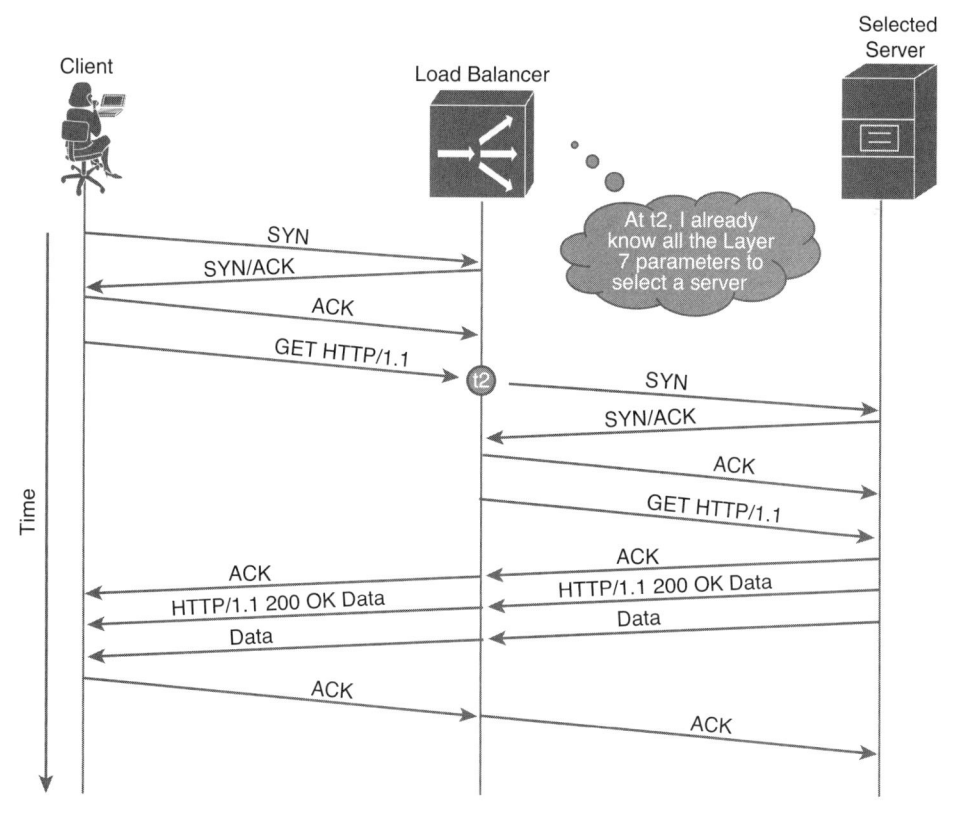

Figure 4-7 *Layer 7 Switching Example*

With Layer 7 switching, a load balancer must perform a decision beyond the transport protocol. Server selection must wait until the client sends relevant information from the session, presentation, or application layer. The load balancer becomes a transparent *TCP proxy*, establishing the connection with the client on behalf of the real servers. This spoofing process is also called *delayed binding* or *proxy connection*.

Connection Management

In a Layer 4 switching scenario, a load balancer must coordinate rewrites on Ethernet, IP, and TCP/UDP information from the original client connection to the communication with the selected server (after all, the client device is connecting to the VIP).

Performing Layer 7 switching, the load balancer needs to control two completely different connections, with distinct parameters such as checksum and sequence calculations. The coordination between these connections is called *splicing*, and it is one of the basic functions of a load balancer.

But some very specific applications might require a different connection management from load balancers. As you will learn, in a few cases, a load balancer can be more useful dispatching the traffic directly to a server and not participating in the communication from the server back to the client.

Figure 4-8 illustrates both ways that load balancers can manage client connections to the servers.

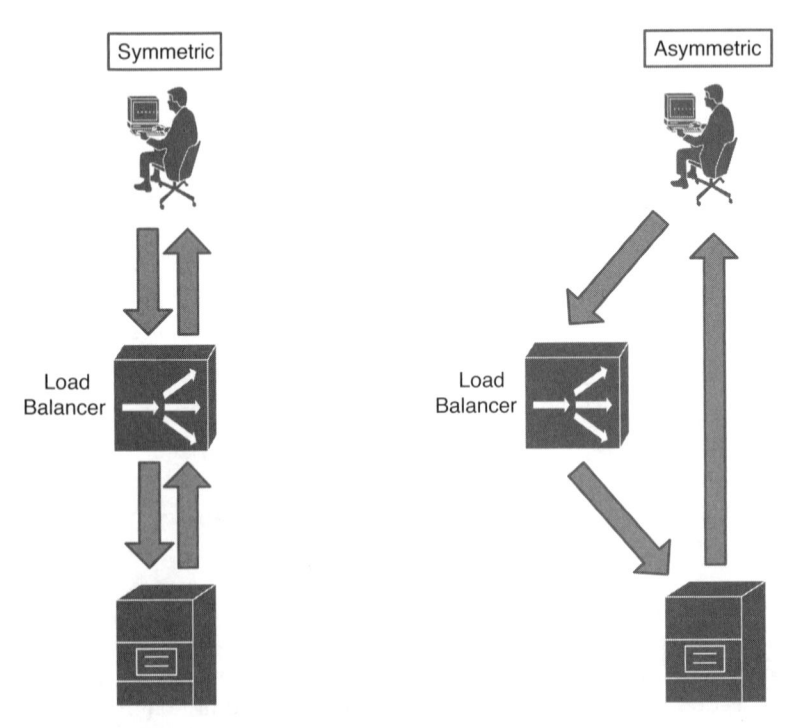

Figure 4-8 *Symmetric Versus Asymmetric Connection Management*

In *symmetric* connection management, all packets, be them from the client or from the selected server, always reach the load balancer. Because the load balancer is aware of the entire communication, it can deploy more advanced server load-balancing features such as Layer 7 switching, IP address translation, and header manipulation. This is by far the most popular connection management method, and both Layer 4 and Layer 7 switching examples from the last section use symmetric connection management.

When only part of the connection traverses the load balancer, the connection management it implements is called *asymmetric*. This method has the advantage of not overloading the load balancer from excessive return traffic from servers (such as video streaming, for example). But as the load balancer can only see one direction of the traffic (from client to server), multiple load-balance features cannot be deployed, such as address and port translation. Timeouts for TCP connections are usually configured in the load balancer because it will never receive connection termination segments (such as FIN) from the servers.

The most known example for asymmetric traffic is **Direct Server Return**, and Figure 4-9 details how this load-balancing technique works.

Tip Asymmetric traffic load-balancing deployment is rare in data centers today, and this technique should only be considered for specific scenarios. This technique is presented here to illustrate the challenges a load balancer implementation faces without connection symmetry.

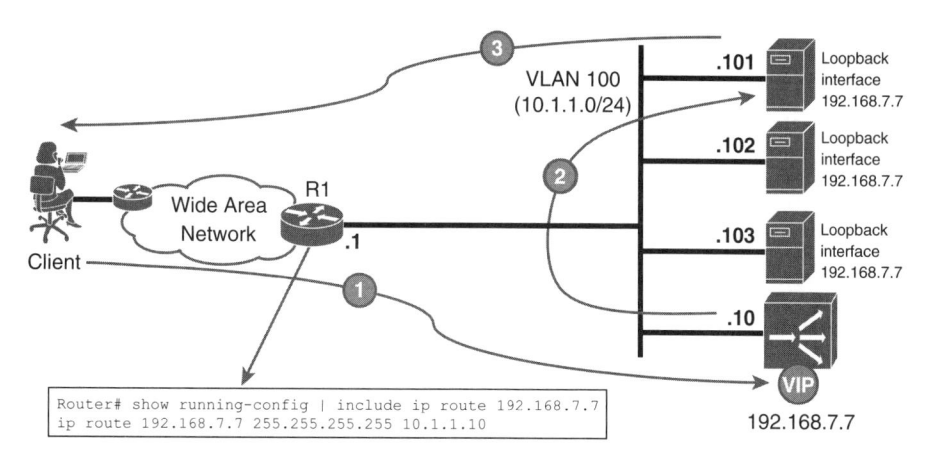

Figure 4-9 *Direct Server Return*

In the example described in Figure 4-9, the Direct Server Return load-balancing process has the following steps:

1. Router R1 forwards the connection packet to the VIP (192.168.7.7) using a static route that points to a load balancer IP address.

2. The load balancer forwards the packet to the selected server, rewriting the destination MAC address in these packets. A preconfigured loopback interface in the server will be able to receive the packet that still has the VIP address as the destination.

3. The server now replies directly to the client because the packet has the original client address.

Note Direct Server Return will work correctly only if the load balancer and servers share a broadcast domain and if each server has a configured virtual interface (loopback) with the same IP address as the VIP. Also, these loopback interfaces must not respond to ARP requests.

Address Translation and Load Balancing

Deploying Network Address Translation (NAT) and Port Address Translation (PAT) is fairly easy for devices that can deal with upper-layer parameters such as HTTP URLs. Actually, load balancers have several modes of address and port translation, and the most common are

- Server NAT
- Dual NAT
- Port redirection
- Transparent

In the following sections, you will examine each one of these translation modes and see their behavior in each phase of a symmetric managed connection: client to load balancer (phase 1), load balancer to server (phase 2), server to load balancer (phase 3), and load balancer back to the client (phase 4).

Server NAT

Server NAT was the first NAT mode deployed by load balancers. Figure 4-10 illustrates how a client sends it connection to the VIP (phase 1) and the load balancer changes the server destination address from its VIP to the IP address of the selected server (phase 2).

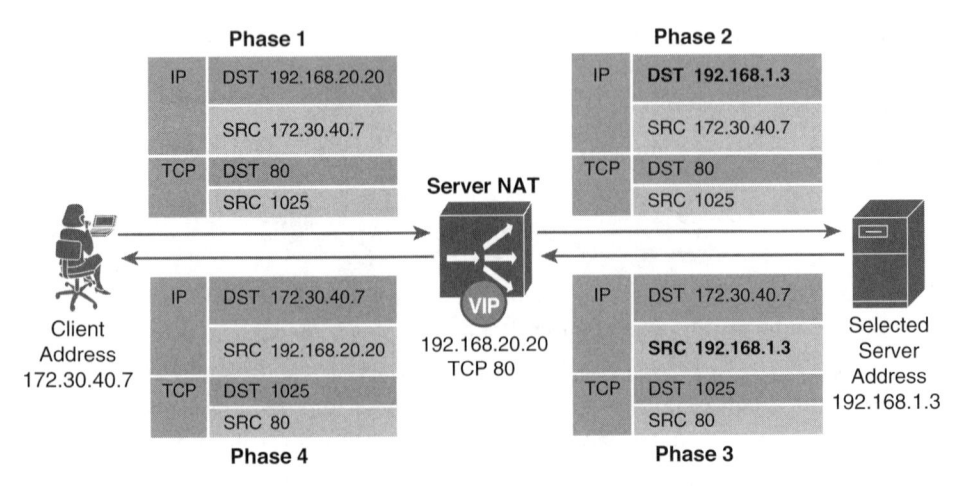

Figure 4-10 *Server NAT Mode*

You can see that the real server sends its responses to the original client IP address (phase 3). Because connection symmetry is mandatory in this scenario, the network infrastructure must force these responses back to the load balancer. Here are some examples of such network configurations:

- The load balancer interface is the default gateway for the real servers.
- Static or dynamic routing inside the data center forwards the traffic from the servers to the load balancer.

> **Tip** In Server NAT mode, the load balancer can protect servers that are on private networks not reachable by the clients (RFC 1918 addresses, for example). Therefore, in this case, only the VIP address needs to have a public address.

Dual NAT

A load balancer deploying *dual NAT* mode changes the source IP address and the destination IP address when it forwards the connection IP packets to a balanced server. Figure 4-11 details this mode of address translation.

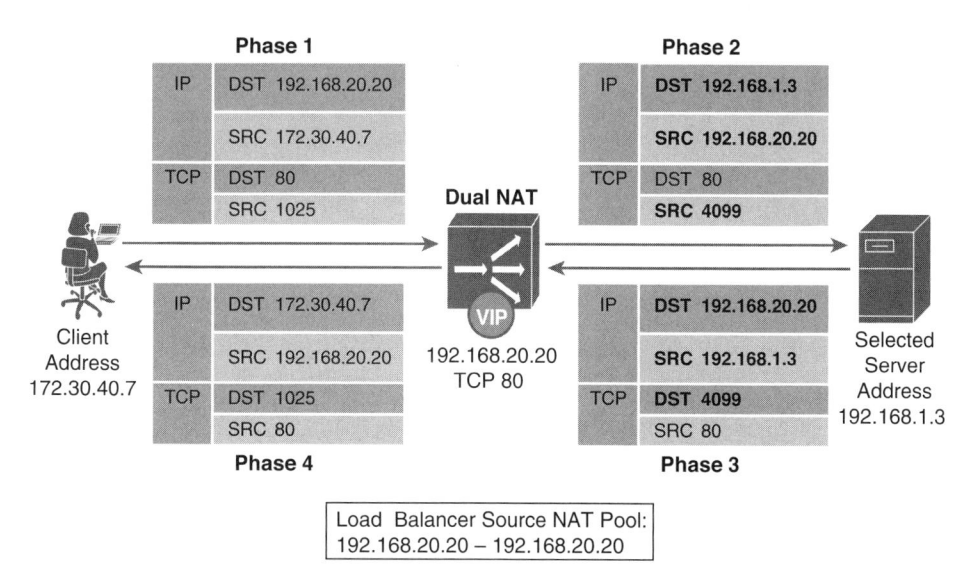

Figure 4-11 *Dual NAT Mode*

In dual NAT mode, the real servers will receive connections as if they were originated by an IP address that belongs to the load balancer (phase 2). Hence, it is certain that the responses from the servers will be directed to the load balancer, and connection symmetry is achieved.

Although the figure uses the VIP address as the source NAT IP address in phase 2, load balancers support the configuration of a range of source NAT IP addresses. Usually this range has fewer addresses than the number of clients, and because of that, the load balancer deploys PAT, changing the TCP (or UDP) source port number to a dynamically generated one.

As you can see in Figure 4-11, the destination port in phase 3 helps the load balancer to identify the original client for this connection.

Port Redirection

Port redirection mode enables the static translation of destination TCP and UDP port addresses. Figure 4-12 depicts this translation method.

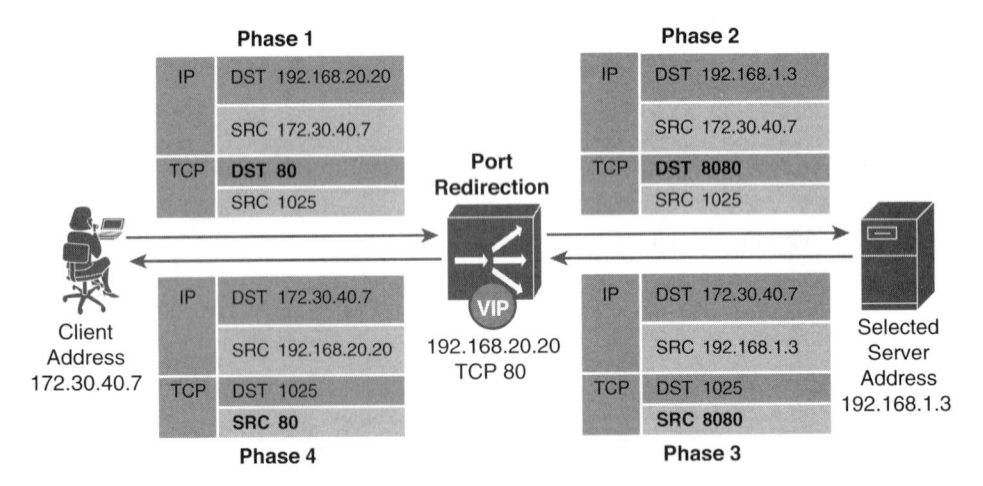

Figure 4-12 *Port Redirection Mode*

This mode can hide from the client the internal complexity of the servers that might receive connections on nontraditional ports.

As shown in Figure 4-12, the client does not need to know that the website accessible through the VIP address 192.168.20.20 (and standard port 80) runs over port 8080 on the real servers.

Transparent Mode

Omission is also a decision. With *transparent mode*, a load balancer does not perform any change on source or destination addresses, as Figure 4-13 exhibits.

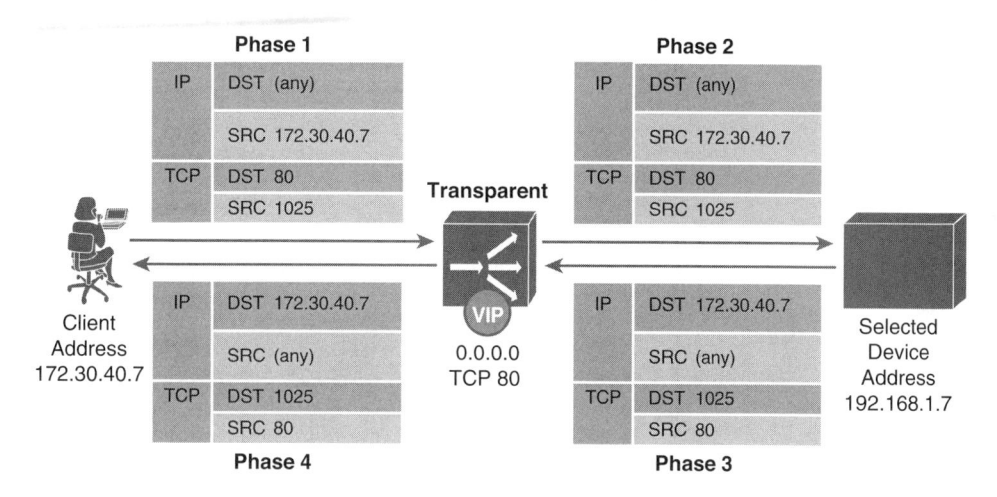

Figure 4-13 *Transparent Mode*

A wise engineer I know once defined such a mode as "super policy-based routing." This comparison makes sense because the load balancer Layer 7 capabilities can redirect traffic in an extremely granular fashion when compared with a router performing policy-based routing (PBR).

The VIP associated with this policy defines the traffic that will be transparently load balanced. Usually the VIP is configured for all destination IP addresses (0.0.0.0, as represented in Figure 4-13) or for a specific IP subnet.

One might ask whether there is any practical use for this mode. Actually, the answer for this question is a big yes. As you will learn in the next section, load balancers usually deploy transparent mode in load-balancing scenarios of devices other than servers.

Other Load-Balancing Applications

Over the years, with the introduction of advanced features such as URL switching and new predictor methods, load balancers began to be applied on other service devices. Placed in the path between a client and a server, the load balancer can redirect the traffic to devices such as web caches, VPN concentrators, WAN accelerators, firewalls, and proxy servers. In the following sections, we will explore aspects of real load-balancing data center designs for two of them.

Firewall Load Balancing

This load-balancing design is used when there is a need to scale out firewall capacity on a network.

Figure 4-14 illustrates the "firewall sandwich" design, with two layers of load balancers distributing client connections among a set of firewall appliances.

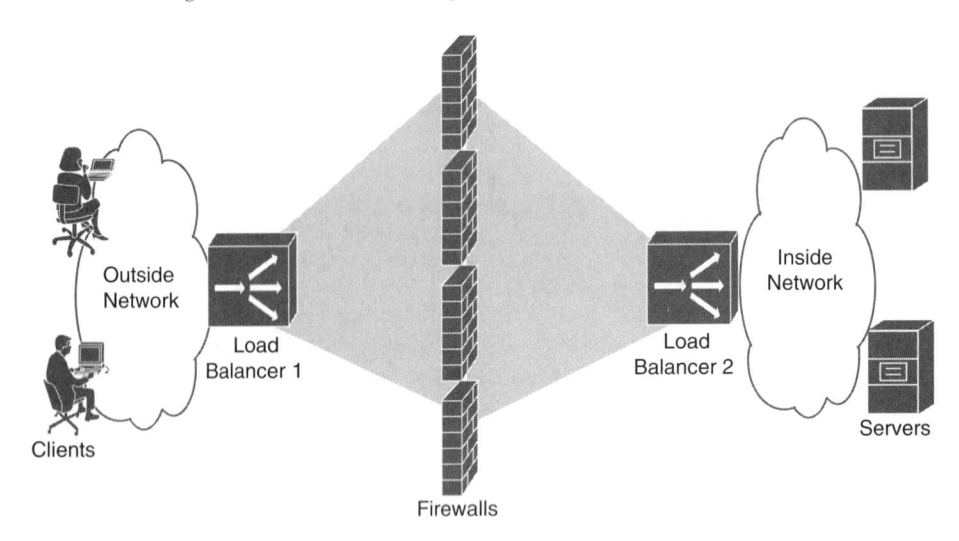

Figure 4-14 *Firewall Load-Balancing Topology*

To work correctly with stateful firewalls, one principle must be maintained by this design: Each client connection must traverse the same firewall on both directions.

Load balancers can achieve this principle using hashing predictors on complementary parameters. As an example, in Figure 4-14, load balancer 1 could use hashing on the *source* IP addresses (from the clients) while load balancer 2 would use hashing on the *destination* IP address (to the clients). Both operations would have the same result, and therefore the same firewall would be used on both directions of a connection.

Transparent translation mode is usually deployed in this design. Probes from both load balancers must also be configured to test the paths through the firewalls, and because of that, rules must be configured on all firewalls to permit their transit.

Firewall load balancing requires a fairly complex configuration on load balancers and firewalls, and for such reason, this design is only recommended in special cases. One applicable scenario can happen when the existing firewalls have a relatively smaller performance if compared with available load balancers.

The load balancer and firewall configuration becomes especially challenging when the firewalls have more than two interfaces (for demilitarized zones, for example).

Reverse Proxy Load Balancing

Proxies are servers that act as intermediaries for client-server connections. They evaluate the client request according to its service rules and provide a request to the appropriate server on behalf of the client.

Proxy servers can provide services such as

- Web security
- Caching
- Email filtering
- Application acceleration

A proxy server is called *reverse proxy* when it is placed in a data center as a front-end service for clients coming from outside networks.

To avoid client-by-client configuration, a load balancer can provide traffic load balancing to a set of reverse proxy servers. Figure 4-15 examines this design in more detail.

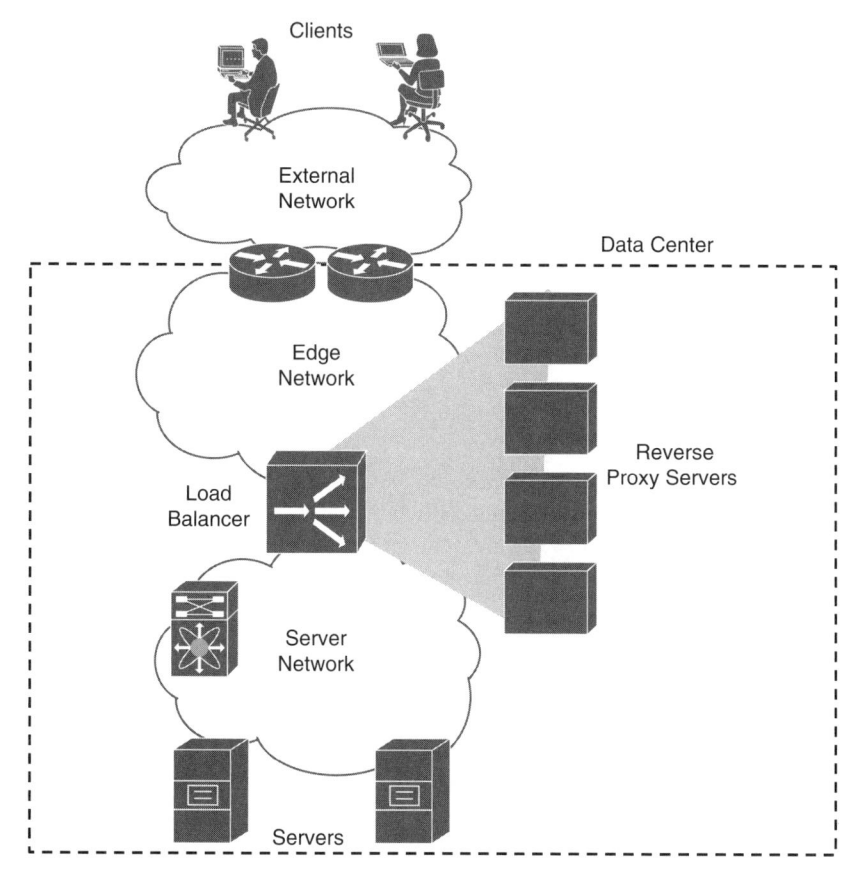

Figure 4-15 *Reverse Proxy Design*

In these designs, the load balancer usually deploys transparent translation mode and probes to evaluate whether the proxy servers are available. Depending on the service provided by the reverse proxies, the load balancer can use predictors such as URL hashing (for web caching) or least-loaded if there is a meaningful SNMP agent active in each proxy.

Offloading Servers

Load balancers can also provide additional services to servers, offloading them from hardware-consuming operations. The most common offload services they provide are encryption, authentication, connection processing, and compression.

Offloading allows the repositioning of server resources to the main application, enabling better response time and performance for the users.

The following sections discuss three advanced offload services that a load balancer can provide for servers:

- Secure Sockets Layer (SSL) offload
- TCP offload
- HTTP compression

Note From the load balancer implementation perspective, server offload features are deployed as Layer 7 switching operations.

SSL Offload

Secure Sockets Layer (SSL) is a protocol, created by Netscape in the 1990s, that provides security for Internet connections. SSL ensures confidentiality, authentication, and integrity for the data transported by it. In 1999, the Internet Engineering Task Force (IETF) proposed a standard version of SSL called Transport Layer Security (TLS) in RFC 2246.

Both SSL and TLS act between the transport layer and the session layer, as Figure 4-16 explains.

After a TCP connection is established between a client and a server, the SSL connection participants perform key exchanges and negotiate an appropriated encryption algorithm.

When an SSL connection is established, the upper-layer protocol can send its data using SSL as its own secure transport layer. The most used protocol over SSL is HTTP.

Note Secure HTTP (HTTPS) is simply HTTP encrypted by SSL.

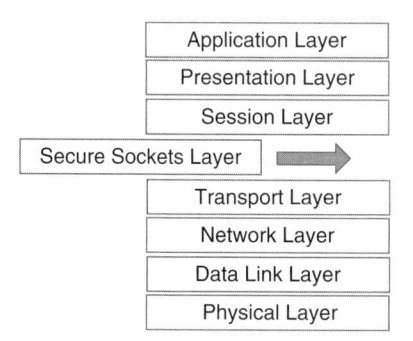

Figure 4-16 *SSL and the OSI Model*

Figure 4-17 details the protocol exchange between an SSL client and an SSL server.

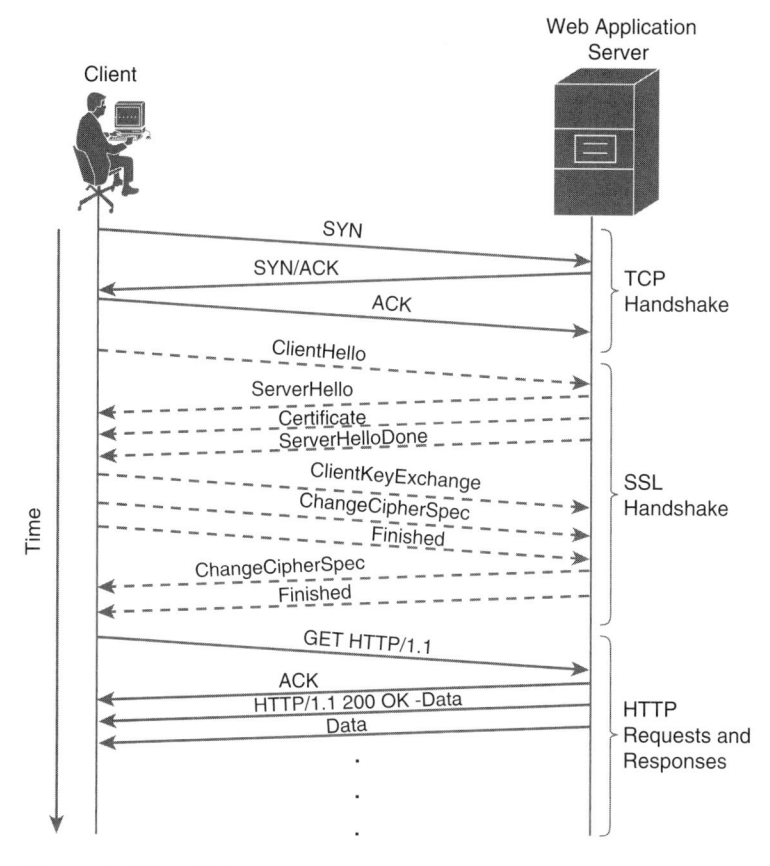

Figure 4-17 *HTTPS Operation*

Note In Figure 4-17, only the server certificate is authenticated. Although the figure does not show that option, it is possible for the server to authenticate the client certificate as well.

A load balancer performing SSL offload can act as an SSL server to the client, an SSL client to the real server, or both. In each of these possibilities, it is possible to obtain advantages from this feature in real-world cases.

Figures 4-18, 4-19, and 4-20 present three deployment options for SSL offload: SSL termination, SSL initiation, and end-to-end SSL.

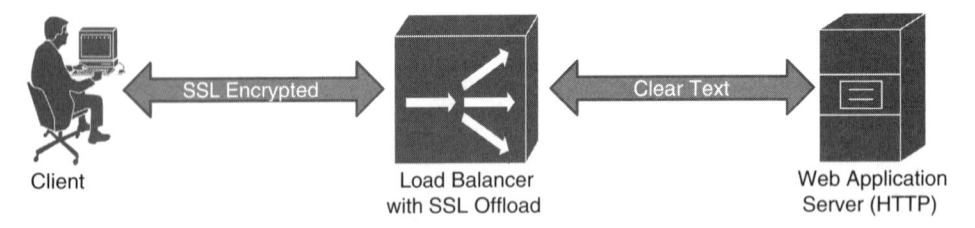

Figure 4-18 *SSL Termination*

SSL termination can completely relieve servers from the intensive encryption processing. This is the most usual deployment of SSL offload and it can bring the following benefits:

- Total offload of encryption from the servers
- Layer 5 to 7 awareness for Layer 7 switching in SSL connections
- Savings on public certificates because only the load balancer (and not the real servers) requires one

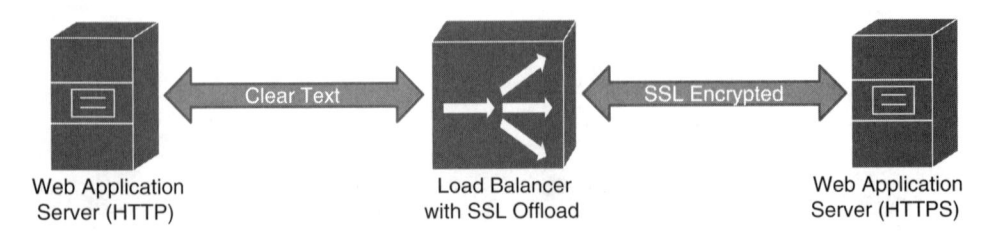

Figure 4-19 *SSL Initiation*

In *SSL initiation*, the load balancer can perform the SSL negotiation and encryption on behalf of the SSL client. This SSL client can be a local data center server exchanging secure data with a remote one.

This design can be especially useful when the SSL server is accessible only through the Internet and the data center administration wants to offload the local servers from the encryption processing. It is possible to avoid spending on unnecessary public certificates because only the load balancer needs one.

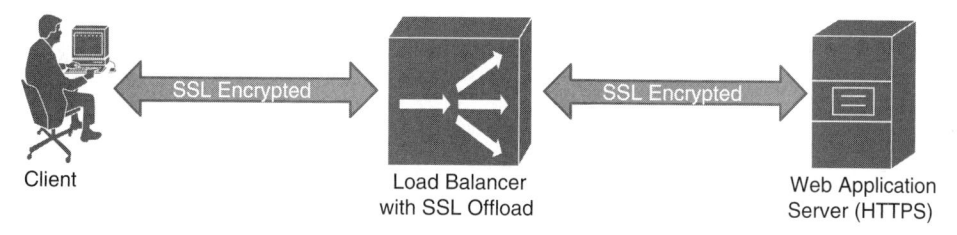

Figure 4-20 *End-to-End SSL*

Some data centers have security policies that simply do not allow the exchange of business traffic in clear text under any circumstance (a bank is a nice example of that). The *end-to-end SSL offload* design can be quite useful because it brings the following possibilities:

- It can deploy a less intensive encryption on the servers (Advanced Encryption Standard [AES] for the SSL clients and Data Encryption Standard [DES] for servers, for example).

- It allows the load balancer to perform Layer 7 switching without losing the connection security.

- Only the load balancer needs a public certificate (servers can use customer-generated private certificates).

TCP Offload

When a server is performing TCP communication with its clients, it must execute the following operations for each connection:

- Connection establishment (three-way handshake)
- Acknowledgment of segments
- Checksum and sequence number calculation
- Sliding window calculation
- Congestion control
- Connection termination

Depending on the number and characteristics of the connections, a server can spend a great part of its resources, such as memory and CPU cycles, on these operations.

A load balancer can use its connection management capabilities to offload web servers from TCP excessive processing. Figure 4-21 illustrates how a load balancer can drastically reduce the number of connections a server is managing.

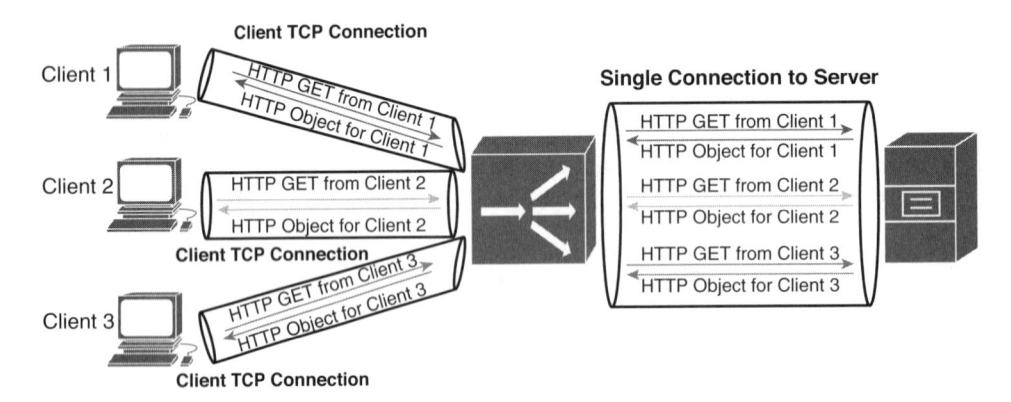

Figure 4-21 *TCP Connection Management Offload*

Instead of dealing with the totality of sessions sent by the users, a load balancer can send all the data from these connections inside one or two connections for this server. This offload service is also called "TCP reuse" or "TCP multiplexing."

> **Note** I recommend that you properly test the web application behavior with TCP offload before you deploy this capability on production servers. Some of these applications might not support this connection handling, and unpredictable results can arise from it.

HTTP Compression

The majority of web servers and browsers have the capability to, respectively, compress and uncompress transmitted objects in order to

- Better use the available bandwidth for both of them
- Improve the web page response time

The most common compression algorithms used by browsers nowadays are *GZIP* and *deflate*. The compress operations usually consume considerable server resources, such as CPU and memory. Depending on the number of simultaneous requests and object sizes, enabling compression can seriously damage the application performance of a web server.

Because the biggest amount of traffic is usually from the server to the client, it is possible for a load balancer, which might be participating in the communication between these two entities, to offload the compression processing from the servers.

In this scenario, the load balancer could observe which types of compression methods a client web browser supports and, on behalf of the web server, compress all objects to this client using a supported algorithm.

Load Balancer Proliferation in the Data Center

As discussed in Chapter 2, "Data Center Network Evolution," load balancers are typically connected to the aggregation layer of a data center network. At this location, these devices can provide network services on VLANs that are accessible to (possibly) thousand of servers.

However, considering that they are so strategically positioned, why is it common for a data center to have tens of these devices? In fact, I know some service provider data centers that have hundreds of them.

I will cite four reasons for this collateral effect:

- Load balancer performance
- Security policies
- Suboptimal traffic avoidance
- Application environment independency

In the next sections, you will be able to examine each factor in detail.

Load Balancer Performance

The most usual performance parameters for stateful network devices (such as load balancers) are

- **Bandwidth:** This measures how many bits per second can go through a load balancer. Unfortunately, this parameter is commonly mistaken as the only one available for sizing.
- **Concurrent connections:** This represents how many user connections the device can serve simultaneously. This parameter is memory dependent and can have different values for Layer 4 and Layer 7 switching.
- **New connections per second (cps):** This parameter shows how fast a load balancer can absorb new client connections. Usually a load balancer has different values for Layer 4 and Layer 7 switching defined by its hardware.

Traditionally, when the traffic submitted to a load balancer saturates one of these performance parameters, the entire device is replaced by one that can support the intended capacity (it does not matter how the other parameters are being utilized). And if the load balancer is being used by multiple server farms, another popular alternative is replacing one device for two or more. You can observe this scale-out of load balancers in Figure 4-22.

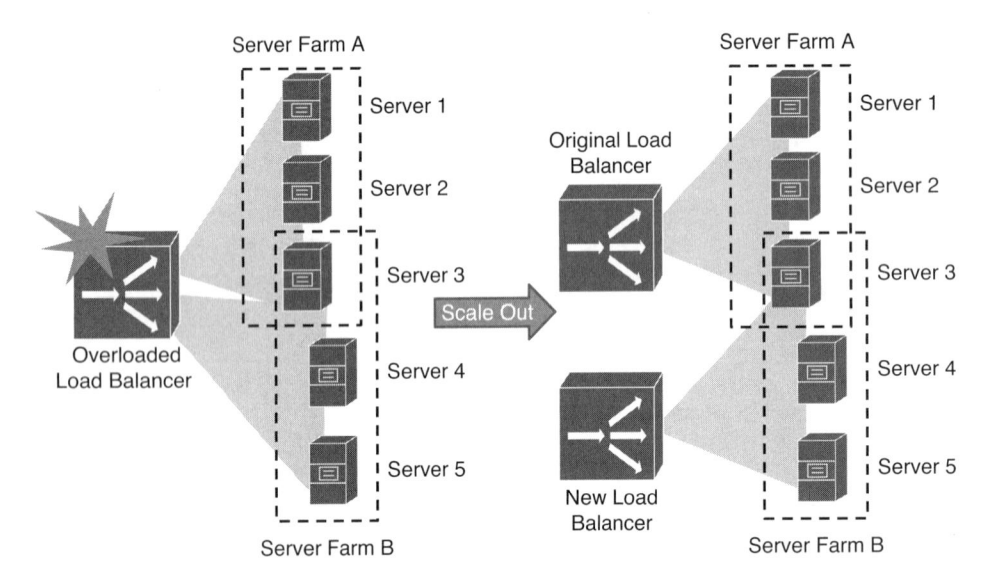

Figure 4-22 *Load Balancers Scaling Out*

This scaling decision might explain why some customers have multiple load balancers in a single application environment. And as you can imagine, configuration complexity grows proportionally with the number of devices, and some design doubts can arise, such as: Which load balancer should be the default gateway for Server 3 in Figure 4-22? How do you guarantee symmetry of traffic for both devices (original and new load balancer)?

Security Policies

Some data centers are simply not allowed to share network devices among different application environments because of security policies. These rules can force network and application administrators to have separate load balancers for different security zones (DMZs) or application importance.

Therefore, security policies can easily multiply the number of load balancers needed in a data center. But on the other hand, you can analyze the complexity of an opposite scenario: load balancer sharing between two security zones separated by a firewall.

In Figure 4-23, a single device load-balances DMZ servers (for Internet users) and intranet servers (for employees inside the company network). In this topology, the firewall rules would have to be configured to allow

- Client–to–load balancer connection (1 and 4)
- Connection from the load balancer to the intranet server (2 and 3)
- Load balance probes to the intranet servers

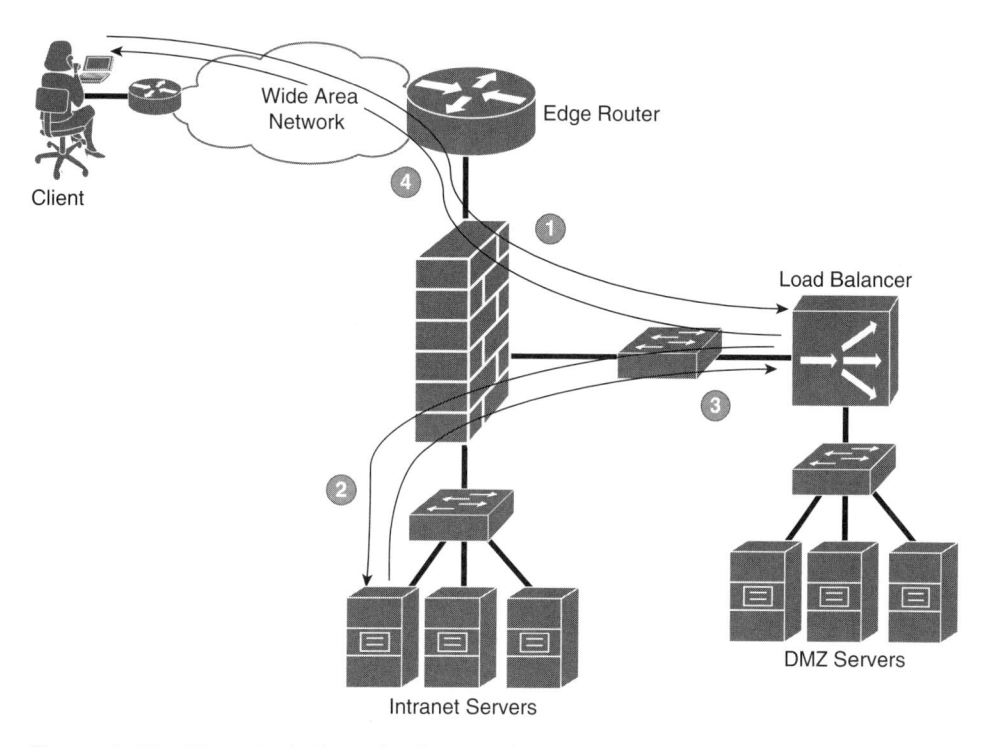

Figure 4-23 *Hypothetical Load Balancer Sharing Between Security Zones*

Also, if the edge router is the default gateway for the firewall, the load balance configuration would have to use some technique, such as dual NAT, to guarantee traffic symmetry.

Hence, configuration complexity grows when there is load balance sharing among firewall security zones of a number of configuration steps. This operational challenge might explain why so many data center architects accept the rule that "every DMZ needs separate load balancers" and why so many of these devices are underutilized.

Suboptimal Traffic

Sometimes the data center network topology justifies the decision to acquire another pair of load balancers. Figure 4-24 illustrates what happens when a load balancer is shared among servers distributed on different aggregation switches.

> **Tip** The devices' uplink connections are not depicted in Figure 4-24 for the sake of clarity.

In such a scenario, although the client connections use a straightforward path to the load balancers (Steps 1 and 4), the connections from the load balancer to the servers that belong to another aggregation pair (Steps 2 and 3) do not share that characteristic. In fact,

138 Data Center Virtualization Fundamentals

as you can observe in Figure 4-24, each data packet from Steps 2 and 3 must traverse the core switches twice, which can negatively affect the uplink usage in this data center network layer and increase the overall application response time to the client.

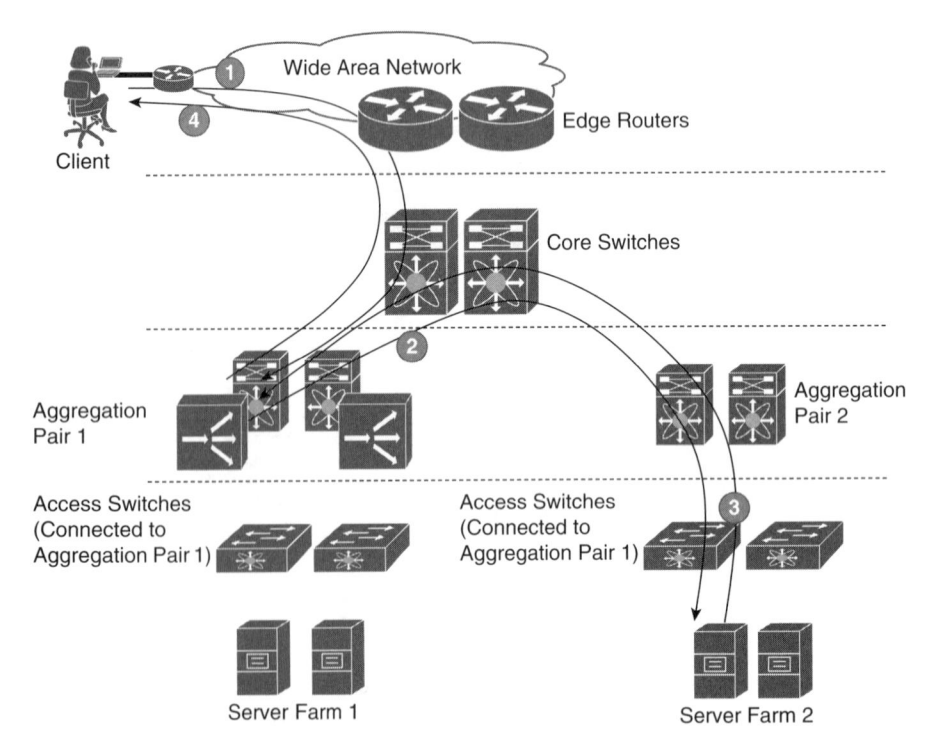

Figure 4-24 *Load Balancer Sharing Between Server Farms Located in Different Aggregation Switches*

Application Environment Independency

Multitier applications are very common in most corporate data centers. This client-server popular architecture separates functions among groups of servers to create a flexible application, where a server tier can be easily replaced or rewritten.

The most deployed application multitier architecture is the three-tier architecture. It encompasses the following group or servers:

- **Presentation tier:** This layer is responsible for the front-end communication with the clients. It generally uses web technologies.

- **Application tier:** This is a group of servers that controls the business logic.

- **Data tier:** This is where the information is stored and retrieved. Database servers are usually the components of this tier.

Depending on the organization of an enterprise, the servers from these tiers can be managed by different teams. And more: Company policies might restrict the level of device sharing among each tier. In the case of load balancers, it can mean that each tier must have its own pair of devices, as illustrated on Figure 4-25.

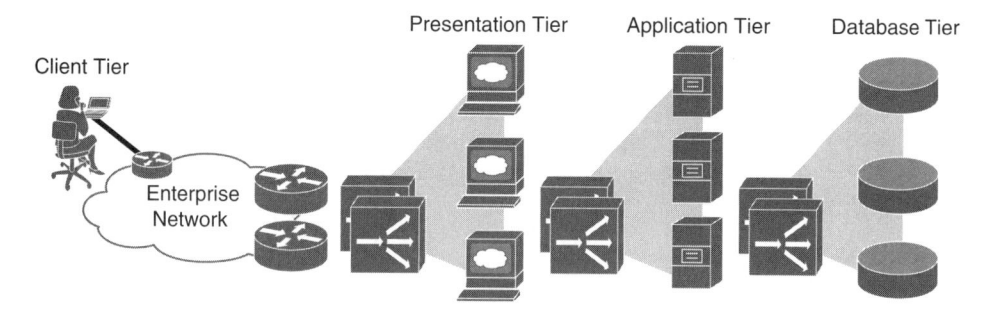

Figure 4-25 *Load Balancers and Multitier Applications Scenario*

When a data center houses lots of independent customers, the number of required load balancers can be even bigger. These are called *multitenant data centers*, and they can belong to service providers and to a parent corporation (holding) that houses different owned companies in the same infrastructure.

Some contracts determine that the customers (or owned companies) can have access to their allocated load balancer configuration. Therefore, these service providers (or parent companies) are obliged to guarantee management isolation.

This requirement can mean separate devices for different customer environments, especially if the deployed load balancers do not have any form of management isolation for configuration elements such as real servers, server farms, probes, and VIPs.

If every different application environment uses a different pair of physical load balancers, there is also a big chance that these devices do not have an optimal resource utilization. That waste of resources is a great challenge for companies that are trying to rationalize their decreasing data center budget.

ACE Virtual Contexts

Cisco created the first hardware-based load balancer in 1996. It was called Cisco Local Director, and it was a success during the early days of e-business. In the 2000s, Cisco continued the evolution of load-balancing hardware and features through the Content Services Switch (CSS) 11000 and the Content Switching Module (CSM) for the Catalyst 6500.

To address the challenges of low utilization and proliferation explained in the last section, Cisco created the concept of *virtual contexts* and applied it in the Application Control Engine (ACE) product series.

An *ACE virtual context* is an abstraction of an independent load balancer with its own interfaces, configuration, policies, and administrators. At the time of this writing, a single ACE physical equipment piece can act as 250 virtual load balancers. However, different from dedicated physical devices, a virtual context can have its performance capacity tailored for a specific environment.

Figure 4-26 illustrates the creation of contexts in a single ACE device.

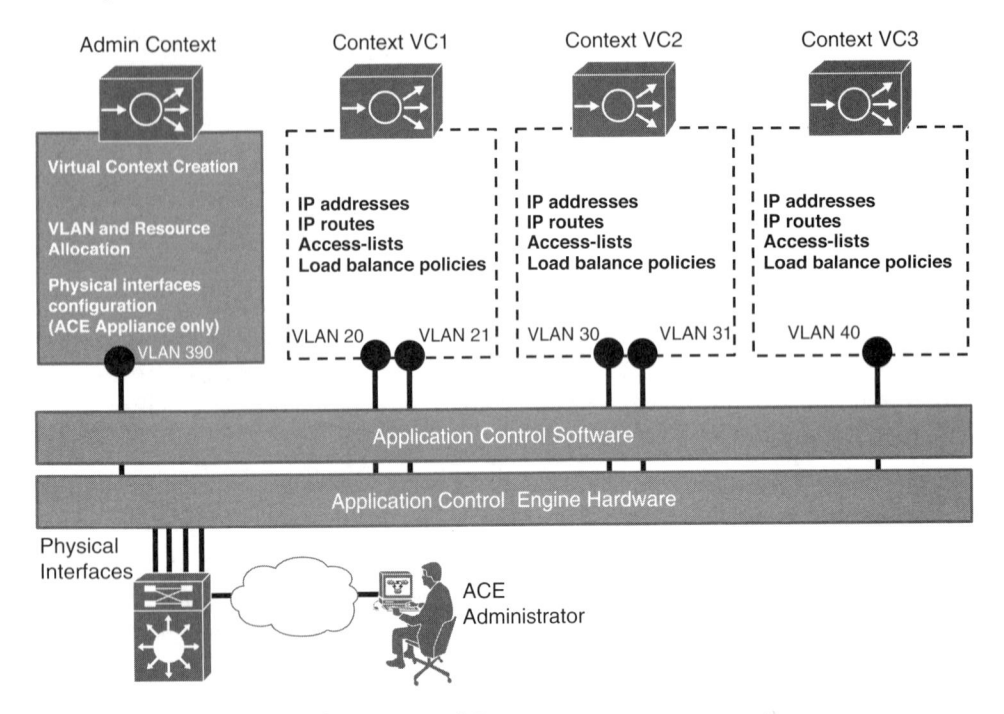

Figure 4-26 *Overview of ACE Virtual Contexts*

The creation and configuration of virtual contexts are done through management access to a built-in *admin context*. The admin context is automatically created when an ACE is configured for the first time. An account called *admin* is created with full configuration authorization (including the creation of virtual contexts). Although it is not recommended, the admin context can be used to perform load balancing as well.

Caution It is possible to configure all your load-balancing policies in the admin context. But you must be aware that management access to the admin context can severely damage, or even destroy, the other contexts.

In Figure 4-26, three other virtual contexts are depicted: VC1, VC2, and VC3. They all have deliberate distinct configurations to demonstrate how flexible the ACE virtualization capabilities are. These contexts will be used in the remaining sections of this chapter.

Application Control Engine Physical Connections

Each ACE form factor has different ways to connect to a network. In the following sections, you will learn how the ACE appliance and the ACE module can be configured to be part of a data center network.

Connecting an ACE Appliance

The ACE 4710 has four 1000BASE-T Gigabit Ethernet interfaces that can be connected to a single switch or up to four different ones. Figure 4-27 illustrates one connectivity scenario for the ACE 4710.

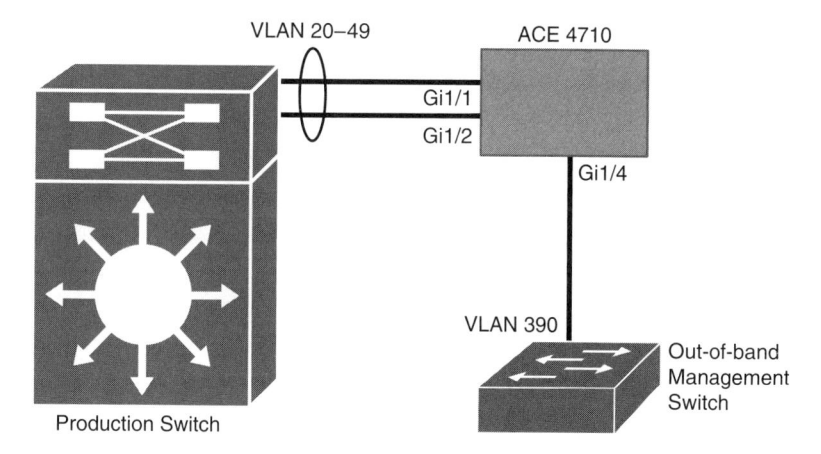

Figure 4-27 *ACE 4710 Network Connection Example*

In the case depicted in Figure 4-27, the appliance has two Gigabit Ethernet interfaces connected to a production switch (and aggregated in a PortChannel) and one interface connected to an out-of-band management switch. The PortChannel is used for the traffic that ACE load-balances (it is a trunk for the VLANs allocated to the virtual contexts), and the lonely interface is used for management purposes only.

Tip PortChannels will be discussed in detail in Chapter 6, "Fooling Spanning Tree." At this time, I just want you to understand that this capability allows the aggregation of multiple Ethernet ports on a virtual interface.

Example 4-1 shows how the physical connection from this figure was configured. As you can see, the ACE operational system (application control software) has an IOS-like command-line interface (CLI).

> **Note** If you are not familiar with the Cisco IOS command-line interface, I highly recommend that you first read Appendix B, "IOS, NX-OS, and Application Control Software Command-Line Interface Basics."

Example 4-1 *ACE 4710 Physical Connection Configuration*

```
ACE/Admin# show running-config interface
Generating configuration....
interface gigabitEthernet 1/1
  channel-group 1
  no shutdown
interface gigabitEthernet 1/2
  channel-group 1
  no shutdown
interface gigabitEthernet 1/3
  shutdown
interface gigabitEthernet 1/4
! Allowing VLAN 390 (out-of-band management)
  switchport access vlan 390
  no shutdown
interface port-channel 1
! Allowing VLANs that will be used by the virtual contexts
  switchport trunk allowed vlan 20-49
  no shutdown
```

Examples 4-2 and 4-3 show the respective configurations of the production and management switch ports.

Example 4-2 *Production Switch Interface Configuration for the ACE Appliance*

```
ProductionSwitch# show running-config interface gigabitEthernet 4/20
Building configuration...

Current configuration : 227 bytes
!
interface GigabitEthernet4/20
 description Connection to ACE-4710 Gi1/1
 no ip address
```

```
  switchport
  switchport trunk encapsulation dot1q
  switchport trunk allowed vlan 20-49
  switchport mode trunk
 ! Enabling PortChannel mode ON
  channel-group 20 mode on
 end


Production# show running-config interface gigabitEthernet 4/21
Building configuration...

Current configuration : 227 bytes
!
interface GigabitEthernet4/21
 description Connection to ACE-4710 Gi1/2
 no ip address
 switchport
 switchport trunk encapsulation dot1q
 switchport trunk allowed vlan 20-49
 switchport mode trunk
 ! Enabling PortChannel mode ON
 channel-group 20 mode on
end
Production# show running-config interface port-channel 20
Building configuration...

Current configuration : 157 bytes
!
interface Port-channel20
 no ip address
 switchport
 switchport trunk encapsulation dot1q
 ! Allowing VLANs 20 to 49 for ACE virtual contexts
 switchport trunk allowed vlan 20-49
 switchport mode trunk
end
```

Example 4-3 *Out-of-Band Management Switch Interface Configuration*

```
ManagementSwitch# show running-config interface fastEthernet 3/15
Building configuration...

Current configuration : 179 bytes
!
```

```
interface FastEthernet3/15
 description Connection to ACE-4710 Gi1/4
 no ip address
 switchport
! Configuring VLAN 390 for out-of-band management traffic
 switchport access vlan 390
 switchport mode access
end
```

Connecting an ACE Module

Because this form factor is already integrated to the Catalyst 6500, an ACE module requires less configuration steps for its physical connection than the ACE appliance. Actually, the Catalyst 6500 automatically configures the module network insertion using its internal Ethernet Out-of-Band Channel (EOBC) connection.

Figure 4-28 depicts the internal Catalyst 6500 connection for the ACE module and the required Catalyst configuration.

```
Catalyst6500# show running-config | include svc
svclc vlan-group 20 20-49
svclc vlan-group 39 390
svc module 5 vlan-group 20,39
svclc multiple-vlan-interfaces
```

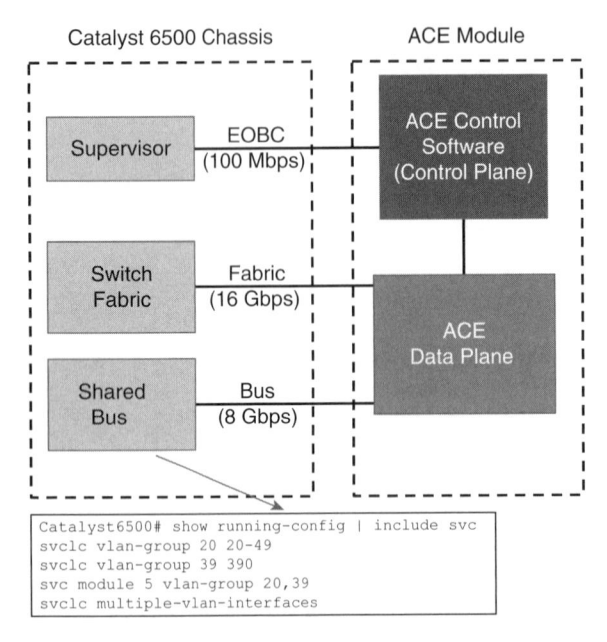

Figure 4-28 *ACE Module Internal Connectivity to Catalyst 6500 and Configuration*

The internal EOBC allows the Catalyst Supervisor to access the ACE module control plane for session command access. The switch fabric and the shared bus connections are responsible for the traffic sent and received by the ACE module data plane.

Note The shared bus interconnect is used only if communication to Catalyst 6500 "classic cards" is required. Refer to Appendix A, "Cisco Data Center Portfolio," for more details.

The IOS commands shown in Figure 4-28 simply create a group of VLANs (20 to 49) and allow this group to use the ACE module internal connections (switch fabric and shared bus) in slot 5. These VLANs are supposed to be handled by the admin context and the virtual contexts in the module.

The **svclc multiple-vlan-interfaces** command allows the creation of multiple Switch Virtual Interfaces (SVI) in the Catalyst 6500 Multilayer Switching Feature Card (MSFC) if they are needed for the virtual contexts. Without this command, IOS permits only one of these VLANs with a Layer 3 interface in the Catalyst MSFC.

With these commands, it is now possible to configure virtual contexts that can use these VLANs as their own communication media.

Creating and Allocating Resources to Virtual Contexts

Both ACE form factors initially have one system-defined admin context and enable the creation of five virtual contexts. With the acquisition of context licenses, the ACE module for Catalyst 6500 can deploy up to 250 virtual contexts, while the ACE 4710 can implement up to 20 contexts.

Virtualization is enabled by default and cannot be disabled on both ACE devices. As described before, the admin context is the default context for ACE administrators, and it is generally used to create virtual contexts and to perform management tasks.

Example 4-4 shows the commands used to create our three example contexts (VC1, VC2, and VC3) in the admin context. In this configuration, you can allocate VLANs to the virtual context. Depending on their configuration, each context can deploy SVIs or Bridge-group Virtual Interfaces (BVI) for the VLANs allocated to it.

Note Aside from network connection configuration and VLAN assignment method, ACE appliance and module configuration is very similar (in fact, they use the same code). The following examples were created in an ACE 4710, but they can also be applied to the ACE module. For the sake of simplicity, I will refer to them as ACE whenever the situation applies to both form factors.

Example 4-4 *Virtual Context Creation and VLAN Allocation*

```
! Accessing ACE command line through console, EOBC session, telnet, or ssh
ACE/Admin# configure terminal
Enter configuration commands, one per line. End with CNTL/Z.
```

```
! Creating virtual context VC1
ACE/Admin(config)# context VC1
ACE/Admin(config-context)# allocate-interface vlan 20
ACE/Admin(config-context)# allocate-interface vlan 21
ACE/Admin(config-context)# exit
! Creating virtual context VC2
ACE/Admin(config)# context VC2
ACE/Admin(config-context)# allocate-interface vlan 30
ACE/Admin(config-context)# allocate-interface vlan 31
ACE/Admin(config-context)# exit
! Creating virtual context VC3
ACE/Admin(config)# context VC3
ACE/Admin(config-context)# allocate-interface vlan 40
ACE/Admin(config-context)# exit
ACE/Admin(config)# exit
```

Tip You do not need to allocate VLANs for the admin context.

The ACE admin context supports management through Console, Telnet, SSH, SNMP, and XML. The ACE appliance supports all of these management protocols and methods and two more: HTTP and HTTPS. Its graphical user interface (GUI) tool is called ACE Device Manager (DM). Figure 4-29 depicts the GUI main page and its configuration options.

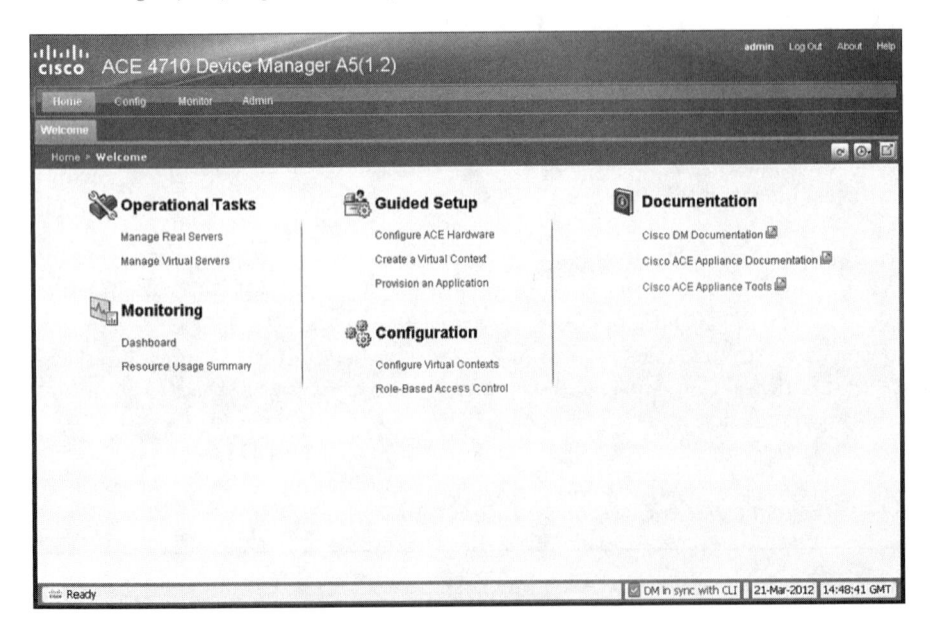

Figure 4-29 *ACE Device Manager Main Page*

Multiple ACE devices can also be managed simultaneously through another GUI named Application Network Manager (ANM). Both graphical interfaces are detailed in Appendix I.

From the admin context EXEC prompt, you can access the virtual contexts command-line interfaces using the **changeto** command, as shown here:

```
ACE/Admin# changeto VC1
ACE/VC1# changeto VC2
ACE/VC2#
```

The context you are configuring, in a given moment, is represented in the prompt, as you can see. Any of the allocated VLANs could as well be used for the virtual context management (independently from the admin context).

Example 4-5 shows how you can verify the contexts creation from the admin context. As you can see, just after the commands from Example 4-4, all the contexts belong to a default resource class.

Example 4-5 *Verifying the Context Creation*

```
ACE/Admin# show context

Number of Contexts = 4
Name: Admin , Id: 0
Config count: 85
Description:
Resource-class: default


Name: VC1 , Id: 1
Config count: 0
Description:
Resource-class: default
Vlans:   Vlan20-21


Name: VC2 , Id: 2
Config count: 0
Description:
Resource-class: default
Vlans:   Vlan30-31


Name: VC3 , Id: 3
Config count: 0
```

```
Description:
Resource-class: default
Vlans:     Vlan40
```

The contexts VC1, VC2, and VC3, created in Example 4-4, can also be verified in ACE DM, as Figure 4-30 illustrates.

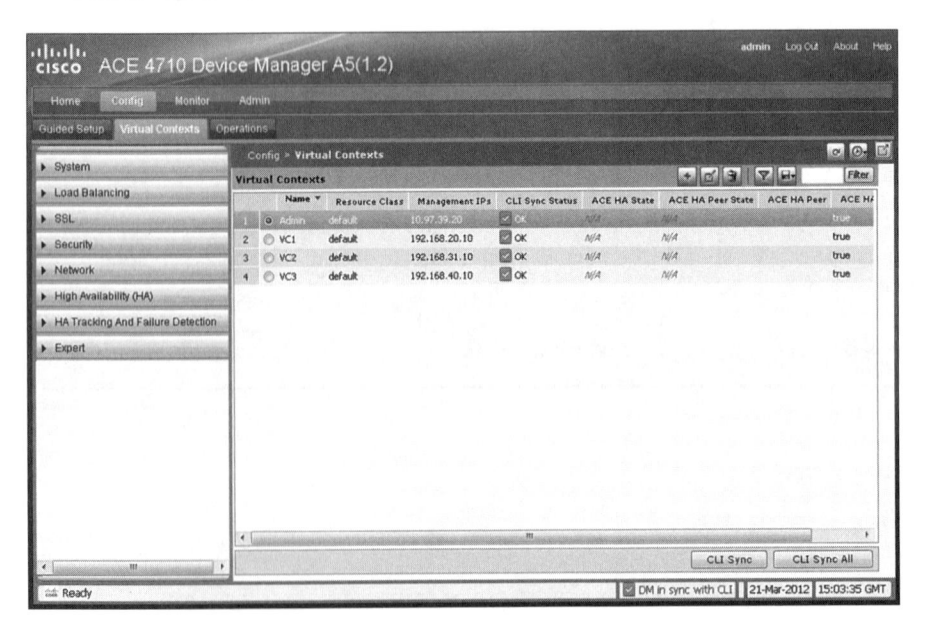

Figure 4-30 *Verifying the Context Creation in ACE Device Manager*

> **Note** All the remaining configurations in this chapter will use the CLI for learning purposes. In real user case scenarios, you can use both methods of configuration and management.

The understanding of context resource control is key for a successful ACE virtualization deployment. A *resource class* defines how the ACE physical resources are allocated to a virtual context. Whenever a virtual context is configured as a member of a resource class, this context receives the performance parameters defined for this class.

There are two types of resources that can be allocated to a virtual context: *memory resources* and *rate resources*. The memory resources are

- Access list entries
- Buffers for syslog messages and TCP out-of-order (OOO) segments
- Concurrent connections through the context

- Management connections to the context
- Proxy connections for Layer 7 switching
- Regular expressions for operations such as URL switching
- Stickiness table entries
- Address translations

And the rate resources are

- Bandwidth through the context
- Connections per second
- Inspected connections from special protocols such as FTP, DNS, HTTP, and ICMP
- HTTP compression performance
- MAC misses for frames for which ACE does not have an ARP entry
- Management connections per second to the context
- SSL connections per second
- Syslog messages per second

The resource class context membership defines the minimum resources a context has and how much more it can claim for itself. As you can see in Figure 4-31, each **limit-resource** command inside a resource class has a minimum and maximum percentage defined. These parameters refer to the total physical device capacity and define the minimum resources a context has and how big it can become.

Figure 4-31 also shows both ways a resource from a context (such as concurrent connections) can have its maximum parameter configured in two resource classes: SMALL (maximum is equal to minimum) and SMALL+ (where maximum is unlimited).

Note In a resource class, you can configure the minimum and maximum for each resource independently. I have used the **limit-resource all** command to simplify the configuration in these examples.

150   Data Center Virtualization Fundamentals

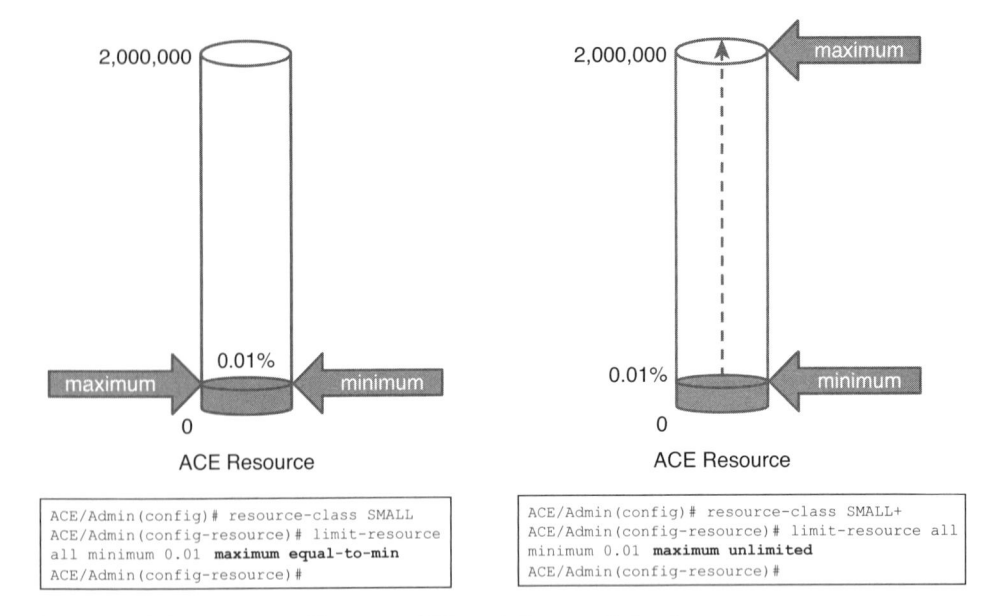

Figure 4-31 *Resource Classes and Virtual Context Behavior*

Example 4-6 shows the required configuration for context VC1 and VC2 to become members of resource classes SMALL and SMALL+, respectively.

Example 4-6 *Allocation of Resources for Context VC1 and VC2*

```
ACE/Admin# configure terminal
Enter configuration commands, one per line. End with CNTL/Z.
ACE/Admin(config)# context VC1
ACE/Admin(config-context)# member SMALL
ACE/Admin(config-context)# exit
ACE/Admin(config)# context VC2
ACE/Admin(config-context)# member SMALL+
ACE/Admin(config-context)#
```

At this point of our configuration sequence, VC1 is allowed to consume up to 0.01 percent of each resource from the hardware and nothing more. However, these resources will always be available for VC1, at any time.

VC2 has a minimum of 0.01 percent reserved resources for it, but differently from VC1, VC2 can use more resources from ACE, as long as they are not being used by other contexts.

To demonstrate the difference between both behaviors, I have submitted contexts VC1 and VC2 to stress traffic that could easily surpass the 0.01 percent of resources allocated to them. Figure 4-32 depicts the test scenario.

Chapter 4: An Army of One: ACE Virtual Contexts   151

Note The contexts' load-balancing configurations for VC1 and VC2 will be analyzed in more detail in future sections in this chapter. Right now, I want you to focus on their resource usage behavior.

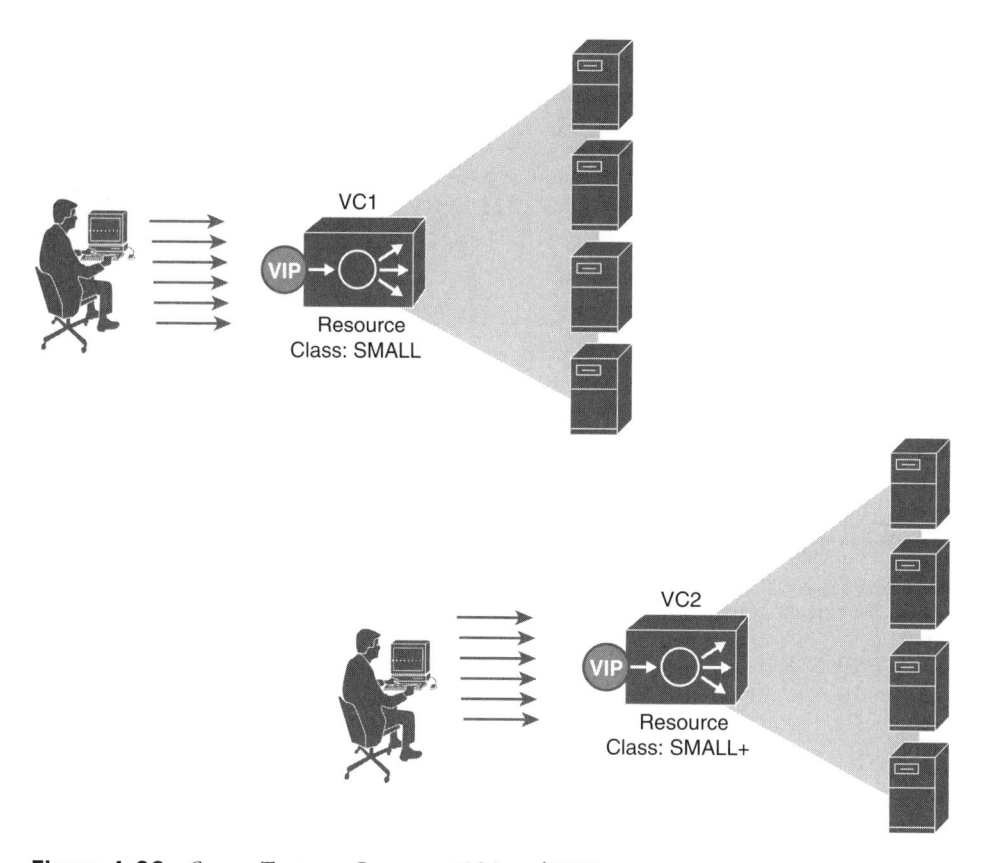

Figure 4-32 *Stress Tests on Contexts VC1 and VC2*

The traffic was based on TCP port 80 connections transporting HTTP sessions, and it was generated by Microsoft's Web Stress Tool. In this test, two parameters were saturated: concurrent connections and connection rate.

In Example 4-7, you can observe what happened to context VC1, member of resource-class SMALL, during the stress test.

Example 4-7 *Context VC1 Resource Usage*

```
ACE/VC1# show resource usage
                                    Allocation
        Resource       Current      Peak      Min      Max      Denied
   -----------------------------------------------------------------
```

```
Context: VC1
  conc-connections       154     200     200     200       49
  mgmt-connections         2       8      10      10        0
  proxy-connections        0       4      26      26        0
  xlates                   0       0       7       7        0
  acc-connections          0       0       0       0        0
  bandwidth             4954   12731   12375 123762375   1254
    throughput          4954   12375   12375    12375    1254
    mgmt-traffic rate      0     356       0 123750000     0
  connection rate          8      12      12      12       28
  ssl-connections rate     0       0       1       1        0
  mac-miss rate            0       0       0       0        0
  inspect-conn rate        0       0       4       4        0
  http-comp rate           0       0   26214   26214        0
  acl-memory            2784    3312    5984    5984        0
  Actual Min:     3904
  sticky                   0       0      81      81        0
  regexp                   0       0     105     105        0
  Actual Min:        0
  syslog buffer            0       0       0       0        0
  syslog rate              2       4      10      10        3
```

As you can see, VC1 started to deny connections when one of the performance parameters (concurrent connections or connection rate) reached its peak.

Now, what happens to context VC2 when it is submitted to the same test traffic? Example 4-8 has the answer to that question.

Example 4-8 *Context VC2 Resource Usage*

```
ACE/VC2# show resource usage
                                        Allocation
        Resource      Current    Peak    Min       Max      Denied
---------------------------------------------------------------------
Context: VC2
  conc-connections       196     204    200   1999700        0
  mgmt-connections         0       6     10     99890        0
  proxy-connections        0       8     26    262117        0
  xlates                   0       0      7     65529        0
  acc-connections          0       0      0       105        0
  bandwidth             2080   18910  12375 247487625        0
    throughput          2080   16586  12375 123737625        0
    mgmt-traffic rate      0    2324      0 123750000        0
  connection rate          5      54     12    119888        0
  ssl-connections rate     0       0      1      7500        0
[output suppressed]
```

In the test, VC2 could achieve 204 concurrent connections and 54 connections per second because there were available resources in the ACE device. In fact, ACE dedicated 0.01 percent of its physical resources to each context, leaving 99.98 percent free for the use of VC2 or other contexts.

When several virtual contexts are created and their minimum allocated resources do not add up to 100 percent of the physical device, the unallocated resources form a *shared area*. A context that belongs to a resource class with unlimited maximum can use the entire shared area for itself (if it is available, of course). *Oversubscription* happens whenever multiple contexts have unlimited maximums and need to simultaneously use the resources available in the shared area.

Tip ACE allocation of shared area resources for contexts follows the first come, first served policy.

But what happens when a context is configured to allocate more resources than those available on the shared area? To demonstrate this ACE behavior, I created a resource class that wants to reserve to itself a minimum of 99.99 percent of the physical resources. You know this is not possible because VC1 and VC2 have each a minimum allocation of 0.01 percent of the physical resources. This configuration is depicted in Example 4-9.

Example 4-9 *Creation of Resource Class BIG and Tentative Allocation of Resources for Context VC3*

```
ACE/Admin(config)# resource-class BIG
ACE/Admin(config-resource)# limit-resource all min 99.99 maximum
equal-to-min
ACE/Admin(config-resource)# exit
ACE/Admin(config)# context VC3
ACE/Admin(config-context)# member BIG
Error: All resources in use
ACE/Admin(config-context)#
```

The error message "All resources in use" states that it is not possible for ACE to dedicate the minimum resources defined in the resource classes. Such a message does not show if VC3 receives 99.98 percent of the remaining resources, as shown in Example 4-10.

Example 4-10 *Adjustment of Resource Class BIG and Allocation of Resources for Context VC3*

```
ACE/Admin(config)# resource-class BIG
ACE/Admin(config-resource)# limit-resource all min 99.98 maximum
equal-to-min
ACE/Admin(config-resource)# exit
```

```
ACE/Admin(config)# context VC3
ACE/Admin(config-context)# member BIG
ACE/Admin(config-context)#
```

With the creation of context VC3, there is no shared area anymore. This happens because the minimum allocated resources for VC1, VC2, and VC3 add up to 100 percent of the ACE resources. Therefore, in this situation, there is no oversubscription.

Figure 4-33 summarizes ACE physical resource distribution before and after context VC3 creation.

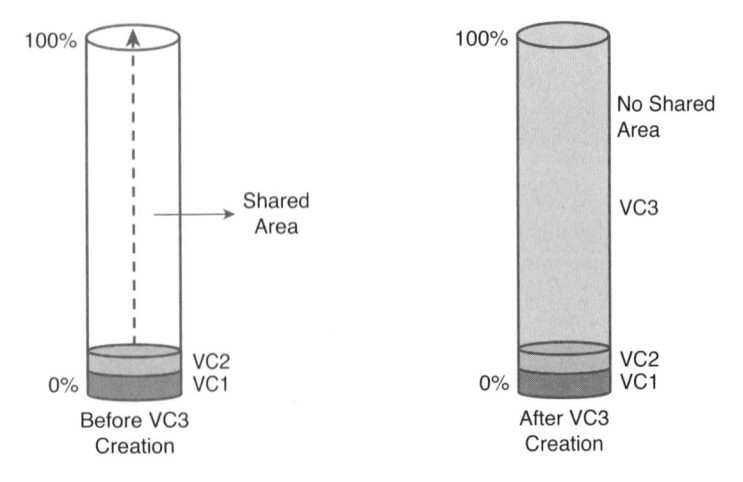

Figure 4-33 *ACE Resource Allocation Before and After the Creation of VC3*

With the creation of VC3, which belongs to resource class BIG, the results for a similar stress test in VC2 are quite different. Example 4-11 shows that without a shared area, VC2 dropped connections just like VC1 did before.

Note VC2 statistics were cleared through the **clear stats resource-usage** command to make the results more visible.

Example 4-11 *Context VC2 Resource Usage After the Creation of VC3*

```
ACE/VC2# clear stats resource-usage
ACE/VC2# show resource usage
                                                 Allocation
        Resource        Current      Peak     Min      Max      Denied
-------------------------------------------------------------------------
Context: VC2
   conc-connections          138      200     200   1599720          73
```

```
  mgmt-connections           2       6      10      10           0
  proxy-connections          0       6      26      26           0
  xlates                     0       0       7       7           0
  acc-connections            0       0       0       0           0
  bandwidth               4628    9693   12375  123762375         0
    throughput            2468    7533   12375   12375           0
    mgmt-traffic rate     2160    2160       0  123750000         0
  connection rate            8      12      12      12          83
  ssl-connections rate       0       0       1       1           0
[output suppressed]
```

ACE virtual contexts can greatly increase efficiency in application rollouts because their creation does not depend on an acquisition and physical installation. And as you can see, resource allocation for ACE virtual contexts is a very powerful tool to increase hardware utilization in data centers. Using this capability, it is possible to create a load balancer completely tailored for an application environment performance and deploy it very quickly.

As a generic example, Figure 4-34 illustrates a resource class where each parameter was defined independently from the others.

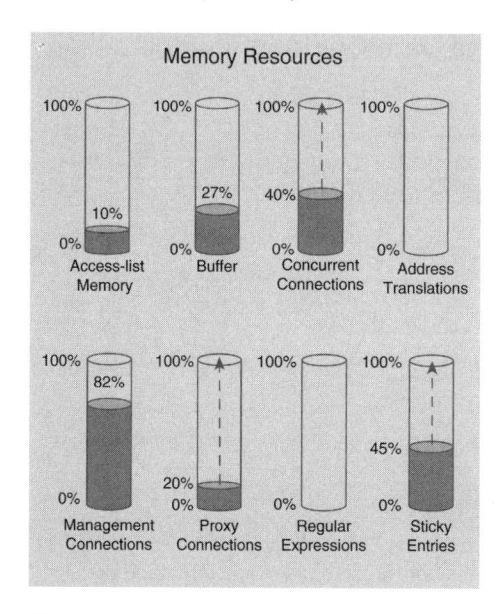

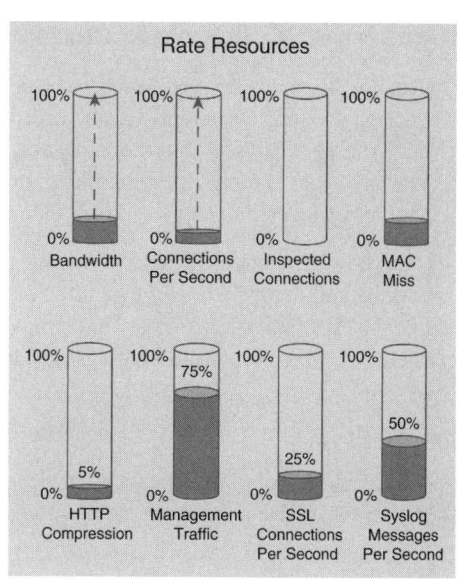

Figure 4-34 *Virtual Context Resource Class Example*

But what can be done when a context runs out of its resources in a load-balancing scenario? Another advantage of the load balance virtualization approach is that you can change the virtual context performance parameters at any time, avoiding unnecessary hardware migrations and configuration. All you have to do is respect the full capacity from the ACE hardware.

For example, if you want to increase the number of concurrent connections from 200 to 1000 on all contexts that are members of resource class SMALL, all you have to do is reconfigure the ACE resource allocation, as shown in Example 4-12.

Example 4-12 *Resource Allocation Change*

```
ACE/Admin# configure terminal
Enter configuration commands, one per line. End with CNTL/Z.
ACE/Admin(config)# resource-class BIG
! Changing the allocation of parameters for context VC3 to free resources
ACE/Admin(config-resource)# limit-resource all minimum 90.00 maximum equal-to-min
ACE/Admin(config-resource)# resource-class SMALL
! Changing only concurrent connections parameters for context VC1
ACE/Admin(config-resource)# limit-resource conc-connections minimum 0.05 maximum
equal-to-min
ACE/Admin(config-resource)#
```

Integrating ACE Virtual Contexts to the Data Center Network

A load balancer, as any network service device, must exchange traffic with a network to function properly. Differently from several physical load balancers, an ACE virtual context has SVIs or BVIs as interfaces. Hence, through VLAN manipulation, you can easily insert a virtual context in a networking environment and deploy it to load-balance servers or other connected devices.

The following sections introduce the three main designs for ACE virtual context networking and describe how they can be configured. In fact, to demonstrate the independency of configuration among contexts, VC1, VC2, and VC3 were configured in a way where each one used a different design (although they belong to the same ACE device).

Routed Design

In this type of topology, the load balancer performs the function of a router, connecting different IP subnets. In Figure 4-35, context VC1 acts according to this design.

In an ACE context configuration, when an SVI is configured (using the **interface vlan** command with an associated IP address), the context automatically enables routed mode. In Example 4-13, VC1 is configured in this fashion.

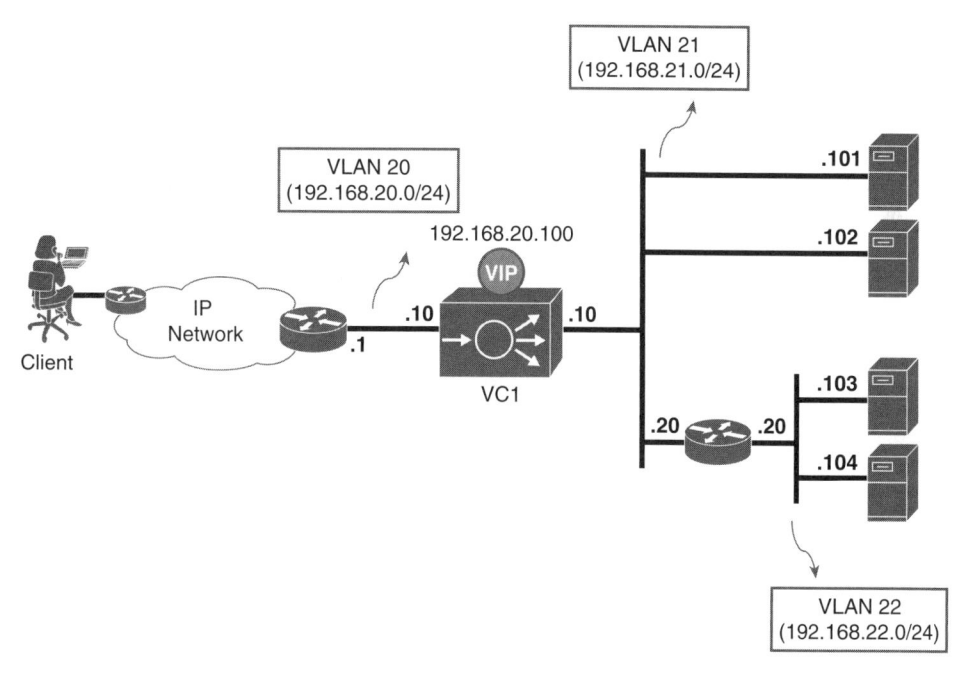

Figure 4-35 *ACE Context VC1 in Routed Mode*

Example 4-13 *ACE Context VC1 Configuration*

```
ACE/VC1# show running-config interface
Generating configuration....
interface vlan 20
  description Client VLAN
  ip address 192.168.20.10 255.255.255.0
  [ output suppressed ]
  no shutdown
interface vlan 21
  description Server VLAN
  ip address 192.168.21.10 255.255.255.0
  no shutdown
ACE/VC1# show running-config | include route
Generating configuration....
! Inserting routes to reach the external IP network and subnet 192.168.22.0
ip route 0.0.0.0 0.0.0.0 192.168.20.1
ip route 192.168.22.0 255.255.255.0 192.168.21.20
```

In a server load-balancing scenario, clients send connections directed to the context VIP. The VIP can belong to either subnet (or even to a different one, similarly to a loopback interface), but it is mandatory that the VIP is a routable address for the client.

According to its configuration and after the server selection, the context sends the request to the selected server. A routing configuration forces the server response to the ACE context that forwards it back to the client, and the connection symmetry is guaranteed.

In Figure 4-35, two examples of routing configuration for connection symmetry are shown:

- Servers 1 and 2 have VC1 IP address (192.168.21.10) in VLAN 21 as their default gateway.
- Servers 3 and 4 will reach the context through the Router R1 routing table that will point to 192.168.21.10 as its gateway toward the clients.

Because the context acts as router between its VLANs, it is possible to assign RFC 1918 private addresses to the internal subnets while only the external subnets and VIP can have public IP address. This can be very useful if we consider that the number of public addresses is continuously becoming scarce.

Note ACE virtual contexts only support static routing.

Bridged Design

In this mode, an ACE virtual context acts similarly to a transparent bridge (although it learns the MAC addresses from devices directly connected through ARP). In Figure 4-36, context VC2 is a bridge between VLANs 30 and 31.

When a BVI interface is configured in a context, it automatically becomes a bridged context. Each context can only bridge two VLANs. In Example 4-14, VC2 is configured in such a mode.

Example 4-14 *ACE Context VC2 Configuration*

```
ACE/VC2# show running-config interface
Generating configuration....
interface vlan 30
  description Client VLAN
  bridge-group 31
  [ output suppressed ]
  no shutdown
interface vlan 31
  description Server VLAN
  bridge-group 31
  no shutdown
interface bvi 31
```

```
  ip address 192.168.31.10 255.255.255.0
  no shutdown
ACE/VC2# show running-config | include route
Generating configuration....
! Default gateway for outside communication
ip route 0.0.0.0 0.0.0.0 192.168.31.1
! Route for probes directed to servers in this network
ip route 192.168.32.0 255.255.255.0 192.168.31.20
```

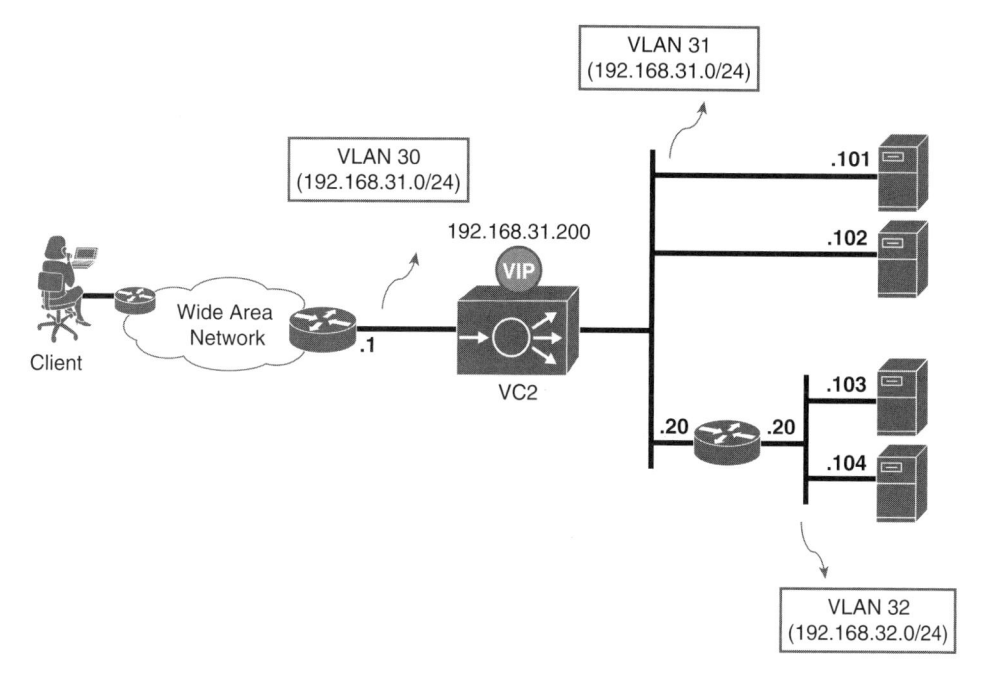

Figure 4-36 *ACE Context VC2 Bridged Mode*

If you remember from Chapter 3, "The Humble Beginnings of Network Virtualization," the concepts of VLANs and subnets are completely distinct. Therefore, the bridge design permits two VLANs to be mapped to a single subnet. This configuration forces the response server traffic to traverse the virtual context, enabling symmetric connection management without routing tweaks.

The configuration mechanism that allows this broadcast domain connection is the BVI. As you can see, this interface has an IP address (192.168.31.10) that is accessible to both VLANs and that can be used for management purposes.

> **Tip** A virtual context can simultaneously deploy one BVI (between two VLANs) and multiple SVIs. In this scenario, hosts in the bridged VLANs can use the BVI IP address as a gateway to reach the routed VLANs.

Data centers that do not have the flexibility to change server IP addresses generally use this design in load balancer rollouts. And yet another advantage of this design is the possibility of routing protocol configuration between the edge router and the internal router. This possibility can eliminate the need for static routing on the data center network.

> **Note** ACE only supports IEEE 802.1D legacy Spanning Tree Protocol.

One-Armed Design

In this topology, only the load-balanced connections are sent to the virtual context (it does not even detect the direct client-server). This design can be really useful when the load-balanced traffic is small if compared with the total traffic directed to the servers.

For symmetric load balancing, one of two methods must be chosen: *dual NAT* or *policy-based routing*.

Figure 4-37 illustrates how dual NAT can be used in this scenario.

The main idea behind this design is that the server detects an IP address from the ACE virtual context as the source IP in the received requests. Therefore, their responses will surely be directed to the context.

The caveat for this design is that the servers cannot detect the IP address from the original requesters, and this might not be allowed by some security policies.

> **Tip** For HTTP connections, an ACE context can insert the original client IP address in the HTTP header. This makes it possible for some scenarios to use the one-arm scenario.

Without the address translation, the client IP address is detected as the source IP for the TCP connections in the server, but it is necessary to deploy some kind of routing mechanism between the servers and the ACE virtual context.

If the servers must receive the original client IP, techniques such as PBR can be used. Figure 4-38 details how PBR acts in such topology.

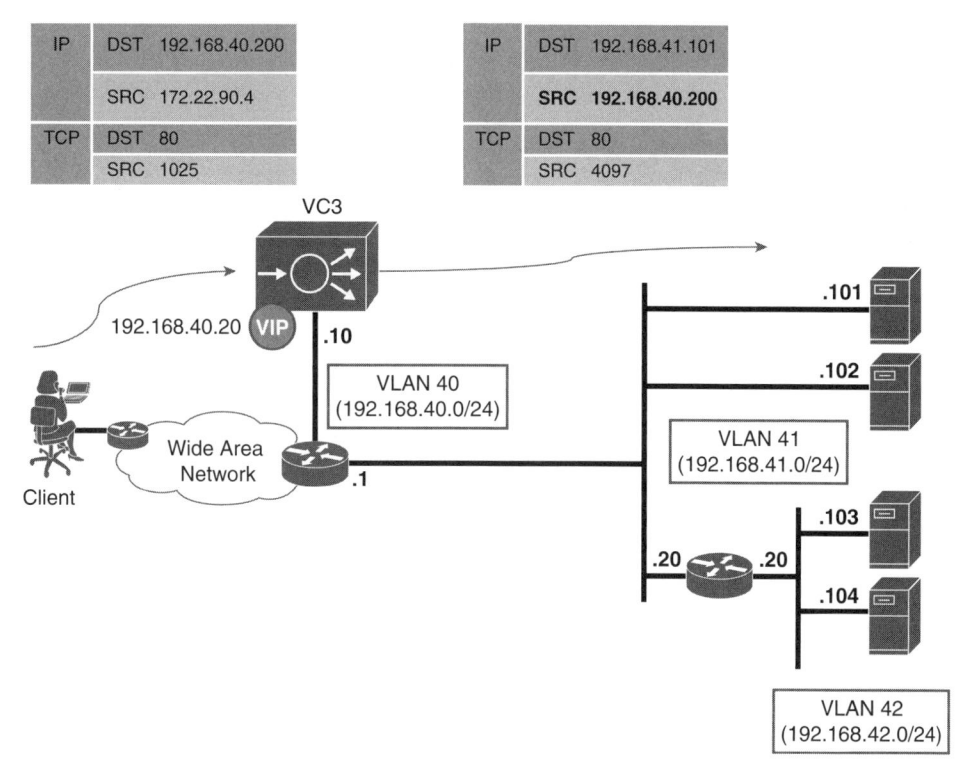

IP	DST	192.168.40.200
	SRC	172.22.90.4
TCP	DST	80
	SRC	1025

IP	DST	192.168.41.101
	SRC	**192.168.40.200**
TCP	DST	80
	SRC	4097

Figure 4-37 *ACE Context One-Arm Topology with Dual NAT for Context VC3*

In Figure 4-38, the traffic is returned to the virtual context when the following characteristics are identified in the traffic:

- Packet is coming from the servers
- Packet has port 80 as the source port

In this scenario, only the TCP port 80 is being load balanced. The rest of the client traffic accesses the servers directly.

The advantage for one-arm load balance topology is that the virtual context is relieved from direct traffic from or to the servers, avoiding unnecessary use of ACE resources.

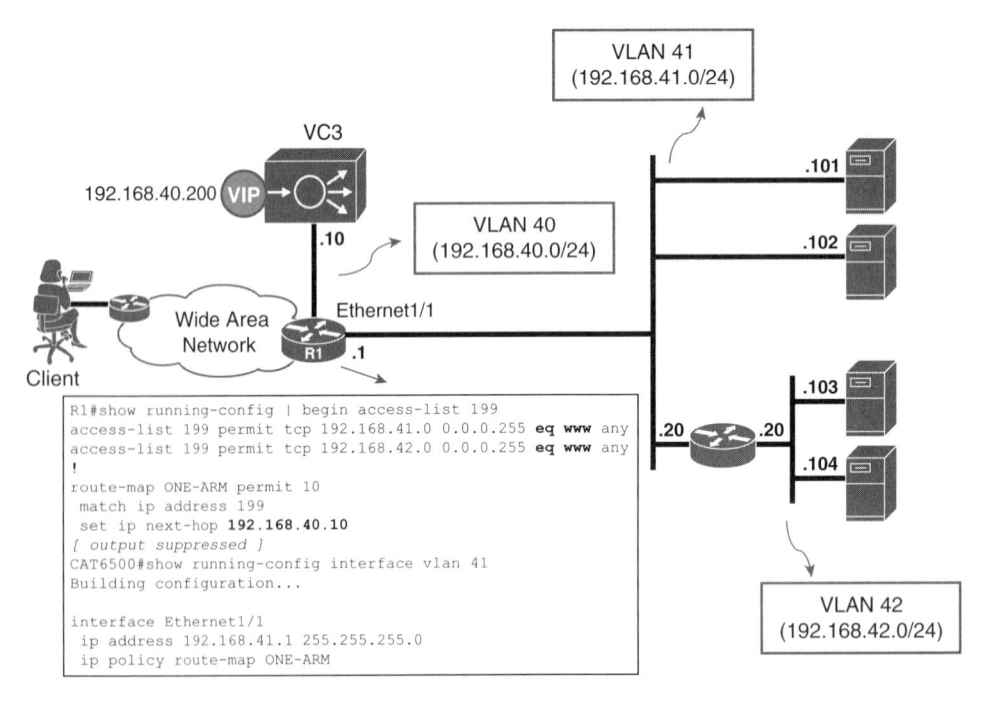

```
R1#show running-config | begin access-list 199
access-list 199 permit tcp 192.168.41.0 0.0.0.255 eq www any
access-list 199 permit tcp 192.168.42.0 0.0.0.255 eq www any
!
route-map ONE-ARM permit 10
 match ip address 199
 set ip next-hop 192.168.40.10
[ output suppressed ]
CAT6500#show running-config interface vlan 41
Building configuration...

interface Ethernet1/1
 ip address 192.168.41.1 255.255.255.0
 ip policy route-map ONE-ARM
```

Figure 4-38 *One-Arm Design with Policy-Based Routing for Context VC3*

Managing and Configuring ACE Virtual Contexts

Any ACE virtual context is created as a "closed" network device, just like a firewall. Therefore, it does not allow any management, control, or data plane communication by default. You must allow it explicitly to make those communications happen in your context.

ACE configuration follows the Modular Policy CLI (MPC) model, which was originally created in IOS to make quality of service configurations easier. MPC is a very powerful tool that allows great flexibility and less configuration commands.

Allowing Management Traffic to a Virtual Context

Allowing management traffic (connections directed to the virtual context) on an interface, you will learn the basic principles of the MPC model. Figure 4-39 explains the steps for this configuration.

These are the configuration steps for management traffic:

1. Create a *management class map* that defines the management protocols ACE will allow.

2. Create a *policy map* that will actually permit these protocols.

3. Apply the policy map to an interface, to a group of interfaces, or to the entire context.

```
                              What?

                          ┌─────────────┐
                          │  Class-map  │──┐
                          │   (Step 1)  │  │
                          └─────────────┘  │
                                           ▼
                                         How?
ACE/VC1# show running-config         ┌─────────────┐
class-map MGMT-PROTOCOLS             │ Policy-map  │──┐
Generating configuration....         │  (Step 2)   │  │
                                     └─────────────┘  │
class-map type management                             ▼
match-any MGMT-PROTOCOLS                            Where?
  description Remote Access
Protocols                      ACE/VC1# show running-config   ┌──────────────┐
  2 match protocol telnet any  policy-map remote-mgmt         │Service-Policy│
  3 match protocol ssh any     Generating configuration....   │   (Step 3)   │
  4 match protocol icmp any                                   └──────────────┘
                               policy-map type management
                               first-match REMOTE-MGMT
                                 class MGMT-PROTOCOLS       ACE/VC1# show running-config
                                   permit                   interface
                                                            Generating configuration....

                                                            interface vlan 20
                                                              description Client VLAN
                                                              ip address 192.168.20.10
                                                            255.255.255.0
                                                              [ output suppressed ]
                                                              service-policy input
                                                            REMOTE-MGMT
                                                              [ output suppressed ]
                                                              no shutdown
```

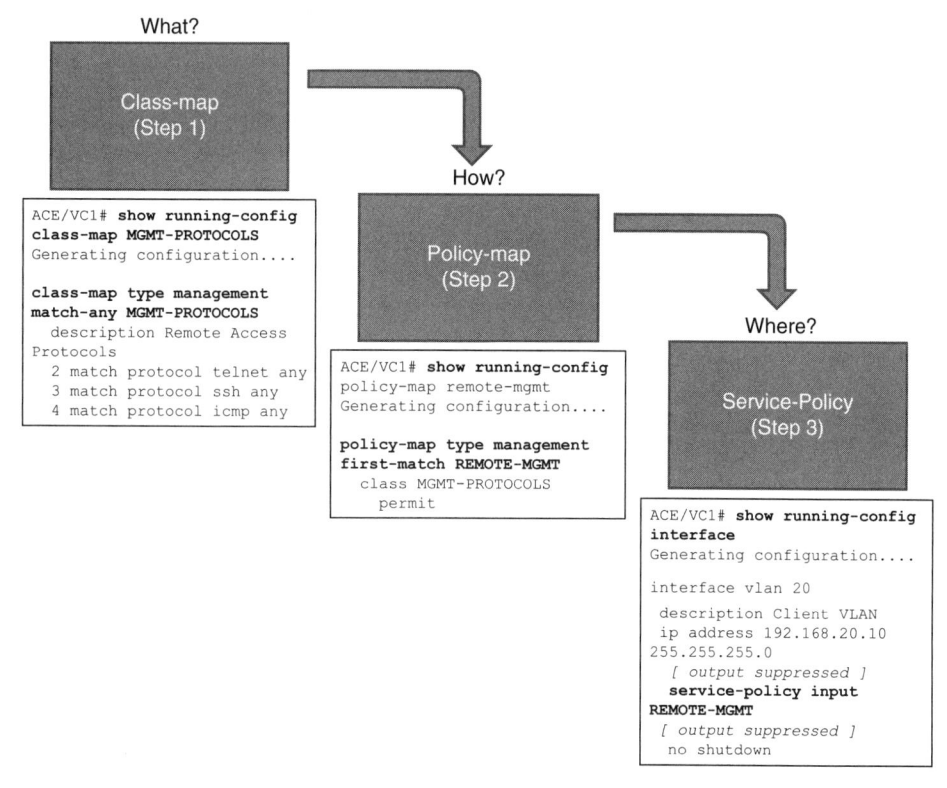

Figure 4-39 *ACE Virtual Context Management Traffic Configuration*

Tip I suggest that you use arbitrary configuration names (such as class maps, policy maps, access lists, and others) in capital letters. This procedure will make the configuration commands easier to read.

Figure 4-39 details the configuration to allow Internet Control Message Protocol (ICMP), Secure Shell (SSH), and Telnet traffic to interface VLAN 20 from context VC1. Other protocols such as SNMP and HTTP can be inserted in class map MGMT-PROTOCOLS as well.

Note The admin context also needs a similar configuration to allow management connections.

Allowing Load Balancing Traffic Through a Virtual Context

Using access lists, a virtual context permits traffic to be processed by the ACE data plane (connection data passing through the context). Example 4-15 details a very simple access list that will allow all kinds of traffic for management and server load balancing for the VC1 VLAN 20 interface.

Example 4-15 *Access List to Permit Traffic to the Context Through an Interface*

```
ACE/VC1# configure terminal
Enter configuration commands, one per line. End with CNTL/Z.
ACE/VC1(config)# access-list ALL extended permit ip any any
ACE/VC1(config)# interface vlan 20
ACE/VC1(config-if)# access-group input ALL
ACE/VC1(config-if)#
```

An ACE virtual context is a stateful device because it keeps track of network connections instead of treating each packet as an independent entity. Therefore, when you apply an access list to permit data traffic on an interface, it is enough for the connection management. Hence, you do not need to configure access lists to allow the connection to be redirected by the context or another one for the server response traffic.

Note ACE treats a UDP flow (exchanged between a client and a server and using the same ports) as a connection. It also treats ICMP echo and ICMP echo reply as members of a single connection by default. You can disable the last behavior through the **no icmp-guard** command.

To configure server load balancing you will use a more sophisticated MPC configuration than the one executed for management traffic. Figure 4-40 clarifies the load-balancing configuration steps for an ACE virtual context.

As a practical exercise, you will analyze the scenario described in Figure 4-35 (VC1-routed design scenario) using the configuration steps in Figure 4-40.

In each step, you will observe the construction of MPC configuration structures such as real servers, probes, server farms, class maps, policy maps, and their relationships.

1. Real Servers and Probes Configuration

In this phase, the context is informed of the servers it can potentially send client requests. Example 4-16 details the configuration of four real servers associated to context VC1.

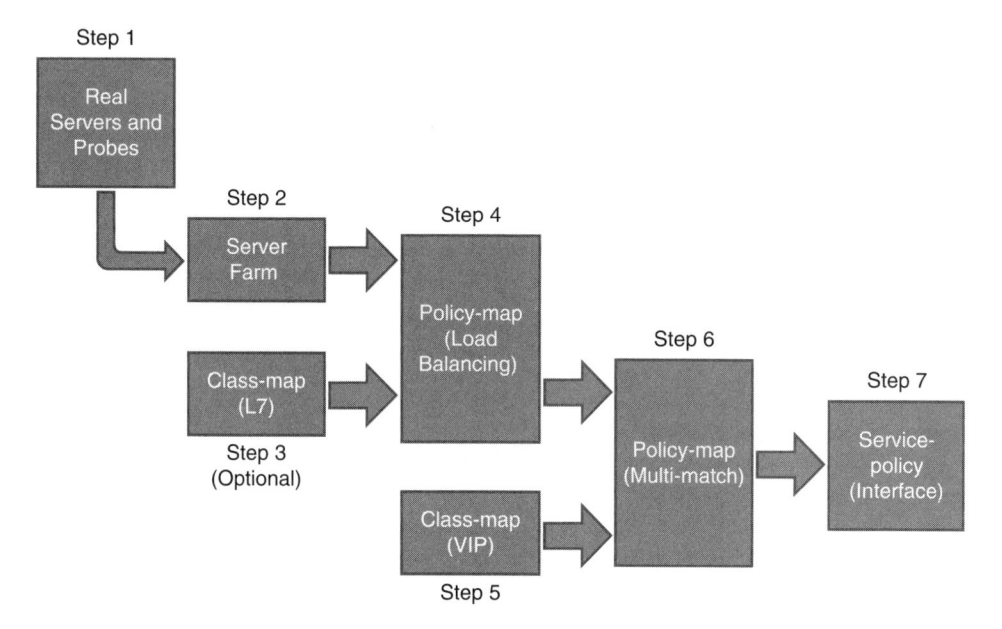

Chapter 4: An Army of One: ACE Virtual Contexts   165

Figure 4-40 *ACE Load-Balancing Configuration Steps*

Example 4-16 *Real Servers Configuration for Context VC1*

```
ACE/VC1# show running-config rserver
Generating configuration....

rserver host SERVER01
   ip address 192.168.21.101
   inservice
rserver host SERVER02
   ip address 192.168.21.102
   inservice
rserver host SERVER03
   ip address 192.168.22.103
   inservice
rserver host SERVER04
   ip address 192.168.22.104
   inservice
```

For VC1, it does not matter if the servers are located in a subnet different from the ones to which it is connected. It is enough that the context has a route pointing to this subnet.

As shown in Example 4-17, two probes were configured:

- An HTTP GET probe that expects a real server response with code 200 as a success
- A simple ICMP probe to test the TCP/IP stack of the real servers

Example 4-17 *ICMP Probe Creation in VC1*

```
ACE/VC1# show running-config probe
Generating configuration....

probe http GET
  expect status 200 200
probe icmp PING
  interval 10
```

These probes were created to allow VC1 to test the server's health. As configured for PING, the interval between probes, when the server is operational, can be changed from the default (15 seconds) to another value (10 seconds). Alternatively, you can also define

- The interval between probes when the server is not operational
- How many probe failures to change the state of a real server from Operational to Failed
- How many probe successes to change the state of a real server from Failed to Operational

2. Server Farms

As explained before, a server farm groups servers that share the same application and, therefore, receives the load-balanced connections.

In the server farm configuration structure, you can define the predictor you want to use and the probes the ACE context will use to check whether each server is available to receive connections.

Example 4-18 shows the server farm configuration on context VC1.

Example 4-18 *Server Farm Configuration for Context VC1*

```
ACE/VC1# show running-config serverfarm SERVERS
Generating configuration....

serverfarm host SERVERS
  probe PING
  rserver SERVER01
    inservice
```

```
    rserver SERVER02
      inservice
    rserver SERVER03
      inservice
    rserver SERVER04
      inservice
```

In the configuration, the servers created in Step 1 are included in the server farm SERVERS, and will receive ICMP probes defined by the probe PING. The **inservice** command inserted in each **rserver** configuration structure allows the context to test it through the defined probe.

> **Note** The default predictor for server farms (thus, not shown in the configuration) is *round-robin*.

It is possible to configure various server farms containing any combination of real servers. In the next (optional) step, you will understand how different server farms can be used in a virtual context load-balancing configuration.

3. (Optional) Layer 7 Class Maps

This step enables Layer 7 switching in a context. Consequently, an ACE context can direct traffic to other server farms depending on parameters from protocols such as

- File Transfer Protocol (FTP)
- Hypertext Transfer Protocol (HTTP)
- Remote Authentication Dial-In User Service (RADIUS)
- Real-Time Streaming Protocol (RTSP)
- Session Initiation Protocol (SIP)

An ACE context can also recognize specific strings in the data payload of TCP or UDP connections using regular expressions. This capability is called *generic data parsing*.

Imagine a scenario where only SERVER03 and SERVER04 can handle mobile phone HTTP connections with a customized website. Example 4-19 shows a simple class map configuration that defines this traffic.

Example 4-19 *Layer 7 Class Map Creation*

```
ACE/VC1# show running-config class-map MOBILE-DEVICES
Generating configuration....

class-map type http loadbalance match-any MOBILE-DEVICES
```

```
    2 match http header User-Agent header-value ".*iphone.*"
    3 match http header User-Agent header-value ".*blackberry.*"
    4 match http header User-Agent header-value ".*android.*"
```

With this class map, VC1 is capable of identifying an HTTP header field called *User Agent*. This field carries the type of browser or device used to initiate the connection.

Now, in Example 4-20, a new server farm is created to receive this traffic.

Example 4-20   *Server Farm for Servers with Websites for Mobile Devices*

```
ACE/VC1# show running-config serverfarm MOBILE
Generating configuration....

serverfarm host MOBILE-SERVERS
  probe GET
  rserver SERVER03
    inservice
  rserver SERVER04
    inservice
```

    4. Load-Balancing Policy Map

The load-balancing policy map links classes of traffic with server farms. For Layer 4 switching, only the configuration shown in Example 4-21 is enough as a linkage between traffic and one server farm.

Example 4-21   *Layer 4–Only Load-Balancing Policy Map*

```
ACE/VC1# show running-config policy-map LB-LOGIC
Generating configuration....

policy-map type loadbalance first-match LB-LOGIC
  class class-default
    serverfarm SERVERS
```

This policy map simply defines for VC1 that all unclassified traffic must be load-balanced to the server farm SERVERS.

Optionally, if you have configured Step 3, you would have to configure a load-balancing policy map that contains the class map MOBILE-SERVERS. Example 4-22 presents this optional configuration.

Example 4-22 *Layer 7 Load-Balancing Policy Map (Optional)*

```
ACE/VC1# show running-config policy-map LB-LOGIC
Generating configuration....

policy-map type loadbalance first-match LB-LOGIC
! HTTP traffic from mobile phones is sent to servers with customized web site
  class MOBILE-DEVICES
    serverfarm MOBILE-SERVERS
! The rest of the traffic is sent to all four servers
  class class-default
    serverfarm SERVERS
```

Because the load-balancing policy map is responsible for the Layer 7 forwarding decision, it is also called the *Layer 7 policy map*.

5. Virtual IP Class Map

This configuration structure allows the creation of the virtual IP addresses in the virtual context. Example 4-23 details the configuration of VIP 192.168.20.100 in VC1.

Example 4-23 *Virtual IP Creation*

```
ACE/VC1# show running-config class-map VIP-100
Generating configuration....

class-map match-all VIP-100
  2 match virtual-address 192.168.20.100 tcp eq www
```

Acting as a front end for the traffic, this VIP will only receive TCP client connections with 80 as their destination port.

6. Multimatch Policy Map

This configuration element links the remaining disconnected configuration structures: the VIP and the load-balancing behavior (Layer 7 policy map). It also defines the final policy that will be finally applied to one of more context interfaces.

Example 4-24 details this policy map configuration.

Example 4-24 *Multimatch Policy Creation*

```
ACE/VC1# show running-config policy-map CLIENT-VIPS
Generating configuration....

policy-map multi-match CLIENT-VIPS
```

```
! Defining the load balancing behavior for VIP 192.168.20.100 TCP port 80
  class VIP-100
    loadbalance vip inservice
    loadbalance policy LB-LOGIC
    loadbalance vip icmp-reply active
```

In this policy, the VIP is defined as active, linked to policy LB-LOGIC and configured to respond to ICMP echo packets if there is at least one active real server in the associated server farms.

This policy is called multimatch because other VIPs could be linked to other load-balancing policies in a single policy map. Therefore, this configuration structure allows several load-balancing configurations to be applied at once on a virtual context interface.

7. Service Policy

This step represents the grand finale for the ACE load-balancing configuration. In this step, the multimatch policy can be applied to an interface, to a group of interfaces, or for the entire context.

Example 4-25 shows how the CLIENT-VIPS multimatch policy could be applied to interface VLAN 20 in context VC1.

Example 4-25 *Service Policy Application to an Interface in Context VC1*

```
ACE/VC1# show running-config interface
Generating configuration....

interface vlan 20
  description Client VLAN
  ip address 192.168.20.10 255.255.255.0
  access-group input ALL
  service-policy input REMOTE-MGMT
  service-policy input CLIENT-VIPS
  no shutdown
interface vlan 21
  description Server VLAN
  ip address 192.168.21.10 255.255.255.0
  no shutdown
```

Tip You can apply the policy map to all context interfaces at once using the **service-policy input** command directly in the context global configuration. But be sure to check whether the access lists on each interface allow the traffic to the VIP.

From now on, VC1 processes TCP connections on port 80 directed to IP address 192.168.20.100. These connections will be load balanced, in a round-robin order (which is the default server farm SERVERS predictor), to servers 192.168.21.101, 192.168.21.102, 192.168.22.103, and 192.168.22.104.

If the Layer 7 policy map from optional Step 3 is configured, HTTP connections from Android mobile devices will be load balanced to servers 192.168.21.103 and 192.168.22.104 only.

Controlling Management Access to Virtual Contexts

As seen in the earlier section "Creating and Allocating Resources to Virtual Contexts," the *admin* user from the admin context can create contexts and enter his command-line interface through the **changeto** command. However, to act like a true load balancer, a virtual context should be able to have its own management users and access rules.

In fact, ACE contexts have flexible Role-Based Access Control (RBAC) capabilities that are explored by this section.

Figure 4-41 illustrates how virtual contexts VC1, VC2, and VC3 can have different local users, as well as completely different authentication, authorization, and accounting (AAA) remote servers.

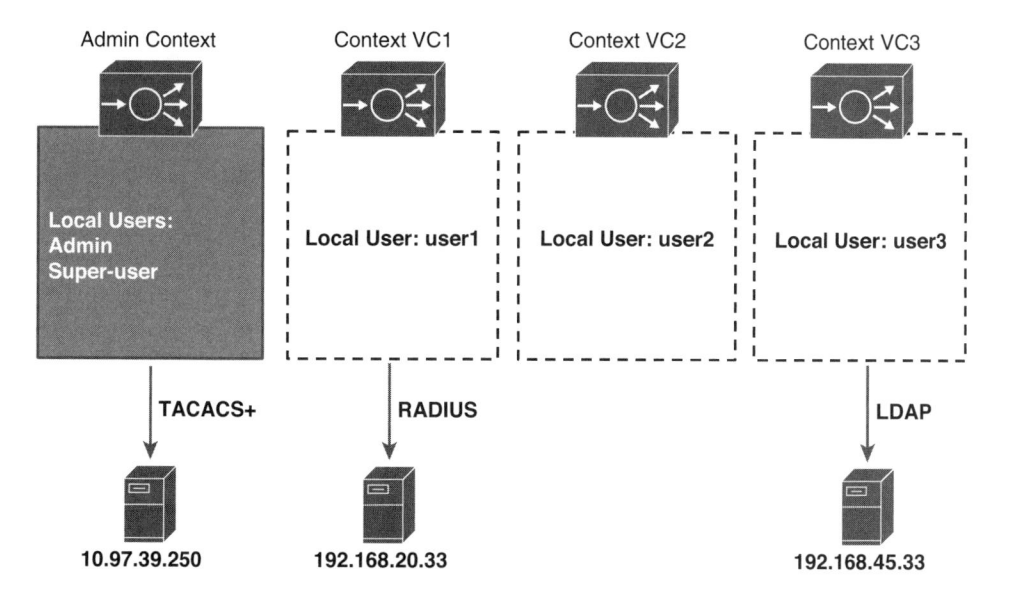

Figure 4-41 *Users and Virtual Contexts*

What exactly each user can manage inside each context is controlled by which role and domain the user belongs to.

A *role* is a set of operations that can be executed on a context. When a virtual context, such as VC3, is created, it already has eight system-defined roles that are depicted in Example 4-26.

Example 4-26 *Virtual Context System-Defined Roles*

```
ACE/VC3# show role

Role: Admin (System-defined)
Description: Administrator
Number of rules: 3
----------------------------------------------
  Rule    Type      Permission       Feature
----------------------------------------------
  1. Permit    Create                 all
  2. Permit    Create             user access
  5. Permit    Create            exec-commands

Role: Network-Admin (System-defined)
Description: Admin for L3 (IP and Routes) and L4 VIPs
Number of rules: 7
----------------------------------------------
  Rule    Type      Permission       Feature
----------------------------------------------
  1. Permit    Create             interface
  2. Permit    Create               routing
  3. Permit    Create             connection
  4. Permit    Create                  nat
  5. Permit    Create                  vip
  6. Permit    Create            config_copy
  8. Permit    Create           exec-commands

Role: Server-Maintenance (System-defined)
Description: Server maintenance, monitoring and debugging
Number of rules: 7
----------------------------------------------
  Rule    Type      Permission       Feature
----------------------------------------------
  1. Permit    Modify                 real
  2. Permit    Debug               serverfarm
  3. Permit    Debug                   vip
  4. Permit    Debug                  probe
  5. Permit    Debug              loadbalance
  7. Permit    Create           exec-commands
  8. Permit    Modify           real-inservice
```

```
Role: Server-Appln-Maintenance (System-defined)
Description: Server maintenance and L7 policy application
Number of rules: 6
-------------------------------------------
Rule    Type       Permission      Feature
-------------------------------------------
  1.   Permit      Create                  real
  2.   Permit      Create              serverfarm
  3.   Permit      Create             loadbalance
  4.   Permit      Create             config_copy
  5.   Permit      Create         real-inservice
  7.   Permit      Create          exec-commands

Role: SLB-Admin (System-defined)
Description: Administrator for all load-balancing features
Number of rules: 10
-------------------------------------------
Rule    Type       Permission      Feature
-------------------------------------------
  1.   Permit      Create                  real
  2.   Permit      Create              serverfarm
  3.   Permit      Create                     vip
  4.   Permit      Create                   probe
  5.   Permit      Create             loadbalance
  6.   Permit      Create                     nat
  7.   Permit      Modify               interface
  8.   Permit      Create             config_copy
  9.   Permit      Create         real-inservice
 11.   Permit      Create          exec-commands

Role: Security-Admin (System-defined)
Description: Administrator for all security features
Number of rules: 8
-------------------------------------------
Rule    Type       Permission      Feature
-------------------------------------------
  1.   Permit      Create             access-list
  2.   Permit      Create                 inspect
  3.   Permit      Create              connection
  4.   Permit      Modify               interface
  5.   Permit      Create                     AAA
  6.   Permit      Create                     nat
  7.   Permit      Create             config_copy
  9.   Permit      Create          exec-commands
```

```
Role: SSL-Admin (System-defined)
Description: Administrator for all SSL features
Number of rules: 5
-------------------------------------------
Rule   Type     Permission      Feature
-------------------------------------------
1.  Permit     Create                   ssl
2.  Permit     Create                   pki
3.  Permit     Modify             interface
4.  Permit     Create           config_copy
6.  Permit     Create         exec-commands

Role: Network-Monitor (System-defined)
Description: Monitoring for all features
Number of rules: 4
-------------------------------------------
Rule   Type     Permission      Feature
-------------------------------------------
1.  Permit    Monitor                   all
3.  Deny      Create          exec-commands
4.  Deny      Create        fault-tolerance
5.  Deny      Create                    pki
```

The system-defined roles were designed to mirror common operational groups in server load-balancing environments.

> **Note** The default role for users is Network-Monitor.

Notwithstanding, you can create your own role to define exactly the tasks a user or group of users can execute. Example 4-27 shows the creation of a simple role called *Server-Operator* in VC3.

Example 4-27 *Server-Operator Role Creation*

```
ACE/VC3# show running-config role Server-Operator
Generating configuration....

role Server-Operator
  description Can Modify Real Servers and Server Farms
  rule 1 permit modify feature rserver
  rule 2 permit modify feature serverfarm
  rule 3 permit monitor
```

In this example, I have created Server-Operator as a role that is capable of modifying the configuration of real servers and server farms. It also has read-only rights (**show** commands) to all other operations, and a user created with such a role would inherit the rights to execute the same operations in VC3.

Another dimension of restriction can be defined by what load balance elements can be managed by a user, such as

- Real servers
- Server farms
- Probes
- Class maps
- Policy maps

Such restriction uses a concept called *domain*, which can be defined as a set of objects that a role can manage.

Example 4-28 presents the creation of a simple domain in context VC3.

Example 4-28 *Domain Creation Example*

```
ACE/VC3# show running-config domain Domain42
Generating configuration....

domain Domain42
  add-object rserver SERVER03
  add-object rserver SERVER04
```

Note The default domain includes all objects created in the context.

Example 4-29 shows the configuration used to create a user account (user3) limited by the role Server-Operator and domain Domain42.

Example 4-29 *User Account Creation*

```
ACE/VC3# show running-config | include username
Generating configuration....
username user3 password [suppressed] role Server-Operator domain Domain42
```

And it is finally time to test these limitations. Example 4-30 shows operations from a user3 login session.

Example 4-30 *User Login in Context VC3*

```
Trying 192.168.40.10 ... Open

ACE login: user3
Password:
Bad terminal type: "network". Will assume vt100.
Cisco Application Control Software (ACSW)
[output suppressed]
ACE/VC3# show running-config
Generating configuration....
! This command works because the role Server-Operator has full monitor feature rights
[ output suppressed ]
ACE/VC3# configure terminal
Enter configuration commands, one per line.End with CNTL/Z.
! An error happens when the user tries to configure an element that is not permitted
in role
ACE/VC3(config)# class-map ?
% invalid command
ACE/VC3(config)# rserver SERVER01
Error: object being referred to is not part of User's domain
ACE/VC3(config)# rserver SERVER03
ACE/VC3(config-rserver-host)# no inservice
ACE/VC3(config-rserver-host)#
```

In the last example, user3 could not enter the real server SERVER01 configuration because it does not belong to Domain42. With these features, it is possible for different teams to share the same virtual context, drastically reducing the risk of misconfiguration, especially in long context configurations.

Note A user that belongs to multiple roles and multiple domains will have configuration rights from all associated roles and access to objects from all associated domains.

When a context is using remote AAA servers (such as TACACS+, RADIUS, and LDAP), it is possible for the servers to authenticate users and send to the virtual context the group and domain each user belongs to.

ACE Virtual Context Additional Characteristics

Although a virtual context emulates, as closely as possible, a physical load balancer, there are some distinct implementation details for these virtual devices. The following sections discuss some of these special virtual context characteristics.

Sharing VLANs Among Contexts

ACE permits that virtual contexts share the same VLAN, as shown in Figure 4-42.

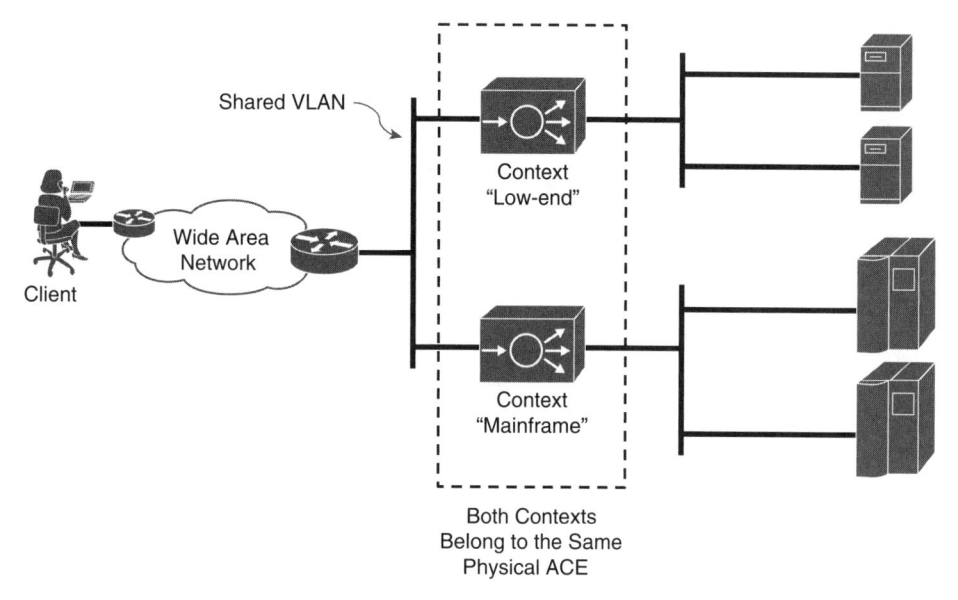

Figure 4-42 *Shared VLAN Between Two Virtual Contexts*

However, unlike a physical load balancer connection, there are some restrictions for shared VLANs between contexts. The most important limitations are

- Each ACE supports up to 1024 shared VLANs.
- Only routed VLAN interfaces (with configured IP addresses) can join shared VLANs.
- Routing between contexts is not allowed.
- Each context receives a randomly generated MAC address in the shared VLAN.

Note It is possible (and highly recommended) to configure different MAC address ranges if more than one ACE physical device participates on a shared VLAN. This configuration can avoid loss of communication because of MAC address conflicts.

Virtual Context Fault Tolerance

The virtual contexts created in an ACE device can be protected against hardware, software, and connectivity failures. ACE fault tolerance is configured between two ACE modules or two ACE appliances. The devices must have the same licenses and software version.

Note Both ACE modules can be installed in the same Catalyst 6500 chassis or in two different chassis.

Figure 4-43 illustrates how this fault tolerance is performed between two ACE devices.

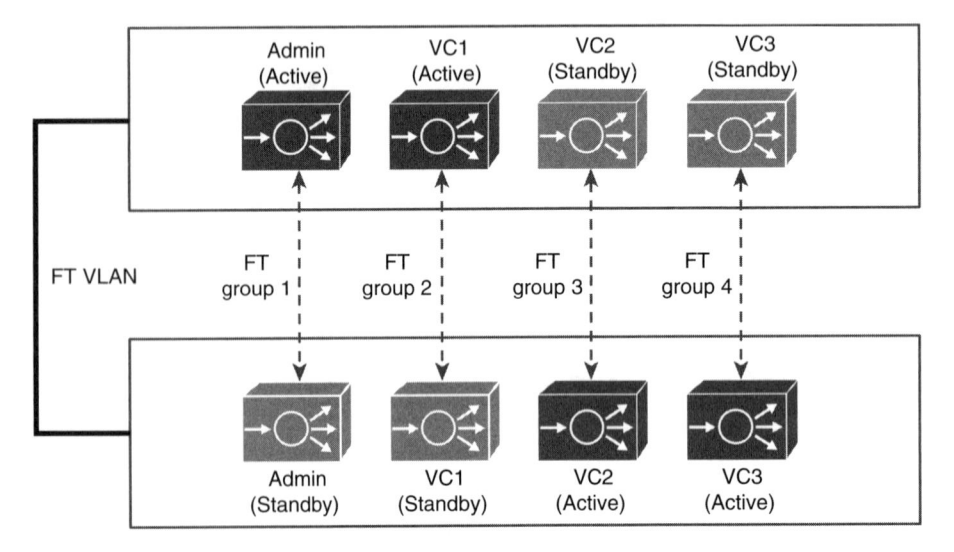

Figure 4-43 *ACE Fault Tolerance Model*

To configure ACE fault tolerance, you should pay attention to the following characteristics:

- Fault tolerance is configured in the admin context.
- There is a fault tolerance (FT) VLAN that is used by the ACE redundancy protocol, keepalives, and configuration synchronization.
- Each fault tolerance group can contain only one context.
- One virtual MAC address is associated with each VLAN on a fault tolerance group. This avoids ARP updates in the case of a failover.
- ACE implements stateful redundancy (standby context is aware of all Layer 4 connections from active context).
- ACE does not support the replication of SSL or proxied (Layer 7) connections.
- In the ACE appliance, it is recommended that you dedicate an interface for FT traffic.

It is highly recommended that every ACE project deploys fault tolerance in a load-balancing scenario. This procedure does not allow ACE to become a single point of failure for user communication to an application hosted in a data center.

Use Case: Multitenant Data Center

Virtual contexts are not exclusive to the Cisco ACE series. In fact, they were first created in the Cisco Firewall Service Module (FWSM) for Catalyst 6500 and continue to exist in the Adaptive Security Appliances (ASA) product line. At the time this book was written, the ASA5585-X and ASA Service Module for Catalyst 6500 could deploy up to 250 security contexts with similar resource allocation and fault tolerance capabilities as the ACE.

Through the use of ACE virtual contexts, ASA security contexts, VRFs, and VLANs, it is possible to build a scenario known as a *multitenant data center*.

In this scenario, multiple customers or application environments can share a common physical infrastructure maintaining characteristics such as

- Logical separation of devices
- IP addresses reuse (same subnet in more than one environment)
- Separate IP routes
- Independent management of firewalls and load balancers

Figure 4-44 reflects the logical view of a multitenant data center.

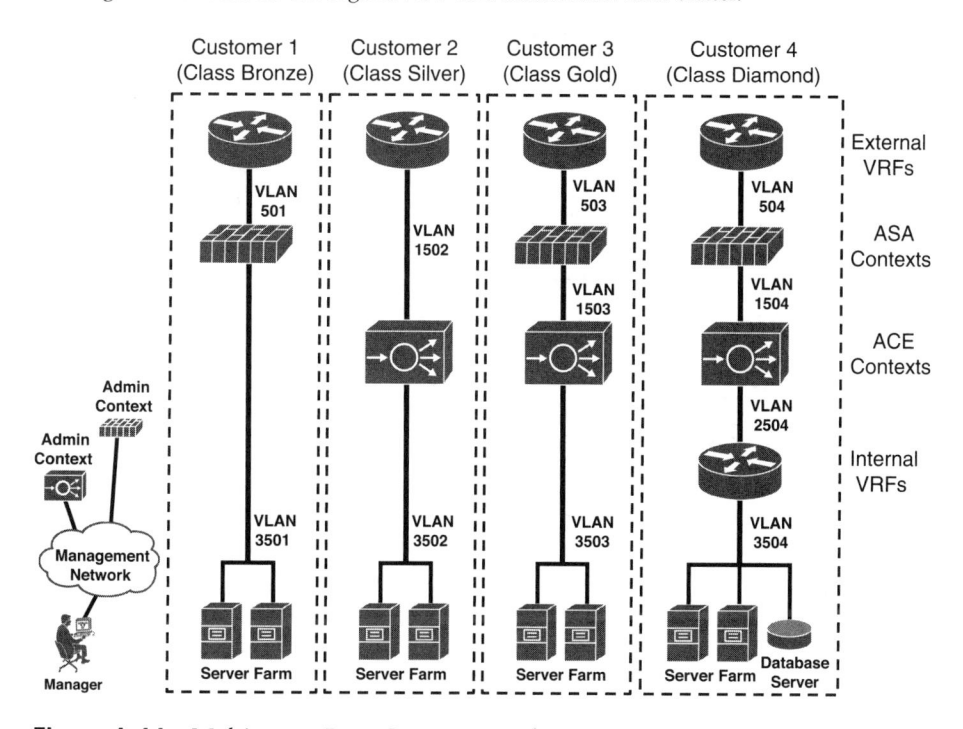

Figure 4-44 *Multitenant Data Center Logical View*

In this specific multitenant data center, the shared infrastructure provides connectivity, security, and server load balancing for four different customers. Each one of them has a different level of service according to the allocated networking services, and naturally, they might be paying different prices for their virtual infrastructure class (bronze, silver, gold, and diamond).

ACE and ASA virtual contexts can be configured in bridged or routed modes. ACE contexts can be configured in a one-arm design if the load-balanced traffic is not as big as the real server traffic.

For class diamond customers, an internal VRF can be deployed to offload the load balancer from direct traffic between application and database servers.

Customized services such as load balancing of DMZ servers can be provided with one more interface for an ASA context and an additional ACE virtual context for these servers.

The VRFs can be provided by the aggregation switches or by the service chassis comprised of the Catalyst 6500 and the ACE and ASA service modules, as shown in Figure 4-45.

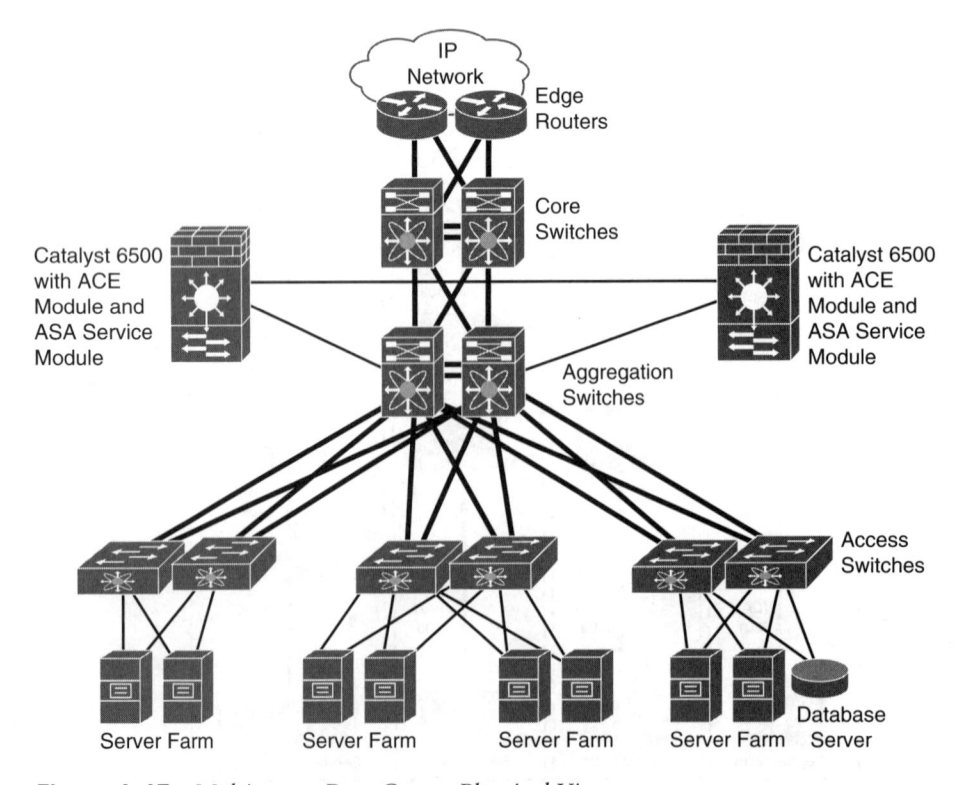

Figure 4-45 *Multitenant Data Center Physical View*

The multitenant data center design is not exclusive for service providers. In fact, acquisitions and merging between corporations might bring the same challenges during a migration period. After all, it can be very hard to change all the servers' IP addresses to install them in another data center infrastructure. The multitenant data center design can provide a new virtual infrastructure to accommodate the acquired company servers without traumatic IP address changes and hardware spending.

You should observe that this design does not address VLAN conflicts between environments, that is, customers that need to deploy the same VLAN ID but should *not* have the same broadcast domain. Other virtualization techniques explained in Chapter 5, "Instant Switches: Virtual Device Contexts," and Chapter 8, "A Tale of Two Data Centers" will address this challenge.

Although the servers that belong to the farms shown in Figures 4-44 and 4-45 are physical servers, they could potentially be virtual machines as well. In fact, the *end-to-end resource virtualization* is the seed to the concept of virtual data centers that will be explored in the chapters of Part IV, "Virtualization in Server Technologies".

Summary

This chapter explored the concept of network services and described how they can be useful for application environments in data centers. As an example of these services, the devices known as load balancers were carefully analyzed and their importance for application scaling explained.

You also have learned

- The main elements of a server load-balancing implementation
- Different load-balancing techniques for connection management and address translation
- Other devices such as firewalls and proxies that can be load balanced as well
- Load balancer server offload techniques such as SSL offload, TCP reuse, and HTTP compression
- The main causes for load balancer proliferation in data centers
- How the Cisco ACE series implements load balancer virtualization with several advantages, such as easy provisioning and performance customization
- The different methods for ACE virtual context insertion in a data center network
- Basic Layer 4 and Layer 7 switching configuration of a virtual context
- Role-Based Access Control for virtual access administrators
- ACE virtual context distinct behavior to topics such as shared VLANs and fault tolerance

- A real-use case (multitenant data center) that can fully use the Cisco ACE series virtual context capabilities along with other solution virtualization techniques, such as Cisco ASA, VRFs, and VLANs

Figure 4-46 graphically differentiates the physical and the logical view of ACE virtual contexts.

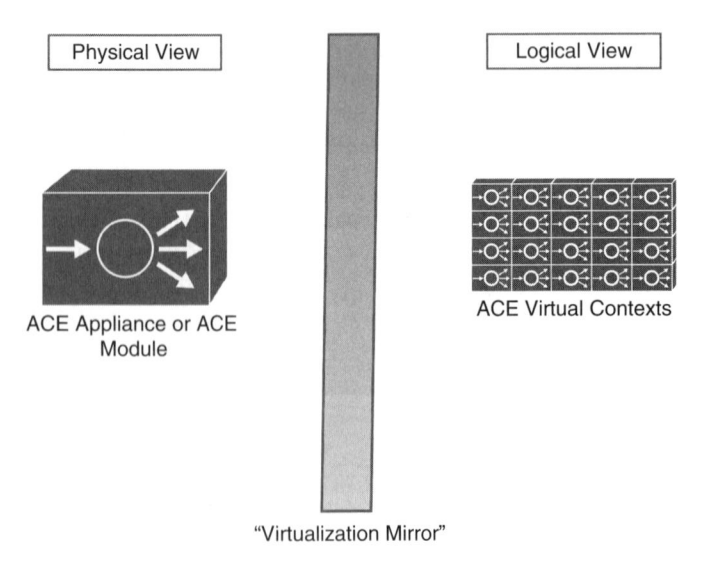

Figure 4-46 *Through the Virtualization Mirror*

Further Reading

Moraes, Alexandre M.S.P. *Cisco Firewalls*. Cisco Press, 2011.

Arregoces, Mauricio and Portolani, Maurizio. *Data Center Fundamentals*. Cisco Press, 2003.

Chapter 5

Instant Switches: Virtual Device Contexts

"Now, here, you see, it takes all the running you can do, to keep in the same place. If you want to get somewhere else, you must run at least twice as fast as that!"
(Lewis Carroll, Through the Looking-Glass*)*

This chapter examines virtual device contexts (VDC) as an evolution of network partitioning virtualization technologies. It covers the following topics:

- Extending Device Virtualization
- Why Use VDCs?
- VDCs in Detail
- Creating and Configuring VDCs
- Allocating Resources to VDCs
- Using Resource Templates
- Managing VDCs
- Global Resources
- Use Case: Data Center Security Zones

Table 5-1 categorizes virtual device contexts in the virtualization taxonomy described in Chapter 1, "Virtualization History and Definitions."

Table 5-1 *VDC Virtualization Classification*

Virtualization Characteristics	VDC
Emulation	Ethernet switch
Type	Partitioning
Subtype	Resource allocation control
Scalability	Up to eight VDCs plus one admin VDC (depending on Nexus 7000 hardware and software)[1]
Technology area	Networking
Subarea	Data, control, and management plane
Advantages	Higher device utilization, device consolidation, and fault isolation

[1] Refer to Appendix A, "Cisco Data Center Portfolio," for more details and to Cisco online documentation for updated information.

A technology is always restricted by its original design and purpose. Hence, it is only natural that deployment cases will continuously test and reach their limits, until a new technology is created to fulfill new demands. This cyclic process is the basis of technology evolution, and it is no different in network virtualization.

In Chapter 3, "The Humble Beginnings of Network Virtualization," I have explained how VLANs and Virtual Routing and Forwarding (VRF) became *the* most popular network virtualization units in the data center, how they can be used in practical scenarios, and what their main limitations are.

In Chapter 4, "An Army of One: ACE Virtual Contexts," I introduced a new style of network partitioning: *virtual contexting*. Such a virtualization technique enables the provisioning of *virtual devices*, which are abstract elements that deploy virtualization in all networking planes (data, control, and management). With virtual contexts, a network designer is no longer forced to deploy a new device if there are unused resources in the data center. And there is an additional advantage: The provisioning of a virtual context is a dynamic and almost instantaneous process.

Virtual device contexts (VDC) are the implementation of virtual contexting in Ethernet switches. As you will learn and experience in this chapter, VDCs are basically virtual Ethernet switches. With VDCs, data center network designers can achieve a higher level of consolidation and isolation that was not possible with other network partitioning technologies, such as VLANs and VRFs.

Extending Device Virtualization

In 2008, Cisco introduced virtual device contexts to its new line of Nexus 7000 data center switches. Taking advantage of this switch software architecture, Cisco's engineering brought innovation to data center networks, meshing two technologies together: virtual contexts (from Application Control Engine [ACE] and Firewall Services Module [FWSM]) and Ethernet switching.

A VDC can be defined as a logical partition of a physical switch that provides, as a result, a virtual entity with separate data, control, and management planes. More specifically:

- Each VDC can be managed by a completely distinct set of administrators (*management plane virtualization*).

- All Layer 2–3 processes and protocol instances are exclusive per VDC (*control plane virtualization*).

- By default, hosts connected to a VDC cannot communicate with others that belong to another VDC, even if they were created in the same physical switch (*data plane virtualization*).

VDCs overlay other network virtualization techniques such as VLANs and VRFs, as illustrated in Figure 5-1.

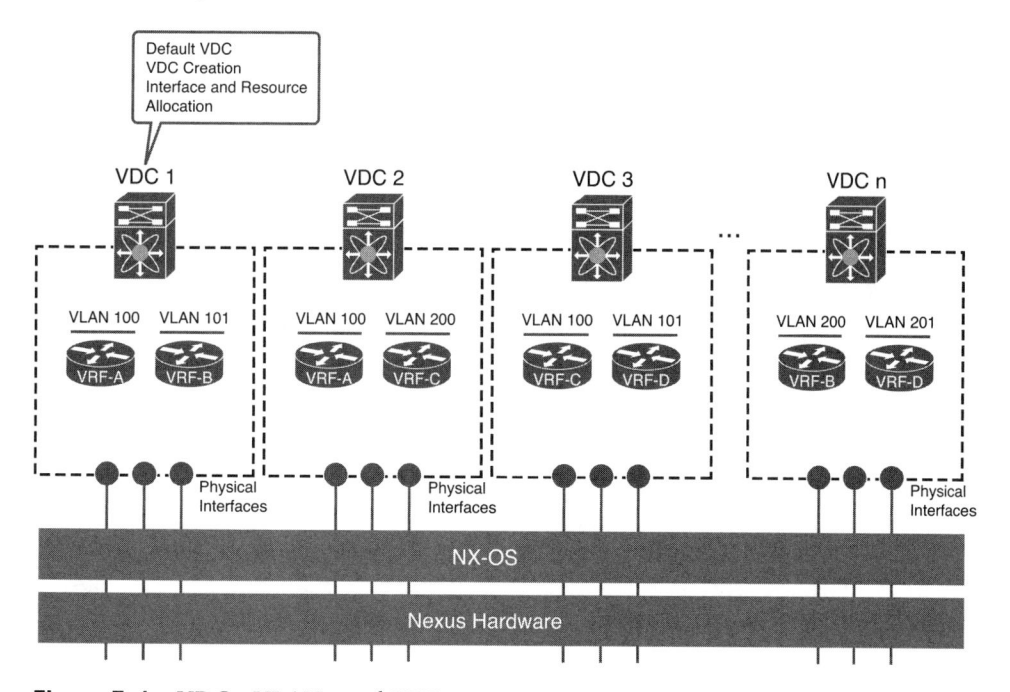

Figure 5-1 *VDCs, VLANs, and VRFs*

Within a VDC, you can create VLANs and VRFs as if you were configuring a physical switch. As a general rule, VLAN 100 from VDC 1 and VLAN 100 from VDC 2 are completely distinct elements from the physical switch perspective. Additionally, if you configure VRFs with the same name on different VDCs, they will characterize distinct virtual elements.

Similarly to ACE virtual contexts, physical hardware resources can be dynamically allocated to VDCs. But unlike the former, a VDC has **physical interfaces** allocated to it. And as another general rule, each Ethernet interface must belong to only one VDC.

> **Note** The Nexus 7000 Fibre Channel over Ethernet (FCoE) implementation creates exceptions to the some of the described VDC behaviors. For example, FCoE VLANs must be unique for all VDCs in a physical switch, and shared FCoE interfaces belong to two VDCs simultaneously. More details about this subject will be presented in Chapter 12, "One Cable to Unite Us All."

The illusion of a virtual Ethernet switch is hardened with the impossibility of internal communication between VDCs created on the same physical device. In fact, if you absolutely need to allow any communication between hosts connected to two different VDCs, you will have to physically interconnect these contexts.

Figure 5-2 portrays this curious scenario.

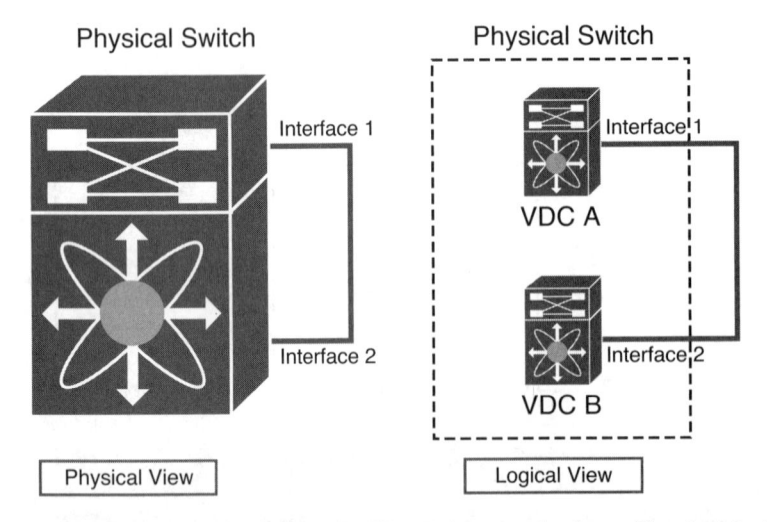

Figure 5-2 *Connecting VDCs That Belong to the Same Physical Switch*

> **Note** If the connection shown in Figure 5-2 is configured as an Ethernet trunk for all VLANs, VLAN x in VDC A shares the same broadcast domain with VLAN x in VDC B. Hence, each VLAN ID will represent the same broadcast domain in both VDCs.

Why Use VDCs?

Simply put, VDCs were created to implement network partitioning where other virtualization techniques might not be suitable solutions. Switch consolidation, hardened secure segmentation, and fault isolation are the most common objectives network designers want to achieve with VDCs.

Nowadays, modular Ethernet switches (such as the Nexus 7000) can have almost 800 Ethernet interfaces. However, it is very common that only a fraction of these ports is effectively used in data centers. This low utilization of resources happens because data center networks usually cannot deploy a switch in more than one environment. Here are some reasons why additional switches have to be deployed in spite of the existence of unused ports available:

- A different team (or company) must exclusively manage these new devices.
- There is an environment that deploys a protocol that is different from the one used in the data center (for example, Multiple Spanning Tree [MST] when the network runs Rapid Per VLAN Spanning Tree Plus [Rapid PVST+]).
- The new switch must deploy VLAN IDs that are already being used in the installed network.

VDCs, created in the existent network, could easily avoid the acquisition of new switches in any of these scenarios. Furthermore, when two or more data centers are being consolidated (merging), and all of these situations are happening simultaneously, VDCs can significantly improve resource utilization.

Figure 5-3 portrays switch consolidation with four different VDCs replacing four physical switches.

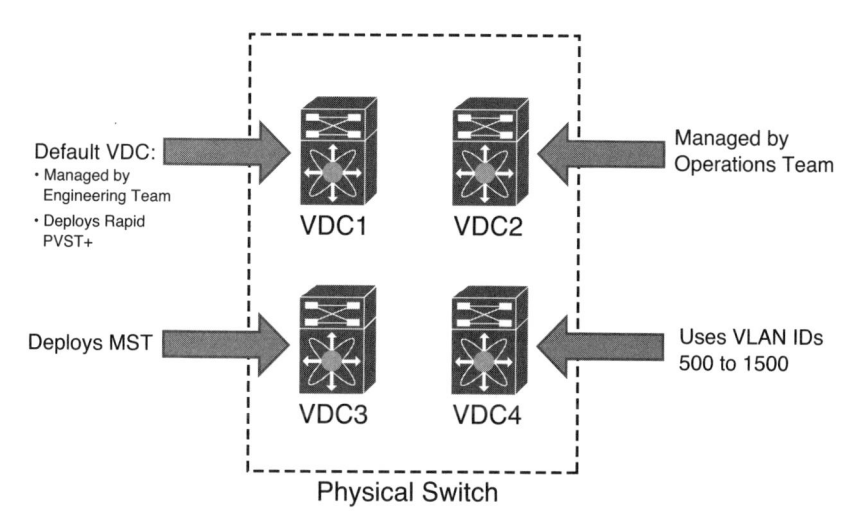

Figure 5-3 *Switch Consolidation Example*

Another level of consolidation can happen between network layers. As an example, Figure 5-4 demonstrates how a single physical switch could envelop core and aggregation network layers with VDCs.

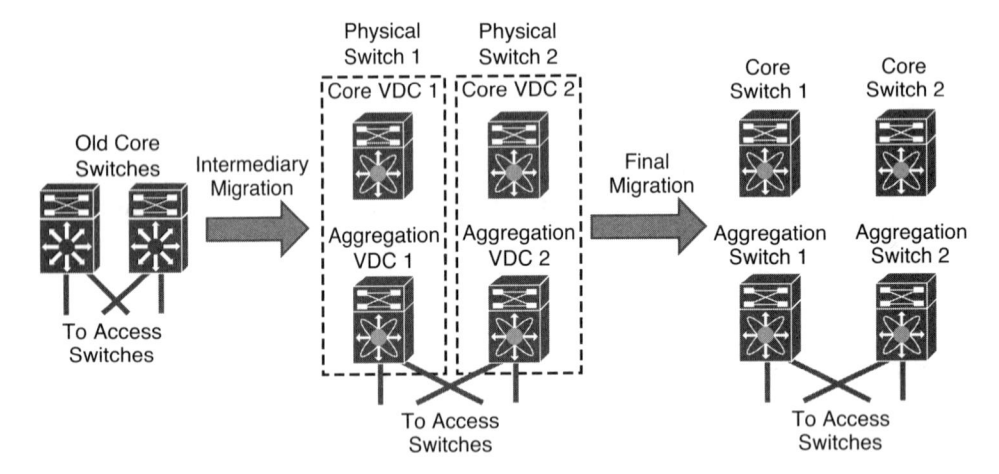

Figure 5-4 *Consolidation of Layers in a Data Center Network*

Although it is not a common application of VDCs, this design can be very useful for a network that is migrating from a two-layer topology (Core-Access) to a three-layer topology (Core-Aggregation-Access).

In Figure 5-4, the old switches are being replaced because they do not support the data center's future growing needs. However, at this moment, two new core switches and two new aggregation switches can result in an excessive number of unused interfaces. As an intermediary migration step, the network designers can deploy core and aggregation VDCs in the same physical switch. And because the core and aggregation VDCs have distinct configurations, the final migration to physical switches will be much easier when the network outgrows the number of ports these VDCs can provide.

Even in the case of an internal process failure (such as a routing protocol freeze) or a configuration error, a VDC does not impact the operation of other VDCs created in the same physical switch. This isolation allows the use of VDCs to limit the fault domain in data centers and helps network designers to build *virtually* segregated test environments.

VDCs in Detail

NX-OS, the Nexus switches operating system, has a modular architecture based on concurrent processes that can be individually started and stopped at any time. NX-OS also prevents each process from accessing memory that is not allocated to it, using a technique called *protected space*.

VDCs take advantage of these robust characteristics to deploy network partitioning with security and stability. In Figure 5-5, you see how VDCs are related to the NX-OS architecture.

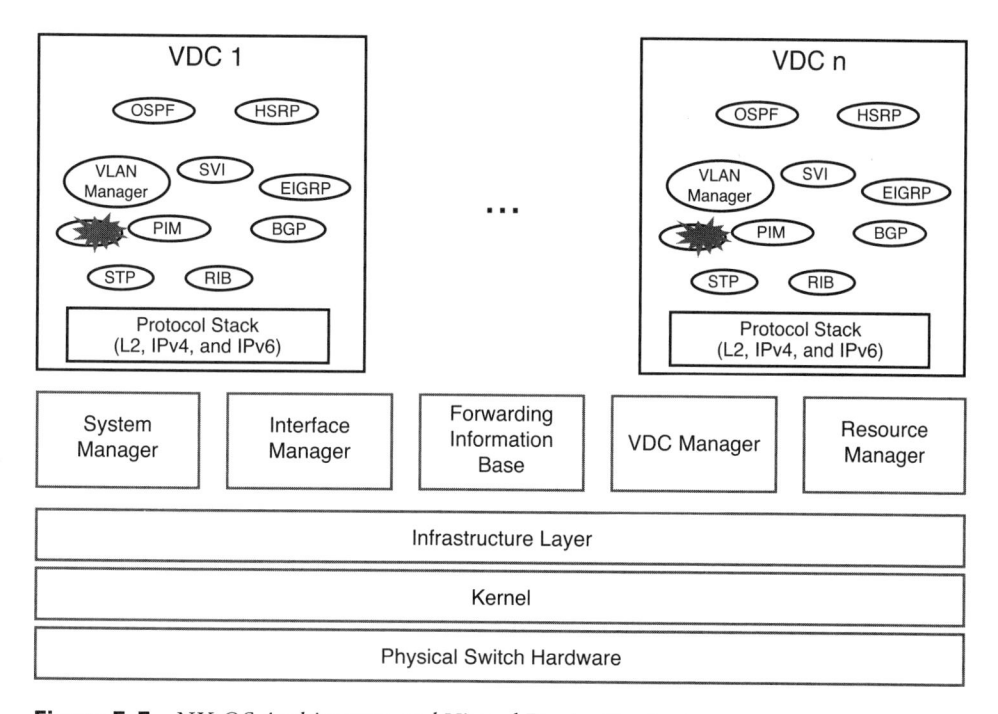

Figure 5-5 *NX-OS Architecture and Virtual Device Contexts*

In Figure 5-5, several processes are shared among all VDCs. Designed to reduce complexity and to scale performance, these processes are responsible for the physical switch hardware control. The main shared processes are

- **Kernel:** This process name is originated from the German word *kern*, which means "core." It is usually the main component of most operating systems and is responsible for the communication between the software processes and the hardware components.

- **Infrastructure layer:** This supports the requests from higher-layer processes that change the switch hardware behavior. It was designed to facilitate NX-OS feature implementation.

- **System Manager:** This launches, monitors, and tears down processes. It is the center of service management and fault recovery.

- **Interface Manager:** This process creates a common namespace for the switch interfaces. It also serves as an information reference map for interfaces owned by other processes.

- **Forwarding Information Base (FIB):** This process represents the hardware implementation of the data plane. It defines how the switch forwards Ethernet frames and IP packets.
- **VDC Manager:** This process is responsible for the creation and deletion of VDCs. It also communicates with the System Manager (for VDC process management) and the Resource Manager (for resource allocation).
- **Resource Manager:** This process is responsible for managing the allocation and distribution of switch resources between VDCs, such as VLANs, VRFs, PortChannels, physical interfaces, CPU shares, and memory for FIB entries.

Note It is not possible to run different versions of NX-OS in distinct VDCs, nor is this the objective of this capability.

Each VDC has Layer 2 and Layer 3 services processes that are started during the boot or through the **feature** command. These exclusive processes guarantee full control and management plane virtualization.

Tip The complete list of processes in a VDC can be viewed through the **show processes vdc** command.

Creating and Configuring VDCs

Even if you do not want to deploy VDCs in an NX-OS switch, you are forced to use at least one: the *default VDC*, or simply *VDC1*. This context is automatically created during the switch boot and actually represents the physical switch by default.

In a switch without *nondefault VDCs*, all interfaces that can share a context are allocated to the default VDC. In Example 5-1, you can verify this initial condition in a Nexus 7000 switch called N7K.

Example 5-1 *Verifying Hardware Modules and Initial Interface Allocation*

```
! Verifying the hardware modules installed in this switch
N7K# show module | head lines 7
Mod  Ports  Module-Type                        Model          Status
---  -----  ---------------------------------  -------------  --------
1    48     10/100/1000 Mbps Ethernet Module   N7K-M148GT-11  ok
5    0      Supervisor module-1X               N7K-SUP1       active *
```

```
6     0      Supervisor module-1X          N7K-SUP1      ha-standby
10    32     10 Gbps Ethernet Module       N7K-M132XP-12 ok


! Verifying the existent VDCs and how the physical interfaces are distributed among
them
N7K# show vdc membership


vdc_id: 0 vdc_name: Unallocated interfaces:

vdc_id: 1 vdc_name: N7K interfaces:
        Ethernet1/1           Ethernet1/2           Ethernet1/3
        Ethernet1/4           Ethernet1/5           Ethernet1/6
[output suppressed]
        Ethernet1/46          Ethernet1/47          Ethernet1/48

        Ethernet10/1          Ethernet10/2          Ethernet10/3
        Ethernet10/4          Ethernet10/5          Ethernet10/6
[output suppressed]
        Ethernet10/31         Ethernet10/32
```

Besides the default VDC, Example 5-1 also exposes another context called *unallocated VDCs* (VDC ID of 0). This nonfunctional context is merely a repository for interfaces that cannot be included in any of the created VDCs, or for interfaces that belonged to VDCs that were erased.

Note Some Nexus 7000 linecards, such as F2-series modules, cannot share the same VDC with other linecards in the same chassis. Therefore, in a heterogeneous module configuration, these module ports are initially allocated in VDC 0.

To observe in detail the consequences of the creation of a VDC, I have designed a simple test, whose logical topology is represented in Figure 5-6.

Although there is no practical reason to deploy such a connection, this absurd scenario will be useful in the exploration of basic VDC concepts. In it, I want you to focus on how the switch reacts with this *looped* connection (although the word by itself is already a surprise spoiler).

Example 5-2 details the operational status of the interconnected interfaces, which were configured as standard trunks for all VLANs.

192 Data Center Virtualization Fundamentals

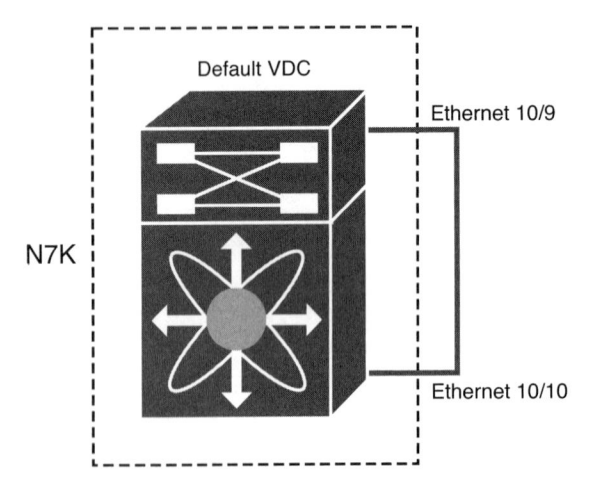

Figure 5-6 *Connection of Ports That Belong to the Same Switch*

Example 5-2 *Verifying the Looped Interface's Status*

```
! Verifying if the interfaces 9 and 10 from module 10 are working
N7K# show interface Ethernet 10/9-10 brief
--------------------------------------------------------------------
Ethernet        VLAN    Type Mode    Status  Reason      Speed       Port
Interface                                                            Ch #
--------------------------------------------------------------------

Eth10/9         1       eth  trunk   up      none        10G(S)  --
Eth10/10        1       eth  trunk   up      none        10G(S)  --
```

The example shows that both interfaces are operational. However, to verify whether these interfaces are actually forwarding data traffic, you need to check the Spanning Tree Protocol (STP) in such a topology.

Example 5-3 details the port's STP conditions in VLAN 1 (which is the only existent VLAN in this switch).

Example 5-3 *N7K Interfaces and Spanning Tree*

```
! Verifying how STP is working in VLAN 1
N7K# show spanning-tree vlan 1


VLAN0001
  Spanning tree enabled protocol rstp
  Root ID    Priority    32769
! This MAC Address represents the switch N7K in the STP topology
             Address     001b.54c2.9c41
```

```
               This bridge is the root
[output suppressed]
! Interface Ethernet 10/9 is Forwarding and 10/10 is Blocked
Interface         Role Sts Cost      Prio.Nbr Type
---------------- ---- --- --------- -------- --------------
Eth10/9           Desg FWD 2         128.1289 P2p
Eth10/10          Back BLK 2         128.1290 P2p
```

Predictably, STP detected a potential loop and reacted to it. In more detail:

- The connection between Ethernet interfaces 10/9 and 10/10 created a segment in which Rapid PVST+ selected one *designated* port to forward traffic.

- Because Ethernet 10/9 has the lowest port ID (128.1289), it became the designated port in this segment (*forwarding* state), while Ethernet 10/10 becomes a backup port (*blocked* state).

A completely different scenario is formed when these ports belong to different VDCs. As mentioned in the earlier section "Extending Device Virtualization," these ports behave as interfaces that belong to different switches.

Figure 5-7 portrays the described scenario.

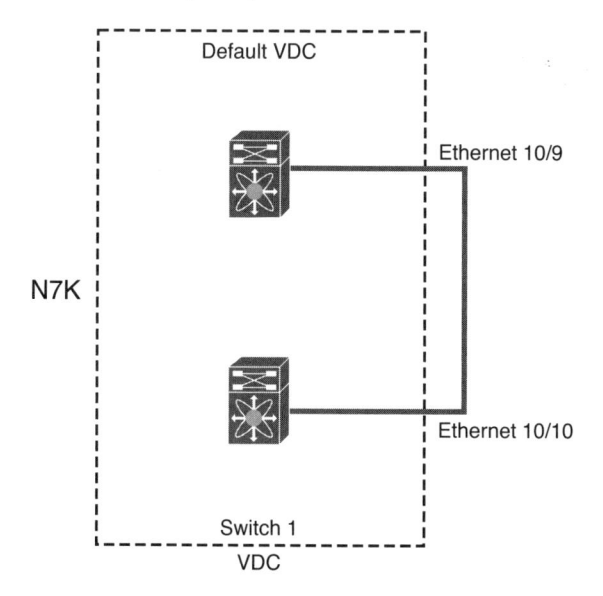

Figure 5-7 *New VDC Creation*

To demonstrate this behavior, I will create a new VDC, creatively named Switch1. Example 5-4 details the Switch1 configuration and interface allocation.

Example 5-4 *VDC Switch1 Creation*

```
! Creating a VDC named Switch1
N7K(config)# vdc Switch1
Note:  Creating VDC, one moment please ...
14:36:07 N7K %$ VDC-1 %$ %VDC_MGR-2-VDC_ONLINE: vdc 2 has come online
! Allocating interface Ethernet 10/10 to Switch1
N7K(config-vdc)# allocate interface ethernet 10/10
! The entire Ethernet 10/10 hardware port-group will be allocated to this VDC
Entire port-group is not present in the command. Missing ports will
be included automatically
Moving ports will cause all config associated to them in source vdc
to be removed. Are you sure you want to move the ports (y/n)?  [yes]
yes

! Verifying the new interface distribution among VDCs
N7K(config-vdc)# show vdc membership

vdc_id: 0 vdc_name: Unallocated interfaces:

vdc_id: 1 vdc_name: N7K interfaces:
        Ethernet1/1         Ethernet1/2         Ethernet1/3
        Ethernet1/4         Ethernet1/5         Ethernet1/6
[output suppressed]
        Ethernet1/46        Ethernet1/47        Ethernet1/48

        Ethernet10/1        Ethernet10/2        Ethernet10/3
        Ethernet10/4        Ethernet10/5        Ethernet10/6
        Ethernet10/7        Ethernet10/8        Ethernet10/9
        Ethernet10/11       Ethernet10/13       Ethernet10/15
        Ethernet10/17       Ethernet10/18       Ethernet10/19
[output suppressed]
        Ethernet10/32

vdc_id: 2 vdc_name: Switch1 interfaces:
        Ethernet10/10       Ethernet10/12       Ethernet10/14
        Ethernet10/16
```

Tip NX-OS automatically assigns the next available identifier (in this case, ID 2) to this new VDC. However, you can change this assignment through the **vdc** *<vdc name>* **id** command.

Although I have allocated only one interface to VDC Switch1, four of them were automatically inserted there because they belong to the same *hardware port group*. A port group shares hardware resources that do not allow distinct configurations among its interfaces (such as different VDCs).

Table 5-2 summarizes how port groups are organized in the Nexus 7000 modules at the time of this writing. However, I recommend that you refer to the Cisco online documentation for more updated information.

Table 5-2 *Nexus 7000 Port Groups*

Module	Port Groups
N7K-F132XP-15	(1,2), (3,4), (5,6), (7,8), (9,10), (11,12), (13,14), (15,16), (17,18), (19,20), (21,22), (23,24), (25,26), (27,28), (29,30), (31,32)
N7K-F248XP-25	(1-4), (5-8), (9-12), (13-16), (17-20), (21-24), (25-28), (29-32)
N7K-F248XP-25E	(1-4), (5-8), (9-12), (13-16), (17-20), (21-24), (25-28), (29-32)
N7K-F248XT-25E	(1-4), (5-8), (9-12), (13-16), (17-20), (21-24), (25-28), (29-32)
N7K-M108X2-12L	No restriction for VDC allocation
N7K-M132XP-12	(1,3,5,7), (2,4,6,8), (9,11,13,15), (10,12,14,16), (17,19,21,23), (18,20,22,24), (25,27,29,31), (26,28,30,32)
N7K-M132XP-12L	(1,3,5,7), (2,4,6,8), (9,11,13,15), (10,12,14,16), (17,19,21,23), (18,20,22,24), (25,27,29,31), (26,28,30,32)
N7K-M148GS-11	No restriction for VDC allocation[1]
N7K-M148GS-11L	No restriction for VDC allocation[1]
N7K-M148GT-11	No restriction for VDC allocation[1]
N7K-M148GT-11L	No restriction for VDC allocation[1]
N7K-M224XP-23L	No restriction for VDC allocation
N7K-M206FQ-23L	No restriction for VDC allocation
N7K-M202-CF-22L	No restriction for VDC allocation

[1] In these modules, interfaces (1-12), (13-24), (25-36), and (37-48) belong to four different ASICs (application-specific integrated circuits). Therefore, some VDC-related operations can impact interfaces in the same ASIC.

Note The way that VDCs are distributed over linecards affects the total number of MAC addresses that can be learned on a physical switch. If a VDC learns a MAC address, its MAC address table entry is only replicated to modules that have interfaces allocated to that specific VDC. Therefore, if a VDC is limited to a set of linecards, it will not consume MAC address space from other modules.

With VDC Switch1 created, it is interesting to check how close to a physical switch its command-line interface (CLI) is. One way to access the VDC Switch1 CLI is through the **switchto vdc** command.

Example 5-5 portrays the first login to Switch1.

Example 5-5 *Entering Switch1 Configuration*

```
! Accessing the VDC Switch CLI
N7K# switchto vdc Switch1



         ---- System Admin Account Setup ----


Do you want to enforce secure password standard (yes/no) [y]: yes
[output suppressed]


Would you like to enter the basic configuration dialog (yes/no): no
Cisco Nexus Operating System (NX-OS) Software
[output suppressed]
! Please notice the prompt below
N7K-Switch1#
```

Tip The **switchto vdc** NX-OS command and the **changeto** ACE command have similar functions: switch to a context's CLI.

In Example 5-5, the first login to the VDC resulted in an initial setup script, as if you were powering up a switch for the first time. The prompt **N7K-Switch1#** denotes that you are accessing the VDC CLI.

Note If you are recognizing this prompt from somewhere else, you are right: N7K-Switch1 and N7K-Switch2 from Chapter 3 were VDCs, not physical switches. Excuse me for the "Neo, you are in the matrix" moment, but isn't *emulation with transparency* the exact description of an effective virtualization technique?

In an NX-OS setup script, the default interface configuration can be defined. As expected, the same occurs within a VDC setup, as you can verify in Example 5-6.

Example 5-6 *Switch1 Interfaces Default Configuration and Status*

```
! Verifying the VDC default configuration for its interfaces
N7K-Switch1# show running-config all | include "system default"
no system default switchport
system default switchport shutdown
[output suppressed]
!Checking the interfaces status in the VDC
N7K-Switch1# show interface brief

--------------------------------------------------------------------
Ethernet      VLAN Type Mode    Status Reason           Speed      Port
Interface                                                          Ch #
--------------------------------------------------------------------
Eth10/10      --   eth  routed  down   Administratively down auto(S) --
Eth10/12      --   eth  routed  down   SFP not inserted     auto(S) --
Eth10/14      --   eth  routed  down   SFP not inserted     auto(S) --
Eth10/16      --   eth  routed  down   SFP not inserted     auto(S) --
```

When an interface is allocated to a VDC, it receives the default configuration defined in the **system default switchport** and **system default switchport shutdown** commands. And as you can see, the VDC interfaces are configured exactly this way (routed and disabled).

Continuing the VDC interconnection test, I have configured interface Ethernet 10/10 as a trunk (for all VLANs) to communicate with Ethernet 10/9 (that still belongs to VDC1). Example 5-7 details how STP reacts to this connection.

Example 5-7 *Interface Ethernet 10/10 Configuration and Status in Switch1*

```
! Checking STP
N7K-Switch1# show spanning-tree vlan 1


VLAN0001
  Spanning tree enabled protocol rstp
!The Default VDC is the Root switch in this network
  Root ID    Priority    32769
             Address     001b.54c2.9c41
             Cost        2
             Port        1290 (Ethernet10/10)
             Hello Time  2  sec  Max Age 20 sec  Forward Delay 15 sec

!VDC Switch1 has a different MAC address
  Bridge ID  Priority    32769  (priority 32768 sys-id-ext 1)
             Address     001b.54c2.9c42
```

```
                       Hello Time   2   sec  Max Age 20 sec   Forward Delay 15 sec
```

```
!VDC Switch1 interface 10/10 is active and is the Root port because it connects the
VDC to the Root
Interface        Role Sts Cost      Prio.Nbr Type
---------------- ---- --- --------- -------- --------------------
Eth10/10         Root FWD 2         128.1290 P2p
```

As expected, interface Ethernet 10/10 is now forwarding traffic because it belongs to another (virtual) switch. More specifically, Ethernet 10/10 is a root port, because the default VDC is the root switch in VLAN1.

VDC Names and CLI Prompts

In a VDC, the switch illusion is maintained when an administrator performs usual tasks, such as changing the host name in the Switch1 VDC, as shown in Example 5-8.

Example 5-8 *Common Tasks Performed in Switch1*

```
! Changing the switch name to "VDC2"
N7K-Switch1(config)# switchname VDC2
N7K-VDC2#
```

Differently from what happens in a physical NX-OS switch, the configuration command **switchname** only changes the second part of the prompt. By default, a prefix N7K (which is the name of VDC1) is added to the prompt of the nondefault VDCs.

Tip If you do not want to hint to an operator that he is not managing a physical switch, it is possible to remove the prompt prefix with the **no vdc combined-hostname** configuration command.

With Example 5-9, it is possible to notice that the CLI prompt *automatically* defines how a VDC is named. Nevertheless, the VDC ID remains the same (2 in the example) when a name change occurs.

Example 5-9 *Verifying the VDC Name*

```
! Although the name of the VDC changed from 'Switch1' to 'VDC2', its Identifier
remains the same
N7K# switchto vdc ?
  N7K       VDC number 1
  VDC2      VDC number 2
```

Virtualization Nesting

Virtual elements such as VLANs and VRFs can be configured and monitored in a virtual device context. Such abstraction recursivity is called *virtualization nesting*.

Figure 5-8 shows a scenario where the VDCs from the previous sections share a VLAN and have distinct VRFs configured with the same name.

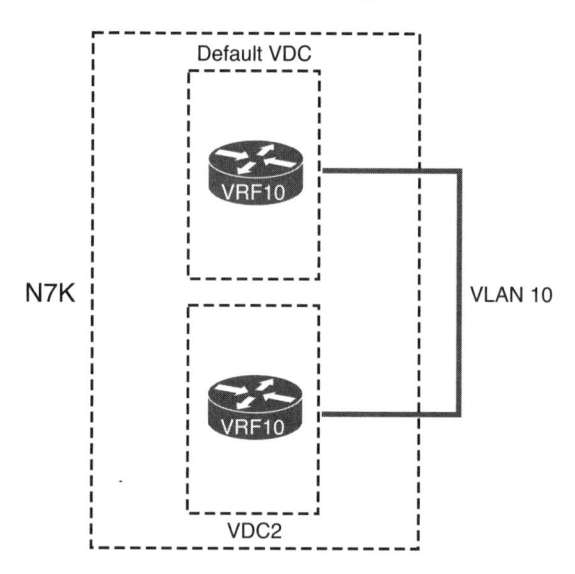

Figure 5-8 *VLAN and VRF Connection Between Two VDCs*

Example 5-10 details the configuration for this scenario in the default VDC. Notice the VLANs and VRFs I am using.

Example 5-10 *Configuring a VRF Named VRF10 in the Default VDC*

```
! Creating VLAN 10 and VRF10 in VDC 1
N7K(config)# vlan 10
N7K(config-vlan)# vrf context VRF10
! Starting process for SVIs in VDC 1
N7K(config-vrf)# feature interface-vlan
! Creating SVI for VLAN10 in VRF10
N7K(config)# interface vlan 10
N7K(config-if)# vrf member VRF10
% Deleted all L3 config on interface Vlan10
N7K(config-if)# ip address 192.168.10.1/24
N7K(config-if)# no shutdown
```

Afterward, I have done the corresponding configuration in VDC2, as detailed in Example 5-11. Observe that the configurations done in the default VDC (VLAN, VRF, SVI) do not exist in VDC2. Again, observe the names and identifiers I am using for the virtual elements.

Example 5-11 *Configuring VRF Also Named VRF10 in VDC 2*

```
! VDC2 does not have VLAN 10 defined yet
N7K-VDC2# show vlan brief

VLAN Name                             Status    Ports
---- -------------------------------- --------- -----------------------
1    default                          active    Eth10/10

! Nor a VRF10
N7K-VDC2# show vrf | include VRF10
N7K-VDC2# configure terminal
Enter configuration commands, one per line.  End with CNTL/Z.
! Creating VLAN 10 and VRF10
N7K-VDC2(config)# vlan 10
N7K-VDC2(config-vlan)# vrf context VRF10
! It is necessary to enable SVIs in VDC too
N7K-VDC2(config)# feature interface-vlan
N7K-VDC2(config)# interface vlan 10
N7K-VDC2(config-if)# vrf member VRF10
% Deleted all L3 config on interface Vlan10
N7K-VDC2(config-if)# ip address 192.168.10.2/24
N7K-VDC2(config-if)# no shutdown
```

To test that both homonymous VRFs are communicating with each other, I have issued an echo request from VDC 2, as shown in Example 5-12.

Example 5-12 *Testing IP Connectivity Between VRF10 in VDC 1 and VRF10 in VDC 2*

```
! Verifying the IP connectivity between VRF10 in VDC1 and VRF10 in VDC2
N7K-VDC2# ping 192.168.10.1 vrf VRF10
PING 192.168.10.1 (192.168.10.1): 56 data bytes
Request 0 timed out
64 bytes from 192.168.10.1: icmp_seq=1 ttl=254 time=1.87 ms
[output suppressed]
```

A VDC can offer flexibilities that are impossible for VLANs, as I have explained in the earlier section "Why Use VDCs?" For example, a separate VDC can provide additional ports and Ethernet connectivity to an MST-based network with no influence on the other

VDCs in the same physical switch. A separate VLAN that belongs to a Rapid PVST+ switch simply cannot provide such connectivity.

To connect to an MST-enabled network, I have created another device context called VDC3 with interfaces Ethernet 1/1 to 1/12 allocated to it. VLAN 2 was enabled in it, and Ethernet 1/1 was configured as a trunk for all VLANs.

Figure 5-9 depicts VDC3 topology, while Example 5-13 details the corresponding MST configuration where

- VDC3 is using the same region name and version from the already installed MST switch.

- An MST instance is created for VLANs 2 to 99.

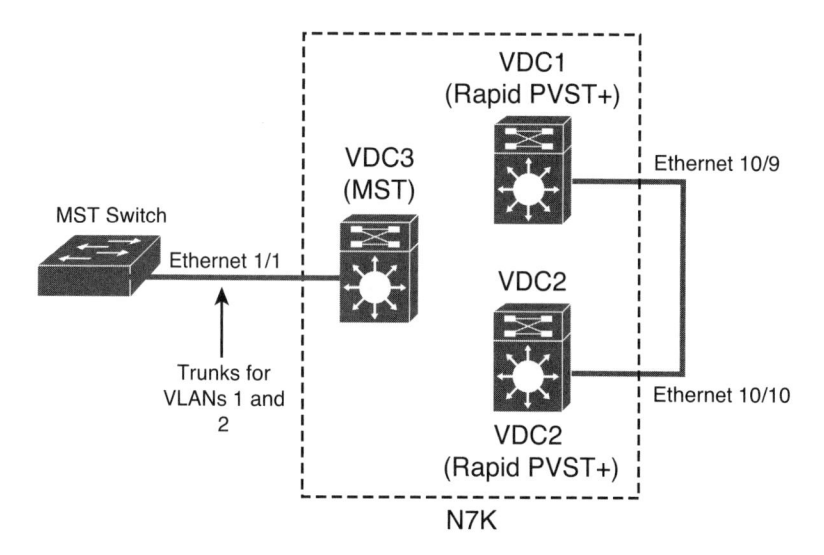

Figure 5-9 *VDC3 Creation, Configuration, and Connection to an MST-Enabled Switch*

Example 5-13 *VDC3 Creation and MST Configuration*

```
! Enabling MST in VDC3
N7K-VDC3(config)# spanning-tree mode mst
! Configuring MST in this VDC
N7K-VDC3(config)# spanning-tree mst configuration
N7K-VDC3(config-mst)# name Region1
N7K-VDC3(config-mst)# revision 1
N7K-VDC3(config-mst)# instance 1 vlan 2-99
```

The STP status can be verified in Example 5-14.

Example 5-14 *Verifying MST in VDC3*

```
! Verifying MST in VLAN 1
N7K-VDC3# show spanning-tree vlan 1
! VLAN 1 belongs to instance 0
MST0000
  Spanning tree enabled protocol mstp
! In this instance MST-switch is the root
  Root ID    Priority    4096
             Address     f025.72a6.8f43
             Cost        0
             Port        129 (Ethernet1/1)
[output suppressed]
Interface        Role Sts Cost      Prio.Nbr Type
---------------- ---- --- --------- -------- ------------------------
Eth1/1           Root FWD 20000     128.129  P2p


N7K-VDC3# show spanning-tree vlan 2
! VLAN 1 belongs to instance 1
MST0001
  Spanning tree enabled protocol mstp
! In this instance VDC3 is the root
  Root ID    Priority    32769
             Address     001b.54c2.9c43
             This bridge is the root
[output suppressed]
Interface        Role Sts Cost      Prio.Nbr Type
---------------- ---- --- --------- -------- ------------------------
Eth1/1           Desg FWD 20000     128.129  P2p
```

Once again, the creation of a VDC avoided the deployment of an additional physical switch. And more importantly, it was done instantaneously.

Allocating Resources to VDCs

When you create VDCs, it is possible to change how they share the available physical resources. Similarly to ACE virtual contexts, you can allocate minimum and maximum resources for each VDC. While NX-OS guarantees the minimum resources to a VDC, it can reclaim more (up to the maximum value), if additional resources are not being used.

At the time this writing, the hardware resources that can be controlled and allocated among existent VDCs are

- **VLANs:** These are bridged broadcast domains, as explained in Chapter 3.
- **Monitor sessions:** These are Switch Port ANalyzer (SPAN) sessions that can replicate the traffic from a port (or a group of ports) to another interface in the same switch for analysis purposes.
- **Encapsulated Remote Switch Port ANalyzer (ERSPAN) destinations:** These are SPAN sessions whose traffic is encapsulated into IP packets and directed to an IP address.
- **VRFs:** These are instances of routing tables and forwarding tables, as explained in Chapter 3.
- **PortChannels:** These are sets of aggregate interfaces that function as a single interface.
- **Memory for IPv4 unicast routes**
- **Memory for IPv4 multicast routes**
- **Memory for IPv6 unicast routes**
- **Memory for IPv6 multicast routes**
- **CPU utilization**

Figure 5-10 exemplifies how these physical resources can be dynamically used by three VDCs in a given instant.

The **limit-resource** command is used to define the minimum and maximum allocation for all resources except CPU percentage, which is defined through the **cpu-share** VDC command.

Tip The percentage of the supervisor CPU utilization a VDC receives can be calculated by dividing the shares assigned to this VDC by the sum of all shares from active VDCs.

Example 5-15 depicts a resource allocation configuration for monitor sessions in VDC2 and VDC3. Because there are only two available SPAN sessions for all the VDCs, it will be easier to verify what happens if a VDC requests one resource that is unavailable.

204 Data Center Virtualization Fundamentals

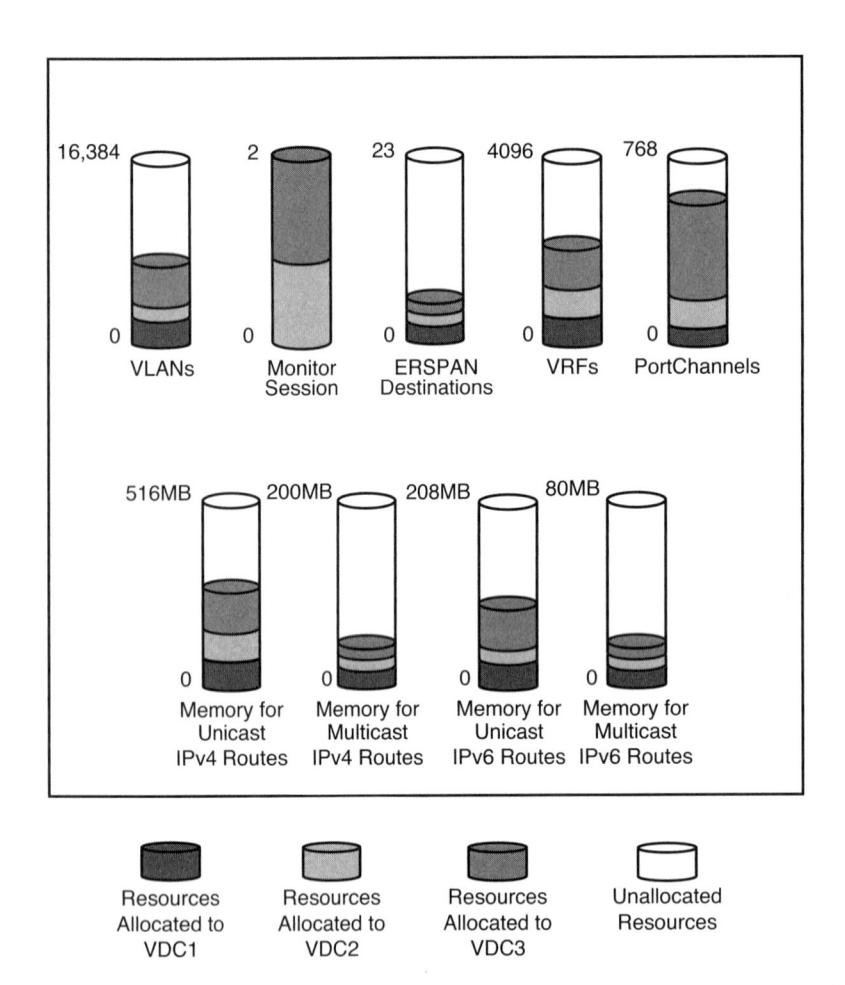

Figure 5-10 *Nexus 7000 Hardware Resources Allocated to Three VDCs*

Example 5-15 *Limiting the Monitor Sessions for VDC2 and VDC3*

```
N7K(config)# vdc VDC2
! Defining that VDC2 must have at least one SPAN session dedicated to it or two, if
there is another unused session
N7K(config-vdc)# limit-resource monitor-session minimum 1 maximum 2
N7K(config-vdc)# vdc VDC3
! Defining that VDC3 must have only one SPAN session dedicated to it
N7K(config-vdc)# limit-resource monitor-session minimum 1 maximum equal-to-min
! Verifying how the SPAN sessions are distributed among the VDCs
N7K(config-vdc)# show vdc resource monitor-session detail

  monitor-session    0 used    2 unused    2 free    0 avail    2 total
  ----------------
```

```
Vdc                     Min        Max        Used       Unused     Avail
---                     ---        ---        ----       ------     -----
N7K                     0          2          0          0          0
VDC2                    1          2          0          1          1
VDC3                    1          1          0          1          1
```

> **Note** Resource allocation configurations are done in the default VDC or in an *admin VDC*, which is exclusively restricted to handle administrative tasks over the other VDCs and the physical hardware. Refer to Appendix A and the Cisco online documentation to verify whether your hardware and software combination supports admin VDCs.

In Example 5-15, at least one SPAN session is guaranteed for VDC2 and VDC3 (minimum is 1 for both). The only difference is that VDC2 can potentially activate two simultaneous sessions. However, this situation will never happen because the other available session is reserved to VDC3.

The Avail column, from the **show vdc resource** command, exposes how many sessions each VDC can actually use. Example 5-16 shows what happens if an administrator tries to configure one monitor session in the default VDC (whose avail value is 0).

Example 5-16 *Default VDC Tries to Allocate and Configure a SPAN Session*

```
! Trying to allocate one session to VDC1
N7K(config)# vdc N7K
N7K(config-vdc)# limit-resource monitor-session minimum 1 maximum equal-to-min
ERROR: required resource cannot be reserved
```

As you can see in Example 5-16, it is not possible to configure a monitor session in the default VDC.

Adversely, a SPAN session configuration is possible in VDC3, as shown in Example 5-17.

Example 5-17 *SPAN Session Configuration in VDC3*

```
N7K-VDC3# show monitor session 1 brief
   session 1
---------------
type              : local
state             : up
source intf       :
   rx             : Eth1/1
   tx             : Eth1/1
   both           : Eth1/1
```

```
destination ports : Eth1/12
[output suppressed]
```

As expected, VDC3 could have only one monitor session configured. Example 5-18 shows how many SPAN sessions are available to each VDC at this moment.

Example 5-18 *Monitor Sessions Status for the VDCs*

```
! Observing what changed in the monitor-session allocation
N7K# show vdc resource monitor-session detail
  monitor-session   1 used    1 unused    1 free    0 avail    2 total
  -----------------
          Vdc              Min         Max         Used      Unused     Avail
          ---              ---         ---         ----      ------     -----
          N7K              0           2           0         0          0
          VDC2             1           2           0         1          1
          VDC3             1           1           1         0          0
```

You can see that, even if VDC2 can potentially have two SPAN sessions, it can only deploy one more (because VDC3 is using the other one).

More abundant physical resources present a different behavior when they are allocated to a VDC. VLANs, for example, must have both a minimum and maximum defined in the range of 16 to 4094. Also, the actual number of VLANs a VDC is using must consider some internal implementation details, as I will explain later in this section.

Example 5-19 shows how one can allocate a minimum of 16 VLANs for both VDC2 and VDC3, where only the former is allowed to use up to 4094 VLANs (if they are available, of course).

Example 5-19 *Allocation of VLAN Resources to VDC2 and VDC3*

```
! Allocating 16 to 4094 VLANs (if available) to VDC2
N7K (config)# vdc VDC2
N7K(config-vdc)# limit-resource vlan minimum 16 maximum 4094
N7K(config-vdc)# vdc VDC3
! Allocating only 16 VLANs to VDC3
N7K(config-vdc)# limit-resource vlan minimum 16 maximum equal-to-min
Verifying the VLANs distribution among the VDCs
N7K(config-vdc)# show vdc resource vlan detail

  vlan    28 used    24 unused    16356 free    16332 avail    16384 total
  ------
          Vdc              Min         Max         Used      Unused     Avail
          ---              ---         ---         ----      ------     -----
```

```
N7K      16     4094    20    0     4074
VDC2     16     4094    4     12    4090
VDC3     16     16      4     12    12
```

Besides the minimum and maximum values configured for each VDC, the output shows a weird result: VDC1, VDC2, and VDC3 are using 20, 4, and 4 VLANs, respectively.

If you do not remember such a high number of VLANs defined in each VDC, you are right. Example 5-20 verifies the defined VLANs in each VDCs.

Example 5-20 *Defined VLANs in Each VDC*

```
N7K# show vlan brief

VLAN Name                             Status    Ports
---- -------------------------------- --------- --------------------
1    default                          active    Eth1/24, Eth10/9
10   VLAN0010                         active    Eth1/24, Eth10/9
! Only two VLANs defined in the default VDC

N7K# switchto vdc VDC2
 [output suppressed]
N7K-VDC2# show vlan brief

VLAN Name                             Status    Ports
---- -------------------------------- --------- --------------------
1    default                          active    Eth10/10
10   VLAN0010                         active    Eth10/10
! Only two VLANs defined in VDC2

N7K-VDC2# switchback
N7K# switchto vdc VDC3
 [output suppressed]
N7K-VDC3# show vlan brief

VLAN Name                             Status    Ports
---- -------------------------------- --------- --------------------
1    default                          active    Eth1/1, Eth1/12
2    VLAN0002                         active    Eth1/1, Eth1/12
! Only two VLANs defined in VDC3
```

Why the difference? What are the additional VLANs shown in the **show vdc resource** command? The answer lies in the way internal VLANs are mapped to *bridge domains*.

A bridge domain (BD) is the internal representation of a VLAN within NX-OS. Deploying BDs, a switch such as the Nexus 7000 can identify and deploy a much higher number of VLANs (16,384) than defined by the IEEE 802.1Q standard (4094). Therefore, VLANs with the same identifier, created in different VDCs, have different bridge domain identifiers.

Example 5-21 details how to unconceal the VLAN-to-BD mapping within each VDC.

Example 5-21 *Bridge Groups Show Internal VLANs*

```
! Verifying how VLANs are mapped to bridge domains in VDC1 (VLANs 4032 to 4059 are reserved)
N7K# show vlan internal bd-info vlan-to-bd all-vlan
VDC Id  Vlan Id  BD Id
------  -------  -------
1        1        1
1        10       36
1        4032     3

1        4033     4
[output suppressed]
1        4059     35
! Total number of VLANs is 19


N7K# switchto vdc VDC2
  [output suppressed]
! Verifying how VLANs are mapped to Bridge Domains in VDC2 (VLAN 4042 is reserved)
N7K-VDC2# show vlan internal bd-info vlan-to-bd all-vlan

VDC Id  Vlan Id  BD Id
------  -------  -------
2        1        17
2        10       20
2        4042     19
! Total number of VLANs is 3

N7K-VDC2# switchback
N7K# switchto vdc VDC3
[output suppressed]
! Verifying how VLANs are mapped to bridge domains in VDC3 (VLAN 4042 is reserved)
N7K-VDC3# show vlan internal bd-info vlan-to-bd all-vlan

VDC Id  Vlan Id  BD Id
------  -------  -------
3        1        37
3        2        40
```

```
3          4042     39
! Total number of VLANs is 3
```

And if you add the reserved VLAN 4095 to each VDC, which is not represented in the **show vlan internal bd-info vlan-to-bd all-vlan** command, it is possible to understand why NX-OS computes that the default VDC, VDC2, and VDC3 are using 20, 4, and 4 VLANs, respectively.

Also, in Example 5-21, it is possible to verify that VLAN 10 in the default VDC and the same VLAN in VDC2 have different BDs (36 and 20, respectively).

Now that you understand how VLANs are calculated as resources, you will observe what happens when a VDC is configured to have more VLANs than its maximum value permits. Example 5-22 describes the results achieved when 20 additional VLANs (101–120) are configured in VDC2 and VDC3.

Example 5-22 *Trying to Configure 20 VLANs in VDC2 and VDC3*

```
! Defining 20 new VLANs in VDC2
N7K-VDC2(config)# vlan 101-120
N7K-VDC2(config-vlan)# end
! Verifying the VLANs Creation
N7K-VDC2# show vlan brief

VLAN Name                             Status    Ports
---- -------------------------------- --------- -----------------------
1    default                          active    Eth10/10
10   VLAN0010                         active    Eth10/10
101  VLAN0101                         active    Eth10/10
  [output suppressed]
120  VLAN0120                         active    Eth10/10


[output suppressed]
! Defining 20 new VLANs in VDC2
N7K-VDC3(config)# vlan 101-120
Warning: VLANs 113-120 - VLAN resource request exceed maximum available
N7K-VDC3(config-vlan)# show vlan brief
! Verifying the created VLANs

VLAN Name                             Status    Ports
---- -------------------------------- --------- -----------------------
1    default                          active    Eth1/1, Eth1/12
2    VLAN0002                         active    Eth1/1, Eth1/12
101  VLAN0101                         active    Eth1/1, Eth1/12
  [output suppressed]
112  VLAN0112                         active    Eth1/1, Eth1/12
```

210 Data Center Virtualization Fundamentals

In Example 5-22, because VDC3 already has four VLANs (and it is restricted to a maximum of 16 VLANs), VLANs 113 to 120 cannot be created.

It also is possible to define how much RAM a VDC can use for each of its routing tables. Through such a class of resources, a VDC can be protected from an excessive use of memory caused by a misconfiguration or a denial-of-service attack.

Table 5-3 shows how many megabytes can be allocated per context for each type of route.

Table 5-3 *Allocated Memory Range for Each Route Type*

Route Type	Configurable Memory Range (MB)
IPv4 unicast	1 to 350
IPv4 multicast	3 to 90
IPv6 unicast	1 to 100
IPv6 multicast	3 to 20

Example 5-23 illustrates how the memory used by an IPv4 unicast routing table in a VDC can be limited to 1 MB.

Example 5-23 *VDC2 and VDC3 Memory Allocation*

```
! Guaranteeing the memory for IPv4 unicast routes in VDC2
N7K(config)# vdc VDC2
N7K(config-vdc)# limit-resource u4route-mem minimum 1 maximum 350
N7K(config-vdc)# exit
N7K(config)# vdc VDC3
! Limiting the memory for IPv4 unicast routes in VDC3
N7K(config-vdc)# limit-resource u4route-mem minimum 1 maximum 1
N7K(config-vdc)# end
! Verifying the resource distribution among the VDCs
N7K# show vdc resource u4route-mem detail

  u4route-mem     112 used     0 unused   404 free   404 avail   516 total
  -------------
          Vdc          Min         Max        Used     Unused       Avail
          ---          ---         ---        ----     ------       -----
          N7K          96          96         1        95           95
          VDC2         1           1          1        0            0
          VDC3         1           1          1        0            0
```

You can observe that, although the **limit-resource u4route-mem** command has minimum and maximum values, the maximum was ignored. This behavior occurs in all VDC memory resource allocations.

> **Note** The actual change of memory allocation will effectively occur after the VDC is reinitialized.

It is highly recommended that constant monitoring is performed to avoid memory allocation errors because of a lack of resources. A very interesting command can be used to estimate the initial quantity of memory a set of routes would consume in a VDC: **show routing ip unicast memory estimate**.

Sample output from this command is detailed in Example 5-24.

Example 5-24 *Memory Estimation for VDC2*

```
N7K-VDC2# show routing ip unicast memory estimate routes 10000 next-hops 2
Shared memory estimates:
  Current max      8 MB;     5197 routes with 16 nhs
          in-use   1 MB;        8 routes with  1 nhs (average)
  Configured max   1 MB;       28 routes with 16 nhs
  Estimate         4 MB;    10000 routes with  2 nhs
[output suppressed]
```

In this example, NX-OS estimates that 4 MB of memory are necessary to deploy 1000 IPv4 unicast routes (with two next hops) in VDC2. The same estimation can be done for multicast routes with the **show routing ip multicast memory estimate** command.

Using Resource Templates

Instead of changing resource allocation in each VDC, it is possible to configure *resource templates* that can be applied to multiple VDCs. Resource templates can be used to decrease the amount of configuration operations and increase standardization.

There are two default resource templates in the Nexus 7000: *global-default* and *vdc-default*. The former only defines memory resources and is automatically applied to the default VDC (VDC1). The latter is applied to all VDCs including the default.

> **Note** The vdc-default and global-default templates cannot be changed.

Although it was possible, I did not change the resource allocation in the default VDC in the previous section. Example 5-25 presents this resource allocation.

Example 5-25 *Default VDC Resource Allocation*

```
N7K# show vdc N7K resource

    Resource                    Min     Max     Used    Unused   Avail
    --------                    ---     ---     ----    ------   -----
    vlan                        16      4094    30      0        4064
    monitor-session             0       2       0       0        0
    monitor-session-erspan-dst  0       23      0       0        23
    vrf                         2       1000    3       0        997
    port-channel                0       768     0       0        768
    u4route-mem                 96      96      1       95       95
    u6route-mem                 24      24      1       23       23
    m4route-mem                 58      58      1       57       57
    m6route-mem                 8       8       1       7        7
```

Resource template *vdc-default* assigns all resource parameters to newly created VDCs. Creating a VDC called VDC4, you can verify how its default resource allocation differs from VDC1 (see Example 5-26).

Note Interfaces Ethernet 10/1, 10/3, 10/5, and 10/7 were also allocated to VDC4.

Example 5-26 *VDC4 Creation and Verification of Allocated Resources*

```
! Verifying the default resource allocation for VDC4
N7K# show vdc VDC4 resource

    Resource                    Min     Max     Used    Unused   Avail
    --------                    ---     ---     ----    ------   -----
    vlan                        16      4094    3       13       4091
    monitor-session             0       2       0       0        0
    monitor-session-erspan-dst  0       23      0       0        23
    vrf                         2       4096    2       0        4086
    port-channel                0       768     0       0        768
    u4route-mem                 8       8       1       7        7
    u6route-mem                 4       4       1       3        3
    m4route-mem                 8       8       1       7        7
    m6route-mem                 5       5       1       4        4
```

Now, let's create a resource template and apply it to VDC4. The template is called SMALL because it restricts every resource to its lowest possible value (except for VLANs). Example 5-27 depicts its configuration and application to VDC4.

Example 5-27 *SMALL Resource Template Creation and Application to VDC4*

```
! Creating resource template
N7K(config)# vdc resource template SMALL
N7K(config-vdc-template)# limit-resource m4route-mem minimum 3 maximum 3
N7K(config-vdc-template)# limit-resource m6route-mem minimum 3 maximum 3
N7K(config-vdc-template)# limit-resource monitor-session minimum 0 maximum equal-to-min
N7K(config-vdc-template)# limit-resource monitor-session-erspan-dst minimum 0 maximum equal-to-min
N7K(config-vdc-template)# limit-resource port-channel minimum 0 maximum equal-to-min
N7K(config-vdc-template)# limit-resource u4route-mem minimum 1 maximum 1
N7K(config-vdc-template)# limit-resource u6route-mem minimum 1 maximum 1
N7K(config-vdc-template)# limit-resource vlan minimum 1000 maximum equal-to-min
N7K(config-vdc-template)# limit-resource vrf minimum 2 maximum equal-to-min
! Applying resource template SMALL to VDC4
N7K(config-vdc-template)# vdc VDC4
N7K(config-vdc)# template SMALL
! Verifying the change of resource allocation in VDC4
N7K (config-vdc)# show vdc VDC4 resource

      Resource                  Min     Max     Used    Unused   Avail
      --------                  ---     ---     ----    ------   -----
      vlan                      1000    1000    3       997      997
      monitor-session           0       0       0       0        0
      monitor-session-erspan-dst 0      0       0       0        0
      vrf                       2       2       2       0        0
      port-channel              0       0       0       0        0
      u4route-mem               1       1       1       0        0
      u6route-mem               1       1       1       0        0
      m4route-mem               3       3       1       2        2
      m6route-mem               3       3       1       2        2
```

Tip Although VDC resource templates look like ACE resource classes, a change in the former does not automatically update any resource allocation. You must reapply the template to the VDC to make such a change happen.

As a visual checkpoint, Figure 5-11 portrays how our logical topology looks after the inclusion of VDC4.

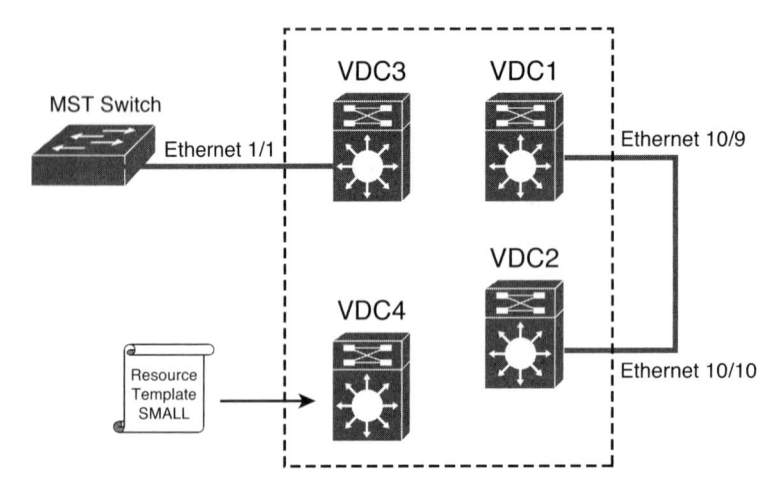

Figure 5-11 *Updated Logical Topology*

Managing VDCs

Because it represents virtualization in the management plane, a VDC can be managed as a physical switch. However, some specific operations have differences when applied to VDCs.

The following sections will discuss some of the particulars a network administrator should be aware of when managing VDCs.

VDC Operations

When a physical switch is reinitialized, it will boot the VDCs (defined in the startup configuration) according to their configured *boot order*. By default, the boot order of any VDC is 1, which means that without any change, all VDCs are booted in their original order of creation.

However, there can be situations when you want to boot a specific VDC only after the others are already operational and stable. Example 5-28 shows how you can postpone VDC2 booting after the others.

Example 5-28 *Boot Order Change in VDC2 and Physical Switch Reload*

```
N7K(config)# vdc VDC2
! Changing the boot order for VDC2
N7K(config-vdc)# boot-order 2
N7K(config-vdc)# end
! Saving the configuration in all VDCs
N7K# copy running-config startup-config vdc-all
[########################################] 100%
```

```
Copy complete, now saving to disk (please wait)...
! Rebooting the physical switch
N7K# reload
This command will reboot the system. (y/n)?  [n] y
2012 May  1 16:49:01 N7K %$ VDC-1 %$ %PLATFORM-2-PFM_SYSTEM_RESET: Manual system
restart from Command Line Interface
[output suppressed]
! Verifying the VDCs boot order
N7K# show logging | include VDC_ONLINE
16:54:56 N7K %VDC_MGR-2-VDC_ONLINE: vdc 1 has come online
16:55:44 N7K %VDC_MGR-2-VDC_ONLINE: vdc 3 has come online
16:56:17 N7K %VDC_MGR-2-VDC_ONLINE: vdc 4 has come online
16:56:45 N7K %VDC_MGR-2-VDC_ONLINE: vdc 2 has come online
```

You can also reload a specific VDC if, for example, you want a memory resource allocation change to be applied. From the default VDC, the **reload vdc** command is used for this operation, as demonstrated in Example 5-29.

Example 5-29 *Reload of VDC2 and Suspension of VDC4*

```
! Reloading a VDC from the default VDC CLI
N7K# reload vdc VDC2
Are you sure you want to reload this vdc (y/n)?  [no] yes
17:24:42 N7K %$ VDC-1 %$ %VDC_MGR-2-VDC_OFFLINE: vdc 2 is now offline
17:24:42 N7K %$ VDC-1 %$ %SYSMGR-STANDBY-2-SHUTDOWN_SYSTEM_LOG: vdc 2 will shut down
soon.
17:25:15 N7K %$ VDC-1 %$ %VDC_MGR-2-VDC_ONLINE: vdc 2 has come online
```

If you are logged in to the VDC CLI, the **reload vdc** command (without the VDC name) is used to reload it.

A physical switch shutdown is emulated with the *suspension* of a VDC. When it is suspended, it is not possible to access or to configure a VDC, as demonstrated in Example 5-30.

Example 5-30 *Suspension of VDC4*

```
! Suspending VDC4
N7K(config)# vdc VDC4 suspend
This command will suspend the VDC. (y/n)?  [no] yes
Note: Suspending vdc VDC4
N7K(config)# 2012 May  1 18:15:43 N7K %$ VDC-1 %$ %VDC_MGR-2-VDC_OFFLINE: vdc 4 is
now offline
! Trying to access a suspended VDC
N7K (config)# switchto vdc VDC4
ERROR: VDC is not ACTIVE cannot SWITCH
```

> **Note** Although I could reactivate VDC4 with the **no vdc VDC4 suspend** command, I will keep VDC4 suspended to present a more colorful set of examples in the next sections.

Processes Failures and VDCs

In the earlier section "VDCs in Detail," I have presented VDCs as an extra layer of software hardening because they can be isolated from process failures on other contexts. Additionally, a VDC has ways to react to internal failures caused by misuse, denial of service attacks, or bugs.

Figure 5-12 shows how a *high-availability (HA) policy* can be applied to a VDC after the System Manager shared process detects a failure in a VDC process.

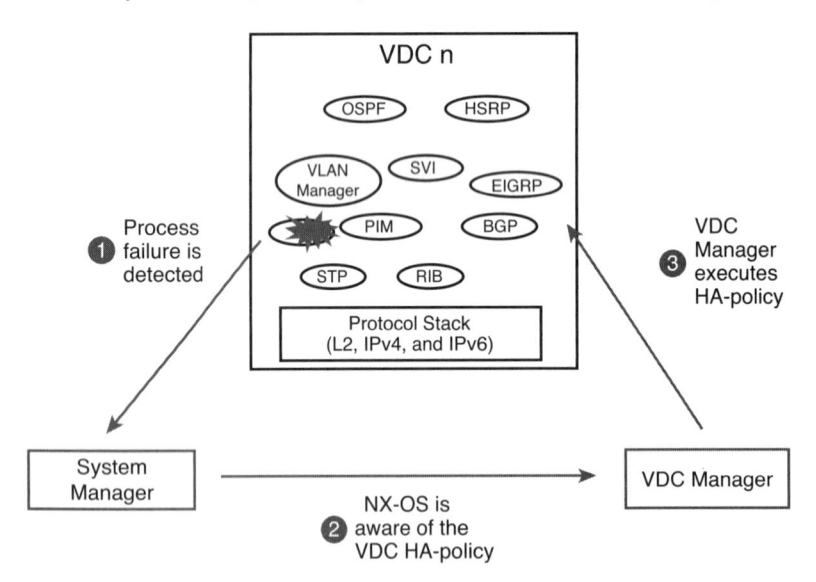

Figure 5-12 *HA Policy in Action*

Each VDC can be configured to behave differently when handling control plane failures. Also, a VDC HA policy includes different behaviors depending on whether the physical switch has supervisor module redundancy.

These are the HA policies that can be applied to each VDC:

- **Bringdown:** The NX-OS puts the VDC in a failed state and waits for a manual reload from the administrator.
- **Restart:** The system shuts down every process in the VDC and automatically restarts the context using its startup configuration.

- **Switchover:** This method is exclusive to dual-supervisor systems. With the detection of a failure, the NX-OS initiates a supervisor switchover (standby supervisor becomes active and vice versa).
- **Reload:** This is an exclusive policy to switches that have a single supervisor. In this case, the entire physical switch is reloaded with the control plane failure identification.

Table 5-4 exposes the default HA policies for VDCs at the time of this writing.

Table 5-4 *Default High-Availability Policies*

VDC Type	Supervisor Redundancy	Default HA Policy
Default VDC	No	Reload
Default VDC	Yes	Switchover
Other VDCs	No	Restart
Other VDCs	Yes	Switchover

Example 5-31 details how VDC3 can have its HA policy changed. Also, this example demonstrates that it is not possible to change the HA policy defined for the default VDC.

Example 5-31 *HA Policy Change Behavior for VDC3 and Default VDC*

```
N7K(config)# vdc VDC3
! Changing both policies to bringdown in VDC3
N7K(config-vdc)# ha-policy dual-sup bringdown single-sup bringdown
N7K(config-vdc)# vdc N7K
! Trying the same configuration in the default VDC
N7K(config-vdc)# ha-policy dual-sup bringdown single-sup bringdown
ERROR: Default vdc is only allowed to have hap reset
```

VDC Out-of-Band Management

Whereas a VDC supports *in-band* management through its routed or SVI interfaces, some organizations require *out-of-band* management, meaning that each data center device has an exclusive interface connected to an isolated management network.

With VDCs, this can be achieved through the creation of a management interface, as detailed in Example 5-32.

Note Intentionally, I have not defined a management interface in VDC4 in this example because it remains suspended.

Example 5-32 *Management Interface Configuration in VDC1, VDC2, and VDC3*

```
! Out-of-band interface configuration in the default VDC
N7K# show running-config interface mgmt0
[output suppressed]
interface mgmt0
  ip address 172.19.19.1/13

N7K# switchto vdc VDC2
[output suppressed]
! Out-of-band interface configuration in VDC2
N7K-VDC2# show running-config interface mgmt0

[output suppressed]
interface mgmt0
  ip address 172.19.19.2/13

N7K-VDC2# switchback
N7K# switchto vdc VDC3
[output suppressed]
! Out-of-band interface configuration in VDC3
N7K-VDC3# show running-config interface mgmt 0
[output suppressed]
interface mgmt0
  ip address 10.3.3.3/24
```

These logical out-of-band interfaces share the physical management Ethernet port in the active supervisor module. As this interface does not support trunking, it should be connected to an access interface on a management switch, as illustrated in Figure 5-13.

Data Center Network Manager (DCNM) for LAN is a graphical user interface tool that can use management interfaces to manage NX-OS devices. DCNM-LAN can be used to facilitate the configuration of physical NX-OS and VDCs in complex data center networks.

In Figures 5-14 and 5-15, you can see how DCNM-LAN manages VDCs using their mgmt0 interface.

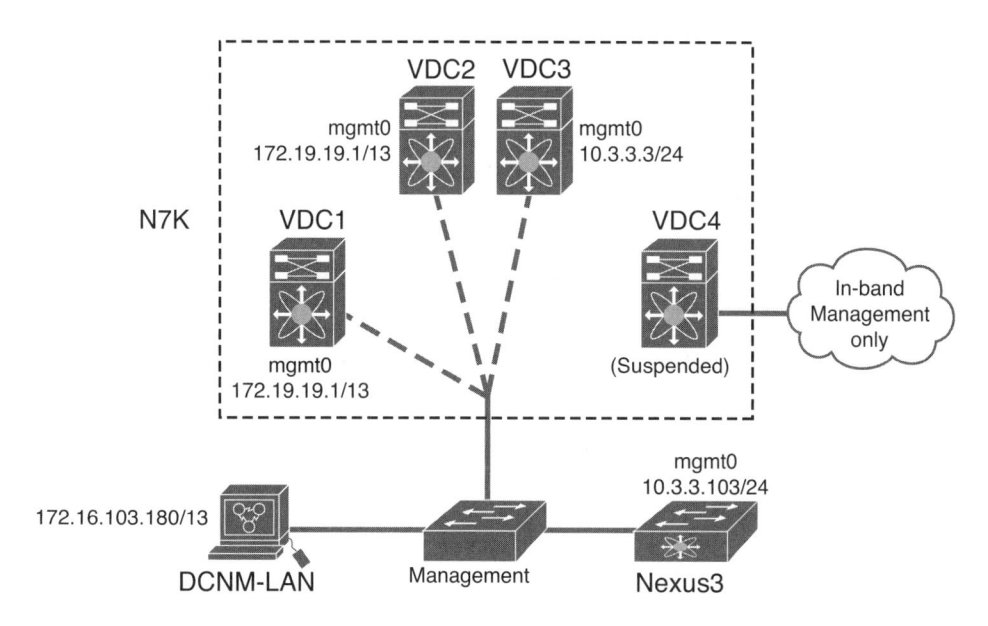

Figure 5-13 *VDC Out-of-Band Management*

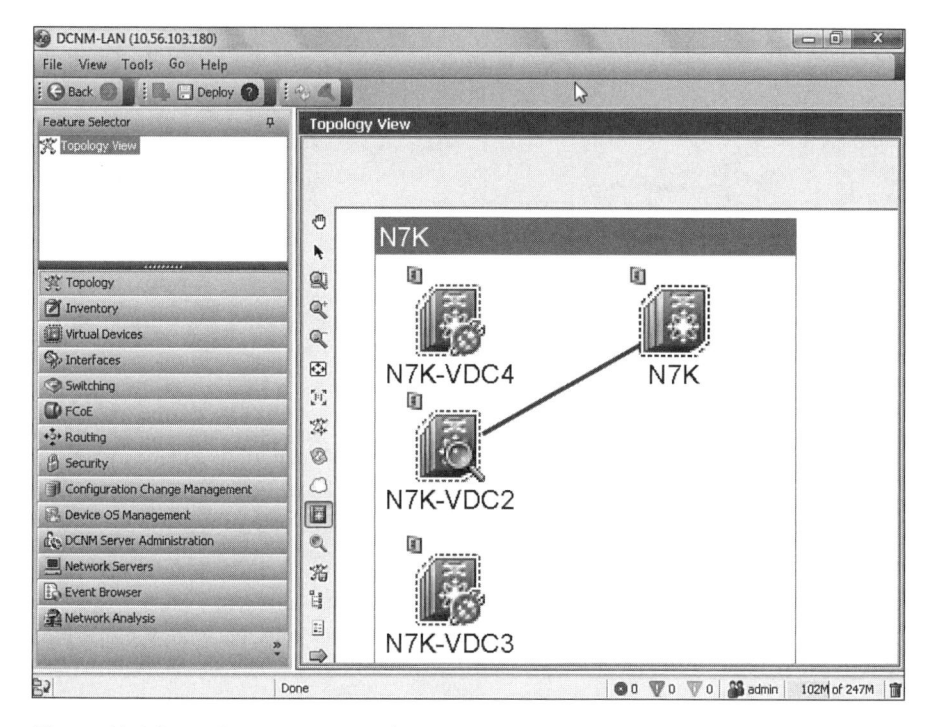

Figure 5-14 *DCNM-LAN Topology View During VDC2 Discovery*

After a discovery process directed to the default VDC management interface (IP address 172.19.19.1/13), DCNM-LAN was able to exhibit all four VDCs in its **Topology** pane. This was possible because the VDCs are configured in the default VDC startup configuration.

As shown in Figure 5-14, DCNM-LAN can only manage VDC1 and VDC2 individually. VDC3 and VDC4 cannot be reached because the former's management interface is in a subnet that is unreachable to DCNM-LAN, and the latter is suspended.

Figure 5-15 shows the DCNM-LAN **Virtual Devices** view, which details the parameters defined for each VDC.

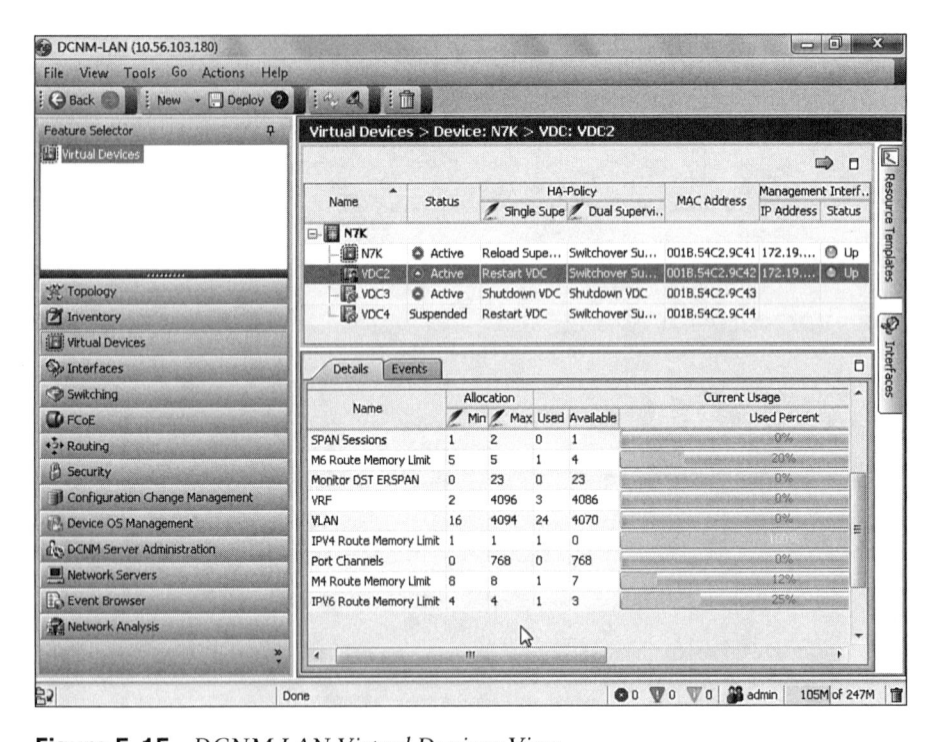

Figure 5-15 *DCNM-LAN Virtual Devices View*

To illustrate how DCNM-LAN can be used in common VDC operations, I have re-created VDC4 exactly as it was defined in the earlier section "Using Resource Templates," but with one additional configuration: its management interface using IP address 172.19.19.4/13.

In the Virtual Devices view, right-clicking VDC4, it is possible to delete VDC4, as shown in Figure 5-16. In this figure, the **Create VDC** wizard is also visible. Through this wizard, I have re-created a new VDC (creatively called NewVDC4), as you can see in Figure 5-17.

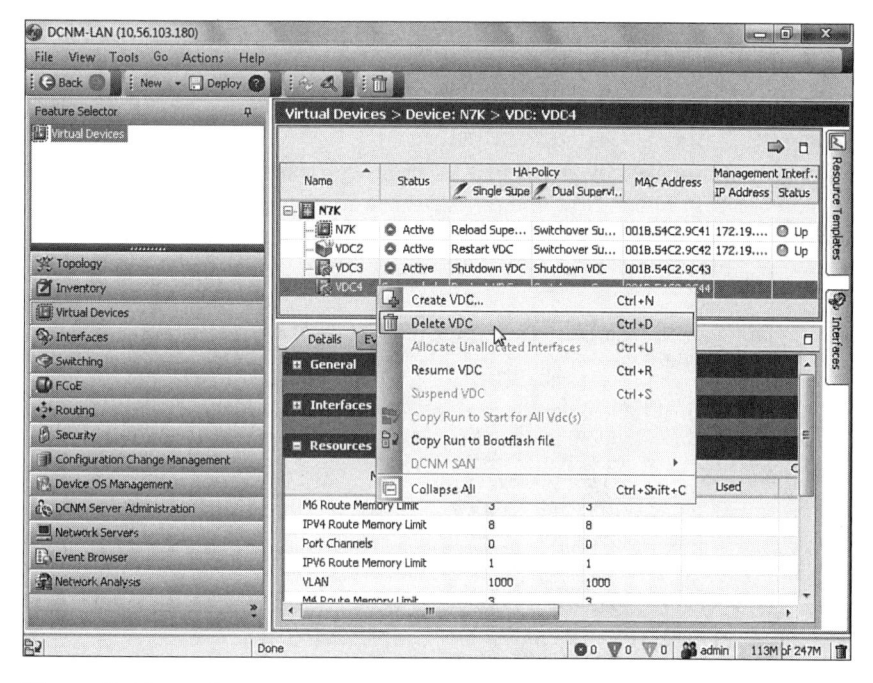

Figure 5-16 *Deleting VDC4 in DCNM-LAN*

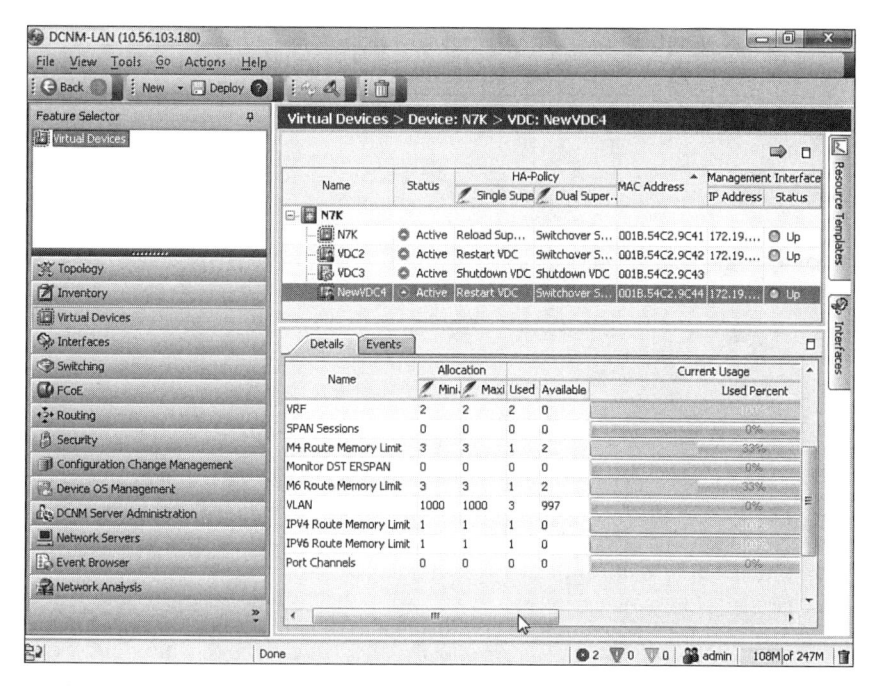

Figure 5-17 *DCNM-LAN Virtual Devices View After NewVDC4 Creation*

> **Note** More details about DCNM-LAN can be found in Appendix A, "Cisco Data Center Portfolio."

VDC3 still remains unmanaged by DCNM-LAN because its management interface belongs to a different IP subnet. However, this VDC can still be managed by different devices that can reach subnet 10.3.3.0/24.

> **Note** A VDC cannot access the mgmt0 of another VDC in the same physical switch.

Figure 5-18 shows our final logical topology after the operations executed in this section.

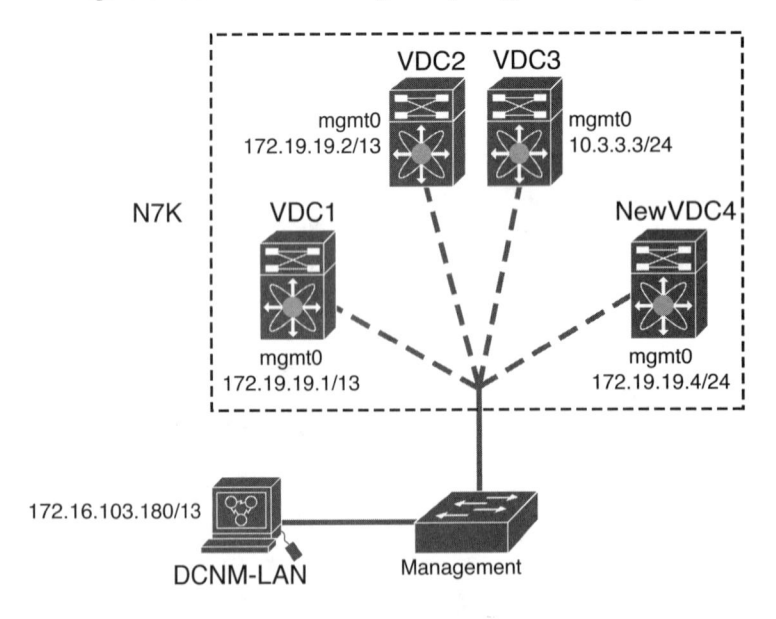

Figure 5-18 *Final Logical VDC Topology*

Role-Based Access Control and VDCs

As a distinct virtual NX-OS switch, each VDC has distinct user accounts, roles, and authentication, authorization, and accounting (AAA) servers. However, in the default VDC, one special role can create, delete, and access VDCs: *network-admin*. Actually, the superuser *admin*, which belongs to the network-admin role, executed all the configurations in this chapter.

Network-operator is another default VDC-exclusive role that can only monitor and view the configurations defined on the default VDC (including the nondefault VDCs).

Within a nondefault VDC, other default roles exist: *vdc-admin* and *vdc-operator*. The former has read and write permissions, while the latter has read-only rights. Both of them can only act over the VDC they belong to.

Example 5-33 shows these role permissions in VDC2.

Example 5-33 *Default Roles and Accounts in VDC2*

```
! Exhibiting the permissions for the vdc-admin role
N7K-VDC2# show role name vdc-admin

Role: vdc-admin
  Description: Predefined vdc admin role has access to all commands within
  a VDC instance
  -------------------------------------------------------------------
  Rule    Perm    Type      Scope             Entity
  -------------------------------------------------------------------
  1       permit  read-write

! Exhibiting the permissions for the vdc-operator role
N7K-VDC2# show role name vdc-operator

Role: vdc-operator
  Description: Predefined vdc operator role has access to all read commands
  within a VDC instance
  -------------------------------------------------------------------
  Rule    Perm    Type      Scope             Entity
  -------------------------------------------------------------------
  1       permit  read
```

Tip The *admin* user account, created during the VDC setup script, belongs to the *vdc-admin* role.

The default VDC also has a vdc-admin and a vdc-operator role, because it is indeed a VDC. However, in practical terms, these roles are equivalent to the network-admin and network-operator roles.

Other roles and accounts can be created inside a VDC exactly as you would do in a physical switch. Similarly, a completely different AAA server can be configured per VDC.

Figure 5-19 illustrates a highly heterogeneous management scenario for our VDC topology where

- VDC1 uses a TACACS+ server reachable through its mgmt0 interfaces.
- VDC2 does not use a AAA server because it has locally defined users.
- VDC3 uses a RADIUS server, also reachable through its mgmt0 interface. However, it uses a completely different network from VDC1 and VDC3 (its management VRF has a distinct default gateway).
- NewVDC4 uses a TACACS+ server reachable through interfaces other than its mgmt0.

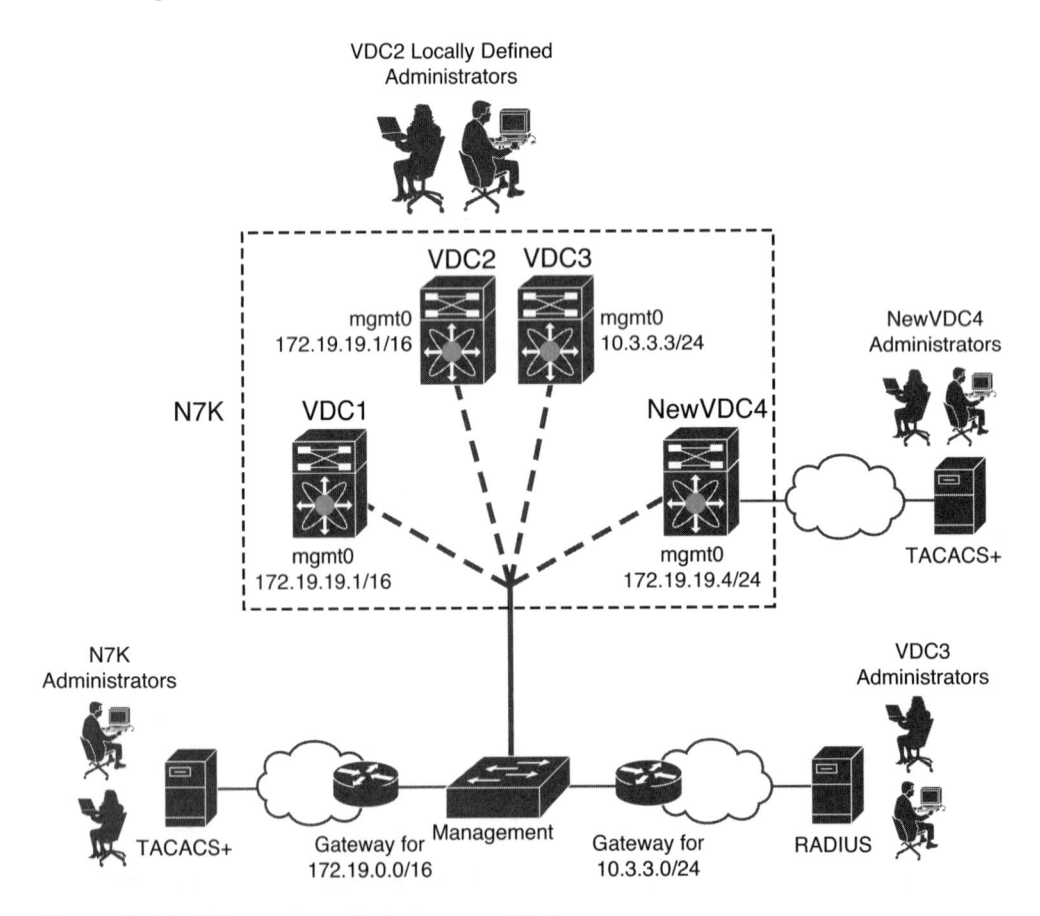

Figure 5-19 *Management Variations per VDC*

In each VDC, you can also configure roles and VLAN and VRF scopes to restrict the operations of an administrator, as demonstrated in Chapter 3 (in the sections "VLAN Specifics" and "VRFs and the Management Plane").

Global Resources

Because VDCs share hardware and some processes in NX-OS (as I have explained in the earlier section "VDCs in Detail"), it is only natural that some configurations are also shared among VDCs.

In that manner, when the following *global resources* are configured, they are executed in all VDCs defined in the same physical switch:

- **Boot configuration:** After all, the VDCs share the same NX-OS.

- **Etheranalyzer session:** This capability allows the visualization (through a tool such as Wireshark) of the traffic directed to the switch control plane.

- **Control Plane Policing:** This feature restricts the amount of traffic directed to the switch control plane.

- **PortChannel load-balancing method:** This configuration is the link aggregation frame distribution algorithm. (I will discuss this topic in detail in Chapter 6, "Fooling Spanning Tree.")

- **Quality of service (QoS) mappings:** These mappings include CoS-to-queue, CoS-markdown, DSCP-to-queue, DSCP-markdown, and DSCP-mutation.

- **Event Embedded Manager (EEM):** This is an automation switch capability that allows a script execution after an event is detected.

These resources are configured in the default VDC or in the admin VDC.

Use Case: Data Center Security Zones

One very usual motivation for separate switch deployment is the existence of demilitarized zones (DMZ). Such a perimeter area is usually a part of the network that contains and exposes applications to external networks and, because of such access, must be protected by special security devices such as firewalls and intrusion prevention systems (IPS).

In Chapter 3, you learned that VLANs can be used to create DMZs. However, some corporate security policies do not allow such implementation, in spite of the consistent VLAN security improvements that were developed over the last decades (private VLANs, port security, and dynamic ARP inspection, for example).

Figure 5-20 illustrates how such companies must deploy separate switches for three security zones in a data center:

- **External:** This zone is connected to an unsecure network such as the Internet.

- **Internal:** This security area comprises servers that are accessed through the DMZ or by other internal servers.

- **DMZ:** This zone contains servers that are accessible externally and require perimeter protection from a firewall.

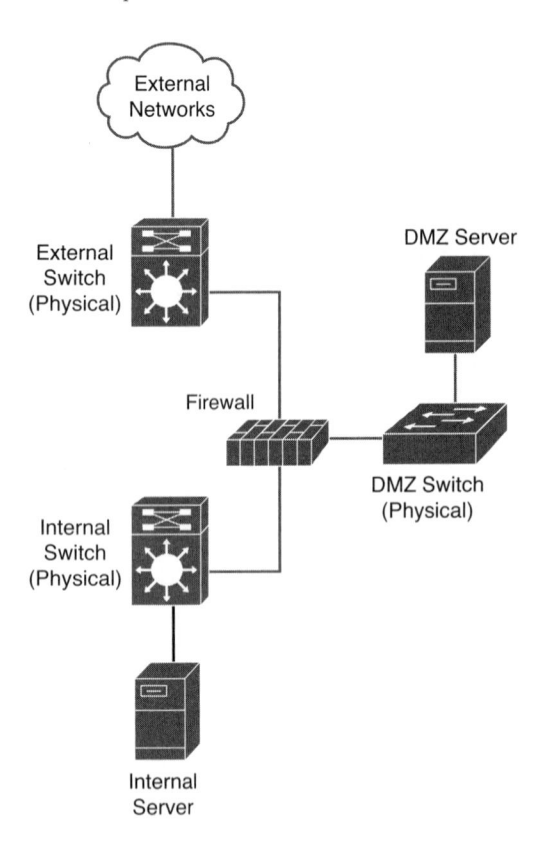

Figure 5-20 *Physical Switches and Security Zones*

As you can see, a firewall separates the security zones to control IP traffic between them, according to predefined rules.

VDCs present an interesting alternative to this scenario. For example, a virtualization-versed network designer can replace the physical switches for VDCs if the security policies require that

- A distinct team can manage each zone switch
- Each switch must not be affected by failures on another switch

This switch consolidation is shown in Figure 5-21. As an advantage, it improves port utilization and provisioning speed in this data center network.

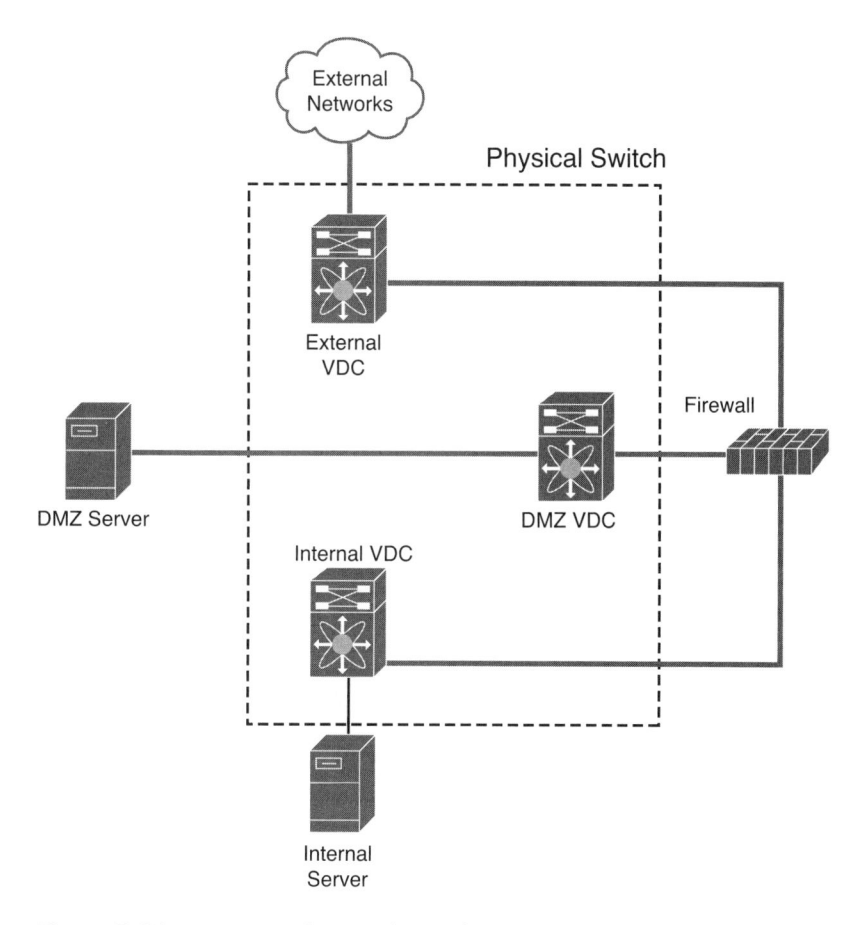

Figure 5-21 *VDCs Replacing Physical Switches*

Nevertheless, it is up to each organization to perform a detailed analysis on VDCs to decide whether this virtualization technology is suitable for its security policies. As a support for this decision, VDCs have achieved several security certifications, such as

- NSS Labs for Payment Card Industry (PCI) Compliant Environments
- U.S. Federal Information Processing Standards (FIPS) Publication 140-2
- Common Criteria Evaluation and Validation Scheme (Certification no. 10349)

Summary

When compared to VLANs and VRFs, virtual device contexts can be considered a more complete network partitioning technique. The main reason for this affirmation is that VDCs deploy virtualization on data, control, and management network planes.

In this chapter, you learned the following:

- With very few exceptions, a physical interface belongs to a single VDC.
- VDCs can provide switch consolidation, secure segmentation, and fault isolation to data center networks.
- NX-OS provides separate Layer 2 and Layer 3 processes for each VDC.
- Through the default VDC or an exclusive admin VDC, an administrator can create and manage other VDCs.
- Each VDC can have minimum and maximum values defined for resources such as SPAN monitor sessions, VLANs, VRFs, PortChannels, and memory reserved for IP routes.
- CPU shares define the percentage of supervisor CPU processing a VDC receives.
- It is possible to use resource templates to reduce and standardize configuration operations.
- VDCs can be managed as physical switches with some specific operations such as boot order and exclusive out-of-band interface.
- There are some resources that are globally configured for all VDCs. Boot and Control Plane Policing are examples of these global resources.
- VDCs can be used in data center security zones to replace separate Ethernet switches.

Figure 5-22 graphically summarizes how VDCs relate to physical Ethernet switches.

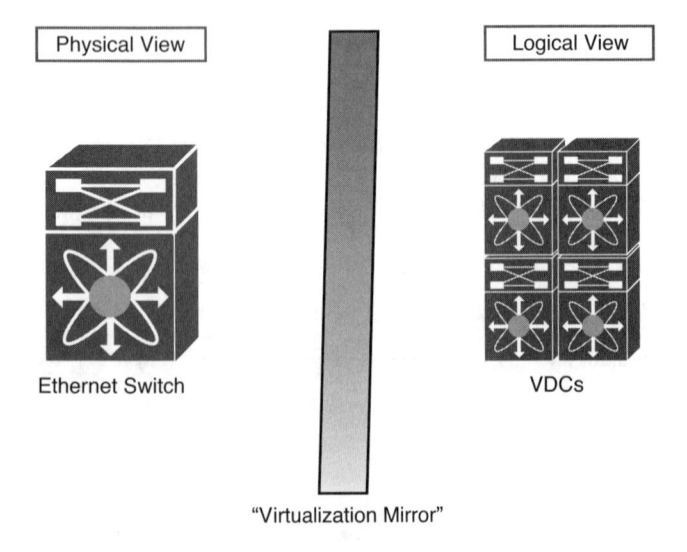

Figure 5-22 *Through the Virtualization Mirror*

Further Reading

Corbin, Kevin. Fuller, Ron. Jansen, David. *NX-OS and Cisco Nexus Switching.* Cisco Press, 2010.

Network Switch Virtualization: Cisco Nexus 7000 Q2 2010

http://www.nsslabs.com/research/network-security/virtualization/cisco-nexus-7000-q2-2010.html

FIPS 140-2 Non-Proprietary Security Policy (Nexus 7010)

csrc.nist.gov/groups/STM/cmvp/documents/140-1/140sp/140sp1533.pdf

FIPS 140-2 Non-Proprietary Security Policy (Nexus 7018)

csrc.nist.gov/groups/STM/cmvp/documents/140-1/140sp/140sp1534.pdf

Validation Report: Cisco Nexus 7000 Switch

http://www.niap-ccevs.org/st/st_vid10349-vr.pdf

Chapter 6

Fooling Spanning Tree

"Everything that deceives may be said to enchant." (Plato)

This chapter will examine virtual PortChannels (vPC) in detail and explore how they can optimize data center networks. It will cover the following topics:

- Spanning Tree Protocols and Link Utilization
- Link Aggregation
- Cross-Switch PortChannels
- Virtual PortChannels
- Layer 2 Multipathing and vPC+
- Use Case: Evolution of Network PODs

Table 6-1 positions virtual PortChannels in the virtualization taxonomy described in Chapter 1, "Virtualization History and Definitions."

Table 6-1 *Virtual PortChannel Virtualization Classification*

Virtualization Characteristics	vPC and vPC+
Emulation	Single Ethernet switch
Type	Pooling
Subtype	Homogeneous
Scalability	Two physical switches
Technology area	Networking
Subarea	Data and control plane virtualization
Advantages	Higher throughput, faster fault recovery, less complexity

Even with a ubiquitous presence in Ethernet networks, Spanning Tree Protocol (STP) does not enjoy an enviable reputation among most data center network designers.

One of the most usual criticisms against this protocol is the fact that it does not allow the use of *multiple active paths* between two defined points in an Ethernet network. By design, STP forces redundant paths to remain dormant, substantially reducing interface and cabling utilization in Layer 2 networks.

Link aggregation technologies, such as Cisco EtherChannel and IEEE 802.3ad, were developed to address that limitation when two Ethernet switches are connected through multiple links. However, they were not as effective in traditional data center networks that deploy multiswitch looped topologies.

This quandary can be mitigated with *virtual PortChannels (vPCs)*: a virtualization technique that allows the deployment of link aggregation on triangle topologies. For this reason alone, vPCs are one of the most valued features on Nexus switches.

This chapter explores vPC concepts, inner workings, configuration, and interaction with other technologies. It also explains how *FabricPath*, the Cisco first Layer 2 multipath protocol, can implement virtual PortChannels in a slightly different manner.

Spanning Tree Protocol and Link Utilization

In a hypothetical protocol popularity contest, I would not be surprised if Spanning Tree Protocol achieved the last place with data center network professionals. Having performed its dues during the last three decades, STP has attained such negative perception for some reasons:

- Lack of convergence speed
- Shared fault domains between data centers
- Waste of interswitch connections

In Chapter 3, "The Humble Beginnings of Network Virtualization," I have explained how Rapid Spanning Tree Protocol (RSTP) has addressed the first point, providing a much faster convergence after a network failure.

In Chapter 8, "A Tale of Two Data Centers," I will discuss some virtualization techniques that lessen the effects of shared fault domains when distinct data centers must connect their Layer 2 networks.

However, one of the most persistent challenges STP presents is the waste of interswitch connection resources. More specifically, in a traditional Ethernet network, it is expected that STP (or any of its later versions) will block *every redundant path* between two Ethernet switches. This behavior is especially expensive in mission-critical data center networks, where every single system and connection must be designed to be fault tolerant.

Allow me to illustrate this STP characteristic with two practical examples. First, if you remember Chapter 3 (in the section "Spanning Tree and VLANs"), I have presented the decision sequence that defines how a switch deploying STP chooses a superior bridge protocol data unit (BPDU). The "BPDU death match" sequence is defined (in order) by

1. Lowest root bridge ID
2. Lowest-path cost to root bridge
3. Lowest sender bridge ID
4. Lowest port ID

Figure 6-1 depicts a double connection between two imaginatively named STP devices: *Switch1* and *Switch2*. Switch1 is the root in this network, and to avoid loops, Switch2 must decide which interface will remain active as its root port (e1/9 or e1/10).

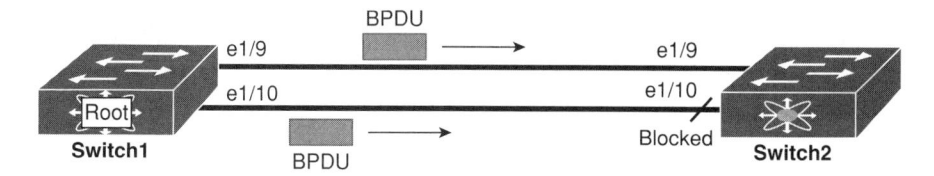

Figure 6-1 *STP in Multiple Connections Between Two Switches*

Following the decision sequence, the interface on Switch1 with the lowest port ID has the superior BPDU and, therefore, has the right to remain active. The result would be the same if more connections were available; after all, Switch2 can only elect one root port.

Example 6-1 further details this scenario using two Nexus switches. In this example, interface Ethernet 1/9 on Switch2 receives the superior BPDU from Switch1.

Example 6-1 *STP in Multiple Connections Between Two Switches*

```
Switch2# show spanning-tree vlan 1
[output suppressed]
! Only one interface is forwarding traffic between both switches
Interface        Role Sts Cost      Prio.Nbr Type
---------------- ---- --- --------- -------- ------------------------
Eth1/9           Root FWD 2         128.137  P2p
Eth1/10          Altn BLK 2         128.138  P2p
```

I also have discussed, in the same chapter and section, how different versions of STP act over triangular switch topologies. Figure 6-2 summarizes that discussion.

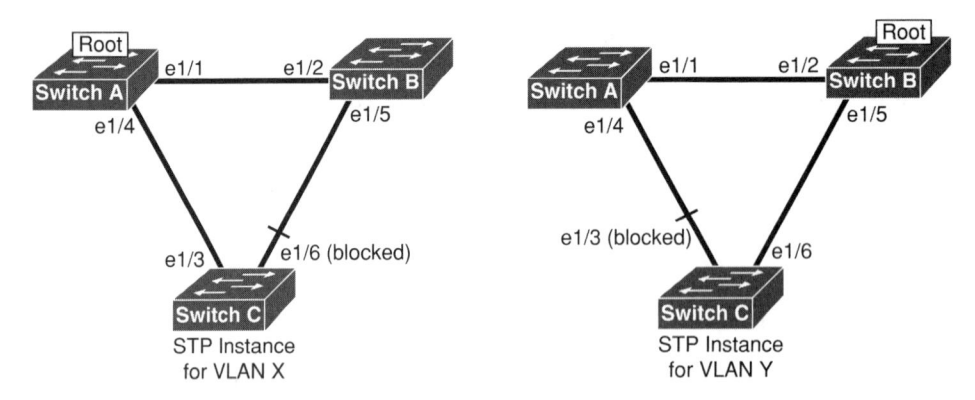

Figure 6-2 *STP in Triangular Topologies*

Yes, it is possible to distribute VLANs between multiple STP instances available through Multiple Spanning Tree (MST) or Rapid Per VLAN Spanning Tree Plus (Rapid PVST+). However, this arrangement must be done manually and can be quite cumbersome in some traffic patterns. For these protocols, loop avoidance and multipathing are still incompatible concepts within a single VLAN.

The interswitch connections exhibited in Figures 6-1 and 6-2 can be considered canonical models for most data center networks topologies. In Figure 6-3, you can find an example for a Layer 2 network that could be deployed in a typical data center. Considering that this network has two aggregation switches and four access switches, it is interesting to observe how STP influences the network utilization.

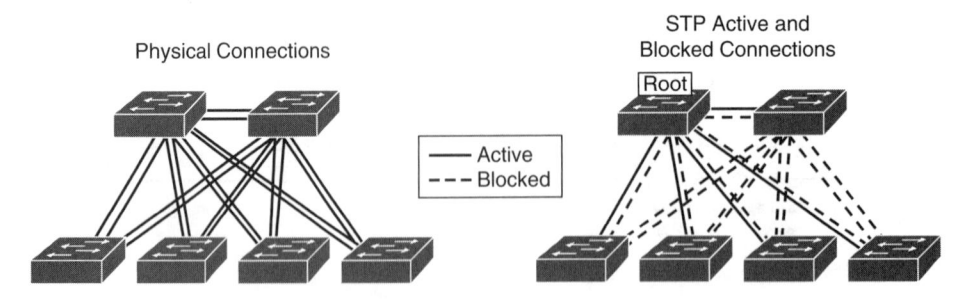

Figure 6-3 *Spanning Tree Protocol and Switch Connection Redundancy*

Statistically speaking, STP disables 13 of the 18 interswitch links available in Figure 6-3. Therefore almost *73 percent of the connection investment*, including cabling, interfaces, and optical adapters, is not being used.

Link Aggregation

Leveraging existent processes and protocols to obtain a technical advantage, virtualization was deployed to "fool" STP during the 1990s. In that period, Cisco developed

EtherChannels to provide link aggregation between two Ethernet devices, as if they were connected with a single (virtual) link. To fulfill the illusion of a single interface between two switches, each interface in an EtherChannel group must

- Have the same physical properties and configuration (such as speed, duplex, flow control, Layer 2 mode, native VLAN, and so on)
- Not flood unknown unicast or forward broadcast frames back to the channel

In 2000, IEEE 802.3ad was published as the link aggregation standard, allowing interoperability of devices from different manufacturers. Nowadays, almost every Ethernet switch supports the standard, including Cisco Nexus data center switches.

Using these technologies, STP only detects one logical interface, while the traffic destined to this interface is load balanced among the active physical links that are part of the channel.

Figure 6-4 illustrates the perspective of STP over a link aggregation.

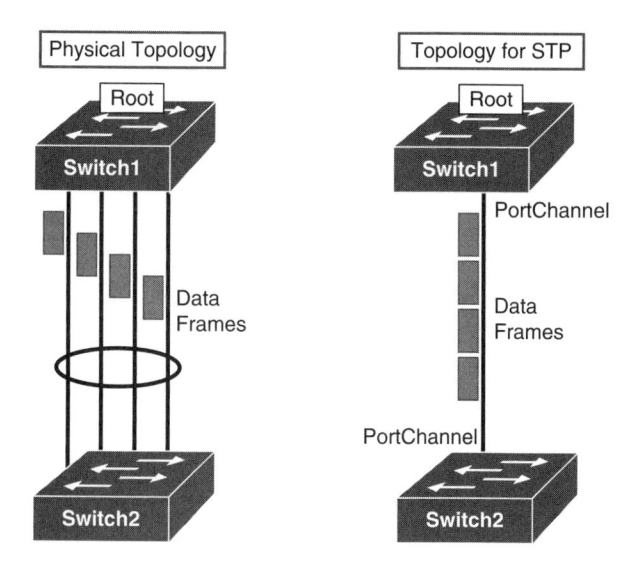

Figure 6-4 *Link Aggregation*

The virtual interface that results from this aggregation is denominated a *PortChannel*. Each PortChannel has a unique identifier to represent it in a switch, and that can be manually or dynamically assigned to it.

Example 6-2 shows the configuration of a PortChannel in the Switch2 from Figure 6-4, considering that the same configuration was done in Switch1. The example also exposes how Spanning Tree reacts to the configuration.

236 Data Center Virtualization Fundamentals

Example 6-2 *PortChannel Configuration and Spanning Tree*

```
! Configuring both interfaces as trunks for all VLANs
Switch2(config)# interface ethernet 1/9-10
Switch2(config-if-range)# switchport
Switch2(config-if-range)# switchport mode trunk
! Creating PortChannel 1 and assigning both interfaces to it using the same command
Switch2(config-if-range)# channel-group 1 mode on
Switch2(config-if-range)# no shutdown
Switch2(config-if-range)# show spanning-tree vlan 1
[output suppressed]
! Spanning Tree is using PortChannel 1 as the only interface to forward traffic to
Switch1
Interface        Role Sts Cost      Prio.Nbr Type
---------------- ---- --- --------- -------- ------------------------
Po1              Root FWD 1         128.4096 P2p
```

Tip If you want to group interfaces whose parameters are not homogeneous (native VLANs, for example), you can use the **channel-group** *<id>* **force** command to overwrite their configuration with the one of a previously created PortChannel interface.

You can observe that Ethernet 1/9 and 1/10 do not exist anymore for STP; only PortChannel 1 does. Also, the PortChannel STP cost is automatically updated to express the available aggregated bandwidth (1 for 20 Gbps).

And so the "Spanning Tree deception initiative" began. . . .

Note It is also possible to create *Layer 3 PortChannels*, which will work as routed interfaces, as portrayed in Example 6-3. In this configuration, the traffic that is routed to the PortChannel is load balanced between interfaces Ethernet 3/21 and 3/22.

Example 6-3 *Layer 3 PortChannel Configuration*

```
! Configuring both interfaces as routed
Switch2(config)# interface ethernet 3/21-22
Switch2(config-if-range)# no switchport
! Creating PortChannel 2 and assigning both interfaces to it using the same command
Switch2(config-if-range)# channel-group 2 mode on
Switch2(config-if-range)# no shutdown
! Assigning an IP address to the layer 3 PortChannel
```

```
Switch2(config-if-range)# interface port-channel 2
Switch2(config-if)# ip address 172.16.35.200/24
```

At the time of this writing, some Nexus switches support up to 16 Ethernet interfaces in a single PortChannel. However, I definitely recommend that you refer to the Cisco online documentation to verify the link aggregation scalability on your hardware and software combination.

Examples 6-2 and 6-3 depict a *static* PortChannel. With this configuration, Ethernet interfaces will only work in a PortChannel, or they will not function at all. They also require that the connected interfaces on the peer switch are configured in the same way.

Nevertheless, it is possible to dynamically provision the aggregation of interfaces between a pair of switches. As part of the IEEE 802.3ad standard, the Link Aggregation Control Protocol (LACP) was created to conduct this negotiation in an interoperable manner.

An interface that implements this protocol sends LACP data unit (LACPDU) frames to verify whether the other side also deploys LACP and how it is configured to aggregate links. Using this LACP, both switches will negotiate and activate a PortChannel (with the correctly configured interfaces).

Tip The **feature lacp** command is necessary to enable the LACP process in NX-OS switches.

There are two LACP modes for an Ethernet interface: *active* or *passive*. In active mode, an interface will automatically preempt the creation of a PortChannel if the connected switch interface simply supports LACP. Adversely, interfaces in passive mode will only aggregate if the other side of the connection is in active mode.

Table 6-2 clarifies the results for different combinations of interface LACP modes in each connected switch.

Table 6-2 *LACP Configuration and Results*

LACP Interface Configuration	LACP Interface Configuration	Result
Active	Active	Link aggregation
Active	Passive	Link aggregation
Passive	Active	Link aggregation
Passive	Passive	Individual links

> **Note** A statically configured interface (ON mode) does not participate in the LACP negotiation. Hence, it will not form a PortChannel with another interface in active or passive mode.

You can also configure how a PortChannel distributes its traffic to member interfaces. When a frame is forwarded to a PortChannel, a hash function is performed on the frame parameters to define which physical interface will actually forward it. The load-balancing algorithms supported on most Nexus switches use the following parameters:

- Destination IP address
- Destination MAC address
- Destination TCP or UDP port
- Source and destination IP addresses (default for Layer 3 PortChannels)
- Source and destination MAC addresses (default for Layer 2 PortChannels)
- Source and destination TCP or UDP ports
- Source IP address
- Source MAC address
- Source TCP or UDP port

> **Note** The PortChannel load-balancing algorithm is configured for the entire switch. It is also a global parameter that is shared by all VDCs. However, Nexus 7000 switches allow you to configure a load-balancing method per module.

Your knowledge of the traffic characteristics defines which one of these methods is the best one for your network. For example, I would not use the source IP address method to load-balance traffic originated from a firewall that is deploying source Network Address Translation (NAT) into a single IP address.

I also recommend that you regularly monitor the traffic on PortChannels to detect *polarized links* (member interfaces that have more traffic than others). A simple change of load-balance method can avoid unnecessary buffering and packet drops in this situation.

Server Connectivity and NIC Teaming

From a connectivity perspective, there is one fundamental difference between servers and desktops: redundancy. Because it is expected that multiple clients access a server, the impact of a connection failure is much smaller on a user workstation. That reason alone justifies extra Ethernet interfaces per server, or even in some critical scenarios, extra network interface cards (NIC).

NIC teaming is an umbrella term that defines how a group of Ethernet interfaces provide fault tolerance and traffic load balancing in a single server.

Figure 6-5 depicts three types of NIC teaming that a server can deploy.

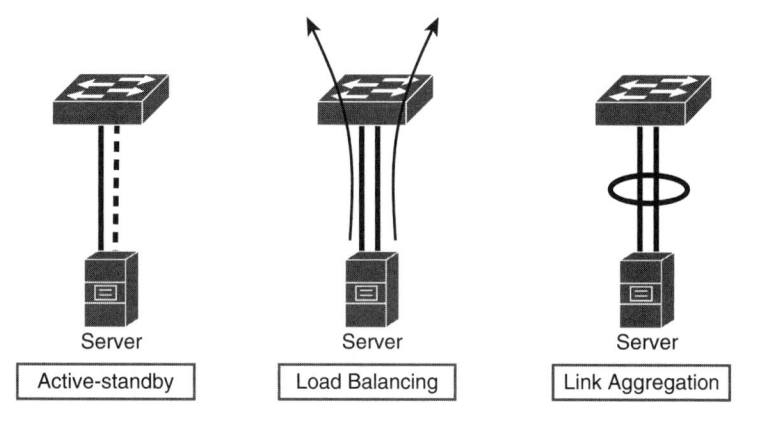

Figure 6-5 *Server Connectivity*

Generally speaking, *active-standby teaming* allows that failures in an active link do not interrupt the server traffic because the standby link can almost immediately replace it. To work seamlessly, the standby interface must assume the former active interface addresses (MAC and IP) and send a broadcast frame to update the switch's MAC address table. This method, however, does not allow an optimal utilization of bandwidth resources.

Load-balancing teaming methods wildly vary among different manufacturers. But it is expected that these methods can, somehow, distribute the traffic among the available active links. Whereas the client MAC, IP, or port address hashing can be used to spread the frames that are leaving the server, it is usually trickier to do provide load balancing for the incoming traffic. That is why these methods are usually applicable to specific scenarios where the outgoing traffic is considerably heavier than the incoming traffic (a file server or a Network Attached Storage, for example).

Caution Some NIC load-balancing methods can cause excessive flooding, link saturation, and frame drop on a network. I highly recommend that you consult the manufacturer's documentation before deploying such load-balancing techniques in your production network.

Even though servers are not expected to implement Spanning Tree protocols, they can leverage PortChannels' aggregated bandwidth, load balancing, and fault tolerance. The requirement for *link aggregation teaming* is that the server operating system, or NIC driver, supports IEEE 802.3ad (and LACP, if you want to deploy a less disruptive aggregation process).

At the time of this writing, several versions of Microsoft Windows and the Linux operating system are already able to aggregate Ethernet interfaces using the standard protocol. If the NIC is providing interface aggregation, only the interfaces on the same NIC will probably be able to connect to a PortChannel.

> **Note** The topologies shown in Figure 6-5 only protect the server against link failures and not switch failures. The next sections will present virtualization techniques that can overcome this limitation.

Cross-Switch PortChannels

To increase fault tolerance on server and switch Ethernet connections, Cisco (and other manufacturers) developed *cross-switch PortChannel* technologies. The idea behind such a concept is allowing link aggregation from a generic device to distinct physical switches.

In the early 2000s, Cisco introduced virtualization techniques that transformed multiple Catalyst switches in a single bridging entity. Consequently, a device could aggregate interfaces connected to this *virtual element* as if they were connecting to a single switch.

Figure 6-6 portrays two variations of this technique in Catalyst switches.

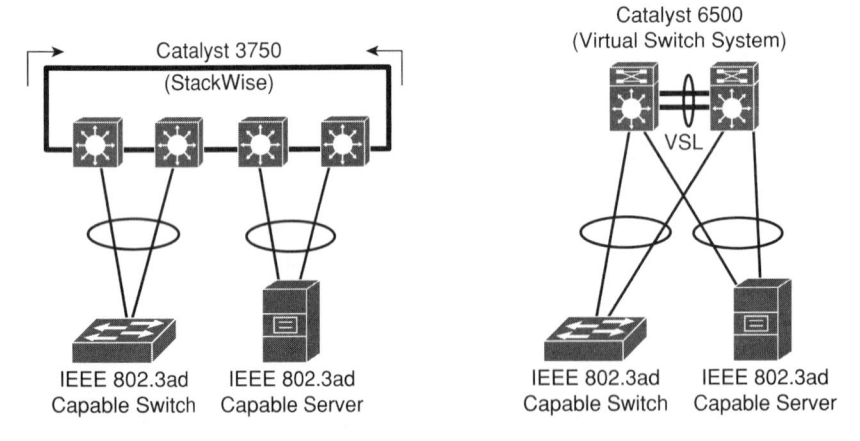

Figure 6-6 *Catalyst 3750 StackWise and Catalyst 6500 Virtual Switch System*

Cisco launched the Catalyst 3750 switches as an evolution over previous stackable switches. Through the *StackWise* and *StackWise Plus* technologies, Catalyst 3750 switches can share up to 64 Gbps on a stack connection. A set of nine Catalyst 3750 switches can act as modules of a virtual chassis, with the StackWise connection functioning as its backplane. Within this virtual switch, one Catalyst 3750 is elected (or configured) as *master* and, therefore, is responsible for configuring and monitoring the remaining switches in the stack. As a result, devices connected to different switches, but on the same virtual chassis, are able to aggregate links.

Some years later, Cisco created the *Virtual Switch System (VSS)* technology, which allowed two Catalyst 6500 switches to behave as a single virtualized chassis. Similar to the StackWise technology, a VSS can provide cross-switch PortChannels to servers and switches.

Acting as a backplane extension for the VSS, the *virtual switch link (VSL)* is actually a PortChannel that transports control information and data traffic between the VSS members. For this reason, Cisco recommends that 10 Gigabit Ethernet interfaces are used in the VSL.

Each Catalyst 6500 switch can have single- or dual-supervisor configurations in a VSS (both of them must have the same number of supervisors). If each switch has two supervisor modules, the overall system is called *Quad-Supervisor VSS* and supports In Service System Upgrade (ISSU).

A VSS can also support service modules such as Application Control Engine (ACE), Adaptive Security Appliance Service Module (ASA-SM), and Network Analysis Module (NAM).

Note There are special requirements for the hardware and software combination that can be used in a VSS. Refer to the Cisco Catalyst 6500 product documentation for more details.

Both StackWise and VSS technologies offer switch virtualization, where all the physical elements share control and management planes. Therefore, all the switches that are part of the *virtual switch* share the same processes.

Virtual PortChannels

Nexus switches can offer Layer 2 multiswitch link aggregation through a feature called *virtual PortChannel (vPC)*.

Differently from two Catalyst 6500 switches operating as a VSS, each Nexus switch maintains its management and control planes separation in a vPC. And as you learn in the following sections, when two switches are configured to deploy vPCs, the communication between their control planes significantly affects how they forward Ethernet frames.

Figure 6-7 illustrates how an IEEE 802.3ad switch and server can aggregate ports that belong to a vPC provided by two Nexus switches.

[Physical Topology] [Logical Topology]

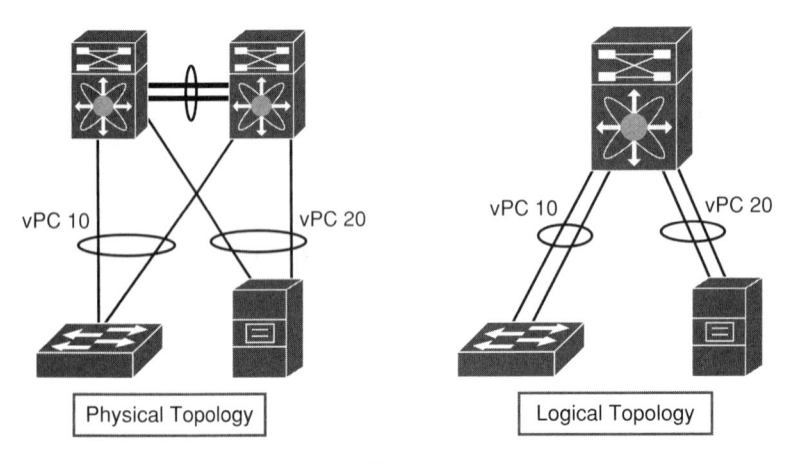

Figure 6-7 *Virtual PortChannel*

Note At the time of this writing, Nexus 7000, 6000, 5000, and 3000 are the NX-OS platforms that support vPC, as described in these sections. Nexus 1000V deploys *vPC Host Mode*, which is a distinct feature, as you will learn in Chapter 15, "Transcending the Rack."

Virtual PortChannel Definitions

Figure 6-8 details the main configuration elements in a virtual PortChannel.

Figure 6-8 *Virtual PortChannel Elements*

The descriptions of these elements are as follows:

- **vPC:** The PortChannel between a device that deploys IEEE 802.3ad link aggregation and two identical NX-OS switches.

- **vPC peer:** A switch (or VDC) of a pair that is configured to implement vPCs. Both peers must belong to the same Nexus switch series.

- **vPC member port:** An interface that belongs to a defined vPC in one of the vPC peers.

- **vPC domain:** A unique identifier (per Layer 2 network) that defines the pair of switches that provides the vPC feature to another devices. Each switch (or VDC) only supports one vPC domain.

- **vPC peer link:** Used to synchronize states and forward traffic between two vPC peers. It is recommended that you use a PortChannel with at least two 10 Gigabit Ethernet connections between the vPC peers.

- **vPC peer keepalive link:** Transports heartbeats between the vPC peers. It is used to explicitly differentiate a vPC peer link failure from a vPC peer failure.

- **Cisco Fabric Services (CFS):** Originated in the MDS 9000 storage switches and directors, this capability is used to synchronize state and configuration between vPC peers. It is automatically enabled in a vPC configuration.

A domain identifies the pair of switches that are deploying a vPC. When you configure a vPC domain on two peers, they both generate a shared MAC address that can be used as a logical switch bridge ID in STP communications. Cisco recommends that you configure unique vPC domains in a Layer 2 network to avoid MAC address conflicts.

> **Tip** Alternatively, you can configure static MACs for the vPC domain. But this is not a mandatory procedure.

Within a vPC domain, each peer is assigned to a role: *primary* or *secondary*. By default, the switch with the lowest MAC address becomes the primary peer, but you can change that behavior using the **role priority** command (where the lowest priority wins).

The vPC-related control plane communication occurs over the vPC peer link. Additionally, Ethernet frames transported over the vPC peer link receive special treatment to avoid loops in the vPC member ports.

Figure 6-9 describes the loop avoidance mechanism that vPC peers apply over an Ethernet broadcast frame.

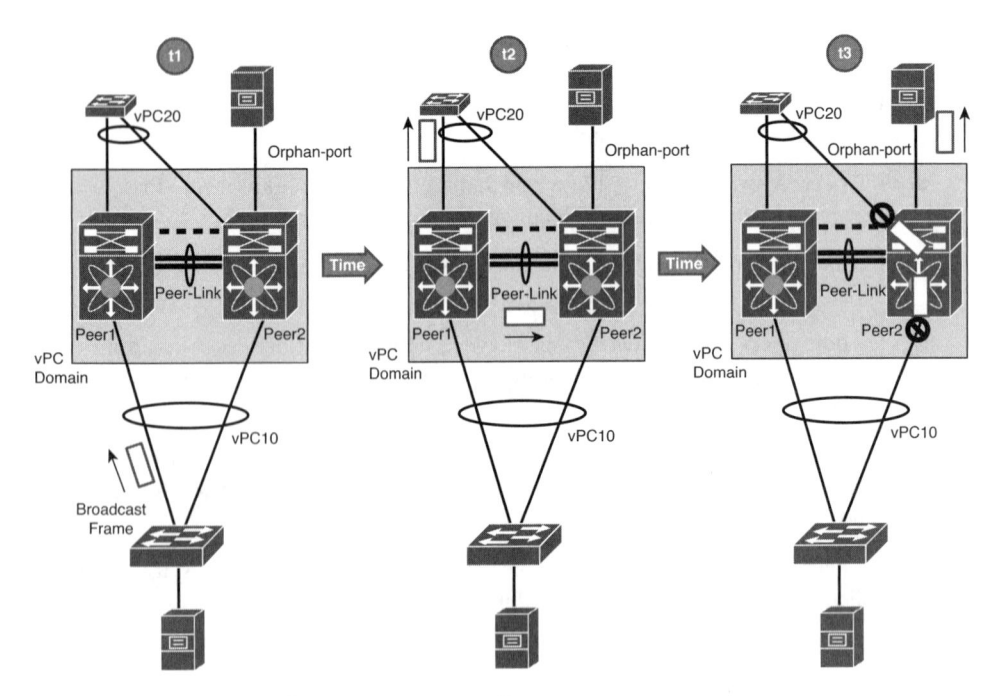

Figure 6-9 *vPC Broadcast Frame Forwarding*

1. At t1, Peer1 receives the broadcast frame and, as expected, forwards it to every interface except the one that received it.

2. At t2, the replicated broadcast frame is sent to these interfaces including the vPC peer link.

3. Peer2 marks this frame at the ingress at t3, and does not forward this frame to vPC member ports.

Under normal conditions, the peer switches never learn MAC addresses from the peer link. The vPC check rule ("*never forward a frame received through the peer link to a vPC member port*") emulates the behavior of a single switch receiving a frame on a standard PortChannel. However, this rule does not block unknown unicast, multicast, and broadcast frames from the peer link to

- Non-vPC interfaces (for example, the orphan port depicted in Figure 6-9)
- vPC member ports that are only active in the receiving peer

Every time a vPC peer switch learns a MAC address from a frame received in a vPC member port, it uses CFS to synchronize its peer's MAC address table. The inserted table entry associates the learned MAC address to its shared vPC interface.

Under normal conditions, the peer link is mostly used for flooding, multicast, broadcast, and control plane traffic. Each vPC peer switch is expected to forward known unicast frames to its directly connected vPC member ports.

Figure 6-10 portrays three expected vPC traffic patterns.

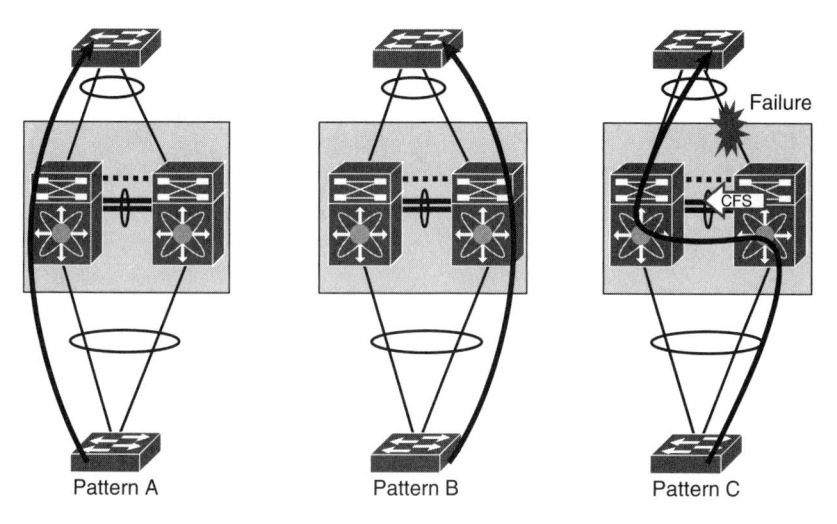

Figure 6-10 *Three vPC Traffic Patterns*

In Figure 6-10, Patterns A and B represent how each vPC peer locally forwards known unicast frames that are being received in a fully operational vPC.

Pattern C occurs if there is a failure on all members of a vPC in a single peer. In this scenario, CFS is used to warn the other peer about this failure, which must no longer block frames received from the peer link to the remaining member ports of the vPC. This pattern continues until at least one failed interface is operational again. Pattern C also explains why 10 Gigabit Ethernet connections are necessary for the peer link: because it is used for data traffic in such a scenario.

The peer keepalive link is a mandatory vPC element that avoids dual-active (or "split-brain") scenarios, where both vPC peers are working as standard STP switches. If a peer link general failure happens, the peer keepalive link can indicate to the secondary vPC peer that the primary peer is still operational.

The vPC peer keepalive link only transports *heartbeats*, which are UDP datagrams sent every second by default. In a peer link failure, the secondary vPC peer ignores heartbeats during a period defined by a timer called *hold timeout*. This timer allows the secondary peer to wait for a network reconvergence, if there is one. After this period, another timer, called *default timeout*, is started, and the secondary vPC peer is now ready to receive keepalive messages. If it receives one, the primary vPC peer is considered operational and, as a result, *all vPC interfaces are disabled in the secondary peer switch*.

Figure 6-11 depicts this specific vPC behavior.

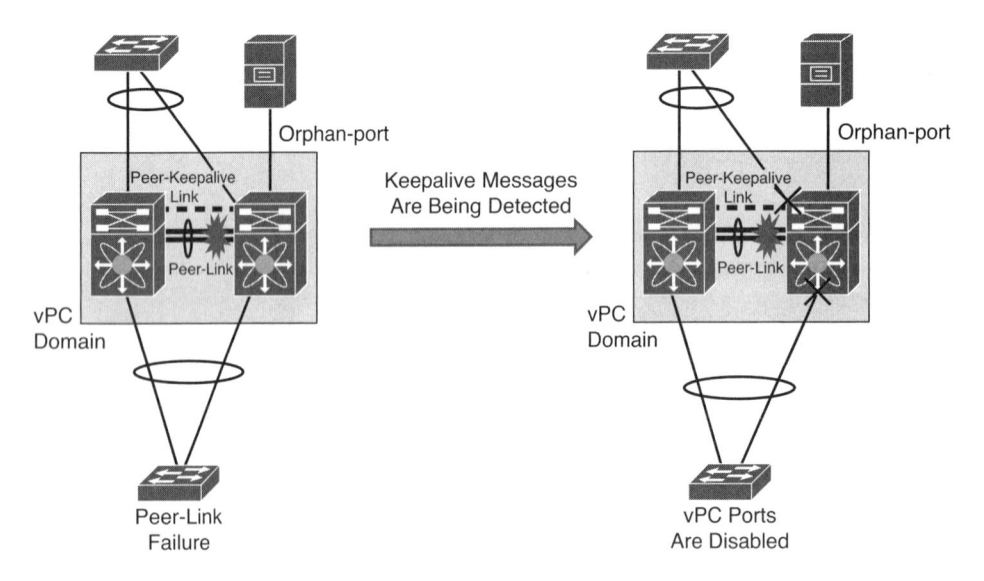

Figure 6-11 *vPC Peer Link Failure Scenario*

Note If no heartbeat is received after both timeouts, the secondary vPC peer has evidence that the primary peer is not active. Therefore, it becomes the primary peer in the vPC domain and all its vPC member ports remain active.

In Figure 6-11, you can also observe what happens to an orphan port in a peer link failure scenario with heartbeats being detected on the keepalive peer link. Contrary to the vPC member ports, the orphan ports remain active in the secondary peer, even though they can be completely isolated from the rest of the network.

Tip If you have devices with a single Ethernet port that must be connected to a vPC peer, I recommend that you configure an additional non-vPC trunk between peer switches to avoid device isolation in failure scenarios.

It is recommended that the vPC peer keepalive link

- Does not use the vPC peer link for heartbeat exchange.
- Uses the mgmt0 interface and the management Virtual Routing and Forwarding (VRF). If this interface is not available, use a routed interface that belongs to an exclusive VRF instead.
- Does not use a direct cable between mgmt0 interfaces to avoid loss of connectivity in a Nexus 7000 supervisor switchover. Because the active supervisor is the one sending heartbeats out of the chassis, a direct connection between an active and a

standby supervisor can result in a false chassis state detection. In this scenario, I recommend that you connect all four mgmt0 interfaces in a Layer 2 or 3 network that can provide any-to-any connectivity between them.

Figure 6-12 clarifies these recommendations.

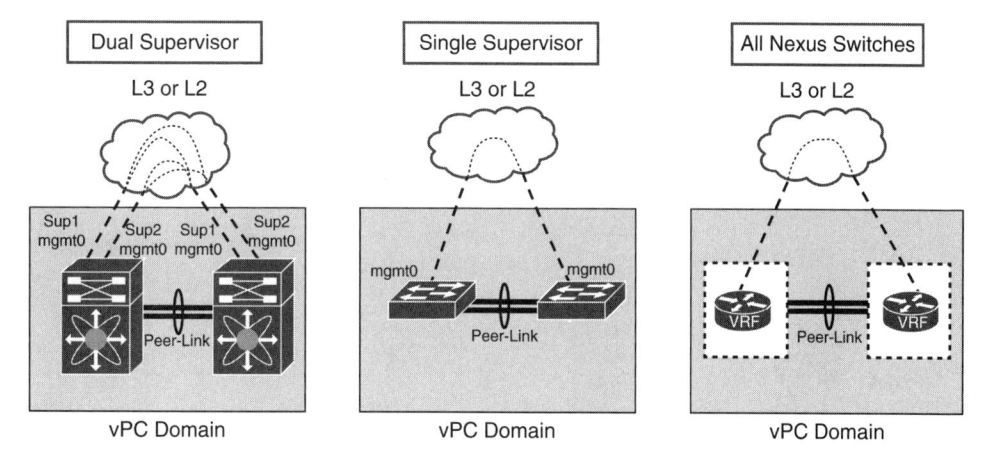

Figure 6-12 *Peer Keepalive Link Options*

Configuring Virtual PortChannels

To correctly configure a virtual PortChannel between identical NX-OS switches, it is highly recommended that you execute the following steps in order:

1. Define the vPC domain.
2. Establish peer keepalive connectivity.
3. Create a peer link.
4. Create a vPC.

The order of these steps is important to follow because each of them depends on the success of its previous one.

Two switches (N7K-1 and N7K-2) will be configured to provide a virtual PortChannel to another switch (Nexus1). A server (Orphan1) is connected to N7K-2 to demonstrate the behavior of an orphan port.

> **Tip** Yes, N7K-1 and N7K-2 are VDCs. However, they were created in different Nexus 7000 chassis, because it is not possible to configure vPCs between VDCs from the same physical device.

Step 1: Defining the Domain

In this step, a vPC domain is defined in both peer switches. A prerequisite for this configuration is the enabling of LACP and vPC to start their respective processes (*LACP Manager* and *VPC Manager*).

As I have explained in section "Virtual PortChannels," it is mandatory that both peers share the same vPC domain identifier (200 in this scenario).

Figure 6-13 portrays the vPC domain configuration in N7K-1 and N7K-2.

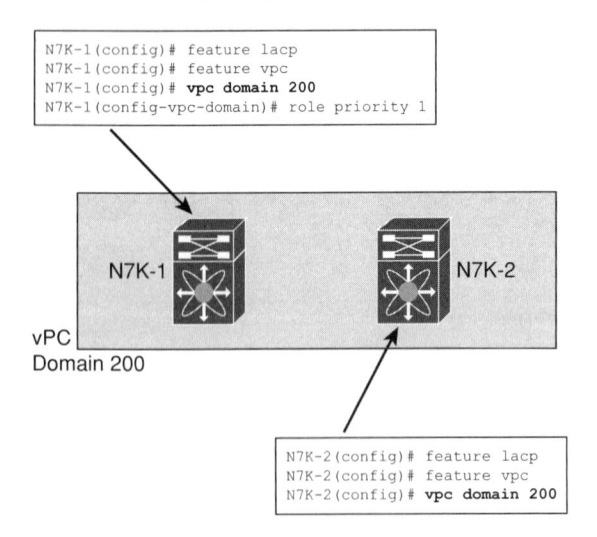

```
N7K-1(config)# feature lacp
N7K-1(config)# feature vpc
N7K-1(config)# vpc domain 200
N7K-1(config-vpc-domain)# role priority 1
```

```
N7K-2(config)# feature lacp
N7K-2(config)# feature vpc
N7K-2(config)# vpc domain 200
```

Figure 6-13 *Creating the vPC Domain*

Notice also that I have forced N7K-1 to become the primary peer in the vPC domain through the **role priority** command. This configuration will be especially useful to explain how BPDUs are generated within a vPC in future sections.

Step 2: Establishing Peer Keepalive Connectivity

To create the peer keepalive link, each switch must be configured with the destination IP address of the interface that will receive keepalive messages on the other vPC peer.

This scenario uses the switch's management interfaces (and consequently, the management VRF) to generate and receive keepalive messages.

Tip In NX-OS, mgmt0 is the default interface for peer keepalive links.

Figure 6-14 shows the specific configuration command required in both switches for this step.

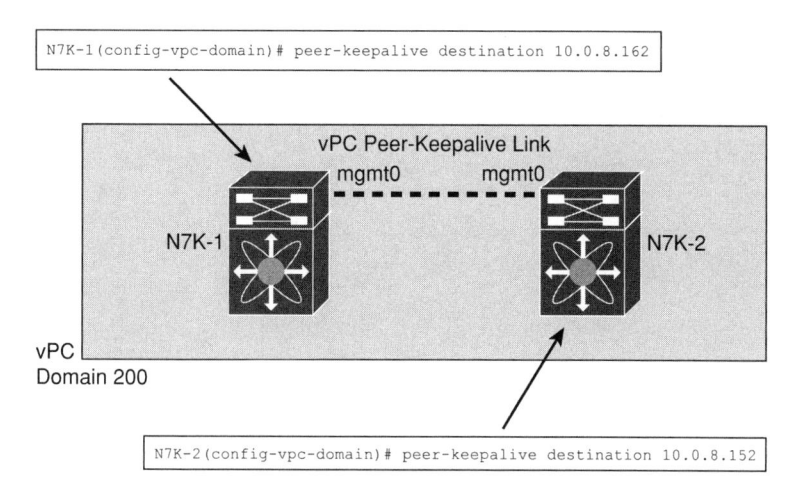

```
N7K-1(config-vpc-domain)# peer-keepalive destination 10.0.8.162
```

```
N7K-2(config-vpc-domain)# peer-keepalive destination 10.0.8.152
```

Figure 6-14 *Establishing Peer Keepalive Connectivity*

After this configuration, both switches start to exchange messages and detect each other. However, as you can see in Example 6-4, none of them are assigned to a role yet.

Example 6-4 *Peer Keepalive Configuration in N7K-2*

```
! Verifying the vPC status
N7K-2# show vpc brief
Legend:
                (*) - local vPC is down, forwarding via vPC peer-link

vPC domain id                     : 200
Peer status                       : peer link not configured
! Both switches are exchanging keepalive messages
vPC keep-alive status             : peer is alive
Configuration consistency status  : failed
Per-vlan consistency status       : failed
Configuration inconsistency reason: vPC peer-link does not exist
Type-2 consistency status         : failed
Type-2 inconsistency reason       : vPC peer-link does not exist
! No primary or secondary peer was defined yet
vPC role                          : none established
[output suppressed]
```

Step 3: Creating the Peer Link

Figure 6-15 exhibits the vPC peer link configuration in N7K-1 and N7K-2. You can notice that the peer link is configured as a standard Layer 2 PortChannel with one addition: the **vpc peer-link** command.

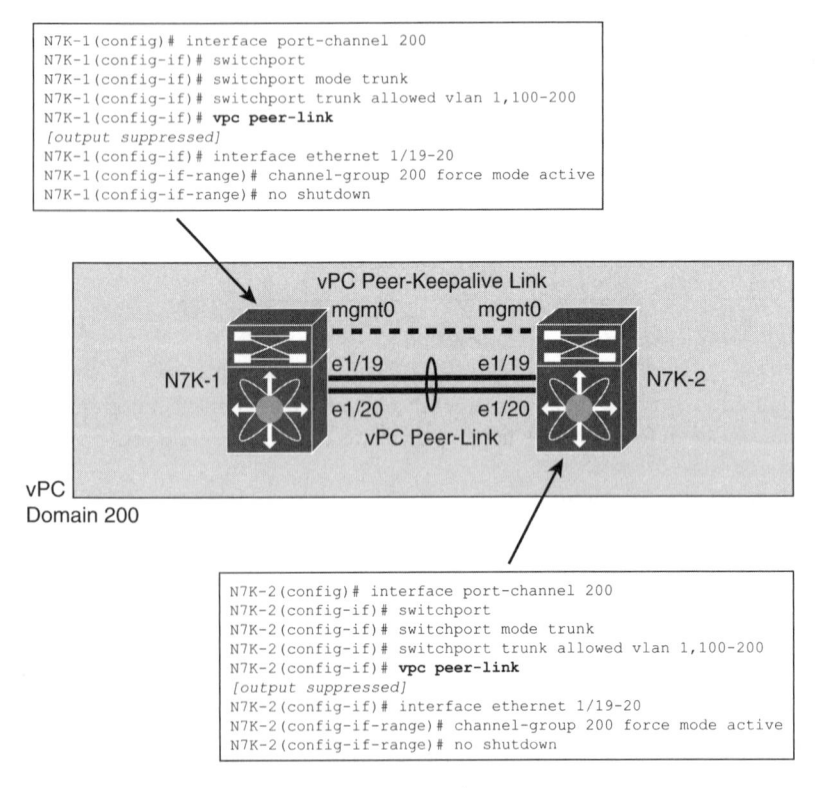

```
N7K-1(config)# interface port-channel 200
N7K-1(config-if)# switchport
N7K-1(config-if)# switchport mode trunk
N7K-1(config-if)# switchport trunk allowed vlan 1,100-200
N7K-1(config-if)# vpc peer-link
[output suppressed]
N7K-1(config-if)# interface ethernet 1/19-20
N7K-1(config-if-range)# channel-group 200 force mode active
N7K-1(config-if-range)# no shutdown
```

```
N7K-2(config)# interface port-channel 200
N7K-2(config-if)# switchport
N7K-2(config-if)# switchport mode trunk
N7K-2(config-if)# switchport trunk allowed vlan 1,100-200
N7K-2(config-if)# vpc peer-link
[output suppressed]
N7K-2(config-if)# interface ethernet 1/19-20
N7K-2(config-if-range)# channel-group 200 force mode active
N7K-2(config-if-range)# no shutdown
```

Figure 6-15 *Creating the vPC Peer Link*

Tip Although I have used the ID 200 for the vPC domain and the peer link PortChannel, these parameters do not need to be the same.

After interfaces Ethernet 1/19 and 1/20 are added to the PortChannel, both switches automatically enable CFS on the peer link and are now capable to detect vPC-related parameters from the other peer. For example, they agree on what will be their respective roles in the vPC (primary or secondary) and how they will deal with STP.

Tip Whenever possible, you should include ports from different interface modules in the vPC peer link. This good practice will raise the peer link availability against hardware malfunctions. But as you can see in Figure 6-15, this is not a mandatory requirement.

Examples 6-5 and 6-6 show the roles that are established and the MAC addresses used by this configuration. N7K-1 is expected to become the primary peer because it was configured with the lowest role priority of the pair in the first step.

These examples also disclose the shared virtual MAC address that was generated when the vPC domain was configured.

Example 6-5 *Verifying vPC Roles in N7K-1*

```
N7K-1# show vpc role

vPC Role status
--------------------------------------------------
! N7K-1 is the primary peer in this vPC domain
vPC role                       : primary
[output suppressed]
! This is the virtual MAC address for the vPC domain
vPC system-mac                 : 00:23:04:ee:be:c8
vPC system-priority            : 32667
! And this is N7K-1 system MAC address
vPC local system-mac           : 00:26:98:0d:53:c3
vPC local role-priority        : 1
```

Example 6-6 *Verifying vPC Roles in N7K-2*

```
N7K-2# show vpc role

vPC Role status
--------------------------------------------------
! N7K-2 is the secondary peer in this vPC domain
vPC role                       : secondary
[output suppressed]
! This is the same virtual MAC address for the vPC domain
vPC system-mac                 : 00:23:04:ee:be:c8
vPC system-priority            : 32667
! And this is N7K-1 system MAC address
vPC local system-mac           : 00:26:98:0d:43:43
vPC local role-priority        : 32667
```

Both switches share the same vPC system MAC address (0023.04ee.bec8) generated when the domain 200 (0xc8 in hexadecimal) was configured.

One additional observation: Notice that the local address in the secondary peer (0026.980d.4343) is lower that the one in the primary peer (0026.980d.53c3). This will be an important detail when I explain how STP is working under the vPC covers.

Step 4: Creating the Virtual PortChannel

In this step, independent PortChannels are created in both switches and reused to define a virtual PortChannel with the **vpc** interface command.

Figure 6-16 shows this configuration applied on four interfaces in each switch.

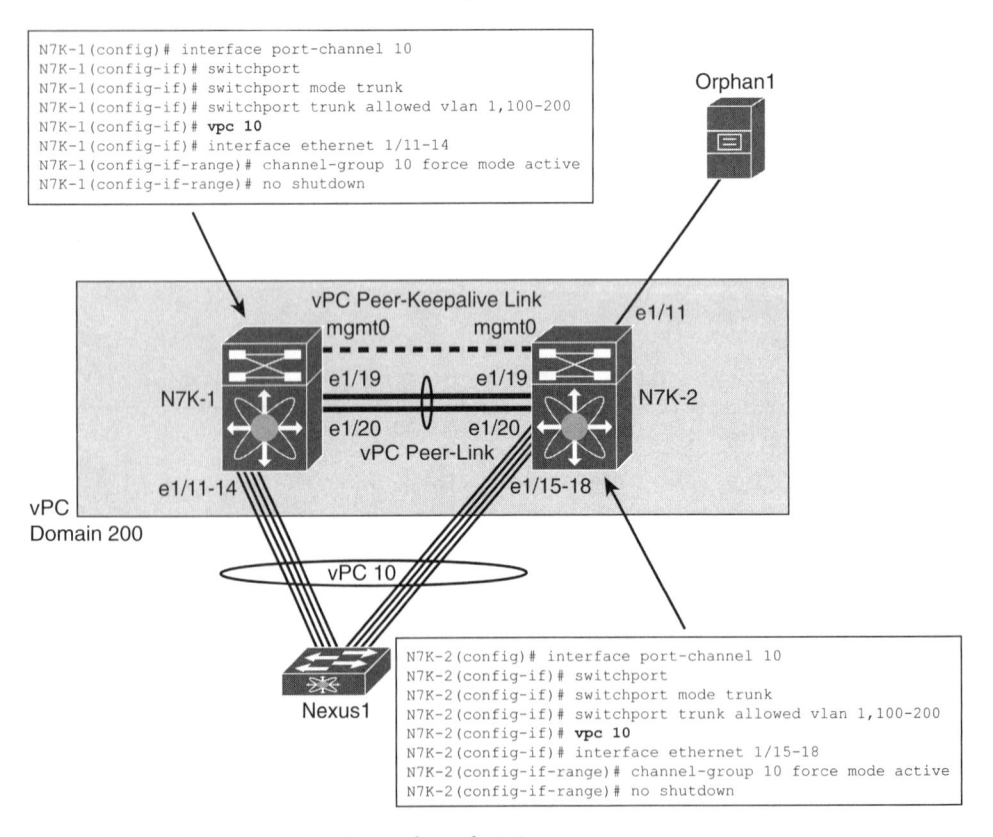

```
N7K-1(config)# interface port-channel 10
N7K-1(config-if)# switchport
N7K-1(config-if)# switchport mode trunk
N7K-1(config-if)# switchport trunk allowed vlan 1,100-200
N7K-1(config-if)# vpc 10
N7K-1(config-if)# interface ethernet 1/11-14
N7K-1(config-if-range)# channel-group 10 force mode active
N7K-1(config-if-range)# no shutdown
```

```
N7K-2(config)# interface port-channel 10
N7K-2(config-if)# switchport
N7K-2(config-if)# switchport mode trunk
N7K-2(config-if)# switchport trunk allowed vlan 1,100-200
N7K-2(config-if)# vpc 10
N7K-2(config-if)# interface ethernet 1/15-18
N7K-2(config-if-range)# channel-group 10 force mode active
N7K-2(config-if-range)# no shutdown
```

Figure 6-16 *Creating PortChannels and vPC*

Both PortChannels must share the same identifier in the **vpc** command (10 in our example). This condition must be met because this identifier has significance in the CFS messages exchanged between vPC peers.

Tip Though it is not mandatory, I have created the PortChannels using the same identifier as the vPC (10) in both switches. I specially recommend this practice to facilitate logging message retrieval during troubleshooting.

With an operational peer link, CFS transmits the local vPC configuration parameters to the remote peer. Then, both switches can perform a *compatibility check* on the vPC member port's configuration and states. vPCs can be partially or fully suspended if the following parameters are not identical in each peer:

- PortChannel mode (on, active, or passive)
- Link speed per PortChannel
- Duplex mode per PortChannel
- Trunk configuration per PortChannel (native VLAN, allowed VLANs, native VLAN tagging)
- Spanning Tree Protocol version (Rapid PVST+ or MST)
- Region configuration (if MST is used)
- VLAN state
- Spanning Tree configuration (global and per PortChannel)
- Maximum transmission unit (MTU)

Tip You can determine whether these parameters are compatible with the **show vpc consistency-parameters** command.

Example 6-7 shows the status of vPC 10 in N7K-2 after the configuration is applied to both peers.

Example 6-7 *Checking vPC Status in N7K-2*

```
! Verifying vPC status
N7K-2# show vpc brief
Legend:
                (*) - local vPC is down, forwarding via vPC peer-link

vPC domain id                     : 200
Peer status                       : peer adjacency formed ok
vPC keep-alive status             : peer is alive
! Mandatory parameters are OK
Configuration consistency status  : success
Per-vlan consistency status       : success
[output suppressed]
! The vPC peer-link is working
vPC Peer-link status
---------------------------------------------------------------------
id    Port   Status Active vlans
```

```
--   ----   ------ -------------------------------------------------
1    Po200  up     1
! And here is the successfully created vPC 10
vPC status
-----------------------------------------------------------------
id   Port   Status Consistency Reason          Active vlans
--   ----   ------ ----------- ------          ------------
10   Po10   up     success     success         1
```

And the mission is accomplished: Target switch Nexus1 has all eight interfaces working within a PortChannel, as shown in Example 6-8.

Example 6-8 *Nexus1 PortChannel Status*

```
Nexus1# show port-channel database
port-channel10
    Last membership update is successful
    8 ports in total, 8 ports up
[output suppressed]
    Ports:   Ethernet1/1     [active ] [up] *
             Ethernet1/2     [active ] [up]
[output suppressed]
             Ethernet1/8     [active ] [up]
```

Spanning Tree Protocol and Virtual PortChannels

It is conceptually wrong to affirm that "vPC eliminates Spanning Tree." In this section, you will observe that behind the illusion created by vPC, STP is alive and well.

Going back to the creation of vPC 10, depicted in Figure 6-16, it is interesting to observe how Spanning Tree Protocol is behaving on the vPC target switch, Nexus1.

Example 6-9 exposes the STP status for VLAN 1 (which, for simplicity, is the only existent VLAN in this network).

Example 6-9 *Checking Spanning Tree Protocol in Nexus1*

```
Nexus1# show spanning-tree vlan 1

VLAN0001
  Spanning tree enabled protocol rstp
  Root ID    Priority    32769
! N7K-2 is the Root
             Address     0026.980d.4343
```

```
                Cost         2
                Port         4105 (port-channel10)
[output suppressed]
Interface          Role Sts Cost      Prio.Nbr Type
---------------    ---- --- --------- -------- ----------------
Po10               Root FWD 1         128.4105 P2p
```

As expected from a switch that is deploying link aggregation, Nexus1 has a single STP interface: *PortChannel 10*. More specifically, this interface is a root port, and the root switch in the network is N7K-2.

That small detail shows how STP is still working in this scenario: N7K-2 has the lowest local MAC address; thus it becomes the root switch in the VLAN 1 STP instance.

But how do vPC peers deal with BPDUs? To explain that, I have enabled a debug that exhibits the BPDUs that each peer is transmitting in Examples 6-10 and 6-11.

Example 6-10 *N7K-1 Transmitted BPDUs*

```
! Enabling sent BPDU debug
N7K-1# debug spanning-tree bpdu_tx
! N7K-1 sends BPDUs to vPC 10 and to the vPC peer-link
19:15:06.578728 stp: RSTP(1): transmitting RSTP BPDU on port-channel10
[output suppressed]
19:15:06.579108 stp: RSTP(1): transmitting RSTP BPDU on port-channel200
```

Example 6-11 *N7K-2 Transmitted BPDUs*

```
! Enabling sent BPDU debug
N7K-2# debug spanning-tree bpdu_tx
! N7K-2 sends BPDUs vPC peer-link and to the orphan-port
19:08:13.409073 stp: RSTP(1): transmitting RSTP BPDU on port-channel200
[output suppressed]
19:08:13.409124 stp: RSTP(1): transmitting RSTP BPDU on ethernet1/11
```

Examples 6-10 and 6-11 exhibit the default behavior STP on vPCs: Even if it is not the root of a network, the primary peer is responsible for all STP communication over the vPCs. And because N7K-2 is the secondary peer, it only generates BPDUs for its non-vPC interfaces (even Ethernet 1/11, because it is not configured as an edge port) as a standard switch would.

Here, it is already possible to foresee a consequence: A failure with the root switch (N7K-2) would demand a new convergence in the network. And during a short period, some traffic would be interrupted within the vPC-connected interfaces.

To avoid exposing target devices to this behavior, vPC can deepen its virtualization illusion through the **peer-switch** command. This feature allows both vPC peer switches to improve the emulation of a single STP bridge, as depicted in Figure 6-17.

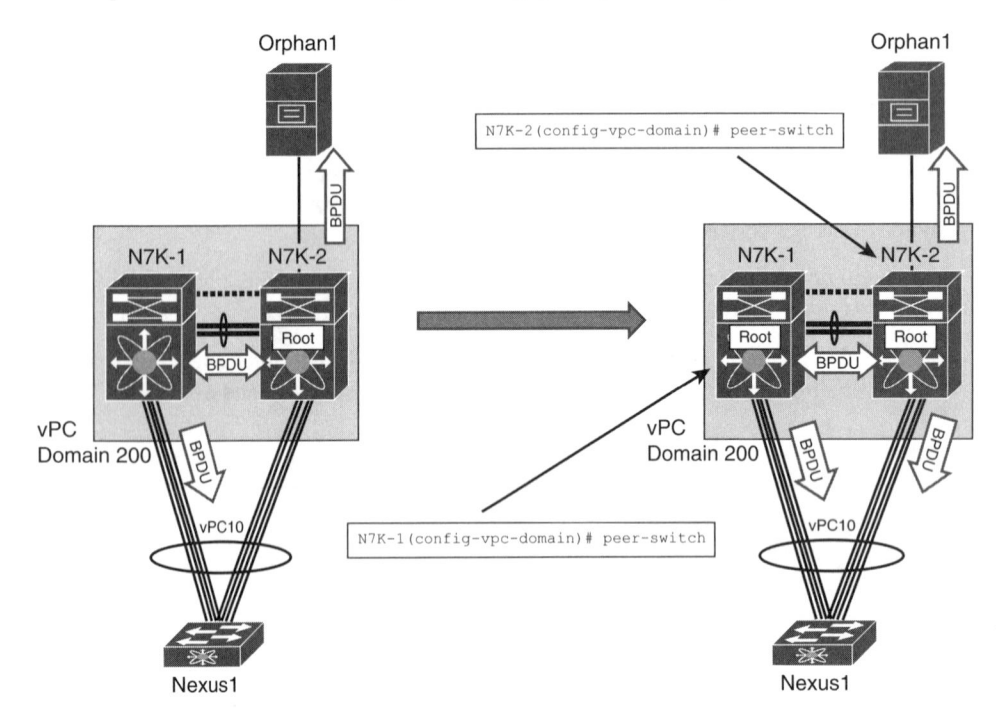

Figure 6-17 *Before and After vPC Peer Switch*

In Examples 6-12 and 6-13, you can verify how the peer switch feature turns both peers into the root switch in VLAN 1.

Example 6-12 *STP in N7K-1 After Peer Switch Configuration*

```
! N7K-1 is the Root for VLAN1
N7K-1# show spanning-tree vlan 1

VLAN0001
  Spanning tree enabled protocol rstp
  Root ID    Priority    32769
             Address     0023.04ee.bec8
             This bridge is the root
[output suppressed]
! Enabling sent BPDU debug
N7K-1# debug spanning-tree bpdu_tx
! N7K-1 sends BPDUs to vPC 10 and to the vPC peer-link
19:37:24.578740 stp: RSTP(1): transmitting RSTP BPDU on port-channel10
```

```
[output suppressed]
19:37:24.579095 stp: RSTP(1): transmitting RSTP BPDU on port-channel200
```

Example 6-13 *STP in N7K-2 After Peer Switch Configuration*

```
! N7K-2 also thinks it is the Root for VLAN1
N7K-2# show spanning-tree vlan 1

VLAN0001
  Spanning tree enabled protocol rstp
  Root ID    Priority    32769
             Address     0023.04ee.bec8
             This bridge is the root
[output suppressed]
! Enabling sent BPDU debug
N7K-2# debug spanning-tree bpdu_tx
! N7K-1 sends BPDUs to vPC 10 and to the vPC peer-link
19:32:35.416221 stp: RSTP(1): transmitting RSTP BPDU on port-channel10
[output suppressed]
19:32:35.416365 stp: RSTP(1): transmitting RSTP BPDU on port-channel200
[output suppressed]
19:32:35.416466 stp: RSTP(1): transmitting RSTP BPDU on Ethernet1/11
```

With the peer switch feature enabled, both switches now send BPDUs down every interface using the same STP bridge ID. The vPC system MAC address is used on the BPDUs, as explained in Example 6-14.

Example 6-14 *STP in Nexus1 After Peer Switch Configuration in N7K-1 and N7K-2*

```
! Verifying the STP status in VLAN 1
Nexus1# show spanning-tree vlan 1

VLAN0001
  Spanning tree enabled protocol rstp
  Root ID    Priority    32769
! The Root Bridge ID has the vPC System-MAC address
             Address     0023.04ee.bec8
[output suppressed]
```

Note Because of the intense development in NX-OS, mapping enhancement features to Nexus platforms is almost like aiming at a moving target. Hence, I recommend that you verify whether the vPC features presented in this chapter are available in your hardware and software combination. My objective here is to explain the key concepts behind virtual PartChannels and not to present an outdated snapshot of Nexus capabilities.

Peer Link Failure and Orphan Ports

As explained in earlier section "Virtual PortChannels," you can expect the following consequences in the secondary vPC peer (N7K-2, in our topology) in a peer link failure:

- All the vPC ports are suspended.
- Orphan ports (Ethernet 1/11, for example) remain operational.

Example 6-15 illustrates this behavior after I have interrupted both connections in the peer link through a **shutdown** command executed in PortChannel 200 on N7K-1.

Example 6-15 *N7K-2 Port Status After Peer Link Failure*

```
! Verifying which interfaces were suspended after a peer-link failure
N7K-2# show interface brief | include vpc
Eth1/15   1   eth   trunk   down   suspended by vpc          auto(D) 10
Eth1/16   1   eth   trunk   down   suspended by vpc          auto(D) 10
Eth1/17   1   eth   trunk   down   suspended by vpc          auto(D) 10
Eth1/18   1   eth   trunk   down   suspended by vpc          auto(D) 10
Po10      1   eth   trunk   down   suspended by vpc          auto(D) lacp
```

No surprises here: N7K-2 is still detecting that N7K-1 is active through the peer keepalive link; therefore, it will suspend every vPC port.

Note SVIs from VLANs present on vPC member ports are also suspended with the peer link failure.

Nevertheless, Ethernet 1/11 is still active, and at this moment, Orphan1 is completely isolated. And even if Orphan1 was deploying an active-standby NIC teaming policy, no failure would be detected in the active link.

To avoid such situations, it is possible to suspend the interface along with the vPC ports in a peer link failure scenario. The idea is that such failure will provoke at least a switchover to the standby interfaces of dual-homed servers.

The **vpc orphan-port suspend** command, configured in the Ethernet 1/11 on N7K-2, produces the result shown in Example 6-16.

Example 6-16 *N7K-2 Port Status After Another Peer Link and Orphan Port Configuration*

```
! Verifying which interfaces were suspended after a peer-link failure
N7K-2# show interface brief | include vpc
Eth1/11   1    eth   trunk   down    vpc peerlink is down    auto(D) --
Eth1/15   1    eth   trunk   down    suspended by vpc        auto(D) 10
Eth1/16   1    eth   trunk   down    suspended by vpc        auto(D) 10
Eth1/17   1    eth   trunk   down    suspended by vpc        auto(D) 10
Eth1/18   1    eth   trunk   down    suspended by vpc        auto(D) 10
Po10      1    eth   trunk   down    suspended by vpc        auto(D) lacp
```

First-Hop Routing Protocols and Virtual PortChannels

Virtual PortChannel peers can also be configured as default gateways, as long as they both deploy Layer 3 capabilities. In truth, first-hop routing protocols (such as Hot Standby Router Protocol [HSRP] and Virtual Router Redundancy Protocol [VRRP]) can leverage the active-active behavior from vPC deployments in a way that was not possible with standard STP switches.

Figure 6-18 clarifies how both vPC peers are able to route IP packets directed to the virtual IP created by HSRP.

Note I had to enable **interface-vlan** and **hsrp** features before this configuration.

In Example 6-17, you can see that N7K-1 can route IP packets directed to the virtual default gateway.

Example 6-17 *N7K-1 MAC Addresses*

```
! Verifying N7K-1 HSRP role
N7K-1# show hsrp brief
                   P indicates configured to preempt.                      |
Interface  Grp Prio P State   Active addr   Standby addr  Group addr
Vlan1       1  255  P Active  local         10.1.1.2      10.1.1.254    (conf)
! Discovering the MAC address for VLAN1 SVI
N7K-1# show interface vlan 1 | include address
  Hardware is EtherSVI, address is  0026.980d.53c3
! Verifying HSRP Virtual MAC
N7K-1# show hsrp group 1 | include mac
  Virtual mac address is 0000.0c9f.f001 (Default MAC)
! Checking which MAC addresses can act as a Gateway in N7K-1
N7K-1# show mac address-table vlan 1
```

```
Legend: * - primary entry, G - Gateway MAC, (R) - Routed MAC, O - Overlay MAC
        age - seconds since last seen,+ - primary entry using vPC Peer-Link
   VLAN   MAC Address      Type      age    Secure NTFY Ports/SWID.SSID.LID
---------+----------------+--------+-------+------+----+------------
G  1     0000.0c9f.f001   static     -       F    F    sup-eth1(R)
*  1     0026.980d.4343   static     -       F    F    vPC Peer-Link
G  1     0026.980d.53c3   static     -       F    F    sup-eth1(R)
[output suppressed]
```

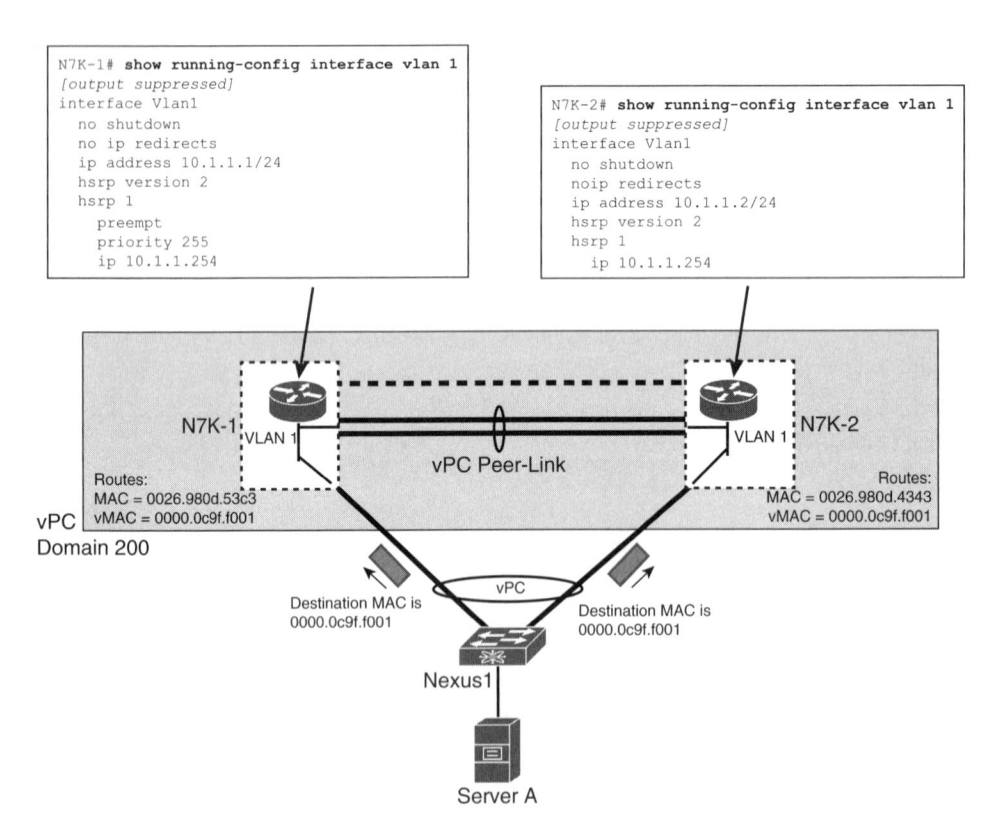

```
N7K-1# show running-config interface vlan 1
[output suppressed]
interface Vlan1
  no shutdown
  no ip redirects
  ip address 10.1.1.1/24
  hsrp version 2
  hsrp 1
    preempt
    priority 255
    ip 10.1.1.254
```

```
N7K-2# show running-config interface vlan 1
[output suppressed]
interface Vlan1
  no shutdown
  noip redirects
  ip address 10.1.1.2/24
  hsrp version 2
  hsrp 1
    ip 10.1.1.254
```

Figure 6-18 *HSRP and vPC*

From the output of the **show mac address-table** command, you can verify that N7K-1 can act as an IP gateway to frames directed to MAC addresses marked with the letter *G*, such as 0000.0c9f.f0001 (HSRP group virtual MAC) and 0026.980d.53c3 (VLAN 1 SVI MAC address in N7K-1).

In the same way, Example 6-18 illustrates that N7K-2 can act as a gateway to frames that are sent to MAC addresses 0000.0c9f.f0001 (HSRP group virtual MAC) and 0026.980d.4343 (VLAN 1 SVI MAC address in N7K-2).

Example 6-18 *N7K-2 MAC Addresses*

```
! Verifying N7K-2 HSRP role
N7K-2# show hsrp brief
                 P indicates configured to preempt.                    |
Interface  Grp Prio P State    Active addr Standby addr    Group addr
Vlan1       1   100   Standby  10.1.1.1    local           10.1.1.254   (conf)
! Discovering the MAC address for VLAN1 SVI
N7K-2# show interface vlan 1 | include address
  Hardware is EtherSVI, address is  0026.980d.4343
! Verifying HSRP Virtual MAC
N7K-2# show hsrp group 1 | include mac
  Virtual mac address is 0000.0c9f.f001 (Default MAC)
! Checking which MAC addresses can act as a Gateway in N7K-2
N7K-2# show mac address-table vlan 1
Legend: * - primary entry, G - Gateway MAC, (R) - Routed MAC, O - Overlay MAC
   age - seconds since last seen,+ - primary entry using vPC Peer-Link
   VLAN    MAC Address     Type      age    Secure NTFY Ports/SWID.SSID.LID
-------+---------------+--------+-------+----+----+----------
G 1     0000.0c9f.f001  static     -      F    F   sup-eth1(R)
G 1     0026.980d.4343  static     -      F    F   sup-eth1(R)
* 1     0026.980d.53c3  static     -      F    F   vPC Peer-Link
[output suppressed]
```

Both Nexus switches can route packets to the HSRP virtual MAC address! As a consequence, the upstream routed traffic will be load balanced through the PortChannel hash algorithm in Nexus1.

However, some host devices deploy nonstandard behavior within their multiple Ethernet connections. For example, some Network Attached Storage (NAS), and servers with particular NIC teaming techniques, might not send any Address Resolution Protocol (ARP) frames to discover MAC addresses; they simply use the MAC address received on the original request to build its response. If such an NAS had its multiple interfaces connected to Nexus1 (from our topology), the replies to external clients would be directed to the *SVI MAC addresses* and not the HSRP MAC address.

This characteristic can generate the undesired vPC behavior described as follows:

- The NAS sends an IP packet directed to MAC address 0026.980d.53c3 (VLAN 1 SVI MAC address in N7K-1) using an interface connected to N7K-2 (because of a PortChannel hash decision).

- N7K-2 switches this frame to N7K-1 using its MAC address table.

- N7K-1 can *block* this packet if it was supposed to be forwarded out to a vPC.

262 Data Center Virtualization Fundamentals

Do you remember the vPC check rule? Some NX-OS switches (Nexus 7000 equipped with M1-series modules, for example) apply this rule for switched and *routed* traffic, causing packet drops when submitted to nonstandard traffic like the one I am describing now.

The *peer gateway* feature was designed to solve this awkward scenario. If both vPC peers are configured with this feature, each one of them will be able to route packets that are directed to its peer MAC address.

Figure 6-19 and Example 6-19 show that with peer gateway enabled, N7K-2 will be able to route the packet sent to the N7K-1 SVI MAC address.

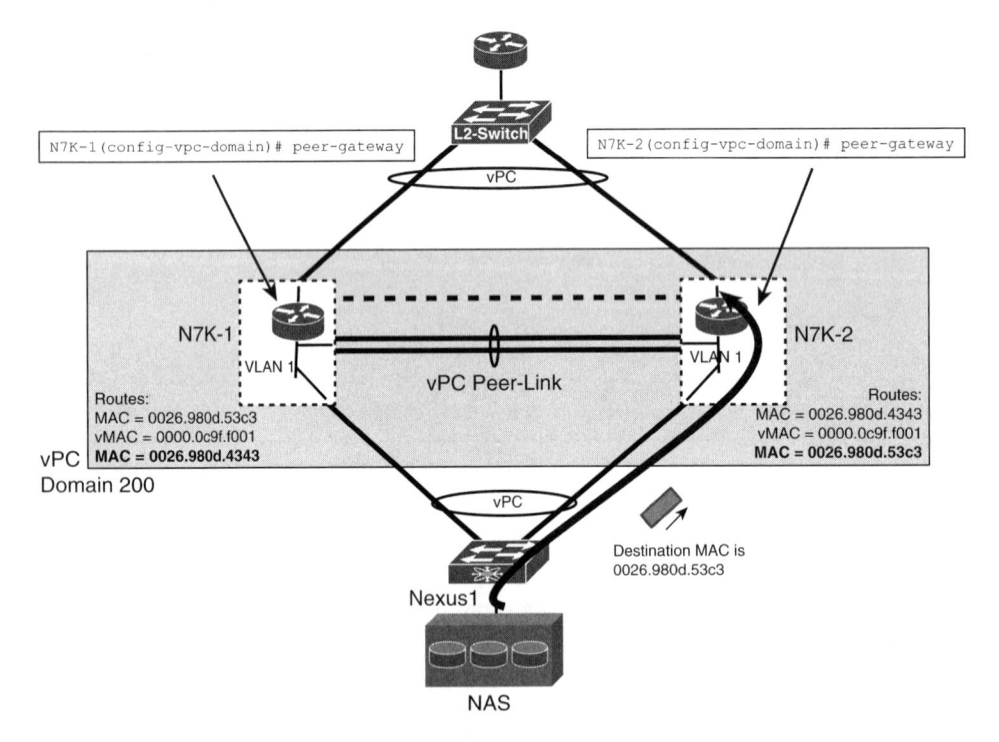

Figure 6-19 *Peer Gateway Configured in N7K-1 and N7K-2*

Example 6-19 *MAC Addresses in N7K-2 After Peer Gateway Is Enabled*

```
! Checking which MAC addresses can now act as a Gateway in N7K-2
N7K-2# show mac address-table vlan 1 | include "G"
        * - primary entry, G - Gateway MAC, (R) - Routed MAC, O - Overlay MAC
   G 1        0000.0c9f.f001     static      -      F      F   sup-eth1(R)
   G 1        0026.980d.4343     static      -      F      F   sup-eth1(R)
   G 1        0026.980d.53c3     static      -      F      F   sup-eth1(R)
```

Of course, the same behavior is expected on N7K-1 regarding frames directed to the N7K-2 SVI MAC address.

> **Note** As previously mentioned, I recommend that you consult the Cisco online documentation to verify how your specific NX-OS device behaves with routed unicast and multicast IP traffic on a vPC.

Routing Protocols and Virtual PortChannelsVirtual PortChannels are a Layer 2 multihop technology whose path decision depends on a hashing algorithm. On the other hand, when a Layer 3 device must choose a gateway among a set of equal-cost possible routers, another hash algorithm is used as well.

When applied to the same device, both independent algorithms can generate unexpected results in some vPC scenarios. For example, consider this hypothetical topology:

- Router1 is connected to our N7K-1 and N7K-2 switches using a vPC. Router1 is sending a packet to a remote subnet connected to another router (Router2).

- Router2 is also using a vPC created by N7K-1 and N7K-2.

- Router1 can use either N7K-1 or N7K-2 as gateways to the remote subnet. This is an equal-cost multipath decision that, for example, could result in a frame with N7K-1 MAC address as its destination.

- However, because Router1 is also using a vPC, the frame directed to the N7K-1 Layer 2 address can use an N7K-2–connected interface.

- N7K-2 switches the frame to N7K-1 SVI through the peer link.

- N7K-1 receives the frame and routes it to the vPC connected to Router2.

- Depending on its hardware characteristics, N7K-1 can apply the vPC check rule to this frame and block it.

This is not a problem of the vPC technology, but simply a design incompatibility between independent decision processes.

Similar to the NAS scenario presented in the previous section, this behavior can be fixed with the peer gateway feature. This capability can avoid the vPC check in N7K-1, because the traffic would be routed in N7K-2.

Although the vPC peer gateway capability can be a good solution to static routing in this case, the feature does not help when a routing protocol is deployed between a vPC-connected router and the vPC peers.

As shown in Figure 6-20, some routing protocols use packets with TTL of one that can be dropped by a vPC peer switch with peer gateway enabled. Hence, the routing protocol communication between the Layer 3 switch and N7K-1, passing through N7K-2 (Layer 2 hash decision), would not happen.

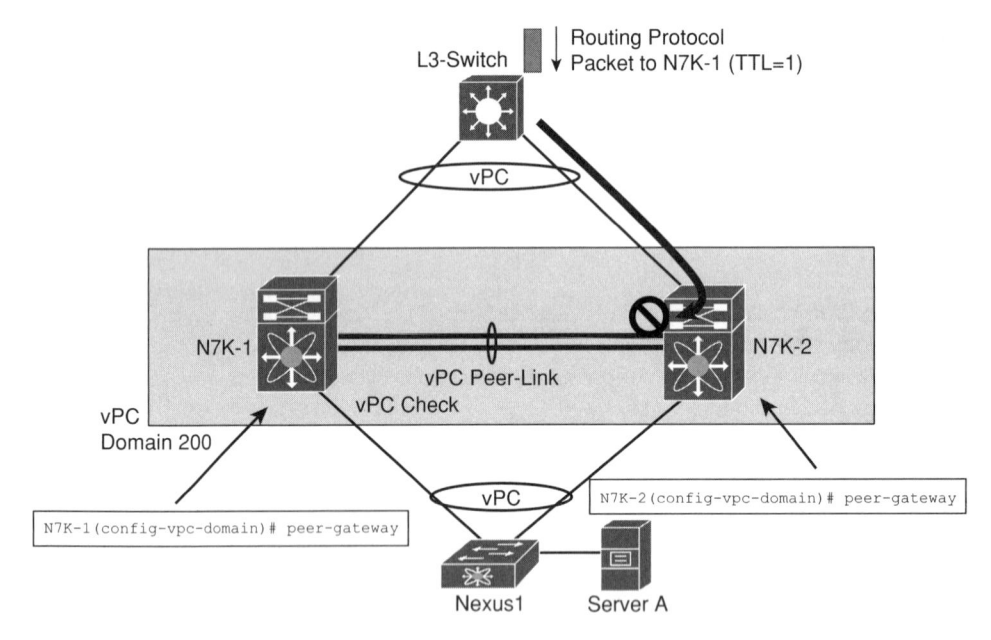

Figure 6-20 *Routing Protocols and vPC 2*

As a general best practice that can be used in most unicast and multicast IP routing scenarios, I recommend that you use *routed ports* or *transit VLANs* to deploy dynamic IP routing between the vPC peers and other Layer 3 devices. And if you want to deploy any kind of dynamic routing between the vPC peers, I also recommend that you use a separate Layer 3 connection.

If you exclude the Layer 2 hash decision from your Layer 3 devices, it is easier to achieve routing behaviors similar to non-vPC network designs.

An implementation of this practice is depicted in Figure 6-21. In this figure, if a packet is supposed to be routed by one of the vPC peers, it will never traverse the peer link and be affected by the vPC check rule.

Examples 6-20 and 6-21 demonstrate how both vPC peers and connected routers can exchange routes normally through the routing protocol shown in Figure 6-21.

Example 6-20 *N7K-1 OSPF Neighbors*

```
! Verifying that both OSPF neighbors are fully operational for N7K-1
N7K-1# sh ip ospf neighbors
 OSPF Process ID 1 VRF default
 Total number of neighbors: 2
 Neighbor ID     Pri State            Up Time  Address         Interface
 37.2.2.2          1 FULL/DR          00:27:50 37.1.1.2        Eth3/11
 10.1.1.2          1 FULL/DR          00:00:06 37.3.3.2        Vlan37
```

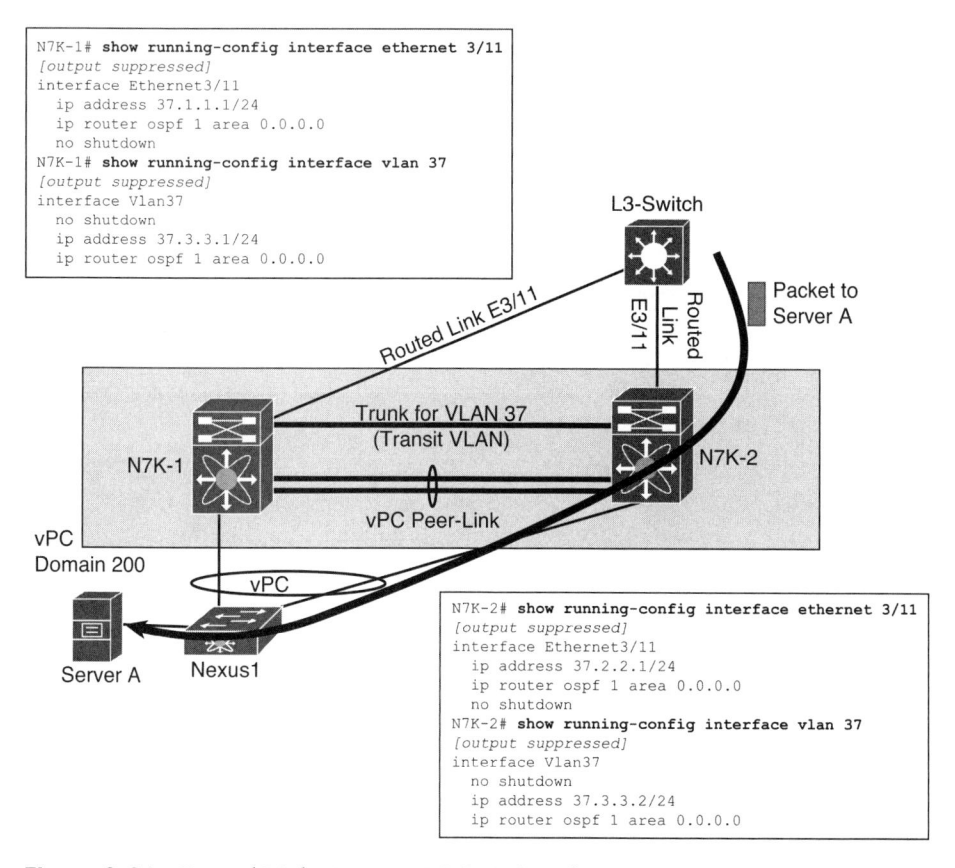

```
N7K-1# show running-config interface ethernet 3/11
[output suppressed]
interface Ethernet3/11
  ip address 37.1.1.1/24
  ip router ospf 1 area 0.0.0.0
  no shutdown
N7K-1# show running-config interface vlan 37
[output suppressed]
interface Vlan37
  no shutdown
  ip address 37.3.3.1/24
  ip router ospf 1 area 0.0.0.0
```

```
N7K-2# show running-config interface ethernet 3/11
[output suppressed]
interface Ethernet3/11
  ip address 37.2.2.1/24
  ip router ospf 1 area 0.0.0.0
  no shutdown
N7K-2# show running-config interface vlan 37
[output suppressed]
interface Vlan37
  no shutdown
  ip address 37.3.3.2/24
  ip router ospf 1 area 0.0.0.0
```

Figure 6-21 *Routed Links Between L3 Switch and vPC Peers*

Example 6-21 *N7K-2 OSPF Neighbors*

```
! Verifying that both OSPF neighbors are fully operational for N7K-2
N7K-2# show ip ospf neighbors
 OSPF Process ID 1 VRF default
 Total number of neighbors: 2
 Neighbor ID    Pri State      Up Time  Address    Interface
 37.2.2.2         1 FULL/DR    00:30:28 37.2.2.2   Eth3/11
 10.1.1.1         1 FULL/BDR   00:03:17 37.3.3.1   Vlan37
```

Layer 2 Multipathing and vPC+

Although some technologies need to fool STP to achieve active-active links in Layer 2, some networks are already celebrating this protocol's retirement.

Over the last years, networking manufacturers and standard organizations have invested research and development time to fulfill the desire of a true *Ethernet multipathing technology* in data center networks.

For sure, the creation of virtual PortChannels was already a firm step in this direction. However, as you have learned in this chapter, vPC-based networks must abide to topologies where traffic is load balanced to a pair of devices.

The creation of a Layer 2 multipathing protocol (L2MP) intends to end the recurring debate over which is more suitable for highly scalable data centers: Layer 2 or Layer 3 networks? The idea behind this initiative is the possibility of using the advantages associated with Layer 3 routing (equal-cost multipath, flexible topologies, traffic control) while keeping the simplicity that Layer 2 switching offers to all kinds of traffic (unicast, multicast, and broadcast).

In 2009, the very same Radia Perlman kick-started the creation of a standard L2MP, coauthoring the informational RFC 5556 ("Transparent Interconnection of Lots of Links (TRILL): Problem and Applicability Statement"). Motivated by this statement of direction, Cisco launched *FabricPath* as the Layer 2 multipath protocol capable of replacing STP in Nexus-based networks. Under FabricPath's hood, a link-state routing protocol called IS-IS (Intermediate System–to–Intermediate System) acts as the control plane decision mechanism to forward Ethernet frames from one FabricPath switch to another (using up to 16 different paths).

With active participation from Cisco engineering, the Internet Engineering Task Force (IETF) publishes RFCs 6325 and 6326 in 2011, defining TRILL as a standard and IS-IS as its underlying routing protocol. At the time of this writing, work is still being done to define remaining TRILL mechanisms. Cisco is fully committed to these efforts and has intentionally derived FabricPath from TRILL to support both protocols in the future.

Note This is not a new strategy for Cisco. The company has always been recognized for its innovation and is used to deploying brand new technology (ISL, HSRP, and PVST+, for example) in its products before standards were even available (IEEE 802.1Q, VRRP, and MST, respectively). After publication, these standards were included in Cisco devices through software or hardware upgrades.

FabricPath interoperates with STP-based switches through standard trunk and access Ethernet interfaces. And, as you will learn shortly, a FabricPath network can provide Layer 2 multipathing to non-FabricPath switches through a virtualization technology called *virtual PortChannel Plus (vPC+)*.

FabricPath Data Plane

When a FabricPath network is fully operational, an Ethernet switch does not forward frames based on destination MAC addresses as transparent bridges would normally do. A FabricPath switch forwards frames based on a *Switch ID* field on a FabricPath header.

The FabricPath frame is used to encapsulate standard Ethernet frames that traverse a FabricPath network, as shown in Figure 6-22.

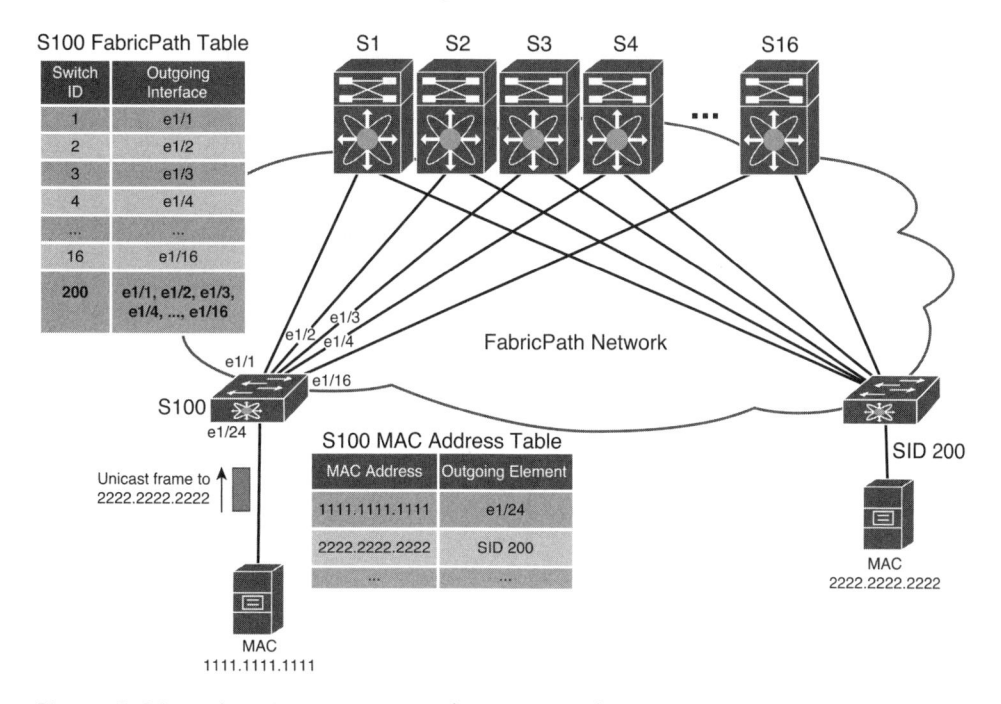

Figure 6-22 *Ethernet Frame Forwarding over a FabricPath Network*

A frame sent from MAC address 1111.1111.1111 to MAC address 2222.2222.2222, and illustrated in Figure 6-22, goes through the following actions during its complete trajectory:

1. When the frame arrives at a *classical* STP Ethernet interface (Ethernet 1/24) on switch S100, it uses its MAC address table to determine where to forward the frame.

2. The MAC address table does not have an interface on the 2222.2222.2222 entry, but a FabricPath switch ID (200) that belongs to switch S200.

3. Consequently, a *FabricPath table* is used to direct the frame to S200. The frame is encapsulated with a FabricPath header and forwarded to one of the available outgoing interfaces that can be used to reach S200 (switches S1 to S16, respectively).

4. These *spine* switches (S1 to S16) use the switch ID in the FabricPath header to forward the frame.

5. When the frame arrives at S200, this switch strips the FabricPath header from the frame and forwards the original frame to 2222.2222.2222.

As a final result, Ethernet traffic from switch S100 to S200 is load balanced among the links that are available in the FabricPath network.

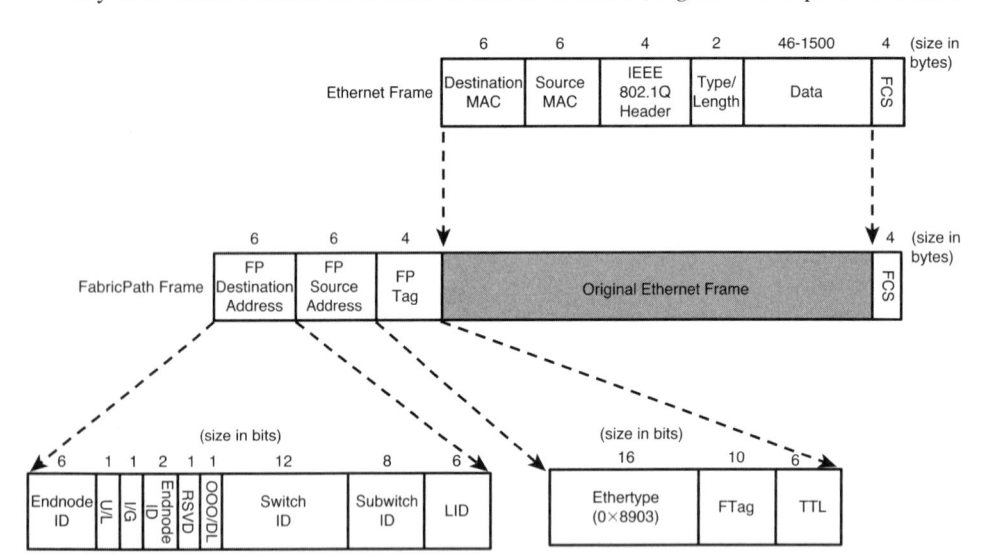

If you are curious about the FabricPath header structure, Figure 6-23 depicts its details.

Figure 6-23 *FabricPath Header*

As shown in the figure, the FabricPath header is comprised of three basic elements: two 6-byte addresses (destination and source) and a tag. Their detailed field description unconceals some of the present and future features of FabricPath:

- **Endnode ID:** This field is reserved for future use. In broadcast and multicast frames, the destination address (DA) Endnode ID field receives the destination MAC address from the original Ethernet frame.

- **Universal or Local (U/L) bit:** Set in all unicast frames, this indicates that MAC addresses have local significance in FabricPath switches that deploy STP ports (FabricPath *edge* switches).

- **Individual or Group (I/G) bit:** This bit identifies whether the frame has one or multiple destinations.

- **Out-of-order or Don't Learn (OOO/DL):** This bit is not used at the time of this writing.

- Switch ID: This is a unique number that identifies each switch in a FabricPath network. It is used for forwarding within a FabricPath network. It populates both MAC and FabricPath tables on edge switches.

- **Subswitch ID:** This field can identify a group of hosts or devices in a FabricPath switch.

- **Local ID (LID):** This value identifies a destination (or source) interface in a FabricPath switch where the frame is directed (or originated).

- **Ethertype:** All FabricPath frames have the value 0x8903 in this field.

- **Forwarding Tag (Ftag):** This tag is a unique number identifying the FabricPath *topology* (for unicast frames) or the *distribution tree* (for multidestination frames). These concepts will be discussed in the next section.

- **Time-to-Live (TTL):** This value is decremented at each switch hop to prevent frames from looping infinitely (if you remember, standard Ethernet does not possess this safety mechanism).

FabricPath Control Plane

Antoine Lavoisier once said, "Nothing is lost, nothing is created, all is transformed." As you will learn in this section, the FabricPath control plane sticks firmly to the French chemist's philosophy.

When a switch starts its FabricPath processes, it automatically assigns to itself a switch ID. This identifier uniquely represents the switch in the FabricPath network.

FabricPath *core interfaces* form adjacencies with other FabricPath switches through the well-known routing protocol IS-IS. If a switch ID conflict is detected in the network, the affected switch automatically chooses another identifier value until all FabricPath switches have distinct switch IDs.

Tip You can also manually assign a switch ID to a FabricPath switch. Obviously, static identifier conflicts must be solved manually.

IS-IS can inform other peers about values other than IP subnets. In a FabricPath network, IS-IS exchanges reachable switch IDs and completely replaces Spanning Tree Protocol with several advantages:

- Using the Shortest Path First (SPF) algorithm, IS-IS allows the use of multiple equal-cost paths between two points of the network.

- It has a faster convergence when compared to any version of STP.

A *topology* represents a subset of interfaces in a FabricPath network, where an interface can belong to more than one topology and each VLAN (or group of VLANs) only belongs to a single topology. Through FabricPath topologies, it is possible to choose the switches and links that each VLAN will be able to use within a network.

Tip It is valid to compare a topology to an instance in MST networks.

FabricPath uses *multidestination trees* to forward broadcast, multicast, and unknown unicast frames inside a topology. These trees are automatically generated and are limited to the capacity of the devices that are part of the network.

Figure 6-24 depicts two multidestination trees from the FabricPath network shown in Figure 6-22.

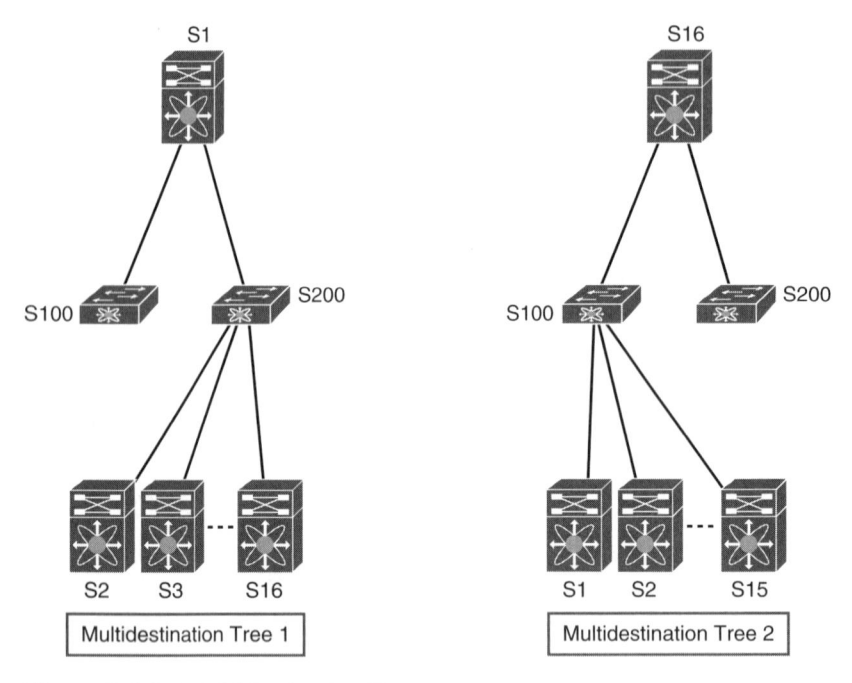

Figure 6-24 *Multidestination Trees*

At the time of this writing, FabricPath-enabled Nexus switches support up to two topologies and two multidestination trees (except Nexus 7000 switches, which support one topology and two multidestination trees). Nexus switches assign flooding and broadcast to one multidestination tree and load-balance multicast traffic between both trees through a hashing algorithm.

Tip Each multidestination tree has a *root switch* that is elected based on the following order of parameters: root priority, system MAC address, and switch ID. Changing these parameters, you can influence the formation of the trees in a FabricPath network.

FabricPath core switches do not need to learn MAC addresses, because they only use the FabricPath header (destination switch ID) in their forwarding decision. A method called *conversational MAC learning* is deployed to populate the MAC address table in the edge switches. Inside these devices

- Local MAC addresses are learned normally in the classical Ethernet ports.

- Remote MAC addresses (from other edge switches) are learned if, and only if, *the destination MAC addresses in the received frames are already in the local edge switch MAC address table.*

Figure 6-25 illustrates FabricPath's conversational learning in two distinct scenarios.

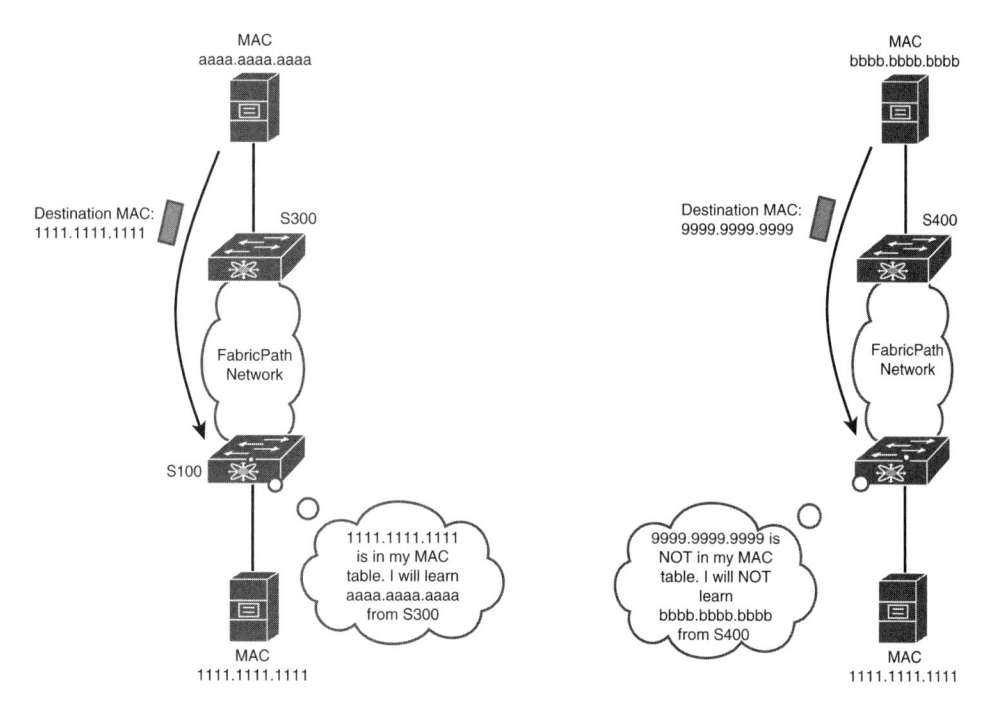

Figure 6-25 *FabricPath Conversational Learning*

In the left scenario, switch S100 inserts the MAC address aaaa.aaaa.aaaa (received from S200) into its MAC address table because the frame is directed to a known local MAC address (1111.1111.1111). In this case, conversational learning assumes that both servers are having a bidirectional exchange of frames.

Conversely, in the other scenario, S100 does not populate its MAC address table with MAC bbbb.bbbb.bbbb (received from S300) because this frame was not sent to a locally learned address. As a result, conversational learning does not waste a MAC address table entry with unknown unicast frames whose destination MAC addresses do not belong to the local STP network.

Tip Broadcast frames sourced from the FabricPath network will not populate the MAC address table in edge switches either.

Compared to transparent bridge learning, FabricPath's conversational learning definitely decreases the number of learned MAC addresses on edge switches. As a consequence, FabricPath translates Layer 2 networks into more scalable, simple, and highly available Ethernet *fabrics*.

FabricPath and Spanning Tree Protocol

Before I explain how a FabricPath network can provide Layer 2 active-active paths to standard switches, first you must learn how this protocol interoperates with STP networks.

There's nothing better than an example: In Figure 6-26, you can see the FabricPath network that will be used to explore this protocol interaction.

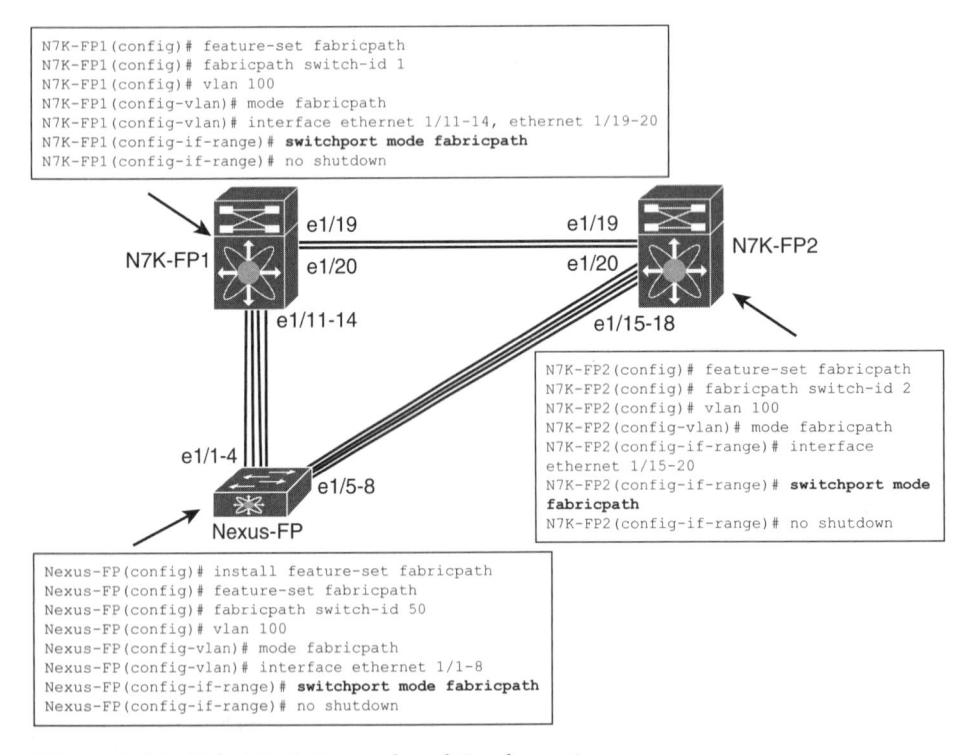

```
N7K-FP1(config)# feature-set fabricpath
N7K-FP1(config)# fabricpath switch-id 1
N7K-FP1(config)# vlan 100
N7K-FP1(config-vlan)# mode fabricpath
N7K-FP1(config-vlan)# interface ethernet 1/11-14, ethernet 1/19-20
N7K-FP1(config-if-range)# switchport mode fabricpath
N7K-FP1(config-if-range)# no shutdown
```

```
N7K-FP2(config)# feature-set fabricpath
N7K-FP2(config)# fabricpath switch-id 2
N7K-FP2(config)# vlan 100
N7K-FP2(config-vlan)# mode fabricpath
N7K-FP2(config-if-range)# interface ethernet 1/15-20
N7K-FP2(config-if-range)# switchport mode fabricpath
N7K-FP2(config-if-range)# no shutdown
```

```
Nexus-FP(config)# install feature-set fabricpath
Nexus-FP(config)# feature-set fabricpath
Nexus-FP(config)# fabricpath switch-id 50
Nexus-FP(config)# vlan 100
Nexus-FP(config-vlan)# mode fabricpath
Nexus-FP(config-vlan)# interface ethernet 1/1-8
Nexus-FP(config-if-range)# switchport mode fabricpath
Nexus-FP(config-if-range)# no shutdown
```

Figure 6-26 *FabricPath Network and Configuration*

The figure also portrays a basic FabricPath configuration for switches N7K-FP1, N7K-FP2, and Nexus-FP. In summary, this configuration requires the execution of the following steps:

1. Enable the FabricPath feature set, because it is comprised of a set of processes. Other switches, such as Nexus 5500, require the installing the feature set before its enablement.

2. Optionally change the switch ID. This is step is executed here to make the outputs clearer.

3. Configure the VLANs that will be used on the FabricPath network (VLAN 100, in our scenario).

4. Include interfaces in the FabricPath network through the **switchport mode fabric-path** command.

Example 6-22 illustrates the immediate results from the configuration shown in Figure 6-26.

Example 6-22 *Interfaces, Multipathing, and STP Status in a FabricPath Switch*

```
! Verifying the FabricPath interface status
Nexus-FP#  show interface ethernet 1/1-8 brief

--------------------------------------------------------------------
Ethernet       VLAN     Type Mode    Status Reason       Speed      Port
Interface                                                            Ch #
--------------------------------------------------------------------
Eth1/1         1        eth  f-path  up     none         10G(D)     --
Eth1/2         1        eth  f-path  up     none         10G(D)     --
Eth1/3         1        eth  f-path  up     none         10G(D)     --
Eth1/4         1        eth  f-path  up     none         10G(D)     --
Eth1/5         1        eth  f-path  up     none         10G(D)     --
Eth1/6         1        eth  f-path  up     none         10G(D)     --
Eth1/7         1        eth  f-path  up     none         10G(D)     --
Eth1/8         1        eth  f-path  up     none         10G(D)     -
! Checking the available layer 2 unicast paths to other FabricPath switches
Nexus-FP# show fabricpath route
FabricPath Unicast Route Table
'a/b/c' denotes ftag/switch-id/subswitch-id
'[x/y]' denotes [admin distance/metric]
ftag 0 is local ftag
subswitch-id 0 is default subswitch-id



FabricPath Unicast Route Table for Topology-Default
! Route to itself
0/50/0, number of next-hops: 0
     via ---- , [60/0], 0 day/s 00:17:50, local
! Four routes to N7K-FP1
1/1/0, number of next-hops: 4
     via Eth1/1, [115/40], 0 day/s 00:18:05, isis_fabricpath-default
     via Eth1/2, [115/40], 0 day/s 00:18:05, isis_fabricpath-default
```

```
              via Eth1/3, [115/40], 0 day/s 00:18:05, isis_fabricpath-default
              via Eth1/4, [115/40], 0 day/s 00:18:05, isis_fabricpath-default
! Four routes to N7K-FP2
1/2/0, number of next-hops: 4
              via Eth1/5, [115/40], 0 day/s 00:03:15, isis_fabricpath-default
              via Eth1/6, [115/40], 0 day/s 00:03:15, isis_fabricpath-default
              via Eth1/7, [115/40], 0 day/s 00:03:15, isis_fabricpath-default
              via Eth1/8, [115/40], 0 day/s 00:03:15, isis_fabricpath-default
! Making sure this VLAN is not running STP
Nexus-FP# show spanning-tree vlan 100
Spanning tree instance(s) for vlan does not exist.
```

With these simple commands, all FabricPath interfaces are active between the switches (something that would not happen if you were using STP without PortChannels and vPC). Also, VLAN 100 does not have an STP instance because FabricPath has replaced this protocol in the network.

Tip As demonstrated in Example 6-22, FabricPath has a default administrative distance of 115 and assigns 40 as the default cost for 10 Gigabit Ethernet connections.

Edge switches permit the connection of a FabricPath and STP networks through classical Ethernet interfaces. In this situation, the FabricPath network appears as a single bridge to all STP switches. This *virtual STP bridge* can be identified with the MAC address c84c.75fa.6000, which is included in all BPDUs sent to STP switches.

Figure 6-27 explains how our FabricPath network is viewed from an STP-enabled switch perspective.

Note All STP interfaces are configured as trunks allowed for all VLANs.

Example 6-23 shows that, in VLAN 100, Nexus-STP is the root and, as expected, all three connections to the FabricPath network are in the forwarding state.

Example 6-23 *Verifying the STP Status in Nexus-STP*

```
Nexus-STP# show spanning-tree vlan 100

VLAN0100
  Spanning tree enabled protocol rstp
  Root ID    Priority    32868
             Address     0005.73ca.f73c
             This bridge is the root
[output suppressed]
```

```
Interface         Role Sts Cost      Prio.Nbr Type
---------------- ---- --- --------- -------- ------------------------
Eth1/1            Desg FWD 2         128.129  P2p
Eth1/5            Desg FWD 2         128.133  P2p
Eth1/9            Desg FWD 2         128.137  P2p
```

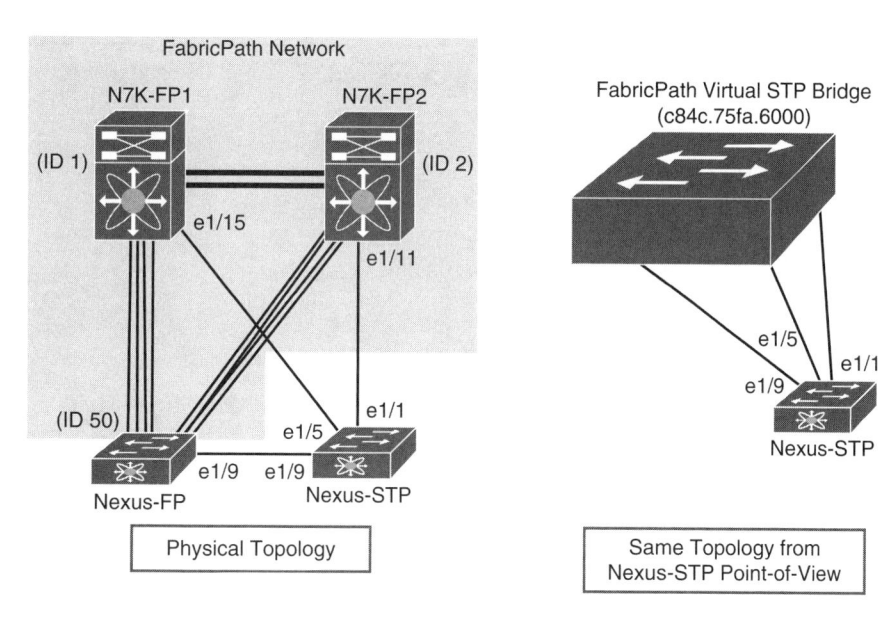

Figure 6-27 *FabricPath and STP Interaction*

However, on the FabricPath switches, all three interfaces are blocked because of protocol inconsistency, as shown in Example 6-24.

Example 6-24 *STP Status in N7K-FP1*

```
! Verifying the inconsistent ports in VLAN 100 STP instance
N7K-FP1# sh spanning-tree vlan 100 inconsistentports

Name            Interface        Inconsistency
--------------- ---------------- ------------------
VLAN0100        Eth1/15          L2 Gateway Backbone Port Inconsistent
```

Interfaces Ethernet 1/11 on switch N7K-FP1 and Ethernet 1/9 on switch Nexus-FP are in the same condition for one reason: **loop avoidance**. In a hypothetical scenario where all these ports were forwarding traffic, you can easily picture how a broadcast frame could form a loop entering and leaving the FabricPath network through Nexus-STP.

To enable traffic between both networks, you must guarantee that the FabricPath network is *selected as the root* for the connected STP network.

Example 6-25 shows the STP status for VLAN 100 in Nexus-STP, after the **spanning-tree vlan 100 priority 8192** command is executed on each FabricPath-enabled switch.

Example 6-25 *Nexus-STP Status After the FabricPath Switches Are Configured as Root*

```
! Verifying how STP converged after the priority change in the FabricPath switches
Nexus-STP# show spanning-tree vlan 100

VLAN0100
  Spanning tree enabled protocol rstp
  Root ID    Priority    8292
! FabricPath virtual STP bridge is the root
             Address     c84c.75fa.6000
[output suppressed]
Interface       Role Sts Cost      Prio.Nbr Type
---------------- ---- --- --------- -------- ------------------------

Eth1/1          Root FWD 2         128.129  P2p
Eth1/5          Altn BLK 2         128.133  P2p
Eth1/9          Altn BLK 2         128.137  P2p
```

This built-in "safety mechanism" against loops also helps to position FabricPath as an interesting option for Layer 2 extension between data centers. As I have mentioned before, Chapter 8 will discuss this in much more depth, with the various alternatives for such connections.

Virtual PortChannel Plus

The FabricPath virtual bridge is a convenient structure to build active-active paths for STP switches. Actually, a feature called *virtual PortChannel Plus (vPC+)* allows an IEEE 802.3ad device to aggregate classical Ethernet links to a pair of FabricPath edge switches.

vPC and vPC+ have many similarities, such as the presence of peer link and peer keepalive links. However, a vPC+ is created with the help of yet another virtual element: an *emulated FabricPath switch*, which actually performs the aggregation per se. As you will verify at the end of this section, this emulated switch guarantees the load balancing of frames directed to virtual PortChannels through the FabricPath network.

Figure 6-28 portrays how vPC+ is viewed from two different perspectives: FabricPath network an STP-enabled switch. In this situation, the STP switch is deploying link aggregation to two FabricPath switches (N7K-FP1 and N7K-FP2).

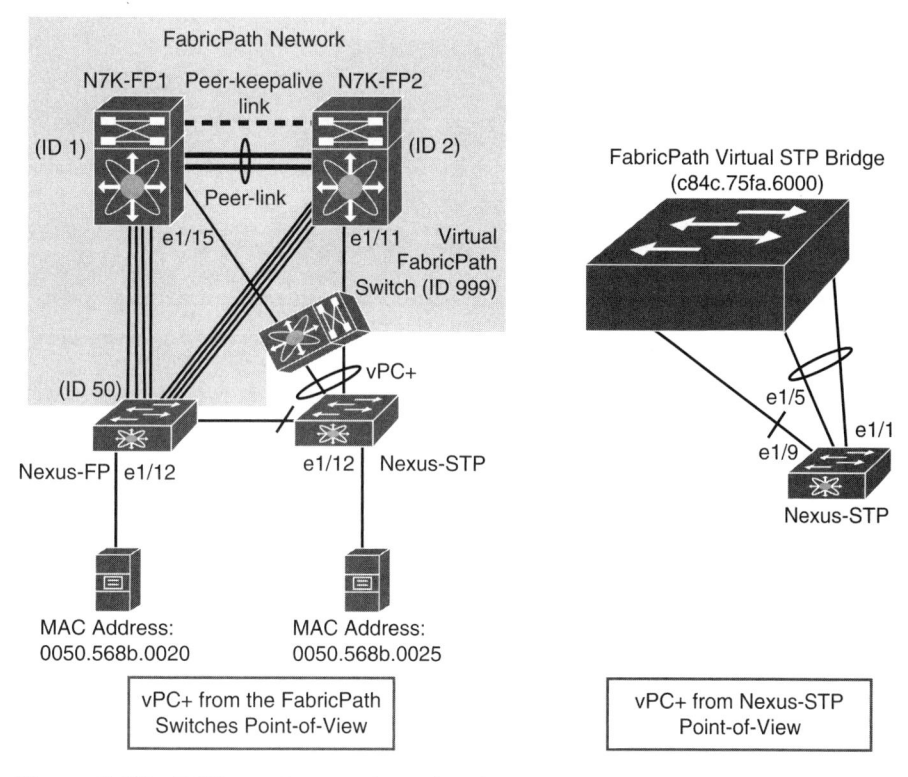

Figure 6-28 *Different Perspectives of vPC+*

The configuration of a vPC+ closely follows the steps presented in the earlier section "Configuring Virtual PortChannels" with a few exceptions:

- The creation of a virtual FabricPath switch (switch ID 999 in Figure 6-28).
- The peer link is comprised of FabricPath interfaces.

Example 6-26 uncovers the vPC+ configuration in N7K-FP1. This configuration is very similar in N7K-FP2 (I will comment the differences in the same example).

Example 6-26 *vPC+ Configuration in N7K-FP1*

```
! Verifying the features necessary for vPC+ implementation
N7K-FP1# show running-config | include feature
feature-set fabricpath
feature lacp
feature vpc
N7K-FP1# show running-config vpc
[output suppressed]
! Step 1: Configuring the vPC domain
```

278 Data Center Virtualization Fundamentals

```
vpc domain 400
! Configuring virtual FabricPath switch is part of Step 1
  fabricpath switch-id 999
! Step 2: In N7K-FP2, the peer-keepalive destination is 10.0.8.172 (N7K-FP1 mgmt0 IP
address)
  peer-keepalive destination 10.0.8.182
[output suppressed]
N7K-FP1# show running-config interface port-channel 40, port-channel 80
output suppressed]
! Step 3: Configuring the vPC+ peer-link (interfaces e1/19 and e1/20 on both
switches)
interface port-channel40
  switchport
  switchport mode fabricpath
  vpc peer-link
! Step 4: Configuring the PortChannel that will be reused in the vPC+ (interface
e1/15 on N7K1 and e1/11 on N7K-2)
interface port-channel80
  switchport
  switchport mode trunk
  vpc 80
```

These configuration commands establish a vPC+ for Nexus-STP. Example 6-27 shows the STP status within this device after PortChannel 80 is configured to aggregate the interfaces that are connected to N7K-1 and N7K-2 (Ethernet 1/5 and 1/1, respectively).

Example 6-27 *STP Status in N5K-STP*

```
Nexus-STP# show spanning-tree vlan 100

VLAN0100
  Spanning tree enabled protocol rstp
  Root ID    Priority    8292
! FabricPath virtual STP bridge remains the Root
             Address     c84c.75fa.6000
             Cost        1
             Port        4175 (port-channel80)
[output suppressed]
Interface        Role Sts Cost      Prio.Nbr Type
---------------- ---- --- --------- -------- ------------------------
Po80             Root FWD 1         128.4175 P2p
Eth1/9           Altn BLK 2         128.137  P2p
```

> **Tip** Similarly to virtual PortChannels, a vPC+ also provides active-active capability for gateway redundancy protocols such as HSRP. Cisco also recommends that a separate Layer 3 link is configured for routing from the vPC+ peer devices.

Now, I will exercise the FabricPath concepts with one simple experiment executed over the established FabricPath network.

First, two servers are connected to classical Ethernet interfaces on Nexus-FP and Nexus-STP (MAC addresses are, respectively, 0050.568b.0020, and 0050.568b.0025). Then, their access interfaces belong to VLAN 100, and they start to exchange ICMP echo packets with each other using the same IP subnet.

Example 6-28 illustrates the MAC address table and the FabricPath routing table in Nexus-FP immediately after they have started their bidirectional "conversation."

Example 6-28 *Nexus-FP MAC Address Table and FabricPath Routes*

```
Nexus-FP# show mac address-table vlan 100
Legend: * - primary entry, G - Gateway MAC, (R) - Routed MAC, O - Overlay MAC
   age - seconds since last seen,+ - primary entry using vPC Peer-Link
    VLAN    MAC Address     Type    age   Secure NTFY Ports/SWID.SSID.LID
---------+---------------+--------+-----+------+----+------------------
! This is a local MAC addresses
*  100     0050.568b.0020 dynamic  0        F    F   Eth1/12
! This is a remote MAC addresses included in the table due to
conversational learning. Observe that switch ID 999 owns the MAC
address.
*  100     0050.568b.0025 dynamic  0        F    F   999.11.417
! Checking the FabricPath Routing Table
Nexus-FP# show fabricpath route
[output suppressed]
FabricPath Unicast Route Table for Topology-Default

0/50/0, number of next-hops: 0
        via ---- , [60/0], 0 day/s 02:28:52, local
! Frames to N7K-1 are load balanced over four links
1/1/0, number of next-hops: 4
        via Eth1/1, [115/40], 0 day/s 02:29:07, isis_fabricpath-default
        via Eth1/2, [115/40], 0 day/s 02:29:07, isis_fabricpath-default
        via Eth1/3, [115/40], 0 day/s 02:29:07, isis_fabricpath-default
        via Eth1/4, [115/40], 0 day/s 02:29:07, isis_fabricpath-default
! Frames to N7K-2 are also load balanced over four links
1/2/0, number of next-hops: 4
        via Eth1/5, [115/40], 0 day/s 02:14:17, isis_fabricpath-default
        via Eth1/6, [115/40], 0 day/s 02:14:17, isis_fabricpath-default
```

```
              via Eth1/7, [115/40], 0 day/s 02:14:17, isis_fabricpath-default
              via Eth1/8, [115/40], 0 day/s 02:14:17, isis_fabricpath-default
! Frames to vPC+ emulated switch are load balanced over eight links
1/999/0, number of next-hops: 8
              via Eth1/1, [115/40], 0 day/s 00:34:53, isis_fabricpath-default
              via Eth1/2, [115/40], 0 day/s 00:34:53, isis_fabricpath-default
[output suppressed]
              via Eth1/8, [115/40], 0 day/s 00:34:53, isis_fabricpath-default
```

Example 6-28 explains why the emulated switch (ID 999) is necessary when a FabricPath network deploys vPC+. If frames originated from the vPC+ were learned in Nexus-FP through N7K-FP1 or N7K-FP2:

- Only half the connections would be used to reach a MAC address behind this vPC+.
- The Nexus-FP MAC address table entry would flap between N7K-FP1 and N7K-FP2 whenever a Nexus-STP–originated frame was load balanced to a different switch.

Finally, Example 6-29 examines the Nexus-STP MAC address table to explain how FabricPath's conversational learning was deployed on Nexus-FP.

Example 6-29 *Nexus-STP MAC Address Table*

```
Nexus-STP# show mac address-table vlan 100
Legend:      * - primary entry, G - Gateway MAC, (R) - Routed MAC, O - Overlay MAC
             age - seconds since last seen,+ - primary entry using vPC Peer-Link
   VLAN     MAC Address      Type     age     Secure NTFY    Ports/SWID.SSID.LID
---------+-----------------+--------+-------+------+----+------------------
! This local MAC address was not learnt in Nexus-FP even though its host sent
several broadcasts
*  100     0015.1757.fd74   dynamic   10      F      F    Eth1/11
! This MAC address was learned over the vPC+
*  100     0050.568b.0020   dynamic   10      F      F    Po80
! This local MAC address was learned in Nexus-FP through the exchanged ICMP Echo
packets.
*  100     0050.568b.0025   dynamic   10      F      F    Eth1/12
```

Comparing Examples 6-28 and 6-29, Nexus-FP only learned a MAC address (0050.568b.0025) that was effectively exchanging frames with a local host (0050.568b.0020). Other MAC addresses (such as 0015.1757.fd74) were not learned in Nexus-FP, even after ARP broadcasts were sent from this address.

Use Case: Evolution of Network PODs

PODs (or "pool of devices") are one of most useful tools for modular data center designs. A POD is defined as a set of equipment grouped in a reusable unit that can be deployed in a data center.

A POD can include servers, switches, routers, storage arrays, cabling, racks, cooling systems, and other devices that are designed to work together. The main advantages of using PODs in data center designs are

- **Replicability:** A POD is a fairly independent design unit that can be redeployed whenever necessary (including in different data centers).
- **Predictability:** It is possible to estimate the physical characteristics of a POD, such as weight, occupied space, cooling needs, and power consumption, before any equipment is acquired.
- **Flexibility:** PODs can be redesigned regularly to facilitate the adoption of new technologies in specific environments, and not in the entire data center.

A data center can have different types of PODs, depending on its characteristics and expansion requirements. For example, a data center can deploy one POD for high-end servers and a different one for low-end servers. Because these PODs have different physical characteristics, the data center facilities can be *gradually prepared* before the installation of each POD.

A *network POD* represents the concept of PODs applied only to data center network devices. Within a network POD, it is usually expected that servers can be able to communicate directly. Hence, it is common to design network PODs as Layer 2 networks formed with two layers of switches (aggregation and access).

Note Network PODs do not necessarily represent aggregation and access switches sharing a Layer 2 network. As a variation example, a data center can use multiple instances of a POD with a single pair of Layer 3 switches each. As I have commented, PODs are flexible design units that can be customized for specific needs.

There is little doubt that the virtualization technologies explained in this chapter can drastically accelerate the evolution of network PODs. And to demonstrate it, I will use a real-world scenario adapted for learning purposes. But first, I need you to imagine the following scenario (enter cue to flashback effects sounds).

After the successful network virtualization designs you have deployed in the company where you worked (and chronicled in Chapter 3), you decide to invest in a network consulting career.

Your first client is a big financial company whose network team employs a friend of yours. Its data center network has *four network PODs*, where each one of them has two aggregation switches (equipped with server load balancing and firewall modules) and 50 access switches with two 10 Gigabit Ethernet uplinks to the aggregation switches.

Because these devices use legacy Spanning Tree Protocol, half of their 10 Gigabit Ethernet uplinks are not being used, and each time a reconvergence happens, the network becomes unavailable during precious seconds.

The size of each network POD was limited by the number of ports on the aggregation switches, and because of some past decisions, the PODs are interconnected through a Layer 3 network. The team's main concern with this design is the fact that it does not allow the insertion of servers from distinct PODs in the same VLAN. That characteristic alone brings the challenge of controlling the number of servers per POD and, at the same time, grouping new servers in a POD.

The company needs you to help it design a new network POD that encompasses all the servers in the same Layer 2 domain, and that can use the uplinks more efficiently.

The network POD design you presented to the company is depicted in Figure 6-29.

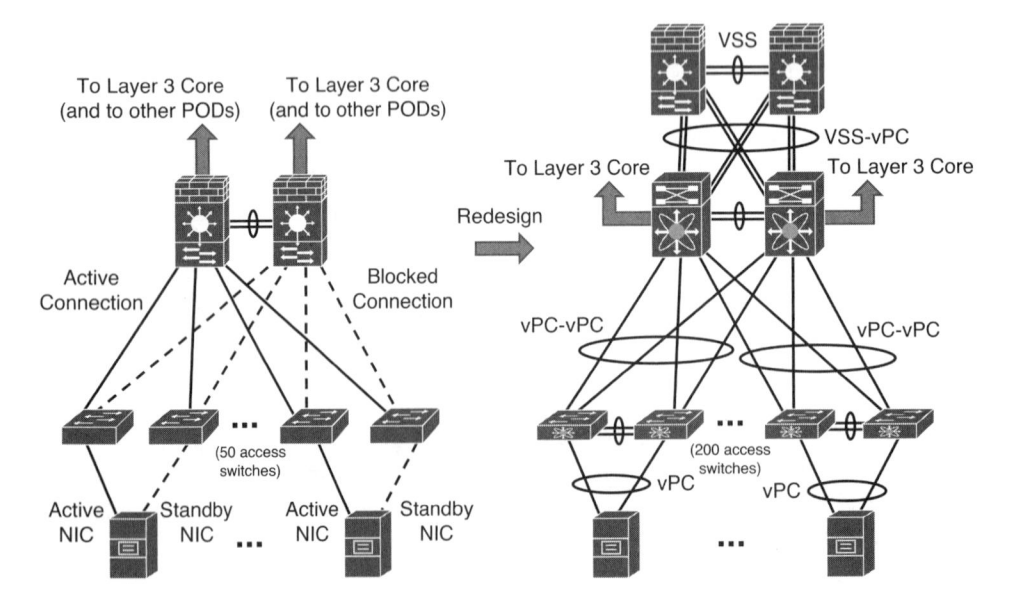

Figure 6-29 *Network POD Redesign with vPCs*

In the new network POD, you have deployed two new Nexus 7000s as the new consolidated aggregation switches. Their number of ports is more than enough to support the 200 access switches from the previous PODs.

You also recommend replacing the access switches for any Nexus platform to deploy *double-sided vPCs* with the aggregation switches. This connection allows all four uplinks from the access switches to remain active and deliver 40 Gbps of bidirectional traffic to the connected servers.

Each pair of access switches is also able to deploy virtual PortChannels to their connected servers, as long as they support standard link aggregation (IEEE 802.3ad). This additional capability can double the available bandwidth to each server and reduce the switchover latency in case of an Ethernet connection failure.

Because the original aggregation devices were Catalyst 6500 switches with ACE and ASA modules, you suggest that the company reuse some of them to build a Virtual Switch System (VSS). This structure behaves as a single virtual chassis that can aggregate links from each switch and is interoperable with a vPC provided by the Nexus aggregation switches. Your design also recommends that the original service modules (and their virtual contexts) are consolidated in these new *service chassis*.

> **Note** The number of links between the Nexus 7000 and the Catalyst 6500 must consider the aggregate performance of the service modules and switch failure scenarios.

The network team is enthusiastically satisfied with your design. They particularly enjoyed how the new RSTP turned into a very simple structure, with only one logical connection between pairs of switches. They also appreciated that the new POD will be able to load-balance routed traffic as well, because both aggregation switches can serve as active HSRP default gateways to all the connected servers.

That is why, two years later, your friend contacts you again, requesting a second modernization in the company's data center network. In his words, your first redesign was considered a true breakaway from the data center because it enabled the adoption of a series of new technologies, including *server virtualization*.

He explains that the increasing adoption of this technology was causing some collateral effects on the network, such as

- With more bandwidth being generated at the servers, the uplinks between aggregation and access switches were almost saturated.
- Each physical server now has multiple MAC addresses (at least one for each virtual server). And because these servers share the same VLAN, all the access switches are overusing their MAC address table with these MAC addresses.

The company wants to hire you to solve these design problems and help it scale its network again. After it agrees to pay your present fees (which are much higher after all these years), you accept the job.

Analyzing the team requirements, you realize that FabricPath, the Cisco Layer 2 multipath protocol (that was not available when you did the first redesign), might be very appropriate in this new project.

Within a couple of weeks, you present the new design portrayed in Figure 6-30.

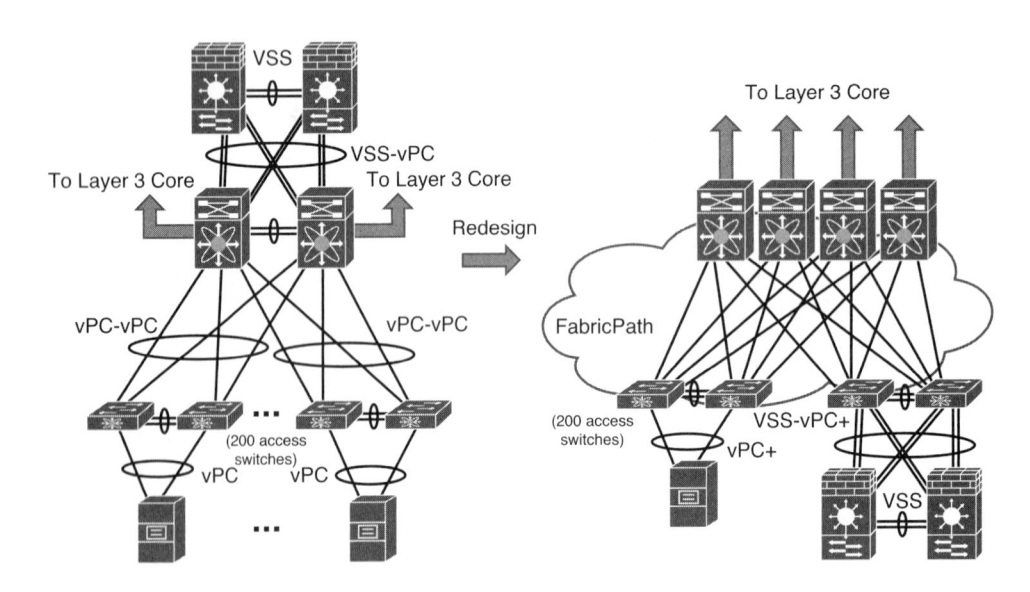

Figure 6-30 *Network POD Redesign with FabricPath and vPC+*

Your new design adds two new Nexus 7000s, also connected to the access switches, and enables FabricPath on all switches (after a software upgrade and license install). In this new design, each pair of access switches has now up to 80 Gbps to the Nexus 7000 switch layer.

You also point out to the team that FabricPath's conversational learning greatly reduces the number of learned MAC addresses in the access switches. With this capability, each access switch will only insert on the tables remote MAC addresses that are actually exchanging traffic with a directly connected server.

The new design also brings the following advantages as bonus:

- Servers continue to aggregate links to the access switches through vPC+.

- All the spine switches can simultaneously be the default gateway for the servers using *Gateway Load Balancing Protocol (GLBP)* as the first-hop routing protocol.

- The VSS service chassis can still provide load balancing and firewall services for the entire POD if they are connected to a pair of access switches (the number of links in the VSS-vPC+ connection must still consider the service module's performance and switch failure scenarios).

- Except in the service chassis connection, STP is no longer running in the network POD.

After this project proves to be a complete success, you continue to interview more candidates for the positions that will soon be available in your consulting company.

Summary

In this chapter, you have learned the following:

- EtherChannel and IEEE 802.3ad were created to transform multiple physical interfaces into a single virtual interface for STP and, therefore, aggregate Ethernet connections between two switches.

- There are different NIC teaming methods to control the behavior of redundant server connections, including standard link aggregation.

- Technologies such as StackWise and VSS have provided cross-switch aggregation to other devices through the creation of a single virtual switch.

- Virtual PortChannels (vPC) are an NX-OS capability that permits the aggregation of links to two different switches.

- FabricPath, the Cisco Layer 2 multipath protocol, appears as a single virtual STP bridge when connected to STP networks.

- FabricPath networks can provide link aggregation to STP switches and hosts through virtual PortChannel Plus (vPC+).

Figure 6-31 graphically depicts the virtualization vPCs provided to Ethernet-connected devices.

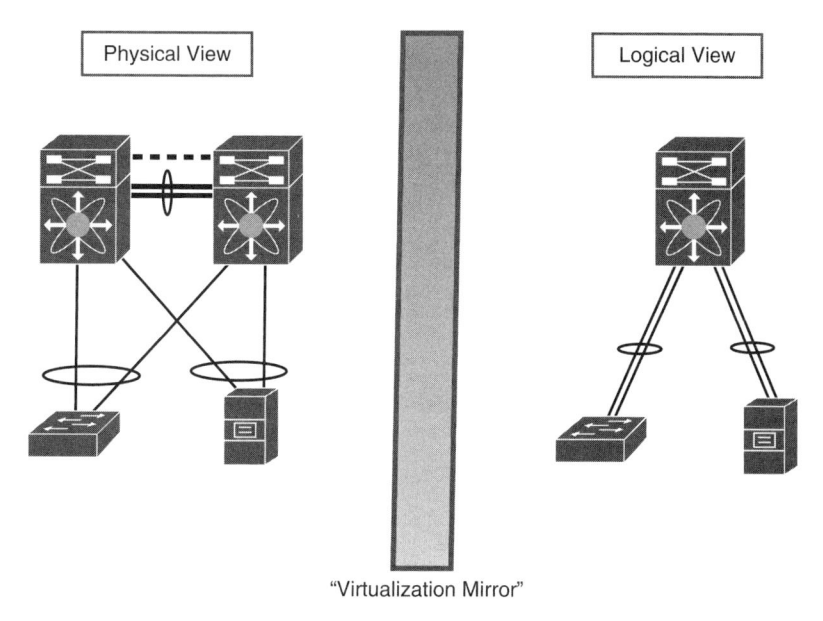

Figure 6-31 *Through the Virtualization Mirror*

Further Reading

Corbin, Kevin. Fuller, Ron. Jansen, David. *NX-OS and Cisco Nexus Switching.* Cisco Press, 2010.

Cisco NX-OS Virtual PortChannel: Fundamental Design, www.cisco.com/en/US/prod/collateral/switches/ps9441/ps9670/design_guide_c07-625857.pdf

FabricPath: Cisco's New Way of Extending Layer 2 Network Without Spanning Tree www.cisco.com/web/services/news/ts_newsletter/tech/chalktalk/archives/201012.html

FabricPath Design Guide, www.cisco.com/en/US/prod/collateral/switches/ps9441/ps9670/guide_c07-690079.html#wp9000280

Chapter 7

Virtualized Chassis with Fabric Extenders

"Form follows function – that has been misunderstood. Form and function should be one, joined in a spiritual union." (Frank Lloyd Wright)

This chapter examines Fabric Extenders and how they optimize cabling and consolidate network management in data centers. It covers the following topics:

- Server Access Models
- Understanding Fabric Extenders
- Fabric Extender Topologies
- Use Case: Mixed Access Data Center

Table 7-1 categorizes Fabric Extenders using the virtualization taxonomy described in Chapter 1, "Virtualization History and Definitions."

Table 7-1 *Fabric Extender Virtualization Classification*

Virtualization Characteristics	Fabric Extender
Emulation	Modular Ethernet access switch
Type	Pooling
Subtype	Heterogeneous
Scalability	Hardware dependent[1]
Technology Area	Networking
Subarea	Data, control, and management planes

Virtualization Characteristics	Fabric Extender
Advantages	Cabling savings, consolidated management

[1] Refer to Appendix A, "Cisco Data Center Portfolio" for more details and the Cisco online documentation for updated information.

In data center projects, cabling is usually one of the first discussed topics. Unfortunately, it is very common that cabling design is defined before any network and server decisions are made. Because of its intrinsic affinity with three traditional data center teams (facilities, network, and server), server access architecture should be a shared decision that kick-starts optimized projects within each technology division.

To exacerbate this situation, one choice in particular does not seem to have a unanimous answer: Where do you position the access switches? Both Top-of-Rack and End-of-Row connectivity models present advantages and shortcomings, and during the last decades, they have attracted as many fans as detractors within the data center community.

Innovating again with its data center portfolio, Cisco introduced the concept of Fabric Extenders with the Nexus 2000 series. These devices are not Ethernet switches, but remote linecards of a virtualized modular chassis. This virtual entity permits server access to achieve the best aspects of both connectivity models.

Fabric Extenders allow scalable topologies that were not previously possible with traditional Ethernet switches. This chapter describes the design and configuration options of these devices and shows how they can optimize the server access layer within data centers.

Server Access Models

In 2005, the Electronic Industries Alliance (EIA) and the Telecommunications Industry Association (TIA) published the first formal specification for data center infrastructure: ANSI/TIA-942. This standard was intended to provide requirements and guidelines for the design and installation of a data center and includes the facility, network, and cabling design.

This specification defines horizontal cabling as the extension from the mechanical termination of the equipment distribution area (servers) to the horizontal distribution area (switches). Compared with backbone cabling (between switches and other communication equipment), horizontal cabling presents a much higher number of connections and, therefore, has a bigger impact over the entire infrastructure.

As discussed in Chapter 2, "Data Center Network Evolution," the ANSI/TIA-942 specification supports the most popular server connectivity models: Top-of-Rack (ToR) and End-of-Row (EoR). These models define where the access layer switches are positioned in relation to the server localization, and consequently, how the horizontal cabling is designed.

In ToR-based networks, access switches (with 1 or 2 rack units) are usually installed at the top position inside the server cabinets. As a result, horizontal cabling is intrarack and can use a great variety of media such as twisted-pair, fiber, or twinax. To allow easier uplink upgrades, fiber is generally used in the redundant connections to upper-layer devices (core, aggregation, or edge routers).

Figure 7-1 depicts a Top-of-Rack access network.

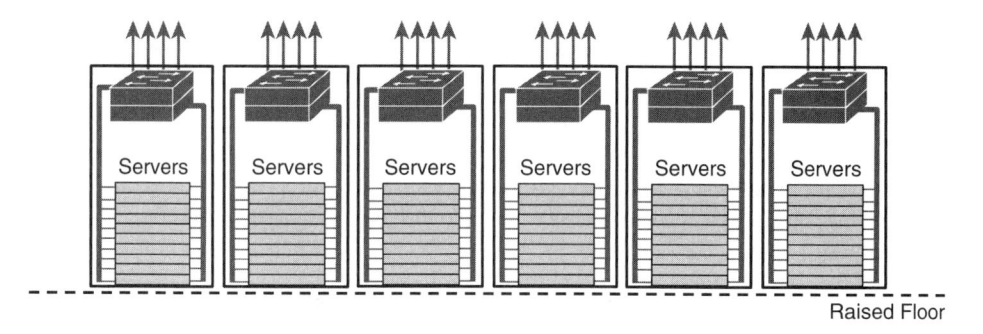

Figure 7-1 *Top-of-Rack Network*

The ToR model permits

- Savings in horizontal cabling (because cable length is reduced)
- Provisioning of fully populated server cabinets
- Per-cabinet migration of connection technologies (Gigabit Ethernet to 10 Gigabit Ethernet, for example).

The number of servers per cabinet heavily influences the port utilization in Top-of-Rack designs. ToR switches usually have 24, 32, 48, or 96 Ethernet interfaces, and if a cabinet does not support a considerable number of servers, some switch interfaces can remain unused.

To increase port utilization on low-populated cabinets, ToR designs can be adapted to other horizontal cabling variations. Figure 7-2 portrays an example where each switch is the "**Top-of-Many-Racks.**"

Note Data center power distribution and cooling capacity usually define how many servers can be installed per cabinet.

A pointed disadvantage for the ToR model is the management effort that must be spent on multiple switches. Because a data center can span hundreds or even thousands of server racks, regular operations (such as the identification of interfaces and firmware upgrades) can become quite challenging.

Alternatively, the EoR model allows the connectivity management of hundreds of servers, which are installed in a row of cabinets, with a pair of devices.

290 Data Center Virtualization Fundamentals

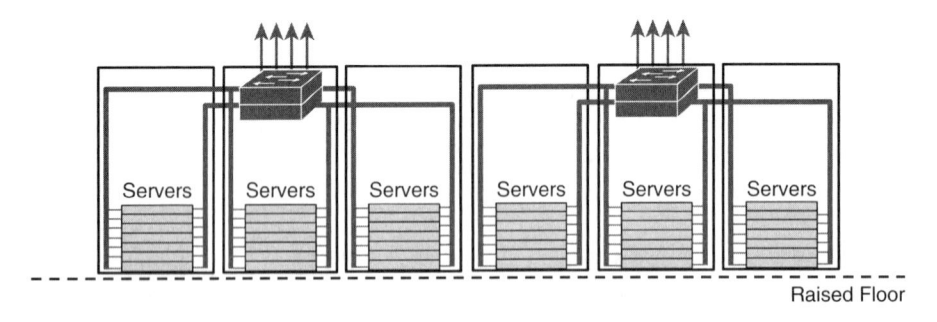

Figure 7-2 *"Top-of-Many-Racks" Network*

EoR switches are typically modular chassis with UTP-based interfaces for horizontal cabling and multiple fiber connections to the network upper-layer devices (core, aggregation, or edge routers).

Figure 7-3 illustrates an End-of-Row access network, while Figure 7-4 portrays a variation called **Middle-of-Row**. The latter decreases the average cable length, which can achieve substantial cost savings depending on the number of cabinets in each row.

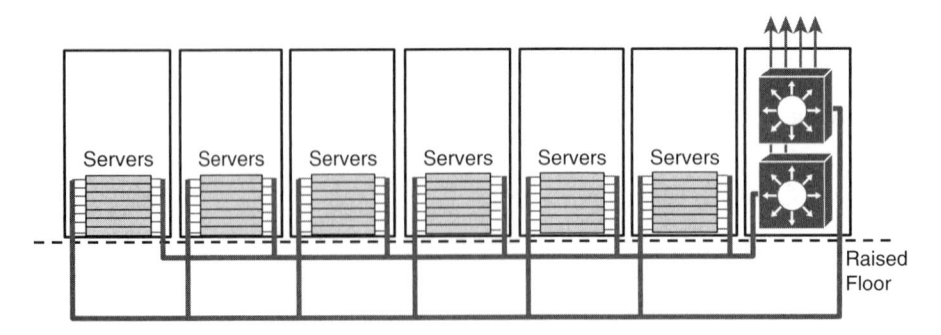

Figure 7-3 *End-of-Row*

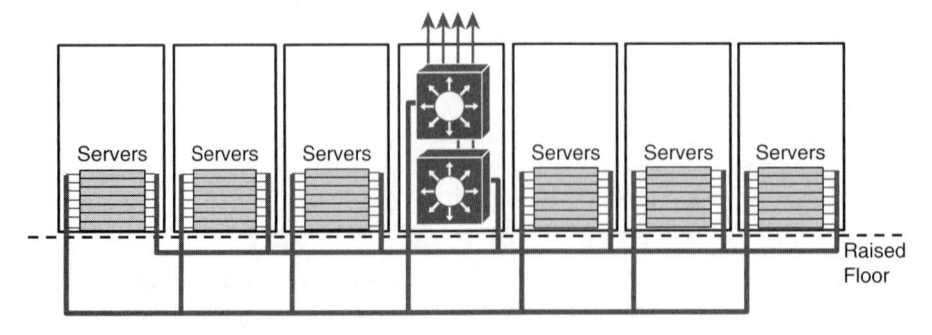

Figure 7-4 *Middle-of-Row*

EoR topologies are more flexible for low-density cabinets, because the horizontal cabling can potentially reach any rack in the row, leveraging the higher number of ports of modular chassis switches.

Cabling sprawl is the main disadvantage of EoR topologies. In a data center, excessive EoR cabling brings consequences such as

   Difficult cable management, troubleshooting, and decommission

   Blockage for air cooling (if it is installed underneath a raised access floor)

Data centers usually invest in structured cabling, preprovisioning a large part of the connections to avoid excessive cable installation. In these situations, EoR-based networks can only adopt new connectivity technologies if they were previously considered in the original cabling design.

Over the last decades, none of the access models were clearly defined as the "best" for cabling implementations. A design decision between ToR or EoR models depends on technical experience, knowledge about the server environment, and investment resources. However, best results should not be expected when there is little interaction between the facilities, network, and server teams.

Understanding Fabric Extenders

In 2009, Cisco launched the Nexus 2000 Fabric Extender series. Not conceived to be used as standalone Ethernet switches, these devices are remote linecards that are managed by a *parent* switch, such as a Nexus 5000, Nexus 6000, UCS Fabric Interconnect, or Nexus 7000 (with appropriate modules).

Fabric Extenders (or FEX) enable a data center to leverage the advantages from both ToR and EoR models because

   Multiple Fabric Extenders can be managed from a single parent switch (similar to EoR).

   A Fabric Extender can be installed inside a server cabinet and decrease cabling costs (similar to ToR).

Figure 7-5 illustrates an example of a server access topology that uses Fabric Extenders.

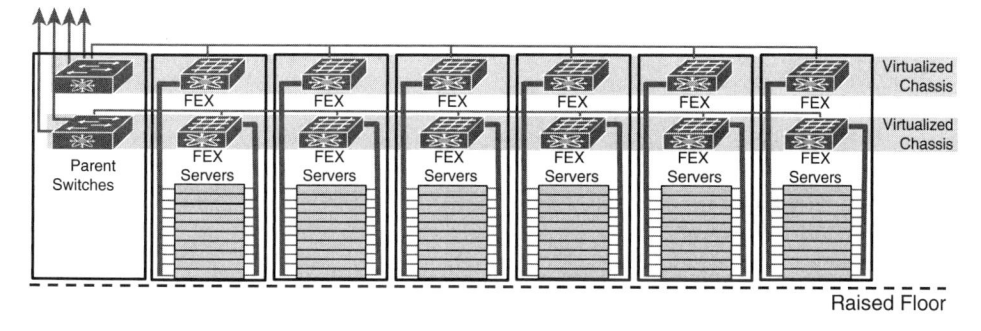

Figure 7-5 *Fabric Extender Topology*

As the figure suggests, a parent switch and multiple Fabric Extenders are elements of a virtualized modular chassis. Inside this virtual structure, every management operation is performed on the parent switch (which performs the role of a supervisor module of such chassis), and Ethernet frames are exchanged on the Fabric Extender interfaces (which represent the chassis interface modules).

The main endeavor of Fabric Extenders is to keep the configuration complexity within the parent switches and drive simplicity toward the server interfaces.

The Fabric Extender architecture introduces new types of ports to the network, including physical and virtual interfaces. Figure 7-6 deals with the interaction between the following FEX-related interfaces:

- **Fabric Interface (FIF):** This is a physical interface created to connect the Fabric Extender to a parent switch. It cannot be used for any other purpose.

- **Host Interface (HIF):** This is a standard physical Ethernet interface designed for server connection.

- **Logical Interface (LIF):** This is a data structure in the parent switch that emulates an Ethernet interface. It carries properties such as VLAN membership, access control list (ACL) labels, and STP states and is mapped to a virtual interface created on a Fabric Extender.

- **Virtual Interface (VIF):** This is a logical entity inside Fabric Extenders that receives its configuration from the parent switch, and it is used to map frames to a switch Logical Interface (LIF).

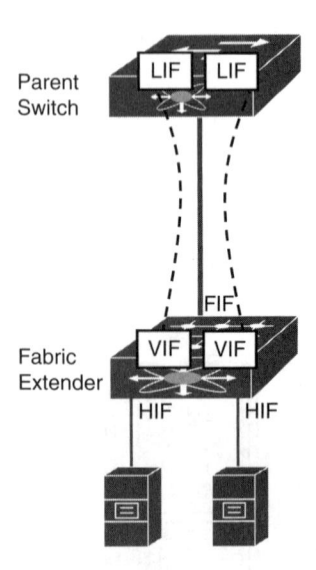

Figure 7-6 *Fabric Extender Interfaces*

The mapping between a parent switch LIF and a Fabric Extender VIF is called a *Virtual Network Link (VN-Link)*, and it is defined through a special tag that is inserted on all Ethernet frames that traverse these physical links. This extra header is called a *Virtual*

Network Tag (VNTag), and its main objective is to differentiate frames received from (or sent to) distinct FEX host interfaces.

Figure 7-7 depicts the 6-byte VNTag header implemented on Cisco Fabric Extenders.

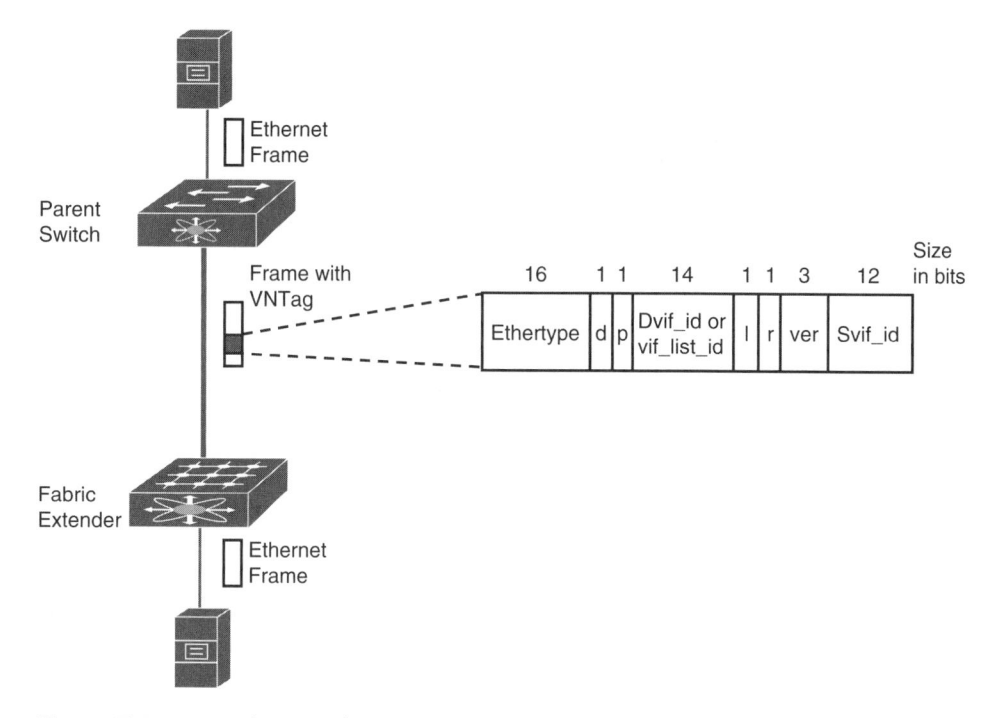

Figure 7-7 *Virtual Network Tag*

The VNTag is inserted between the source MAC address and the IEEE 802.1Q fields from the original Ethernet frame. The VNTag fields are

- **Ethertype:** This field identifies a VNTag frame. IEEE reserved the value 0x8926 for Cisco VNTag.

- **Direction bit (d):** A 0 indicates that the frame is traveling from the FEX to the parent switch. A 1 means that the frame is traveling from the parent switch to the FEX.

- **Pointer bit (p):** A 1 indicates that a Vif_list_id is included in the tag. A 0 signals that a Dvif_id is included in the frame.

- **Virtual Interface List Identifier (Vif_list_id):** This is a 14-bit value mapped to a list of host interfaces to which this frame must be forwarded.

- **Destination Virtual Interface Identifier (Dvif_id):** This is a 12-bit value mapped to a single host interface to which an Ethernet frame will be forwarded.

- **Looped bit (l):** This field indicates a multicast frame that was forwarded out the switch port and later received. In this case, the FEX checks the Svif_id and filters the frame from the corresponding port.

- **Reserved bit (r):** This bit is reserved for future use.

- **Version (ver):** This value is currently set to 0. It represents the version of the tag.

- **Source Virtual Interface Identifier (Svif_id):** This is a 12-bit value mapped to the host interface that received this frame (if it is going from the FEX to the parent switch).

When an Ethernet frame is received on a host interface,

> The Fabric Extender adds a VNtag to the frame and forwards it to one of the fabric interfaces.
>
> The parent switch recognizes the logical interface that sent the frame (through the Svif_id field), removes the tag, and forwards it according to its MAC address table.

Tip The parent switch MAC address table is updated if an unknown MAC address originates the frame received on an HIF. The new entry points to the logical interface index.

In the other direction (parent switch receives a frame that is destined to a FEX host interface),

> The parent switch reads the frame destination MAC address and forwards it to a logical interface index in its MAC address table.
>
> The switch inserts the VNtag associated with the logical interface and forwards it to the correct FEX.
>
> Receiving this frame, the FEX recognizes the associated VIF (through the Dvif_id), removes the VNTag, and sends it to the mapped host interface.

From a data plane perspective, forwarding in Fabric Extender host interfaces completely depends on the parent switch. Consequently, a frame exchange between two host interfaces always traverses the parent switch, even if they are located in the same Fabric Extender.

Note Because of its hardware simplicity, Nexus 2000 Fabric Extenders have a very low latency (as low as 500 nanoseconds at the time of this writing) when compared to traditional Ethernet switches.

Multidestination VNTag frames (such as flooding, broadcast, and multicast) are characterized with the Pointer bit and Vif_list_id fields. When such a frame is being forwarded from the parent switch to the Fabric Extender, it is replicated inside the FEX to reduce the fabric interface traffic.

> **Note** Cisco has been shipping VNTag as a prestandard port extension protocol since 2009. This additional header is intended to deliver the same capabilities defined in the IEEE 802.1BR (formerly IEEE 802.1Qbh) standard, which was published in July 2012. At the time of this writing, Cisco is expected to deliver products that fully support a VNTag and standards-based solutions.

Fabric Extender Options

Cisco has launched several Fabric Extender models since the Nexus 2148T was first shipped in 2009. Subsequent Cisco Fabric Extender products differ from each by factors such as

- **Fabric interfaces:** Most Cisco Fabric Extenders have four or eight 10 Gigabit Ethernet interfaces, which can use fiber (10GBASE-ER, 10GBASE-LR, Fabric Extender transceivers) or twinax cables. At the time of this writing, the Nexus 2248PQ exclusively supports 4 QSFP+ fabric interfaces that can deploy four 40-gigabit Ethernet connections or, using breakout cables, sixteen 10-gigabit Ethernet connections.

- **Host interfaces:** 8, 24, 32, or 48 Ethernet ports, which can be fixed (1000BASE-T, 100BASE-TX/1000BASE-T, 10GBASE-T) or SFP based (10GBASE-ER, 10GBASE-LR, twinax, 1000BASE-T).

- **Memory buffer:** Some models have larger shared buffers for applications such as large databases, shared storage, and video editing.

- **Form factor:** Fabric Extenders can be accommodated in server cabinets or in select blade server chassis (the latter option includes the UCS I/O Module).

- **Network capabilities:** These factors include multiple PortChannel members, number of quality of service (QoS) queues, and Fibre Channel over Ethernet (FCoE).

- **Choice of airflow:** Some models offer the choice to alternatively deploy front-to-back or back-to-front airflow.

A virtualized chassis can have different Fabric Extenders depending on server access requirements. This flexibility facilitates technology evolution, because migrations can be executed per server cabinet or even per server connection.

Devices as the Nexus 7000, Nexus 6000, Nexus 5000, and UCS Fabric Interconnect can act as parent switches to Fabric Extenders. Each one of these supports distinct Fabric Extender features and has different scalability characteristics.

> **Note** For more details about Cisco Fabric Extenders models (and their parent switches), you can read Appendix A, "Cisco Data Center Portfolio." If you want to verify the capabilities supported on your hardware and software combination, also refer to the Cisco online documentation for the most recent information.

Connecting a Fabric Extender to a Parent Switch

When there is one active connection between them, a Fabric Extender and its parent switch use Satellite Discovery Protocol (SDP) periodic messages to discover each other. After this formal introduction, the Fabric Extender deploys a Satellite Registration Protocol (SRP) request to register itself to the parent switch.

Figure 7-8 illustrates the FEX discovery and registration process when a switch interface is configured with the **switchport mode fex-fabric** command.

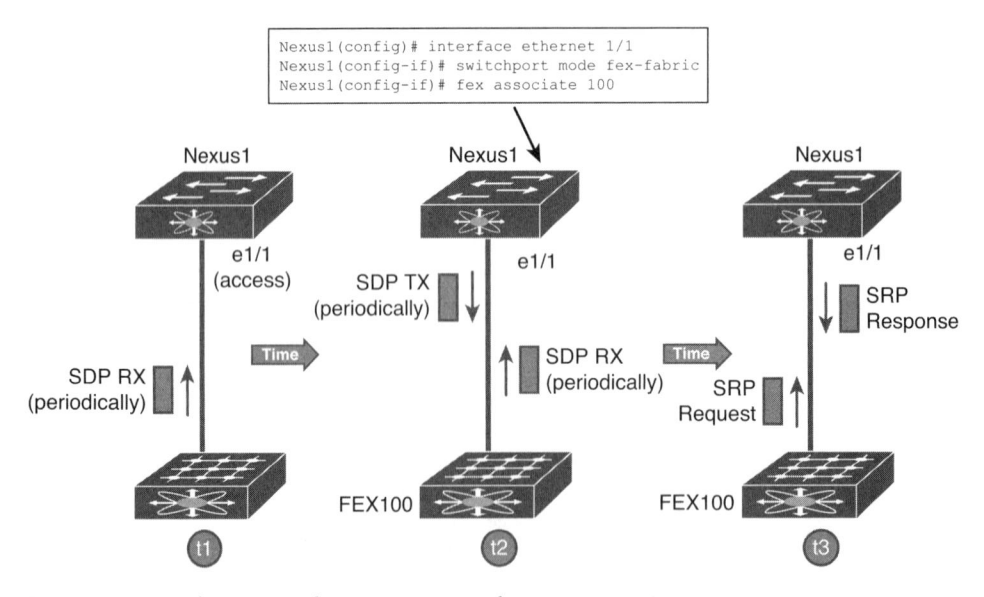

Figure 7-8 *Fabric Extender Discovery and Registration Process*

Example 7-1 shows a sample of the SDP messages sent from the Fabric Extender before any FEX configuration is executed in Nexus1 (at instant t1). As expected, the Fabric Extender automatically sends SDP messages as soon as it has an active fabric interface.

Example 7-1 *SDP Frames Sent at t1*

```
! Enabling the Fabric Extender processes in Nexus1
Nexus1# feature fex
! Enabling the tracing of SDP and SRP packets
Nexus1# debug fex pkt-trace
```

```
! Sample SDP Message received at interface Ethernet 1/1 (and repeated every 3
seconds)
08:35:03.086490 fex: Sdp-Rx: Interface: Eth1/1, Fex Id: 0, Ctrl Vntag: -1, Ctrl
Vlan: 1
08:35:03.086511 fex: Sdp-Rx: Refresh Intvl: 3000ms, Uid: 0x80a3e61d9cc8, device:
Fex, Remote link: 0x20000080
08:35:03.086523 fex: Sdp-Rx: Vendor: Cisco Systems  Model: N2K-C2232PP-10GE Serial:
JAF1509ECGT
[output suppressed]
```

In these SDP messages, the Fabric Extender exposes the VLAN from which it expects to receive control commands, SDP refresh interval (3 seconds), and hardware information.

After interface e1/1 in Nexus1 is configured with the **switchmode fex-fabric** and **fex associate** commands (instant t2 in Figure 7-8), this interface starts to send SDP packets, and both devices discover each other.

Example 7-2 details the Fabric Extender discovery process from the parent switch perspective.

Tip Fabric Extender identifiers must belong to the 100–199 range.

Example 7-2 *SDP Frames Sent After Ethernet 1/1 Configuration*

```
! SDP Messages sent from interface Ethernet 1/1 with Control VNTag -1 and Control
VLAN 4042
08:36:27.007428 fex: Sdp-Tx: Interface: Eth1/1, Fex Id: 100, Ctrl Vntag: -1, Ctrl
Vlan: 4042
08:36:27.007445 fex: Sdp-Tx: Refresh Intvl: 3000ms, Uid: 0xc03cc7730500, device:
Switch, Remote link: 0x1a000000
2012 Jun  4 08:36:27.007456 fex: Sdp-Tx: Vendor:   Model:   Serial: ----------
[output suppressed]
! SDP Messages sent from interface Ethernet 1/1 with new VNTag (zero)
08:36:27.101688 fex: Sdp-Tx: Interface: Eth1/1, Fex Id: 100, Ctrl Vntag: 0, Ctrl
Vlan: 4042
08:36:27.101704 fex: Sdp-Tx: Refresh Intvl: 3000ms, Uid: 0xc03cc7730500, device:
Switch, Remote link: 0x1a000000
08:36:27.101715 fex: Sdp-Tx: Vendor:   Model:   Serial: ----------
! Notice how the SDP Messages received from the FEX have changed
08:36:27.125135 fex: Sdp-Rx: Interface: Eth1/1, Fex Id: 0, Ctrl Vntag: 0, Ctrl Vlan:
4042
08:36:27.125153 fex: Sdp-Rx: Refresh Intvl: 3000ms, Uid: 0x80a3e61d9cc8, device:
Fex, Remote link: 0x20000080
08:36:27.125164 fex: Sdp-Rx: Vendor: Cisco Systems  Model: N2K-C2232PP-10GE Serial:
JAF1509ECGT
[output suppressed]
```

After the discovery is complete, the Fabric Extender sends an SRP Request message and waits for an SRP Response from the parent switch (instant t3). The registration process completes the FEX detection on the parent switch, and SDP messages continue to be exchanged between both devices after the registration.

Example 7-3 shows the registration process and describes how the Fabric Extender becomes operational for Nexus1.

Example 7-3 *SRP Registration and FEX Becoming Operational*

```
! FEX sens an SRP Request
08:36:30.114980 fex: Srp Req: Interface: Eth1/1, Uid: 0x80a3e61d9cc8, Card Id: 82,
IPC ver: 21
08:36:30.114992 fex: Srp Req: Version: 5.1(3)N2(1a), Interim Version: 5.1(3)N2(1a)
! Nexus1 sends an SRP Response confirming that FEX firmware is
supported . . .
08:36:30.116726 fex: Srp Resp: Interface: Eth1/1, Fex id: 100 Ver Chk: Compatible,
Img Uri:
! . . . and assigns an internal IP address for the FEX
08:36:30.116744 fex: Srp Resp: MTS addr: 0x2102, IP addr: 127.15.1.100/0 Switch MTS:
0x101, Switch Ip: 127.15.1.250
! After that the parent switch has a new remote linecard
08:26:16 5548P-3-174 %$ VDC-1 %$ %SATCTRL-FEX100-2-SOHMS_ENV_ERROR: FEX-100 Module
1: Check environment alarms.
[output suppressed]
08:36:33 5548P-3-174 %$ VDC-1 %$ %PFMA-2-FEX_STATUS: Fex 100 is online
```

From this moment on, the Fabric Extender is a remote linecard for the parent switch's supervisor module. Example 7-4 shows how the FEX interfaces can be seen and controlled on Nexus1.

Example 7-4 *Verifying the Fabric Extender Status*

```
! Verifying the operational Fabric Extenders
Nexus1# show module fex
FEX Mod Ports Card Type                          Model             Status.
--- --- ----- ------------------------------    ---------------   -------
100  1   32   Fabric Extender 32x10GE + 8x10G   N2K-C2232P-10GE   present
[output suppressed]
! Verifying the available FEX interfaces
Nexus1# show interface brief
[output suppressed]
--------------------------------------------------------------------------
Ethernet      VLAN    Type Mode  Status  Reason         Speed Port
Interface                                                     Ch #
--------------------------------------------------------------------------
```

```
! Notice that all interfaces have the FEX ID and that interface e100/1/1 is down
Eth100/1/1      1    eth  access  down     SFP not inserted  10G(D) --
Eth100/1/2      1    eth  access  down     SFP not inserted  10G(D) --
[output suppressed]
Eth100/1/32     1    eth  access  down     SFP not inserted  10G(D) --
```

Nexus1 logical interfaces (LIF) can be recognized through the FEX ID/slot/port index format. And because these interfaces are within Nexus1 configuration reach, its default configuration is applied to the FEX interfaces as well (**switchport mode access** and **no shutdown** commands, in this case).

With a control VLAN (4042) and an internal IP address (127.15.1.100), the Fabric Extender is configured through the Virtual Interface Configuration (VIC) protocol after its operationalization. Based on command/response messages, this protocol is also responsible for configuring the forwarding tables inside each FEX. The parent switch uses the VIC protocol to assign the Dvif_id to each virtual interface in the FEX and retrieve the FEX virtual interface list identifiers (Vif_list_id) for multidestination traffic.

Note Chapter 15, "Transcending the Rack," discusses a VNTag-based technology called Virtual Machine Fabric Extender (VM-FEX), where specialized adapters use the VIC protocol to dynamically request the creation, deletion, enabling, and disabling of logical interfaces in the parent switch.

Fabric Extended Interfaces and Spanning Tree Protocol

In the previous section, you learned that FEX host interfaces can be visualized as any other interface on the parent switch. These interfaces can also inherit various features from the same switch, justifying the concept of the virtualized modular chassis.

Example 7-5 illustrates the enablement of interface Ethernet 100/1/1, which is using a 1000BASE-T Small Form Pluggable (SFP) transceiver.

Example 7-5 *FEX Interface Configuration*

```
! Configuring interface Ethernet 100/1/1 to accept the GigabitEthernet SFP
Nexus1(config)# interface ethernet 100/1/1
Nexus1(config-if)# speed 1000
! Verifying the interface status
Nexus1(config-if)# show interface ethernet 100/1/1 brief

--------------------------------------------------------------------
Ethernet        VLAN     Type Mode    Status  Reason       Speed     Port
Interface                                                             Ch #
```

```
Eth100/1/1      1       eth   access  up      none             1000(D)   --
```

Nevertheless, there are some differences on how a host interface behaves in the Spanning Tree Protocol context. In Example 7-6, you can spot three commands that expose this distinct behavior.

Example 7-6 *Fabric Extender Interface and Spanning Tree Protocol*

```
! Verifying the STP status on the Fabric Interface
Nexus1# show spanning-tree interface ethernet 1/1
No spanning tree information available for Ethernet1/1
! Verifying the STP status on FEX interface
Nexus1# show spanning-tree interface ethernet 100/1/1

Vlan              Role Sts Cost      Prio.Nbr Type
---------------- ---- --- --------- -------- --------------------------------
VLAN0001          Desg FWD 4         128.1025 Edge P2p
! Verifying the BPDU features on the FEX interface
Nexus1# show spanning-tree interface e100/1/1 detail | include Bpdu
   Bpdu guard is enabled
   Bpdu filter is enabled by default
Nexus1# show spanning-tree interface e100/1/1 detail | include BPDU
   BPDU: sent 11, received 0
```

From the example, it is possible to infer that

- The interface connected to the Fabric Extender (Ethernet 1/1) does not participate in STP, because from the Nexus1 perspective, it is considered a "backplane connection."
- The host interfaces on the FEX are configured as RSTP edge point-to-point ports.

By default, host interfaces are configured with bridge protocol data unit (BPDU) filter and BPDU guard. These configurations mean, respectively, that the interfaces will not process any received BPDUs, and will actually be disabled if such a frame arrives at them. Nevertheless, as a safeguard mechanism, these interfaces do send some BPDUs when they are activated to avoid loops that can be caused with a mistakenly direct connection between two host interfaces.

As a conclusion, the parent switch controlling Fabric Extenders as linecards forms a virtualized chassis designed for host connections. In my opinion, a correct characterization for the virtualization technique detailed in this chapter would be *virtualized modular access switch*.

> **Caution** Although Fabric Extenders are primarily designed for server connections, they also support switches connected to host interfaces as long as you disable STP on these devices. In consequence, to eliminate loops in redundant active connections, the switches must deploy a redundancy mechanism that is not STP dependent (Cisco Flex Link, for example).

Fabric Interfaces Redundancy

A Fabric Extender with multiple connections to a parent switch can have two different behaviors in the case of a fabric interface failure. By default, a FEX deploys an interface pinning policy to control which host interfaces are shut in the case of such a failure.

The objective of static pinning is to keep the exact amount of bandwidth at the host ports in the case of a fabric interface failure. Hence, for the remaining available host interfaces, there is no oversubscription increase.

Example 7-7 shows how a fabric interface (Ethernet 1/1) is "pinned" to an active host interface (Ethernet 100/1/1).

Example 7-7 *Static Pinning*

```
Nexus1# show fex 100 detail
FEX: 100 Description: FEX0100   state: Online
[output suppressed]
  Fabric interface state:
    Eth1/1 - Interface Up. State: Active
    Eth1/2 - Interface Up. State: Active
! Interface Ethernet 100/1/1 is active as long as Ethernet 1/1 is active
  Fex Port        State   Fabric Port
       Eth100/1/1    Up        Eth1/1
       Eth100/1/2    Down      None
[output suppressed]
       Eth100/1/32   Down      None
```

The example output exhibits the host interface status dependence whether or not its associated fabric interface is active. If Ethernet 1/1 fails, Ethernet 100/1/1 is automatically disabled, and hopefully, the connected server should activate a fault tolerance mechanism (NIC teaming).

Example 7-8 portrays the host interface behavior when the fabric interface is disabled. Notice that Ethernet 100/1/1 fails too, ignoring the fact that another fabric interface (Ethernet 1/2) is still active.

Example 7-8 *Failure in Static Pinning*

```
! Disabling fabric interface e1/1
Nexus1(config)# interface ethernet 1/1
Nexus1(config-if)# shutdown
! Vefifying e100/1/1 status
Nexus1(config-if)# show fex 100 detail
FEX: 100 Description: FEX0100   state: Online
[output suppressed]
Pinning-mode: static    Max-links: 1
[output suppressed]
  Fabric interface state:
    Eth1/1 - Interface Down. State: Configured
    Eth1/2 - Interface Up. State: Active
  Fex Port        State   Fabric Port
      Eth100/1/1  Down       Eth1/1
      Eth100/1/2  Down       None
[output suppressed]
      Eth100/1/32 Down       None
```

The **pinning max-link** command divides the host interfaces among a maximum number of fabric interfaces. With our 32-port Fabric Extender, if you issue the **pinning max-link 4** command, eight interfaces will be disabled if a fabric port fails.

In static pinning, host interface assignment follows the fabric interface order of configuration. However, if you reload the parent switch or execute the **fex pinning redistribute** command, the host interface groups will be reassigned to the fabric interface numerical order.

Table 7-2 illustrates this exact scenario, where the order of configuration for the fabric interfaces was Ethernet 1/3, Ethernet 1/2, Ethernet 1/4, and Ethernet 1/1.

Table 7-2 *Fabric Extender Pinning Example*

Parent Switch Interface	Associated Host Interfaces (Following Order of Configuration)	Associated Host Interfaces (After Reload or Redistribution)
e1/1	25 to 32	1 to 8
e1/2	9 to 16	9 to 16
e1/3	1 to 8	17 to 24
e1/4	17 to 24	25 to 32

> **Tip** Both the **pinning max-link** and **fex pinning redistribute** commands are disruptive to the Fabric Extender host interfaces.

Alternatively, the configuration of a PortChannel between the parent switch and the Fabric Extender guarantees that every host interface remains operational if a fabric interface fails. However, the remaining bandwidth to the parent switch will be shared by all host ports (increasing the oversubscription).

Example 7-9 presents the results from a PortChannel configuration on the fabric interfaces (shown later in Figure 7-9).

Example 7-9 *PortChannel Configuration*

```
! Verifying how FEX 100 uses PortChannel 100 as its fabric interface
Nexus1# show fex 100 detail
FEX: 100 Description: FEX0100   state: Online
[output suppressed]
! When using PortChannel Max-links must be one
Pinning-mode: static    Max-links: 1
[output suppressed]
  Fabric interface state:
    Po100 - Interface Up. State: Active
    Eth1/1 - Interface Up. State: Active
    Eth1/2 - Interface Up. State: Active
  Fex Port        State   Fabric Port
       Eth100/1/1     Up       Po100
       Eth100/1/2     Down     None
[output suppressed]
       Eth100/1/32    Down     None
```

When fabric interfaces are aggregated, the max-link pinning must be set to 1 (because it is not possible to have more than one upstream PortChannel per FEX), and the interface must be configured in mode ON because Fabric Extenders do not support Link Aggregation Control Protocol (LACP).

Example 7-10 demonstrates that a failure in Ethernet 1/1 does not have any effect over interface Ethernet 100/1/1 when the fabric interfaces are aggregated. As expected, PortChannel 100 remains operational if a single member interface is active (Ethernet 1/2).

Example 7-10 *Failure in Ethernet 1/1*

```
! Disabling fabric interface e1/1
Nexus1(config)# interface ethernet 1/1
Nexus1(config-if)# shutdown
```

```
! Vefifying e100/1/1 status
Nexus1(config-if)# show fex 100 detail
FEX: 100 Description: FEX0100    state: Online
[output suppressed]
Pinning-mode: static    Max-links: 1
 [output suppressed]
  Fabric interface state:
    Po100 - Interface Up. State: Active
    Eth1/1 - Interface Down. State: Configured
    Eth1/2 - Interface Up. State: Active
! PortChannel is still operational
  Fex Port        State   Fabric Port
       Eth100/1/1    Up        Po100
       Eth100/1/2  Down        None
 [output suppressed]
       Eth100/1/32 Down        None
```

Figure 7-9 exhibits the behavior for both fabric interface redundancy options (static pinning and PortChannel) and details the configuration required in each one.

```
Nexus1(config)# fex 100
Nexus1(config-fex)# pinning max-links 2
Change in Max-links will cause traffic disruption.
Nexus1(config)# interface ethernet 1/1-2
Nexus1(config-if-range)# switchport mode fex-fabric
Nexus1(config-if-range)# fex associate 100
```

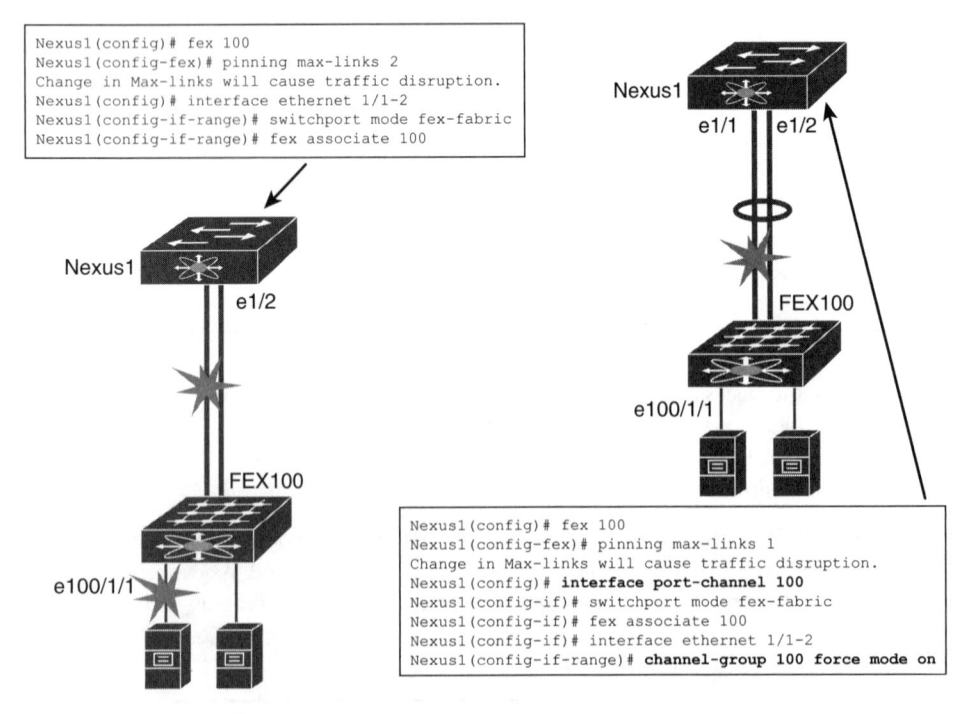

```
Nexus1(config)# fex 100
Nexus1(config-fex)# pinning max-links 1
Change in Max-links will cause traffic disruption.
Nexus1(config)# interface port-channel 100
Nexus1(config-if)# switchport mode fex-fabric
Nexus1(config-if)# fex associate 100
Nexus1(config-if)# interface ethernet 1/1-2
Nexus1(config-if-range)# channel-group 100 force mode on
```

Figure 7-9 *Static Pinning Versus PortChannel: Configuration and Host Interface Behavior*

Fabric Extender Topologies

In the previous section, you were presented with simple scenarios that demonstrated basic functionalities of a Fabric Extender connected to one parent switch. Nevertheless, it is paramount that you understand the principles behind highly available FEX topologies.

There are basically two classes of topologies that provide fault tolerance in Fabric Extender designs:

Straight-through: Where a Fabric Extender is connected to a single parent switch

Dual-homed: Where a Fabric Extender is connected to a pair of parent switches

An example of each of these topologies is presented in Figure 7-10.

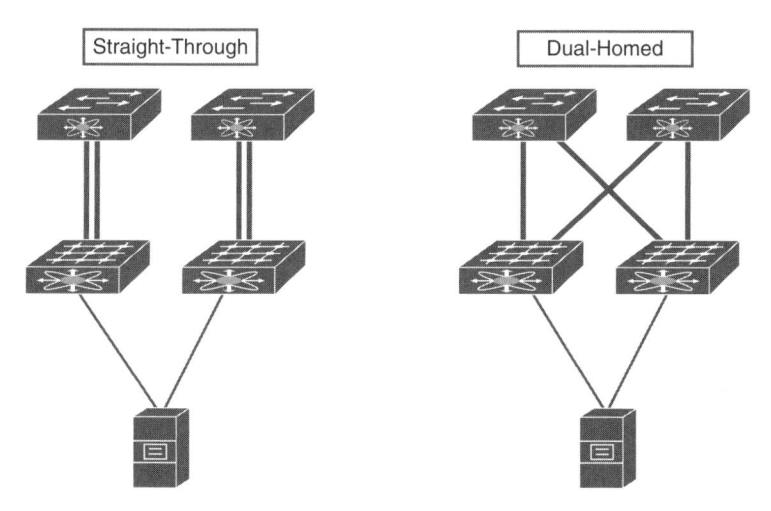

Figure 7-10 *Fabric Extender Topology Types*

Note In the next sections, I will discuss topologies whose support varies depending on the parent switch and Fabric Extender hardware models and software versions. Because of the NX-OS constant state of evolution, I will avoid transcribing a matrix of supported topologies that will be quickly outdated. I highly recommend that you refer to the Cisco online documentation for the most recently supported FEX topologies.

Straight-Through Topologies

In straight-through topologies, it is recommended that each host has interfaces connected to Fabric Extenders that are managed by distinct parent switches. This practice avoids the total of loss of connectivity for a server in case of a switch failure.

Straight-through designs create a pair of NX-OS virtualized chassis with a single supervisor module in each. Likewise, IEEE 802.3ad–compatible servers can leverage active-active connections using virtual PortChannels (vPCs).

Figure 7-11 demonstrates how vPCs can be deployed in a straight-through topology comprised of two switches (Nexus1 and Nexus2) and two Fabric Extenders (FEX110 and FEX120). In the figure, each Fabric Extender uses two aggregated fabric connections to its parent switch. Both server interfaces are connected to access interfaces in VLAN 50 (e110/1/1 in Nexus1 and e120/1/1 in Nexus2) which will be vPC 10 member ports.

Tip Notice that Nexus1 is configured to be the primary vPC peer, using the **role priority 1** command.

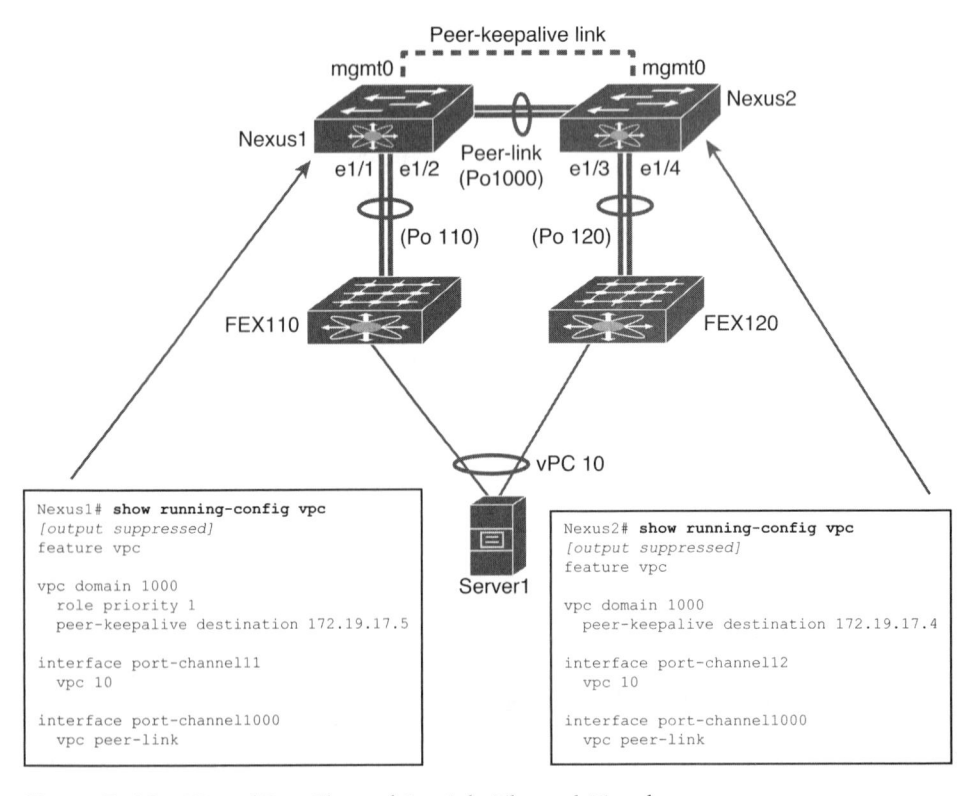

```
Nexus1# show running-config vpc
[output suppressed]
feature vpc

vpc domain 1000
  role priority 1
  peer-keepalive destination 172.19.17.5

interface port-channel11
  vpc 10

interface port-channel1000
  vpc peer-link
```

```
Nexus2# show running-config vpc
[output suppressed]
feature vpc

vpc domain 1000
  peer-keepalive destination 172.19.17.4

interface port-channel12
  vpc 10

interface port-channel1000
  vpc peer-link
```

Figure 7-11 *Virtual PortChannel Straight-Through Topology*

For clarification, the PortChannel configuration options in this topology are explained in Table 7-3.

Table 7-3 *PortChannel Options*

Switch	PortChannel ID	Interfaces	Remote Peer	LACP
Nexus1	11 (vPC 10)	e110/1/1	Server A	Depends on peer
Nexus1	110	e1/1, e1/2	FEX110	No
Nexus1	1000	e1/31, e1/32	Nexus2	Depends on peer
Nexus2	12 (vPC 10)	e120/1/1	Server A	Depends on peer
Nexus2	120	e1/3, e1/4	FEX120	No
Nexus2	1000	e1/31, e1/32	Nexus1	Depends on peer

Note PortChannels 110 and 120 are not mandatory for this configuration because static pinning would work as well.

In Examples 7-11 and 7-12, you can verify the status of the virtual PortChannel created to aggregate Server1 Ethernet interfaces.

Example 7-11 *Virtual PortChannel 10 Status in Nexus1*

```
! Verifying vPC 10 status
Nexus1# show vpc 10
vPC status
----------------------------------------------------------------
id      Port        Status Consistency Reason                    Active vlans
------  ----------  ------ ----------- ------------------------- ----
10      Po10        up     success     success                   50
```

Example 7-12 *Virtual PortChannel Status in Nexus2*

```
! Verifying vPC 10 status
Nexus1# show vpc 10
vPC status
----------------------------------------------------------------
id      Port        Status Consistency Reason                    Active vlans
------  ----------  ------ ----------- ------------------------- ----
10      Po10        up     success     success                   50
```

In a straight-through vPC topology, the consequences of peer link total failure are the same as expected in a standard vPC configuration: All vPC member ports in the secondary vPC peer are automatically disabled. Example 7-13 exhibits this situation in Nexus2, when PortChannel 1000 is disabled on Nexus1 (through a **shutdown** command in the PortChannel).

Example 7-13 *Peer Link Effect on Nexus2*

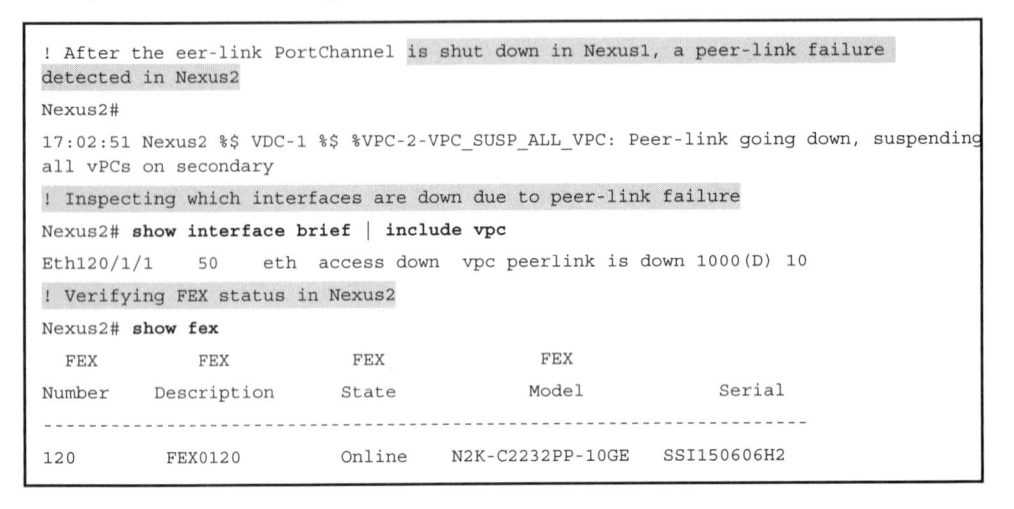

```
! After the eer-link PortChannel is shut down in Nexus1, a peer-link failure
detected in Nexus2
Nexus2#
17:02:51 Nexus2 %$ VDC-1 %$ %VPC-2-VPC_SUSP_ALL_VPC: Peer-link going down, suspending
all vPCs on secondary
! Inspecting which interfaces are down due to peer-link failure
Nexus2# show interface brief | include vpc
Eth120/1/1     50      eth   access down  vpc peerlink is down 1000(D) 10
! Verifying FEX status in Nexus2
Nexus2# show fex
    FEX         FEX            FEX           FEX
    Number      Description    State         Model              Serial
    ---------------------------------------------------------------------
    120         FEX0120        Online        N2K-C2232PP-10GE   SSI150606H2
```

As expected, even though FEX120 is still operational, only vPC member ports are disabled because of the peer link failure.

Orphan ports, connected only to the secondary peer, can also be isolated in straight-through vPC topologies. The same recommendations I have described in Chapter 6, "Fooling Spanning Tree," apply for these interfaces.

Figure 7-12 depicts other possible straight-through topologies available at the time of this writing.

Tip I usually recommend straight-through topologies for scenarios that require higher access port scalability (because they can deploy a twofold increase in the number of Fabric Extenders that a single parent switch supports).

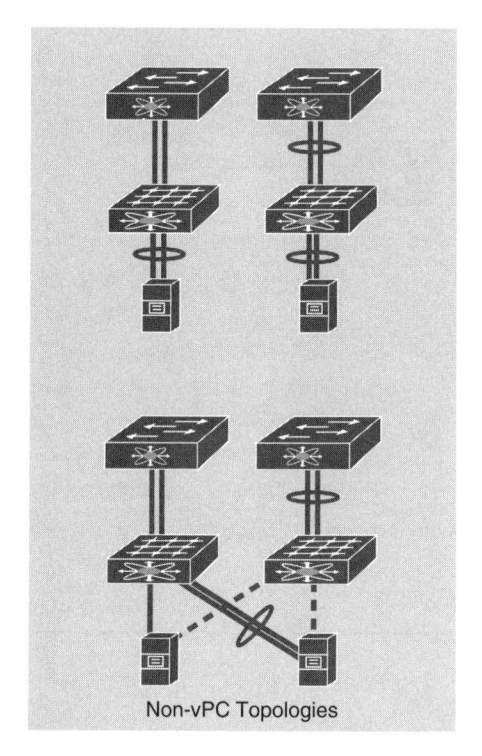

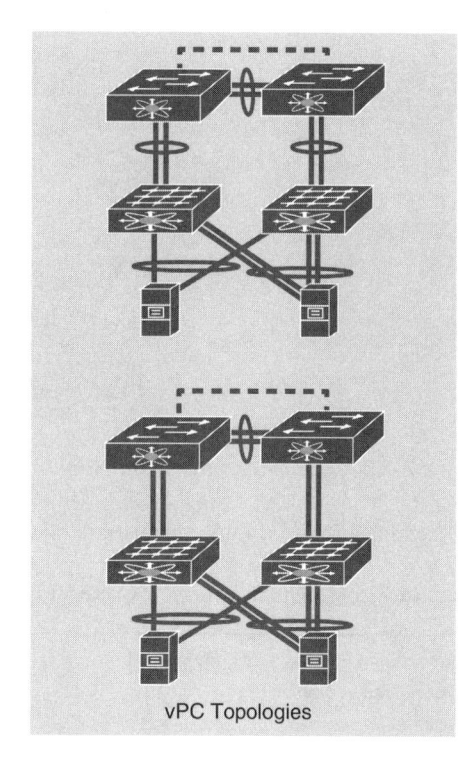

Figure 7-12 *Straight-Through Topologies*

Dual-Homed Topologies

In a classical modular Ethernet switch, redundant supervisor modules can control the installed linecards. In a virtualized access switch, the same redundancy can be achieved with the connection of two parent switches to a single Fabric Extender. However, you should not expect that the straightforward FEX configuration is sufficient to build a dual-homed topology: By default, a Fabric Extender can only be managed by a single parent switch.

To illustrate this behavior, consider the topology and configuration detailed in Figure 7-13. There, the Fabric Extender is connected and registered to Nexus1, and afterward, connected to Nexus2.

```
Nexus1(config)# interface ethernet 1/1
Nexus1(config-if)# switchport mode fex-fabric
Nexus1(config-if)# fex associate 180
```

```
Nexus2(config)# interface ethernet 1/1
Nexus2(config-if)# switchport mode fex-fabric
Nexus2(config-if)# fex associate 180
```

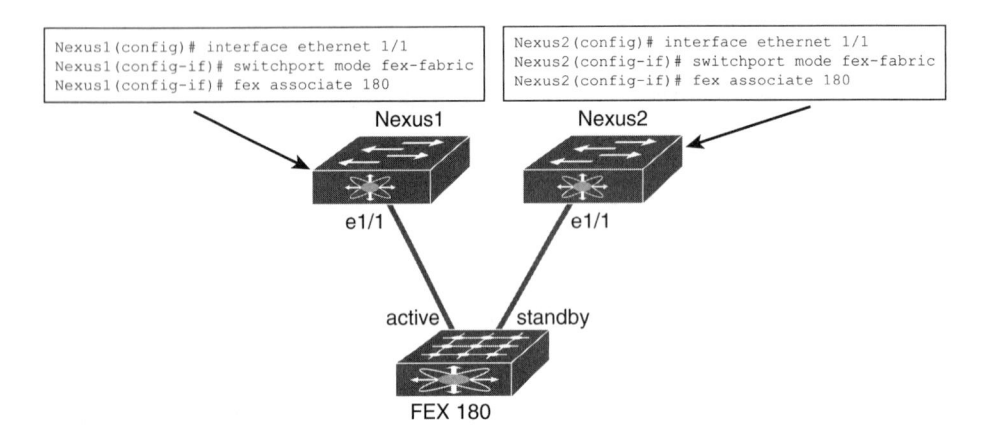

Figure 7-13 *Active-Standby Dual-Homed Topology*

Examples 7-14 and 7-15 demonstrate how each switch detects FEX180.

Example 7-14 *Fabric Extender Connected on Two Parent Switches*

```
! Verifying FEX status in Nexus1
Nexus1# show fex
  FEX         FEX          FEX         FEX
  Number    Description    State       Model            Serial
------------------------------------------------------------------
  180       FEX0180        Online      N2K-C2232PP-10GE SSI150606J3
```

Example 7-15 *Single FEX Connected on Two Parent Switches*

```
! Verifying FEX status in Nexus2
Nexus2# show fex
  FEX         FEX          FEX         FEX
  Number    Description    State       Model            Serial
------------------------------------------------------------------
  ---       --------       Connected   N2K-C2232PP-10GE SSI150606J3
```

The Fabric Extender remains in the **Connected** state (and not **Online**) in Nexus2 because it is already registered to Nexus1. Therefore, Nexus2 and the Fabric Extender only discover each other, without advancing to the registration phase.

If the connection to Nexus1 fails, the Fabric Extender registers itself to Nexus2 and remains in that state (even if the connection to Nexus1 is reactivated).

However, after the parent switch transition, the host interfaces would remain unconfigured. The reason is simple: Before the FEX is completely operational on Nexus2, it is not possible to configure any host interfaces because they simply do not exist yet!

Example 7-16 shows what happens if you try to configure a host interface in Nexus2 before FEX180 is online. The example also details how you can enable *Fabric Extender preprovisioning* to fix this behavior and effectively provide active-standby parent switches to a Fabric Extender.

Example 7-16 *Fabric Extender Preprovisioning*

```
! Trying to configure a host interface in FEX180 (which is not operational in Nexus2)
Nexus2(config)# interface ethernet 180/1/1
                                 ^
Invalid range at '^' marker.
! Pre-provisioning FEX180 in Nexus2
Nexus2(config)# slot 180
Nexus2(config-slot)# provision model N2K-C2232P
! Now you can pre-configure a host interface in FEX180
Nexus2(config-slot)# interface ethernet 180/1/1
Nexus2(config-if)# speed 1000
```

Tip The preprovisioning configuration must be done on both switches if you want the host interfaces to be enabled after a switchover from any parent switch to the other.

From a control plane perspective, it might be enough that a single parent switch manages a Fabric Extender while the other waits for a failure. Nevertheless, there are two drawbacks in an active-standby dual-homed topology that challenge its application in real-world scenarios:

- The connection to the standby parent switch is not used for data traffic.
- The transition from one parent switch to the other must wait almost 40 seconds before the Fabric Extender is online.

Figures 7-14 clarifies how virtual PortChannels can overcome both drawbacks and enable active-active dual-homed topologies for Fabric Extenders.

Example 7-17 depicts the vPC configuration in Nexus1. The same configuration was issued in Nexus2, except for the peer keepalive destination IP address that was pointed to 172.19.17.4 (Nexus1 mgmt0 interface).

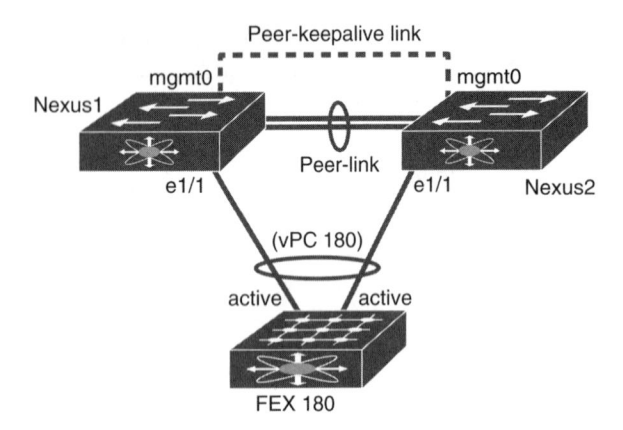

Figure 7-14 *Active-Active Dual-Homed Fabric Extender*

Example 7-17 *Nexus1 vPC Configuration*

```
! Observing all vPC configuration parameters in Nexus1
Nexus1# show running-config vpc
[output suppressed]

feature vpc
! Step 1: Configuring vPC domain
vpc domain 1000
  role priority 1
! Step 2: Configuring peer-keepalive link (IP address 172.19.17.4 in Nexus2)
  peer-keepalive destination 172.19.17.5
[output suppressed]
! Step 3: Configuring peer-link (interfaces e1/31 and e1/32)
Nexus1# show running-config interface port-channel 1000, port-channel 180
[output suppressed]
interface port-channel1000
  switchport mode trunk
  spanning-tree port type network
  vpc peer-link
! Step 4: Configuring and reusing PortChannels (interface e1/1 on both switches)
interface port-channel180
  switchport mode fex-fabric
  fex associate 180
  vpc 180
```

In active-active dual-homed scenarios, each Fabric Extender is online for both parent switches, and Examples 7-18 and 7-19 portray this status.

Example 7-18 *Verifying Fabric Extender Status in Nexus1*

```
Nexus1# show fex 180 detail
FEX: 180 Description: FEX0180    state: Online
[output suppressed]
  Fabric interface state:
    Po180 - Interface Up. State: Active
    Eth1/1 - Interface Up. State: Active
  Fex Port        State   Fabric Port
! Interface e180/1/1 is configured and operational in Nexus1
      Eth180/1/1    Up        Po180
      Eth180/1/2    Down      None
[output suppressed]
```

Example 7-19 *Verifying Fabric Extender Status in Nexus2*

```
Nexus2# show fex 180 detail
FEX: 180 Description: FEX0180    state: Online
[output suppressed]
  Fabric interface state:
    Po180 - Interface Up. State: Active
    Eth1/1 - Interface Up. State: Active
  Fex Port        State   Fabric Port
! Interface e180/1/1 is configured and operational in Nexus2
      Eth180/1/1    Up        Po180
      Eth180/1/2    Down      None
[output suppressed]
```

In active-active topologies, a parent switch failure does not affect the host interfaces on the Fabric Extender because both vPC peers manage it simultaneously. However, it is a requirement that the FEX configuration (including the host interfaces) is the same on both switches.

> **Tip** You can use the *configuration synchronization* NX-OS feature to replicate selected parts of a configuration to a peer switch (if it is available in your software and hardware combination).

I usually recommend active-active dual-homed topologies for scenarios that require minimum failure effects on server connectivity (such as servers that have only one Ethernet connection, for example).

During a period, it was not possible to deploy vPCs on host interfaces connected to dual-homed active-active Fabric Extenders. Notwithstanding, Enhanced virtual PortChannel (EvPC) capability surpassed that limitation, maintaining a simple configuration principle: Because in active-active dual-homed topologies, the host interfaces are configurable on both parent switches, you only need to deploy a PortChannel for the server interfaces you want to aggregate.

Figure 7-15 depicts the EvPC scenario derived from our topology with the inclusion of another Fabric Extender (FEX190).

Note Consider that the FEX190 configuration on both switches is exactly the same as the one issued for FEX180.

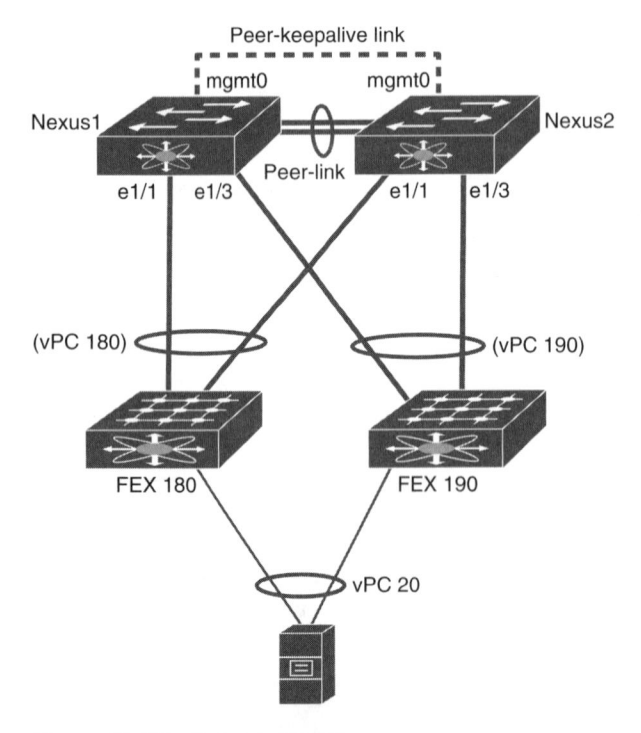

Figure 7-15 *Enhanced vPC*

The EvPC configuration on Nexus1 is detailed in Example 7-20. As mentioned previously, Nexus2 received the same configuration.

Example 7-20 *Enhanced vPC Configuration in Nexus1*

```
Nexus1# show running-config interface port-channel 20
[output suppressed]
! Configuring the EvPC
interface port-channel20
  switchport access vlan 50


Nexus1# show running-config interface ethernet 180/1/1, ethernet 190/1/1
[output suppressed]
interface Ethernet180/1/1
  switchport access vlan 50
  speed 1000
! Including Ethernet 180/1/1 in the EvPC
  channel-group 20 mode active

interface Ethernet190/1/1
  switchport access vlan 50
  speed 1000
! Including Ethernet 190/1/1 in the EvPC
  channel-group 20 mode active
```

Use Case: Mixed Access Data Center

After your imaginary career achieves the sequential successes described in previous chapters, you are requested to design the server access network of a midrange data center.

This data center is acquiring 160 new rack-mountable servers with two 10 Gigabit Ethernet interfaces (for redundancy), where each server consumes approximately 450 watts. But the design must also support 96 legacy servers that will be decommissioned over the next two years. These old servers have only one Gigabit Ethernet interface and very similar power requirements (although only one-third of the performance).

This company's CIO requires that three principles orient your project: scalability, high availability, and physical optimization. He also presents two boundary conditions:

   Only 7.5 kilowatts can be provided per server cabinet.

   The network cannot have an oversubscription higher than 5:1, even in moments of a connection failure.

Believing that an FEX-based virtualized chassis can be customized to support the specific requirements of most server environments, you present the design depicted in Figure 7-16.

316 Data Center Virtualization Fundamentals

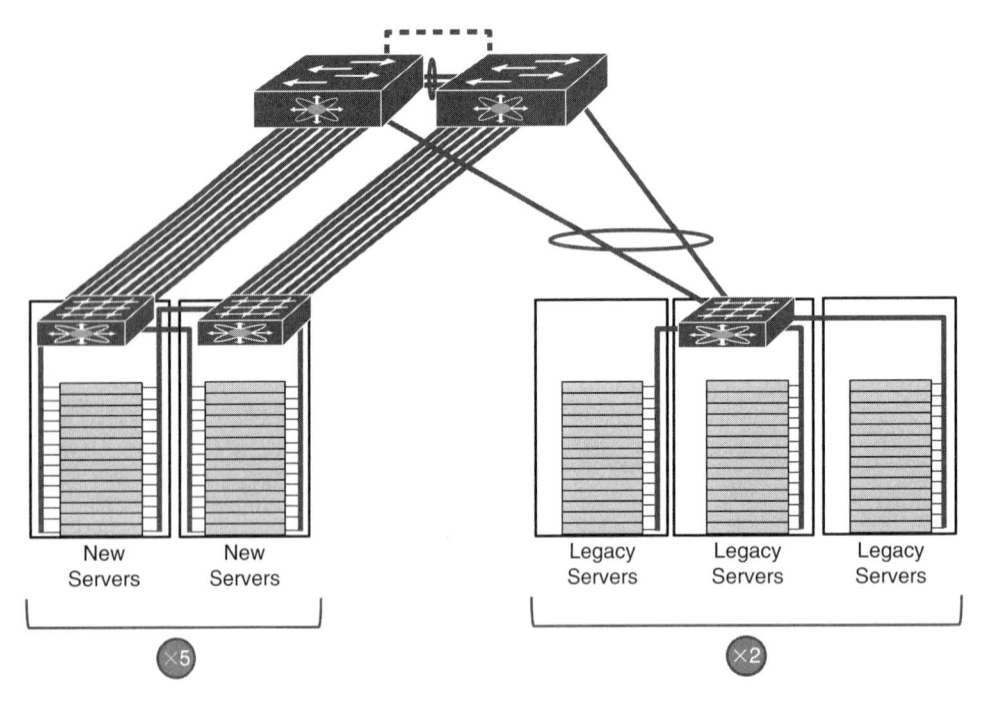

Figure 7-16 *Mixed Access Data Center*

In your design, each server cabinet can accommodate up to 16 servers because these devices consumes together 7.2 kW (leaving 300 W for the Fabric Extender). A pair of Nexus 2232PP Fabric Extenders (with eight 10 Gigabit Ethernet fabric interfaces and 32 10 Gigabit Ethernet host interfaces) can support and optimize the cabling of two server cabinets.

Within these cabinets, each new server is connected to two different Nexus 2232PP Fabric Extenders in a straight-through topology. The fabric interfaces do not use PortChannels to maintain the bandwidth oversubscription of 4:1 if there is a connection failure. Optionally, these servers can leverage vPCs to deploy 20 Gbps of bandwidth with aggregated interfaces.

For the legacy servers, you also consider 16 servers in each cabinet. However, you select one Nexus 2248TP-E Fabric Extender (with four 10 Gigabit Ethernet fabric interfaces and 48 10 Gigabit Ethernet host interfaces) to provide connectivity to three server cabinets and increase high availability through an active-active dual-homed topology. This design assures the network team that, even in the case of a fabric interface failure, the host interface's maximum oversubscription is 4.8:1.

Next, you select a pair of Layer 3 Nexus switches capable of deploying both FEX topologies and acting as the default gateway for the servers. The team is happy to know that only two virtualized switches will be able to manage their entire data center.

During lunch, they reveal that you have just designed their backup data center for the next three years. And later, you are invited to lead their main data center project.

Summary

In this chapter, you have learned that

- Both Top-of-Rack and End-of-Row server access models have advantages and shortcomings. Fabric Extenders leverage the best of both models (cabling optimization and consolidated management, respectively).
- A parent switch connected to one or more Fabric Extenders forms a virtualized access chassis.
- Parent switches and Fabric Extenders use VNTag to deploy virtual interfaces for each FEX host interface.
- FEX host interfaces are RSTP edge ports with BPDU filter and BPDU guard enabled.
- Fabric Extenders can have fabric interface redundancy through static pinning or PortChannels.
- There are two classes of Fabric Extender redundant topologies: straight-through and dual-homed.
- It is possible to provide link aggregation to servers connected to Fabric Extenders in straight-through topologies (standard vPC) and dual-homed topologies (Enhanced vPC).

Figure 7-17 graphically summarizes how Fabric Extenders (connected to a parent switch) can emulate a virtualized modular chassis for a server connection.

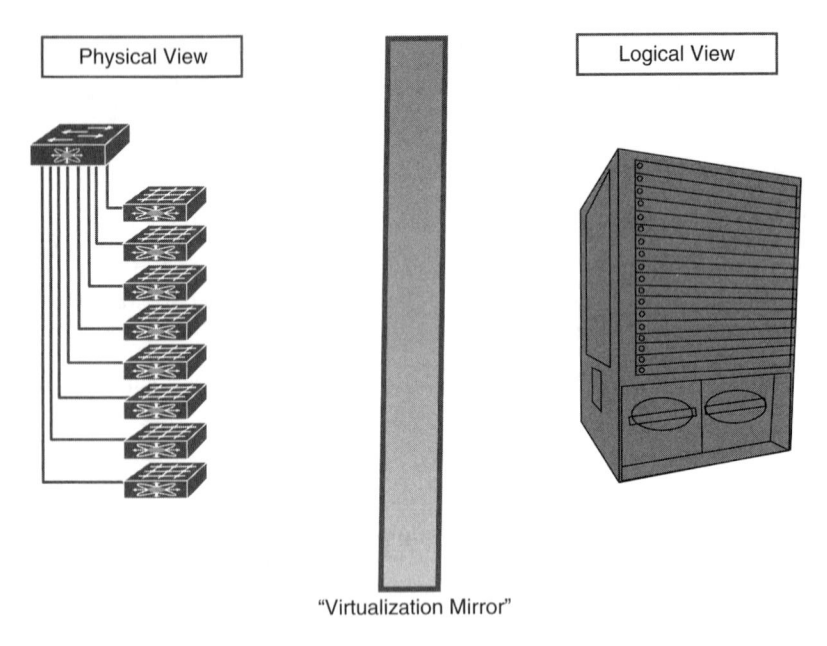

Figure 7-17 *Through the Virtualization Mirror*

Further Reading

Gai, Silvano and DeSanti, Claudio. *I/O Consolidation in the Data Center*. Cisco Press, 2009.

VNTag 101
www.ieee802.org/1/files/public/docs2009/new-pelissier-vntag-seminar-0508.pdf

White Paper: Virtual Machine Networking: Standards and Solutions
www.cisco.com/en/US/prod/collateral/switches/ps9441/ps9902/whitepaper_c11-620065.pdf

IEEE Standards Association
standards.ieee.org/getieee802/download/802.1BR-2012.pdf

Chapter 8

A Tale of Two Data Centers

"Success depends upon previous preparation, and without such preparation there is sure to be failure." (Confucius)

This chapter discusses Layer 2 extension technologies, such as Ethernet over MPLS (EoMPLS), Virtual Private LAN Service (VPLS), and Overlay Transport Virtualization (OTV). It covers the following topics:

- A Brief History of Distributed Data Centers
- The Case for Layer 2 Extensions
- Ethernet Extension over Optical Connections
- Ethernet Extension over MPLS
- Ethernet Extension over IP
- VLAN Identifiers and Layer 2 Extensions
- Internal Routing in Connected Data Centers
- Use Case: Active-Active Greenfield Data Centers

Table 8-1 compares EoMPLS, VPLS, and OTV using the taxonomy described in Chapter 1, "Virtualization History and Definitions".

Table 8-1 *Layer 2 Extension Virtualization Classification*

Virtualization Characteristics	EoMPLS	VPLS	OTV
Emulation	Ethernet connection	Ethernet bridge	Overlay Ethernet network
Type	Abstraction	Abstraction	Abstraction

Virtualization Characteristics	EoMPLS	VPLS	OTV
Subtype	Structural	Structural	Structural
Scalability	Hardware and software dependent	Hardware and software dependent	Hardware and software dependent
Technology Area	Networking	Networking	Networking
Subarea	Data plane	Data plane	Data and control planes
Advantages	Layer 2 extension, simplicity, transparency	Layer 2 extension, multipoint connections, loop avoidance within MPLS network	Layer 2 extension, multipoint, transport independence, loop avoidance

Nowadays, it is very rare to find a company that hosts all of its applications in a single data center facility. With a lonesome site, as business results become more dependent on IT processes, an hour-long failure can represent the quickest way to bankruptcy.

Consequently, building at least two separate data centers is considered mandatory for an organization that seriously contemplates a disaster recovery plan. To lessen the probability that both sites share the same risks, it became usual to separate these structures by a certain distance. Some companies must even adhere to industry compliance rules that define a minimum distance between sites, as well as other specific localization criteria.

Whereas prudence suggests dispersing data centers as widely as possible, data transport services, application requirements, and available budget define the natural boundaries for such a decision.

From a networking perspective, distributed data centers should also be as independent as possible. For years, best practices recommended that networks from distinct data centers should be connected through Layer 3 (routing), isolating known Layer 2 turmoils such as flooding, loops, and reconvergences. However, it is the way applications provide fault tolerance that actually defines the connectivity requirements between distributed data centers.

Some applications simply require that Layer 2 domains are *extended* over multiple data centers. For network teams, designing such extensions is similar to walk a tightrope between control and connectivity. After all, how do you provide this kind of communication avoiding problems that can be extended to all sites as well?

During the last decades, Cisco has developed a wide array of Layer 2 extension virtualization solutions to help with distinct challenge scenarios. This chapter details their mechanisms and describes how each of them can be optimally applied.

A Brief History of Distributed Data Centers

Availability can be defined as the ability of a system to perform its agreed function when required. It can be measured by the time such system takes from moving a business transaction from one failed component to another one that is working.

Nevertheless, available components do not translate into application availability, because the lack of coordination among these mechanisms can easily result in a total system failure. An organization should base its high-availability strategy on more general planning activities, such the disaster recovery plan and the business continuity plan.

Generically speaking, a *disaster recovery plan* is responsible for the response to the total loss or major failure of an IT system, while a *business continuity plan* defines the management processes that will be executed for each identified threat (IT related or not) and its business impacts. Commonly, these plans define two metrics for each application environment, reflecting their influence on business results. They are

- **Recovery Point Objective (RPO):** The maximum tolerable amount of time in which data can be lost from an IT service because of a major incident.

- **Recovery Time Objective (RTO):** The maximum tolerable amount of time after a major incident after which an IT service must be operational.

It is paramount that these values are very well characterized to avoid ineffective "best effort" reactions to disasters or excessive expenses on their avoidance. Usually, as an application requires a smaller RPO or RTO, more sophisticated recovery technologies are likely to be used.

The development of these recovery solutions was molded by the distinct application architectures they were supposed to serve. Actually, if you consider the history of distributed data centers, it is much easier to understand the expectations that created each recovery technology.

In the next sections, I will present a chronological account of how distributed data centers were mainly used during the last four decades. It does not mean that companies should only deploy the latest recovery solutions to their systems. In contrast, I would say that smart IT teams should always apply the best technologies for each distinct application environment, independently of how many years ago they were created.

The Cold Age (Mid-1970s to 1980s)

During this period, data centers were still referred to as computer rooms and they mainly housed mainframe systems. A backup facility was characterized by a remote secure location where stored data could be transported and recovered.

Applications were based on *batch processing*, running periodically whenever input data was loaded into the systems. RPO and RTO could span days or even weeks, depending on these application periods, and recovery technologies were focused on data backup and retrieval.

Data was usually stored on *tapes*, and connectivity was represented by the physical transport of such tapes to the backup site. Not preposterously, this method of data transport was sometimes called PTAM, or "Pick-up Truck Access Method."

Depending on how small an application RTO was, a company used a *cold-standby* or a *warm-standby* site. A cold-standby site required software (and sometimes hardware) installation before data could be retrieved and delivered to the application. Alternatively, a warm-standby site had software and hardware already prepared for the data loading. Nonetheless, both of these scenarios required manual intervention to satisfy the desired recovery objectives.

With such expectations, some companies simply preferred not to invest in additional facilities. In general, they decided to hire specialized providers, such as SunGard and IBM, to comprise these services instead.

The Hot Age (1990s to Mid-2000s)

This period encompasses the Internet boom and the advent of electronic business. Then, online applications were characterized by the need of *real-time responses*. Consequently, employed recovery technologies were primarily focused on *service availability*, where an extended downtime of an IT system could easily represent the demise of a company.

It was expected that a remote data center site was able to react very quickly to a major failure on the main facility. Therefore, the sum of RPO and RTO for these applications was generally confined to hours, or even minutes.

Hence, companies preferred to deploy *hot-standby* remote sites. Basically, these were data centers that were ready to automatically respond to a major incident in the primary data center (in some cases, a minimal manual intervention was recommended to avoid erroneous behaviors).

To satisfy such requirements, the concept of *geographic clusters* (or geoclusters) was created during this period. A geocluster is usually comprised of a set of application servers (or nodes) installed on at least two geographically separated sites. Within these extended server clusters, a detected failure on the active node triggers an automatic switchover to a standby node, which from this moment on processes the application transactions.

Figure 8-1 depicts an example of a geocluster.

In a generic geocluster, the active node processes the client requests received on the public interface, saves the operation data in a nonvolatile storage device, and (optionally) informs the standby node about this operation. Meanwhile, the standby node constantly checks whether the active node is working properly to decide whether a switchover is necessary. If the standby node becomes active, it should be able to access the stored data in the primary data center, or a copy of this data already located in the secondary data center.

Some examples of geoclusters are Microsoft Windows Server Failover Cluster, Veritas Cluster Server, and Oracle Real Application Cluster (RAC).

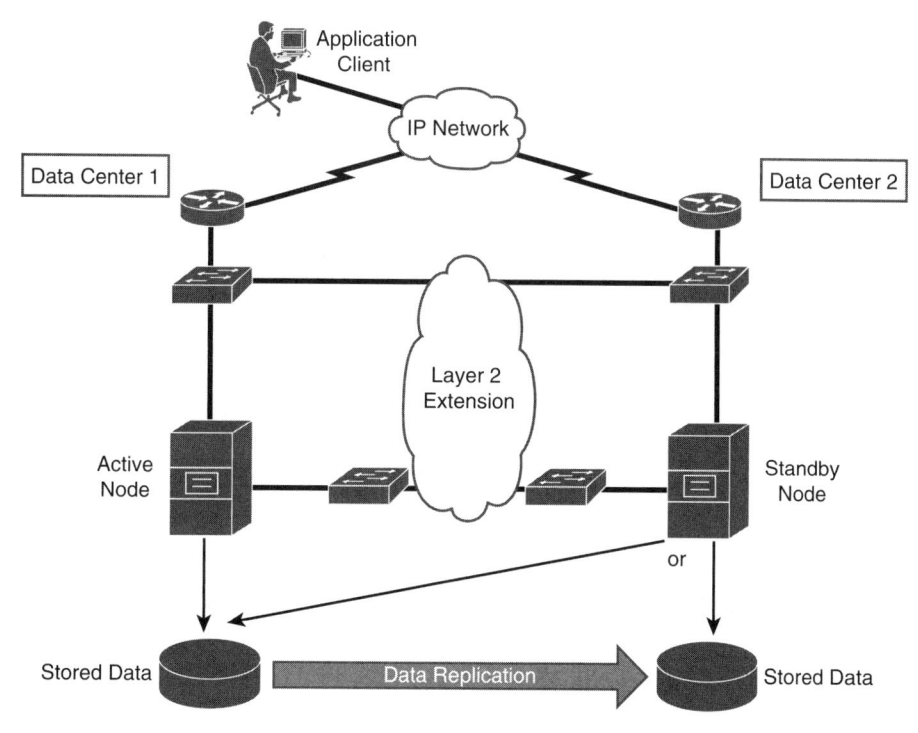

Figure 8-1 *Geocluster*

Note Geocluster internal mechanisms can vary wildly depending on the software version and vendor. My intention with this definition is to offer a theoretical model that can include all these variations, independently from their idiosyncrasies.

Geoclusters generally require data replication to the hot-standby site. In *synchronous replications*, the storage device on the primary site only confirms a server-requested data change (or *write*) if this change was already copied to the secondary site. Thus, to avoid latency-related issues, data centers that deploy synchronous replication are usually apart by tens of kilometers.

On the other hand, *asynchronous replications* are a more relaxed recovery solution because data is periodically copied from the primary to the secondary site. Hence, the intended RPO for an application defines its replication period.

Note Storage replication will be further explored in Chapter 9, "Storage Evolution."

Network availability between the sites is critical for the transport of different types of geocluster communication, such as

- "Heartbeat" communication, which is used by the cluster servers to verify the state of other nodes

- Application state information that should be shared by all cluster nodes (for example, cached data for database servers)

- Client traffic, especially if the nodes share the same virtual IP (VIP) address.

> **Tip** The complete set of solutions used to transport data between geographically dispersed sites is generically referred as *Data Center Interconnect (DCI)*.

The Active-Active Age (Mid-2000s to Today)

By definition, a *hot-standby* site houses hardware and software resources that are ready to be used in the case of a major failure at the main site. However, these resources are expected to be activated for a small amount of time per year, because some critical applications require very short recovery objectives (RPO of 0 and RTO of some seconds). Consequently, several companies decided that they simply could not afford the luxury of unused sites and expressed their intention to deploy *active-active* data center facilities.

Within such design principles, applications are expected to use resources from all distributed sites. To avoid the waste of hardware and software resources, new technologies were developed to support this behavior. More specifically

- Server clusters that can deploy several active nodes dispersed over multiple data centers

- Server and storage virtualization technologies that provide automatic and quick workload mobility between sites

Although they can increase resource utilization, active-active designs also challenge the scalability and flexibility of several established DCI technologies. And in the next section, I will address one of the most discussed topics among data center network designers: Layer 2 extensions between remote sites.

The Case for Layer 2 Extensions

To decrease fate sharing in distributed data centers, Cisco generically recommends that Layer 3 connections are deployed in DCI. This principle allows the reduction of Layer 2 environments to their smallest possible scope and isolates each site from remote network instabilities.

Notwithstanding, some applications simply cannot function under these conditions. More specifically, the majority of geoclusters require *Layer 2 adjacency between their nodes*.

There are basically two reasons why geographic clusters require broadcast domain extension between data centers:

- Heartbeat and connection state communications are usually directed to multiple destinations (from one node to the others). For simplicity, cluster manufacturers prefer to define this communication as broadcast, multicast, or even unknown unicast Ethernet frames (flooding).
- Active and standby nodes usually share the same virtual IP and MAC address to facilitate traffic handling in the case of a failure.

Note Some cluster vendors, such as Microsoft and Veritas, also offer geocluster solutions that can communicate over Layer 3 networks. Nonetheless, they do not represent the general case.

Server migration from one data center to another also justifies the extension of VLANs between sites. Some applications do not support IP readdressing because these values are already embedded in their codes, or simply because it can generate painstakingly complex operations.

Tip I am referring both to physical server migration and to virtual server online migration. The latter will be further explored in Chapter 13, "Server Evolution."

Data center expansion can also require that Layer 2 communication between sites continue to happen. This situation is very common when a data center has reached a physical limitation (such as power or space) and when a company hires a colocation service from an outsourcing data center.

As a result, data center network designers started to deploy standard Layer 2 connections to provide extended VLANs over multiple data centers. Unsurprisingly, they have faced various difficulties in this endeavor.

Challenges of Layer 2 Extensions

The risks related to VLAN extensions between data centers mirror some of the annoyances that Ethernet and Spanning Tree Protocol bring to LAN designers.

Although *flooding* and *broadcast* are necessary for IP communication in Ethernet networks, they can become quite dangerous in data center interconnections. If unknown unicast or broadcast frames are not controlled, the loops over the Layer 2 extensions can be easily formed, threatening the network availability on all connected data centers.

While loop avoidance mechanisms can control the effects of multidestination traffic over Layer 2 extensions, they can also disrupt the operation of multiple data centers at the same time. More precisely, a spanning tree instance that spans multiple sites presents formidable challenges, such as

- **Scalability:** *STP diameter* can be defined as the number of hops between two switches that belong to a spanning tree. When data centers are connected, the Spanning Tree Protocol (STP) diameter can easily surpass the IEEE-recommended value of 7, bringing unexpected results.

- **Isolation:** When an STP instance is extended to multiple sites, only one of them will contain the root switch. If this device fails, or if a topology change happens, all VLANs within that instance will be affected by a reconvergence. And because STP is a conservative protocol, preferring connectivity loss over temporary loops, traffic can be interrupted on all sites during the entire process.

- **Multihoming:** Because STP elects a single path between the root and any other switch in the spanning tree, multiple DCI links between sites will simply not be used for data communication.

Figure 8-2 illustrates these challenges in a Layer 2 connection between two data centers.

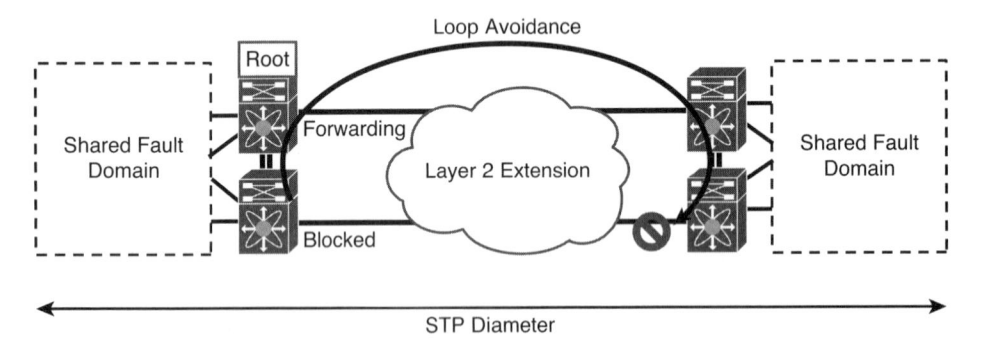

Figure 8-2 *STP Challenges in DCI*

Another collateral effect called *tromboning* can be formed between data centers, when nonoptimal internal routing happens within extended VLANs. Figure 8-3 illustrates this effect in an active-active geocluster scenario.

In the figure, outgoing traffic from both servers zig-zags between data centers whenever a Layer 3 device forwards IP packets from the servers. As you can observe, the uncontrolled state of an active-standby pair of devices (default gateways, load balancers, firewalls, and routers) is the cause for this potential waste of DCI resources.

Data confidentiality is also a challenge that some companies must address when using communication channels that are not totally under their control. Some industries have compliance rules that mandate strict forms of encryption in their data center interconnect to minimize the risk of data leakage.

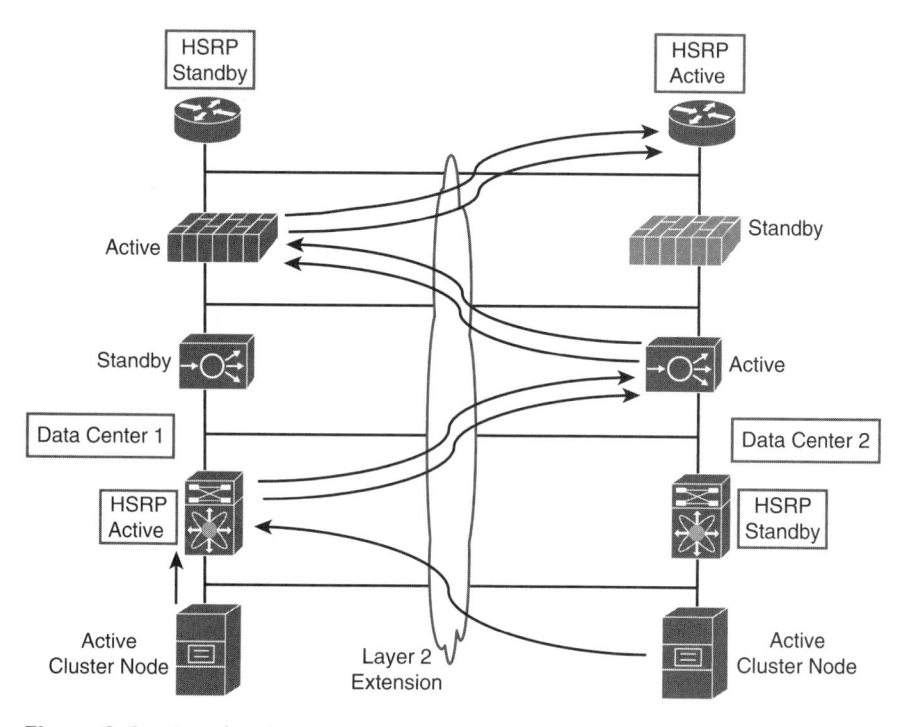

Figure 8-3 *Tromboning in Action*

There is no panacea, or unique solution, that solves every challenge presented in this section on all available scenarios. Different designs and features must be applied to each customer case, according to the communication resources available for the DCI solution.

Virtual PortChannels, FabricPath, Ethernet over MPLS, Virtual Private LAN Service, and Overlay Transport Virtualization are examples of virtualization technologies that can be used in Layer 2 extension between data centers. As you will see in the next sections, all these techniques aim to leverage traditional processes without exposing remote sites to undesirable risky behaviors.

Ethernet Extensions over Optical Connections

Optical connections can prove be an excellent option for data centers that are separated by less than a few hundred kilometers.

In this context, the term *dark fiber* refers to a fiber-optic pair that can be used to connect networking devices from a service provider or a private customer. A dark fiber transport capacity can be increased with the use of *wavelength-division multiplexing (WDM)* technologies. WDM allows multiple optical carrier signals to be multiplexed on a single optical fiber through the use of distinct wavelengths for each carrier. These solutions can also provide native redundancy through the use of *ring topologies*, which automatically react to a physical connection failure.

The most popular WDM technologies are as follows:

- **Coarse wavelength-division multiplexing (CWDM):** This technology can multiplex eight optical carrier signals. Usually, special switch transceivers provide the carrier signal transformation.
- **Dense wavelength-division multiplexing (DWDM):** This is capable of aggregating a higher number of optical carrier signals (128, for example). Generally, the carrier signal transformation is provided by the DWDM equipment itself.

Unsurprisingly, Cisco provides DWDM solutions, such as the ONS 15000 line of products. The company also offers switch transceivers that can directly send a transformed carrier to a DWDM device, avoiding the installation of multiplexing circuits on this equipment.

Because dark fiber and WDMs are basically communication solutions that belong to Layer 1 of the OSI model, they can transport any data-link protocol, including, of course, Ethernet.

Virtual PortChannels

As you have learned in Chapter 6, "Fooling Spanning Tree," vPCs can greatly simplify the way STP behaves inside a data center. In Layer 2 extensions, vPCs can also transform multiple Ethernet links into a single-switch STP connection.

Figure 8-4 exhibits how a double-sided vPC can optimize a Layer 2 extension provided by a pair of DWDM devices.

> **Tip** The switches depicted in Figure 8-4 can represent aggregation switches, or exclusive switches that are being used to extend VLANs from multiple network PODs (Pool of Devices). From now on, I will use the term *DCI switch* to refer to both of them.

In the figure, the left topology shows that STP does not allow Ethernet traffic on all the links between DCI switches. Also, an STP instance is spread over both sites, which are now sharing any internal topology change or reconvergence.

Alternatively, the topology on the right in Figure 8-4 shows how a virtual PortChannel positioned between DCI switches can leverage the following benefits to this scenario:

- Multihoming is enabled because all connections between data centers are being used (and load balanced).
- Spanning tree topology is simplified, because there is only one connection between sites.
- Optionally, if the vPC peer switch feature is deployed on the DCI switches, a device failure will not result in a reconvergence.
- At the time of this writing, the M-series modules on the Nexus 7000 support native encryption of Ethernet frames through the IEEE 802.1AE standard. This implementation uses Advanced Encryption Standard (AES) cipher and a 128-bit shared key.

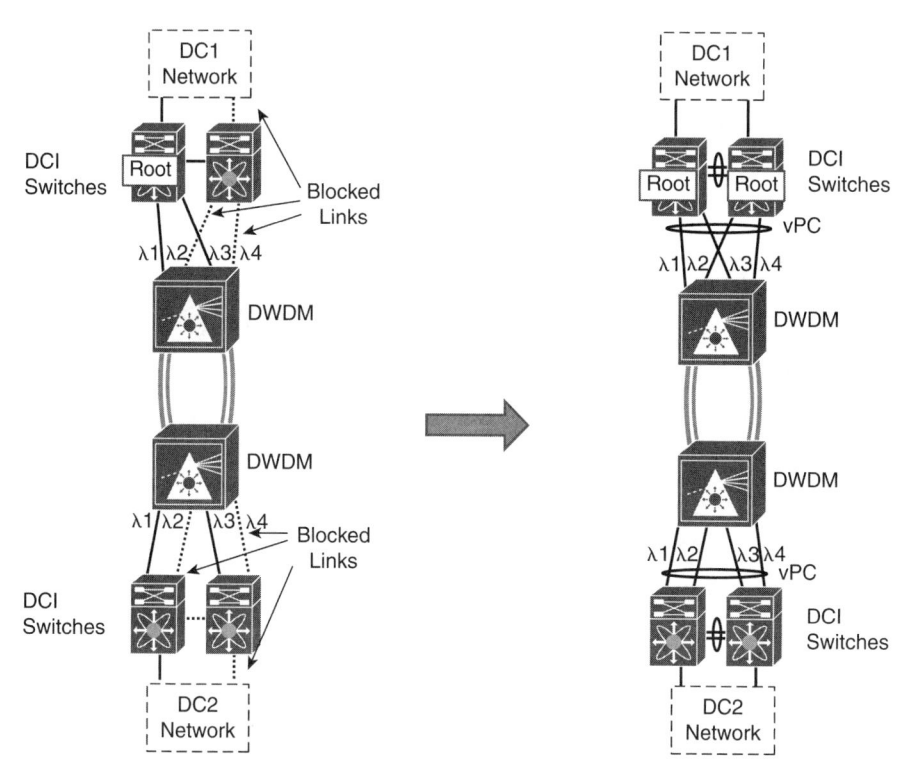

Figure 8-4 *Virtual PortChannel on a Layer 2 Extension*

Loops are formed when a classical Ethernet network has multiple active paths between two switches. Because the double-sided vPC characterizes a single connection from the STP perspective, disjoint STP instances can be deployed in each data center. Such isolation can be achieved with bridge protocol data unit (BPDU) filtering on DCI interfaces or the configuration of a distinct Multiple Spanning Tree (MST) region on each site.

vPC recommendations and best practices still apply to Layer 2 extensions. For example, it is still recommended that you use different vPC domains for each site and that Layer 3 communication between vPC peers is performed on dedicated routed links.

Note Although I am focusing on virtual PortChannels in DCI deployments, other cross-switch aggregation techniques, such as Virtual Switch Systems (VSS), can also be used on these scenarios.

Unfortunately, vPCs cannot help full-mesh extensions among three or more data centers as easily. Because vPCs can form a logical looped topology, these scenarios must abide by a hub-and-spoke formation to deploy disjoint STP instances per site.

Figure 8-5 exhibits a multisite vPC connection example scenario, where STP isolation is enabled on all DCI switches.

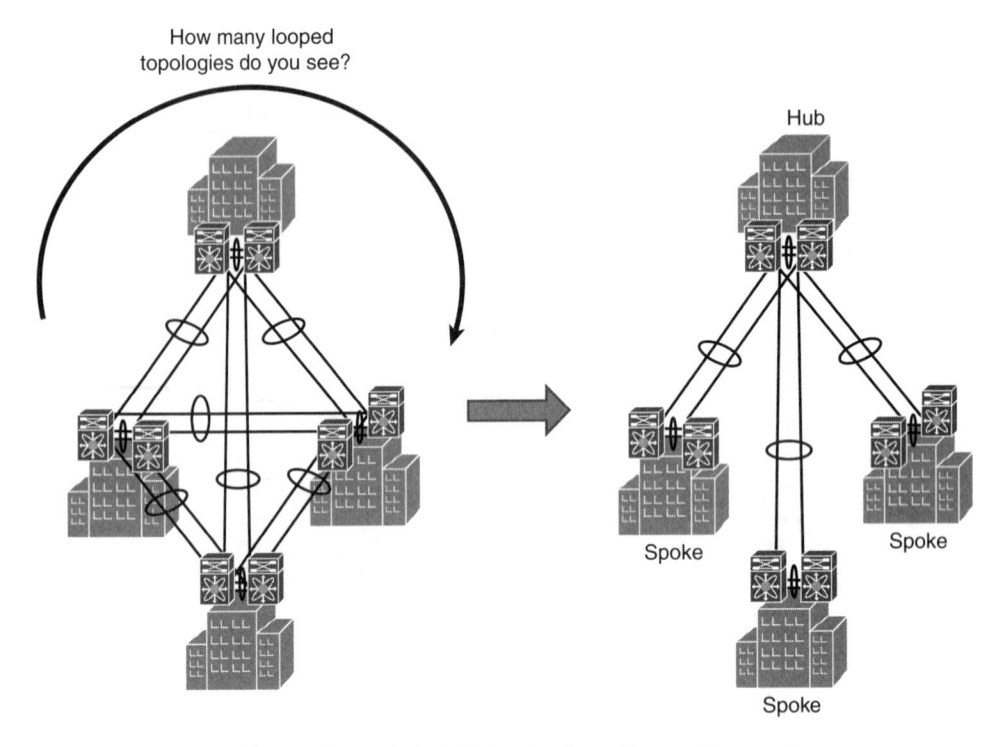

Figure 8-5 *Virtual PortChannels in Multipoint Data Center Connections*

In the figure, the hub-and-spoke topology was manually enforced to avoid loops in the Layer 2 extension. Traffic between spoke data centers must traverse the hub site, which can be quite cumbersome depending on each site location and available link resources.

In all discussed topologies, if the DCI switches deploy vPCs on Nexus 7000 M-series module interfaces, data can be encrypted through the IEEE 802.1AE standard.

FabricPath

The characteristics of FabricPath make it a special candidate for data center interconnection over optical connections. As you have also learned in Chapter 6, FabricPath can bring the following benefits to Layer 2 extensions between data centers:

- FabricPath has a built-in loop avoidance mechanism based on Intermediate System–to–Intermediate System (IS-IS).

- Contrarily to STP, FabricPath can use all available paths to *route* Ethernet traffic between two sites, with considerable configuration easiness (the **switchport isis metric** interface command can be used to control the traffic between sites).

- Conversational learning optimizes the use of the MAC address tables on FabricPath edge switches.

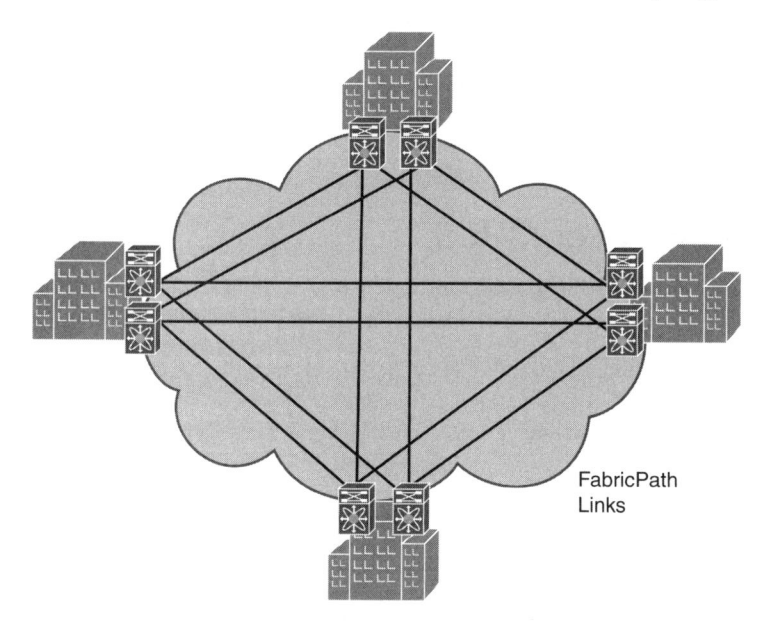

Figure 8-6 shows how FabricPath acts over a multisite topology.

Figure 8-6 *FabricPath in a Multisite Interconnection*

If STP is still being used on the internal networks, with the **spanning-tree domain** command, FabricPath can create completely disjoint STP instances for each site. And if FabricPath DCI switches on different sites are configured with distinct STP domains, Topology Change Notifications (TCN) are not transported over the FabricPath network, and fault isolation between sites is increased.

FabricPath demands special attention to unknown unicast, multicast, and broadcast traffic between sites. Because the protocol deploys multidestination trees to avoid loops caused by this type of traffic, link *polarization* (unbalancing) can become an unwanted collateral effect depending on this traffic amount.

To mitigate this situation, you should check the availability of multiple FabricPath topologies in your network devices. With this possibility, extended VLANs can be distributed among these topologies to avoid that multidestination traffic overuse a single optical connection.

Although Nexus 7000 switches can offer both technologies, at the time of this writing, they cannot deploy FabricPath and IEEE 802.1AE encryption in the same interface.

Note In any FabricPath design, it is very important that this protocol scalability and characteristics are observed and respected. I recommend that you refer to the Cisco online documentation to find the most recent values for your software and hardware combination. For example, at the time of this writing, the Nexus 7000 FabricPath implementation supports 2000 VLANs, 256 switch IDs, and one topology. On the other hand, Nexus 6000 and Nexus 5500 switches support up to 4000 VLANs, 128 switch IDs, and two topologies.

Ethernet Extensions over MPLS

Originated from the Cisco tag switching, *Multiprotocol Label Switching (MPLS)* has enabled a series of new services in service provider and enterprise networks.

MPLS provides packet forwarding based on *labels* inserted between the Layer 2 and the Layer 3 headers. This is why MPLS is sometimes referred as a "Layer 2.5" technology and is the main reason for its independence from Layer 2 and Layer 3 transport protocols. In truth, MPLS permits the transport of any type of data, including Ethernet frames.

Figure 8-7 details the 32-byte MPLS label structure and shows how it is inserted in a standard protocol data unit.

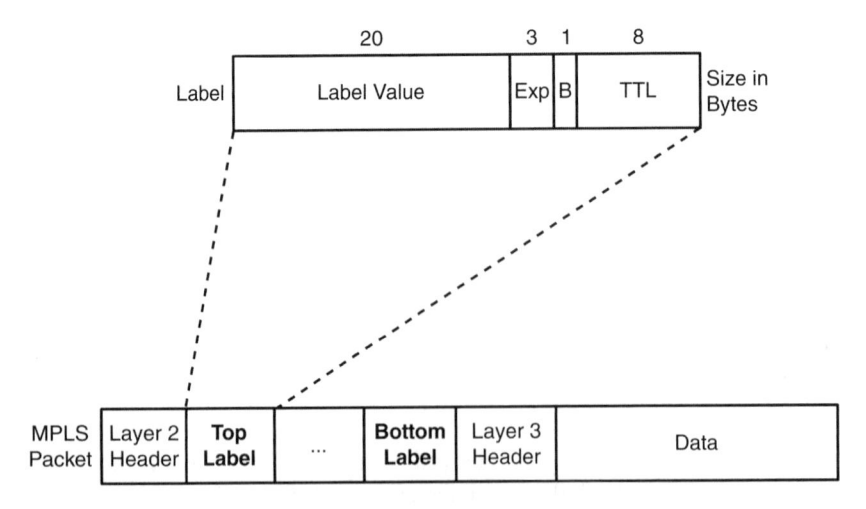

Figure 8-7 *MPLS Label and MPLS Packet*

Each MPLS label has the following header fields:

- **Label Value:** Unstructured data that represents *how* an MPLS device should handle this packet.

- **Experimental (Exp):** Originally designed for experimental use, this field is currently used to define quality of service classes in MPLS networks.

- **Bottom of Stack (B):** Signals that this frame is the bottom of the label stack.
- **Time to Live (TTL):** Designed to mitigate loops within an MPLS network. By default, this field is decremented by 1 for every hop it traverses in the MPLS network. When it reaches the value of 0, the packet is discarded.

The original motivation of MPLS was to avoid the longest prefix match software-based routers had to deploy when forwarding IP packets. Although this is no longer a limitation for hardware-based modern routers, the architecture of MPLS allowed a myriad of services that determined its longevity.

More precisely, the capability of stacking labels on a single MPLS packet defines this protocol flexibility. This label structure permits the implementation of different MPLS services, such as

- **Traffic Engineering (TE):** Permits the use of alternative network paths that would not be used in standard routing protocol implementations. With this service, unidirectional tunnels are explicitly configured and defined by a specific *tunnel label*, which is pushed to the top of the stack to override the routing protocol decision.
- **Layer 3 Virtual Private Networks (VPN):** This service allows an MPLS network to be able to connect different VPNs, which are set of sites that can communicate with each other and are under the same administrative policies. In this service, an inner label represents the VPN a packet belongs to, whereas the top label is used to route traffic between sites that belong to the same VPN.
- **Any Transport over MPLS (AToM):** Allows the transport of Layer 2 frames over an MPLS network. In this service, the inner label represents a *virtual circuit (VC)* that forwards the frame between two edges of the MPLS network.

Note L3 VPNs use Virtual Routing and Forwarding (VRF) to deploy different routing and forwarding tables for each customer VPN. These virtual structures are also used for slightly different purposes within data center networks, as discussed previously in Chapter 3, "The Humble Beginnings of Network Virtualization."

AToM provides the basis for Layer 2 extensions over MPLS. As you will learn in the next sections, MPLS networks can provide two types of transport methods for Ethernet frames: *Ethernet over MPLS (EoMPLS)* and *Virtual Private LAN Service (VPLS)*. However, to explain their intricacies, I must explore some MPLS concepts first.

MPLS Basic Concepts

A group of MPLS packets that share the same label is called *Forwarding Equivalence Class (FEC)*. In an MPLS network, an FEC is handled distinctively by two types of routers: *label edge routers (LER)* and *label switch routers (LSR)*.

Figure 8-8 illustrates how these devices are defined by their position in an MPLS topology.

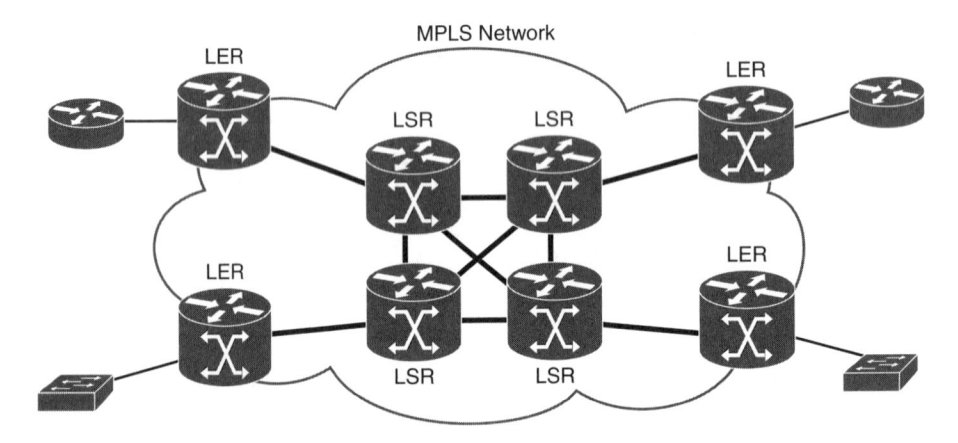

Figure 8-8 *Sample MPLS Topology*

Positioned at the border of an MPLS network, an LER classifies protocol data units, *pushes* (imposes) labels to these units, and forwards them to a next-hop LSR. Each LSR forwards MPLS packets inside the MPLS backbone based on the top label on the stack, and labels can be swapped along the path. When a packet finally arrives at its proper egress LER, this device *pops* (removes) the labels and forwards the packet to a non-MPLS-connected device.

Note To reduce the load on edge MPLS routers, the majority of LSRs remove the outmost label right before delivering it to the egress LER. This technique is called *Penultimate Hop Popping (PHP)*.

MPLS networks depend on a previously established routing protocol to define their IP address reachability. Protocols such as Open Shortest Path First (OSPF), IS-IS, or Border Gateway Protocol (BGP) are therefore used to generate a Routing Information Base (RIB), a Forwarding Information Base (FIB), and a resulting *Label Forwarding Information Base (LFIB)*, which is mapped to MPLS interfaces.

The *Label Distribution Protocol (LDP)*, defined in RFCs 3035 and 3036, is the principal mechanism for label distribution within an MPLS network. This protocol also allows the discovery of MPLS devices through UDP port 646, using TCP port 646 for session establishment and actual label assignment.

Note Other protocols, such as BGP, can also distribute labels for other MPLS services (Layer 3 VPNs, for example).

In summary, a basic MPLS network deployment should include the following elements on each MPLS router:

- A loopback interface, to improve reachability in the network (because it does not depend on the operational state of a physical interface).

- A routing protocol, to advertise connected subnets (including the one configured on the loopback) to the other MPLS routers.

- LDP, to enable device discovery and label distribution. Preferably, the loopback interface is configured as a router identifier on these messages.

- MPLS interfaces between routers. The **mpls ip** command enables label-based forwarding.

To effectively illustrate these configuration elements, Figure 8-9 represents a sample MPLS network with three MPLS routers.

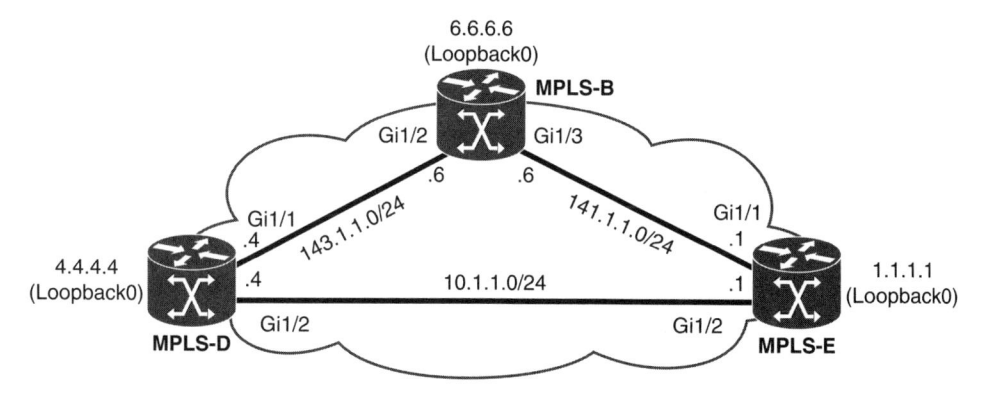

Figure 8-9 *Example MPLS Network*

Example 8-1 details router MPLS-B configuration.

Note I have used Catalyst 6500 switches, equipped with SUP-2T, to deploy all the MPLS configurations presented in this chapter.

Example 8-1 *MPLS-B Configuration and MPLS Interface Status*

```
! Displaying all the interfaces configuration
MPLS-B# show running-config interface loopback 0 | begin interface
interface Loopback0
 ip address 6.6.6.6 255.255.255.255
end
MPLS-B# show running-config interface gigabitEthernet 1/2 | begin interface
```

```
interface GigabitEthernet1/2
 description Connected to MPLS-D
 ip address 143.1.1.6 255.255.255.0
! Enabling MPLS on interface Gi1/2
 mpls ip
end
MPLS-B# show running-config interface gigabitEthernet 1/3 | begin interface
interface GigabitEthernet1/3
 description Connected to MPLS-E
 ip address 141.1.1.6 255.255.255.0
! Enabling MPLS on interface Gi1/2
 mpls ip
end
! OSPF is configured as a routing protocol to define address
reachability inside the MPLS network
MPLS-B# show running-config | begin router
router ospf 100
 router-id 6.6.6.6
 network 6.6.6.6 0.0.0.0 area 0
 network 141.1.1.6 0.0.0.0 area 0
 network 143.1.1.6 0.0.0.0 area 0
!
[output suppressed]
! Configuring LDP globally in MPLS-B
MPLS-B# show running-config | include ldp
! This command allows that this device maintains its forwarding label
bindings if the LDP session is interrupted (default timer is 120
seconds)
mpls ldp graceful-restart
! Forcing the LDP messages to use the loopback0 as source address
mpls ldp router-id Loopback0 force
! Verifying the MPLS interface status when similar configurations are
deployed to MPLS-D and MPLS-E
MPLS-B# show mpls interfaces
Interface           IP          Tunnel   BGP Static Operational
GigabitEthernet1/2  Yes (ldp)   No       No  No     Yes
GigabitEthernet1/3  Yes (ldp)   No       No  No     Yes
```

For brevity, I will not show the configurations applied to MPLS-D and MPLS-E. They are very similar to the MPLS-B configuration, except for interface names and IP addresses that are already described in Figure 8-9.

Example 8-2 details the labels used in MPLS-D to forward IP packets inside this network (when all devices are configured as described).

Note I have tweaked MPLS-D's routing table a bit to force MPLS-B to be its next hop for packets directed to MPLS-E.

Example 8-2 *Sample Label Binding in MPLS-D*

```
! Changing the route to 1.1.1.1 to use MPLS-B as the next hop
MPLS-D(config)# interface gigabitEthernet 1/2
MPLS-D(config-if)# ip ospf cost 65535
MPLS-D(config-if)# exit
! Verifying the label used to forward packets to route 1.1.1.1/32
(MPLS-E loopback0 interface)
MPLS-D# show mpls ip binding 1.1.1.1 32
  1.1.1.1/32
! This binding is used when packets with label 19 are received (from MPLS-B)
        in label:     19
! Penultimate Hop Popping is performed to forward packets direcly to
MPLS-E. This binding is not actually being used to
forward packets to 1.1.1.1
        out label:    imp-null   lsr: 1.1.1.1:0
! Label 20 is inserted on packets to 1.1.1.1 that are routed through
MPLS-B. This binding is actually being used to
forward packets to 1.1.1.1
        out label:    20         lsr: 6.6.6.6:0           inuse
```

In Example 8-2, you can see that labels were assigned to every route generated by the routing protocol to destination 1.1.1.1. Because I have increased the OSPF cost on the MPLS-D interface connected to MPLS-E, an IP packet received in MPLS-D with destination 1.1.1.1 will be forwarded to MPLS-B with a label value of 20. MPLS packets received with label 19 will receive the same treatment.

Example 8-3 details the label binding for the same packets directed to 1.1.1.1, but in MPLS-B.

Example 8-3 *Sample Label Binding in MPLS-B*

```
! Verifying the label used to forward packets to route 1.1.1.1/32
(MPLS-E loopback0 interface)
MPLS-B# show mpls ip binding 1.1.1.1 32
  1.1.1.1/32
! This binding is used when packets with label 20 are received (from MPLS-D)
        in label:     20
! This binding is actually being used to forward packets to 1.1.1.1
and Penultimate Hop Popping is performed to forward packets directly
```

```
to MPLS-E.
        out label:      imp-null  lsr: 1.1.1.1:0           inuse
! Alternative route where Label 19 is inserted on packets to 1.1.1.1
that are routed through MPLS-D
        out label:      19        lsr: 4.4.4.4:0
```

In Example 8-3, it is clear that MPLS packets received with label 20 (remember them?) will be forwarded to MPLS-E without any label ("implicit null" means that MPLS-D is performing Penultimate Hop Popping).

This basic configuration provides the foundation where MPLS services such as EoMPLS and VPLS can be defined, as you will see in the next two sections.

Ethernet over MPLS

EoMPLS is arguably the most deployed AToM technology today. For many years, EoMPLS was also referred as "draft-martini" because it was defined on a draft RFC submitted to the Internet Engineering Task Force (IETF) by Cisco employee Luca Martini. In 2007, RFC 4095 ("Encapsulation Methods for Transport over Layer 2 Frames over MPLS") finally standardized the protocol.

In essence, EoMPLS encapsulates Ethernet frames within MPLS packets, which will be transported, decapsulated, and delivered as they were, at the egress of an MPLS network.

A *virtual circuit (VC)* is established between two LERs, and one VC identifier is used to differentiate circuits that are defined on the same edge device. Therefore, each EoMPLS packet has a label stack comprised of a *VC label*, which characterizes its virtual circuit, and a *path label*, which routes the packet from the ingress LER to the egress LER.

Tip Both labels must be accounted for in the maximum transmission unit (MTU) interface configuration within the MPLS network.

The standard describes two types of virtual circuits for Ethernet frames:

- **VLAN-based (VC Type 4)**: Transports frames without the IEEE 802.1Q tag
- **Port-based (VC Type 5)**: Transports frames with the IEEE 802.1Q tag

EoMPLS-enabled networks provide a virtual connection referred to as a *pseudowire*. This entity is basically the emulation of an Ethernet cable between customer edge (CE) devices that are connected to distinct LERs, which can be also called provider edge (PE) devices.

Through the MPLS topology built in the previous section, Figure 8-10 demonstrates the configuration of an EoMPLS pseudowire enabling the exchange of frames between two switches connected to MPLS-D and MPLS-E.

```
SUP2T-D#show running-config interface
gigabitEthernet 1/3 | begin interface
interface GigabitEthernet1/3
 no ip address
 no keepalive
 xconnect 1.1.1.1 1 encapsulation mpls
end
```

```
SUP2T-E#show running-config interface
gigabitEthernet 1/7 | begin interface
interface GigabitEthernet1/7
 no ip address
 no keepalive
 xconnect 4.4.4.4 1 encapsulation mpls
end
```

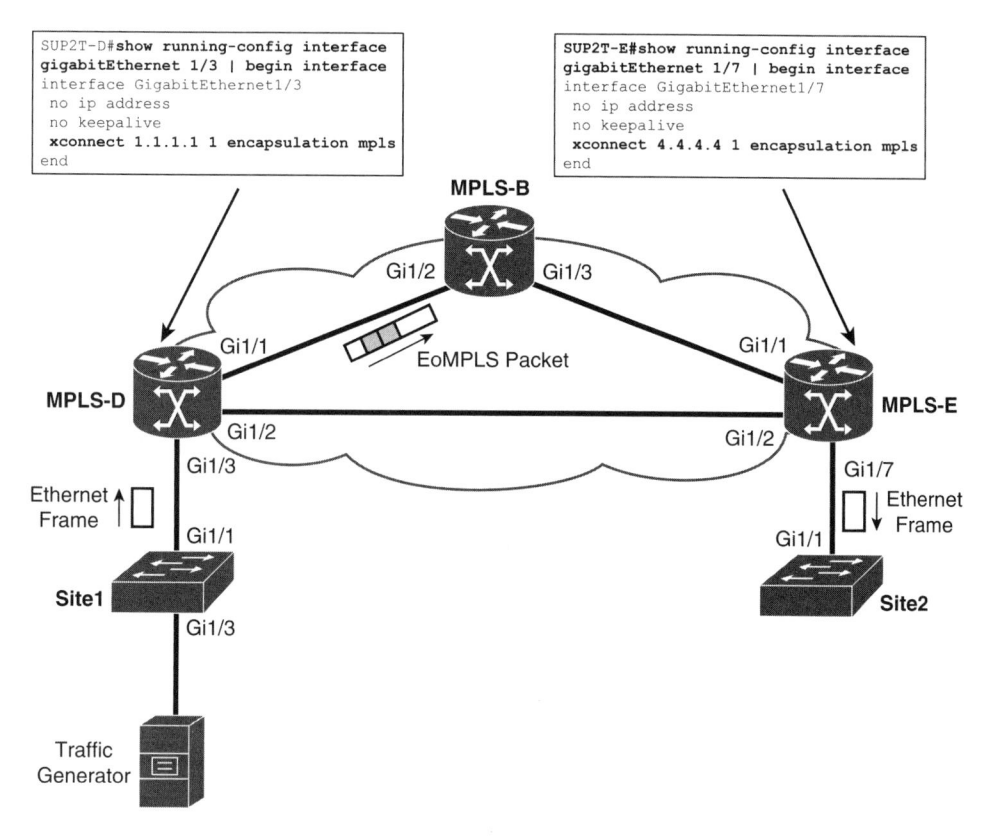

Figure 8-10 *EoMPLS Configuration*

In this specific scenario, I have configured a port-based virtual circuit because I have used the **xconnect** command directly in interfaces Gigabit Ethernet 1/3 on MPLS-D and Gigabit Ethernet 1/7 on MPLS-E.

Tip VLAN-based virtual circuits could be configured if the same command were applied to *subinterfaces* defined for a specific VLAN (for example, interfaces GigabitEthernet 1/3.50 and GigabitEthernet 1/7.50 for VLAN 50 in MPLS-D and MPLS-E, respectively).

The status of the virtual circuits created in MPLS-D and MPLS-E can be examined in Examples 8-4 and 8-5, respectively.

Example 8-4 *Virtual Circuit Status in MPLS-D*

```
MPLS-D# show mpls l2transport vc

Local intf     Local circuit          Dest address     VC ID       Status
-------------  ---------------------  ---------------  ----------  ------
Gi1/3          Ethernet               1.1.1.1          1           UP
```

Example 8-5 *Virtual Circuit Status in MPLS-E*

```
MPLS-E# show mpls l2transport vc

Local intf     Local circuit          Dest address     VC ID       Status
-------------  ---------------------  ---------------  ----------  ------
Gi1/7          Ethernet               4.4.4.4          1           UP
```

As you can see, Figure 8-10 exhibits a basic EoMPLS configuration intended to demonstrate its deployment simplicity. Although I have not demonstrated them here, the following enhancements can be added to an EoMPLS configuration:

- **Traffic Engineering:** MPLS allows explicitly defined paths to be used to transport EoMPLS packets. For example, a path with the lowest possible latency between PEs can be configured.

- **Fast reroute:** If Traffic Engineering is being used, this feature can protect EoMPLS traffic from a device or link failure in the main path.

- **Quality of service:** Reserves bandwidth resources for EoMPLS traffic.

In the topology shown in Figure 8-10, the formation of the pseudowire allows *every* Ethernet frame to be encapsulated in an MPLS packet, exactly as a physical wire would do. Consequently, this emulation also applies to the transport of unknown unicast frames and BPDUs.

Example 8-6 demonstrates that EoMPLS-connected devices still depend on flood-based MAC address learning, as a traffic generator connected to interface Gigabit Ethernet 1/3 in Site1 transmits unknown unicast frames. These frames were directed to MAC address 0000.0800.0002 and used 0000.0600.0002 as their source address.

Tip On switches Site1 and Site2, I have configured VLAN 101 and allowed this VLAN on the trunks connected to interface Gigabit Ethernet 1/3 in MPLS-D and interface Gigabit Ethernet 1/7 in MPLS-E.

Example 8-6 *MAC Address Table in Site2 After Flooding*

```
Site2# show mac address-table dynamic vlan 101
Legend: * - primary entry
        age - seconds since last seen
        n/a - not available

  vlan    mac address     type        learn     age        ports
------+----------------+--------+-----+----------+------------------
```

```
Active Supervisor:
*  101    0000.0600.0002    dynamic   Yes              0      Gi1/1
```

To understand how EoMPLS affects the STP behavior in CE devices, Examples 8-7 and 8-8 detail this protocol status in switches Site1 and Site2 from the same topology.

Example 8-7 *STP Status in Site1*

```
Site1# show spanning-tree vlan 101

VLAN0101
  Spanning tree enabled protocol rstp
  Root ID    Priority    32869
             Address     000b.45a9.7580
             This bridge is the root
[output suppressed]
! Traffic can be forwarded through the pseudowire
Interface           Role Sts Cost      Prio.Nbr Type
------------------- ---- --- --------- -------- --------------------
Gi1/1               Desg FWD 4         128.1    P2p
```

Example 8-8 *STP Status in Site2*

```
Site2# show spanning-tree vlan 101

VLAN0101
  Spanning tree enabled protocol rstp
  Root ID    Priority    32869
! Site1 is the Root
             Address     000b.45a9.7580
             Cost        4
             Port        1 (GigabitEthernet1/1)
             Hello Time  2 sec  Max Age 20 sec  Forward Delay 15 sec

  Bridge ID  Priority    32869  (priority 32768 sys-id-ext 101)
             Address     0013.5f1c.6600
             Hello Time  2 sec  Max Age 20 sec  Forward Delay 15 sec
             Aging Time 300
! BPDU forwarding is happening through the pseudowire
Interface           Role Sts Cost      Prio.Nbr Type
------------------- ---- --- --------- -------- --------------------
Gi1/1               Root FWD 4         128.1    P2p
```

Consequently, EoMPLS pseudowires bring to DCI switches the same challenges related to loop avoidance and STP isolation as optical connections. And as I have explained in the earlier section "Ethernet Extensions over Optical Connections," virtual PortChannels can help surpass both obstacles with simplicity.

Figure 8-11 details a highly available vPC-over-EoMPLS design between two data centers. The same recommendations apply in this scenario: Peers on different sites should use distinct vPC domains, and BPDU filtering (or distinct MST regions) should be deployed on DCI switches.

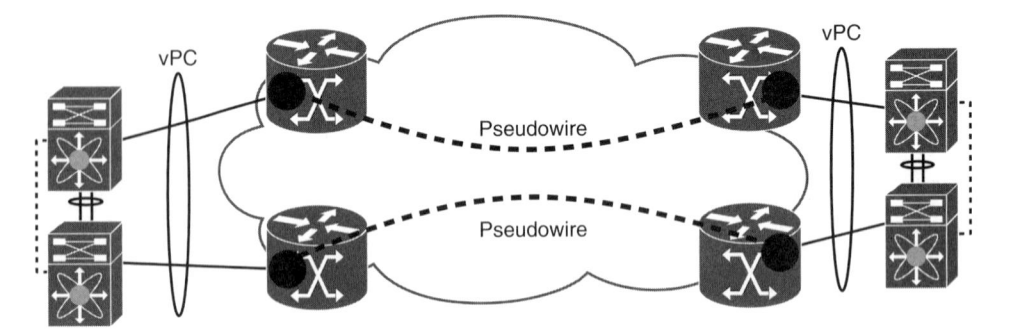

Figure 8-11 *Virtual PortChannel and EoMPLS*

Note Other cross-switch aggregation techniques, such as VSS, will also work in these scenarios.

Unsurprisingly, vPC over EoMPLS is not recommended in multisite scenarios. Although hub-and-spoke topologies could be also deployed in these cases, their drawbacks can be avoided with another MPLS Layer 2 extension service with intrinsic multipoint capabilities.

Virtual Private LAN Service

Virtual Private LAN Service (VPLS) is a VPN service that offers Layer 2 connectivity between sites that belong to the same customer.

A more sophisticated service than EoMPLS, VPLS provides emulation of a single giant virtual Ethernet bridge connected to all customer sites. In essence, VPLS is also deployed on MPLS provider edge devices whose configuration is comprised by the following elements:

- **Virtual Forwarding Instance (VFI):** Defines an Ethernet VPN domain within a provider edge MPLS router. It contains the addresses from other MPLS routers that are providing VPLS for a defined Layer 2 VPN.

- **Virtual circuits (VC):** Can be seen as pseudowires that are used to connect VPLS-enabled PEs.

- **Attachment interfaces:** Standard Layer 2 interfaces that are connected to a customer device.

A set of attachment interfaces, VFIs with the same VPN ID, and connecting pseudowires form a *VPLS instance*. The virtual bridge created by VPLS permits a VLAN to be connected between data centers, creating a single shared broadcast domain.

Conversely to EoMPLS, pseudowires are only used to connect VFIs, and not CE devices. BPDUs are not transported between different customer sites, and as a consequence, STP instances are local to each site.

To further explore the VPLS relationship to STP, Figure 8-12 presents a VPLS topology (originated from the same MPLS basic configuration shown in the earlier section "MPLS Basic Concepts").

Tip The last paragraph was just a nicer way to say that I have erased the EoMPLS configuration from Figure 8-10.

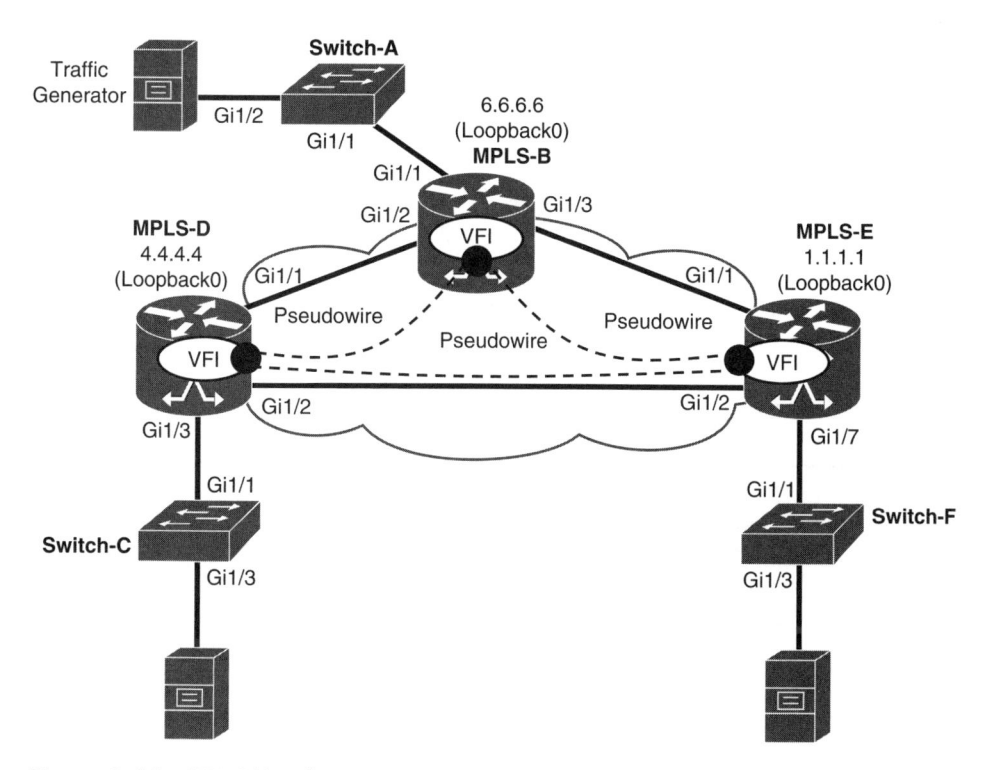

Figure 8-12 *VPLS Topology*

In this topology, all three MPLS routers are configured as VPLS PEs to represent a multisite scenario. The configuration of this service is only required on PEs because backbone MPLS routers are not aware of the services generated on edge devices. Analogous to EoMPLS, provider (P) routers must only forward the MPLS packets generated at the ingress PE.

A single VLAN extension over multiple sites requires the following at each VPLS PE:

- The creation of the VLAN

- A VFI configuration (defining the VPN ID and neighbors that deploy VFIs for the same VPLS instance)

- A Switch Virtual Interface (SVI) creation to bind the extended VLAN to the VFI.

Example 8-9 details this configuration for MPLS-D.

Example 8-9 *MPLS-D VPLS Configuration*

```
! Creating VLAN 202 that will be extended to MPLS-B and MPLS-E
MPLS-D# show running-config vlan 202 | include vlan
vlan 202
! Creating Virtual Forwarding Instance VPLS_202
MPLS-D# show running-config | begin 12
l2 vfi VPLS_202 manual
 vpn id 2
 neighbor 1.1.1.1 encapsulation mpls
 neighbor 6.6.6.6 encapsulation mpls
!
[output suppressed]
! Binding VLAN 202 to VFI
MPLS-D# show running-config interface vlan 202 | begin interface
interface Vlan202
 no ip address
 xconnect vfi VPLS_202
end
```

MPLS-B and MPLS-E share the same configuration (except they use different neighbor addresses in their VFI definitions) as MPLS-D. Afterward, I have connected the customer edge devices (Switch-A, Switch-C, and Switch-F) to attachment trunk interfaces in each PE, as depicted in Figure 8-12.

Examples 8-10, 8-11, and 8-12 demonstrate that, after each site individual convergence, the STP processes in the CE devices are only aware of the directly connected PE routers.

Example 8-10 *STP Status in Switch-A*

```
Switch-A# show spanning-tree vlan 202
! This switch is the Root in VLAN 202
VLAN0202
  Spanning tree enabled protocol rstp
  Root ID    Priority    32768
             Address     001d.7064.628a
             This bridge is the root
[output suppressed]
! All interfaces are in the forwarding state (as one would expect in a Root switch)
Interface           Role Sts Cost      Prio.Nbr Type
Gi1/1               Desg FWD 4         128.1    P2p
Gi1/2               Desg FWD 4         128.2    P2p
```

Example 8-11 *STP Status in Switch-C*

```
Switch-C# show spanning-tree vlan 202
! This switch is also a Root for VLAN 202!
VLAN0202
  Spanning tree enabled protocol rstp
  Root ID    Priority    32768
             Address     0021.d8c6.604a
             This bridge is the root
[output suppressed]
! All interfaces are in the forwarding state
Interface           Role Sts Cost      Prio.Nbr Type
------------------- ---- --- --------- -------- --------------------
Gi1/1               Desg FWD 4         128.1    P2p
Gi1/3               Desg FWD 4         128.3    P2p
```

Example 8-12 *STP Status in Switch-F*

```
Switch-F# show spanning-tree vlan 202
! This switch is not the root. But observe this device, the root ID
does not belong to Switch-A or Switch-C.
VLAN0202
  Spanning tree enabled protocol rstp
  Root ID    Priority    32768
! This is MPLS-E MAC address
             Address     0021.d8b2.2fca
             Cost        4
```

```
                    Port          1 (GigabitEthernet1/1)
                    Hello Time    2 sec  Max Age 20 sec  Forward Delay 15 sec

  Bridge ID  Priority    32768
             Address     0021.d8c5.e04a
             Hello Time    2 sec  Max Age 20 sec  Forward Delay 15 sec
             Aging Time 300
! All interfaces are forwarding
Interface              Role Sts Cost       Prio.Nbr Type
-------------------    ---- --- ---------  -------- --------------------
Gi1/1                  Root FWD 4          128.1    P2p
Gi1/3                  Desg FWD 4          128.3    P2p
```

The last three examples clearly show that VPLS provides, by default, STP isolation for customer sites.

Tip   To increase the isolation among customer and provider devices, it is recommended that edge trunk ports (with BPDU filtering) are configured in the attachment interfaces. In fact, STP can even be disabled on PE devices (with the **no spanning-tree vlan** command).

In VPLS, CEs and PEs learn MAC addresses transparently through their data plane. To demonstrate this behavior, I have used a traffic generator to insert Ethernet frames on interface Gigabit Ethernet 1/2 on Switch-A. These soon-to-be-flooded frames had a MAC source address of 0000.0500.0001 and an unknown unicast destination address of 0000.0100.0001.

Examples 8-13, 8-14, and 8-15 depict how this source MAC address is learned on each VPLS PE device (MPLS-B, MPLS-D, and MPLS-E).

Example 8-13   *Local MAC Addresses Learned in MPLS-B*

```
MPLS-B# show mac address-table dynamic vlan 202

Legend: * - primary entry
        age - seconds since last seen
[output suppressed]
Displaying entries from active supervisor:
! Locally learned address (Switch-A has flooded the frames)
    vlan    mac address    type     learn    age              ports
----+----+---------------+--------+------+----------+--------------------
*    202  0000.0500.0001  dynamic  Yes         0      Gi1/1
```

Example 8-14 *Remote MAC Address Learned in MPLS-D*

```
MPLS-D# show mac address-table dynamic vlan 202
[output suppressed]
Displaying entries from active supervisor:
! Remotely learned address (MPLS-B has flooded the frames)
    vlan   mac address      type     learn   age              ports
----+----+----------------+--------+-------+----------+-----------------------------
 *    202 0000.0500.0001   dynamic  Yes        0       VPLS peer 6.6.6.6(2:2)
```

Example 8-15 *Remote MAC Address Learned in MPLS-E*

```
MPLS-E# show mac address-table dynamic vlan 202
[output suppressed]
Displaying entries from DFC linecard [1]:
! Remotely learned address (MPLS-B has flooded the frames)
    vlan   mac address      type     learn   age              ports
----+----+----------------+--------+-------+----------+-----------------------------
 *    202 0000.0500.0001   dynamic  Yes        0       VPLS peer 6.6.6.6(2:1)
[output suppressed]
```

VPLS deploys an internal loop avoidance method based on a routing technique called *split horizon*. Enabled by default on PEs, split horizon does not allow a VPLS packet received from a virtual circuit to be forwarded to another connected VC.

Using our already configured VPLS network (Figure 8-12 and Example 8-9), you can observe that virtual circuits are automatically created to all neighbors, forming a full-mesh VC topology.

Example 8-16 exhibits the virtual circuit status in MPLS-B. Note the default split horizon state in this device.

Example 8-16 *Virtual Circuits in MPLS-B*

```
! All VCs are up and running
MPLS-B# show mpls l2transport vc
Local intf     Local circuit              Dest address    VC ID Status
-------------  -------------------------  -------------   -----------
VFI VPLS_202   VFI                        1.1.1.1           2    UP
VFI VPLS_202   VFI                        4.4.4.4           2    UP
! Verifying if split-horizon is enabled in each VC
MPLS-B# show vfi

Legend: RT=Route-target, S=Split-horizon, Y=Yes, N=No
```

```
VFI name: VPLS_202, state: up, type: multipoint
  VPN ID: 2
  Local attachment circuits:
    Vlan202
  Neighbors connected via pseudowires:
  Peer Address     VC ID       S
  4.4.4.4          2           Y
  1.1.1.1          2           Y
```

Note You can disable split horizon in a PE to build hub-and-spoke VPLS topologies, but you need to be careful about internal loops in these scenarios. As a matter of fact, *Hierarchical VPLS (H-VPLS)* designs are a good example of hub-and-spoke topologies being used securely in highly scalable VPLS networks.

As Figure 8-13 illustrates, a fully redundant VPLS deployment with dual PEs per site presents two immediate consequences:

- Because of split horizon, all PEs must be connected through a full mesh of pseudowires (except between PEs that belong to the same site).

- "Customer-provided" loops can occur when flooded (or broadcast) frames leave the VPLS network and return to it through an external Layer 2 network.

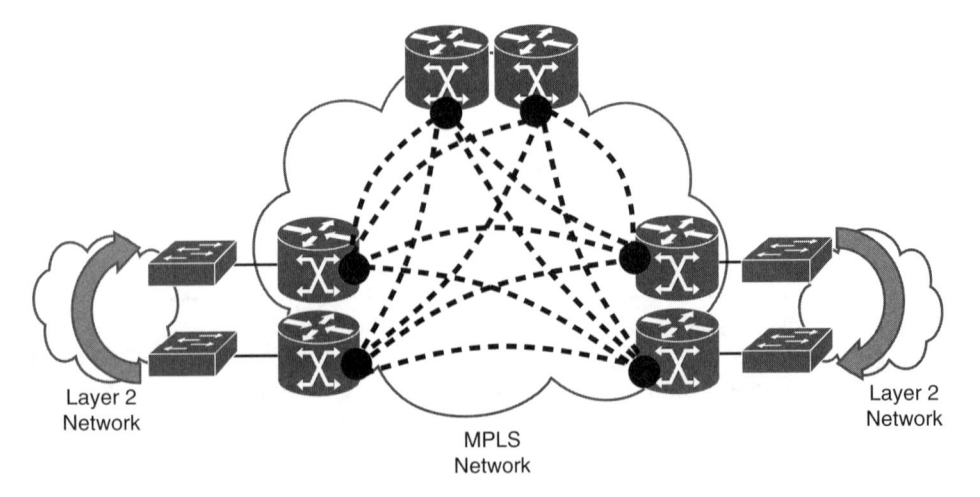

Figure 8-13 *Redundant VPLS Deployment*

Although the high number of virtual circuits can be difficult for management and troubleshooting, "customer-provided" loops are a much more unsettling problem for VPLS network administrators. But during the last few years, a diverse set of methods was developed to avoid such a situation.

These external loop avoidance solutions can be provided solely by CEs or can depend on some PE special capabilities. First, allow me to present a method that belongs to the first group of solutions.

Embedded Event Manager (EEM) is a powerful scripting tool available in several IOS and NX-OS switching platforms. EEM encompasses *policies* that are triggered by monitored *events* (interface status, route presence, and so on) and that executes a set of *actions* such as

- Logging
- Shutdown of some modules
- Reload
- Send an e-mail
- Execute a set of CLI commands

In fully redundant VPLS networks, EEM can force only one PE to be used on each site, disabling all Ethernet connections on redundant PEs. In the case of a device failure (PE or DCI), EEM activates the site connection to the secondary PE.

Figure 8-14 illustrates how EEM can provide a single active PE connection per site, disabling all attachment interfaces to the secondary PEs.

> **Note** All pseudowires remain active within the MPLS network. However, EEM implies that only a subset of these circuits is effectively used.

Although I will not exhibit the required EEM configuration, the following procedure is a possible deployment for redundant VPLS scenarios:

1. An SVI is created on the primary DCI switch, and it is associated to an exclusive VLAN between this device and the primary PE. Because of the autostate feature, this VLAN will go down if a failure occurs in the connection to the PE.

2. This SVI subnet is advertised to the secondary DCI switch through a routing protocol.

3. The secondary DCI switch executes a script that enables its connection to the secondary PE should this route disappear from its routing table.

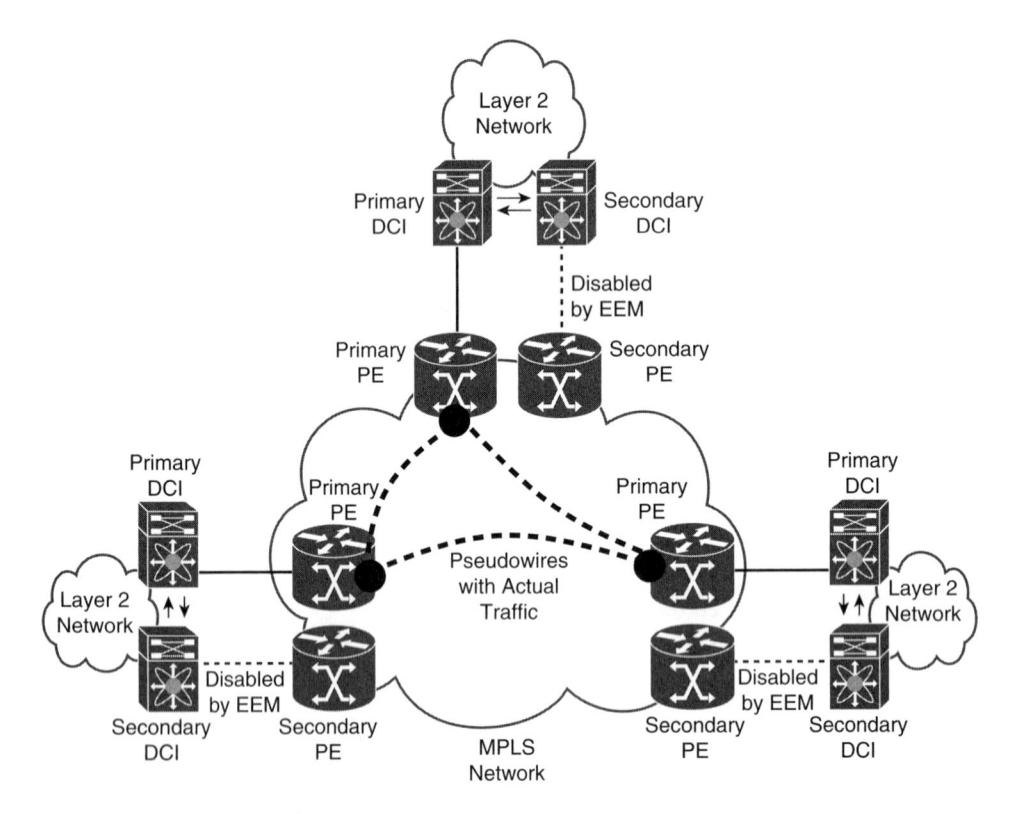

Figure 8-14 *EEM and VPLS*

The following additional details should also be considered in these EEM scripts:

- The preemption of the primary PE when its connection to the PE is operational again.
- Establishment of delays to avoid unnecessary flapping.
- Depending on the monitored elements (routes generated by an SVI), vPCs should be avoided because they can hide the specific failures that EEM must detect.
- Manual load balancing of VLANs to increase pseudowire utilization. For example, EEM can force even VLANs to use primary devices and odd VLANs to use secondary devices.

Advanced VPLS (A-VPLS) is another external loop avoidance solution in a scenario where there is some administrative control over the VPLS PEs (you can imagine a customer-owned MPLS backbone). Besides its concise configuration and pseudowire load-balancing features, this Catalyst 6500 feature allows redundant PEs to establish a Virtual Switching System (VSS).

Such capability radically simplifies the connection to vPC-enabled (or VSS-enabled) DCI switches. Using IEEE 802.3ad standard link aggregation, a link or device failure does not interrupt the connectivity between CEs and PEs, enabling much faster failover actions.

Figure 8-15 exhibits how A-VPLS can optimize a fully redundant VPLS deployment.

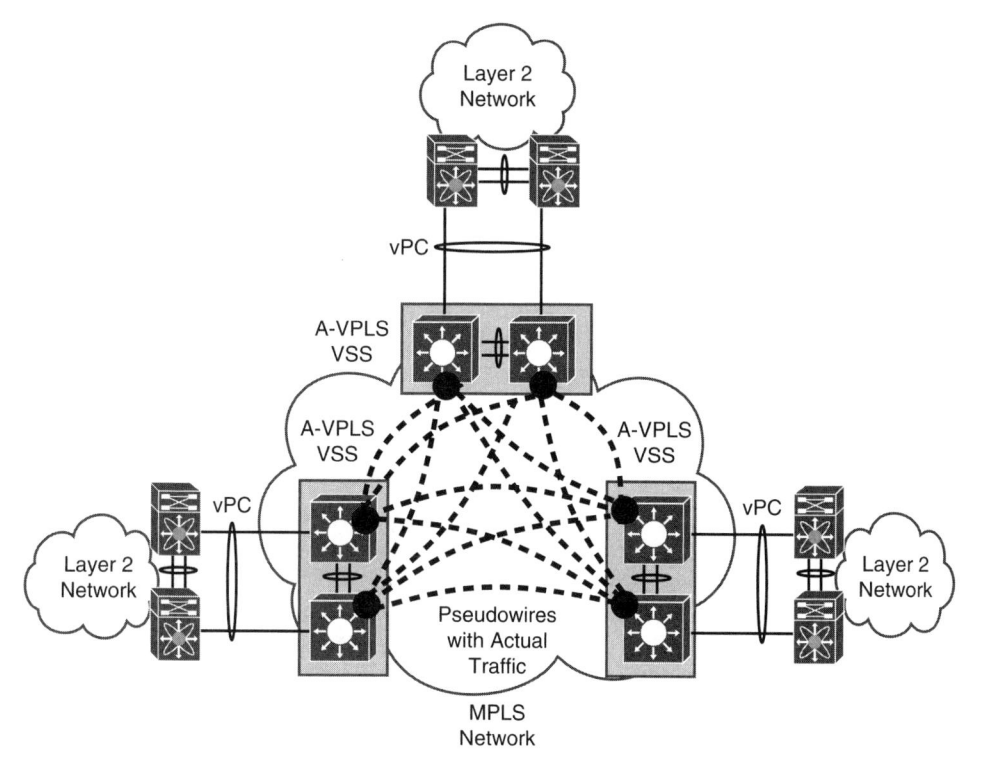

Figure 8-15 *Advanced VPLS Redundant Topology*

Additional redundant VPLS design options, such as *Multi-Chassis Link Aggregation Group (MC-LAG)*, are also available on other Cisco routing equipment.

Note In any EoMPLS or VPLS design, it is very important that scalability is observed and respected. I recommend that you refer to the Cisco documentation to find the most recent values for your software and hardware combination. At the time of this writing, the Catalyst 6500 VPLS implementation supports 4096 VFIs, 250 PEs per VFI, and more than 12,000 VCs.

Ethernet Extensions over IP

It is not always possible to use optical or MPLS connections to extend Layer 2 domains across data centers. Depending on the facilities' locations and mutual distance, such services might not be even available for purchase. On the other hand, some companies simply cannot afford the costs involved with a private DWDM or MPLS implementation.

Notwithstanding, Internet Protocol (IP) connectivity is ubiquitous all over the third planet from the sun. Since its inception, IP permits transport of data over *any* connection infrastructure, be it based on dark fiber, DWDM, ATM, Frame Relay, MetroEthernet, MPLS, and so on. And as a result, the flexibility and relatively lower costs of IP can provide a reasonable solution for data center interconnect traffic, *including Layer 2 extension*.

When IP is used to transport Ethernet traffic, the OSI model is curiously inverted, because Layer 3 packets will now envelop Layer 2 frames. And because these scenarios require a traditional IP network between sites, it is up to the DCI switches to deploy this encapsulation.

MPLS Services over GRE and *Overlay Transport Virtualization* are two popular Layer 2 extension methods for IP-connected data centers. Both of them will be respectively discussed in the next two sections.

Note It is very important that you understand that the available connections between data center sites represents an indication of the possible Layer 2 extension technologies in a scenario. As I have mentioned before, one solution does not fit all cases. Consequently, there is no specific reason to disqualify EoMPLS, VPLS, MPLS over GRE, or Overlay Transport Virtualization as suitable Ethernet extension solutions over optical connections, if it is considered adequate for the deployment.

MPLS over GRE

Generic routing encapsulation (GRE) allows generic data units to be encapsulated in an IP packet. This protocol works with the establishment of *GRE tunnels* between two IP routers, which are basically virtual back-to-back connections between these devices.

MPLS over GRE Layer 2 extension solutions are based on a straightforward idea: "What if I deploy my own MPLS backbone over GRE tunnels between data centers connected through IP?" Consequently, such a valid concept permits an MPLS Layer 2 extension technology, such as EoMPLS and VPLS, to be deployed over pure IP networks.

Tip A virtual data plane (and optionally, other network planes) created over an underlying networking infrastructure is commonly referred as an *overlay network*.

Figure 8-16 exhibits a sample configuration where an MPLS connection is built over an IP network represented by two routers. As you can observe, tunnel interfaces are created in each device to deploy and control this virtual connection.

```
MPLS-D#show running-config interface tunnel 99 |
begin interface
interface Tunnel99
 ip address 192.168.99.4 255.255.255.0
 mpls ip
 tunnel source GigabitEthernet1/3
 tunnel destination 141.1.1.1
end
MPLS-D#show running-config | include 1.1.1.1
ip route 1.1.1.1 255.255.255.255 192.168.99.1
```

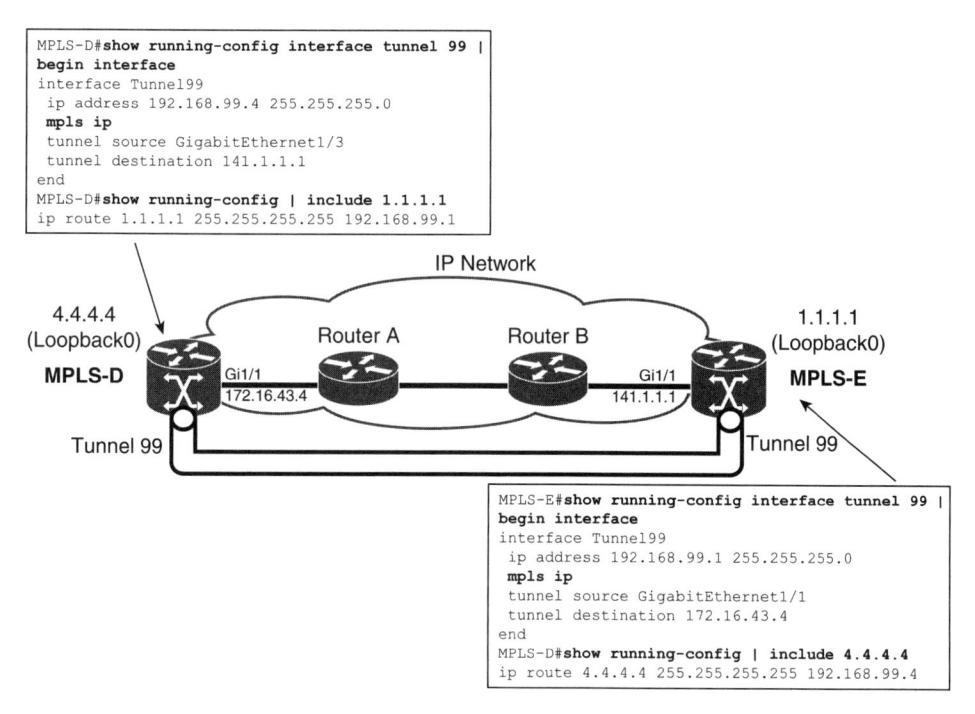

```
MPLS-E#show running-config interface tunnel 99 |
begin interface
interface Tunnel99
 ip address 192.168.99.1 255.255.255.0
 mpls ip
 tunnel source GigabitEthernet1/1
 tunnel destination 172.16.43.4
end
MPLS-D#show running-config | include 4.4.4.4
ip route 4.4.4.4 255.255.255.255 192.168.99.4
```

Figure 8-16 *MPLSoGRE Scenario*

In the figure, a GRE tunnel is configured on both MPLS-capable routers. MPLS is actually deployed in this back-to-back connection between MPLS-D and MPLS-E.

Note I have nserted the static routes for a reason: to force traffic destined to the MPLS loopback interfaces through the GRE tunnel.

Example 8-17 demonstrates how the MPLS connection is established on both routers.

Example 8-17 *MPLS Connections and Label Binding*

```
! Checking which interfaces are deploying MPLS
MPLS-D# show mpls interfaces
Interface            IP           Tunnel   BGP Static Operational
Tunnel99             Yes (ldp)    No       No  No     Yes
! Verifying MPLS label binding for the loopback0 IP reachability
MPLS-D# show mpls ip binding 1.1.1.1 32
```

```
1.1.1.1/32
     in label:      17
     out label:     imp-null  lsr: 1.1.1.1:0          inuse
```

With such a configuration replicated between MPLS-capable DCI devices, EoMPLS and VPLS can be implemented over GRE tunnels. However, you should always refer to Cisco online documentation to verify whether your hardware and software combination supports EoMPLSoGRE or VPLSoGRE.

EoMPLSoGRE and VPLSoGRE share the same recommendations related to loop avoidance and STP isolation from traditional EoMPLS and VPLS designs.

Also, GRE introduces 24 bytes (20 bytes for the IP header and 4 bytes for the GRE header) of overhead to an EoMPLS packet. Therefore, the MTU should be adjusted accordingly in the IP backbone to avoid undesired discards.

Furthermore, GRE also facilitates data encryption on Layer 2 extensions because IPsec can be applied to the tunnel interfaces.

Overlay Transport Virtualization

In 2009, Cisco introduced to its Nexus 7000 series another method for Layer 2 extension: *Overlay Transport Virtualization (OTV)*. At the time of this writing, OTV is deployed in Nexus 7000 and ASR 1000 platforms.

Similarly to MPLS over GRE techniques, OTV provides Ethernet connectivity over IP infrastructures through the creation of a virtual data plane (overlay). However, OTV presents a clear differentiation from any other Layer 2 extension technology discussed in this chapter: Remote MAC addresses are not learned through the data plane (flooding and broadcast) because OTV actually uses IS-IS updates to exchange MAC address reachability (thus, defining a virtual control plane).

Figure 8-17 illustrates how an OTV-capable switch (OTV1) advertises MAC addresses to other data center sites connected by an IP network.

Figure 8-17 switches OTV2 and OTV3 learn MAC address X through the following process:

   a. Server with MAC address X sends frames that are flooded or broadcasted within site 1.
   b. OTV1 learns MAC X and populates its MAC address table.
   c. OTV1 advertises MAC X with an IS-IS update.
   d. OTV2 and OTV3 become aware that MAC X can be reached through OTV1 and populate their MAC address tables using the virtual Layer 2 interface called *Overlay*.

The effective Ethernet frame transport is demonstrated in Figure 8-18.

Chapter 8: A Tale of Two Data Centers   355

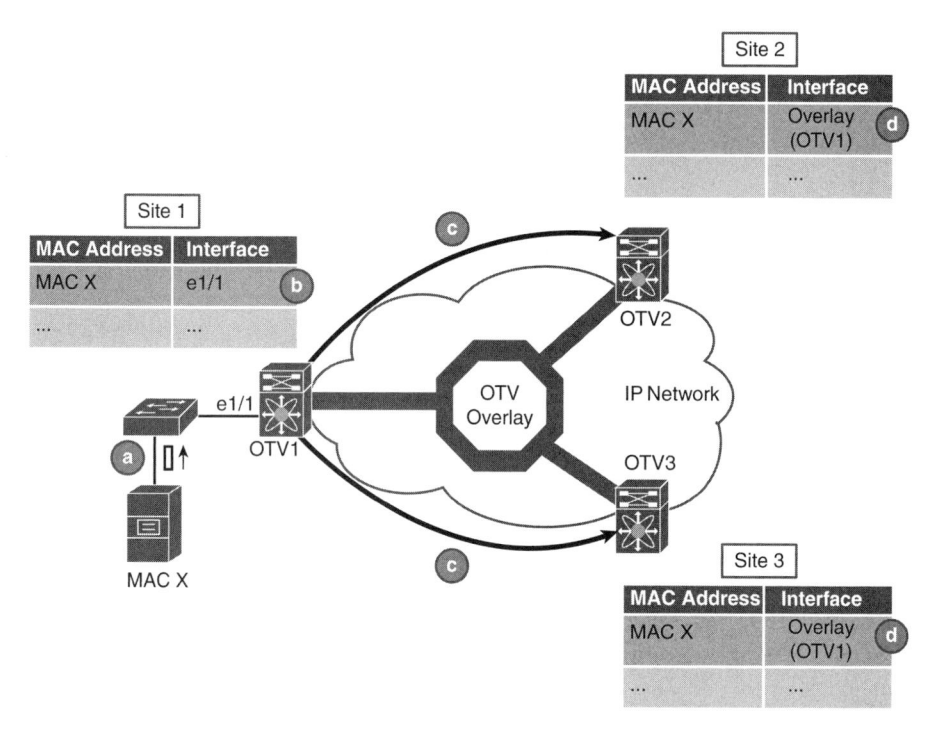

Figure 8-17 *OTV Control Plane MAC Learning*

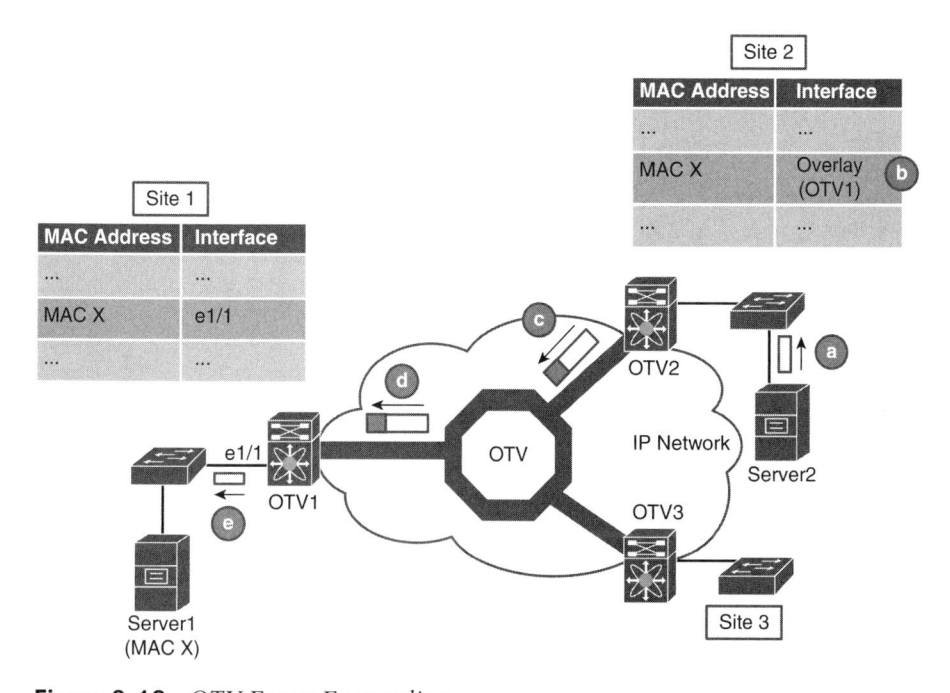

Figure 8-18 *OTV Frame Forwarding*

In Figure 8-18, a frame can be transported from site 2 to site 1 through OTV in the following manner:

a. Server2 sends a unicast frame destined to MAC X that is flooded to OTV2.

b. OTV2 checks its MAC address table and realizes that the MAC X entry points to an Overlay interface.

c. Internally in OTV2, this Overlay interface provides a mapping to OTV1's IP address. As a result, the unicast frame is encapsulated into an IP packet directed to OTV1.

d. OTV1 receives the IP packet and decapsulates it, recovering the original Ethernet frame sent by Server2.

e. OTV1 uses its local MAC address table to forward the frame to Server1.

As you can observe, OTV suppresses the management operations needed by GRE tunnels and MPLS pseudowires. Because OTV does not require source and destination static configurations, it is referred to as a *dynamic encapsulation* technology.

Figure 8-19 details the OTV packet encapsulation of an Ethernet frame.

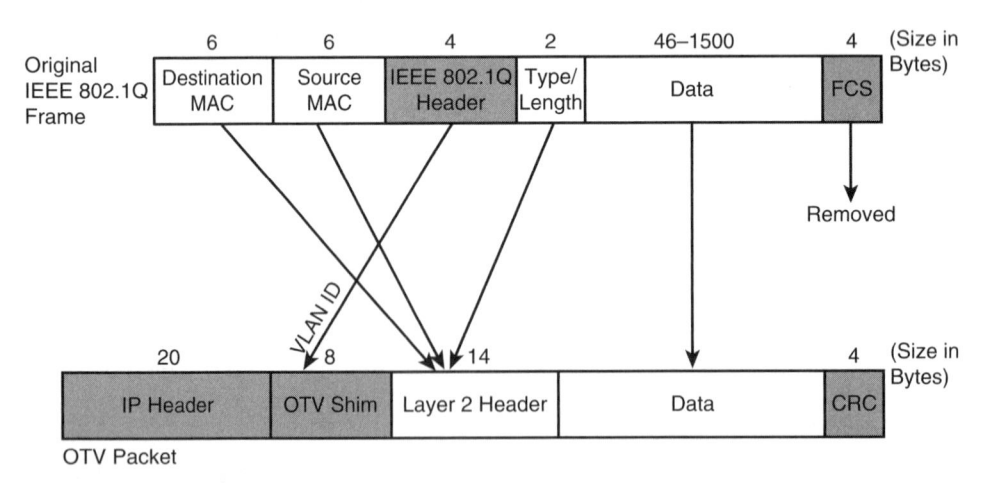

Figure 8-19 *OTV Encapsulation*

Tip A more detailed description of this encapsulation can be found in the OTV draft submitted to the IETF in 2010 (see the "Further Reading" section, later in this chapter).

Because OTV generates IP packets with the DF (Don't Fragment) bit set to 1, an OTV packet must contain a single Ethernet frame. Therefore, the MTU must be configured accordingly in the IP network to avoid discards.

OTV has a simple way of dealing with spanning tree: It simply does not. Just like VPLS, OTV does not transport BPDUs between different sites, providing STP isolation and separate fault domains.

Additionally, OTV provides built-in *multihoming*, which allows Layer 2 traffic to be load balanced through different IP WAN links.

OTV Terminology

As a protocol designed from ground up, OTV introduces new elements that are pictured in Figure 8-20.

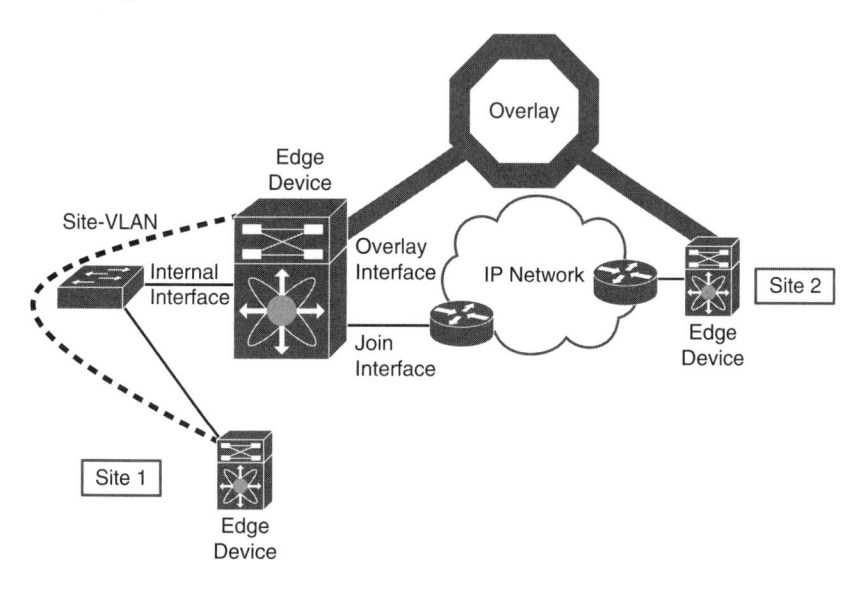

Figure 8-20 *OTV Elements*

The main OTV elements are as follows:

- **Edge device:** This is the network equipment that is actually deploying OTV. Invariably, this device should be connected to a Layer 2 network (to process Ethernet frames) and to the Layer 3 network (to send or receive OTV packets). A minimum of two edge devices are recommended in each data center.

- **Internal interface:** An edge device's interface that is connected to a Layer 2 network. It participates in the STP processes, learns MAC addresses transparently, and is usually configured as a trunk. PortChannels are recommended to increase fault tolerance on this interface.

- **Join interface:** An edge device's routed interface that is connected to an IP network. Its IP address is used as the source of generated OTV packets. Because it is responsible for the discovery of other edge devices and maintenance of their adjacency, PortChannels are highly recommended to increase fault tolerance on these interfaces.

- **Overlay interface:** This is a virtual Layer 2 interface that represents an OTV Layer 2 extension to other edge devices. Therefore, it is used on their MAC address tables as the interface associated to remote MAC addresses. In an edge device, an overlay interface is always associated to a join interface.
- **Site:** An isolated Layer 2 network that is connected to other sites through OTV.
- **Site VLAN:** A dedicated VLAN that is used for discovery and adjacency maintenance between edge devices on the same site. It should not be extended to other sites.
- **Overlay:** This is a virtual Layer 2 network that consists of two or more OTV edge devices that exchange MAC reachability information.

Edge devices can discover each other and exchange MAC address reachability information using IP *multicast* or *unicast* communication. Using IP multicast, OTV edge devices act as members of a single multicast group. Therefore, when a MAC update must be sent to all other edge devices, a single update is transmitted to such multicast group address. This address is called *control-group*, and it defines whether overlay interfaces belong to the same overlay.

Because all edge devices can also be multicast sources, the Internet Group Management Protocol (IGMP) Join messages sent by each join interface use an *Any Source Multicast (ASM)* group. With a multicast-enabled control plane, the replication of OTV packets is completely outsourced from the edge devices to the IP network.

If an IP multicast network is not available to connect OTV edge devices, they can deploy their control plane communication within IP unicast packets. For the reason that multicast control-groups are not used, adjacency between edge devices is determined by the overlay interface identifier (Overlay3, for example) in a unicast control plane scenario.

Also, in a unicast-enabled control plane, one OTV edge device must be configured as an *adjacency server*. Such a device is responsible for receiving registration requests from each edge device that is configured to join a specific overlay. After processing these registrations, the adjacency server builds an *OTV Neighbor List (ONL)* that is sent periodically to all other edge devices. From this list, each edge device can find the IP addresses necessary to generate OTV packets.

Tip A secondary adjacency server is highly recommended to increase fault tolerance in a unicast-enabled overlay.

Using a unicast-enabled control plane, an edge device is forced to create multiple updates to inform its neighbors about a new learned MAC address.

OTV Basic Configuration

Compared to other Layer 2 extension methods, OTV has a much shorter configuration. To justify this statement, I will configure OTV, using its multicast-enabled control plane, over the topology portrayed in Figure 8-21.

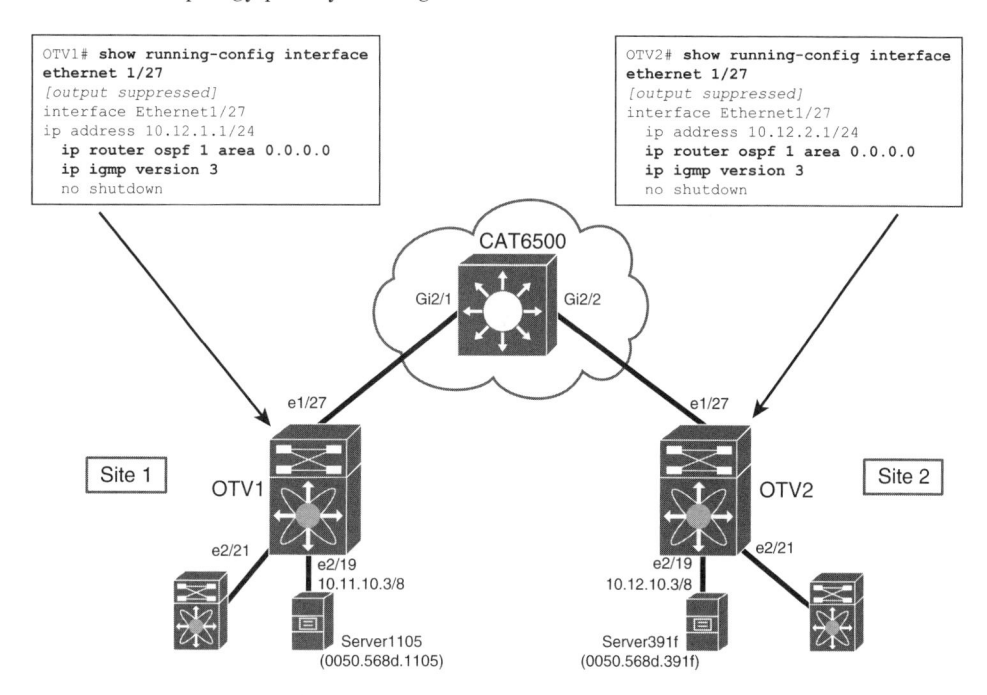

```
OTV1# show running-config interface
ethernet 1/27
[output suppressed]
interface Ethernet1/27
 ip address 10.12.1.1/24
  ip router ospf 1 area 0.0.0.0
  ip igmp version 3
  no shutdown
```

```
OTV2# show running-config interface
ethernet 1/27
[output suppressed]
interface Ethernet1/27
 ip address 10.12.2.1/24
  ip router ospf 1 area 0.0.0.0
  ip igmp version 3
  no shutdown
```

Figure 8-21 *OTV Topology*

Figure 8-21 also details the join interface configuration (Ethernet 1/27 on both edge devices). As you can see, each switch advertises its IP subnets through OSPF and uses IGMP version 3 to send multicast Join messages.

Note A Catalyst 6500 switch performs the role of an IP network in this topology. It is configured to receive IGMP version 3 Join messages from the edge devices and to advertise multicast routes through Protocol Independent Multicast (PIM) sparse mode.

Examples 8-18 and 8-19 detail the required configuration to enable OTV on edge devices OTV1 and OTV2, respectively.

Example 8-18 *OTV1 Configuration*

```
OTV1# show running-config otv
[output suppressed]
! Enabling otv processes
```

```
feature otv
! Defining the VLAN that will be used for edge devices communication in the same
site
otv site-vlan 111
! Creating an overlay interface
interface Overlay1
! Defining the Layer 3 interface that will be used as source IP address on OTV
packets
  otv join-interface Ethernet1/27
! Defining the ASM group that will be used for control plane communication between
edge devices in the same overlay
  otv control-group 239.1.1.1
! Defining Source Specific Multicast (SSM) groups that will be used to carry Layer 2
multicast traffic
  otv data-group 232.1.1.0/28
! Declaring which VLANs will be extended through OTV to other sites
  otv extend-vlan 300
! Enabling the Overlay interface
  no shutdown
! Explicitly identifying the site. This configuration is mandatory after NX-OS
version 5.2(1)
otv site-identifier 0x1
```

Example 8-19 *N7K2 Commented OTV Configuration*

```
OTV2# show running-config otv
[output suppressed]
feature otv
! A different site VLAN since this device belongs to a is on a different OTV site
otv site-vlan 112
! Although this is not necessary with multicast control plane, I have
used the same Overlay interface identifier for simplicity
interface Overlay1
  otv join-interface Ethernet1/27
! But the ASM group must be the same from OTV1
  otv control-group 239.1.1.1
  otv data-group 232.1.1.0/28
! Extending the same VLAN
  otv extend-vlan 300
  no shutdown
! Assuring that OTV1 and OTV2 are on different sites
otv site-identifier 0x2
```

Both configurations define OTV1 and OTV2 as belonging to different sites (0x1 and 0x2, respectively) and that VLAN 300 must be extended through their overlay interfaces.

Example 8-20 exhibits the multicast routes for the ASM control group (239.1.1.1) reachability from the Catalyst 6500 perspective.

Example 8-20 *Verifying Control Group Multicast Routes*

```
CAT6500# show ip mroute 239.1.1.1 summary
[output suppressed]
(*, 239.1.1.1), 00:25:09/stopped, RP 0.0.0.0, OIF count: 2, flags: DC
! Join interfaces on OTV1 and OTV2 are members of this multicast group
  (10.12.1.1, 239.1.1.1), 00:24:56/00:02:53, OIF count: 1, flags: T
  (10.12.2.1, 239.1.1.1), 00:23:37/00:02:53, OIF count: 1, flags: T
```

This connectivity status establishes the OTV adjacency between both edge devices, which are now capable of sending MAC reachability information to each other.

Example 8-21 details the output of two OTV commands that can be used to verify whether an edge device is ready to forward Ethernet traffic to remote sites.

Example 8-21 *OTV1 OTV Status*

```
! Verifying OTV adjacency status to other edge devices
OTV1# show otv adjacency detail
Overlay Adjacency database
! OTV1 has established an adjacency with OTV2
Overlay-Interface Overlay1 :
Hostname                    System-ID        Dest Addr        Up Time     State
OTV2                        0022.5579.f744   10.12.2.1        00:24:57    UP
HW-St: Up Peer-ID: 1
! Verifying the extended VLAN status
OTV1# show otv vlan detail
OTV Extended VLANs and Edge Device State Information (* - AED)
Legend: F - Forwarding B - Blocked
! VLAN 300 is being extended to other sites
VLAN   Auth. Edge Device                    Vlan State   Overlay
----   ----------------------------------   ----------   -------
300*   OTV1                                 active       Overlay1
[output suppressed]
```

Tip Although not depicted, the same commands applied to OTV2 show very similar results.

With this groundwork laid, both edge devices are ready to extend VLAN 300 to each other. To test this extension, I have issued an ICMP Echo message from Server1105 in site 1 to Server391f in site 2 (both servers belong to VLAN 300 and share the same IP subnet).

Examples 8-22 and 8-23 exhibit the MAC address table in OTV1 and OTV2, after these ping operations were successful. For more clarity, because these tables only point to the overlay interfaces, I have also included the OTV routes from both edge devices to both examples. These OTV routes expose the edge devices that have generated the MAC reachability information.

Example 8-22 *OTV1 MAC Address Table for VLAN 300 and OTV Routes*

```
! Verifying the MAC address table in VLAN 300
OTV1# show mac address-table vlan 300
Legend:
        * - primary entry, G - Gateway MAC, (R) - Routed MAC, O - Overlay MAC
        age - seconds since last seen,+ - primary entry using vPC Peer-Link
   VLAN     MAC Address      Type      age     Secure NTFY Ports/SWID.SSID.LID
---------+-----------------+--------+---------+------+----+----------
! Server1105 is a local MAC address
* 300       0050.568d.1105   dynamic   0        F     F    Eth2/19
! Server391f is reachable through Overlay1
O 300       0050.568d.391f   dynamic   0        F     F    Overlay1
[output suppressed]
! Verifying the OTV routes
OTV1# show otv route

OTV Unicast MAC Routing Table For Overlay1
! OTV2 has advertised Server391f MAC address
VLAN MAC-Address       Metric  Uptime    Owner     Next-hop(s)
---- ---------------   ------  --------  --------- -----------
 300 0050.568d.1105    1       00:38:01  site      Ethernet2/19
 300 0050.568d.391f    42      00:38:01  overlay   OTV2
[output suppressed]
```

Example 8-23 *OTV2 MAC Address Table for VLAN 300 and OTV Routes*

```
! Verifying the MAC address table in VLAN 300
OTV2# show mac address-table vlan 300
Legend:
        * - primary entry, G - Gateway MAC, (R) - Routed MAC, O - Overlay MAC
        age - seconds since last seen,+ - primary entry using vPC Peer-Link
   VLAN     MAC Address      Type      age     Secure NTFY Ports
---------+-----------------+--------+---------+------+----+----------
```

```
! Server1105 is reachable through Overlay1
O 300     0050.568d.1105    dynamic   0       F    F   Overlay1
! Server391f is  a local MAC address
* 300     0050.568d.391f    dynamic   0       F    F   Eth2/19
[output suppressed]
! Verifying the OTV routes
OTV2# show otv route
OTV Unicast MAC Routing Table For Overlay1
! OTV1 has advertised Server391f MAC address
VLAN MAC-Address       Metric  Uptime    Owner    Next-hop(s)
---- ---------------   ------  --------  -------- -----------
 300 0050.568d.1105    42      00:38:43  overlay  OTV1
 300 0050.568d.391f    1       00:38:43  site     Ethernet2/19
[output suppressed]
```

By default, each OTV edge device forwards broadcast frames to the entire overlay. Examples 8-22 and 8-23 discreetly demonstrate this behavior, because both servers exchanged ARP requests and replies before the ICMP Echo messages.

To decrease the rate of ARP messages within the overlays, OTV deploys *ARP caching* by default. This mechanism basically stores in the local edge device the ARP reply values (IP and MAC addresses) received from a remote host. Subsequent ARP requests for the same IP address will be handled by the local edge device for a defined interval.

Examples 8-24 and 8-25 exhibit the ARP cache tables in OTV1 and OTV2 after Server1105 and Server 391f exchanged ICMP Echo messages.

Example 8-24 *OTV1 ARP Cache*

```
OTV1# show otv arp-nd-cache
OTV ARP/ND L3->L2 Address Mapping Cache

Overlay Interface Overlay1
VLAN  MAC Address         Layer-3 Address    Age        Expires In
300   0050.568d.391f      10.12.10.3         00:05:08   00:04:51
```

Example 8-25 *OTV2 ARP Cache*

```
OTV2# show otv arp-nd-cache
OTV ARP/ND L3->L2 Address Mapping Cache

Overlay Interface Overlay1
VLAN  MAC Address         Layer-3 Address    Age        Expires In
300   0050.568d.1105      10.11.10.3         00:03:30   00:04:31
```

Note This feature can also cache the Neighbor Discovery (ND) protocol results for IPv6 hosts. The **otv suppress-arp-nd** command disables ARP and ND caching in an overlay interface.

It is very important that the ARP cache aging timer is set to lower values than the MAC address table aging timer. This practice minimizes local ARP replies with a remote MAC address that might not be present in the MAC address table (because edge devices drop unknown unicast frames). By default, these timers on the Nexus 7000 are 480 and 1800 seconds, respectively.

Silent hosts, or cluster nodes that depend on flooding to receive Layer 2 traffic, represent a challenge to OTV MAC address learning behavior. Because they do not send Ethernet frames, these hosts cannot be reached from remote OTV sites. Because OTV does not transmit unknown unicast frames on the overlay, the protocol could be disruptive to clusters with silent nodes.

A work-around for this situation is the manual insertion of the silent host in the local edge devices MAC address table. Examples 8-25 and 8-26 explain that this procedure guarantees that frames to this address are correctly delivered.

Example 8-25 *Static MAC Address Configuration in OTV1*

```
OTV1(config)# mac address-table static 0a0a.0a0a.0a0a vlan 300 interface ethernet
2/19
```

Example 8-26 *Static MAC Address Detection in OTV2*

```
OTV2# show mac address-table vlan 300 address 0a0a.0a0a.0a0a
Legend:
        * - primary entry, G - Gateway MAC, (R) - Routed MAC, O - Overlay MAC
        age - seconds since last seen,+ - primary entry using vPC Peer-Link
   VLAN     MAC Address      Type        age     Secure NTFY Ports
---------+-----------------+--------+---------+------+----+---------
O 300      0a0a.0a0a.0a0a   dynamic     0          F    F  Overlay1
```

In Examples 8-25 and 8-26, MAC address 0a0a.0a0a.0a0a is inserted in OTV1's MAC address table and is automatically detected on OTV2.

Note Any static configuration tends to be forgotten over time. If no control is applied to this specific configuration, traffic to MAC address 0a0a.0a0a.0a0a will always be forwarded OTV1, even if the silent host is no longer located in its site.

OTV Loop Avoidance and Multihoming

Besides blocking unknown unicast traffic between edge devices, OTV avoids loops provoked by multidestination traffic (broadcast and multicast) through the *authoritative edge device (AED)* concept.

By default, OTV elects a single AED per site to be responsible for the MAC address reachability in each VLAN. Consequently, such AED will be the only edge device on a site that will handle unicast, multicast, and broadcast traffic for that VLAN.

Figure 8-22 details how authoritative edge devices provide loop avoidance in a single extended VLAN.

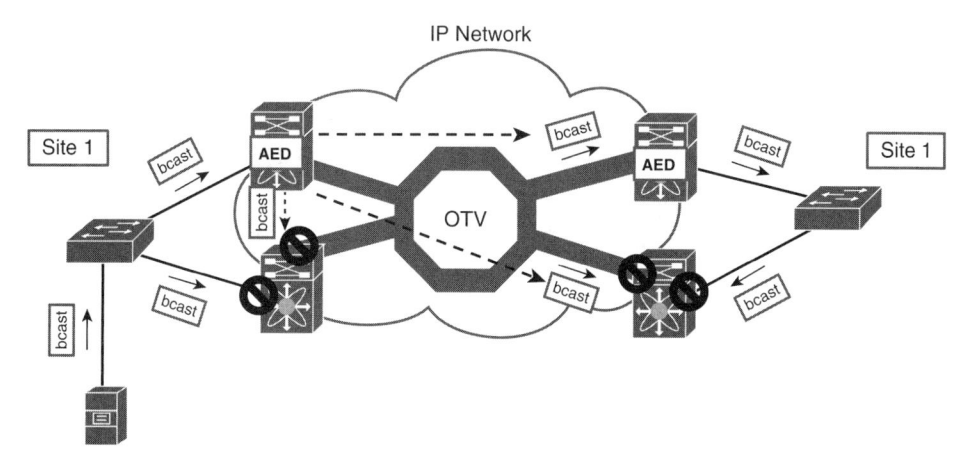

Figure 8-22 *Authoritative Edge Device and Loop Avoidance*

In the figure, if a server from site 1 sends a broadcast frame in the OTV-extended VLAN, only the site's assigned AED can forward this frame to other edge devices in the overlay. In unison, only site 2's AED is allowed to decapsulate these frames and forward them to their respective internal interfaces. Acting as "broadcast gatekeepers" for each site, AEDs provide loop avoidance for OTV-connected networks.

The election of AED involves all the OTV edge devices that belong to the same site. Starting from NX-OS 5.2(1), a Nexus 7000 switch only becomes a candidate for the AED role when it has Layer 2 (internal site-VLAN) and Layer 3 (site identifier used between join interfaces) connectivity assured and advertised between the site peers. These prerequisites avoid multiple AEDs from being active in a single site (in the case of a disjoint site-VLAN, for example).

Considering the traffic pattern that AEDs impose in an overlay, at the time of this writing, OTV multihoming is achieved in OTV with three situations:

- Automatic distribution of the VLANs among the available AED candidates (a hashing function is used to deploy this distribution).

- For unicast egress traffic, OTV can be load balanced among all the equal-cost Layer 3 paths to remote edge devices. Multidestination egress and ingress traffic can only use the join interface.

- Layer 3 PortChannels (between AED and a single device or one deploying VSS).

Figure 8-23 illustrates such multihoming options.

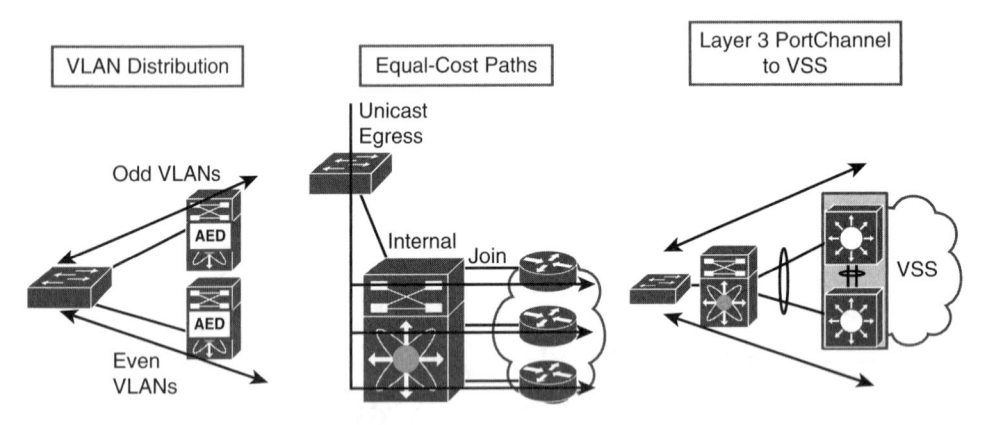

Figure 8-23 *OTV Multihoming Options*

Note At the time of this writing, OTV cannot use loopback interfaces to generate OTV packets.

Migration to OTV

Without preparation or proper care, the concurrent deployment of OTV and another Layer 2 extension technology can generate Ethernet loops. This situation can occur in a migration from such a Layer 2 extension to OTV, as illustrated in Figure 8-24.

In Figure 8-24, both AEDs are responsible for forwarding broadcast frames to each other. However, the overlay is not detected as an active path because it does not forward BPDUs or participate in other loop avoidance methods (such as VPLS split horizon or FabricPath's virtual STP bridge). Consequently, two active Layer 2 paths for broadcast frames might welcome our old annoying acquaintance, the loop.

During a migration from any Layer 2 extension to OTV, a step-by-step procedure can be used to avoid this active-active path situation. As this best practice leverages the concept of authoritative edge devices, I also find it very useful to explain their mechanisms and behavior.

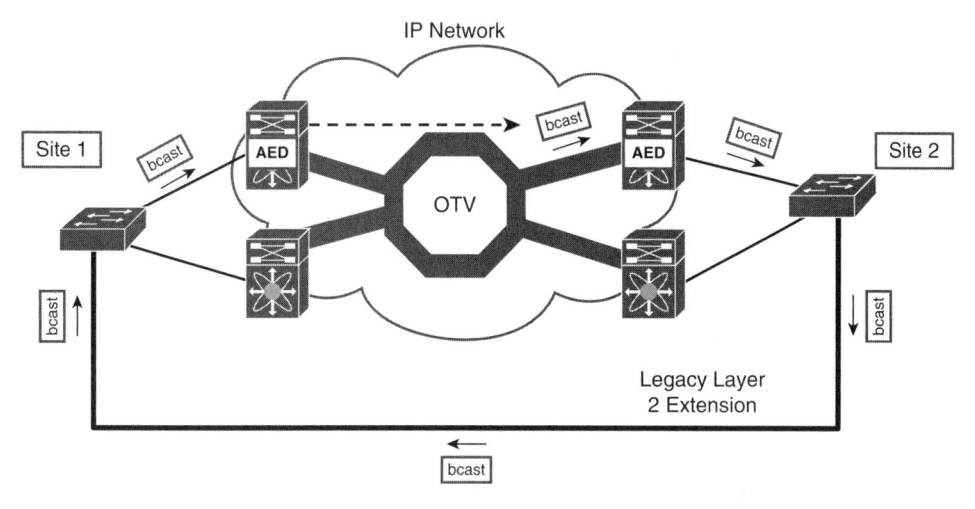

Figure 8-24 *OTV Migration Loop*

Figure 8-25 illustrates a topology that represents two data centers whose legacy Layer 2 extension is performed by PortChannel 200.

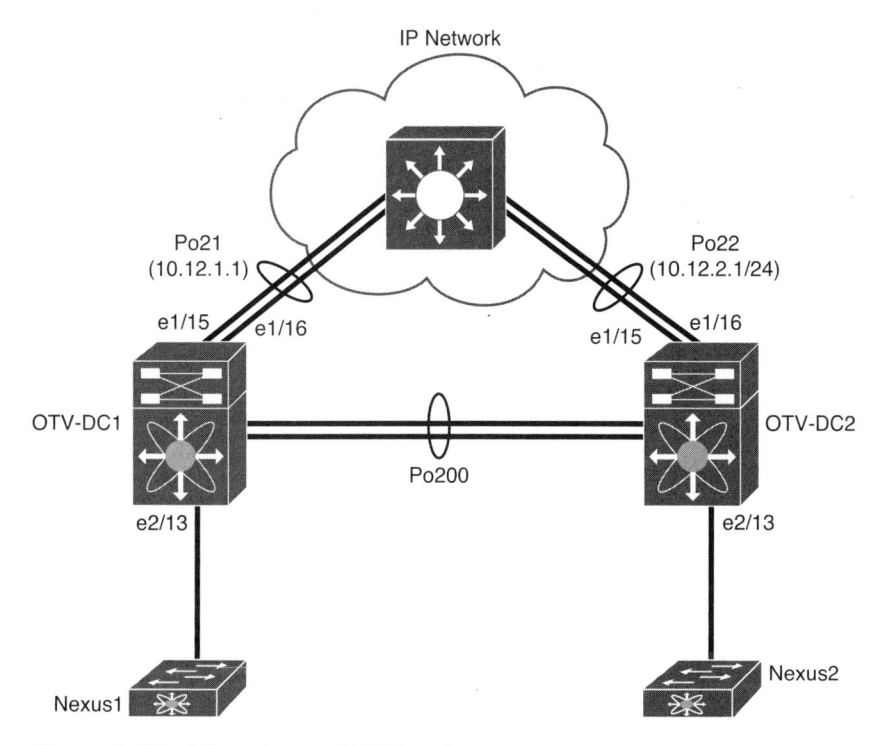

Figure 8-25 *Migration to OTV Topology*

The idea behind this phased procedure is to transform both data centers in *a single OTV site first*. In this state, the native OTV loop avoidance mechanisms can guarantee that no edge device will be able to send broadcasts through the overlay interfaces until the legacy extension is disabled.

The following steps describe the migration procedure:

1. Extend the site VLAN through the Layer 2 extension. In this phase, the site VLAN (200) and the data VLANs (1 to 8) are extended between both sites. PortChannel 200 is using STP to expose the fact that the site VLAN is active on both sites, as Examples 8-27 and 8-28 detail.

Example 8-27 *STP Status in OTV Site1*

```
OTV-DC1# show spanning-tree vlan 200
! OTV-Site1 is the Root
VLAN0200
  Spanning tree enabled protocol rstp
  Root ID    Priority    4296
             Address     0024.f714.c243
             This bridge is the root
[output suppressed]
Interface        Role Sts Cost      Prio.Nbr Type
---------------- ---- --- --------- -------- ------------------------
Po200            Desg FWD 1         128.4295 P2p
Eth2/13          Desg FWD 2         128.269  P2p
```

Example 8-28 *STP Status in N7K12*

```
OTV-DC2# show spanning-tree vlan 200
! OTV-Site1 is the Root
VLAN0200
  Spanning tree enabled protocol rstp
[output suppressed]
Interface        Role Sts Cost      Prio.Nbr Type
---------------- ---- --- --------- -------- ------------------------
Po200            Root FWD 1         128.4295 P2p
Eth2/13          Desg FWD 2         128.269  P2p
```

2. Make sure that both OTV edge devices share the same site identifier.

   In this step, OTV is configured on both edge devices (OTV-DC1 and OTV-DC2) with the same OTV site identifier (0xa) and site VLAN (200).

Examples 8-29 and 8-30 detail such configurations on each OTV edge device.

Example 8-29 *OTV Site VLAN and Identifier in OTV-DC1*

```
OTV-DC1(config)# feature otv
OTV-DC1(config)# otv site-vlan 200
OTV-DC1(config-site-vlan)# otv site-identifier 0xa
```

Example 8-30 *OTV Site VLAN and Identifier in OTV-DC2*

```
OTV-DC2(config)# feature otv
OTV-DC2(config)# otv site-vlan 200
OTV-DC2(config-site-vlan)# otv site-identifier 0xa
```

3. Configure overlays on both edge devices without extending any VLANs yet.

   As a variation from previous OTV configuration examples, I will use the unicast control plane to deploy OTV adjacency between OTV-DC1 and OTV-DC2.

   In Examples 8-31 and 8-32, you can observe that both devices use interface Overlay2 in their OTV configuration (which is necessary for the unicast-enabled adjacency) and OTV-DC1 is the adjacency server.

Example 8-31 *Overlay Interface Configuration in OTV-DC1*

```
! Configuring interface Overlay2
OTV-DC1(config)# interface overlay 2
OTV-DC1(config-if-overlay)# otv join-interface port-channel21
! Enabling unicast control plane
OTV-DC1(config-if-overlay)# otv adjacency-server unicast-only
```

Example 8-32 *Overlay Interface Configuration in OTV-DC2*

```
OTV-DC2(config)# interface overlay 2
OTV-DC2(config-if-overlay)# otv join-interface port-channel22
OTV needs join interfaces to be configured for IGMP version 3
! Enabling unicast control plane
OTV-DC2(config-if-overlay)# otv adjacency-server unicast-only
! Defining OTV-DC1 as the Adjacency Server. Another IP address could
also be included in this command to define a secondary Adjacency
Server.
OTV-DC2(config-if-overlay)# otv use-adjacency-server 10.12.1.1 unicast-only
```

4. After the internal adjacency is achieved, extend the data VLANs.

   After the overlay interfaces are successfully configured, Examples 8-33 and 8-34 show that OTV-DC1 and OTV-DC2 established a same-site adjacency. This situation permits a secure extension of VLANs 1 to 8, because each VLAN can only have one AED per site.

Example 8-33 *Verifying OTV Adjacency in OTV-DC1 and Extending Data VLANs*

```
OTV-DC1(config-if-overlay)# show otv adjacency
Overlay Adjacency database

Overlay-Interface Overlay2 :
Hostname                        System-ID         Dest Addr      Up Time     State
OTV-DC2                         0022.5579.f743    10.12.2.1      00:09:40    UP
! Extending the data VLANs through OTV
OTV-DC1(config-if-overlay)# otv extend-vlan 1-8
```

Example 8-34 *Verifying OTV Adjacency in OTV-DC2 and Extending Data VLANs*

```
OTV-DC2(config-if-overlay)# show otv adjacency
Overlay Adjacency database

Overlay-Interface Overlay2 :
Hostname                        System-ID         Dest Addr      Up Time     State
OTV-DC1                         0024.f714.c243    10.12.1.1      00:10:03    UP
! Extending the data VLANs through OTV
OTV-DC2(config-if-overlay)# otv extend-vlan 1-8
```

This is the "gotcha" moment for the entire migration procedure. Because both data centers constitute a single OTV site, only one AED will be active per extended VLAN. Therefore, no data VLAN is being extended through the overlay and the legacy extension simultaneously.

In Examples 8-35 and 8-36, you can observe how the data VLANs are distributed among both edge devices.

Example 8-35 *Active VLANs for OTV-DC1*

```
! Displaying OTV extended VLANs
OTV-DC1(config-if-overlay)# show otv vlan

OTV Extended VLANs and Edge Device State Information (* - AED)
! OTV-DC1 is the AED for Odd VLANs
VLAN   Auth. Edge Device           Vlan State              Overlay
```

```
   ----  ----------------------     ----------       -------
    1*   OTV-DC1                    active           Overlay2
    2    OTV-DC2                    inactive(Non AED)Overlay2
    3*   OTV-DC1                    active           Overlay2
    4    OTV-DC2                    inactive(Non AED)Overlay2
    5*   OTV-DC1                    active           Overlay2
    6    OTV-DC2                    inactive(Non AED)Overlay2
    7*   OTV-DC1                    active           Overlay2
    8    OTV-DC2                    inactive(Non AED)Overlay2
```

Example 8-36 *Active VLANs for OTV-DC2*

```
! Displaying OTV extended VLANs
OTV-DC2(config-if-overlay)# show otv vlan

OTV Extended VLANs and Edge Device State Information (* - AED)
! OTV-DC1 is the AED for Even VLANs
   VLAN  Auth. Edge Device          Vlan State       Overlay
   ----  ----------------------     ----------       -------
    1    OTV-DC1                    inactive(Non AED)Overlay2
    2*   OTV-DC2                    active           Overlay2
    3    OTV-DC1                    inactive(Non AED)Overlay2
    4*   OTV-DC2                    active           Overlay2
    5    OTV-DC1                    inactive(Non AED)Overlay2
    6*   OTV-DC2                    active           Overlay2
    7    OTV-DC1                    inactive(Non AED)Overlay2
    8*   OTV-DC2                    active           Overlay2
```

As a matter of fact, the hashing algorithm has assigned odd VLANs to AED OTV-DC1, while OTV-DC2 is the AED for even VLANs.

5. Disable the legacy Layer 2 extension solution.

   In our topology, this step can be executed with the **shutdown** command in interfaces Ethernet 2/11 on any edge device.

   Example 8-37 exhibits how the OTV adjacency established between OTV-DC1 and OTV-DC2 reacts when the site VLAN is not extended on both sites (and the edge devices cannot communicate through it). Nevertheless, a *partial adjacency* also guarantees that the legacy Layer 2 extension has been fully disabled!

Example 8-37 *Legacy Extension Disabling and Adjacency Status in OTV-DC1*

```
! Disabling the legacy extension (PortChannel 200)
OTV-DC1(config-if-overlay)# interface PortChannel 200
```

```
OTV-DC1(config-if)# shutdown
! Verifying the OTV adjacency status
OTV-DC1(config-if)# sh otv site

Dual Adjacency State Description
    Full    - Both site and overlay adjacency up
    Partial - Either site/overlay adjacency down
    Down    - Both adjacencies are down (Neighbor is down/unreachable)
[output suppressed]
Hostname        System-ID           Adjacency-          Adjacency-      AED-
                                    State               Uptime          Capable
-------------------------------------------------------------------------------
OTV-DC2         0022.5579.f743      Partial (!)         00:30:01        Yes
```

> **Note** At this point, Layer 2 traffic is briefly interrupted between sites. I also recommend that you double-check to see whether the extended VLANs are really disjoint, verifying whether they have different roots for their respective spanning trees.

A very similar output is found on OTV-DC2, so I will not depict it here.

6. Change the site identifier and site VLAN on the secondary site.

   This final step enables data traffic to finally be forwarded through the overlay. When the site identifier is changed on OTV-DC2, both edge devices become the AED for all VLANs as they now belong to distinct OTV sites.

   Example 8-38 portrays this result when OTV-DC2 is configured with a different site identifier (0xb).

Example 8-38 *OTV-DC2 Site Identifier Change and OTV Traffic Enablement*

```
! Changing OTV site identifier
OTV-DC2(config-if)# otv site-identifier 0xb
% Site Identifier mismatch will prevent  overlays from forwarding traffic.
! Verifying extended VLAN status
OTV-DC2(config)# show otv vlan

OTV Extended VLANs and Edge Device State Information (* - AED)
! All VLANs are now forwarded through interface Overlay2
VLAN    Auth. Edge Device           Vlan State          Overlay
----    ---------------------       ----------          -------
  1*    OTV-DC2                     active              Overlay2
  2*    OTV-DC2                     active              Overlay2
[output suppressed]
  8*    OTV-DC2                     active              Overlay2
```

Example 8-39 demonstrates that OTV-DC1 is also forwarding Layer 2 traffic from all data VLANs.

Example 8-39 *N7K11*

```
! Verifying extended VLAN status
OTV-DC1(config-if-overlay)# sh otv vlan


OTV Extended VLANs and Edge Device State Information (* - AED)
! All VLANs are now forwarded through interface Overlay2
VLAN    Auth. Edge Device         Vlan State        Overlay
----    ----------------------    ----------        -------
   1*   OTV-DC1                   active            Overlay2
   2*   OTV-DC1                   active            Overlay2
[output suppressed]
   8*   OTV-DC1                   active            Overlay2
```

At this time, each data center has a single OTV edge device. It is recommended that one more edge device is added to each site to increase the overlay fault tolerance.

Although this is a minimally disruptive migration procedure, it definitely helps to avoid loops during a migration to OTV (which, believe me, can be much more disruptive and obnoxious).

OTV Site Designs

Although OTV is fairly easy to configure, its deployment demands careful planning. A main factor justifies this statement: At the time of this writing, an OTV edge device cannot deploy Switched Virtual Interfaces (SVI) using switch an extended VLAN.

Example 8-40 exposes this behavior in OTV-DC1 from the last section.

Example 8-40 *Trying to Configure OTV and SVI on the Edge Device*

```
OTV-DC1(config)# feature interface-vlan
! Configuring SVI for VLAN 8
OTV-DC1(config)# interface vlan 8
ERROR: Vlan 8 is OTV Extended VLAN
                  ^
Invalid range at '^' marker.
```

As you have learned from Chapter 5, "Instant Switches: Virtual Device Contexts," VDCs are elegantly handy when a single physical switch cannot support two incompatible features. Avoiding the acquisition of additional switches, a single physical device can create one VDC for the SVIs and another one for OTV.

> **Tip** Only the OTV VDC must be created when the default VDC is already deploying SVIs as default gateways for the connected servers.

An OTV VDC must have at least one internal interface and a join interface. How its join interface is connected to the IP network defines whether the OTV VDC follows the *appliance-on-a-stick* or the *inline appliance* model.

Figure 8-26 portrays both possibilities.

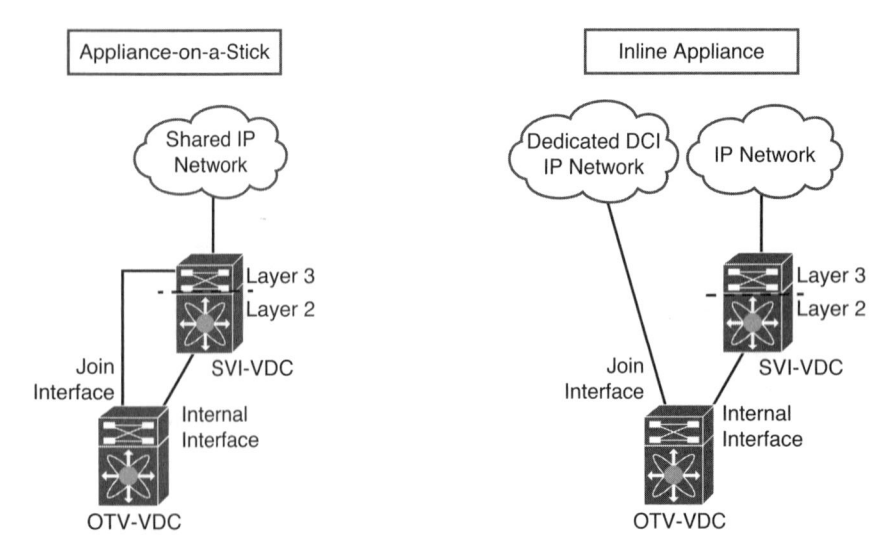

Figure 8-26 *OTV VDC Models of Insertion*

The appliance-on-a-stick model can be used whenever OTV traffic can share the data center IP network with other Layer 3 traffic. On the other hand, the inline appliance model is ideal for Layer 2 extension scenarios that require an exclusive IP network (for service-level agreement [SLA] reasons, for example).

A redundant OTV design must also define how the OTV VDC internal interfaces will be connected to the site's Layer 2 network.

Figure 8-27 demonstrates two options: *dual-homing based on STP* and *virtual PortChannels*.

vPCs can surely help availability and provide load balancing of Layer 2 traffic. However, as a general recommendation, I suggest that the internal interface connection mimics the access switch's design. This best practice avoids excessive use of the vPC peer link in scenarios such as the following:

- N7K1 is the root switch for the Layer 2 network.
- The access switch is connected through a vPC to N7K1 and N7K2 while the OTV VDCs are using STP without any aggregation.

- A server sends Ethernet frames that must be transported through OTV to a remote data center, and the access switch hashing decision sends these frames to N7K2.
- If the AED for this VLAN is OTV-VDC1, traffic must traverse the peer link to reach the root switch and, afterward, the AED.

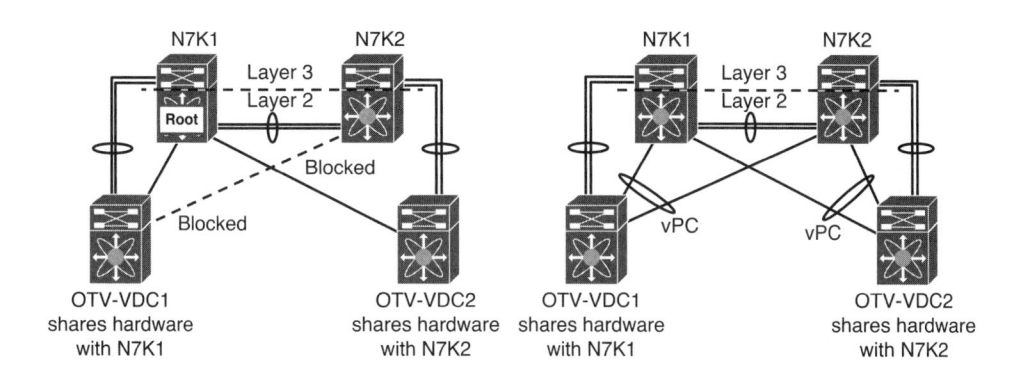

Figure 8-27 *OTV Redundant Layer 2 Connection*

A similar situation can also occur if the OTV VDCs are connected through a vPC while the access switches are not.

Logically, the optimal position of the OTV VDCs in a data center network topology is as close as possible to the border between Layer 3 and Layer 2 networks. In a traditional core-aggregation-access data center POD, the aggregation switches usually are the "sweet spot" for OTV deployment.

Although multiple OTV arrangements are possible, I will focus on two specific topologies that illustrate the main OTV design principles, at the time of this writing. They also represent, in my opinion, the majority of OTV customer scenarios.

At first, Figure 8-28 exhibits a sample site design where OTV uses the data center Layer 3 network to deploy Ethernet reachability to other sites. Note that this design can only extend any VLAN that is connected to the pair of aggregation switches.

If more than one aggregation POD must extend its VLANs to other sites, the OTV VDCs can be connected to multiple pairs of aggregation switches.

Figure 8-29 portrays such scenario, where the OTV internal interfaces are connected to a vPC aggregation POD (formed with VDCs from the same pair of Nexus 7000s) and to an already installed STP-based aggregation POD. For clarity (and because the OTV VDCs are using an exclusive IP network for VLAN extension), the core switches are not pictured in Figure 8-29.

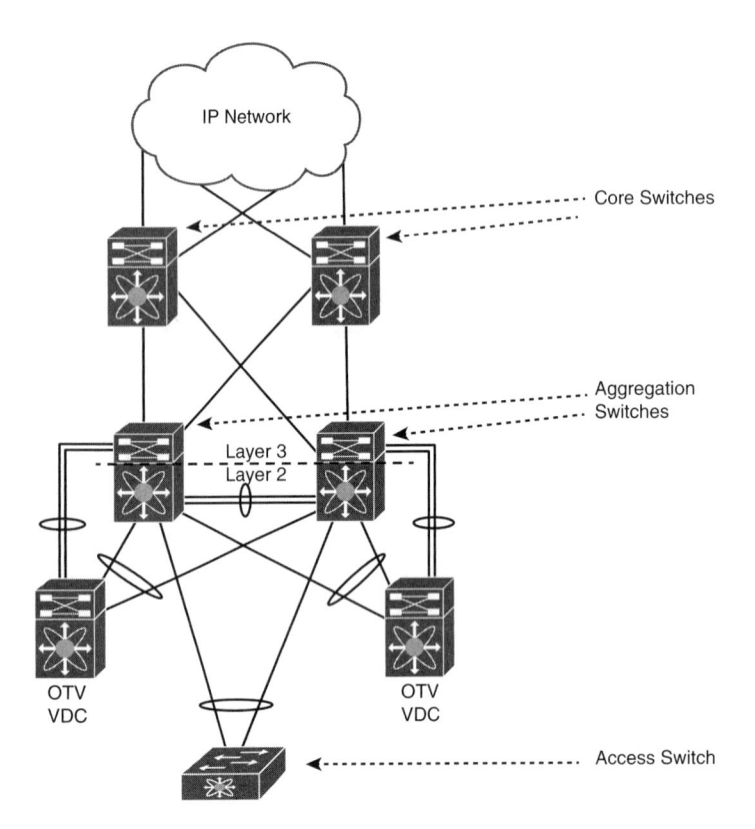

Figure 8-28 *OTV Design in a Single Aggregation POD*

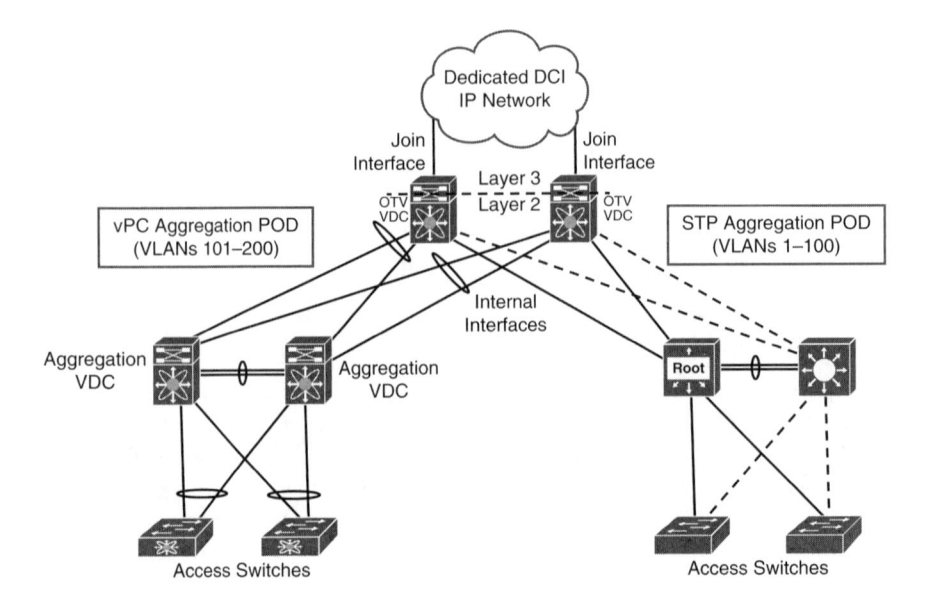

Figure 8-29 *Shared OTV VDC Design*

In Figure 8-29, you should also observe two other aspects:

- If these aggregation PODs are not supposed to share broadcast domains, they should deploy distinct VLAN IDs. After all, they are connected to the same OTV VDCs.

- It is highly recommended that each aggregation POD runs distinct STP instances. This best practice avoids unnecessary fate sharing between both PODs.

To see additional variations of OTV designs, refer to the "Further Reading" section, later in this chapter.

Note In any OTV design, it is paramount that this protocol scalability is observed and respected. I recommend that you refer to the Cisco documentation to find the most recent values for your software and hardware combination. At the time of this writing, the Nexus 7000 OTV implementation supports 256 VLANs, six sites, 16,000 MAC addresses, and two edge devices per site.

VLAN Identifiers and Layer 2 Extensions

In Chapter 3, you have learned that the IEEE 802.1Q frame format allows 4094 usable VLANs within an Ethernet domain. However, if distinct Layer 2 environments are extended to a single data center facility, it is highly probable that the same VLAN ID will be used in both environments.

For example, imagine that environments A and B represent different customers that already deploy VLAN 10 inside their data centers. If both of them desire to extend this VLAN to a service provider data center, how can this provider network differentiate VLAN 10 from customer A and VLAN from customer B? This scenario characterizes what is referred to as *VLAN ID collision*.

Note VLAN ID collision is not an exclusive service provider challenge. It can also happen on private data centers during corporate mergers or acquisitions.

A possible approach could be the deployment of distinct Layer 2 networks, one for each different environment, inside the shared data center. Not surprisingly, this could be quite challenging if one considers the cost involved in the acquisition of multiple Layer 2 devices, including DCI switches. In this section, I will present three options that allow these Layer 2 devices to be shared by environments with colliding VLAN IDs.

Virtual device contexts can be used to avoid the acquisition of additional Layer 2 devices in VLAN ID collision scenarios. As an example, one VDC can be used to extend VLAN 10 from customer A, whereas another VDC can take care of another VLAN 10.

VDCs can be very useful for vPC, FabricPath, and OTV Layer 2 extensions, because these technologies are also available on Nexus 7000 switches. Therefore, you should be aware that the maximum number of VDCs per switch limits the number of environments that a single physical device can support.

IEEE 802.1Q Tunneling, or simply "Q-in-Q", is yet another capability created to handle VLAN ID collision with elegance and scalability. Its concept is based on the additional tagging of IEEE 802.1Q Ethernet frames in a stack, where

- The inner tag represents the original VLAN the frame belongs to (*customer VLAN*).

- The outer tag relates to a VLAN provided to envelop the traffic from a specific environment, differentiating it inside the provider network (*provider VLAN*).

Figure 8-30 depicts the Ethernet frame encapsulation in a Q-in-Q frame. Potentially, a Q-in-Q-enabled network can support more than 16 million (4094 times 4094) distinct broadcast domains.

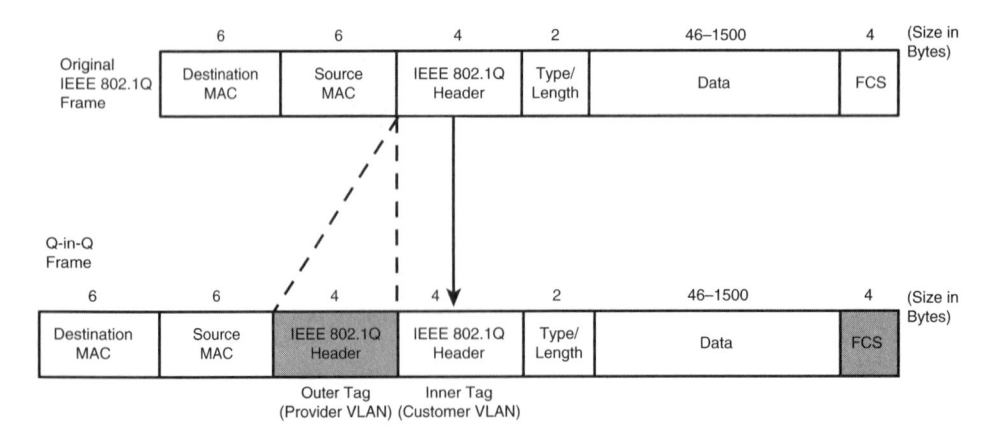

Figure 8-30 *Q-in-Q Frame Encapsulation*

Nexus 7000 switches support Q-in-Q, and Example 8-41 shows how the **switchport mode dot1q-tunnel** command defines a *tunnel port* in such switches. These interfaces insert (and remove) the outer tag and are usually connected to customer trunk interfaces.

Example 8-41 *Q-in-Q Tunnel Interface Configuration*

```
N7K# show running-config interface ethernet 2/3
[output suppressed]
interface Ethernet2/3
  switchport
! Defining a Q-in-Q tunnel interface
  switchport mode dot1q-tunnel
! This is the VLAN ID from the outer tag
  switchport access vlan 100
```

```
! BPDU filtering enabled by default on tunnel interfaces
  spanning-tree bpdufilter enable
  no shutdown
```

> **Tip** BPDUs can be transparently transported between Q-in-Q tunnel interfaces with the **l2protocol tunnel stp** interface command.

Layer 2 extensions through vPC, EoMPLS, and VPLS support double tagging to allow the sharing of DCI switches (and other network devices) between different environments. Although OTV and FabricPath can transport double-tagged frames (the inner tag can be viewed as mere data payload), Cisco does not support Q-in-Q over these protocols at the time of this writing. Nevertheless, I recommend that you refer to the Cisco online documentation for updated information.

VLAN translation is another useful technique that can help with VLAN ID collision scenarios. In Layer 2 extensions, a VLAN ID is translated to another one that has global significance in the shared infrastructure. Although VLAN translation is a relatively simple solution, it is generally treated as a last resort collision avoidance technique because the shared network continues to support 4094 VLANs and requires meticulous management of VLAN identifiers.

Figure 8-31 portrays all three described solutions for VLAN collisions on Layer 2 extension solutions.

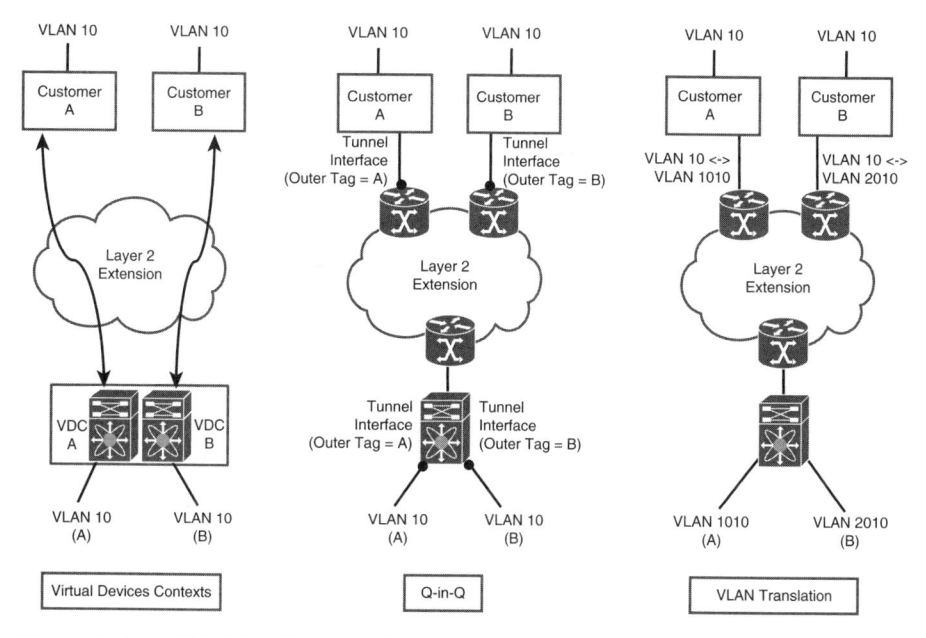

Figure 8-31 *VLAN Collision Solutions*

Internal Routing in Connected Data Centers

As I have presented in the earlier section "Challenges of Layer 2 Extensions," tromboning can happen in Layer 2–connected data centers, when IP packets "ping-pong" between sites before they reach their final destination. Although some distributed data centers do not worry about such behavior, others prefer not to waste their scarce DCI resources with this phenomenon.

Some simple design choices can decrease, or even eliminate, tromboning between data centers. These options are mainly related to how network services, first-hop redundancy protocols (FHRP), and coupled applications are deployed in connected data centers.

If network services, such as load balancers and firewalls, deploy active-standby availability, it is highly recommended that a pair of each of these devices is installed in each data center. This design guarantees that a network service device is always active on all sites, not requiring packets to be sent to another site for proper handling.

FHRPs usually rely on multicast communication to define active default gateways in a broadcast domain. However, if access control lists (ACL) are applied to Layer 2 extensions to specifically block the communication of these protocols, at least one default gateway will be active per site.

Tip A description of Hot Standby Router Protocol (HSRP) is included in Chapter 1 if you want to review how an FHRP works.

For brevity, I will not show these ACL configurations. Instead, Table 8-2 summarizes the traffic that should be blocked for three FHRPs: Hot Standby Router Protocol (HSRP), Virtual Router Redundancy Protocol (VRRP), and Gateway Load Balance Protocol (GLBP).

Table 8-2 *First-Hop Routing Protocol Traffic Characterization*

Protocol	Hello Address	Hello Transport	Virtual MAC Address[1]
HSRPv1	224.0.0.2	UDP port 1985	0000.0c07.acXX
HSRPv2	224.0.0.102	UDP port 1985	0000.0c9f.f0XX
VRRP	224.0.0.18	IP protocol 112	0000.5e00.01XX
GLBP	224.0.0.102	UDP port 3222	0007.b4XX.XXXX

[1] These values should be used to suppress Ethernet frames and gratuitous ARPs between sites (XX represents any hexadecimal number between 00 and ff).

These ACLs are sufficient when FHRP virtual MAC addresses are only learned through the data plane over the Layer 2 extension. Nevertheless, OTV demands an additional step to avoid these addresses from being advertised to other sites through the OTV control plane protocol (IS-IS).

Example 8-42 explains how you can select specific MAC addresses that will not be advertised through IS-IS. In this example, HSRPv1 and HSRPv2 traffic is filtered with a route map, as a subnet would be in a routing protocol configuration.

Example 8-42 *OTV HSRP MAC Reachability Filtering*

```
OTV-Site1# show running-config | begin mac-list
! Characterizing the vMACs used by HSRPv1 and HSRPv2
mac-list OTV_HSRP_VMAC_deny seq 10 deny 0000.0c07.ac00 ffff.ffff.ff00
mac-list OTV_HSRP_VMAC_deny seq 11 deny 0000.0c9f.f000 ffff.ffff.f000
mac-list OTV_HSRP_VMAC_deny seq 20 permit 0000.0000.0000 0000.0000.0000
!
! Prohibitting the advertisement of such vMACs in a filter
Route-map OTV_HSRP_filter permit 10
Match mac-list OTV_HSRP_VMAC_deny
!
[output suppressed]
OTV-Site1# show running-config | begin otv-isis
otv-isis default
! Applying the filter to Overlay1 in this switch
vpn Overlay1
redistribute filter route-map OTV_HSRP_filter
[output suppressed]
```

In addition, FabricPath links do not support FHRP filtering at the time of this writing. However, one possible work-around for STP networks connected through a FabricPath DCI network is to use a FHRP shared authentication key to block FHRP discovery and negotiation between switches from distinct sites.

With local clustering for network services and FHRP filtering, it is expected that internal traffic will not traverse the Layer 2 extension between data centers unnecessarily.

Figure 8-32 shows that even traffic from active-active geoclusters can benefit from these practices.

Similarly, if tiered applications (for example, presentation, business logic, and database servers) are clustered and distributed on connected data centers, traffic between instances from different clusters can also cause tromboning. There are basically two ways to avoid this situation:

- All application clusters should have at least one active node in each site.
- If there is a switchover in one of the clusters, all other applications should fail over to the same site.

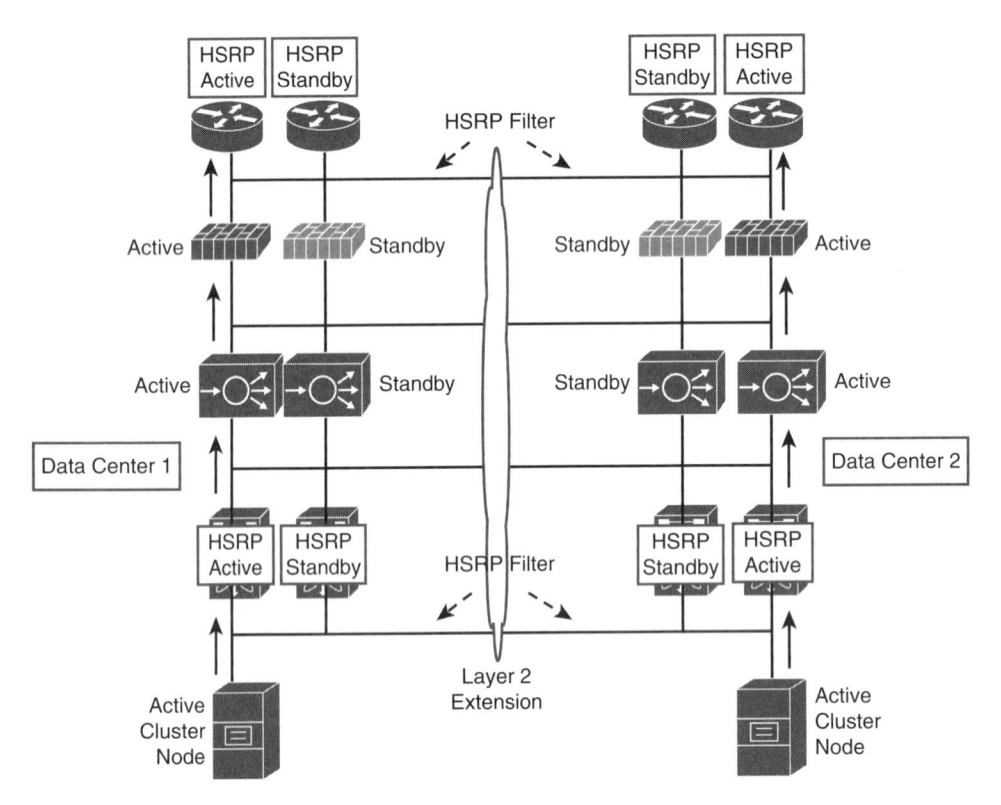

Figure 8-32 *Localization of Traffic in Connected Data Centers*

As these implementations vary wildly among clustering solutions, I recommend that you refer to their documentation for more details.

> **Note** As you have probably noticed, I have not addressed how a data center site is selected to support an external client request. To leverage some server virtualization concepts that will be explained in the future, I have saved this discussion for Chapter 16, "Moving Targets."

Use Case: Active-Active Greenfield Data Centers

After your consulting firm delivers a series of successful projects for a big company, its management team decides it is time to disclose its new project: two completely new (greenfield) data centers that it will build in the next three years. At present, the company has two sites: one legacy site and an international site (which are 500 kilometers apart).

The company's greenfield data centers will be located 40 kilometers from the legacy site and will be very close to each other (less than 5 kilometers apart). Multiple pairs of dark fiber are already available between these sites.

The company has planned that these new facilities will host applications clusters that can be active in either site. Each greenfield data center and the international site will be capable of handling the entire company's IT needs.

Six months after the greenfield data centers are fully operational, the legacy site will be deactivated (IT thinks it is enough time for the complete data migration), and the international site will be used as a disaster recovery site.

The company wants to hire your services to solve the Layer 2 extension problems it has been facing for some years: EoMPLS is currently being used to extend unicast traffic over 100 VLANs and, unfortunately, whenever a convergence happens in the international site, it provokes serious instabilities in the legacy site. Also, STP does not allow the company to use both available EoMPLS connections, which is considered a waste of money.

Definitely, the company does not want these problems to occur after its new sites are working. You realize that your proposal must be robust enough to handle any type of Layer 2 control protocol within the sites. It is already known that the legacy and international sites will continue to use Rapid PVST+ while the greenfield data centers will probably use a Layer 2 multipath technology (this choice was not made yet). Additionally, the company wants to avoid "zig-zag" traffic to the international site (the phenomenon is not considered a critical problem between the greenfield and legacy facilities).

Immediately, you explain that these problems are not caused by EoMPLS alone, but for the company's lack of a fault isolation strategy. Although these problems can immediately be solved with the positioning of a cross-switch link aggregation (for example, vPCs) and BPDU filtering, these techniques are not appropriate if these VLANs must be extended to more than two sites.

After one week, you propose the topology depicted in Figure 8-33.

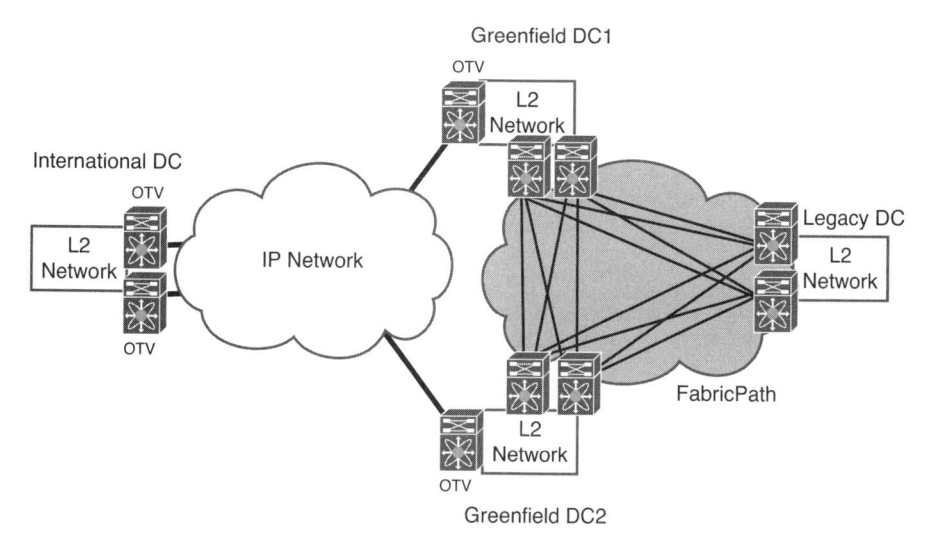

Figure 8-33 *Hybrid Layer 2 Extension Solution*

During the design presentation meeting, you highlight the following details from your solution:

- The greenfield and legacy sites can use FabricPath as a DCI technology to use all the bandwidth resources during the migration period. Different spanning tree domains will be used to completely isolate STP between the sites (if the greenfield data centers use STP internally).

- OTV will be used to extend the VLANs to the international site over its IP network.

- Each greenfield data center will have a single OTV edge device because they will constitute a single OTV site (it will share a site VLAN and a site identifier). This procedure guarantees that each VLAN will use a single authoritative edge device to reach the international site.

- Classical Ethernet (using STP) will be used in the greenfield sites to extend each VLAN between the FabricPath network and its corresponding OTV AED.

- Tromboning can be avoided in the OTV connection with FHRP filtering. This traffic phenomenon is not considered a problem between the greenfield and legacy sites.

During the rest of the meeting, you explain how your design provides fault isolation, loop avoidance, and multihoming to future sites, during and after the migration phase. Very impressed, the executives ask whether your company also designs storage-area networks.

Summary

In this chapter you have learned that

- Geographically distributed data centers are part of the disaster recovery and business continuance plans of a company.

- Geoclusters and the migration of servers (physical or virtual) demand that Layer 2 domains are extended between two or more data centers.

- Loop avoidance, fault isolation, and multihoming are the most typical challenges for Layer 2 extensions.

- Several Layer 2 extension virtualization techniques are available to address these challenges. Their characteristics, at the time of this writing, are summarized in Table 8-3.

Table 8-3 *Data Center Interconnection Summary*

Characteristic	vPC or VSS	FabricPath	EoMPLS	VPLS	OTV
Transport	Optical or EoMPLS	Optical	MPLS or IP (GRE)	MPLS or IP (GRE)	IP
Loop Avoidance Mechanisms	Multichassis link aggregation	IS-IS	Multichassis link aggregation	Split horizon	IS-IS and AED
STP Isolation	BPDU filter or MST region	STP domain	BPDU filter or MST region	Native	Native
Multihoming	PortChannel hashing	ECMP	PortChannel hashing	PortChannel hashing (A-VPLS)	VLAN distribution
Encryption	IEEE 802.1ae	Not supported	IEEE 802.1ae or IPsec (GRE)	IPsec (GRE)	IPsec (with external device)
Added Bytes to Original Ethernet Frame	No	22 bytes	30 or 54 bytes (GRE)	30 or 54 bytes (GRE)	42 bytes
Q-in-Q	Yes	Not supported	Yes	Yes	Not supported

- VDCs, Q-in-Q, and VLAN translation are three different methods of avoiding VLAN ID collisions on a shared network.
- Tromboning can be minimized with FHRP filtering and localization of network service active-standby clusters.

Figure 8-34 illustrates how Ethernet over MPLS, Virtual Private LAN Service, and Overlay Transport Virtualization can be logically represented when providing Layer 2 extensions to a pair of data center interconnect switches.

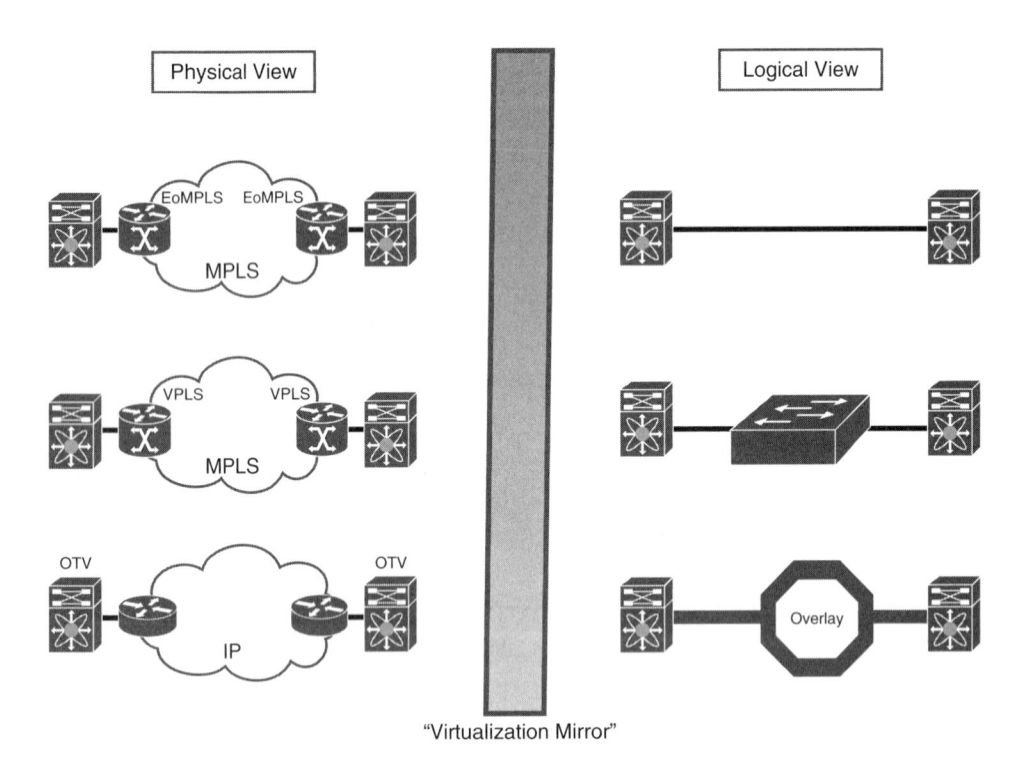

Figure 8-34 *Through the Virtualization Mirror*

Further Reading

Darukhanawalla, Nash and Bellagamba, Patrice. *Interconnecting Data Centers Using VPLS*. Cisco Press, 2009

Data Center Interconnect

www.cisco.com/go/dci

Overlay Transport Virtualization IETF Draft

http://tools.ietf.org/html/draft-hasmit-otv-03

Chapter 9

Storage Evolution

"The palest ink is better than the best memory." (Chinese proverb)

This chapter examines the core aspects of modern data center storage technologies, as well as their intrinsic relationship with virtualization concepts. It contains the following topics:

- Data Center Storage Devices
- Accessing Data in Rest
- Storage Virtualization

Storage technologies epitomize the word *data* in data centers. With access to the same hardware and software solutions, it can be said that the main difference between two data centers corresponds to the actual information they gather and generate.

Permanent storage technologies were developed concurrently with data processing, because their relationship has a direct impact on application performance and effectiveness. And from punch cards to solid-state drives, these technologies have come a long way in improving capacity, increasing speed, and reducing size.

In this chapter, I discuss the most common storage devices and access methods found in data center installations today. Unsurprisingly, I also address how virtualization has continually improved availability, serviceability, and provisioning in these devices and their associated systems.

Data Center Storage Devices

Throughout computer science history, data storage technologies have been segregated into classes that characterize their role on compute systems. These classes are commonly known as

- **Primary storage:** Also referred to as memory, these volatile storage mechanisms can be directly accessed by a computer's central processing unit (CPU). They usually have small capacity but are very fast when compared to other storage technologies.

- **Secondary storage:** Not directly accessible to the CPU, these devices require input and output (I/O) channels to transport their data to the primary storage. They deploy nonvolatile data, have more capacity than primary memory, provide slower access times, and are also known as auxiliary memory.

- **Tertiary storage:** Refers to removable mass storage media whose data access time is much longer than secondary storage. These solutions present the lowest cost per data unit among all storage types and provide the required capacity for large long-term data sets.

In the next sections, I focus on secondary and tertiary storage devices that are most commonly found in modern data centers. Because primary storage devices are more related to server systems, I delay their discussion to Chapter 13, "Server Evolution."

Hard Disk Drives

The first *hard disk drive (HDD)* was commercialized by IBM in 1956. Derived from the magnetic drum memory concept (which was a rotating metal cylinder covered in ferromagnetic recording material that allowed static heads to read and write data), modern disk drives are based on multiple platters (disks) spinning around a common axis at a constant speed. Electromagnetic movable heads are positioned above and below each disk, moving toward their center or edge to read or write data.

In HDDs, data is stored in concentric *sectors*, which are the atomic data units of a disk and usually accommodate 512 bytes. A *track* aggregates all sectors that a single head can access when it is motionless. Outer disk tracks are less densely populated with data then the inner ones, fixing a constant amount of data per track that can be accessed at a defined period of time.

There are usually 1024 tracks on a single disk, and all corresponding tracks from all disks define a cylinder. Consequently, if a specific sector must be retrieved from a hard disk drive, it must be referenced through a three-part address comprised of *cylinder/head/sector* information.

Figure 9-1 illustrates how these elements integrate the structure of a hard disk drive.

After an I/O operation (for example, read) requests data from a defined cylinder/head/sector position, a mechanical actuator positions the disk drive heads at the requested cylinder, where they remain still until the required sector is accessible to them. The time interval for the dislocation of the heads is called *seek time*, and the one related to the localization of a sector is called *rotational latency*. Added to the disk drive processing and transfer intervals, they form the overall system *access time*. Most server internal disk drives spin at a fixed rate of 10,000 or 15,000 revolutions per minute, and their access time ranges between 3 and 12 milliseconds.

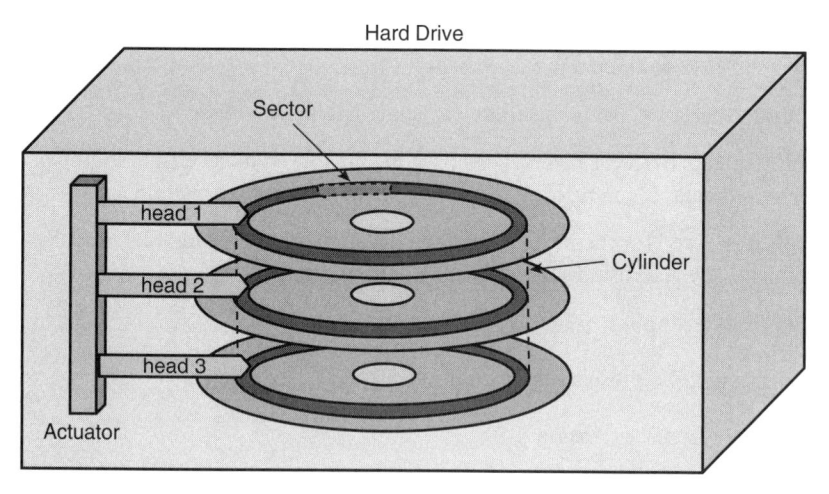

Figure 9-1 *Hard Disk Drive Element*

I/O operations for a single sector are a rare occurrence on disk drives. Commonly, these requests refer to multiple *sector clusters*, which consist of two, four, or another exponent of two, contiguous sectors. I/O operations targeted at nonconsecutive sectors will increase access time and consequently slow application performance.

Although *solid-state drives (SSDs)* were created several decades ago, it was just around the late 2000s that they have achieved a cost that was compatible with their advantages over HDDs. Because most SSDs use flash memory to store data persistently through power outages, SSDs have a lower access time (less than 100 microseconds) when compared to electromechanical hard drives. As a consequence, these devices are usually positioned for application environments that require superior I/O performance.

Disk Arrays

Regardless of their underlying technology, hard drives truly constitute the secondary storage of choice in most computer systems today. However, there is not much use for data on an internal disk that lives inside a server in the case of a hardware failure. Besides, the storage demands of corporate data centers certainly cannot be satisfied with a single hard drive.

Broadly speaking, the decoupling of hard drives and servers can be made through two different devices: JBODs (Just a Bunch of Disks) or disk arrays. JBODs are basically hard drives assembled together in a unit that can be accessed remotely by application servers. Because each server must individually control their assigned HDDs, JBODs generally cannot match the level of management, availability, and capacity required in enterprise and service provider facilities.

Adversely, a *disk array* contains multiples disks that can be administered as a scalable resource pool shared among several application environments. The main components of a disk array are

- **Controllers:** Manage the array hardware resources (such as disks) and coordinate the server access to data contained in the device.

- **Access ports:** Interfaces that are used to exchange data with servers.

- **Cache:** RAM (random-access memory) or flash memory used to accelerate I/O operations for stored data. It can be located at the controller or on expansion modules.

- **Disk enclosures:** Used for the physical accommodation of HDDs and SSDs. Usually, a disk enclosure gathers disk drives with similar characteristics.

- **Redundant power supplies.**

The left side of Figure 9-2 represents these components.

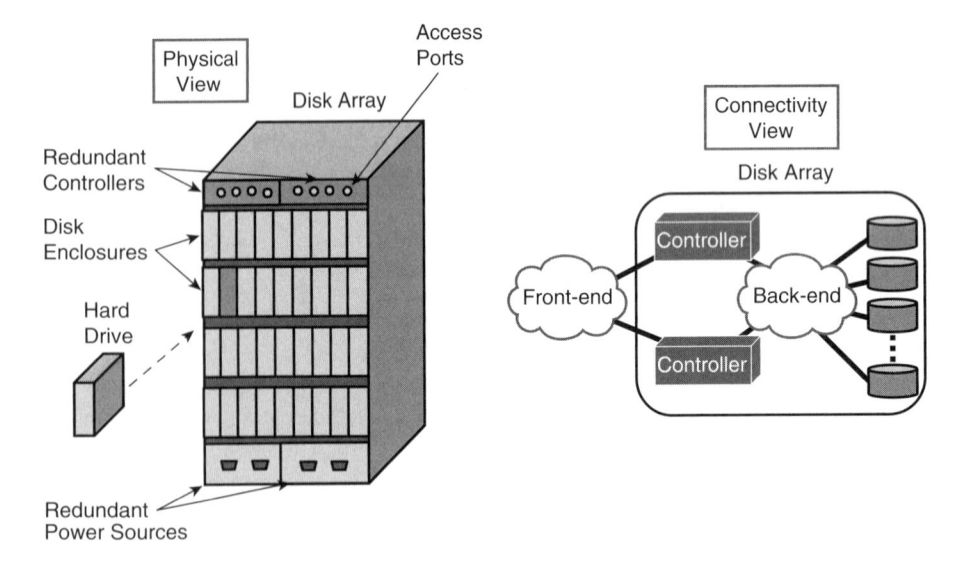

Figure 9-2 *Disk Array Components*

At the right side of Figure 9-2, you can visualize both types of disk array interconnections: *front-end* (used for server access) and *back-end* (used for disk connection to the controller). Both ports support a great variety of communication protocols and physical media, as you will learn in the next sections.

With their highly redundant architecture and management features, disk arrays have become the workhorse of permanent storage in modern data centers. At the time of this writing, the main disk array vendors are EMC Corporation, Hitachi Data Systems (HDS), IBM, and NetApp Inc.

Tape Drives and Libraries

Magnetic tapes are a storage medium made of magnetizable coating on a long strip of plastic film. They are usually inserted into a motorized *tape drive* that can wind the tape to a desired point and use its magnetic heads to read, write, or erase data as the tape moves.

Tape drives were first available in 1951, with the UNIVAC I systems. Afterward, they were able to replace decades of punch cards and punch tapes with more speed and storage capacity.

Before the popularization of hard disk drives, magnetic tapes were the leading secondary storage technology in computer rooms. And because of their cost and durability, they still remain the preferred choice for tertiary storage in most data centers today.

Because tape drives require human manipulation of media, it is more common to find them on *tape libraries*. These devices are basically systems that can contain thousands of tape drives with multiple slots to hold tape cartridges, a bar-code reader to identify these cartridges, and a robot that can move cartridges to tape drives.

As you can infer, when compared to hard disk drives, tape libraries present significantly slower access times. Because the library robot must first locate the correct tape, manipulate it physically to a tape drive, and finally forward the tape head up to the desired data, it can take minutes before data is finally retrieved to a computer system.

Modern tape libraries can store hundreds of petabytes, and their main vendors are IBM and Oracle (after the acquisition of Sun Microsystems). They are mostly used for data archiving and backup, where they can implement advanced features such as data encryption and tape life cycle management.

Accessing Data in Rest

To save or retrieve data from a permanent storage device, a computer system must implement a communication protocol that is compatible with such a device. During the decades of storage evolution, several methods were developed in parallel with differing objectives and results. Notwithstanding, it is possible to classify these methods into three different categories, depending on the data structure that they are based on.

Blocks are simply a sequence of bytes, with a defined length (block size), that embody the smallest container for data in a storage device (tape, hard drive, or flash memory). As an illustration, a hard drive block can be mapped to a disk sector.

Files are a set of contiguous data bytes that are stored persistently on a storage device. Besides containing proper user data, files also contain *metadata*, which symbolizes attributes such as name, owner, permissions of access, date of creation, date of last revision, and many other details. Each operating system has a different method of creating files, depending on their defined metadata structure.

Records are similar structures to files, but present highly structured data that simplifies database queries. Broadly speaking, files and records are simply an abstraction applied over data blocks, requiring an additional layer of software on end devices to establish a rather sophisticated access method to stored data.

Block-Based Access

Block-based storage devices provide direct access to data blocks that will be commonly controlled by a server. In that generic scenario, a server software piece called *Logical Volume Manager (LVM)* will normally create local volumes and perform I/O operations on the storage device on behalf of the server applications.

The methods of data block exchange between a computer and its storage device vary widely depending on the chosen components of a scenario. And as you will see in the next sections, they can be based on

- Proprietary or standard protocols
- Dedicated connections, shared buses, or storage area networks (SANs)

Small Computer Systems Interface

The set of standards that define the *Small Computer Systems Interface* (SCSI, pronounced *scuzzy*) were developed by the International Committee for Information Technology Standards (INCITS) Technical Committee T10. Originated from the work of Larry Boucher (from Shugart Associates), SCSI essentially defines how data is transferred between computers and peripheral devices. With that intention, SCSI describes commands, protocols, and physical interfaces aiming to provide compatibility between different vendors.

Before delving further into the details of the SCSI standards, allow me to take you for a walk down memory lane. The year is 1986, Run D.M.C is redefining pop music with "Walk This Way," and SCSI-1 (or SCSI First Generation) is a recently ratified standard. Then, a typical SCSI implementation followed the physical topology illustrated in Figure 9-3.

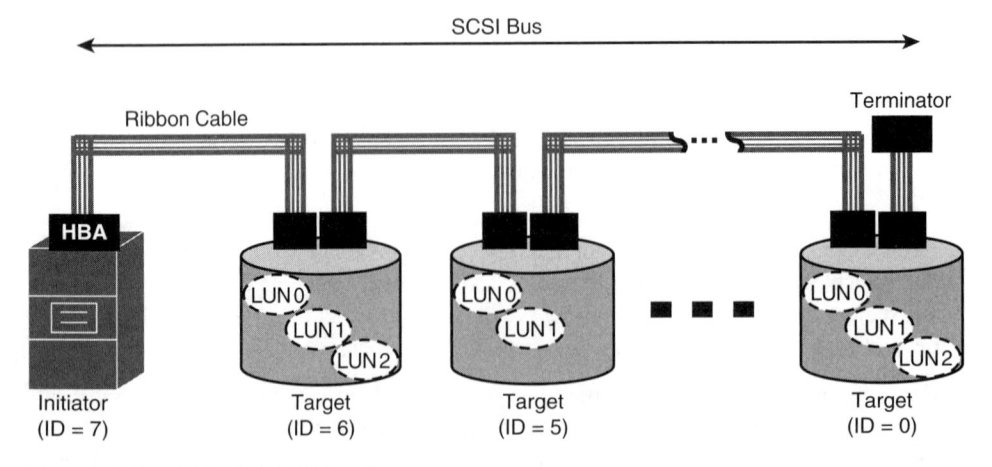

Figure 9-3 *SCSI Parallel Topology*

Figure 9-3 depicts a SCSI *initiator*, or simply a computer system that accessed seven hard drives (SCSI *targets*). In this particular topology, a bus was formed with a daisy-chain arrangement that required two parallel ports on each external target and several ribbon cable segments. The bus also needed a *terminator* connection at the end devices to avoid signal reflection and loss of connectivity. Some devices could deploy termination through manual configuration or even automatically (as is the case of the initiator from Figure 9-3).

The communication inside this SCSI parallel bus was half-duplex, meaning that only one device can transmit on the bus at a time. SCSI *identifiers* (ID) were assigned to devices connected to the bus representing the access priority over the shared transmission media. These IDs had to be configured manually (through jumpers or software), and it was recommended that the initiator always had the maximum priority (7, in the depicted scenario).

In this arrangement, the initiator communicated with *logical units (LU)* defined at each target device and identified with a *logical unit number (LUN)*. Whereas most devices only supported a single LUN, more sophisticated peripherals, such as some hard drives, could deploy multiple logical storage devices.

After it earned the rights to transmit in the bus, the initiator sent SCSI commands a target using a *bus/target/LUN* address. Using this triad, a logical device could be uniquely located even if the initiator deployed more than one SCSI host bus adapter (HBA) and had several targets at each bus.

In SCSI, I/O operations and control commands was sent using *command descriptor blocks (CDB)*, whose first byte symbolized the command code and the remaining data, its parameters.

Table 9-1 illustrates some SCSI command codes and their actions over SCSI peripherals.

Table 9-1 *SCSI Command Codes*

Command	Code (Hexadecimal)	Initiator Action
Test Unit Ready	00	Asks whether target device is ready to process data transfers
Inquiry	12	Asks for basic device information
Send Diagnostic	1d	Requests a self-test operation
Read	08, 28, a8, 88, 7f, 3e	Requests data from a target
Write	0a, 2a, aa, 8a, 7f, 3f, 9f	Requests storing data on one target
Read Capacity	25	Requests target size information
Format Unit	04	Prepares medium for use

As you might infer, the vast majority of commands in a SCSI bus communications were *read* and *write* operations. All their associated commands were intended to interact with a selected part of the LUN and define an I/O operation. To express the exact block location of the operation on a LUN, a SCSI command indicates two values:

- **Logical Block Address (LBA):** Signals the data block within the LUN where the operation will start.
- **Transfer length:** Announces how many blocks will be transported in this particular I/O operation.

To further clarify how these SCSI parameters are handled in I/O operations, Figure 9-4 illustrates the exchange of data during a read and a write command.

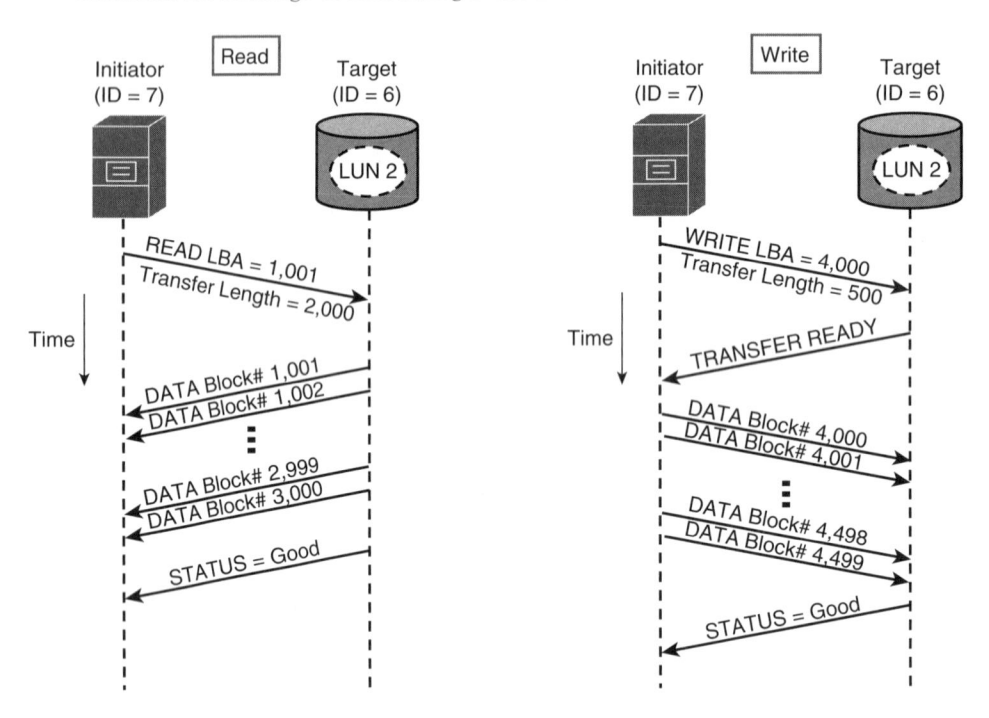

Figure 9-4 *Read and Write SCSI Operations*

On the left side of Figure 9-4, a sample SCSI read operation from an initiator requires 2000 blocks from the data stored on LUN 2 starting at LBA 1,001. After the target receives the command, it sends the requested data to the initiator and finalizes the operation with a status code confirming its correct execution (status=Good).

On the right side of the figure, a SCSI write is sent to the same target requesting that the same LUN stores 500 blocks starting at LBA 4,000. After receiving an acknowledgment that the target is ready to receive the data blocks, the initiator transmits them and waits for a confirmation from the successful operation (status=Good).

The SCSI parallel architecture was incrementally stretched to its limits with several enhancements in its transmission media and control protocol, achieving speeds of 640 Mbps and having up to 16 devices on a bus. Still, the communication remained half-duplex and connections could not surpass 25 meters because of known difficulties in parallel communications, such as clock skew (signals that do not arrive simultaneously at the other end of the connection) and interference from adjacent connections.

To support future SCSI interfaces and cabling, T10 has envisioned the separation between physical components and elements related to higher-level software. And as a result, the *SCSI Architectural Model (SAM)* was created.

Figure 9-5 illustrates the structure of this model.

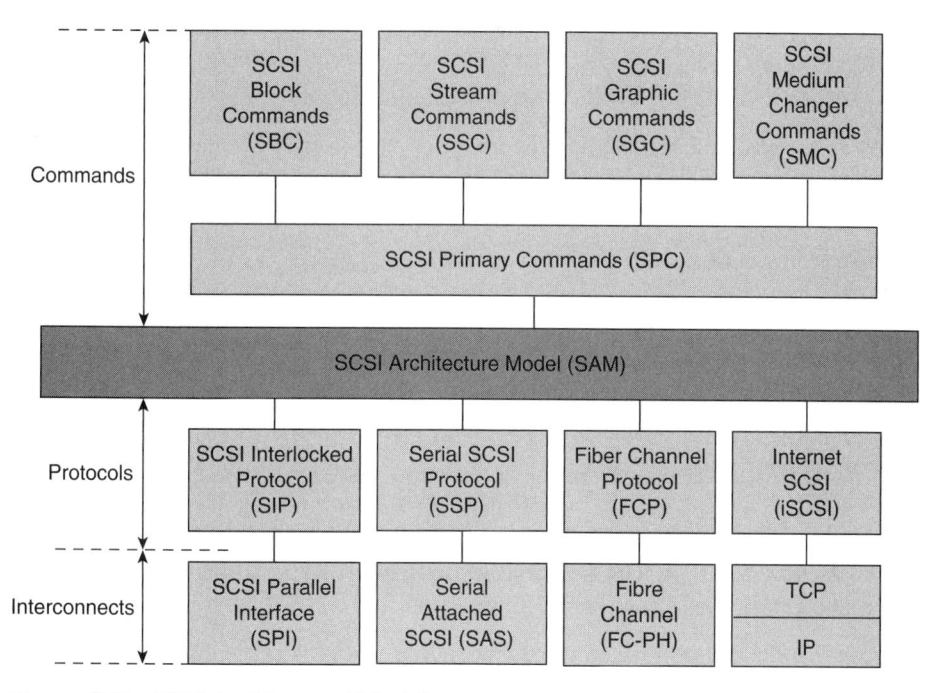

Figure 9-5 *SCSI Architectural Model*

Based on standard SCSI-3, SAM literally segregates SCSI commands (primary and specific for each peripheral) from their physical layer implementations. Similarly to Ethernet, this model abstracted the physical layers for SCSI and allowed its portability to other types of interconnects. One of them, *Serial Attached SCSI (SAS)*, was specifically designed to overcome the bandwidth and scalability limitations of the SCSI parallel interface.

In summary, SAS can be defined as point-to-point serial connection that attaches two devices through a maximum speed of 6 Gbps and distances shorter than 10 meters. This standard has achieved popularity with internal hard drives and is also commonly used in back-end connections in disk arrays.

Another famous interconnect option, *Fibre Channel* is a series of protocols defined by INCITS Technical Committee T11 that provide high-speed data communication between computer systems. Fibre Channel has established itself as the leading SAN protocol, with speeds of up to 16 Gbps, 10-km reach, and potentially more than 16 million connected hosts in a single fabric (network).

> **Tip** I discuss Fibre Channel and its core mechanisms in Chapter 10, "Islands in the SAN."

Internet SCSI (iSCSI) is essentially the transport of SCSI commands and data over a TCP connection, with destination port 3260. An iSCSI session can be directed to an iSCSI port on a storage array or a Fibre Channel switch that will act as a gateway between the iSCSI initiator and the SAN-connected storage devices.

The SCSI Architectural Model also supports other physical layer standards such as IEEE 1394 (also known as FireWire) and IBM's Serial Storage Architecture (SSA).

Mainframe Storage Access

The history of storage access on IBM mainframes (formally referred to as Central Electronics Complex, or CEC) is interwoven with the creation and development of storage in general. In these environments, peripherals such as storage control units (CU) were connected to CECs through *I/O channels*, which were essentially dedicated processors for data transfer between primary memory and the peripherals.

In the 1960s, the mainframe I/O channel architecture was called *Bus&Tag* and, in hindsight, shared several similarities with parallel SCSI. Bus&Tag communication was also based on ribbon cables that carried data (bus) and control (tag) information. Bus&Tag also implemented a daisy-chain arrangement that permitted a bus cable length of 60 meters and a shared bandwidth of 4.5 Mbps.

In the early 1990s, IBM introduced *Enterprise System Connection (ESCON)* as the next evolution for mainframe I/O channels. The architecture included ESCON directors, which were switching devices that enabled the sharing of a peripheral between multiple channels. ESCON deployed optical fibers to connect channels and control units, achieving 17 Mbps and maximum unrepeated distances of 3 km over mulitmode fiber (MMF) or 43 km over single-mode fiber (SMF). Still, the communication between end devices remained half-duplex.

In 2002, IBM released *Fiber Connectivity (FICON)*, a new I/O channel architecture using Fibre Channel as its underlying transport protocol and, consequently, inheriting most Fibre Channel physical characteristics such as bandwidth, reach, and evolution. Similarly to ESCON, FICON supports point-to-point and cascaded topologies, with a maximum of two FICON directors between channels and CUs. Notwithstanding, FICON only deploys communication over single-mode fibers.

> **Note** At the time of this writing, FICON supports 8-Gbps connections and up to 100-km distances.

Although modern zSeries mainframes support SCSI over Fibre Channel connectivity (for example, when they are deploying IBM's version of Linux: Linux on system z), they commonly use a proprietary I/O control protocol called *Single-Byte Command Code Set (SBCCS)*. Combined with FICON, SBCCS supports multiple concurrent I/O operations per channel, and it is one of the best-performing storage access protocols today.

Advanced Technology Attachment

Parallel Advanced Technology Attachment (PATA) was created in 1986 to connect IBM PC/AT microcomputers to their internal hard disk drives. Also known as *Integrated Drive Electronics (IDE)*, this still-popular interconnect can achieve up to 133 Mbps with ribbon parallel cables.

As its name infers, an IDE disk drive has integrated controllers. From a data access perspective, each IDE drive is an array of 512-byte blocks reachable through a simple command interface (*basic ATA command set*) that is defined by the INCITS T13 Technical Committee.

In the mid-1990s, the Small Form Factor (SFF) committee introduced *ATA Packet Interface (ATAPI)* that extended PATA to other devices, such as CD-ROMs, DVD-ROMs, and tape drives. More importantly, ATAPI allowed an ATA physical connection to carry SCSI commands and data, serving as an alternative interconnect for this widespread standard.

Serial Advanced Technology Attachment (SATA) constitutes the evolution of ATA architecture for internal hard drive connections. First standardized in 2003 (also by the T13 Technical Committee), SATA can achieve 6 Gbps and remains a popular internal hard disk connection for servers and disk arrays.

SAS offer compatibility with SATA disks through the SATA Tunneling Protocol (STP). Therefore, in a rather interesting way, ATA commands can be carried over SCSI media (with STP) and vice versa (with ATAPI).

Both PATA and SATA received multiple enhancements that have resulted in standards such as ATA-2 (Ultra ATA), ATA-3 (EIDE), external SATA (eSATA), and mSATA (mini-SATA).

File Access

Comprised of software, hardware, and permanent storage, a *file system* can be defined as a hierarchical structure designed to store, retrieve, and update a set of files. Although file systems can be built on servers with standard operating systems such as Linux and Windows (*file servers*), larger data center implementations generally employ specialized storage devices named *Network Attached Storage (NAS)*.

Besides all the usual components of a disk array, an *NAS appliance* also incorporates file systems that can serve multiple remote clients with performance and scalability. These devices can also be implemented through an *NAS head* (or NAS gateway), which basically decouples the file system function from the disk arrays.

An NAS (or file server) has exclusive access to the file system metadata and is especially built to offer file access through network file-sharing protocols. In essence, this storage device works as single point of arbitration to remote client systems, providing file locks and permissions.

NASs are commercialized through various vendors, such as EMC Corporation and NetApp Inc. These devices support multiple network file-sharing protocols, the most common being *Network File System (NFS)* and *Common Internet File System (CIFS)*.

Network File System

NFS is a file-sharing protocol mostly used on computers running UNIX and Linux operating systems. When directories are shared on an NFS server, an NFS client can associate it to its local file structure (or "mount"), allowing local applications and users to access files on the server.

Since Sun Microsystems created NFS in 1984, it has been released through various versions, with the last one being standardized in RFC 3530 (NFS version 4). Ratifying the use of UDP or TCP (both on port 2049) as transport layer protocols, the RFC also introduces built-in security into the protocol, allowing authentication of both client and servers through Kerberos, LIPKEY, and SPKM-3 standards.

Common Internet File System

CIFS is an updated version of the Microsoft Server Message Block (SMB) network file-sharing protocol. With CIFS, virtually any Windows-based machine can map a network drive to a CIFS file server or NAS. Nonetheless, other operating systems can also use CIFS to share files, including Linux and its open CIFS implementation (Samba).

CIFS is specified by Microsoft, and it can use TCP port 445 connections or Microsoft NetBIOS as its transport protocols. CIFS provides client and server Active Directory (AD) authentication through NT LAN Manager (NTLM) version 2 and Kerberos.

Record Access

A *database* is a collection of highly organized information (records) that allows the retrieval and saving of select portions of data. Probably the best known analogy for a database is the telephone book, where each record has at least three types of data: name, address, and telephone number.

A *database management system (DBMS)* provides access to one or multiple database records through queries defined in specialized access protocols, such as

- Open DataBase Connectivity (ODBC)
- Java DataBase Connectivity (JDBC)
- Structured Query Language (SQL)

Database management systems are generally comprised of one or more *database servers* controlling storage devices (where data is actually saved) and providing record access to other applications. The most popular DBMSs are Oracle Database and Microsoft SQL Server.

> **Note** With the scaling and cost reduction of main memory, *in-memory databases* such as SAP HANA are becoming an attractive option. Because these systems provide access to records without relying on I/O operations in a disk-based storage device, they deliver a more powerful performance. Nonetheless, in-memory database implementations also require a secondary storage device to avoid loss of data in the case of a server failure.

Storage Virtualization

Virtualization is deeply ingrained in storage technologies. Similarly to the seven network layers of the OSI model, storage abstractions are recursive and embody different meanings and behaviors according to its "consumer" software layer.

To further clarify this statement, note that I have already discussed two data structure abstractions in this chapter:

- A *file*, which can be seen as an assembly of data and metadata that can be manipulated by the operating system or remote file system clients
- A *logical unit*, which represent a virtual partition of a SCSI storage device

Other virtualization techniques have also been absorbed into data center storage tasks. *LUN translation*, for example, transforms a LUN from its original assignment to another identifier when it is accessed by a particular server. The translation to LUN 0 is a particularly useful operation, because some operating systems select the lowest LUN as a boot device.

Another virtualization technology, *Redundant Array of Independent Disks (RAID)*, is arguably the most common abstraction in modern storage systems today. In summary, RAID aggregates data blocks from multiple HDDs to achieve storage high availability, performance, or capacity. Moreover, a *RAID group* basically produces the illusion of a single virtual hard disk drive.

> **Note** RAID was formally defined in the 1988 paper "A Case for Redundant Arrays of Inexpensive Disks (RAID)," by David A. Patterson, Garth A. Gibson, and Randy Katz, from the University of California. A small curiosity: The acronym currently stands for both definitions "Redundant Array of Independent Disks" and "Redudant Array of Inexpensive Disks."

Figure 9-6 portrays some popular RAID levels, each one representing a different block aggregation scheme for the involved disk drives.

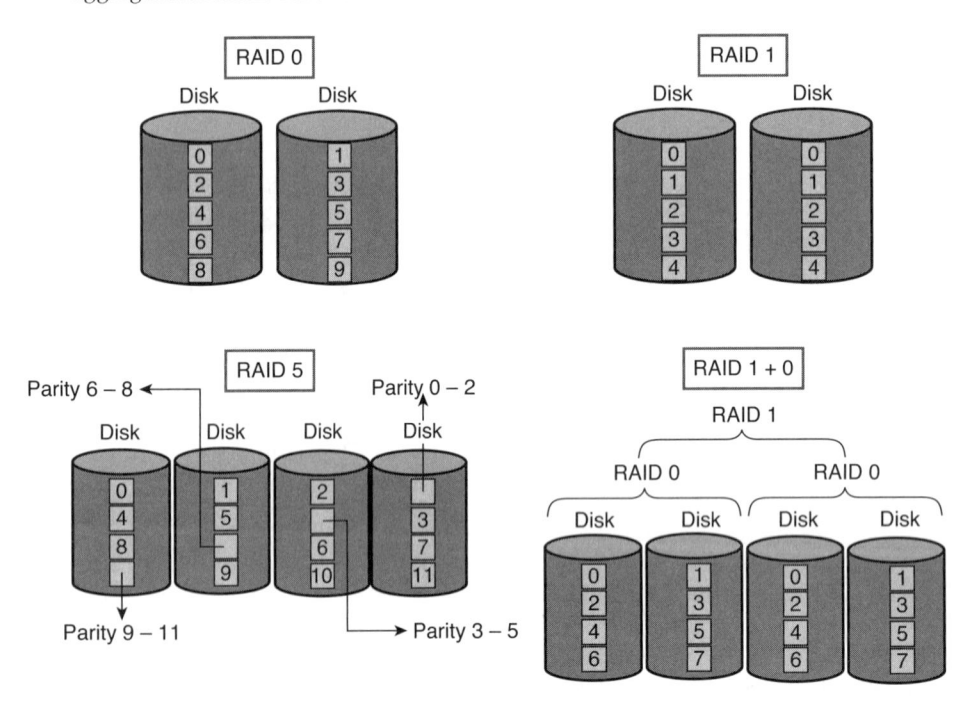

Figure 9-6 *RAID Levels*

In a group of disks deploying *RAID level 0*, sequential blocks of data are written across them, in an operation called "striping." Figure 9-6 depicts a sequence of ten blocks being striped between two disks, which is the minimum quantity of devices for this level. RAID level 0 does not deploy any data redundancy, because a disk failure results in total data loss. However, when compared to a lonely disk drive with similar capacity, this RAID level improves I/O performance because it supports simultaneous reads or writes on all disks.

RAID level 1, also known as "mirroring," requires at least two disks simply because every write operation at one device must be duplicated to another. Hence, if one of the disks fails, data can be completely recovered from its mirrored pair. This RAID level adds latency for write operations, because they must be executed on both disks and reduces by 50 percent the overall capacity of the disk group.

RAID level 5 is a very popular method mainly because it nicely balances capacity and I/O performance when compared with other RAID levels. In summary, it deploys data block striping over a group of disks (minimum of three) and builds additional *parity blocks* that can be used to recover an entire sequence of blocks in the absence of a disk. Contrary to other parity-based methods, RAID 5 distributes the parity blocks evenly among the disks, minimizing I/O bottlenecks (because the write operation generates a change in its corresponding parity block).

One of the main complaints about RAID 5 is that it can take too long to reestablish the block aggregation arrangement in the case of a disk failure (all blocks from a lost disk must be recalculated and saved on a replacement disk). RAID level 6 avoids this situation, creating two parity blocks in different disks for each sequence and providing fault tolerance for two sequential drive failures.

RAID level 1+0 is a hybrid block aggregation method that was not contemplated in the original RAID level definition. A group of disks employing RAID 1+0 essentially mirror groups of striped disks, leveraging the best characteristics of each level: redundancy and performance without the use of parity processing.

As discussed in Chapter 1, "Virtualization History and Definitions," storage virtualization techniques can be deployed in three different "locations" or subareas: *host*, *storage device*, or *interconnect*. In modern data centers, disk arrays most commonly deploy RAID groups. However, this virtualization technique can also be implemented through server controller adapters (*RAID adapters*) managing internal or JBOD disks.

To illustrate the normalcy of abstraction on storage technologies, allow me to present the deployment steps of a standard file server installation that is using block data access from a disk array:

1. Physically install the disk array, all *disks*, and remaining components, while connecting it to the SAN.

2. Configure a disk *RAID group* to achieve the file server application recommended redundancy, capacity, and performance.

3. Create *LUNs* on this RAID group for SCSI I/O operations, and make the LUNs available to the correct server.

4. Prepare the SAN to transport data between the initiator and target.

5. Configure the server Logical Volume Manager to control the exposed LUNs and transform them into local *volumes*.

6. Activate the file server application to manage *files* on the local volumes.

And as you can see, each step used an extra layer of abstraction over the data structure from the previous step (disk, RAID group, LUN, volume, and file).

Tip In Chapter 10, you learn how Step 4 actually happens in real-world scenarios.

Rising apart from these everyday abstractions, a new wave of storage virtualization technologies has hit the data center shores around the turn of the century. Designed to increase resource utilization, such innovative technologies also targeted the lack of flexibility, integration, and performance in storage installations.

In the next sections, I will outline some of these virtualization solutions, their characteristics, and the benefits they bring to the daily tasks of storage professionals. And because each vendor has different implementations for these solutions, in the next three sections I will aggregate their most common features using the level of data abstraction they act upon.

Note As an useful exercise, I recommend that you use the virtualization taxonomy explained in Chapter 1 to categorize each storage virtualization technology at the end of each section.

Virtualizing Storage Devices

Disk array virtualization can be currently deployed partitioning a single device or grouping several of them. Through *partitioning*, a physical disk array can be subdivided into logical devices, with assigned resources such as disks, cache, memory, and ports. Using the array as a pool of these resources, each virtual array partition can create exclusive LUNs or file systems to different departments, customers, or applications. Protecting data access between partitions and controlling hardware resources for each one of them, this style of virtualization encourages storage consolidation and resource optimization in multitenant data centers.

Storage virtualization also allows multiple physical arrays to work together as a single system, bringing advantages such as data redundancy and management consolidation. For example, *array-based data replication* illustrates how two distinct disk arrays can work in coordination to provide fault tolerance for the stored data transparently to hosts that might be accessing them.

There are two basic methods to deploy array-based replication, as Figure 9-7 illustrates.

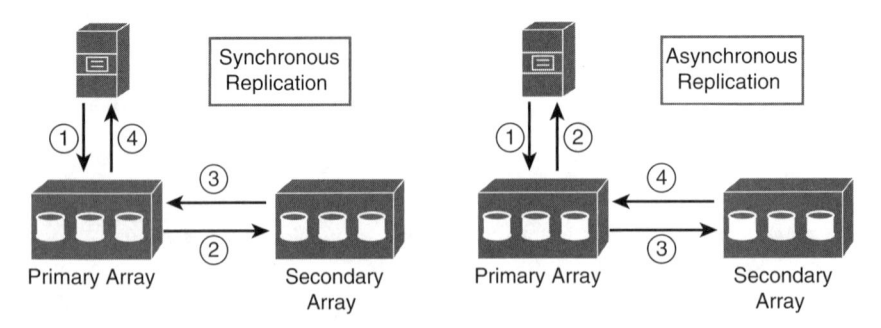

Figure 9-7 *Synchronous Versus Asynchronous Replication*

On the left side of Figure 9-7, both disk arrays are implementing synchronous replication. As the figure shows, this method of storage redundancy will always trace the following actions:

1. A write operation is received on the primary disk array.
2. The primary array delays confirmation of the write to the server, initiating another one to the secondary array.
3. After the new data is successfully stored on the secondary array, it sends a confirmation to the primary array.
4. Finally, a confirmation is sent to the server.

With synchronous replications, there is a guarantee that every single piece of data on the primary array is present on the secondary array, which can be located at a different site location to satisfy disaster recovery objectives. Nonetheless, this method is very dependent on the latency between arrays. To maintain acceptable levels of application performance (measured in I/O per second, or IOPS), both distances between sites and WAN resources must be correctly evaluated.

Asynchronous replications, as the right side of Figure 9-7 demonstrates, do not require a confirmation from the secondary array to acknowledge a write operation to the server. In fact, the primary array will maintain new data queued to be copied to the secondary device at a later time (after a time interval is reached). But as this replication method relieves the server from a performance impact, replication to the secondary storage is delayed, probably resulting in data loss after an array or WAN link failure.

As discussed on Chapter 8, "A Tale of Two Data Centers," in the section "A Brief History of Distributed Data Centers," the recovery objectives (RPO and RTO) of each application will help define the replication method that should be applied to it.

Various replication technologies are available from array vendors, such as EMC Symmetrix Remote Data Facility (SRDF), HDS TrueCopy, IBM Peer-to-Peer Remote Copy (PPRC), and NetApp SnapMirror. In general, these methods are proprietary and cannot be shared among arrays from different manufacturers. Commonly, these replication technologies do not permit write I/Os on the replicated data from the secondary array either.

Array clustering technologies permit a step further into the pooling of disk arrays as single device. For example, *tightly coupled array clusters* allow the scale of I/O performance and storage capacity through a proprietary back-end connection. Such an architecture enables the addition of more controllers, access ports, or disk enclosures within the same management domain according to the environment demand. EMC Symmetrix VMAX is an example of this kind of array clustering.

Loosely coupled array clusters, on the other hand, enable the aggregation of multiple disk arrays from heterogeneous architectures. Using standards and deploying an array hierarchy, products such as HDS USP-V can consolidate the management of multiple distinct arrays.

Disk arrays are also an integral part of the virtualization of tape libraries. In these solutions, such a device acts as a **virtual tape library** *(VTL)* for the backup and archive servers, leveraging its performance in comparison with real tape libraries.

Figure 9-8 illustrates a generic tape library virtualization design.

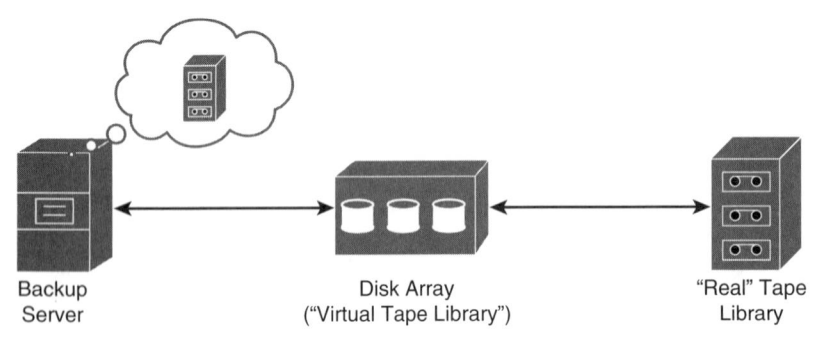

Figure 9-8 *Virtual Tape Library*

In the figure, a backup server is retrieving and sending data to the disk array, using the same processes and protocols it would deploy with a traditional tape library. Consequently, a disk array imports and exports streams of data to the tape library, acting as a "cache" mechanism for the latter.

The most common VTL vendors are IBM, FalconStor, and Oracle. Some of the available VTLs can reduce the number of stored data through a compression technique called *data deduplication*, which eliminates duplicate copies of the same data sequence. Through this feature, a redundant chunk of data is replaced by a small reference that points to the only-once stored chunk. In real-world scenarios, deduplication can obliterate up to 95 percent of stored data on both the VTL and tape library.

Virtualizing LUNs

Chances are that a discussion about storage virtualization will invariably bring up LUN virtualization as the key topic. Because LUNs usually represent the final deliverable element from the storage team to its main consumer (server team), their management has been under rigorous scrutiny since the origins of SCSI.

Here are some examples of the LUN management challenges faced by array administrators:

- LUNs are statically defined in a single disk array.
- The migration of LUNs to another disk array is a rather complicated task, and it generally demands application interruption.
- Servers rarely utilize the requested size of their LUNs, raising capital and operational costs and severely decreasing device utilization.
- The resizing of a LUN is usually a disruptive operation.

In most LUN virtualization deployments, a *virtualizer* element is positioned between a host and its associated target disk array (in-path I/O interception). This virtualizer generates a *virtual LUN (vLUN)* that proxies server I/O operations while hiding specialized data block processes that are occurring in the pool of disk arrays under its "jurisdiction."

Figure 9-9 exemplifies how vLUNs can enhance block-based storage environments.

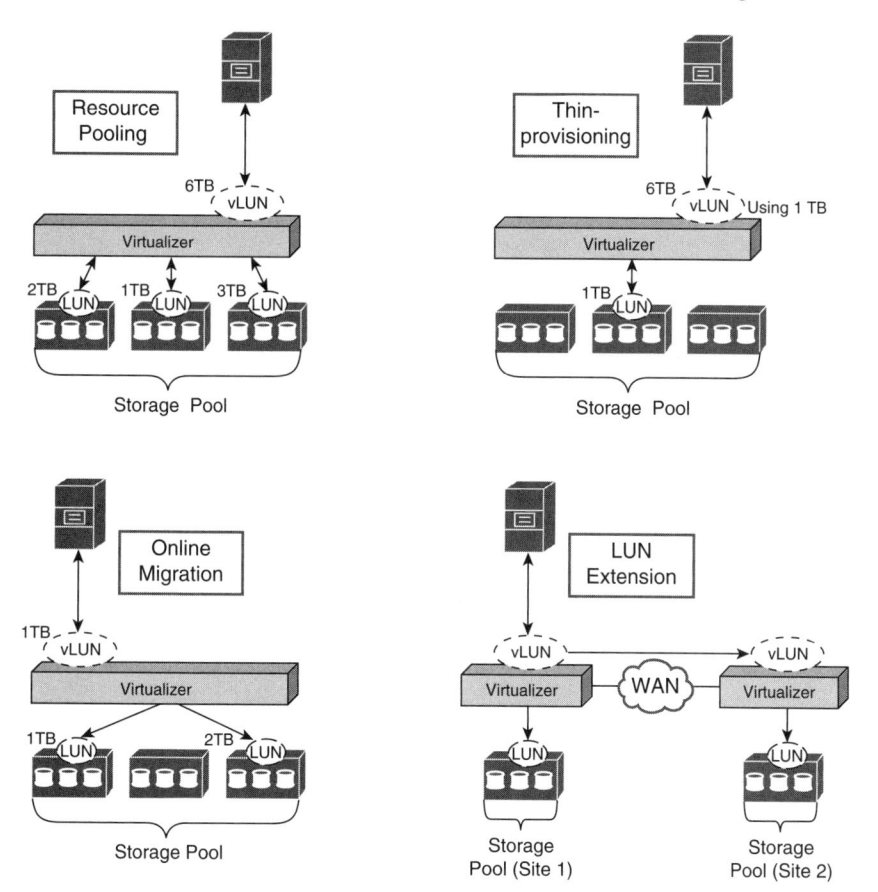

Figure 9-9 *Virtual LUN Applications*

The upper-left corner of Figure 9-9 demonstrates how a virtualizer can deploy *storage resource pooling*, where a physical group of devices is treated as a single repository of data block resources. With this specific feature, a vLUN can be generated through the use of smaller LUNs distributed over different physical arrays. In general terms, storage resource pooling increases device utilization and consolidates storage management.

Thin-provisioning, represented in the upper-right corner of the figure, is a LUN virtualization feature that helps reduce the waste of block storage resources. With this technique, although a server can detect a vLUN with a "full" size; only blocks that are present in the vLUN are actually saved on the storage pool. This feature brings the concept of oversubscription to data storage, consequently demanding special attention to the ratio between "declared" and actually used resources.

Also shown in Figure 9-9 (left-lower corner), vLUNs can also enable *data online migration* between different arrays or types of disk drivers in a non-disruptive manner. This virtualization feature actually unlocks several possibilities such as non-disruptive LUN resizing and storage tiering. As an illustration, defining distinct tiers of storage, vLUNs from high-performance applications could be automatically migrated from SATA HDDs ("bronze") to SSDs ("gold").

Also, through the employment of virtualizers at different data center sites, *LUN extension* permits mirroring between heterogeneous storage resources with a bonus: Both virtualizers declare the same vLUN, enabling write operations on both sites. As you can infer, this specific LUN virtualization feature is extremely useful for geocluster switchovers and server migrations between data center locations.

As previously mentioned, each storage vendor has a different LUN virtualization solution, generally presenting a subset of the features explained in this section (or additional ones, such as point-in-time copies). These solutions also diverge on the device (storage subarea, according to our virtualization taxonomy) that actually generates the virtual LUNs. For example:

- **Disk array:** HDS USP-V
- **SAN appliance:** IBM SAN Volume Controller, EMC VPLEX (LUN extension), NetApp V-series
- **SAN switch:** EMC Invista running within Cisco MDS 9500 directors
- **Server:** VMware vSphere (which intercepts requests from virtual machines to physical LUNs)

Virtualizing File Systems

A *virtual file system* is basically an abstraction layer that allows client applications using heterogeneous file-sharing network protocols to access a unified pool of storage resources.

These systems are based on a global file directory structure that is contained on dedicated file metadata servers. Whenever a file system client needs to access a file, it must retrieve information about the file from the metadata servers first. Among the information controlled by these specialized servers, I can cite

- The location of the file data on a physical or virtual LUN
- File locking status
- File attributes (owner, permission, size, among others)

Figure 9-10 illustrates the architecture of a virtual file system.

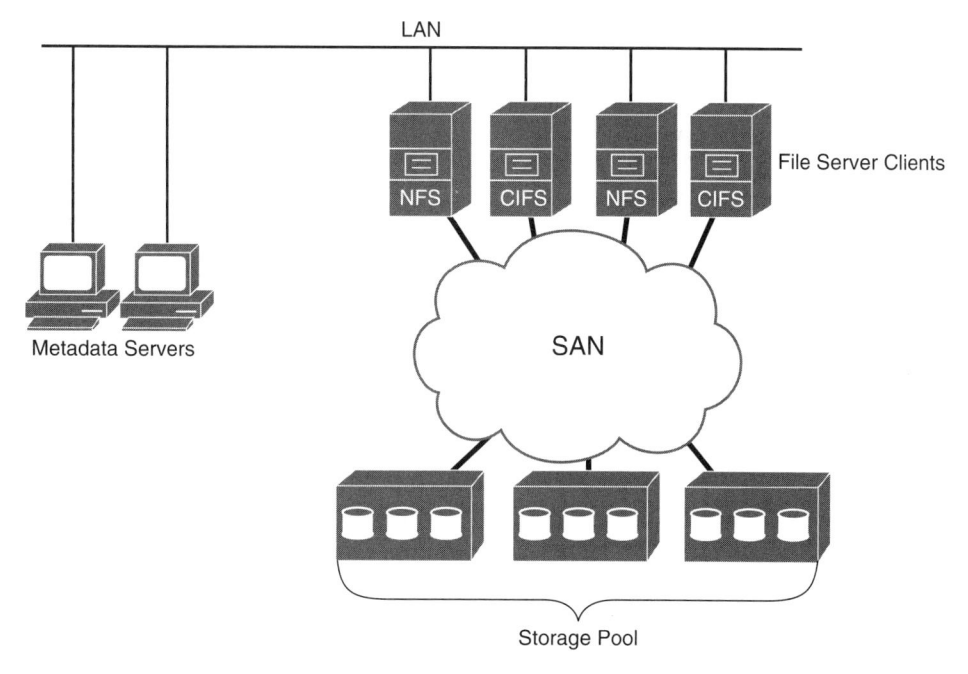

```
                              LAN
    ──┬─────────┬──────┬──────┬──────┬──────┬──
                      [NFS] [CIFS] [NFS] [CIFS]   File Server Clients

   [PC]  [PC]
   Metadata Servers              ( SAN )

                         [disks] [disks] [disks]
                         ╰──────Storage Pool──────╯
```

Figure 9-10 *File System Virtualization*

> **Note** Figure 9-10 depicts an **out-of-band** virtualization system because only control information is handled by the virtualization device (metadata servers).
>
> Adversely, virtualization systems that directly act upon the exchanged data are known as **inband** virtualizers.

Besides extending a consolidated file system to multiple different clients, a virtual file system can also leverage a performance boost through SAN block access. IBM TotalStorage SAN File System is an example of a virtual file system solution.

Virtualizing SANs

Considering that storage area networks are critical components in modern storage environments, it is no surprise that they can also benefit from virtualization features.

Cisco entered the Fibre Channel switch market in 2003 with its MDS 9000 directors and fabric switches series. Since then, the company has applied its experience and resources to enable multiple virtualization features within intelligent SANs.

In truth, this very subject characterizes the core content of the remaining chapters of Part III, "Virtualization in Storage Technologies":

- Chapter 10, "Islands in the SAN," will discuss SAN partitioning with virtual SANs.
- Chapter 11, "Secret Identities," will examine identity virtualization on SANs through Fibre Channel over IP (FCIP), Inter-VSAN Routing (IVR), and Node Port Virtualization (NPV).
- Chapter 12, "One Cable to Unite Us All," will detail how Ethernet-based networks can deploy storage-area networks through Fibre Channel over Ethernet (FCoE) and Data Center Bridging (DCB).

Summary

In this chapter, you learned the following:

- The evolution of storage technologies blends itself with the history of computer science.
- The most popular permanent storage devices in data centers today are disk drives, disk arrays, and tape libraries.
- Storage data can be accessed in three canonical forms: block, file, or record.
- Data blocks can be retrieved from storage devices through direct connections or storage-area networks. A common communication protocol between host and storage device, such as SCSI, is also necessary.
- Remote file access demands a network file-sharing protocol (for example, NFS and CIFS) on both the client and server.
- Database servers provide access to highly structured data through record queries sent by other applications.
- Most storage-manageable elements, such as RAID groups, LUNs, and files, are established layered abstractions.
- A new wave of virtualization technologies has brought numerous benefits to storage environments, such as data fault tolerance, multitenancy, management consolidation, performance, resource optimization, and active-active configurations.

Further Reading

Long, James. *Storage Networking Protocol Fundamentals (Volume 2)*. Cisco Press, 2006.

Clark, Tom. *Storage Virtualization*. Addison-Wesley, 2005.

SCSI Standards Architecture, www.t10.org/scsi-3.htm

Technical Committee T13 AT Attachment, www.t13.org

Network File System (NFS) version 4 Protocol, www.ietf.org/rfc/rfc3530.txt

Common Internet File System Specification, http://msdn.microsoft.com/en-us/library/ee442092.aspx

Chapter 10

Islands in the SAN

"For the rest of it, the last and greatest art is to limit and isolate oneself."
(Johann Wolfgang von Goethe)

This chapter will introduce virtual storage-area networks (VSANs) and the advantages of creating isolated logical fabrics in a physical Fibre Channel SAN. It will cover the following topics:

- Some Fibre Channel Definitions
- Fabric Processes
- Defining and Exploring VSANs
- Use Case: SAN Consolidation

Table 10-1 classifies VSANs in the virtualization taxonomy described in Chapter 1, "Virtualization History and Definitions."

Table 10-1 *Virtual Storage-Area Network Classification*

Virtualization Characteristics	VSAN
Emulation	Fibre Channel fabric
Type	Partitioning
Subtype	No resource control
Scalability	Hardware dependent[1]
Technology Area	Storage networking
Subarea	Data and control planes
Advantages	SAN island consolidation, scalability, multitenancy, traffic engineering, and fault isolation

[1] Refer to Appendix A, "Cisco Data Center Portfolio," for more details and the Cisco online documentation for updated information.

Created in 1988, Fibre Channel is the general name for a series of integrated protocols that provide high-speed data communication between computer systems. Since its ratification in 1994, Fibre Channel has become one of the most popular protocols for enterprise and service provider storage-area networks.

Fibre Channel was originally conceived to offer different types of data transport services to its connected nodes, such as delivery confirmation and connection emulation. Because these services can be fulfilled per host request, it is said that interconnected Fibre Channel communication devices form special kind of network called *fabric*.

Within data centers, Fibre Channel fabrics were originally deployed as separate networks that connect servers (equipped with host bus adapters) to storage devices. Recent developments in Ethernet have permitted both protocols to share the same cabling and networking equipment.

Tip This convergence will be dealt with Chapter 12, "One Cable to Unite Us All."

Cisco launched its family of Fibre Channel switches in 2003, with the Cisco Multilayer Data Switch (MDS) 9000 series. Also deploying NX-OS as their operating system, these devices continue to bring innovations to Fibre Channel SANs. One innovation in particular has been helping to scale and protect these critical environments: *virtual storage-area networks*, or simply *VSANs*.

Because VSANs are logical Fibre Channel fabrics defined over a single physical structure, this chapter will first concentrate on the explanation of Fibre Channel basic concepts and processes. Using this background, the chapter will examine how VSANs work and their advantages over nonvirtualized SANs.

Some Fibre Channel Definitions

Fibre Channel was developed by the T11 Technical Committee of the International Committee for Information Technology Standards (INCITS), which is accredited by the American National Standards Institute (ANSI). Fibre Channel was created to provide higher speeds (starting at 1 Gbps) and several different transport services to higher-level protocols such as Small Computer System Interface (SCSI), IBM's Single Byte Command Code Set (SBCCS), and IP.

These services and speeds are defined in the T11 Fibre Channel standards, which are very detailed inter-referenced documents. The following list presents some of the most important T11 Fibre Channel standards:

- Fibre Channel Physical and Signaling Interface (FC-PH)
- Fibre Channel Physical Interface (FC-PI)

- Fibre Channel Framing and Signaling (FC-FS)
- Fibre Channel Generic Services (FC-GS)
- Fibre Channel Arbitrated Loop (FC-AL)
- Fibre Channel Fabric and Switch Control Requirements (FC-SW)
- Fibre Channel Protocol for SCSI (SCSI-FCP)
- Single Byte Command Code Sets Mapping for Fibre Channel (FC-SB)
- Transmission IPv4 and ARP Packets over Fibre Channel (IPv4FC)

Within INCITS T11, each family of standards can be complemented (not superseded) by a new-generation document. For example, FC-SW-2 introduced new definitions to FC-SW, and FC-SW-3 did the same for both.

Note If you are interested in Fibre Channel standards that are not cited in this chapter, refer to the "Further Reading" section, later in this chapter.

Fibre Channel Layers

Unsurprisingly, as the majority of networking architectures, Fibre Channel does not follow the Open Systems Interconnection (OSI) model. However, it also divides its protocols into hierarchical layers with predefined responsibilities. From the bottom up, each Fibre Channel layer can be described as follows:

- **FC-0:** Specifies the physical components of a Fibre Channel connection, such as media (fiber or copper), connectors, and transmission parameters.
- **FC-1:** Defines encoding and error control. Some Fibre Channel connections (1-, 2-, 4-, and 8-Gbps) use the *8B/10B* transmission encoding, where 10 bits are transmitted to represent an 8-bit symbol. This method intends to achieve DC balance (an equal number of transmitted 0s and 1s) and clock recovery in serial transmissions.

Note 8B/10B encoding is also used in some Ethernet connections (Ethernet and Fast Ethernet). On the other hand, Gigabit Ethernet and 16-Gbps Fibre Channel implement 64B/66B encoding.

- **FC-2:** Presents the signaling protocol's description, which includes the frame structure and byte sequences.
- **FC-3:** Describes the set of services that are common across a Fibre Channel fabric, such as time distribution and security capabilities.

- **FC-4:** Defines the mapping between an *upper-layer protocol (ULP)*—such as SCSI, SBCCS, and IP—and the other Fibre Channel layers.

Figure 10-1 is a graphical representation of how some T11 standards fit into Fibre Channel's layer model.

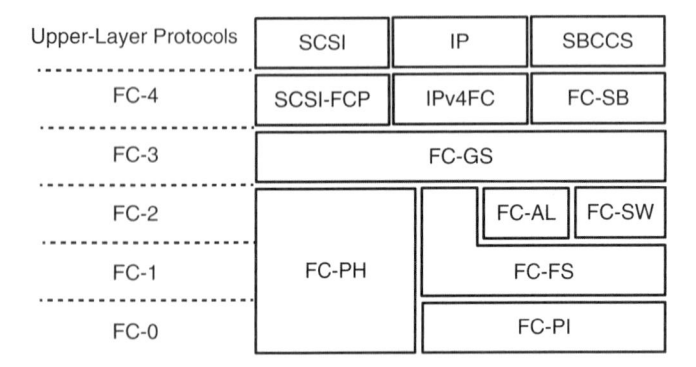

Layer			
Upper-Layer Protocols	SCSI	IP	SBCCS
FC-4	SCSI-FCP	IPv4FC	FC-SB
FC-3	FC-GS		
FC-2		FC-AL	FC-SW
FC-1	FC-PH	FC-FS	
FC-0		FC-PI	

Figure 10-1 *Fibre Channel Layers and Standards*

Fibre Channel Topologies and Port Types

Fibre Channel supports three types of topologies:

- **Point-to-point:** Connects two Fibre Channel–capable hosts without the use of a communication device, such as a switch or hub.

- **Arbritrated loop:** Permits up to 127 devices to communicate with each other in a looped connection. Fibre Channel hubs were constructed to improve reliability in these topologies, but with the higher adoption of switches, Fibre Channel loop interfaces are more likely to be found on legacy storage devices such as JBODs (just a bunch of disks) or legacy tape libraries.

- **Fabric:** Comprises Fibre Channel devices that exchange data with the Fibre Channel switches. Theoretically, up to 16 million devices can be connected to a Fibre Channel fabric. This chapter focuses on these topologies.

Figure 10-2 illustrates these topologies and introduces the port types that are defined in each one of them.

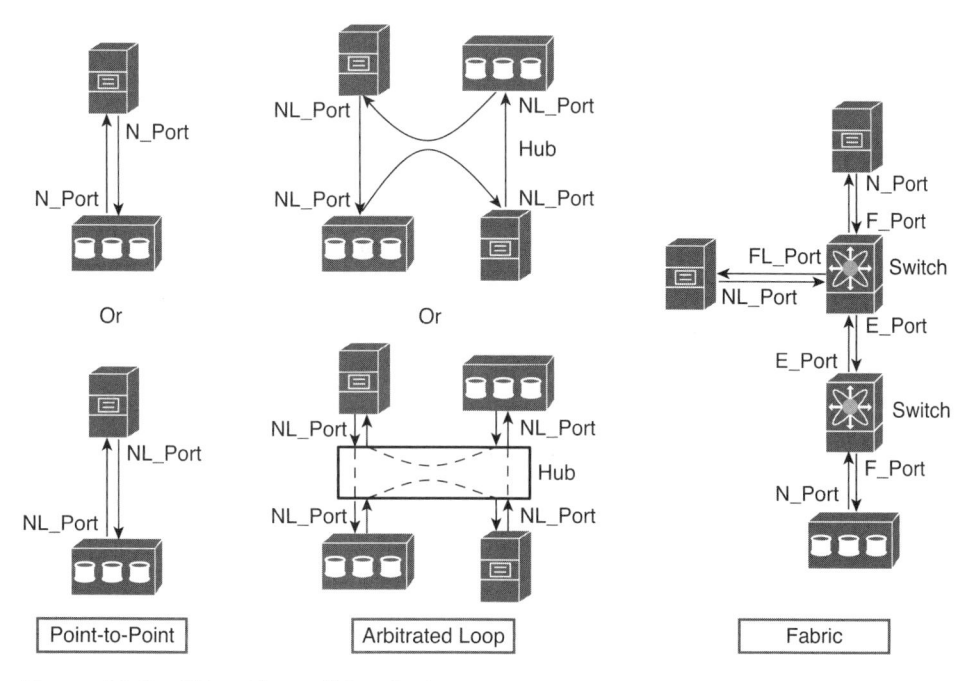

Figure 10-2 *Fibre Channel Topologies*

Depending on the Fibre Channel topology, an interface can be assigned to one of the following port types:

- **Node Port (N_Port):** Interface that belongs to a Fibre Channel end host in a point-to-point or fabric topology.

- **Node Loop Port (NL_Port):** Interface that is installed in a Fibre Channel end host connected to an arbitrated loop topology.

- **Fabric Port (F_Port):** Fibre Channel switch interface that is connected to an N_Port.

- **Fabric Loop Port (FL_Port):** Fibre Channel switch interface that is connected to a public loop. Per definition, a private loop does not have a fabric connection.

- **Expansion Port (E_Port):** Interface that connects to another E_Port to create an Inter-Switch Link (ISL) between Fibre Channel switches.

Fibre Channel Addressing

In fabric topologies, Fibre Channel devices can have two types of addresses: *World Wide Names (WWN)* and *Fibre Channel Identifiers (FCID)*.

A WWN is a unique 8-byte identifier that is usually predefined at the time of manufacturing. This book will represent WWNs as colon-separated bytes (10:00:00:00:c9:76:fd:31, for example).

MDS 9000 switches support three WWN formats, which can be identified by the WWN's first nibble. These first 4 bits are also referred to as the *network address authority (NAA)*.

Figure 10-3 portrays these formats.

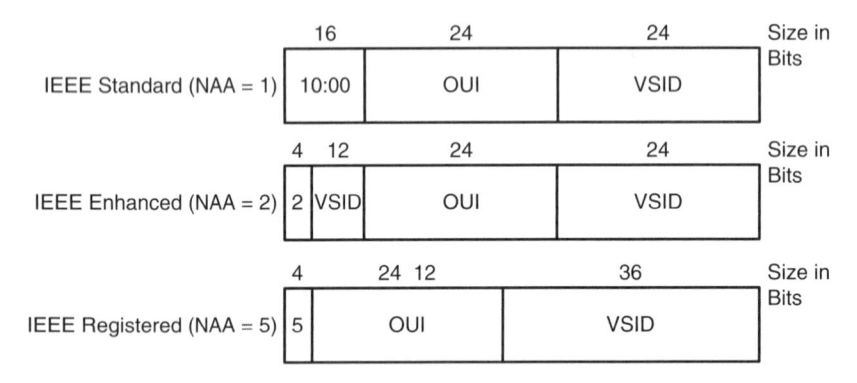

	16	24	24	Size in Bits
IEEE Standard (NAA = 1)	10:00	OUI	VSID	

	4	12	24	24	Size in Bits
IEEE Enhanced (NAA = 2)	2	VSID	OUI	VSID	

	4	24 12	36	Size in Bits
IEEE Registered (NAA = 5)	5	OUI	VSID	

Figure 10-3 *World Wide Name Formats*

IEEE controls and distributes *Organizational Unique Identifiers (OUIs)* to network manufacturers to avoid two different devices from being produced with the same WWN (for example, Cisco has the following OUIs: 00:00:0c, 00:01:42, 00:01:43, 00:01:63, 00:01:64, 00:01:96, 00:01:97, and many others). Afterward, each manufacturer should choose a *vendor-specific identifier (VSID)* to uniquely characterize each produced device.

A Fibre Channel device can have hundreds of WWNs, where each address represents a part of the device. For example:

- **Port WWN (pWWN):** Identifies one interface from a Fibre Channel node and characterizes an N_Port.
- **Node WWN (nWWN):** Represents the node (or a host bus adapter [HBA]) that contains more than one port.
- **Switch WWN (sWWN):** Uniquely identifies a Fibre Channel switch.
- **Fabric WWN (fWWN):** Identifies a switch interface and distinguishes an F_Port.

FCIDs are administrative addresses that are assigned to N_Ports and actually inserted in Fibre Channel frame headers. An FCID is comprised of 3 bytes, as shown in Figure 10-4.

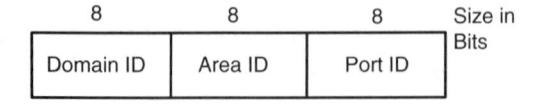

8	8	8	Size in Bits
Domain ID	Area ID	Port ID	

Figure 10-4 *Fibre Channel Identifier Format*

Each byte has a specific meaning in an FCID:

- **Domain ID:** Represents the switch where this device is connected.
- **Area ID:** Can represent a set of devices connected to a switch or NL_Ports connected to an FL_Port.
- **Port ID:** Assigned to differentiate a device within an area.

Mimicking NX-OS commands, this book represents FCIDs with contiguous hexadecimal bytes preceded with the "0x" symbol (for example, 0x01ab9e).

> **Tip** Depending on your original area of work, you are probably making parallel comparisons between WWNs and MAC addresses, as well as FCIDs and IP addresses. Although these are valid analogies, I recommend that you refrain from using further Ethernet and IP comparisons with Fibre Channel from now on. Trust me on that to avoid future confusions.

Frames, Sequences, and Exchanges

When connected to a fabric, it is expected that N_Ports exchange data that is confined within *Fibre Channel frames*. Additionally, the Fibre Channel standards dictate that these frames are structured in a hierarchical scheme when an initiator node wants to communicate with a target node (or server and storage devices in SCSI environments, respectively).

A *sequence* is a set of one or more related data frames transmitted unidirectionally between two N_Ports. Each sequence has an identifier (SEQ_ID) that is generated by the initiator node. Also, each frame in a sequence has a sequence counter (SEQ_CNT) that represents its order of transmission.

An *exchange* is comprised of one or more nonconcurrent sequences, and it can be unidirectional or bidirectional. A ULP data transfer (for example, a SCSI read or write) is performed using an exchange as transport unit. Each exchange is identified by an Originator Exchange_Identifier (OX_ID) and a Responder Exchange_Identifier (RX_ID), which are respectively generated by the initiator and the target nodes. The initiator node can start multiple concurrent exchanges, whereas each one must use a unique OX_ID.

Figure 10-5 illustrates how these Fibre Channel data structures are organized.

A Fibre Channel frame is the atomic data unit that N_Ports send and receive. A frame can transport up to 2048 bytes of data, and its header identifies the exchange and sequence it belongs to, as shown in Figure 10-6.

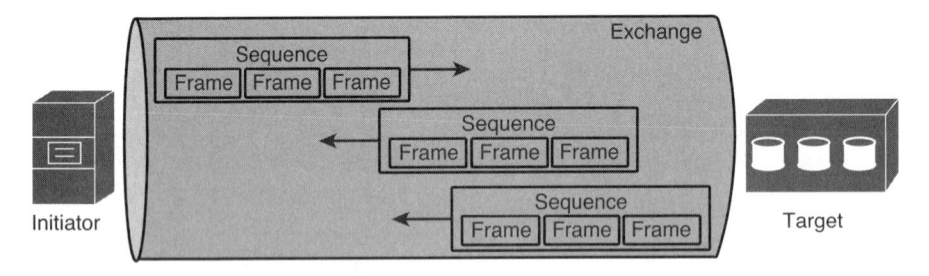

Figure 10-5 *Fibre Channel Building Blocks*

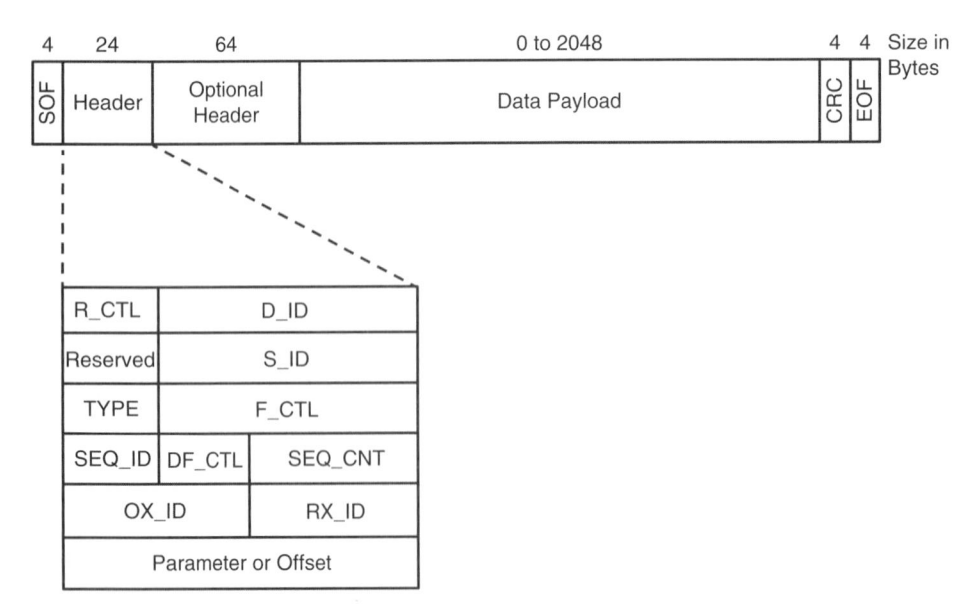

Figure 10-6 *Fibre Channel Frame*

Besides the already discussed exchange- and sequence-related identifiers (OX_ID, RX_ID, SEQ_ID, and SEQ_CNT), a Fibre Channel header also presents the following fields:

- **Route Control (R_CTL):** Categorizes the frame function. When it is used in combination with the TYPE field, it provides information about the frame content (for example, ULP and FC-4 information) to the N_Port.

- **Destination Identifier (D_ID):** The FCID from the destination N_Port. Fibre Channel switches use this field to route a frame.

- **Source Identifier (S_ID):** Identifies the FCID from source N_Port.

- **TYPE:** Identifies the upper-layer protocol that the frame is carrying (for example, SCSI uses values 0x08 and 0x09).

- **Frame Control (F_CTL):** Denotes frame information such as the first or last frame in a sequence.

- **Data Field Control (DF_CTL):** Specifies the presence (and size) of the optional header at the beginning of the data payload.

- **Relative Offset (optional):** Contains specific information for control frames, or the relative displacement of the first byte of the payload of a data frame from the base address specified by the ULP.

As shown in Figure 10-6, a frame is defined by two predefined 4-byte structures: *start of frame (SOF)* and *end of frame (EOF)*. Another 4-byte field called cyclic redundancy check (CRC) is used to verify the integrity of the frame header and the data field when it is received on each Fibre Channel device. The optional header can perform security services or enclose network addresses to be used by specialized Fibre Channel devices such as gateways.

Flow Control

As a protocol capable of providing lossless transport of data, a Fibre Channel device must determine whether there are enough resources to process a frame before its reception. For this reason, flow control mechanisms are required to avoid frame discarding within a Fibre Channel fabric.

Fibre Channel natively provides flow control with credit-based strategies between directly connected ports and between end nodes. On both methods, the receiver is always in control, and the transmitter only sends a frame if it is sure that the receiver has available resources to handle this frame.

Buffer-to-buffer Credits (BB_Credits) flow control deals only with directly connected ports (for example, N_Port to F_Port, N_Port to N_Port, or E_Port to E_Port). In summary, this method works as follows:

1. Each port is aware of how many buffers are available to receive a frame at the other end of the connection (BB_Credit).

2. Each port has a counter (BB_Credit_CNT) that, starting at 0, is increased by 1 if a frame is transmitted.

3. Frames are only transmitted if BB_Credit_CNT is lower than BB_Credit.

4. If one more buffer becomes available, the receiving port sends a 4-byte *Return Ready* (R_RDY) signal that decreases by 1 the BB_Credit_CNT in its neighbor.

BB_Credit counters usually have low values when both connected ports belong to the same data center (around 12 credits). However, in some data center interconnections, a small number of BB_Credits can result in an abysmal utilization of a communication link.

To illustrate this situation, imagine a 2-Gbps ISL between two switches that are connected with a 100-km fiber. Considering that light travels inside a fiber with a speed of

200,000 kilometers per second, a bit takes 500 microseconds to get from one end of the connection to the other. Additionally, a typical Fibre Channel frame, which is carrying 2048 bytes of payload plus the header (36 bytes) and 24 bytes of IDLE communication between frames, takes 9.92 microseconds to be serialized on an interface with a clock frequency of 2.125 GHz.

If the receiving interface signals a BB_Credit value of 1, it would take 509.92 microseconds to completely receive a full-size frame (serialization plus transmission plus deserialization). Also, the R_RDY (if we consider that its serialization is close to 0) would take 500 microseconds to reach the transmitting interface. Therefore, in this extreme scenario, each 2-Gbps interface can only transmit a frame every 1009.92 microseconds, resulting in a disappointing performance of less than 20 Mbps!

Therefore, to efficiently use long-latency data center interconnections, a Fibre Channel interface must present a minimum value of BB_Credits. This number of credits allows each transmitting port to "fill the pipe" with frames. Consequently, this can be calculated if you realize how many frames an interface can potentially transmit before it receives the first R_RDY from its distant neighbor.

Using the previously described scenario, Figure 10-7 demonstrates how many BB_Credits are necessary to fill this specific pipe.

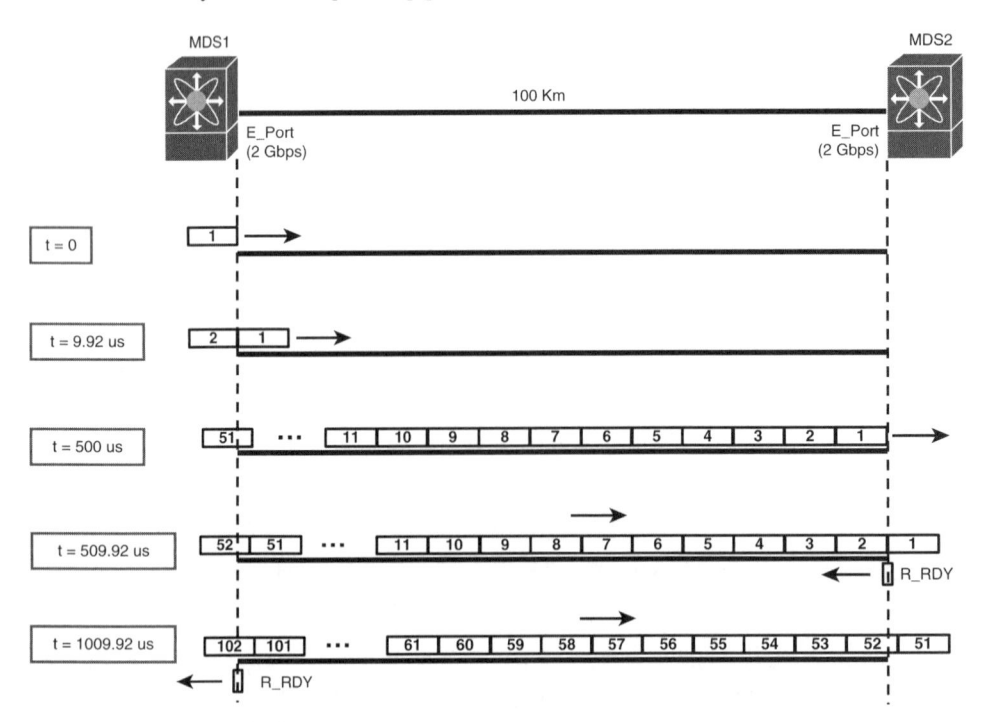

Figure 10-7 *Buffer-to-buffer Credits Calculation on a 100-km Fiber Link*

- At **t=0**, the first bit from Frame 1 is put on the fiber. Its last bit is transmitted after 9.92 microseconds.
- At **t=500 microseconds**, the first bit from Frame 1 reaches MDS2.
- MDS2 processes Frame 1 at **t=509.92 microseconds** (I have only considered the deserialization time in its processing). Again, I have assumed that the R_RDY is a very small frame and that it is almost immediately generated and put on the wire.
- At **t=1009.92 microseconds**, the first R_RDY reaches MDS1. During this interval, the E_Port on MDS1 could have serialized 101.8 frames. As a result, 102 BB_Credits are necessary on the E_Port on MDS2 to guarantee maximum performance in this scenario.

The general formula to calculate the number of required credits for optimal performance in a long distance link is

Credits = (Round-trip time + Processing time) / Serialization time

To save you some calculations, Table 10-2 depicts the minimum number of BB_Credits needed to optimize the communication in ISLs with different distances.

Table 10-2 *Minimum Buffer-to-Buffer Credits*

Distance (km)	1 Gbps	2 Gbps	4 Gbps	8 Gbps
10	7	12	22	42
50	27	52	102	203
1000	52	102	203	405

The *End-to-End Credits (EE_Credits)* flow control method regulates the transport of frames between source and destination N_Ports. With a very similar mechanism to BB_Credits, this mechanism allows a sender node to obtain the delivery confirmation of frames from the receiver node.

Deploying this method, two N_Ports negotiate a number of EE_Credits before any communication happens. This value represents the number of buffers that are available on the receiver for this transmission.

An End-to-End Credit Counter (EE_Credit_CNT) starts at 0 and is increased by 1 with the transmission of a frame at each end. This counter is also decreased by 1 with the arrival of an *acknowledgment control frame (ACK)*.

Because the sender never transmits a frame if its EE_Credit_CNT reaches the EE_Credit value, it only knows that all transmitted frames were delivered if it receives all the corresponding ACKs from the receiver device.

Classes of Service

Theoretically, a Fibre Channel fabric can provide a great variety of transport services to its connected nodes. Several *classes of service*, with distinct characteristics, have already been defined in the T11 standards to deploy these services. These classes are as follows:

- **Class 1:** Provides a dedicated connection between two N_Ports, maintaining the order and confirming each frame's delivery. It only uses end-to-end flow control, and it is not widely supported.

- **Class 2:** A connectionless service with the fabric multiplexing frames where the order is not guaranteed but delivery is always confirmed. It uses buffer-to-buffer and end-to-end flow control methods.

- **Class 3:** Called a *datagram service* because it does not provide connection-oriented or delivery confirmation. It is the most used class in Fibre Channel SANs, and it only uses buffer-to-buffer flow control.

- **Class 4:** Provides a fractional bandwidth virtual circuit (connection-oriented) between two N_Ports with delivery confirmation.

- **Class 5:** Not yet defined.

- **Class 6:** Provides connection-oriented multicast delivery with confirmation.

- **Class F:** Provides packet-switched delivery services with confirmation. It is used for interswitch communication.

Class of Service 3 is used by most upper-layer protocols, such as SCSI. Because this class does not provide connection or delivery assurance, it is up to the upper-layer protocol to manage lost and out-of-order frames.

Fabric Processes

The Fibre Channel standards define a *fabric* as the "entity that interconnects various N_Ports attached to it and is capable of routing frames by using only the D_ID information in an FC-2 frame header." But from a pure lexical meaning, such a definition does not really distinguish a fabric from a network.

Nevertheless, more attentive minds have noticed that during the last few years, the networking industry has chosen the term *fabric* to represent the concept of a "better network." Arguably, Fibre Channel has inspired other networking technologies (including Ethernet) to deploy characteristics such as simplicity, reliability, flexibility, minimum operation overhead, and support of new applications without disruption.

Many of these characteristics refer to this protocol as native *fabric services*. Such services are basic functions that can be accessed through certain well-known addresses (FCIDs from 0xfffff0 to 0xffffff) and that provide specific information and operations to connected devices.

As an illustration, Table 10-3 depicts some of these fabric services and their respective well-known addresses, as defined in the Fibre Channel standards.

Table 10-3 *Some Fibre Channel Fabric Services*

Fibre Channel Service	Well-Known Address
Broadcast Alias	0xffffff
Fabric Login Server	0xfffffe
Fabric Controller	0xfffffd
Name Server	0xfffffc
Management Server	0xfffffa
Reserved	0xfffff4 to 0xfffff0

The **Broadcast Alias** service can be accessed in a fabric switch if a Fibre Channel frame is sent to address 0xffffff. Frames delivered to this address are replicated and delivered by the fabric to all other available N_Ports at a given instant.

The **Login Server** service is the logical entity within each fabric switch that receives and responds to *Fabric Login (FLOGI)* frames sent by N_Ports. This procedure is used to discover the operating characteristics associated with a fabric or a fabric element. The Login Server also assigns, confirms, or reassigns the FCID for the N_Port.

The **Fabric Controller** service is the logical entity responsible for the operation of the fabric. It has the characteristics of an N_Port, though it is not an external device. The fabric controller also executes functions such as

- Fabric initialization
- Parsing and routing of frames directed to well-known addresses
- Setup and tear down of dedicated connections
- General frame routing
- Generation of fabric error responses

The **Name Server** service maintains tables that store information about the known N_Ports, including WWNs, FCIDs, and FC operating parameters (such as supported ULP and requested classes of service). These tables can be used by nodes to discover an FCID given the knowledge of a WWN and vice versa.

Tip As you will see in the section "Zoning," later in this chapter, the name server also deploys soft zoning by performing WWN lookups.

The **Management Server** service is a read-only service that is used to collect and report information on link usage, errors, link quality, and so on.

In a fabric, *Extended Link Service (ELS)* frames represent requests between N_Ports and a Fibre Channel switch. An ELS reply is expected after an ELS request, and this communication is formalized in the Fibre Channel Link Services (FC-LS) family of standards.

On the other hand, the communication between switches is comprised of *Switch Internal Link Service (SW_ILS)* frames. These frames belong to the Class F service and, consequently, must always be confirmed or rejected by the receiving switch. SW_ILSs are described in the Fibre Channel Switch Fabric (FC-SW) family of standards.

Fabric Initialization

A fabric must be fully operational before it can successfully transport Fibre Channel frames between N_Ports. This process depends on a key figure called the *principal switch*.

Such a device is responsible for domain ID distribution within the fabric, and its selection depends on the priority assigned to each switch (1 to 254, where the lower value wins), and if a tie happens, on its switch WWN (sWWN).

A principal switch shall be selected whenever at least one ISL is formed. Each switch on the fabric has a *principal ISL* that is used to communicate with the principal switch because it points toward it.

The principal switch selection is a very detailed process. In Figure 10-8, for the sake of simplicity, I have summarized its phases in a two-switch sample fabric.

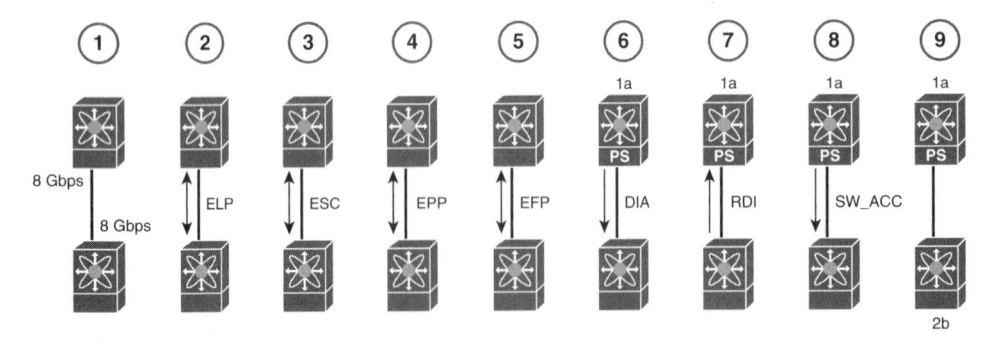

Figure 10-8 *Fabric Initialization*

As shown in Figure 10-8, the principal switch selection phases are as follows:

1. A switch detects a valid connection to another switch and begins *link initialization* at this port. If the port is capable of operating at more than one speed, it can perform speed negotiation.

2. When two E_Ports are connected and the link is initialized, they begin the *Exchange Link Parameters (ELP)* phase. Information about the interfaces is exchanged between both fabric controller addresses (0xfffffd) using the Class F service. Supported classes of service, timers, and buffer-to-buffer credits are also traded using the ELP frame (ISL isolation can occur because of a mismatch of FC timers).

3. The *Exchange Switch Capabilities (ESC)* phase occurs when neighboring fabric controllers agree upon a common routing protocol and recognize the switch vendor ID.

4. If these are Cisco MDS 9000 devices, they exchange a proprietary *Exchange Peer Parameter (EPP)* frame. This is used for Cisco-specific feature negotiations such as virtual SAN trunks (as you will learn later in this chapter).

5. During the *Exchange Fabric Parameters (EFP)* phase, the principal switch is selected.

6. In this phase, the principal switch assigns a domain ID to itself (based on a configured domain ID list) and floods the fabric with *Domain ID Identifier (DIA)* frames with such information.

7. Each connected switch that receives the DIA requests a domain ID from the principal switch, sending a request domain identifier (RDI) to the principal switch. The request can contain a preferred (or static) domain ID, depending on the device configuration.

8. The principal switch grants a domain ID to the request. It can be the requested domain ID or another from its domain ID list.

9. The downstream switch accepts the domain ID (if it is the same as the static ID or it belongs to its domain ID list), and a fabric is finally formed. If the downstream switch does not accept the domain, it becomes an isolated switch.

Note If an unconfigured switch (or fabric) is joined to an already configured fabric, the principal switch will perform an address assignment normally.

The principal switch selection can be triggered by a switch boot, a *Build Fabric (BF)* frame, or a *Reconfigure Fabric (RCF)* frame. A BF frame requests a nondisruptive reconfiguration of the entire fabric, without connectivity loss of or change of addressing. An RCF frame requests a disruptive reconfiguration of the entire fabric and can cause addresses allocated to a switch to change. RCF must be used with caution because it causes all traffic in the fabric to stop.

A BF can be manually initiated or sent to all other switches in a fabric if

- A principal ISL experiences link failure or transition to offline.

- A configured fabric is joined to another configured fabric and their domain IDs do not overlap.

ISL isolation occurs if

- A configured fabric is joined to another configured fabric, and a domain ID overlap is detected.

- A reconfiguration caused by a BF frame fails for any reason.

To completely restart the fabric (and solve an isolation issue), a fabric reconfiguration procedure can be manually initiated with RCF frames sent to all other switches in a fabric. Additionally, RCFs can be configured to be automatically generated after any isolation occurs. However, for security measures, this automatic option is disabled by default on Cisco MDS 9000 switches.

Tip Cisco MDS switches can also reject RCFs in an E_Port selectively to prevent a compromised switch from causing fabric outages.

Fabric Shortest Path First

After the domain ID assignment phase is complete, routing tables must be built within the fabric to correctly route frames between N_Ports. Such a process guarantees that all switches are able to route Fibre Channel frames, based on their destination FCID, and using the best available path.

Fibre Channel uses the *Fabric Shortest Path First (FSPF)* protocol to advertise addresses to other switches so that they can build their routing tables. As a link-state path selection protocol, FSPF keeps track of the state of the links on all switches in the fabric and associates a cost with each link. The protocol computes paths from a switch to all other switches in the fabric by adding the cost of all the links traversed by the path, and choosing the path with the lowest cost. The collection of link states (including cost) of all the switches in a fabric constitutes the *topology database*.

In a nutshell, FSPF has four major components:

- A **Hello protocol**, used to establish connectivity with a neighbor switch and to exchange FSPF parameters and capabilities.

- A replicated **topology database**, which uses link-state records (LSR) for complete synchronization whenever a switch is initialized or an ISL comes up.

- A loop-free path computation algorithm.

- **Link-state updates (LSU)**, which happen periodically or with a link-state change.

All FSPF messages use Switch Internal Link Service (SW_ILS) and Class F service. Additionally, LSUs are transmitted by a mechanism called *reliable flooding*, which transmits this message to all other switches and expects an acknowledgment from each one of them.

FSPF computes the least-cost path based on link speed and number of hops. The default cost of each link is calculated using the following formula:

Link cost = S * (1.0625e12 / Baud rate)

where S is an administratively set factor. By default, S is set to 1, respectively assigning the values 1000, 500, 250, and 125 to 1-, 2-, 4-, and 8-Gbps links. You can also manually assign the cost of an ISL.

Figure 10-9 illustrates how path costs are used to route frames between N_Ports.

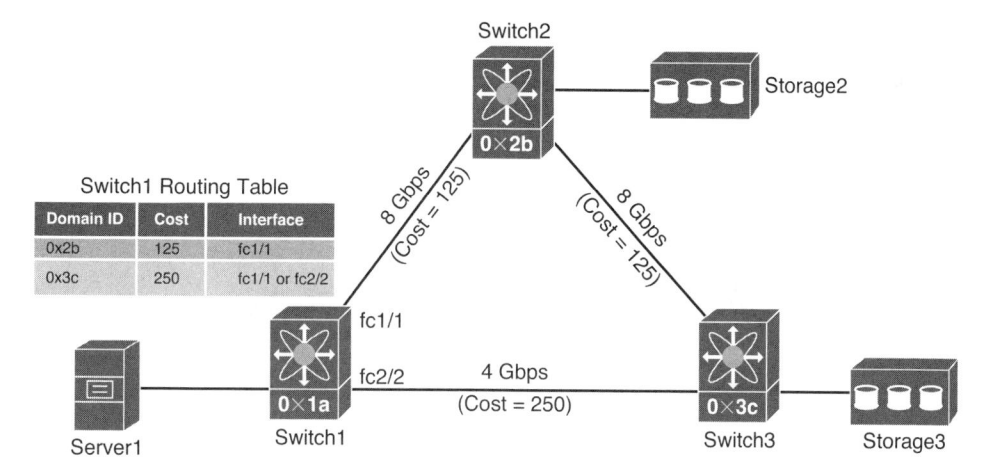

Figure 10-9 *FSPF Costs in a Fabric*

According to the routing table on Switch1 in Figure 10-9, frames from Server1 to Storage2 will be routed to Switch2 through interface fc1/1 on Switch1. The path calculation algorithm has chosen the least-cost path (Switch1 to Switch2 with cost 125) over the Switch1-Switch3-Switch2 path that has a cost of 375.

However, an interesting situation arises with frames that must be routed from Server1 to Storage3. In Switch1, there are two equal-cost paths to Switch3: a 4-Gbps path (Switch1-Switch3) and an 8-Gbps path (Switch1-Switch2-Switch3).

According to the Fibre Channel standards, it is up to each manufacturer to decide how a switch forwards frames in the case of equal-cost paths. Cisco NX-OS devices, including MDS 9000 switches, can load-balance traffic on up to 16 equal-cost paths using one of the following behaviors:

- **Flow-based:** Each pair of N_Ports only uses a single path (for example, traffic from Server1 to Storage3 will only use the path Switch1-Switch3). The path choice is based on a hash operation over the device's source and destination FCIDs.

- **Exchange-based:** Exchanges from each pair of N_Ports are load balanced between both paths. The path choice is based on a hash operation over the device's source and destination FCIDs, plus the Originator Exchange Identifier (OX_ID).

As you can notice, FSPF does not take into account the available bandwidth or utilization of the paths for its calculation. That is why FSPF planning is a typical task for SAN administrators, to avoid bottlenecks and nonoptimal routing scenarios.

It is only natural that a SAN administrator would want to deploy ISL redundancy between switches. However, whenever an LSU is sent to all FSPF switches, a general route recomputation can bring unstable effects to the fabric, including traffic loss and downtime. *PortChannels* can help reduce these risks with the creation of logical connections, comprised of multiple aggregated ISLs.

Figure 10-10 depicts the distinct fabric behaviors with a failure on a nonaggregated ISL and a failure on an ISL that is part of a PortChannel.

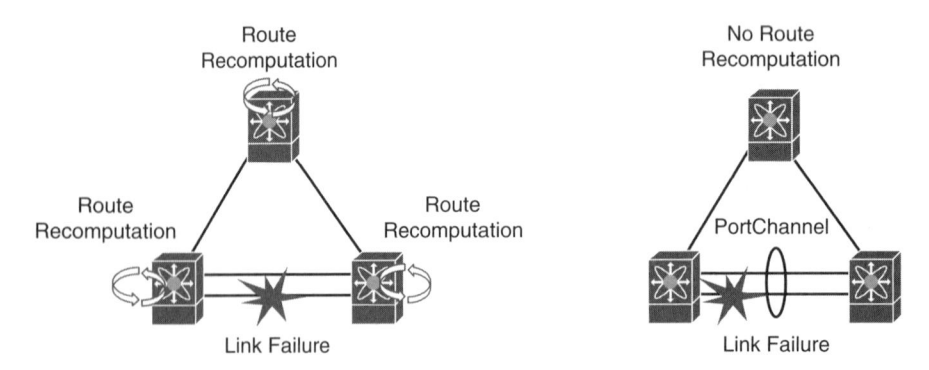

Figure 10-10 *FSPF and PortChannels*

When PortChannels are not being deployed, a link failure will always cause route recomputation. With PortChannels, such a failure is confined to the logical ISL, not causing any FSPF change in the fabric if at least one PortChannel member is operational. In summary, PortChannels increase the fabric reliability and simplify its operation, reducing the number of available paths between switches.

Cisco MDS 9000 devices support up to 16 interfaces in a PortChannel defined between two switches. Traffic is load balanced among the members of a PortChannel using the same FSPF equal-cost load balance–chosen algorithm.

Register State Change Notification

A Fibre Channel fabric can notify connected N_Ports about internal changes, such as an ISL state alteration or the addition of an N_Port.

The **Registered State Change Notification** (RSCN) is the service that provides this information, and it is managed by the fabric controller. Nodes can receive this information by sending a *State Change Registration (SCR)* frame. As a result, the fabric controller transmits RSCN commands to registered N_Ports when a fabric state change occurs.

Fibre Channel Logins

An N_Port must execute three basic login processes in an operational fabric before it can exchange frames with another N_Port. These login processes are as follows:

- **Fabric Login (FLOGI):** A process where an N_Port obtains an FCID and discovers the operating characteristics associated with a fabric or switch. The Login Server within a switch receives and responds to FLOGI frames using the well-known address 0xfffffe. In a public loop, each NL_Port performs a fabric login with the switch that contains the FL_Port.

- **Port Login (PLOGI):** A process where two N_Ports discover their mutual capabilities and operating parameters.

- **Process Login (PRLI):** A process used to establish a session between two FC-4 level logical processes (ULP) between the devices that have recently performed a PLOGI.

Figure 10-11 details a FLOGI process between a server HBA and a Fibre Channel switch, and both PLOGI and PRLI processes between the same HBA and a storage array port. For the sake of clarity, I have not depicted the FLOGI process from the storage array port.

Each step from the login processes portrayed in Figure 10-11 is explained as follows:

1. After the connection between the node and the switch is initialized, the node sends a FLOGI request frame containing information about itself (such as its WWNs). The source address is 0x000000, and it is directed to the Login Server's well-known address (0xfffffe).

2. The switch issues an ACCEPT message to the received FLOGI. It contains the node FCID as its destination FCID.

3. The N_Port sends a PLOGI to the name server (0xfffffc) as if it were an N_Port. This exposes the node's intention to use the name server from now on.

4. The switch name server accepts the port login.

5. The node registers itself with the name server. From now on, this N_Port can be discovered on the fabric.

6. The name server accepts the registration.

7. The node registers to receive RSCNs whenever a change in the fabric is detected.

8. The switch accepts the State Change Registration.

9. The N_Port queries the name server about other devices that are available for it to communicate with.

428 Data Center Virtualization Fundamentals

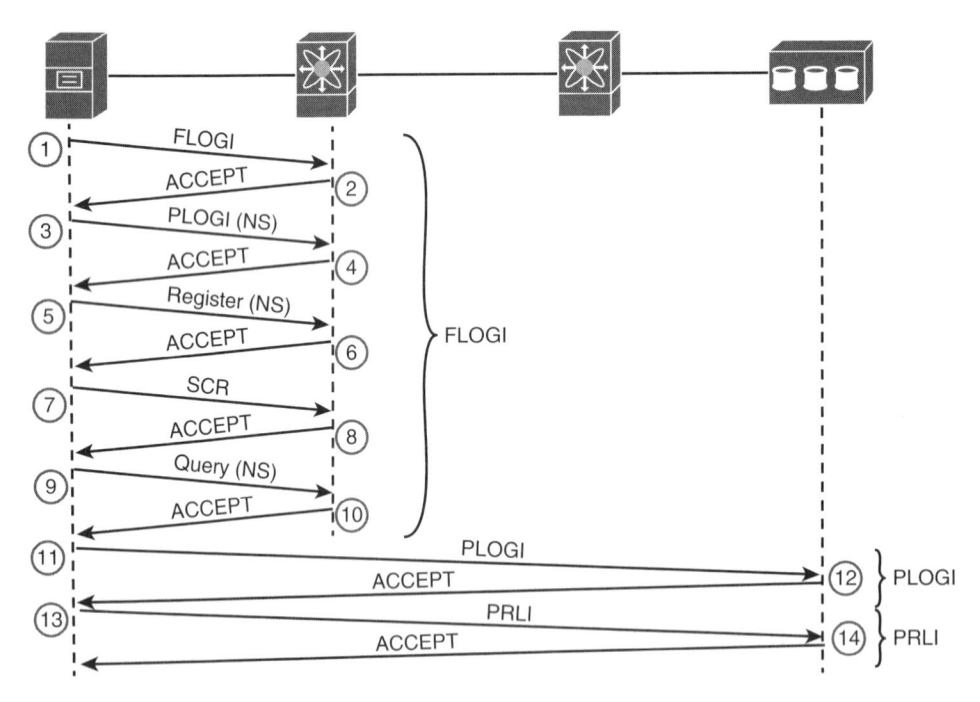

Figure 10-11 *Login Processes*

10. In response to the query, the name server returns a list of FCIDs of nodes that share common *zones* (and declared FC-4 parameters) with the device.

Tip In the next section, I will explore the concept of zoning. For now, I just want you to understand that if two devices are zoned together, they are capable of discovering each other through the name server, and the fabric will not block data frames exchanged between these devices.

11. The node tries to perform a PLOGI with a target N_Port FCID that was returned by the name server. It sends a PLOGI frame that contains its operating parameters.

12. The target N_Port replies with an ACCEPT frame that specifies its operating parameters (supported classes of service, for example). An N_Port can be logged in to multiple N_Ports simultaneously.

13. The initiator N_Port tries to establish a session between two FC-4 processes (PRLI). It sends information about its ULP support.

14. The target responds with an ACCEPT frame with its ULP support parameters.

After all these negotiations, both devices are ready to proceed with their upper-layer protocol communication.

Zoning

According to the Fibre Channel standards, a *zone* is a collection of N_Ports in a fabric that are aware of each other, but not of devices outside the zone. In a zone, each *zone member* can be specified by a port on a switch, WWN, FCID, or human-readable alias (also known as FC-Alias).

Zones can also be understood as Virtual Private Networks defined within in a fabric. They are deployed to increase network security, introduce storage access control, and prevent data loss. For example, the zoning processes can avoid a situation where servers with different operating systems access the same storage resource, which can be hazardous for their stored data.

In Fibre Channel fabrics, there are two methods of zoning. *Soft zoning* consists of members that are made visible to each other only through name server queries. On the other hand, *hard zoning* is enforced as a hardware function on the fabric, which in turn will only forward frames among members of a zone.

Tip Modern Fibre Channel switches and directors only deploy hard zoning. In NX-OS devices, you can also configure the switch behavior when frames between unzoned members are received. For the sake of data security, blocking is the recommended behavior for unzoned N_Ports.

One or more zones that can be activated or deactivated as a group are called a *zone set*. A fabric can have multiple zone sets, but only one can be active at a time. The active zone set is present in all switches from a fabric.

The **Zone Server** service is used to manage zones and zonesets. Implicitly, it includes all the well-known addresses on every zone.

Figure 10-12 illustrates how zones and an active zone set can be understood in a sample fabric.

In Figure 10-12, each zone contains two or three members, but more hosts could be included in a zone if desired. When performing a name service query, each device receives the FCID addresses from members in the same zone. Therefore, to avoid unintentional initiator-initiator (or target-target) accesses, it is recommended that each zone includes only two members.

When two operational fabrics are connected, information is exchanged between border switches to verify that active zone sets are do not conflict with each other (no duplicate domain IDs, same zone set name, and zones with same names have identical members). If there is compatibility, the resulting active zone set is a single structure containing zone definitions from both fabrics. If not, the newly connected E_Ports become isolated.

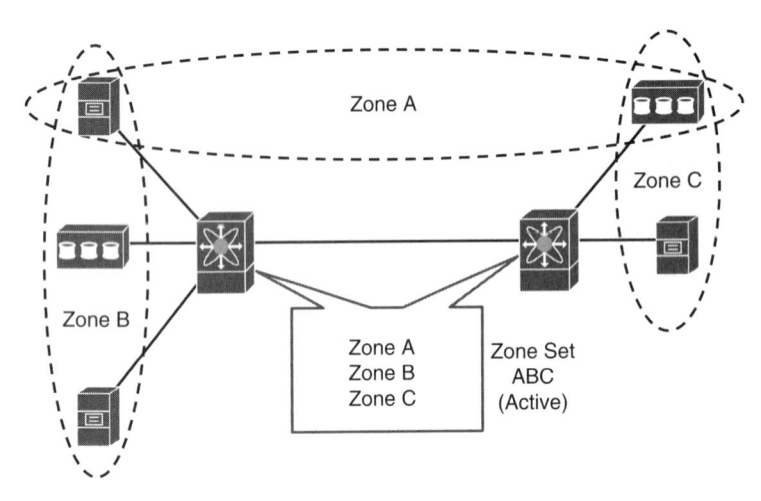

Figure 10-12 *Zones and Zone Sets*

Defining and Exploring VSANs

A *virtual storage-area network (VSAN)* can be defined as a set of N_Ports (or NL_Ports) that share the same Fibre Channel fabric processes in a single physical SAN. For that reason, fabric services such as Name Server, Zone Server, and Login Server are replicated per VSAN.

VSANs permit the consolidation of different fabrics in the same physical infrastructure. As you will see in the next sections, they provide data and control plane isolation without the shortcomings of maintaining physically segmented fabrics.

SAN Islands

You already know that zoning is used to provide basic security in a Fibre Channel fabric. It restricts visibility and connectivity between nodes and helps filter nonrelevant information (such as N_Ports that do not belong to a zone) to some nodes.

However, devices that belong to different zones in the same SAN still share fabric services such as the Name Server, Login Server, and (obviously) Zone Server. Hence, such nodes are subject to fabric-wide disruptive events such as a sent RCF, an FSPF route recomputation, or even an unintentional misconfiguration in any of these services.

In the late 1990s, storage administrators started to deploy *SAN islands* to connect servers and storage devices to avoid these situations. Their concept was really simple: independent and relatively small fabrics that could confine such problems in a single environment.

SAN islands typically scaled to a mesh of small fabric switches where ISLs were deployed whenever an expansion was needed. The fact that these switches were generally included in a storage device acquisition further aggravated this "accidental" architecture.

Figure 10-13 exemplifies two sample SAN islands from that not-so-distant era (actually, I know several customers who still use such structures).

> **Tip** In SAN designs, it is typical to deploy two independent fabrics if the servers and storage devices have more than one N_Port. This best practice increases the storage access availability (because there are two paths between each server and a storage device) and scalability (if multipath I/O software is installed on the servers).

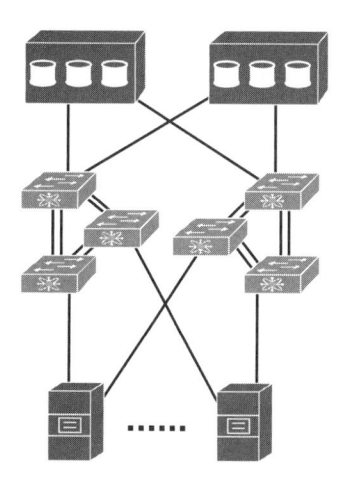

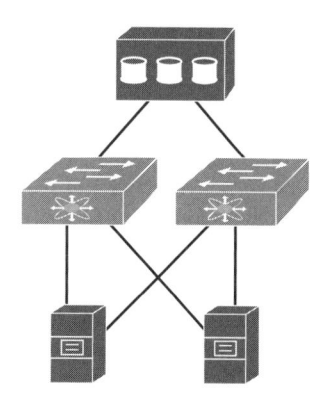

Figure 10-13 *SAN Islands*

The deployment of SAN islands produced some architectural challenges, such as

- Lower utilization of resources (switches and storage arrays)
- Larger number of management points
- Considerable number of ports used for ISLs
- Unpredictable traffic oversubscription on ISLs

In the beginning of the 2000s, some data centers ignited SAN consolidation projects to mitigate these effects. At that time, *director-class switches*, with fully redundant hardware components, modular architecture and hundreds of ports, were the natural candidates for these projects.

But how to consolidate SAN islands without the formation of a single fabric with shared services? As an answer to that question, Cisco introduced the concept of VSANs. Originally, this virtualization technique was created to permit the consolidation of SAN islands within a shared physical Fibre Channel fabric. Notwithstanding, as you will learn in the next sections, VSANs can bring additional advantages to SAN administrators.

> **Note** MDS 9000 switches and directors deploy VSANs in hardware. Therefore, the use of this feature does not affect the device performance.

VSAN Creation

The **VSAN Manager** is the NX-OS process that maintains VSAN attributes and port membership. It also possesses a database that contains information on each VSAN, such as its unique name, administrative state (suspended or active), operational state (up, if there is at least one active interface), FSPF and PortChannel load-balance algorithm, and Fibre Channel timers.

In an NX-OS device, there are two predefined virtual SANs:

- **Default (VSAN 1):** This cannot be deleted (only suspended) and contains all the ports when a switch is first initialized.

- **Isolated (VSAN 4094):** This receives the ports from deleted VSANs and actually does not work. It exists to avoid involuntary inclusion of ports in a VSAN and it cannot be deleted either.

I believe that the best way to learn chess is to play the game. For that reason, to illustrate what VSANs really are, I will present an evolving SAN topology where you can easily observe "how this stuff works."

Let's start with Figure 10-14, which depicts a single switch that will deploy two VSANs. The figure also portrays the interface configuration needed for this configuration.

> **Note** For learning purposes, I will ignore all interface automatic default behavior and include all the commands required to define each interface's intended mode and state.

```
MDS-CORE(config)# interface fc1/1, fc2/1
MDS-CORE(config-if)# switchport mode Fx
MDS-CORE(config-if)# no shutdown
```

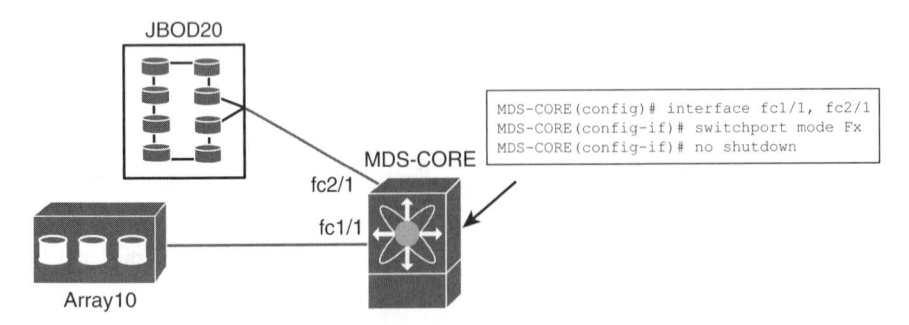

Figure 10-14 *Soon-to-Be Virtualized Fibre Channel Switch*

In Figure 10-14, both interfaces (fc1/1 and fc2/1) were configured with the **switchport mode Fx** command. This configuration means that they can only become F_Ports or

FL_Ports, depending on their connected devices. From now on, consider that this will be the configuration used in our fabric for all host and storage ports.

Example 10-1 exhibits the creation of VSANs 10 and 20 and the MDS-CORE FLOGI database after both nodes join their respective virtual fabrics.

Example 10-1 *VSAN Creation and FLOGI Database in MDS-CORE*

```
! Entering the VSAN configuration database
MDS-CORE(config)# vsan database
! Creating VSAN 10
MDS-CORE(config-vsan-db)# vsan 10
! Including interface fc1/1 in VSAN 10
MDS-CORE(config-vsan-db)# vsan 10 interface fc1/1
! If this interface is already operational and working on a VSAN the
following message is sent to the administrator
Traffic on fc1/1 may be impacted. Do you want to continue? (y/n) [n] y
! Creating VSAN 20
MDS-CORE(config-vsan-db)# vsan 20
! Interface fc1/1 is included in VSAN 20
MDS-CORE(config-vsan-db)# vsan 20 interface fc2/1
Traffic on fc2/1 may be impacted. Do you want to continue? (y/n) [n] y
! Verifying the interfaces status
MDS-CORE(config-vsan-db)# show interface fc1/1, fc2/1 brief

-------------------------------------------------------------------
Interface  Vsan   Admin   Admin   Status  SFP  Oper   Oper    Port
                  Mode    Trunk                Mode   Speed   Channel
                          Mode                               (Gbps)
-------------------------------------------------------------------
! Interface fc1/1 is connected to an N_Port
fc1/1      10     FX      on      up      swl  F      4       --
! Interface fc1/1 is connected to an Public Loop
fc2/1      20     FX      on      up      swl  FL     1       --
MDS-CORE(config-vsan-db)# show flogi database
-------------------------------------------------------------------
INTERFACE        VSAN    FCID       PORT NAME                NODE NAME
-------------------------------------------------------------------
! Storage Device is connected to domain 0xd4
fc1/1            10      0xd40000   50:00:40:21:03:fc:6d:28  20:03:00:04:02:fc:6d:28
! JBOD contains 8 NL_Ports (disks) and is connected to domain 0xed
fc2/1            20      0xed00da   22:00:00:04:cf:92:8b:ad  20:00:00:04:cf:92:8b:ad
fc2/1            20      0xed00dc   22:00:00:0c:50:49:4e:d8  20:00:00:0c:50:49:4e:d8
fc2/1            20      0xed00e0   22:00:00:04:cf:92:86:8e  20:00:00:04:cf:92:86:8e
fc2/1            20      0xed00e1   22:00:00:04:cf:92:7a:b7  20:00:00:04:cf:92:7a:b7
fc2/1            20      0xed00e2   22:00:00:0c:50:49:4e:30  20:00:00:0c:50:49:4e:30
```

```
fc2/1              20      0xed00e4   22:00:00:0c:50:49:4e:cf 20:00:00:0c:50:49:4e:cf
fc2/1              20      0xed00e8   22:00:00:04:cf:92:85:0e 20:00:00:04:cf:92:85:0e
fc2/1              20      0xed00ef   22:00:00:0c:50:49:4e:35 20:00:00:0c:50:49:4e:35

Total number of flogi = 9.
```

In Example 10-1, you can observe that VSANs 10 and 20 have different domain IDs (0xd4 and 0xed, respectively) that were randomly chosen from the VSANs' domain ID list (1 to 239, by default). Additionally, the VSAN *distinct* Login Servers have, accordingly, assigned FCIDs to the connected storage devices. As expected, from the storage devices' perspective, they are connected to different switches.

Note NX-OS switches automatically include the FCID-to-WWN mapping in their startup configuration (to be saved across reboots). Although not recommended, this behavior can be disabled per VSAN.

VSAN Trunking

VSANs were not designed to be confined within a single switch. They can be extended to other switches, spreading a virtual Fibre Channel fabric over multiple devices. Although E_Ports can also be configured to extend a single VSAN, a *trunk* is usually the recommended extension between VSAN-enabled switches. By definition, a Trunk Expansion Port (TE_Port) can carry the traffic of several VSANs over a single *Enhanced Inter-Switch Link (EISL)*.

In an EISL, an 8-byte VSAN header is included between the Start of Frame (SOF) and the frame header. Although this header structure is not depicted in this book, you should know that it includes a 12-bit field that identifies the VSAN that a frame belongs to.

Note The VSAN header is standardized in FC-FS-2 section 10.3 ("VFT_Header and Virtual Fabrics").

Figure 10-15 shows an EISL configured between two switches (one of them is MDS-CORE). The figure also depicts the nonautomatic interface configuration in MDS-CORE.

```
MDS-CORE(config)# interface fc2/14
MDS-CORE(config-if)# switchport rate-mode dedicated
MDS-CORE(config-if)# switchport speed 2000
MDS-CORE(config-if)# switchport mode E
MDS-CORE(config-if)# switchport trunk mode on
MDS-CORE(config-if)# switchport trunk allowed vsan 10
MDS-CORE(config-if)# switchport trunk allowed vsan add 20
MDS-CORE(config-if)# no shutdown
```

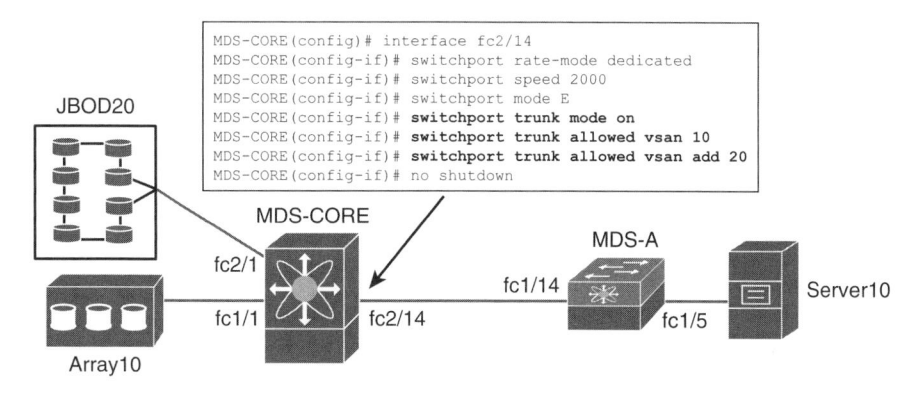

Figure 10-15 *Trunk Between MDS-CORE and MDS-A*

Interface fc2/14 on MDS-CORE is configured as a trunk interface for VSANs 10 and 20 only (because by default, a trunk allows the traffic for all VSANs). The **switchport rate-mode dedicated** command is mandatory on oversubscribed modules or switches because ISLs must be configured on full-rate interfaces.

Tip For the sake of simplicity, I am only presenting the configuration from one side of the EISL. From now on, consider that the interface on the other side has exactly the same configuration.

In MDS-A, interface fc1/5 (that is connected to an HBA in Server10), is assigned to VSAN 10.

Example 10-2 exhibits VSAN configuration and the EISL status in MDS-A.

Example 10-2 *VSAN Creation and Trunk Status in MDS-A*

```
! Creating VSAN 10 and 20 and assigning interface fc1/5 to VSAN 10
MDS-A(config)# vsan database
MDS-A(config-vsan-db)# vsan 10
MDS-A(config-vsan-db)# vsan 10 interface fc1/5
Traffic on fc1/5 may be impacted. Do you want to continue? (y/n) y
MDS-A(config-vsan-db)# vsan 20
! Checking the trunk status
MDS-A(config-vsan-db)# show interface fc1/14
! VSAN trunking is working
fc1/14 is trunking
    Hardware is Fibre Channel, SFP is short wave laser w/o OFC (SN)
    Port WWN is 20:0e:00:0d:ec:22:c1:00
    Peer port WWN is 20:4e:00:05:9b:7c:94:40
    Admin port mode is E, trunk mode is on
```

```
    snmp link state traps are enabled
    Port mode is TE
! Even as a trunk, the interface does belong to a VSAN
    Port vsan is 1
[output suppressed]
! VSAN Status in the Trunk
    Trunk vsans (admin allowed and active)  (10,20)
    Trunk vsans (up)                         (10,20)
    Trunk vsans (isolated)                   ()
    Trunk vsans (initializing)               ()
    5 minutes input rate 1616 bits/sec, 202 bytes/sec, 1 frames/sec
[output suppressed]
```

As depicted in Example 10-2, interface fc1/14 on MDS-A still belongs to VSAN 1, even if it can transport traffic from other VSANs. Although their original VSAN is not allowed in the trunk, the connected ports are up simply because this VSAN is active on both switches.

Figure 10-16 exhibits the placement of MDS-B in our fabric. This switch has an EISL with MDS-CORE and a PortChannel aggregating three interfaces (fc1/7, fc1/8, and fc1/9) with MDS-A.

```
MDS-B(config)# interface fc1/7-9
MDS-B(config-if)# switchport rate-mode dedicated
MDS-B(config-if)# switchport speed 2000
MDS-B(config-if)# switchport mode E
MDS-B(config-if)# switchport trunk mode on
MDS-B(config-if)# switchport trunk allowed vsan 10
MDS-B(config-if)# switchport trunk allowed vsan add 20
MDS-B(config-if)# channel-group 10 force
[output suppressed]
MDS-B(config-if)# no shutdown
```

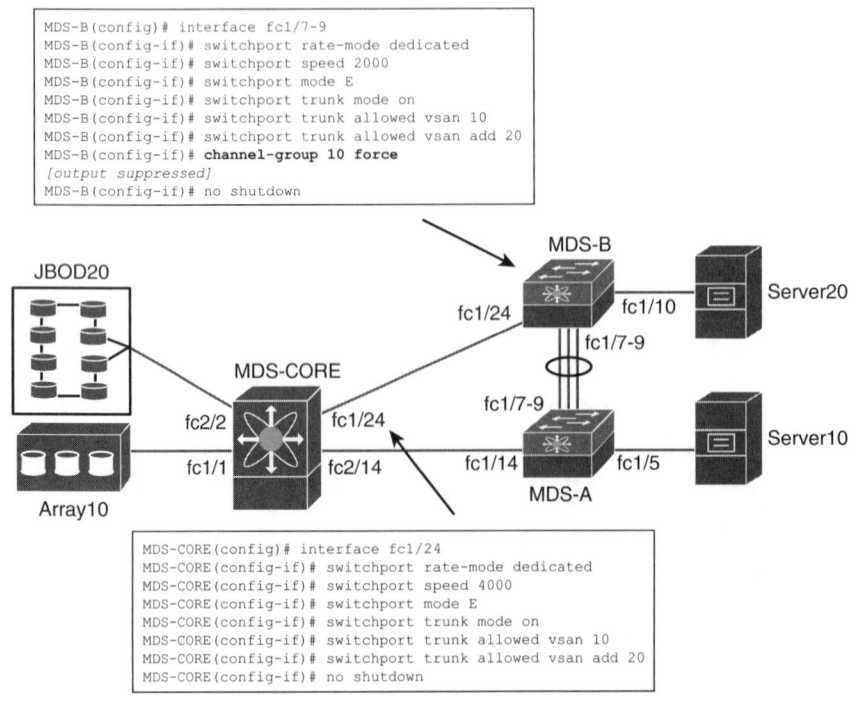

```
MDS-CORE(config)# interface fc1/24
MDS-CORE(config-if)# switchport rate-mode dedicated
MDS-CORE(config-if)# switchport speed 4000
MDS-CORE(config-if)# switchport mode E
MDS-CORE(config-if)# switchport trunk mode on
MDS-CORE(config-if)# switchport trunk allowed vsan 10
MDS-CORE(config-if)# switchport trunk allowed vsan add 20
MDS-CORE(config-if)# no shutdown
```

Figure 10-16 *PortChannel Configuration on MDS-B and Trunk Configuration on MDS-CORE*

> **Tip** PortChannels can also be automatically created between two switches using the **channel-group auto** command.

Example 10-3 shows the creation of VSANs 10 and 20 in MDS-B, which now shares both virtual fabrics with MDS-CORE and MDS-A. The same example also displays the Fibre Channel Name Server databases, as seen from MDS-B.

Example 10-3 *FLOGI and Name Service in MDS-B*

```
! Creating VSANs 10 and 20 and assigning interface fc1/10 to VSAN 20
MDS-B(config)# vsan database
MDS-B(config-vsan-db)# vsan 10
MDS-B(config-vsan-db)# vsan 20
MDS-B(config-vsan-db)# vsan 20 interface fc1/10
Traffic on fc1/10 may be impacted. Do you want to continue? (y/n) y
! Verifying Fibre Channel Name Service database on both VSANs
MDS-B(config)# show fcns database
! VSAN 10 has two N_Ports (Server10 connected to MDS-A and the Disk Array connected
to MDS-CORE)
VSAN 10:
--------------------------------------------------------------------------
FCID        TYPE  PWWN                    (VENDOR)        FC4-TYPE:FEATURE
--------------------------------------------------------------------------
0x710000    N     10:00:00:00:c9:2e:66:00 (Emulex)        scsi-fcp:init
0xd40000    N     50:00:40:21:03:fc:6d:28                 scsi-fcp:target

Total number of entries = 2
! VSAN 20 has one N_Port (Server20 conntected to MDS-B) and 8 NL_Ports (JBOD
connected to MDS-CORE)
VSAN 20:
--------------------------------------------------------------------------
FCID        TYPE  PWWN                    (VENDOR)        FC4-TYPE:FEATURE
--------------------------------------------------------------------------
0x140000    N     10:00:00:00:c9:73:9c:2c (Emulex)        scsi-fcp:init
0xed00da    NL    22:00:00:04:cf:92:8b:ad (Seagate)       scsi-fcp:target
0xed00dc    NL    22:00:00:0c:50:49:4e:d8 (Seagate)       scsi-fcp:target
[output suppressed]
Total number of entries = 9
```

The name service provides information about the connected devices, including FCID, port type, pWWN, vendor, and FC-4 capabilities. In Example 10-3, the FCIDs also expose how the domain IDs are distributed among the switches in each VSAN.

As explained in earlier section "Fabric Processes," each VSAN went through the phases of fabric initialization, including principal switch selection and domain ID distribution.

The **show fcdomain domain-list** command exhibits the domain ID distribution and principal switch selection decision in each virtual fabric, as shown in Example 10-4.

Example 10-4 *Domain ID Distribution*

```
! Verifying the Domain ID distribution in VSAN 10
MDS-CORE# show fcdomain domain-list vsan 10
Number of domains: 3
Domain ID              WWN
---------              -----------------------
! MDS-A is the Principal Switch in this VSAN
0x71(113)    20:0a:00:0d:ec:22:c1:01 [Principal]
! This is the local switch (MDS-CORE)
0xd4(212)    20:0a:00:05:9b:7c:94:41 [Local]
! And this is MDS-B
 0x47(71)    20:0a:00:0d:ec:47:e7:41
! Verifying the Domain ID distribution in VSAN 10
MDS-CORE# show fcdomain domain-list vsan 20
Number of domains: 3
Domain ID              WWN
---------              -----------------------
! MDS-A is also the Principal Switch in this VSAN
0x1e(30)     20:14:00:0d:ec:22:c1:01 [Principal]
! This is the local switch (MDS-CORE)
0xed(237)    20:14:00:05:9b:7c:94:41 [Local]
! And this is MDS-B
 0x14(20)    20:14:00:0d:ec:47:e7:41
```

Because all switches are using the default priority of 128, the principal switch in each fabric was decided through the sWWN in each VSAN. Also, observe that the second byte of the sWWN contains the VSAN identifier in hexadecimal.

In our scenario, MDS-A has the lowest sWWNs on both VSANs and, therefore, was selected as their principal switch. However, the fabric initialization processes from both VSANs were completely independent from each other.

Tip You can change a switch priority in a VSAN with the **fcdomain priority** command. A nondisruptive restart (the **fcdomain restart vsan** command) is also required for a new principal switch selection in this VSAN if you do not want to provoke any domain ID change.

Zoning and VSANs

Two steps are necessary to present a SCSI storage volume (or Logical Unit Number [LUN]) to a server, after both of them are logged to a common fabric:

- In the storage arrays, a LUN must be configured to be accessed by a server pWWN. This process is also called *LUN masking* and is not necessary on JBODs.
- Both device ports must be zoned together in the Fibre Channel fabric.

In our continuously evolving SAN topology, I have already masked a 20-GB LUN to Server10's pWWN. I will not depict this procedure because it varies a lot depending on the array manufacturer and model.

Example 10-5 details the zoning configuration that joins Server10's HBA (whose pWWN is 10:00:00:00:c9:2e:66:00) to the disk array port (50:00:40:21:03:fc:6d:28).

> **Tip** Because the zone service is a distributed fabric process, I could have chosen any switch for this configuration.

Example 10-5 *Server10 to Disk Array Zoning*

```
! Creating a zone in VSAN 10
MDS-A(config)# zone name SERVER10-ARRAY10 vsan 10
! Including Server10 pWWN in the zone
MDS-A(config-zone)# member pwwn 10:00:00:00:c9:2e:66:00
! Including Array10 pWWN in the zone
MDS-A(config-zone)# member pwwn 50:00:40:21:03:fc:6d:28
! Creating a zone set and including zone SERVER10-ARRAY in it
MDS-A(config-zone)# zoneset name ZS10 vsan 10
MDS-A(config-zoneset)# member SERVER10-ARRAY10
! Activating the zone set
MDS-A(config-zoneset)# zoneset activate name ZS10 vsan 10
Zoneset activation initiated. check zone status
! At this moment, all switches in VSAN 10 share the same active zone set
MDS-A(config)# show zoneset active vsan 10
zoneset name ZS10 vsan 10
  zone name SERVER10-ARRAY10 vsan 10
  * fcid 0x710000 [pwwn 10:00:00:00:c9:2e:66:00]
  * fcid 0xd40000 [pwwn 50:00:40:21:03:fc:6d:28]
```

The stars on the side of each zone member signal that these nodes are logged in and present in the VSAN 10 fabric. Finally, they are zoned together.

Figure 10-17 exhibits the 20-GB disk array volume detected on Server10, which uses Windows 2003 as its operating system. From this moment on, Windows can manage this volume through standard SCSI commands.

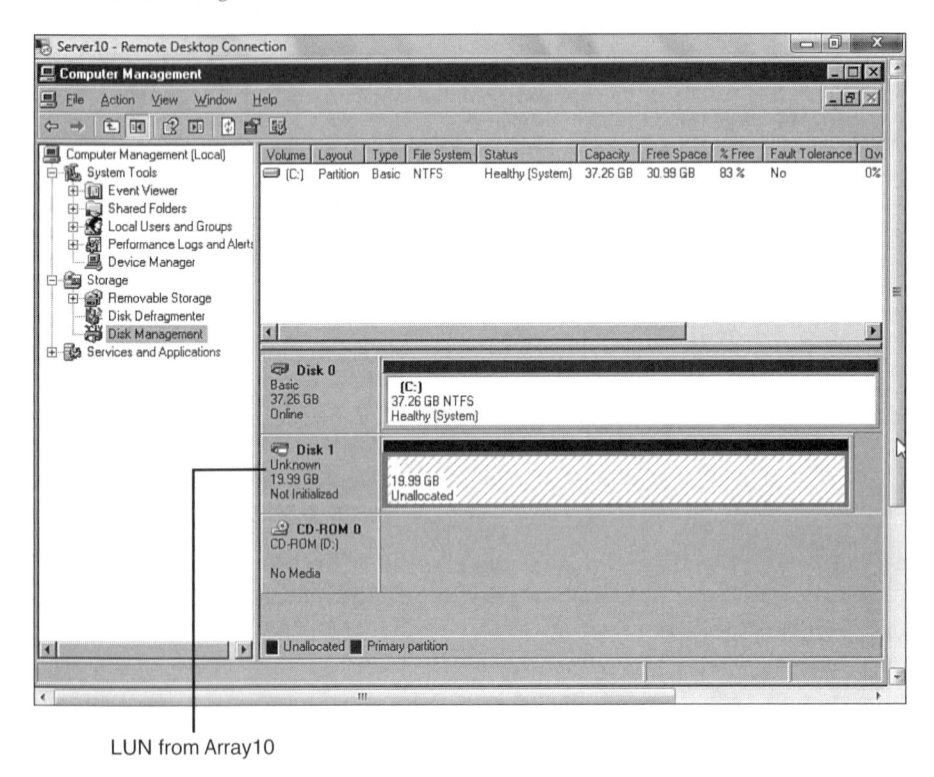

Figure 10-17 *New Volume Detected in Server10*

In Example 10-5, I have chosen pWWNs to characterize both devices in the zone because these values will remain the same, wherever they are connected in the fabric. Nevertheless, other methods can be used to include a device in a zone.

For example, you can include a *switch interface* to a zone. This option frees the SAN administrator from knowing what is being connected to this interface (other devices that belong to the same zone will automatically become visible to this device). Alternatively, you can also include FCIDs in a zone to facilitate migrations if your SAN suffers from too many device replacements. In summary, the choice of device characterization really depends on the flexibility you want to impose on the zoning process.

Back in VSAN 20, nothing related to zones and zone sets really occurred. Actually, Example 10-6 demonstrates that the zone service processes for the VSANs are completely independent.

Example 10-6 *Zoning in VSAN20*

```
!Creating zone in VSAN 20
MDS-B(config)# zone name FC1-10-JBOD20 vsan 20
! Including interface fc1/10 (connected to Server20 at the moment) to the zone
MDS-B(config-zone)# member interface fc1/10
! Inserting a disk from JBOD20 into the zone
MDS-B(config-zone)# member pwwn 22:00:00:04:cf:92:8b:ad
! Creating zone set in VSAN 20
MDS-B(config-zone)# zoneset name ZS20 vsan 20
! Including the created zone into the zone set
MDS-B(config-zoneset)# member FC1-10-JBOD20
! Activating the zone set
MDS-B(config-zoneset)# zoneset activate name ZS20 vsan 20
Zoneset activation initiated. check zone status
! Verifying the active zone set status in VSAN 20
MDS-B(config)# show zoneset active vsan 20
zoneset name ZS20 vsan 20
  zone name FC1-10-JBOD20 vsan 20
  * fcid 0x140000 [interface fc1/10 swwn 20:00:00:0d:ec:47:e7:40]
  * fcid 0xed00da [pwwn 22:00:00:04:cf:92:8b:ad]
```

In Example 10-6, it is possible to verify that VSAN 20's zone service is unaware of the recent zone set activated in VSAN 10. Also, for the sake of diversity, I have included an interface zone FC1-10-JBOD20 to illustrate how this information is advertised within VSAN 20 (FCID 0x140000 is distributed to the entire virtual fabric along with the sWWN plus the interface index).

Note If you connect another HBA to interface fc/10 on MDS-B, the FCID registered on the active zone set will automatically change, in the entire VSAN, to the new one assigned during the new FLOGI. Remember: MDS 9000 switches deploy hard zoning; hence, they block or forward frames if their source and destination FCIDs match the active zone set.

Because each VSAN deploys distinct zones and zone sets, they can also help the scalability of physical SANs. For example, imagine that a non-Cisco fabric switch, which can deploy a maximum of 100 zones, will be connected to an MDS 9000 fabric. In this scenario, this switch can be connected through a standard ISL to a VSAN with less than 100 zones and become unaware of other VSAN zone sets. Also, this VSAN can be configured in a compatible interoperability mode (with specific timers and service parameters) without affecting the other virtual fabrics.

FSPF and VSANs

The zoning process from the last section allowed the exchange of Fibre Channel frames between Server10 and the disk array. In this section, you will observe how FSPF defines the path these frames are taking in the SAN.

As a start, Example 10-7 exhibits the MDS-CORE routing table for unicast traffic in VSAN 10 (we will deal with VSAN 20 later). More specifically, I want you to pay attention to the route to MDS-A, where Server10 is connected.

Example 10-7 *MDS-CORE Routing Table*

```
! Verifying unicast routes in VSAN 10
MDS-CORE# show fcroute unicast vsan 10


D:direct   R:remote   P:permanent   V:volatile   A:active   N:non-active
                                                          # Next
Protocol   VSAN     FC ID/Mask          RCtl/Mask      Flags  Hops  Cost
--------   ----     --------- --------  ---- ----      -----  ----  ----
! Route to MDS-B
fspf       10       0x470000 0xff0000   0x00 0x00      D P A  1     250
! Route to MDS-A
fspf       10       0x710000 0xff0000   0x00 0x00      D P A  1     416
! Route to locally connected Disk Array
local      10       0xd40000 0xffffff   0x00 0x00      D P A  1     1
! Let's dig further into the route to MDS-A
MDS-CORE# show fcroute unicast 0x710000 0xff0000 vsan 10


D:direct   R:remote   P:permanent   V:volatile   A:active   N:non-active
                                                          # Next
Protocol   VSAN     FC ID/Mask          RCtl/Mask      Flags  Hops  Cost
--------   ----     --------- --------  ---- ----      -----  ----  ----
! MDS-CORE is using the EISL to MDS-B to reach MDS-A
fspf       10       0x710000 0xff0000   0x00 0x00      D P A  1     416
    fc1/24  Domain  0x47(71)
```

Example 10-7 exposes two very interesting points:

- The total cost to MDS-A is 416. This value is the sum of the costs from the 4-Gbps EISL between MDS-CORE and MDS-A (250) and the 6-Gbps PortChannel between MDS-B and MDS-A (166).

- The traffic from MDS-CORE (domain ID 0xd4 in VSAN10) to MDS-A (domain ID 0x71 in VSAN10) goes through MDS-B because it has a smaller cost (416) than the 2-Gbps EISL between MDS-CORE and MDS-A (500).

Symmetrically, the traffic from MDS-A to MDS-CORE will also pass through MDS-B. It is important to notice that these path decisions were defined by FSPF default behavior and costs.

However, imagine a situation where a SAN administrator does not want the 2-Gbps EISL between MDS-CORE and MDS-A switches to remain unused. Actually, he wants this EISL to transport frames between VSAN 10 devices that are connected to both switches.

Such traffic "hairpinning" can be executed with the manual adjustment of FSPF costs. Example 10-8 illustrates how such a configuration can be done in MDS-CORE.

Example 10-8 *FSPF Cost Setting*

```
MDS-CORE(config)# int fc2/14
! Changing the EISL cost for VSAN 10 only
MDS-CORE(config-if)# fspf cost 100 vsan 10
Checking the route to MDS-A
MDS-CORE(config-if)# show fcroute unicast 0x710000 0xff0000 vsan 10
D:direct   R:remote   P:permanent   V:volatile   A:active   N:non-active
                                                            # Next
Protocol   VSAN       FC ID/Mask            RCtl/Mask    Flags  Hops  Cost
--------   ----       ---------- --------   ---- ----    -----  ----  ----
fspf       10         0x710000 0xff0000     0x00 0x00    D P A  1     100
    fc2/14   Domain   0x71(113)
```

If the same configuration is performed on MDS-A, VSAN 10 traffic to MDS-CORE will use the same 2-Gbps EISL, thus becoming symmetric. Figure 10-18 represents how both FSPF cost configurations affected the traffic between Server10 and the array.

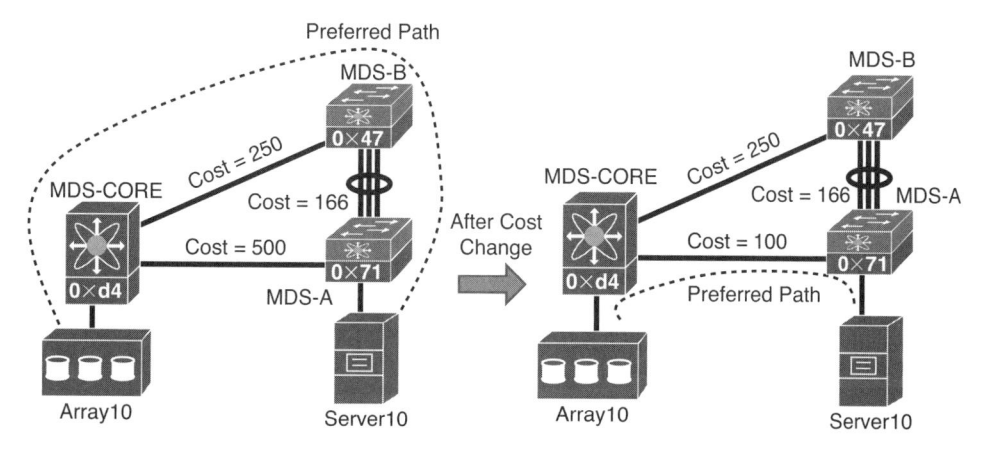

Figure 10-18 *Traffic Engineering in VSAN 10*

On purpose, I have picked 100 as the cost for the 2-Gbps EISL. This value guarantees that traffic between MDS-B and MDS-CORE continues to use their direct 4-Gbps EISL (cost 250) instead of the path through MDS-A (cost 266).

Example 10-8 detailed VSAN 10 configurations only. Other virtual fabrics, such as VSAN 20, will continue to use the FSPF paths defined by their default costs, even if one PortChannel member fails!

Example 10-9 shows that nothing changed for traffic in VSAN 20. This example also exhibits the FSPF behavior when two links from PortChannel 10 are disabled.

Example 10-9 *MDS-A Routing Table for VSAN 20 and Link Failure*

```
! Verifying VSAN 20 routing table
MDS-A(config)# show fcroute unicast vsan 20

D:direct   R:remote   P:permanent   V:volatile   A:active   N:non-active
                                                       # Next
Protocol   VSAN      FC ID/Mask          RCtl/Mask     Flags   Hops   Cost
--------   ----      ----------------    ---------     -----   ----   ----
! Route to MDS-B
fspf       20        0x140000 0xff0000   0x00 0x00     D P A   1      166
! Route to MDS-CORE
fspf       20        0xed0000 0xff0000   0x00 0x00     D P A   1      416
! Disabling two interfaces from PortChannel 10
MDS-A(config)# interface fc1/8-9
MDS-A(config-if)# shutdown
! A failure within a PortChannel does not change in the FSPF routes
MDS-A(config-if)# show fcroute unicast vsan 20

D:direct   R:remote   P:permanent   V:volatile   A:active   N:non-active
                                                       # Next
Protocol   VSAN      FC ID/Mask          RCtl/Mask     Flags   Hops   Cost
--------   ----      ----------------    ---------     -----   ----   ----
fspf       20        0x140000 0xff0000   0x00 0x00     D P A   1      166
fspf       20        0xed0000 0xff0000   0x00 0x00     D P A   1      416
```

Differently from Ethernet PortChannels, Fibre Channel PortChannels do not change their cost values when individual links fail. As a result, fabric overall stability is increased with ISL aggregation.

The fact that each VSAN is running its own FSPF process brings great flexibility to SAN administrators. More specifically, it presents a simple way to deploy traffic engineering over physical fabrics.

VSAN Scoping

NX-OS does not deploy management plane virtualization on VSANs, because its configuration shell process is shared by all virtual fabrics. However, to avoid misconfiguration and nonauthorized access, it is possible to restrict which VSANs an administrator (or administrative team) can access.

For example, imagine that you want to assign a team configuration access to VSANs 10 to 19. In this case, a *role* can be configured to restrict their configuration commands to such VSANs.

Example 10-10 details a sample role configuration (VSAN1X-ADMIN) and a sample console access for a user that belongs to this role (admin1x).

Example 10-10 *VSAN Scope in MDS-CORE*

```
! Creating role VSAN1X-ADMIN
MDS-CORE# show running-config | begin "role name VSAN1X-ADMIN" next 9
! Allowing all commands for this role
role name VSAN1X-ADMIN
  rule 5 permit show
  rule 4 permit exec
  rule 3 permit debug
  rule 2 permit config
  rule 1 permit clear
! Allowing only VSANs 10 to 19 for this role
  vsan policy deny
    permit vsan 10-19
username admin password [suppressed] role network-admin
! Creating user admin20 that belongs to role VSAN1X-ADMIN
username admin1x password [suppressed]  role VSAN1X-ADMIN
! Leaving the session and logging in as user admin10
MDS-CORE# exit
User Access Verification
MDS-CORE login: admin1x
Password:
Cisco Nexus Operating System (NX-OS) Software
[output suppressed]
! This user can only configure parameters from VSANs 10 to 19
MDS-CORE(config)# zone name test vsan 20
% VSAN permission denied
MDS-CORE(config)# interface fc1/24
MDS-CORE(config-if)# fspf cost 99 vsan 20
% VSAN permission denied
SAN-CORE(config-if)# zone name test vsan 10
SAN-CORE(config-zone)# exit
```

```
SAN-CORE(config)# interface fc1/24
SAN-CORE(config-if)# fspf cost 99 vsan 10
SAN-CORE(config-if)#
```

Consequently, VSANs can also help SAN administrators to deploy distinct management domains. Configuration access through graphical user interfaces, such as the Cisco Prime Data Center Network Manager for SAN (DCNM-SAN), can be also restricted by VSAN scopes.

Figures 10-19 and 10-20 propose an interesting "spot-the-difference" game for you. Figure 10-19 depicts the DCNM-SAN client "All VSANs" view for an administrative user account that has no VSAN restrictions.

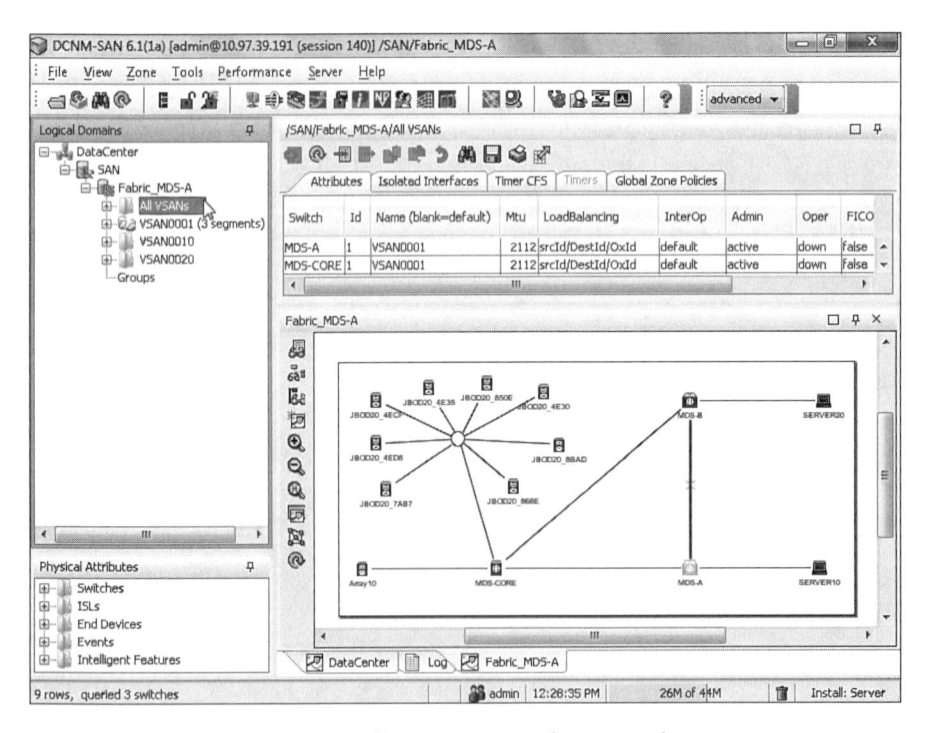

Figure 10-19 *DCNM-SAN "All VSANs" View for User admin*

User admin1x (which is associated with role VSAN1X-ADMIN on all switches) has a distinct All VSANs view, as shown by Figure 10-20.

Differently from users without any VSAN scoping, user admin1x can only visualize and configure VSANs defined in the 10 to 19 range. Therefore, only VSAN 10 is available on our current fabric configuration for this user DCNM-SAN client session.

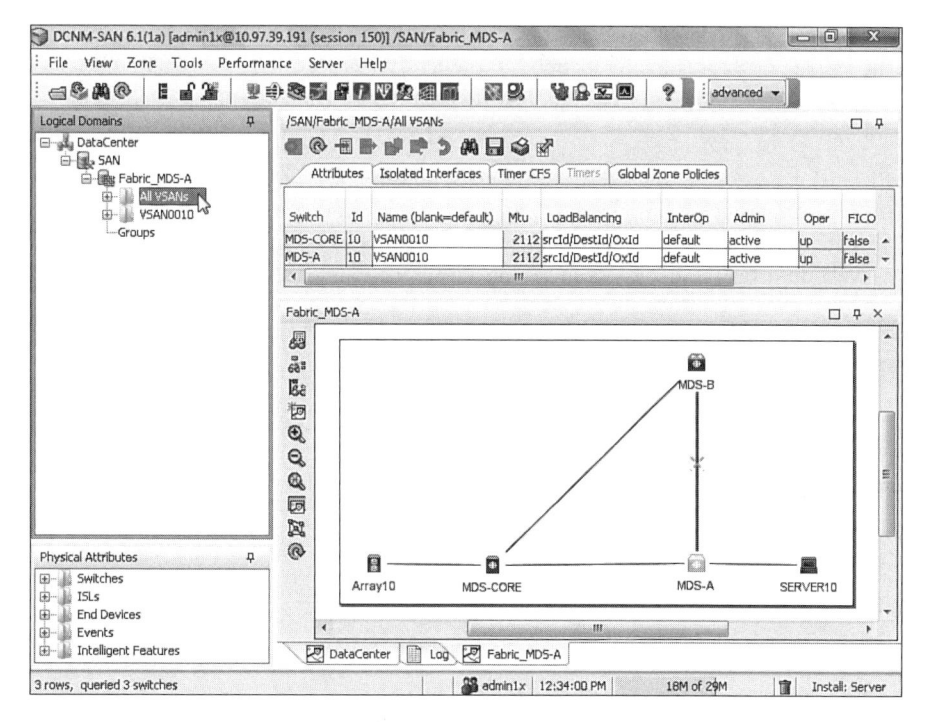

Figure 10-20 *DCNM-SAN "All VSANs" View for User admin1x*

> **Note** To reduce operational tasks and increase security on a SAN administration, I highly recommend that you deploy centralized user administration through authentication, authorization, and accounting (AAA) servers, such as RADIUS or TACACS+.

Use Case: SAN Consolidation

Because the *N* in SAN stands for *network*, the management team from a well-known company wants to hire your network consulting firm to help them consolidate their multiple SAN islands. This is a strategic customer for your company, therefore you accept the challenge by yourself.

After the current topology presentation meeting, you realize that almost all of the customer's SAN islands follow the traditional design of two physical fabrics. Here is the summary of your meeting notes:

- **Production SAN:** This is the company's workhorse SAN. It provides redundant access to the production storage array and contains the largest number of servers. It has been suffering scalability problems because it is built with interconnected 24-port switches. It is controlled by the storage administration team.

- **Backup SAN:** Also controlled by the storage team, this single-switch island connects selected production servers to a tape library with one NL_Port.

- **Database SAN:** This is maintained by the Database team. Because the FCID from the storage ports are already mapped to the RISC server's operating system, both 16-port switches must not change their domain ID (0x01 and 0x02) after the consolidation.

- **Extension SAN:** This is used for the synchronous replication of data on both arrays to a secondary site 50 kilometers away. The 2-Gbps Fibre Channel switches on the secondary site will not be consolidated, and they should maintain their domain IDs as well (unfortunately, they also use domain IDs 0x1 and 0x2).

Figure 10-21 is a slide taken from the customer presentation. It represents a view from its current SAN islands.

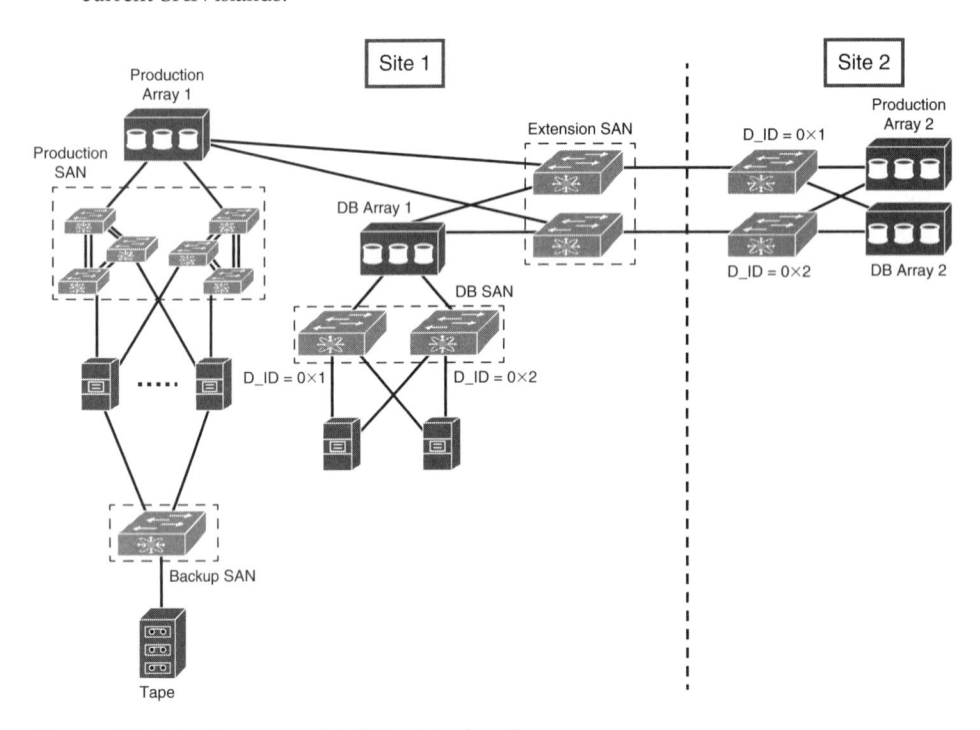

Figure 10-21 *Customer SAN "Archipelago"*

After one week, you advise the customer that it is possible to consolidate all its SAN islands into a pair of MDS 9000 directors. You defend that this decision will maintain their redundant physical fabric configuration, eliminate internal ISLs, and increase the overall SAN scalability to more than 1000 ports.

As the basis for your solution, VSANs must be deployed to guarantee the distinct environment requirements on each (virtual) SAN island. For example:

- **Production VSAN:** Its growth can benefit from the director's modular scalability. One VSAN is defined on each director to deploy this environment.

- **Backup VSAN:** This virtual SAN must be only present on a single director.
- **Database VSAN:** This VSAN is present on both switches and controlled by a completely different group of administrators (a role with a VSAN scope can be created on both switches to control a single VSAN in each director). It has static domain addresses (0x01 and 0x02) defined with the **fcdomain domain** command. The FLOGI for the storage ports is also statically assigned within each VSAN.
- **Extension VSAN:** This virtual SAN is present on both switches and has 2-Gbps ISLs (with more than 52 BB_Credits in each port) with legacy switches. This VSAN must be configured with the interoperability mode recommended in the most recent MDS interoperability matrix.

Figure 10-22 portrays your proposal to the company's new consolidated SAN.

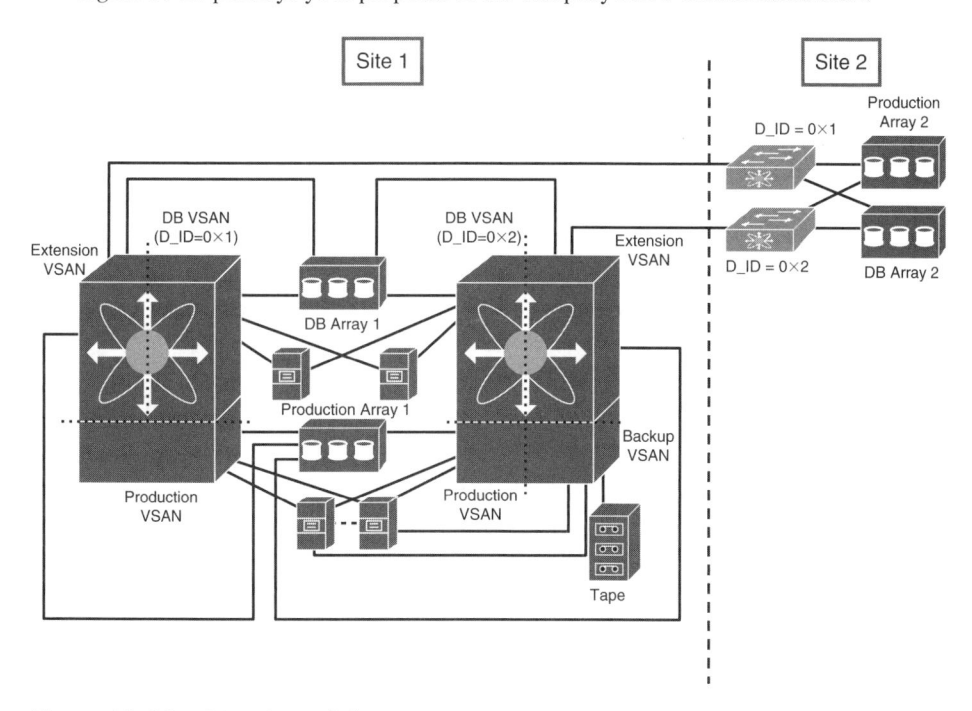

Figure 10-22 *SAN Consolidation*

You also recommend to the company that each VSAN must have a unique identifier (for example, the VSAN 101 is the production VSAN in one director and VSAN 201 performs the same function on the other). This procedure avoids any fabric merge problems should someone mistakenly connect both directors with an EISL.

In the company's opinion, your design brings elegance to its SAN environment because all its storage access communication runs over two very reliable director-class switches. The executives also remark that ISL bottlenecks will no longer have to be handled.

After you leave the room, your "nailed it!" scream is almost heard by the members of the storage team.

Summary

In this chapter you learned the following:

- Fibre Channel protocols are organized into five layers and use physical and administrative addresses (WWNs and FCIDs, respectively).

- Fibre Channel fabrics deploy distributed processes such as fabric initialization, state change notification, name service, routing, and zoning.

- SAN islands are usually deployed to guarantee isolation between different application environments.

- VSANs are virtual fabrics deployed in hardware on NX-OS switches. They allow SAN islands to be consolidated within the same physical fabric.

Figure 10-23 illustrates how VSANs can be logically understood from a logical perspective.

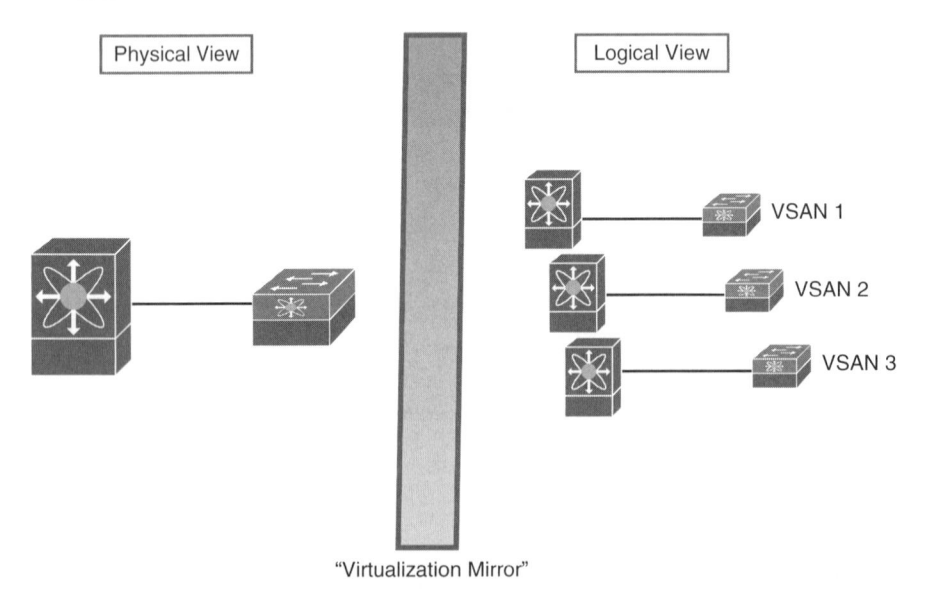

Figure 10-23 *Through the Virtualization Mirror*

Further Reading

Farley, Marc. *Storage Networking Fundamentals.* Cisco Press, 2004.

Clark, Tom. *Designing Storage Area Networks (2nd Edition).* Addison-Wesley Professional, 2003.

T11 Fibre Channel Standards Guest Page

www.t11.org/t11/hps.nsf/guesthome766kx

Cisco Data Center Interoperability Support Matrix

www.cisco.com/en/US/docs/switches/datacenter/mds9000/interoperability/matrix/intmatrx.html

Chapter 11

Secret Identities

"The value of identity of course is that so often with it comes purpose."
(Richard R. Grant)

This chapter explores three SAN virtualization techniques that can help enable data protection, increase storage device utilization, and scale Fibre Channel fabrics. They are

- Fibre Channel over IP (FCIP)
- Inter-VSAN Routing (IVR)
- N_Port Virtualization (NPV)

Table 11-1 positions FCIP, IVR, and NPV in the virtualization taxonomy described in Chapter 1, "Virtualization History and Definitions."

Table 11-1 *Virtualization Techniques Classification*

Virtualization Characteristics	FCIP	IVR	NPV
Emulation	Fibre Channel physical media	N_Ports from local VSAN	Host bus adapter
Type	Abstraction	Abstraction	Abstraction
Subtype	Structural	Structural with optional address remapping (FCID)	Structural with optional address remapping (pWWN)
Scalability	Three tunnels per Gigabit Ethernet interface	20,000 IVR zone members, 8000 zones, 32 IVR zone sets per physical fabric[1]	105 NPV switches per core, 2000 FLOGIs per core, 400 FLOGIs per linecard[1]

Virtualization Characteristics	FCIP	IVR	NPV
Technology Area	Storage networking	Storage networking	Storage networking
Subareas	Data plane	Control and data plane	Control and data plane
Advantages	SAN extension over great distances, optical media offload, lower cost	Device port sharing over multiple VSANs, failure domain isolation in SAN extensions	Domain ID reduction, operation simplicity, switch interoperability simplification

[1] Values at the time of this writing. Please refer to Appendix A, "Cisco Data Center Portfolio," for more details and the Cisco online documentation for updated information.

Like superheroes, sometimes Fibre Channel fabric switches must disguise themselves to provide protection and stability to the ones close to them. And during the last decade, Cisco and other industry manufacturers have developed a series of "dissimulation" techniques that help storage-area networks (SAN) to reach distances and scale that were previously unimaginable.

Fibre Channel over IP (FCIP) allows the creation of another type of Fibre Channel interface: the Virtual Expansion Port (VE_Port). Such entities permit SANs to be extended using IP backbones, with several advantages over standard optical connections.

Inter-VSAN Routing (IVR) zones and connects specific nodes that reside on distinct VSANs as if they belonged to the same Fibre Channel fabric. Although IVR provides connectivity beyond the boundaries of a virtual SAN, it continues to maintain its control plane isolation.

Finally, N_Port Virtualization (NPV) scales the supported number of fabric switches in a single Fibre Channel fabric. With this virtualization technique, an edge switch emulates a simple server host bus adapter (HBA) to its connected fabric, suppressing processes such as Inter-Switch Link (ISL) formation and domain ID distribution.

As this chapter explains these technologies in detail, it will also present use cases to illustrate their applicability in data center SANs.

Fibre Channel over IP

Broadly speaking, SANs from different data center sites are connected to provide stored data availability. Through cross-site Fibre Channel ISLs, storage devices can replicate and back up critical data to remote secure locations, only to be accessed or restored in the case of a failure in the main facility.

However, Fibre Channel connections over optical media raise some practical challenges to SAN administrators, such as

- Cost
- Lack of service offer between sites
- Switch transceivers that support few tens of kilometers (for example, a long-wave transceiver can reach up to 10 km)
- Dense Wavelength Division Multiplexing (DWDM) systems distance limitations

These difficulties can be overcome (or, at least, be lessened) through Fibre Channel over IP (FCIP) tunnels, which are basically TCP connections that encapsulate Fibre Channel frames between two fabrics.

In 2004, IETF ratified FCIP with RFC 3821 (Fibre Channel over TCP/IP). At the same time, the T11 committee included FCIP on its FC-BB-2 (Fibre Channel Backbone 2nd Generation) standard.

Note The FC-BB standards define the function and mappings necessary to integrate Fibre Channel to networks that deploy other protocols, such as IP, Ethernet, or ATM.

Both publications dictate that an FCIP tunnel must be transparent to the SANs connected to each FCIP device. They also detail that an FCIP-enabled device must implement the following components:

- **FCIP Entity:** Responsible for the FCIP protocol exchanges on the IP network.
- **FC Entity:** The Fibre Channel–specific functional component that combines with an FCIP Entity to form an interface between a Fibre Channel fabric and an IP network.
- **FCIP Data Engine (FCIP_DE):** Part of an FCIP Entity that handles Fibre Channel frame encapsulation, decapsulation, and transmission of FCIP frames over a single TCP connection.
- **FCIP Link Endpoint (FCIP_LEP):** Element of an FCIP Entity that handles a single FCIP link and contains one or more FCIP_DEs.
- **Virtual E_Port (VE_Port):** Data-forwarding component of the FC Entity that emulates an E_Port.
- **Virtual ISL:** A logical ISL that connects two VE_Ports across a non–Fibre Channel link.
- **IP Network Interface:** Physical element that provides IP connectivity for the FCIP Entity.

Figure 11-1 portrays the elements of a sample connection between two FCIP-enabled switches. The figure also exhibits the protocol structure used in each part of the communication.

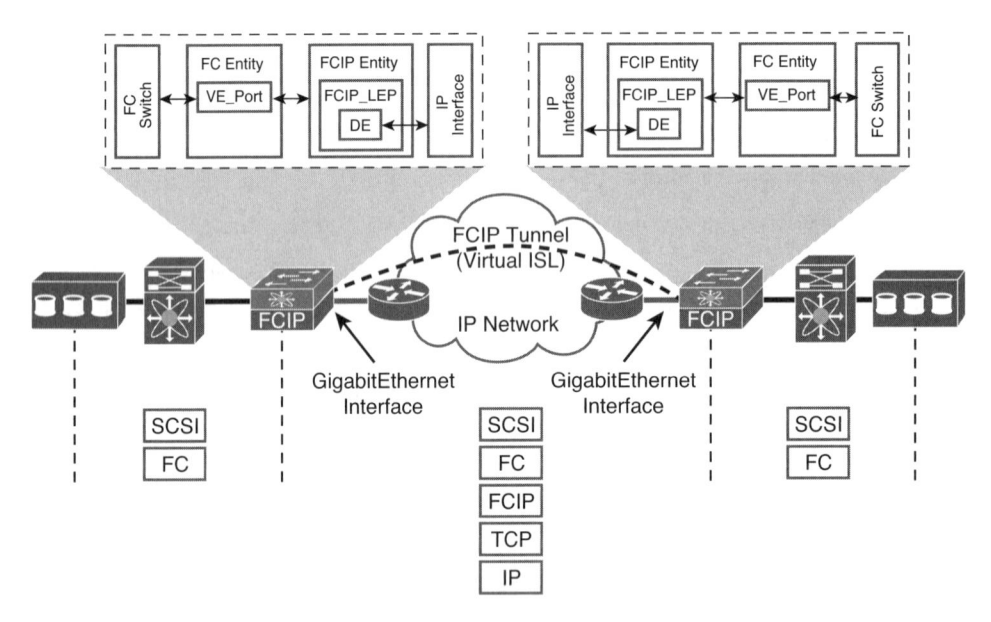

Figure 11-1 *FCIP Elements and Protocol Structure*

Tip Although the figure depicts Fibre Channel frames encapsulating SCSI communication, FCIP can also transport other upper-layer protocols such as IBM's Single-Byte Command Code Set (SBCCS).

On MDS 9000 switches, FCIP is deployed through Gigabit Ethernet interfaces that behave just like hosts connected to an IPv4 or IPv6 network. At the time of this writing, these interfaces can be found in modular fabric switches (such as MDS 9222i), or modules for MDS 9200 and 9500 series (such as SSN-16 and MSM-18/4).

Each of these interfaces can deploy up to three FCIP tunnels each, defined through different TCP ports. On each end device, an FCIP tunnel configuration demands two distinct elements:

- An **FCIP Profile**, which defines the IP tuning parameters of an FCIP tunnel.
- An **FCIP interface**, which represents a VE_Port. It refers to the FCIP profile that should be used, as peer information, and Fibre Channel ISL parameters (such as trunking mode and allowed VSAN list).

An FCIP interface has two TCP connections by default: one connection for data frames and another for Fibre Channel control frames. However, if desired, you can configure an FCIP interface to use a single TCP connection for both types of frames.

Figure 11-2 portrays two MDS 9000 switches that will soon negotiate and form an FCIP Virtual ISL. In the figure, the required IP routing configuration (interface IP address and a static route) is also displayed. And as you can verify, each switch is using a local router as an IP gateway to reach the remote switch's Gigabit Ethernet interface.

```
MDS-CORE# show running-config interface gigabitethernet 2/1
[output suppressed]
interface GigabitEthernet2/1
  ip address 192.168.1.1 255.255.255.0
  no shutdown
MDS-CORE# show running-config | include route
ip route 192.168.2.0 255.255.255.0 192.168.1.254 interface GigabitEthernet2/1
```

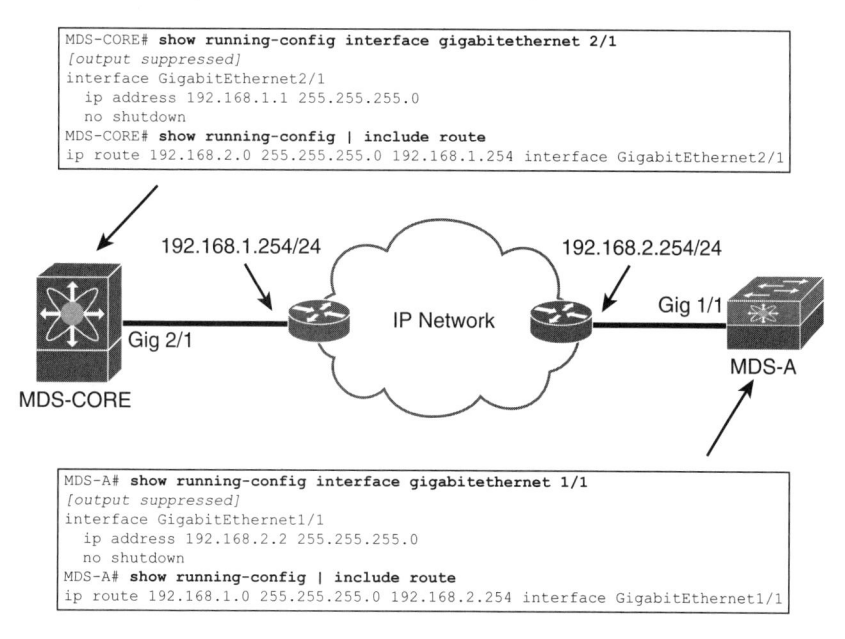

```
MDS-A# show running-config interface gigabitethernet 1/1
[output suppressed]
interface GigabitEthernet1/1
  ip address 192.168.2.2 255.255.255.0
  no shutdown
MDS-A# show running-config | include route
ip route 192.168.1.0 255.255.255.0 192.168.2.254 interface GigabitEthernet1/1
```

Figure 11-2 *FCIP Topology and Configuration Prerequisites*

Against this backdrop, Example 11-1 details a basic FCIP configuration in switch MDS-CORE.

> **Note** Although DCNM-SAN provides a very good wizard that facilitates FCIP tunnel configuration, in my opinion, the NX-OS command-line interface is a more effective tool to expose what is really happening "behind the scenes."

Example 11-1 *FCIP Configuration in MDS-CORE*

```
! Enabling FCIP processes in NX-OS
SAN-CORE(config)# feature fcip
! Creating an FCIP profile to define IP parameters
SAN-CORE(config)# fcip profile 1
! Linking the profile to interface GigabitEthernet 2/1
SAN-CORE(config-profile)# ip address 192.168.1.1
! Creating the VE_Port
SAN-CORE(config-profile)# interface fcip 100
! Using IP parameters defined in FCIP profile 1
SAN-CORE(config-if)# use-profile 1
```

```
! Defining the remote peer IP address (GigabitEthernet 1/1 on MDS-A)
SAN-CORE(config-if)# peer-info ipaddr 192.168.2.2
! Enabling the VE_Port
SAN-CORE(config-if)# no shutdown
```

Meanwhile, on the other side of the IP network, a very similar configuration is performed in MDS-A. Example 11-2 exhibits such a procedure, as well as the resulting FCIP interface status.

Example 11-2 *FCIP Configuration and FCIP Interface Status in MDS-A*

```
! Very similar configuration, except for the IP addresses and interface indexes
MDS-A(config)# feature fcip
MDS-A(config)# fcip profile 2
MDS-A(config-profile)# ip address 192.168.2.2
MDS-A(config-profile)# interface fcip 200
MDS-A(config-if)# use-profile 2
MDS-A(config-if)# peer-info ipaddr 192.168.1.1
MDS-A(config-if)# no shutdown
! Consequently, the Virtual ISL is active and using the default parameters of a E_
Port
MDS-A# show interface fcip 200 brief

-------------------------------------------------------------------------------
Interface  Vsan  Admin  Admin    Status     Oper   Profile  Eth Int           Port-channel
                 Mode   Trunk               Mode
                        Mode
-------------------------------------------------------------------------------
fcip200    1     auto   on       trunking   TE     2        GigabitEthernet1/1  --
```

From this moment on, you can configure each FCIP interface as a standard Fibre Channel E_Port. To demonstrate that, Example 11-3 disables trunk negotiation on interface fcip100 (on MDS-CORE) and restricts the VSANs that are allowed to use this interface.

Tip Consider that VSANs 1 (default VSAN for the VE_Ports), 10, and 20 are already operational on both switches.

Example 11-3 *FCIP Configuration in MDS-CORE*

```
! Configuring interface fcip 100 as a trunk VE_Port allowing VSANs 10 and 20
MDS-CORE(config)# interface fcip 100
MDS-CORE(config-if)# switchport mode E
```

```
MDS-CORE(config-if)# switchport trunk mode on
MDS-CORE(config-if)# switchport trunk allowed vsan 10
MDS-CORE(config-if)# switchport trunk allowed vsan add 20
```

If a similar configuration is executed in interface fcip200 on MDS-A, it is possible to monitor which VSANs are using the FCIP tunnel as an ISL.

Example 11-4 exhibits the status of interface fcip100 on MDS-CORE. It also unveils very interesting details about the established FCIP tunnel.

Example 11-4 *Interface fcip100 Status in MDS-CORE*

```
MDS-CORE# show interface fcip 100
fcip100 is trunking
    Hardware is GigabitEthernet
[output suppressed]
! This speed is used for default FSPF cost calculation
    Speed is 1 Gbps
! VSAN status on the trunk
    Trunk vsans (admin allowed and active)  (10,20)
    Trunk vsans (up)                        (10,20)
    Trunk vsans (isolated)                  ()
    Trunk vsans (initializing)              ()
[output suppressed]
! This fcip tunnel is using two connections
    TCP Connection Information
      2 Active TCP connections
        Control connection: Local 192.168.1.1:65395, Remote 192.168.2.2:3225
        Data connection: Local 192.168.1.1:65397, Remote 192.168.2.2:3225
[output suppressed]
```

From Example 11-4, you can observe that this 1-Gbps ISL is allowing VSANs 10 and 20 to merge. Additionally, the **show interface** command exposes the number of TCP connections the FCIP interface is using, as well as the involved IP addresses and TCP ports.

Even if the **show interface** command output in Example 11-4 were shown in its complete form, you would not find any reference to the number of buffer-to-buffer credits of an FCIP interface (in truth, you cannot configure it either). The reason is simple enough: Although the FCIP standards recommend that both TCP and BB_Credits flow control methods should work in concert, TCP is actually the transport protocol that will provide reliability to the encapsulated data (Fibre Channel). With another protocol handling error detection and retransmission, the VE_Ports are preset by default with enough BB_Credits to fill any supported TCP connection "pipe."

Note Cisco MDS 9000 switches support up to 100 milliseconds of round-trip time and 0.5% of packet drop probability on FCIP connections.

An FCIP profile configuration in MDS 9000 allows an admirable control over the IP parameters of a tunnel, such as

- FCIP TCP port configuration
- Minimum amount of time TCP waits before a segment retransmission
- Tunnel keepalive timeout
- Maximum number of times a segment is retransmitted before TCP decides to close the connection
- Automatic maximum transfer unit (MTU) path discovery (RFC 1191)
- Selective acknowledgments of isolated segments on a transmitted window (RFCs 2018 and 2883)
- Maximum bandwidth and minimum available bandwidth for the connection (traffic shaping)
- Hardware-based data compression with deflate algorithm (RFC 1951) and encryption with IPsec (RFC 4301 and many others)
- FCIP Write Acceleration and Tape Acceleration to minimize the high latency effects of IP links for such ULP operations.

The detailed explanation of each parameter configuration is beyond the scope of this book. Therefore, I recommend that you refer to Cisco online documentation for more specific information.

FCIP High Availability

In FCIP, the simultaneous use of two network technologies (Fibre Channel and IP) permit SAN administrators to choose between two redundancy mechanisms. Consequently, *Virtual Router Redundancy Protocol (VRRP)* and *Fibre Channel PortChannels* can be used to increase the availability of FCIP tunnels on MDS 9000 switches.

Deploying VRRP, a SAN administrator can select another Gigabit Ethernet interface (in the same switch or not) to work as a standby port, should a failure occur with an active interface. For that intent, a VRRP group must be configured on both interfaces, defining a virtual IP address that will be used by other FCIP peers.

Tip Currently standardized in RFC 5798, VRRP is a first-hop routing protocol (FHRP) that shares a lot of similarities with the Cisco Hot Standby Router Protocol (HSRP). If you want to review how an FHRP works, a more detailed description of HSRP is included on Chapter 1.

Figure 11-3 shows the required configuration of two Gigabit Ethernet interfaces, from distinct switches, sharing a VRRP group. Using the same topology from previous examples, another FCIP tunnel was established between MDS-CORE (using FCIP interface 101) and MDS-A (using FCIP interface 201). An additional switch (MDS-BACKUP) has a Gigabit Ethernet interface that will act as a backup for Gigabit Ethernet 2/2 on MDS-CORE.

```
MDS-CORE# show running-config interface gigabitethernet 2/2
[output suppressed]
interface GigabitEthernet2/2
  ip address 10.1.1.1 255.255.255.0
  no shutdown
  vrrp 1
    priority 1
    address 10.1.1.100
    no shutdown
```

```
MDS-BACKUP# show running-config interface gigabitethernet 2/3
[output suppressed]
interface GigabitEthernet2/3
  ip address 10.1.1.11 255.255.255.0
  no shutdown
  vrrp 1
    priority 254
    address 10.1.1.100
    no shutdown
```

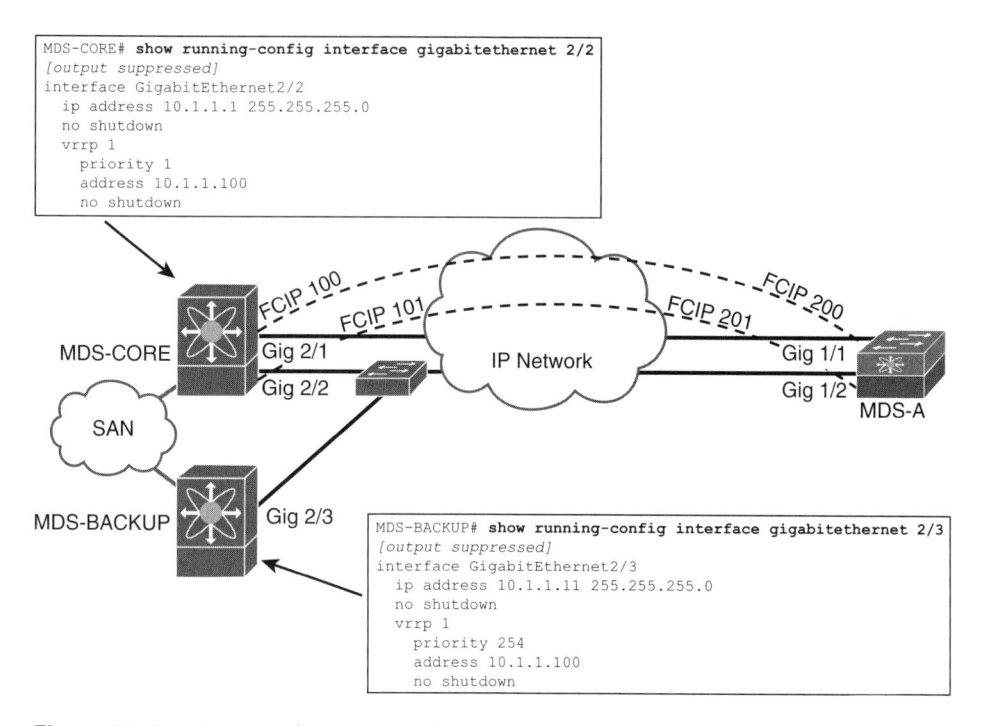

Figure 11-3 *VRRP and FCIP Tunnels*

Because it has a higher priority value (254), interface Gigabit Ethernet 2/3 on MDS-BACKUP will become the active member of VRRP group 1 if, for any reason, interface Gigabit Ethernet 2/2 on MDS-CORE fails. In this situation, MDS-BACKUP assumes the traffic sent to the virtual IP address 10.1.1.100.

Hence, to provide redundancy to the newly added FCIP tunnel, MDS-CORE and MDS-BACKUP must include the **ip address 10.1.1.100** command in their corresponding FCIP profiles. Also, the FCIP interface configuration for the second Virtual ISL in MDS-A must have the **peer-info ipaddr 10.1.1.100** command.

With these arrangements, MDS-BACKUP can provide FCIP redundancy between MDS-A and the SAN located on the left side of Figure 11-3. Other VRRP features, such as interface tracking and preemption, are also available on MDS 9000 Gigabit Ethernet interfaces.

Additionally, VE_Ports can also be bundled in PortChannels to increase the availability of an FCIP-based SAN extension. Figure 11-4 portrays the configuration of PortChannel 50, which aggregates both established FCIP tunnels between MDS-CORE and MDS-A.

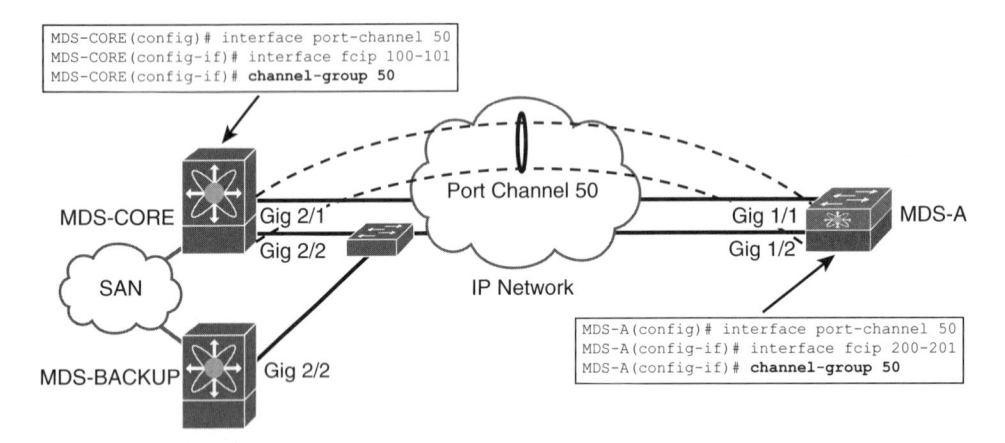

```
MDS-CORE(config)# interface port-channel 50
MDS-CORE(config-if)# interface fcip 100-101
MDS-CORE(config-if)# channel-group 50
```

```
MDS-A(config)# interface port-channel 50
MDS-A(config-if)# interface fcip 200-201
MDS-A(config-if)# channel-group 50
```

Figure 11-4 *FCIP PortChannels*

The same prerequisites for standard Fibre Channel PortChannels apply here (the interfaces must have the same configuration, such as VSAN, trunk mode, and so on). The default Fabric Shortest Path First (FSPF) cost (which is 500, in this scenario) is also derived from the total aggregated interface bandwidth, and the load balance method (flow or exchange-based) is similarly defined per VSAN.

In Figure 11-4, as a final result, a failure in interface Gigabit Ethernet 2/2 on MDS-CORE will activate an FCIP tunnel between MDS-BACKUP and MDS-A. Meanwhile, PortChannel 50 will remain active, because another Virtual ISL is still operational between MDS-CORE and MDS-A.

Use Case: SAN Extension with Traffic Engineering

From an FSPF perspective, an FCIP tunnel works exactly as a 1-Gbps Fibre Channel ISL. However, considering that IP connections can reach tens of milliseconds of latency, they might not be appropriate for every single data protection solution (for example, synchronous replications).

This characteristic should not stop you from using FCIP Virtual ISLs for other disaster recovery techniques, such as asynchronous replication or backup. Actually, if you concurrently use Fibre Channel and FCIP in your SAN extension, chances are you will spend less money on the entire solution.

Illustrating this argument, Figure 11-5 exhibits a single extension fabric connecting SANs that belong to two different sites. In the figure, VSAN 10 is defined to transport the synchronous replication traffic, while VSAN 20 is connecting the asynchronous replication and backup-related devices.

> **Tip** For the sake of clarity, Figure 11-5 does not depict the recommended redundant SAN extension fabric.

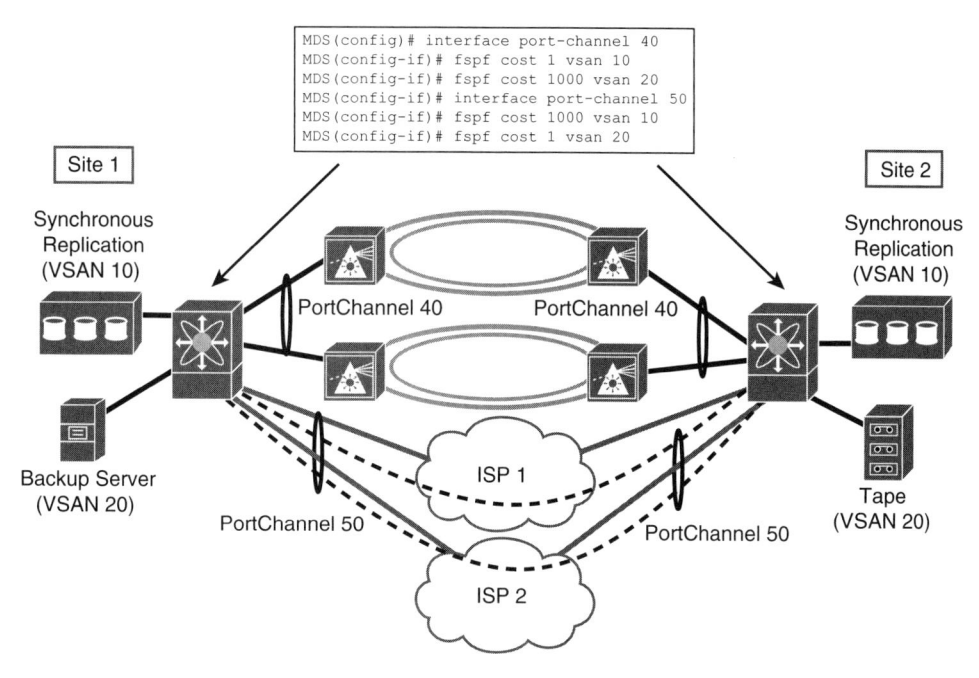

```
MDS(config)# interface port-channel 40
MDS(config-if)# fspf cost 1 vsan 10
MDS(config-if)# fspf cost 1000 vsan 20
MDS(config-if)# interface port-channel 50
MDS(config-if)# fspf cost 1000 vsan 10
MDS(config-if)# fspf cost 1 vsan 20
```

Figure 11-5 *FCIP and Traffic Engineering*

As you can notice, the extension fabric in Figure 11-5 is primed for maximum availability because it is using redundant optical paths and separate IP service providers (ISP) for FCIP tunnels.

In this design, PortChannel 40 aggregates two Fibre Channel links that are using both DWDM systems (which also have ring redundancy, in case of a path failure). Similarly, PortChannel 50 is comprised of two FCIP Virtual ISLs that are using one service provider each.

> **Tip** If a single private network is providing IP connectivity in your scenario, I recommend that you configure routing protocols to form at least two distinct paths for each FCIP tunnel on a PortChannel.

Because both PortChannels are configured as trunks, they can transport traffic from VSAN 10 (synchronous replication) and VSAN 20 (which is responsible for the VSAN backup). Notwithstanding, if you tweak their FSPF costs exactly as shown in Figure 11-5, the following traffic behavior would be achieved:

- Synchronous replication traffic will preferentially use the low-latency path (PortChannel 40), because it has the lowest cost for VSAN 10.

- VSAN 20 is routed through the FCIP PortChannel.

As I have implied before, this design can save expensive DWDM resources for traffic that really requires their low-latency characteristics, while cheaper IP connections can be used for traffic that does not. In addition, the overall solution robustness is increased with PortChannels that are deployed on both connection types.

You must also be aware that FSPF will detour VSAN 20 traffic to PortChannel 40 if there is a general failure in the IP network. In this situation, I recommend that a quality of service (QoS) policy is deployed in the fabric to protect the synchronous replication traffic from bandwidth starvation.

Inter-VSAN Routing

As you have learned in Chapter 10, "Islands in the SAN," VSANs were primarily designed to define *virtual SAN islands* in a shared Fibre Channel infrastructure. Their control plane isolation guarantees that these virtual fabrics deploy distinct fabric processes, avoiding fate-sharing in the case of a failure or abnormal behavior.

However, a host or storage N_Port can only belong to a single VSAN. And this condition can force multiple access ports whenever servers from different VSANs are supposed to access a storage device.

To improve the utilization of storage array ports and enable the sharing of single-port devices (such as older tape libraries) between different VSANs, MDS 9000 switches can employ a feature called *Inter-VSAN Routing (IVR)*.

In a nutshell, IVR allows the transport of Fibre Channel frames between a pair of devices from distinct VSANs. Although IVR permits communication between selected nodes *without merging both virtual fabrics*, minimal control plane traffic is exchanged between them to allow selected device discovery, such as:

- Name service information

- Registered State Change Notification (RSCN)

- FSPF routing information

Figure 11-6 illustrates how two devices can transcend the reach of their VSANs through IVR.

In Figure 11-6, Array A and Server B must exchange Fibre Channel frames as if they were zoned together in the same fabric. Consequently, an *IVR zone* is built and activated in an *IVR zone set*. As a result, the IVR-enabled switch creates virtual devices in each VSAN and automatically zones them with the real devices to provide Fibre Channel visibility.

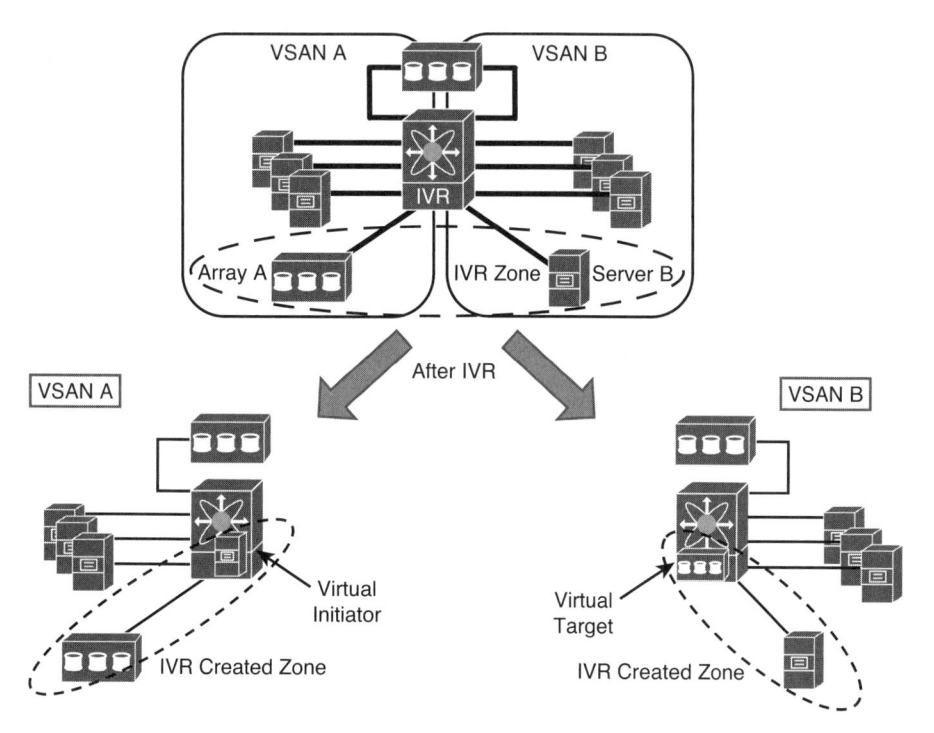

Figure 11-6 *Inter-VSAN Routing Example*

> **Note** IVR only uses port world wide name (pWWN) addresses to select devices from different VSANs and is completely compliant with the Fibre Channel standards.

To maintain the illusion to the devices that they are connected to the same fabric, the IVR-enabled switch *proxies* all communication received on a virtual device to its real counterpart from another VSAN. And as you will learn in the next sections, it can also adapt these frames before forwarding them.

IVR Infrastructure

Exploring the innards of IVR, I will use a configuration example. Our workbench is the topology shown in Figure 11-7, where the VSANs are already created on both MDS 9000 switches, and all depicted interfaces are configured accordingly.

In this topology, MDS-CORE will deploy IVR to transport Fibre Channel frames between Server30 (which is in VSAN 30) and Array10 (unsurprisingly, in VSAN 10). MDS-CORE can be also referred as a *border switch*, because it will be configured as an IVR-enabled switch that is a member of more than one VSAN.

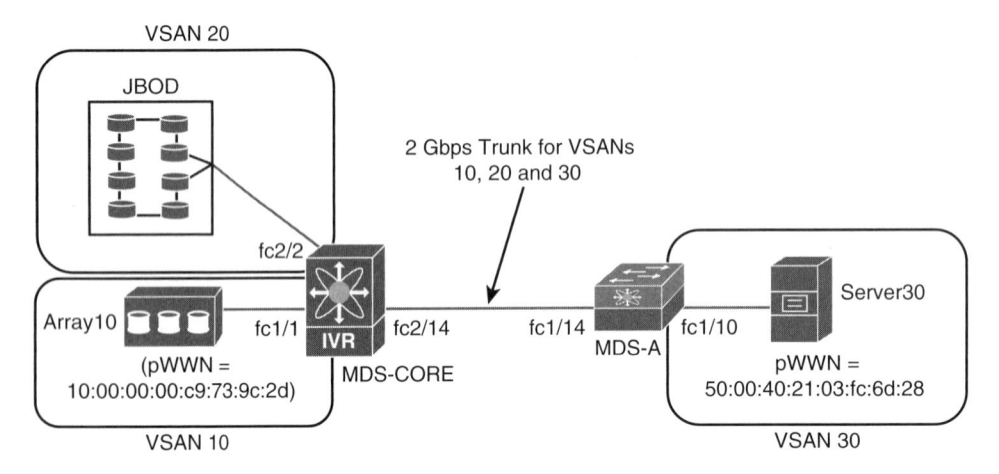

Figure 11-7 *IVR Topology*

Notwithstanding, before any IVR zoning operation, a SAN administrator must first configure the *IVR infrastructure* of a physical fabric. There are four steps involved with this procedure:

1. Enable the IVR processes on all border switches.

2. Enable *Cisco Fabric Services (CFS)* configuration distribution for IVR (this step is optional if there is only one border switch in the fabric).

> **Tip** If you recall from Chapter 6, "Fooling Spanning Tree," CFS is also used on the configuration virtual PortChannels (vPC). Actually, this protocol was designed to provide configuration synchronization for selected features on a SAN with multiple MDS 9000 switches. With CFS enabled on every IVR-enable switch, any additional IVR configuration must only be executed on a single device.

3. Enable IVR Network Address Translation (NAT) to avoid routing problems because of domain ID overlapping between different VSANs.

4. Create the IVR VSAN topology.

A *VSAN topology* defines the switches that provide a "meeting point" for the VSANs. This mapping permits the correct exchange of FSPF information about IVR-zoned nodes.

All four steps are detailed on Example 11-5, where MDS-CORE is configured as the only IVR-enabled switch in the fabric. Note that the example also exhibits the resulting VSAN topology.

> **Note** Although DCNM-SAN has a wizard to facilitate IVR configuration, I find that the NX-OS command-line interface is more effective in explaining what is really happening "behind the scenes."

Example 11-5 *IVR Infrastructure Configuration and IVR VSAN Topology*

```
! STEP 1: Enabling IVR on NX-OS
MDS-CORE(config)# feature ivr
! STEP 2: Enabling CFS distribution for IVR
MDS-CORE(config)# ivr distribute
! STEP 3: Enabling IVR NAT
MDS-CORE(config)# ivr nat
! If a new IVR configuration is performed on the fabric, CFS locks
all other border switches IVR configuration until an 'ivr
commit'command (or 'ivr abort') is performed.
fabric is now locked for configuration. Please 'commit' configuration when done.
! STEP 4: Automatically creating an IVR VSAN topology
MDS-CORE(config)# ivr vsan-topology auto
! Executing the IVR configuration on all border switches that are
using CFS and releasing the fabric from the configuration lock
MDS-CORE(config)# ivr commit
Verifying the discovered VSAN topology (* marks this switch sWWN)
MDS-CORE(config)# show ivr vsan-topology

AFID   SWITCH WWN                  Active    Cfg. VSANS
--------------------------------------------------------
   1   20:00:00:05:9b:7c:94:40 *   yes       no   1,10,20,30


Total:   1 entry in active and configured IVR VSAN-Topology
```

The **show ivr vsan-topology** command exposes that MDS-CORE (represented by its switch world wide name [sWWN] and marked with a star) is now the only border switch in the fabric. Furthermore, it is capable of actually deploying IVR between nodes on VSAN 1, 10, 20, or 30.

IVR Zoning

In our topology, because MDS-CORE was already defined as the "meeting point" of several VSANs, the fabric is already prepared to zone Server30 (from VSAN 30) and Array10 (from VSAN 10) together.

Before that operation, I suggest we proceed with an overview of both VSANs' status. For example, Example 11-6 exhibits their distributed name server information, as seen by MDS-CORE.

Example 11-6 *Name Server Database in VSANs 10 and 30*

```
MDS-CORE(config)# show fcns database vsan 10


VSAN 10:
--------------------------------------------------------------------------
FCID        TYPE   PWWN                     (VENDOR)        FC4-TYPE:FEATURE
--------------------------------------------------------------------------
! Array10 is connected to MDS-CORE (Domain ID is 0xd4 in VSAN 10)
0xd40000    N      50:00:40:21:03:fc:6d:28                  scsi-fcp:target

Total number of entries = 1
MDS-CORE(config)# show fcns database vsan 30


VSAN 30:
--------------------------------------------------------------------------
FCID        TYPE   PWWN                     (VENDOR)        FC4-TYPE:FEATURE
--------------------------------------------------------------------------
! Server30 is connected to MDS-A (Domain ID is 0x6b in VSAN 30)
0x6b0000    N      10:00:00:00:c9:73:9c:2d  (Emulex)        scsi-fcp:init

Total number of entries = 1
```

Example 11-7 details the required IVR zoning configuration. As you can see, this operation was designed to mimic the standard zoning operation on Cisco MDS 9000 switches.

Example 11-7 *IVR Zoning Configuration*

```
! Configuring an IVR zone
MDS-CORE(config)# ivr zone name SERVER30-ARRAY10
fabric is now locked for configuration. Please 'commit' configuration when done.
! Including Array10 in the IVR zone
MDS-CORE(config-ivr-zone)# member pwwn 50:00:40:21:03:fc:6d:28 vsan 10
! Including Server30 to the IVR zone
MDS-CORE(config-ivr-zone)# member pwwn 10:00:00:00:c9:73:9c:2d vsan 30
! Creating an IVR zone set
MDS-CORE(config-ivr-zone)# ivr zoneset name IVR-ZS
! Including IVR zone into the IVR zone set
MDS-CORE(config-ivr-zoneset)# member SERVER30-ARRAY10
! Activating IVR zone set
```

```
MDS-CORE(config-ivr-zoneset)# ivr zoneset activate name IVR-ZS
! Executing IVR configuration on all CFS-enabled border switches (only MDS-CORE, in
our scenario)
MDS-CORE(config)# ivr commit
commit initiated. check ivr status
! Verifying active IVR zone set on the physical fabric
MDS-CORE(config)# show ivr zoneset active
! Both devices are already logged to their respective VSANs, are
zoned together, and are using the  discovered VSAN topology
zoneset name IVR-ZS
  zone name SERVER30-ARRAY10
    * pwwn 50:00:40:21:03:fc:6d:28         vsan   10 autonomous-fabric-id  1
    * pwwn 10:00:00:00:c9:73:9c:2d         vsan   30 autonomous-fabric-id  1
```

After the IVR zone set is activated with the **ivr commit** command, several operations are executed automatically within the physical fabric:

- MDS-CORE chooses two virtual domains whose identifiers are not present at any VSAN. These identifiers will be used by IVR NAT in VSAN 10 and VSAN 30.
- Two FCIDs, derived from these domain IDs, are assigned to the virtual initiator in VSAN 10 and the virtual target in VSAN 30.
- Both virtual nodes are logged in to each VSAN, using the characteristics of the actual devices.
- An additional zone, between a virtual and physical device, is inserted in the active zone sets of each VSAN.

Example 11-8 shows all of these operations in VSANs 10 and 30 through a single command.

Tip Both VSANs must have previous active zone sets to accept the IVR zone insertion.

Example 11-8 *Zones Inserted by IVR on Each VSAN Active Zone Set*

```
! Verifying the active zone set in VSAN 10
MDS-CORE# show zoneset active vsan 10
[output suppressed]
! Inserted IVR zone
  zone name IVRZ_SERVER30-ARRAY10 vsan 10
! This is the real target
  * fcid 0xd40000 [pwwn 50:00:40:21:03:fc:6d:28]
! This is the virtual initiator. Please notice that its FCID was
translated by IVR NAT (from 0x6b0000 to 0xb10001)
```

```
  * fcid 0xb10001 [pwwn 10:00:00:00:c9:73:9c:2d]
! Verifying the active zone set in VSAN 30
MDS-CORE# show zoneset active vsan 30
zoneset name ZS30 vsan 30
[output suppressed]
! Inserted IVR zone
  zone name IVRZ_SERVER30-ARRAY10 vsan 30
! This is the virtual target. Please notice that its FCID was
translated by IVR NAT (from 0xd40000 to 0xc2c07b)
  * fcid 0xc2c07b [pwwn 50:00:40:21:03:fc:6d:28]
! This is the real initiator
  * fcid 0x6b0000 [pwwn 10:00:00:00:c9:73:9c:2d]
```

Enabling IVR between VSANs 10 and 30, MDS-CORE proxies all the communication between Server30 and Array10 through the virtual devices created by the IVR process. It must also advertise these new domain IDs into the FSPF process of each VSAN. This automatic operation guarantees that the frames can be correctly routed to MDS-CORE before they are transported to another VSAN.

Example 11-9 reveals how the virtualization trick is executed from a VSAN 10 perspective.

Example 11-9 *FSPF Route to Server30 in VSAN 10*

```
! Analyzing the route to Server30's translated Domain ID in VSAN 10
MDS-CORE# show fcroute unicast 0xb10000 0xff0000 vsan 10
! Domain ID 0xb1 is reachable through the IVR process (since MDS-CORE
is connecting both VSANs). IVR adds value 1 to the original cost
between MDS-CORE and MDS-A (500).
D:direct  R:remote  P:permanent  V:volatile  A:active  N:non-active
                                                    # Next
Protocol   VSAN      FC ID/Mask         RCtl/Mask     Flags   Hops   Cost
--------   ----      ---------------    ---------     -----   ----   ----
fspf       10        0xb10000 0xff0000  0x00 0x00     D P A    1     501
   ivr 212:177    Domain  0xb1(177)
```

Example 11-9 shows IVR NAT in action in VSAN 10. To reach Server30 (FCID 0xb10001), MDS-CORE must send frames directly to domain 0xb1 that is only reachable through the IVR process.

Pay attention to the fact that FSPF has injected this route into VSAN 10 with a cost value of 501: IVR always adds one unit to the total path cost of imported routes from other VSANs (think of it as a "toll tax" for the IVR "meeting point").

I have included Figure 11-8 as a visual aid to represent the VSAN 10 logical perspective from MDS-CORE.

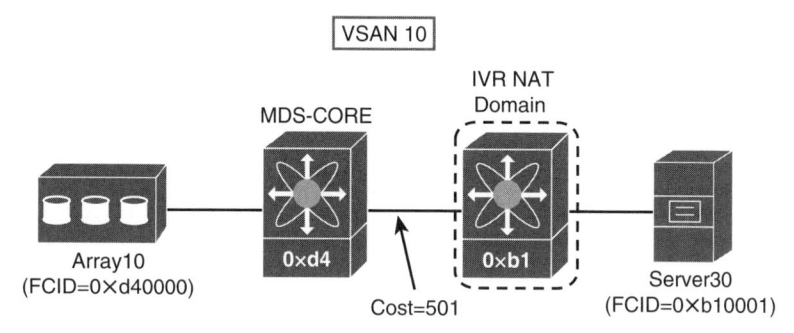

Figure 11-8 *VSAN 10 Perspective*

A little bit weird, right? Nevertheless, understand that this illusion is enough to make Server30 visible on VSAN 10.

Things are a little bit clearer if you observe the same consequences from a VSAN 30 perspective. For example, Example 11-10 exhibits the FSPF route generated by IVR in the MDS-A routing table.

Example 11-10 *FSPF Route to Array10 in VSAN 30*

```
! VSAN 30 routing table
MDS-A# show fcroute unicast vsan 30


D:direct   R:remote   P:permanent   V:volatile   A:active   N:non-active
                                                           # Next
Protocol   VSAN      FC ID/Mask          RCtl/Mask    Flags  Hops Cost
--------   ----      --------- --------  ---- ----    -----  ---- ----
local      30        0x6b0000  0xffffff  0x00 0x00    D P A  1    1
! IVR-generated route
fspf       30        0xc20000  0xff0000  0x00 0x00    R P A  1    501
! Route to MDS-CORE Domain ID in VSAN 30 (0xc7)
fspf       30        0xc70000  0xff0000  0x00 0x00    D P A  1    500
! Analyzing the route to Server30's translated Domain ID in VSAN 10
MDS-A# show fcroute unicast 0xc20000 0xff0000 vsan 30
! Domain ID 0xc2 is reachable through interface fc1/14 and Domain ID
0xc7. IVR adds value 1 to the original cost between MDS-CORE and MDS-A (500).
D:direct   R:remote   P:permanent   V:volatile   A:active   N:non-active
                                                           # Next
Protocol   VSAN      FC ID/Mask          RCtl/Mask    Flags  Hops Cost
--------   ----      --------- --------  ---- ----    -----  ---- ----
fspf       30        0xc20000  0xff0000  0x00 0x00    R P A  1    501
    fc1/14  Domain   0xc7(199)
```

In Example 11-10, you can find routes that point to the following VSAN 30 domains:

- **0x6b:** MDS-A domain in VSAN 30.
- **0xc2:** Domain generated by IVR NAT in MDS-CORE to contain the virtual target.
- **0xc7:** MDS-CORE's actual domain in VSAN 30.

Therefore, to reach domain 0xc2, MDS-A must send frames to domain 0xc7 first. And as expected, the injected FSPF route to 0xc2 is "taxed" with an additional cost of 1.

To help me explain how IVR NAT is working on VSAN 30, Figure 11-9 logically represents this MDS-A's point of view within this virtual fabric.

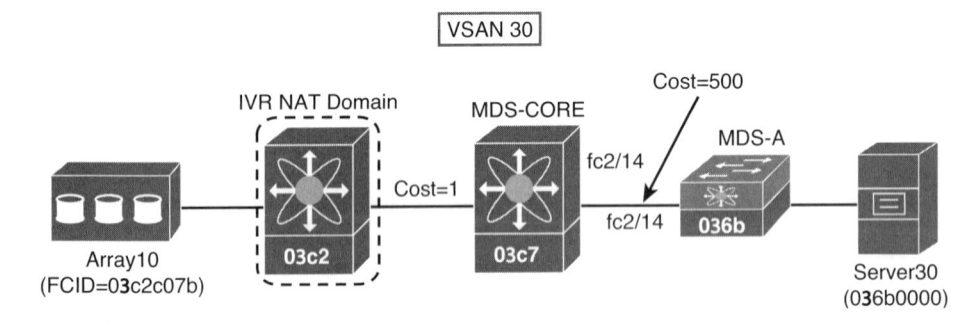

Figure 11-9 *VSAN 30 Perspective*

As with many other virtualization techniques, IVR executes several operations to transparently offer Fibre Channel connectivity between selected nodes from different VSANs. And more importantly, it does that without affecting the intended isolation of virtual SAN islands.

> **Note** You should always refer to the Cisco online documentation to check IVR (or any other MDS feature) configuration limits. At the time of this writing, MDS 9000 fabrics support 32 IVR zone sets, 8000 IVR zones, and 20,000 IVR zone members.

Use Case: Transit VSAN

Standard SAN extensions usually suffer from one paradoxical side effect: Fibre Channel fabric processes are shared between the main data center and its disaster recovery sites. This lack of isolation means that any control plane erratic behavior, caused by humans or not, can be extended to a remote location. In addition, an extension link failure can provoke fabric reinitialization and reconvergences, because the extended fabric principal switch can be only located at one site.

IVR provides an interesting way to provide the isolation between SANs from distinct sites. Through the use of *transit VSANs*, local virtual fabrics at each site (or edge

VSANs) are connected by another logical fabric that does not possess any real target or initiator. This entity simply supplies a data path for communication between both virtual SAN islands.

As an example, Figure 11-10 illustrates two edge VSANs (100 and 200) that contain storage arrays deploying data replication from Site 1 to Site 2. These devices are connected through a transit VSAN (999), which is only defined on the extension ISL.

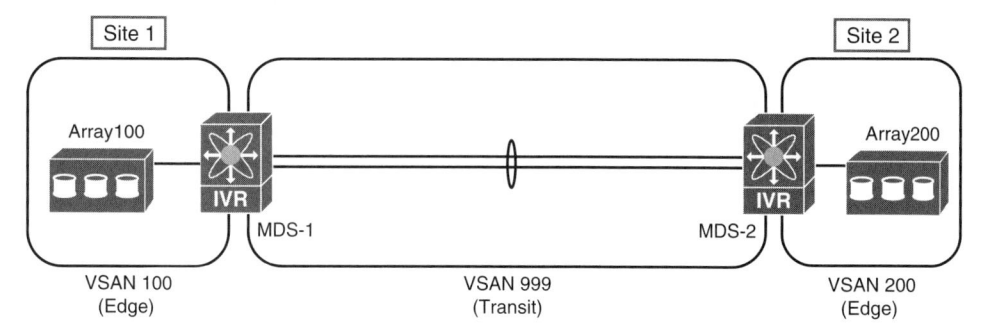

Figure 11-10 *SAN Extension with Transit VSAN*

At each data center site, a border switch will enable communication between its local and the transit VSAN. In Figure 11-10, while MDS-1 offers Fibre Channel connectivity for the arrays between Edge VSAN 100 and Transit VSAN 999, MDS-2 binds them between Transit VSAN 999 and Edge VSAN 200.

This design presents the following advantages over standard SAN extensions:

- Easy configuration based on IVR zoning of device pairs.
- Complete isolation of fabric processes between edge VSANs.
- It can be applied to any SAN extension media (optical or FCIP).
- Failures on transit VSAN do not imply instabilities on edge VSANs.
- IVR NAT guarantees that no domain ID overlapping occurs within the physical fabric.

N_Port Virtualization

In an exercise in humility, a Fibre Channel switch can scale the number of ports in a SAN when it is no longer a switch. But allow me to elaborate on this silicon-based existential crisis.

According to the INCITS T11 Fibre Channel standards, the number of domain IDs in a fabric is theoretically limited to 239. Nevertheless, there are much more strict limits in real-world scenarios, such as

- Legacy switches and directors with a limited number of supported domain IDs (up to 16 or 31) in the same fabric
- Storage and SAN manufacturer matrices defining an upper limit for the number of switches in a SAN (varying between 50 and 80)

Around the early 2000s, these values represented very reasonable boundaries for SANs. However, SAN administrators started to approach such limits in Core-Edge fabrics with top-of-rack and blade switches.

Figure 11-11 illustrates a Core-Edge SAN, where two types of edge switches are represented: top-of-rack and blade server switches.

Tip Note that I have depicted the blade server internal structure to show the similarities between both edge switch models.

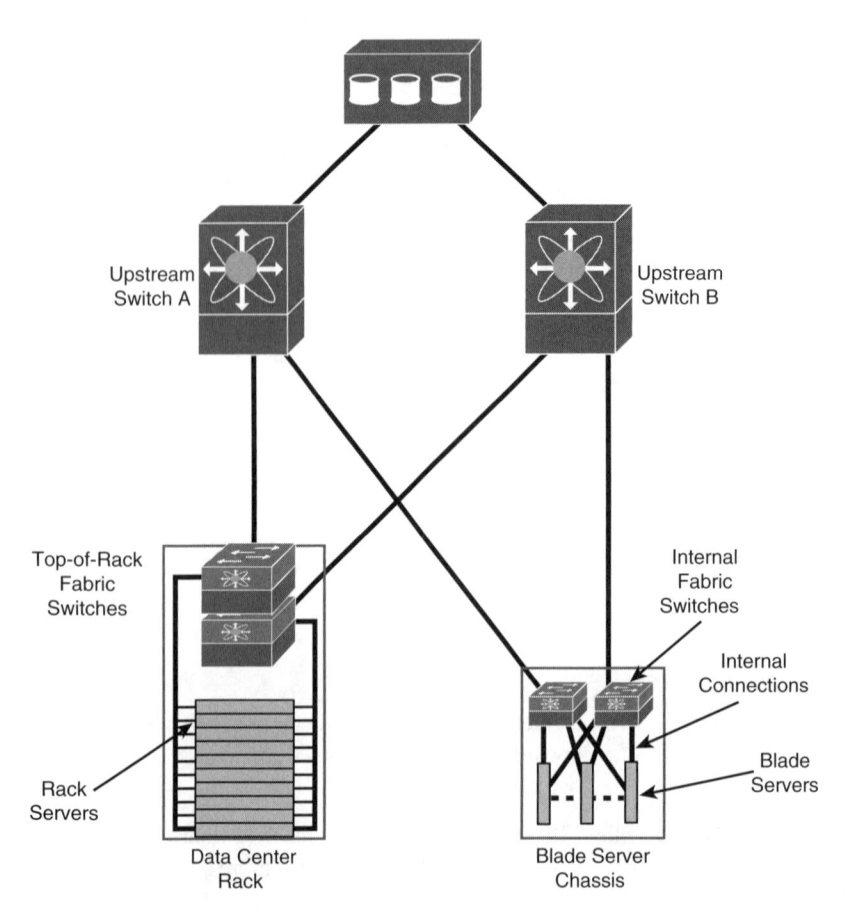

Figure 11-11 *Core-Edge SAN with Top-of-Rack and Blade Switches*

As discussed in Chapter 7, "Virtualized Chassis with Fabric Extenders," network cabling can be greatly simplified with top-of-rack designs. SANs can also leverage this advantage with the placement of fabric switches within the server racks. Also, blade server chassis have become an extremely popular solution because of their data center space savings and quick server provisioning features. These modular structures usually have internal fabric switches that offer external storage connectivity to their accommodated servers.

On both models, a fabric switch has the responsibility to connect tens of servers to one (or more) upstream Fibre Channel switches. Considering that modern directors can potentially have hundreds of Fibre Channel interfaces, it is fairly easy that a fabric can dangerously border on the aforementioned domain IDs limits.

N_Port Virtualization (NPV) is a mode that some NX-OS devices can deploy to avoid domain ID explosion in a fabric. Running in NPV mode, a fabric switch can emulate an N_Port connected to an upstream switch F_Port, hence, not deploying an ISL or spending an additional domain ID in the fabric.

Note At the time of this writing, the following Cisco fabric switches supported NPV mode: MDS 9100 Series, Cisco Fabric Switch for HP c-Class BladeSystem, Cisco Fabric Switch for IBM Blade Center, Nexus 5000, 5500, and 6000 switches.

Figure 11-12 details the differences between a standard ISL and an NPV connection.

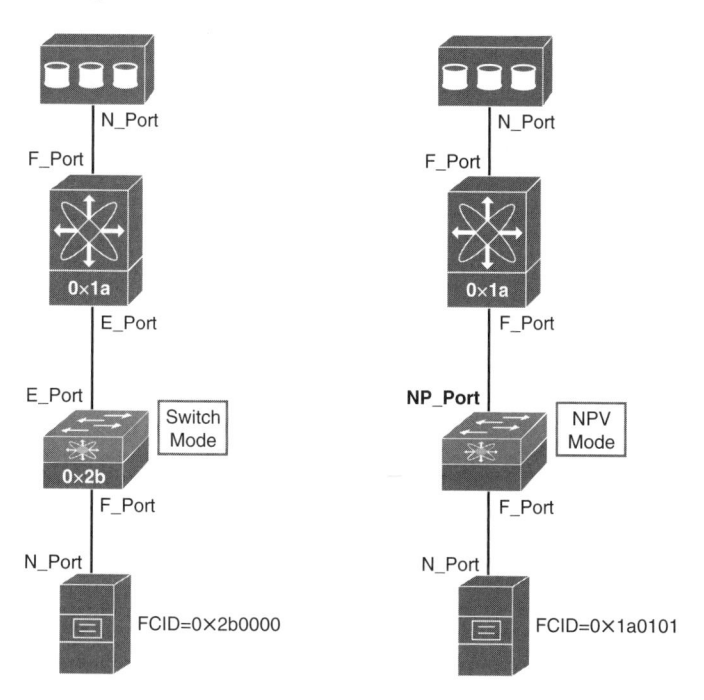

Figure 11-12 *Comparing ISLs to NPV Connections*

Unlike a standard ISL, an NPV-mode switch performs a fabric login (FLOGI) in an upstream switch through a Node Proxy Port (NP_Port), which receives an FCID in the upstream switch in response. Afterward, the NPV-mode switch uses this NP_Port to forward all FLOGIs from connected servers to the upstream switch. (In Figure 11-12, it is clear that the host connected to the NPV-mode switch received FCID 0x1a0101, which is derived from the core switch domain ID.)

An NPV connection requires that an upstream F_Port can receive and process more than one fabric login. To support such behavior, the upstream switch must deploy a capability called *N_Port ID Virtualization (NPIV)*. In an NPIV-enabled switch, a single F_Port can process one FLOGI from an N_Port and additional FDISCs (Discover F_Port service parameters) as if they were FLOGI frames from other N_Ports.

> **Note** NPIV is defined in the T11 Fibre Channel Link Services (FC-LS) standard series. It was originally created to permit logical partitions from a host to share the same physical HBA.

Therefore, the basic requirements of a NPV connection are

- The upstream switch must deploy NPIV.
- The NP_Port on the NPV-mode switch must perform a FLOGI in the upstream switch.
- All FLOGIs from nodes connected to the NPV-mode switch must be translated into FDISCs.

From an upstream switch perspective, the servers connected to the NPV-mode switch are seen as directly connected N_Ports. Meanwhile, the NPV-mode switch can be considered as a mere "bump in the road" for its connected nodes, not participating in any fabric process, such as zoning or FSPF.

One observation though: Traffic originated from a node connected to an NPV-mode switch is always forwarded to the upstream switch. Because NPV-mode switches do not deploy local switching of frames, the connection of locally accessed targets is not recommended.

Configuring N_Port Virtualization

Figure 11-13 depicts a fabric topology where MDS-CORE is the upstream switch and MDS-B will be configured in NPV mode. After MDS-B is correctly connected to MDS-CORE, the SAN administrator wants to zone Array10 (on VSAN 10) and Server10 (also on VSAN 10) together to provide storage access to the latter. Also, he expects to zone a second server to JBOD20 on VSAN 20 at a later time.

Chapter 11: Secret Identities 477

```
MDS-CORE(config)# feature npiv
MDS-CORE(config)# interface fc1/24
MDS-CORE(config-if)# switchport mode F
MDS-CORE(config-if)# no shutdown
```

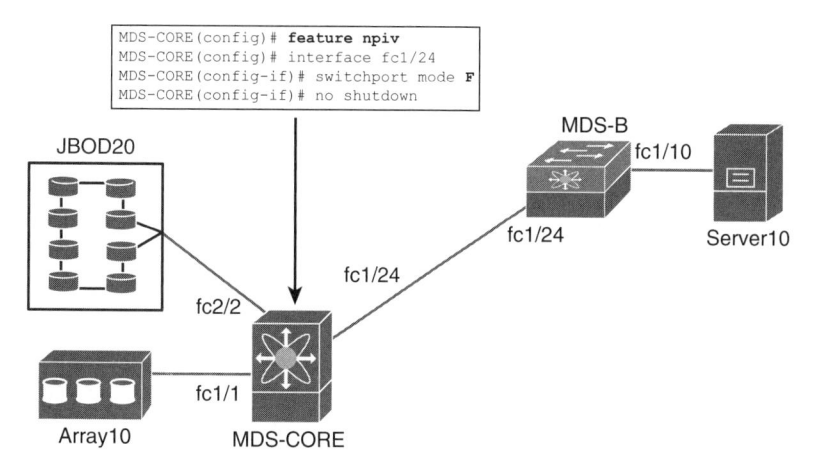

Figure 11-13 *NPV Topology and MDS-CORE Configuration*

In Figure 11-13, MDS-CORE is already configured to support the MDS-B FLOGI and subsequent FDISCs (which, from now on, I will generically refer to as FLOGIs) from its soon-to-be-connected servers.

Tip Although negotiable configurations (**switchport mode auto** or **switchport mode Fx**) are also supported on MDS-CORE, I will configure each port in nonautomatic mode to provide a clearer explanation of the process.

First, let's put MDS-B in NPV mode. Example 11-11 exhibits the output collected from a console access during this conversion.

Tip In an operational fabric switch, it is highly recommended that you previously save the running configuration before enabling NPV mode.

Example 11-11 *NPV Configuration and Status Checking*

```
! Enabling NPV mode in MDS-B
MDS-B(config)# feature npv
Verify that boot variables are set and the changes are saved.
Changing to npv mo
de erases the current configuration and reboots the switch in npv mode. Do you w
ant to continue? (y/n):y
! Switch reboots after confirmation

>> MDS-Bootloader-01.00.19 (Feb  1 2010 - 15:13:26), Build: 01.00.19
```

```
[output suppressed]
! After the boot, MDS-B still maintains its host name and admin credentials
User Access Verification
MDS-B login: admin
Password:
[output suppressed]
MDS-B#
```

Although the NPV-mode activation erases the device running configuration, several settings are preserved:

- Management interface IP address and default gateway
- Device name
- Local administrative accounts

Continuing the MDS-B NPV configuration, Example 11-12 depicts the configuration of two MDS-B interfaces: fc1/24 (as an NP_Port connected to MDS-CORE) and fc1/10 (as the F_Port connected to Server10).

Example 11-12 *NP_Port and F_Port Configuration and NPV-FLOGI Table in MDS-B*

```
! Configuring interface fc1/24 as Node Proxy Port to MDS-CORE
MDS-B(config)# interface fc1/24
MDS-B(config-if)# switchport mode NP
MDS-B(config-if)# no shutdown
! Configuring interface fc1/10 as Fabric Port to Server10 (FX or FL
configurations are not supported)
MDS-B(config-if)# interface fc1/10
!
MDS-B(config-if)# switchport mode F
MDS-B(config-if)# no shutdown
! Verifying how MDS-B handled Server10's FLOGI
MDS-B(config-if)# show npv flogi-table
--------------------------------------------------------------------------------
SERVER                                                             EXTERNAL
INTERFACE VSAN FCID         PORT NAME                NODE NAME      INTERFACE
--------------------------------------------------------------------------------
fc1/10     1    0x480021 10:00:00:00:c9:73:9c:2c 20:00:00:00:c9:73:9c:2c fc1/24
! Server belongs to VSAN 1 and is using fc1/24 as its associated NP_Port
Total number of flogi = 1.
```

Because MDS-CORE was already primed to receive FLOGIs from MDS-B, both MDS-B interfaces are active and Server10 is already visible through the **show npv flogi-table** command.

On the other side of the fiber, MDS-CORE receives both FLOGIs on the same interface, as shown in Example 11-13.

Example 11-13 *FLOGI and Name Server Database in MDS-CORE*

```
! Verifying FLOGI database
MDS-CORE# show flogi database
--------------------------------------------------------------------------------
INTERFACE        VSAN    FCID        PORT NAME                NODE NAME
--------------------------------------------------------------------------------
fc1/1            10      0xd40000    50:00:40:21:03:fc:6d:28  20:03:00:04:02:fc:6d:28
! Both FLOGIs in interface fc1/24 belong to VSAN 1
fc1/24           1       0x480020    20:18:00:0d:ec:47:e7:40  20:01:00:0d:ec:47:e7:41
fc1/24           1       0x480021    10:00:00:00:c9:73:9c:2c  20:00:00:00:c9:73:9c:2c
[output suppressed]
Total number of flogi = 11.
! Verifying Name Server database in VSAN 1
MDS-CORE# show fcns database vsan 1

VSAN 1:
--------------------------------------------------------------------------------
FCID         TYPE   PWWN                    (VENDOR)         FC4-TYPE:FEATURE
--------------------------------------------------------------------------------
! This entry was created during the FLOGI of interface fc1/24 on MDS-B...
0x480020     N      20:18:00:0d:ec:47:e7:40  (Cisco)          npv
! ... while this entry was generated by Server10's FLOGI
0x480021     N      10:00:00:00:c9:73:9c:2c  (Emulex)         scsi-fcp:init

Total number of entries = 2
```

It might be said that the NPV configuration has worked because interface fc1/24 on MDS-CORE accepted the FLOGIs from MDS-B NP_Port (fc1/24) and Server10. However, as you can observe, all mentioned interfaces remain on their default VSAN (1).

Although IVR could be deployed to zone Server10 and Array10 in this situation, the SAN administrator does not want to use VSAN 1 because of company policy reasons. Hence, the simplest way to connect both devices is to relocate Server10 to VSAN10.

Example 11-14 depicts the FLOGI database on MDS-CORE when its interface fc1/24 is placed on VSAN 10 (without any other additional changes on MDS-B).

Example 11-14 *Inserting Interface fc1/24 into VSAN 10*

```
MDS-CORE(config)# vsan database
MDS-CORE(config-vsan-db)# vsan 10 interface fc1/24
Traffic on fc1/24 may be impacted. Do you want to continue? (y/n) [n] y
! Checking updated FLOGI database
MDS-CORE(config-vsan-db)# show flogi database interface fc1/24
INTERFACE        VSAN     FCID         PORT NAME                  NODE NAME
--------------------------------------------------------------------------------
fc1/24           10       0xd40020     20:18:00:0d:ec:47:e7:40    20:0a:00:0d:ec:47:e7:41

Total number of flogi = 1.
```

If you are questioning yourself about the Server10 FLOGI, Example 11-15 presents the answer you are looking for.

Example 11-15 *Interface Status in MDS-B*

```
MDS-B# show interface fc1/10, fc1/24 brief

--------------------------------------------------------------------------------
Interface  Vsan  Admin   Admin   Status           SFP    Oper   Oper    Port
                 Mode    Trunk                           Mode   Speed   Channel
                         Mode                                   (Gbps)
--------------------------------------------------------------------------------
fc1/10     1     F       off     npmExtLinkDown   swl    --     --      --
fc1/24     1     NP      off     init             swl    --     --      --
```

Example 11-15 shows that, because fc1/24 on MDS-B does not belong to the same VSAN from MDS-CORE, it cannot become fully active and remains in the "init" state. Consequently, without an operational NP_Port, internal F_Port fc1/10 is disabled.

The insertion of interfaces fc1/10 and fc1/24 into VSAN 10 would certainly solve this problem. And as a matter of fact, I would recommend this procedure if the core switch could not deploy VSANs.

However, if you remember, the SAN administrator also wants to connect a server in VSAN 20 in the near future. Thus, if he does not feel like spending an NP_Port for each new enabled VSAN on MDS-B, *F-Trunks* can provide an interesting solution. Using this capability, a single F_Port can transport frames from multiple VSANs at the same time.

Figure 11-14 depicts the required configuration on both switches to allow the fabric connection of N_Ports that belong to VSANs 10 and 20. In the figure, I have also included interfaces fc1/10 and fc1/24 on MDS-B on VSAN 10.

```
MDS-CORE(config)# feature fport-channel-trunk
[output suppressed]
MDS-CORE(config)# interface fc1/24
MDS-CORE(config-if)# switchport trunk mode on
MDS-CORE(config-if)# switchport trunk allowed vsan 10
MDS-CORE(config-if)# switchport trunk allowed vsan add 20
```

```
MDS-B(config)# vsan database
MDS-B(config-vsan-db)# vsan 10
MDS-B(config-vsan-db)# vsan 10 interface fc1/10, fc1/24
[output suppressed]
MDS-B(config-vsan-db)# interface fc1/24
MDS-B(config-if)# switchport trunk mode on
MDS-B(config-if)# switchport trunk allowed vsan 10
MDS-B(config-if)# switchport trunk allowed vsan add 20
```

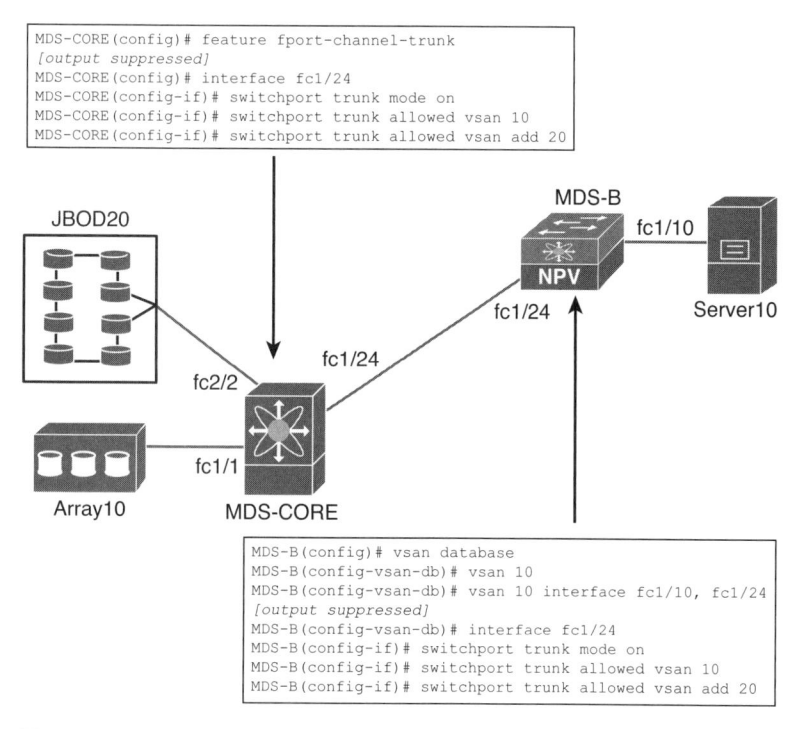

Figure 11-14 *F-Trunk Configuration on MDS-CORE and MDS-B*

Tip The F-Trunk capability is enabled by default on switches running in NPV mode.

After this step, MDS-CORE is connected to MDS-B through a *Trunk Fabric Port (TF_Port)*, as shown in Example 11-16. The example also shows that Server10 is now correctly logged in to VSAN 10.

Example 11-16 *Interface fc1/24 Status and FLOGI Database in MDS-CORE*

```
MDS-CORE# show interface fc1/24 brief
-------------------------------------------------------------------------------
Interface   Vsan    Admin   Admin    Status         SFP     Oper    Oper    Port
                    Mode    Trunk                           Mode    Speed   Channel
                            Mode                                    (Gbps)
-------------------------------------------------------------------------------
fc1/24      10      F       on       trunking       swl     TF      4       --
MDS-CORE# show flogi database vsan 10
-------------------------------------------------------------------------------
INTERFACE          VSAN    FCID         PORT NAME              NODE NAME
```

```
fc1/1              10    0xd40000    50:00:40:21:03:fc:6d:28 20:03:00:04:02:fc:6d:28
! FLOGI from interface fc1/24 from MDS-B
fc1/24             10    0xd40020    20:18:00:0d:ec:47:e7:40 20:0a:00:0d:ec:47:e7:41
! FLOGI from Server10
fc1/24             10    0xd40021    10:00:00:00:c9:73:9c:2c 20:00:00:00:c9:73:9c:2c

Total number of flogi = 3.
```

At this time, Server10 and Array10 can be zoned together on VSAN 10 as if they were N_Ports connected to the same switch.

Note You should always refer to the latest Cisco MDS 9000 documentation to verify the scalability limits that are related to NPV scenarios. For example, at the time of this writing, a core switch can support up to 105 connected NPV switches and 400 FLOGIs per linecard.

NPV Traffic Management

Before giving any theoretical discussions about how NPV-mode switches distribute server traffic among their NP_Ports, allow me to show you their default behavior first.

In Figure 11-15, MDS-CORE and MDS-B are connected with a similarly configured F-Trunk between their respective fc1/23 interfaces. Also, the new server (Server20) is already connected to interface fc1/5 on MDS-B and included in VSAN 20.

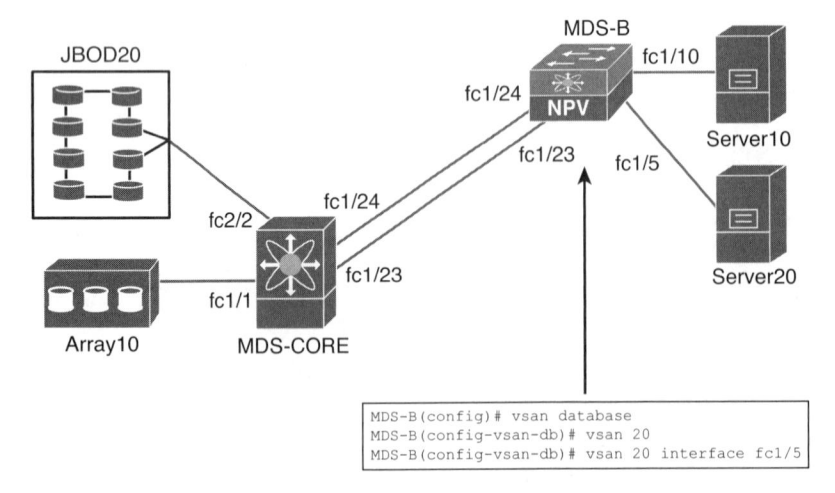

Figure 11-15 *Additional NP Link and Server20 Insertion in VSAN 20*

Since both F-Trunks to MDS-CORE are operational, you will observe how MDS-B distributes the server FLOGIs (and additional traffic) between them.

Example 11-17 demonstrates this default behavior.

Example 11-17 *MDS-B Traffic Distribution*

```
MDS-B# show npv flogi-table
--------------------------------------------------------------------------------
SERVER                                                                  EXTERNAL
INTERFACE VSAN FCID        PORT NAME               NODE NAME            INTERFACE
--------------------------------------------------------------------------------
fc1/5     20   0xed0100  10:00:00:00:c9:2e:66:00 20:00:00:00:c9:2e:66:00 fc1/23
fc1/10    10   0xd40021  10:00:00:00:c9:73:9c:2c 20:00:00:00:c9:73:9c:2c fc1/24

Total number of flogi = 2.
```

The distribution process on MDS-B can be described as follows:

1. Server10 was already using NP_Port fc1/24 as an external interface (as seen in the last section).

2. When the Server20 interface was brought up on interface fc1/5, MDS-B selects an operational NP_Port with **minimum traffic load** and binds fc1/5 to it.

3. Server20 FLOGI, and subsequent traffic, is carried over fc1/23.

By default, the NPV switch will always keep the original distribution unless there is a failure on one of the NP_Ports. This behavior guarantees that network disruptions are minimally perceived on the connected servers.

Example 11-18 illustrates this behavior in more detail, when external interface fc1/4 on MDS-B is brought down and activated again.

Example 11-18 *NP_Port Flapping in MDS-B*

```
! Disabling interface fc1/24
MDS-B(config)# interface fc1/24
MDS-B(config-if)# shutdown
! After a new FLOGI, Server20 is now sharing interface fc1/23 with Server10
MDS-B(config-if)# show npv flogi-table
--------------------------------------------------------------------------------
SERVER                                                                  EXTERNAL
INTERFACE VSAN FCID        PORT NAME               NODE NAME            INTERFACE
--------------------------------------------------------------------------------
fc1/5     20   0xed0100  10:00:00:00:c9:2e:66:00 20:00:00:00:c9:2e:66:00 fc1/23
fc1/10    10   0xd40021  10:00:00:00:c9:73:9c:2c 20:00:00:00:c9:73:9c:2c fc1/23
```

```
Total number of flogi = 2.

! Enabling interface fc1/24 back
MDS-B(config-if)# no shutdown
! MDS-B maintains the distribution even if another NP_Port becomes operational
MDS-B(config-if)# show npv flogi-table
--------------------------------------------------------------------------------
SERVER                                                                  EXTERNAL
INTERFACE VSAN FCID          PORT NAME                NODE NAME         INTERFACE
--------------------------------------------------------------------------------
fc1/5     20   0xed0100 10:00:00:00:c9:2e:66:00 20:00:00:00:c9:2e:66:00 fc1/23
fc1/10    10   0xd40021 10:00:00:00:c9:73:9c:2c 20:00:00:00:c9:73:9c:2c fc1/23

Total number of flogi = 2.
```

You can conclude that, by default, a Cisco NPV-mode switch load-balances server FLOGIs between all available NP_Ports. And as you have observed, it will only force new N_Port FLOGIs to servers that were previously using a failed external interface (even if a new external interface is activated).

Alternatively to the default automatic mode, NPV-capable switches can also deploy one of the following traffic management methods:

- **Traffic-map:** Where an administrator can statically select the external interface for each F_Port. A failure on an NP_Port disables its associated server interfaces (for that reason, this method is not recommended for single-homed servers).

- **Disruptive load balance:** Where all server interfaces are reinitialized whenever a new external interface is brought up. Beforehand, you should check whether the applications installed on these servers have an issue with such behavior.

The burden of choosing which method of NPV traffic management on Cisco NPV-mode switches can be lessened with the use of *F-Trunk PortChannels*.

As standard ISL PortChannels, these entities allow the aggregation of NP_Port-to-F_Port trunk connections on a single virtual connection. Using any method of NPV traffic management, an F_Port PortChannel can

- Maintain the server FLOGI in the event of a physical connection failure
- Load-balance traffic of a single server over multiple physical connections (provided that its VSAN is using exchange-based load balancing)

In our continuously evolving topology, Figure 11-16 details an F-Trunk PortChannel configuration on both NPV connections available between MDS-CORE and MDS-B.

```
MDS-CORE(config)# interface fc1/23-24
MDS-CORE(config-if)# channel-group 60 force
fc1/23 fc1/24 added to port-channel 60 and disabled
please do the same operation on the switch at the other end of the port-channel,
then do "no shutdown" at both ends to bring it up
MDS-CORE(config-if)# no shutdown
MDS-CORE(config-if)# interface port-channel 60
MDS-CORE(config-if)# channel mode active
```

```
MDS-B(config)# interface fc1/23-24
MDS-B(config-if)# channel-group 60 force
[output suppressed]
MDS-B(config-if)# no shutdown
MDS-B(config-if)# interface port-channel 60
MDS-B(config-if)# channel mode active
```

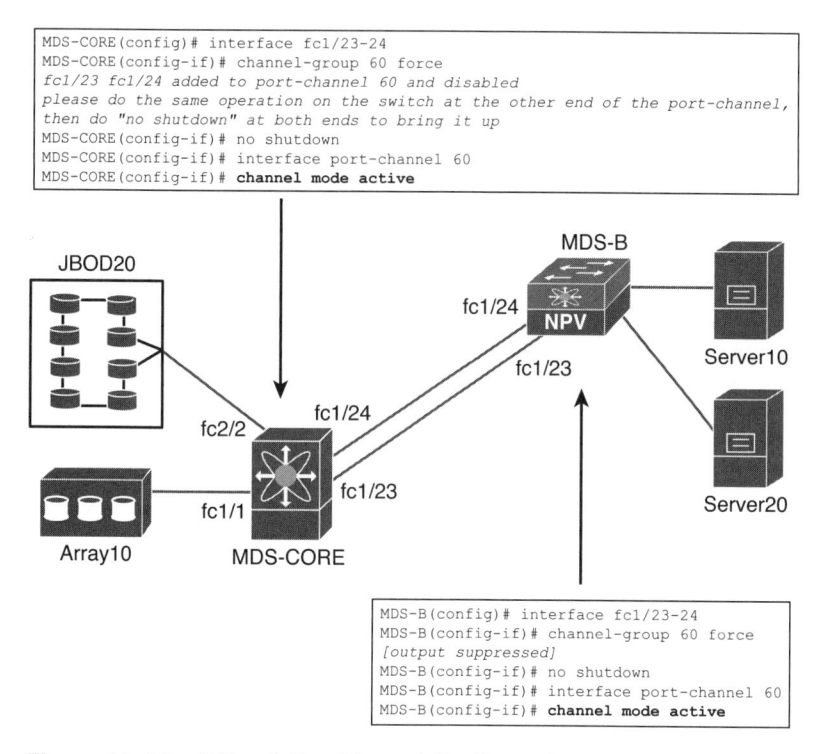

Figure 11-16 *F-Trunk PortChannel Configuration*

Tip F-Trunk ports can only deploy PortChannels with the negotiation protocol enabled by the **channel-group active** command. This restriction allows the NP_Ports to remain operational if the aggregation is not possible for any reason (misconfiguration, for example).

On each switch, a PortChannel virtual interface is created with inherited parameters from the physical interfaces (for example, their allowed VSANs).

Examples 11-19 and 11-20 depict the results from the PortChannel configurations displayed in Figure 11-16. First, Example 11-19 shows the FLOGIs received on the PortChannel in MDS-CORE.

Example 11-19 *FLOGI Database in MDS-CORE*

```
MDS-CORE# show flogi database interface port-channel 60
--------------------------------------------------------------------------------
INTERFACE         VSAN    FCID           PORT NAME               NODE NAME
--------------------------------------------------------------------------------
! FLOGI from Server10
```

```
port-channel 60   10      0xd40021  10:00:00:00:c9:73:9c:2c 20:00:00:00:c9:73:9c:2c
! FLOGI from PortChannel60 on MDS-B (observe that it has a different
pWWN from the physical interfaces)
port-channel 60   10      0xd40060  24:3c:00:0d:ec:47:e7:40 20:0a:00:0d:ec:47:e7:41
! FLOGI from Server20
port-channel 60   20      0xed0100  10:00:00:00:c9:2e:66:00 20:00:00:00:c9:2e:66:00

Total number of flogi = 3.
```

Example 11-20 shows that both servers are assigned to the PortChannel interface.

Example 11-20 *FLOGI Table in MDS-B*

```
MDS-B# show npv flogi-table
--------------------------------------------------------------------------------
                                                                       EXTERNAL
SERVER
INTERFACE VSAN FCID        PORT NAME               NODE NAME           INTERFACE
--------------------------------------------------------------------------------
! This is Server20...
fc1/5     20   0xed0100 10:00:00:00:c9:2e:66:00 20:00:00:00:c9:2e:66:00 Po60
! ... and this is Server10
fc1/10    10   0xd40021 10:00:00:00:c9:73:9c:2c 20:00:00:00:c9:73:9c:2c Po60

Total number of flogi = 2.
```

As a result, a single link failure will not bring the PortChannel interface down. Consequently, PortChannels are also deployed to harden NPV connections on Cisco NPV connections.

Deploying Port WWN Virtualization on NPV

Although N_Port virtualization can greatly simplify and scale SANs, this technology can offer some operational challenges when compared to fabric switches running in standard mode. One of these characteristics is the loss of *interface-based zoning* on the upstream switches, because an NPV-mode switch does not participate on such fabric process.

Without this zoning method, every time an HBA or blade server is replaced, a SAN administrator is required to perform changes in the fabric active zone set.

The *Flex-Attach* functionality can help in such scenarios, virtualizing physical addresses of servers connected to NPV switches. Also known as "WWN-NAT," Flex-Attach basically replaces the pWWN of a server with a **virtual pWWN** on all communications to the upstream switch. Because this virtual address can be assigned to an internal interface, it can be used on zoning and LUN masking procedures to represent any device that is connected to this specific interface.

Example 11-21 demonstrates Flex-Attach on interface fc1/5 on MDS-B from our NPV topology. With this configuration, any device connected to fc1/5 on MDS-B will present a specific pWWN (01:02:03:04:05:06:07:08) on its FLOGI to the MDS-CORE.

Example 11-21 *Flex-Attach Configuration*

```
MDS-B(config)# interface fc1/5
! Server interface must be disabled for Flex-Attach configuration
MDS-B(config-if)# shutdown
MDS-B(config-if)# exit
! Assigning virtual pWWN to any node connected to interface fc1/5
MDS-B(config)# flex-attach virtual-pwwn 01:02:03:04:05:06:07:08 interface fc1/5
! Flex-attach is a CFS distributed feature by default. Hence, you
must commit it to complete its execution.
MDS-B(config)# flex-attach commit
! Enabling interface fc1/5
MDS-B(config)# interface fc1/5
MDS-B(config-if)# no shutdown
```

Flex-Attach requires CFS as a configuration aid to avoid the creation of the same virtual pWWN in two different NPV-mode switches. And because NPV-mode switches do not deploy ISLs, CFS must be transported over IP through their management interfaces.

Example 11-22 demonstrates how the virtual pWWN from interface fc1/5 on MDS-B is detected on MDS-CORE.

Example 11-22 *FLOGI Database in MDS-CORE*

```
MDS-CORE# show flogi database interface port-channel 60
--------------------------------------------------------------------------------
INTERFACE        VSAN    FCID       PORT NAME                NODE NAME
--------------------------------------------------------------------------------
port-channel 60  10      0xd40021   10:00:00:00:c9:73:9c:2c  20:00:00:00:c9:73:9c:2c
port-channel 60  10      0xd40060   24:3c:00:0d:ec:47:e7:40  20:0a:00:0d:ec:47:e7:41
! A new virtual device is born
port-channel 60  20      0xed0101   01:02:03:04:05:06:07:08  20:00:00:00:c9:2e:66:00

Total number of flogi = 3.
```

From this moment on, this pWWN can be used for zoning, IVR, LUN masking, and any other operation that can involve the device that might be connected to interface fc1/5 on MDS-B.

Although static virtual pWWN assignments are very illustrative, they can be quite tiresome to configure and manage in scalable scenarios. As an alternative, you can use automatic virtual pWWN assignment with the **flex-attach virtual-pwwn auto** command. In this method, virtual pWWNs are derived from the switch WWN to avoid address conflicts in the Fibre Channel fabric.

> **Tip** Flex-Attach also permits one virtual pWWN to be assigned to a specific physical pWWN to facilitate server migrations.

Use Case: Blade Server Hosting Data Center

A service provider has achieved reasonable success in renting exclusive physical servers and storage arrays to customers while providing shared network services (Ethernet, IP, and Fibre Channel) for these devices. Six months from now, the company will introduce a similar hosting service (tentatively named "Blades of Glory"), based on blade servers and with a much more aggressive service-level agreement, promising 99.999 percent availability per year and requested changes execution within 24 hours.

The service provider's storage team has requested you to design its new SAN for this new service. In summary, the team wants to avoid the following insurmountable problems dealt with on a daily basis with its legacy SAN:

- All customers are using the same physical fabric. Hence, they are all affected with a misconfiguration or when a fabric process starts to behave erratically.

- Some of the legacy switches do not support more than 16 domain IDs in a single fabric (the shared SAN was out of service during some hours when someone inserted the 17th switch into the fabric). Although the team members will not use these switches in the new project, they are really worried about this kind of "surprise" limitation.

- Not all array manufacturers support the number of fabric switches they will need in future service. The storage team does not want to deploy more than two redundant physical fabrics because it needs to increase device utilization, simplify server provisioning, and reduce cabling management (whenever a customer changes his environment).

The company's server team has already decided to build this service with a 16-slot blade server chassis. And by contract, each server HBA interface should have at least 1 Gbps of average traffic over the SAN (a 4:1 oversubscription rate, considering that each server is equipped with two 4-Gbps Fibre Channel ports). The team hopes to scale this project to 200 customers that will be distributed over 100 blade chassis.

Two weeks later, the SAN design you propose to the storage team is depicted in Figure 11-17.

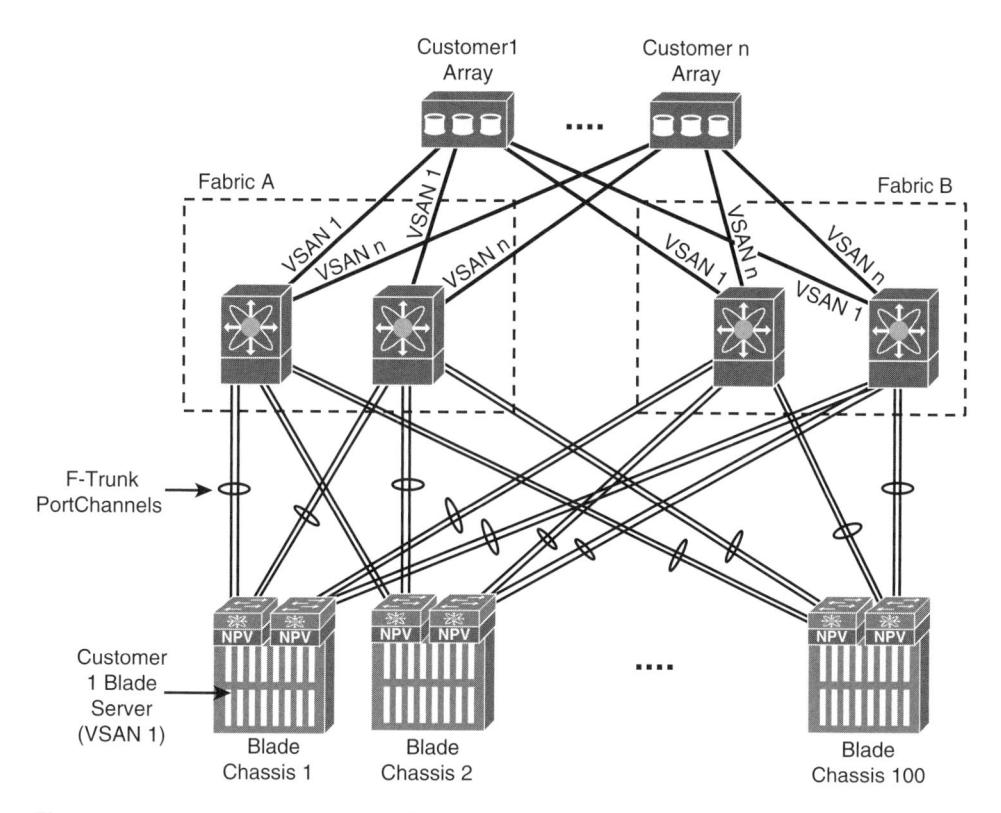

Figure 11-17 *Service Provider Blade Hosting SAN*

Your design recommends the use of three essential SAN virtualization techniques: VSANs, NPV, and Flex-Attach. Each customer will earn a dedicated VSAN to avoid fate sharing in the case of a fabric process or misconfiguration.

To avoid physical management of cabling, these VSANs will be defined in the blade chassis switches as well. Such devices will run in NPV mode to decrease the number of fabric domain IDs to the minimum (two directors per physical fabric).

To reach 1 Gbps per server Fibre Channel port, at least four 4-Gbps NP_Ports will be activated per blade chassis switch. Each of these blade switches is connected to two core switches with at least 400 Fibre Channel ports: 200 for the blade switch connections and 200 for the storage device connections. To improve load balancing and server availability, you also suggest that an F-Trunk PortChannel is configured between each blade server and core switch.

Moreover, you detail that the storage team can also benefit from the activation Flex-Attach on the blade switches. Through this capability, each blade switch server port will be advertised to the fabric with a virtual pWWN, which will be used for all LUN masking and zoning operations. As a result, the following operations will require a much smaller amount of time:

- HBA or server replacement
- Server upgrade or migration between chassis
- New customer provisioning

After making sure that your project is formally approved, you also recommend that the team change the name of the service as soon as possible (though marketing is not your original area of expertise).

Summary

In this chapter, you learned the following:

- An IP network can emulate Fibre Channel physical media with an FCIP tunnel established between two switches. This technology is mostly used to provide flexibility and global reach in SAN extensions.
- Inter-VSAN Routing (IVR) is a SAN virtualization technique that allows the communication of devices that belong to distinct VSANs. Because IVR does not merge virtual fabrics, it can also help to isolate data center sites with transit VSANs.
- N_Port Virtualization allows the scaling of connected switches in a Fibre Channel fabric. To their upstream NPIV-enabled switches, NPV-mode switches behave as N_Ports.
- On a fabric with NPV-mode switches, Flex-Attach can accelerate host provisioning and change operations that are related to pWWNs.

Figure 11-18 exhibits the logical perspective of FCIP, IVR, and NPV in Fibre Channel fabrics.

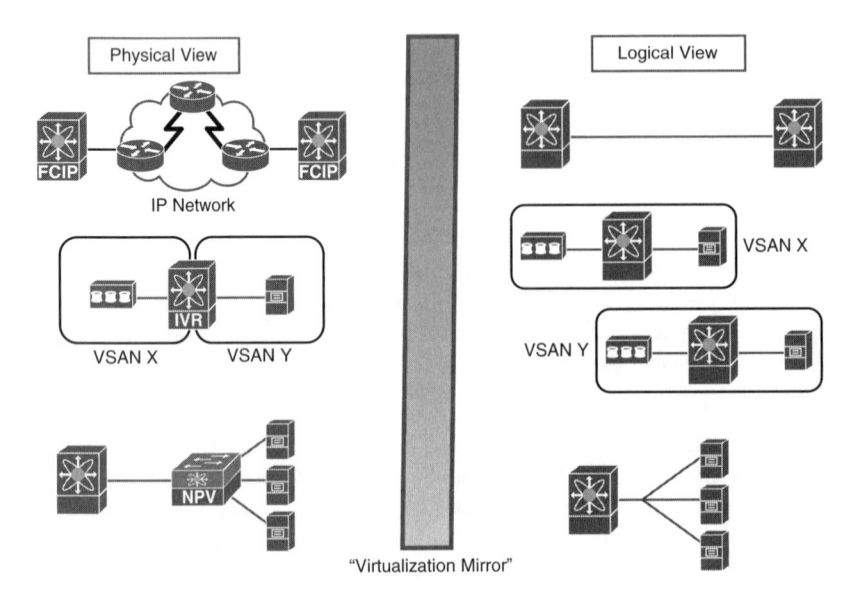

Figure 11-18 *Through the Virtualization Mirror*

Further Reading

Mason, Seth and Kirishnamurthyi, Venkat. *Cisco Storage Networking Cookbook: For NX-OS release 5.2 MDS and Nexus Families of Switches.* CreateSpace Independent Publishing Platform, 2011.

IETF Request for Comment 3821 (Fibre Channel over TCP/IP)

http://tools.ietf.org/html/rfc3821

T11 Fibre Channel Standards Guest Page: www.t11.org/t11/hps.nsf/guesthome766kx

Chapter 12

One Cable to Unite Us All

"When there is no enemy within, the enemies outside cannot hurt you."
(Winston Churchill)

This chapter examines I/O consolidation, the virtualization aspects of Data Center Bridging (DCB), and how Fibre Channel over Ethernet (FCoE) helps data centers to achieve network convergence. It contains the following topics:

- The Case for Data Center Networking Convergence
- Data Center Bridging
- Introducing Fibre Channel over Ethernet
- Deploying Unified Server Access
- Deploying Multihop FCoE
- Unified Fabric Designs
- FCoE and SAN Extension
- Use Case: LAN and SAN Management Separation

Table 12-1 classifies FCoE using the virtualization taxonomy described in Chapter 1, "Virtualization History and Definitions."

Table 12-1 *Virtualization Techniques Classification*

Virtualization Characteristics	FCoE
Emulation	Fibre Channel media
Type	Abstraction
Subtype	Structural

Virtualization Characteristics	FCoE
Scalability	Hardware dependent[1]
Technology area	Storage networking
Subarea	Data and control plane[2]
Advantages	Hardware consolidation (network devices, cabling and server adapters), operation simplification, resource usage optimization

[1] Refer to Appendix A, "Cisco Data Center Portfolio," for more details and the Cisco online documentation for updated information.

[2] Storage VDCs on Nexus 7000 platforms additionally deploy FCoE management plane virtualization.

While the sheer number of servers grows inside data center facilities, manufacturers and standards organizations have deployed considerable time and effort to decrease the total cost of ownership related to these devices. One of these initiatives, known as *I/O consolidation*, intends to bring operational simplicity, resource optimization, and cost savings to server environments.

Although previous I/O consolidation technologies, such as Infiniband, proved to be technically functional, they have failed to achieve a wider adoption on enterprise and service provider data centers. In truth, time has shown that new technologies usually reach popularization when they also consider the human aspects of their implementation, not offering a complete disruption to the daily operations of the technical teams.

As discussed in Chapter 2, "Data Center Network Evolution," 10 Gigabit Ethernet is quickly becoming the most common network access option for servers. As an incremental innovation alone, 10 Gigabit Ethernet easily enables the consolidation of Gigabit Ethernet connections. An important barrier fell in 2011, when IEEE ratified and published several protocol enhancements, collectively known as *Data Center Bridging (DCB)*. Among other innovations, these enhancements introduced to 10 Gigabit Ethernet the capability to emulate the lossless behavior of Fibre Channel. And as a result, DCB provided the necessary background for *Fibre Channel over Ethernet (FCoE)*.

Already defined in the INCITS T11 FC-BB-5 standard in 2009, FCoE enables the *convergence* of Fibre Channel fabrics and Ethernet networks. And even before its standardization, this technology had already fulfilled the early promises of I/O consolidation on multiple data centers all over the world.

This chapter will explain why I/O consolidation and network convergence are such important topics for data center architects today. It will also detail the design and deployment options of DCB and FCoE through basic concepts and real-world scenarios.

The Case for Data Center Networking Convergence

Generally speaking, a standard server presents different input/output (I/O) communication demands. Traditionally, these traffic loads are characterized by separate physical connections, such as

- **Public interfaces:** Responsible for receiving application client requests.
- **Private interfaces:** Used for internal communication between servers from a cluster or between servers in a multitier application structure (presentation-application-database, for example).
- **Management interfaces:** Deployed to support server operations, such as software installation, firmware upgrades, health monitoring, and so on.
- **Backup interfaces:** Used to copy files, databases, or entire computer images to a nonvolatile media (such as magnetic tapes). Ethernet or Fibre Channel connections can be deployed for this traffic.
- **Storage access interfaces:** Responsible for external storage access. Ethernet (for Internet Small Computer System Interface [iSCSI] or Network File System [NFS]) or Fibre Channel is generally used on these connections.

While some data center teams might resist remembering it, a single server connection has three distinct elements: *an adapter interface*, *a cable*, and *a network device port*. Consequently, at each new server connection, at least three different operations must be harmonically coordinated. And as each server generation increases its processing capacity and average number of connections, these operations can become quite complex, error-prone, and slow.

Unconsolidated connections also mean the formation of "bandwidth islands" within each server. Hence, even if a connection is not using its available bandwidth, it cannot provide resources for other interfaces that might need it. In these scenarios, an additional physical connection will probably have to be provisioned, resulting in the waste of server, cabling, network, and human resources.

Facing the challenges brought by discrete server connections, data center architects have craved for I/O consolidation solutions during the last decade. Figure 12-1 illustrates the concept of I/O consolidation on a server.

Through this process, multiple physical connections are severely reduced to only two (if redundancy is desired) on each server. Such cabling approach is also known as "wire once and walk away" because it enables data centers to quickly add any type of I/O access to a server without any extra physical changes.

I/O consolidation and network convergence are complementary concepts, especially considering that the server access layer presents the highest number of cables within the data center network infrastructures. Consequently, a *Unified Fabric* (or converged network) should possess sufficient resources to support all distinct traffic loads that a server might require. A Unified Fabric should also allocate these resources fairly among these loads, creating a "virtual network" for each one of them.

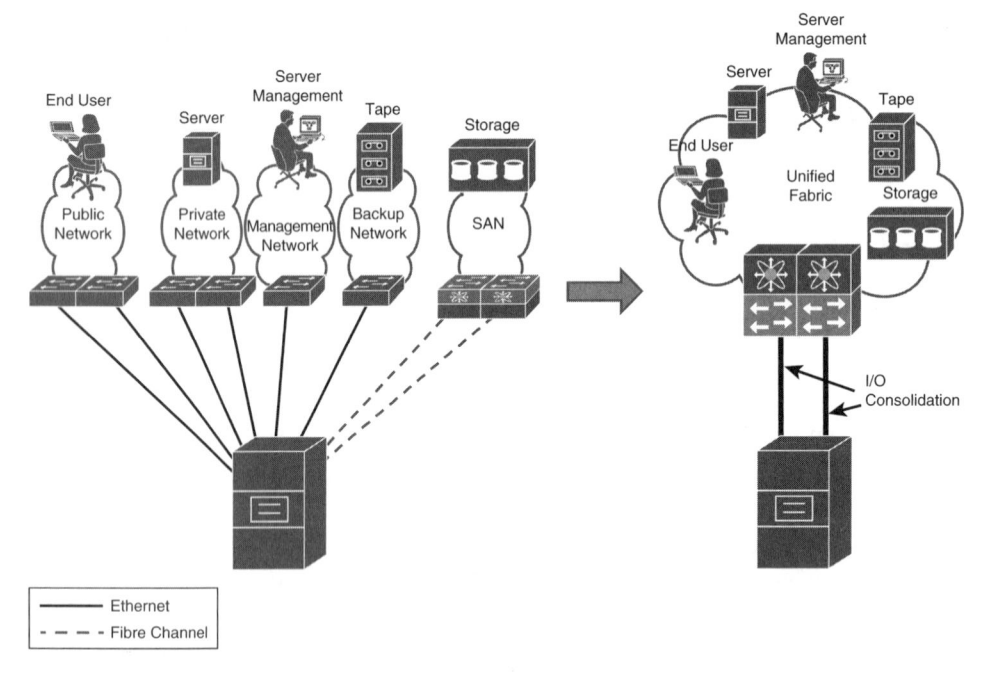

Figure 12-1 *I/O Consolidation Example*

When I/O consolidation is deployed over a Unified Fabric, a data center can

- Reduce the number of interfaces and adapters per server
- Avoid excessive cabling
- Decrease the number of network devices
- Increase resource utilization
- Permit traffic loads to peak beyond its defined share, if resources are available
- Consolidate management points
- Simplify scaling and capacity planning because it does not demand several different resource pools

And, almost as a collateral effect, converged infrastructures use less power, cooling, and space when compared to unconsolidated facilities.

The popularization of 10 Gigabit Ethernet on server access has provided a straightforward way to group multiple Gigabit Ethernet interfaces into a single connection. Because of its admirable longevity and scaling capacity (reaching 100 Gbps at the time of this writing), Ethernet surely presents itself as an extremely viable technology for future-proof I/O consolidation processes.

10 Gigabit Ethernet can easily consolidate IP-based storage access loads such as NFS and iSCSI. Nevertheless, its best-effort transport characteristics would simply break the reliability that a Fibre Channel fabric must provide. Therefore, to encapsulate a lossless protocol such as Fibre Channel, Ethernet had to deploy such characteristics as well.

And in 2008, it did.

Data Center Bridging

"Gentlemen, we can rebuild it. We have the technology. We have the capability to build the world's first Unified Fabric. Ethernet will be that fabric. Better than it was before. Better, stronger, faster." (Excerpt from a completely fictional IEEE meeting)

Even after the use of highly reliable transmission media and the elimination of collisions with full-duplex links, standard Ethernet networks can still introduce loss to their transported data. Broadly speaking, IP-based applications do not expect an Ethernet frame to receive all the proper resources (such as interface buffers) to reach its final destination. For that reason, these applications mostly employ transport mechanisms, such as TCP, to handle discards and enforce retransmission of data.

Although Ethernet has a flow control mechanism, in the form of IEEE 802.3x PAUSE frames, it is usually not used in data center networks because it can affect the performance of *all traffic loads* that might be traversing an Ethernet link.

On the other hand, Fibre Channel Class of Service 3 employs a credit-based flow control method between connected ports. This buffer-to-buffer mechanism offers the guarantee to upper-layer protocols (such as SCSI) that a Fibre Channel frame is only transmitted if resources are available for it.

To become *the* converged transport protocol in data centers, Ethernet has to present the same nondiscarding behavior to select traffic loads. Resulting from a series of innovations that Cisco kick-started in 2008, IEEE has published a group of standards that define how an Ethernet network can support multiple distinct traffic loads, including highly loss sensitive ones such as Fibre Channel.

Collectively known as *Data Center Bridging (DCB)*, these standards are actually enhancements that allow lossless transport, resource allocation, automated configuration of devices, and congestion notification over full-duplex 10 Gigabit Ethernet networks. And as stated in its name, DCB was designed for data center environments, which are characterized by limited bandwidth-delay switches and relatively fewer hop counts.

Note *Data Center Ethernet (DCE)* and *Converged Enhanced Ethernet (CEE)* are prestandard initiatives led by two different groups of manufacturers. After the publication of the DCB standards, these terms were deprecated to avoid further confusion.

Priority-Based Flow Control

Published in 2011, IEEE 802.1Qbb (*priority-based flow control*, or simply PFC) enables flow control per traffic class on full-duplex Ethernet links, with each class identified by its VLAN tag priority values. In a nutshell, PFC intends to eliminate frame loss caused by contention, with a mechanism similar to the IEEE 802.3x PAUSE, but over individual priorities.

> **Note** IEEE 802.1Qbb is an amendment to IEEE 802.1Q.

In a PFC-enabled interface, a frame of a *lossless* (or no-drop) priority is not available for transmission if that priority is paused on that port. And similarly to the buffer-to-buffer credits mechanism from Fibre Channel, PFC is defined on a pair of full-duplex interfaces connected by one point-to-point link.

Figure 12-2 illustrates how an IEEE 802.3x PAUSE standard Ethernet link contrasts with a PFC-enabled point-to-point connection.

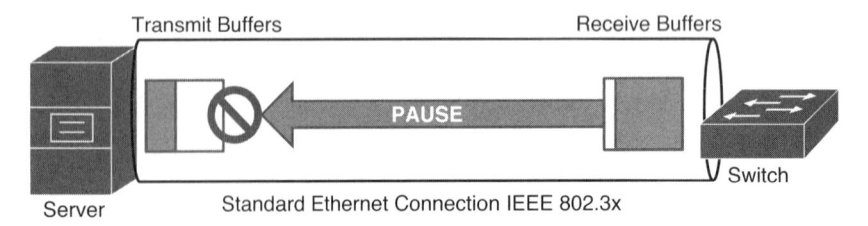

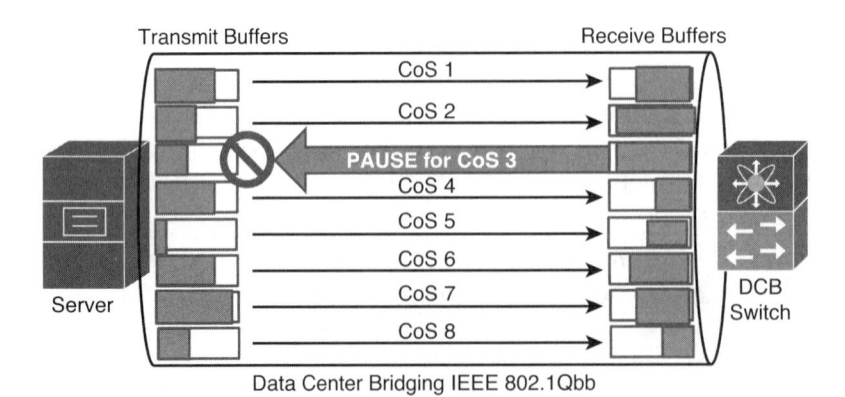

Figure 12-2 *IEEE 802.3x and IEEE 802.1Qbb Compared*

As Figure 12-2 shows, PFC blends two well-known technologies (the aforementioned IEEE 802.3x PAUSE and IEEE 802.1p CoS priority bits) to offer a per-priority lossless behavior to select classes of service (CoS 3 in Figure 12-2). Traffic loads that do not required this characteristic will traverse the PFC-enabled link as if it were a standard Ethernet connection.

As IEEE 802.3x, a PFC PAUSE is invoked through a frame with Ethertype 0x8808 directed to multicast MAC address 0180.c200.0001. This frame also details how much time each no-drop class transmission buffer should hold before transmitting again. However, PFC receivers mostly rely on the PAUSE/UNPAUSE mechanism instead of following strict timer values, which are set to a large interval to enable this behavior.

With a PFC-enabled class of service, a loss-sensitive protocol such as Fibre Channel can be transported in such a class, preventing an encapsulated frame from being dropped because of resource starvation.

Notwithstanding, PFC presents an essential distinction to credit-based flow control methods: The PFC-enabled *receiving port* pauses the sender after a certain condition is met (such as buffer threshold). If you remember from Chapter 10, "Islands in the SAN," after it uses all its BB_Credits to send Fibre Channel frames, a *sender port refrains itself* from transmitting more data until it receives a clear statement from the receiving port about an available buffer (R_RDY). Hence, an interface that deploys PAUSE mechanisms should always provision sufficient ingress buffer space for two sets of data *after it sends a PAUSE frame*:

- Frames that were in "on the wire," meaning that were already serialized but not yet received
- Frames that were transmitted during the time a PAUSE frame left the sender and were processed by the transmitter

Figure 12-3 further details this exact situation when a PAUSE frame is sent at instant t1, is received at t2, and the last transmitted frame is received at t3.

The size of this buffer space depends on several variables, such as bandwidth, speed of signal transmission, and latency between the connected interfaces. Hence, this sizing must be taken into account when PFC is used on longer distances (such as data center interconnections, as you will see in the later section "FCoE and SAN Extension").

Note Latency is one of the difficulties for PFC-enabled applications over 10GBASE-T cabling. For that reason, Cisco only supports Fibre Channel over Ethernet on 10GBASE-T connections that are shorter than 30 meters at the time of this writing. Refer to the latest Cisco online product documentation for updated information about this support.

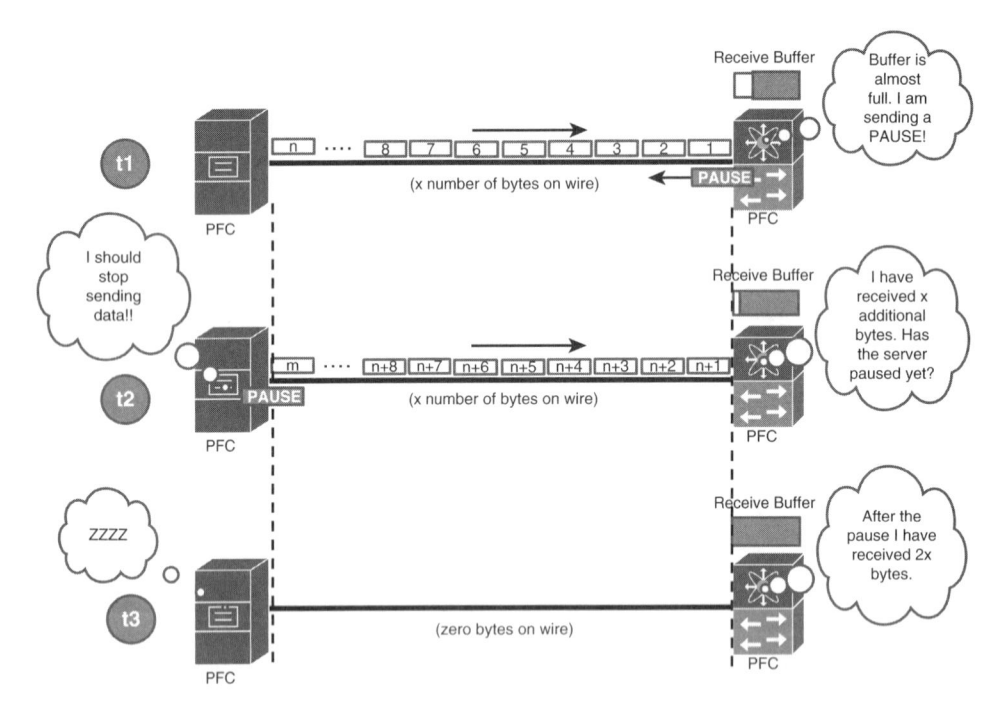

Figure 12-3 *Additional Buffer Space After PAUSE Is Sent*

Enhanced Transmission Selection

Considering that IEEE 802.1p class of service enables the creation of eight *virtual wires* on each Ethernet link, another Ethernet extension was brought into existence to define the resource allocation for each of these wires.

Also published in 2011, IEEE 802.1Qaz (*Enhanced Transmission Selection*, or ETS) controls the allocation of bandwidth among classes of service. In an ETS-enabled connection, when a traffic class is not using its allocated bandwidth, ETS will allow other traffic classes to use the available bandwidth (also according to their allocation percentages).

According to the IEEE 802.1Qaz standard, an ETS bridge must support at least three traffic classes (one with enabled PFC, one without PFC, and one with strict priority), a minimum percentage granularity of 1 percent, and allocation with a minimum precision of 10 percent.

Figure 12-4 illustrates a scenario where three classes of service share the same 10-Gbps ETS-enabled connection with the following predefined percentages:

- CoS 1: 60 percent
- CoS 2: 20 percent
- CoS 3: 20 percent

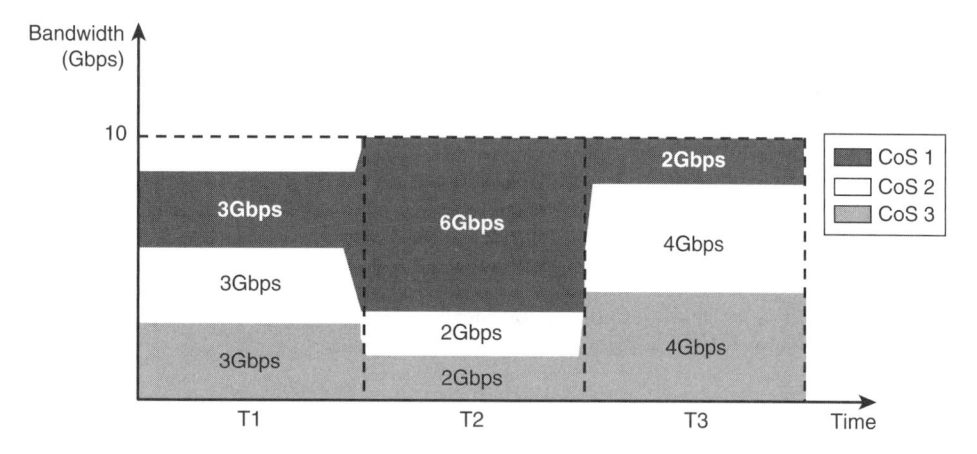

Figure 12-4 *Enhanced Transmission Selection in Action*

In Figure 12-4:

- During interval T1, all classes are transmitting 3 Gbps, hence not saturating the 10-Gbps link.

- In T2, when the offered traffic reaches the 10-Gbps limit of the connection, ETS is activated to distribute the traffic with the predefined percentages (60, 20, and 20 for CoS 1, CoS 2, and CoS 3, respectively).

- During T3, CoS 1 only requires 2 Gbps of traffic, thus enabling CoS 2 and CoS 3 to share the unused bandwidth equally, because they were assigned with the same percentage.

Although ETS dictates that bandwidth must be divided between classes of service, the queueing method or allocation algorithm bandwidth is not defined in the standard.

Data Center Bridging eXchange Protocol

I hope a small, but decisive, detail has not escaped your attention: PFC and ETS are implemented on both ends of a connection. Hence, network devices *and host adapters* must adhere to the DCB policies defined for each class of service.

One can only imagine that the benefits DCB brings to data center networks might also provoke a mammoth task of configuring potentially thousands of server adapters. Fortunately, these multiple operations are avoided with the *Data Center Bridging eXchange Protocol (DCBX)*. In summary, DCB-enabled devices use DCBX to

- Discover DCB capabilities in a peer port
- Exchange configuration information with directly connected peers
- Detect wrong configuration parameters

Also defined in the IEEE 802.1Qaz standard, DCBX is mainly used for ETS, PFC, and application priority policy enforcement on DCB-enabled devices. DCBX uses *Link Layer Discovery Protocol (LLDP)*, defined in the IEEE 802.1AB standard, to exchange attributes between two link peers.

DCBX attributes are transmitted through LLDP TLVs (Type-Length-Values), and they can be

- **Informational,** if there is no negotiation or participation of a DCBX state machine
- **Asymmetric,** if the sent configuration for the remote peer does not have to match the local peer configuration
- **Symmetric,** if the configuration must be the same on both peer ports

Also, according to the standard, a *data center environment* is defined by the reach of DCBX, as shown in Figure 12-5.

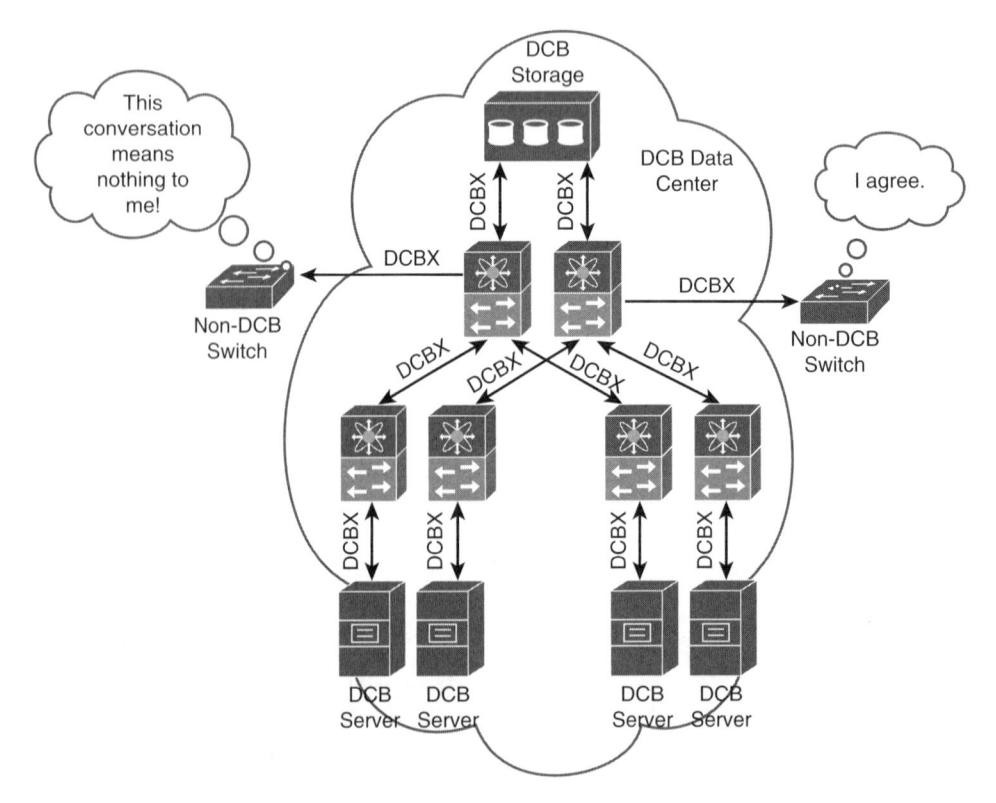

Figure 12-5 *Data Center Environment*

> **Note** On NX-OS devices, DCBX is responsible for Fibre Channel over Ethernet (FCoE) enablement, PFC negotiation, and logical link up/down (if an interface changes its virtual storage-area network [VSAN] membership, for example).

Congestion Notification

In 2010, IEEE included *Quantized Congestion Notification (QCN)* to the DCB initiative with the 802.1Qau standard. QCN is basically a feedback method for end-to-end congestion notification in data center networks.

A Layer 2 bridge can signal a congestion condition through *congestion notification messages (CNM)* addressed to the source of the frames. These messages contain information about the extent of congestion at the QCN-enabled switch (also referred to as *congestion point*, or simply CP).

Based on congestion parameters transported in a received message, a *rate limiter (RL)* associated with a frame source decreases its sending rate. Afterward, the RL increases its rate *unilaterally* to recover lost bandwidth and probe for extra available bandwidth.

Figure 12-6 depicts an example of a QCN-enabled switch generating congestion notification messages to two different RLs.

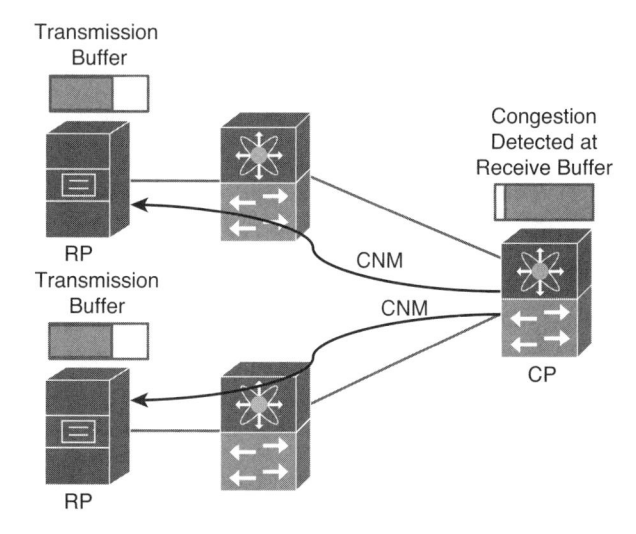

Figure 12-6 *Quantified Congestion Notification*

> **Note** Although QCN could potentially reduce the frequency with which PFC is invoked, its implementation is not mandatory for Fibre Channel over Ethernet topologies at the time of this writing.

Introducing Fibre Channel over Ethernet

Parallel to the development of the DCB Ethernet enhancements, the first application for a PFC lossless virtual wire was also being produced.

Fibre Channel over Ethernet (FCoE or FC-BB_E) is a protocol mapping defined in 2009 in the INCITS T11 FC-BB-5 (Fibre Channel Backbone 5th Generation) standard. In a nutshell, FCoE allows the transport of Fibre Channel over a lossless Ethernet network, thus leveraging some of the DCB efforts described in the last section.

FCoE simply encapsulates byte-encoded Class 2, 3, or F Fibre Channel frames into appropriate Ethernet frames. An FCoE frame has a unique Ethertype (0x8906), and its structure is detailed in Figure 12-7.

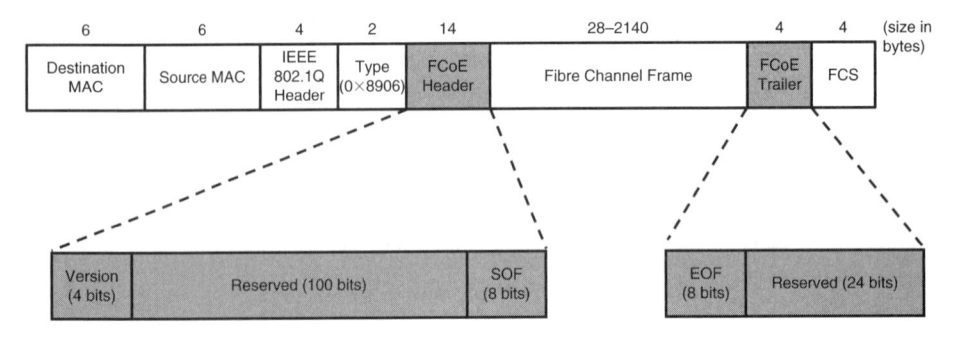

Figure 12-7 *FCoE Frame Format*

According to Figure 12-7, FCoE frames must support a maximum transmission unit (MTU) of 2140 bytes to avoid fragmentation. Frames around this size are also informally referred as "mini-jumbo."

From a Fibre Channel perspective, FCoE works as another flavor of physical media that can carry Fibre Channel frames between *Virtual Fibre Channel (VFC)* ports.

Tip In Chapter 11, "Secret Identities", you have already seen an example of a Virtual Fibre Channel port from Fibre Channel over IP (FCIP): VE_Ports.

To highlight this virtualization technique, Figure 12-8 compares the Fibre Channel and FCoE layer models.

In Figure 12-8, the FC-2 sublevels are also presented to expose which of its elements are reused or completely redesigned in the FCoE layer model. According to the Fibre Channel standards, the FC-2 sublevels are

- **FC-2V**: Defines functions and facilities that a Virtual Fibre Channel port can provide, regardless of the used physical media.

- **FC-2M:** Handles the multiplexing of traffic between different Virtual Fibre Channel ports that might be using the same physical connection.

- **FC-2P:** Is responsible for frame formatting and control functions necessary for information transfer, such as BB_Credit flow control.

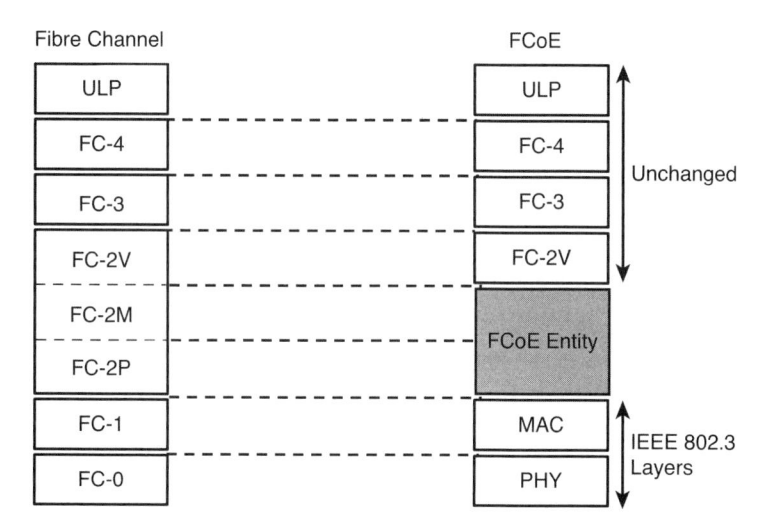

Figure 12-8 *Fibre Channel and FCoE Layers*

FCoE Elements

According to FC-BB-5, the *FCoE Entity* is the element that provides the interface between a Virtual Fibre Channel port and a lossless Ethernet network. The standard also presents the following definitions:

- **Lossless Ethernet Media Access Controller (MAC):** A full-duplex Ethernet MAC implementing extensions that avoid frame loss because of congestion (for example, the PAUSE mechanism [IEEE 802.3-2008] or the priority-based flow control mechanism [IEEE 802.1Qbb]).

- **ENode (FCoE Node):** A Fibre Channel node that can transmit FCoE frames using one or more lossless Ethernet MACs.

- **FCoE Controller:** A functional entity that is coupled with a lossless Ethernet MAC, instantiating (creating) and deinstantiating (deleting) Virtual Fibre Channel ports and FCoE link endpoints. It also performs the FCoE Initialization Protocol (FIP).

- **FCF (FCoE Forwarder):** A Fibre Channel switching element that is able to forward FCoE frames across one or more Media Access Controllers and that optionally includes one or more lossless Ethernet bridging elements and a Fibre Channel fabric interface.

- **FCF-MAC:** A lossless Ethernet MAC coupled with an FCoE controller in an FCF.

- **Lossless Ethernet Bridging Element:** An Ethernet bridging function operating across lossless Ethernet MACs.

- **FCoE Link End-Point (FCoE_LEP):** The data-forwarding component of an FCoE Entity that handles FC frame encapsulation and decapsulation, and the exchange of encapsulated frames with another FCoE_LEP.

- **Virtual Link:** The logical link connecting two FCoE_LEPs.

- **VE_Port (Virtual E_Port):** An instance that communicates with another VE_Port and that is dynamically instantiated on a successful completion of a FIP Exchange Link Parameter (ELP) exchange.

- **VF_Port (Virtual F_Port):** An instance that communicates with one or more VN_Ports and that is dynamically instantiated on a successful completion of a FIP Fabric LOGIn (FLOGI) exchange.

- **VN_Port (Virtual N_Port):** An instance that operates as an N_Port and is dynamically instantiated on successful completion of a FIP FLOGI exchange.

- **Fibre Channel Switching Element:** A functional entity performing Fibre Channel switching among E_Ports, F_Ports, VE_Ports, and VF_Ports on an FCF. Its behavior is specified in the FC-SW standard series.

Figure 12-9 details the relationship among the aforementioned elements.

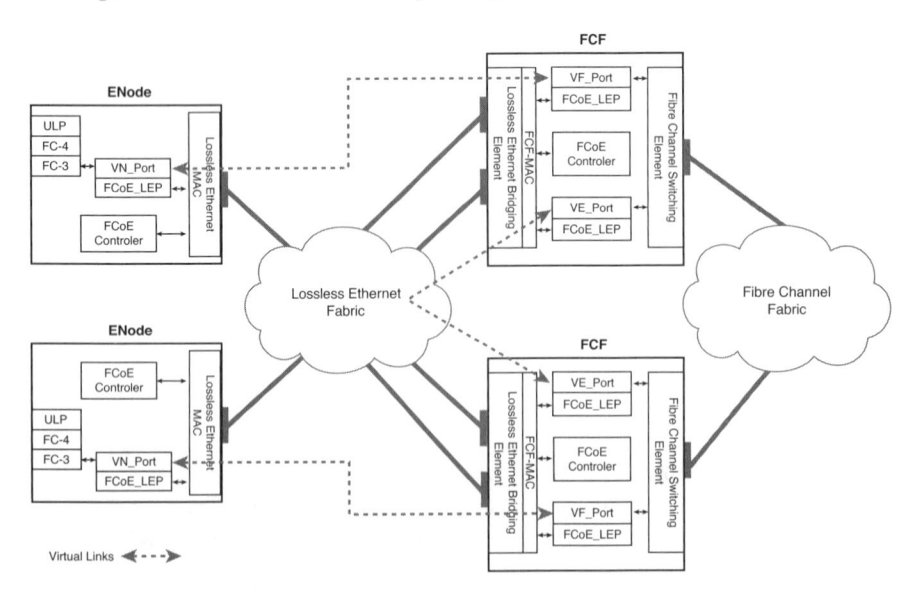

Figure 12-9 *FCoE Functional Model*

The functional model presented in 12-9 is intentionally vague regarding whether the virtual links from the same FCF are using the same lossless Ethernet port. In truth, FC-BB-5 permits the sharing of a single lossless Ethernet interface for multiple virtual links.

FCoE Initialization Protocol

Before any FCoE frame is effectively transported between Virtual Fibre Channel ports, each FCoE device must perform a kick-start ritual coordinated by the FCoE Initialization Protocol (FIP). This protocol is used to perform the functions of FCF detection, FCoE VLAN discovery, virtual link initialization, and connection maintenance.

All FIP frames use a distinct Ethertype (0x8914) and each ENode uses its original MAC address on all FIP frames (except on FIP keepalive frames, which use the instantiated VN_Port MAC address). On FCFs, the FCF-MAC address is used as the source for all FIP frames. Multicast MAC addresses such as All-FCoE-MACs (0110.1801.0000), All-ENode-MACs (0110.1801.0001), and All-FCF-MACs (0110.1801.0002) are also used in select negotiations.

Figure 12-10 illustrates the four FIP negotiation phases between an ENode and an FCF.

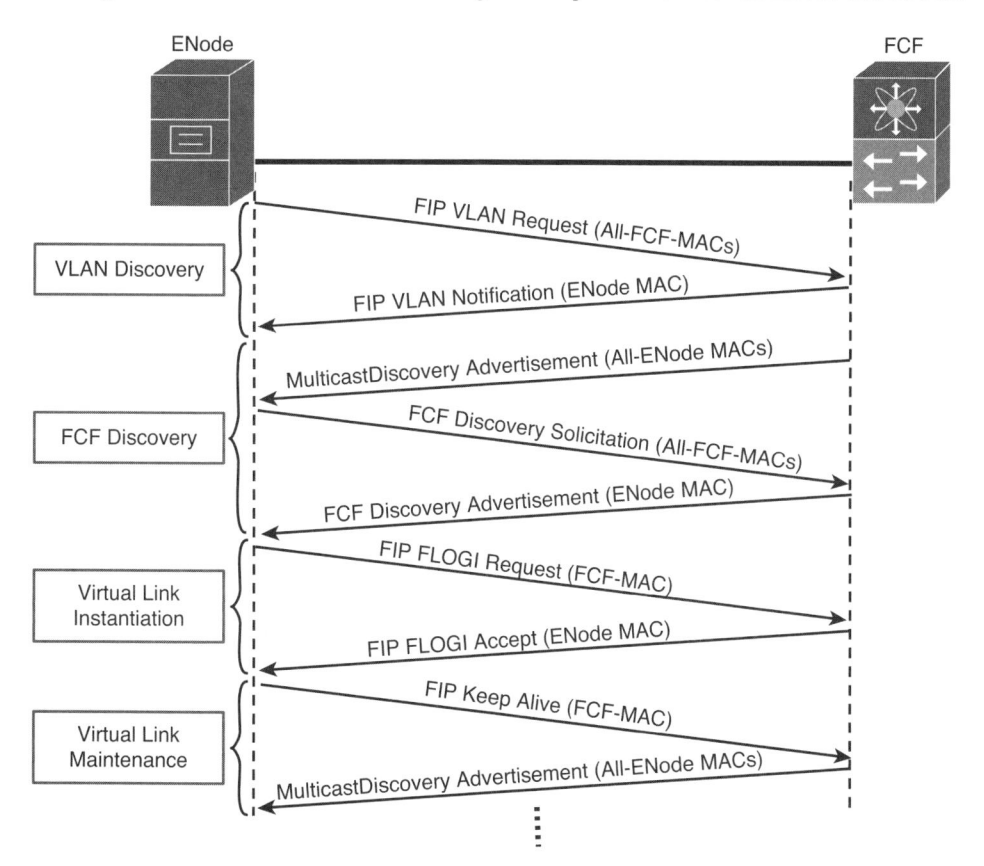

Figure 12-10 *FIP Login Phases*

As described in Figure 12-10, the four FIP negotiation phases are

1. **FIP VLAN discovery:** Begins when the ENode sends a FIP VLAN request frame on its native VLAN to All-FCF-MACs. Each reachable FCF responds with a unicast FIP VLAN notification frame over the same VLAN, stating a list of VLAN IDs that offer FCoE services.

2. **FIP FCF discovery:** This phase is performed independently in each discovered FCoE VLAN. It starts when FCFs periodically send multicast Discovery Advertisements to the All-ENode-MACs group to announce its FCoE capabilities (such as availability for Fabric LOGIn and *FCoE address assignment* available methods). After selecting one FCF, the FCoE controller of an ENode transmits to it a unicast Discovery Solicitation that shall be responded to with a unicast Discovery Advertisement.

3. **FCoE virtual link instantiation:** In this phase, the FCoE controller of an ENode instantiates a VN_Port to a VF_Port located at the chosen FCF. The ENode indicates the *FCoE address assignment* method it intends to use to exchange FCoE frames. Usually, as soon as the virtual link is established, FCoE frames are used to complete the Fibre Channel logins and start frame exchange.

4. **FCoE virtual link maintenance:** In this phase, each FCoE controller from an ENode and its corresponding VF_Port transmit FIP keepalive frames to continuously verify the state of the virtual link. A fault that can occur in a lossless Ethernet network results in the deinstantiation of Virtual Fibre Channel interfaces.

VE_Ports, which will form a virtual link between two FCFs, also perform all four FIP negotiation phases in a similar way as a VN_Port and VF_Port pair. However, the virtual link instantiation phase is dependent of a successful completion of a *FIP ELP request*, instead of a FIP FLOGI request. Furthermore, the virtual link maintenance phase mainly consists of the transmission and reception of multicast Discovery Advertisements from each VE_Port.

As you might have noticed, during the FIP virtual link instantiation, the MAC address that is effectively used in the FCoE communication on a virtual link is assigned. FC-BB-5 defines two methods of FCoE address assignment:

- **Server-Provided MAC Address (SPMA):** A MAC address that is assigned *by an ENode* to a single one of its ENode MACs, and is not assigned to any other MAC within the same Ethernet VLAN. An SPMA can be associated with more than one VN_Port at an ENode MAC.

- **Fabric-Provided MAC Address (FPMA):** MAC address that is assigned *by an FCF* to a single VN_Port at one ENode MAC. A properly formed FPMA is one in which the 24 most significant bits correspond to the *FC Mapped Address Prefix (FC-MAP)* value, and the least significant 24 bits are mapped to the Fibre Channel Identifier (FCID) assigned to the VN_Port by an FCF. This process guarantees that FPMAs are unique within an FCoE fabric.

The FC-MAP value for the upper 24 bits of an FPMA is checked by the FIP Discovery Protocol to ensure that it is consistent across the fabric. It can use a default value or another one in the range from 0x0efc00 to 0x0efcff.

One example of FPMA can be illustrated when an FCF with an FC-MAP of **0x0efc00** assigns the FCID **0x100101** to a VN_Port in response to the ENode's FIP FLOGI frame. Consequently, all FCoE frames from such a Virtual Fibre Channel port will use the FPMA **0efc.0010.0101**.

Note To avoid overlapping of FPMAs on a single broadcast domain, FC-BB-5 does not support multiple virtual fabrics on a single VLAN. And because NX-OS deploys FPMAs, these devices only deploy one VSAN per FCoE VLAN.

Deploying Unified Server Access

In 2008, Cisco shipped its first FCoE-capable switch (Nexus 5020), before any of the previously explained standards were even published. Since then, Cisco has leveraged its real-world experience to actively participate and lead both DCB and FCoE standardization initiatives. (Special acknowledgments must be given to Cisco engineers Claudio DeSanti and Joe Pelissier, who helped develop both initiatives.)

Cisco has complemented its Unified Fabric portfolio with additional switches (Nexus 5010, 4000, 5500, and 6000), Fabric Extenders (Nexus 2232 and blade module B22), and directors (MDS 9500 and Nexus 7000). Simultaneously, other manufacturers such as Emulex, QLogic, and Intel have launched server adapters that could fulfill the promise of cost-effective I/O consolidation with DCB and FCoE.

There are basically two ways to transform a server into an FCoE ENode: through an FCoE software driver (running on its CPU) or through a specialized hardware-based adapter called a *converged network adapter (CNA)*. Although software-based FCoE is becoming more attractive as CPUs get more powerful and servers are already shipped with 10 Gigabit Ethernet LAN-on-motherboard interfaces, the majority of Cisco FCoE deployments use CNAs at the time of this writing.

Generically speaking, a CNA combines the properties of an Ethernet network interface card (NIC) and a Fibre Channel host bus adapter (HBA) on a single adapter card. In fact, prestandard CNAs (also known as Generation 1) had three distinct circuits to deploy a NIC, an HBA, and the FCoE_LEP. Even after the fully standardized Generation 2 CNAs consolidated all these circuits on a single one, operating systems still view the Ethernet and Fibre Channel components as completely separate entities.

Figure 12-11 portrays an example of this perspective, when a Windows-based server detects two Ethernet interfaces and two Fibre Channel ports on a dual-port Generation 2 CNA.

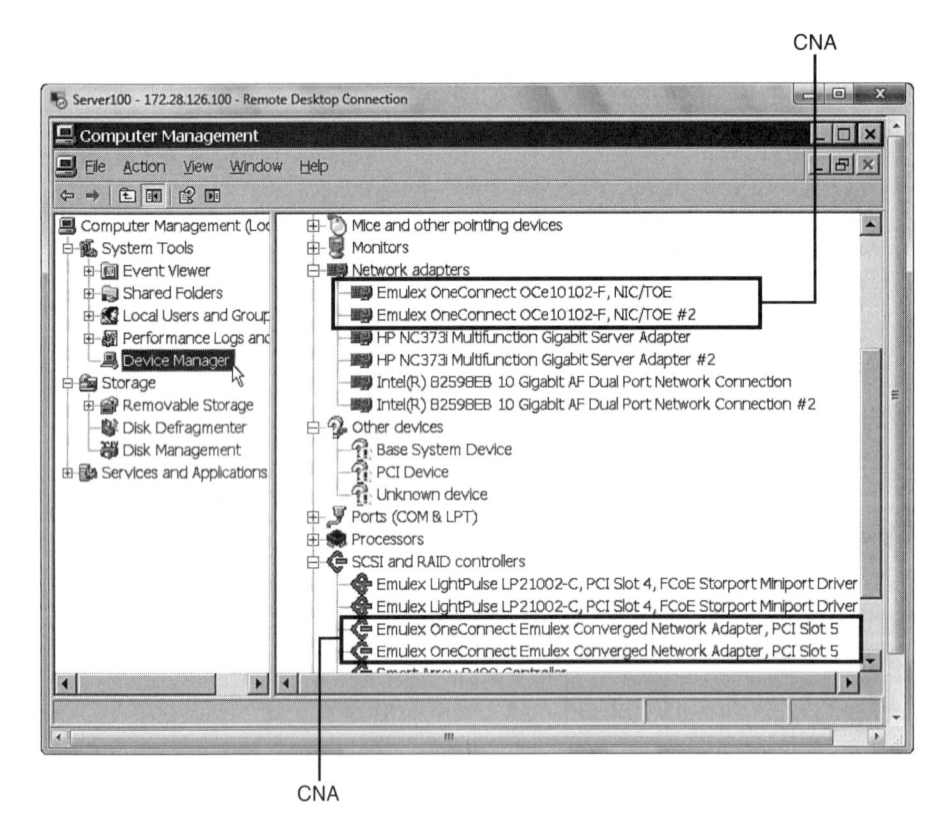

Figure 12-11 *Operating System Perspective of a Converged Network Adapter*

Within the Cisco FCoE portfolio, there are two distinct classes of FCFs that can provide Unified Access (Ethernet and FCoE) to servers: *single-context switches* (such as the such as Nexus 5000, 5500, and 6000) and *VDC-capable switches* (such as the Nexus 7000). In the next sections, you will learn the configuration differences and similarities when these devices are deploying Unified Access to servers.

Configuring Unified Server Access on Single-Context Switches

In single-context converged devices, the Ethernet and the FCoE processes share device's management plane. This arrangement enables a comparatively low number of configuration steps to provide FCoE access for a server with a CNA or an FCoE software driver.

In these switches, four steps are necessary to instantiate an operational VF_Port:

1. Enable the FCoE processes on the device.
2. Create an FCoE VLAN, which is mapped to a single VSAN.

3. Configure and enable an Ethernet physical interface as an IEEE 802.1Q trunk, to transmit and receive FCoE frames from a predefined class of service (the default CoS for FCoE in NX-OS devices is 3).

4. Create and enable a *Virtual Fibre Channel* interface in the correct VSAN to process the encapsulated Fibre Channel traffic.

To demonstrate this procedure, examine how N5K, our soon-to-be FCF, is already preconfigured in the topology shown in Figure 12-12. It has two active 4-Gbps Fibre Channel Inter-Switch Links (ISL) with a Fibre Channel director called MDS. This figure also details the required configuration on both devices to establish a standard Fibre Channel virtual fabric (VSAN 100).

Tip The Fibre Channel interfaces fc1/7 and fc1/8 on MDS have the exact same configuration as interfaces fc2/1 and fc2/2 on N5K.

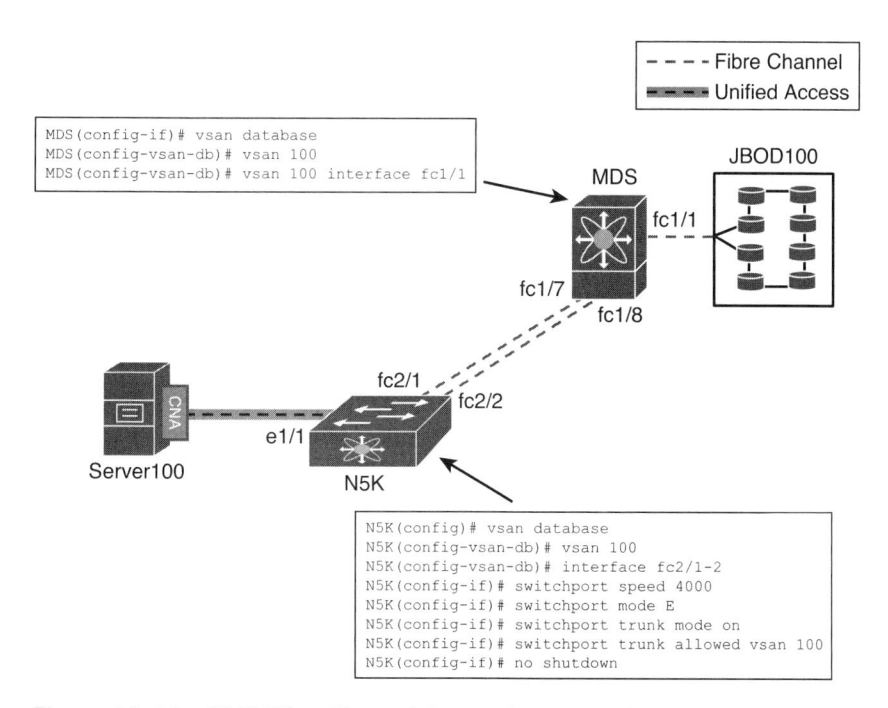

Figure 12-12 *N5K Fibre Channel Connection to MDS*

Shall we get started then? Example 12-1 describes the first three steps from the cited configuration procedure on N5K.

Example 12-1 *Preparing an Ethernet Interface to Create a VF_Port*

```
! STEP 1: Enabling FCoE
N5K(config)# feature fcoe
FC license checked out successfully
! STEP 2: Creating FCoE VLAN 1100 which is mapped to VSAN 100
N5K(config)# vlan 1100
N5K(config-vlan)# fcoe vsan 100
! STEP 3: Configuring an Ethernet interface as a trunk for the FCoE
VLAN (and all pure Ethernet VLANs)
N5K(config-vlan)# interface ethernet 1/1
N5K(config-if)# switchport mode trunk
N5K(config-if)# switchport trunk allowed vlan 1,1100
! It is always recommended to configure host ports as STP edge trunks.
N5K(config-if)# spanning-tree port type edge trunk
[output suppressed]
```

After enabling FCoE, creating the FCoE VLAN (1100), and configuring an Ethernet interface (Ethernet 1/1) trunking the FCoE VLAN, I have also configured the interface as an STP edge trunk because no bridge protocol data unit (BPDU) exchange is expected on it. Although this configuration is not a mandatory procedure for FCoE-enabled servers, it is recommended for host access Ethernet interfaces in general.

In Example 12-2, the Virtual Fibre Channel interface (vfc 11) is finally created. You can observe on this configuration that the VFC is bounded to the physical interface because this is a *point-to-point* topology (where there is a direct connection between the CNA and FCF).

Servers directly connected to FCoE-capable Fabric Extenders (such as the Nexus 2232PP) also form an FCoE point-to-point topology. As explained in Chapter 7, "Virtualized Chassis with Fabric Extenders," the interfaces on a Fabric Extender (FEX) are similarly configured as a local port on a parent switch.

Note At the time of this writing, Nexus 5000, 5500, and 6000 switches support FCoE connections with selected Fabric Extenders.

Back in our configuration, the VFC interface can be handled exactly as a standard NX-OS Fibre Channel interface.

Example 12-2 *Creating and Configuring the Virtual Fibre Channel Interface*

```
! STEP 4: Creating the Virtual Fibre Channel interface
N5K(config-if)# interface vfc 11
! Binding the virtual interface to a physical interface
```

```
N5K(config-if)# bind interface ethernet 1/1
! Configuring the virtual interface as a VF_Port and enabling it
N5K(config-if)# switchport mode F
N5K(config-if)# no shutdown
! Including the virtual interface to VSAN 100
N5K(config-if)# vsan database
N5K(config-vsan-db)# vsan 100 interface vfc 11
```

Tip Depending on your hardware and software combination, you can configure the VFC index as an integer (from 1 to 8192) or as an x/y pair of integers (where x belongs to the 1–8192 range and y to the 1–127 range). I recommend that you try to replicate the physical Ethernet interface index on the VFC interface to facilitate your future management operations.

A CNA in Server100 automatically tries to proceed with its FIP negotiation and Fibre Channel FLOGI. And as you can verify in Example 12-3, it was successful with this endeavor.

Example 12-3 *Verifying FLOGI Database in N5K*

```
N5K# show flogi database
--------------------------------------------------------------------
INTERFACE       VSAN    FCID        PORT NAME                NODE NAME
--------------------------------------------------------------------
vfc11           100     0x110000    10:00:00:00:c9:9c:f7:03  20:00:00:00:c9:9c:f7:03
! N5K Domain ID in VSAN 100 is 0x11
Total number of flogi = 1.
```

Server100 has instantiated a VN_Port that is now part of the VSAN 100 fabric. As a result, it can be viewed on MDS as a standard Fibre Channel N_Port on VSAN 100, as demonstrated in Example 12-4. Further illustrating this status, the example also depicts a standard zoning operation between the VN_Port and a disk from JBOD100.

Example 12-4 *Zoning CNA Server to a Disk from the JBOD100*

```
! Displaying the Name Server database in VSAN 100
MDS# show fcns database

VSAN 100:
--------------------------------------------------------------------
FCID         TYPE     PWWN                    (VENDOR)     FC4-TYPE:FEATURE
--------------------------------------------------------------------
```

```
! Here is the VN_Port from Server100
0x110000    N    10:00:00:00:c9:9c:f7:03 (Emulex)  ipfc scsi-fcp:init
! And here is the disk you will zone to Server100
0xc700cd    NL   22:00:00:0c:50:01:e5:9c (Seagate) scsi-fcp:target
! By the way, MDS is Domain ID 0xc7 on VSAN 100
0xc700ce    NL   22:00:00:0c:50:03:10:bf (Seagate) scsi-fcp:target
[output suppressed]
Total number of entries = 15
! Zoning Server100 and disk from JBOD
MDS(config)# zone name SERVER100-JBOD100 vsan 100
MDS(config-zone)# member pwwn 10:00:00:00:c9:9c:f7:03
MDS(config-zone)# member pwwn 22:00:00:0c:50:01:e5:9c
MDS(config-zone)# zoneset name ZS100 vsan 100
MDS(config-zoneset)# member SERVER100-JBOD100
MDS(config-zoneset)# zoneset activate name ZS100 vsan 100
Zoneset activation initiated. check zone status
! Verifying the zoneset status on VSAN 100
MDS(config)# show zoneset active vsan 100
zoneset name ZS100 vsan 100
  zone name SERVER100-JBOD100 vsan 100
  * fcid 0x110000 [pwwn 10:00:00:00:c9:9c:f7:03]
  * fcid 0xc700cd [pwwn 22:00:00:0c:50:01:e5:9c]
! "I see stars everytime we are zoned together (and logged to the fabric)..."
```

Note As explained in Chapter 10, besides zoning the CNA and the array ports together, logical unit number (LUN) masking would have to be performed on an array to permit the CNA access to a preconfigured LUN.

That is just about it: Server100 is already accessing a remote storage Fibre Channel disk through a 10 Gigabit Ethernet connection to N5K.

I invite you to hang out on N5K a little bit more to further analyze how exactly FCoE is functioning on this device. As a starter, Example 12-5 portrays the output from the **show fcoe** command.

Example 12-5 *FCoE Status on N5K*

```
! Verifying FCoE status on N5K
N5K# show fcoe
Global FCF details
! MAC address used on the FIP operations
     FCF-MAC is 00:05:9b:74:b6:40
! Default FC-MAP to be used on Server100 FPMA
```

```
        FC-MAP is 0e:fc:00
! Priority is not a relevant parameter on point-to-point topologies
        FCF Priority is 128
! FIP Keep Alive period
        FKA Advertisement period for FCF is 8 seconds
! And vfc11 is using the exact same FCF-MAC
VFC MAC details
        vfc11 FCF-MAC is 00:05:9b:74:b6:40
```

As you can see, several FCoE elements, such as FCF-MAC and FC-MAP, are exposed through this command. Also, with the FCID shown in Example 12-3 and N5K FC-MAP in Example 12-5, you can deduce that the VN_Port on Server100 has an FPMA of 0efc.0011.0000.

Tip Although you can change the FC-MAP, FCF priority, and FIP keepalive period parameters, I will use their default values for the sake of simplicity.

In addition, Example 12-6 demonstrates that Spanning Tree Protocol is not enabled on the FCoE VLAN.

Example 12-6 *Spanning Tree on FCoE VLANs*

```
N5K# show spanning-tree vlan 1100
Spanning tree instance(s) for vlan does not exist.
```

Before you ask whether disabling STP on the FCoE VLAN was a wise decision, you should remember that an FCF does not *bridge* an FCoE frame. In truth, an FCF must decapsulate and *route* the inner Fibre Channel frame through its FSPF-generated routes, exactly like a Fibre Channel switch.

Tip It is not wrong to compare FCoE to Layer 3 switching, where a routing protocol actually defines packet forwarding.

Traffic from non-FCoE VLANs are allowed on Ethernet 1/1. And as Example 12-7 details, after some IP traffic is sent through the CNA port, N5K learns the CNA original MAC address on its native VLAN.

Example 12-7 *VLAN 1 MAC Address Table on N5K*

```
N5K# show mac address-table vlan 1
Legend:
```

```
            * - primary entry, G - Gateway MAC, (R) - Routed MAC, O - Overlay MAC
            age - seconds since last seen,+ - primary entry using vPC Peer-Link
   VLAN     MAC Address      Type       age     Secure NTFY   Ports/SWID.SSID.LID
---------+-----------------+--------+---------+------+----+------------------
* 1        0000.c99c.f702   dynamic    10        F      F    Eth1/1
```

Continuing our FCoE "biopsy," Example 12-8 exposes N5K default PFC and ETS definitions. In the example, you will notice that NX-OS devices also deploy modular QoS CLI syntax based on class maps ("what?"), policy maps ("how?"), and service policies ("where?").

Example 12-8 *Default N5K Priority-Based Flow Control and Enhanced Transmission Selection Configuration*

```
! Checking the default Class Maps
N5K# show class-map
  Type qos class-maps
  ===================
[output suppressed]
! FCoE frames are recognized as CoS 3
    class-map type qos match-any class-fcoe
      match cos 3
! All other unicast traffic is assigned to a separate Class Map
    class-map type qos match-any class-default
      match any
[output suppressed]
! Checking how the defined Class Maps are handled on N5K QoS Policy
N5K# show policy-map
! This Policy Map selects the hardware queue for each Class Map
  Type qos policy-maps
  ====================
[output suppressed]
! The type "qos" Policy Map inserts each class on a hardware ingress queue
  policy-map type qos default-in-policy
    class type qos class-fcoe
      set qos-group 1
    class type qos class-default
      set qos-group 0
! FCoE traffic is given 50% of the bandwidth. The remaining resources
(50%) are assigned to the default traffic
  Type queuing policy-maps
  ========================
! For ingress traffic...
  policy-map type queuing default-in-policy
    class type queuing class-fcoe
```

```
      bandwidth percent 50
    class type queuing class-default
      bandwidth percent 50
! ...and egress
  policy-map type queuing default-out-policy
    class type queuing class-fcoe
      bandwidth percent 50
    class type queuing class-default
      bandwidth percent 50
! In this Policy Map type, PFC and appropriate MTUs are assigned per Class Map
  Type network-qos policy-maps
  ================================
! PFC is enabled and MTU adjusted for FCoE traffic
  policy-map type network-qos default-nq-policy
    class type network-qos class-fcoe
      pause no-drop
      mtu 2158
! And the remaining traffic does not get any special treatment
    class type network-qos class-default
      mtu 1500
! The queueing algorithm used on N5K is Weighted Round Robin
N5K# show queuing interface ethernet 1/1
Ethernet1/1 queuing information:
  TX Queuing
    qos-group  sched-type  oper-bandwidth
        0      WRR         50
        1      WRR         50
! Since default "service-policy" commands do not appear show
configuration, I will use the show running-config all option to disclose them
N5K# show running-config all | include "service-policy"
  service-policy type queuing input default-in-policy
  service-policy type queuing output default-out-policy
  service-policy type qos input default-in-policy
  service-policy type network-qos default-nq-policy
```

To sum up, Example 12-8 shows that N5K

- Recognizes Ethernet CoS 3 frames as FCoE
- Allocates 50 percent of interface bandwidth to FCoE
- Enables PFC for FCoE

Obviously, these parameters can be changed to fit whatever requirements a data center network might deploy in its DCB interfaces. However, this customization is subject to some restrictions such as:

- System-defined class maps (class-fcoe and class-default) cannot be deleted.
- The default policy maps (default-in-policy, default-out-policy, and default-nq-policy) cannot be changed.

Through this topology, it is also possible to observe how DCBX silently configures the connected DCB interface on Server100. For example, Figure 12-13 displays the CNA Management Software DCB configuration for Port0 (which is the one connected to e1/1 on N5K).

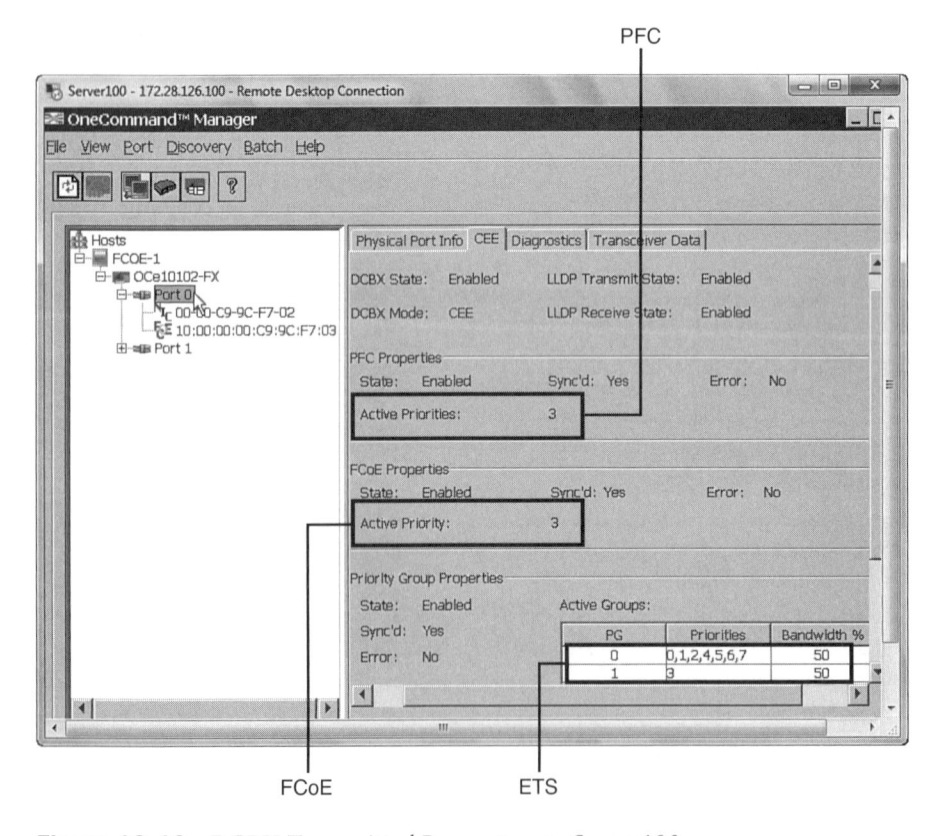

Figure 12-13 *DCBX Transmitted Parameters to Server100*

In Figure 12-13, you can verify that both N5K and the CNA port have agreed ("sync'd") on the values described in Example 12-7. Therefore, the CNA is using the fabric-defined DCB parameters in Port0.

> **Tip** If it is really necessary, you can change the CoS value for FCoE traffic on NX-OS devices using the **match cos** class map command. Note that this value must be consistent on FCoE multihop paths.

Configuring Unified Server Access with Storage VDCs

As explored in Chapter 5, "Instant Switches: Virtual Device Contexts," a virtual device context (VDC) deploys segmentation on all network planes (management, control, and data), creating a virtual Ethernet switch within a physical device. VDC-capable switches (such as the Nexus 7000) can deploy an FCF in a dedicated *storage virtual device context*.

For that reason, a different concept should be applied to Unified Fabric **server** ports on these devices. Because such connections were originally conceived to transport Ethernet and FCoE frames, their corresponding interfaces must belong to *two different VDCs* (Ethernet and storage VDCs). These ports are referred as *shared interfaces*, and their received traffic is split between VDCs according to each frame Ethertype. Hence, FCoE and FIP frames are directed to the storage VDC while the remaining frames are forwarded to the other standard VDC.

Allow me to present a VF_Port configuration on this exact scenario to further clarify the shared interface concept. First, Example 12-9 exposes the available modules on a physical switch (N7K is its default VDC).

Example 12-9 *Hardware Modules on N7K*

```
! Verifying the hardware modules on N7K (default VDC)
N7K# show module
Mod   Ports   Module-Type                    Model              Status
---   -----   ----------------------------   ----------------   ----------
1     32      10 Gbps Ethernet Module        N7K-M132XP-12      ok
2     32      1/10 Gbps Ethernet Module      N7K-F132XP-15      ok
5     0       Supervisor module-1X           N7K-SUP1           active *
6     0       Supervisor module-1X           N7K-SUP1           ha-standby
[output suppressed]
```

Example 12-9 shows that the physical switch has two linecards: one N7K-M132XP-12 on slot 1 and an N7K-F32XP-15 on slot 2. Because F1-, F2-, and F2E-series modules can actually deploy FCoE on Nexus 7000, I will prepare interfaces Ethernet 2/9 to 2/32 for unified server access.

Example 12-10 details the creation of a storage VDC and the allocation of shared interfaces to both VDCs (default and storage VDC).

Example 12-10 *Creating the Storage VDC and Allocating Shared Ports*

```
! Enabling all the NX-OS processes related to FCoE
N7K(config)# install feature-set fcoe
! Creating the Storage VDC. Please notice the VDC type
N7K(config)# vdc Storage-VDC type storage
```

```
Note:  Creating VDC, one moment please ...
N7K %$ VDC-1 %$ %VDC_MGR-2-VDC_ONLINE: vdc 2 has come online
! Limiting the use of F1-series modules (such as the one on slot 2) to the Storage
VDC
N7K(config-vdc)# limit-resource module-type f1
This will cause all ports of unallowed types to be removed from this vdc. Continue
(y/n)? [yes] yes
! Allowing the FCoE processes to be executed on the Storage VDC
N7K(config-vdc)# allow feature-set fcoe
! Allocating VLAN IDs from the default VDC that will be used as FCoE VLANs
N7K(config-vdc)# allocate fcoe-vlan-range 1100,1200 from vdcs N7K
! Allocating interfaces Ethernet 2/9 to 2/32 to both VDCs
N7K(config-vdc)# allocate shared interface ethernet 2/9-32
Ports that share the port group of the interfaces you have specified
will be affected as well. Continue (y/n)? [yes] yes
```

Note Because shared interfaces must trunk FCoE VLANs, their VLAN identifier has global significance for both VDCs. Consequently, the VLAN IDs used on the FCoE VLANs in the storage VDCs must be different than any other VLAN used on the Ethernet VDC.

After the configuration in Example 12-10 is performed, both VDCs own each interface from the allocated range. If a CNA port on Server200 is connected to Ethernet 2/9, its standard Ethernet configurations (such as IEEE 802.1Q trunking) must be executed on the Ethernet VDC, as demonstrated in Example 12-11.

Example 12-11 *Preparing and Testing Interface Ethernet 2/9 for Pure Ethernet Traffic*

```
! Configuring interface Ethernet 2/9 as a trunk for VLANs 1 to 10
N7K(config-vdc)# interface ethernet 2/9
N7K(config-if)# switchport mode trunk
N7K(config-if)# switchport trunk allowed vlan 1-10
! It is always recommended to configure host ports as STP edge
trunks. This is not mandatory, though...
N7K(config-if)# spanning-tree port type edge trunk
[output suppressed]
! Enabling the interface
N7K(config-if)# no shutdown
! After Server200 sends some IP traffic through the CNA port, the
default VDC learns its Ethernet MAC Address
N7K# sh mac address-table vlan 1
Legend:
        * - primary entry, G - Gateway MAC, (R) - Routed MAC, O - Overlay MAC
```

```
               age - seconds since last seen,+ - primary entry using vPC Peer-Link,
           (T) - True, (F) - False
   VLAN     MAC Address      Type        age     Secure NTFY Ports/SWID.SSID.LID
---------+-----------------+--------+---------+------+----+------------------
* 1        0000.c99c.f704   dynamic    60         F    F    Eth2/9
```

As you can see, interface Ethernet 2/9 can already bridge standard Ethernet traffic received on its trunked VLANs (including the native).

On the other hand, you should configure the storage VDC as an FCF for Server200. Example 12-12 shows the required configuration on the storage VDC to insert Server200 in VSAN 200.

Tip As you will notice, the configuration is similar to the one demonstrated in the earlier section "Configuring Unified Server Access on Single-Context Switches." Therefore, I will use the same four-step procedure.

Example 12-12 *Configuring the Storage VDC*

```
! Accessing Storage-VDC CLI
N7K# switchto vdc Storage-VDC
! Since it is the first time the VDC is accessed, it offers the setup
script to generate an initial running configuration. Allow me to skip
the boring parts for you (since none is related to storage configurations).
 [output suppressed]
Cisco Nexus Operating System (NX-OS) Software
! This is the VDC CLI in exec mode. Just another jump...
 [output suppressed]
N7K-Storage-VDC# configure terminal
Enter configuration commands, one per line.  End with CNTL/Z.
! STEP1: Enabling FCoE-related processes on this VDC
N7K-Storage-VDC(config)# feature-set fcoe
! STEP2: Creating FCoE VLAN 1200 and mapping it to VSAN 200
N7K-Storage-VDC(config)# vlan 1200
N7K-Storage-VDC(config-vlan)# fcoe vsan 200
! STEP 3: Configuring a shared interface as a trunk for the FCoE VLAN
N7K-Storage-VDC(config-vsan-db)# interface ethernet 2/9
N7K-Storage-VDC(config-if)# switchport trunk allowed vlan 1200
N7K-Storage-VDC(config-if)# no shutdown
```

Note At the time of this writing, Nexus 7000 switches do not support FCoE connections with Fabric Extenders.

With this background, the storage VDC can instantiate a VF_Port and bind it to shared interface Ethernet 2/9. As Example 12-13 demonstrates, the VFC configuration is also very similar to the one executed on N5K.

Example 12-13 *Configuring the Virtual Fibre Channel Interface on Storage VDC*

```
! STEP 4: Creating vfc 2/9 as a VF_Port and assigning it to VSAN 200
N7K-Storage-VDC(config-if)# interface vfc 2/9
N7K-Storage-VDC(config-if)# bind interface ethernet 2/9
N7K-Storage-VDC(config-if)# switchport mode F
N7K-Storage-VDC(config-if)# no shutdown
N7K-Storage-VDC(config-if)# vsan database
N7K-Storage-VDC(config-vsan-db)# vsan 200
N7K-Storage-VDC(config-vsan-db)# vsan 200 interface vfc2/9
```

At last, the CNA port on Server200 can proceed with its FIP FLOGI and Fibre Channel operations. Actually, Example 12-14 shows the VN_Port inserted in the storage VDC FLOGI database.

Example 12-14 *Verifying the FLOGI Database*

```
N7K-Storage-VDC# show flogi database
--------------------------------------------------------------------------------
INTERFACE        VSAN    FCID        PORT NAME                NODE NAME
--------------------------------------------------------------------------------
vfc2/9           200     0x400000    10:00:00:00:c9:9c:f7:05  20:00:00:00:c9:9c:f7:05
! The storage VDC Domain ID in VSAN 200 is 0x40
Total number of flogi = 1.
```

Drilling down in the storage VDC, Example 12-15 depicts its FC-MAP and FPMA assigned to Server200.

Example 12-15 *Storage VDC FC-MAP and MAC Address Table on VLAN 1200*

```
! Verifying the VDC FC-MAP
N7K-Storage-VDC# show fcoe | include FC-MAP
        FC-MAP is 0e:fc:00
! Checking Server200's derived FPMA
N7K-Storage-VDC# show mac address-table vlan 1200
```

```
Legend:
        * - primary entry, G - Gateway MAC, (R) - Routed MAC, O - Overlay MAC
        age - seconds since last seen,+ - primary entry using vPC Peer-Link,
        (T) - True, (F) - False
   VLAN     MAC Address      Type        age      Secure NTFY Ports/SWID.SSID.LID
---------+-----------------+--------+---------+------+----+------------------
* 1200     0efc.0040.0000   static      -         F    F   Eth2/9
```

As expected, the fabric-provided MAC address results from the concatenation of the VDC FC-MAP (**0x0ffc00**) and the VN_Port FCID (**0x400000**).

As a graphical summary, Figure 12-14 represents the status achieved with Examples 12-9 through 12-12.

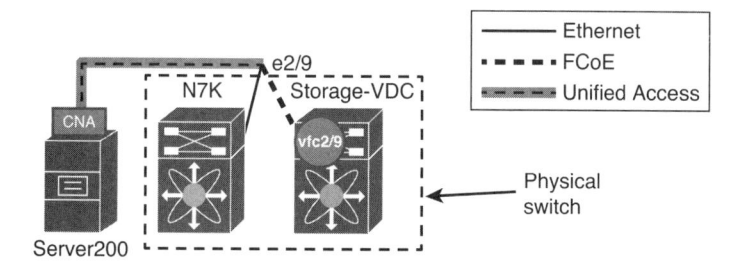

Figure 12-14 *Shared Interface Between VDCs N7K and Storage VDC*

Configuring Multihop FCoE

In the section "Introducing Fibre Channel over Ethernet," earlier in this chapter, you learned that the FC-BB-5 standard also defines virtual links between two VE_Ports from distinct FCFs. And on NX-OS converged switches, these VE_Ports are also deployed through Virtual Fibre Channel interfaces.

Figure 12-15 represents the physical connection between interface Ethernet 2/8 on N7K and Ethernet 1/15 on N5K. With this 10 Gigabit Ethernet uplink, Storage-VDC and N5K will form an (FCoE) Enhanced ISL (EISL).

Figure 12-15 also details preliminary configurations I have done in MDS and N5K. With these configurations, MDS and N5K are also prepared to merge with VSAN 200 on Storage-VDC (where Server200 is logged in to).

Let's start with the configuration of the VE_Port on Storage-VDC. Example 12-16 depicts the migration of *dedicated* Ethernet interfaces from the default VDC to Storage-VDC. It also shows how one of these interfaces can be prepared to transport two FCoE VLANs.

524 Data Center Virtualization Fundamentals

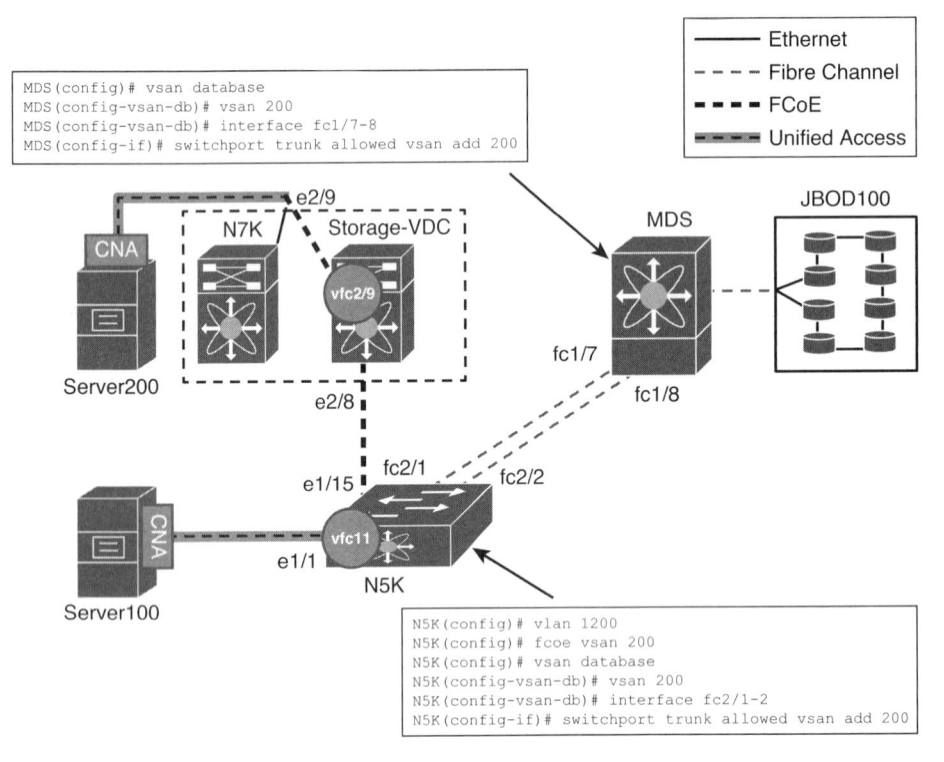

```
MDS(config)# vsan database
MDS(config-vsan-db)# vsan 200
MDS(config-vsan-db)# interface fc1/7-8
MDS(config-if)# switchport trunk allowed vsan add 200
```

```
N5K(config)# vlan 1200
N5K(config)# fcoe vsan 200
N5K(config)# vsan database
N5K(config-vsan-db)# vsan 200
N5K(config-vsan-db)# interface fc2/1-2
N5K(config-if)# switchport trunk allowed vsan add 200
```

Figure 12-15 *Physically Connecting N7K and N5K and Configuring VSAN 200 on MDS and N5K*

Example 12-16 *Inserting Dedicated Interfaces into Storage VDC and Preparing Storage VDC for the VSAN Trunk Creation*

```
! Migrating interfaces Ethernet 2/1 to 2/8 to Storage-VDC
N7K(config)# vdc Storage-VDC
N7K(config-vdc)# allocate interface ethernet 2/1-8
Moving ports will cause all config associated to them in source vdc
to be removed. Are you sure you want to move the ports (y/n)?  [yes]
yes
! Accessing Storage-VDC CLI
N7K(config-vdc)# switchto vdc Storage-VDC
Cisco Nexus Operating System (NX-OS) Software
[output suppressed]
N7K-Storage-VDC# configure terminal
Enter configuration commands, one per line.  End with CNTL/Z.
! Creating FCoE VLAN 1100 and mapping it to VSAN 100
N7K-Storage-VDC(config)# vlan 1100
N7K-Storage-VDC(config-vlan)# fcoe vsan 100
! Creating VSAN 100 on the Storage VDC
```

```
N7K-Storage-VDC(config-vlan)# vsan database
N7K-Storage-VDC(config-vsan-db)# vsan 100
! Preparing interface Ethernet 2/8 to trunk both FCoE VLANs (1100, 1200)
N7K-Storage-VDC(config)# interface ethernet 2/8
N7K-Storage-VDC(config-if-range)# switchport mode trunk
N7K-Storage-VDC(config-if-range)# switchport trunk allowed vlan 1100,1200
N7K-Storage-VDC(config-if-range)# no shutdown
```

Note At the time of this writing, only dedicated (nonshared) interfaces can be configured as VE_Ports on storage VDCs.

An FCoE VLAN can only contain a single virtual fabric. Therefore, interface Ethernet 2/8 must allow FCoE VLANs 1100 and 1200 to enable a VSAN trunk with their corresponding VSANs (100 and 200, respectively).

In Example 12-17, the VE_Port vfc2/8 is finally instantiated on the storage VDC.

Example 12-17 *Creating the VFC Interface on Storage-VDC*

```
! Creating and enabling a VE_Port and allowing VSANs 100 and 200
N7K-Storage-VDC(config-if-range)# interface vfc2/8
N7K-Storage-VDC(config-if)# bind interface ethernet 2/8
N7K-Storage-VDC(config-if)# switchport mode E
N7K-Storage-VDC(config-if)# switchport trunk allowed vsan 200
N7K-Storage-VDC(config-if)# switchport trunk allowed vsan add 100
N7K-Storage-VDC(config-if)# no shutdown
```

Note By default, all VFC interfaces on NX-OS devices are configured as VSAN trunks, and that mode cannot be disabled.

Example 12-17 denotes the virtual link configuration on the storage VDC. As expected, single-context switches require a slightly simpler, but very similar configuration.

Example 12-18 depicts the instantiation of a VE_Port (vfc115) that is bound to interface Ethernet 1/15 on N5K.

Example 12-18 *Creating the VFC Interface on N5K*

```
! Configuring interface Ethernet 1/15 as a trunk for VLANs 1100 and 1200
N5K(config)# interface ethernet 1/15
N5K(config-if)# switchport mode trunk
```

```
N5K(config-if)# switchport trunk allowed vlan 1100,1200
N5K(config-if)# no shutdown
! Creating interface vfc 115 and allowing VSANs 100 and 200
N5K(config)# interface vfc 115
N5K(config-if)# bind interface ethernet 1/15
N5K(config-if)# switchport mode E
N5K(config-if)# switchport trunk allowed vsan 200
N5K(config-if)# switchport trunk allowed vsan add 100
N5K(config-if)# no shutdown
```

With both VE_Ports configured, a virtual link is established between both FCFs.

Example 12-19 depicts this status. This FCoE EISL permits VSANs 100 and 200 to merge on all three switches (Storage-VDC on N7K, N5K, and MDS).

Example 12-19 *Checking Interface vfc 2/8 Status on Storage VDC*

```
N7K-Storage-VDC# show interface vfc 2/8
! This is the default unchangeable trunk mode
vfc2/8 is trunking
    Bound interface is Ethernet2/8
    Hardware is Ethernet
    Port WWN is 20:48:00:26:98:0d:51:80
    Admin port mode is E, trunk mode is on
    snmp link state traps are enabled
    Port mode is TE
! This port belongs to VSAN 1 but it does not trunk it
    Port vsan is 1
! Virtual ISL speed is important to FSPF path computation
    Speed is 10 Gbps
! VSANs 100 and 200 are merged between Storage-VDC and N5K
    Trunk vsans (admin allowed and active) (100,200)
    Trunk vsans (up)                       (100,200)
    Trunk vsans (isolated)                 ()
    Trunk vsans (initializing)             ()
[output suppressed]
```

Note For the sake of brevity, I will not describe the similar output from interface vfc115 on N5K.

At this stage, all three devices are forming virtual Fibre Channel fabrics over two different "media": optical fiber (between N5K and MDS) and Ethernet (between N5K and the storage VDC). Demonstrating that both VSANs (100 and 200) are active on these devices, Example 12-20 depicts their assigned domain IDs from the perspective of the MDS.

Example 12-20 *Physical Fabric VSANs and Domains*

```
! Domain IDs in VSAN 100
MDS# show fcdomain domain-list vsan 100


Number of domains: 3
Domain ID          WWN
---------          -----------------------
! MDS Domain ID
0xc7(199)    20:64:00:05:73:a8:16:41 [Local] [Principal]
! This is N5K (do you remember Server100's FLOGI?)
 0x11(17)    20:64:00:05:9b:74:b6:41
! And by exclusion, This is Storage-VDC
0x8b(139)    20:64:00:26:98:0d:51:81
! Domain IDs in VSAN 200
MDS# show fcdomain domain-list vsan 200


Number of domains: 3
Domain ID          WWN
---------          -----------------------
! Respectively: MDS, N5K, and Storage-VDC
 0x2e(46)    20:c8:00:05:73:a8:16:41 [Local] [Principal]
 0x4f(79)    20:c8:00:05:9b:74:b6:41
 0x40(64)    20:c8:00:26:98:0d:51:81
```

In addition, Example 12-21 curiously confirms that the FCoE ISL between N5K and Storage-VDC has an FSPF cost of 100 (which is the default cost of a 10-Gbps link).

Example 12-21 *Verifying the Fibre Channel Routing Table in N5K*

```
N5K# show fcroute unicast vsan 100

D:direct   R:remote   P:permanent   V:volatile   A:active   N:non-active
                                                   # Next
Protocol   VSAN       FC ID/Mask           RCtl/Mask    Flags   Hops  Cost
--------   ----       --------- --------   ---- ----    -----   ----  ----
local      100        0x110000 0xffffff    0x00 0x00    D P A   1     1
fspf       100        0x8b0000 0xff0000    0x00 0x00    D P A   1     100
fspf       100        0xc70000 0xff0000    0x00 0x00    D P A   2     250
```

The storage VDC on N7K is also capable of performing other functions as an FCoE director. For example, I have configured and activated an Inter-VSAN Routing (IVR) zone between Server200 on VSAN200 and another disk in JBOD100.

Because the IVR configuration is extremely similar to the one I have explained in the section "Inter-VSAN Routing" from Chapter 11, Example 12-22 only details the IVR status on Storage-VDC.

Example 12-22 *IVR Status Between Server200 and Disk on JBOD100*

```
! Exposing Storage-VDC sWWN
N7K-Storage-VDC# show wwn switch
Switch WWN is 20:00:00:26:98:0d:51:80
! Verifying IVR VSAN-topology enabled by Storage-VDC
N7K-Storage-VDC# show ivr vsan-topology


AFID   SWITCH WWN                   Active    Cfg. VSANS
-----------------------------------------------------------
   1   20:00:00:26:98:0d:51:80 *    yes       no   1,100,200
The star


Total:   1 entry in active and configured IVR VSAN-Topology
! Verifying active IVR zone set
N7K-Storage-VDC# show ivr zoneset active
zoneset name IVRZS
  zone name SERVER200-JBOD100
    * pwwn 10:00:00:00:c9:9c:f7:05         vsan 200 autonomous-fabric-id 1
    * pwwn 22:00:00:0c:50:03:10:bf         vsan 100 autonomous-fabric-id 1
```

Configuring Virtual Fibre Channel PortChannels

Besides DCB-enabled Ethernet interfaces, Virtual Fibre Channel interfaces can also be bound to Fibre Channel PortChannels, providing redundancy and load balancing for virtual links between FCFs. These structures are called *VFC-PortChannels*.

Figure 12-16 portrays two connections between N7K and MDS (with a licensed FCoE eight-port module installed in slot 5). In this section, I will use both to further explore the VFC-PortChannel basic concept and its consequences on a mixed Fibre Channel and FCoE fabric.

Basically, a VFC-PortChannel is a VE_Port bound to a standard Ethernet PortChannel, such as the one demonstrated in Example 12-23.

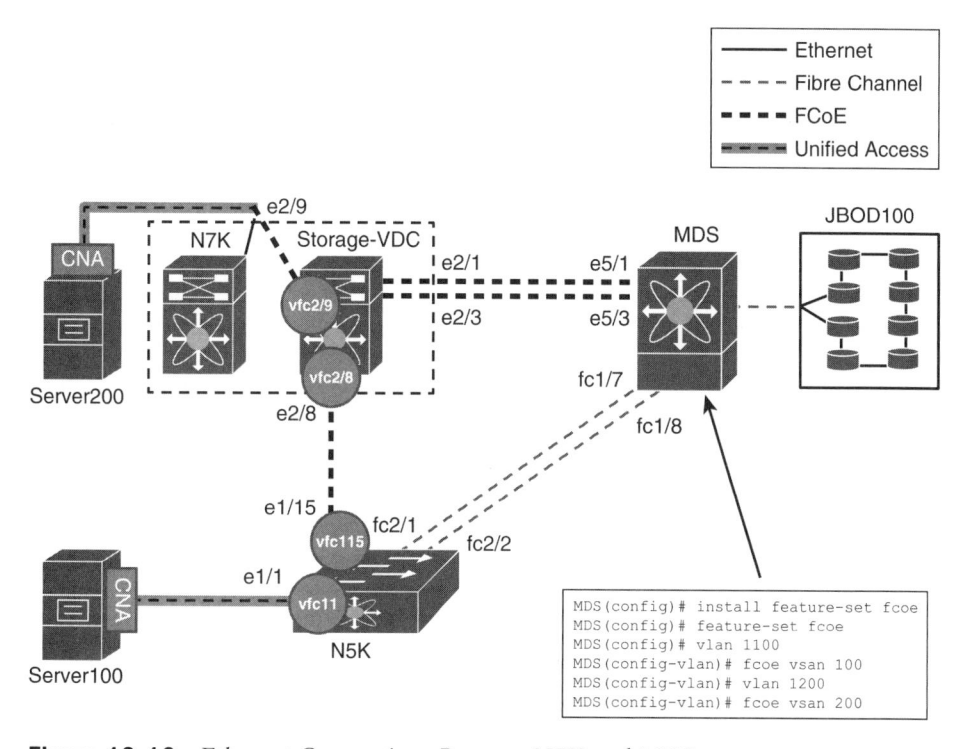

Figure 12-16 *Ethernet Connections Between N7K and MDS*

Example 12-23 *Configuring FCoE on MDS*

```
! Aggregating interfaces ethernet 5/1 and 5/3 on a PortChannel
MDS(config-vlan)# interface ethernet 5/1, ethernet 5/3
MDS(config-if-range)# switchport mode trunk
MDS(config-if-range)# switchport trunk allowed vlan 1100,1200
MDS(config-if-range)# channel-group 300 force mode on
MDS(config-if-range)# no shutdown
```

With the same configuration on interfaces Ethernet 2/1 and 2/3 on the storage VDC, Ethernet PortChannel 300 becomes operational (MDS 9000 allows Ethernet PortChannel IDs from 257 to 4095).

Example 12-24 shows the Ethernet PortChannel 300 status on the storage VDC.

Example 12-24 *Verifying PortChannel 300 Status on Storage-VDC*

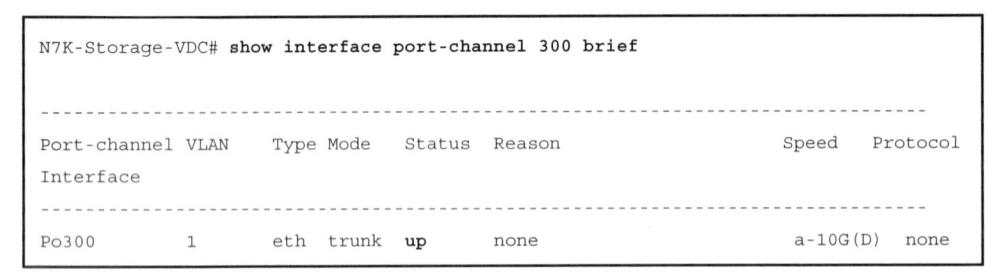

```
N7K-Storage-VDC# show interface port-channel 300 brief

--------------------------------------------------------------------------------
Port-channel VLAN    Type Mode   Status  Reason                  Speed      Protocol
Interface
--------------------------------------------------------------------------------
Po300        1       eth  trunk  up      none                    a-10G(D)   none
```

At this time, it is possible to create a VFC-PortChannel and bind it to PortChannel 300 on both devices. Example 12-25 deals with such a configuration on MDS and shows its results (considering that N7K was similarly configured).

Example 12-25 *Configuring and Verifying the Status of a Virtual Fibre Channel PortChannel on MDS*

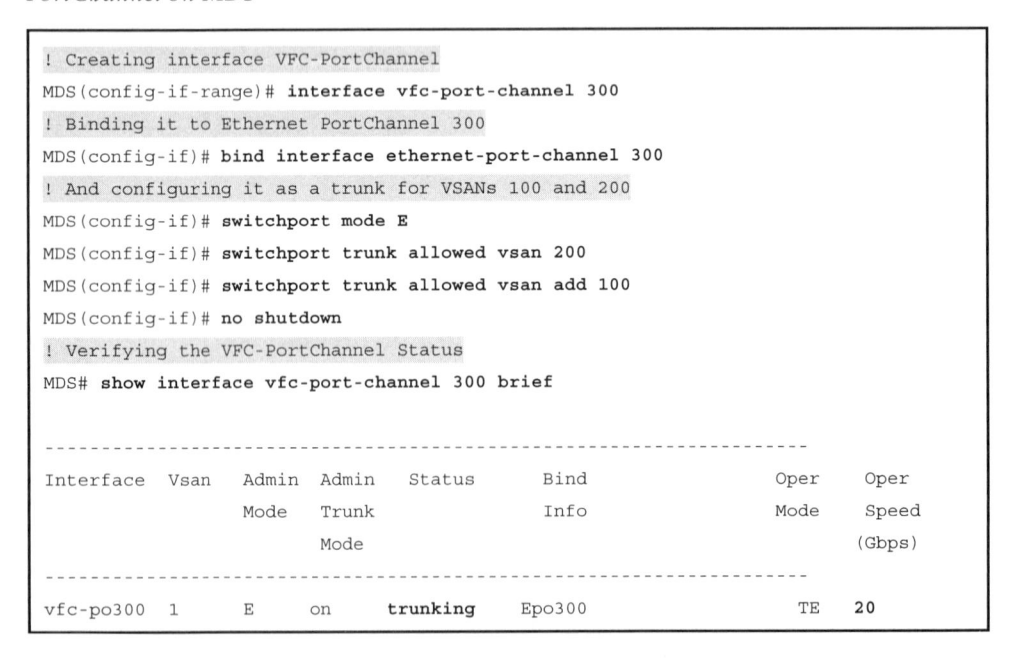

```
! Creating interface VFC-PortChannel
MDS(config-if-range)# interface vfc-port-channel 300
! Binding it to Ethernet PortChannel 300
MDS(config-if)# bind interface ethernet-port-channel 300
! And configuring it as a trunk for VSANs 100 and 200
MDS(config-if)# switchport mode E
MDS(config-if)# switchport trunk allowed vsan 200
MDS(config-if)# switchport trunk allowed vsan add 100
MDS(config-if)# no shutdown
! Verifying the VFC-PortChannel Status
MDS# show interface vfc-port-channel 300 brief

--------------------------------------------------------------------------------
Interface    Vsan   Admin   Admin   Status    Bind        Oper    Oper
                    Mode    Trunk             Info        Mode    Speed
                            Mode                                  (Gbps)
--------------------------------------------------------------------------------
vfc-po300    1      E       on      trunking  Epo300      TE      20
```

Because this 20-Gbps path has a default FSPF cost of 50, Storage-VDC becomes the preferred path from traffic between MDS and N5K. Figure 12-26 demonstrates this new FSPF-generated path through N5K's Fibre Channel routing table.

Example 12-26 *Routing Table on N5K*

```
N5K# show fcroute unicast vsan 100


D:direct   R:remote   P:permanent   V:volatile   A:active   N:non-active
                                                     # Next
Protocol   VSAN      FC ID/Mask          RCtl/Mask      Flags   Hops   Cost
--------   ----      ---------- -------  ----- -----    -----   ----   ----
local      100       0x110000   0xffffff  0x00  0x00    D P A    1      1
fspf       100       0x8b0000   0xff0000  0x00  0x00    D P A    1      100
! The path to MDS Domain ID in VSAN 100 has a new cost of 100 (10Gbps) plus 50
(20Gbps)
fspf       100       0xc70000   0xff0000  0x00  0x00    D P A    1      150
```

To summarize what was configured on MDS, Storage-VDC, and N5K, Figure 12-17 depicts the resulting fabric topology as seen on DCNM-SAN. You will notice that in DCNM-SAN, FCoE virtual links are represented with bracketed lines.

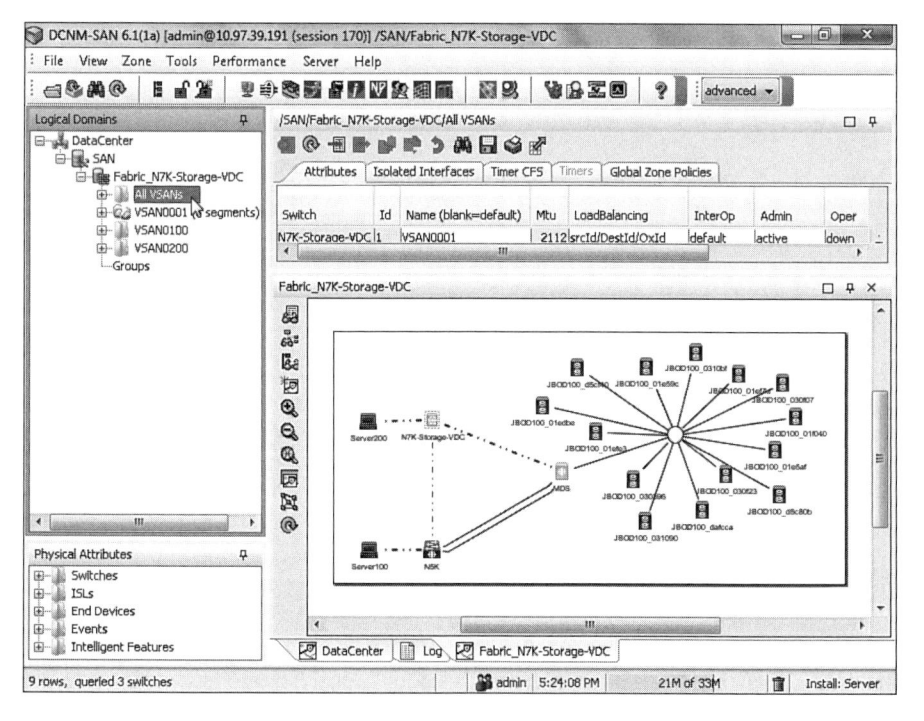

Figure 12-17 *DCNM-SAN Topology*

FCoE N_Port Virtualization

As discussed in Chapter 11, Nexus 5000, 5500, and 6000 switches can also run in N_Port Virtualization (NPV) mode, relieving a Fibre Channel fabric from an additional domain ID and other fabric processes. As you have learned, a switch running in NPV mode emulates an HBA, transforming received FLOGIs into FDISCs (Discover F_Port service parameters) and directing them to upstream F_Ports on Fibre Channel switches configured with N_Port ID Virtualization (NPIV).

These switches can also deploy *FCoE NPV*, mirroring this exact behavior on FCoE fabrics. Actually, FCoE leverages the FC-BB-5 definition of *FIP NPIV FDISCs* to allow multiple VN_Ports to share an FCF VN_Port.

> **Tip** A switch running in FCoE NPV mode is still an FCF because it still must instantiate VF_Ports for attached hosts to forward their FIP and FCoE frames to upstream switches.

Running in FCoE NPV mode, a switch must proxy all communication between directly connected hosts and upstream switches through *Virtual Node Proxy ports (VNP_Ports)*. As with any NX-OS Virtual Fibre Channel interface, VNP_Ports are also configured as VSAN trunks by default.

There are two ways to enable FCoE NPV in a Nexus switch:

- **Enable FCoE and then enable NPV mode.** This conversion method permits the coexistence of FCoE VNP_Ports and Fibre Channel NP_Ports. The switch needs a reload, as explained in Chapter 11.

- **Enable FCoE NPV,** where no reload is required if FCoE is not yet enabled on the device. However, this method does not allow the configuration of NP_Ports.

To further explore the similarities of FCoE NPV and NPV, I will use the first method to convert N5K. Figure 12-18 shows the physical connection between N5K and Storage-VDC, which is already primed to become the upstream switch.

In Figure 12-18, you can see that two additional configurations were performed on the storage VDC:

- I have enabled NPIV.
- I have configured interface vfc 2/8 as an F-Trunk for VSANs 100 and 200.

Example 12-27 details N5K behavior when NPV mode is enabled on the switch.

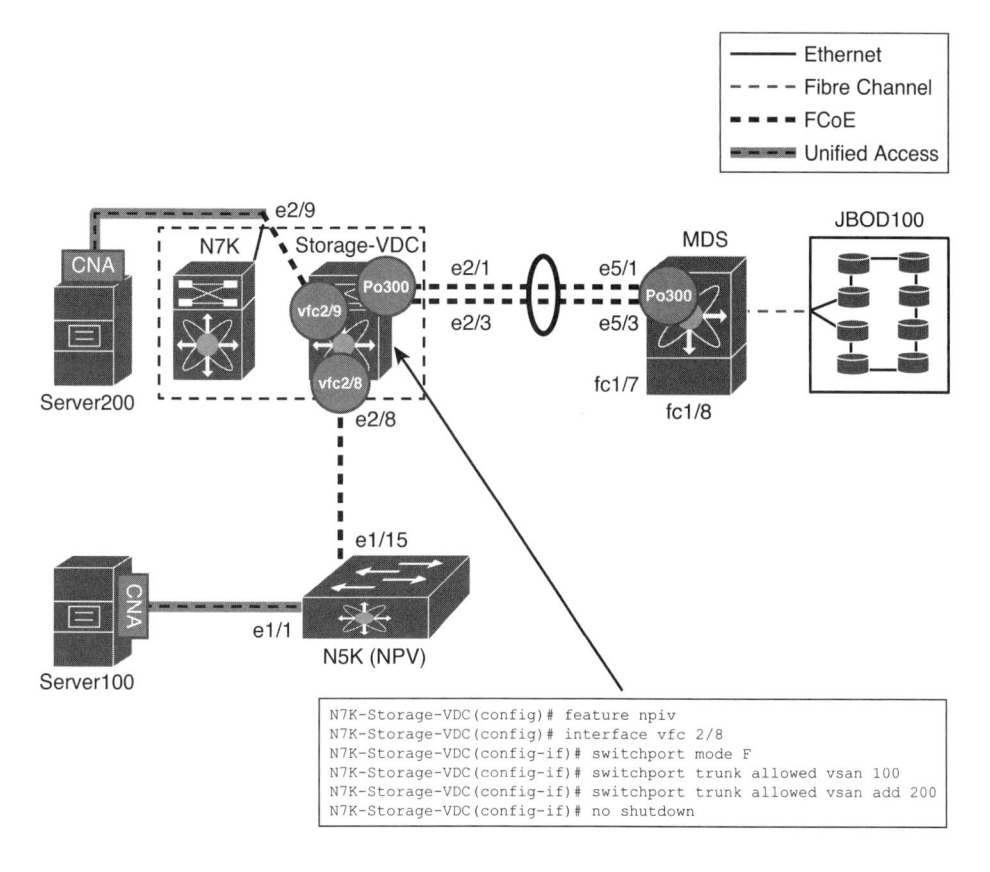

Figure 12-18 *FCoE NPV Topology*

Example 12-27 *Enabling NPV on N5K*

```
N5K(config)# feature npv
Verify that boot variables are set and the changes are saved.
Changing to npv mode erases the current configuration and reboots the
switch in npv mode. Do you want to continue? (y/n):y
%KERN-0-SYSTEM_MSG: Shutdown Ports.. - kernel
! The switch reboots with an erased configuration...
[output suppressed]
! But it maintains its host name, local user database, and management interface
configuration
Nexus 5000 Switch
login: admin
Password:
Cisco Nexus Operating System (NX-OS) Software
[output suppressed]
N5K#
```

After the reboot, you can establish FCoE connectivity to Server100 with the same four-step procedure described in the earlier section "Configuring Unified Server Access on Single-Context Switches." For that reason, I will not repeat it.

Nevertheless, this VF_Port will remain nonoperational until a VNP_Port is configured and activated. Therefore, Example 12-28 details the configuration of a VNP_Port on N5K.

Example 12-28 *Creating a VNP_Port on N5K*

```
! Configuring Ethernet 1/15 as a trunk for both FCoE VLANs (1100 and 1200)
N5K(config)# interface ethernet 1/15
N5K(config-if)# switchport mode trunk
N5K(config-if)# switchport trunk allowed vlan 1100,1200
N5K(config-if)# no shutdown
! Configuring interface vfc115 as a VNP_Port
N5K(config-if)# interface vfc115
N5K(config-if)# bind interface ethernet 1/15
N5K(config-if)# switchport mode NP
N5K(config-if)# switchport trunk allowed vsan 100
N5K(config-if)# switchport trunk allowed vsan add 200
N5K(config-if)# no shutdown
```

As interface vfc115 is in trunk mode, you do not need to worry if it is on VSAN 1 (as long as it is operational on the switch).

Example 12-29 shows the operational status of both VFC interfaces on N5K.

Example 12-29 *Interface Status on N5K*

```
N5K-FCoE# show interface vfc115, vfc11 brief
-------------------------------------------------------------------------
Interface  Vsan   Admin   Admin    Status      SFP    Oper   Oper    Port
                  Mode    Trunk                       Mode   Speed   Channel
                          Mode                               (Gbps)
-------------------------------------------------------------------------
vfc11      100    F       on       trunking    --     TF     auto    --
vfc115     1      NP      on       trunking    --     TNP    auto    --
N5K-FCoE# show npv flogi-table
-------------------------------------------------------------------------
                                                              SERVER
                                                              EXTERNAL
INTERFACE VSAN FCID         PORT NAME              NODE NAME              INTERFACE
-------------------------------------------------------------------------
vfc11     100  0x8b0000  10:00:00:00:c9:9c:f7:03 20:00:00:00:c9:9c:f7:03 vfc115

Total number of flogi = 1.
```

In Example 12-29, you can also observe that vfc11 has provided an FCID (0x8b0000) derived from the Storage-VDC domain ID in VSAN 100 (0x8b). Therefore, the CNA FIP FLOGI was directed to the upstream switch (Storage-VDC), which also provided an FPMA for it.

The NPV illusion is finally complete: The CNA in Server100 is logically logged on to Storage-VDC, which is now responsible for conducting Fibre Channel processes involving the VN_Port, such as zoning.

An FCoE NPV switch lets the same three methods control how the internal VN_Ports will be distributed among the active VNP_Port: *automatic load balancing*, *static traffic mapping*, and *disruptive load balancing*. Each of these methods shares the same characteristics from its Fibre Channel NPV counterpart.

Unified Fabric Designs

When designing Unified Fabrics, a data center architect must be aware that Ethernet networks and Fibre Channel fabrics traditionally deploy distinct network availability designs. Clearly speaking:

- An Ethernet network usually comprises a *single physical structure*, where a pair of switches of each layer connects to all switches that belong to the upper layer. The underlying theme on Ethernet network designs is usually "connectivity," where a network should recover as quickly as possible in the case of a link or device failure. Upper-layer protocols such as TCP or the applications are expected to handle frame discards provoked by reconvergences and instabilities.

- A Fibre Channel storage area network (SAN) is usually deployed with *two distinct physical fabrics*. The motto for SAN design is "robustness," where at least one path to the storage device should always available, regardless of instabilities that might be happening on the other physical fabric. Initiators are expected to react to path unavailability and deploy load balancing between active paths.

Both models are portrayed in Figure 12-19. The figure also demonstrates exactly how a server can leverage multiple connections to Ethernet networks and Fibre Channel fabrics: aggregating Ethernet links with virtual PortChannels, and using multipath I/O software to use Fibre Channel fabrics A and B (alternatively or simultaneously).

The reconciliation of both models on a Unified Fabric requires the understanding that FCFs can virtualize a Fibre Channel fabric within a Data Center Bridging network. Consequently, the main principle that compels converged designs is that *distinct FCoE VLANs define different fabrics*, which should not cross from side A to side B (or vice versa) within a Unified Fabric.

Using a bottom-up approach, I will explain how Unified Fabric designs can simultaneously preserve the required availability characteristics deployed on Ethernet and Fibre Channel infrastructures.

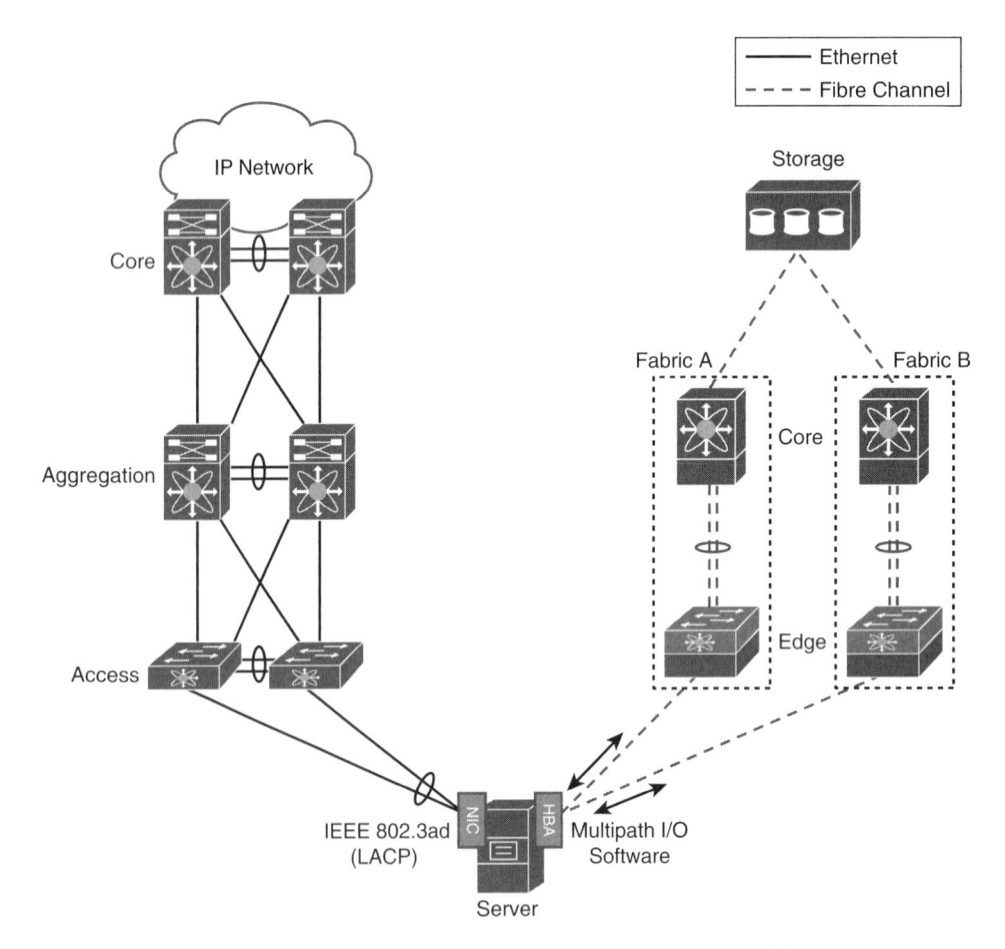

Figure 12-19 *Ethernet and Fibre Channel Traditional Design Models*

Server Access Layer Unified Designs

In the section "The Case for Data Center Networking Convergence," earlier in this chapter, I explained how the server access layer usually leverages more benefits from I/O consolidation and network convergence. Actually, cabling can be drastically reduced on such a layer because it naturally utilizes a higher number of connections when compared to other data center network layers (such as aggregation and core).

Figure 12-20 presents two general point-to-point server access models.

In Figure 12-20, a server can be directly attached to a pair of FCFs or to a pair of FCF-managed Fabric Extenders. As explained in Chapter 7, these devices can help scale the number of server ports within a single management domain.

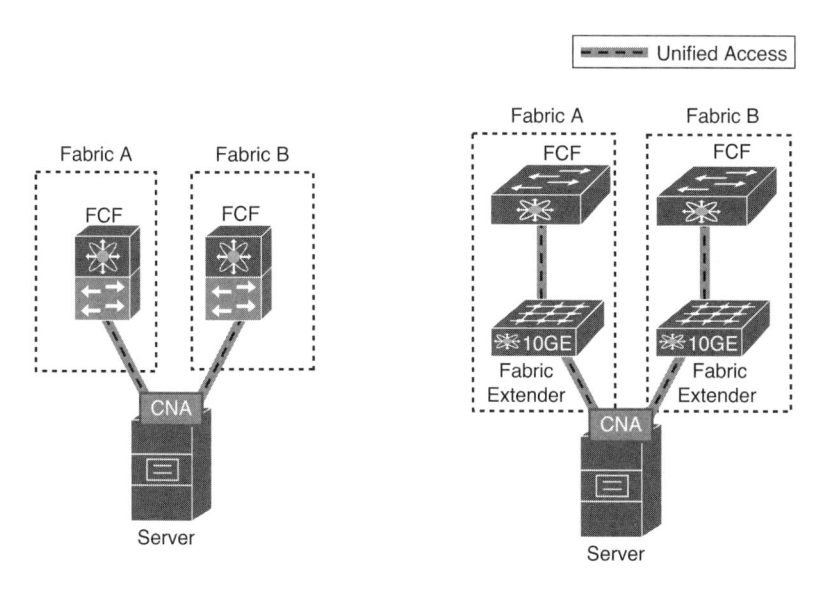

Figure 12-20 *Point-to-Point Server Access Models*

Generically speaking, pass-through FEX topologies are recommended to deploy the Fabric A and B separation down to the Fabric Extenders. However, starting at NX-OS 5.1(3)N1(1), Nexus 5500 switches can also deploy FCoE over dual-homed Fabric Extenders. Figure 12-21 illustrates how such a design leverages enhanced virtual PortChannels and distinct configurations on parent switches to deploy Fabric A and B segmentation.

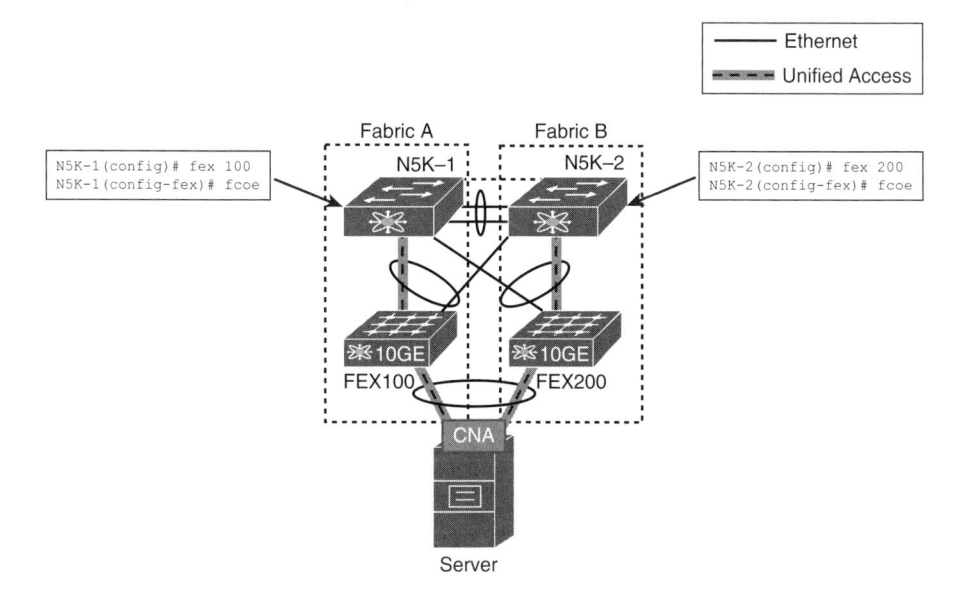

Figure 12-21 *FCoE on Dual-Homed Fabric Extenders*

Tip Although Figure 12-21 depicts a vPC joining both server Unified Access connections, this configuration does not affect the FCoE virtual links between the CNA and the FCFs, as I will explain in the next section.

One last observation: A single pair of Nexus 5000 or 5500 switches can completely support midsize data centers through direct attachments to (Fibre Channel or FCoE) storage devices and with Fabric Extenders scaling the converged network to its servers.

FCoE and Virtual PortChannels

From a pure Ethernet standpoint, servers with two Unified Access connections can offer active-standby behavior with ease. Notwithstanding, virtual PortChannels (vPC) can also be leveraged on these servers without any interference on the FCoE traffic.

Figure 12-22 portrays a logical representation of a dual-port CNA. The figure explains how a standard IEEE 802.3ad aggregation can be applied solely to the server Ethernet connections and the vPC configuration on each NX-OS access switch.

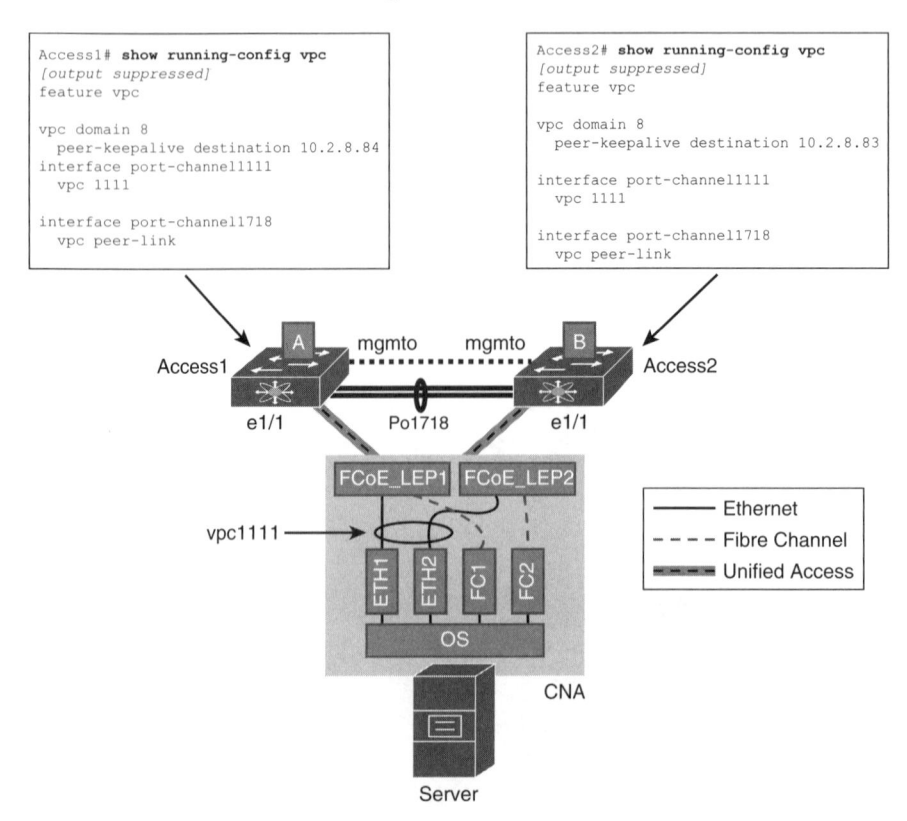

```
Access1# show running-config vpc
[output suppressed]
feature vpc

vpc domain 8
  peer-keepalive destination 10.2.8.84
interface port-channel1111
  vpc 1111

interface port-channel1718
  vpc peer-link
```

```
Access2# show running-config vpc
[output suppressed]
feature vpc

vpc domain 8
  peer-keepalive destination 10.2.8.83
interface port-channel1111
  vpc 1111

interface port-channel1718
  vpc peer-link
```

Figure 12-22 *vPC on Converged Server Access*

As you can see, the FCoE traffic is simply encapsulated and decapsulated on the CNA component that implements FCoE encapsulation on Ethernet.

From a networking perspective, the following recommendations should be observed on these designs:

- The access switches should *not* deploy the same FCoE VLAN to reinforce Fabric A and Fabric B segmentation.
- The Virtual Fibre Channel interfaces should be configured on each switch and bound to the physical interfaces. This procedure benefits servers that might be deploying boot through the SAN (which should not wait for link aggregation negotiation and establishment).

Examples 12-30 and 12-31 detail the VFC configuration on switches Access1 and Access2 from Figure 12-22.

Example 12-30 *FCoE over vPC Members on Access1*

```
! VLAN 11 is mapped to VSAN 11 only on Access1 (Fabric A)
Access1# show vlan fcoe
Original VLAN ID         Translated VSAN ID       Association State
----------------         ------------------       -----------------

     11                          11                   Operational
! VF_Port is bounded to the physical interface (and not PortChannel111)
Access1# show running-config interface vfc2
[output suppressed]
interface vfc2
  bind interface Ethernet1/1
  no shutdown
! Verifying the VN_Port FLOGI to VSAN 11
Access1# show flogi database
--------------------------------------------------------------------------
INTERFACE        VSAN    FCID         PORT NAME                NODE NAME
--------------------------------------------------------------------------
vfc2             11      0xa40000     21:00:00:c0:dd:14:cd:ad  20:00:00:c0:dd:14:cd:ad

Total number of flogi = 1.
```

Example 12-31 *FCoE over vPC Members on Access2*

```
! VLAN 12 is mapped to VSAN 12 only on Access2 (Fabric B)
Access2# show vlan fcoe
Original VLAN ID         Translated VSAN ID       Association State
```

```
               ----------------         -----------------         ------------------
                      12                        12                    Operational
! VF_Port is bounded to the physical interface (and not PortChannel111)
Access2# show running-config interface vfc2
[output suppressed]
interface vfc2
  bind interface Ethernet1/1
  no shutdown
! Verifying the VN_Port FLOGI to VSAN 12
ACCESS2# show flogi database
--------------------------------------------------------------------------------
INTERFACE        VSAN    FCID          PORT NAME                NODE NAME
--------------------------------------------------------------------------------
vfc2             12      0x090000      21:00:00:c0:dd:14:cd:af 20:00:00:c0:dd:14:cd:af

Total number of flogi = 1.
```

And as described on the last section, Nexus 5000, 5500, and 6000 will switches also support this configuration over FCoE-capable Fabric Extenders.

Note At the time of this writing, vPC is not supported on shared interfaces on storage VDCs or on first-generation CNAs. Nevertheless, always refer to the Cisco online documentation for updated information.

With Access1 and Access2 providing two distinct Fibre Channel paths to a server, a multipath I/O software should also be used to establish high availability or load balancing between the FCoE-enabled server and a storage device.

Allow me to call your attention to a very important aspect of Unified Fabrics: *The operational tasks and procedures are extremely similar to traditional Ethernet and Fibre Channel implementations*. These similarities are completely intentional to enable a smooth migration from traditional to converged networks.

FCoE and Blade Servers

Much like rack-mountable servers, blade servers can also leverage the advantages of I/O consolidation and network device convergence. With CNAs or software FCoE drivers, these devices can achieve optimal bandwidth management and cabling savings too.

At the time of this writing, Cisco supports three connectivity models to deploy FCoE on third-party blade server chassis. Figure 12-23 details each model, depicting how the internal chassis connections can be logically understood.

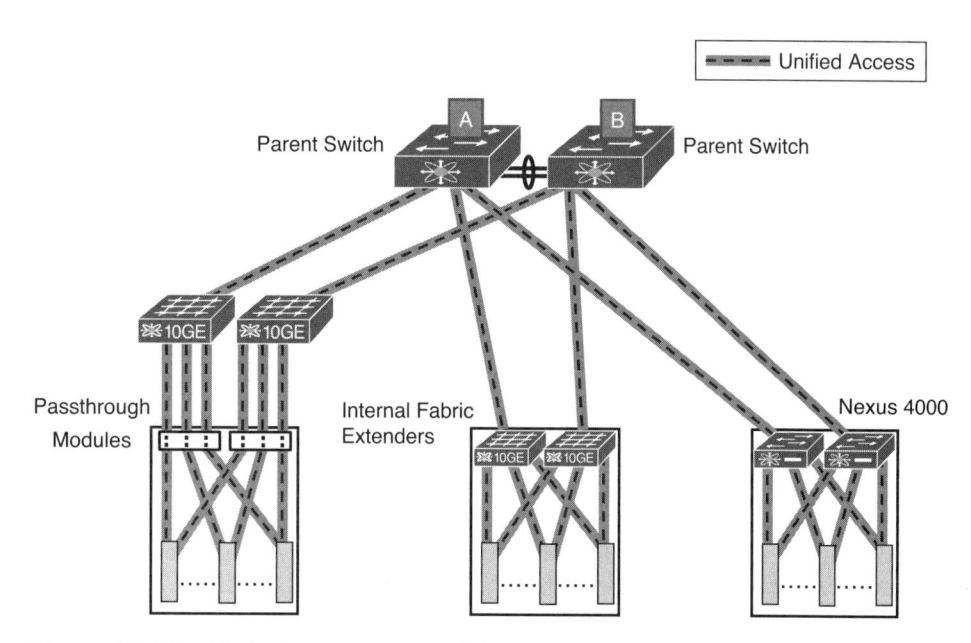

Figure 12-23 *Blade Server I/O Consolidation Connectivity Models*

When a blade service chassis is not compatible with any Cisco Unified Fabric blade device, *pass-through modules* can be used to expose each blade internal connection to the outer world. In this model, each server can be directly connected to a pair of FCFs or to a pair of FCoE-capable Fabric Extenders (in a more scalable model). Obviously, all recommendations related to FCoE on Fabric Extenders should be followed in this design.

With the *Internal Fabric Extender* model, an FCoE-capable Fabric Extender (such as Nexus B22) acts as an internal point of connection for FCoE-enabled blade servers. In a similar way, the connection between these internal FEX and the parent switches must also follow the most recent recommendations.

At last, a Cisco *Nexus 4000* blade switch series can provide Unified Fabric access to a blade server, forwarding all Ethernet frames to an upstream FCF. In these scenarios, the VFCs are bound to ENode MAC addresses instead of physical Ethernet interfaces.

Differently from a Fabric Extender, or a switch running in FCoE NPV mode, Nexus 4000 is the first Cisco DCB switch that can *bridge* FCoE traffic to an upstream FCF.

To securely perform this task, Nexus 4000 deploys a feature called *FIP snooping*, which is an implementation of a group of FC-BB-5 security recommendations from FC-BB-5 (Annexes C and D).

In summary, FIP snooping aims to provide the same level of robustness achieved with point-to-point topologies, because it

- Analyzes FIP FLOGI frames to access information such as FPMAs
- Allows autoconfiguration of access control lists, only permitting FIP and FCoE traffic between pairs of ENodes and FCFs

To maintain Fabric A and B segmentation, each Nexus 4000 should only deploy DCB connections (containing FCoE traffic) to "a single upstream FCF, as depicted in Figure 12-23.

> **Note** FCoE is also a component of the Cisco family of blade servers (Unified Computing System B-series). This aspect of the solution will be explained in more detail in Chapter 13, "Server Evolution," and Chapter 14, "Changing Personalities."

Beyond the Access Layer

Several design options can be deployed to connect a Unified Access server to upstream LAN and SAN resources. In this section, I examine two basic designs, with varying levels of network convergence.

Converged Access Model

Usually considered the first step in I/O consolidation, this model only deploys network convergence in the server access layer. From an upstream connectivity perspective, the converged switches function as access layer switches for the Ethernet aggregation switches *and* edge switches for the SAN core switches.

Figure 12-24 represents this network convergence model.

With this design:

- Converged access switches can deploy vPCs, vPC+, or a Layer 2 multipath protocol (such as FabricPath) to deploy active-active uplinks to the Ethernet aggregation layer
- Converged access switches can run in NPV mode to avoid domain ID explosion on both Fibre Channel fabrics

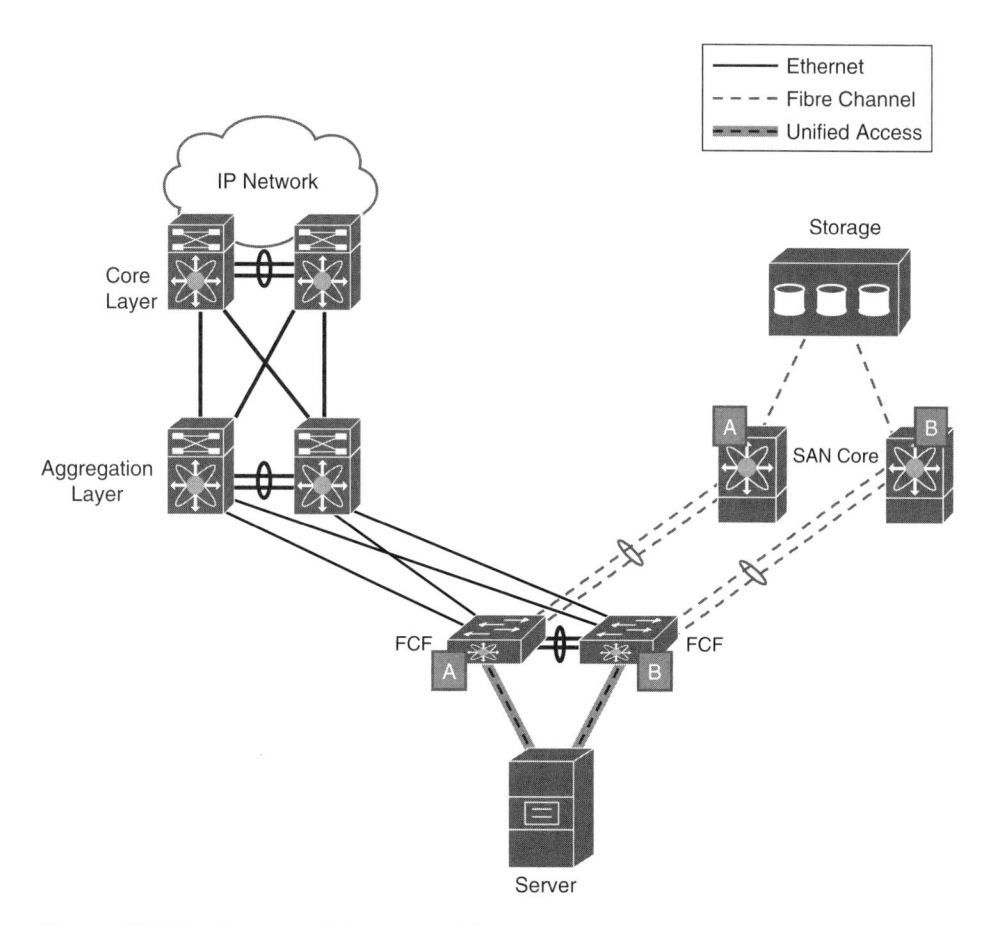

Figure 12-24 *Converged Access Model*

Converged Aggregation Model

In this design, an Ethernet aggregation switch and SAN core switch can share the same converged device. Actually, depending on the number of ports and device redundancy requirements, a Nexus 7000 switch (with a storage VDC), a Nexus 6000, or a Nexus 5000 can perform this role.

Figure 12-25 generically portrays the converged aggregation design.

In Figure 12-25, you might have noticed one important detail: the physical separation between FCoE ISLs and Ethernet uplinks. There are several reasons for deploying these separated switch connections:

1. The FCoE VLANs from Fabric A and Fabric B must remain on separate devices to deploy a Fibre Channel–equivalent network design.

2. Fibre Channel ISLs and Ethernet uplinks usually present much higher bandwidth utilization than server connections. Therefore, a hypothetical consolidation of these connections will not bring significant savings in cabling.

3. SAN and LAN teams can deploy independent bandwidth capacity planning with separate ISLs and uplinks, respectively.

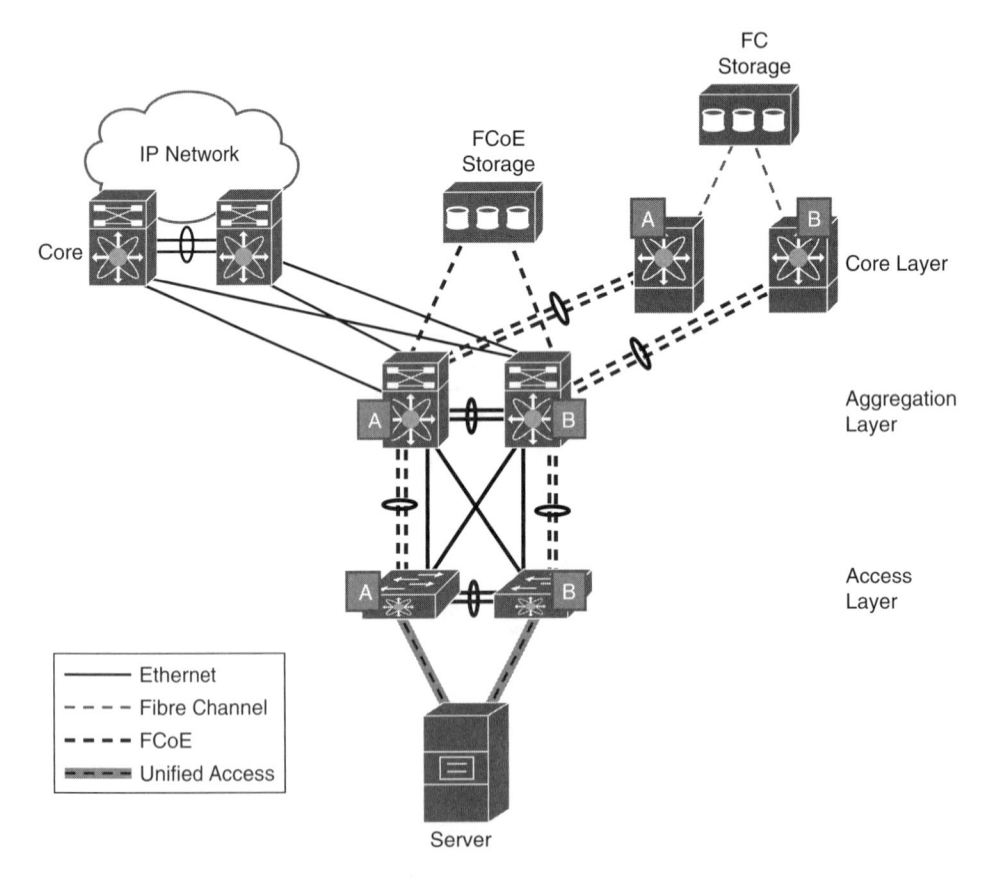

Figure 12-25 *Converged Aggregation and Access Model*

Additionally, this design allows that

- Converged access switches can deploy vPCs, vPC+, or a Layer 2 multipath protocol (such as FabricPath) to deploy active-active uplinks to the Ethernet aggregation layer.

- Converged access switches can deploy FCoE NPV mode on their FCoE connections to the aggregation.

- Storage devices with FCoE access ports can connect directly to the converged aggregation.

- The converged aggregation switches can deploy FCoE ISLs to FCoE-capable SAN directors to provide access to Fibre Channel SANs.

Although FCoE ISLs and Ethernet uplinks are separated on this supported design, it does not mean that they will remain completely segmented in the future. In truth, at the time of this writing, there are several efforts under way to converge FCoE traffic into Ethernet multipathing fabrics.

FCoE and SAN Extension

Since the advent of the first FCoE-enabled switch, several corporations started to demonstrate interest in using such technology as a form of SAN extension between data centers. And although FCoE was originally created to be deployed inside a data center, Cisco has verified that such a technology can also be applied to connect SAN from different locations, with some boundary conditions.

As explained in the earlier section "Data Center Bridging", buffer sizing is especially critical in the deployment of priority-based flow control over connections with higher latency. For that reason, Cisco supports limited distances for FCoE virtual links over optical media.

Table 12-2 portrays the maximum distances for lossless connections that were verified in NX-OS devices, at the time of this writing.

Table 12-2 *FCoE SAN Extension*

NX-OS Device	Maximum Distance (km)	Sharing with Ethernet VLANs
Nexus 5000	3	Yes
Nexus 7000[1]	20	No
MDS 9500	10	No

[1] Verified on F1-series modules.

Additionally, the table also details whether these FCoE connections can share the same 10-Gbps link with pure Ethernet traffic.

Note Always refer to the latest Cisco online documentation for updated support information.

Use Case: LAN and SAN Management Separation

A company has decided to build a new data center using Unified Fabric concepts. After some very successful proof-of-concept tests that your consulting firm has developed for it (described in Examples 12-1 to 12-29 in this chapter), the company's management team has invited you to an impromptu meeting after lunch.

The meeting subject was the "*Homo sapiens factor*" of Unified Fabric. During the tests, it was clear that the executives have understood that FCoE was designed to deploy Fibre Channel fabric within a DCB network virtual wire, preserving the existent knowledge and processes from its LAN and SAN teams. However, from lessons learned in previous virtualization processes, consolidation without control can increase the probability of human-caused misconfigurations. And the managers are really worried about this class of problems because they were responsible for 40 percent of the IT systems' failures in the last fiscal year.

At the end of the meeting, the company's CIO formally indicated his will to extend your consulting contract for one more project: to harden the converged network devices to reduce the occurrence of inappropriate access from the LAN team over SAN resources, and vice versa.

You schedule several interviews with key members of both LAN and SAN teams to correctly understand their operational processes. After observing that both teams are already working together on the I/O consolidation project, you conclude that their operations are very well customized for the project. Notwithstanding, you enlist the following recommendations that must be dealt from a switch management perspective:

- The LAN team should not have access to SAN-related commands and vice-versa.
- Both teams should not get access to operations that can impact the entire switch, such as licensing and rebooting.
- The LAN team can only enable and disable non-FCoE traffic on Ethernet interfaces, while the SAN team can only do the same with FCoE traffic.
- ETS and PFC policies should not be changed to benefit one traffic load to the detriment of others.

Using device contexts and Role-Based Access Control (RBAC) capabilities, you affirm that it is possible to deploy a complete separation for the operations of each team. After all, these features were created to allow different teams to continue to work as if they still have distinct physical devices.

You schedule a presentation to introduce your findings to the managers of both teams. When the day finally arrives, you begin your presentation by suggesting that three teams should manage the converged devices:

- **The LAN team:** Manages Ethernet-only-related operations such as VLANs and trunks.

- **The SAN team:** Manages FCoE VLANs, Virtual Fibre Channel interfaces, and fabric operations (such as zoning and VSANs).

- **An infrastructure team:** Responsible for operations that can affect both LAN and SAN teams, such as licensing, firmware upgrades, authentication, bandwidth allocation, and so on.

After arguing that this organizational change fits the company's virtualization approach, you divide the management separation demonstration in two parts: *VDC-capable switches* and *single-context switches*.

In Part I, you explain that VDCs already provide management plane segmentation between SAN (storage VDC) and LAN (remaining VDCs) operations on a converged network device.

To demonstrate such management separation, you will use the very same Nexus 7000 switch from the proof-of-concept tests (N7K), using the following interface allocation per VDC:

- Ethernet 1/1 to 1/32 on a new Ethernet VDC
- Ethernet 2/1 to 2/32 on the previously created Storage-VDC

Because the company's new data center will not deploy Nexus 7000 switches on the server access layer, you do not include any shared interface in your demonstration.

Although you have used the default VDC on the proof-of-concept tests, you recommend that a different VDC is defined as an Ethernet-only aggregation switch, increasing the management separation between the LAN and the infrastructure team.

Example 12-32 shows the creation of an Ethernet-only VDC called Ethernet-VDC.

Example 12-32 *Ethernet-Only VDC Creation*

```
! Creating additional Ethernet-only VDC
N7K(config)# vdc Ethernet-VDC
Note:  Creating VDC, one moment please ...
! Limiting the modules that may have allocated interfaces to this VDC
N7K(config-vdc)# limit-resource module-type m1 m1xl m2xl f1
! Allocating interfaces to this VDC
N7K(config-vdc)# allocate interface ethernet 1/1-32
Moving ports will cause all config associated to them in source vdc
to be removed. Are you sure you want to move the ports (y/n)?  [yes]
! Accessing the VDC CLI prompt
N7K# switchto vdc Ethernet-VDC


          ---- System Admin Account Setup ----
[output suppressed]
```

```
Cisco Nexus Operating System (NX-OS) Software
[output suppressed]
N7K-Ethernet-VDC#
```

Continuing the hardening of Ethernet-VDC, Example 12-33 details the configuration of a LAN-ADMIN role defined on Ethernet-VDC.

Example 12-33   *LAN-ADMIN Role Configuration on Default VDC*

```
N7K-Ethernet-VDC# show running-config | begin "role name LAN-ADMIN" next 3
! This role can execute any command on this VDC
role name LAN-ADMIN
  rule 1 permit read-write
username admin password [suppressed]   role vdc-admin
! Creating Local user that belongs to LAN-ADMIN role
username lanuser password [suppressed]   role LAN-ADMIN
```

Although the LAN-ADMIN role has the same rights as the vdc-admin default role, you have created a separate role to allow new restrictions that might come in the future.

Example 12-34 portrays the configuration of a SAN-ADMIN role in Storage-VDC. During the demonstration, you comment that a user who belongs to this role can only configure Storage-VDC-allocated resources, such as interfaces Ethernet 2/1 to 2/32.

Example 12-34   *SAN-ADMIN Role Configuration on Storage VDC*

```
N7K-Storage-VDC# show running-config | begin "role name SAN-ADMIN" next 3
role name SAN-ADMIN
! This role can execute every command over this Storage VDC allocated interfaces and
VLANs
  rule 1 permit read-write
username admin password [suppressed]   role vdc-admin
! Local VDC user that belongs to SAN-ADMIN role
username sanuser password [suppressed]   role SAN-ADMIN
```

Then, you demonstrate how much protection these VDCs provide against improper management accesses. Examples 12-35 and 12-36 show live tests you have performed during the presentation.

In Example 12-35, you try to access resources on both VDCs using *lanuser* credentials.

Example 12-35 *LAN Admin Telnet Session*

```
! When the user access a Telnet session at Storage VDC, his
login/password combination results in authentication failure (they
are not defined on Storage-VDC)
User Access Verification
login: lanuser
Password:
Login incorrect
! But he can access the Ethernet VDC
User Access Verification
login: lanuser
Password:
Cisco Nexus Operating System (NX-OS) Software
[output suppressed]
! User cannot reload switch (only the VDC), access the default VDC, or access any
FCoE interfaces
N7K-Ethernet-VDC# reload ?
  vdc  Restart the current vdc
N7K-Ethernet-VDC# switchback
! Displaying the interfaces that can be configured on this VDC
N7K-Ethernet-VDC# show interface brief
--------------------------------------------------------------------------------
Port   VRF          Status IP Address                                Speed    MTU
--------------------------------------------------------------------------------
mgmt0  --           up     172.28.126.152                            1000     1500


--------------------------------------------------------------------------------
Ethernet      VLAN   Type Mode   Status Reason                       Speed    Port
Interface                                                                     Ch #
--------------------------------------------------------------------------------
Eth1/1        --     eth  routed down   Administratively down        auto(S)  --
Eth1/2        --     eth  routed down   Administratively down        auto(S)  --
[output suppressed]
Eth1/32       --     eth  routed down   SFP not inserted             auto(S)  --
```

Example 12-36 details your attempts to access the same resources, using *sanuser* credentials.

Example 12-36 *SAN Admin Telnet Session*

```
! sanuser cannot even access the Ethernet-VDC CLI
User Access Verification
login: sanuser
Password:
Login incorrect
! But it can access the Storage VDC and all of its allocated resources
User Access Verification
login: sanuser
Password:
Cisco Nexus Operating System (NX-OS) Software
[output suppressed]
! User cannot reload switch (only the VDC), access the default VDC, or access any
FCoE interfaces
N7K-Storage-VDC# reload ?
  vdc  Restart the current vdc
N7K-Storage-VDC# switchback
N7K-Storage-VDC# show interface brief
[output suppressed]
--------------------------------------------------------------------------------
Port   VRF          Status IP Address                                Speed    MTU
--------------------------------------------------------------------------------
mgmt0  --           up     172.28.126.53                             1000     1500


--------------------------------------------------------------------------------
Ethernet      VLAN   Type Mode   Status Reason                      Speed      Port
Interface                                                                      Ch#
--------------------------------------------------------------------------------
Eth2/1        1      eth  trunk  up     none                        10G(D)     --
Eth2/2        1      eth  access down   SFP not inserted            auto(D)    --
Eth2/3        1      eth  trunk  up     none                        10G(D)     --
[output suppressed]
Eth2/8        1      eth  trunk  up     none                        10G(D)     --
[output suppressed]
Eth2/32       1      eth  trunk  down   SFP not inserted            auto(D)    --


--------------------------------------------------------------------------------
Interface  Vsan   Admin  Admin   Status   Bind           Oper    Oper
                  Mode   Trunk            Info           Mode    Speed
                         Mode                                    (Gbps)
--------------------------------------------------------------------------------
vfc2/8     100    E      on      trunking Eth2/8         TE      10
vfc-po300  1      E      on      trunking Epo300         TE      20
```

To take care of all administrative operations that can impact both LAN and SAN teams, the infrastructure team can be associated to the network-admin role in the default VDC. Nevertheless, a more restrictive role can be created to include specific operations for this team, such as licensing and software upgrades.

The second part of your demonstration concerns single-context converged switches, which present refined RBAC capabilities that can overcome the lack of management plane segmentation between LAN and SAN resources.

This topic is extremely important for the company's Unified Fabric project, because single-context devices will be deployed on the server access layer, where the same physical interface contains elements from both SAN and LAN teams.

You continue the demonstration presenting the concept of *feature groups*, which can aggregate commands from different features in a single RBAC rule.

Example 12-37 shows how you have customized three feature groups in switch N5K: *LAN-FEATURES*, *SAN-FEATURES*, and *INFRA-FEATURES*.

Tip You have used the **role feature-group** command to perform this configuration.

Example 12-37 *Configured Feature Groups*

```
N5K# show role feature-group
! This feature group owns features that may affect both LAN and SAN operations
feature group: INFRA-FEATURES
aaa             (AAA service related commands)
cdp             (Cisco Discovery Protocol related commands)
radius          (Radius configuration and show commands)
syslog          (Syslog related commands)
tacacs          (TACACS configuration and show commands)
install         (Software install related commands)
license         (License related commands)
callhome        (Callhome configuration and show commands)
platform        (Platform configuration and show commands)
! This feature group owns all the Ethernet and IP related features
feature group: LAN-FEATURES
arp             (ARP protocol related commands)
l3vm            (Layer 3 virtualization related commands)
ping            (Network reachability test commands)
access-list     (IP access list related commands)
svi             (Interface VLAN related commands)
hsrp            (Hot Standby Router Protocol related commands)
igmp            (Internet Group Management Protocol related commands)
msdp            (Multicast Source Discovery Protocol related commands)
```

```
dot1x             (DOT1X related commands)
ipfib             (IP Forwarding Information Base related commands)
eth-span          (Ethernet SPAN related commands)
router-bgp        (Border Gateway Protocol related commands)
router-rip        (Routing Information Protocol related commands)
ethanalyzer       (Ethernet Analyzer)
router-ospf       (Open Shortest Path First protocol related commands)
router-eigrp      (Enhanced Interior Gateway Routing Protocol related commands)
spanning-tree     (Spanning Tree protocol related commands)
! This feature group owns all Fibre Channel related features
feature group: SAN-FEATURES
acl               (FC ACL related commands)
sfm               (ISCSI flow related commands)
sme               (Storage Media Encryption feature related commands)
fcns              (Fibre Channel Name Server related commands)
fcsp              (Fibre Channel Security Protocol related commands)
fdmi              (FDMI related commands)
fspf              (Fabric Shortest Path First protocol related commands)
rlir              (Registered Link Incident Report related commands)
rscn              (Registered State Change Notification related commands)
span              (SPAN session relate commands)
vsan              (VSAN configuration and show commands)
wwnm              (WorldWide Name related commands)
zone              (Zone related commands)
fcanalyzer        (FC analyzer related commands)
sme-kmc-admin     (SME commands authorized to kmc admin)
sme-stg-admin     (SME commands authorized to storage admin)
vsan-assign-intf(Assign interfaces to vsan)
sme-recovery-officer(SME commands authorized to recovery officer)
```

You make a very important observation to your audience: All features that should be configured by all teams (such as **vlan** and **snmp**) were not included in any feature group. Therefore, to create a team role, you have used a *negative logic*: excluding what should not be accessed by a role and implicitly allowing the remaining features.

Example 12-38 details the configuration of the LAN-ADMIN role in N5K.

Example 12-38 *LAN-ADMIN Role Configuration in N5K*

```
! Displaying LAN-ADMIN role configuration
N5K# show running-config | begin "role name LAN-ADMIN" next 15
role name LAN-ADMIN
! This role cannot change any ETS or PFC configuration
  rule 6 deny command configure terminal ; policy-map *
! It can only shut the LAN traffic on Ethernet interfaces
```

```
  rule 5 permit command configure terminal ; interface * ; shutdown lan
  rule 4 deny command configure terminal ; interface * ; shutdown
! It cannot access any feature that may be exclusive to INFRASTRUCTURE and SAN teams
  rule 3 deny read-write feature-group INFRA-FEATURES
  rule 2 deny read-write feature-group SAN-FEATURES
  rule 1 permit read-write
! This role cannot change the configuration on any FCoE VLAN (1100 to 1200)
  vlan policy deny
    permit vlan 1-1099
    permit vlan 1201-3967
    permit vlan 4048-4093
! And it is restricted to configure the available Ethernet interfaces
  interface policy deny
    permit interface Ethernet1/1-20
    permit interface Ethernet2/1-4
username admin password [suppressed] role network-admin
! Creating local user that belongs to role SAN-ADMIN
username lanuser password [suppressed] role LAN-ADMIN
```

Likewise, Example 12-39 depicts the creation of the SAN-ADMIN role in N5K.

Example 12-39 *SAN-ADMIN Role Configuration in N5K*

```
! Displaying SAN-ADMIN role configuration
N5K# show running-config | begin "role name SAN-ADMIN" next 12
role name SAN-ADMIN
! This role cannot change any ETS or PFC configuration
  rule 4 deny command configure terminal ; policy-map *
! It cannot access any feature that may be exclusive to INFRASTRUCTURE and LAN teams
  rule 3 deny read-write feature-group INFRA-FEATURES
  rule 2 deny read-write feature-group LAN-FEATURES
  rule 1 permit read-write
! It can only configure predefined FCoE VLANs...
  vlan policy deny
    permit vlan 1100-1200
! ... and all Fibre Channel and Virtual Fibre Channel interfaces
  interface policy deny
    permit interface fc2/1-4
    permit interface vfc1-8192
 [output suppressed]
! Creating local user that belongs to role SAN-ADMIN
username sanuser password [suppressed] role SAN-ADMIN
```

After you explain, line by line, all the configurations you have performed on N5K, you demonstrate how a fictional access from a LAN-ADMIN user would work on the single-context switch. Example 12-40 details a Telnet session where *lanuser* credentials were used.

Example 12-40 *LAN Admin Telnet Session*

```
! User can log in to N5K
Nexus 5000 Switch
login: lanuser
Password:
Cisco Nexus Operating System (NX-OS) Software
[output suppressed]
! User cannot reload, change FCoE VLANs, access Fibre Channel
interfaces, create zones, or disable the physical Ethernet interfaces
completely
N5K# reload
% Permission denied
N5K# configure terminal
Enter configuration commands, one per line.  End with CNTL/Z.
N5K(config)# vlan 1100
% VLAN permission denied
N5K(config)# interface fc2/1
% Interface permission denied
N5K(config)# zone name TEST vsan 100
                    ^
% Invalid command at '^' marker.
N5K(config)# interface vfc 11
% Interface permission denied
N5K(config)# interface ethernet 1/1
N5K(config-if)# switchport trunk allowed vlan remove 1100
% VLAN permission denied
N5K(config-if)# shutdown
% Permission denied
N5K(config-if)# shutdown lan
N5K(config-if)#
```

Therefore, the negative logic you have applied to the LAN-ADMIN role has worked because no forbidden operation for this role was successful.

Example 12-41 portrays a Telnet session to the same device, but using *sanuser* credentials instead.

Example 12-41 *SAN Admin Telnet Session*

```
! User can log in
Nexus 5000 Switch
login: sanuser
Password:
Cisco Nexus Operating System (NX-OS) Software
[output suppressed]
! User cannot reboot the switch, access non-FCoE VLANS, physical
Ethernet interfaces, change ETS configurations
N5K# reload
% Permission denied
N5K# configure terminal
Enter configuration commands, one per line.  End with CNTL/Z.
N5K(config)# vlan 999
% VLAN permission denied
N5K(config)# interface ethernet 1/1
% Interface permission denied
N5K(config)# policy-map type queuing TEST
% Permission denied
! But it can create and change zones and configure Fibre Channel interfaces
N5K(config)# zone name TEST vsan 100
N5K(config-zone)# interface vfc 11
N5K(config-if)# no shutdown
N5K(config-if)# interface fc2/1
N5K(config-if)# no shutdown
```

In these switches, you add that the infrastructure team can also be associated to the default network-admin role or use a customized role, if desired.

In your final remarks, you emphasize that

- The configuration you have demonstrated is only a demonstration of each device's management isolation capabilities. The final configuration depends on further tests that should include as many daily operations as possible.

- Although you have used local users in your demonstration, it is highly recommended that the infrastructure team deploys remote AAA (authentication, authorization, and accounting) servers to centralize user account management.

Summary

In this chapter, you learned the following:

- I/O consolidation and network convergence can bring multiple benefits to data centers, such as cost savings, agile provisioning, and optimal resource utilization.
- Data Center Bridging (DCB) is a set of IEEE standards that introduce lossless transport of data, bandwidth allocation, configuration of connected devices, and congestion notification to 10 Gigabit Ethernet connections.
- Fibre Channel over Ethernet (FCoE) is an INCITS T11 standard that allows the encapsulation of Fibre Channel traffic over a lossless Ethernet network.
- NX-OS switches permit different forms of FCoE configuration, leveraging VDCs and standard Fibre Channel commands.
- Cisco Data Center portfolio supports a great variety of Unified Fabric designs (from converged access to end-to-end FCoE).
- SAN extension projects can also use FCoE connections, if Cisco-supported limits are observed.
- VDCs and Role-Based Access Control (RBAC) features can help streamline which converged switch resources can be accessed by each operational team.

Figure 12-26 graphically summarizes the virtualization that FCoE brings to data center networks.

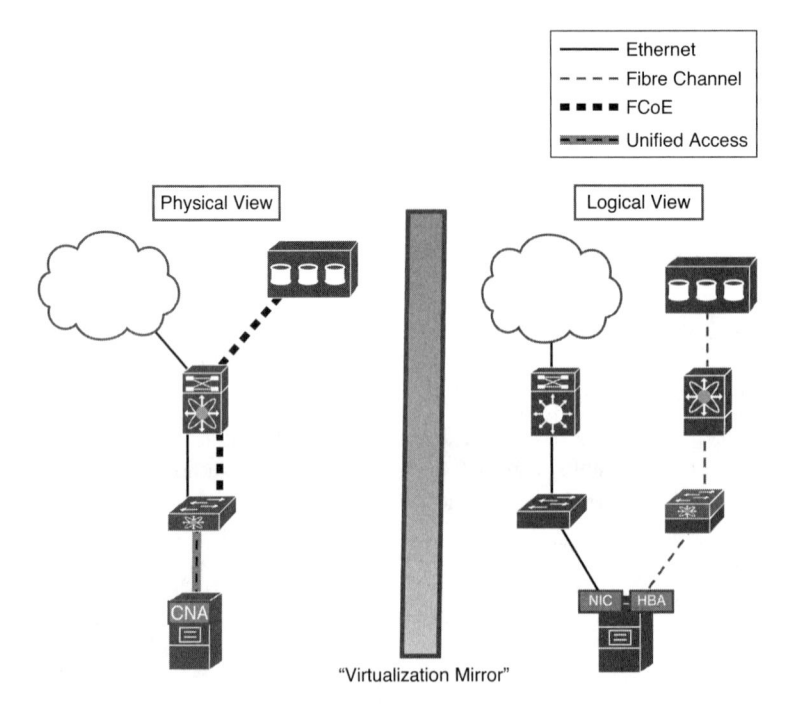

Figure 12-26 *Through the Virtualization Mirror*

Further Reading

Gai, Silvano and DeSanti, Claudio. *I/O Consolidation in the Data Center.* Cisco Press, 2009.

www.t11.org/ftp/t11/pub/fc/bb-5/09-056v5.pdf

http://standards.ieee.org/findstds/standard/802.1Qaz-2011.html

http://standards.ieee.org/findstds/standard/802.1Qbb-2011.html

Chapter 13

Server Evolution

"The best way to find yourself is to lose yourself in the service of others."
(Mahatma Gandhi)

This chapter addresses the main server technologies found in data centers today, focusing on x86 hardware development and presenting concepts such as server virtualization and unified computing. It contains the following topics:

- Server Architectures
- x86 Hardware Evolution
- Introducing x86 Server Virtualization
- Unified Computing

During the early 1990s, a great shift in software architecture aspired to abandon the centralized processing model of mainframes toward *client-server applications*. In this model, personal computers equipped with "client" software accessed resources from centralized "servers" employing standard protocols.

Because server applications could also be running on personal computers, the client-server model proved to be extremely affordable and flexible. And in fact, it has indirectly supported the Internet boom in its heyday.

With the majority of applications departing mainframe environments, server hardware demanded special attention because of its increasing critical role for business. Hence, specialized computers were designed to exhibit the following characteristics:

- **Reliability:** Consistently producing trusted results with acceptable performance.
- **Availability:** Presenting extremely low downtime per year.
- **Serviceability:** Requiring simple and fast operations to recover from a failure.

In a way, the server market has performed for personal computers the role that Formula One plays for commercial vehicles: creating and delivering cutting-edge technologies focused on performance and dependability.

For data center architects, servers represent the *raw material* that defines how a facility is designed and operated. In truth, a data center is only considered active after its servers, and their applications, go into production.

With the Internet bubble burst in 2000, cracks were already visible in the reign of the dedicated server hardware. Running a single application on a computer meant lower resource utilization and higher operational costs, which were simply not compatible with the new directives of IT management. Inspired by the mainframe virtualization technologies, VMware and other software vendors started another paradigm shift. And a new unit from the modern data center was defined: the virtual machine.

This thunder is still resounding today, as physical resources such as compute, network, and storage are being rethought to support server virtualization. And the best example might be the Cisco Unified Computing System, whose architecture further blurs the boundaries between these technology areas to offer simplification, control, and easy deployment.

Server Architectures

Much like cities, corporate data centers rarely rip and replace entire environments overnight. Actually, new technologies are usually deployed in complementary environments while existing "regions" are always handled with care and minimal disruption. In that way, old downtown can coexist with modern condominiums in urbanistic harmony.

Representing different neighborhoods, three different server architectures are usually present in Data Center City: *mainframes*, *RISC*, and *x86*. Although the latter's presence is increasing its footprint, the examination of all architectures paints a more realistic scenario for these facilities.

Mainframes

Mainframes are computers whose origins go back to the beginnings of business computing, in the 1940s. From that period until the 1970s, a computer room was commonly occupied with a single processing structure occupying thousands of square meters and consuming hundreds of kilowatts. For our grandparents, they were not the largest computers; they were the only computers.

Through the development achievements of IBM and other manufacturers (such as Burroughs, Remington, and DEC), mainframes incrementally introduced concepts that have elevated computer science to its present level. Although any list would be short, I can cite achievements such as electronic processors, storage of programs in memory, real-time processing, direct-access memory, system compatibility, and operating systems.

With the prevalence of the client-server model, IBM responded with changes that adapted its mainframes to these new requirements while leveraging the best characteristics from such platforms: stability and performance. Through features such as support for web and online applications, logical partitions (LPAR) running modern operating systems, and geographic clustering, mainframes still remain an important part of several corporate data centers.

Maintaining compatibility with software developed in previous generations, these machines are capable of bridging the past and the present under the same management domain, running thousands of simultaneous transactions and I/O operations over distributed sites.

The zSeries products represent IBM's current mainframe architecture. At the time of this writing, a single mainframe platform occupies the area of four consecutive data center cabinets, supporting up to 120 microprocessors running at a clock speed of 5.5 GHz, with 3 TB of real memory.

RISC Servers

Reduced Instruction Set Computing (RISC) servers are a set of computers that share a common characteristic: Their processing design is based on simplified instructions that spend only one clock cycle on execution time, avoiding recursive interactions with the memory. Adding pipelining and a larger number of registers to its architecture, RISC platforms were prepared to provide relatively more performance when compared to *Complex Instruction Set Computing (CISC)* computers such as x86 servers and even mainframes.

Although the first projects occurred in the late 1970s, RISC servers achieved great popularity in the 1990s due their good performance/price ratio over other architectures. The main RISC vendors were Sun Microsystems, DEC, Hewlett-Packard, and IBM, with each one deploying its own version of UNIX on its platforms (Solaris, Digital UNIX, HP-UX, and AIX, respectively). At the same time, RISC workstations were also highly popular with users who required higher processing power for their local applications.

At the time of this writing, RISC computers are still a significant presence in most data centers. A typical RISC server occupies an entire server cabinet, supporting up to 256 processors running at 4 GHz with 16 TB of memory.

With the vertiginous development of x86-based hardware, the application performance and reliability that can be achieved by both architectures has approached a similar level. Consequently, multiple customers already have migrated enterprise applications from these proprietary platforms to the more cost-effective open universe of x86.

Curiously, the twenty-first century has seen an extremely high adoption of RISC processors in smartphones and tablets.

x86 Servers

The rather loose term "x86" refers to computers that inherited the basic architecture from the Intel 8086 processor and its descendents (80286, 80386, 80486, and so on). The lineage started in 1981, when IBM released a one-user platform called the IBM Personal Computer, or simply the PC.

Even establishing the PC as an industry standard, the influence of IBM on the microcomputer market lessened with time as other manufacturers such Compaq and Dell introduced cheaper "IBM PC–compatible" models (also known as *clones*). And with their success, functions such as bus connections and memory management were being redesigned without any participation from the company.

The combination of the Intel processors and the dominance of the Microsoft Windows operating system have both named the architecture as "Wintel" during the 1990s. Nevertheless, with the introduction of competing processor manufacturers (Advanced Micro Devices, or AMD) and other operating systems (Linux and Mac OS X), the architecture was informally rebranded to "x86."

The client-server application model has subtly hinted the possibility of servers based on x86 computers. With the advent of hardware RAS (Reliability, Availability, and Serviceability) features and more robust operating systems, x86 servers continue their number supremacy through the twenty-first century, replacing mainframes and RISC servers in the process. Undoubtedly, the architecture's main strength remains its openness, which allows fierce competition and quick development, while leveraging a wide range of software components developed during the last 30 years.

x86 Hardware Evolution

The progress and variety of x86 servers make it very difficult to pinpoint a generic architectural model for these computers. With sequential enhancements accumulated since their inception, these devices quickly change how each one of their components performs its functions.

Notwithstanding, Figure 13-1 presents a computer design (or *microarchitecture*) that I will use as a reference point to the architecture of x86 servers.

According to Figure 13-1, the main components of an x86 server are

- **Central processing unit (CPU):** Certainly the most important component of any computer, it is responsible for the majority of processing jobs and calculations. Also referred as the processor, the CPU is the x86 component that has experienced the fastest evolution.

- **Memory:** The CPU uses these fast volatile storage devices to directly access data retrieved from files and programs that are being worked on.

- **Memory controller:** Component that controls how data is exchanged with the memory.

- **Bus:** Medium that transports data between components of an x86 computer. There are multiple types of buses such as *memory bus* (connects the memory to its controller), *system bus* (provides higher-speed connections between components), and *expansion bus* (connects adapters and peripherals).

- **Dedicated processor:** Assists the CPU in the execution of specialized functions such as graphics, encryption, and I/O control.

- **Clock generator:** Provides a timing signal for the synchronization of operations between two or more components.

- **Chipset:** Controls data exchange between the CPU and the majority of elements of an x86 computer. It is ultimately designed to work with a specific family of CPU chips and can provide some integrated controllers, peripherals, and connections.

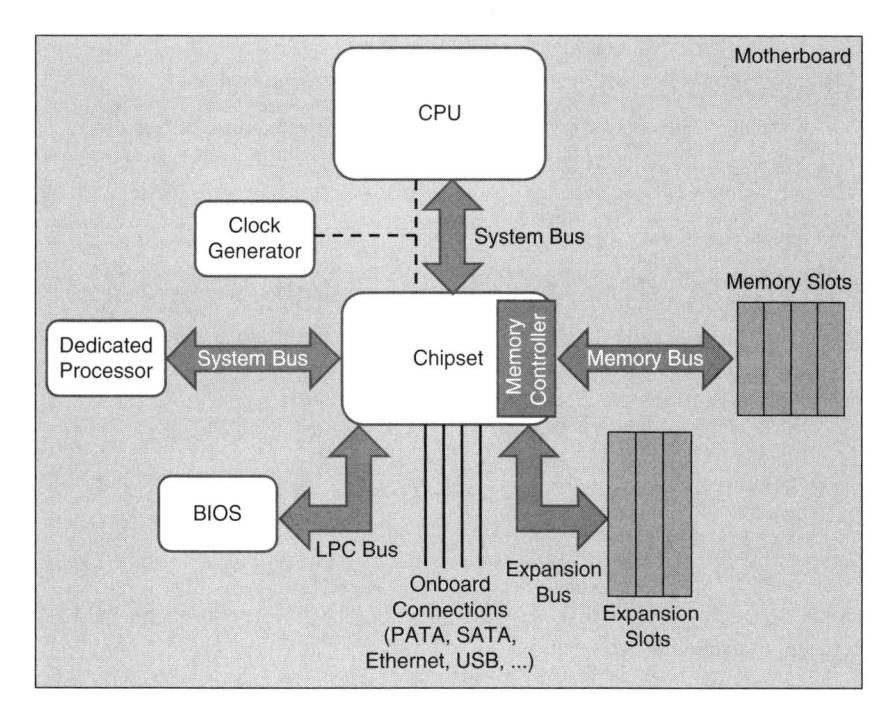

Figure 13-1 *x86 Microarchitecture Example*

Tip On some Intel microarchitectures, the chipset is split in two different circuits: the **Northbridge** (which links the CPU to high-speed devices such as dedicated processors) and the **Southbridge** (which takes care of the expansion bus and other lower-speed connections).

- **Basic input/output system (BIOS):** A nonvolatile memory that carries the first software that will be executed when the computer is powered on. Such software verifies all hardware components, loading the operating system afterward. The BIOS normally possesses a setup program that allows the configuration of several options (such as boot device and CPU settings), and it is usually connected to the chipset through a connection known as *low pin count (LPC)*.

- **Motherboard:** Circuit board that physically contains all the computer components, providing appropriate connection slots for them.

CPU Evolution

Because x86 servers are CISC-based computers with multicycle instructions, their performance relies less on software design (and more on hardware power) if compared to RISC servers. Nevertheless, time has been kind to this architecture because x86 CPUs have tremendously improved their processing capacity over the last three decades.

In his 1965 paper, Intel cofounder Gordon Moore stated that the number of transistors on integrated circuits doubles approximately every two years. And his prediction (also known as Moore's Law) has been kept by processor manufacturers, such as AMD and, of course, Intel.

Following Moore's Law, x86 CPUs have improved with a clock speed from 4.77 MHz in the 8086 to 4.4 GHz in the current Intel Xeon processors. These CPUs, as all other components, have also increased the size of their data path widths from 16 to 64 bits, considerably optimizing data transport within the computers and decreasing the number of clock cycles per operation.

Multiprocessing has also been used in the evolution of CPUs. Since the mid 2000s, x86 CPU manufacturers have simultaneously used two methods to scale out the number of processors in a single CPU microarchitecture:

- **Cores:** Multiple individual processors coexisting in a single CPU chip.
- **Sockets:** Physical connectors that allow the insertion of multiple chips connected through a high-bandwidth connection.

With tens of processors available for parallel use, it was up to the applications and operating system vendors to employ these multiple resources to their benefit.

Although a description of every CPU enhancement in the history of x86 servers is out of the scope of this book, the examination of sequential families of CPU chips can adequately illustrate this process. With that intent, Figure 13-2 depicts three two-socket Intel Xeon microarchitectures.

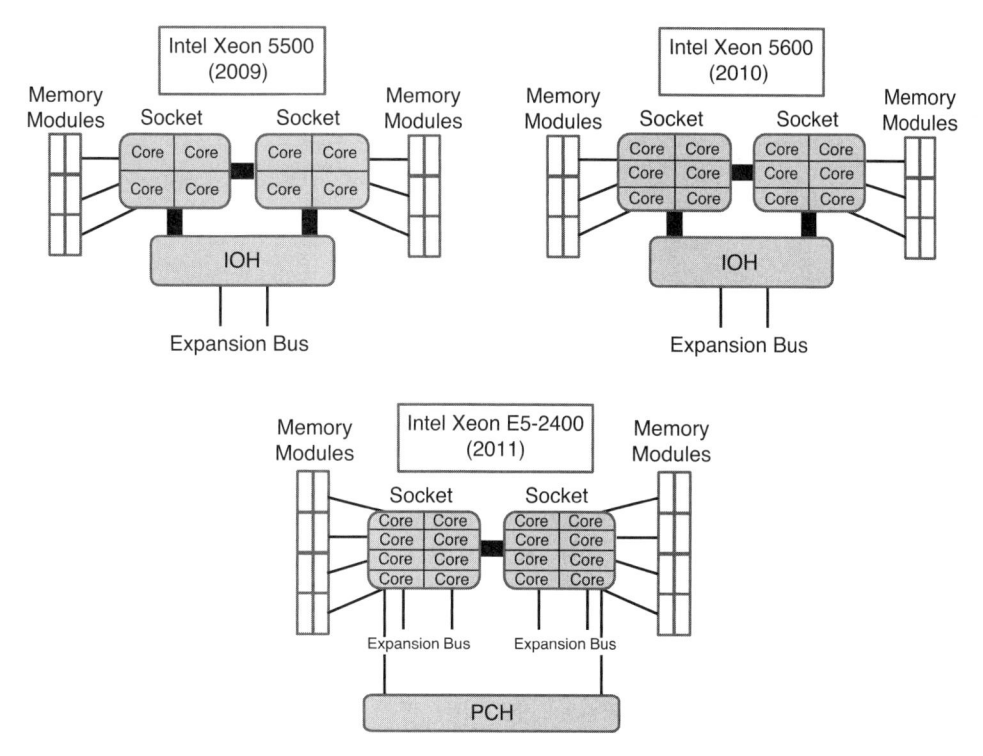

Figure 13-2 *Intel Xeon Microarchitecture Examples (Printed by permission of Intel Corporation.)*

Observe that Figure 13-2 portrays microarchitectures that differ from the one shown in Figure 13-1. In these processors, the memory controller is now part of the CPUs, which deploy multiple channels to access memory. This behavior exemplifies how specific circuits can be "absorbed" by the CPU as they evolve over time.

Displayed in the upper-left corner of Figure 13-2, an Intel Xeon 5500 microarchitecture is comprised of two different CPU chips (sockets) with up to four cores each, totaling eight different processors per server. As the number of cores is increased in the Intel Xeon 5600 family, its microarchitecture achieves up to 12 independent processors per server. Both families employ an I/O Hub (IOH) chipset to perform Southbridge tasks and a system bus between CPU sockets and the IOH called *QuickPath Interconnect (QPI)*. This connection can offer a bandwidth of 8 gigatransfers per second, where a transfer can be defined as 64 bits of data every two clock cycles in each direction.

Also notice at the bottom of Figure 13-2 that the Intel Xeon E5-2400 simultaneously increased the maximum number of cores per socket while deploying a different CPU microarchitecture. In this new design, the expansion bus is now controlled by the CPU chips, leaving all the remaining Southbridge functions to the Platform Controller Hub (PCH) chipset.

> **Note** The transition shown in Figure 13-2 exemplifies the two-year "tick-tock" cycle that Intel has followed since 2007. In this process, a "tick" represents the shrinking of process technology in enhancing a preestablished architecture (Intel Xeon 5500 to 5600). On the other hand, a "tock" describes a change of microarchitecture (Intel Xeon 5600 to E5-2400).

Multiprocessing microarchitectures can be classified according to the way they can get access to memory. Therefore, they can be

- **Symmetric Multi Processing (SMP):** Where multiple processors are connected to a single memory pool that can be accessed equally and uniformly.
- **Massive Parallel Processing (MPP):** Where memory is not shared between processors.
- **Non-Uniform Memory Access (NUMA):** Where each processor has access to its local memory pool and also to the memory from other processors, with added latency.

All microarchitectures from Figure 13-2 are based on the NUMA architecture, illustrating a current trend in x86 CPUs. Most operating systems for these machines are NUMA-aware because they are able to distinctively handle data that should be stored on the processor local memory as well as data that does not have that requirement.

Memory Evolution

Supposing that you are a computer CPU, you can picture the memory as your office desk, where documents recently retrieved from the filing cabinets (auxiliary storage) are available for your analysis. After you finish your work on these documents, they are stored back in the cabinets to free your desk for other tasks.

Throughout computer history, memory has evolved from vacuum tubes to the modern random-access memory (RAM) chips, whose name invokes the fast access they provide to any of their available addresses.

RAM chips are essentially simple structures that contain transistors and capacitor sets that are capable of processing and storing a single bit during a certain period of time. Because the energy stored in the capacitor leaks, its information must be constantly refreshed, characterizing the most common type of memory used today: *dynamic RAM (DRAM)*.

> **Note** Although static RAM (SRAM) chips do not require constant energy charging, they are comparatively more complex to build, requiring more transistors per stored bit than DRAMs.

A memory controller is a specialized circuit that controls how data is inserted and retrieved from memory. To perform this function, it applies an exclusive clock signal to the memory chips to synchronize the data exchange. *Single Data Rate (SDR)* RAM chips can only provide one data exchange during a memory clock cycle. Meanwhile, *Double Data Rate (DDR)* chips can provide two data exchanges at each clock cycle.

Figure 13-3 illustrates the distinction between SDR and the hugely popular DDR RAM chips.

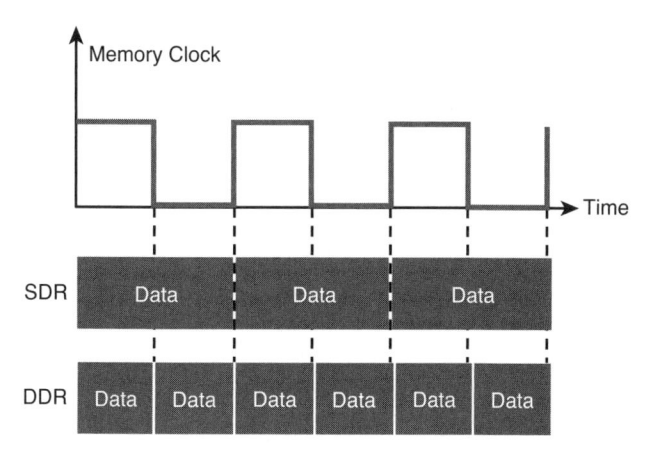

Figure 13-3 *Single and Double Data Rate*

There are currently three different DDR technologies (DDR, DDR2, and DDR3), whose distinctive performance characteristics are detailed in Table 13-1.

Table 13-1 *Double Data Rate Memory Technologies*

Characteristic	DDR	DDR2	DDR3
Typical voltage (volts)	2.5	1.8	1.5
Memory clock frequency (megahertz)	100 to 200	200 to 533	400 to 800
Maximum theoretical transfer rate (megabytes per second)	3200	8533	12,800
Typical latency (clock cycles)	3	5	7
Latency (nanoseconds)	15 to 30	9 to 25	8 to 18

Two values comprise the naming system for DDR RAM chips: their DDR technology and another one symbolizing their nominal frequency (which is twice the memory clock). Examples of memory chip names are DDR2-400 (memory clock is 200 MHz) and DDR3-1600 (memory clock is 800 MHz).

In the first x86 computers, memory chips were directly inserted on the motherboard, wasting a considerable area in this component and offering difficult access during maintenance. *Memory modules* were designed to solve both challenges, as Figure 13-4 illustrates.

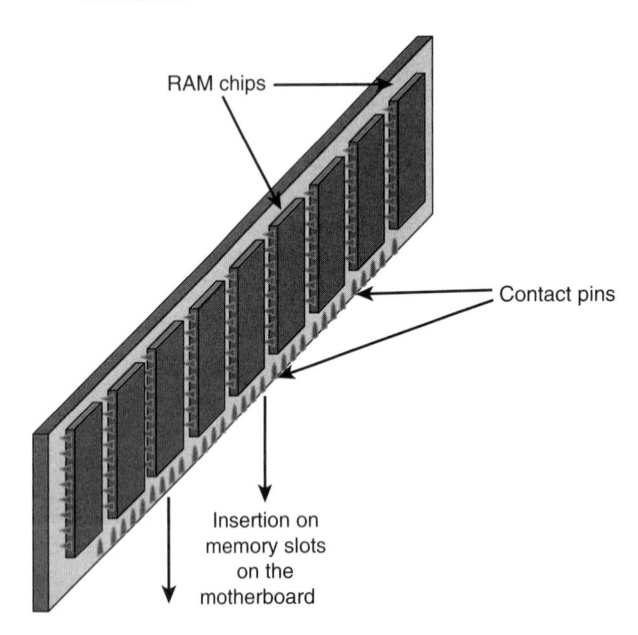

Figure 13-4 *Memory Module*

Memory modules include a variable number of RAM chips. *Single In-line Memory Modules (SIMM)* only have RAM chips on one side, while *Dual In-line Memory Modules (DIMM)* use both sides to populate RAM chips (with separate electrical contacts on each side of the module). To follow the current x86 architecture data path width, current memory modules deploy 64-bit transfers.

The naming system for memory modules follows the *PCx-yyyy* syntax, where x refers to the chip's DDR technology and *yyyy* refers to their chips transfer rate in megabytes per second (MBps). Examples of memory modules are PC2-3200 and PC3-12800, which are respectively comprised of DDR2-400 and DDR3-1600 memory chips.

Tip DDR, DDR2, and DDR3 memory modules deploy different connection pin schemes to avoid incorrect insertion.

In a single-memory module, one, two, or four *memory ranks* can share the same 64-bit-wide data path. Therefore, although the inclusion of additional ranks increases the capacity of a module, only one rank can be accessed at a time. As a result, a single-rank memory module is faster than a dual- or a quad-rank module.

Memory modules are also classified into *Unregistered DIMMs (UDIMM)* and *Registered DIMMs (RDIMM)*. Conversely from UDIMMs, RDIMMs have a buffer mechanism that stands between the DRAM chips and the memory controller, relieving the controller from the memory capacitor's electrical load. This reliability, however, taxes one additional clock cycle at each memory access when compared to UDIMMs.

> **Tip** RDIMMs are generally used on servers because of their higher scalability and stability.

Although memory quality has improved significantly over the years, an error on any capacitor, chip, or module can seriously impact a server, causing loss of data or even application outages. To overcome this situation, memory controllers can employ different RAS methods, such as

- **Parity:** An additional bit is also stored to represent the parity derived from a byte (8 bits). This method is not used very often because it cannot correct detected errors.
- **Error Correction Code (ECC):** As stated in its name, this method is capable of detecting and correcting single-bit data errors. Hence, it stores extra bits (up to 4) obtained in memory controller processing.
- **RAM mirroring:** Every bit is copied to two different modules, basically deploying RAID level 1 in memory chips. This method provides total data redundancy, but as a drawback, it reduces the usable memory by 50 percent.

The CPU responds to a superior clock when compared to the memory system. Consequently, at each memory access, it must literally wait for several CPU clock cycles until data is correctly retrieved or saved. To avoid wasting precious resources in this process, modern x86 CPUs deploy *memory caches* that can store the recent memory data in low-latency registers.

Modern CPUs deploy hierarchical layers of memory cache, with decreasing size and increasing latency. The memory cache levels are

- **L1:** The fastest cache and usually associated to each core.
- **L2:** A set of cores can share this memory cache layer.
- **L3:** Usually shared by all cores from a CPU chip.

Expansion Bus Evolution

In the evolution of the x86 architecture, several expansion bus technologies were created and sometimes simultaneously used on a single computer. The invention of a new bus technology usually mirrored the increasing speeds of CPUs and peripherals in a game of catch-up, where the bus would invariably remain as the last bottleneck.

These main expansion bus technologies (and their developers) were

- Industry Standard Architecture (ISA): IBM.
- Micro Channel Architecture (MCA): IBM.
- Extended Industry Standard Architecture (EISA): Compaq, Epson, Hewlett-Packard, NEC, and others.
- VESA Local Bus (VLB): Video Electronics Standards Association.
- Peripheral Component Interconnect (PCI): Intel.
- Accelerated Graphics Port (AGP): Intel.
- Peripheral Component Interconnect Extended (PCI-X): Compaq, IBM, and HP.

Table 13-2 illustrates the characteristics of these parallel bus technologies.

Table 13-2 *Parallel Expansion Buses*

Bus	Year	Width (Bits)	Maximum Clock Speed (Megahertz)	Maximum Bandwidth (Megabytes per Second)	Number of Pins
ISA	1981	8 and 16	8.33	8.33	98
MCA	1987	16 and 32	10	66	172
EISA	1988	32	8.33	33	198
VLB	1992	32	33	133	112
PCI	1993	32 and 64	66	533	124
AGP	1996	32	66	2133	132
PCI-X	1998	64	66	1064	184

Even if these bus technologies were sequentially replacing each other with higher speeds and adding features such as Direct Access Memory (DMA) and peripheral plug-and-play, they still were based on shared bus parallel topologies. Consequently, these technologies were submitted to contention and other challenges that are common in parallel communications such as clock skew (signals that do not arrive simultaneously at the other end of the connection) or interference from adjacent connections.

In 2004, Intel and other companies proposed a radical redesign with *PCI Express (PCIe)*, a serial connection between endpoints that could be peripherals or specialized PCIe communication circuits. Avoiding the communication limitations of parallel connections and leveraging dedicated pairs of unidirectional connections known as *lanes*, PCIe has superseded all other expansion bus technologies. Actually, it is the standard internal peripheral connection found on current x86 servers.

A PCIe device deploys a set of lanes (one, two, four, eight, or sixteen) to transfer data within a computer. Each connection is named through an *x* prefix and its number of lanes (for example, an x2 PCIe connection employs two lanes). At the time of this writing, a single PCIe lane can achieve almost 2 gigabytes per second.

PCIe is a true network stack, with transaction, data link, and physical layers standardized by PCI-SIG (PCI Special Interest Group), an industry organization formed in 1992 that maintains all PCI definitions and standards. It is also capable of implementing network virtualization: PCI-SIG has standardized *single-root I/O virtualization (SR-IOV)*, which allows a single PCIe I/O endpoint (such as a network adapter) to emulate multiple "lightweight" PCIe endpoints. Nonetheless, because these virtual adapters cannot be directly configured as their physical counterparts, SR-IOV requires support from the operating system (or hypervisor).

Physical Format Evolution

Nowadays, it is possible to find x86 servers built in three different formats: tower, rack-mountable, and blade chassis.

Figure 13-5 illustrates these server formats.

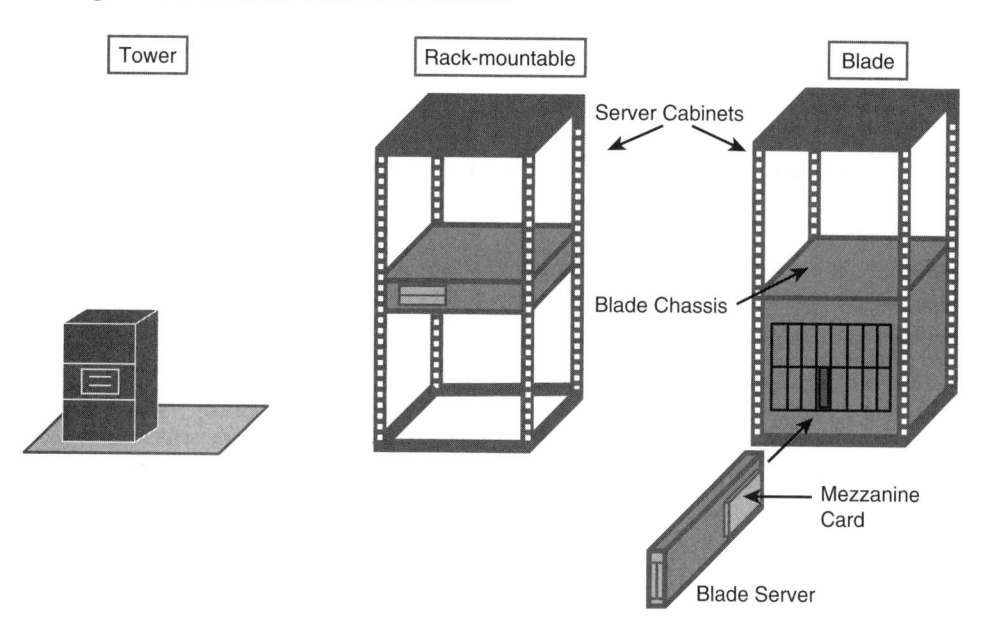

Figure 13-5 *Traditional Server Formats*

Tower servers resemble x86 desktops so much that I have heard some customers referring to them as "desk servers." These devices can be easily accommodated on any surface and do not require any special physical infrastructure (cabinets) for their installation. They are still used in remote branches or any environment with a low number of servers. These machines are not as popular in data center environments because they do not optimize space when in large numbers, and their installation in data center server cabinets requires rather cumbersome adaptations.

As stated in the name, *rack-mountable servers* are self-sufficient x86 computers that can be directly installed in standard 19-inch server cabinets. Each rack-mountable server demands individual management, and they usually occupy from one to eight rack units (RU).

> **Tip** Each rack unit is 1.75 inches or 44.45 mm high.

Briefly mentioned in Chapter 11, "Secret Identities," *blade servers* can be considered a space-optimized evolution from the rack-mountable server format. By definition, these machines are inserted in slots from a blade chassis that can deploy the following redundant elements:

- Ethernet switches
- Fibre Channel fabric switches
- Power sources
- Management modules

A blade chassis can occupy up to 10 RUs of a server cabinet. A single blade server can consume one or more chassis slots, receiving from the chassis the necessary power to work as well as Ethernet and Fibre Channel "electrical back plane" wires.

> **Note** These internal media connecting blade server interfaces to the chassis internal switches are specified in the IEEE 802.3ap, IEEE 802.3ba, and the T11 FC-PI family of standards.

Because of their higher server density and management features, blade servers currently have a higher adoption rate among all three formats. Nonetheless for the same reason, blade server deployments clearly demand special care from a power and cooling distribution perspective.

When space is optimized on a server, some hardware flexibility is lost. Consequently, rack-mountable and tower servers support more adapters and local storage devices than blade servers. Blade servers, however, have included a considerable variety of *mezzanine* cards to their portfolio. These connectivity adapters bear this name because they are stacked over the blade motherboard like a theater balcony.

Introducing x86 Server Virtualization

In the early 2000s, x86 computers were established as the prevalent server architecture in most data centers. As discussed in the previous section, intense hardware development enabled the support of mission-critical applications that were hardly imaginable a few years earlier.

Nevertheless, the shock of reality that was originated from the Internet bubble burst seriously challenged the *one-server-per-application* design that was very common in this period. As servers were sized to support sporadic performance peaks (such as an e-mail server at 9 a.m. on weekdays), they were poorly used during the remaining periods.

Such low resource utilization significantly affected all other technology areas in the data center. After all, a server working at 20 percent of its capacity still allocates 100 percent of space, storage, cabling, and network ports.

In hindsight, it can be said that the x86-based data center was in a similar situation as the mainframe computer room in the 1970s: At a great cost, hardware resources were being deployed but barely used.

In 2001, the three-year-old company VMware launched two products that proposed different solutions for this problem: *VMware GSX* and *VMware ESX*. Both products deployed server virtualization in distinct ways, as Figure 13-6 details.

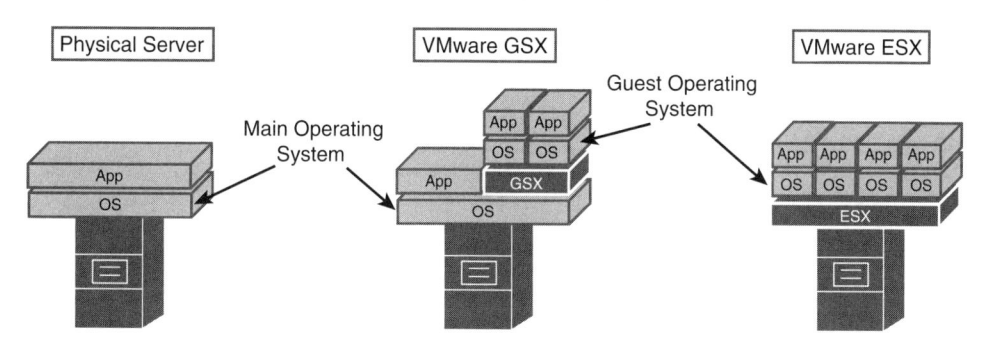

Figure 13-6 *Physical Server and VMware Solutions in 2001*

Figure 13-6 compares both solutions with a standard dedicated x86 server, with its operating system and its sole application. In the middle of the figure, VMware GSX runs over the server operating system as another application. As a *hypervisor*, GSX can create virtual hardware (including the processor, memory, storage, networking, and all other aspects) for the installation of a *guest operating system*. After applications are installed over the guest OS, these new virtual servers can consume the free resources from the physical machine.

The differences between this model and the installation of additional applications over the main operating system are

- The guest operating system is not necessarily the same software that is actually controlling the physical server hardware. Therefore, applications running over the guest OS can overcome compatibility issues with the main OS.

- VMware GSX has some level of hardware control over the virtual hardware that is being perceived by the guest operating systems.

Notwithstanding, it is the main operating system that ultimately controls the hardware resources in the case of VMware GSX. For that reason, this software is considered a *Type 2 hypervisor* according to the classification that was developed by Gerald J. Popek and Robert P. Goldberg in their 1974 article "Formal Requirements for Virtualizable Third Generation Architectures."

On the right side of Figure 13-6, VMware ESX is installed directly over the server hardware. With this privileged access to the physical resources, ESX is considered a *Type 1 hypervisor* for x86 computers.

VMware ESX not only leveraged unused hardware resources as GSX, but it also could employ them in a unique and optimized way.

Note As an exercise, I recommend that you use the virtualization taxonomy explained in Chapter 1, "Virtualization History and Definitions," to categorize VMware GSX and ESX.

Virtualization Unleashed

Both aforementioned VMware hypervisors were based on the management of *virtual machines (VM)*, which can be defined as software computers running an operating system and associated applications. For these solutions, a virtual machine is comprised of a set of specification and configuration manageable files, such as

- Emulated hardware definition file
- Virtual disk data
- VM BIOS

The clever decision to summon a VM through a set of files consequently defines the virtual machine flexibility when compared to physical server installations. For example, through a simple file copy operation, a virtual machine state can be saved and cloned on a different host (physical server).

Using ESX as its basis, VMware has built a *virtualization infrastructure*, where a VM manager controlled a group of virtualized hosts. Initially called *Virtual Center* (later *vCenter*), this software was able to coordinate features that were not envisioned by the forefathers of computer virtualization.

Figure 13-7 depicts the virtualization infrastructure architecture.

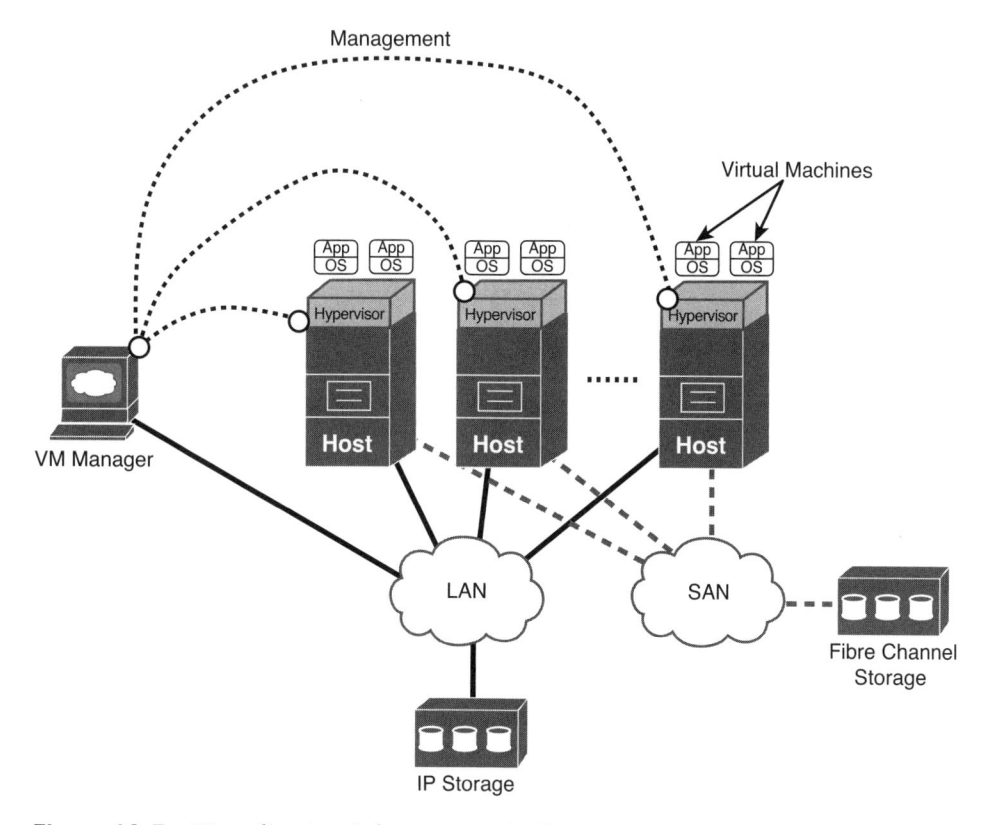

Figure 13-7 *Virtualization Infrastructure Architecture*

The figure shows the VM manager controlling Type 1 hypervisors installed in a group of physical hosts that defined a *virtualization cluster*. Accessing this management software, an administrator can create and control VMs as well as monitor the resource utilization on all hosts, including CPU, memory, network, and storage.

Tip In true virtualization form, the VM manager can be installed in a VM from the virtualization cluster it is managing.

Shared storage structures, such as a SAN or NAS, are crucial to allow hosts in a virtualization cluster to share VM files. For example, when accessing logical unit numbers (LUN), any ESX host can format with the Virtual Machine File System (VMFS) to store the VM files in a specialized way.

VMware VMFS also allows multiple hosts to access the same file concurrently, unlike other lock-based file systems such as common internet file system (CIFS). To further optimize the use of storage, recent versions of ESX can deploy storage thin-provisioning, where the virtual disk file only stores what the VMs are effectively using.

> **Tip** Thin-provisioning was discussed in Chapter 9, "Storage Evolution."

Broadly speaking, a server virtualization infrastructure enables data center features through a software layer, with multiple operational advantages. For example, it can provide *high availability (HA)* for virtual machines without relying on their own clustering capabilities. With HA, the VM files that were running on failed host are accessed by another host from the cluster, which can automatically reinitiate the VM.

Provisioning can also be streamlined through the use of *VM templates*, which define patterns for the "industrialization" of virtual machines. With VM templates, the creation of a VM is only a mouse click away, because it includes resource settings, installed applications, and common configurations such as Domain Name System (DNS) servers.

But it was the online migration of virtual machines (VMware vMotion) that provided the basic element for the large changes that were about to come. Using vMotion, a VM can be transferred from one host without any application interruption, as shown in Figure 13-8.

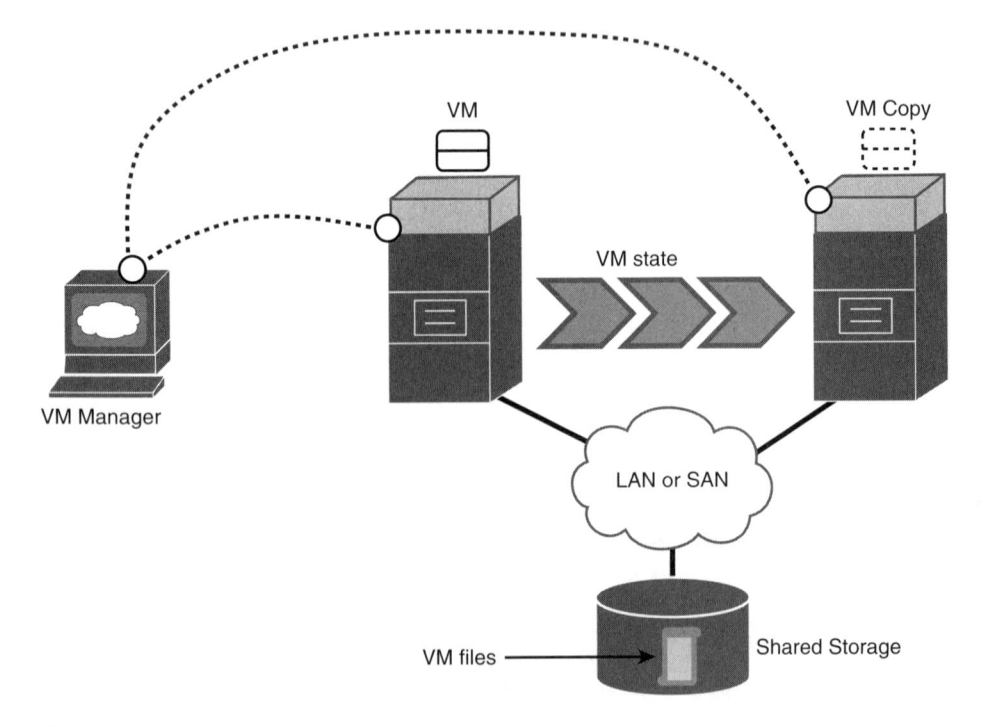

Figure 13-8 *Virtual Machine Online Migration*

Under its "hood," VMware vMotion works as follows:

- When the VM manager orders a VM migration between two hosts, the destination host creates a copy of this VM using its files that are available on the shared storage.

- The VM state (memory) is then copied to this empty VM container, until both virtual machines are fully synchronized with each other.

- Finally, the VM is quietly paused and decommissioned in the source host while its copy starts working at the destination host.

With vMotion, virtual machines are free to roam to any of the cluster hosts, using their combined hardware elements as a resource pool. In truth, a distinct infrastructure feature called *Distributed Resource Scheduling (DRS)* can automatically transfer VMs from an overloaded host to achieve a more balanced use of the hardware resource pool. Using server management protocols such as IPMI (Intelligent Platform Management Interface), the VM manager can also put servers in energy-saving mode if the total power load from the VMs does not require all hosts from a virtualization cluster to be active at the same time.

As an interesting variation of online migration, a feature called *Fault Tolerance (FT)* can offer stateful redundancy for VMs in a virtualization infrastructure. If FT is enabled for a VM, a "shadow" machine is created in another host, and through constant updates, it will always be synchronized with the active machine. Should the VM host fail for any reason, the "shadow" machine will nondisruptively assume its duties.

Figure 13-9 further illustrates both DRS and FT at work in a virtualization infrastructure.

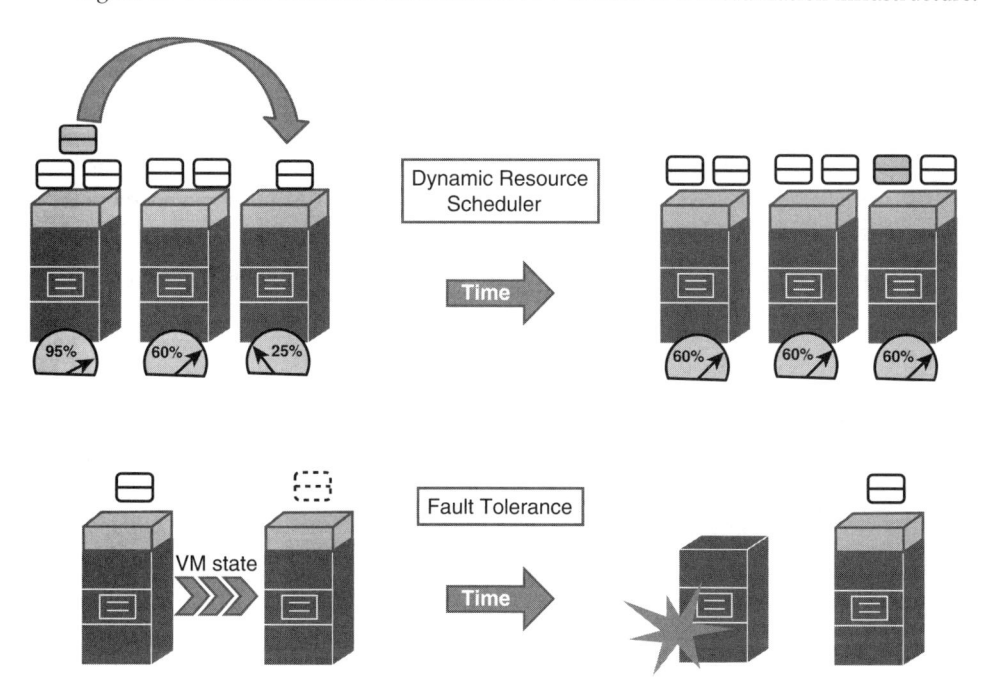

Figure 13-9 *VMware Dynamic Resource Scheduler and Fault Tolerance in Action*

> **Tip** Although FT is not disruptive, it invariably requires twice the resources of the protected VM from the hardware resource pool.

As the 2000s approached their end, the benefits brought by VMware virtualization infrastructures (rebranded VMware vSphere in 2009) inspired the development of other Type 1 hypervisors such as Microsoft Hyper-V, Citrix XenServer, and Linux KVM.

With a multitude of other features still being developed on these structures, *virtual networking* has emerged as a very important piece in the x86 server virtualization puzzle. Cisco has made significant contributions to virtual networking, which will be the subject of Chapter 15, "Transcending the Rack," and Chapter 16, "Virtual Network Services."

Unified Computing

In 2009, Cisco entered the x86 server market with the Unified Computing System (UCS). Not a standard server solution, Cisco UCS was designed with a systemic view to address the following challenges related to critical x86 server deployments:

- Deployment simplification
- Management consolidation
- Easier interaction with other teams (server virtualization, storage, and networking)

In essence, *unified computing* can be defined as the harmonic coalition of server, storage, network, and virtualization technologies in the same compute architecture. Cisco UCS actually materialized this concept, aggregating several virtualization technologies that were already discussed in this book.

To illustrate how UCS simplifies server deployments, Figure 13-10 compares a traditional blade server environment with a Cisco UCS B-series deployment.

In the upper-left corner of Figure 13-10, the traditional blade server deployment achieves a considerable level of management and connectivity consolidation for the servers installed in the same chassis. However, as the number of blade enclosures grows, manageability for servers in different chassis is considerably challenged. After all, the chassis internal modules (LAN, SAN, and management) demand operations that must be repeated at each enclosure.

On the other hand, UCS enables the management of hundreds of servers as if they are part of the same structure. The software called *UCS Manager* fulfills this task while running on a crucial UCS component named *Fabric Interconnect*.

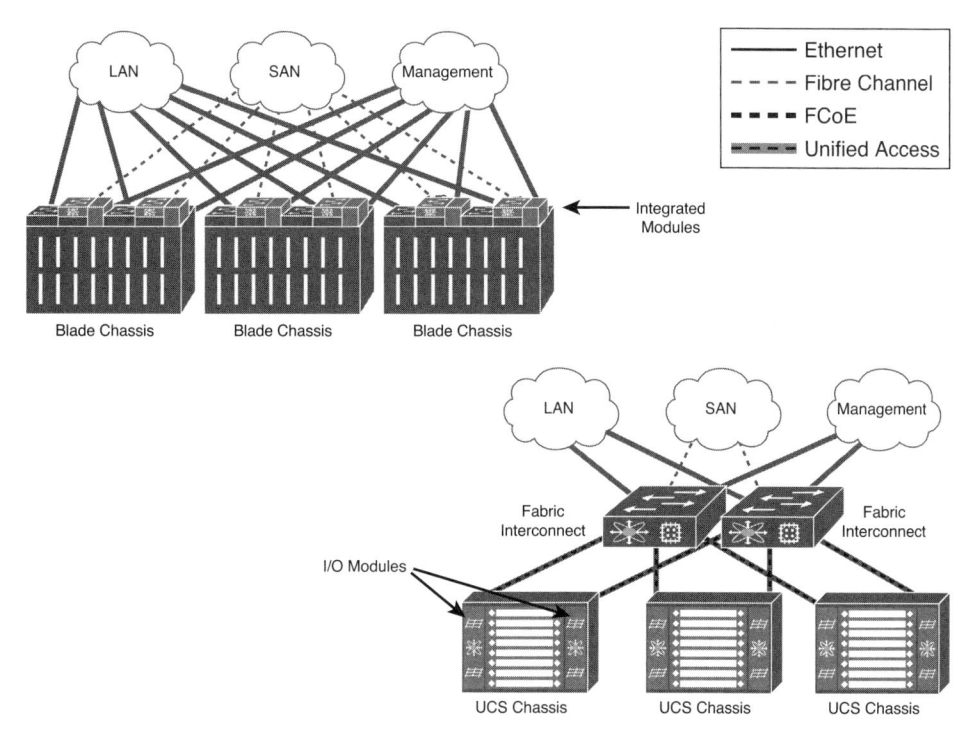

Figure 13-10 *Traditional Blade Environment and Unified Computing System*

Considered by many customers as the amalgamation of a server management platform with a converged Nexus switch, UCS Fabric Interconnect actually runs NX-OS and provides similar connectivity flexibility to these data center switches (for example, Ethernet, Fibre Channel, and DCB/FCoE ports). As depicted at the lower-right corner of Figure 13-10, Fabric Interconnects perform the role of "connectivity portals" for the servers in the UCS architecture. Through these elements, server operations, such as the inclusion of a new chassis, are isolated from the outer world (LAN, SAN, management networks) and vice versa.

Connectivity is further simplified in UCS Blade chassis through internal Fabric Extenders called I/O Modules (IOM). These components allow the consolidation of all interfaces of a system on two virtual access chassis, reducing cabling and improving serviceability.

Besides implementing I/O convergence, Fabric Extenders, and server management in the same infrastructure, Cisco UCS provides additional enhancements to physical and virtual server environments. Two chapters from Part IV, "Virtualization in Server Technologies," will examine in detail the following features:

- Chapter 14, "**Changing Personalities**": UCS service profiles.
- Chapter 15, "**Transcending the Rack**": Virtual Machine Fabric Extender (VM-FEX).

Summary

In this chapter, you learned the following:

- Servers can be found in three different architectures: mainframe, RISC, and x86.
- x86 computers have undergone an impressive hardware evolution in all of their components, including CPU, memory, and expansion bus.
- x86 servers are available in three basic formats: tower, rack-mountable, and blade.
- Server virtualization in x86 servers has initially improved hardware utilization. Afterward, it has truly revolutionized data center operations with flexible features such as online migration and VM high availability.
- Unified Computing simplifies x86 server operations through the consolidation of server, storage, networking, and virtualization elements in a single integrated architecture.

Further Reading

Morimoto, Carlos E. *Hardware, o Guia Definitivo*. SUL Editores, 2007.

Introduction to the New Mainframe: z/OS Basics, www.redbooks.ibm.com/redpieces/abstracts/sg246366.html

Intel Xeon Processor 5500 Series, www.intel.com.br/content/dam/www/public/us/en/documents/product-briefs/xeon-5500-brief.pdf

Intel Xeon Processor 5600 Series, www.intel.com.br/content/dam/www/public/us/en/documents/product-briefs/xeon-5600-brief.pdf

Intel Xeon Processor E5-2400 Series-Based Platforms for Intelligent Systems, www.intel.com.br/content/dam/www/public/us/en/documents/marketing-briefs/xeon-e5-2400-for-intelligent-systems-brief.pdf

VMware vSphere Documentation, www.vmware.com/support/pubs/vsphere-esxi-vcenter-server-pubs.html

Server - Unified Computing, www.cisco.com/go/ucs

Chapter 14

Changing Personalities

"The measure of intelligence is the ability to change." (Albert Einstein)

This chapter explores service profiles and how they can simplify, accelerate, and automate physical server provisioning in Unified Computing Systems (UCS). It contains the following topics:

- Server Provisioning Challenges
- Unified Computing and Service Profiles
- Building Service Profiles
- Industrializing Server Provisioning
- Use Case: Seasonal Workloads

Table 14-1 categorizes service profiles in the virtualization taxonomy described in Chapter 1, "Virtualization History and Definitions."

Table 14-1 *Service Profile Virtualization Classification*

Virtualization Characteristics	Service Profile
Emulation	Server hardware identifiers and settings
Type	Abstraction
Sub-type	Address remapping
Scalability	160 associated service profiles per Unified Computing System[1]
Technology area	Server

Virtualization Characteristics	Service Profile
Subarea	Hardware
Advantages	Fast physical server provisioning, physical workload migration, server automation

[1]Refer to Appendix A, "Cisco Data Center Portfolio," for more details and Cisco Unified Computing System online documentation for updated information.

Many end users consider server provisioning the single most visible of all data center operations. Adding importance to this process, the number of physical servers in a data center continues to be a popular method of comparing the size of different facilities.

Fully activating a physical server builds on efforts that involve purchasing of hardware, transportation, physical installation, cabling, networking, storage provisioning, software installation, and many other customizations. Intending to increase control over IT resources, industry best practices and governance standards have, in some cases, raised the complexity on server provisioning processes. And as a result, it is not uncommon that *weeks*, or even *months*, are spent before the first client can finally access the application hosted on the provisioned server.

On traditional server architectures, multiple provisioning tasks are dependent on hardware identifiers such as World Wide Names (WWNs) and MAC addresses, which in many cases are only gathered after the server is somehow accessible. Post-installation operations, such as migrations and adapter upgrades, are also heavily challenged by these hardware identifiers. After all, a single address change can require several adaptations from the data center infrastructure and software images.

With the widespread popularity of x86 servers, tasks such as BIOS settings and firmware updates can substantially increase the "time to market" of a data center in the same way. On the other hand, business is becoming even less tolerable to such delays. Moreover, demanding end users are invariably forcing service providers and internal IT teams to respond much faster than they used to.

Leveraging the opportunity to build a completely new server architecture from the ground up, Cisco has also revolutionized server provisioning through the creation of *service profiles* in Unified Computing Systems. Essentially, a service profile brings the possibility of activating servers within minutes. And other service profile–related functions, such as policies, cloning, pools, and templates, can further accelerate the creation of physical servers. Together, these elements enable data center *industrialization* characteristics that are only comparable to server virtualization environments.

This chapter will examine the intricacies of traditional server provisioning and the inner mechanisms of UCS service profiles, and how these elements can be applied to improve service implementation agility.

Server Provisioning Challenges

Server provisioning is the process of readying a server for production use. Generally speaking, the activation of a physical server depends on numerous tasks that are performed by different data center teams:

- Rack or blade chassis installation (facilities team)
- Power and cooling provisioning (facilities team)
- Physical connection for LAN, storage-area network (SAN), management, and other required connectivity traffic (cabling team)
- Configuration of access switches, interfaces, VLANs, and routing (networking team)
- Logical unit number (LUN) provisioning and masking, SAN zoning, Internet Small Computer System Interface (iSCSI) mapping, and Network Attached Storage (NAS) permissions (storage team)
- BIOS settings, firmware management, operating system installation, licensing, and configuration (server team)
- Application software installation, licensing, and customization (application team)

Consequently, server provisioning involves multiple operations that are spread over distinct control areas (cabling, network switches, SAN switches, storage arrays, and the servers themselves). Such characteristics challenge the efficiency of IT departments, which must deal with incompatibility scenarios, inconsistent policies, and poor integration in a daily basis.

To avoid operational mistakes and sponsor standardization, a large number of companies rely on governance certifications defined in frameworks such as COBIT (Control Objectives for Information and Related Technologies). However, as more control processes are introduced to server provisioning, the longer it can take to activate a server for production.

For corporations that require almost immediate responses from their IT team, this latency can be simply unbearable. And although additional layers of provisioning tools have tried to insert little order to this equation, their integration to highly heterogenous x86 environments is considered a formidable challenge among server teams.

As an illustration, Figure 14-1 enlists some of the usual tasks that are executed whenever a new x86 server is provisioned in a data center.

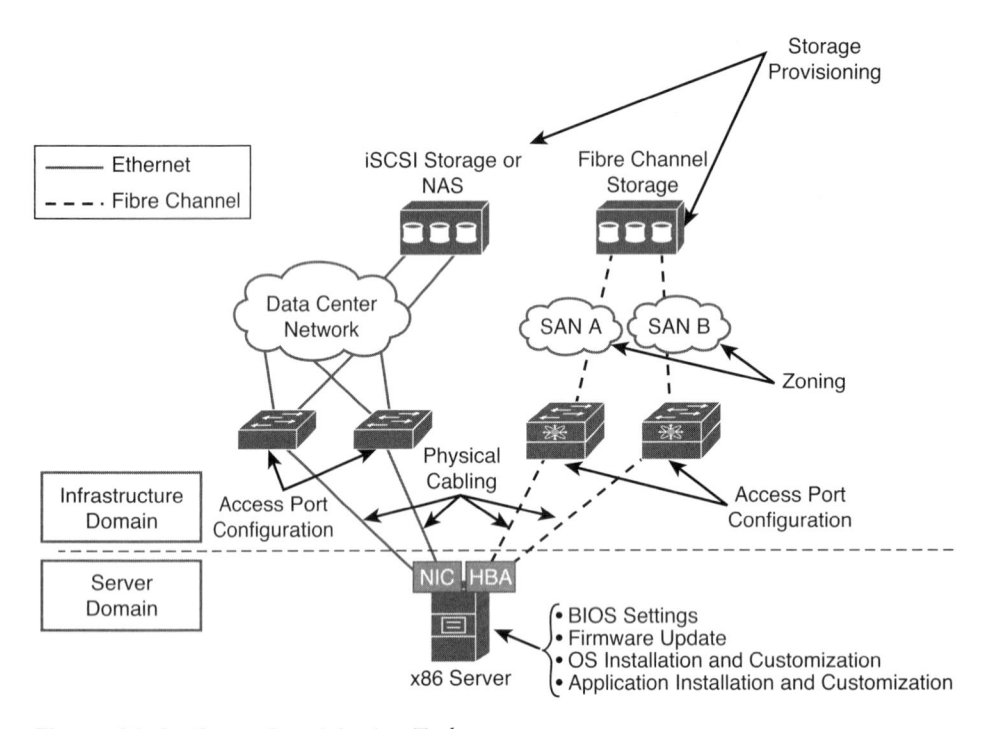

Figure 14-1 *Server Provisioning Tasks*

In Figure 14-1, you can see that the provisioning tasks are divided into two domains:

- **Server domain:** Tasks that are performed directly on the server hardware by the server and application teams.

- **Infrastructure domain:** Tasks that are performed by other teams on devices and elements such as switches, storage arrays, and cables.

Each operational domain has its own characteristics and challenges, as I will elaborate in next two sections.

Server Domain Operations

Server domain tasks are only concerned with the customization of hardware and software components of a server. Arguably, the operating system and the application installations are the most well-known of the server domain tasks.

While some server operators might still prefer to carry DVDs and step-by-step manuals through data center corridors, software installation tasks have been highly simplified with techniques such as

- **Scripting:** Where a script (or "answer file") allows the automation of the installation steps without manual intervention. Depending on the installed software, scripted installation can take hours, and careful maintenance over the script versions is usually necessary. Because hardware detection is generally performed during a scripted installation, this technique is more adaptable to the unique identifiers (addresses and names) of a server.

- **Imaging:** In this method, the base installation of the operating system on a storage device (local or external) can be derived into identical copies that are customized to work on other servers. Although this technique might be faster when compared to scripting, it demands more control over the resulting images. Additionally, imaging is highly dependent on unique identifiers (addresses and names) of a server.

Operating systems and applications normally present compatibility restrictions with some BIOS settings and firmware versions from adapters and controllers. And these dependencies demand considerable effort from server teams, because BIOS configuration and firmware updates are usually manual operations.

Discrepancies in identifiers and firmware versions also challenge the migration of software between two servers. Besides dealing with incompatibilities, the server team must also be aware of licenses that can be bound to unique identifiers, such as an adapter MAC address. In these scenarios, it might not even be possible to reinstall the software on a new server without a new license.

Infrastructure Domain Operations

The activation of a physical server also depends on tasks that are executed outside the server carcass. Although power, cooling, cabling, and networking can all be pre-provisioned for a server, other infrastructure tasks are completely dependent on identifiers that are only known through some kind of local access to the device. For example:

- LUN masking and SAN zoning usually require the previous knowledge of the Port WWN from a host bus adapter (HBA) (or converged network adapter [CNA]).
- DHCP servers can use IP-to-MAC address mappings to increase automation on server provisioning processes.

Changing, updating, repurposing, or replacing hardware components can also increase complexity of these processes. The new hardware identifiers usually require a complete reconstruction of hardware-dependent infrastructure domain operations, raising both operational costs and maintenance windows.

Although server virtualization (as discussed in Chapter 13, "Server Evolution,") has elegantly streamlined many of these tasks, not all servers in a data center are virtualized. Besides, a hypervisor is also an operating system that requires proper physical server installation and customization.

Definitely, extreme coordination among all teams is mandatory as server environments become larger and more complex. But in archaic data center architectures, error-prone and morose infrastructures are the direct result of uncoordinated management islands.

Unified Computing and Service Profiles

As explained in Chapter 13, the Cisco Unified Computing System (UCS) integrates technologies that were already available in other data center solutions, such as Fabric Extenders, I/O consolidation, N_Port Virtualization (NPV), and many others. Moreover, Cisco UCS architecture literally "raises the bar" between infrastructure and server domains, grouping several network, SAN, and server tasks under the same point of control.

Figure 14-2 portrays this discreet but essential structural characteristic of Cisco UCS.

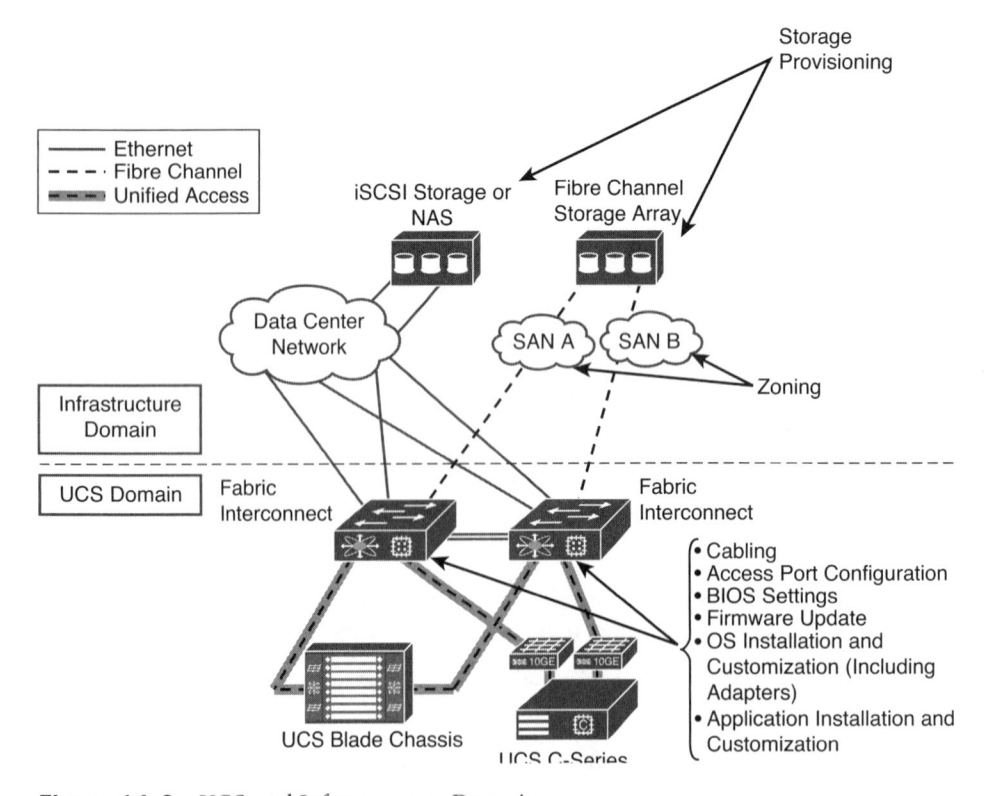

Figure 14-2 *UCS and Infrastructure Domains*

In Figure 14-2, you can observe that the UCS Manager software (embedded on both Fabric Interconnects) increases the opportunity for process standardization and agility. Its native Role-Based Access Control (RBAC) capabilities also provide the necessary separation among tasks that should belong to different data center teams.

Cisco UCS also includes a virtualization technique that primarily groups a huge number of server provisioning tasks into a single assignment, while releasing unique identifier dependencies on all operational domains. A *service profile* is a self-contained logical entity that maintains configuration information about a server hardware, interfaces, fabric connectivity, and identifiers. Because it is centrally stored inside the UCS Manager, a service profile can be associated to server hardware that belongs to a UCS domain.

A blade or rack-mountable UCS server *must* be associated to a service profile to run an operating system and upper-layer applications. Each associated service profile has a one-to-one relationship with a server, and when a service profile is disassociated from a server, its configuration is reset to the factory defaults.

In a UCS domain, all server-related tasks are performed on the service profile, providing a logical separation between a server "personality" and its hardware. When a service profile is associated with a server, both Fabric Interconnects and server components (such as adapters and BIOS) are configured according to the data in the profile. For example, a service profile can contain the following:

- Fabric Interconnect virtual interfaces (Ethernet and Fibre Channel)
- Unique server identifier
- LAN connectivity attributes, such as MAC address and quality of service (QoS) policies
- SAN connectivity attributes, such as WWN and QoS policies
- Firmware packages and versions
- Operating system boot order and configuration
- Management IP address

Figure 14-3 portrays the association of a service profile to a blade server that is inserted in a UCS blade chassis.

The association of service profiles is performed as a simple, single operation that only takes a few minutes to complete. Because a service profile is a virtual entity within UCS Manager, one can observe that it effectively enables migration of unique identifiers (and many other customizations) between servers without requiring any manual configuration changes.

But more than moving identifiers and settings between servers, service profiles enable the concept of *stateless computing*, in which the underlying hardware can be made completely transparent to the operating system and applications that run on it. By design, stateless computing overcomes the challenges described in the last section.

Tip Stateless computing cannot support operating system data stored on internal disks, because they would require physical removal and insertion in another server. Consequently, in stateless computing, server boots are executed using external storage devices.

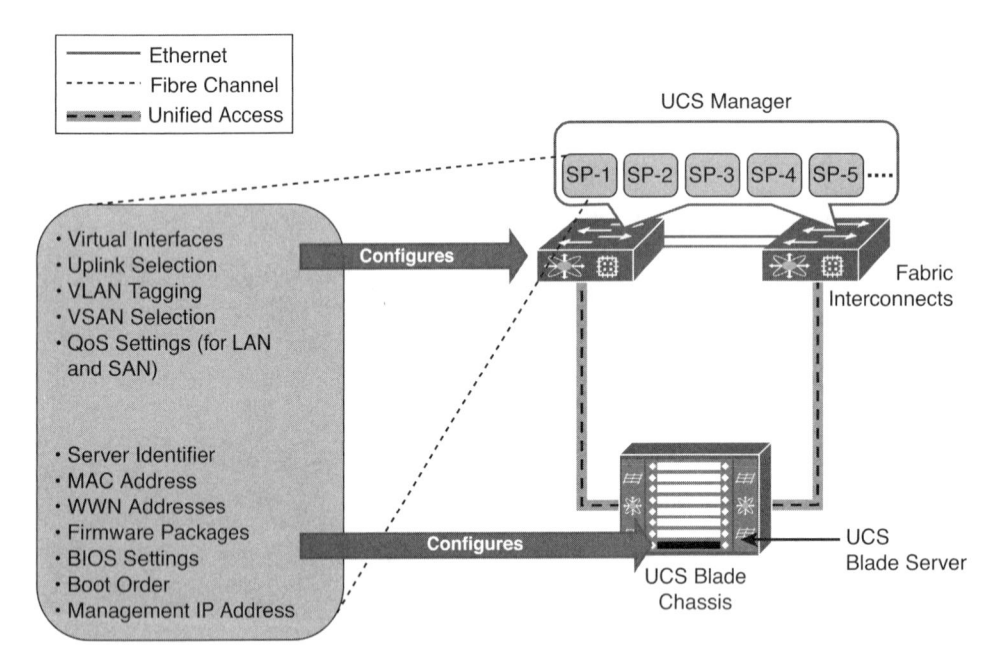

Figure 14-3 *Associating a Service Profile to a Blade Server*

As you will learn in the following sections, service profiles allow the infrastructure domain tasks to be completed before a server is even purchased. They are also strong management tools that can define all pre-OS server settings and firmware versions on a provisioned server.

Building Service Profiles

The UCS Manager uses service profiles to properly configure the Fabric Interconnects (and consequently, their associated Fabric Extenders) and server components. While each Fabric Interconnect is configured through commands applied to different software components (such as NX-OS), it also configures one specific non-installable circuit on UCS servers: the *Cisco Integrated Management Controller (CIMC)*. Through its CIMC, a UCS server can provide hardware status, a configuration interface to UCS Manager, and remote access to server administrators.

In a UCS domain, each Fabric Extender (or I/O module [IOM] on a UCS blade chassis) provides out-of-band connectivity between UCS Manager and the CIMC of its managed servers. In the case of UCS blade chassis, this out-of-band network is comprised of a *chassis management switch (CMS)* that interconnects the IOM, the *chassis management circuit (CMC)*, and the CIMC chip on the blade servers. Each CMS has eight Fast Ethernet interfaces to the CIMCs and one Gigabit Ethernet interface to the IOM. Additionally, this internal switch supports several infrastructure VLANs, such as

- **DCOS Network (VLAN 4042):** Connects the Fabric Interconnects NX-OS to the IOMs and to the adapters that can be implementing Virtual Machine Fabric Extender (VM-FEX), as I will discuss in Chapter 15, "Transcending the Rack". A curiosity: DCOS was the original name of NX-OS inside Cisco.

- **Adapter Management Network (VLAN 4043):** Connects the Fabric Interconnect and the adapter cards to allocate resources, change identifiers, and monitor performance.

- **Infrastructure Network (VLAN 4044):** This is used to configure the CMCs and the CIMCs.

- **PXE Network (VLAN 4047):** This is used to provide Preboot Execution Environment (PXE) for the Cisco UCS Utility OS (UUOS).

> **Note** These infrastructure VLANs must also be provided when UCS C-series rack-mount servers are managed by UCS Manager. At the time of this writing, this design requires the connection of Nexus 2232 Fabric Extenders to the C-series management interfaces ("dual-wire" option) or to special adapters such as the UCS VIC 1225 ("single-wire" option). Notwithstanding, refer to Cisco online documentation for updated information about this design.

After a server is associated to a service profile, its CIMC boots the UUOS agent to execute changes defined in the profile. This "pre-OS configuration agent" system boot is completely transparent to the server administrator and takes only approximately two minutes to complete.

A service profile can be configured through the UCS Manager graphical user interface (GUI) or command-line interface. Generally speaking, because the former provides an easier experience, it is usually preferred over the latter by the majority of UCS administrators. The UCS Manager GUI is accessible through an HTTP or HTTPS session directed to a Fabric Interconnect IP address. In dual Fabric Interconnect topologies, this access is usually targeted to a virtual IP address configured on both devices to provide management high availability.

Figure 14-4 portrays the UCS Manager access to the virtual IP address (10.97.39.225) of a Unified Computing System.

Figure 14-4 also highlights the button that downloads and executes the UCS Manager client file. Launching UCS Manager and authenticating yourself, you have access to the Java-based GUI that allows the configuration of the entire system.

Figure 14-5 shows a sample screen capture of the GUI.

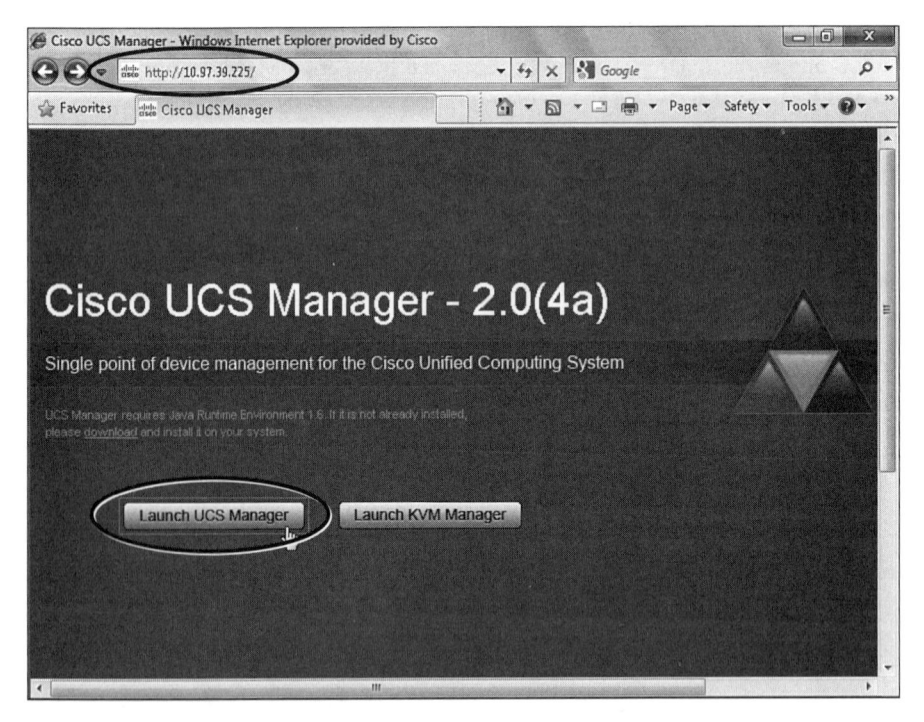

Figure 14-4 *UCS Manager Web Access*

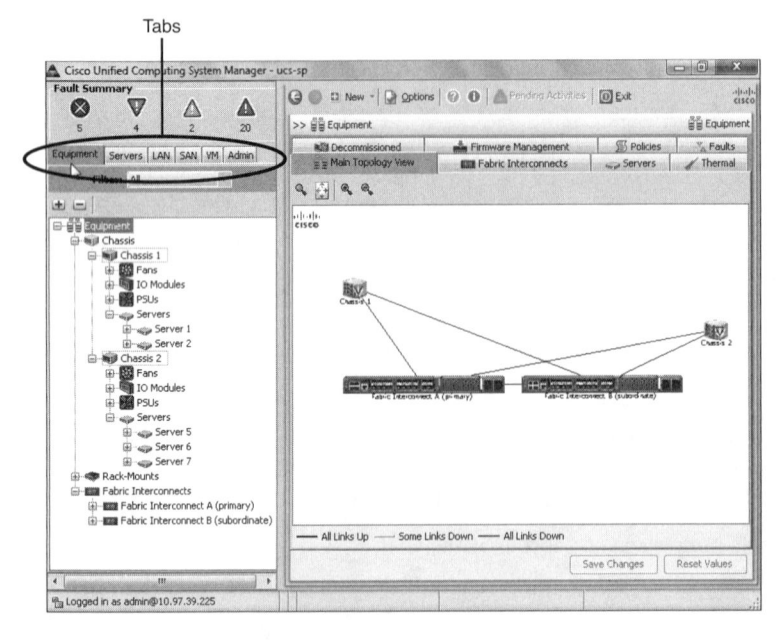

Figure 14-5 *UCS Manager Topology View*

In the upper-left corner of Figure 14-5 there are six main tabs available for the system configuration. They can be described as follows:

- **Equipment:** Where you can configure the physical inventory of the UCS components such as Fabric Interconnects, chassis, servers, and so on. A system or server administrator is usually responsible for the configuration of the elements in this tab.

- **Servers:** Contains all configuration related to servers, such as service profiles, policies, pools, and templates. It is expected that a server administrator controls this tab (which will be the basis for this chapter).

- **LAN:** Comprises the components related to LAN configuration, such as VLANs, QoS classes, and Ethernet uplinks. This tab was designed with the LAN administrator tasks in mind.

- **SAN:** Encompasses the creation and control of SAN elements such as VSANs and external connectivity. Its administration can be offloaded to the SAN administrator.

- **VM:** Contains the components required to configure VM-FEX for servers with virtualized adapters. The contents of this topic will be analyzed in detail in Chapter 15.

- **Admin:** Configures system-wide settings, such as user account management and call home. The system administrator typically accesses and manages the components on this tab.

Tip On each main tab, you can also select a filter that allows a cleaner visualization of a single part of the tab parameters.

In Figure 14-6, you can also observe that this specific UCS is comprised of two Fabric Interconnects and two chassis. Chassis 1 has two servers (in slots 1 and 2), and chassis 2 has three (in slots 5, 6, and 7).

In truth, this system is already primed to create service profiles. Figure 14-6 details how this particular system is connected to an Ethernet network and a Fibre Channel SAN.

In the topology shown in Figure 14-6, both Fabric Interconnects (ucs-sp-a and ucs-sp-b) are running in NPV mode and respectively using MDS-A (VSAN 10) and MDS-B (VSAN 20) as upstream switches. From a pure Ethernet perspective, ucs-sp-a and ucs-sp-b are configured in *End-Host mode*, which basically means that

- Ethernet interfaces are classified into two distinct behaviors (uplink or virtual Ethernet [vEth]).

- An uplink interface is directly connected to an upstream Ethernet switch.

- A virtual Ethernet interface is directly connected to a server. In UCS, a vEth corresponds to a Logical Interface (LIF) on a Fabric Extender.

- A virtual Ethernet interface is associated (or *pinned*) to an uplink port, using it for nonlocal traffic (frames not directed to another vEth interface).

- Uplink interfaces do not learn MAC addresses from external switches. Virtual Ethernet interfaces can learn MAC addresses.

- Uplink ports and virtual Ethernet interfaces do not participate in the Spanning Tree Protocol (STP) processes.

- To avoid loops, frames received on an uplink port are never forwarded to another uplink. Additionally, frames sourced from a MAC address that is associated to a vEth interface are not received on an uplink.

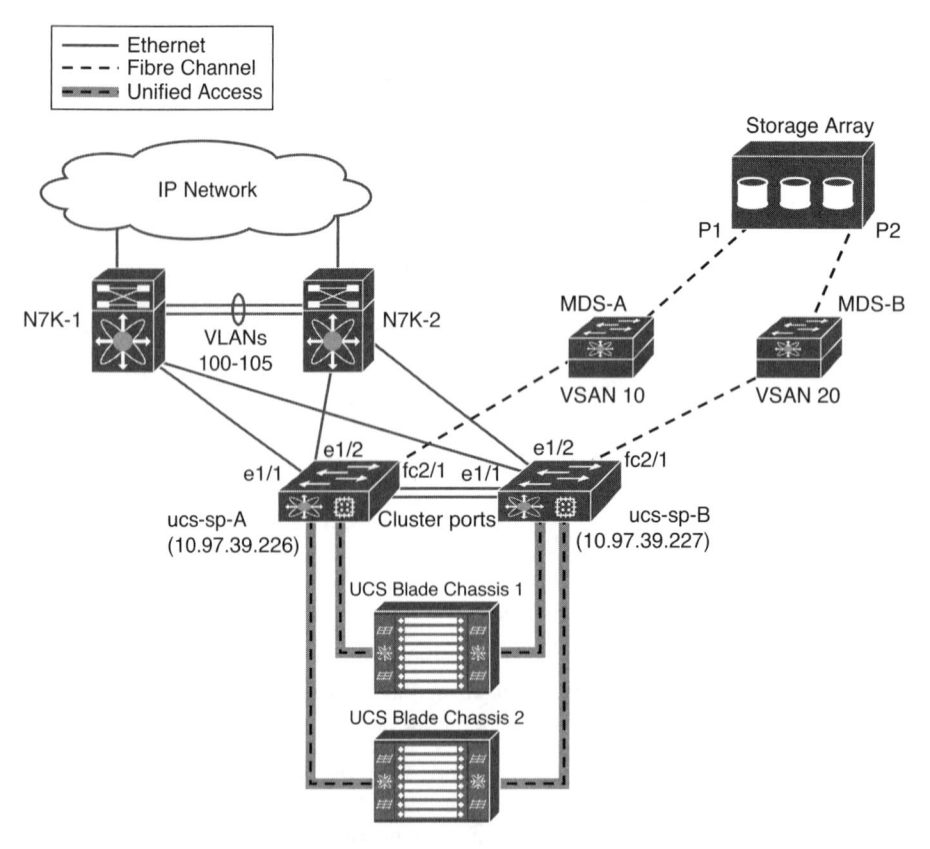

Figure 14-6 *Our UCS Topology*

Tip End-Host mode can be understood as a similar hardware implementation of a virtual switch behavior, such as the Nexus 1000V.

Both forwarding modes (NPV and End-Host) allow the entire system to be perceived as a simple server from their upstream SAN and LAN switch's point of view. Although a Fabric Interconnect can be configured to function in *switch mode* (for both Fibre Channel and Ethernet), for simplicity's sake, I have not done that in our scenario.

Additionally, I have configured VLANs 100 to 105 on the Fabric Interconnects and the Ethernet network, defining the uplink interfaces as trunks for these VLANs.

Coming back to the UCS Manager GUI, a new service profile is about to be created. After selecting the Servers tab, its toolbar and a work pane are displayed to allow you to perform service profile–related actions and observe their results (as shown in Figure 14-7).

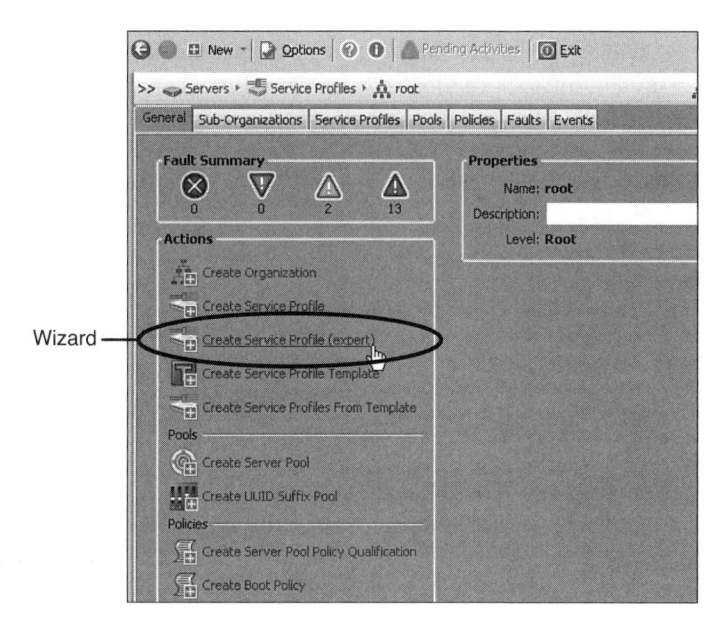

Figure 14-7 *Servers Tab View*

As it is common with graphical interfaces, there are multiple ways to perform the same task in UCS Manager GUI. I will use a specific tool to explain how service profiles can be built: the Create Service Profile (expert) wizard. In my opinion, this step-by-step guided procedure permits a better learning experience about service profile concepts and its possibilities.

The link that activates the Create Service Profile (expert) wizard is highlighted in Figure 14-7. This wizard has eight steps, which I will use to explain the elements of a service profile and the myriad parameters that can be included in it.

> **Note** Each of the next sections will deal with one step of the wizard. Do not consider that these procedures are the best possible practices. In these configurations, I will be as direct as possible, emphasizing concepts instead of every single configuration tweak (you can access Cisco online documentation for that). Also, for the sake of simplicity, I will only create service profiles in the root organization.

Identifying a Service Profile

In Step 1 of the Create Service Profile (expert) wizard, you must provide unique identifiers for this service profile. For example, it must have a unique name within its organization (which is root in our scenario).

This identification string represents all the configurations that are part of the service profile (which will be called SP-1).

Another identity attribut defined on this step is the *Universally Unique Identifier (UUID)*, which is generally used in software development, and it is also known as the *Globally Unique Identifier (GUID)*. This 128-bit value basically guarantees uniqueness across space and time without requiring a central registration process.

Note UUIDs were originally used in the Apollo Network Computing System, later in the Open Software Foundation's (OSF) Distributed Computing Environment (DCE) and then in Microsoft Windows platforms. Today, UUIDs are defined in the ISO/IEC 9834-8:2004 and RFC 4122 standards.

Because this identifier can be later inserted into the server image (or licensing) during the operating system and application installations, it is useful that this is part of a service profile. In UCS manager, a UUID is represented in the format XXXXXXXX-XXXX-XXXX-XXXX-XXXXXXXXXXXX (where X represents any hexadecimal value between 0 and F). You can assign a UUID to a service profile using one of the following methods:

- **Hardware default:** Where a service profile will use the original UUID from its associated server. Therefore, if this service profile is migrated between servers, a UUID change will certainly happen.

- **UUID suffix pool:** Where you can use a value from a preconfigured range of UUIDs that share the same 64-bit suffix.

- **Manual:** Where you can manually define the UUID of a service profile.

To explore the concept of a service profile, I will use the manual method to assign a UUID to SP-1. And as shown in Figure 14-8, I have chosen UUID 01234567-89AB-CDEF-0123-456789ABCDEF.

Tip As a cautionary action, I have verified that this specific UUID was not already being used by another service profile. However, this checking is only performed on a single UCS Manager domain.

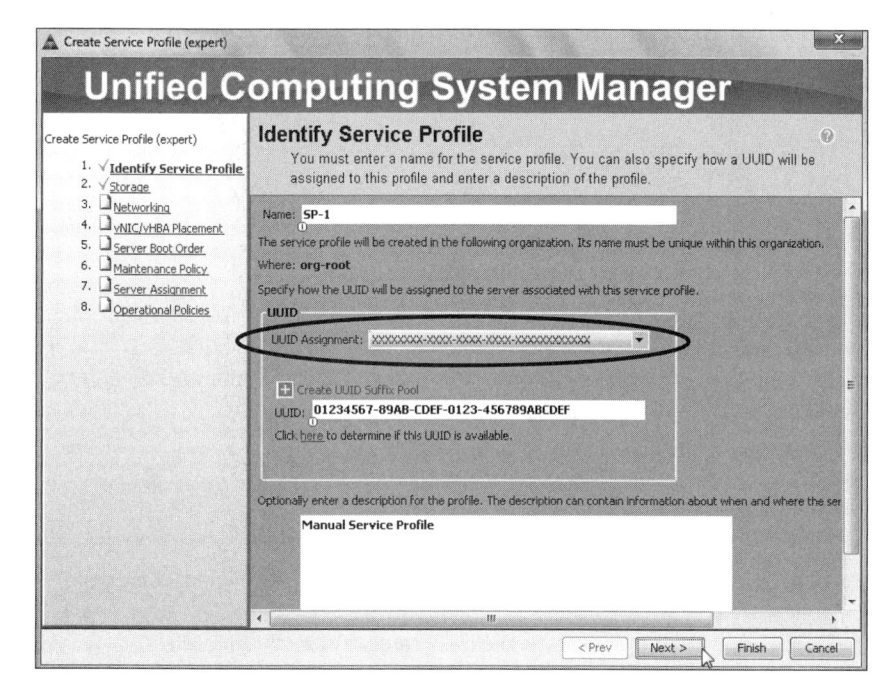

Figure 14-8 *Identifying Service Profile SP-1*

Storage Definitions

In the wizard's second step, two important data storage definitions are configured in a service profile: *local disk policies* and *virtual host bus adapter (HBA) assignment*.

When defining how the local disks on a service profile will behave, you can use a previous protected configuration that resides on the disk or change this behavior. With the Any Configuration option, chances are you will not destroy the disks' content.

On the other hand, if you want to deploy new data to the local disks after the associate server boots, you should choose a mode among the following options:

- **No local storage:** Configuration for diskless servers only (it should not contain any disks). Consequently, this server must deploy a remote boot method (for example, SAN or iSCSI).

- **RAID 0 striped:** Data is distributed (or striped) among all disks in the array, providing high throughput but without any redundancy.

- **RAID 1 mirrored:** The same data is stored on two disks, providing redundancy in the case of a disk failure.

- **No RAID:** Removes the RAID and leaves the disk data and *master boot record* (which is a special type of boot sector that defines the how logical partitions are organized on that medium) unchanged.

- **RAID 5 striped parity:** Data is striped across all disks in the array, and each RAID member stores parity information that can be later used to rebuild the data set in the case of a disk failure.

- **RAID 6 striped dual parity:** Data is striped across all disks in the array, and two parity disks are used to provide protection against the failure of up to two physical disks.

- **RAID 10 mirrored and striped:** Uses mirrored pairs of disks to provide complete data redundancy.

Therefore, the chosen option essentially configures the associated server internal storage controller. I have selected a specific storage policy for SP-1 (RAID 0 with no protection). However, as you will verify later, I will not use the local disks as boot devices to deploy stateless computing.

Tip The Redundant Array of Independent Disk (RAID) levels were discussed in Chapter 9, "Storage Evolution."

The Protection Configuration option assures that the server retains the local disk configuration policy even if the service profile is no longer associated with it. When a new service profile is associated to this server, the protected setting takes precedence over the service profile configuration.

Next in this step, you can configure virtual HBAs (vHBA) that will be instantiated on the server CNA. There are four ways to define vHBAs in the wizard:

- **Simple:** Allows you to create a maximum of two vHBAs (with minimal options).

- **Expert:** Permits that you to create multiple vHBAs. A service profile with multiple vHBAs should be only associated to servers with adapters that deploy I/O virtualization such as the Cisco M81KR, P81E, VIC 1225, VIC 1240, and VIC 1280 (collective known as *virtual interface cards*).

- **No vHBAs:** This option does not define any vHBAs in the service profile. It is usually associated to servers with a local disk or LAN-based boot.

- **Hardware inherited:** Uses the original Fibre Channel characteristics from the associated server's CNA.

For SP-1, I will use the expert option. Before creating any interface per se, a Node WWN must be defined for the profile (it is referred to as "WWNN" in the wizard). Configuring it statically, you can choose from three different formats: 20:00:00:25:b5:XX:XX:XX, 20:XX:XX:XX:XX:XX:XX:XX, or 5X:XX:XX:XX:XX:XX:XX:XX (where X represents a hexadecimal digit between 0 and F).

Figure 14-9 shows that I have chosen 20:00:00:25:b5:00:00:01 as SP-1's Node WWN.

Note Although the UCS Graphical User Interface represents World Wide Names using uppercase letters, I will use lowercase letters in the text to maintain consistency with the format used in previous chapters.

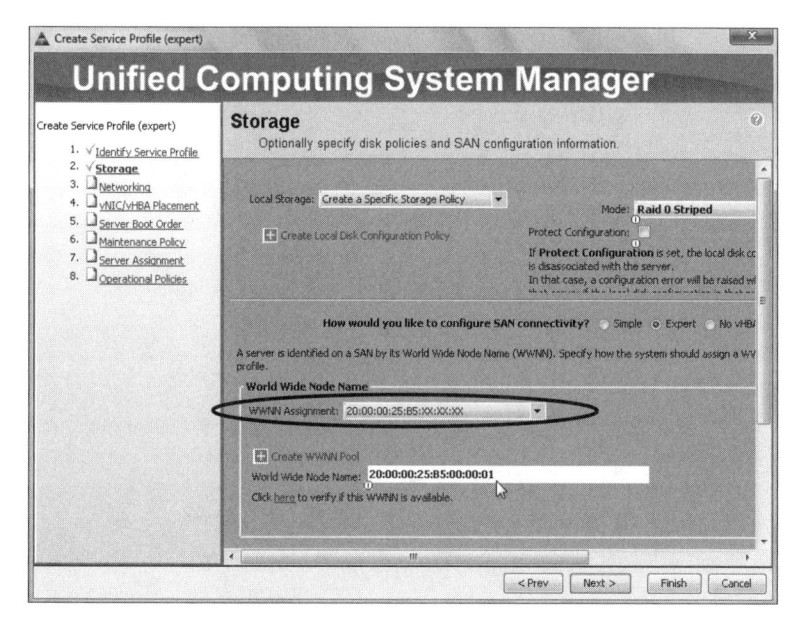

Figure 14-9 *SP-1 Local Disk Policy and Node WWN*

> **Note** The OUI 00:25:b5 is reserved for Cisco. Although you can verify whether a WWN is available, this check is performed on this system domain only. I recommend that you are extra attentive to WWN collisions that can occur in the SAN with preexistent WWNs.

Next, you can finally create the vHBAs. Clicking **Add**, you reach the vHBA configuration screen that is portrayed in Figure 14-10.

As you can verify, I have chosen the value of 20:00:00:25:b5:1a:1a:1a as the Port WWN for a vHBA called fc0. This vHBA belongs to VSAN 10 on Fabric A (meaning that its Virtual Fibre Channel interface will be created on Fabric Interconnect ucs-sp-a).

Figure 14-10 also unveils some other options that can be set on a vHBA, such as

- **Pin Group:** Where you can choose a specific external interface to send the traffic from this vHBA. This configuration can be useful if the ucs-sp-a were connected to distinct Fibre Channel fabrics.

- **Persistent Binding:** The vHBA guarantees that the storage device pWWN, SCSI bus, and SCSI ID will remain the same after the system is rebooted (some operational systems and applications require this characteristic to work properly).

- **Fibre Channel Adapter Policy:** Where you can define queues (transmit, receive, SCSI I/O) and their ring size, timeouts, and retries values.

- **QoS Policy:** Where you can use a predefined policy comprised of class, burst size, and rate (kbps).

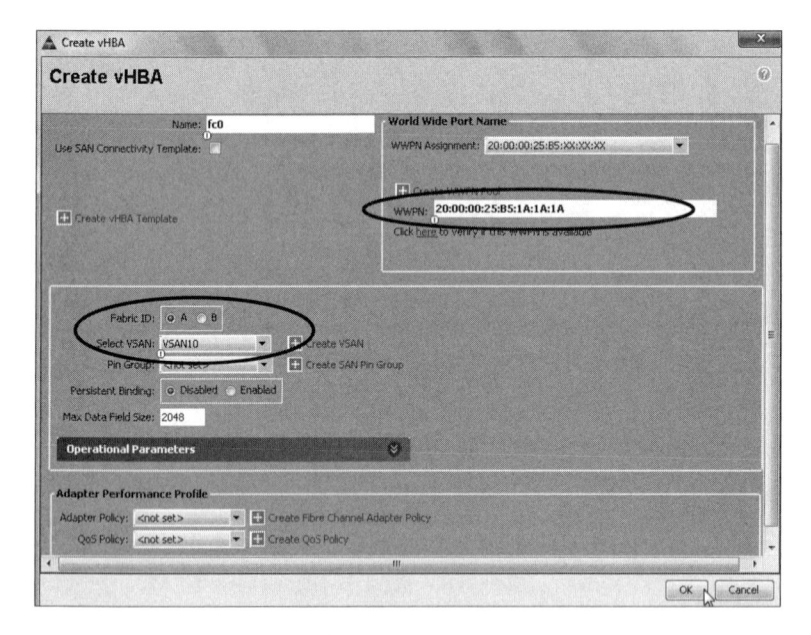

Figure 14-10 *vHBA Configuration in SP-1*

In Figure 14-11, the final SP-1 vHBAs (fc0 and fc1) can be visualized.

Note Refer to Cisco documentation to find out how many vHBAs your adapter supports. A service profile association will fail if its number of vHBAs is greater than the adapter limit.

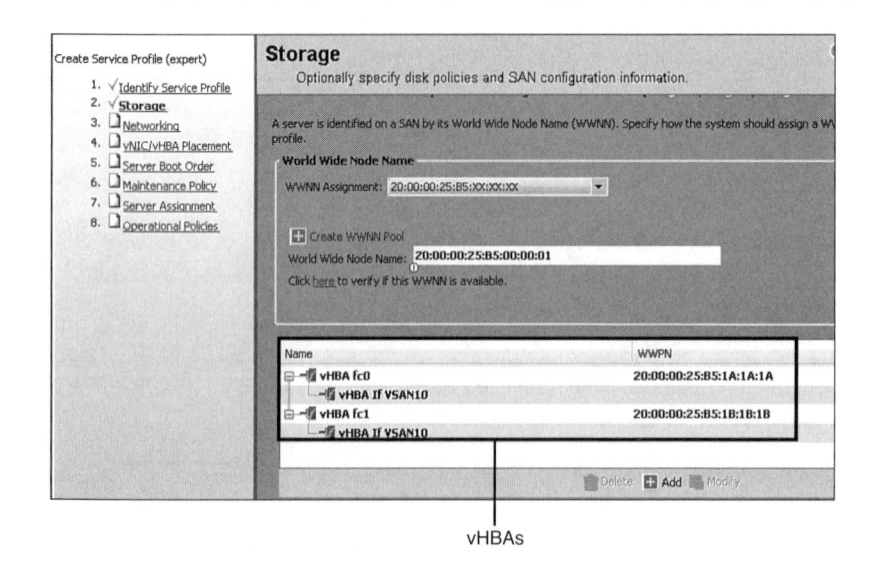

Figure 14-11 *SP-1 vHBAs*

Network Definitions

One step later, we arrive at the SP-1 network configuration. In this part, you can define the *Dynamic vNIC Connection Policy* (VM-FEX) and the virtual network interface cards for this service profile.

I will not delve much deeper into the VM-FEX configuration because this topic will be dealt with in much more detail in Chapter 15. Notwithstanding, you can understand that a *dynamic virtual network interface card (vNIC)* is a virtual Ethernet interface that is dynamically instantiated on an virtualized adapter and defined by a server virtualization cluster manager (such as VMware's vCenter) for virtual machine connectivity. On SP-1, I will use the default option, which does not deploy any dynamic vNICs.

The process of creating a "static" vNIC is very similar to a vHBA. And in fact, the wizard displays the same methods of configuration for a vNIC:

- **Simple:** Allows the creation of two vNICs in a service profile, one for each fabric (with minimal options).
- **Expert:** Allows the creation of multiple vNICs and iSCSI boot vNICs.
- **No vNICs:** This option does not include any vNICs for connections to a LAN in the service profile (this is a rare scenario).
- **Hardware inherited:** Uses the original characteristics from the associated server's NIC.

Likewise, I will use the expert option to create two vNICs (one for each fabric) on SP-1.

Figure 14-12 depicts the configuration done for a vNIC called eth0.

In Figure 14-12, vNIC eth0 is created using a static MAC address of 0025.b51a.1a1a. The definition of a MAC address is very important for stateless computing because some software licenses can be bound to specific MAC addresses (such as Cisco Data Center Network Manager).

Note Although the UCS Graphical User Interface represents MAC addresses using uppercase letters and bytes separated with colons, I will use lowercase letters in the text leveraging the same format used in previous chapters.

A Fabric Failover option can also be enabled per vNIC. Such an option represents a very powerful feature in which servers with nonredundant NICs can leverage the high availability of a dual-fabric Unified Computing System.

Figure 14-13 illustrates how Fabric Failover works for a vNIC within a UCS B-series system.

With Fabric Failover, vNICs that are associated to a Fabric Interconnect (meaning that their VNTag is associated with a virtual Ethernet interface in this device) can migrate to the other Fabric Interconnect in the case of a connectivity problem (Fabric Interconnect, IOM, or IOM uplink failure).

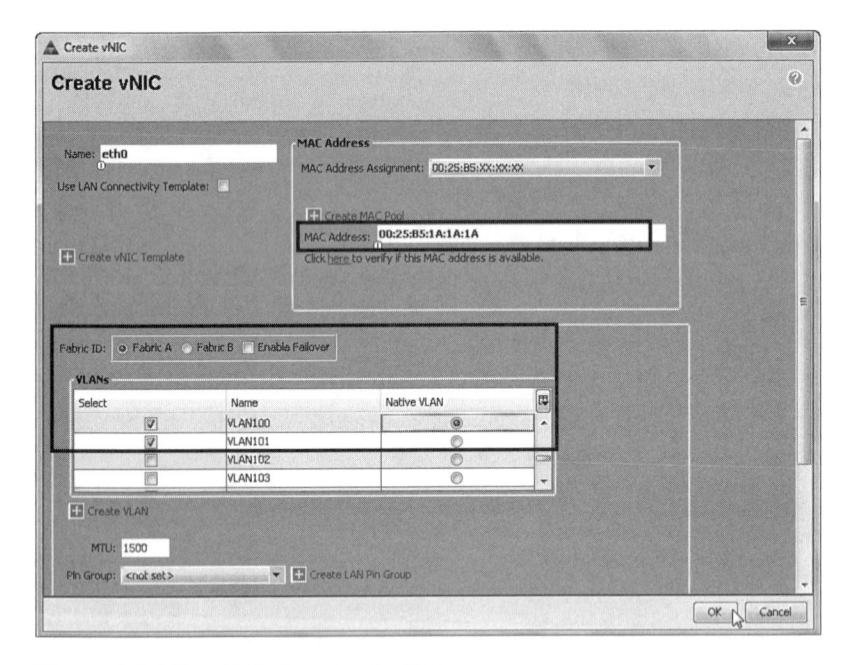

Figure 14-12 *vNIC Creation in SP-1*

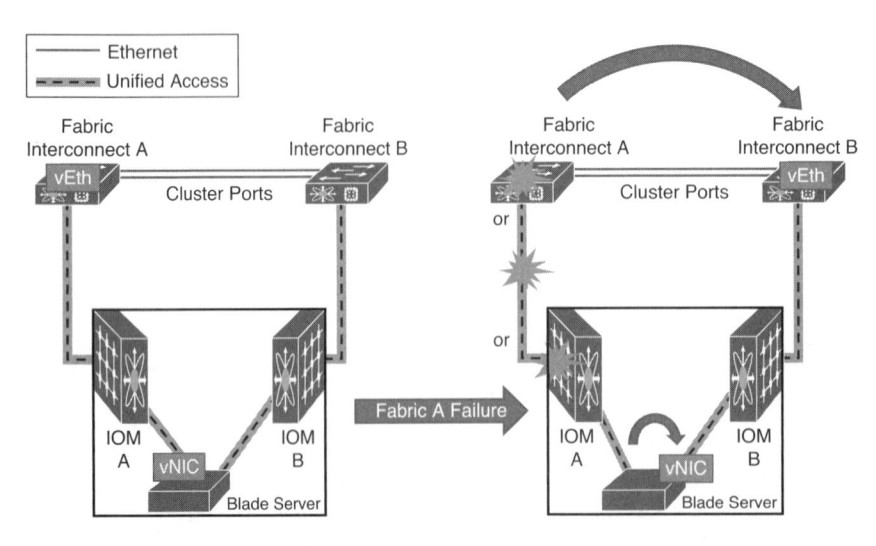

Figure 14-13 *Fabric Failover*

Note At the time of this writing, to implement Fabric Failover, the Fabric Interconnects must be running in End-Host mode and the vNIC must be deployed on an adapter that supports the feature (such as the Cisco VICs). The underlying structure used in Fabric Failover will be further detailed in Chapter 15, in the section "Migrating Virtual Machines to VM-FEX."

Besides choosing VLANs 100 (as native) and 101 for vNIC eth0, Figure 14-12 also depicts other options that I have not configured on SP-1, such as

- **MTU:** Set to 1500 by default, but it can be customized.
- **Pin Group:** Where you can define the Ethernet uplink interface that will be used by this vNIC.
- **Ethernet Adapter Policy:** Where you can define the number of queues (transmit, receive, and completion) and ring size. Also, offload settings (checksum, TCP segmentation, and TCP large receive) can be enabled.
- **QoS Policy:** Where you can use a predefined policy comprised of class, burst size, rate (kbps), and host control. (if you want to trust the Class of Service [CoS] markings from the server)
- **Network Control Policy:** Which enables Cisco Discovery Protocol (CDP), MAC register mode (native VLAN only or all host VLANs), reaction to uplink failure in End-Host mode (link down or warning), and MAC security.

Afterward, I have similarly created vNIC eth1 to provide connectivity to Fabric B (ucs-sp-b). Figure 14-14 shows the final configuration for both vNICs.

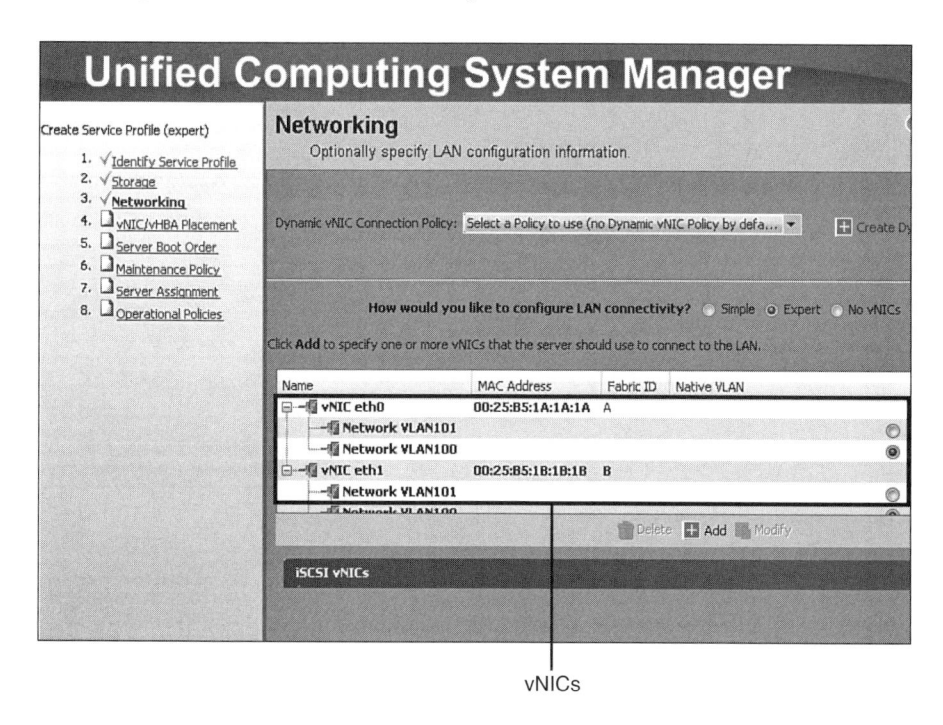

Figure 14-14 *SP-1 Networking Configuration*

Note Refer to the Cisco online documentation to find out how many vNICs your adapter can support. A service profile association will fail if its number of vNICs is greater than the adapter limit.

Virtual Interface Placement

This Create Service Profile (expert) wizard step refers to vNIC and vHBA placement over the physical adapters from the server that will be associated with SP-1. Because the number of adapters can vary among servers on a UCS domain, a placement policy contains four *virtual network interface connections (vCons)*, which are logical representations of the physical adapters.

vCons are basically a way to provide a hardware-independent vNIC and vHBA distribution to service profiles. When a service profile is associated to a server, a predefined mapping between the service profile's vCons and the server physical adapters is used to guide UCS Manager on where to place each vNIC and vHBA.

Table 14-2 portrays the default mapping between vCons and the physical adapters of UCS servers.

Table 14-2 *vCon-to-Physical Adapter Mapping*

Number of Adapters on a Server	vCon1 Assignment	vCon2 Assignment	vCon3 Assignment	vCon4 Assignment
1	Adapter 1	Adapter 1	Adapter 1	Adapter 1
2	Adapter 1	Adapter 2	Adapter 1	Adapter 2
3	Adapter 1	Adapter 2	Adapter 3	Adapter 2
4	Adapter 1	Adapter 2	Adapter 3	Adapter 4

Note B250-M1 and B250-M2 blades have a different mapping between vCons and their two adapters: Adapter 1 is assigned vCon2 and vCon4, while Adapter 2 is assigned vCon1 and vCon3.

Back to the wizard, there are three options for this assignment: It can be left to the system decision, follow a placement policy, or be explicitly defined.

Figure 14-15 shows that I have configured SP-1 using the last method.

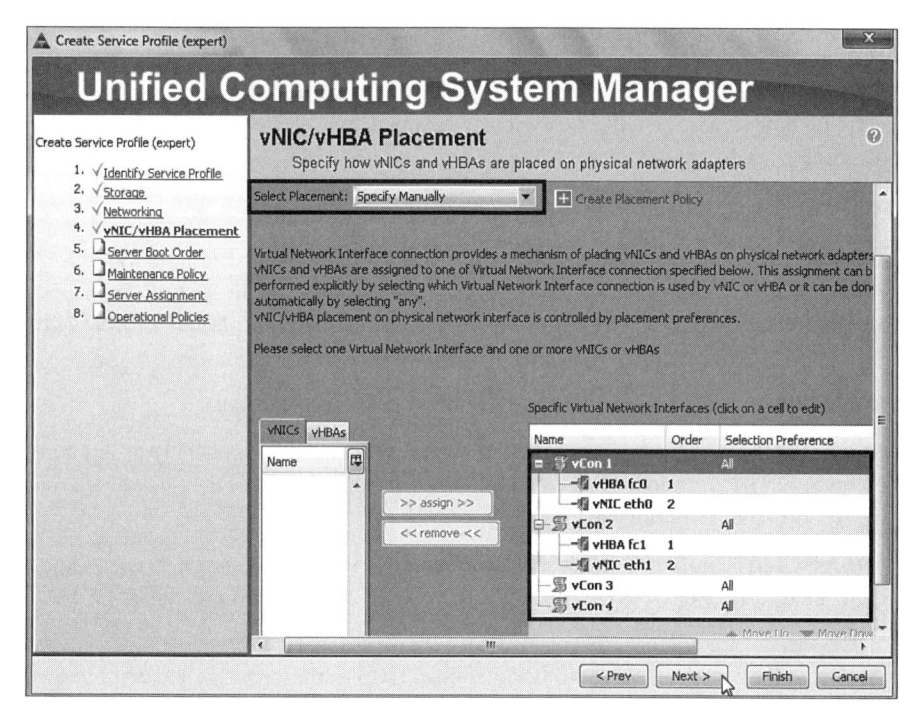

Figure 14-15 *SP-1 vNIC/vHBA Placement*

Using such a configuration, if SP-1 is associated to a single adapter server, fc0, fc1, eth0, and eth1 will be obviously assigned to this adapter. However, if a two-adapter server (different from B250-M1 or B250-M2) is associated to SP-1, UCS Manager will assign fc0 and eth0 to its Adapter 1 and fc1 and eth1 to its Adapter 2.

I have also configured the selection preference All for each vCon on SP-1. This option basically means that any type of vNIC or vHBA can be assigned to the vCons. Alternatively in a vCon, you can restrict the types of vNICs and vHBAs using other selection preferences, such as

- **Assigned-only:** In which a vCon is reserved for vNICs and vHBAs that are explicitly assigned to it, excluding dynamic vNICs and unassigned vNICs or vHBAs.

- **Excluded-unassigned:** Assigned vNICs or vHBAs and dynamic vNICs can use a vCon. Unassigned vNICs or vHBAs cannot.

- **Exclude-dynamic:** Only assigned and unassigned vNICs and vHBAs can use a vCon.

These selection preferences are especially useful when servers can have heterogeneous adapters with distinct capabilities, such as VM-FEX support.

Server Boot Order

In its fifth step, the wizard enables the configuration of the boot order of a service profile, defining how its associated server will use its storage and network resources to load a boot image.

At the time of this writing, several options can be used to define this order:

- **Virtual Media:** Mimics the insertion of a physical CD-ROM disc (read-only) or a floppy disk (read-write) into a server. As I will demonstrate in the section "Installing an Operating System," later in this chapter, the UCS KVM tool permits a local file to be mapped to a virtual CD-ROM.

- **Local Disk:** When the server will boot from its internal hard drives.

- **vNICs:** Can be used to perform a PXE installation. This option generally uses a combination of DHCP, to locate the appropriate boot server, and TFTP, to download the initial bootstrap program and all subsequent files.

- **vHBAs:** Used to boot the server with an operating system image located on a SAN-connected storage device. This option can include a primary and a secondary SAN boot (if the primary boot fails).

- **iSCSI vNICs:** Enables a server to boot from an iSCSI target machine located remotely on an Ethernet network. Not all adapters can perform iSCSI boot; therefore, refer to Cisco online documentation for updated information about this specific subject.

Note Cisco recommends that the boot order in a service profile includes either a local disk *or* a vHBA, but not both, to avoid the possibility of the server booting from the wrong type of storage.

Because I want to deploy stateless computing with SP-1, I have configured the boot order steps shown in Figure 14-16.

In summary, the service profile boot order depicted in Figure 14-16 will guide the server associated to SP-1 to

1. Try to boot through a CD-ROM (virtual media), thus permitting a scripted installation.

2. If a CD-ROM installation file is not available, try to boot through LUN 0 located at pWWN 50:06:01:60:41:e0:b3:d3 and reachable through vHBA fc0.

3. If this LUN is not available either, try to boot through LUN 0 located on pWWN 50:06:01:61:41:e0:b3:d3 and reachable through vHBA fc1.

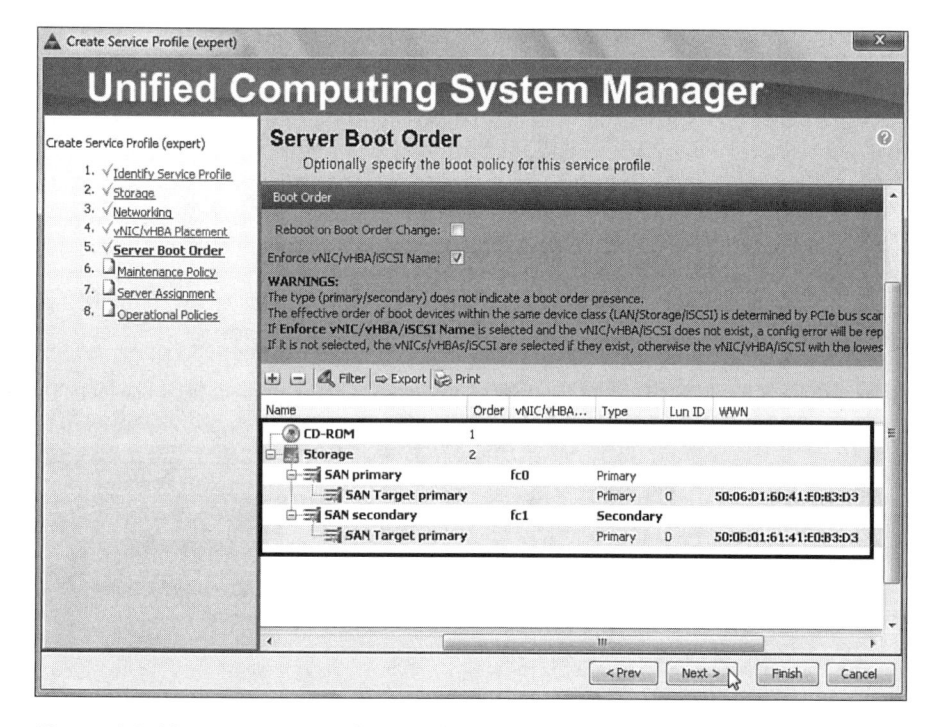

Figure 14-16 *SP-1 Boot Order Configuration*

These Port WWNs are respectively the ports of a storage array connected to MDS-A and MDS-B (from the topology illustrated in Figure 14-6). In this array, I have previously masked two LUNs to fc0 and fc1 pWWNs: a 15-GB LUN (that will be used for the operating system image installation) and a 50-GB LUN (that will be used later for generic data).

Tip It is generally good practice to define a boot LUN with an ID of 0 because some operating systems can only boot from this ID and others always choose the lowest ID for their boot process. By the way, I have also configured the storage array to allow access to both LUNs through ID 0 (with a process called "LUN translation").

Additionally, SP-1 contains the following boot definitions:

- I have not selected **Reboot on Order Change** to preserve the server operational state if any parameter is changed.

- I have enforced the vHBA names to this policy. Therefore, other vHBAs will not be able to use this boot configuration.

Maintenance Policy

At this part of the wizard, you must decide *when* UCS Manager should reboot the server if a disruptive change (such as a firmware upgrade) is applied to a service profile. In summary, a maintenance policy specifies one of the following options:

- Reboot immediately (which is the default method).

- Reboot when a user with administrative privileges acknowledges the reboot.

- Reboot automatically at the time specified in a schedule, which can be configured to reflect a data center maintenance window.

In Figure 14-17, you can verify that I have not selected any maintenance policy, which results in an immediate reboot after a disruptive change is applied to SP-1.

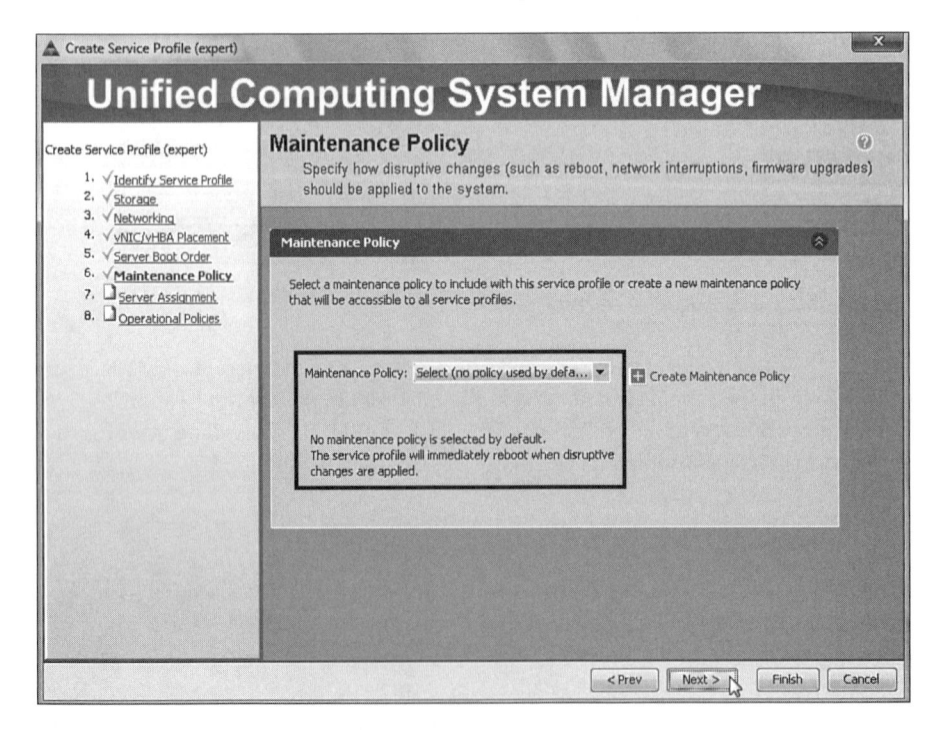

Figure 14-17 *SP-1 Maintenance Policy*

Server Assignment

You can define a service profile association within the Create Service Profile (expert) wizard. In fact, you have the following options to perform this action:

- **Preprovision a slot:** Where any server that is installed on a certain chassis bay will be associated to this service profile.

- **Select existing server:** Where the administrator will select a specific server that already belongs to a UCS domain.

- **Select from a pool:** Where the system will choose from an available server on a default or created server pool. (I will explore this concept later in the section "Industrializing Server Provisioning.")

In our scenario, I will not associate SP-1 to a server yet because I want you to observe some of the operations executed during its association. Hence, I will choose the Assign Later option, as depicted in Figure 14-18.

In the figure, also notice that I have chosen that a server associated to SP-1 should remain in the Down state until it is configured otherwise.

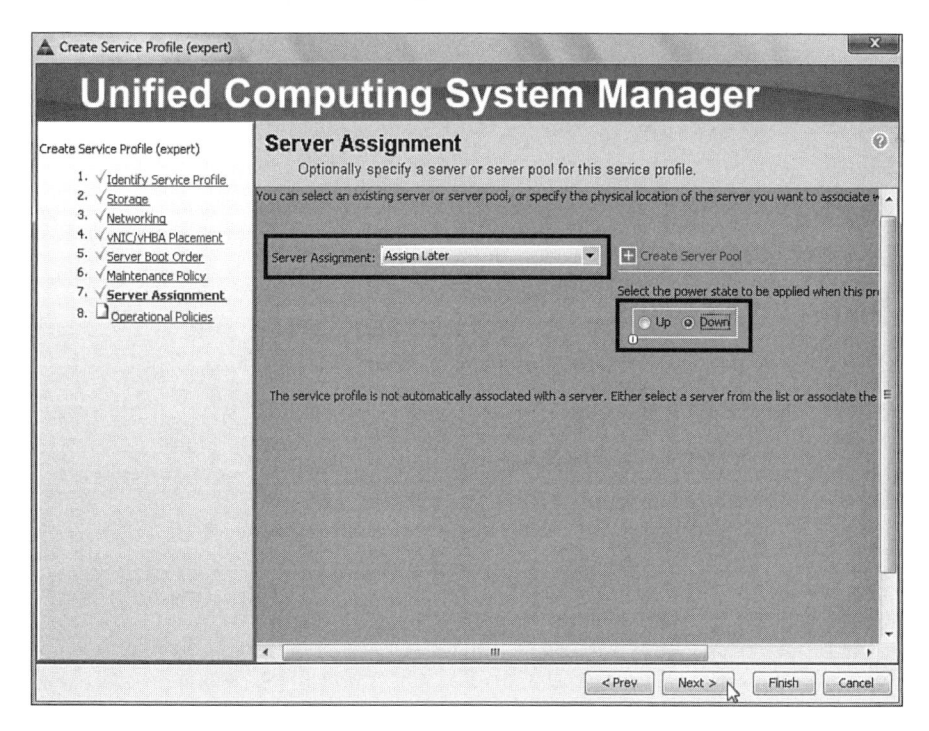

Figure 14-18 *SP-1 Server Assignment*

> **Note** Although it is not visible in the figure (you need to scroll down the screen to find it), the "Server Assignment" step also permits the association of firmware policies to the service profile. Because these policies will be explained in more details in the "Firmware Policies" section, I have not defined anything during the wizard iteration.

Operational Policies

While it might be the last, this step is one of the most powerful in the Create Service Profile (expert) wizard. In it, you will be able to specify operational configurations such as BIOS settings, server management protocols, monitoring thresholds, among other parameters.

In the next four sections I will discuss the main configuration parameters from the "Operational Policies" step.

Configuration

This operation permits that you define *in detail* the BIOS settings of a server that will be associated with this service profile. For this endeavor, you will create a *BIOS policy* that can contain configuration elements such as

- Reboot on BIOS Settings Change
- Quiet Boot
- Post Error Pause
- Intel Turbo Boost
- Enhanced Intel Speedstep
- Intel Hyper Threading
- Core Multi Processing
- Execute Disabled Bit
- Intel Virtualization Technology (VT)
- Intel VT for Directed IO
- Memory Reliability, Availability, and Serviceability (RAS) Configuration

The explanation of these BIOS parameters is beyond the scope of this book (you can easily find them in Cisco online UCS documentation). However, I want you to notice that they can be predefined in a service profile when that is necessary.

Figure 14-19 shows the Create BIOS Policy link, which allows you to create a reusable BIOS policy during the wizard.

In the figure, you can also verify that I have not chosen any policy, and consequently, SP-1 will not enforce any BIOS configuration over its associated server.

> **Tip** If for now, you can only admire the potential of a BIOS policy, in the section "Using Policies," later in this chapter, you will be able to see this policy in action.

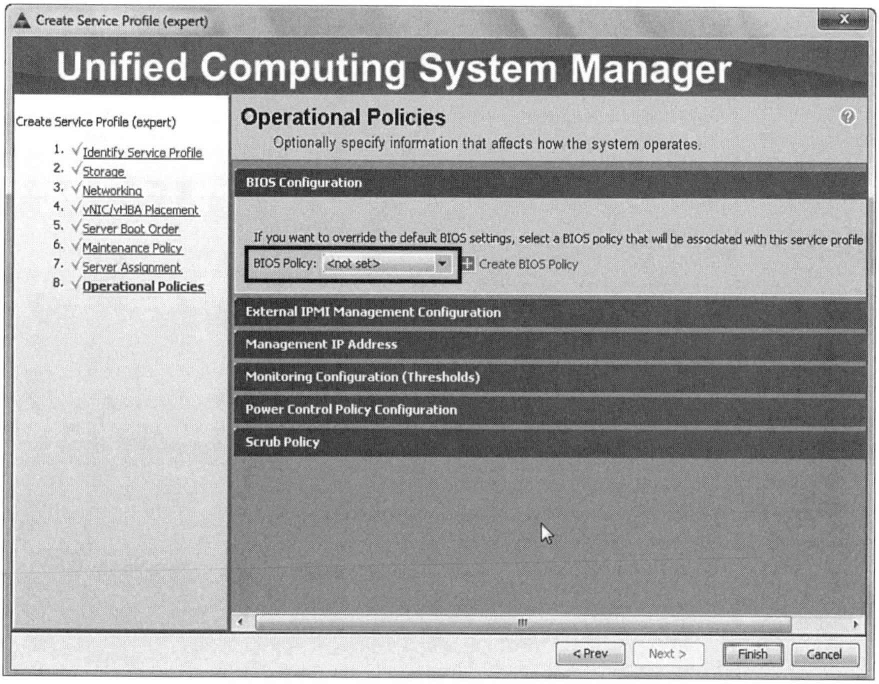
Create Service Profile (expert)
Unified Computing System Manager
Create Service Profile (expert)
1. Identify Service Profile
2. Storage
3. Networking
4. vNIC/vHBA Placement
5. Server Boot Order
6. Maintenance Policy
7. Server Assignment
8. Operational Policies
Operational Policies
Optionally specify information that affects how the system operates.
BIOS Configuration
If you want to override the default BIOS settings, select a BIOS policy that will be associated with this service profile
BIOS Policy: <not set>
Create BIOS Policy
External IPMI Management Configuration
Management IP Address
Monitoring Configuration (Thresholds)
Power Control Policy Configuration
Scrub Policy
< Prev
Next >
Finish
Cancel

Figure 14-19 *SP-1 BIOS Policy Configuration*

External IPMI Management Configuration

Intelligent Platform Management Interface (IPMI) is an Intel-led standard protocol that allows management and monitoring of a computer system. IPMI is currently on version 2.0 and is supported by hundreds of server manufacturers (including Cisco).

IPMI does not require an operating system to work, and on UCS servers, it is deployed by the CIMC, which communicate with other systems through

- **Serial over LAN** (whereas serial console output can be remotely viewed over a SSH session)
- **KVM over IP** (emulating local access to the server)
- **Remote virtual media** (as you already have seen in SP-1's boot order)

Figure 14-20 portrays the IPMI policy (creatively called IPMI-Policy) that was built for SP-1. It also shows a Serial over LAN (SoL) policy called SoL-Active, which activates this serial interaction with the CIMC from the associated server.

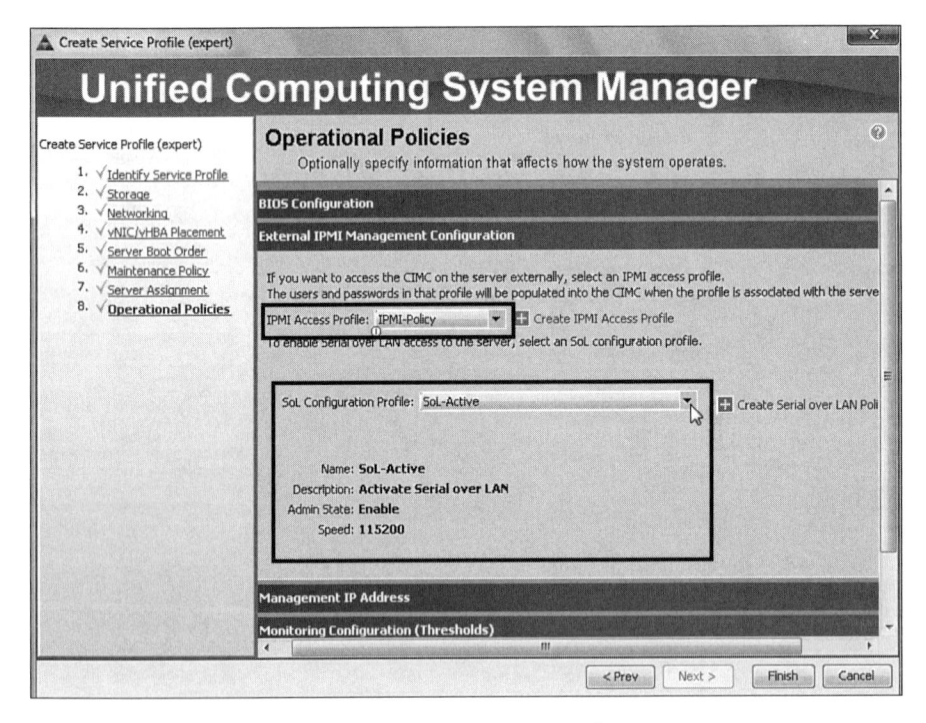

Figure 14-20 *SP-1 IPMI and Serial over LAN Configuration*

Not depicted is a user called ipmi that I have exclusively created for IPMI-Policy.

Management IP Address

UCS Manager also allows you to choose the management IP address that is bound to a service profile, regardless of the server it is associated with.

As portrayed in Figure 14-21, I have assigned static IP address 10.97.39.101 (with subnet mask 255.255.255.0 and default gateway 10.97.39.1) to SP-1. After its association, the Fabric Interconnect management (mgmt0) interfaces will provide connectivity to this IP address.

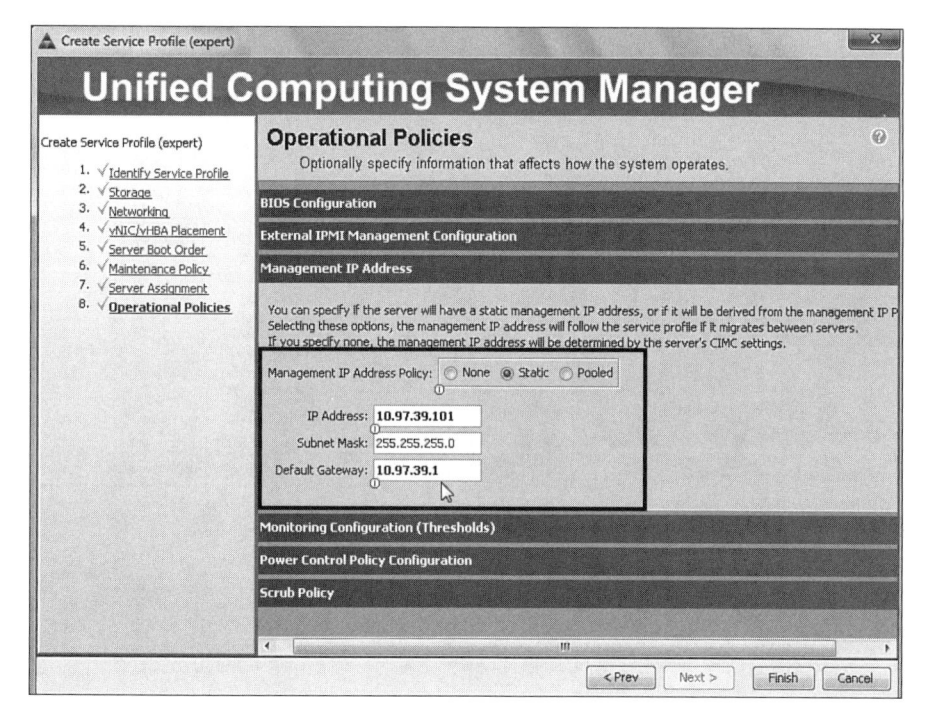

Figure 14-21 *SP-1 Management IP Address*

Additional Policies

Finally, the wizard permits you configure three additional policies:

- Monitoring policy
- Power control policy
- Scrub policy

A *monitoring policy* defines thresholds for parameters that will be monitored by UCS Manager. Among the monitored elements are Ethernet interfaces, vNICs, motherboards, memory, CPU, PCIe, buffers, and processor. For SP-1, I have selected the default monitoring policy.

Each time a service profile is associated or disassociated, UCS Manager recalculates the power allotment for each blade server within the chassis. Furthermore, with a *power control policy*, UCS Manager can control the maximum power consumed by a server, a chassis, or a set of chassis installed in one or more data center racks.

A *scrub policy* determines what happens to local data and to the BIOS settings on a server when it is disassociated from this service profile. In summary, if Disk Scrub is enabled, all data on any local drives is destroyed (otherwise it is preserved). On the other hand, if BIOS Scrub is enabled, it erases all BIOS settings for the server and resets them to the BIOS defaults for that server type and vendor.

Because they are beyond this book scope, I have not selected a power control policy or a scrub policy, as depicted in Figure 14-22.

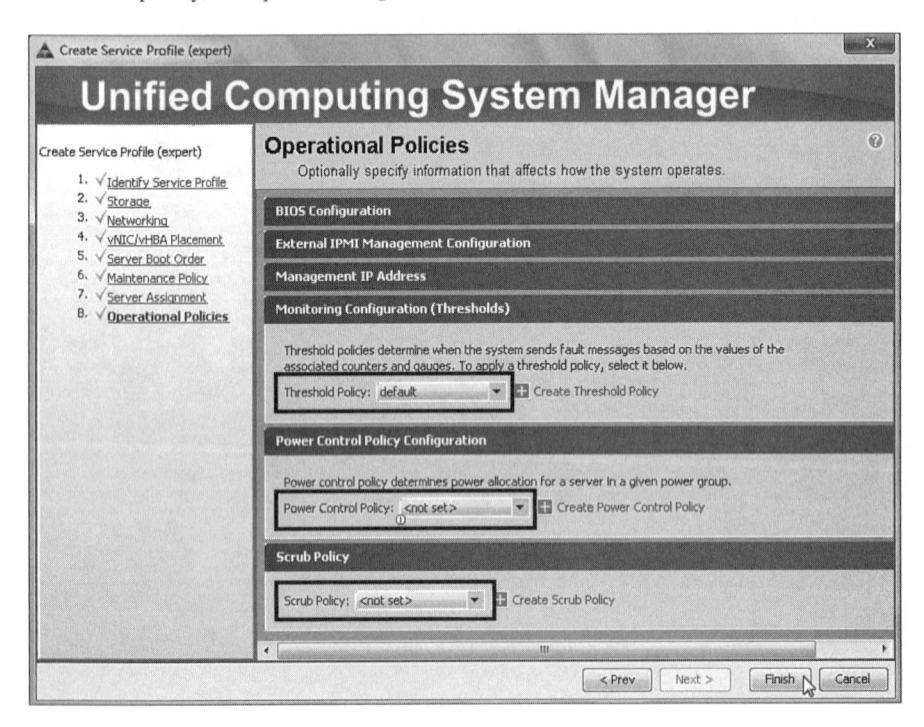

Figure 14-22 *SP-1 Additional Policies*

Clicking **Finish**, the service profile SP-1 is finally created within the UCS Manager.

Associating a Service Profile to a Server

After the service profile configuration, it is possible to associate it to a server (blade or rack-mount) that belongs to a Unified Computing System.

Figures 14-23 describes one method to associate SP-1 to an available server.

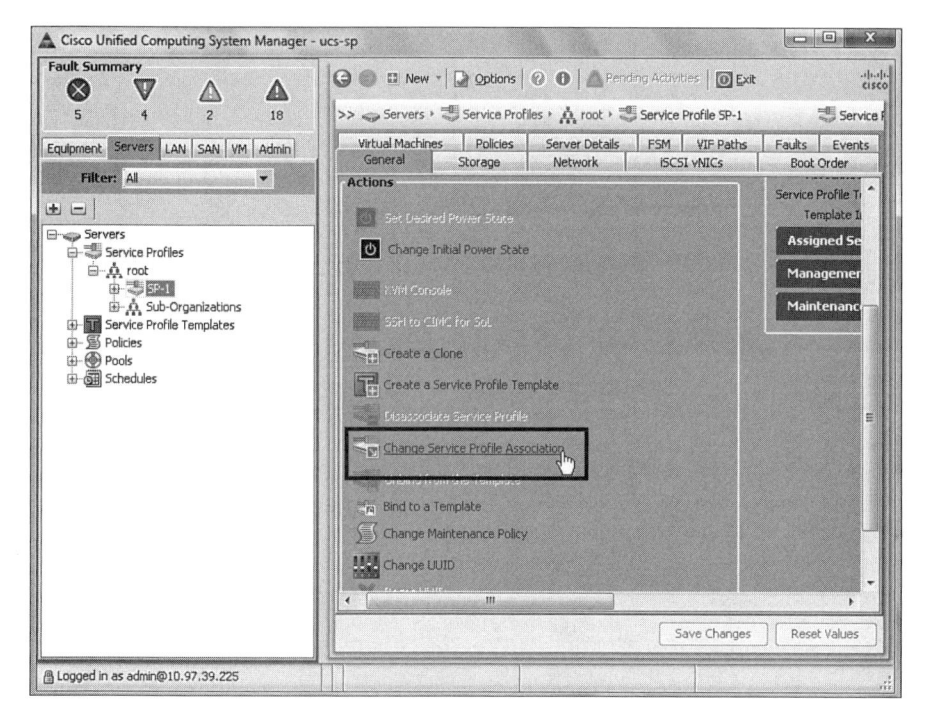

Figure 14-23 *Changing Service Profile Association*

After selecting SP-1 and clicking **Change Service Profile Association,** you can choose one server from a set of available hardware, as shown in Figure 14-24.

> **Caution**   It is also possible to select a server that is already associated to another service profile. However, in this case, UCS Manager will disassociate such service profile to insert SP-1 in its place.

To associate SP-1, I have chosen the blade server that is currently installed in slot 1 from chassis 1 (or simply, server 1/1).

Figure 14-25 depicts the General tab from SP-1 after its association to server 1/1 is initiated. On this screen, you can activate an SSH session to the server CIMC. As you might remember from the previous section, SP-1 has a Serial over LAN policy (SoL-Active) that allows a direct terminal session to the server 1/1 CIMC.

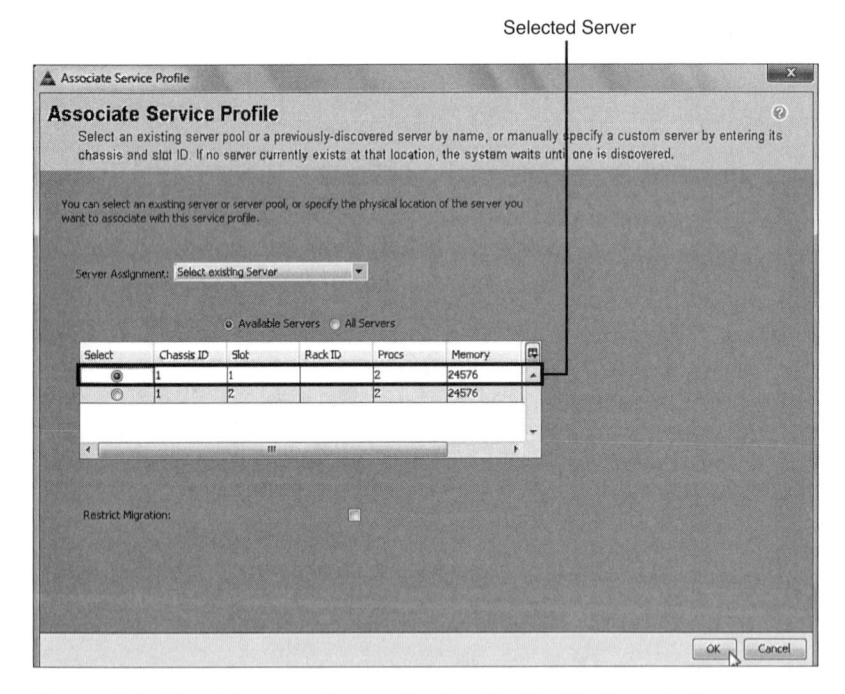

Figure 14-24 *Selecting a Server for Service Profile Association*

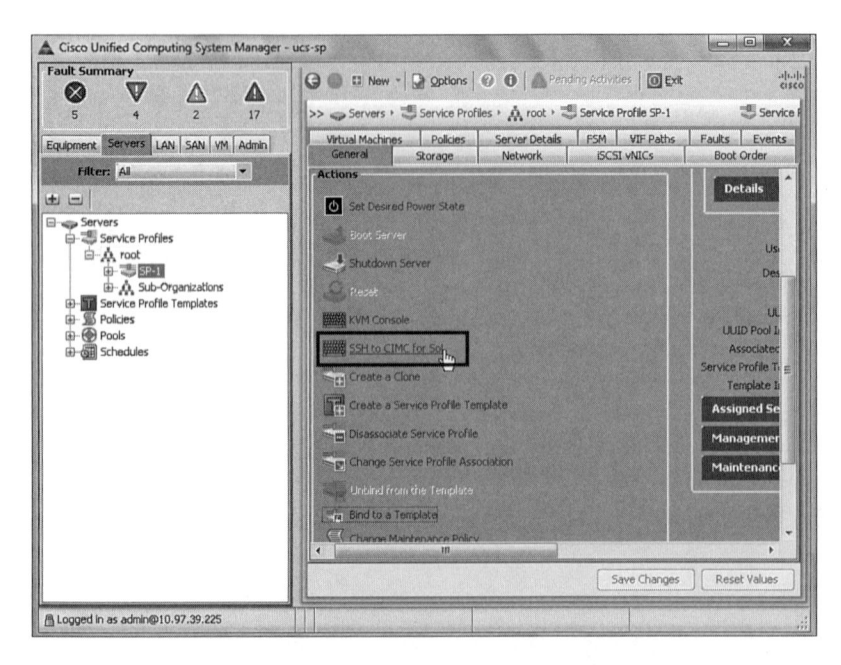

Figure 14-25 *Accessing the Serial over LAN Interface*

Example 14-1 outlines this SSH session output, uncovering some of the procedures that are executed on the server during a service profile association. In the example, you will notice that the server loads UUOS as a preboot operating system to assist in the configurations defined on SP-1.

Example 14-1 *Serial over LAN Output During SP-1 Association*

```
! UUOS is being loaded through PXE from UCS Manager
ISOLINUX 3.72 2008-09-25  Copyright (C) 1994-2008 H. Peter Anvin
Loading /vmlinuz............................
Loading
/pnuosimg.cgz.....................................................
..................................................................
..................................................................
..................................................................
..................................................................
..................................................................
..............................................ready.
! Executing UUOS
Linux version 2.6.29.6 (UCS@CiscoSystemsInc) () #1 SMP Wed Sep 5 09:18:40 PDT 2012
KERNEL supported cpus:
  Intel GenuineIntel
[output suppressed]
INIT: version 2.86 booting

[output suppressed]
! UUOS detects Adapter 1 on server 1/1 (please observe that it is using version 1.4.1.5)
[    6.636108] enic: Cisco VIC Ethernet NIC Driver, ver 1.4.1.5
[output suppressed]
! UUOS detects two 300GB Local Disks on server 1/1
[   22.020856] scsi 0:0:0:0: Direct-Access     SEAGATE  ST9300603SS      0004 PQ: 0 ANSI: 5
[   22.042340] scsi 0:0:0:0: mptscsih: ioc0: qdepth=64, tagged=1, simple=1, ordered=0, scsi_level=6, cmd_que=1
[   22.061760] sd 0:0:0:0: [sda] 585937500 512-byte hardware sectors: (300 GB/279 GiB)
[output suppressed]
[   23.240847] scsi 0:0:1:0: Direct-Access     SEAGATE  ST9300603SS      0004 PQ: 0 ANSI: 5
[   23.263072] scsi 0:0:1:0: mptscsih: ioc0: qdepth=64, tagged=1, simple=1, ordered=0, scsi_level=6, cmd_que=1
[   23.282492] sd 0:0:1:0: [sdb] 585937500 512-byte hardware sectors: (300 GB/279 GiB)
[output suppressed]
! Preparing network interface cards to receive SP-1 configurations from UCS Manager
```

```
Setting up networking....
Configuring network interfaces...done.

INIT: Entering runlevel: 2

Starting enhanced syslogd: rsyslogd.
Starting ACPI services....
Starting internet superserver: inetd.
/opt/Cisco /
/
[   27.338523] enic 0000:08:00.0: eth0: Link UP
[   27.354467] enic 0000:09:00.0: eth1: Link UP
**********************************************************************
*              Booting of UCS Utility OS Completed                    *
**********************************************************************
! UUOS Configuration Agent starts
Starting Cisco UCS Agent: [OK]

[output suppressed]
! Configuring RAID 0 on local disks as defined on SP-1
[   34.636038] mptbase: ioc0: RAID STATUS CHANGE for PhysDisk 0 id=0
[   34.652194] mptbase: ioc0:   PhysDisk has been created
[   34.672040] target0:0:0: mptsas: ioc0: RAID Hidding:
fw_channel=0, fw_id=0, physdsk 0, sas_addr 0x5000c5001db76339
[   35.084033] mptbase: ioc0: RAID STATUS CHANGE for PhysDisk 1 id=1
[   35.097202] mptbase: ioc0:   PhysDisk has been created
[   35.116036] target0:0:1: mptsas: ioc0: RAID Hidding:
fw_channel=0, fw_id=1, physdsk 1, sas_addr 0x5000c5001db768dd
[   36.975951] mptbase: ioc0: RAID STATUS CHANGE for VolumeID 0
[   36.989699] mptbase: ioc0:   volume has been created
[   37.175975] mptsas: ioc0: attaching raid volume, channel 1, id 0
[   37.194748] scsi 0:1:0:0: Direct-Access     LSILOGIC Logical Volume   3000 PQ: 0 ANSI: 2
[   37.215985] scsi 0:1:0:0: mptscsih: ioc0: qdepth=64, tagged=1,
simple=1, ordered=0, scsi_level=3, cmd_que=1
[   37.237788] sd 0:1:0:0: [sda] 1167966208 512-byte hardware sectors: (597 GB/556 GiB)
[   37.255300] sd 0:1:0:0: [sda] Write Protect is off
[output suppressed]
In the meanwhile, UCS Manager has directly configured the adapters through VLAN 4043
[   45.200633] enic 0000:08:00.0: eth0: Link DOWN
[   45.752609] enic 0000:09:00.0: eth1: Link DOWN
```

At this moment, server 1/1 is prepared to load a proper operating system image or an installation file.

During the SP-1 association process, UCS Manager has also configured both Fabric Interconnects. To illustrate these "hidden" procedures, Examples 14-2 and 14-3 reveal how the virtual interfaces from SP-1 are seen by the resident NX-OS on both devices.

Example 14-2 *SP-1 Interfaces on Fabric Interconnect A*

```
! SSH session to ucs-sp-a
Cisco UCS 6100 Series Fabric Interconnect
ucs-sp-a login: admin
Password:
[output suppressed]
! UCS Manager CLI session connection options
ucs-sp-a# connect
  adapter      Mezzanine Adapter
  cimc         Cisco Integrated Management Controller
  clp          Connect to DMTF CLP
  iom          IO Module
  local-mgmt   Connect to Local Management CLI
  nxos         Connect to NXOS CLI


! Connecting to this Fabric Interconnect NX-OS CLI
ucs-sp-a# connect nxos
Cisco Nexus Operating System (NX-OS) Software
[output suppressed]
! Checking MAC Address Table in VLAN 100
ucs-sp-a(nxos)# show mac address-table vlan 100
Legend:
        * - primary entry, G - Gateway MAC, (R) - Routed MAC, O - Overlay MAC
        age - seconds since last seen,+ - primary entry using vPC Peer-Link
   VLAN     MAC Address      Type       age     Secure NTFY    Ports
---------+-----------------+--------+---------+------+----+----------
! Static entry for vNIC eth0 on a virtual Ethernet interface
*  100     0025.b51a.1a1a   static    0            F    F   Veth1838
! Checking NPV FLOGI Table in VLAN 10
ucs-sp-a(nxos)# show npv flogi-table vsan 10
--------------------------------------------------------------------------
SERVER                                                           EXTERNAL
INTERFACE VSAN FCID    PORT NAME            NODE NAME            INTERFACE
--------------------------------------------------------------------------
[output suppressed]
! FLOGI from vHBA fc0 directed to MDS-A through interface fc2/1
vfc1840   10   0x0a0204 20:00:00:25:b5:1a:1a:1a 20:00:00:25:b5:00:00:01 fc2/1

Total number of flogi = 4.
```

Example 14-3 *SP-1 Interfaces on Fabric Interconnect B*

```
ucs-sp-b(nxos)# show mac address-table vlan 100
Legend:
        * - primary entry, G - Gateway MAC, (R) - Routed MAC, O - Overlay MAC
        age - seconds since last seen,+ - primary entry using vPC Peer-Link
   VLAN     MAC Address      Type      age     Secure NTFY    Ports
---------+-----------------+--------+---------+------+----+------------------
! Static entry for vNIC eth1 on a virtual Ethernet interface
*  100     0025.b51b.1b1b    static    0        F      F    Veth1839
! Checking NPV FLOGI Table in VLAN 20
ucs-sp-b(nxos)# show npv flogi-table vsan 20
--------------------------------------------------------------------------------
SERVER                                                              EXTERNAL
INTERFACE VSAN FCID         PORT NAME                NODE NAME      INTERFACE
--------------------------------------------------------------------------------
[output suppressed]
! FLOGI from vHBA fc1 directed to MDS-B through interface fc2/1
vfc1841    20   0x140204  20:00:00:25:b5:1b:1b:1b 20:00:00:25:b5:00:00:01 fc2/1

Total number of flogi = 4.
```

Note Although you can connect to the NX-OS CLI on a Fabric Interconnect, you are not allowed to perform any configurations.

From the last two examples, you could see that both vNICs eth0 and eth1 have corresponding virtual Ethernet interfaces on both Fabric Interconnects (Veth1838 and Veth1839, respectively). Even under a slightly different naming, you might recognize that these interfaces are actually Fabric Extender LIFs (logical interfaces) that are defined by exclusive VNTags.

Tip Fabric Extender, LIFs, and VNTag concepts were discussed in Chapter 7, "Virtualized Chassis with Fabric Extenders."

An interesting question one might ask is, "Which device is actually imposing VNTags to upstream Ethernet frames?" In fact, the answer to this question unveils the true nature of adapter I/O virtualization.

Figure 14-26 illustrates how VNTags are imposed on servers with standard and virtualized adapters in a Unified Computing System.

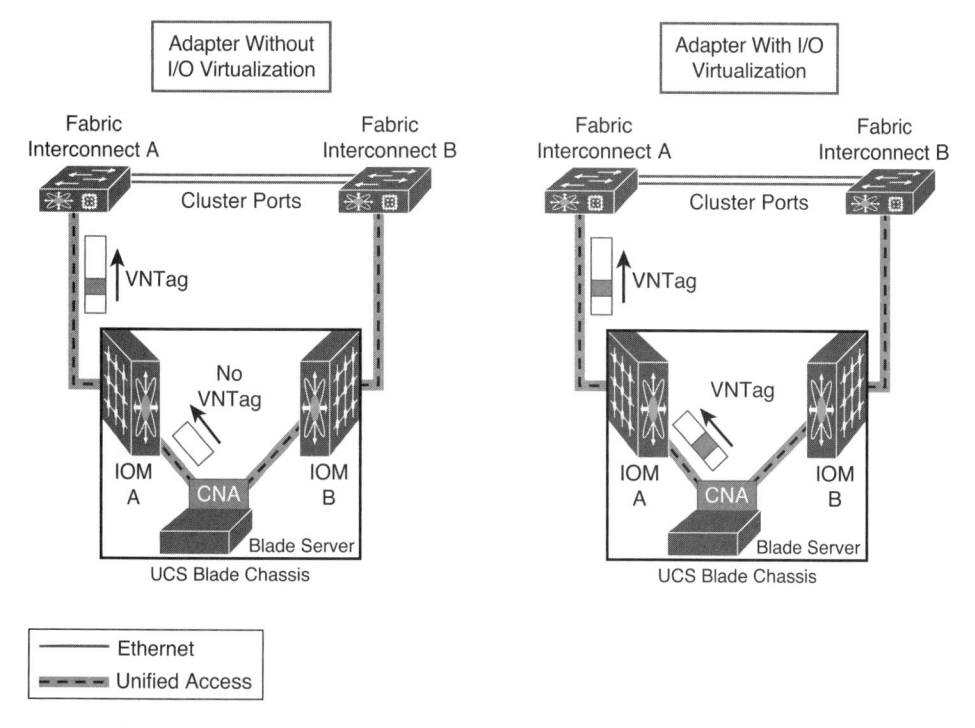

Figure 14-26 *VNTag Imposing Comparison*

On the left side of Figure 14-26, a server equipped with a nonvirtualized adapter sends a standard Ethernet frame to the chassis IOM, which acts exactly as a Fabric Extender would (inserting a VNTag to the frame before forwarding it to the Fabric Interconnect).

On the right side of the same figure, the server adapter with I/O virtualization *inserts* the VNTag in the upstream Ethernet frames to permit the differentiation of traffic from distinct vNICs on the Fabric Interconnect. In this case, the IOM only forwards the tagged frames to the uplinks.

> **Tip** For this reason, the deployment of static vNICs on virtualized adapters is also referred to as "Adapter-FEX."

In the Fibre Channel world, vHBAs fc0 and fc1 are likewise mapped to Virtual Fibre Channel interfaces on the Fabric Interconnects (vfc1840 and vfc1841, respectively), as you would expect from a standard FCoE connection.

Installing an Operating System

The General tab from SP-1, shown in Figure 14-25, also contains a link to a remarkable graphical tool: *the KVM*. In a nutshell, KVM allows the exchange of keyboard, video, and mouse instructions directly to the server as if you were accessing it locally.

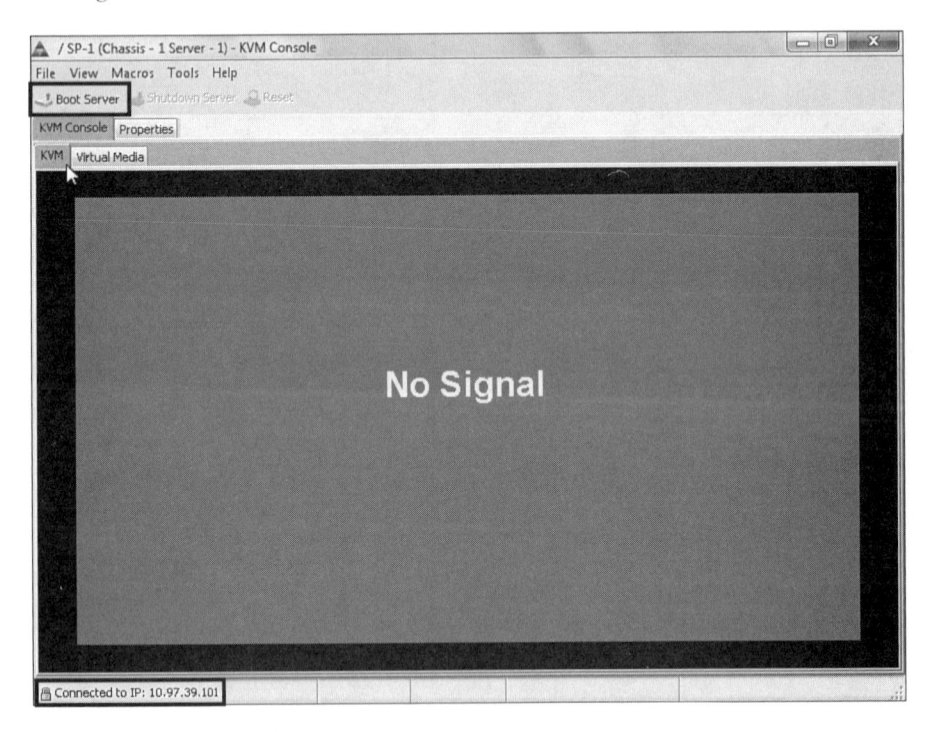

Figure 14-27 illustrates the KVM screen from SP-1 as it is seen for the first time.

Figure 14-27 *KVM Screen*

Tip Following the UCS provisioning model, server-related operations, including accessing the KVM, are executed in the service profile.

In Figure 14-27, two details deserve your attention:

- The server is currently down, according to the option defined in the server assignment step (Figure 14-18).
- KVM accesses IP address 10.97.39.101, which was defined for SP-1 (See Figure 14-21).

Chapter 14: Changing Personalities 621

If you remember the SP-1's configuration, a boot inflicted to the server will first trigger the detection of an image on a CD-ROM, and if this media is not available, SP-1 will try to boot from an image available on LUN 0 from predefined Port WWNs in a storage array.

Because I do not want to use the data that is currently stored in the LUN, I will deploy KVM to map a local installation file to a virtual CD player (and save a visit to the freezing data center room).

Figure 14-28 details the mapping of a VMware vSphere installer to the SP-1 virtual CD-ROM drive.

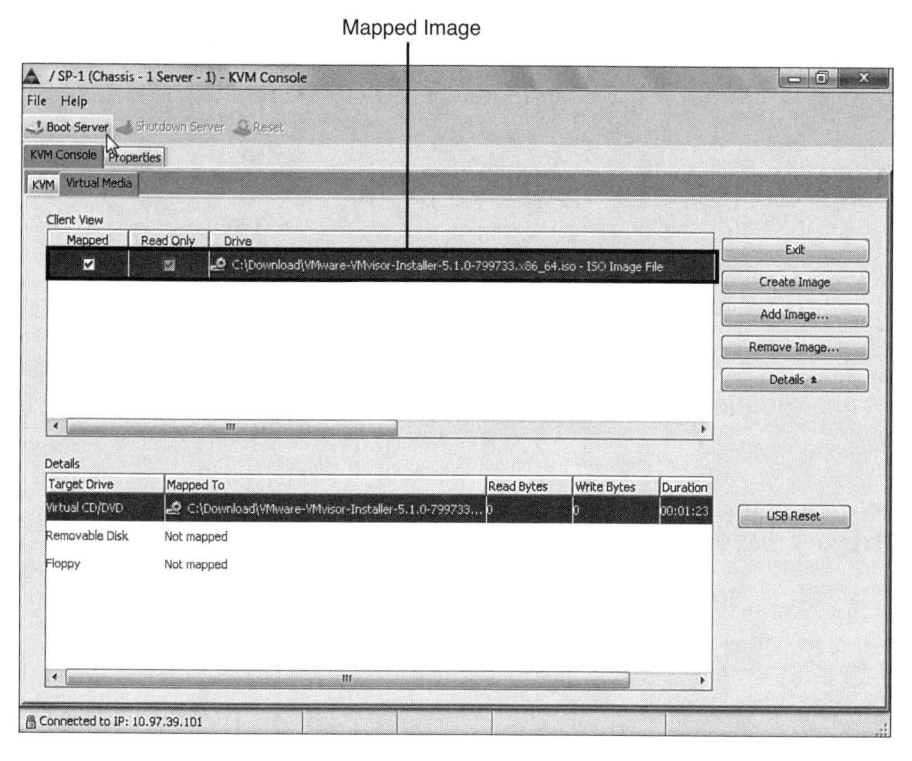

Figure 14-28 *Virtual Media Mapping*

As soon as the server is booted through the KVM tool, the installer is loaded into the server memory according to SP-1's boot order.

Figure 14-29 portrays this process, as viewed from the KVM tool.

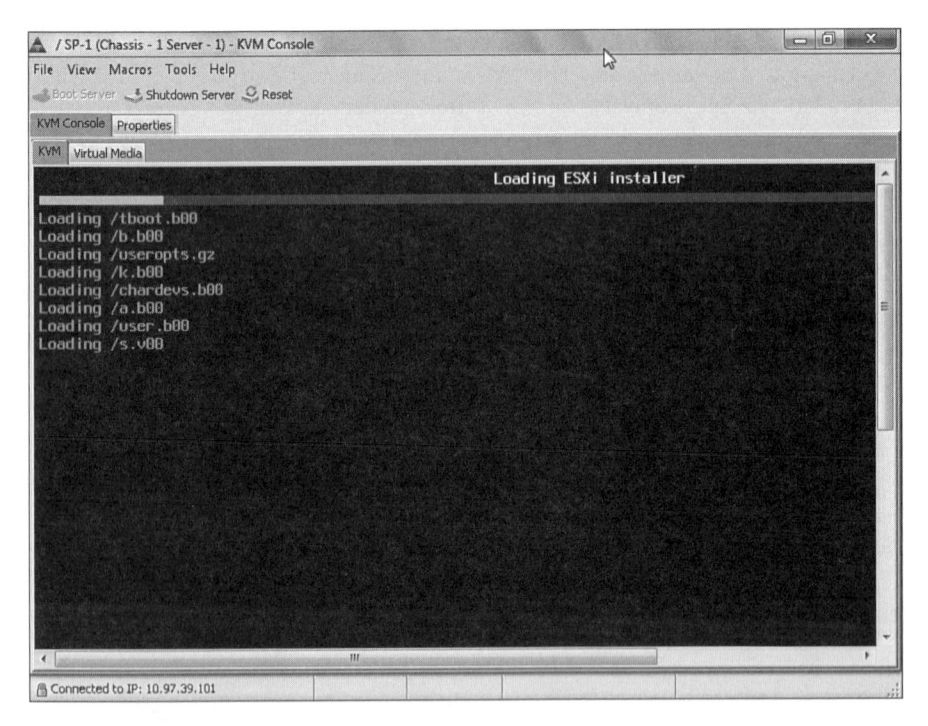

Figure 14-29 *vSphere Installation from Virtual Media*

After all necessary files are loaded, the vSphere installation halts. At this point, a writable nonvolatile media is necessary to actually build the server image. Consequently, the server searches for all SCSI media that are available to it, and Figure 14-30 portrays the results from this discovery.

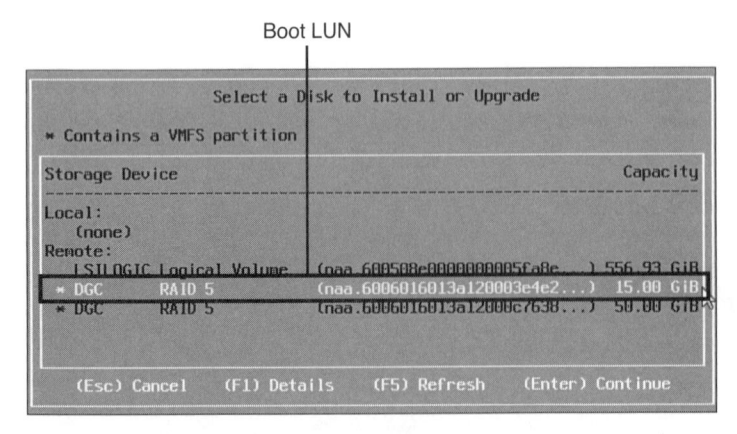

Figure 14-30 *Available Storage for the Installation*

Figure 14-30 depicts all three storage devices: the local RAID 0 group disk (LSILOGIC) and two remote LUNs (15- and 50-GB). Because I have prepared the 50-GB LUN as a data repository, I will choose the 15-GB LUN for the actual operating system installation.

> **Note** The stars on the left of both LUNs show that previous VMware Virtual Machine File System (VMFS) partitions were detected on both LUNs.

After the choice is made, the installation continues until the installation process requests a server reinitialization. Fortunately during this process, the KVM tool automatically unmaps the installer from the virtual CD-ROM driver to avoid going through this installation process again.

After the reboot, an adapter is customized to function as a management interface for the server (or vmnic0, in VMware lingo), as shown in Figure 14-31.

With an accessible management interface, a VMware *virtual interface client* can be used to manage the hypervisor installed on the server.

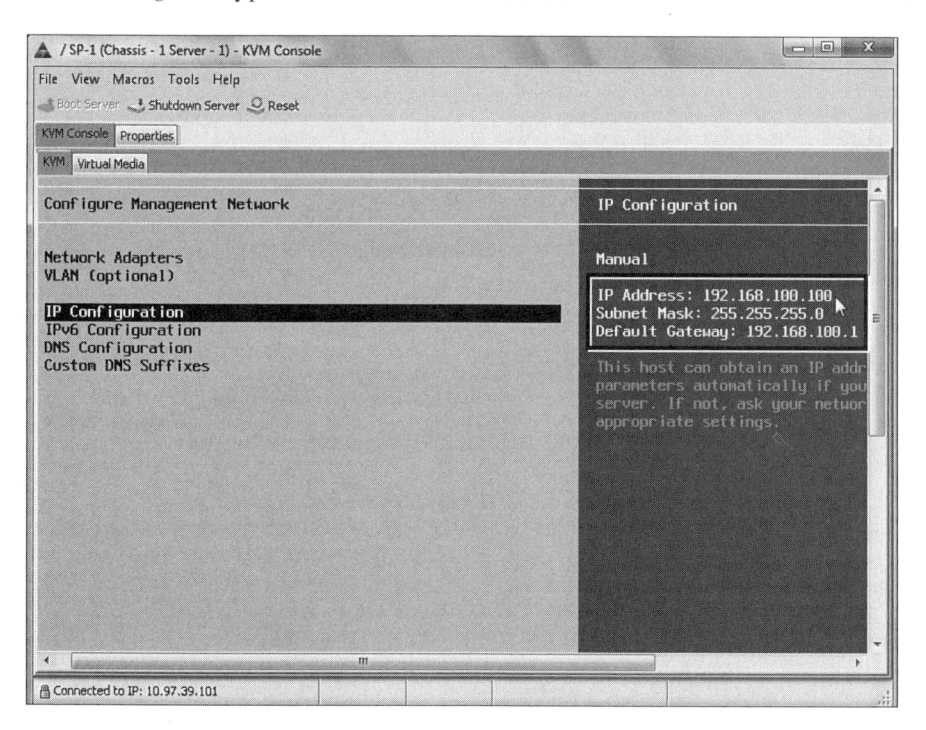

Figure 14-31 *vSphere Management Configuration*

Both Figures 14-32 and 14-33 depict screen captures from this client, and simultaneously reveal the MAC addresses and WWNs that were detected during the hypervisor installation (and were defined on SP-1).

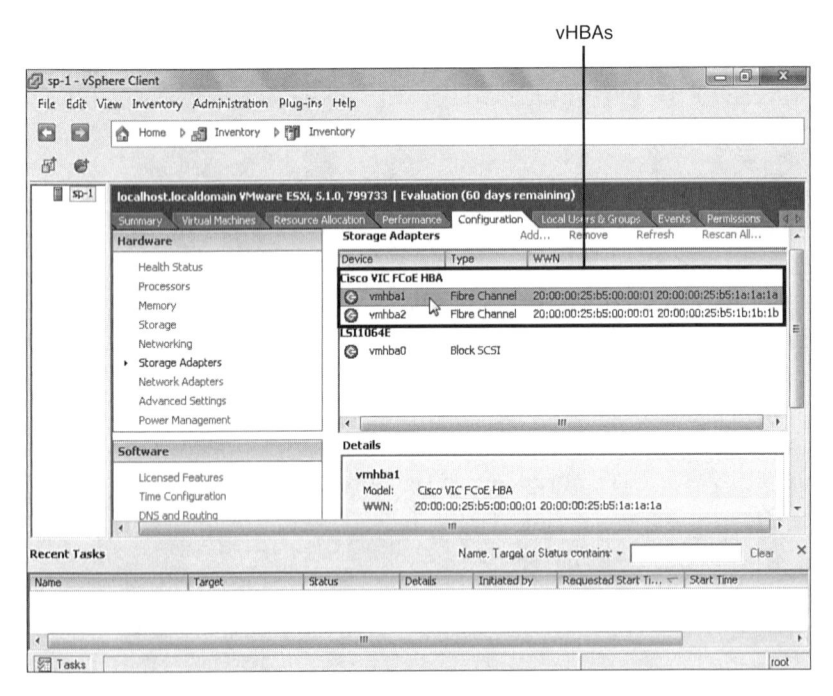

Figure 14-32 *Fibre Channel Interfaces*

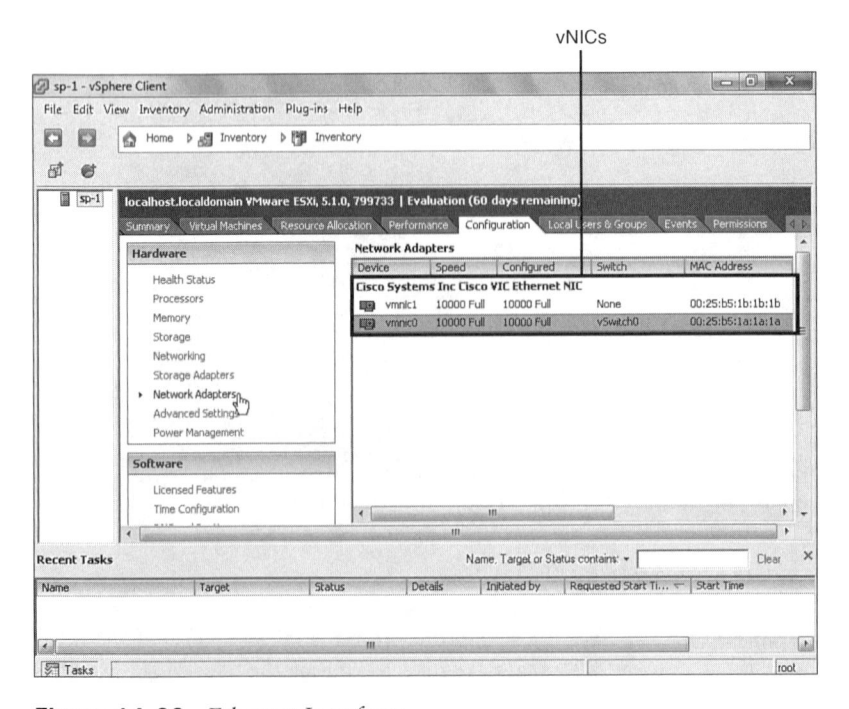

Figure 14-33 *Ethernet Interfaces*

Verifying Stateless Computing

As I have mentioned before, SP-1 was designed to be a fully stateless server. Because I have not used the local disks on server 1/1 in the installation procedure examined in the previous section, SP-1 can migrate to another server with extreme ease.

UCS Manager allows the migration of a complete physical server with a single operation, which is by clicking the same **Change Service Profile** link again and selecting another server to be associated with SP-1.

Therefore, I will change SP-1's association from server 1/1 to server 1/2 (blade 2 on chassis 1) and observe the resulting effects on its installed operating system. As you can imagine, this procedure comprises a rather complex set of internal configurations that are fortunately hidden from the server operating system point of view.

Figure 14-34 depicts yet another method where a UCS administrator can monitor the execution of service profile operations, such as this migration: the *Finite State Machine (FSM)* tab.

In Figure 14-34, the FSM tab shows that the adapter from server 1/2 is being configured to boot the UUOS agent. Consequently, when the progress status bar reaches 100%, SP-1 is completely migrated to server 1/2.

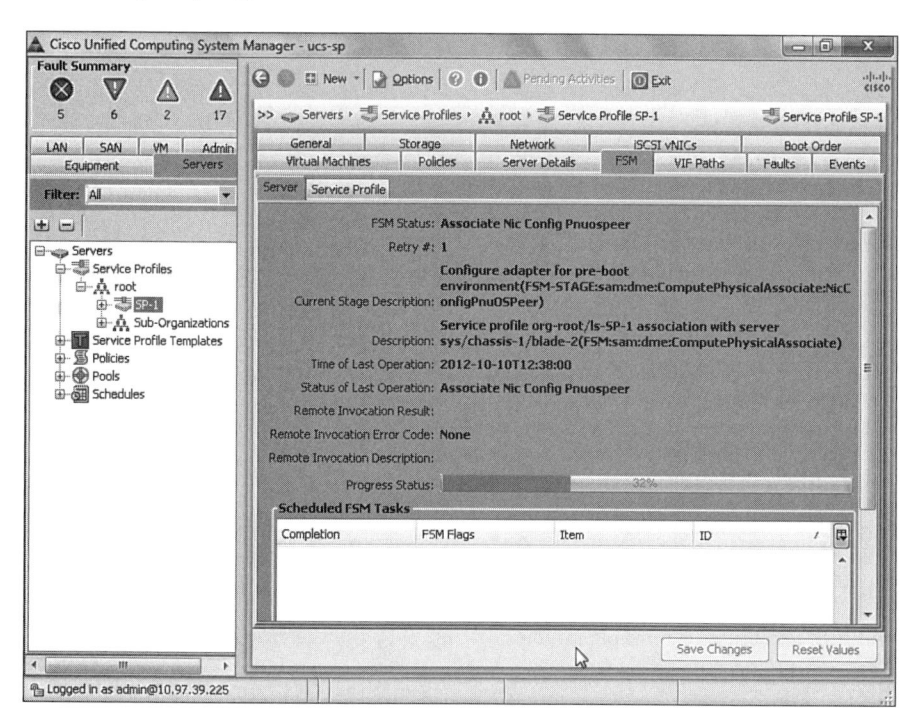

Figure 14-34 *SP-1 Finite State Machine Tab*

Figure 14-35 depicts a KVM session to SP-1 after its migration to server 1/2 and a successful boot from the intact 15-GB LUN.

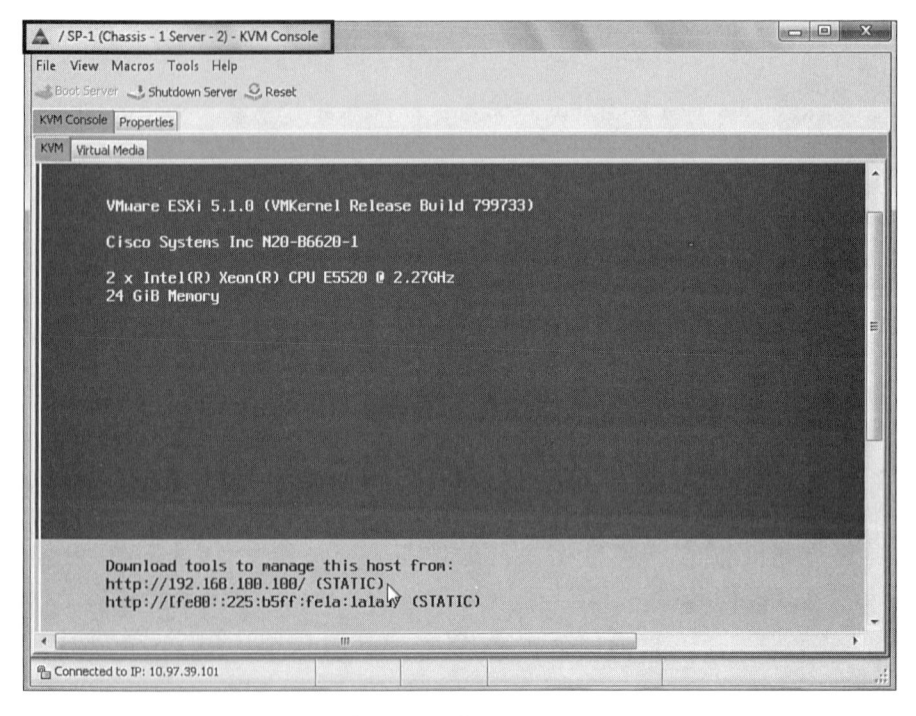

Figure 14-35 *KVM Session for SP-1 After Its Migration*

The upper-left corner of Figure 14-35 reveals that that our previous installation of VMware vSphere is now running on server 1/2. However, both the hypervisor and infrastructure (LAN, SAN, and storage array) are completely oblivious of the migration.

Using Policies

Policies define how a service profile selects or uses UCS resources. In essence, they enclose a set of configurations that can be shared among multiple service profiles.

For SP-1, I have configured many exclusive policies to conclude the wizard as briefly as possible. However, as you might remember, I also had to configure some *reusable* policies, such as IPMI-Policy and SoL-Active.

Naturally, the creation of reusable policies can simplify the creation of new service profiles. As an example, other Create Service Profile (expert) wizard interactions can easily refer to the aforementioned policies to define service profiles with the same IPMI and Serial over LAN configurations.

The following list contains some of the UCS policies that can be used to streamline and standardize service profile creation:

- Adapter policies
- BIOS policies
- Boot policies
- Firmware package policies
- IPMI access profiles
- Local disk configuration policies
- Maintenance policies
- Power control policies
- Scrub policies
- Serial over LAN policies
- Server pool policies
- Server pool policy qualifications
- Threshold policies
- iSCSI authentication profiles
- vNIC/vHBA placement policies

In the next two sections, I will focus on two special policies that can greatly optimize server provisioning: *BIOS setting* and *firmware package policies*.

BIOS Setting Policies

In the earlier section "Server Domain Operations," it was discussed that manually setting BIOS parameters can become an incredibly time-consuming task. UCS BIOS policies further facilitate configuration and standardization in data centers and can easily change BIOS parameters on several servers with a single operation.

To better clarify the potential of BIOS policies, I propose we go back to SP-1 (which was last seen running on server 1/2 on our topology). Through UCS Manager GUI, I will selectively change one of the original BIOS settings detected by the hypervisor (acting as our sample operating system).

In Figure 14-36, the VMware Virtual Interface client allows you to verify that server 1/2 is configured to enable Intel Hyper Threading, which allows operating systems to execute threads in parallel within each processor core. With this technology, a single physical processor core can act as two logical processors.

As you might remember, I did not set any BIOS policy on SP-1 during its creation. Consequently, SP-1 is using the server 1/2 default BIOS policy.

Figure 14-37 describes how this parameter is defined on BIOS Defaults (server 1/2 is a B200-M1 blade server).

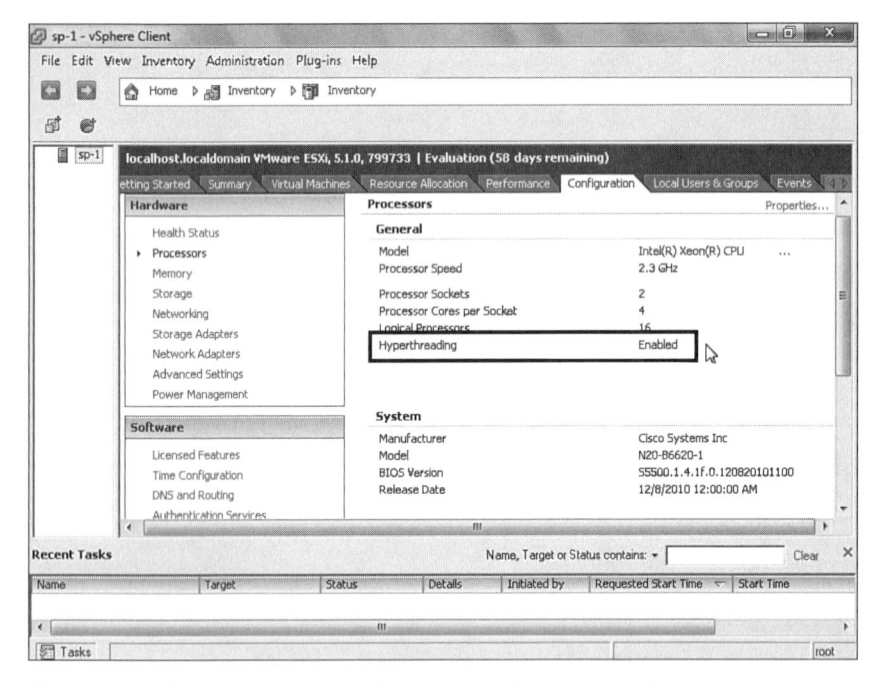

Figure 14-36 *BIOS Parameter Detected by VMware vSphere*

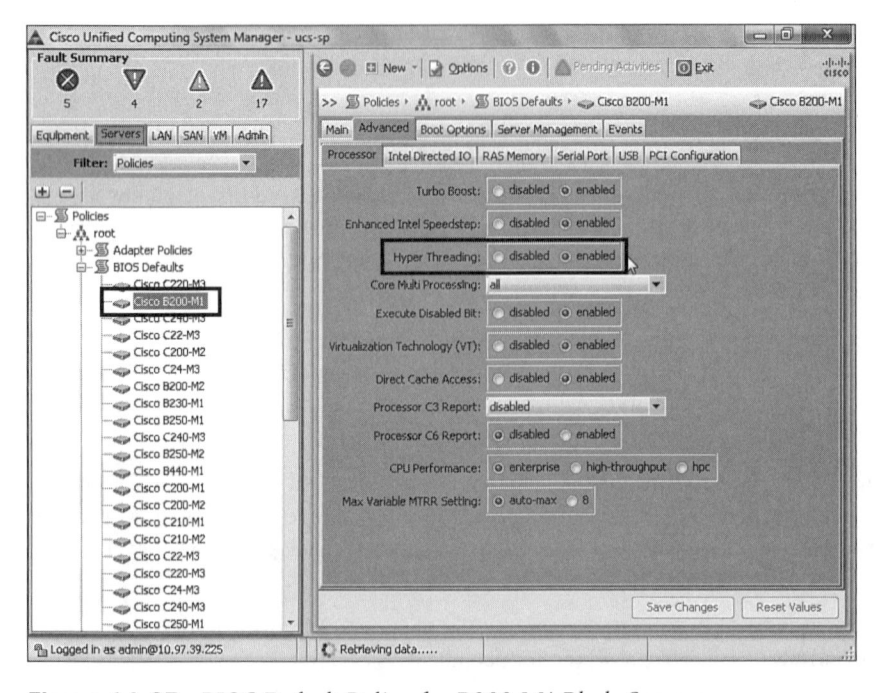

Figure 14-37 *BIOS Default Policy for B200-M1 Blade Servers*

I invite you to imagine the following situation: Suppose that you do not want to use this resource on your servers for some reason (for example, you might want to deploy extremely CPU-intensive virtual machines). Hence, to satisfy your needs, a BIOS policy called BIOS-Policy-noHT will be created.

Figure 14-38 details how the Create BIOS Policy wizard can be accessed by right-clicking **BIOS Policies** on the Servers main tab.

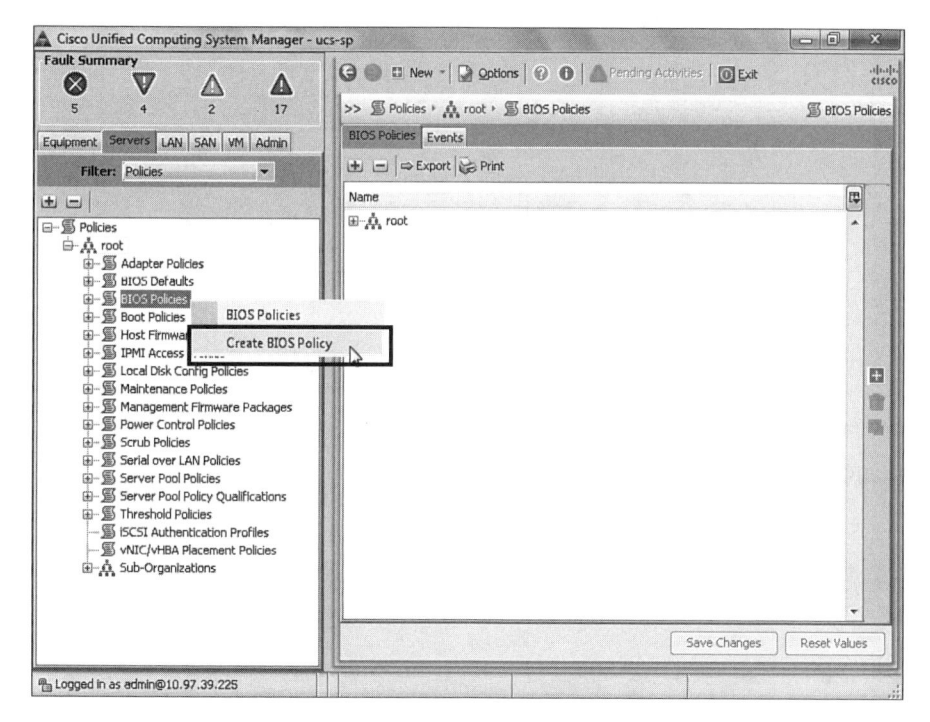

Figure 14-38 *Accessing the Create BIOS Policy Wizard*

> **Tip** From the background of Figure 14-38, you can also observe that other types of policies can be created in a similar way.

Figure 14-39 represents the first step of this wizard, where I have named the policy accordingly and left all the other parameters at the Platform Default option. Also notice that I have not selected the Reboot on BIOS Settings Change check box, meaning that changes in the policy will not be applied until the server is manually rebooted.

Going forward, Figure 14-40 portrays the Create BIOS Policy wizard second step, in which I have explicitly disabled Hyper Threading and, again, left all other parameters at the Platform Default option.

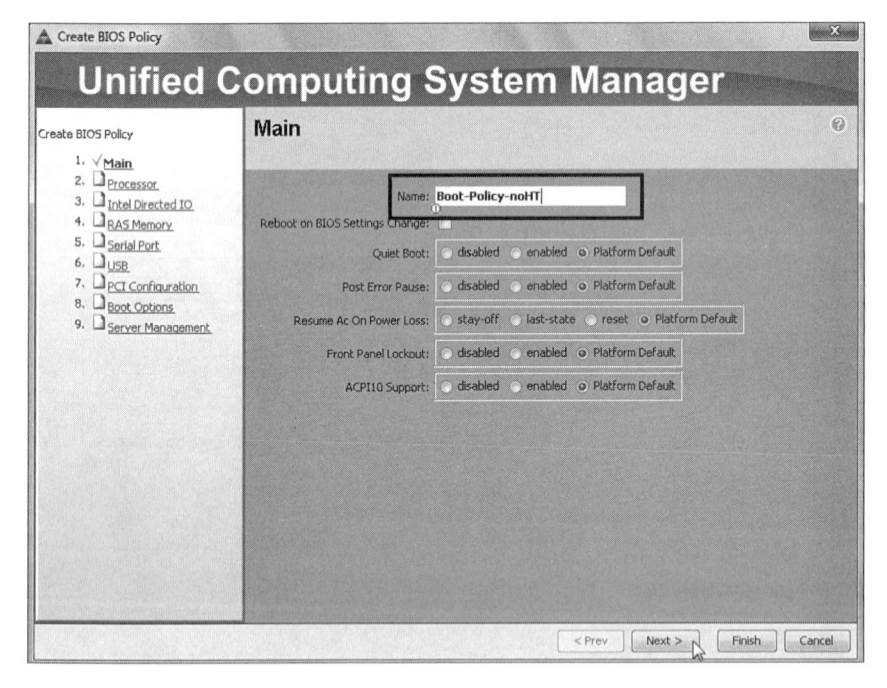

Figure 14-39 *BIOS Policy Main Configuration*

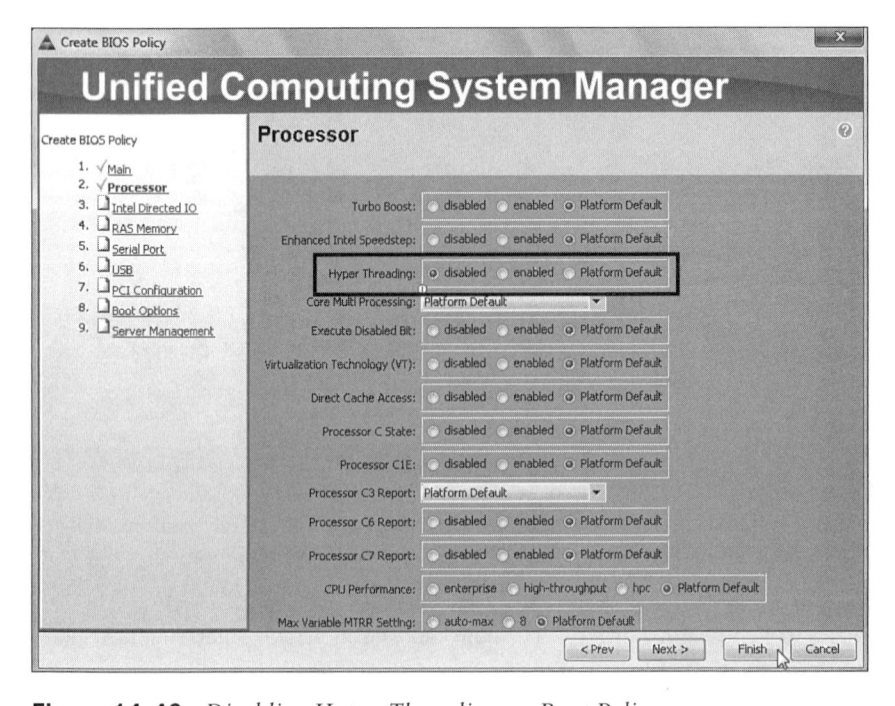

Figure 14-40 *Disabling Hyper Threading on Boot Policy*

Clicking **Finish** at this step guarantees that every other parameter will inherit the configuration that is defined in the hardware default BIOS policy.

> **Note** The discussion of every option of this wizard is beyond the scope of this book. My intention is to show the effects of a policy application on a service profile.

Figure 14-41 shows that BIOS-Policy-noHT can be selected on SP-1, and as mentioned, its BIOS settings will only be activated after a reboot.

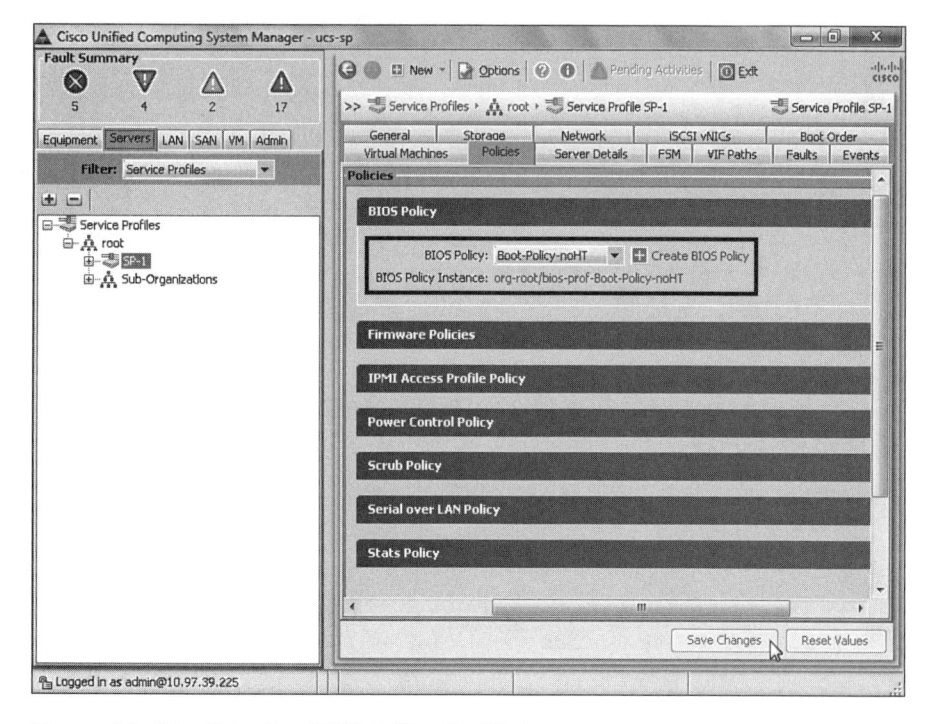

Figure 14-41 *Selecting BIOS Policy for SP-1*

Accessing the KVM for SP-1, it is possible to proceed with the server shutdown, as shown in Figure 14-42.

> **Tip** To avoid data loss or damage to the operating system, I highly recommend that you always use the "Graceful Shutdown" option on server shutdown and reboot operations. In this case, UCS Manager sends an ACPI (Advanced Configuration and Power Interface) signal to the server operating system, which reacts by safely turning itself off.

Booting the server again, you can observe that UCS Manager has indeed changed the BIOS settings on SP-1.

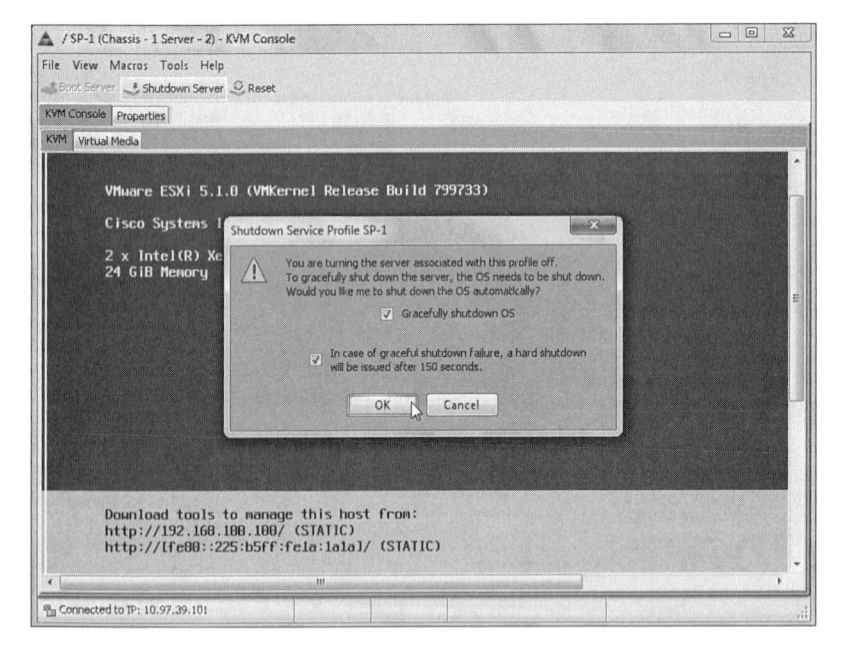

Figure 14-42 *Gracefully Shutting Down SP-1*

Figure 14-43 portrays how this change is perceived by the operating system after the server reboots with the new BIOS policy.

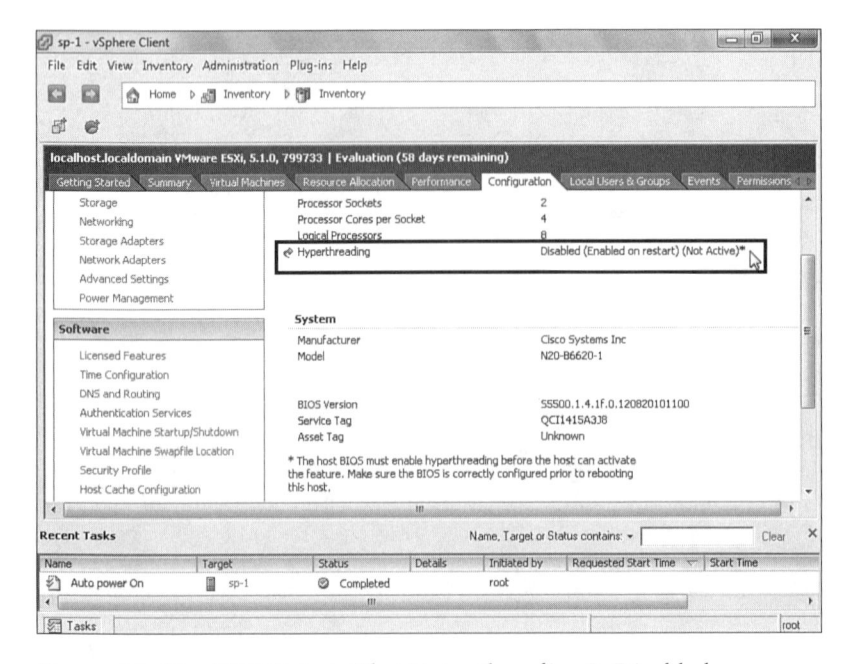

Figure 14-43 *ESXi Detects That Hyperthreading Is Disabled*

Because this policy is reusable, if it is assigned to more than one service profile, any change in the policy is transmitted to all service profiles and activated after a reboot.

Note The operating system has also detected version S5500.1.4.1f.0.120820101100 for the server BIOS. This parameter will be important in the next section.

Firmware Policies

The effort spent on firmware updates can be greatly reduced with *firmware package policies*, without requiring any management software installed on the server's operating system.

In a UCS domain, there are two types of firmware policies:

- **Host software package:** This includes adapter, BIOS, board, and storage controller firmware.

- **Management firmware package:** This includes CIMC firmware.

Figure 14-44 shows how these firmware policies can be accessed and created on the Policies tab from SP-1.

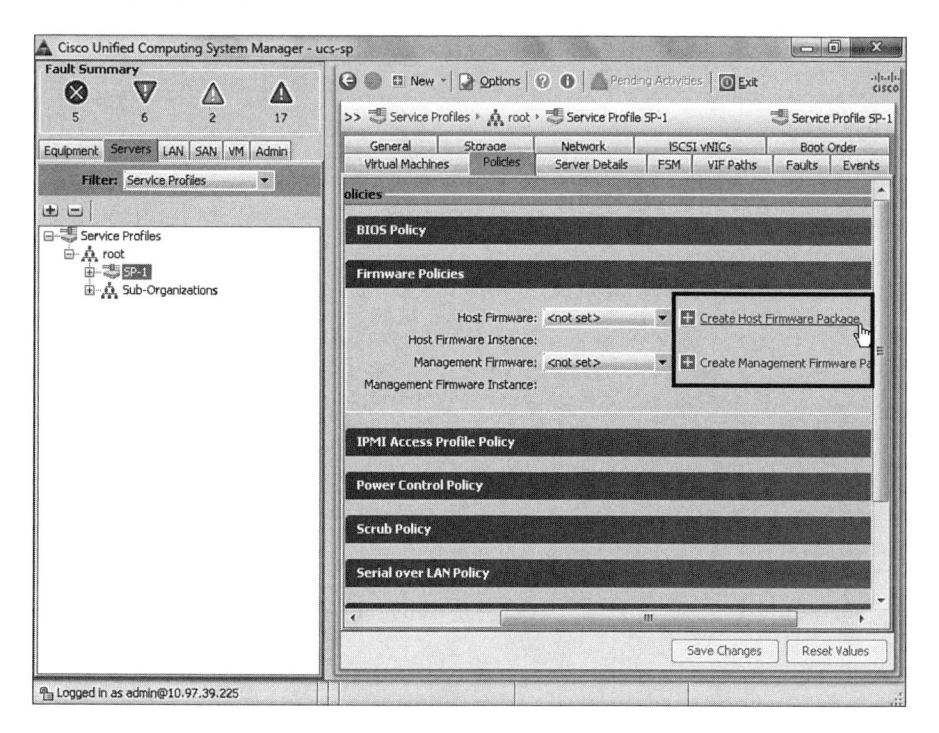

Figure 14-44 *Accessing the Firmware Policies in SP-1*

Clicking **Create Host Firmware Package**, a wizard is started to allow the selection of firmware versions that will be actually deployed on the server that is associated to SP-1.

Figure 14-45 shows the creation of firmware policy HOST-B200M1-VIC and the selection of version 2.0(4a) for the UCS M81KR virtual interface card adapter, which is installed on all servers from our topology.

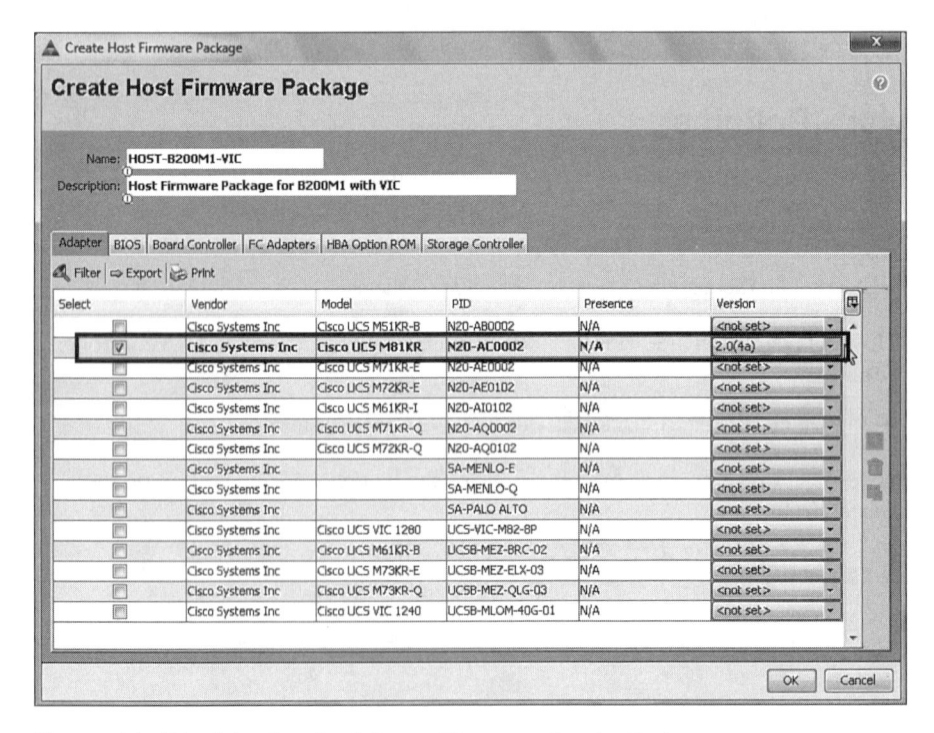

Figure 14-45 *Selecting the Adapter Firmware for the Package*

Furthermore, Figure 14-46 portrays the selection of BIOS version S5500.2.0.3.0.050720121819 for SP-1.

Although I will not describe the other tabs, consider that I have selected the most updated firmware versions for all components that can be installed on a UCS server (board controller, FC adapters, HBA option ROM, and storage controller). Then, clicking **Finish**, I have finally created the host firmware policy.

A management firmware package can also be constructed from SP-1's General tab (see Figure 14-44). And in fact, Figure 14-47 shows the creation of MGMT-B200M1-VIC with CIMC version 2.0(4a).

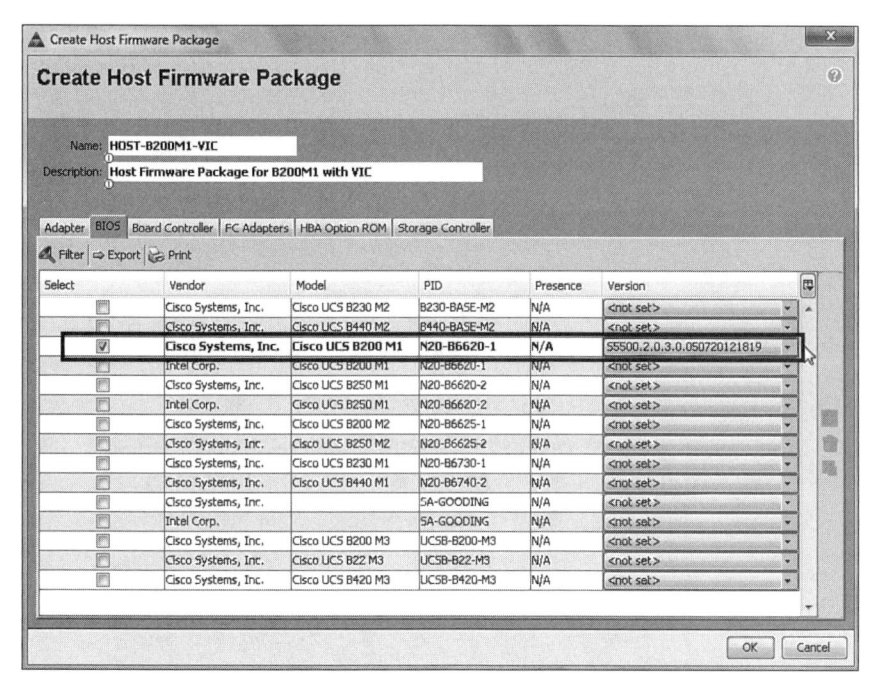

Figure 14-46 *Selecting the BIOS Firmware for the Package*

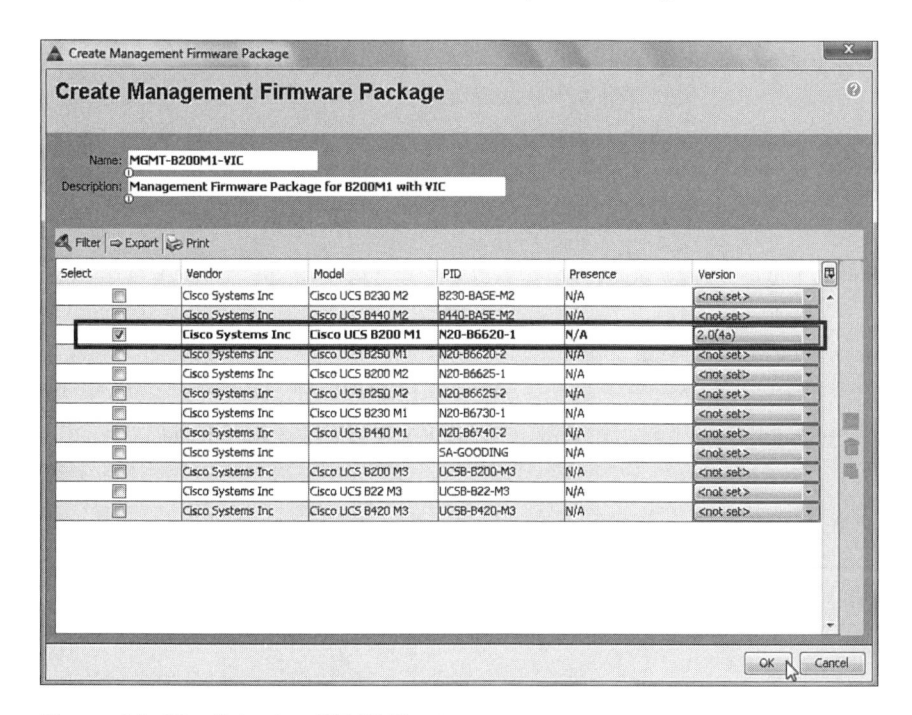

Figure 14-47 *Selecting CIMC Version*

Selecting both firmware policies for SP-1, UCS Manager will reboot the server associated with SP-1. And as usual, you can follow the changes that UCS Manager is performing on the hardware through the FSM tab.

As an illustration, Figure 14-48 captures the moment that the server BIOS is being updated.

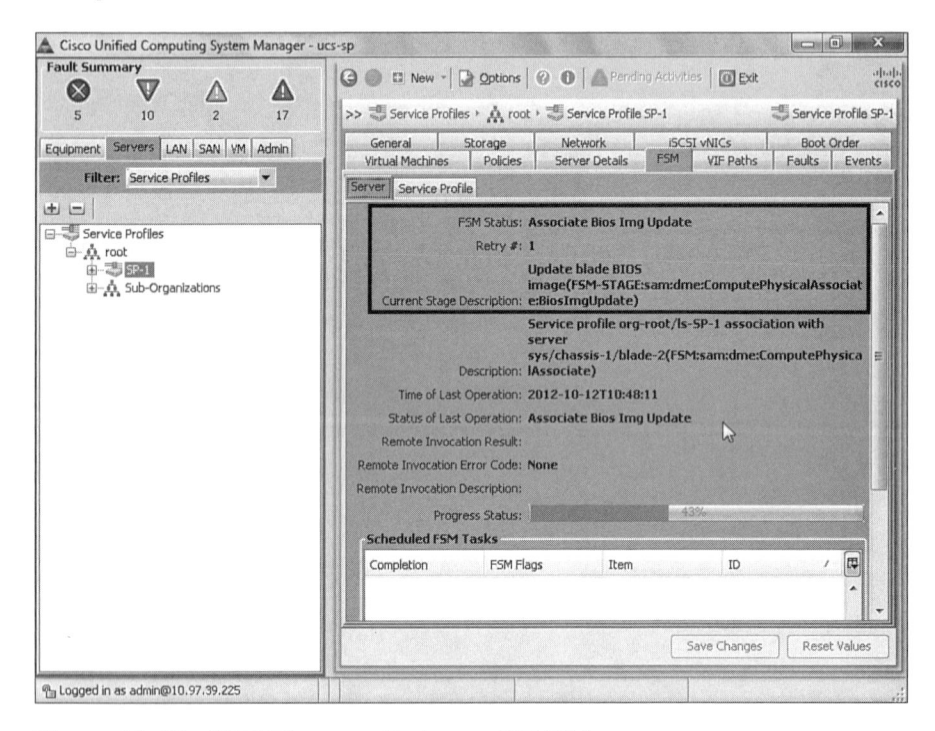

Figure 14-48 *BIOS Firmware Update on FSM Tab*

After all the changes are complete, the server boots with the versions selected on both firmware policies.

Confirming the BIOS firmware update, Figure 14-49 shows the version detected by the vSphere hypervisor installed on server 1/2.

Example 14-4 verifies the running firmware versions on the server 1/2 VIC adapter and CIMC.

Example 14-4 *Adapter and CIMC Version Verification*

```
! Connecting to adapter 1 from server in slot 2 from chassis 1 CLI
ucs-sp-a# connect adapter 1/2/1
! Checking adapter firmware version
adapter 1/2/1 # show-fwlist
[0]:  APP Version 1.4(1m)
```

```
[1]: APP Version 2.0(4a)                [STARTUP, RUNNING]
[2]: BOOT Version 1.0(1e)
[3]: DIAG Version 1.0.4.3
adapter 1/2/1 # exit
! Connecting to CIMC from server 1/2
ucs-sp-a# connect cimc 1/2
[output suppressed]
CIMC Debug Firmware Utility Shell [ support ]
! Checking CIMC firmware version
 [ help version]# version
ver: 2.0(4a)
RAMFS Build Time [ Wed Sep 12 08:27:03 PDT 2012 ]
U-Boot version:  2.0(4a).17
```

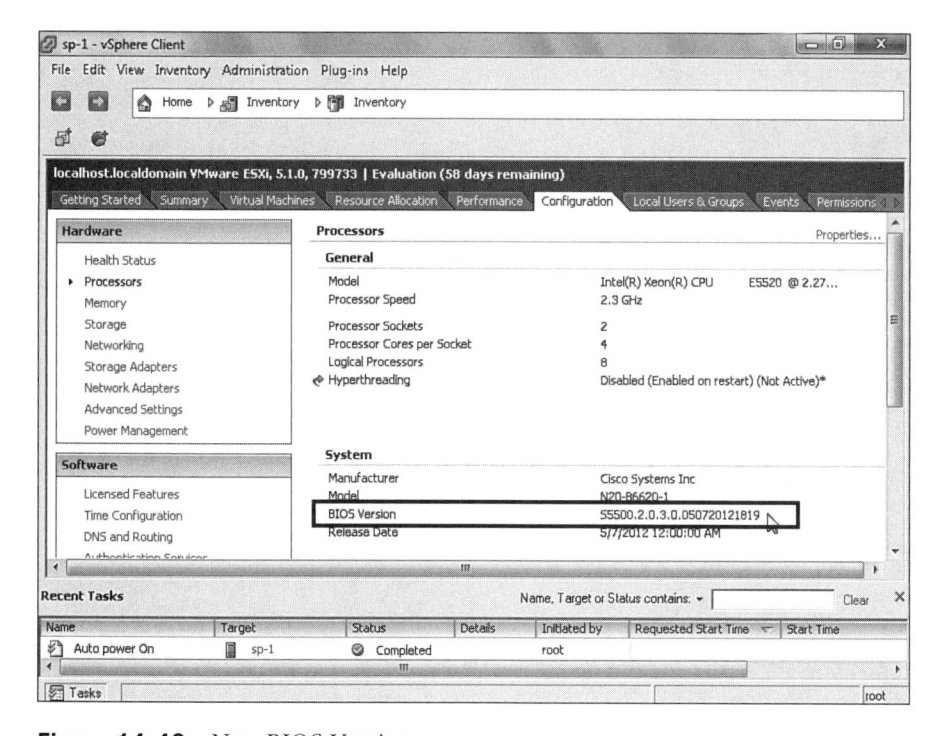

Figure 14-49 *New BIOS Version*

Industrializing Server Provisioning

Service profiles were originally created to consolidate physical server provisioning tasks into a single operation. But although it can be very appropriate for learning purposes, using the Create Service Profile (expert) wizard to instantiate one service profile per time severely underestimates the automation capabilities of UCS Manager.

Because service profiles are essentially logical entities, operations such as **cloning, pools,** and **templates** are capable of defining standards that can be used to quickly build other service profiles. With such *industrialization techniques*, it is possible to create and associate tens of service profiles within minutes.

Cloning

Cloning dramatically reduces the number of tasks of building a service profile. After clicking the **Create a Clone** link on a service profile General tab, all a clone needs is a name before UCS Manager creates a close-as-possible copy of this service profile.

Nevertheless, after a service profile clone is created, additional changes are usually required before it is associated to a UCS blade or rack-mount server.

To further elaborate this statement, review Figure 14-50.

SP-1

UUID: 01234567-89ab-cdef-0000-456789abcdef
Node WWN: 20:00:00:25:b5:00:00:01
Local Disk: RAID 0 Striped (no protection)
vHBA fc0
- Port WWN: 20:00:00:25:b5:1a:1a:1a
- Fabric: A
- VSAN: 10

vHBA fc1
- Port WWN: 20:00:00:25:b5:1b:1b:1b
- Fabric: B
- VSAN: 20

vNIC eth0
- MAC Address: 00:25:b5:1a:1a:1a
- Fabric: A
- VLAN: 100 and 101

vNIC eth1
- MAC Address: 00:25:b5:1b:1b:1b
- Fabric: B
- VLAN: 100 and 101

Boot order: CD, SAN (50:06:01:60:41:e0:b3:d3 LUN 0 or 50:06:01:61:41:e0:b3:d3 LUN 0)
Policies
    Boot-Policy-noHT
    HOST-B200M1-VIC
    MGMT-B200M1-VIC
    IPMI-Policy
    SoL-Active
Management IP Address: 10.97.39.101

→ Cloning →

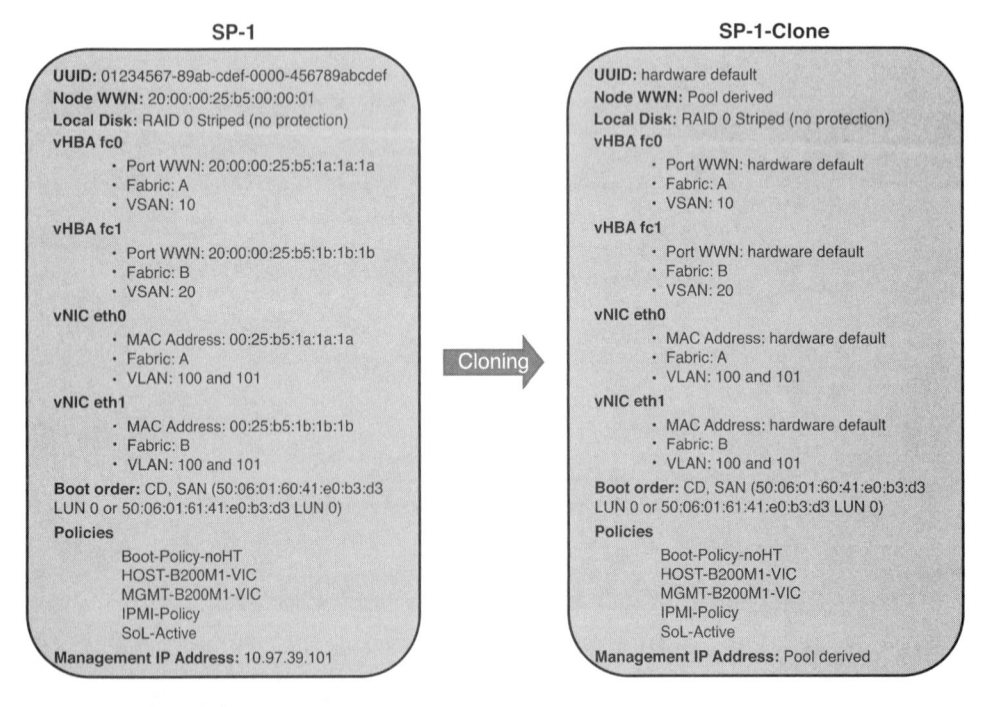

SP-1-Clone

UUID: hardware default
Node WWN: Pool derived
Local Disk: RAID 0 Striped (no protection)
vHBA fc0
- Port WWN: hardware default
- Fabric: A
- VSAN: 10

vHBA fc1
- Port WWN: hardware default
- Fabric: B
- VSAN: 20

vNIC eth0
- MAC Address: hardware default
- Fabric: A
- VLAN: 100 and 101

vNIC eth1
- MAC Address: hardware default
- Fabric: B
- VLAN: 100 and 101

Boot order: CD, SAN (50:06:01:60:41:e0:b3:d3 LUN 0 or 50:06:01:61:41:e0:b3:d3 LUN 0)
Policies
    Boot-Policy-noHT
    HOST-B200M1-VIC
    MGMT-B200M1-VIC
    IPMI-Policy
    SoL-Active
Management IP Address: Pool derived

Figure 14-50 *Cloning SP-1*

Figure 14-50 compares the parameters of SP-1 with a clone (SP-1-Clone) immediately after its creation. Comparing both service profiles, you can observe that while the cloning process leverages all the policies and configurations from the **parent** service profile, it cannot do the same with SP-1 unique identifiers (UUID, WWNs, MACs, management IP addresses). Hence, by default, UCS Manager provides replacement addresses from default pools or derived from the server hardware to service profile clones.

> **Tip** To deploy stateless computing, you will have to manually change the identifiers of a clone to a nonderived address. Additionally, hardware addresses cannot be derived from Cisco virtualized interface card (VIC) adapters.

Pools

The distribution of unique identifiers among service profiles can be optimized through the use of *pools*. In essence, pools are collections of identities of physical or logical resources that are available in a UCS domain.

For example, considering our original scenario, I have created the following pools (with 15 identifiers each):

- **UUID-Pool:** UUIDs from 01234567-89AB-CDEF-0000-000000000001 to 01234567-89AB-CDEF-0000-00000000000F.

- **nWWN-Pool:** Node WWNs from 20:00:00:25:b5:00:01:01 to 20:00:00:25:b5:00:01:0f.

- **pWWN-Pool-A:** Port WWNs from 20:00:00:25:b5:00:0a:01 to 20:00:00:25:b5:00:0a:0f.

- **pWWN-Pool-B:** Port WWNs from 20:00:00:25:b5:00:0b:01 to 20:00:00:25:b5:00:0b:0f.

- **MAC-Pool-A:** MAC addresses from 0025.b500.0a01 to 0025.b500.0a0f.

- **MAC-Pool-B:** MAC addresses from 0025.b500.0b01 to 0025.b500.0b0f.

- **Management IP Pool:** IP addresses from 10.97.39.111 to 10.97.39.125 (with mask 255.255.255.0 and default gateway 10.97.39.1).

These pools were created on different UCS Manager main tabs: Servers (UUID-Pool), SAN (nWWN-Pool, pWWN-Pool-A, and pWWN-Pool-B), LAN (MAC-Pool-A and MAC-Pool-B), and Admin (Management IP Pool).

With these elements, instead of manually defining each identifier on a service profile (and controlling its availability in the system), a UCS administrator can simply refer to an appropriate pool whenever he needs to assign an identifier to a service profile.

For example, if these pools are applied to SP-1-Clone, this service profile will use the values shown in Figure 14-51.

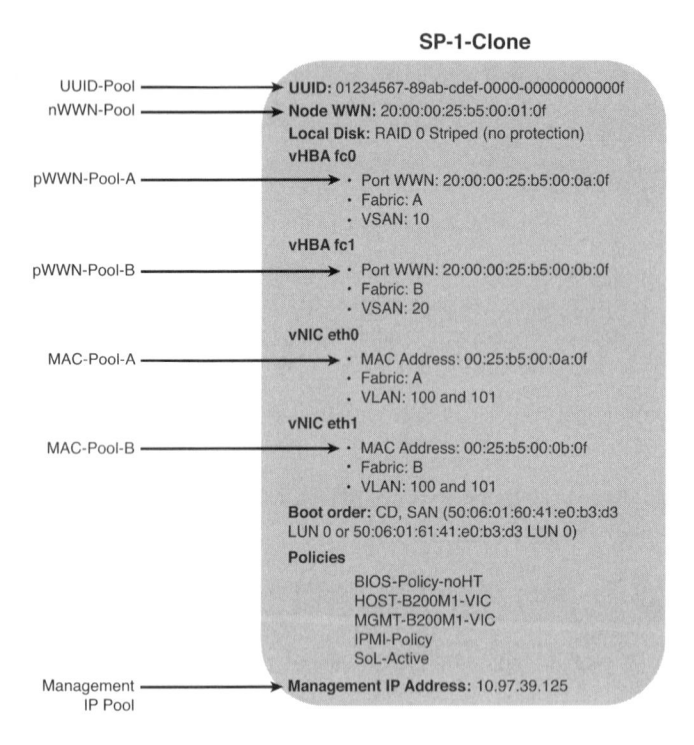

```
                              SP-1-Clone
UUID-Pool ─────────────▶ UUID: 01234567-89ab-cdef-0000-00000000000f
nWWN-Pool ─────────────▶ Node WWN: 20:00:00:25:b5:00:01:0f
                         Local Disk: RAID 0 Striped (no protection)
                         vHBA fc0
pWWN-Pool-A ───────────▶  • Port WWN: 20:00:00:25:b5:00:0a:0f
                          • Fabric: A
                          • VSAN: 10
                         vHBA fc1
pWWN-Pool-B ───────────▶  • Port WWN: 20:00:00:25:b5:00:0b:0f
                          • Fabric: B
                          • VSAN: 20
                         vNIC eth0
MAC-Pool-A ────────────▶  • MAC Address: 00:25:b5:00:0a:0f
                          • Fabric: A
                          • VLAN: 100 and 101
                         vNIC eth1
MAC-Pool-B ────────────▶  • MAC Address: 00:25:b5:00:0b:0f
                          • Fabric: B
                          • VLAN: 100 and 101
                         Boot order: CD, SAN (50:06:01:60:41:e0:b3:d3
                         LUN 0 or 50:06:01:61:41:e0:b3:d3 LUN 0)
                         Policies
                             BIOS-Policy-noHT
                             HOST-B200M1-VIC
                             MGMT-B200M1-VIC
                             IPMI-Policy
                             SoL-Active
Management ────────────▶ Management IP Address: 10.97.39.125
  IP Pool
```

Figure 14-51 *Applying Pools to SP-1 Clone*

> **Tip** UCS Manager uses descending order to consume the elements of a pool.

Service Profile Templates

Without a doubt, you can deploy service profile cloning if you want to create a small number of service profiles. However, if you want to build a true server provisioning "production line" within your UCS domains, I thoroughly recommended that you use *service profile templates* instead.

A service profile template can be defined as the grouping of policies, pools, and element definitions (such as the number of vNICs and vHBAs) in a single configuration element that can quickly create service profiles with the same common characteristics and distinct identifiers. Not by coincidence, the UCS Manager GUI has a wizard that allows a step-by-step configuration of a service profile template (which, from now on, I will simply refer to as a *template*).

Figure 14-52 portrays how this wizard can be activated on the Servers main tab from UCS Manager.

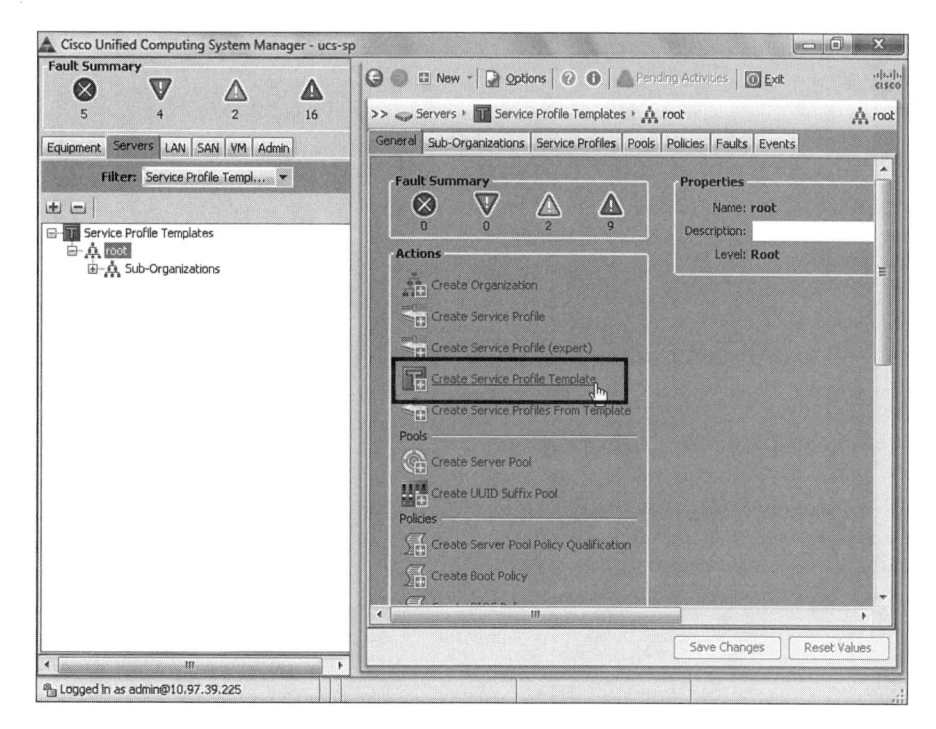

Figure 14-52 *Accessing the Create Service Profile Template Wizard*

After the wizard is started, it has a very similar structure to the Create Service Profile (expert) wizard. Consequently, to avoid unnecessary repetitions, I will focus on the difference between both wizards.

In the first step of the template wizard, after naming the service profile template (Template-1 in our scenario), you have to decide what kind of relation this template will have with its spawned service profiles. You can choose from the following two options:

- **Initial:** Where the service profiles inherit all the properties from the template, but without a "configuration connection" between them. Hence, a change in the template does not cause a modification in its service profiles (which must be changed individually).

- **Updating:** Where service profiles inherit all the properties of the template and remain connected to it. As a consequence, a change in the template automatically updates all of its generated service profiles.

Figure 14-53 shows that I have defined Template-1 as an updating template.

In Figure 14-53, I have also selected pool UUID-Pool as the source of Universally Unique Identifiers for service profiles spawned from Template-1.

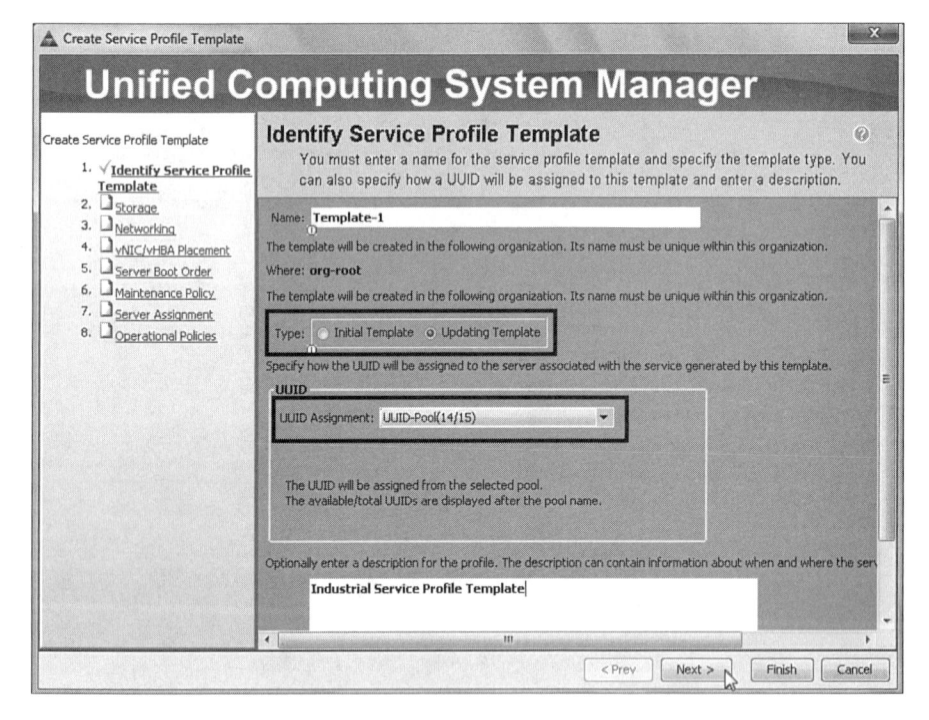

Figure 14-53 *Identifying Template-1*

Generally speaking, whenever you have to define an identifier from a template, you can choose an address pool or derive it from the hardware. And for reasons discussed before, if you want to deploy stateless computing with service profile templates, using pools is mandatory.

Differently from the creation of SP-1, I have used *virtual interface templates* to define fc0, fc1, eth0, and eth1 in Template-1. Using vHBA and vNIC templates, you can further increase the configuration "recycling" in a UCS domain, because virtual interface templates can also be used in the creation of other service profiles and service profile templates.

Figure 14-54 portrays a vHBA template example, where fc0-Template is described through several definitions, such as the use of Fabric A (VSAN10) and pWWN-Pool-A as source of Port WWN addresses.

Tip The fc0-Template is also an *updating vHBA template*, meaning that a change in the template will be carried on to all service profiles that are using it.

After fc0-Template is created, it can be easily referred to on any vHBA definition, including the one on Template-1, as shown in Figure 14-55.

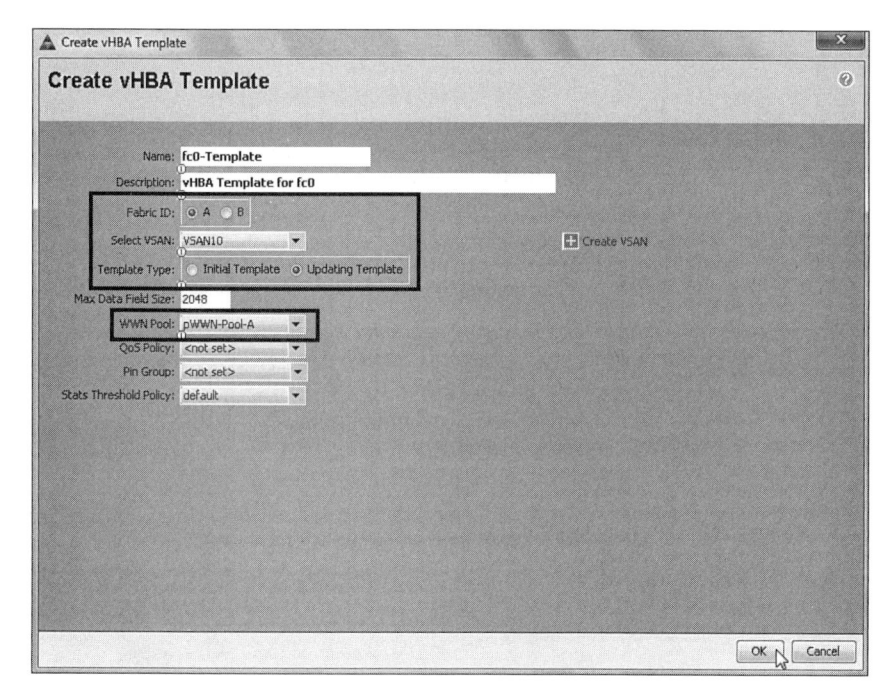

Figure 14-54 *Creating vHBA Template fc0-Template*

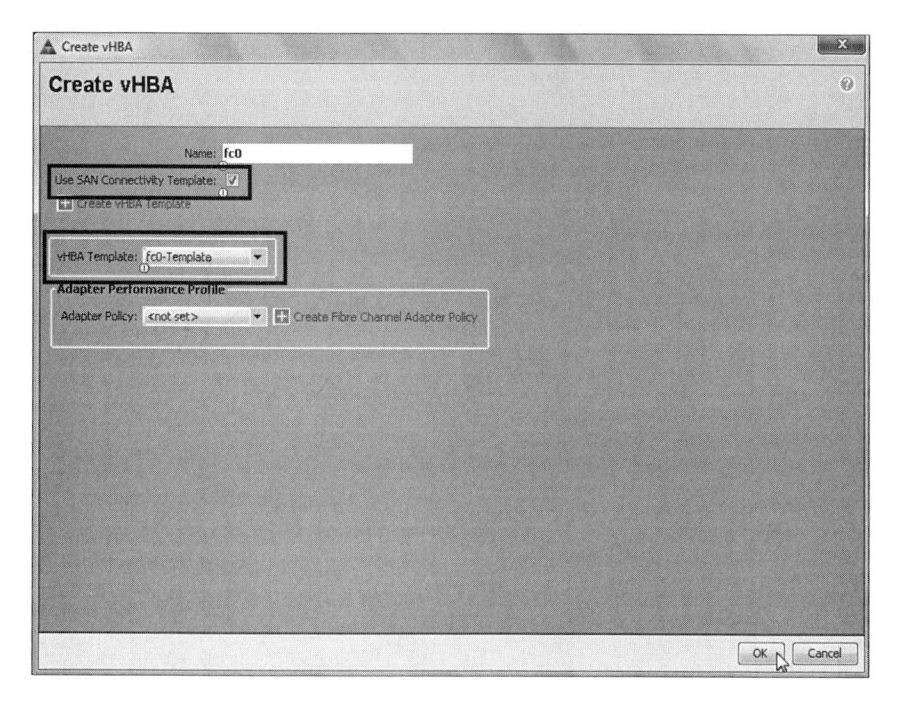

Figure 14-55 *Creating fc0 on Template-1*

In the remaining Create Service Profile wizard steps, I have created reusable policies that mirror the characteristics of SP-1. The policies are as follows:

- **Disk-Policy-1:** Configures both disks in RAID 0 with no protection.
- **vCON-Policy-1:** Assigns fc0 and eth0 to vCon1, and fc1 and eth1 to vCon2 (with option All for all four vCons).
- **Boot-Policy-1:** First boots from CD-ROM and then from a SAN-reachable LUN 0 (on 50:06:01:60:41:e0:b3:d3 or 50:06:01:61:41:e0:b3:d3) with interface name enforcement and no reboot on order change.
- No maintenance policy.
- No server assignment. However, the server must remain down when a service profile created from Template-1 is associated to it.
- **BIOS-Policy-noHT:** Disables Intel Hyper Threading and uses the server hardware default BIOS settings on the remaining parameters.
- Default monitoring policy.
- No power control policy.
- No scrub policy.

Additionally, I have reused IPMI-Policy and SoL-Active policies from SP-1.

Figure 14-56 summarizes the Template-1 configuration defined through my recent interaction with the Create Service Profile Template wizard.

> **Note** As I did during the SP-1 creation, I have not set any firmware policies. However, the same firmware packages created before could also be applied to Template-1 after the wizard's completion.

Using service profile templates, you can reach the highest level of server provisioning industrialization within a Unified Computing System. Figure 14-57 justifies this statement with the simultaneous creation of two service profiles from Template-1.

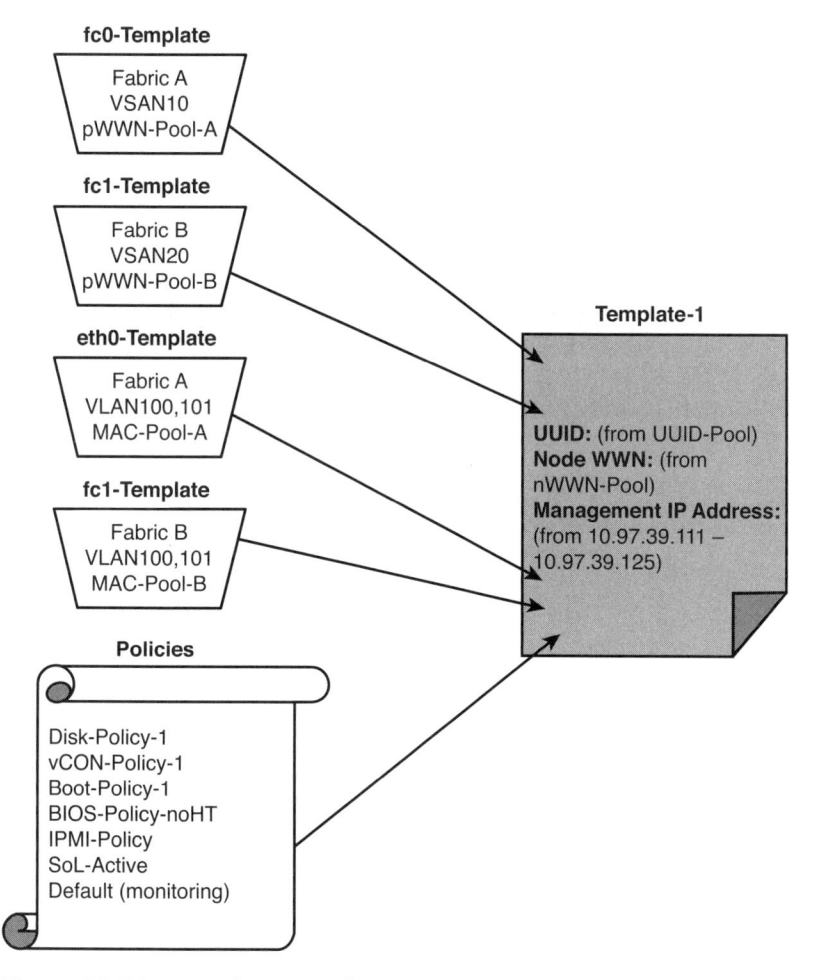

Figure 14-56 *Template-1 Configuration*

On the template General tab, selecting **Create Service Profile from Template**, and afterwards, defining prefix FromTemplate-1-SP, I have created two service profiles in a few seconds: FromTemplate-1-SP1 and FromTemplate1-SP2.

Figure 14-58 depicts both spawned service profiles.

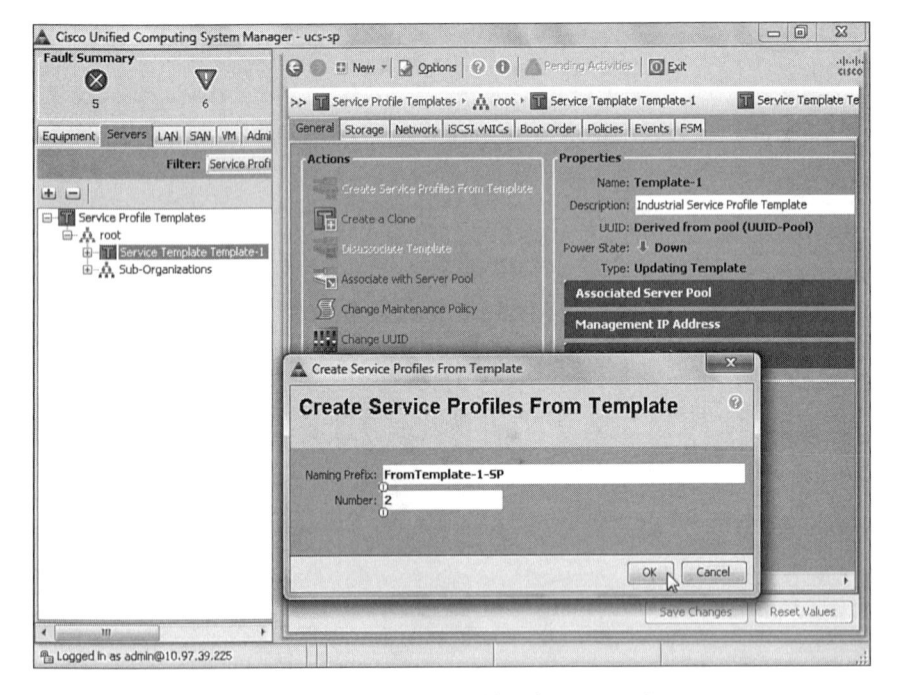

Figure 14-57 *Creating Two Service Profiles from Template-1*

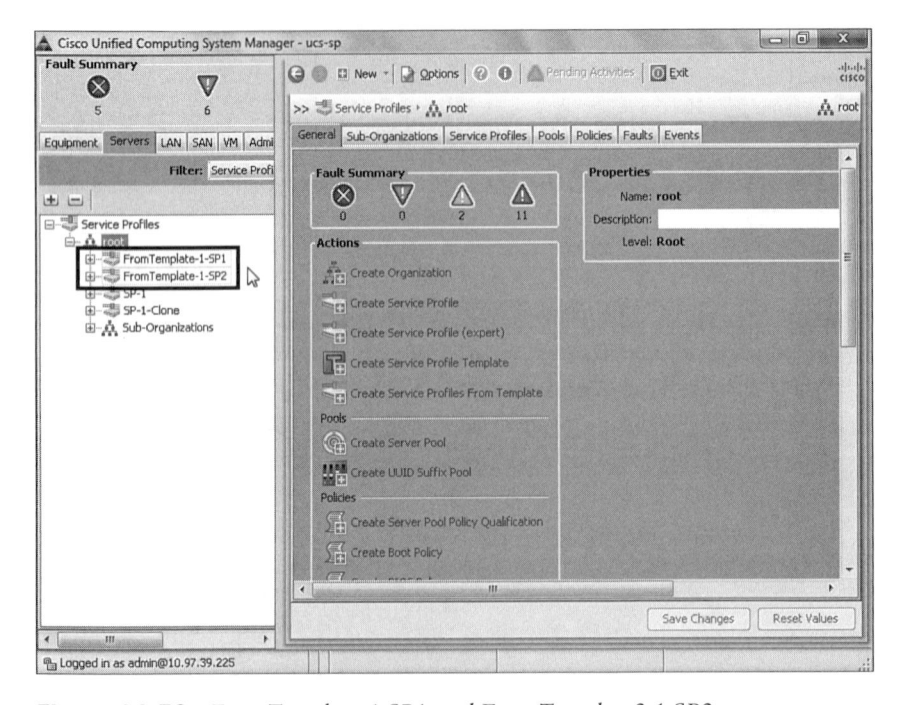

Figure 14-58 *FromTemplate-1-SP1 and FromTemplate2-1-SP2*

Because Template-1 belongs to the organization *root*, both service profiles are automatically included in the same organization. However, a UCS administrator can use Template-1 to instantiate service profiles in a sub-organization.

The characteristics of both service profiles are represented in Figure 14-59. And as you can observe, the identity pools continue to be consumed in descending order.

Template-1

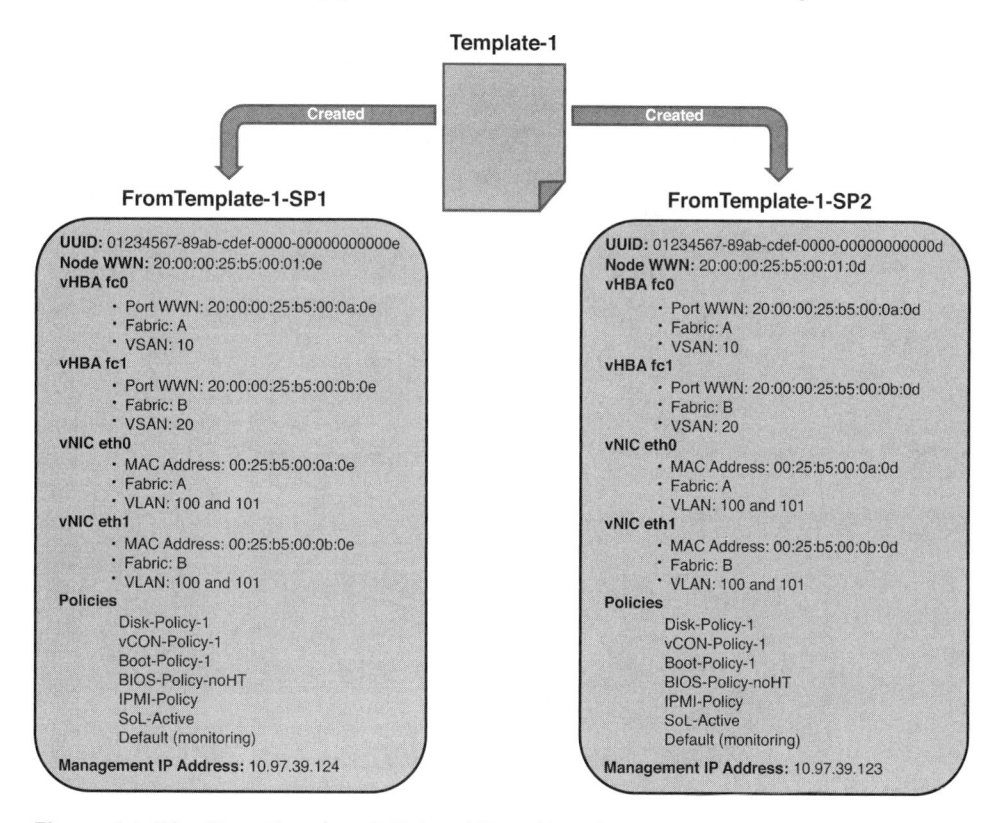

Created → **FromTemplate-1-SP1**
- **UUID:** 01234567-89ab-cdef-0000-00000000000e
- **Node WWN:** 20:00:00:25:b5:00:01:0e
- **vHBA fc0**
  - Port WWN: 20:00:00:25:b5:00:0a:0e
  - Fabric: A
  - VSAN: 10
- **vHBA fc1**
  - Port WWN: 20:00:00:25:b5:00:0b:0e
  - Fabric: B
  - VSAN: 20
- **vNIC eth0**
  - MAC Address: 00:25:b5:00:0a:0e
  - Fabric: A
  - VLAN: 100 and 101
- **vNIC eth1**
  - MAC Address: 00:25:b5:00:0b:0e
  - Fabric: B
  - VLAN: 100 and 101
- **Policies**
  - Disk-Policy-1
  - vCON-Policy-1
  - Boot-Policy-1
  - BIOS-Policy-noHT
  - IPMI-Policy
  - SoL-Active
  - Default (monitoring)
- **Management IP Address:** 10.97.39.124

Created → **FromTemplate-1-SP2**
- **UUID:** 01234567-89ab-cdef-0000-00000000000d
- **Node WWN:** 20:00:00:25:b5:00:01:0d
- **vHBA fc0**
  - Port WWN: 20:00:00:25:b5:00:0a:0d
  - Fabric: A
  - VSAN: 10
- **vHBA fc1**
  - Port WWN: 20:00:00:25:b5:00:0b:0d
  - Fabric: B
  - VSAN: 20
- **vNIC eth0**
  - MAC Address: 00:25:b5:00:0a:0d
  - Fabric: A
  - VLAN: 100 and 101
- **vNIC eth1**
  - MAC Address: 00:25:b5:00:0b:0d
  - Fabric: B
  - VLAN: 100 and 101
- **Policies**
  - Disk-Policy-1
  - vCON-Policy-1
  - Boot-Policy-1
  - BIOS-Policy-noHT
  - IPMI-Policy
  - SoL-Active
  - Default (monitoring)
- **Management IP Address:** 10.97.39.123

Figure 14-59 *FromTemplate-1-SP1 and FromTemplate-1-SP2 Summary*

Because Template-1 is an updating template, it propagates any change to service profiles FromTemplate-1-SP1 and FromTemplate-1-SP2. As a quick demonstration, I have created a BIOS Policy called BIOS-Policy-1 with all its settings configured to Platform Default.

Figure 14-60 depicts BIOS-Policy-1 replacing BIOS-Policy-noHT in Template-1.

After saving this change on Template-1, Figure 14-61 shows that service profile FromTemplate-1-SP2 was automatically updated.

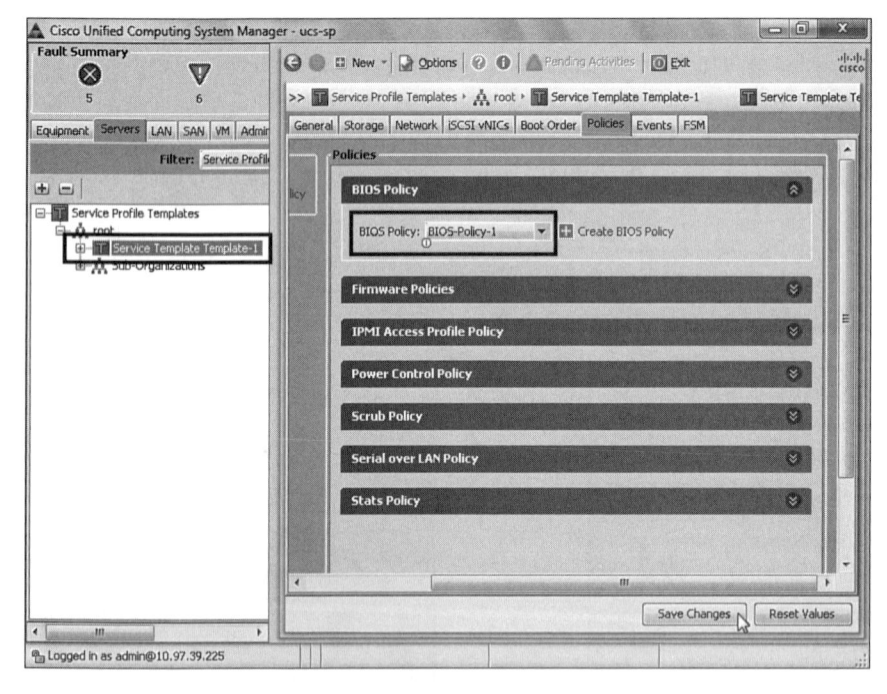

Figure 14-60 *Changing BIOS Policy on Template-1*

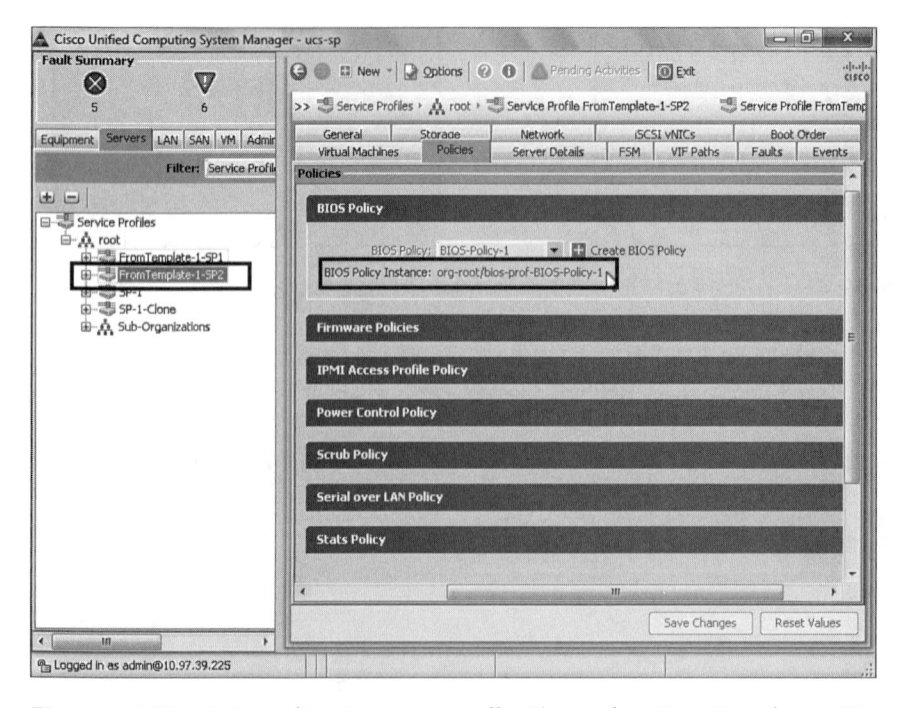

Figure 14-61 *BIOS Policy Is Automatically Changed on FromTemplate-1-SP2*

The binding between an updating template and its resulting service profiles can easily accelerate changes on servers that belong to a UCS domain. Besides, uniformity is enforced because direct changes are not allowed on these service profiles.

Server Pools

A *server pool* is a collection of servers from a UCS domain that share common characteristics (such as memory size and local storage characteristics) or are manually grouped together. Using server pools, UCS Manager can automatically associate a service profile to a server that meets predefined qualifications.

To understand how this automatic association works, imagine that the service profiles created from Template-1 are also supposed to be applied to future VMware vSphere hosts. And because of your company's internal policies, these service profiles must be associated to servers with more than 20 GB of memory.

Intending to increase automation in your data center, you create an empty pool, which you call Server-Pool-vSphere. Afterward, you create a server pool policy qualification called Minimum-20GB that will automatically include servers with more than 20 GB of memory, as shown in Figure 14-62.

As Figure 14-62 reveals, you can also include other qualification factors in the policy, such as

- Adapters (virtualized, non-virtualized, FCoE, and other characteristics)
- Chassis
- CPU or core definitions (processor architecture, processor product identifier [PID], minimum and maximum number of cores and threads, CPU speed and stepping)
- Storage characteristics (diskless, number of blocks, block size, minimum and maximum capacity, units, per-disk capacity)
- Server product identifier (PID)
- Power group
- Rack

Afterward, you create a server pool policy that includes in the (empty) target server pool (Server-Pool-vSphere) all the servers that share characteristics described in a qualification policy (Minimum-20GB).

Figure 14-63 portrays the creation of SrvPool-Policy-1, which links both Server-Pool-vSphere and Minimum-20GB policies.

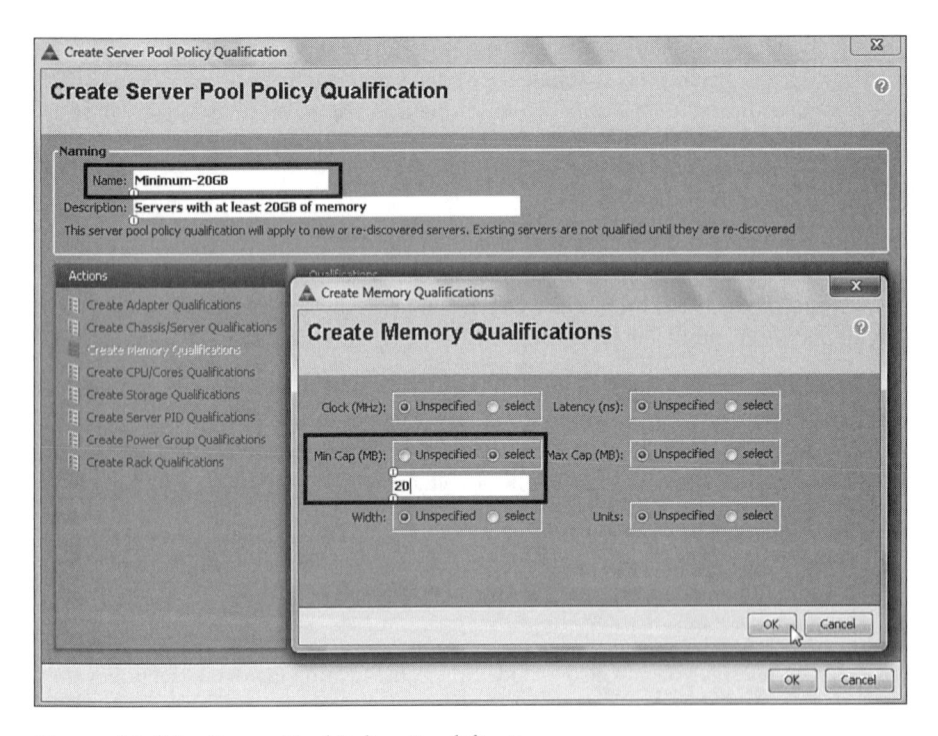

Figure 14-62 *Server Pool Policy Qualification*

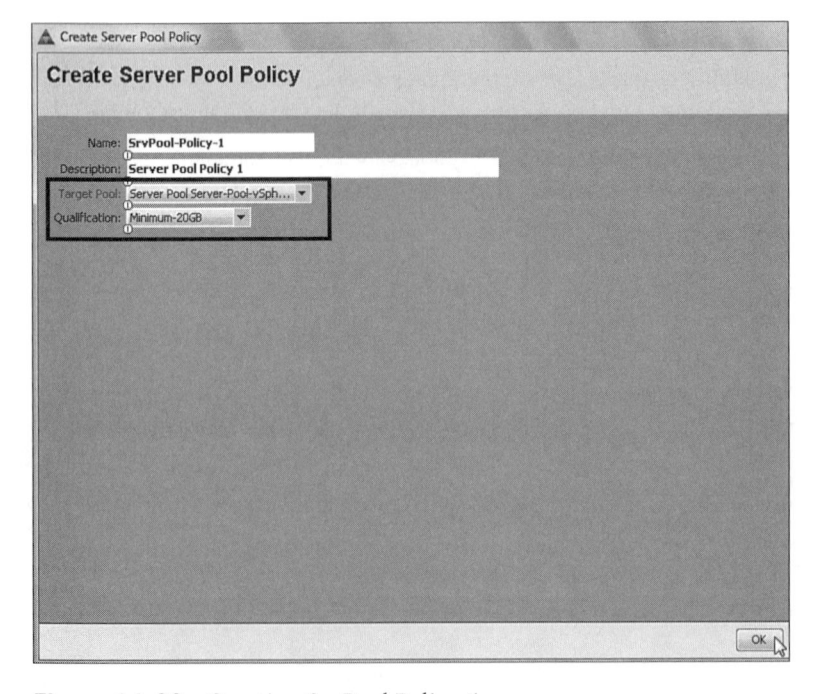

Figure 14-63 *Creating SrvPool-Policy-1*

After SrvPool-Policy-1 is created, all UCS servers that contain more than 20 GB of RAM are automatically inserted into Server-Pool-vSphere, as depicted in Figure 14-64.

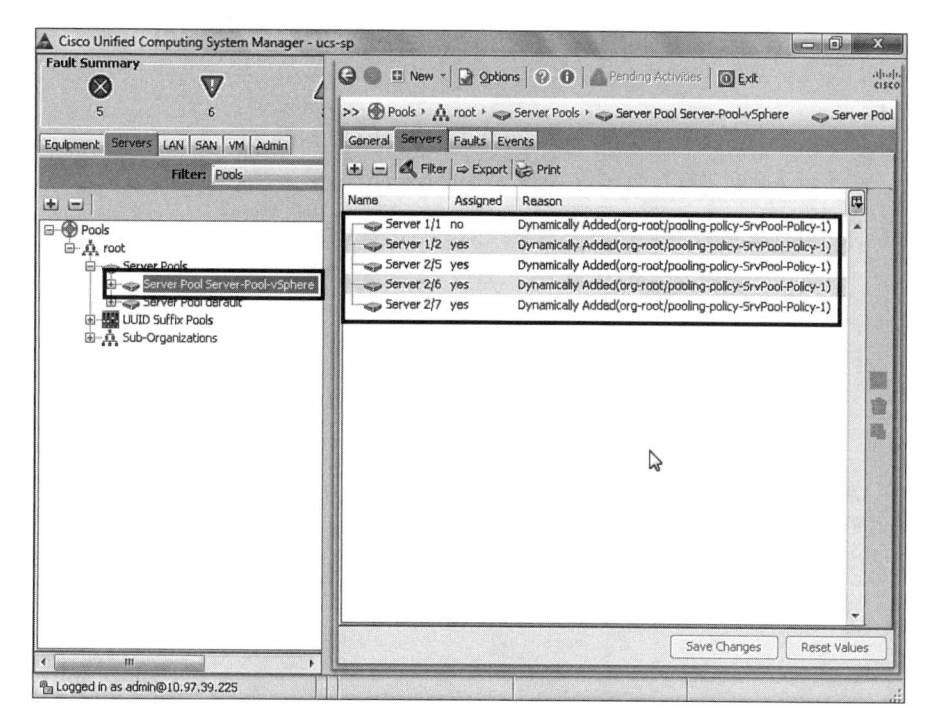

Figure 14-64 *SrvPool-Policy-1 Automatically Assigned Servers*

In Figure 14-64, all five servers from the UCS domain fit right into the qualification policy. However, only server 1/1 is currently not associated with a service profile.

Finally, to deploy automatic service profile association, you assign Server-Pool-vSphere to a service profile template, as Figure 14-65 demonstrates for Template-1.

As highlighted in Figure 14-65, you can also change the server power state to Up after the association. Hence, immediately after the service profile association, the server will automatically boot.

And as Figure 14-66 shows, FromTemplate-1-SP2 was automatically associated to the last available server on Server-Pool-vSphere (which is server 1/1).

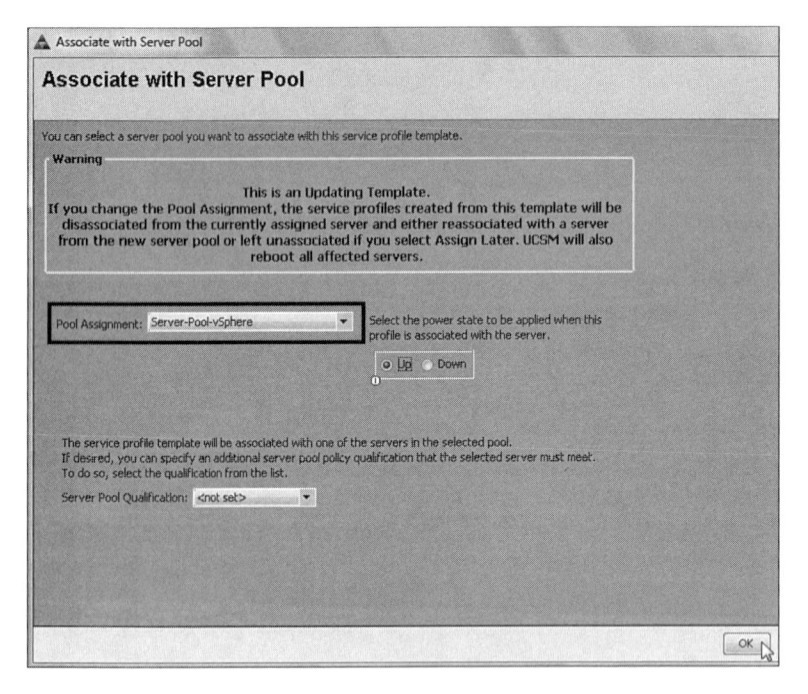

Figure 14-65 *Changing Template-1 Server Association*

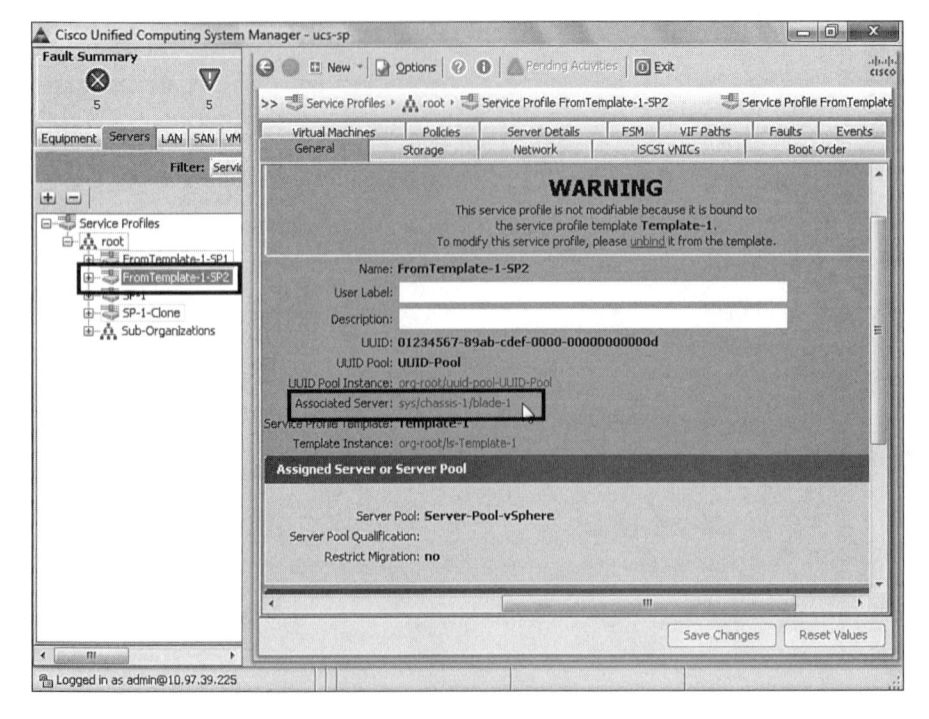

Figure 14-66 *FromTemplate-1-SP2 Association*

From this moment on, you can expect that if other UCS servers are included in the pool, FromTemplate-1-SP1 (and additional service profiles created from Template-1) will also be automatically associated to the newly added servers.

Use Case: Seasonal Workloads

During the last few years, your little consulting firm has transformed itself into a very lucrative and well-respected IT services company. At this time, you are close to hiring your 500th employee, who will join a team of consultants, instructors, technicians, and administrative staff.

To better serve your customers, your company owns a small but very decent data center within your headquarters building. Currently, your disaster recovery site is located at a service provider data center.

Considering that one of your company cultural mottos is "walk the talk" it is not even questioned that the data center must work with the same level of technology that you have been preaching about in projects, conferences, and blogs.

On one given morning, your Chief Information Officer, who manages a very slim team of two people, has approached you with the physical server requirements for the next fiscal year (which coincides with the calendar year). As he elaborates, the company basically deploys four types of physical servers:

- **Enterprise Resource Planning (ERP):** It is the heart of your company, managing all the economic operations. Each server also deploys an instance of a database cluster.

- **E-mail:** A very weird application that simultaneously serves business, silly entertainment, and pure boredom.

- **E-learning:** A multimedia application that provides online training sessions for external customers. Its content is internally generated because it is 100 percent based on the experience of your technical team.

- **Virtualization:** Servers that host all other applications from the company, especially test servers from the employees.

To improve standardization and optimized operations within the data center, all servers must be identical in size and model. Also, according to his previous experiences in other IT environments, the quantity of servers is usually derived from the maximum number of servers for each workload, plus one spare server per server farm. Hence, this traditional capacity planning method results in a grand total of 31 servers (considering that ERP, E-mail, E-learning, and virtualization, respectively, will reach peaks of six, three, ten, and eight servers in the next year).

However, both of you are aware of the flexibility and agility that UCS service profiles can bring to a server environment. An as a result, you decide to explore the workload seasonality to your advantage.

During the meeting, your CIO explains that the ERP system normally needs two servers throughout the fiscal year and three at end of quarters (March, June, and September), but that six will be necessary during the last month of the fiscal year (December). E-mail will require three servers during the year and only two during the vacation months (January and July). E-learning trainings are usually more popular in months after customer budget closure (January, February, July, and August), when ten servers will be necessary and the remaining months need about three servers. Finally, the virtualization servers will require six servers during the first three quarters and eight during the last quarter. He calculates that only two virtualized servers will be used during the vacation months.

As a visual aid, the number of servers per application per month is detailed in Table 14-3.

Table 14-3 *Seasonal Applications Server Requirements*

Application	J	F	M	A	M	J	J	A	S	O	N	D
ERP	2	2	3	2	2	3	2	2	3	2	2	6
E-mail	2	3	3	3	3	3	2	3	3	3	3	3
E-learning	10	10	3	3	3	3	10	10	3	3	3	3
Virtualization	2	6	6	6	6	6	2	6	6	8	8	8
Total	16	21	15	14	14	15	16	21	15	16	16	20

With the help of Table 14-3, both of you arrive at the conclusion that the maximum number of simultaneous servers your company really requires during a month is 21 (in February and August). Hence, with an additional pair of servers to form a shared pool of spare servers for all applications, it is possible to support all applications with a set of 23 servers (saving your company money that would be spent on eight more servers).

Figure 14-67 depicts how UCS Manager can deploy the service profiles that will be deployed during the next year.

With the structure shown in Figure 14-67, 27 service profiles will be built to define all the servers that can be activated and deactivated according to the demand described in Table 14-3 (or to a spare server after a hardware failure). Additionally, boot LUNs will be provisioned on a storage array to deploy stateless computing for all 27 service profiles.

To further increase standardization and governance in the data center, updating templates will be used to create service profiles from the same application, and maintenance policies will be used to automate the provisioning (and unprovisioning) of each workload.

After he realizes that these monthly maintenance windows will only take a couple of minutes, you both laugh, remembering the good old times of all-night server installations, bad pizza, and CD-ROM suitcases.

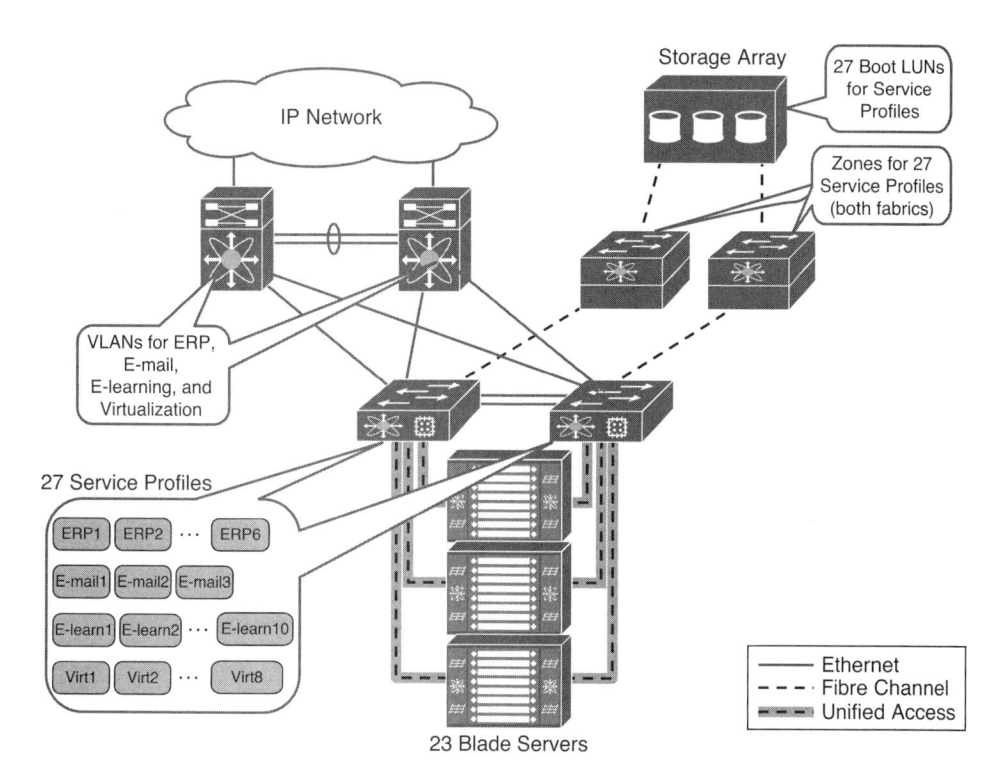

Figure 14-67 *UCS Project for Your Environment*

Summary

In this chapter, you learned the following:

- In traditional data center architectures, server provisioning is a complex and time-consuming operation.

- Server provisioning involves tasks distributed between the server domain (such as BIOS settings and software installation) and the infrastructure domain (such as access interface configuration and SAN zoning).

- Cisco Unified Computing System consolidates several infrastructure and server operations into one management domain.

- Service profiles leverage the UCS architecture, grouping multiple server provisioning tasks under the same point of control, which can be assigned to a server through a single operation.

- A service profile can abstract the server hardware identifiers (such as UUIDs, WWNs, and MAC addresses), and hardware settings and firmware versions (for adapters and BIOS, for example) among servers in a Unified Computing System.

- Service profiles allow the implementation of stateless computing, where the server hardware can be made completely transparent to the operating system and applications that run on it.

- Policies, cloning, pools, and templates can drastically reduce the server provisioning time to market and improve standardization in a data center.

Figure 14-68 graphically summarizes how service profiles can be understood from a logical perspective.

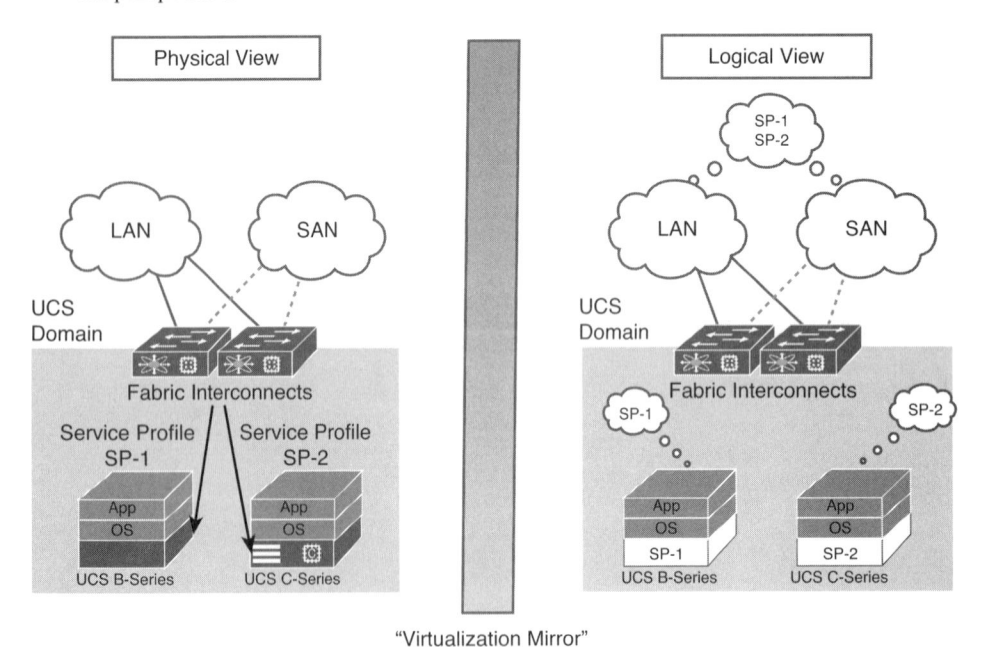

Figure 14-68 *Through the Virtualization Mirror*

Further Reading

Gai, Silvano, Salli, Tommi, and Andersson, Roger. *Cisco Unified Computing Architecture (UCS)*. Cisco Press, 2010.

Cisco Unified Computing

www.cisco.com/go/ucs

Chapter 15

Transcending the Rack

"You cannot solve a problem with the same level of consciousness that created it."
(Carl Gustav Jung)

This chapter addresses two Cisco virtual networking solutions, Nexus 1000V and Virtual Machine Fabric Extender (VM-FEX), and will explain how both connectivity models can bring intelligence and simplicity to server virtualization environments. It contains the following topics:

- Introduction to Virtual Networking
- Cisco Nexus 1000V Architecture
- Deploying Nexus 1000V
- NX-OS Features in the Virtual World
- Online Migrations and Nexus 1000V
- Virtual Extensible Local Area Networks
- Introducing Virtual Machine Fabric Extender
- Use Case: Data Center Merging

Table 15-1 places Nexus 1000V and VM-FEX in the virtualization taxonomy described in Chapter 1, "Virtualization History and Definitions."

Table 15-1 *Nexus 1000V and VM-FEX Virtualization Classification*

Virtualization Characteristics	Nexus 1000V	VM-FEX
Emulation	Ethernet switch	Fabric Extender
Type	Abstraction	Abstraction
Sub-type	Structural	Structural
Scalability	Software version-dependent[1]	Hardware and software version dependent[2]
Technology area	Server	Server
Subarea	Operating system (Type 1 hypervisor)	Hardware
Advantages	Dynamic provisioning, NX-OS features, and integration with physical networking	Dynamic provisioning, networking consolidation, I/O performance (hypervisor bypass)

[1] Refer to Appendix A, "Cisco Data Center Portfolio," for more details and Nexus 1000V online documentation for updated information.

[2] Refer to Cisco UCS and Nexus 5500 and 6000 switches product documentation for updated information.

While server virtualization has increased resource utilization, speed, and automation in computing environments, it has also preserved several operational processes from bare-metal server installations. This decision originally intended to leverage existent knowledge on physical servers to virtual machines.

VMware, the leading x86 server virtualization vendor, introduced virtual switches back in the early 2000s. Besides defining how virtual machines can communicate with each other and with external resources, VMware also kick-started an entirely new area of networking, which is currently referred to as *virtual networking*.

Collaborating actively with VMware, Cisco has applied its experience to innovate virtual networking with the Nexus 1000V and VM-FEX. This chapter will discuss both Cisco solutions and their main concepts and characteristics.

Introduction to Virtual Networking

In its early stages of development, server virtualization in x86 environments faced an interesting challenge: *How can multiple virtual machines share the same physical network interface card (NIC)?*

Figure 15-1 illustrates this particular challenge.

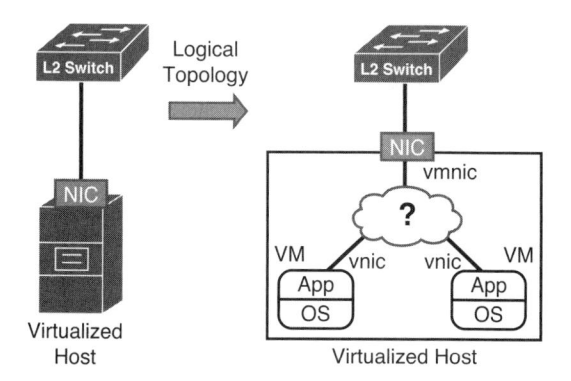

Figure 15-1 *Virtual Machine Networking Challenge*

In the figure, both virtual machines (VMs) should ideally

- Share the physical NIC to communicate with resources connected to the Layer 2 switch
- Communicate with each other through the same broadcast domain

Considering that these VMs are emulating physical servers, they have virtual NICs (vnics) and their recurring elements, such as IP addresses and software drivers. Consequently, a VM should not fully control the standard physical NIC without making this resource unavailable for other VMs. Actually, it would be ideal if this important shared resource were controlled by the hypervisor itself (as other resources such as CPU and memory).

In another analysis, imagine the situation where the hypervisor would carelessly forward VM traffic to the physical network (and vice versa). In this theoretical scenario, Ethernet communication between the VMs would be impossible because the upstream Layer 2 switch could not forward a frame to the same interface on which it was received.

VMware has ingeniously solved this ruse with the creation of the Virtual Switch (vSwitch), which is a hypervisor element that emulates the behavior a Layer 2 switch. In summary, the vSwitch provides access ports to the virtual machine vnics and uplinks to the host physical NICs (or as VMware defines, vmnics). It also deploys IEEE 802.1Q VLAN tagging and a MAC address table to forward Ethernet frames based on their destination MAC addresses.

Figure 15-2 further illustrates the vSwitch concept.

The VMware vSwitch also offers exclusive definitions such as *port group*. This network label defines common connectivity characteristics that can be used by virtual or physical adapters. For example, a port group can contain

- A VLAN identifier
- Security properties (such as promiscuous mode and VM MAC address change detection)

- Traffic shaping (defining average bandwidth, peak bandwidth, and burst size)
- Physical NIC teaming (specifying vmnic load balancing, network failover detection, switch notification, failback, and fail order)

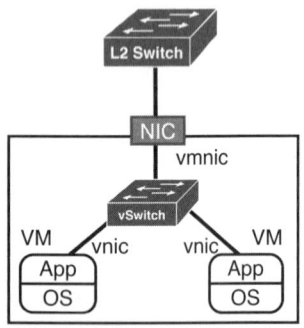

Figure 15-2 *VMware Virtual Switch*

When a port group is assigned to a vnic, the VM carries its characteristics regardless of the physical server it is hosted on. Therefore, in contrast with physical switches, the device interface (vnic) owns the connectivity parameters, instead of the switch port.

Note The VMware standard vSwitch provides two unusual values for port group VLAN identifiers: VLAN ID 0 (which disables any tagging inside the vSwitch) and VLAN ID 4095 (which permits the VM to control the VLAN tags within their vnics).

Virtual Switch Challenges

From a pure networking perspective, the vSwitch transformed the physical access port into an uplink. And without a doubt, it completely redefined the data center network perimeter. However, as more virtualized servers were deployed in data centers, vSwitches presented additional challenges to the daily tasks of their operational teams.

Operational scalability was one of these first difficulties. As online migration of VMs (vMotion) became a "killer app" within virtualization environments, administrators were forced to configure every port group in every host vSwitch. And naturally, as these environments scaled, errors could easily occur.

Network integration was another obstacle found with the extensive use of vSwitches. For example:

- Access ports from physical and virtual servers running the same application could not share the same network settings.

- Because the networking team was basically controlling IEEE 802.1Q uplinks to the virtualized hosts, and not the access ports, it was very difficult to provide the same level of perimeter security for physical and virtual networks.

- The network team could not use its regular management and monitoring tools to obtain information about the traffic within the vSwitch.

- Collaboration between virtualization and networking teams was based on manual processes such as emails, and spreadsheets.

In 2009, VMware released the concept of a Distributed Virtual Switch (DVS), which addressed the operational scalability challenge. Essentially, a DVS allows the simultaneous creation of port groups on multiple hosts as if they are connected to the same vSwitch.

DVS also includes several enhancements over the standard vSwitch, such as private VLANs and third-party integration with other vendors. Using such programming interfaces, Cisco and VMware collaborated closely to provide the solution for the networking integration vSwitch challenge.

Cisco Nexus 1000V Architecture

The Cisco Nexus 1000V switch was primarily conceived to be a non-disruptive and extensible virtual networking platform. Although Nexus 1000V does not share code base with VMware DVS, it leverages the the DVS Application Programmable Interface (API) from VMware vCenter to deploy NX-OS features in server virtualization environments.

From a management plane point of view, Nexus 1000V simultaneously offers

- A DVS management interface for virtualization administrators

- An NX-OS management experience (command-line interface and graphical user interface with DCNM-LAN) for network administrators

Note The minimum requirements for Nexus 1000V installation are VMware vSphere version 4.0 or later and 1-Gbps Ethernet connections (or higher).

Nexus 1000V has two basic components: the *Virtual Supervisor Module (VSM)* and the *Virtual Ethernet Module (VEM)*. The Nexus 1000V VEM is a lightweight software component that runs within the hypervisor kernel (only one VEM is supported per physical host). Because it deploys the Nexus 1000V data plane, VM traffic can be completely handled by a VEM instance, including inter-VM frames and Ethernet traffic between a VM and external resources.

Both control and management planes of the Nexus 1000V reside on the VSM, which executes its own version of NX-OS.

> **Tip** It is completely valid to compare the Nexus 1000V VSM to a Nexus 7000 supervisor module and a VEM to an I/O linecard from such switch.

There are two methods to host a VSM:

- As a standard virtual machine on a virtualized host
- As a "virtual blade" on dedicated Nexus 1010 or 1100 Virtual Services Appliances (VSA)

This choice of VSM hosting really depends on the independency from the server virtualization infrastructure you want to offer the VSMs. While a VSM-as-VM can inherit most capabilities from a virtualization cluster (such as online migration and VM templates), as a virtual blade, it can be protected from problems that might occur within this environment.

Like any supervisor module, the VSM monitors the states of all switch elements, including interfaces and MAC address table. In fact, as Nexus 7000 and MDS platforms, Nexus 1000V employs the very same Message and Transaction System (MTS) and Asynchronous Inter-Process Communication (AIPC) as "backplane protocols."

The Nexus 1000V VSM also communicates with a virtualization management tool (VM manager), such as the VMware vCenter. This connection between management domains provides configuration synchronization and automation between networking and server virtualization administration domains.

The VSM virtual machine (or virtual blade) has three Ethernet interfaces:

- **Control (Network Adapter 1):** Responsible for the communication with another VSM and the configuration of the VEMs.
- **Management (Network Adapter 2):** Related to the management interface (mgmt0) on physical switches. It is used for system login and communication with VMware vCenter server.
- **Packet (Network Adapter 3):** Used when the VEM must send packets to the VSM to be further analyzed (for example, CDP, LACP, IGMP snooping, SNMP, and NetFlow).

Nexus 1000V can deploy active-standby redundancy with two different VSMs. With this option, both modules remain constantly synchronizing each other to provide stateful failover in the event of an active VSM failure.

The VSM-to-VSM "heartbeat" communication enables the detection of VSMs in the same broadcast domain. In a Nexus 1000V implementation, the first VSM to boot declares itself as active, while a detection of a prior VSM (with the same configured domain) automatically puts the module into standby state.

After both VSMs negotiate their state, they transmit unicast heartbeat messages to each other at each second. Periods without the detection of these messages can characterize a degraded communication state (3 seconds) or loss of communication (6 seconds), when theoretically the standby VSM should be activated. "Split-brain" situations are avoided with two channels of communication between VSMs (which are the control and management interfaces).

Note Starting with NX-OS version 4.2(1)SV2(1.1), Nexus 1000V supports split active and standby VSMs across two data centers (with maximum latency of 10 milliseconds) to implement control plane high availability for extended virtualization clusters.

The VSM maintains a 2-second heartbeat with each VEM with a timeout of six seconds before loss of connectivity between VSM and VEM is declared. Notwithstanding, a VEMs does not depend on this connectivity with the VSM to perform traffic switching. In truth, these data plane modules are capable of running the last good configuration state received from a lost VSM pair.

Note The maximum latency between VSMs and VEMs is 100 milliseconds. Therefore, a VSM can potentially control virtual machine traffic outside the data center (branch offices, for example).

Nexus 1000V Communication Modes

There are two available options to implement the communication between the active VSM and the VEMs on a Nexus 1000V. They are as follows:

- **Layer 2 control mode:** The VSM control interface shares broadcast domains (VLANs) with the VEMs.

- **Layer 3 control mode:** The VEMs and the VSM can belong to different IP subnets. Each VEM requires a designated *VMkernel interface (vmknic)* to communicate with the VSM.

Layer 2 control mode was originally available on the first released version of Nexus 1000V. Then, it was very common to find designs where each VSM would be connected to three different broadcast domains (control, management, and packet VLANs). In those scenarios, control and packet VLANs demanded special attention from the networking team because all networking devices between the active VSM and the VEMs should contain these VLANs.

To increase simplicity, it became a best practice to consolidate control and packet traffic in the same VLAN. And in some cases, even management traffic could be included in such a consolidated VLAN.

Nevertheless, at the time of this writing, Cisco recommends Layer 3 control mode for most Nexus 1000V deployments. This recommendation is based on the fact that this mode requires less configuration tasks in the physical networking infrastructure, simplifying the switch deployment.

Note Nevertheless, in both modes, the active and standby VSM control interfaces should always be connected to the same VLAN.

Port Profiles and Dynamic Interface Provisioning

A single-instance Nexus 1000V can implement thousands of interfaces, which could potentially turn port configuration into an operational nightmare. Fortunately, through a mechanism called *port profile*, Nexus 1000V avoids this situation.

A port profile can be defined as a collection of interface-level configuration commands that are combined to create a complete network policy. With port profiles, a network administrator can optimize and standardize the configuration of interfaces in a switch.

Port profiles are not exclusive to Nexus 1000V. They are also present on other NX-OS devices and, in fact, share several similarities with Smart Port Macros from Catalyst switches.

To illustrate the use of these mechanisms on a physical switch, Example 15-1 details the creation of a port profile for Ethernet interfaces that will be connected to vSphere hosts.

Example 15-1 *Creating a Port Profile on a Nexus 5000 Switch*

```
N5K-A(config)# port-profile type ethernet VSPHERE-HOST
! Defining the commands of the port profile
N5K-A(config-port-prof)# switchport mode trunk
N5K-A(config-port-prof)# switchport trunk allowed vlan 200-205
N5K-A(config-port-prof)# no shutdown
! Enabling the use of this port profile on available interfaces
N5K-A(config-port-prof)# state enabled
```

Note Depending on the NX-OS platform, a port profile for other types of interfaces, such as PortChannel, Switch Virtual Interfaces (SVI), loopback, and tunnel, can also be created.

After a port profile is enabled, an interface or a group of interfaces can inherit its configuration, as demonstrated in Example 15-2.

Example 15-2 *Inheriting Port Profile VSPHERE-HOST*

```
! Interfaces Ethernet 1/10 to 1/13 will receive the configuration defined in port
profile VSPHERE-HOST
N5K-A(config-if)# interface ethernet 1/10-13
N5K-A(config-if-range)# inherit port-profile VSPHERE-HOST
! Displaying the switching characteristics of interface Ethernet 1/10
N5K-A(config-if-range)# show interface ethernet 1/10 switchport
Name: Ethernet1/10
  Switchport: Enabled
  Switchport Monitor: Not enabled
  Operational Mode: trunk
  Access Mode VLAN: 1 (default)
  Trunking Native Mode VLAN: 1 (default)
  Trunking VLANs Allowed: 200-205
[output suppressed]
```

In Example 15-2, you can see how port profiles can optimize the task of configuring multiple interfaces at the same time. Actually, port profiles can drastically reduce the configuration efforts in a switch because a change in a profile is reflected on all interfaces that inherit its configuration. Notwithstanding, it is also possible to change the settings of a single port (the most specific configuration always takes priority).

In the Nexus 1000V architecture, the VSM connection to vCenter provides a one-to-one relationship between a port profile and a port group. Consequently, the port profile inheritance is automatically defined when the vCenter administrator assigns a port group to a vmnic, vmknic, or vnic.

Figure 15-3 further details the Nexus 1000V interface configuration flow.

As Figure 15-3 illustrates, the connection between the active VSM and vCenter server enables

- The automatic creation of a DVS port group after a port profile is correctly configured in the VSM

- The automatic provisioning of VEM interfaces after this port group is assigned to a vnic, vmnic, or VMkernel interface (vmknic), such as the vSphere host management interface

At the bottom of Figure 15-3, you can also see both types of interfaces that are supported on a VEM: **Ethernet interfaces** for physical adapters (vmnics) and **virtual Ethernet (vEthernet) interfaces** to be used on virtual adapters (vnics and vmknics). Each of these interfaces inherits the characteristics of port profiles from the same type.

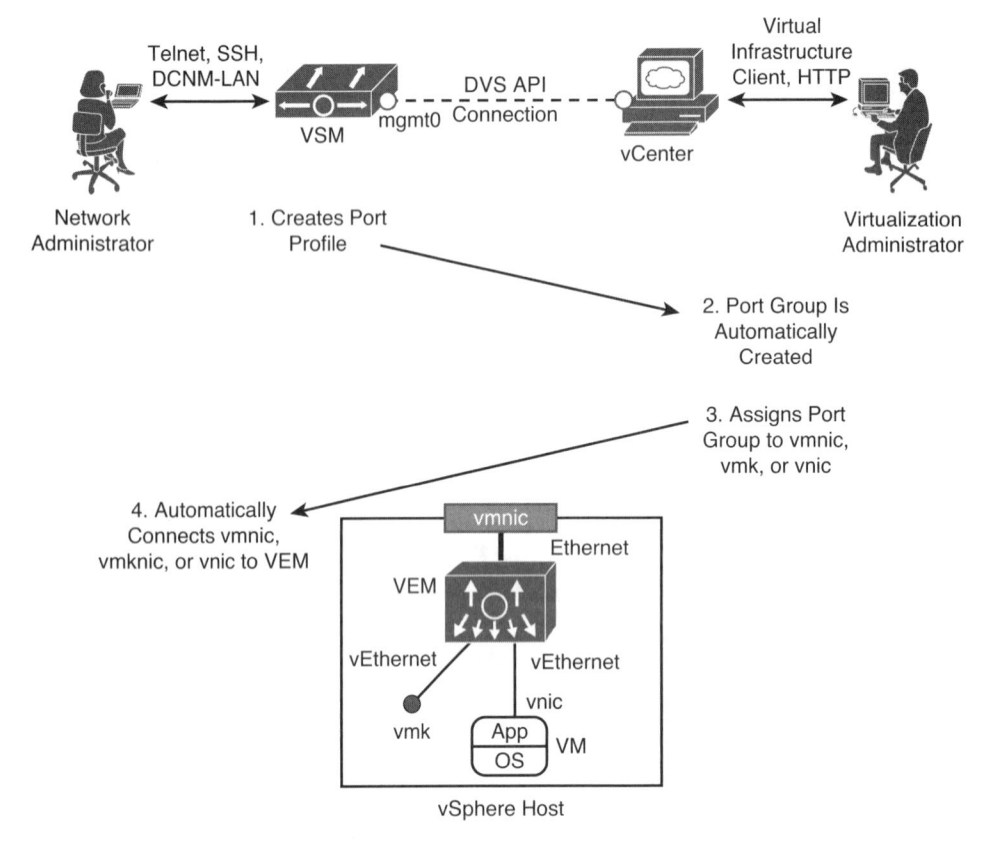

Figure 15-3 *Nexus 1000V Interface Configuration Flow*

With this automatic and collaborative model, Nexus 1000V preserves the interface-provisioning process for the vCenter administrator, where the assignment of a port group to an interface generates the creation of a DVS port. And for the network administrator, Nexus 1000V port profiles are created using the same commands and policies that are available on physical switches.

Deploying Nexus 1000V

Nexus 1000V can be installed on a virtualization structure through different procedures. However, my intention in this section is not to enlist every single Nexus 1000V deployment option. Instead, I will describe a sample installation and highlight concepts that can explain the how this virtual switch works.

As usual, I have prepared a real structure to develop the configurations contained in this chapter. Figure 15-4 depicts the physical view of this topology.

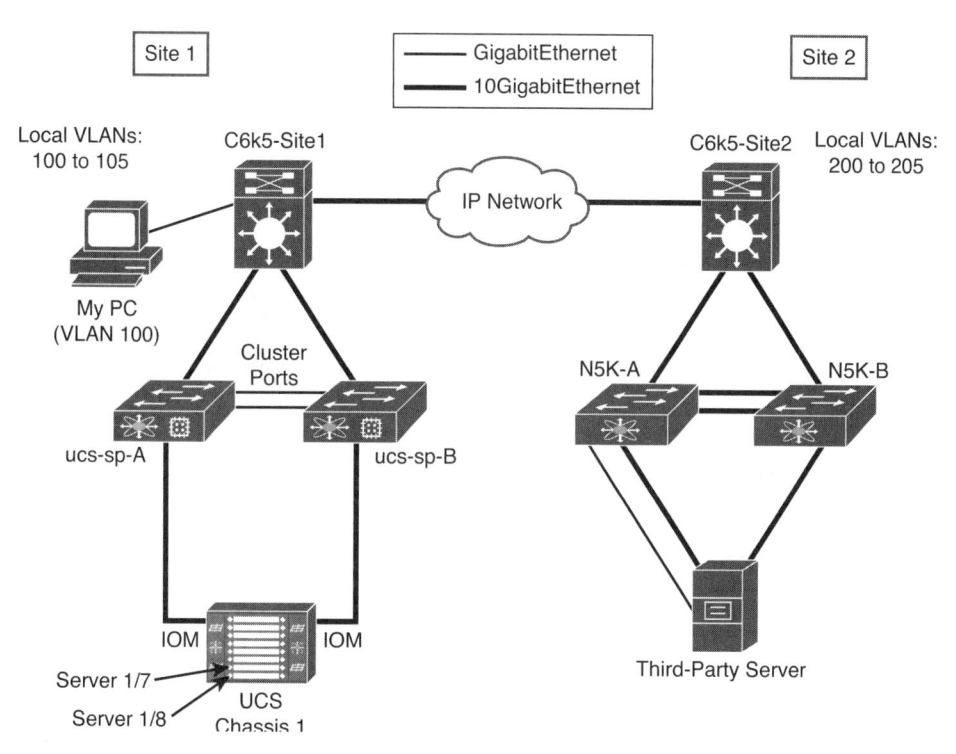

Figure 15-4 *Topology Physical Network View*

As portrayed in Figure 15-4, three servers will be used in our Nexus 1000V deployment: two UCS B-series blade servers on site 1 and a third-party server on site 2.

Although all physical connections are depicted in Figure 15-4, the way this topology is presented is clearly not suitable for the study of virtual connectivity. As demonstrated in previous figures, a different style of drawing is required for this intent. Therefore, I present Figure 15-5, which contains a virtual networking perspective of the same topology.

As Figure 15-5 displays, a VMware vSphere infrastructure is already established in the topology, with three hosts (host10, host11, and host20) and vCenter deployed as a virtual machine running on host10 on site 1. Additionally, every host already has two VMkernel interfaces:

- **vmk0:** Implements host management.
- **vmk1:** Permits the exchange of memory state with another host to provide online migration of VMs (vMotion).

The topology also defines two independent sites that are separated by a Layer 3 network. Because each site deploys distinct local VLANs, all IP addresses from virtual and physical interfaces from distinct sites are located in different IP subnets.

668 Data Center Virtualization Fundamentals

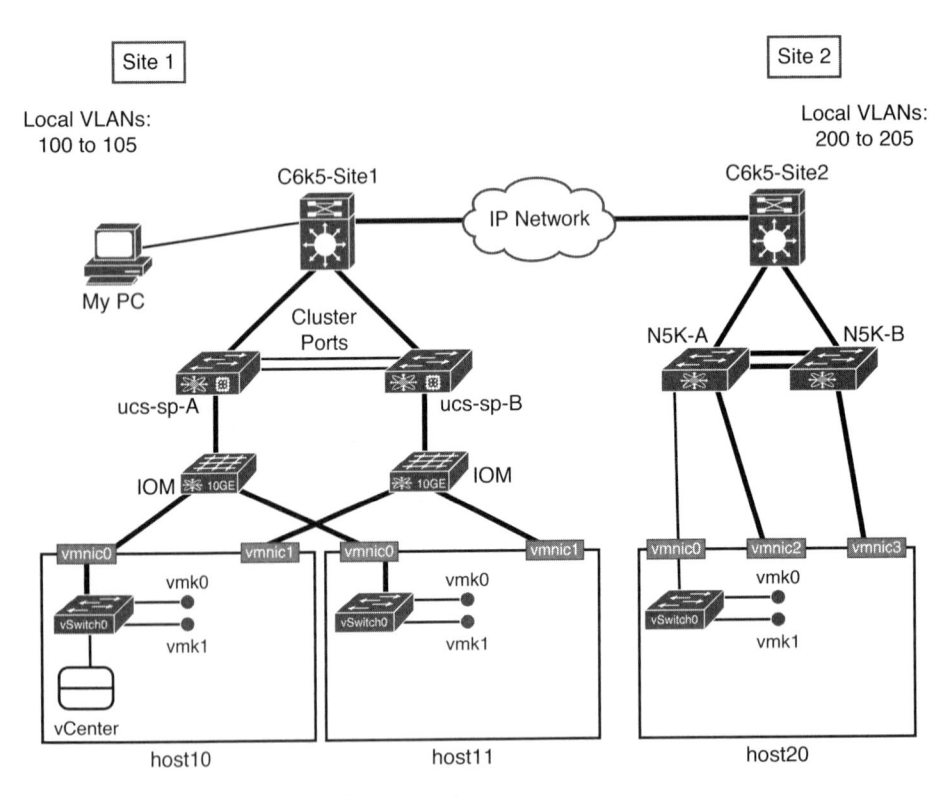

Figure 15-5 *Virtual Networking Topology*

Table 15-2 summarizes the network settings for all adapters and interfaces from the topology depicted in Figure 15-5.

Table 15-2 *Virtualization Cluster IP Addresses*

Device	Interface	VLAN	IP Address	vSwitch Port Group
host10	vmk0	100	192.168.100.10/24	Management
host10	vmk1	101	192.168.101.10/24	vMotion
host11	vmk0	100	192.168.100.11/24	Management
host11	vmk1	101	192.168.101.11/24	vMotion
host20	vmk0	200	192.168.200.20/24	Management
host20	vmk1	201	192.168.201.20/24	vMotion
vCenter	vnic0	100	192.168.100.2/24	Management
C6K5-Site1	SVI 100	100	192.168.100.1/24	—
C6K5-Site1	SVI 101	101	192.168.101.1/24	—
C6K5-Site2	SVI 200	200	192.168.200.1/24	—
C6K5-Site2	SVI 201	201	192.168.201.1/24	—

> **Tip** The Switched Virtual Interfaces (SVI) on both Catalyst 6500 switches work as default gateways for hosts and VMs in each site VLAN.

Figure 15-6 demonstrates the current networking configuration of host10, as seen from vCenter.

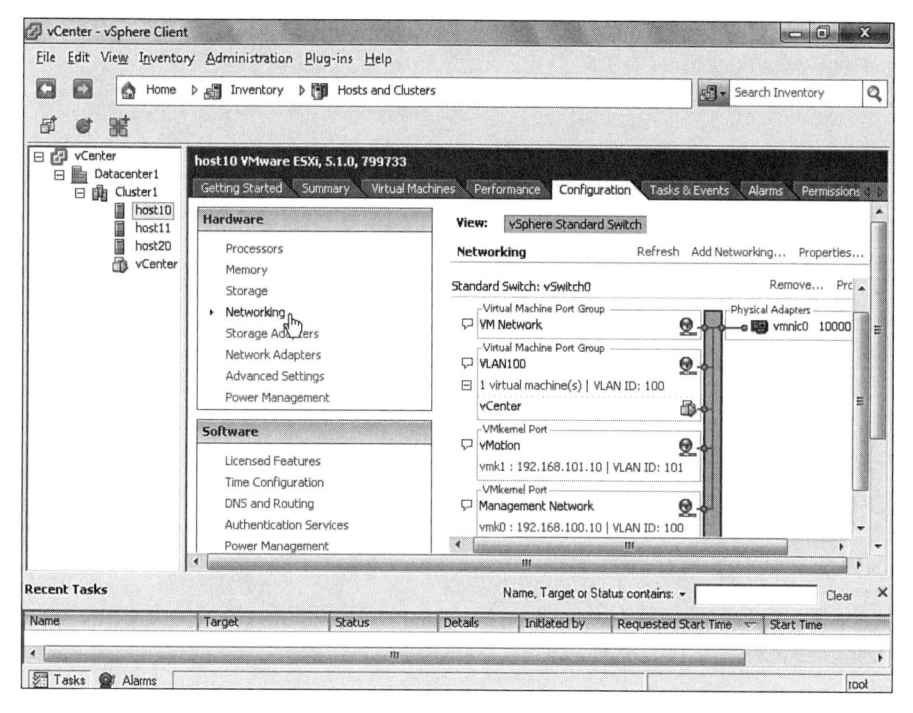

Figure 15-6 *host10 vSwitch Configuration*

Figure 15-6 also shows that the hosts and virtual machine are contained within two vSphere definitions:

- **Datacenter1:** This component is basically a repository of objects such as hosts, VMs, data stores, and virtual switches.
- **Cluster1:** This element encompasses a set of hosts that can share vSphere features such as Dynamic Resource Scheduling and vMotion between different processor architectures.

For the Nexus 1000V installation, I will use its **Installer app**, which is a Java application that can process a complete Nexus 1000V deployment with ease and visibility. The Installer app, and all necessary files for the installation, can be downloaded from www.cisco.com in a single ZIP file.

Figure 15-7 depicts the first screen from the Nexus 1000V Installer app on my personal computer.

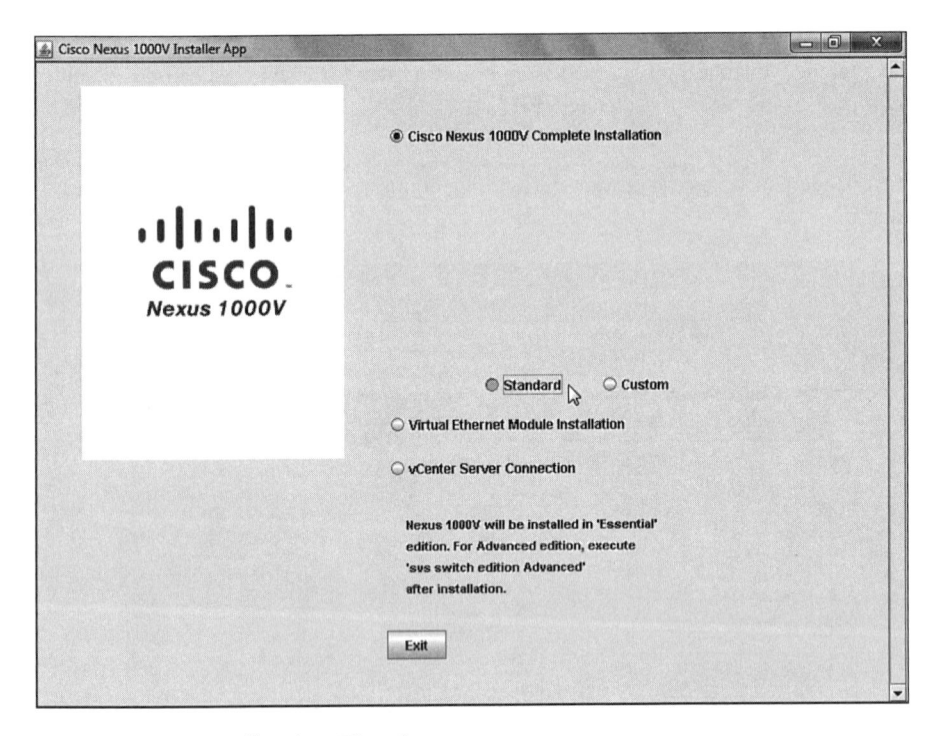

Figure 15-7 *Installer App First Screen*

At this screen, the app can perform

- A Nexus 1000V complete installation, including the deployment of VSMs, vCenter connection, and VEM installation
- A VEM installation in a host or set of hosts
- The VSM connection to vCenter

Selecting the first option, the app presents a wizard that requests parameters for the installation.

Although the app custom installation option permits a wider variety of parameters, I have chosen the standard mode because it is very suitable for our intended scenario. Through the standard installation, only Layer 3 communication mode is available between VSM and VEMs, all VSM interfaces will share the same VLAN, and the switch host name will share the name with the VSM virtual machine.

Figure 15-8 highlights installation parameters for both VSMs.

As Figure 15-8 shows, the app permits you to browse vCenter to select objects for the VSM installation, such as the hosts and data stores (storage volumes) that will host each VSM. The app also allows the following definitions:

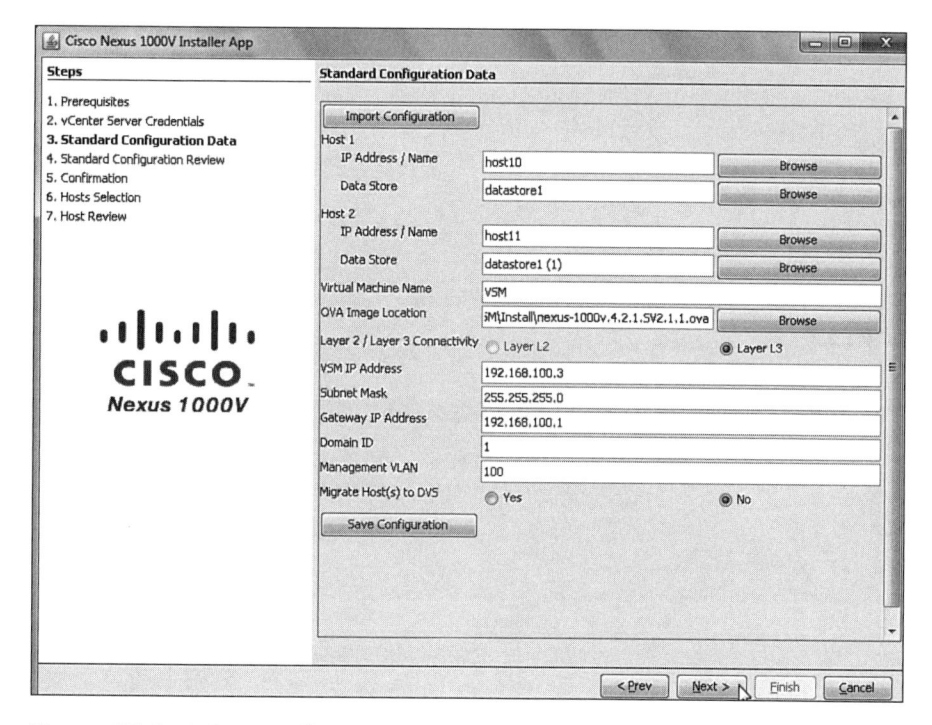

Figure 15-8 *VSM Installation Parameters*

- VSM virtual machine name (which is "VSM").

- Open Virtualization Appliance (OVA) file location at my PC.

- VSM IP address (192.168.100.3), subnet mask (255.255.255.0), and default gateway (192.168.100.1). Only the active VSM answers to traffic destined to this IP address.

- VSM domain ID (1), which differentiates multiple Nexus 1000V installations whose pair of VSMs share the same broadcast domains.

- Consolidated VLAN where the VSMs will connect their management, control, and packet interfaces (VLAN 100).

- Whether the app should insert hosts into Nexus 1000V (I have chosen "no" to further detail this procedure later).

After both VSMs are installed on host10 and host11, and the connection to vCenter is established, the Installer app asks whether more modules (VEMs) should be added to your Nexus 1000V. Figure 15-9 demonstrates that the app can also install *vSphere Installation Bundle* (VIB) files to selected hosts. These files enclose the VEM processes that will be executed at kernel level at each host.

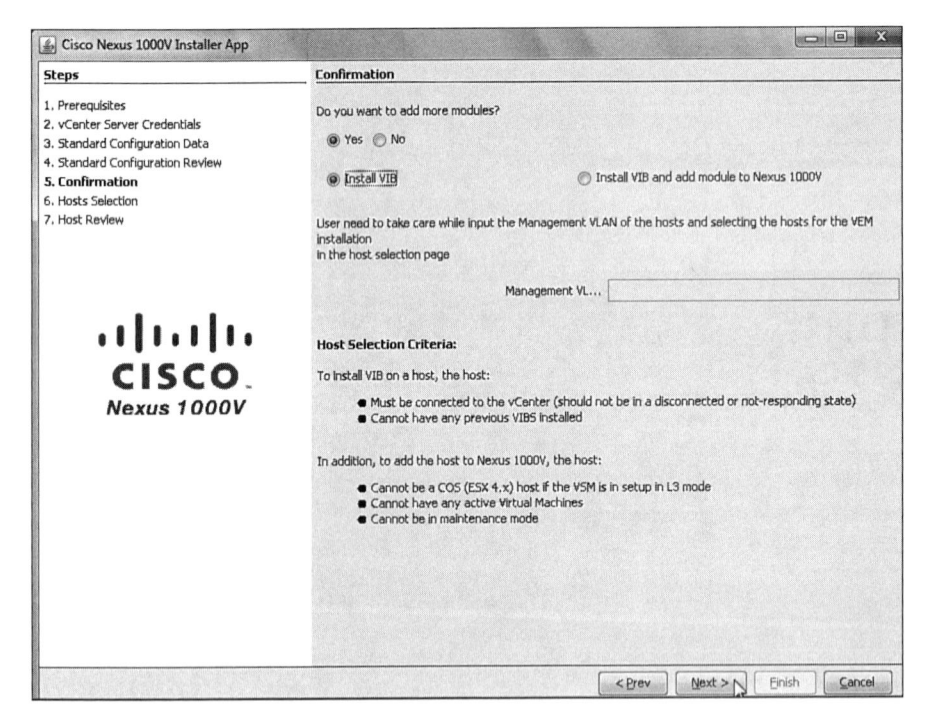

Figure 15-9 *VEM Installation*

Tip The app requires that no VM is active on a host while the VIB file is being installed. Because vCenter is a VM in our scenario, I have used vMotion to transport it out of the host while the VEM installation was being performed.

During the installation process, the app automatically selected the correct VIB file that is compatible with the vSphere version installed on the hosts.

After the Installer app wraps up completely, it is possible to observe how it has modified our topology. For example, Figure 15-10 shows exactly how VSM-1 is connected to vSwitch0 on host10.

As shown in the figure, the VSM-1 interfaces are connected to vSwitch0 through two port groups in VLAN 100: **n1kv-ctrl** (which is assigned to the control and packet interfaces) and **n1kv-mgmt** (which is assigned to the management interface).

Figure 15-11 summarizes the state of the topology after the aforementioned installation procedures.

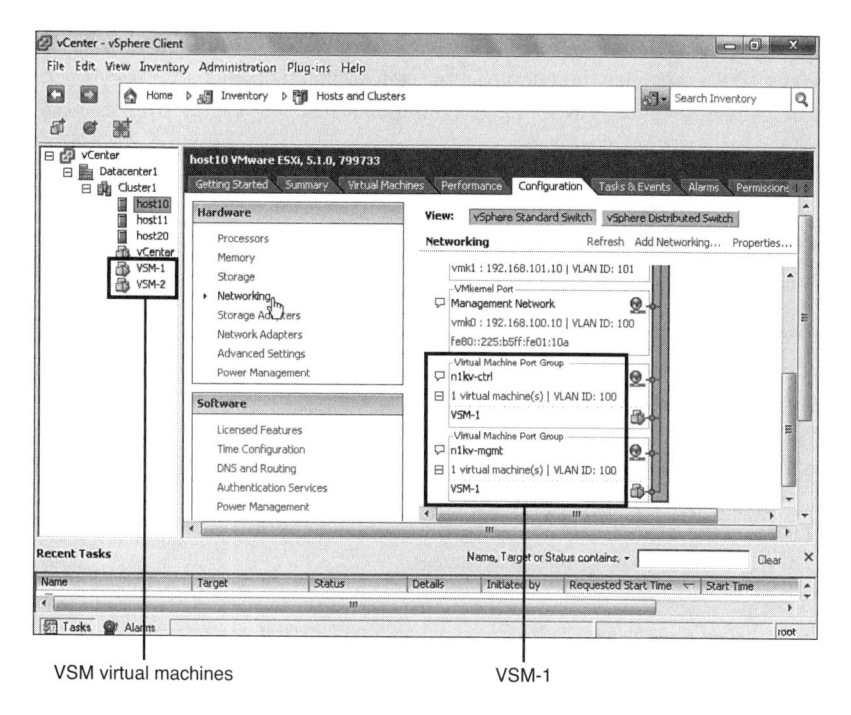

Figure 15-10 *host10 vSwitch Configuration*

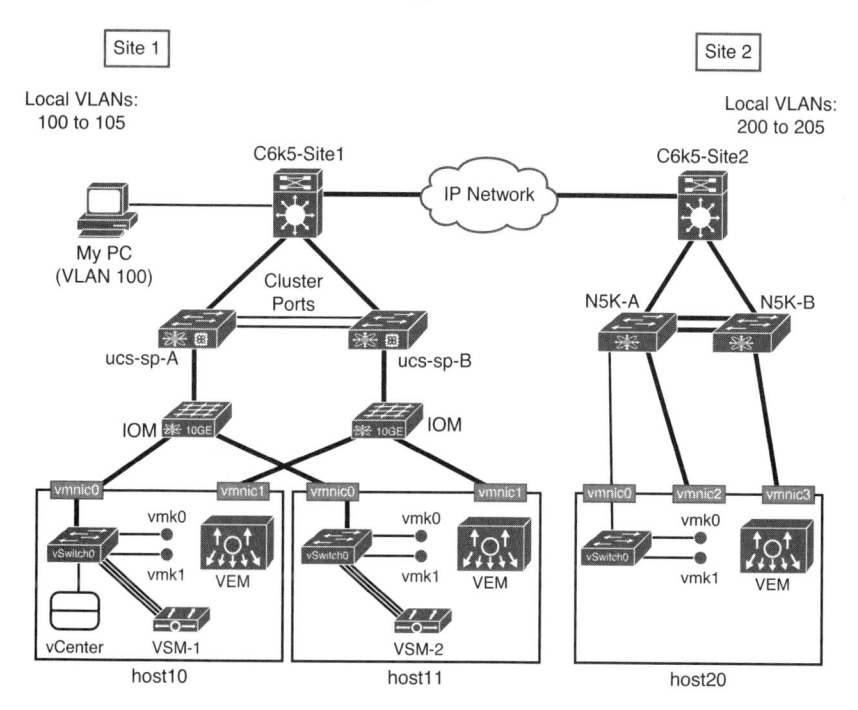

Figure 15-11 *Virtual Networking Topology After VIB Files Installation*

As you can see in Figure 15-11, even if the VEMs are installed on all hosts, they are not yet part of Nexus 1000V because they do not share any connectivity with the VSMs yet. Nevertheless, the VSMs are already working as a redundant pair, as Example 15-3 demonstrates.

Example 15-3 *SSH to the Active VSM*

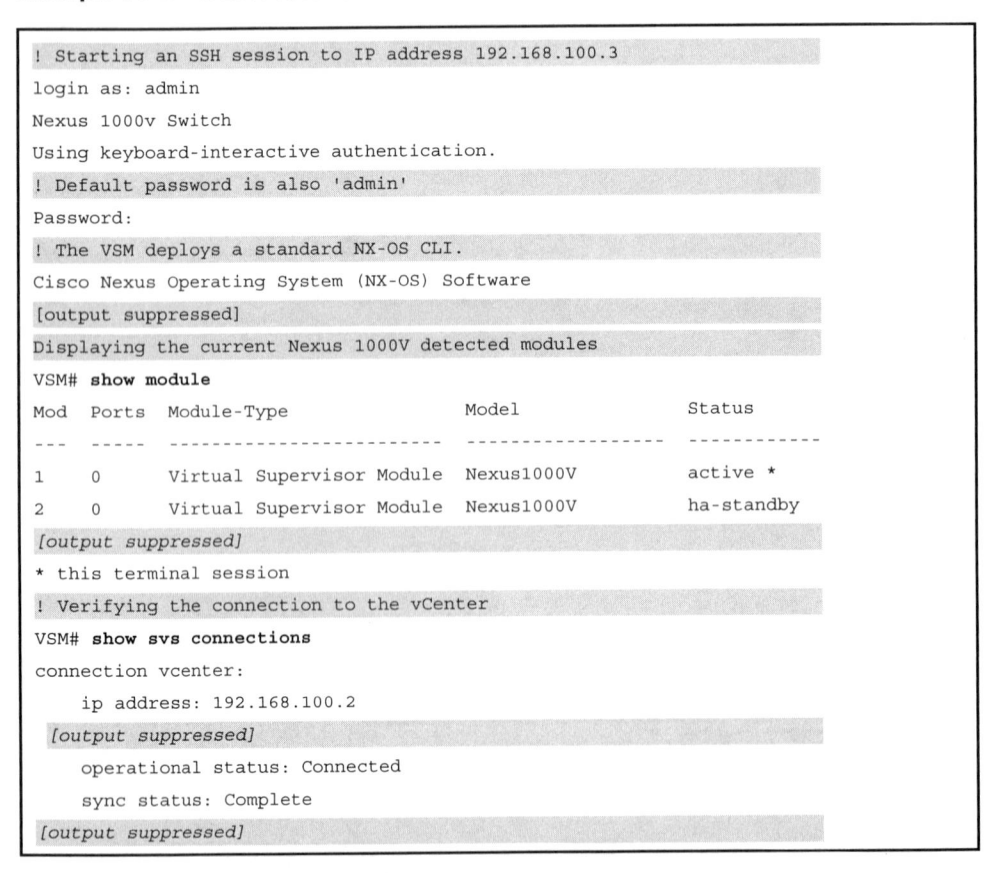

```
! Starting an SSH session to IP address 192.168.100.3
login as: admin
Nexus 1000v Switch
Using keyboard-interactive authentication.
! Default password is also 'admin'
Password:
! The VSM deploys a standard NX-OS CLI.
Cisco Nexus Operating System (NX-OS) Software
[output suppressed]
Displaying the current Nexus 1000V detected modules
VSM# show module
Mod    Ports    Module-Type                    Model           Status
---    -----    ------------------------       -------------   -----------
1      0        Virtual Supervisor Module      Nexus1000V      active *
2      0        Virtual Supervisor Module      Nexus1000V      ha-standby
[output suppressed]
* this terminal session
! Verifying the connection to the vCenter
VSM# show svs connections
connection vcenter:
    ip address: 192.168.100.2
 [output suppressed]
    operational status: Connected
    sync status: Complete
[output suppressed]
```

In our scenario, the connectivity between VSM and VEMs must be established with the creation of an "uplink" in each host, linking the VEMs and the physical network. And, as you remember from the section "Port Profiles and Dynamic Interface Provisioning," earlier in this chapter, Nexus 1000V relies on port profiles to define physical or virtual interfaces.

Example 15-4 details the creation of two "uplink" port profiles, one for each site. Later, these will be used to connect a vmnic to each VEM.

Example 15-4 *Creating Uplink Port Profiles for Each Site*

```
! Configuring VLANs for Nexus 1000V DVS
VSM(config)# vlan 100-105,200-205
! Creating port profile for uplinks in Site 1
VSM(config-vlan)# port-profile type ethernet N1KV-UPLINK-SITE1
VSM(config-port-prof)# switchport mode trunk
VSM(config-port-prof)# switchport trunk allowed vlan 100-105
VSM(config-port-prof)# no shutdown
! Defining that interfaces inheriting this port profile must forward traffic even if
the VSM has not yet programmed this VEM
VSM(config-port-prof)# system vlan 100
! Characterizing this port profile as a VMware port group
VSM(config-port-prof)# vmware port-group
! Enabling the use of this port profile
VSM(config-port-prof)# state enabled
! Configuring a similar port profile for Site 2
VSM(config-port-prof)# port-profile type ethernet N1KV-UPLINK-SITE2
VSM(config-port-prof)# switchport mode trunk
VSM(config-port-prof)# switchport trunk allowed vlan 200-205
VSM(config-port-prof)# no shutdown
VSM(config-port-prof)# system vlan 200
VSM(config-port-prof)# vmware port-group
VSM(config-port-prof)# state enabled
```

The system VLAN configurations on both port profiles from Example 15-4 solve a "chicken-and-the-egg" problem: How can a VEM communicate with the active VSM if the former has not received any control instructions from the latter?

As explained in the example, a system VLAN guarantees that traffic will be forwarded even if the VEM has not been configured by the VSM yet. It is highly recommended that you declare system VLANs for port profiles that will be applied to host management interfaces, VSM interfaces, VEM uplinks that carry control traffic, and IP storage (Internet Small Computer System Interface [iSCSI] or Network File System [NFS]).

Note Port profiles that contain system VLANs are programmed into VEMs as *opaque data* (configuration parameters that are delivered to a VEM through the connection between VSM and vCenter. I do not recommend that you use this special configuration in data VLANs because system VLANs are available in lower numbers than standard VLANs. Besides, they can conflict with some VSM-defined security features during the VEM initialization.

The Installer app has established that our installation will use Layer 3 communication mode between VSM and VEMs. Consequently, it is also necessary to configure a special port profile that provides proper Layer 3 communication between both modules.

A port profile with Layer 3 capability provides UDP encapsulation for control plane traffic that is directed to the VSM. While these packets are sourced from the host vmknic IP address, the VSM IP address is provided to each VEM through *opaque data*.

Example 15-5 shows the configuration of these special port profiles that will be later applied to the hosts' VMkernel interfaces.

Example 15-5 *Creating Layer 3 Control Port Profiles for the VEMs*

```
VSM(config-port-prof)# port-profile type vethernet N1KV-L3-CONTROL-SITE1
! Deploys Layer 3 communication to the VSM using a vmknic
VSM(config-port-prof)# capability l3control
VSM(config-port-prof)# switchport mode access
! Uses management VLAN in Site1
VSM(config-port-prof)# switchport access vlan 100
VSM(config-port-prof)# no shutdown
! Interface must forward traffic before VSM programming
VSM(config-port-prof)# system vlan 100
VSM(config-port-prof)# vmware port-group
VSM(config-port-prof)# state enabled
! Configuring identical port profile for Site2
VSM(config-port-prof)# port-profile type vethernet N1KV-L3-CONTROL-SITE2
VSM(config-port-prof)# capability l3control
VSM(config-port-prof)# switchport mode access
! Site 2 has a distinct management VLAN
VSM(config-port-prof)# switchport access vlan 200
VSM(config-port-prof)# no shutdown
VSM(config-port-prof)# system vlan 200
VSM(config-port-prof)# vmware port-group
VSM(config-port-prof)# state enabled
```

Because the active VSM (VSM-1) and vCenter are connected and synchronized, all port profiles configured in Examples 15-4 and 15-5 automatically generate four port groups in a vSphere Distributed Virtual Switch named "VSM" in vCenter.

Figure 15-12 depicts these port groups in the vCenter **Networking** inventory.

As previously mentioned, Nexus 1000V keeps up the appearance of a DVS to deploy its data plane within vSphere hosts. Therefore, the DVS shown in Figure 15-12 essentially defines how the vCenter sees Nexus 1000V.

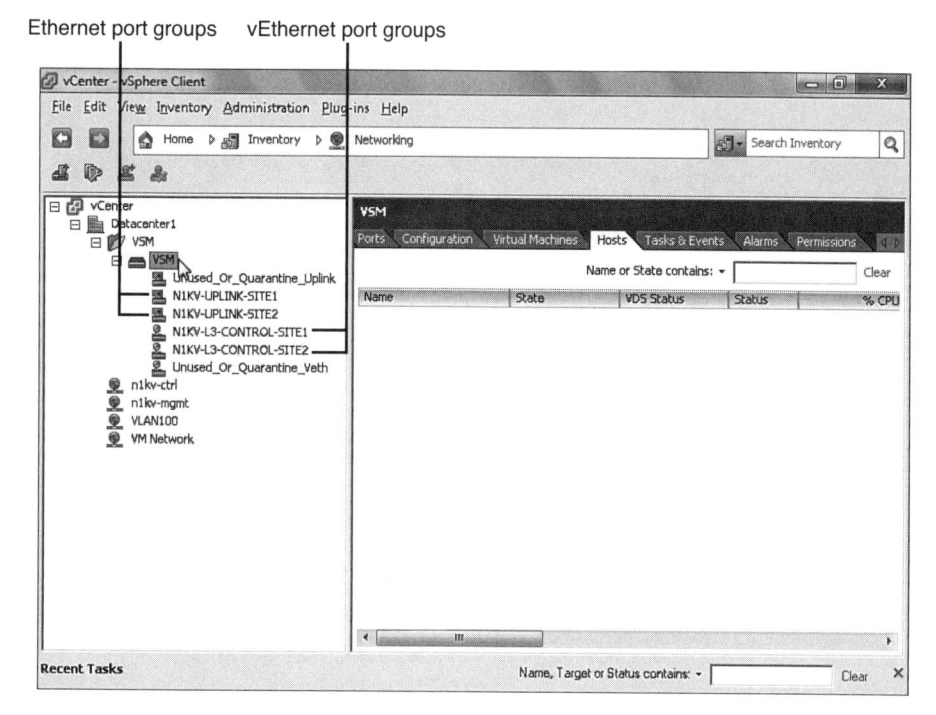

Figure 15-12 *Port Groups Automatically Created in vCenter.*

Right-clicking the VSM DVS, it is possible to access the Add Host wizard, which helps in selecting physical and virtual interfaces to be added to Nexus 1000V. Figure 15-13 illustrates one of the steps of this wizard, where vmnic1 on host10 and host11, and vmnic3 on host20, are assigned to the uplink port groups that were created in Example 15-4 (N1KV-UPLINK-SITE1 and N1KV-UPLINK-SITE2).

Proceeding with the wizard, I have also assigned port groups N1KV-L3-CONTROL-SITE1 and N1KV-L3-CONTROL-SITE2 to the management interfaces (vmk0) of each host, according to their site location.

Figure 15-14 portrays this assignment.

Note The use of the management interface (vmk0) for the VEM Layer 3 connectivity is suitable for small deployments, such as the one demonstrated in this chapter. In bigger scenarios, I recommended that another VMkernel interface is dedicated to this function. This best practice avoids host management traffic from interfering with the control communication between VSM and VEM.

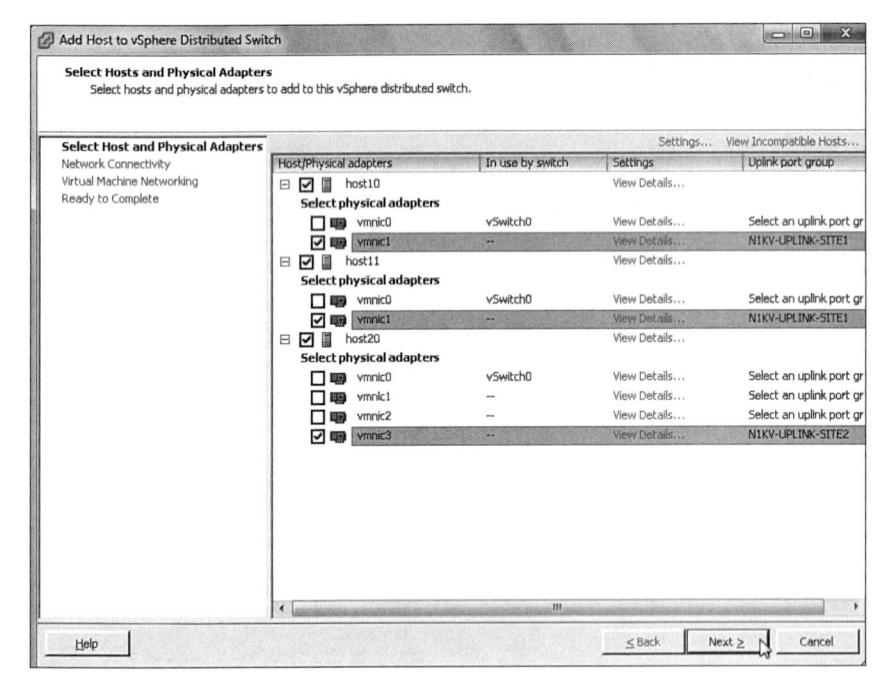

Figure 15-13 *VEM Uplink Selection*

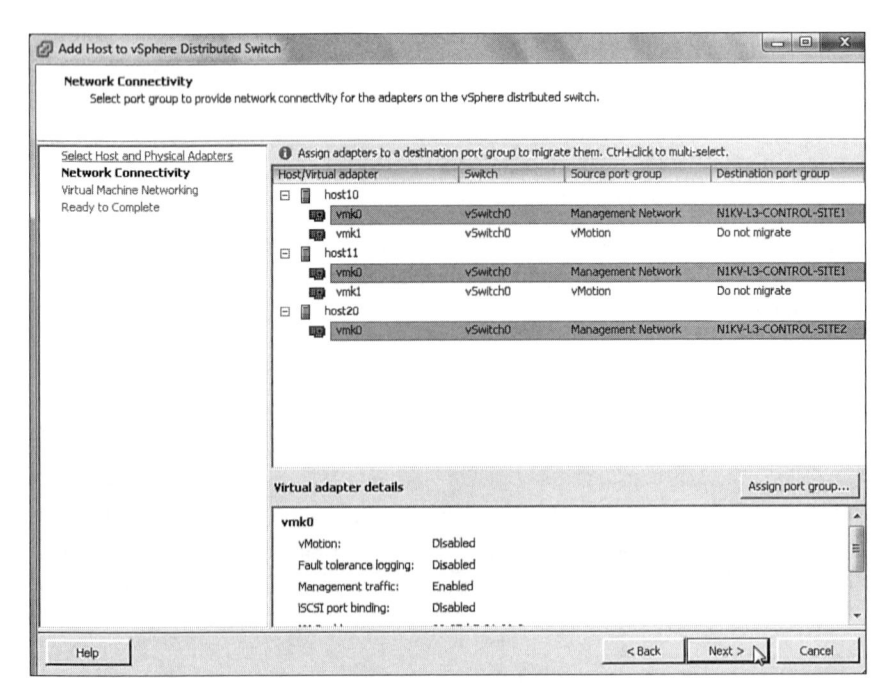

Figure 15-14 *VMkernel Interface Selection for Layer 3 Connectivity Mode*

Because no virtual machine will be migrated to Nexus 1000V just yet, I have concluded the wizard without further modifications. And as Figure 15-15 shows, from a vCenter perspective, all three hosts are now part of Nexus 1000V ("VSM" DVS).

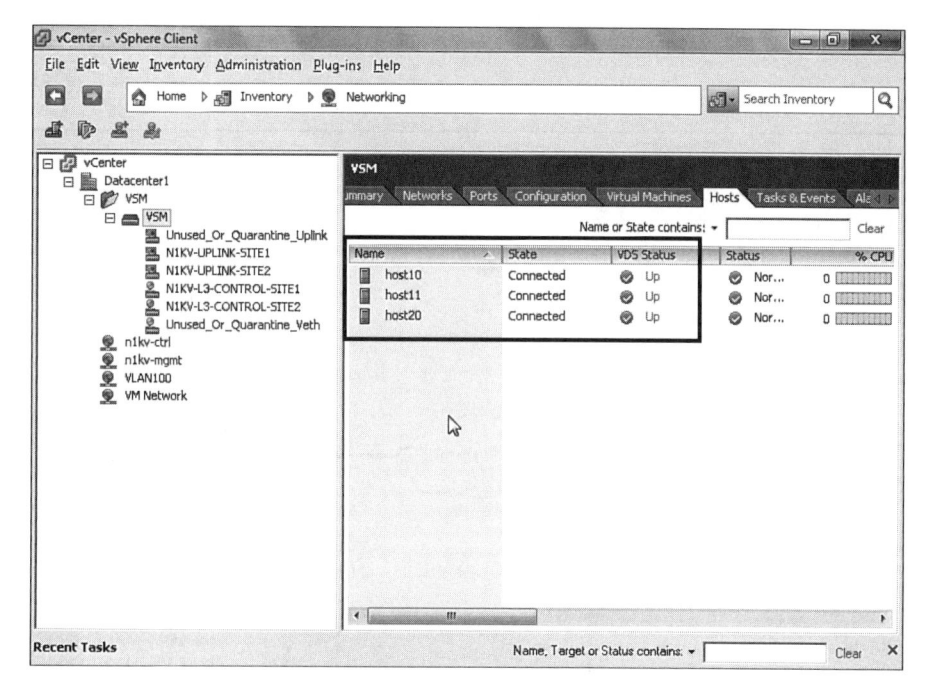

Figure 15-15 *Hosts Included on Nexus 1000V*

The same information can be also retrieved directly from the VSM. Example 15-6 details how each VEM is seen as an I/O module in Nexus 1000V.

Example 15-6 *Verifying the Nexus 1000V Modules*

```
VSM# show module
! These are the VEMs from each host
Mod  Ports  Module-Type                     Model        Status
---  -----  ------------------------------  -----------  ----------
1    0      Virtual Supervisor Module       Nexus1000V   active *
2    0      Virtual Supervisor Module       Nexus1000V   ha-standby
3    248    Virtual Ethernet Module         NA           ok
4    248    Virtual Ethernet Module         NA           ok
5    248    Virtual Ethernet Module         NA           ok
[output suppressed]
! More details about the VEMs are also presented with this command (including the
host UUID)
Mod  Server-IP       Server-UUID                         Server-Name
---  --------------- ----------------------------------  -------------
```

```
1      192.168.100.3     NA                                      NA
2      192.168.100.3     NA                                      NA
3      192.168.100.10    01234567-89ab-cdef-0000-000000000001    host10
4      192.168.100.11    01234567-89ab-cdef-0000-000000000002    host11
5      192.168.200.20    41483531-3241-5553-4538-30344e385836    host20

* this terminal session
```

Figure 15-16 illustrates the evolution of our topology when the VEMs were "inserted" into Nexus 1000V.

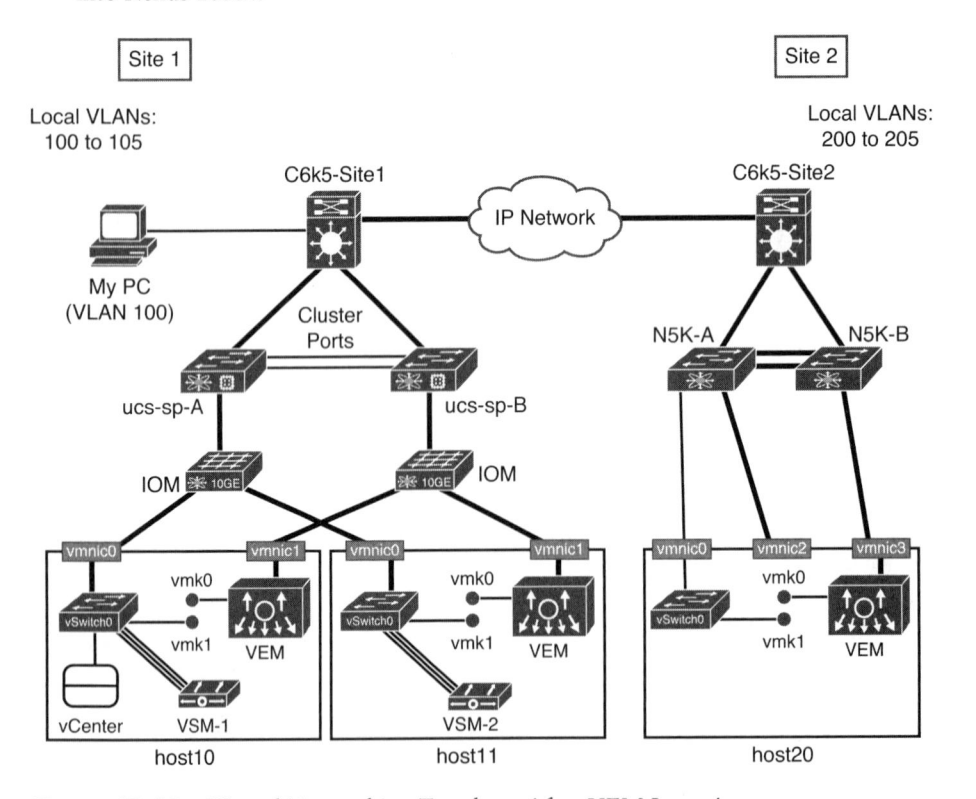

Figure 15-16 *Virtual Networking Topology After VEM Insertion*

In Figure 15-16, you can see that the communication between the active VSM and VEMs currently traverses host10's vSwitch0 and the physical network. Nevertheless, vCenter and the VSMs can also be connected to a VEM because they are virtual machines. To achieve this objective, I have created two port profiles, as shown in Example 15-7.

Example 15-7 *Creating Management and Control Port Profiles*

```
! Configuring port profile that will be applied to the vCenter and VSM management
interfaces
VSM# show running-config port-profile N1KV-MGMT-SITE1
[output suppressed]
port-profile type vethernet N1KV-MGMT-SITE1
  vmware port-group
  switchport mode access
  switchport access vlan 100
  no shutdown
  system vlan 100
  state enabled
! Configuring port profile that will be applied to the VSM control and packet
interfaces
VSM# show running-config port-profile N1KV-CTRL-SITE1
[output suppressed]
port-profile type vethernet N1KV-CTRL-SITE1
  vmware port-group
  switchport mode access
  switchport access vlan 100
  no shutdown
  system vlan 100
  state enabled
```

The migration of vCenter and VSM interfaces can be performed directly in their vCenter virtual machine properties window (which is accessible by right-clicking a VM and selecting the **Edit Virtual Machine Settings** option).

Figure 15-17 illustrates how the VSM-1 virtual machine adapters (vnics) can be connected to the host10 VEM through the assignment of N1KV-MGMT-SITE1 (management interfaces) and N1KV-CTRL-SITE1 (control and packet interfaces).

Tip You can compare this process to a server network cable that is disconnected from one physical switch and connected to another.

The same procedure can be performed on VSM-2 to connect its interfaces to the VEM in host11. Similarly, vCenter can be migrated to Nexus 1000V through the assignment of N1KV-MGMT-SITE1 to its sole interface.

Actually, all virtual networking within a host can be performed by Nexus 1000V. Therefore, I will also connect all vMotion VMkernel interfaces (vmk1) to Nexus 1000V.

Example 15-8 details the port profile configuration for vMotion interfaces for hosts from both sites.

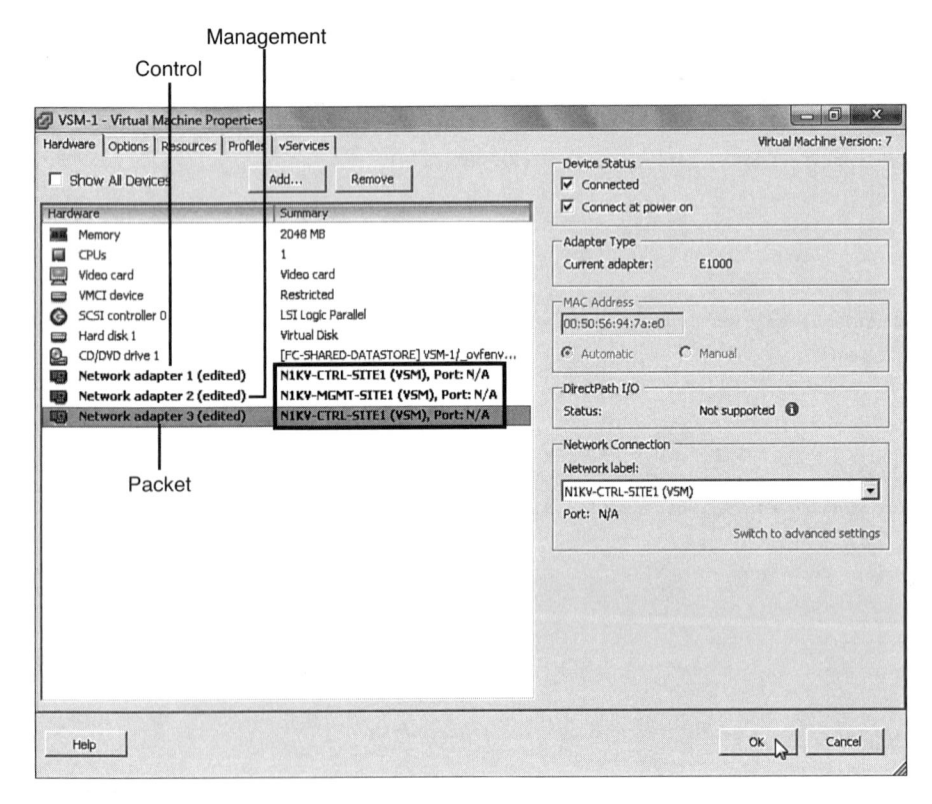

Figure 15-17 *Migrating VSM-1 Interfaces*

Example 15-8 *Creating vMotion Port Profiles*

```
VSM# show running-config port-profile N1KV-VMOTION-SITE1
[output suppressed]
port-profile type vethernet N1KV-VMOTION-SITE1
  vmware port-group
  switchport mode access
  switchport access vlan 101
  no shutdown
  state enabled
VSM# show running-config port-profile N1KV-VMOTION-SITE2
[output suppressed]
port-profile type vethernet N1KV-VMOTION-SITE2
  vmware port-group
  switchport mode access
  switchport access vlan 201
  no shutdown
  state enabled
```

Right-clicking the Nexus 1000V DVS in vCenter and using its Manage Hosts wizard, you can migrate these VMkernel interfaces in a single operation. Figure 15-18 portrays the wizard step where the port groups (inserted by the Nexus 1000V) are assigned to the vmk1 interfaces from each host.

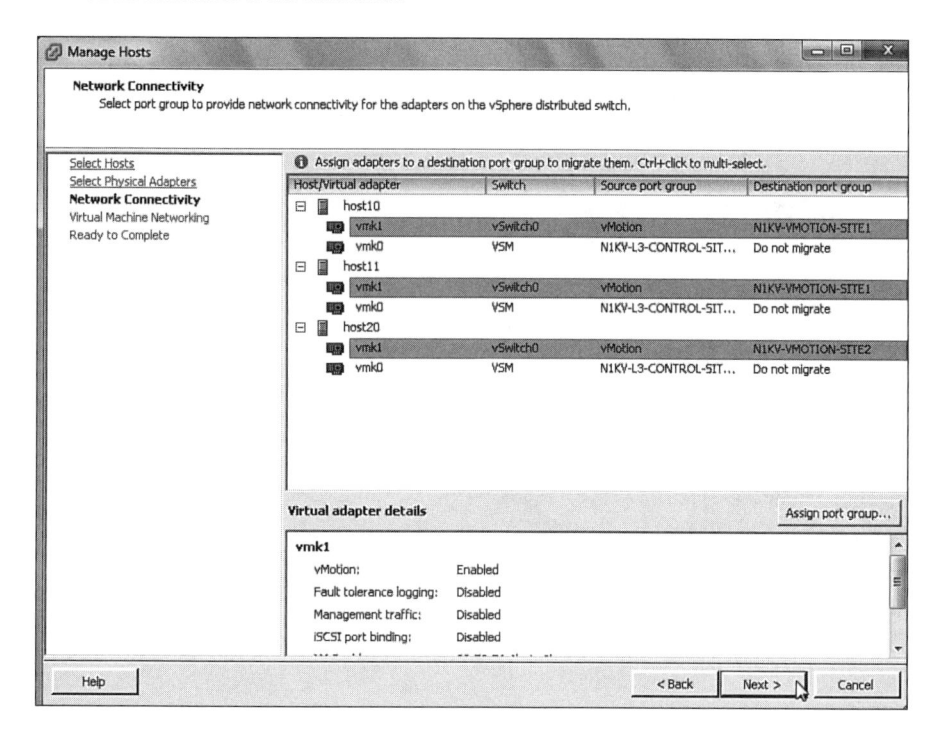

Figure 15-18 *Migrating vMotion Interfaces*

As a visual aid, Figure 15-19 illustrates the results of all virtual adapter migrations.

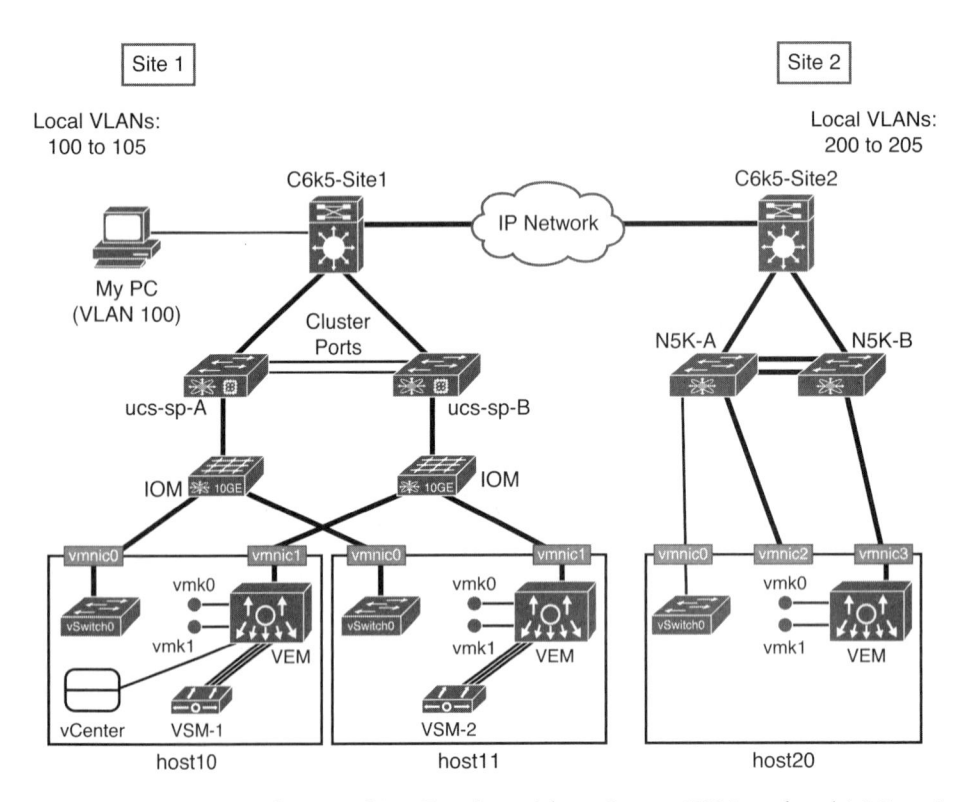

Figure 15-19 *Virtual Networking Topology After vCenter, VSM, and vmk1 Migrations*

External Connectivity and Link Aggregation

Despite the fact that a virtual machine only requires one VEM uplink to exchange Ethernet frames with the physical network, it is a beneficial action to provide redundancy for this connection, especially considering that the VEM-VSM control traffic is also using this lonely interface.

But before I discuss the methods of uplink high availability in Nexus 1000V, you should understand that this switch does not act as a standard Layer 2 physical switch from a Spanning Tree Protocol (STP) perspective. Actually, Nexus 1000V exhibits a behavior called *End-Host mode*, where each VEM can avoid loops without having to rely on STP.

Figure 15-20 justifies this statement by illustrating three Nexus 1000V VEM characteristics that exempt these modules from Layer 2 loops.

As shown in Figure 15-20, each VEM implements

- **BPDU blocking:** Where STP bridge protocol data units (BPDU) are dropped on any VEM port.

- **No external switching:** Where physical Ethernet interfaces do not switch traffic received from the network.

- **Local MAC checking:** Where frames sourced from local virtual machines are dropped if received from physical interfaces.

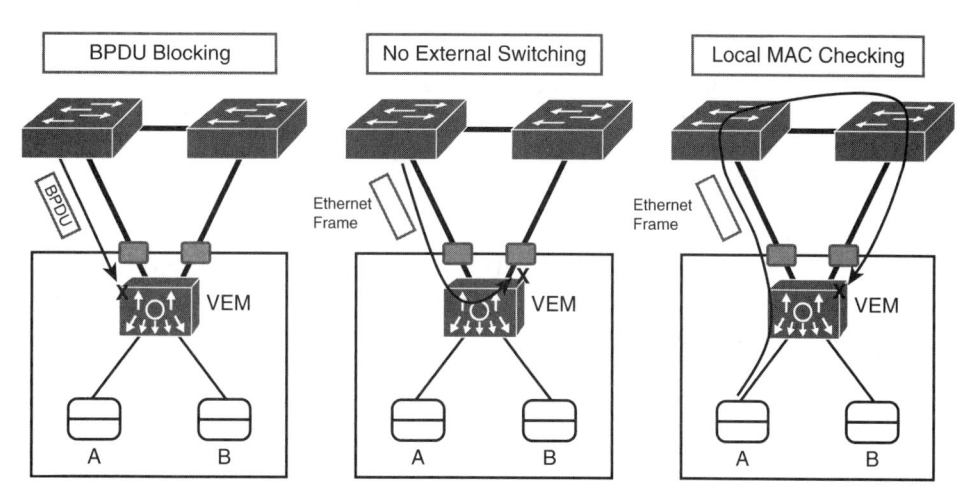

Figure 15-20 *Nexus 1000V Loop-Avoidance Mechanisms*

End-Host mode is essentially based on the distinction between access ports (virtual Ethernet interfaces) and uplinks (Ethernet interfaces). And such predictability allows potential loops to be immediately identified and mitigated.

Nevertheless, there are points that require observation when a VEM deploys more than one uplink connection with the physical network, such as traffic load balancing. If a VM is sending Ethernet frames to the external world, the frames should not be "spread" on more than one interface, or the external switches might detect a MAC flapping phenomenon. And worse: Depending on its configuration, a physical switch can simply block all interfaces where a single VM MAC address is being learned alternatively.

This connectivity quandary can be solved through Nexus 1000V PortChannels, which can aggregate up to eight uplinks in a single VEM. Through this capability, the traffic from virtual adapters is load balanced across a single logical interface, from a physical switch perspective.

Ideally, to improve connection availability, a VEM should also be connected to more than one physical switch. And depending on the aggregation capabilities of these devices, it can deploy the following Nexus 1000V PortChannel modes:

- **Virtual PortChannel Host-Mode (vPC-HM):** Assembles connections to multiple upstream switches where uplinks to the same switch are aggregated into a subgroup. In vPC-HM, the VM-originated traffic is only forwarded to the links of a subgroup (unless it fails and all VMs are relocated to another subgroup). A subgroup can be dynamically formed through Cisco Discovery Protocol (CDP) detection or through manual configuration.

- **MAC pinning:** No aggregation configuration is required from the upstream physical switches. Each virtual machine MAC address is "pinned" to an uplink (in a round-robin fashion), and remains there until a failure happens and the MAC is reallocated to another uplink.

- **Link Aggregation Control Protocol (LACP):** Where LACP can be used to negotiate and establish IEEE 802.3ad aggregation of its uplinks. If two switches are used to provide device high availability, they must deploy a cross-switch link aggregation technology, such as virtual PortChannel (vPC).

Going back to our topology, you can observe different upstream conditions at each site. Because Unified Computing System (UCS) Fabric Interconnect currently does not support vPCs, Nexus 1000V cannot deploy PortChannels in LACP mode on host10 or host11. Consequently, I will change N1KV-UPLINK-SITE1 to provide *automatic aggregation of uplinks* using MAC pinning mode whenever more than one uplink inherits it.

Example 15-9 details the PortChannel mode configuration on N1KV-UPLINK-SITE1.

Example 15-9 *Deploying PortChannel on N1KV-UPLINK-SITE1 Port Profile*

```
! Configuring MAC Pinning mode for uplinks in site 1
VSM(config)# port-profile type ethernet N1KV-UPLINK-SITE1
VSM(config-port-prof)# channel-group auto mode on mac-pinning
```

In contrast, two vPC-capable Nexus 5000 switches are connected to vmnic2 and vmnic3 on host20. For that reason, its VEM can deploy a PortChannel in LACP mode.

Example 15-10 details N1KV-UPLINK-SITE2 port profile configuration to deploy LACP.

Example 15-10 *Changing N1KV-UPLINK-SITE2 Port Profile*

```
! Enabling LACP in the Nexus 1000V
VSM(config)# feature lacp
! Configuring LACP mode active on interfaces that will inherit this port profile
VSM(config)# port-profile type ethernet N1KV-UPLINK-SITE2
VSM(config-port-prof)# channel-group auto mode active
```

From now on, as more vmnic interfaces inherit port profiles N1KV-UPLINK-SITE1 and N1KV-UPLINK-SITE2, they will be automatically aggregated in a PortChannel at each VEM.

Using the Manage Hosts vCenter wizard, Figure 15-21 portrays the selection of vmnics that will be migrated to Nexus 1000V, triggering the automatic link aggregation at each VEM.

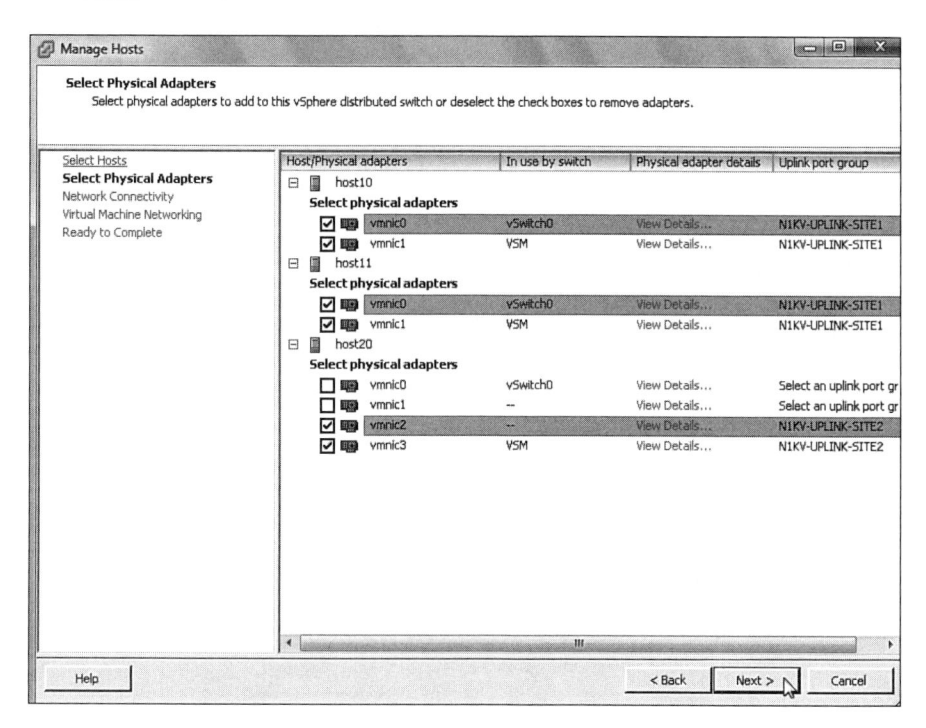

Figure 15-21 *Migrating Additional Physical Interfaces to Nexus 1000V*

Example 15-11 depicts the established PortChannels, right after a vPC is configured on N5K-A and N5K-B and the vmnics migration is completed.

Example 15-11 *Verifying Nexus 1000V PortChannels*

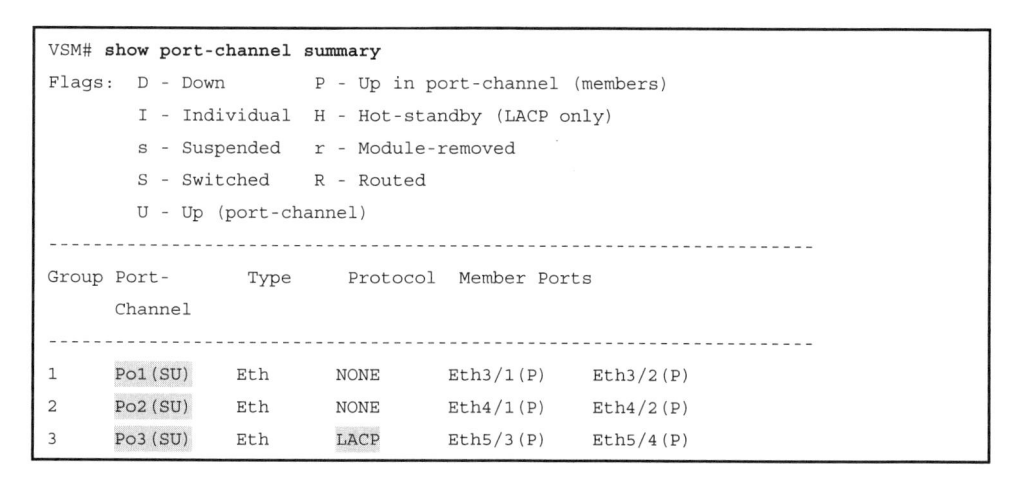

```
VSM# show port-channel summary
Flags:  D - Down        P - Up in port-channel (members)
        I - Individual  H - Hot-standby (LACP only)
        s - Suspended   r - Module-removed
        S - Switched    R - Routed
        U - Up (port-channel)
-------------------------------------------------------------------
Group Port-       Type      Protocol  Member Ports
      Channel
-------------------------------------------------------------------
1     Po1(SU)     Eth       NONE      Eth3/1(P)   Eth3/2(P)
2     Po2(SU)     Eth       NONE      Eth4/1(P)   Eth4/2(P)
3     Po3(SU)     Eth       LACP      Eth5/3(P)   Eth5/4(P)
```

Tip You can find out how MAC pinning has distributed the vEthernet interfaces to the uplinks with the **show interface virtual pinning** command.

A PortChannel load-balancing method can also be configured per Nexus 1000V or per VEM. Each method essentially selects an individual uplink for the egress traffic based on a hashing operation on parameters such as MAC addresses (source MAC address is the default), IP addresses, VLAN ID, TCP or UDP port number, and DVS generated port identifier (Port ID).

NX-OS Features in the Virtual World

In broad terms, Nexus 1000V is an NX-OS Layer 2 switch that can implement the same switching features from its physical counterparts. Therefore, in this section, I will explore some of the Nexus 1000V similarities and particularities in comparison with other Nexus switches through actual virtual machine traffic.

Figure 15-22 presents some new faces in our virtual networking topology.

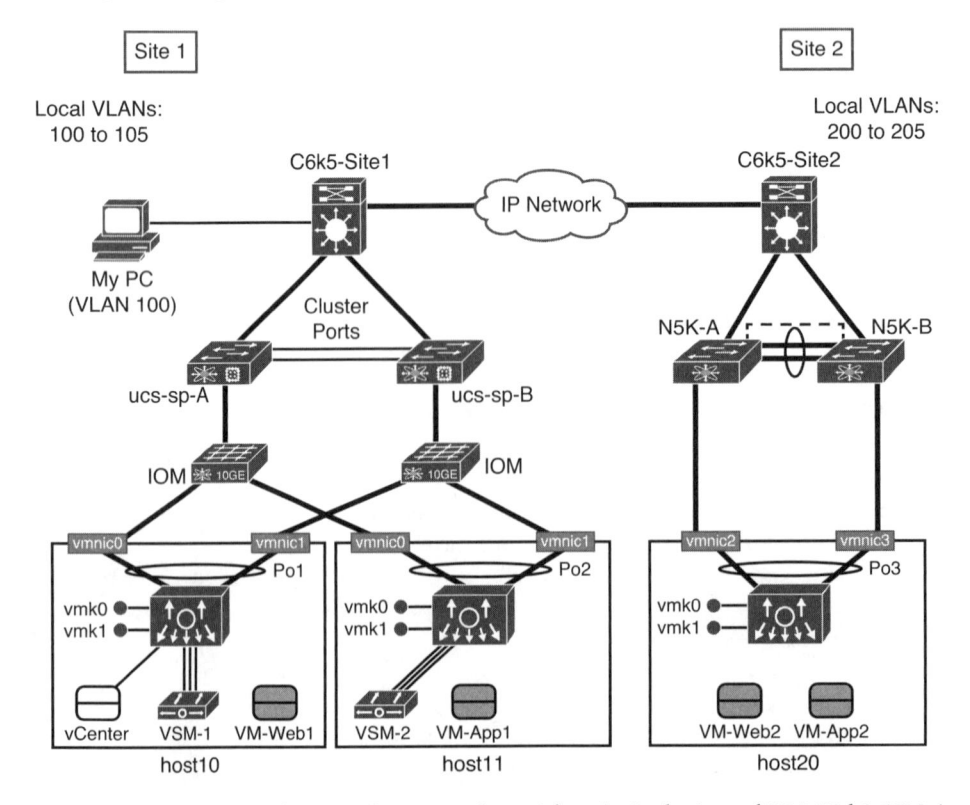

Figure 15-22 *Virtual Networking Topology After the Inclusion of VM-Web1, VM-App1, VM-Web2, and VM-App2*

The figure introduces four new virtual machines: VM-Web1 in host10, VM-App1 in host11, and VM-Web2 and VM-App2 in host20.

> **Note** Although I have not removed the vSwitches from the vSphere hosts, I will not show them to save some "real estate" in the figures.

Because I intend to insert the site 1 VMs into VLAN 105 and the site 2 VMs into VLAN 205, Example 15-12 details the port profile configurations that will be used on these VMs.

Example 15-12 *Port Profile Configuration for the New VMs*

```
! Port Profile for Web servers located in site 1
VSM# show running-config port-profile N1KV-WEB-SITE1
[output suppressed]
port-profile type vethernet N1KV-WEB-SITE1
  vmware port-group
  switchport mode access
  switchport access vlan 105
  no shutdown
  state enabled
! Port Profile for Web servers located in site 2
VSM# show running-config port-profile N1KV-WEB-SITE2
! Port Profile for Web servers located in site 1
port-profile type vethernet N1KV-WEB-SITE2
  vmware port-group
  switchport mode access
  switchport access vlan 205
  no shutdown
  state enabled
! Port Profile for Application servers located in site 1
VSM# show running-config port-profile N1KV-APP-SITE1
[output suppressed]
port-profile type vethernet N1KV-APP-SITE1
  vmware port-group
  switchport mode access
  switchport access vlan 105
  no shutdown
  state enabled
! Port Profile for Application servers located in site 2
VSM# show running-config port-profile N1KV-APP-SITE2
! Port Profile for Web servers located in site 1
port-profile type vethernet N1KV-APP-SITE2
```

```
vmware port-group
switchport mode access
switchport access vlan 205
no shutdown
state enabled
```

Note Although it is not a common procedure, Nexus 1000V also permits the creation of trunk virtual Ethernet interfaces with the **switchport mode trunk** port profile command. Of course, this configuration demands that the connected vnic supports the IEEE 802.1Q protocol.

Afterward, through the Edit Virtual Machine Settings option and vCenter console access, each VM was configured according to the characteristics described in Table 15-3.

Table 15-3 *Virtual Machine Characteristics*

Virtual Machine	Adapter	VLAN	IP Address	DVS Port Group
VM-Web1	Net Adapter 1	105	192.168.105.180/24	N1KV-WEB-SITE1
VM-App1	Net Adapter 1	105	192.168.105.181/24	N1KV-APP-SITE1
VM-Web2	Net Adapter 1	205	192.168.205.180/24	N1KV-WEB-SITE2
VM-App2	Net Adapter 1	205	192.168.205.181/24	N1KV-APP-SITE2

And as expected, each machine is consequently connected to a vEthernet interface after its port group association is performed by vCenter, as shown in Example 15-13.

Example 15-13 *Verifying Virtual Interfaces*

```
VSM# show interface virtual
-------------------------------------------------------------------
Port        Adapter         Owner              Mod Host
-------------------------------------------------------------------
[output suppressed]
! Recently created virtual interfaces for the new VMs
Veth14      Net Adapter 1   VM-Web1            3   host10
Veth15      Net Adapter 1   VM-App1            4   host11
Veth16      Net Adapter 1   VM-Web2            5   host20
Veth17      Net Adapter 1   VM-App2            5   host20
```

In Example 15-13, you can further verify the exchange of information between the VSM and vCenter. For that reason, Nexus 1000V is aware of several virtual machine characteristics such as name, connected vnic, and location (host).

> **Tip** By default, the DVS port group name on vCenter will share its name with the Nexus 1000V port profile. However, you can change this behavior by inserting a distinct port group name right after the **vmware port-group** command. Nonetheless, for the sake of simplicity, I will only use the default option in this chapter.

MAC Address Table

An interesting distinction between standard physical switches and Nexus 1000V is how the latter deals with its MAC address table. Example 15-14 illustrates this distinction by depicting the Nexus 1000V MAC address table on VLAN 105. In our topology, VM-Web1 is communicating with VM-App1 and its default gateway (an SVI configured in C6K5-Site1 with IP address 192.168.105.1).

Example 15-14   *Nexus 1000V MAC Address Table in VLAN 105*

```
VSM# show mac address-table vlan 105
VLAN      MAC Address       Type      Age        Port                Mod
---------+-----------------+--------+----------+-------------------+---
! This static entry represents VM-Web1 vnic in VEM 3 (host10)
105       0050.5694.dc60    static    0          Veth14              3
! This dynamic entry refers to VM-App1 vnic MAC address learned by VEM 3 (host 10)
105       0050.5694.c0f4    dynamic   199        Po1                 3
! This is C6K5-Site1 SVI MAC address
105       00d0.7992.dc00    dynamic   14         Po1                 3
! This static entry represents VM-App1 vnic in VEM 4 (host11)
105       0050.5694.c0f4    static    0          Veth15              4
! This dynamic entry refers to VM-Web1 vnic MAC address learned by VEM 4 (host 11)
105       0050.5694.dc60    dynamic   14         Po2                 4
Total MAC Addresses: 5
```

The double entries for MAC addresses in Example 15-14 reveal a very important aspect of the Nexus 1000V data plane: Each VEM acts as an independent Ethernet bridge. Therefore, even if these modules are coordinated by a centralized control plane (VSM), each VEM deploys dynamic learning for remote MAC addresses (*including VMs that connected to other VEMs*).

And as the example shows, a VEM creates static MAC entries for local machines because it does not make much sense to learn addresses that are already assigned by vCenter itself.

Access Lists

Although Nexus 1000V is strictly a Layer 2 switch, it can process Layer 3 and 4 information through capabilities such as IP access control lists (ACL).

To demonstrate how ACLs can be configured on Nexus 1000V, consider that the web pages on VM-Web1 and VM-Web2 can be accessed from any point of the physical network (including my PC). Also imagine that, because of compliance rules, the access to these web servers must be restricted to the traditional HTTP and HTTPS TCP ports.

Because Nexus 1000V is providing connectivity for both VLANs, IP ACLs can be applied to the virtual interfaces that are connected to both VMs.

Example 15-15 details the creation of an IP access list and its application to both web server VMs.

Example 15-15 *IP Access List for Web TCP Ports*

```
! Creating an ACL that only permits traffic on TCP ports 80 and 443
VSM(config)# ip access-list WEB
VSM(config-acl)# permit tcp any any eq 80
VSM(config-acl)# permit tcp any any eq 443
! Applying ACL to a port profile
VSM(config-acl)# port-profile N1KV-WEB-SITE1
VSM(config-port-prof)# ip port access-group WEB out
! Applying ACL to VM-Web2 interface only
VSM(config-port-prof)# interface vethernet 16
VSM(config-if)# ip port access-group WEB out
```

After the ACL is associated to the egress traffic on port profile N1K-WEB-SITE1 and interface vEthernet 16, both VMs stop receiving any other IP communication that is different from the TCP ports defined in the ACL.

Although both methods of ACL enforcement shared the same results in our simple example, they do have a different impact on Nexus 1000V. In more detail: While ACL WEB can affect the traffic of all VMs that are associated to port group N1KV-WEB-SITE1, other VMs (besides VM-Web2) that are associated to port group N1KV-WEB-SITE2 will not have their traffic filtered.

Other NX-OS features can be deployed in similar ways on Nexus 1000V, such as quality of service (QoS), Switch Port ANalyzer (SPAN), Encapsulated Remote Switch Port ANalyzer (ERSPAN), NetFlow, Private VLANs, port security, IP source guard, Dynamic ARP inspection, and DHCP snooping.

In my opinion, there lies the main strength of Nexus 1000V: the consistency and integration between physical and virtual networking. Solutions such as Cisco Prime Network Analysis Module (NAM) can consolidate traffic visibility from both types of networks, adding vMotion and VM-to-VM exchanges to its wide monitoring scope.

Online Migrations and Nexus 1000V

One of the most famous features of vSphere is vMotion, which enables the migration of live VMs between two different hosts. As briefly discussed in Chapter 13, "Server Evolution," this feature is currently performed through the exchange of VM memory states through vMotion-enabled VMkernel adapters in each host (such as vmk1 interfaces in our topology).

Note At the time of this writing, VMware vMotion also requires that the VM-stored data is located at an external storage device that is accessed by both vSphere hosts.

vMotion can be manually activated in vCenter by right-clicking a VM and selecting the Migrate wizard. After validating the provided choices, vCenter initiates the VM memory state copy between the hosts and completes the migration.

Cisco Nexus 1000V fully supports vMotion through the seamless migration of virtual Ethernet interfaces between Virtual Ethernet Modules. Example 15-16 demonstrates that after VM-Web1 is migrated from host10 to host11.

Example 15-16 *VM-Web1 Migration Aftermath*

```
! Displaying the vEthernet interface from VM-Web1
VSM# show interface virtual vm VM-Web1
! VM-Web1 is now located at host11 (VEM 4)
-------------------------------------------------------------------
Port         Adapter         Owner                  Mod Host
-------------------------------------------------------------------
Veth14       Net Adapter 1   VM-Web1                4   host11
```

Example 15-16 also explains how Nexus 1000V deals with the VM mobility to deploy its networking features. Because vEthernet interfaces are intrinsically joined to a virtual machine, its networking settings are capable of following the VM wherever it might roam.

An emerging topic of discussion in the data center community has been Long Distance vMotion, which allows a virtual machine to be migrated between two different data center locations. For IT departments, such capability enables

- Resource load balancing among multiple active data center facilities

- Disaster avoidance for virtual workloads, because critical VMs can be moved to other sites before a known event can affect the operation of a data center site

Obviously there are limitations for such an operation. For example, at the time of this writing, VMware only offers support for the migration of machines for hosts that have a maximum round-trip time of 10 milliseconds (called Metro vMotion). Additionally, the migrated VM must be able to access its stored data when it arrives at the remote site. In this case, the VM might have to use one of the following methods:

1. Access its stored data in the original site, significantly restricting the distance between both sites.
2. Access a storage virtualization system that permits active-active access on both sites.

Note Storage virtualization solutions were discussed in Chapter 9, "Storage Evolution."

Contributing to the support of Long Distance vMotion, Nexus 1000V can also be spread among multiple sites if the minimum communication requirements between modules (latency and reliability) are respected. For an extended Nexus 1000V switch, a migrated VM will still carry the vEthernet definitions to the other site, assuring connectivity maintenance (if the physical network is prepared accordingly).

From a networking perspective, a VM that has been migrated keeps all its networking characteristics such as network addresses (IP and MAC), ARP tables, and default gateway. Consequently, as it expects a compatible network infrastructure in its new "home." It is mandatory to extend a broadcast domain between both sites to guarantee that the VM continue to access all the resources that were available in its origin site.

Tip Right after a vMotion, a VM always sends a Reverse ARP frame to update all switch MAC address tables that share the VLANs that the VM is connected to.

The situation can be further understood if you picture the topology we have been dealing in this chapter. If VM-App1, which belongs to VLAN 105, migrates to host20, it will not be able to communicate with any other resource because this VLAN simply does not exist on site 2.

To illustrate how a vMotion between different sites could work from a Nexus 1000V perspective, I have created a virtual machine (VM-Nomad) that will be connected to an extended VLAN between sites 1 and 2. Figure 15-23 depicts our updated topology, with the inclusion of this VM.

Tip VM-Nomad has IP address 10.30.30.30/24 and default gateway 10.30.30.1 (which refers to a Hot Standby Router Protocol [HSRP] group deployed by SVIs on both Layer 3 switches).

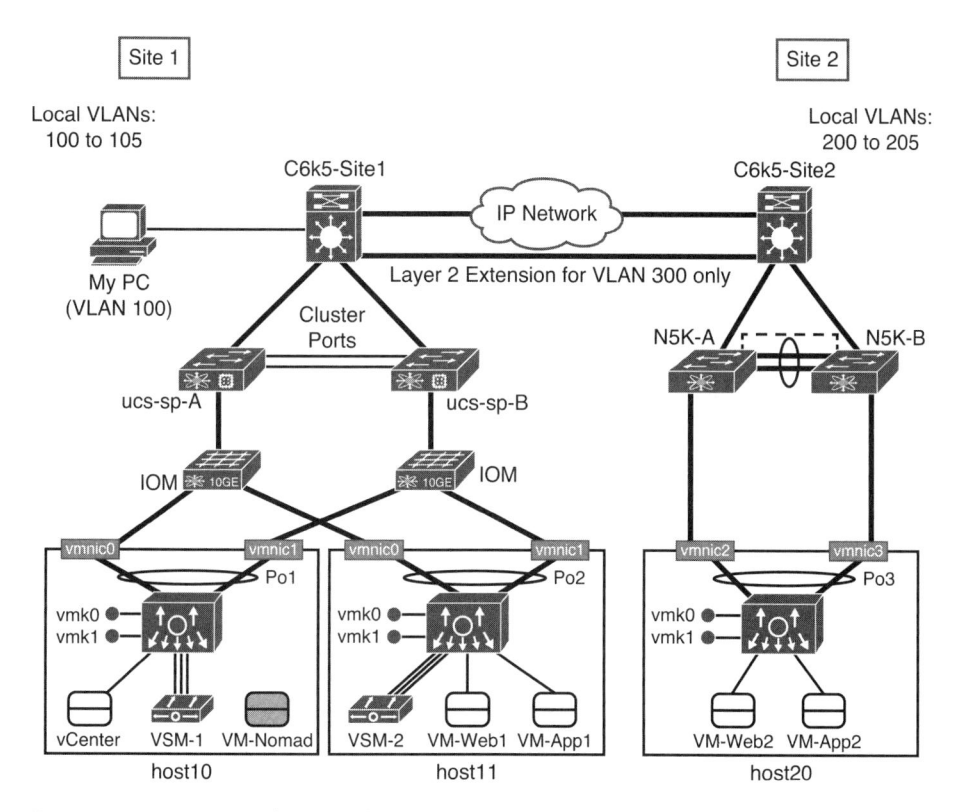

Figure 15-23 *Virtual Networking Topology After the Insertion of VM-Nomad*

> **Note** I have used a simple physical Ethernet connection for the VLAN 300 extension between both sites. Chapter 8, "A Tale of Two Data Centers," offers a detailed discussion of the characteristics of other Layer 2 extension methods and their applicability.

Considering that VLAN 300 is correctly configured in the physical network, it is also necessary to prepare the virtual networking infrastructure for this VLAN deployment.

Example 15-17 details the configuration of Nexus 1000V that is required for the movement of VM-Nomad to the other site.

Example 15-17 *Preparing to Launch VM-Nomad*

```
! Configuring VLAN 300 in Nexus 1000V
VSM(config)# vlan 300
! Including VLAN 300 on all uplink Ethernet interfaces on both sites
VSM(config-vlan)# port-profile N1KV-UPLINK-SITE1
VSM(config-port-prof)# switchport trunk allowed vlan add 300
```

```
VSM(config-port-prof)# port-profile N1KV-UPLINK-SITE2
VSM(config-port-prof)# switchport trunk allowed vlan add 300
```

Example 15-18 creates the port profile that will provide connectivity for VM-Nomad on both sites.

Example 15-18 *Port Profile Configuration for VM-Nomad*

```
VSM# show running-config port-profile N1KV-VLAN300
[output suppressed]
port-profile type vethernet N1KV-VLAN300
  vmware port-group
  switchport mode access
  switchport access vlan 300
  no shutdown
  state enabled
```

After the port profile N1KV-VLAN300 corresponding port group is assigned to VM-Nomad's vnic, Nexus 1000V assigns a virtual Ethernet interface to the VM.

Example 15-19 displays the characteristics of this specific vEthernet interface.

Example 15-19 *VM-Nomad Virtual Ethernet Before the Migration*

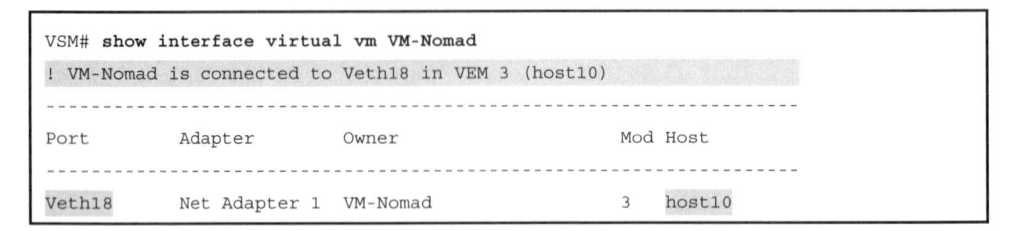

```
VSM# show interface virtual vm VM-Nomad
! VM-Nomad is connected to Veth18 in VEM 3 (host10)
-----------------------------------------------------------------
Port       Adapter         Owner                  Mod Host
-----------------------------------------------------------------
Veth18     Net Adapter 1   VM-Nomad               3   host10
```

As vCenter completes the VM-Nomad migration (only a single Internet Control Message Protocol [ICMP] Echo reply message from the VM to my PC was lost during the process), Example 15-20 demonstrates that VM is now located at host20.

Example 15-20 *VM-Nomad Virtual Ethernet After the Migration*

```
VSM# show interface virtual vm VM-Nomad
! VM-Nomad is connected to Veth18 in VEM 5 (host20)
-----------------------------------------------------------------
Port       Adapter         Owner                  Mod Host
-----------------------------------------------------------------
Veth18     Net Adapter 1   VM-Nomad               5   host20
```

The successful migration hides a small detail that can cause a common confusion to virtualization and network administrators. Erroneously, many believe that the VMkernel adapters from different hosts *must* share the same VLAN to deploy vMotion. But as Example 15-20 has shown, this statement is simply not true (host10's and host20's vmk1s belong to VLANs 101 and 201, respectively).

During the vMotion of VM-Nomad, host10 has used its default gateway (192.168.100.1) to reach host20 vmk1 and establish a TCP connection in port 8000 to transmit VM-Nomad's memory state information. Similarly, host20 has used its configured default gateway (192.168.200.1) to access host10's vmk1.

Note Nevertheless, you should always refer to your hypervisor vendor documentation to find out whether your intended design is supported.

Virtual Extensible Local Area Networks

While VLANs provide a simple way to logically isolate VMs in server virtualization implementations, they also offer some operational obstacles to the scaling of these environments, such as

- Limitation of 4094 broadcast domains
- Requirement of Layer 2 extensions between different data center sites that must share these logical networks

And as server virtualization evolves its applicability toward multitenant environments, the possibility of creating and distributing virtual machines on demand (and regardless of location) is also bound by the aforementioned VLAN constraints.

To overcome these challenges, vendors such as Cisco, VMware, Citrix, and Red Hat have designed a virtual networking technology called *Virtual eXtensible Local Area Network*, or simply VXLAN. In essence, VXLAN consists in a Layer 2 overlay method that supports vastly more logical networks than VLANs and allows "stretching" over a Layer 3 network.

A *VXLAN segment* defines an overlay that permits Layer 2 communication between two or more virtual machines. Each VXLAN segment is defined by a 24-bit segment ID called a VXLAN Network Identifier (VNI). Consequently, this technology has a theoretical limit of more than *16 million broadcast domains*.

Tip VXLAN was submitted to IETF as a draft, which can be located in the "Further Reading" section, later in this chapter.

A virtual machine is completely unaware whether it is connected to a VXLAN or a VLAN. When two virtualized hosts are sharing a VXLAN segment, they must encapsulate standard Ethernet frames sent by a VM into *VXLAN frames*, whose format is detailed in Figure 15-24.

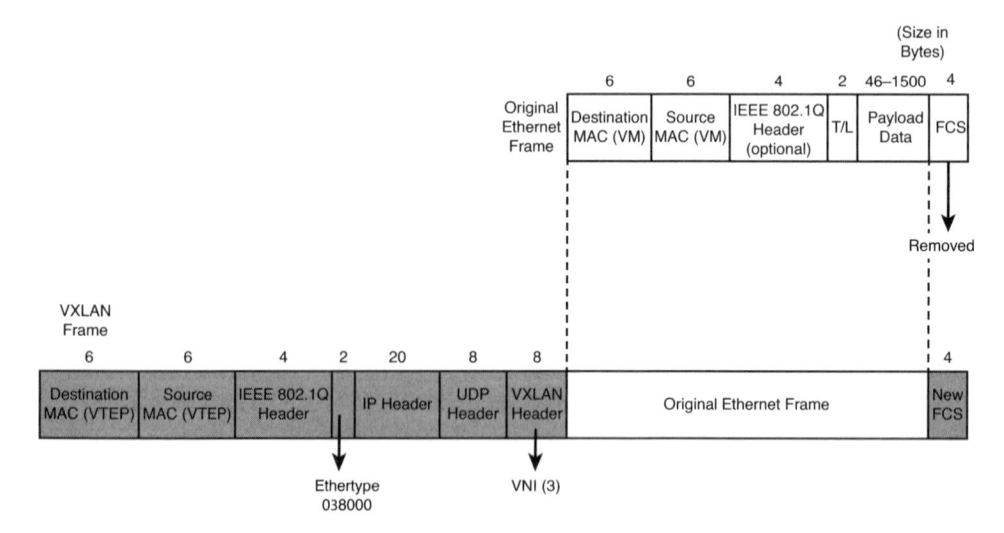

Figure 15-24 *VXLAN Frame Format*

Figure 15-24 shows that a VXLAN frame is basically comprised of a UDP datagram (with destination port 8472), a VXLAN header, and a transported Ethernet frame. Within a VXLAN-capable host, the entity that performs the encapsulation (and decapsulation) is called a *VXLAN Tunnel Endpoint (VTEP)*. A VTEP is used whenever a local VM wants to communicate with a remote VM within the same VXLAN segment.

In the Nexus 1000V VXLAN implementation, each VEM can act as a VTEP to share segments with other VEMs (regardless of whether they are controlled by the same VSM or not).

Figure 15-25 illustrates how the communication between VMs in the same VXLAN segment happens in Nexus 1000V.

In Figure 15-25, virtual machines A, B, and D have vnics connected to VXLAN 5000. Therefore, if A wants to send an Ethernet frame to B, VEM West will simply behave as a transparent bridge, forwarding the frames directly to B as soon as it learns its MAC address. However, if A wants to send an Ethernet frame directly to D, VEM West will encapsulate the original frame into a VXLAN frame and send it through the IP network to VEM East.

In this scenario, VEM West is aware that MAC address D is located at VEM East because it has previously received Ethernet frames from this VM. However, if an address is not present in its MAC address table, a VEM will normally flood frames to other VEMs that share the same VXLAN using multicast IP packets. And in fact, all multidestination traffic will use the same transport mechanism.

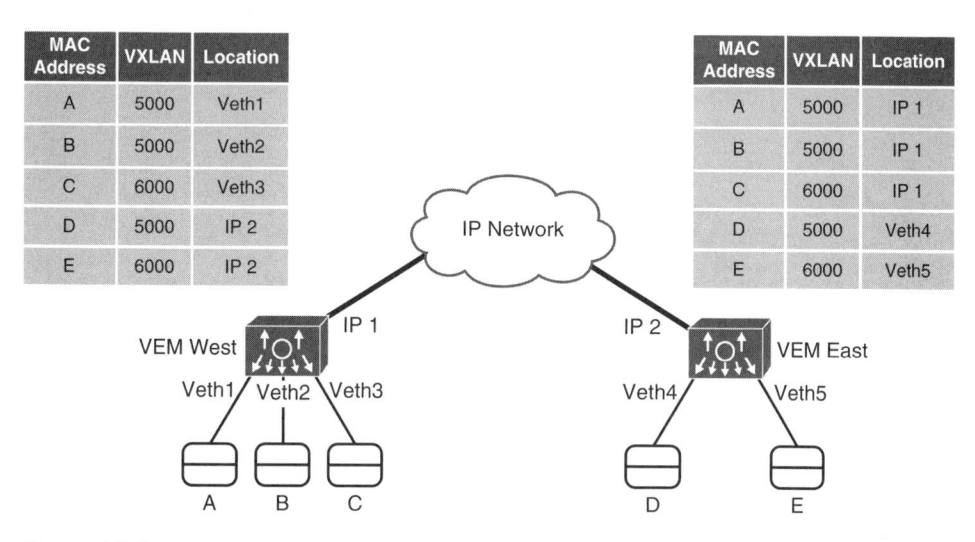

MAC Address	VXLAN	Location
A	5000	Veth1
B	5000	Veth2
C	6000	Veth3
D	5000	IP 2
E	6000	IP 2

MAC Address	VXLAN	Location
A	5000	IP 1
B	5000	IP 1
C	6000	IP 1
D	5000	Veth4
E	6000	Veth5

Figure 15-25 *VXLAN Segments Deployed in Two VEMs*

Consequently, a VXLAN segment requires

- An associated IP multicast address group
- IP multicast routing between VTEPs

If the number of IP multicast address groups available in a network is limited, multiple VXLAN segments can be mapped to a single IP multicast address. In this scenario, a VTEP will only forward a received VXLAN frame to an internal interface that shares the same VXLAN segment.

Therefore, VMs C and E can also communicate with each other through a completely different Layer 2 domain (VXLAN 6000, for example) that might use the same IP multicast address as VXLAN 5000. However, you should be aware that if more than one VXLAN segment is sharing the same IP multicast address group, a VEM will receive multidestination traffic from these VXLAN segments, regardless of whether it has VMs on all of them.

Going back to our virtual networking topology used in the previous sections, imagine that VM-App1 and VM-App2 are part of an application cluster that synchronizes all operations through updates sent in the same broadcast domain. However, for security reasons, these cluster vnics cannot use extended VLAN 300.

Figure 15-26 highlights both VMs in our updated topology.

As you can see, a VXLAN segment can easily connect additional vnics on both VMs. However, before any configuration is done on Nexus 1000V, the IP network infrastructure must be prepared to route the VXLAN multicast traffic.

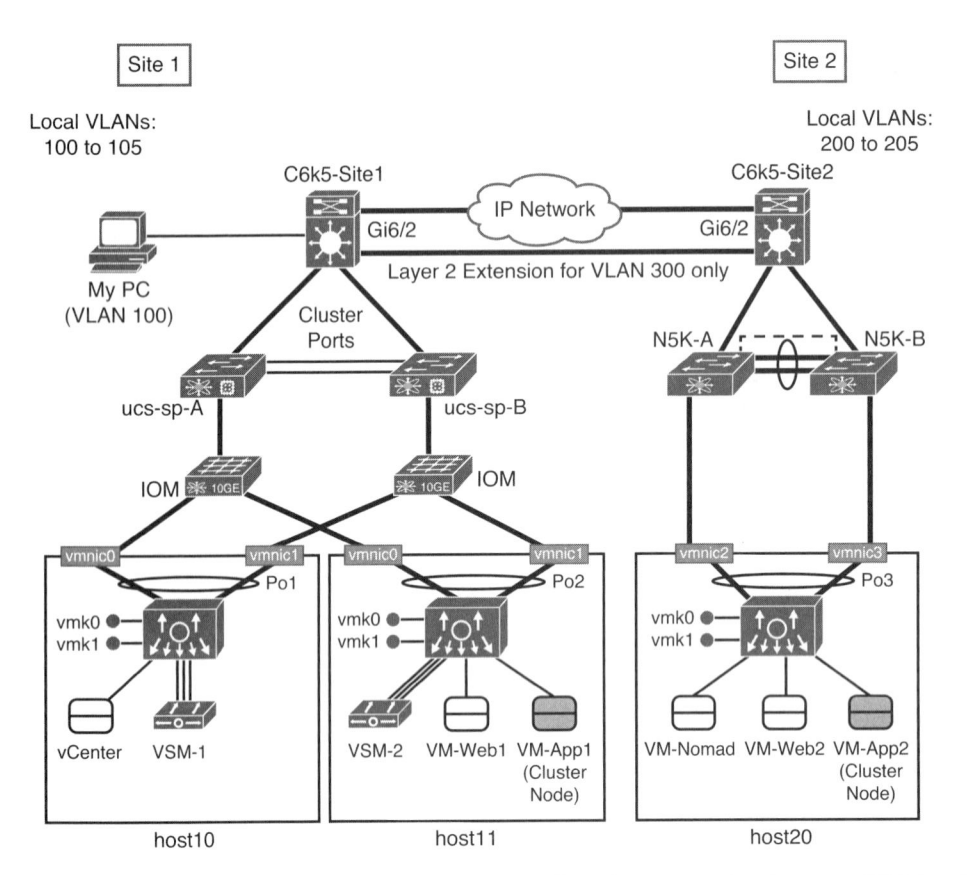

Figure 15-26 *Virtual Networking Topology Before the Connection Between VM-App1 and VM-App2's Cluster Interfaces*

Example 15-21 details the configuration done on the Catalyst 6500 switch from site 1. I will use VLAN 102 in site 1 and VLAN 202 in site 2 to carry VXLAN traffic between sites.

Example 15-21 *Preparing the Infrastructure*

```
! Enabling IP multicast routing
C6K5-Site1(config)# ip multicast-routing
! Configuring the SVI that will receive VXLAN traffic from Site 1
C6K5-Site1(config)# interface vlan 102
C6K5-Site1(config-if)# ip address 192.168.102.1 255.255.255.0
C6K5-Site1(config-if)# no shutdown
! Proxy ARP is required on SVIs that transport VXLAN traffic
C6K5-Site1(config-if)# ip proxy-arp
! Configuring MTU to support VXLAN 50-byte overhead
C6K5-Site1(config-if)# mtu 1550
! Enabling IGMP version 3 and PIM
```

```
C6K5-Site1(config-if)# ip igmp version 3
C6K5-Site1(config-if)# ip pim sparse-mode
! Configuring the IP interface to receive VXLAN traffic from Site 2
C6K5-Site1(config)# interface GigabitEthernet6/2
! Configuring MTU to support VXLAN 50-byte overhead
C6K5-Site1(config-if)# mtu 1550
! Enabling PIM Sparse Mode
C6K5-Site1(config-if)# ip pim sparse-mode
```

Tip Proxy Address Resolution Protocol (ARP) is a technique where a router interface answers ARP requests intended to a said host. Impersonating its identity, the router accepts IP packets to route them to this host. Proxy ARP is defined in RFC 1027.

A very similar configuration was applied to switch C6K5-Site2 for VLAN 202 and Layer 3 interface Gigabit Ethernet 6/2. Additionally, to avoid fragmentation and performance degradation, I have adjusted the MTU on all physical network interfaces that will carry VXLAN traffic (including the VEMs uplinks).

When a VEM is deploying VXLAN, it uses a VMkernel adapter IP address to encapsulate and transport VXLAN frames to another VEM. Also, through this interface, each VEM will initiate an ARP for all remote VEM IP addresses, regardless of whether they are on the same subnet or not. For that reason, the Proxy ARP feature was enabled on the C6K5-Site1 interface.

Example 15-22 details the creation of two special port profiles that will be assigned to the VMkernel adapters from each host.

Example 15-22 *Port Profiles for VXLAN VMkernel Interface*

```
! Port profile for VMkernel interfaces on site 1 (transported in VLAN 102)
VSM# show running-config port-profile N1KV-VMKNIC-VXLAN-SITE1
[output suppressed]
port-profile type vethernet N1KV-VMKNIC-VXLAN-SITE1
  vmware port-group
  switchport mode access
  switchport access vlan 102
  capability vxlan
  no shutdown
  state enabled
! Port profile for VMkernel interfaces on site 2 (transported in VLAN 202)
VSM# show running-config port-profile N1KV-VMKNIC-VXLAN-SITE2
[output suppressed]
port-profile type vethernet N1KV-VMKNIC-VXLAN-SITE2
```

```
vmware port-group
switchport mode access
switchport access vlan 202
capability vxlan
no shutdown
state enabled
```

While there are many ways to create a vmknic, Figure 15-27 represents the final step in a wizard that was started when the **Manage Virtual Adapters** link was accessed on host10.

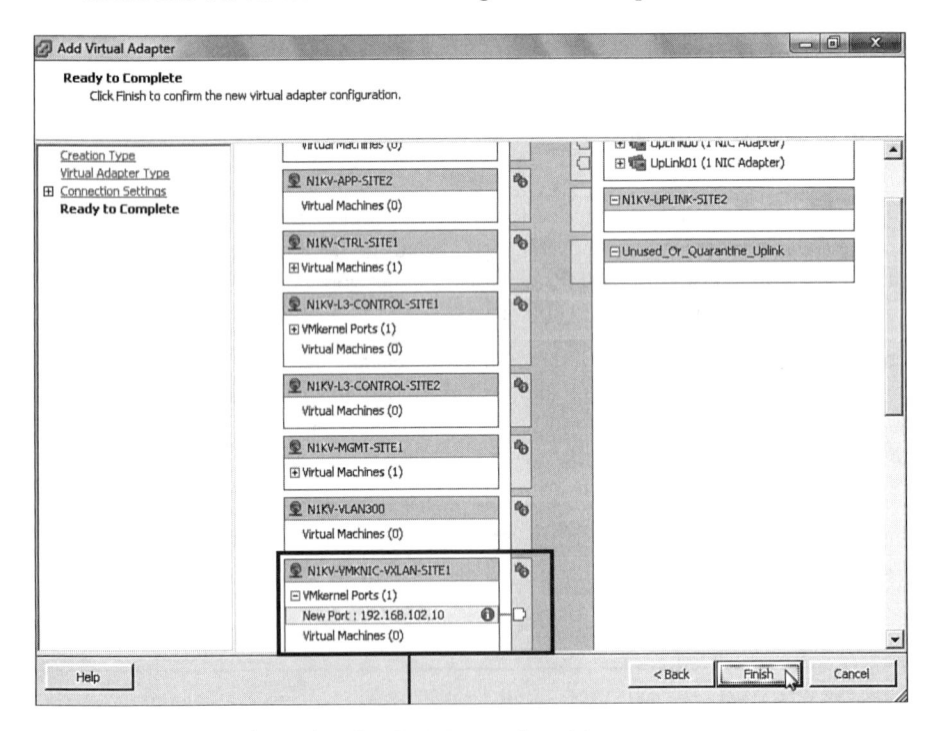

Figure 15-27 *VMkernel vmk2 Creation on host10*

As you can see in Figure 15-27, vmk2 in host10 was assigned to port group N1KV-VMKNIC-VXLAN-SITE1 and configured with IP address 192.168.102.10. The same port group was assigned to vmk2 on host11 (IP address 192.168.102.11).

On the other hand, host20's vmk2 interface was assigned to port group N1KV-VMKNIC-VXLAN-SITE2 and configured with IP address 192.168.202.20.

Because the assignment has connected all vmk2s to Nexus 1000V, we can finally configure a VXLAN segment on this switch, as Example 15-23 details.

Example 15-23 *Configuring VXLAN*

```
! Enabling VXLAN on Nexus 1000V
VSM(config)# feature segmentation
! Creating one VXLAN bridge domain to connect the cluster interfaces from VM-App1
and VM-App2
VSM(config)# bridge-domain VXLAN-CLUSTER-APP
! Assigning a segment ID (VNI) and an IP multicast address to this VXLAN
VSM(config-bd)# segment id 4096
VSM(config-bd)# group 239.1.1.1
```

Example 15-23 demonstrates that the configuration of a VXLAN somehow follows a VLAN-like configuration structure, but with additional parameters such as segment identifier (VNI) and mapped IP multicast group address.

Example 15-24 details the creation of a port profile that will spawn virtual Ethernet access interfaces in VXLAN 4096 (which is the first available VXLAN ID).

Example 15-24 *Configuring VXLAN 4096 Port Profile*

```
VSM# show running-config port-profile N1KV-VXLAN4096
[output suppressed]
! Creating a port-profile for an access port that belongs to VXLAN 4096
port-profile type vethernet N1KV-VXLAN4096
  vmware port-group
  switchport mode access
  switchport access bridge-domain VXLAN-CLUSTER-APP
  no shutdown
  state enabled
```

The cluster vnics can finally be connected to this segment. Figure 15-28 depicts the assignment of port group N1KV-VXLAN4096 to a new added network adapter in VM-App1 (the VM was powered off before this operation).

After the same port group is assigned to VM-App2 (and both VMs are powered on), Layer 2 cluster traffic from both VMs is already traversing VXLAN 4096.

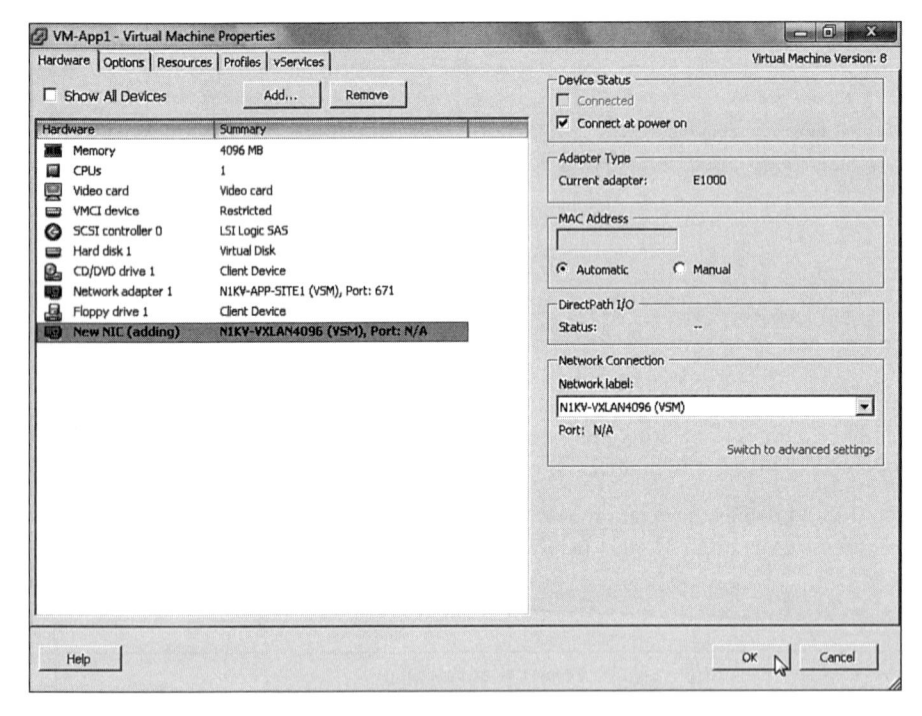

Figure 15-28 *Connecting VM-App1 Cluster vnic to VXLAN 4096*

Example 15-25 verifies the status and the MAC address table of VXLAN segment 4096.

Example 15-25 *VXLAN 4096 Status and MAC Address Table*

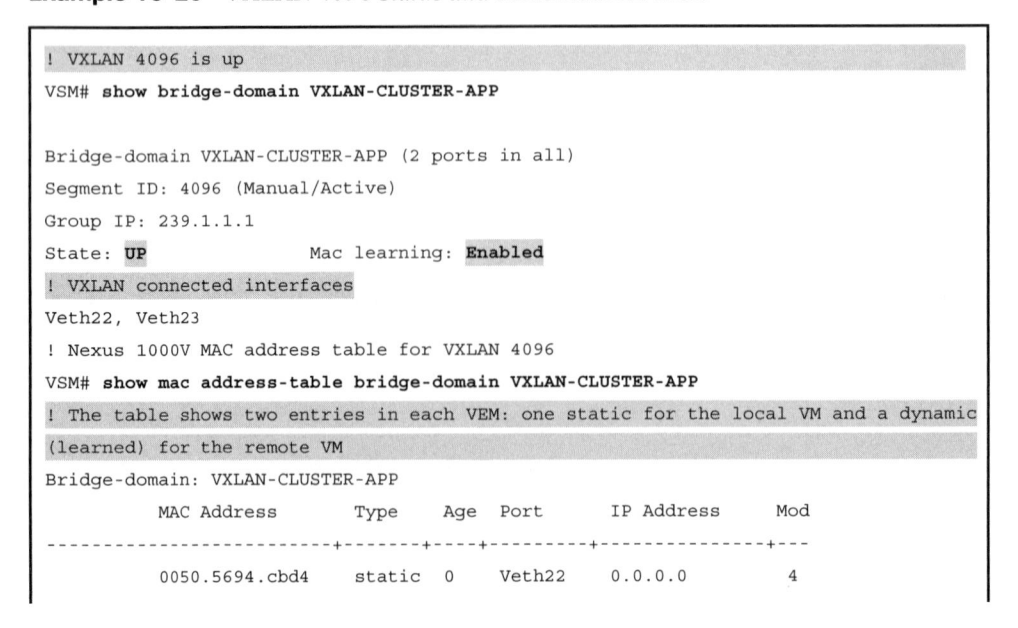

```
! VXLAN 4096 is up
VSM# show bridge-domain VXLAN-CLUSTER-APP


Bridge-domain VXLAN-CLUSTER-APP (2 ports in all)
Segment ID: 4096 (Manual/Active)
Group IP: 239.1.1.1
State: UP                Mac learning: Enabled
! VXLAN connected interfaces
Veth22, Veth23
! Nexus 1000V MAC address table for VXLAN 4096
VSM# show mac address-table bridge-domain VXLAN-CLUSTER-APP
! The table shows two entries in each VEM: one static for the local VM and a dynamic
(learned) for the remote VM
Bridge-domain: VXLAN-CLUSTER-APP
             MAC Address      Type    Age  Port         IP Address       Mod
---------------------------+-------+----+---------+---------------+---
             0050.5694.cbd4   static  0    Veth22       0.0.0.0          4
```

```
              0050.5694.03bf    dynamic 0    Po2      192.168.202.20   4
              0050.5694.03bf    static  0    Veth23   0.0.0.0          5
              0050.5694.cbd4    dynamic 0    Eth5/4   192.168.102.11   5
Total MAC Addresses: 4
```

Should any of these VMs migrate to another host, Nexus 1000V will guarantee that the VXLAN characteristics of the interface are also migrated to the destination VEM.

Besides the scaling of bridge domains and their extension over Layer 3 networks, another VXLAN advantage can be observed on the sizes of the MAC address tables on the physical network. While the deployment of traditional VLANs demands that all STP-based switches learn the MAC address from all VMs, VXLAN will only include the VTEP MAC addresses in their tables.

Introducing Virtual Machine Fabric Extender

As you have learned in this chapter, Nexus 1000V offers the abstraction of an NX-OS switch in server virtualization environments, providing the same level of control and visibility to virtual machine traffic.

Bridging again the chasm between physical and virtual worlds, Cisco has pioneered yet another virtual networking technology: *Virtual Machine Fabric Extender (VM-FEX)*. In essence, VM-FEX emulates a Fabric Extender inside a virtualized host, providing connectivity to its virtual machines.

If you remember the concepts explained in Chapter 7, "Virtualized Chassis with Fabric Extenders," a Fabric Extender is a device that acts as a remote linecard for a parent switch, extending a virtualized chassis to multiple server racks while reducing the number of management points in the data center.

Mimicking its physical counterparts, VM-FEX consolidates the networking infrastructure, enabling configuration, management, and monitoring of virtual and physical connectivity in the same device. With VM-FEX deployed on a server virtualization environment

- Each virtual machine has a dedicated virtual Ethernet interface on the parent switch.
- All virtual machine traffic is sent straight to this interface on the parent switch.
- Software-based switching can be eliminated because the parent switch will handle all VM-related traffic.

Cisco *virtualized interface cards (VIC)* are an integral part of the VM-FEX architecture. Besides creating virtual PCIe I/O devices, these adapters enable the deployment of VNTags in hardware, allowing a parent switch to recognize Ethernet frames from distinct virtual machines.

> **Note** Although single-root I/O virtualization (SR-IOV) embodies a similar principle (the creation of virtual PCIe I/O devices), a Cisco VIC creates fully functional unique and independent PCIe adapters (such as network interface cards [NICs] and host bus adapters [HBAs]) that do not rely on special feature support from operating systems or hypervisors.

There are several options to implement VM-FEX with Cisco Data Center products. At the time of this writing, the following hardware combinations are supported:

- Nexus 5500 or 6000 switches with UCS C-Series servers equipped with VIC adapters (directly connected or through a Fabric Extender [Nexus 2232PP or 2248PQ])
- UCS Fabric Interconnect with UCS C-series servers equipped with VIC adapters, and connected through a Nexus 2232PP Fabric Extender
- UCS Fabric Interconnect with UCS B-series servers equipped with VIC adapters

Figure 15-29 presents the virtual networking view of each VM-FEX deployment option.

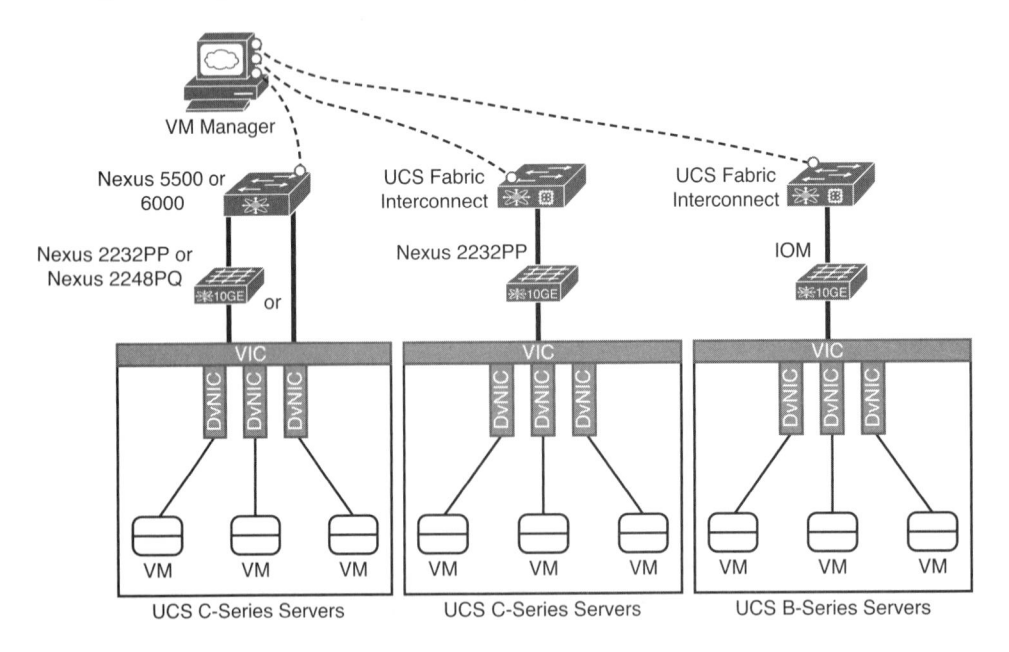

Figure 15-29 *VM-FEX Deployment Options*

Figure 15-29 also deals with the interface provisioning principle behind VM-FEX: As soon as a VM manager (such as VMware vCenter) assigns a port group to a virtual machine, the VIC adapter automatically connects a *dynamic virtual NIC (vNIC)* to this VM. This vNIC will work as an FEX Host Interface (HIF), which has a unique VNTag that will define a virtual Ethernet interface in the parent switch.

> **Tip** In VM-FEX topologies, the UCS IOM or Nexus 2000 Fabric Extenders do not generate VNTags for the dynamic vNICs. They simply forward frames from these adapters based on this parameter.

VM-FEX makes it possible for a physical networking device to define exclusive treatment, such as quality of service and security, for a virtual machine virtual adapter as if it were a directly connected physical host.

At the time of this writing, VM-FEX is available for VMware vSphere, Microsoft Hyper-V, and Red Hat KVM hypervisors. In this chapter, I will focus on its integration with VMware vSphere to allow an accurate comparison between VM-FEX and Nexus 1000V.

Deploying VM-FEX

To explore the concepts of VM-FEX, I will leverage some of the UCS configurations we have developed together in Chapter 14, "Changing Personalities."

The following steps are required for a VM-FEX deployment in a Unified Computing System:

1. Enable dynamic vNICs on a UCS service profile.
2. Prepare a vSphere host for VM-FEX.
3. Use the UCS VMware configuration wizard.
4. Migrate virtual machines to VM-FEX.

Enabling Dynamic vNICs on a UCS Service Profile

If you recall from Chapter 14, UCS servers use service profiles to abstract hardware identifiers, install firmware versions, and define settings. Additionally, these configuration entities also dictate whether a server VIC will generate dynamic vNICs.

To enable VM-FEX on UCS, a dynamic vNIC connection policy must be created on UCS Manager to define how many interfaces will be created per service profile, their adapter policy, and how these vNICs will be "protected" from a fabric failure. In more detail, you have the following options for dynamic vNIC failover behavior:

- **Protected Pref A:** Dynamic vNICs will attempt to use Fabric Interconnect A with backup to B.
- **Protected Pref B:** Dynamic vNICs will attempt to use Fabric Interconnect B with backup to A.
- **Protected:** Dynamic vNICs will attempt to use whichever fabric is available.

Figure 15-30 depicts the dynamic vNIC policy DvNIC-Policy-1, which defines eight virtual interfaces per service profile, adapter policy VMware for these interfaces, and their preference for fabric A.

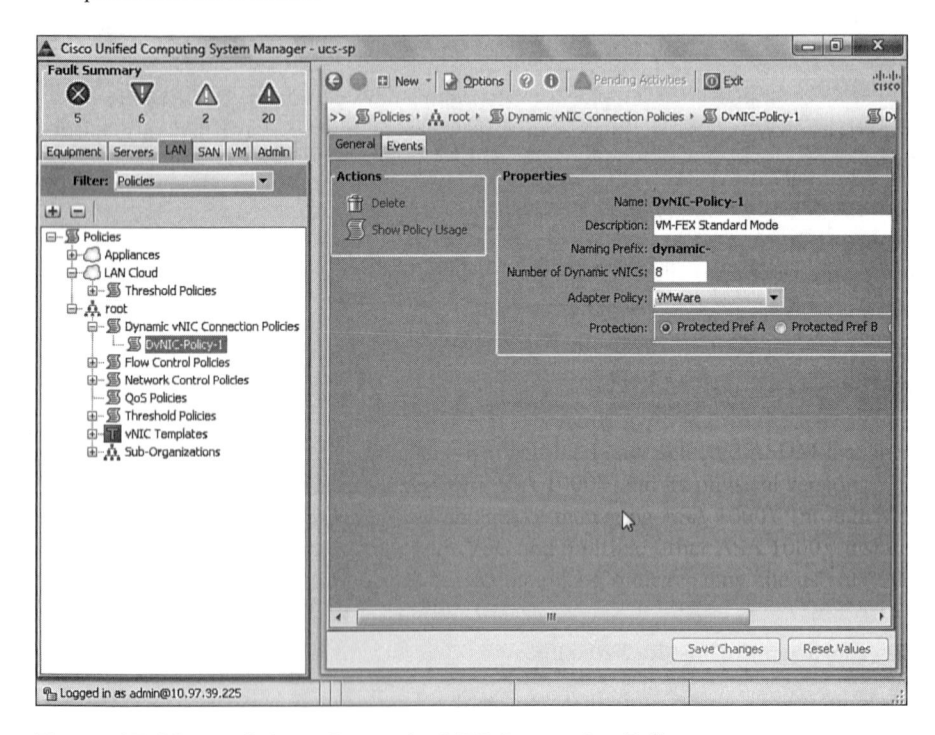

Figure 15-30 *Defining a Dynamic vNIC Connection Policy*

After its creation, you should apply this policy to a service profile that will deploy VM-FEX. As if you have any choice, I propose we use our mutual acquaintance from Chapter 14, service profile SP-1.

> **Tip** To refresh your memory, SP-1 was a pretty straightforward service profile that resulted from one interaction with the Create Service Profile (expert) wizard. At this moment, SP-1 is associated to server 1/1 in our UCS domain.

Through the UCS Manager, right-clicking SP-1 on the Server tab, you can change its dynamic vNIC policy and apply DvNIC-Policy-1 without any disruption to the server.

Figure 15-31 shows the created dynamic vNICs in SP-1 after the DvNIC-Policy-1 is applied to it (the dynamic vNICs are right above the original static vNICs).

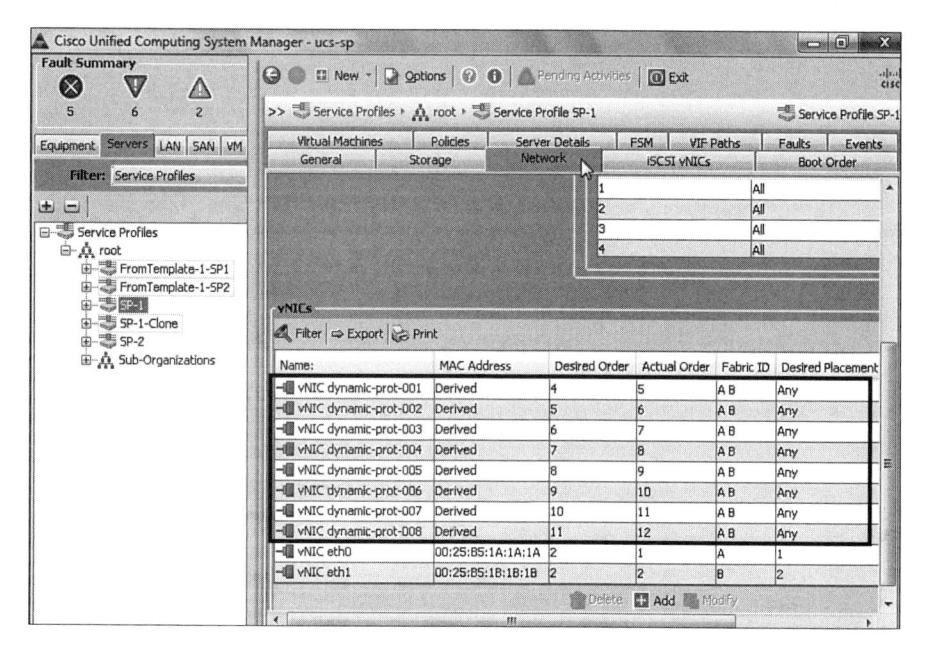

Figure 15-31 *Dynamic vNICs in SP-1*

> **Note** The maximum number of supported dynamic vNICs per server depends on the Fabric Interconnect, IOM, and VIC models. This value is also a factor of the number of uplinks between the IOM and the Fabric Interconnect. Refer to the UCS online product documentation for more details.

I have also cloned SP-1 to deploy a new service profile (SP-2) to implement VM-FEX in server 1/2. Consequently, DvNIC-Policy-1 will also be applied to SP-2.

Preparing VMware vSphere Host to Deploy VM-FEX

Continuing our VM-FEX deployment, the vSphere hosts must also be primed to handle the dynamic vNICs on SP-1 and SP-2. Analogously to Nexus 1000V, a vSphere Installation Bundle (VIB) file is also required for this operation.

The VIB installation should start with a thorough verification of the compatibility of your hardware (server and VIC) and software (vSphere version and VIC drivers) components.

Cisco publishes hardware compatibility lists whenever a new UCS software version is released. In this deployment, I am using a B200-M1 blade with M81KR VIC adapter, which required vSphere 5.0 Update 1, UCS Manager version 2.0(4), Ethernet driver 2.1.2.22, Fibre Channel 1.5.0.8, and VM-FEX VIB file version v132-4.2.1.1.4.1.0-3.0.4. Although I am pretty sure you will use completely different versions in your future deployments, trust me when I recommend that you should be really methodic in this process.

> **Tip** All the referred files can be obtained from different sources, such as Cisco and VMware websites. Additionally, the VIB files can be downloaded from the UCS Fabric Interconnect HTTP server.

To install the VIB, I have enabled Secure Shell (SSH) on both vSphere hosts (using the Troubleshooting options from the server console) and copied the file to their temporary folder (tmp) through SCP (Secure Copy Protocol). After putting the host into Maintenance mode (using the vSphere client), I have initiated an SSH session each host, as Example 15-26 illustrates for host100 (IP address 192.168.100.100).

Example 15-26 *Installing VIB in vSphere host100*

```
login as: root
Using keyboard-interactive authentication.
Password:
[output suppressed]
! Checking if the VIB file is really in the tmp folder
~ # cd tmp
/tmp # ls
cross_cisco-vem-v132-4.2.1.1.4.1.0-3.0.4.vib
! Installing the VIB file
/tmp # esxcli software vib install -v /tmp/cross_cisco-vem-v132-4.2.1.1.4.1.0-
3.0.4.vib
Installation Result
   Message: Operation finished successfully.
   Reboot Required: false
   VIBs Installed: Cisco_bootbank_cisco-vem-v132-esx_4.2.1.1.4.1.0-3.0.4
   VIBs Removed:
   VIBs Skipped:
```

You are probably surprised that VIB file has also installed a **Virtual Ethernet Module (VEM)** on host100 and host101 (IP address 192.168.100.101). Although it uses the same kernel process name, the VM-FEX VEM agent works very differently than the Nexus 1000V VEM agent. As you will see in the next sections, the VIB I have just installed will provide the liaison between the virtual machine adapters (vnics) and the service profile dynamic vNICs.

> **Note** At the time of this writing, you cannot install both VM-FEX and Nexus 1000V VEM agents on the same vSphere host.

Using the UCS Manager VMware Integration Wizard

With hardware (service profiles) and software (vSphere) ready for VM-FEX implementation on both servers, UCS Manager and VMware vCenter can be connected to deploy configuration synchronization and automatic connectivity provisioning.

Fortunately, UCS Manager has a wizard that can assist with this task. Figure 15-32 shows how this wizard can be activated when you access the VM tab from UCS Manager.

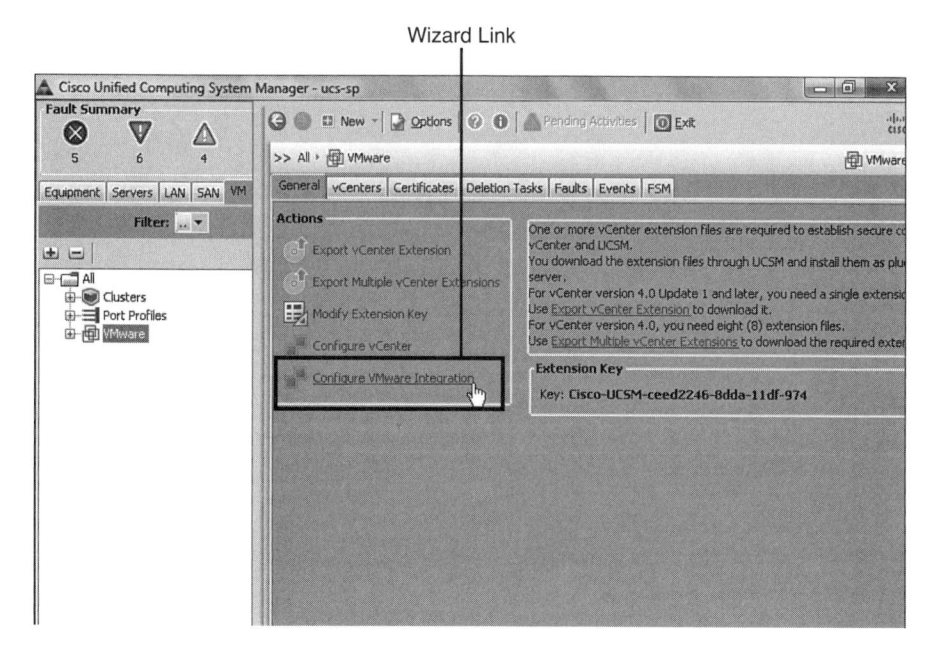

Figure 15-32 *Accessing the UCS VMware Integration Wizard*

In the first step of the wizard, UCS Manager offers to export a vCenter plug-in file. These plug-ins can be defined as software modules that extend the management capabilities of vCenter to provide more features and functionality (such as VM-FEX).

Figure 15-33 depicts the wizard step where you can obtain the UCS VM-FEX plug-in for vCenter.

After the plug-in is installed, vCenter is able to recognize UCS Manager as an associated management tool. The UCS VM-FEX plug-in installation can be performed in vCenter through the **Manage Plug-ins** option, as depicted in Figure 15-34.

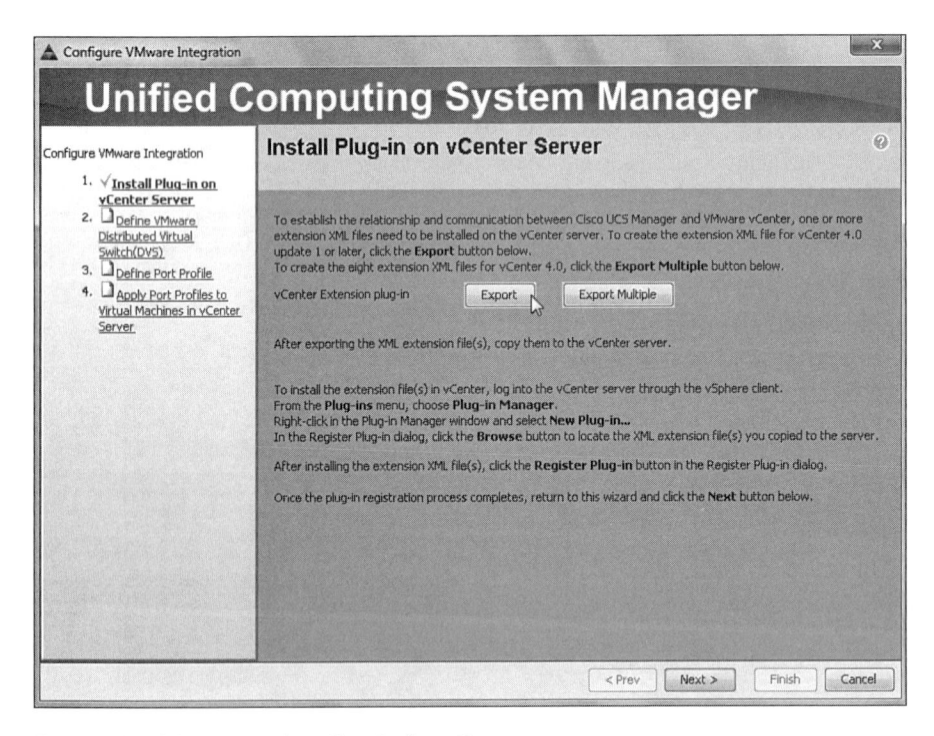

Figure 15-33 *Exporting Plug-in for vCenter*

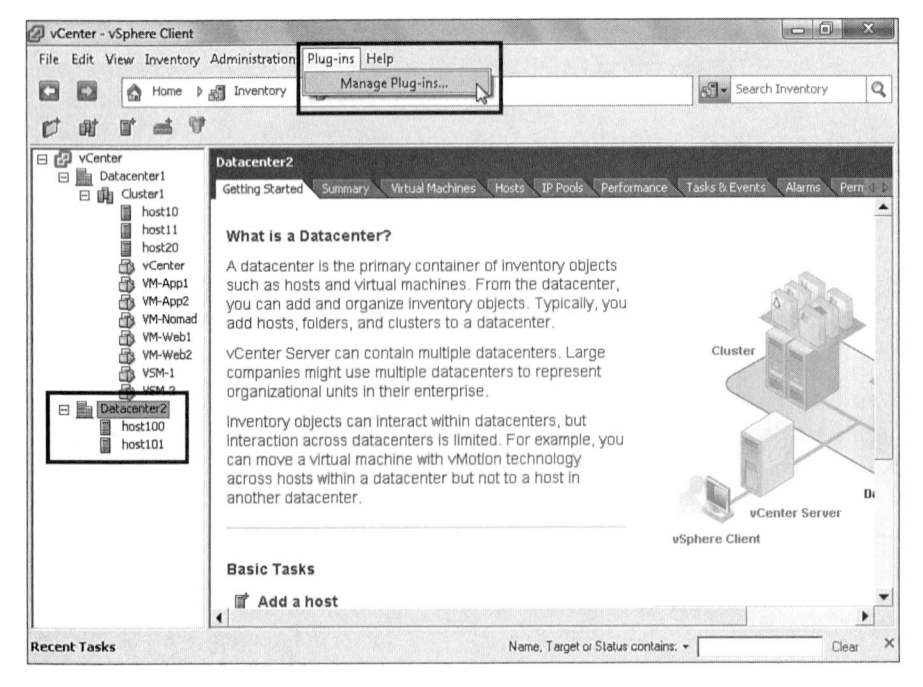

Figure 15-34 *Importing Plug-in in vCenter*

Figure 15-34 also shows the following:

- I will use the same vCenter server from previous sections to deploy VM-FEX.
- This vCenter instance is already managing host100 and host101. Both vSphere hosts belong to a new vCenter data center (Datacenter2), created to achieve a better isolation of resources between the Nexus 1000V and VM-FEX implementations.

After the plug-in is installed (right-clicking in the screen and importing the UCS VM-FEX plug-in), vCenter provides its details, as shown in Figure 15-35.

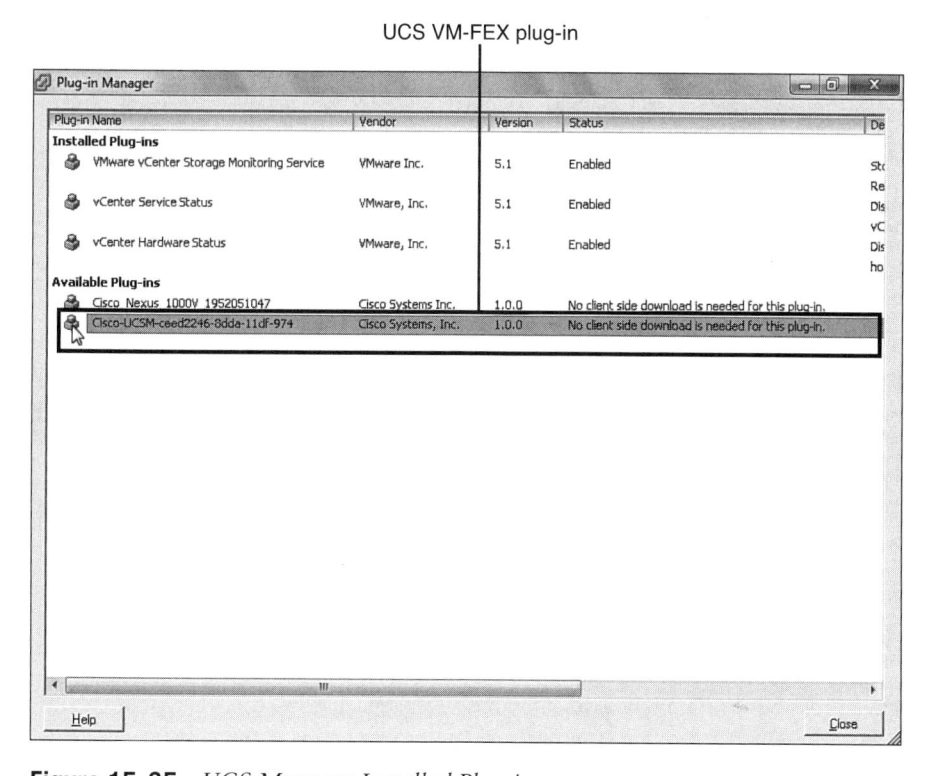

Figure 15-35 *UCS Manager Installed Plug-in*

Advancing to the next step in the UCS Manager wizard, it is time to declare the vCenter parameters that will be used in VM-FEX. All the used vCenter parameters (IP address, Datacenter, Folder, and Distributed Virtual Switch) are defined at this stage, as illustrated in Figure 15-36.

As shown in Figure 15-36, VM-FEX will also leverage the vSphere Distributed Virtual Switch API as its background infrastructure on the vSphere hosts. However, the resulting Distributed Virtual Switch will not behave as an ordinary DVS or a Nexus 1000V. Actually, because it will be controlled by the VM-FEX VEM agent, this DVS will merely provide a a one-to-one connection infrastructure between VM vnics and VIC dynamic vNICs.

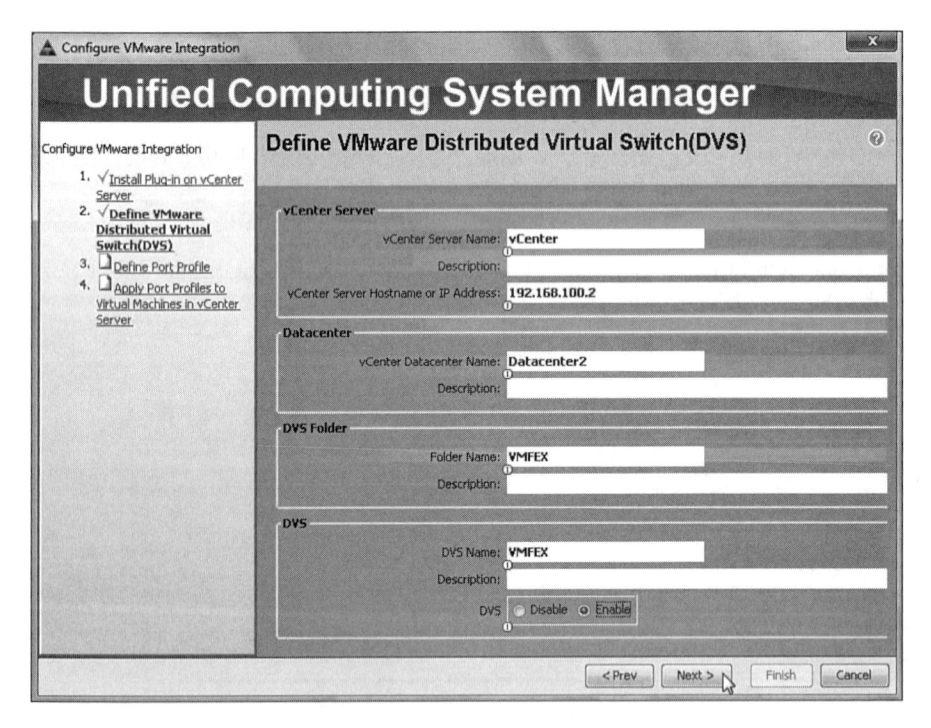

Figure 15-36 *Defining the vCenter Distributed Virtual Switch for VM-FEX*

Similarly to Nexus 1000V, VM-FEX automatically creates VMware port groups through the configuration of port profiles. And in fact, the next wizard step allows you to create a first VM-FEX port profile.

Figure 15-37 displays the port profile VMFEX-VLAN105 settings, which basically provide access connectivity for VLAN105 (note that I have selected VLAN 105 as the port profile native VLAN because I do not expect 802.1Q tags from the VMs).

Although I have not configured them, other interface parameters, such as Quality of Service, Network Policy Control, and Pin Groups could also be configured in this port profile.

The final wizard step applies the previous settings to the selected vCenter and preconfigured Datacenter2. As shown in Figure 15-38, the VM tab on UCS Manager is now populated with a vCenter structure that contains Datacenter2, a VMFEX folder, and a DVS (also named VMFEX).

The VMFEX DVS contains three port profiles: VMFEX-VLAN105 (manually created during the integration wizard interaction), deleted-pg-VMFEX (created automatically to store vNICs from deleted port profiles), and uplink-pg-VMFEX (also created automatically; its use will be explained later).

Because UCS Manager and vCenter are correctly connected and synchronized, a very similar DVS structure can be observed in vCenter networking inventory, as depicted in Figure 15-39.

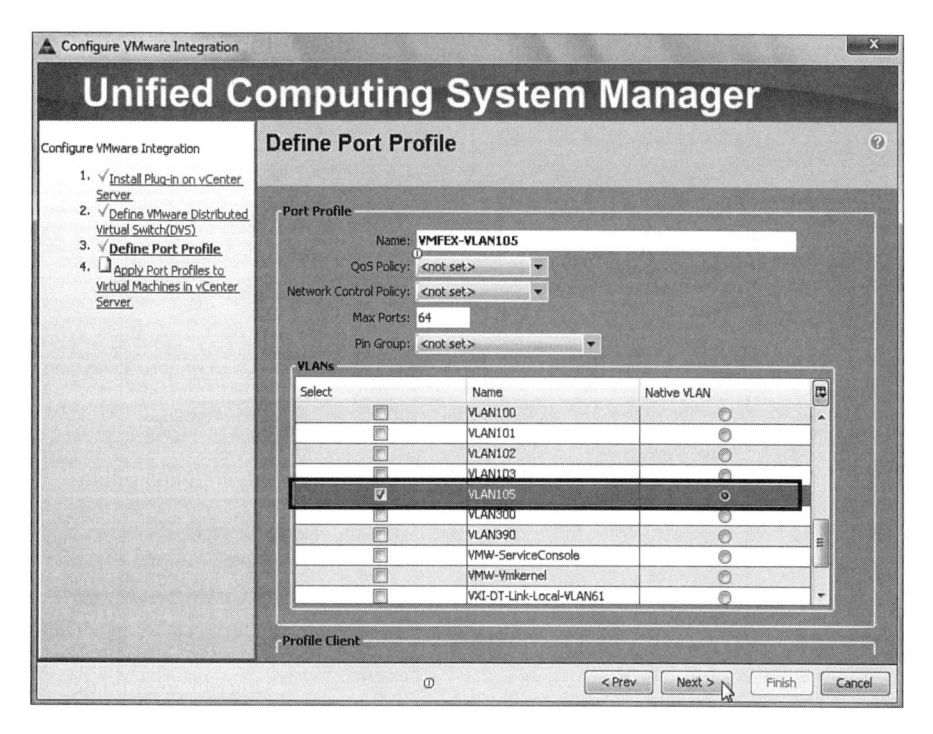

Figure 15-37 *Creating the VMFEX-VLAN105 Port Profile*

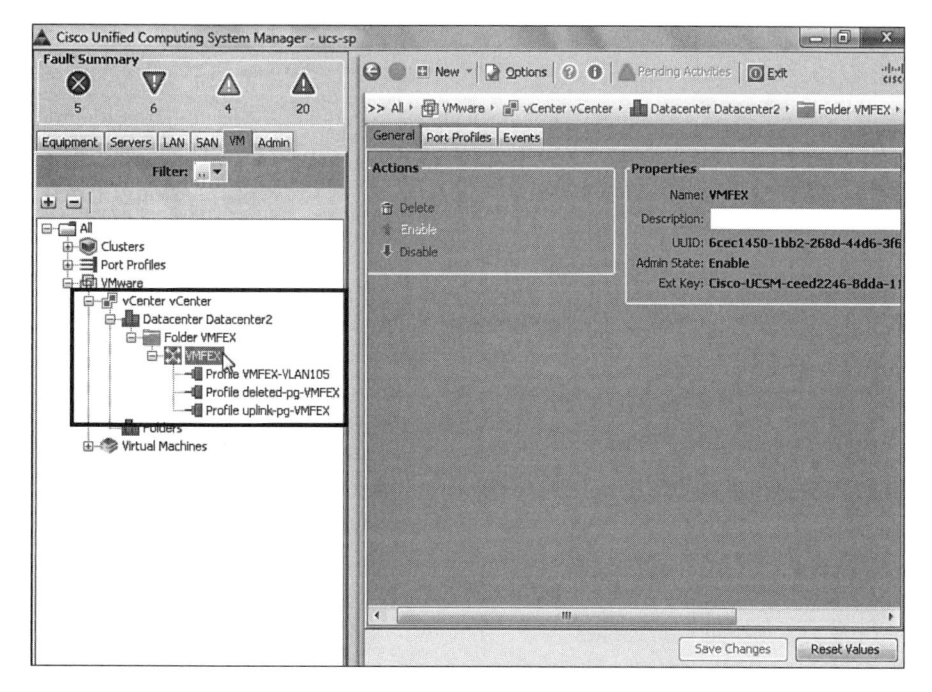

Figure 15-38 *VMFEX DVS" to "VM-FEX vCenter Structure*

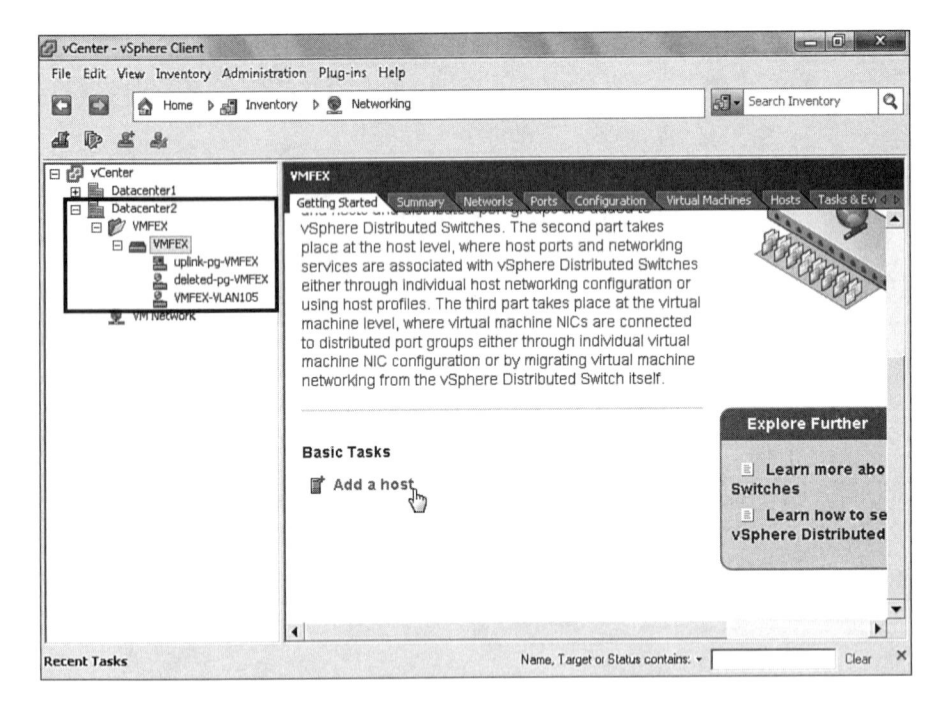

Figure 15-39 *VM-FEX Structure in vCenter*

Nevertheless, the VMFEX DVS does not have any hosts connected to it yet. Clicking the **Add a host** link, also shown in Figure 15-39, both host100 and host101 can be inserted into this DVS through the same wizard that was demonstrated for Nexus 1000V.

VMware vSphere requires a "dummy" uplink (such as vmnic0) to also be migrated to any DVS to enable its activation. This virtual connection does not have any operational significance because it does not carry VM-FEX traffic. But in our scenario, I have migrated vmnic0 on both hosts to the VMFEX DVS using the automatically created port group **uplink-pg-VMFEX**.

At this point, both hosts are ready to connect dynamic vNIC interfaces to VM vnics (or VMkernel interfaces). And as expected, the VMFEX DVS will proxy a one-to-one linkage between both elements.

Migrating Virtual Machines to VM-FEX

In this section, virtual machines will be connected through VM-FEX at last. And with that in mind, I have prepared the virtual networking topology displayed in Figure 15-40.

As you can notice in the figure, I have provisioned two virtual machines (VM-DB1 on host100 and VM-DB2 on host101) that are connected to VLAN 105 through a port group from a vSwitch in each vSphere host.

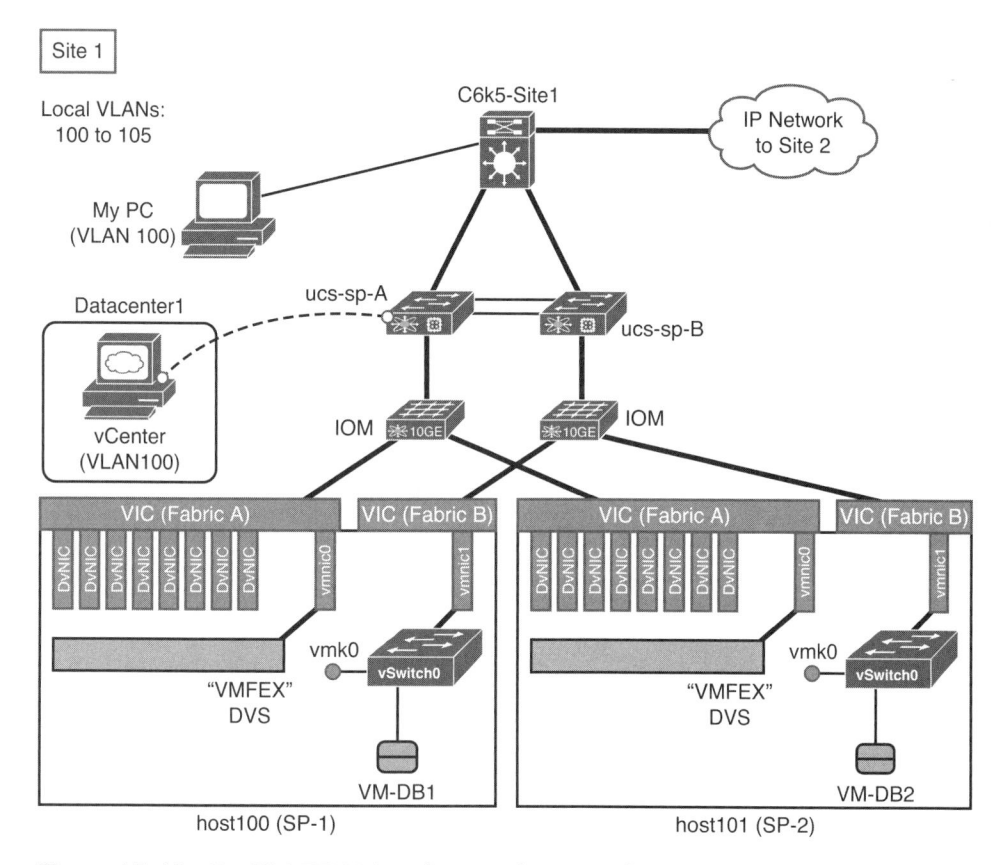

Figure 15-40 *Pre-VM-FEX Virtual Networking Topology*

Because port profile VMFEX-VLAN105 is already a port group from VMFEX DVS in vCenter, all we must do to connect this virtual machine to the virtual Fabric Extender is assign the VMFEX-VLAN105 port group from VMFEX DVS.

Figure 15-41 exhibits this assignment on the virtual machine properties of VM-DB1.

Tip Note that VM-DB1 network adapter 1 has 0050.5694.97d8 as its MAC address. This information will be important in the near future.

After I have performed the same setting on VM-DB2, both virtual machines are visible on the UCS Manager VM tab, as depicted in Figure 15-42.

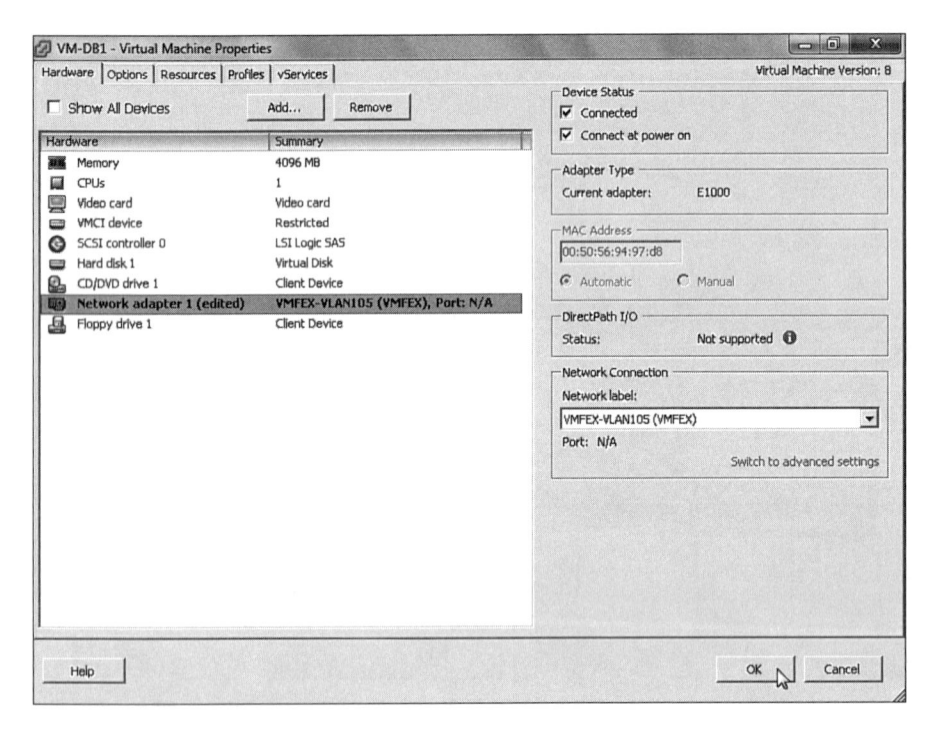

Figure 15-41 *Changing the Port Profile for VM-DB1 Network Adapter 1*

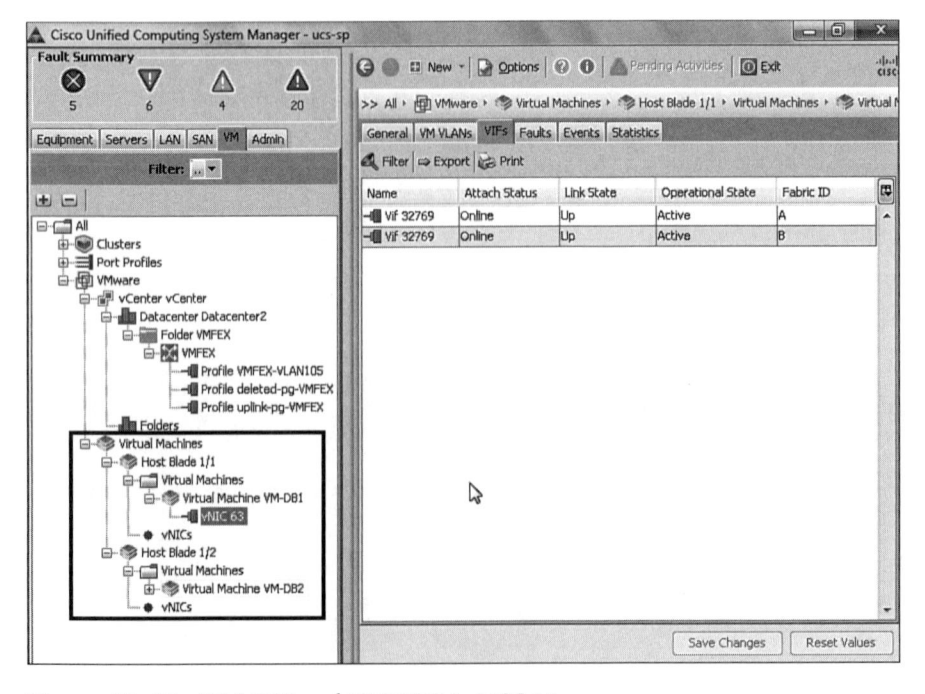

Figure 15-42 *VM-DB1 and VM-DB2 in UCS Manager*

Figure 15-42 also exhibits important details about the UCS implementation of VM-FEX. For example, VM-DB1 is connected to vNIC 63 (which is the port ID from the vSphere DVS) that is mapped to two virtual interfaces with an identifier of 32769. The meaning of these interfaces can be understood through SSH sessions to both Fabric Interconnects, as shown in Examples 15-27 and 15-28.

Example 15-27 *Virtual Ethernet Interfaces and MAC Address Table for VLAN 105 on Fabric Interconnect ucs-sp-a*

```
! Displaying the virtual ethernet interfaces for VM-DB1 and VM-DB2
ucs-sp-a(nxos)# show interface brief
[output suppressed]
--------------------------------------------------------------------
Vethernet     VLAN    Type Mode    Status    Reason        Speed
--------------------------------------------------------------------
[output suppressed]
Veth32769     105     eth  trunk   up        none          auto
Veth32770     105     eth  trunk   up        none          auto
! Verifying the static MAC addresses from VLAN 105
ucs-sp-a(nxos)# show mac address-table static vlan 105
Legend:
        * - primary entry, G - Gateway MAC, (R) - Routed MAC, O - Overlay MAC
        age - seconds since last seen,+ - primary entry using vPC Peer-Link
   VLAN     MAC Address      Type      age     Secure NTFY    Ports
---------+-----------------+--------+---------+------+----+------------------
! VM-DB1 MAC Address and associated virtual Ethernet interface
* 105      0050.5694.97d8    static    0        F      F    Veth32769
! VM-DB2 MAC Address and associated virtual Ethernet interface
* 105      0050.5694.a851    static    0        F      F    Veth32770
```

Example 15-28 *Virtual Ethernet Interfaces and MAC Address Table for VLAN 105 on Fabric Interconnect ucs-sp-b*

```
! Displaying the virtual ethernet interfaces for VM-DB1 and VM-DB2
ucs-sp-b(nxos)# show interface brief
[output suppressed]
--------------------------------------------------------------------
Vethernet     VLAN    Type Mode    Status    Reason        Speed
--------------------------------------------------------------------
[output suppressed]
Veth32769     105     eth  trunk   up        none          auto
Veth32770     105     eth  trunk   up        none          auto
! Although virtual interfaces exist on ucs-sp-b, the virtual machines are not using
them
ucs-sp-b(nxos)# show mac address-table static vlan 105
ucs-sp-b(nxos)#
```

Together, Examples 15-27 and 15-28 demonstrate that both service profiles SP-1 and SP-2 are following the "Protect Pref A" option from policy DvNIC-Policy-1. Although all VMs are primarily connected to Fabric A, virtual Ethernet interfaces are already provisioned on Fabric B to provide a quick failover for them if Fabric A fails for any reason.

Tip To guarantee Ethernet connectivity to a protected vNIC, gratuitous ARPs sourced with its MAC address are sent through the Fabric B uplinks after the fabric failover.

Online Migrations and VM-FEX

VM-FEX also supports the migration of "living" virtual machines. From a parent switch perspective, a migration of a VM-FEX VM does not really change much because the interface's VNTag is also carried on to the destination host.

To demonstrate this behavior in our scenario, each host will need a VMkernel interface to carry vMotion traffic. These interfaces will be also connected to the VM-FEX infrastructure, and thereby, I will create a port profile for them on the VM tab from UCS Manager.

Figure 15-43 portrays the creation port profile VMFEX-vMotion that will be used on the future vMotion VMkernel interfaces.

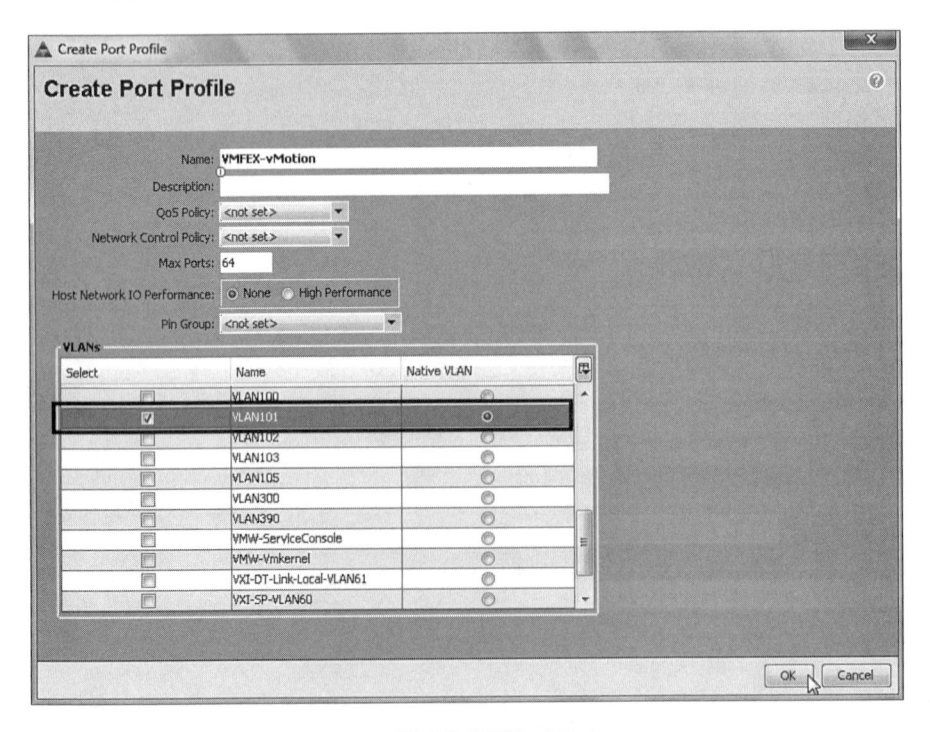

Figure 15-43 *Creating Port Profile VMFEX-vMotion*

After a port profile is configured, UCS Manager also requires a profile client to be created for this port profile. This configuration basically defines the target DVS that will deploy the port profile (if more than one DVS is being implemented). In this chapter, I have selected the **All** option, which invariably "sends" the port profile to VMFEX DVS.

Consequently, a port group named VMFEX-vMotion is created at VMFEX DVS. From this moment on, a new VMkernel interface can be created and assigned to this port group.

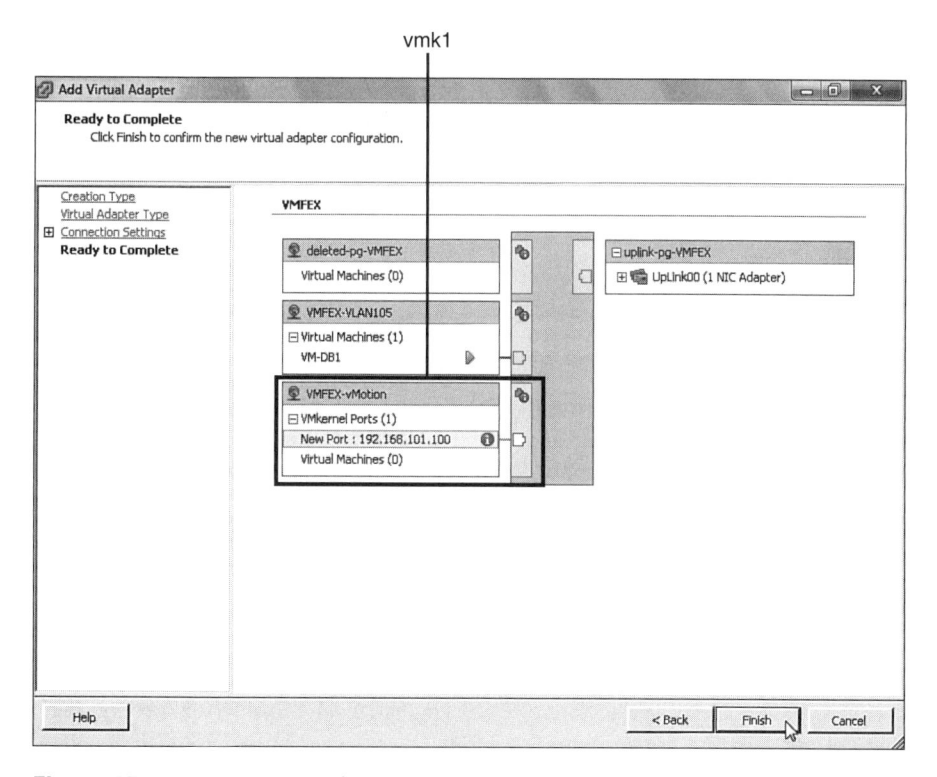

Figure 15-44 represents the last step of the Add Virtual Adapter wizard on host100.

Figure 15-44 *Creating vmk1 on host100*

I have proceeded in the same way with host101, assigning IP address 192.168.101.101 to its vmk1 adapter.

With both vmknic interfaces connected to UCS dynamic vNICs, it is now possible to perform a vMotion of VM-DB2 from host101 to host100. After the vMotion is completed, both VMs can be visualized on server 1/1, as shown Figure 15-45.

Also in Figure 15-45, you can observe that that the vmk1 interfaces have received DVS Port IDs 1730 (host100) and 1731 (host101).

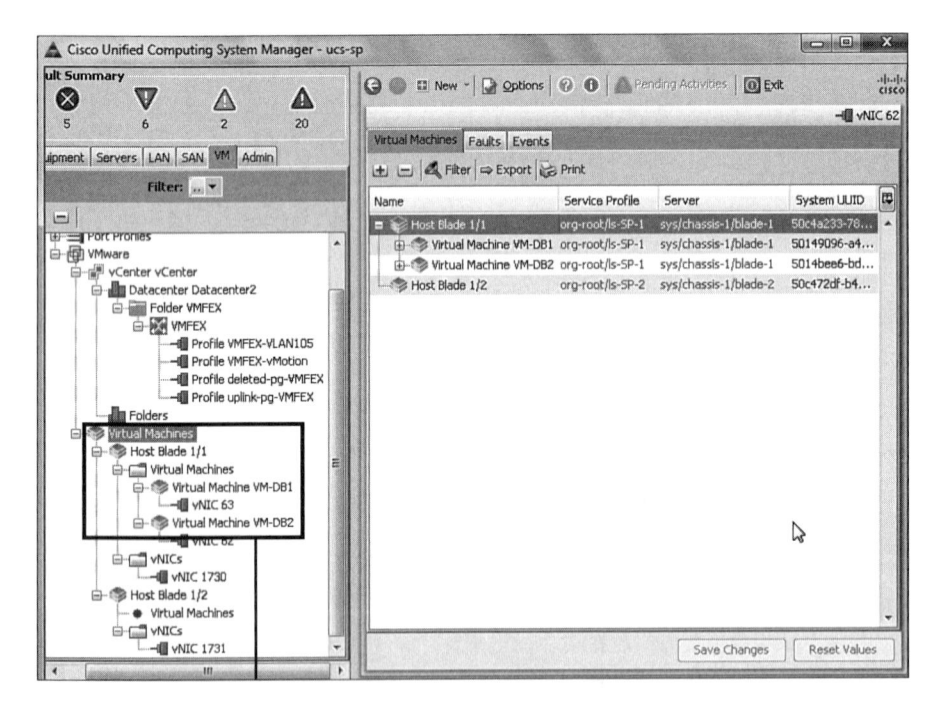

Figure 15-45 *Virtual Machine Location in UCS Manager*

Besides demonstrating VM-FEX support of virtual machine online migrations, this little experience also demonstrates that VMkernel interfaces can also be connected to dynamic vNICs. Hence, to consolidate all virtual networking from our VM-FEX scenario, I have configured a similar port profile (VMFEX-MGMT) to provide connectivity in VLAN 100 for both management virtual adapters (vmk0). Furthermore, I have also migrated vmnic1 to VMFEX DVS to provide connectivity redundancy to the mandatory "dummy" uplink.

I will not show these configurations because I have already explained very similar procedures in this chapter. Nonetheless, Figure 15-46 summarizes the final virtual networking topology of our VM-FEX scenario.

In the figure, I have not pictured the standard vSwitches because they will not be used anymore.

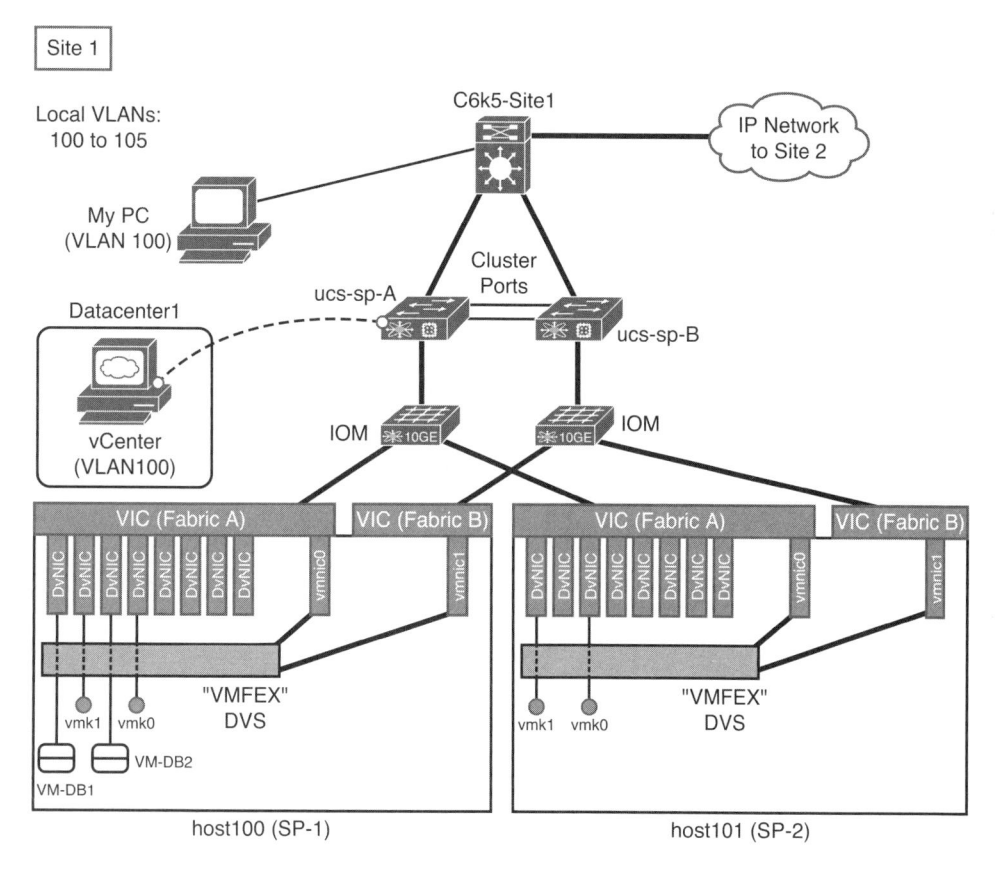

Figure 15-46 *VM-FEX Topology After Virtual Adapters Migration*

VM-FEX High-Performance Mode

Software-based virtual networking solutions, such as VMware vSwitch and Cisco Nexus 1000V, consume server CPU and memory resources to handle virtual machine network traffic. While these solutions expend an extremely small portion of host resources, they invariably add overheads that affect virtual machine I/O performance.

This effect can be fully understood if you consider that the data path between a VM vnic and the physical NIC must be handled by the hypervisor itself. After all, the virtual switching solution must emulate a switch interface to the VM and also control the physical NIC driver to process its traffic. For that reason, several organizations are still reluctant to virtualize I/O-intensive applications such as database and ERP servers.

VMware offered a solution to this problem with the vSphere VMDirectPath I/O feature, which allows a VM guest operating system to directly access a physical PCI or PCIe device on a host. Without a doubt, VMDirectPath I/O demands more strict compatibility requirements from the hardware used in the system. For example, the host CPU must support Intel Virtualization Technology for Directed I/O (VT-d), and the physical Ethernet adapter must support this vSphere feature.

Cisco VIC adapters are fully compatible with VMware VMDirectPath I/O. And when VM-FEX and VMDirectPath I/O are deployed simultaneously, it is said that VM-FEX is running in High-Performance mode.

Figure 15-47 compares the network I/O data path between VM-FEX standard and High-Performance modes.

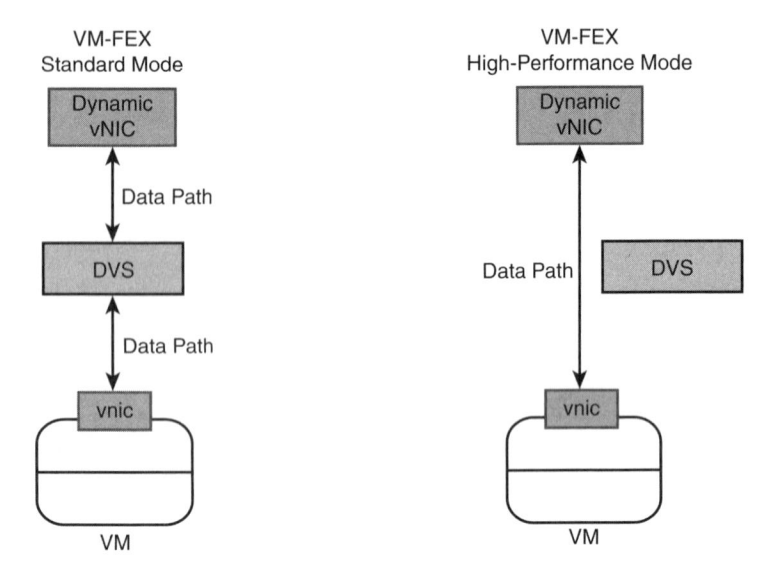

Figure 15-47 *VM-FEX Modes Comparison*

Note Performance studies, based on benchmarks such as Transaction Process Performance Council's TPC-H, have demonstrated that VM-FEX High-Performance mode can increase the I/O throughput of database systems by 30 percent and reduce database request time by almost 30 percent. You will find some of these studies in the "Further Reading" section at the end of this chapter.

To activate High-Performance mode on a VM-FEX standard mode implementation, some specific configurations must be customized on both UCS and vSphere.

First, the dynamic vNIC policy applied to both service profiles must be changed to support High-Performance mode. With that intention, I have created another policy (DvNIC-HiPerf-1), which is portrayed in Figure 15-48.

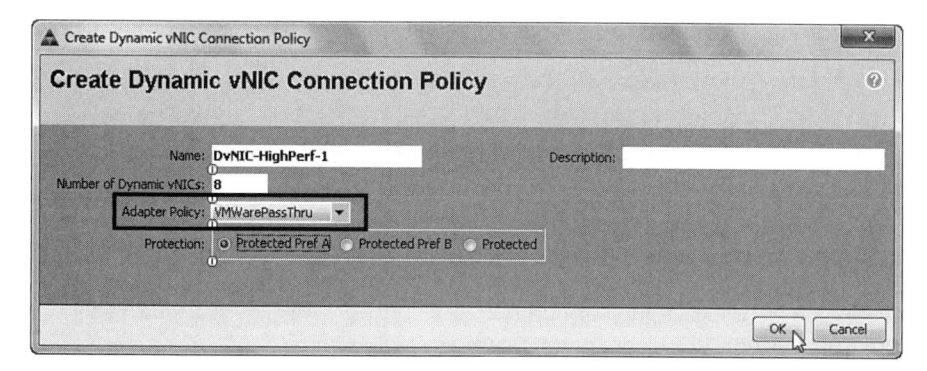

Figure 15-48 *Creating a High-Performance-Enabled Dynamic vNIC Policy*

As you can see, the only difference between this policy and the previous one (DvNIC-Policy-1) is the use of default adapter policy VMWarePassthru, which essentially implements more queues and enables *Receive Side Scaling (RSS)* on the dynamic vNICs.

> **Tip** RSS allows the receive side from a network adapter to be shared across multiple processors, allowing operating systems to take advantage of multi-CPU and multicore architectures.

DvNIC-HiPerf-1 was then assigned to SP-1 and SP-2, without any disruption to the servers. Afterward, the BIOS settings must be changed to enable CPU support for VMDirectPath I/O. In our scenario, this task was executed with the creation of a reusable BIOS Policy called BIOS-HighPerf. This policy enables the following BIOS settings related to Intel VT-d:

- **Virtualization Technology (VT):** Allows the processing of multiple operating systems in independent partitions (virtual machines).

- **Direct Cache Access:** Allows the processor to increase I/O performance, placing data from I/O devices directly into the processor cache.

- **VT For Directed IO:** Assigns I/O devices to VMs, extending the protection and isolation properties of VMs for I/O operations.

- **Interrupt Remap:** Uses Intel VT-d Interrupt Remapping as required, supporting isolation and routing of interrupts from devices and external interrupt controllers to appropriate VMs.

- **Coherency Support:** Uses Intel VT-d Coherency as required.

- **ATS Support:** Supports Intel VT-d Address Translation Services (ATS) as required, allowing caching of device specific Direct Memory Access (DMA) translations in the endpoint devices.

- **Pass Through DMA Support:** The processor uses Intel VT-d Pass-Through Direct Memory Access as required.

Because the change of BIOS policy on a service profile will only be activated after a reboot, I have applied BIOS-HighPerf one server at a time, migrating VM-DB1 and VM-DB2 to the other server before each graceful reinitialization.

As a last operation on UCS, I have created a VM-FEX port profile that will preempt the port group assigned to activate VMDirectPath I/O.

Figure 15-49 depicts the creation of port profile VMFEX-VLAN105-OPT, which will activate High-Performance mode for its assigned virtual machines.

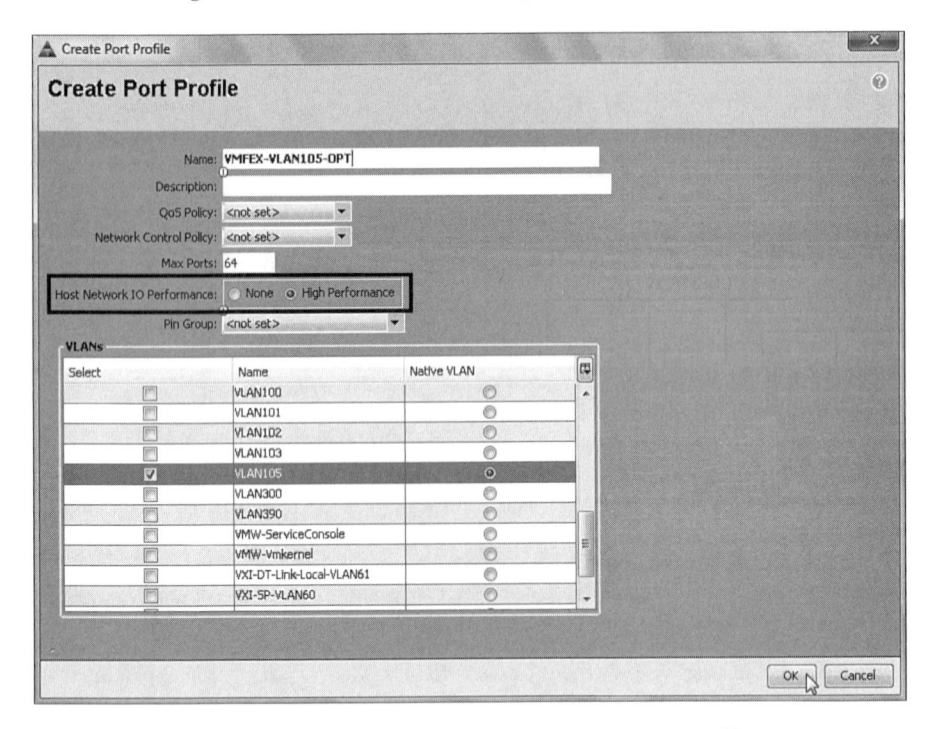

Figure 15-49 *Creating a VM-FEX High-Performance Port Profile*

We are now able to move to the vSphere customizations that are required to activate VMDirectPath I/O. As a first measure, vSphere should be able to identify which PCI or PCIe devices are available for traffic pass-through.

As Figure 15-50 displays, this configuration is available as a **Configure Passthrough** vCenter link on a host Configuration tab (Advanced Settings). This link gives you access to all "raw" PCI devices that are capable of deploying hypervisor bypass.

Figure 15-51 shows that I have marked all eight dynamic vNICs presented to host100 by the VIC.

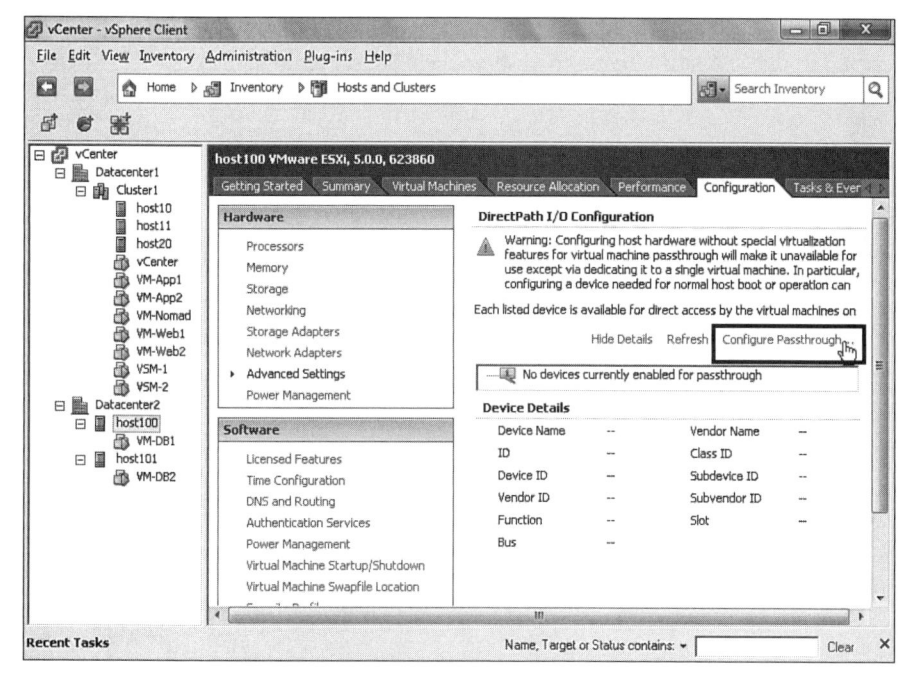

Figure 15-50 *Accessing VMDirectPath I/O Configuration*

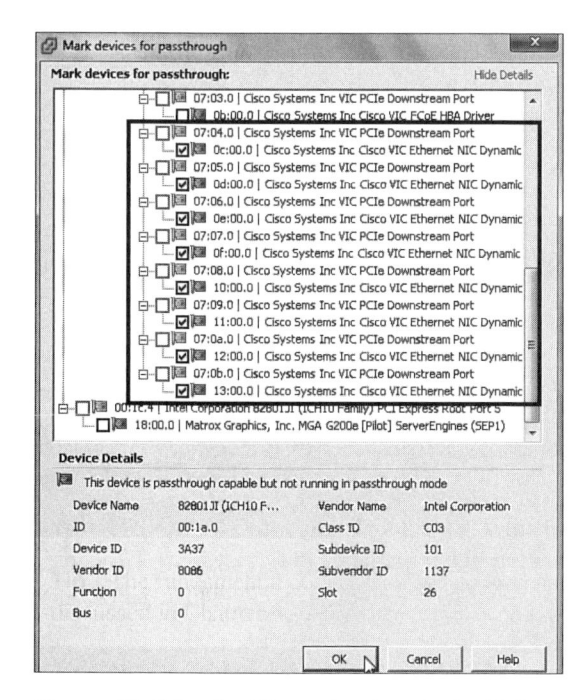

Figure 15-51 *Enabling VMDirectPath I/O for Dynamic vNICs*

In a precocious (but illustrative) attitude, I will assign the High-Performance-enabled port group to the VM-DB1 adapter to observe the results. Figure 15-52 depicts VM-DB1 properties after VMFEX-VLAN105-OPT is assigned to VM-DB1 Network Adapter 1.

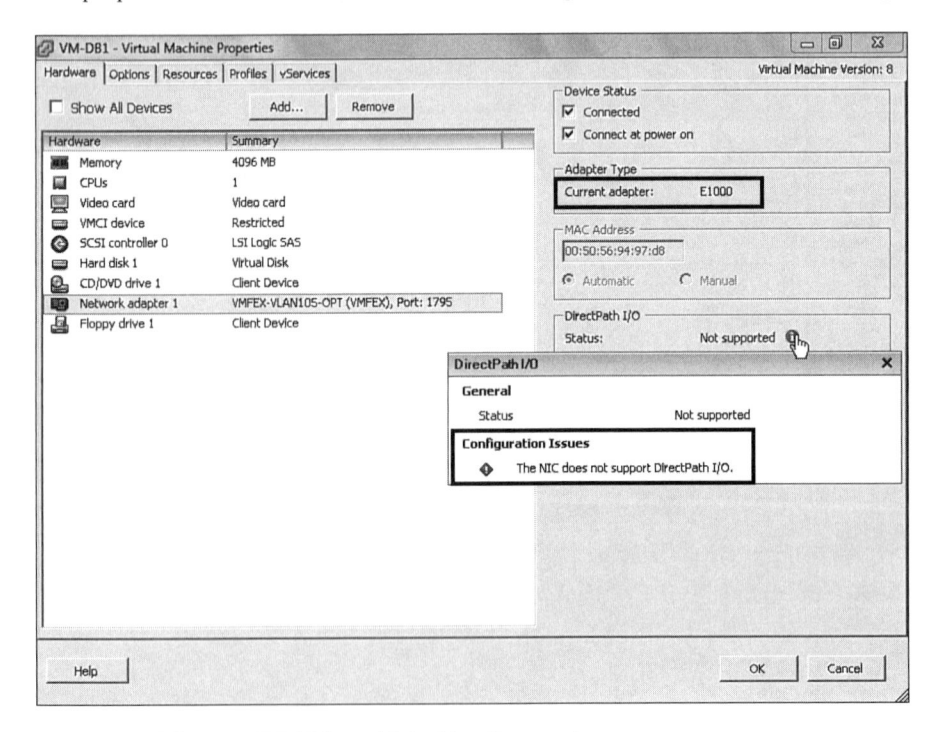

Figure 15-52 *VM-DB1 Virtual Machine Properties*

> **Tip** Also notice that the port group change has also modified the vnic DVS port ID from 63 to 1795 because this is a different DVS connection from the vCenter perspective.

In the figure, it is possible to observe that VMDirectPath I/O is not yet enabled for this connection because the deployed virtual NIC (E1000) is not compatible with this technology. E1000 is an emulated version of the Intel 82545EM Gigabit Ethernet NIC, which is already included on the majority of operating systems (such as Windows 2003 and later versions).

Because it does not support VMDirectPath I/O, I will replace it with a VMXNET3 virtual adapter, which can implement the pass-through technology. Besides, Cisco VIC adapters support the exact data path format of VMXNET3, and this compatibility is necessary to enable VM-FEX High-Performance mode.

After removing Network Adapter 1 from VM-DB1 properties, I have added a VMXNET3 network adapter to the same VM. As the guest OS on the VM did not have a VMXNET3 driver, I have installed VMware Tools before the change. (Right-clicking the VM, you will have access to the Install/Upgrade VMware Tools option.)

After this installation and the replacement of the emulated NIC, VMDirectPath is finally enabled for the VM-DB1 sole network connection, as shown in Figure 15-53.

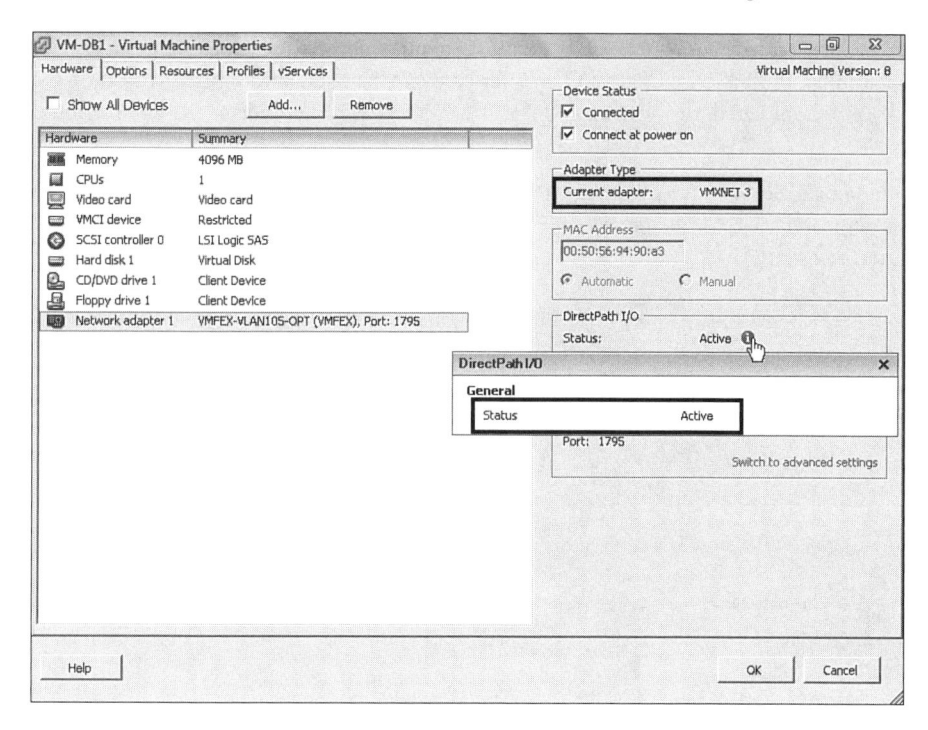

Figure 15-53 *VMDirectPath I/O Status on VM-DB1*

I also have done the same procedures on host101 and VM-DB2, with similar results.

> **Note** I have presented a simple way to enable VMDirectPath I/O from a UCS and vSphere perspective, but other factors must also be observed if you want to reach the desired level of performance. For example:
>
> The guest OS must deploy the correct VMXNET3 driver version.
>
> The guest OS VMXNET3 driver should be correctly configured (interrupts, queues, RSS) to match the dynamic vNIC adapter policy (VMwarePassThru).
>
> The VM must have memory reserve enabled in its properties. This mandatory measure guarantees that the VM has enough hardware resources to run in High-Performance mode.
>
> The number of interfaces in VM-FEX High-Performance connections must respect the overall UCS system support, which depends on the number of supported virtual HBAs and virtual NICs (static and dynamic) per adapter, use of RSS, number of queues, and guest operating system.

In VM-FEX in High-Performance mode, a virtual machine first connects the VMFEX DVS in standard mode and then migrates its data path to the assigned dynamic vNIC. During this transition, the VXMNET3 adapter is paused and its saved state is transferred from the DVS receiving interface to the dynamic vNIC.

Beginning with vSphere version 5.0, VMDirectPath I/O supports vMotion through a clever adaptation in the technology: Because an online migration requires hypervisor data path handling, the VMDirectPath I/O adapter is reverted to standard mode. After the migration is completed, the adapter is put in VMDirectPath I/O mode at the destination host.

As a demonstration of VM-FEX High-Performance mode support of vMotion, Figure 15-54 depicts the UCS Manager VM-FEX management screen after both VMs were migrated to host101.

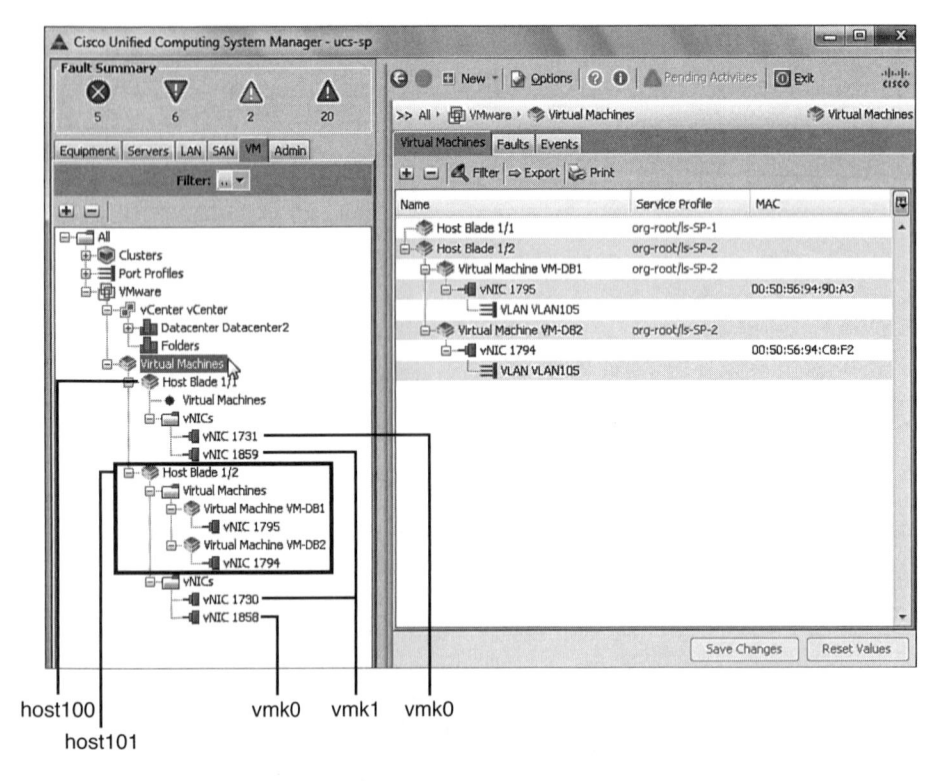

Figure 15-54 *UCS Manager and High-Performance Mode VMs*

To increase clarity, I have also marked the VMware hosts and VMkernel adapters in Figure 15-54 (which were obtained through further navigation on vCenter).

Use Case: Data Center Merging

After your consulting services firm has taken the lead in the IT services market in its region, you decide to expand the business, merging your company with a Cisco product distributor. With this movement, the resulting company will be able to offer end-to-end turnkey (insert other marketing buzzwords here) solutions.

After the merging business phase reaches its conclusion, the consolidated IT team (which is under your leadership) has to plan how to integrate the hardware and software resources from both companies.

Because each former organization had a single data center location with disaster recovery sites located at the same service provider, each site has different networking and server gear. For example, while your service company data used Nexus 7000 as aggregation switches and deployed UCS B-series servers, the "product" data center network has Catalyst 6500 and Nexus 5500 switches to connect third-party servers.

Besides the difference in hardware, one aspect is generating heated discussions within the team: the server virtualization strategy. The main discussion revolves around simplicity and resource optimization, because each data center is obviously deploying distinct VMware vSphere domains.

After further analysis, you realize that the product data center has a very low rate of server virtualization when compared to the service facility. And as some veterans from the product company explained for you, their critical applications (ERP and database) did not present good performance results in virtualized environments. That bad experience ended up relinquishing this technology for nonproduction workloads.

Because resource optimization is the main priority in IT strategy of the consolidated company, you are certain that server virtualization can bring more results at this stage without bringing abrupt hardware changes.

With the short latency obtained by the WAN between sites (luckily they are very close to each other), you decide that both facilities will act as active-active data centers for all virtualized workloads. Therefore, selected virtual machines will be able migrate to any site according to the vCenter Dynamic Resource Scheduler decision.

Your proposal for the architecture of the merged data center is laid out in Figure 15-55.

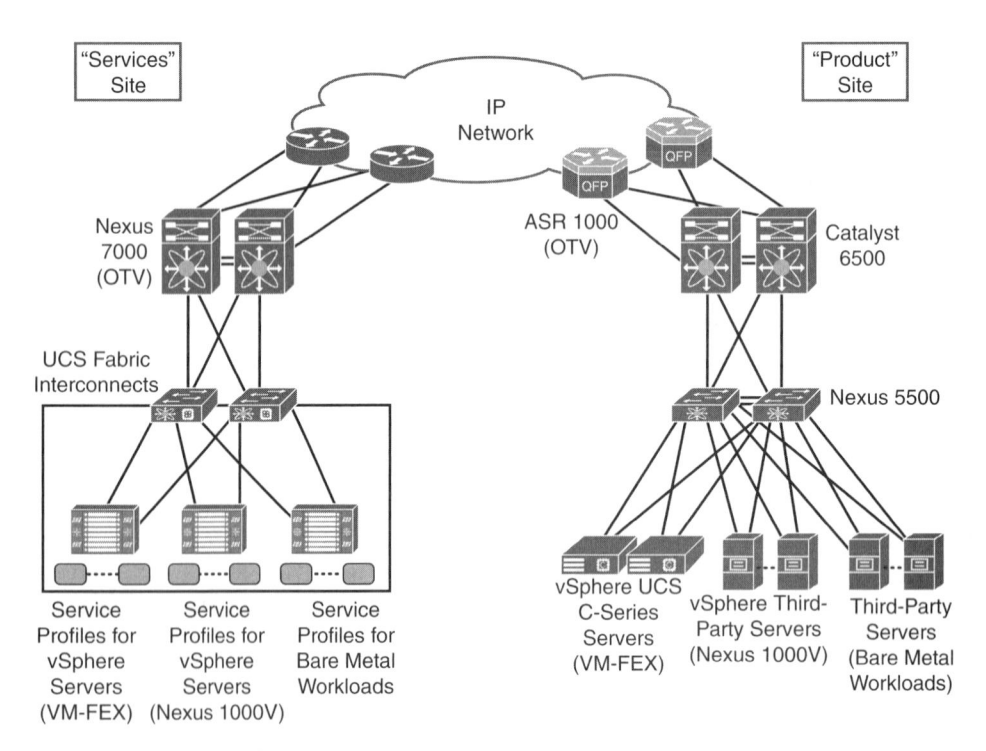

Figure 15-55 *Final Data Center Architecture*

During the architecture presentation, you also detail that

- Separation between sites will be provided through a low-latency multicast-enabled Layer 3 WAN.
- All virtualized hosts will be managed by a single vCenter (protected through vSphere high availability).
- A single Nexus 1000V will span both sites, creating a Distributed Virtual Switch that is integrated into the physical network management. Each site will have a VSM to increase high availability.
- All virtual server VLANs will be extended through Overlay Transport Virtualization (OTV) between both sites because these VMs need to communicate with physical servers, default gateways, and network service devices at both sites. Nexus 7000 core switches will deploy OTV at the services site. A pair of ASR 1000 sites will be deployed at the product site to enable this feature.
- All virtualized hosts will access a storage virtualization solution to enable Long Distance vMotion and higher I/O performance in each site (this solution is not depicted in Figure 15-55).

- Because the application strategy for the consolidated company will take longer to be defined, there will be no radical changes to the application architecture from both original organizations in the 12 months.

- All critical application servers (from both original organizations) will be virtualized and will use VM-FEX High-Performance mode. Two UCS C-series will be acquired for the product site to deploy this technology.

- No vMotion between sites will be supported for VM-FEX virtual machines. However, their applications will be deployed as a geocluster distributed on both sites.

- VXLAN can be used whenever the server virtualization team wants to deploy a broadcast domain that does not depend on the deployment of new VLANs.

And now what you were expecting is really happening: Not only the IT team, but also the entire company, is seriously engaged with the virtualization strategy. After all, this is the merged company's first project.

Summary

In this chapter, you learned the following:

- Virtual networking has solved the challenge of controlling virtual machine traffic within virtualized hosts.

- Cisco Nexus 1000V is a Distributed Virtual Switch whose redundant Virtual Supervisor Modules (VSM) control Virtual Ethernet Modules (VEM) installed in virtualized servers.

- Cisco Nexus 1000V deploys NX-OS features in virtualized environments and improves the collaboration between server virtualization and networking administrators.

- Cisco VM-FEX brings the Fabric Extender model to virtual networking, where each VM interface is directly connected to a virtual Ethernet interface on a parent switch.

- Cisco VM-FEX High-Performance mode allows the I/O operations of a virtual machine to bypass the hypervisor and achieve higher levels of performance.

Figure 15-56 illustrates how Nexus 1000V and VM-FEX virtualization technologies can be graphically summarized.

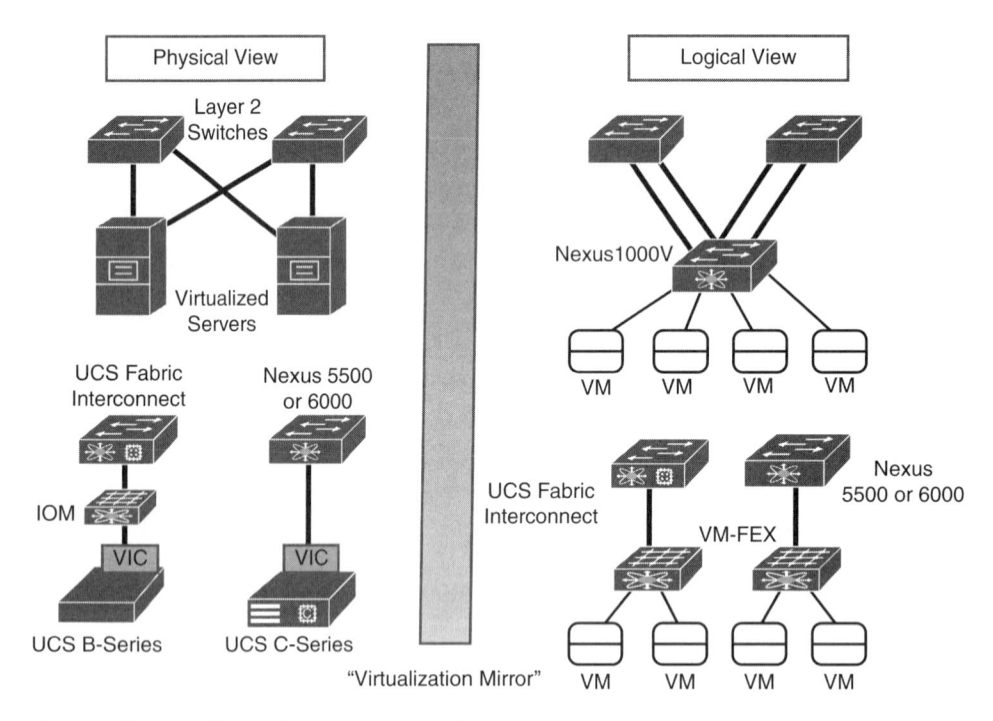

Figure 15-56 *Through the Virtualization Mirror*

Further Reading

Corbin, Kevin. Fuller, Ron. Jansen, David. *NX-OS and Cisco Nexus Switching*. Cisco Press, 2010.

VMware Virtual Networking Concepts: www.vmware.com/files/pdf/virtual_networking_concepts.pdf

Cisco Nexus 1000V Support Page: www.cisco.com/en/US/products/ps9902/tsd_products_support_series_home.html

VXLAN: A Framework for Overlaying Virtualized Layer 2 Networks over Layer 3 Networks: http://datatracker.ietf.org/doc/draft-mahalingam-dutt-dcops-vxlan

Cisco Data Center Virtual Machine Fabric Extender: www.cisco.com/go/vmfex

Intel Virtualization Technology for Directed I/O: http://download.intel.com/technology/computing/vptech/Intel%28r%29_VT_for_Direct_IO.pdf

Microsoft SQL Server 2012 on Cisco UCS with iSCSI-Based Storage Access in VMware ESX Virtualization Environment: Performance Study: www.cisco.com/en/US/prod/collateral/ps10265/ps10281/whitepaper_c11-711915.html

Virtualized SAP: Optimize Performance with Cisco Data Center Virtual Machine Fabric Extender and Red Hat Enterprise Linux and Kernel-Based Virtual Machine: www.cisco.com/en/US/solutions/collateral/ns340/ns517/ns224/ns944/whitepaper_c11_703103.pdf

Chapter 16

Moving Targets

"Those who desire to give up freedom in order to gain security will not have, nor do they deserve, either one." (Benjamin Franklin)

This chapter will examine the concept of *virtual network services*, their diversity in the Cisco product portfolio, and their relevance to server virtualization environments. It contains the following topics:

- Virtual Network Services Definitions
- Virtual Network Services Data Path
- vPath-enabled Virtual Network Services
- Routing in the Virtual World
- Site Selection and Virtual Machine Migration
- Use Case: Virtual Data Center

Table 16-1 generically classifies virtual network services in the taxonomy described in Chapter 1, "Virtualization History and Definitions."

Table 16-1 *Virtual Network Services Virtualization Classification*

Virtualization Characteristics	Virtual Network Services
Emulation	Network service devices
Type	Abstraction
Subtype	Structural
Scalability	Software version dependent[1]
Technology	Server

Virtualization Characteristics	Virtual Network Services
Technology specifics	Operating system (Type 1 hypervisor)
Advantages	Mobility, dynamic provisioning, traffic optimization, and integration with physical solutions

[1] Refer to Appendix A, "Cisco Data Center Portfolio," for more details and the Cisco online documentation of each virtual network service solution for updated information.

In hindsight, it can be said that virtual networking came into existence to supply policy-driven connectivity for server virtualization environments. However, the mere transportation of Ethernet frames between virtual machines (VM) might not satisfy the other data center networking requirements, such as security and application performance. And because of their large scaling and dynamic behavior, server virtualization network traffic can be even harder to pinpoint than its physical counterparts.

As you have learned from Chapter 15, "Transcending the Rack," the adoption of Cisco Nexus 1000V opens up new opportunities for virtual machine traffic control. Moreover, a very important one is fulfilled with the introduction of virtual network services such as *Virtual Security Gateway (VSG)*, *Adaptive Security Appliance (ASA) 1000V*, *Virtual Wide Area Application Services (vWAAS)*, and the *Cloud Services Router (CSR) 1000V*.

This chapter will analyze these solutions and explain how they can help data centers step into their next stage of evolution.

Virtual Network Services Definitions

Chapter 4, "An Army of One: ACE Virtual Contexts," explored the importance of *network services* for data center environments. As a quick reminder, network services are reusable functionalities that specialized network devices can provide to application traffic. With a strategic placement in the network, they can transparently offload servers and clients from repetitive and performance-intensive operations.

Information security is arguably the most popular network service in data centers. Because these facilities were basically created to provide application access, it is unthinkable to expose them to internal and external malicious use without proper protection.

Integral parts of any complete security solution, *firewalls* are network devices whose main objective is to control traffic between network segments. Based on preconfigured rules, these devices analyze data packets and decide if they should be allowed through or not.

Nowadays, firewalls are seriously challenged with server virtualization because it defines a new network control perimeter: the virtual machine connection. During the first years of virtualization on x86 servers, security departments have always considered this "invisible link" a soft spot for attacks simply because it lacked consistency with traditional physical network processes.

Security policies might even collide head on with the original purpose of server virtualization. For example, a lot of time has been spent inside corporations to decide whether a virtualization cluster might or might not host virtual machines from demilitarized zones (DMZ). In fact, I have personally witnessed organizations that were forced to deploy additional hardware resources on new clusters to satisfy network security policies.

Generally speaking, all physical network services suffer from two additional difficulties when dealing with server virtualization:

- VM-to-VM communication must leave the virtual access layer to reach the network service appliances, which are usually located at the network aggregation layer.
- Network services usually rely on the use of VLANs for traffic manipulation, which are becoming very scarce as virtual environments grow.

Cisco has again combined its experience and innovation capacity in the creation of new *virtual network services*. Leveraging the Nexus 1000V programmability and flexibility, the company has released virtual firewalls (VSG and ASA 1000V), virtual WAN accelerators (vWAAS), and virtual routers (CSR 1000V). And as you can infer, these services are deployed as virtual machines at virtualization clusters, naturally acting on traffic "closer" to the other VMs.

It is important to observe that these new solutions were not developed to completely replace physical network service devices. Actually, both formats have complementary advantages that suggest their simultaneous use in data centers.

Figure 16-1 illustrates the placement for physical and virtual network services in a generic data center network structure.

In Figure 16-1, physical network services devices are ideally located at the aggregation layer, theoretically guaranteeing access to the IP-routed network and all site VLANs. Such a position also assures that these nodes can easily intercept "north-south" traffic (between external clients and internal servers).

Tip In Layer 2 multipath spine-leaf topologies, such as the use case explained in Chapter 6 ("Fooling Spanning Tree"), physical network service appliances can also be positioned in a service leaf node.

On the other hand, server-to-server traffic ("east-west") can be especially suitable for virtual network service devices, optimizing such communication without the need of "neck-breaking" traffic manipulations to external devices.

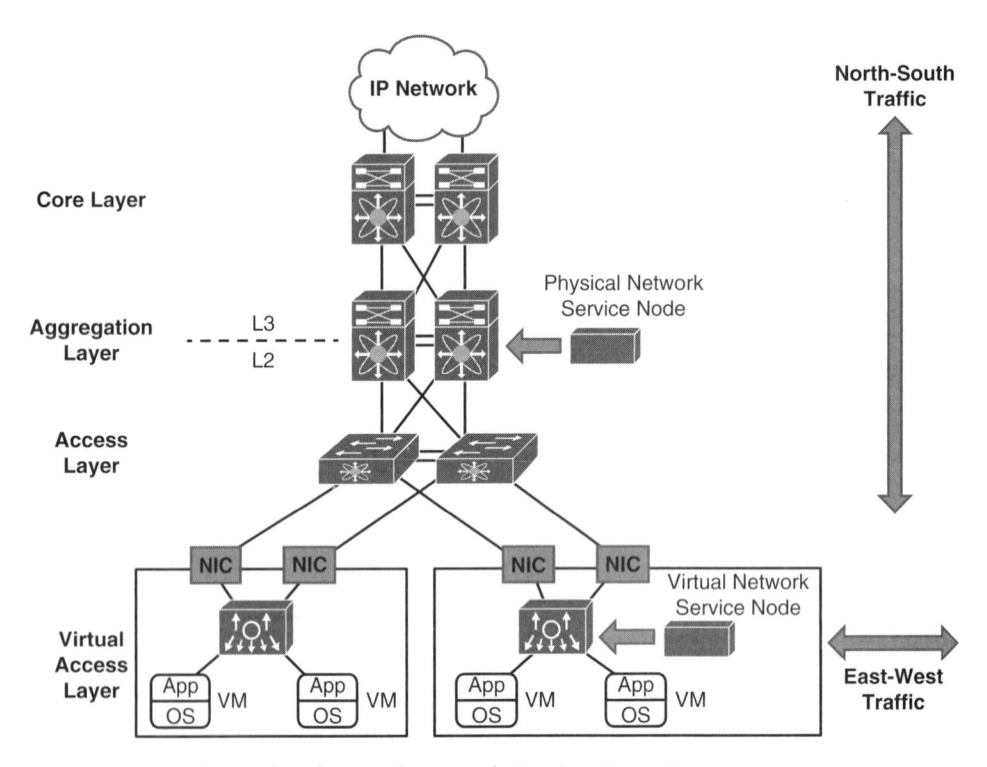

Figure 16-1 *Physical and Virtual Network Services Insertion*

The majority of Cisco virtual network services are offered as *virtual appliances*, which are basically preconfigured virtual machines that permit an extremely quick deployment. Because these highly specialized virtual machines require a lower level of customization when compared to standard VMs, they perfectly mirror how physical appliances are inserted in a network.

Note Some Cisco virtual service nodes explained in this chapter can also be deployed as "virtual blades" in dedicated Nexus 1010 or 1100 virtual service appliances. Refer to Appendix A and Cisco online documentation for more details.

Virtual Network Services Data Path

Virtual Network Services Data Path, or simply vPath, is a Nexus 1000V functionality that allows tighter integration between virtual networking and virtual network services. In essence, such a technology is a programmable framework that provides transparent steering of VM traffic to virtual network service nodes.

Figure 16-2 illustrates how vPath establishes *overlay tunnels* between Nexus 1000V Virtual Ethernet Modules (VEMs) and virtual service nodes, avoiding VLAN manipulations that are so common in inline service implementations.

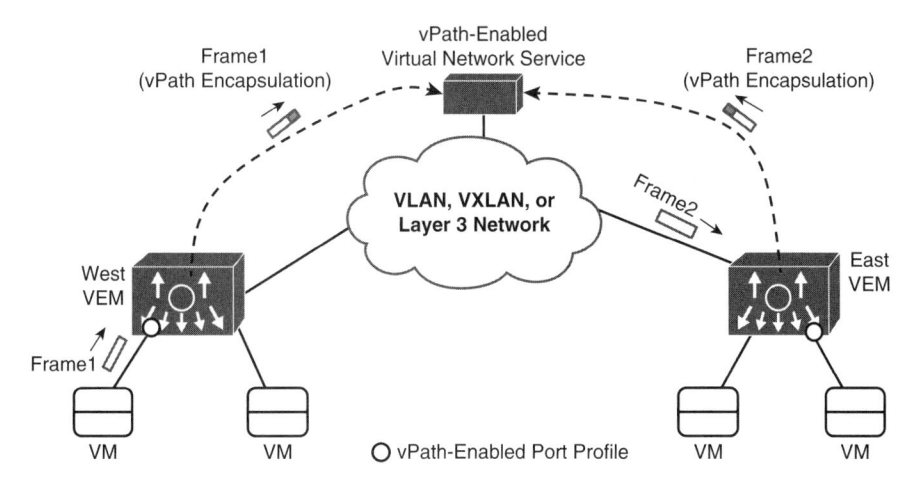

Figure 16-2 *vPath in Action*

In Figure 16-2, you can see how two VEMs are employing vPath in a slightly different manner. First, West VEM has a vEthernet interface that has inherited a vPath-enabled port profile. Because the service node associated to the port profile is alive and well, the VEM can send a *received* frame on this interface to the node through a vPath encapsulation tunnel for further analysis and policy enforcement.

On the East VEM, traffic *destined* to an interface associated to the same port profile can also be encapsulated in vPath-tagged frames and sent to the same virtual network service node (regardless of whether the frame originated from the physical network or from another VM).

It is very important that you understand that vPath redirection, by definition, has priority over the Nexus 1000V standard Layer 2 switching. This hierarchy defines the flexibility of vPath: *Service policy supersedes standard connectivity*, enabling network services to be applied on traffic between VMs that might even belong to the same VLAN!

A vPath-enabled service node does not have to be located at the same host, cluster, or virtual switch as the VMs it is serving. In truth, vPath only requires *proper* connectivity between the virtual machine's VEM and the service node. For example, depending on the vPath-enabled virtual service node, Nexus 1000V can deploy the following methods of frame encapsulation:

- **VLAN mode:** Service node shares a VLAN with the VEMs.
- **VXLAN mode:** Service node is connected to a Virtual eXtensible Local Area Network (VXLAN) present on the VEMs.
- **Layer 3 mode:** A VEM can reach the service node through IP packets.

Note As with any encapsulation technique, I highly recommend that you adjust the maximum transmission unit (MTU) on the network path between the VEMs and the service node to avoid fragmentation and performance loss. Nexus 1000V vPath adds an overhead of 62 bytes using VLAN mode, 112 bytes with VXLAN mode, and 82 bytes with Layer 3 encapsulation mode.

The VEM distinct behavior for each type of network service shows the adaptability of vPath. For example, a virtual service node can

- Program the VEM to permit or block all subsequent frames from the same flow (identified with the same IP addresses, transport protocol, and ports)
- Only use the information from the vPath frame to identify security policies for the VM
- Process the data on the frame and return the resulting frame to the VEM to be forwarded to its original destination

vPath-Enabled Virtual Network Services

At the time of this writing, Cisco Nexus 1000V supports three vPath-enabled virtual network services: VSG, ASA 1000V, and vWAAS. To demonstrate both the simplicity of vPath and the features these services bring to virtualization environments, I will use the Nexus 1000V network infrastructure from Chapter 15.

Figure 16-3 is intended to remind you of this virtual networking topology.

In the topology, a Nexus 1000V switch spans three vSphere hosts on two different sites with distinct local VLANs. Eight virtual machines are connected to the virtual switch, and their connectivity characteristics are described in Table 16-2.

Table 16-2 *Topology Virtual Machine Connectivity Characteristics*

Virtual Machine	vnic ID	VLAN or VXLAN ID	IP Address[1]	DVS Port Group (Nexus 1000V Port Profile)	Nexus 1000 Interface
vCenter	1	100	192.168.100.2	N1KV-MGMT-SITE1	Veth 13
VSM-1[2]	2	100	192.168.100.3	N1KV-MGMT-SITE1	Veth 11
VSM-2[2]	2	100	192.168.100.3	N1KV-MGMT-SITE1	Veth 8
VM-Web1[3]	1	105	192.168.105.180	N1KV-WEB-SITE1	Veth 14
VM-App1	1	105	192.168.105.181	N1KV-APP-SITE1	Veth 15
VM-App1	2	4096	172.16.1.1	N1KV-VXLAN4096	Veth 22
VM-Web2[3]	1	205	192.168.205.180	N1KV-WEB-SITE2	Veth 16
VM-App2	1	205	192.168.205.181	N1KV-APP-SITE2	Veth 17

Virtual Machine	vnic ID	VLAN or VXLAN ID	IP Address[1]	DVS Port Group (Nexus 1000V Port Profile)	Nexus 1000 Interface
VM-App2	2	4096	172.16.1.2	N1KV-VXLAN4096	Veth 23
VM-Nomad	1	300	10.30.30.30	N1KV-VLAN300	Veth 18

[1] All IP addresses use 255.255.255.0 as their subnet mask.

[2] The Nexus 1000V VSMs are deployed in Layer 3 mode using their management interface.

[3] The IP access list configuration presented in Chapter 15 (in the section "NX-OS Features in the Virtual World") was removed from the virtual Ethernet interfaces.

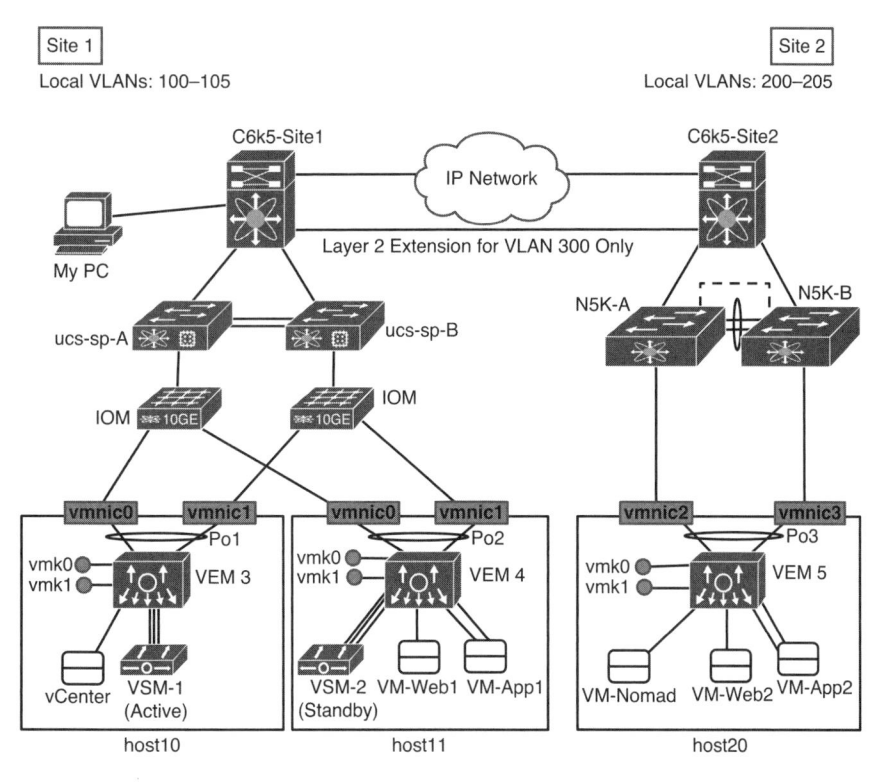

Figure 16-3 *Nexus 1000V Virtual Networking Topology*

Although this knowledge is not essential for the next sections, the configuration of the port profiles mentioned on Table 16-2 can be found in Chapter 15.

Cisco Virtual Security Gateway: Compute Virtual Firewall

The Cisco Virtual Security Gateway (VSG) is an NX-OS-based virtual network service node that provides policy-based traffic access control to server virtualization environments. This virtual appliance is designed to meet the requirements of highly dynamic and scalable virtual networks.

Because it is primarily focused on VM-to-VM communication, VSG is also referred to as a *compute firewall*. It integrates itself to Nexus 1000V and to another virtual appliance named *Virtual Network Manager Center (VNMC)*, which is the main repository of security policies and the management interface for security administrators.

Figure 16-4 summarizes VSG management and control plane architecture.

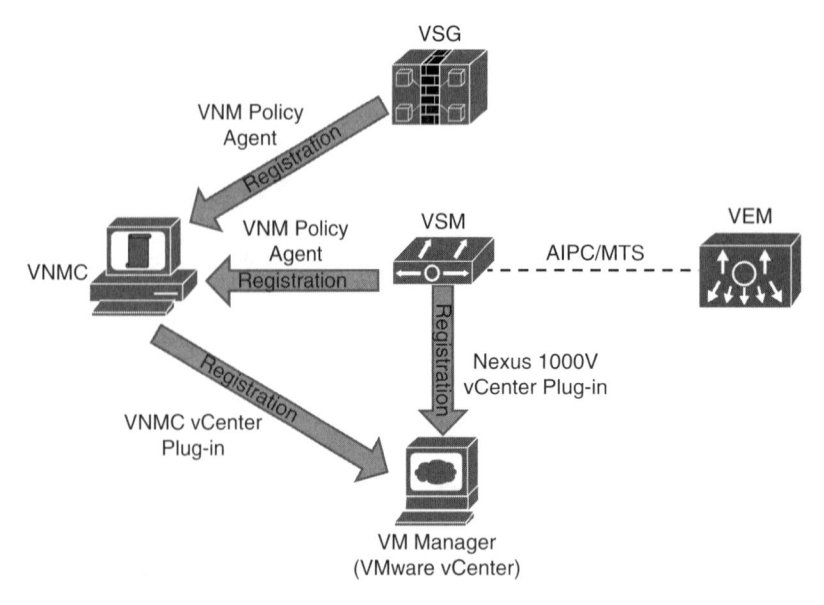

Figure 16-4 *Virtual Security Gateway Management and Control Plane Architecture*

In Figure 16-4, VNMC extends itself to a VM manager such as VMware vCenter management through an XML plug-in. This management connection assures that VNMC can collect VM attributes from vCenter to use them as security policy parameters.

> **Tip** The VNMC plug-in installation procedure in vCenter is very similar to the Unified Computing System (UCS) Virtual Machine Fabric Extender (VM-FEX) plug-in discussed in Chapter 15.

Both VSM and VSG register themselves to VNMC through a native policy agent. With these connections, VNMC can push *security policies* to both VSG and VSM, assuring coherency when vPath traffic will be exchanged between the VEMs and the virtual service node.

Installing Virtual Security Gateway

You can install VSG and VNMC as standard virtual machines using bootable ISO files or through *Open Virtualization Format (OVF)* files. Besides containing the virtual appliance software, the latter file format facilitates the installation encoding the complete specification of the VM, including CPU, memory, vnics, and storage.

A VMware vCenter wizard allows the deployment of a virtual appliance from an OVF file (**Deploy OVF Template**). Depending on each OVF file, this wizard permits the definition of some settings before the virtual appliance is even powered on.

Figure 16-5 illustrates this possibility, depicting a single wizard step from the installation of VNMC.

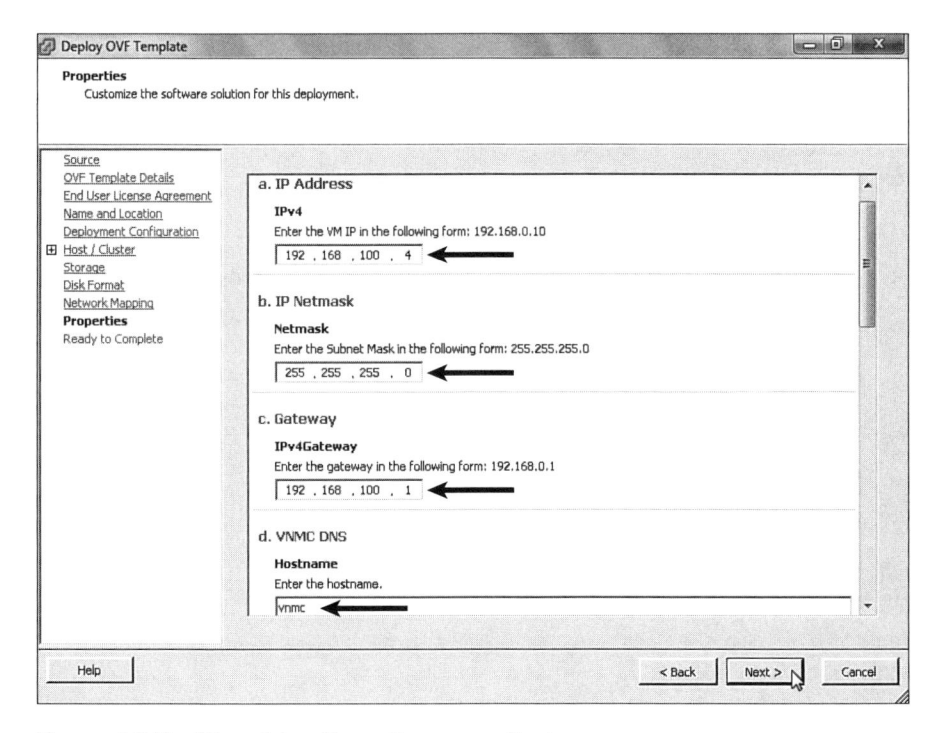

Figure 16-5 *Virtual Appliance Parameter Settings*

In addition to the VNMC interface IP settings shown in Figure 16-5, the Deploy OVF Template wizard was also used to define the virtual appliance location (host10), data store, Nexus 1000V port group (N1KV-MGMT-SITE1), DNS server IP address, and administration password. The wizard also permits the definition of a very important VNMC parameter called *shared-secret*, which is used during the registration of the VNMC policy agents.

Consequently, after the VNMC is correctly installed and initialized, it is possible to register the Nexus 1000V VSM to it, as I demonstrate in Example 16-1.

Example 16-1 *VSM Registration into VNMC and Port Profile Creation for VSG*

```
! Entering the VNMC policy agent configuration
VSM(config)# vnm-policy-agent
! Defining VNMC IP address, shared-secret, and agent image version
(it is on VSM bootflash by default)
VSM(config-vnm-policy-agent)# registration-ip 192.168.100.4
VSM(config-vnm-policy-agent)# shared-secret [suppressed]
VSM(config-vnm-policy-agent)# policy-agent-image bootflash:/vnmc-vsmpa.2.0.0.38.bin
! Verifying the agent registration status
VSM(config-vnm-policy-agent)# show vnm-pa status
VNM Policy-Agent status is - Installed Successfully. Version 2.0(0.38)-vsm
```

Before installing VSG, some arrangements should be made to provide correct connectivity for this virtual appliance. By definition, a VSG instance has three interfaces:

- **Management:** Used for communication with VNMC.
- **Data:** Receives vPath traffic from the Nexus 1000V VEMs.
- **High availability:** Used for state synchronization between a pair of active-standby VSGs.

Note The VSG redundancy mechanism is very similar to the one deployed by Nexus 1000V VSM. However, I will not deploy redundant VSG virtual appliances to focus on its core concepts.

The connectivity of a standalone VSG depends on one port profile for its management interface (N1KV-MGMT-SITE1 will be used again) and another one for its data interface.

Example 16-2 describes the configuration of the port profile that will be associated to the data interface on VSG.

Example 16-2 *Port Profile Configuration for VSG Data Interface*

```
VSM# show running-config port-profile N1KV-VSG-DATA
[output suppressed]
! Creating a standard port profile in VLAN 103
port-profile type vethernet N1KV-VSG-DATA
  vmware port-group
  switchport mode access
  switchport access vlan 103
  no shutdown
  state enabled
```

> **Tip** From now on, to avoid unnecessary repetition of commands, I will use the term "plain" port profile to refer to port profiles that only define access interfaces on a VLAN (similarly to the one configured in Example 16-2).

Using the same **Deploy OVF Template** vCenter wizard, I have defined the following settings for VSG:

- **Host:** host10
- **Management IP Address:** 192.168.100.5/24.
- **Management Default Gateway:** 192.168.100.1 (which is the C6K5-Site1 Switch Virtual Interface [SVI] for VLAN 100)

During the VSG wizard iteration, I was also able to configure the VNMC IP address (192.168.100.4) and its shared-secret. Therefore, as VSG booted up, it is already registered to VNMC.

Creating Security Policies

As I have previously mentioned, VNMC is designed to be the management cockpit for security administrators, enabling the creation of security policies that will be pushed to VSG.

At the time of this writing, a single VNMC instance can support up to 128 VSG nodes. Consequently, VNMC is designed to take advantage of such scalability, deploying a hierarchical multitenant tree structure that can distribute security resources (firewall instances and policies) among different administrative organizations.

In VNMC, five hierarchical levels can be used to house security resources: *root*, *Tenant*, *Virtual Data Center (vDC)*, *Virtual Application (vApp)*, and *Tier*. The resources created at the root level are available to all organizations in a VNMC instance. On the other hand, any resource associated to a different organization below the root level (root/Tenant2/vDC3, for example) is only available to itself and to its subdivisions. Such separation assures that virtual machines belonging to different organizations are logically isolated.

For our VSG deployment, I have instantiated a VNMC Tenant creatively named Tenant1. Within such an organization, I have also created a *security profile,* as Figure 16-6 exhibits.

Security profiles are VNMC-distributed entities that bind two configurations: VSG policies and Nexus 1000V port profiles. In Figure 16-6, SecurityProfile-App was created with an ACL policy set (ACLPolicySet1), containing an ACL policy (ACLPolicy1) with a single rule (ACLPolicyRule-App1). By the way, VNMC has automatically assigned an identifier for this security profile (which is 3).

Consequently, any Nexus 1000V port profile associated to SecurityProfile-App will only allow TCP port 3389 connections from IP address 192.168.105.180 (VM-Web1).

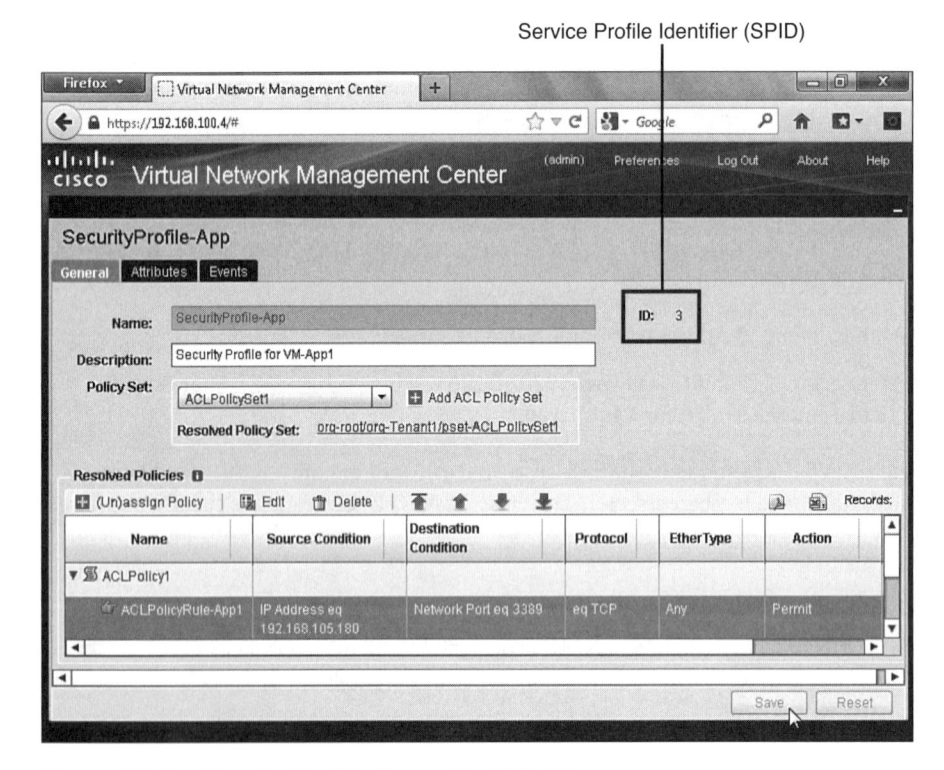

Figure 16-6 *Security Profile Created in VNMC*

Next, using the Resource Managed tab under Managed Devices from VNMC's GUI, I have added a compute firewall called VSG, as depicted in Figure 16-7.

Figure 16-7 *Compute Firewall VSG Configuration*

Figure 16-7 also portrays the compute firewall data interface IP address (192.168.103.5/24).

Afterward, the configuration contained in compute firewall VSG was manually assigned to the discovered registered device we have just installed (192.168.100.5). By design, the assignment operation permits a compute firewall configuration to be quickly ported to another registered VSG node.

Example 16-3 demonstrates that, because both compute firewall VSG and SecurityProfile-App belong to the *same suborganization* (root/Tenant1), VNMC has automatically pushed the security policies defined on root and Tenant1 to our virtual appliance.

Example 16-3 *SSH Session to VSG*

```
! Checking security configurations on VSG
VSG# show running-config | begin security
! VSG has received the security profiles from VNMC with their associated
ACL Policy Sets (From Tenant1 and Root)
security-profile SecurityProfile-App@root/Tenant1
  policy ACLPolicySet1@root/Tenant1
[output suppressed]
security-profile default@root
  policy default@root
[output suppressed]
! The ACL policy rule permits traffic from 192.168.105 to TCP port 3389
rule ACLPolicy1/ACLPolicyRule-App1@root/Tenant1
  condition 10 dst.net.port eq 3389
  condition 11 src.net.ip-address eq 192.168.105.180
  condition 12 net.protocol eq 6
  action 10 permit
! The default rule from the root organization drops any packet
rule default/default-rule@root
  action 10 drop

! ACL policy set contains rules from both organizations
Policy ACLPolicySet1@root/Tenant1
  rule ACLPolicy1/ACLPolicyRule-App1@root/Tenant1 order 101
Policy default@root
  rule default/default-rule@root order 2
[output suppressed]
```

Sending Data Traffic to VSG

With VSG already prepared to enforce security policies, it is time to send vPath traffic into its data interface. Example 16-4 details the configuration on the Nexus 1000V VSM that accomplishes this task.

Example 16-4 *Nexus 1000V vPath Configuration*

```
! Configuring virtual service node globally for Nexus 1000V
VSM(config)# vservice node VSG type vsg
VSM(config-vservice-node)# ip address 192.168.103.5
VSM(config-vservice-node)# adjacency l2 vlan 103
VSM(config-vservice-node)# fail-mode close
! Enabling vPath for interfaces associated with port profile
VSM(config-vservice-node)# port-profile N1KV-APP-SITE1
VSM(config-port-prof)# org root/Tenant1
VSM(config-port-prof)# vservice node VSG profile SecurityProfile-App
```

Example 16-4 defines two different Nexus 1000V configurations. First, VSG is declared as a vPath-enabled service node, prompting Nexus 1000V to start sending ARP requests to IP address 192.168.103.5 on VLAN 103. If the service node is not detected, port profiles associated to this virtual service node must drop packets (fail-mode close is the default behavior for the vPath configuration for VSG nodes).

In that way, we cannot use VEM 5 (host20) to send vPath traffic for VSG because VLAN 103 simply does not exist on site 2.

Tip VSG also supports vPath in Layer 3, as the section "Use Case: Virtual Data Center," later in this chapter, will demonstrate.

In the second part of Example 16-4, port profile N1KV-APP-SITE1 (which is associated to VM-App1's vnic 1) is defined as part of the VNMC organization root/Tenant1, and it is associated to SecurityProfile-App.

From this moment on, VEMs that are connected to VLAN 103 can potentially send vPath frames to VSG. And they will do that as long as traffic is sent or received on interfaces associated to N1KV-APP-SITE1.

Figure 16-8 examines the data path for the first frame of a connection from VM-Web1 to VM-App1.

As detailed in Figure 16-8, Nexus 1000V and VSG act as follows:

a. VEM 4 receives the Ethernet frame destined to an interface associated with a vPath-enabled port profile (N1KV-APP-SITE1). The VEM's vPath flow manager process indicates that this frame contains the first packet from a flow.

b. Because this VEM has Layer 2 connectivity to VSG, it sends the frame to the service node in a vPath Layer 2 encapsulated frame.

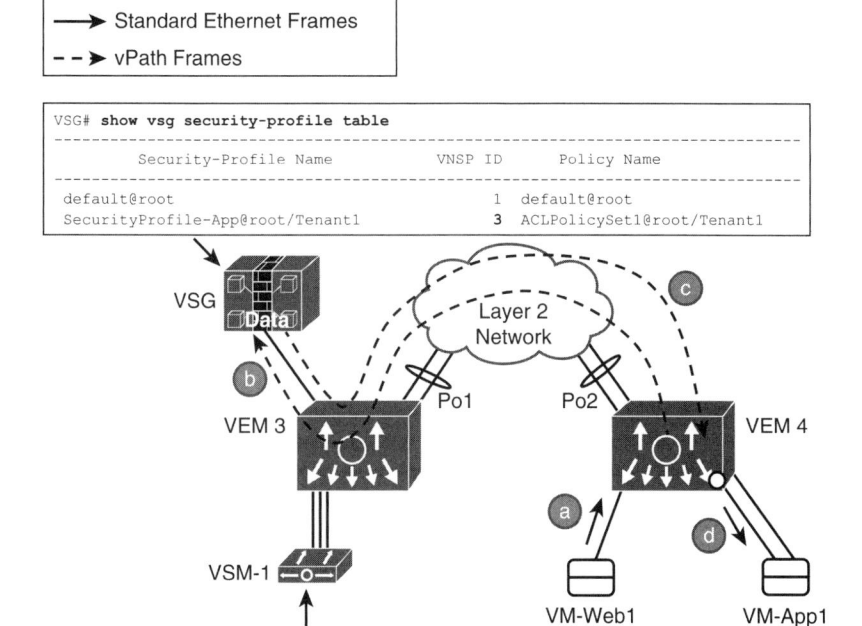

```
                    O   Port Profile N1KV-APP-SITE1
                    ──▶ Standard Ethernet Frames
                    --▶ vPath Frames
```

```
VSG# show vsg security-profile table
-----------------------------------------------------------------
        Security-Profile Name          VNSP ID     Policy Name
-----------------------------------------------------------------
default@root                              1        default@root
SecurityProfile-App@root/Tenant1          3        ACLPolicySet1@root/Tenant1
```

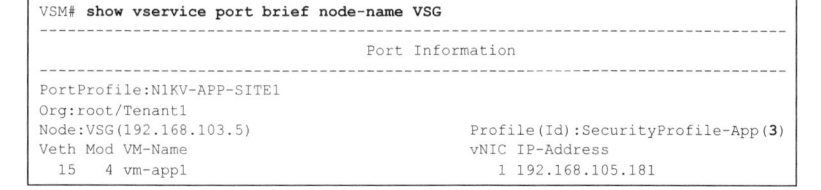

```
VSM# show vservice port brief node-name VSG
-----------------------------------------------------------------
                            Port Information
-----------------------------------------------------------------
PortProfile:N1KV-APP-SITE1
Org:root/Tenant1
Node:VSG(192.168.103.5)                 Profile(Id):SecurityProfile-App(3)
Veth Mod VM-Name                        vNIC IP-Address
  15   4  vm-app1                         1  192.168.105.181
```

Figure 16-8 *VSG Data Path for the First Frame of a Connection*

    c. VSG uses the Security Profile Identifier (SPID 3) on the vPath tag to select the security policies that should be applied to this frame. If its ACL policy set permits this traffic, VSG sends the frame back to the VEM and programs the latter to allow direct communication (pass-through) for the remaining frames from this specific flow.

    d. VEM 4 forwards the frame to VM-App1 and programs its vPath flow manager process with information from the allowed flow.

In Figure 16-8, I have also included two illustrative commands (from VSG and Nexus 1000V) that detail how VNMC has assigned SPID 3 to SecurityProfile-App on both devices.

During the establishment of this TCP connection from VM-Web1 to VM-App1, I have also initiated a series of ICMP Echo messages between the same hosts. As these messages are not allowed on SecurityProfile-App, their discarding is also offloaded to VEM 4, as Example 16-5 demonstrates.

Example 16-5 *Verifying VSG Offloaded Traffic on Nexus 1000V*

```
VSM# show vservice connection node-name VSG
Actions(Act):
! Actions on CAPITAL LETTERS represent connections that were offloaded to the VEMs
d - drop                              s - reset
p - permit                            t - passthrough
r - redirect                          e - error
n - not processed                     upper case - offloaded
Flags:
A - seen ack for syn/fin from src     a - seen ack for syn/fin from dst
E - tcp conn established (SasA done)
F - seen fin from src                 f - seen fin from dst
R - seen rst from src                 r - seen rst from dst
S - seen syn from src                 s - seen syn from dst
T - tcp conn torn down (FafA done)    x - IP-fragment connection
! VEM 4 is forwarding frames from the TCP connection from VM-Web1 to VM-App1...
#Port-Profile:N1KV-APP-SITE1                      Node:VSG
#Module 4
Proto SrcIP[:Port]          SAct    DstIP[:Port]         DAct    Flags      54264 Bytes
 tcp  192.168.105.180:49176         192.168.105.181:3389  P
... but is dropping ICMP messages sent from VM-App1 to VM-Web1
 icmp 192.168.105.181       D        192.168.105.180                                148
```

Nexus 1000V has defined timeouts for the offloading traffic entries configured by VSG. For example, after a FIN or RST is seen on a TCP connection, the VEM automatically purges this specific offload entry. On the other hand, the VEM will continue to drop Internet Control Message Protocol (ICMP) traffic on behalf of VSG for another 2 seconds. Inactivity will also cause the deletion of the offloaded path in any case (36–60 seconds for TCP connections and 8–12 seconds for connectionless traffic, such as ICMP and UDP).

> **Note** VSG does not offload to the VEM the handling of some protocols that require stateful packet inspection, such as File Transfer Protocol (FTP), Trivial File Transfer Protocol (TFTP), and Remote Shell (RSH).

As explained in the section "Virtual Network Services Data Path," earlier in this chapter, vPath architecture does not depend on the location of the VMs as long as the virtual service node is reachable through the defined encapsulation mode (VLAN, VXLAN, or

Layer 3). Hence, in our scenario, VSG supports the migration of any VMs between VEM 3 and 4, including VSG itself.

As an illustration, Example 16-6 depicts the virtual service status of node VSG after VM-App1 is migrated from host11 (VEM 4) to host10 (VEM 3).

Example 16-6 *Checking Virtual Service Node Status*

```
VSM# show vservice node brief name VSG
------------------------------------------------------------------
                          Node Information
------------------------------------------------------------------
! vPath is now being processed on VEM 3
  ID Name              Type    IP-Address      Mode    State   Module
   1 VSG               vsg     192.168.103.5   v-103   Alive   3,
```

Virtual Machine Attributes and Virtual Zones

VSG and VNMC introduce a collaborative model among virtualization, network, and security administrators. Table 16-3 portrays the recommended distribution tasks (and management platforms) between these administrative domains.

Table 16-3 *VSG Management Model*

Role	Management Platform	Access Method	Connectivity Element
Server Virtualization Administrator	VMware vCenter	Virtual Infrastructure Client and Web GUI	Port Group
Network Administrator	Nexus 1000V	Telnet, SSH, or DCNM-LAN	Port Profile
Security Administrator	VNMC	Web GUI	Security Profile

As described in Table 16-3, security administrators manage security profiles on VNMC, while connectivity settings are defined in Nexus 1000V port profiles by the network administrators, and applied through port groups by the VM administrators on vCenter.

The management plane connections between these entities assure coherency and automation in their daily tasks.

Note All three management platforms support Role-Based Access Control (RBAC) features that control what each administrator user can configure and visualize. On vCenter,

> for example, the use of a port group can be limited to a single administrator (or team) to avoid misuse and security breaches.

Although security officers might be used to firewall rules based on IP prefixes and port ranges, the integration between VNMC and vCenter considerably improves security policy writing for virtual machines.

For example, regarding the current policies for SecurityProfile-App, only traffic from IP address 192.168.105.180 to TCP port 3389 is permitted on interfaces associated to port profile N1KV-APP-SITE1. Nonetheless, the creation of this rule demanded the previous knowledge of VM-Web1 IP address, which in real-world scenarios would require the management of a database similar to Table 16-2 (but probably much bigger).

Figure 16-9 illustrates how ACLPolicyRule-App1 can be changed on VNMC to refer to a *virtual machine name* rather than an IP address.

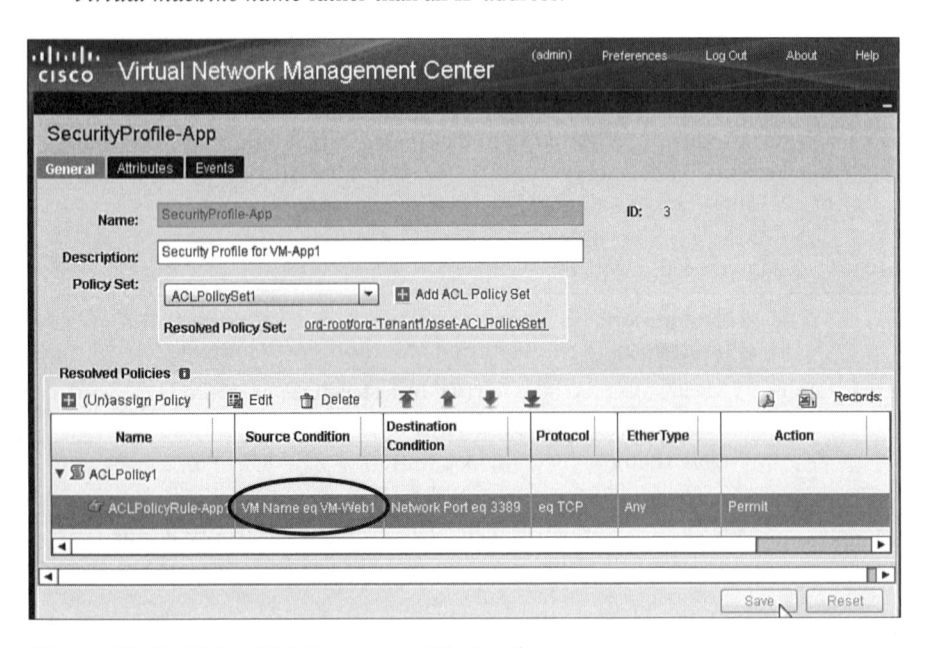

Figure 16-9 *Using VM Names as ACL Attributes*

As a consequence, Example 16-7 portrays how this change on VNMC automatically updates the security policies on VSG.

Example 16-7 *Verifying Policies and Virtual Machine IP Addresses on VSG*

```
! ACL Policy Rule has changed
VSG# show running-config | begin rule
rule ACLPolicy1/ACLPolicyRule-App1@root/Tenant1
  condition 10 dst.net.port eq 3389
```

```
    condition 11 src.vm.name eq VM-Web1
    condition 12 net.protocol eq 6
    action 10 permit
[output suppressed]
! Verifying the VNMC-pushed mapping between VM names and IP addresses
VSG# show vsg ip-binding vm
----------------------------------------------------------------
    VM IP address      VM Name              Port Profile Name
----------------------------------------------------------------
    192.168.105.181    vm-app1              N1KV-APP-SITE1
    192.168.105.180    vm-web1              N1KV-WEB-SITE1
```

The example also portrays some VNMC-provided bindings between VM names and IP address. With this mapping, VSG is capable of retrieving parameters that should be analyzed on vPath-encapsulated frames.

Tip To allow VSG to receive the VM-Web1 attributes from VNMC, the **org root/Tenant1** command was also required in the N1KV-WEB-SITE1 port profile. This command included the port profile in the same VNMC organization as VSG.

VNMC supports firewall rules with other VM attributes, such as VMware cluster name, guest operating system, host, application, port profile, VMware resource pool, and VM DNS name. Moreover, VNMC also allows the use of regular expressions and operators such as **contains**, **equals**, **not equals**, and **prefix** to recognize parts of any VM attribute.

Virtual Zones (vZone) are yet another VNMC resource that facilitates security policy writing. This entity basically defines a logical group of VMs with common attributes that can be referred, as a single parameter, on any ACL policy rule.

Figure 16-10 illustrates the creation of Virtual Zone vZone-Web, which aggregates all VMs whose names start with the prefix "VM-Web" and IP addresses belong to the range between 192.168.105.100 and 192.168.105.254.

Afterward, vZone-Web can be used on any ACL rule, including ACLPolicyRule-App1. Actually, it can replace the source condition with the same results on our scenario.

vZones provide an excellent mechanism for configuration automation: If a virtual machine is created matching vZone-Web conditions, it will be automatically included in all rules that employ this vZone.

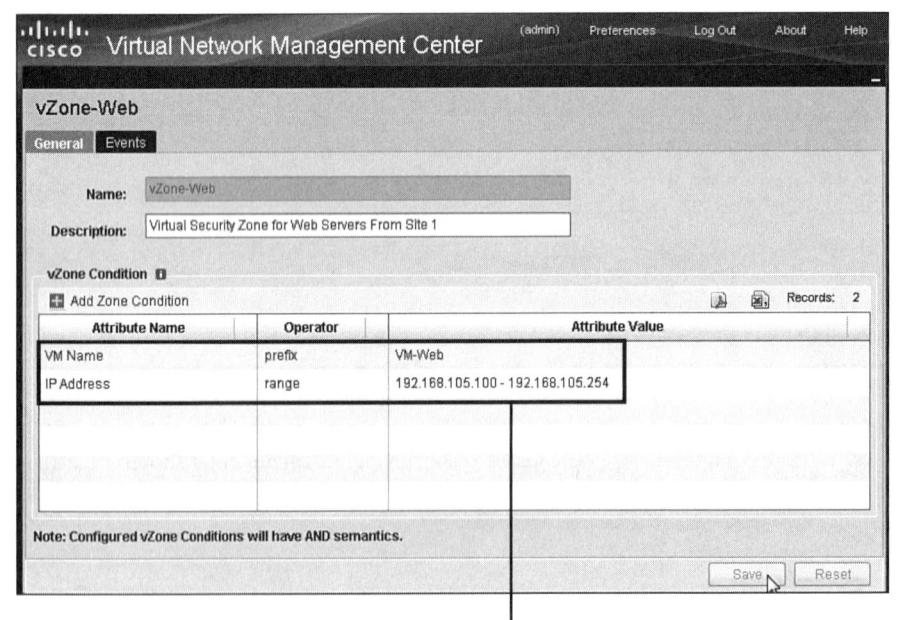

Figure 16-10 *vZone-Web Configuration*

Cisco ASA 1000V: Edge Virtual Firewall

The Cisco ASA 1000V is a virtual network service appliance designed to provide border security to a set of virtual machines. Based on Cisco Adaptive Security Appliances (ASA) 5500 software, ASA 1000V implements edge protection functionalities such as

- Stateful access protection against network-based attacks
- Network Address Translation (NAT)
- Application inspection (DNS, FTP, H.323, HTTP, ICMP, LDAP, MGCP, NetBIOS over IP, PPTP, RADIUS, RSH, RTSP, SIP, SCCP, SMTP, SNMP, SQL*Net, Sun RPC, TFTP, among others)
- Default gateway and Dynamic Host Control Protocol (DHCP) for its protected VMs

Integrated with both Nexus 1000V and VNMC, Cisco ASA 1000V employs *edge security profiles* that can characterize the network security level of a group of protected virtual machines. But contrary to VSG, ASA 1000V uses these security profiles to specify the communication with an external network, not acting over VM-to-VM traffic.

Figure 16-11 represents the ASA 1000V management and control architecture.

From the figure, you can notice that ASA 1000V has a similar management architecture to VSG. Notwithstanding, security administrators also have the option to write ASA 1000V security policies through its *Adaptive Security Device Manager (ASDM)* management software, as if it were a physical ASA device.

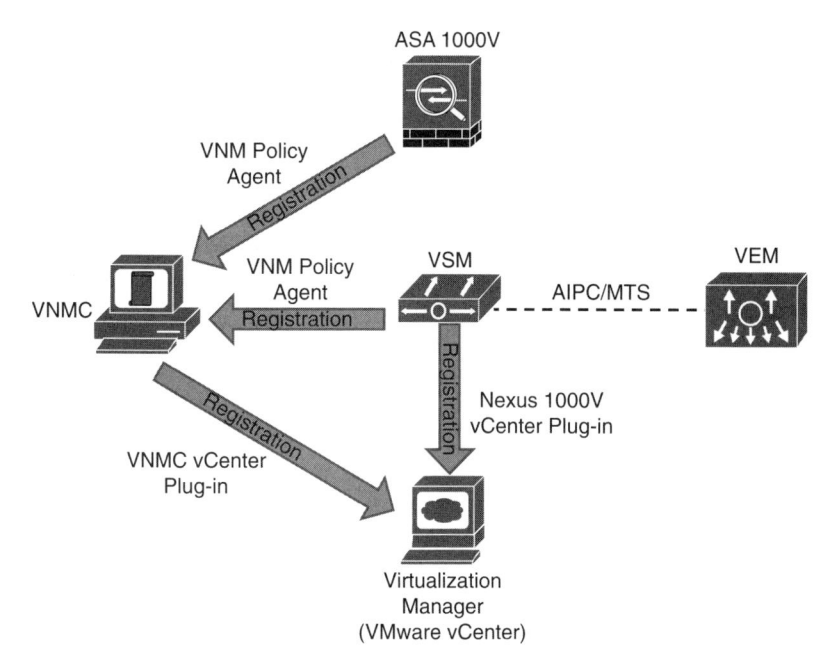

Figure 16-11 *ASA 1000V Management and Control Architecture*

The choice of managing ASA 1000V with VNMC or ASDM is mutually exclusive and must be defined at the time of the virtual appliance installation.

Installing ASA 1000V

An ASA 1000V instance has four interfaces: management 0/0 and Gigabit Ethernet 0/0 to 0/3. On an ASA 1000V installation through an OVF file, these interfaces respectively assume the following roles by default:

- **Management 0/0:** Used for ASDM and VNMC policy agent communication.
- **Gigabit Ethernet 0/0 (inside):** The default gateway for protected VMs and data interface for vPath traffic.
- **Gigabit Ethernet 0/1 (outside):** Connected to an unprotected external network.
- **Gigabit Ethernet 0/2 (failover):** Used for the exchange of connection states and failure detection on an active-standby ASA 1000V pair.

To demonstrate how ASA 1000V protects VM traffic, I will use it to shield VM-Web2 and VM-App2. Table 16-4 depicts the "plain" port profiles and other parameters that were used during the ASA 1000V installation (with the **Deploy OVF Template** vCenter wizard) and posterior configuration.

Table 16-4 *ASA 1000V OVF Parameters*

ASA 1000V Interface	VLAN	DVS Port Group (Nexus 1000V Port Profile)
Management 0/0	200	N1KV-ASA-MGMT-SITE2
Gigabit Ethernet 0/1	205	N1KV-ASA-INT-SITE2
Gigabit Ethernet 0/2	300	N1KV-VLAN300
Gigabit Ethernet 0/3	Unused	Unused_Or_Quarantine_Veth

Besides the management IP address (192.168.200.6/24) and port group assignment, I have also defined the following parameters during the wizard iteration: management default gateway (192.168.200.1, which is the VLAN 200 SVI on switch C6K5-Site2), allowed management IP address (192.168.100.99, which is my PC), and management through ASDM.

Tip Because you are already familiar with VNMC, I have selected ASDM management mode to highlight the similarities between ASA 1000V and its physical versions. Notwithstanding, there are several advantages of managing ASA 1000V through VNMC, such as management consolidation with VSG and multiple other ASA 1000V instances, rapid provisioning of shared policies between devices, multitenancy, the use of VM attributes on rules, and Virtual Security Zones.

After ASA 1000V is installed and powered on host20, it is possible to access its command-line interface through the vCenter VM console. In fact, I have used this method to register the ASA 1000V VNMC policy agent to the previously used VNMC instance (192.168.100.4).

The registration procedure is somewhat similar to the Nexus 1000V registration process, as Example 16-8 details.

Example 16-8 *Registering ASA 1000V in VNMC*

```
ASA# show running-config vnmc
! Defining shared secret and username that will perform configurations on VNMC
vnmc policy-agent
 registration host 192.168.100.4
 shared-secret *****
 login username admin password *****
! Defining the ASA 1000V organization on VNMC
vnmc org root/Tenant1
```

The configurations shown in Example 16-8 will be genuinely useful for the following reasons:

- ASA will be incorporated into organization root/Tenant1.
- ASA can also generate security profiles on VNMC, which will define an SPID for each profile and assure their distribution to both data path devices (ASA and Nexus 1000V).

After its installation, you can also manage ASA through ASDM. This management tool is accessed when a browser is pointed to the ASA management interface IP address (192.168.200.6, in our case). Figure 16-12 illustrates our recently installed ASA 1000V being managed through ASDM.

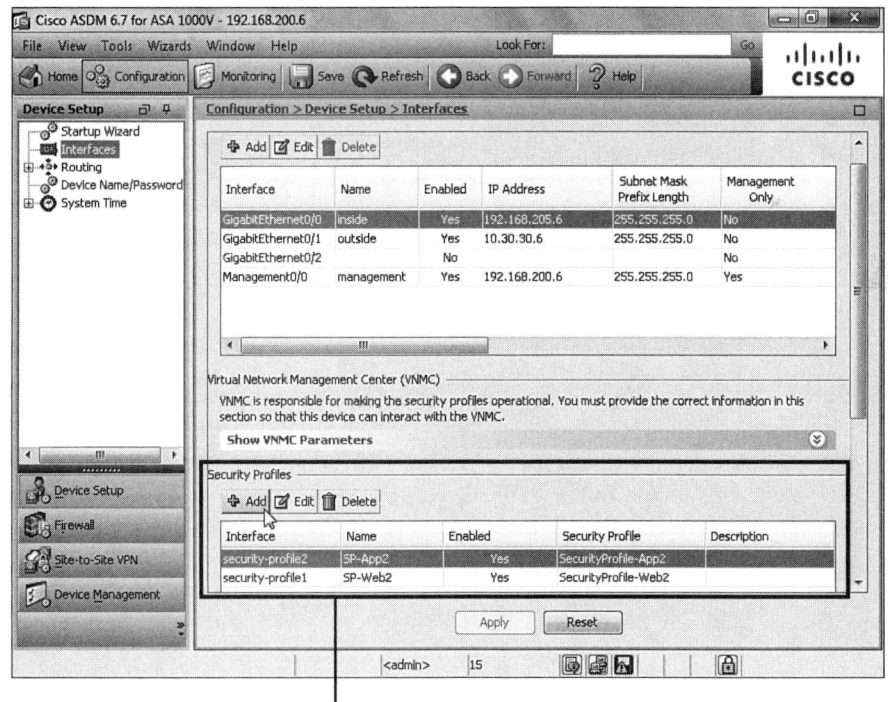

Figure 16-12 *ASA 1000V Security Profile Interfaces*

Figure 16-12 shows that I have configured all required ASA interfaces (management, outside, and inside) according to the port profiles that were associated to them during the installation.

At the bottom of the figure, I have also added two *security profile interfaces* (SP-App2 and SP-Web2) to ASA 1000V. These logical interfaces are abstract constructs that process vPath-tagged frames on the ASA 1000V inside interface.

Sending Data Traffic to ASA 1000V

The ASA 1000V data plane relies on the configuration of vPath on the VEMs that are connected to its protected VMs. Example 16-9 depicts the Nexus 1000V configuration that will correctly forward traffic to ASA 1000V.

Example 16-9 *Nexus 1000V vPath Configuration*

```
! Creating an ASA 1000V virtual service node
VSM(config)# vservice node ASA type asa
! Defining ASA reachability parameters  (IP address, vPath
encapsulation mode, and Nexus 1000V behavior in the case of node failure)
VSM(config-vservice-node)# ip address 192.168.205.6
VSM(config-vservice-node)# adjacency l2 vlan 205
VSM(config-vservice-node)# fail-mode close
! Assigning VM-App2 and VM-Web2 port profiles to ASA organization and Security
Profile
VSM(config-vservice-node)# port-profile N1KV-APP-SITE2
VSM(config-port-prof)# org root/Tenant1
VSM(config-port-prof)# vservice node ASA profile SecurityProfile-App2
VSM(config-vservice-node)# port-profile N1KV-WEB-SITE2
VSM(config-port-prof)# org root/Tenant1
VSM(config-port-prof)# vservice node ASA profile SecurityProfile-Web2
```

As described in the example, Nexus 1000V reaches ASA through its inside interface using Layer 2 encapsulation on VLAN 205. In addition, if Nexus 1000V is not capable of reaching ASA, it will drop traffic that should be steered to this node through vPath.

Tip Close is also the default fail mode for ASA 1000V virtual service nodes in Nexus 1000V.

From now on, an allowed outbound connection from each VM will follow the data path behavior detailed in Figure 16-13.

The figure describes the following:

a. VM-Web2 starts a connection directed to an outer network, sending a frame that is directed to its default gateway (which *must* be the ASA 1000V inside interface).

b. Because VEM 5 receives this frame from a vPath-enabled port profile (N1KV-WEB-SITE2), it is encapsulated on a vPath frame whose tag contains the SPID provided by VNMC.

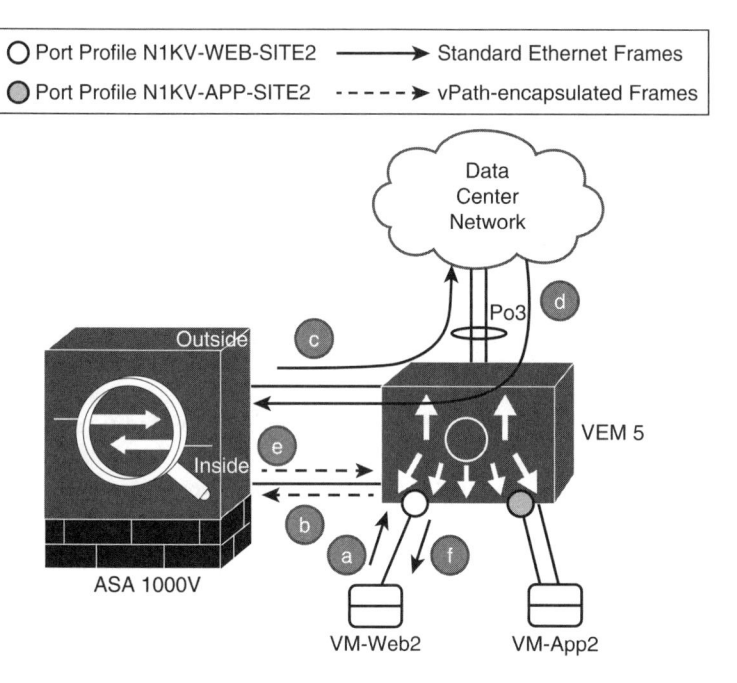

Figure 16-13 *ASA 1000V Data Path for Outgoing Connection*

   c. After ASA 1000V receives the vPath-tagged frame, it applies the policies that are associated to the source interface (which is logical service profile interface SP-Web2). Consequently, ASA 1000V creates a flow for the connection and routes the packet to the outside network (without any vPath tag).

   d. The connection reply packet arrives at ASA's outside interface.

   e. ASA looks up its flow table and forwards the packet to the VEM through a vPath-encapsulated frame that is using the cached SPID.

   f. The VEM removes the tag and forwards it normally to VM-Web2.

In this scenario, it is possible to observe how differently vPath behaves for ASA 1000V and VSG. Rather than consulting the flow manager process before sending vPath-tagged frames to the virtual service node (as was the case of VSG), the VEM will only tag frames whose destination MAC address corresponds to the ASA 1000V inside interface.

Note Broadcast frames (such as ARP and DHCP) are not vPath-tagged for ASA 1000V and are handled by the inside interface itself. If this interface receives other non-tagged frames, they will be dropped.

ASA 1000V deploys an analogous behavior pattern for an allowed incoming connection to a protected VM. For example, if ASA receives a packet from the outside interface, it does the following:

- Applies its configured policies to the packet
- Consults the VM IP address–to–service profile binding database received from VNMC
- Creates forward and reverse flows for the packet connection
- Adds a vPath tag (with the corresponding SPID) and forwards the packet to the destination VM

As you can see, the correct assignment of SPIDs and VM IP addresses to both ASA 1000V and Nexus 1000V is crucial for their correct policy enforcement. For that reason, VNMC is a mandatory component in the ASA 1000V architecture, even if it is managed through ASDM.

Examples 16-10 and 16-11 prove this statement, showing the bindings sent from VNMC on both virtual devices.

Example 16-10 *Checking VNMC Bindings on ASA 1000V*

```
ASA# show vsn
! ASA policies are controlled through ASDM
Configuration through VNMC : disabled
! Security Profiles, SPIDs, and Logical Interfaces association
vsn security-profile info :
security-profile : SecurityProfile-Web2
SPID             : 10
Interface        : SP-Web2


security-profile : SecurityProfile-App2
SPID             : 12
Interface        : SP-App2
! IP Addresses, Security Profiles, and Logical Interfaces association
IP               : 192.168.205.180
security-profile : SecurityProfile-Web2
Interface        : SP-Web2

IP               : 192.168.205.181
security-profile : SecurityProfile-App2
Interface        : SP-App2
```

Example 16-11 *Verifying VNMC Bindings on Nexus 1000V*

```
VSM# show vservice port brief node-name ASA
[output suppressed]
! VNMC has delivered the same parameters to Nexus 1000V
PortProfile:N1KV-WEB-SITE2
Org:root/Tenant1
Node:ASA(192.168.205.6)                     Profile(Id):SecurityProfile-Web2(10)
Veth Mod VM-Name                            vNIC IP-Address
  16   5  vm-web2                             1  192.168.205.180
PortProfile:N1KV-APP-SITE2
Org:root/Tenant1
Node:ASA(192.168.205.6)                     Profile(Id):SecurityProfile-App2(12)
Veth Mod VM-Name                            vNIC IP-Address
  17   5  vm-app2                             1  192.168.205.181
```

Configuring Security Policies on ASA 1000V

All Cisco Adaptive Security Appliances (ASA) employ *interface security levels* from 0 to 100 to enforce security policies between network segments. When an ASA is deciding whether a packet should be forwarded between two interfaces, the comparison between their security levels defines which interface is considered **untrusted** (lower security level) and **trusted** (higher level).

By design, ASA implicitly permits traffic from a trusted interface to an untrusted interface. On the other hand, rules must be explicitly configured to allow traffic from an untrusted interface to a trusted one.

During its installation, the ASA inside interface was configured by default with a security level of 100, while both management and outside received level 0. During their creation, I have also assigned the following levels to the security profile interfaces:

- SP-App2 (SecurityProfile-App2): level 90
- SP-Web2 (SecurityProfile-Web2): level 50

This arrangement permits ASA 1000V to apply distinct security policies for VMs that are connected to the same VLAN. As an example, Figure 16-14 depicts the ASDM view of two explicit inbound access rules: one that permits that hosts on the outside network access VM-Web2 through HTTP and ICMP, and another that permits my PC to initiate an application access (TCP port 3389) to VM-App2.

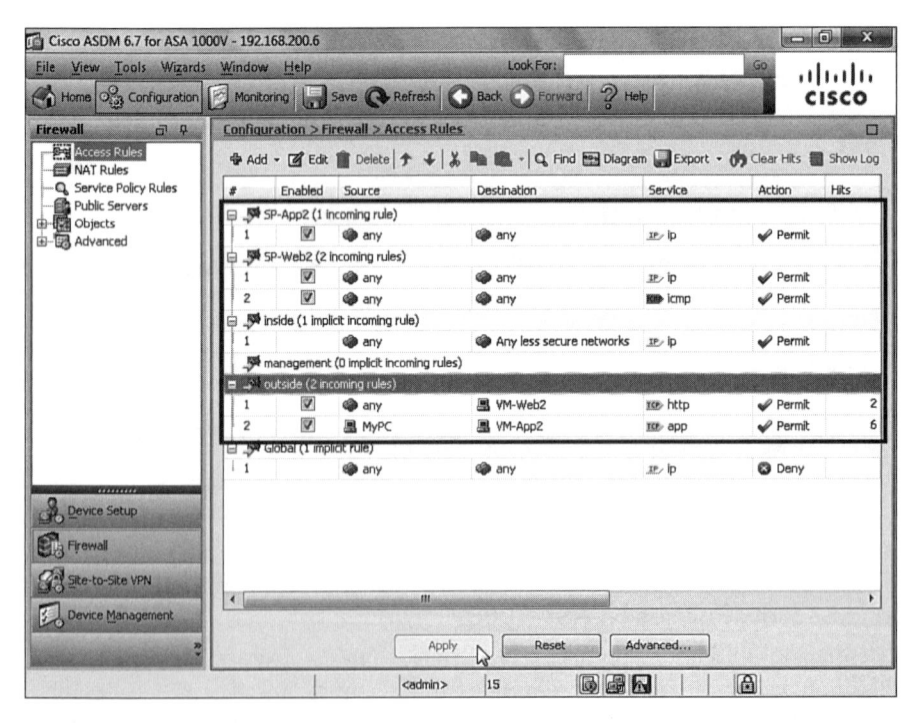

Figure 16-14 *ASA 1000V Access Rules*

In Figure 16-14, you can also observe that distinct outbound permissions can also be assigned to logical interfaces SP-Web2 (IP and ICMP) and SP-App2 (only IP).

To enable the income rules shown in Figure 16-14, I have also configured the following:

- A route to external networks through IP gateway 10.30.30.1 (Hot Standby Router Protocol [HSRP] virtual IP address formed by the Catalyst switchs' SVIs on VLAN 300)

- Dynamic IP address assignment with DHCP for both VMs (VM-Web2 received original IP address 192.168.205.180, and VM-App2 received 192.168.205.181)

- Network Address Translation (NAT), creating external IP address 10.30.30.180 for VM-Web2 and 10.30.30.181 for VM-App2.

As an edge firewall, ASA does not control the traffic between VM-Web2 and VM-App2 because vPath for ASA 1000V only tags frames that are destined to the virtual service node's inside interface MAC address. Consequently, VSG and ASA 1000V perform complementary roles in virtual machine security.

Tip This joint positioning will be further explored in the section "Use Case: Virtual Data Center," later in this chapter.

Application Acceleration

The transmission characteristics of wide-area networks (WAN) can provide dismal performance on some applications. Besides generally having lower bandwidth when compared to LAN connections, long-distance links also present a higher latency that can turn simple file transfers into a snail race.

Chatty file-sharing protocols, such as Common Internet File System (CIFS) and Network File System (NFS), usually exchange lots of small messages during each file transfer. In these operations, the sender must receive an acknowledgment of message delivery before transmitting another one, elapsing a total transmission time directly proportional to the connection latency.

For example, imagine that a file is translated into 5000 protocol messages. If two hosts are connected through an Ethernet LAN connection with a round-trip time (RTT) of 1 millisecond, the file transfer will theoretically be completed after five seconds, if we do not consider processing and serialization time. However, should the same file be transferred over a WAN link with an RTT of 50 milliseconds, it will take 250 seconds (or near eternity, in Internet terms).

TCP, a protocol designed in the late 1960s, also suffers from performance drawbacks when it is submitted to higher latencies. On Windows-based personal computers, the maximum amount of data that can be transmitted without a confirmation from the receiver (TCP window size) is limited to 64 KB. Therefore, in the same 50-millisecond RTT link, a TCP connection throughput cannot reach a value higher of 10.5 Mbps (64 KB, or 525,288 bits, divided by 50 ms), *regardless of the WAN link bandwidth*.

Several enhancements, such as Windows Scaling (RFC 1323) and Selective Acknowledgment Options (RFC 2018), were created to overcome high-latency effects on TCP connections. However, their implementation depends on updates that must be executed on both servers and clients. As any other protocol "boosting" would also suffer from the same scale problem, opportunity knocked for the creation of another network service: application acceleration over WAN links (or simply, WAN acceleration).

Figure 16-15 describes the architecture of the Cisco WAN acceleration solution, Wide Area Application Services (WAAS), and its main components.

Cisco WAAS is a symmetrical acceleration solution, because it demands the presence of one accelerator at each end of a WAN link (one close to the client and another one in the vicinity of the application server). With that arrangement, application connections between hosts are intercepted by both WAAS devices, which in turn apply acceleration algorithms to decrease the application response time and increase the WAN link capacity.

In summary, WAAS offers the following acceleration algorithms:

- **TCP Flow Optimization (TFO):** Where each WAAS device acts as a TCP proxy and automatically employs TCP enhancements (such as large initial windows, selective acknowledgments, short slow start, and lesser degradation in the case of segment loss) to the intercepted connections.

- **Data Redundancy Elimination (DRE):** In which WAAS inspects TCP traffic to identify redundant data patterns at the byte level and quickly replace them with 6-byte signatures that are automatically indexed and recognized by both WAAS devices.

- **Persistent Lempel-Ziv (PLZ) Compression:** Complements the data reduction achieved by DRE.

- **Specific accelerators:** Optimizes the transmission behavior of SSL, HTTP, CIFS, NFS, MAPI, and Citrix ICA on WAN links, providing acceleration for applications such as Microsoft Exchange, Microsoft SharePoint, Oracle, SAP, and virtual desktops.

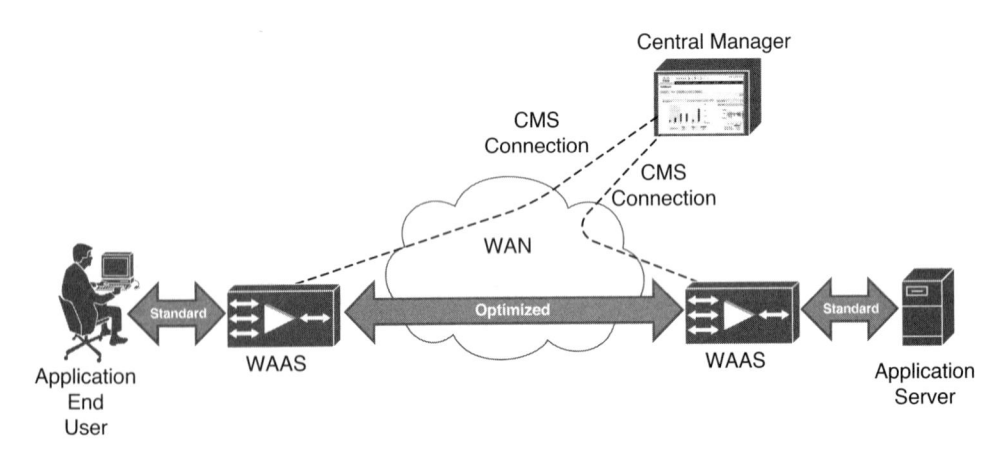

Figure 16-15 *Cisco WAAS Architecture*

> **Note** Although a *desktop virtualization* analysis is beyond the scope of this book, it uses several virtualization technologies described in this publication. In summary, a virtual desktop exists on a virtual machine running an end-user operating system and applications. These desktop VMs are centrally managed and usually accessed through thin clients (or software clients) deploying display protocols such as Citrix ICA (Independent Computing Architecture) or Teradici PCoIP (PC over IP).
>
> Besides the aforementioned components, desktop virtualization architectures usually comprise authentication servers, brokers, WAN accelerators, and specialized automation tools.

Multiple accelerators comprise a Cisco WAAS system, which is managed by at least one *central manager* device. This management tool provides consolidated configuration, provisioning, real-time monitoring, logging, and customized reporting through SSL connections initiated by the Centralized Management Subsystem (CMS) on each accelerator.

WAAS deploys a mechanism called *auto-discovery* that permits that two accelerators between end hosts can discover each other dynamically. The discovery occurs during the three-way handshake of actual application connections, when each WAAS device inserts a small amount of data into the TCP options in the SYN, SYN/ACK, and ACK messages. Through auto-discovery, the pair of devices that stand closer to the connection hosts will negotiate and apply the proper acceleration algorithms (while intermediate appliances or unique devices will let these flows pass through them).

Full WAAS services can be deployed in two different physical formats: *Wide Area Virtualization Engine (WAVE)* appliances and service modules for ISR (Integrated Service Routers). On these devices, network traffic interception must be performed through one of following methods:

- **Policy-Based Routing (PBR):** In which a router selects the WAAS device as the next-hop gateway based on preconfigured traffic policies (ACLs).

- **Inline (WAVE appliances only):** Where a WAAS device is capable of analyzing and optimizing traffic that traverses a special network adapter. Each pair of interfaces on such an adapter can turn into a pass-through connection in the case of a software or hardware failure.

- **Web Cache Control Protocol (WCCP):** Where a router or switch is capable of intercepting and sending traffic to the accelerator. WAAS uses version 2 of this popular protocol.

- **Application delivery controllers:** Devices such as Cisco ACE can select traffic that must be optimized in the data center.

- **AppNav:** Pools WAN optimization resources in the data center into one elastic resource with flexibility, performance monitoring, automation, and high availability. AppNav is a WAAS clustering solution that provides hardware-based classification and can scale to more than 1 million TCP connections.

Note Select IOS routers can also deploy a feature called *WAAS Express*, which implements a smaller set of WAAS acceleration algorithms.

With the release of vWAAS, vPath has been integrated into the range of WAAS-supported interception methods. As with other virtual service nodes, Nexus 1000V can steer VM traffic to a vWAAS instance to be accelerated.

WAAS Central Manager is also available as a virtual appliance (vCM), and both vWAAS and vCM can be installed through OVF files.

Table 16-5 summarizes the VLANs, IP addresses, and "plain" port profile names that were used for vWAAS (and vCM) implementation in our virtual network topology.

Table 16-5 *vWAAS and vCM Connectivity Parameters*

Virtual Machine	VLAN	IP Address	DVS Port Group (Nexus 1000V Port Profile)
vCM	200	192.168.200.7	N1KV-vWAAS-MGMT-SITE2
vWAAS	203	192.168.203.8	N1KV-vWAAS-SERVICE

After both virtual appliances were installed on host20, I configured them using the same procedures that a WAAS device and a central manager require. Though I will not fully describe these procedures here, I will sum them up as follows:

- Using VMware vCenter to access to each VM console, I have executed the initial WAAS setup script, which defines IP address, subnet, default gateway, host name, DNS server, domain name, and NTP server on each virtual appliance.

- During the setup script on vWAAS, I have also pointed the central manager IP address and defined vPath as its interception method.

- Finally, I have executed the **cms enable** configuration command on vWAAS to enable the management subsystems on both virtual appliances.

Tip Refer to WAAS installation guides for more details about these procedures.

With vCM already managing vWAAS, I have also configured vPath on the Nexus 1000V to redirect traffic related to port profile N1KV-VLAN300.

Example 16-12 details this configuration.

Example 16-12 *vPath Configuration for WAAS*

```
! Configuring virtual service node vWAAS
VSM(config)# vservice node vWAAS type vwaas
VSM(config-vservice-node)# ip address 192.168.203.8
VSM(config-vservice-node)# adjacency l2 vlan 203
VSM(config-vservice-node)# fail-mode open
! Enabling vPath for vWAAS on interfaces associated to port profile
VSM(config-vservice-node)# port-profile N1KV-VLAN300
VSM(config-port-prof)# vservice node vWAAS
```

In Example 16-12, because vWAAS does not require the use of security profiles or VNMC organizations, its configuration is simpler when compared to VSG and ASA 1000V. Also contrary to these other vPath services, vWAAS deploys open fail mode by default, maintaining connectivity in the case of a vWAAS node failure.

> **Note** vWAAS relies on the VMware High Availability (HA) feature to deploy acceleration failover. And if the original vWAAS was storing its DRE data in a SAN-based storage, the restarted VM will resume the acceleration operation with the same level of data compression.

Figure 16-16 exhibits the topology elements that are related to the assembled vWAAS deployment.

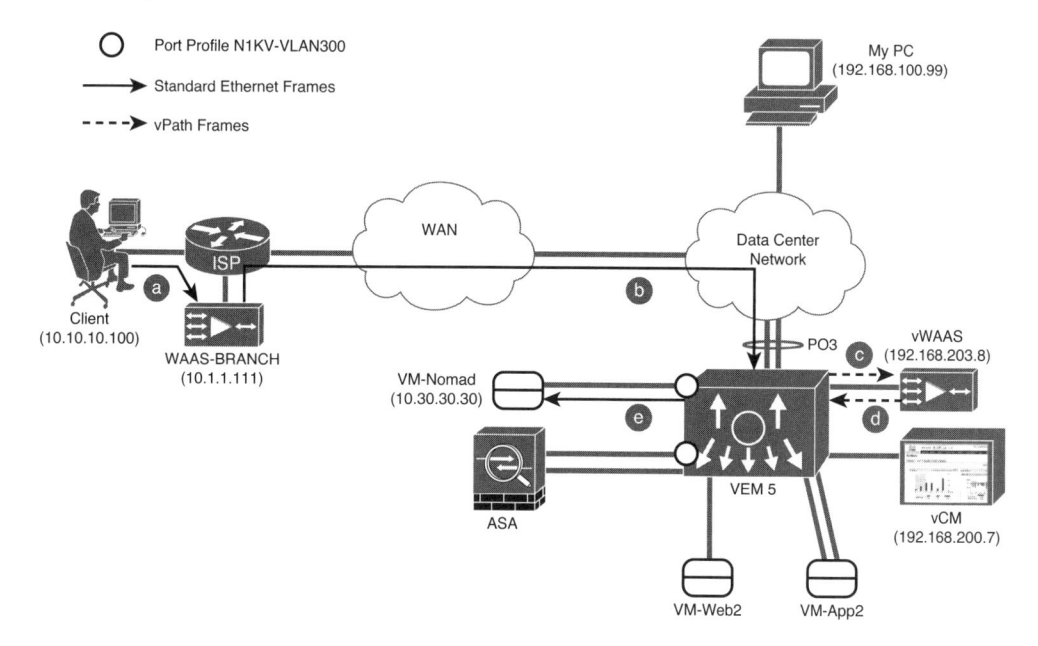

Figure 16-16 *vWAAS Scenario*

In this vWAAS scenario, I have also set up a remote branch to characterize our WAN. This branch is connected to our data center through an ISR router and a two-interface server that is emulating a WAN connection with 2 Mbps and an RTT of 200 milliseconds.

In the ISR, traffic is being intercepted to the WAAS-BRANCH appliance through WCCP. I have also used the same WAAS setup script, vCM IP address, and **cms enable** command to include WAAS-BRANCH in the WAAS system.

Above all, Figure 16-16 details the data path of a connection accelerated by vWAAS and WAAS-BRANCH. Its path can be broken into the following pieces:

   a. The client sends data to VM-Nomad. Enabling WCCP on its ingress Ethernet interface, ISR intercepts the packets and sends them to WAAS-BRANCH.

b. WAAS-BRANCH applies the negotiated acceleration algorithms and sends the traffic back to ISR. Because WAAS does not change the packets IP header, ISR routes them normally towards VM-Nomad (through the WAN and the data center network).

c. VEM 5 (on host 20) realizes that the traffic is destined to a virtual interface associated with port profile N1KV-VLAN300. Consequently, it sends the associated frames to vWAAS using vPath Layer 2 encapsulation.

d. vWAAS applies the acceleration algorithm negotiated with WAAS-BRANCH for this connection and sends the traffic back to VEM 5 (inside vPath frames, because vWAAS is not on the same VLAN as VM-Nomad).

e. VEM sends the resulting frames to VM-Nomad.

As you can see, vWAAS requires a VEM vPath behavior that somehow resembles VSG. For vWAAS, traffic to virtual interfaces associated to a vservice profile is always conducted to vWAAS for analysis. Afterward, vWAAS sends the processed data back to the VEM and optionally use vPath offload to avoid receiving subsequent frames that belong to a non-accelerated connection (pass-through).

To demonstrate this vPath behavior, I have initiated four distinct connections:

- An HTTP session from the client to VM-Nomad
- An FTP file transfer from VM-Nomad to the client
- An HTTP session from the client to the ASA 1000V NAT address for VM-Web2 (10.30.30.180)
- An HTTP session from my PC to VM-Nomad

Example 16-13 depicts how vPath is handling these connections on Nexus 1000V.

Example 16-13 *vPath Connections*

```
VSM# show vservice connection node-name vWAAS
[output suppressed]
#Port-Profile:N1KV-VLAN300                    Node:vWAAS
#Module 5
Proto SrcIP[:Port]           SAct  DstIP[:Port]         DAct  Flags      Bytes
! Lowercase 'p' means that connection is being redirected to vWAAS
 tcp  10.10.10.100:56879           10.30.30.30:80        p     s       88800000
! Uppercase 'P' means that this connection is offloaded and not sent to vWAAS
 tcp  192.168.100.99:59397          10.30.30.30:80        P     E       23400879
 tcp  10.10.10.100:56923            10.30.30.180:80       p     Sas         7533
 tcp  10.10.10.100:56924            10.30.30.30:21        P     E           3669
 tcp  10.30.30.30:20         p     10.10.10.100:56926           Sas     224275515
```

As you can see in Example 16-13, vPath is redirecting all TCP connections to vWAAS, except two that cannot be accelerated:

- HTTP from my PC (using auto-discovery, vWAAS has detected that it was the sole accelerator in the network path between my PC and VM-Nomad)
- FTP control connection (which it is not accelerated according to the WAAS default acceleration policy)

Accessing the vWAAS console, Example 16-14 details which algorithms are actually accelerating the other connections.

Example 16-14 *vWAAS Optimized Connections*

```
vWAAS# show statistics connection optimized
[output suppressed]
D:DRE,L:LZ,T:TCP Optimization RR:Total Reduction Ratio
A:AOIM,C:CIFS,E:EPM,G:GENERIC,H:HTTP,I:ICA,M:MAPI,N:NFS,S:SSL,W:WAN SECURE,V:VID
EO
X: SMB Signed Connection
! vWAAS is applying TFO, HTTP, DRE, and LZ acceleration algorithms to the web
browser connections
ConnID        Source IP:Port           Dest IP:Port           PeerID Accel RR
     2    10.10.10.100:56879       10.30.30.30:80  00:0f:fe:df:3c:f8 THDL  90.7%
    32    10.10.10.100:56923      10.30.30.180:80  00:0f:fe:df:3c:f8 THDL  84.2%
! And applying TFO, DRE, and LZ to the FTP file transfer
    34      10.30.30.30:20     10.10.10.100:56926  00:0f:fe:df:3c:f8  TDL  99.5%
```

In the example, the Total Reduction Ratio (RR) values were achieved because the transferred data was already mapped out on the DRE databases on both accelerators (vWAAS and WAAS-BRANCH) during previous similar sessions.

WAN Acceleration and Online Migration

VM-Nomad, as its name hints, can migrate between site 1 and site 2 of our topology because its only vnic is connected to an extended VLAN (300). However, vWAAS uses VLAN 203 (which is confined to site 2) to send traffic to vWAAS. Therefore, if VM-Nomad migrates from host20 to any host on site 1, vWAAS will not be reachable to vPath frames.

To rectify this situation, VLAN 203 must be extended between both sites, as represented in Figure 16-17.

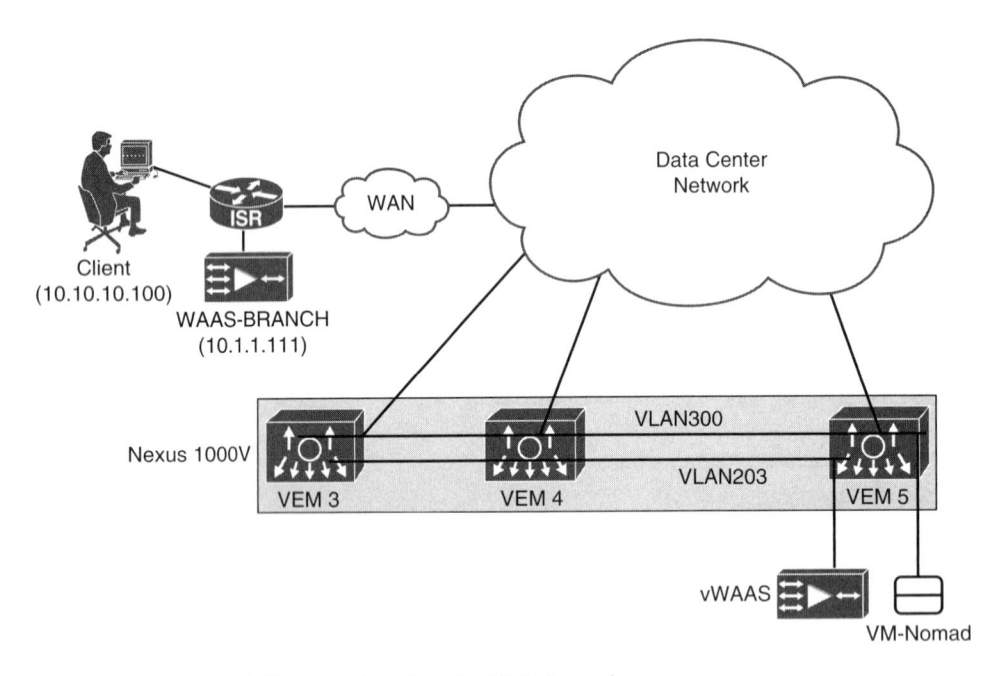

Figure 16-17 *Enabling Acceleration for VM-Nomad*

Figure 16-17 portrays a simplified topology view, where Nexus 1000V is shown as a rectangle spanning all hosts and broadcast domains are represented as straight lines crossing VEMs that are connected to them. Such a "bridging domain" view helps visualize that VLAN 203's extension enables the migration of VM-Nomad and vWAAS to any other host without any loss of connectivity or acceleration services.

In fact, Example 16-15 portrays the status of vWAAS after VM-Nomad is migrated to host11 and vWAAS to host10.

Example 16-15 *vWAAS Service Node Status After VM-Nomad and vWAAS Migration*

```
! VM-Nomad activated vPath on VEM 4 (host11) and vWAAS service remains active
VSM# show vservice node brief name vWAAS
[output suppressed]
ID Name                 Type    IP-Address      Mode    State    Module
 3 vWAAS                vwaas   192.168.203.8   v-203   Alive     4
! vWAAS is located at VEM 3 (host10)
VSM# show interface virtual vm vWAAS
--------------------------------------------------------------------
Port        Adapter          Owner               Mod Host
--------------------------------------------------------------------
Veth43      Net Adapter 1    vWAAS                3  host10
```

Service VLAN extension is not the only solution that unleashes the migration of VMs and virtual service nodes to any host on a virtualization environment. Actually, at the time of this writing, other virtual network services can forward and receive vPath traffic over a VXLAN (such as VSG and ASA 1000V) or to another IP subnet (VSG only).

Note Leveraging the flexibility of vPath architecture, Cisco has announced its intention to also integrate third-party virtual appliances, such as Imperva's SecureSphere Web Application Firewall (WAF) and Citrix's NetScaler VPX virtual Application Delivery Controller (vADC).

Routing in the Virtual World

The broad Cisco product portfolio provides a large horizon for virtual network services, where many hardware solutions can be transformed into virtual appliances. For example, with virtual networking being essentially based on Layer 2 forwarding, there are multiple advantages of deploying routers as virtual machines, such as

- Traffic optimization
- Separation of broadcast domains within virtualization environments
- Router interface scalability
- Leveraging of virtualization features such as cloning, online migration, and templates

The CSR 1000V router fulfills this opportunity, bringing the wide array of IOS intelligent features to virtual networks. Based on the IOS XE modular code, CSR 1000V can securely deploy multiple protocols and functionalities, including MPLS, ACL, HSRP, VPN, NAT, AAA, IP SLA, Layer 3 Firewall, SNMP, Syslog, among many others. CSR 1000V can even provide traffic interception for vWAAS through WCCP and AppNav.

As with other Cisco virtual appliances, CSR 1000V installation is pretty straightforward, leveraging the use of OVF or ISO files. At the time of this writing, CSR 1000V requires that the VM Guest OS is based on Linux 2.6 (just like NX-OS, IOS XE's kernel is based on this operating system), four vCPUs, 4 GB of memory, a virtual hard disk of 8 GB, and a virtual CD/DVD boot device mapped to the IOS XE ISO file.

In a single CSR 1000V instance, you can create up to ten vNICs (which is the current limit for a virtual machine in vSphere). The adding or removing of a vNIC requires a reload, and interface mapping can change if an interface is removed.

To demonstrate its applicability in virtual networks, I have deployed a three-interface CSR 1000V instance on host11 from our virtual topology.

Its virtual connectivity characteristics are described on Table 16-6.

Table 16-6 *CSR 1000V Connectivity Parameters*

CSR 1000V Interface	VLAN	DVS Port Group (Nexus 1000V Port Profile)
Gigabit Ethernet 0	100	N1KV-CSR-MGMT
Gigabit Ethernet 1	300	N1KV-CSR-VLAN300
Gigabit Ethernet 2	600	N1KV-CSR-VLAN600

After the virtual machine is created and powered on, it is possible to access the CSR "console" through a vCenter console session, as portrayed on Figure 16-18.

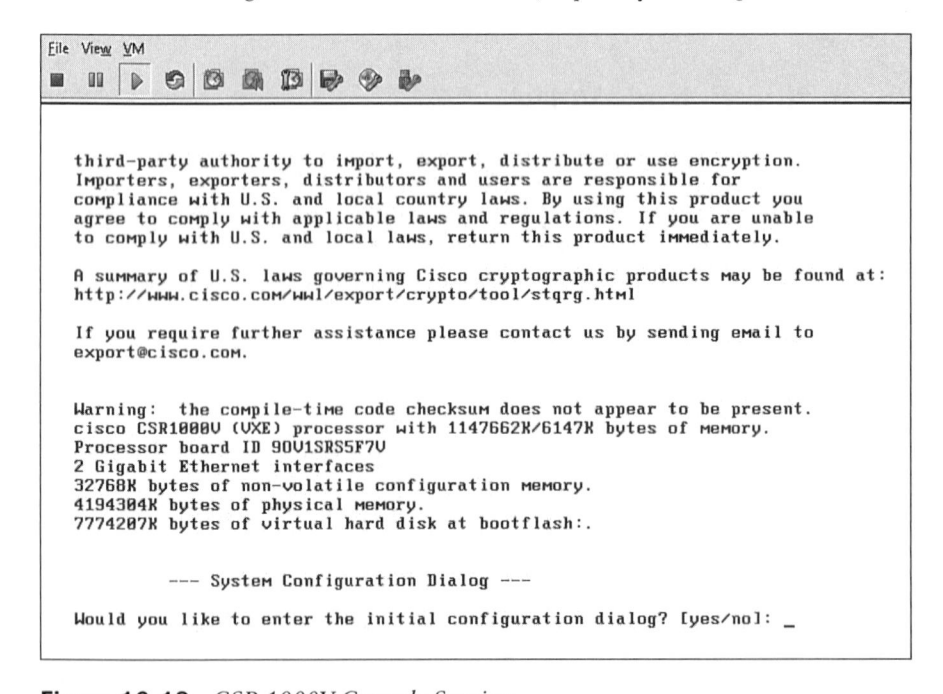

Figure 16-18 *CSR 1000V Console Session*

In the session, a familiar IOS setup script is waiting for you. And by using that dialog box, I have configured interface Gigabit Ethernet 0 with IP address 192.168.100.9/24.

Tip By default, interface Gigabit Ethernet 0 on CSR 1000V is reserved for management purposes. For security reasons, IOS XE places this interface on a dedicated VRF named *Mgmt-intf*.

After the management interface is correctly activated, all CSR 1000V configurations can be executed through a standard Telnet session. In fact, from a pure operational perspective, CSR is practically indistinguishable from a standard IOS-based router.

Example 16-16 explores the potential of CSR 1000V with some configurations will affect the established routing between the branch router and the virtual machines accessible in VLAN 300 (VM-Nomad and ASA 1000V's outside interface).

Example 16-16 *CSR Configuration*

```
! Entering configuration mode
CSR# configure terminal
Enter configuration commands, one per line.  End with CNTL/Z.
! Configuring interface IP address and enabling it to become the active HSRP member
on VLAN 300
CSR(config)# interface GigabitEthernet 1
CSR(config-if)# ip address 10.30.30.9 255.255.255.0
CSR(config-if)# standby 1 ip 10.30.30.1
CSR(config-if)# standby 1 priority 255
CSR(config-if)# standby 1 preempt
CSR(config-if)# no shutdown
! Defining interface IP address
CSR(config-if)# interface GigabitEthernet2
CSR(config-if)# ip address 10.20.20.9 255.255.255.0
CSR(config-if)# no shutdown
CSR(config-if)# exit
! Adding a static route to 192.168.0.0 networks and enabling OSPF on
both non-management interfaces (Gi1 and Gi2)
CSR(config)# ip route 192.168.0.0 255.255.0.0 10.30.30.200
CSR(config)# router ospf 1
CSR(config-router)# redistribute static subnets
CSR(config-router)# network 10.20.20.0 0.0.0.255 area 0
CSR(config-router)# network 10.30.30.0 0.0.0.255 area 0
```

Figure 16-19 represents the "bridging domain" view of VLANs 100, 205, 300, and 600 after CSR is inserted in the topology.

As Example 16-17 demonstrates, CSR has become the default gateway for VM-Nomad and ASA 1000V after it has "hijacked" the HSRP group virtual IP address (10.30.30.1) from both Catalyst 6500 switches. Additionally, CSR is exchanging OSPF routes with ISR while providing Layer 3 connectivity for traffic between IP subnets 10.10.10.0 and 10.30.30.0.

Example 16-17 *CSR 1000V HSRP and OSPF Status*

```
CSR# show standby brief
                     P indicates configured to preempt.
                     |
Interface   Grp  Pri P State    Active       Standby      Virtual IP
Gi1         1    255 P Active   local        10.30.30.200 10.30.30.1
```

```
CSR# show ip ospf neighbor
Neighbor ID      Pri   State       Dead Time   Address        Interface
10.20.20.254       1   FULL/DR     00:00:34    10.20.20.254   GigabitEthernet2
```

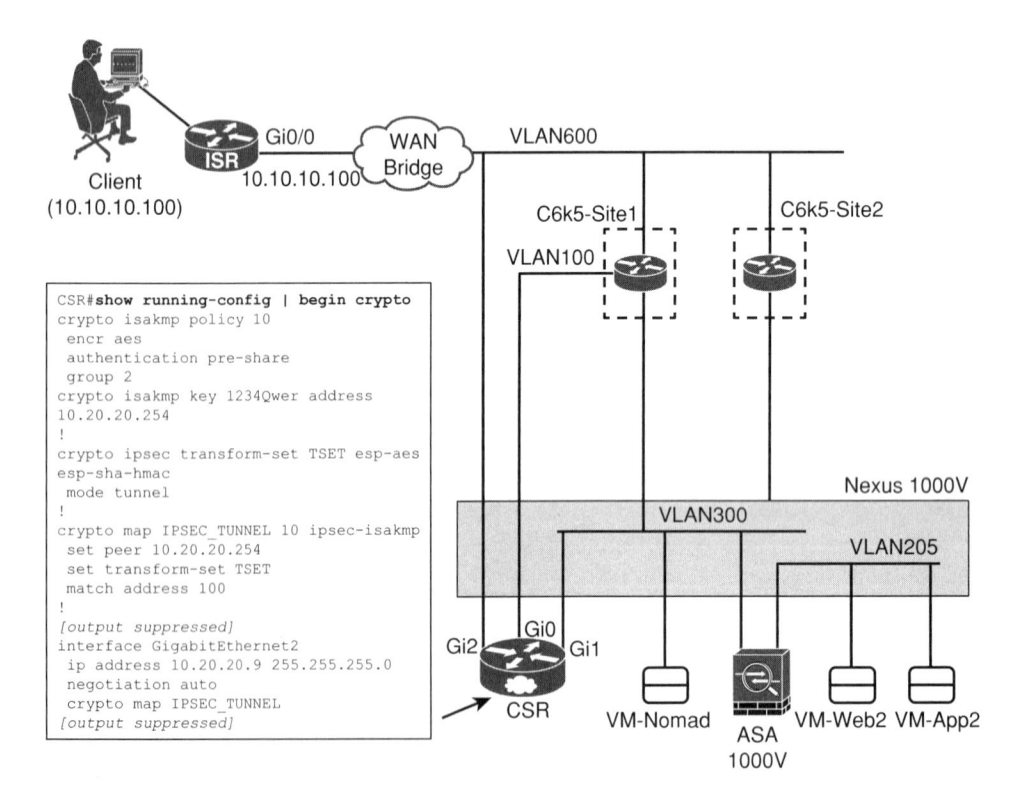

```
CSR#show running-config | begin crypto
crypto isakmp policy 10
 encr aes
 authentication pre-share
 group 2
crypto isakmp key 1234Qwer address
10.20.20.254
!
crypto ipsec transform-set TSET esp-aes
esp-sha-hmac
 mode tunnel
!
crypto map IPSEC_TUNNEL 10 ipsec-isakmp
 set peer 10.20.20.254
 set transform-set TSET
 match address 100
!
[output suppressed]
interface GigabitEthernet2
 ip address 10.20.20.9 255.255.255.0
 negotiation auto
 crypto map IPSEC_TUNNEL
[output suppressed]
```

Figure 16-19 *CSR 1000V Insertion*

Figure 16-19 also depicts an IPsec tunnel configuration that was performed on CSR to encrypt traffic between subnets 10.10.10.0 and 10.30.30.0. And in fact, Example 16-18 describes the tunnel status after ISR receives a similar configuration.

Example 16-19 *IPsec Tunnel Status*

```
CSR# show crypto isakmp sa
IPv4 Crypto ISAKMP SA
dst              src              state            conn-id status
10.20.20.9       10.20.20.254     QM_IDLE             1001 ACTIVE

IPv6 Crypto ISAKMP SA
```

Although CSR 1000V is not a vPath-enabled service node, it undoubtedly holds immense potential for server virtualization environments. For example, CSR 1000V can

- Provide routing between VLANs and VXLANs
- Facilitate IPv4-to-IPv6 migration
- Integrate virtual machines to MPLS Layer 3 VPNs

Site Selection and Server Virtualization

In Chapter 8, "A Tale of Two Data Centers," I discussed a traffic effect called *tromboning*. Under such a condition, a single data packet can traverse VLAN extensions between data centers several times before it is finally routed to an external network or reaches its destination server.

While First Hop Routing Protocol (FHRP) filtering and active network services at each site can minimize tromboning, these techniques act upon packets that are already inside a data center network. Therefore, the missing piece for network traffic efficiency is routing each client to the most adequate data center location. And, providing optimized site selection is a veritable challenge when a server can migrate to another site at any time.

As you must be already used to, significant data center obstacles are usually surmounted through myriad methods with varying advantages and shortcomings. For that reason, I will briefly discuss three client routing network services in the next sections: *Route Health Injection (RHI)*, *Global Server Load Balance (GSLB)*, and *Location ID/ Separation Protocol (LISP)*.

These solutions are not only restricted to online migration of VMs between sites. In fact, they were originally developed to support geoclusters and disaster recovery scenarios. Nevertheless, I will present them from the former perspective to adhere to this chapter's objective.

Route Health Injection

Route Health Injection (RHI) is a site selection technique that relies on server load balancers, such as Cisco Application Control Engine (ACE). In RHI scenarios, a virtual context on an ACE module generates a static host route (with subnet mask 255.255.255.255) in its Catalyst 6500 routing table whenever a virtual IP address (VIP) is active (meaning that it has at least one active real server in its associated server farm).

Tip The fundamental concepts of server load balancing and ACE virtual contexts were discussed in Chapter 4, "An Army of One: ACE Virtual Contexts."

Figure 16-20 details how RHI works when a virtual machine can migrate between two sites (West and East) at any time.

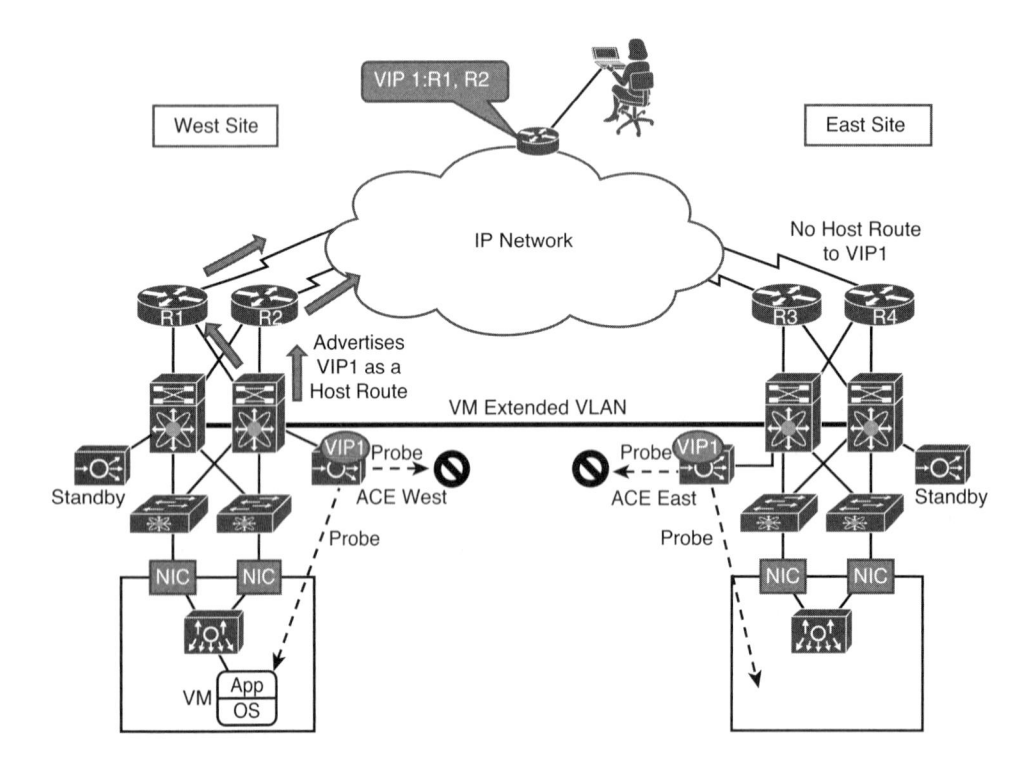

Figure 16-20 *Route Health Injection*

With the VM still on the West site, an ACE virtual context (ACE West) detects its presence using application probes. Receiving a positive probe response, ACE West automatically injects the VIP1 host route into its Catalyst 6500 routing table. Through routing protocols, this route to VIP1 is advertised to the WAN routers, assuring that ingress traffic for VIP1 will arrive at the West site.

Note ACE 4710 currently does not support route injection. A work-around can be achieved through the configuration of IP service-level agreement (SLA) agents and object tracking on IOS routers such as R1, R2, R3, and R4 from Figure 16-20.

Observe that the probes from the active ACE virtual contexts at each site are filtered and, therefore, can only detect the VM if it is hosted on its local site.

Should the VM migrate to the East site, ACE East will detect the VM and activate its VIP1 (which shares the same IP address from site A). Consequently, ACE East will inject a VIP1 host route that will be distributed to the entire WAN, attracting the ingress traffic to East site.

In the meantime, the host route to VIP1 will no longer be advertised because ACE West probes are filtered in the VLAN extension.

While RHI is relatively easy to deploy, this site selection technique deserves some important considerations:

- RHI does not depend on Domain Name System (DNS), and therefore can be appropriate for applications that have hard-coded IP addresses.
- RHI depends on the distribution of host routes (subnet mask 255.255.255.255) into an IP network, which is not suitable for Internet routing.
- RHI does not support active-active scenarios.
- Immediately after the VM migration, the client will probably have to reinitiate the TCP connection because ACE East is not aware of it.

The majority of web applications are usually not affected with the situation described in the last item. But if you have to avoid a connection reset at any cost, you should start by not filtering the probe from ACE West in the VLAN extension and assigning a higher cost to the ACE East RHI route. Using Source NAT, ACE West would still maintain the connections to the VM, even if it were on the East site. Nonetheless, client traffic would continue to be received on the West site and would necessarily traverse the VLAN extension to reach the VM.

Global Server Load Balancing

Global Server Load Balancing (GSLB) is recommended to client applications that use DNS for IP server address resolution. In GSLB scenarios, the DNS structure of a data center is configured to forward select requests to a GSLB device, which in turn is capable of verifying the application status at each data center location.

Cisco ACE Global Site Selector (GSS) is a GSLB solution that integrates with an ACE server load-balancing infrastructure. In essence, ACE GSS serves as a "load balancer of load balancers," sending application probes to ACE VIPs on distinct sites and deciding which IP address should be advertised in DNS responses.

Figure 16-21 illustrates how ACE GSS can optimize client ingress traffic for a moving VM between two sites (East and West).

As Figure 16-21 shows, if ACE probes are filtered on the VLAN extension, an ACE VIP will only be active if the VM is present on its site. Because each ACE GSS in a cluster is sending probes to ACE VIPs configured on both sites, they are able to answer client DNS requests using addresses of active VIPs.

Consequently, when an application client requests the IP address of the VM URL (vm.mycompany.com, for example), the request is forwarded through the DNS infrastructure to one of the members of an ACE GSS cluster. The IP address in this DNS response will be VIP1 if the VM is on the West site, or VIP2 if it is on the East site.

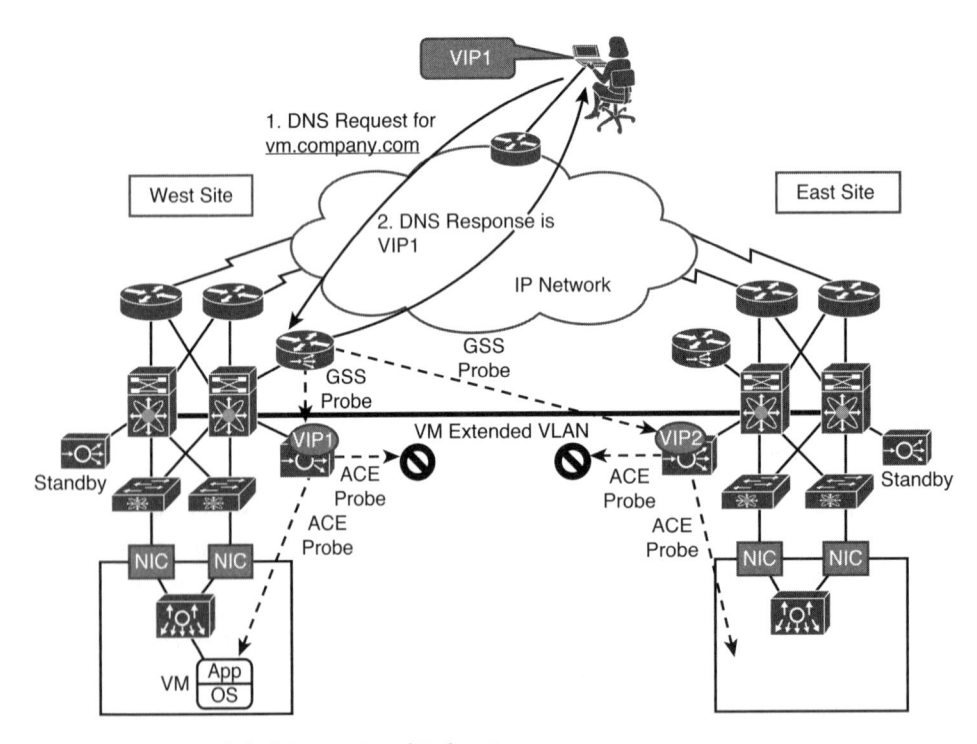

Figure 16-21 *Global Server Load Balancing*

Here are some general considerations about the applicability of this method for VM migration between sites:

- GSLB provides load balancing, which leverages active-active sites in the case of multiple VMs for a single application.

- ACE GSS can distribute client sessions between active VIPs through multiple load-balancing algorithms such as least loaded, round robin, ordered list, among others.

- Some browsers cache DNS entries during a defined *Time to Live (TTL)* interval. This behavior can send users to inactive VIPs during this period.

- ACE GSS can monitor the state, such as health and performance, from individual VMs or server load balancing VIPs using ICMP, TCP, HTTP-header, and SNMP probes (or a combination of them). Alternatively, it can also use a specialized *Keepalive Appliance Protocol (KAL-AP)* to obtain more granular VIP and real server availability information from ACE virtual contexts.

Using source NAT on both ACE virtual contexts and not filtering the ACE probes in the VLAN extension, both VIPs will be advertised by the ACE GSS devices. As a result, ACE GSS can direct clients to reach the VM using both sites, and migration would not force the client to reset his connections in the case of a site migration.

Location/ID Separation Protocol

It can be said that IP routing is essentially based on the assumption that a subnet is contained in a single site. For that reason, routing tables rely on prefix routes directing traffic to hosts that belong to these IP subnets. However, with extended VLANs spanning data centers located in different hemispheres, this hypothesis might no longer be appropriate.

As stated in its name, *Location/ID Separation Protocol (LISP)* proposes a distinction between identity and location addresses. In summary, LISP introduces two numbering spaces that are syntactically identical to IP addresses:

- **Endpoint Identifier (EID):** Assigned independently from the network topology and used on end devices. This value identifies hosts (servers and clients) and is usually obtained through a DNS lookup.
- **Routing Locator (RLOC):** Assigned to network attachment points (routers) and used for routing and forwarding of packets through the IP network.

Through this separation, it is possible to optimize traffic destined to an IP prefix that can be present in different locations. After end hosts are mapped to different locations, the packets they exchange (containing EIDs as source and destination IP addresses) are encapsulated into packets between LISP routers (containing RLOCs as source and destination IP addresses).

In a LISP deployment, a router can perform one or more roles from the following list of definitions:

- **Ingress Tunnel Router (ITR):** Receives IP packets destined to a remote EID and provides LISP encapsulation for its associated RLOC.
- **Egress Tunnel Router (ETR):** Receives and decapsulates LISP packets directed to one of its own RLOCs. Afterward, the ETR strips the "outer" header and forwards the packet based on the next IP destination (which is usually a local EID).
- **xTR:** A router that deploys both ITR and ETR functions.
- **Map-Server (MS):** Registers EID prefixes sent from ETRs. An MS advertises aggregated EID prefixes into a LISP network.
- **Map-Resolver (MR):** Receives EID-to-RLOC requests.

At the time of this writing, LISP is standardized in RFCs 6830 through 6836 and is deployed on Nexus 7000 and the majority of IOS-based routers (including CSR 1000V). In particular, Nexus 7000 switches offer *VM-Mobility*, which applies LISP to virtual machines that are able to migrate between different sites.

Figure 16-22 illustrates the core principles of LISP VM-Mobility.

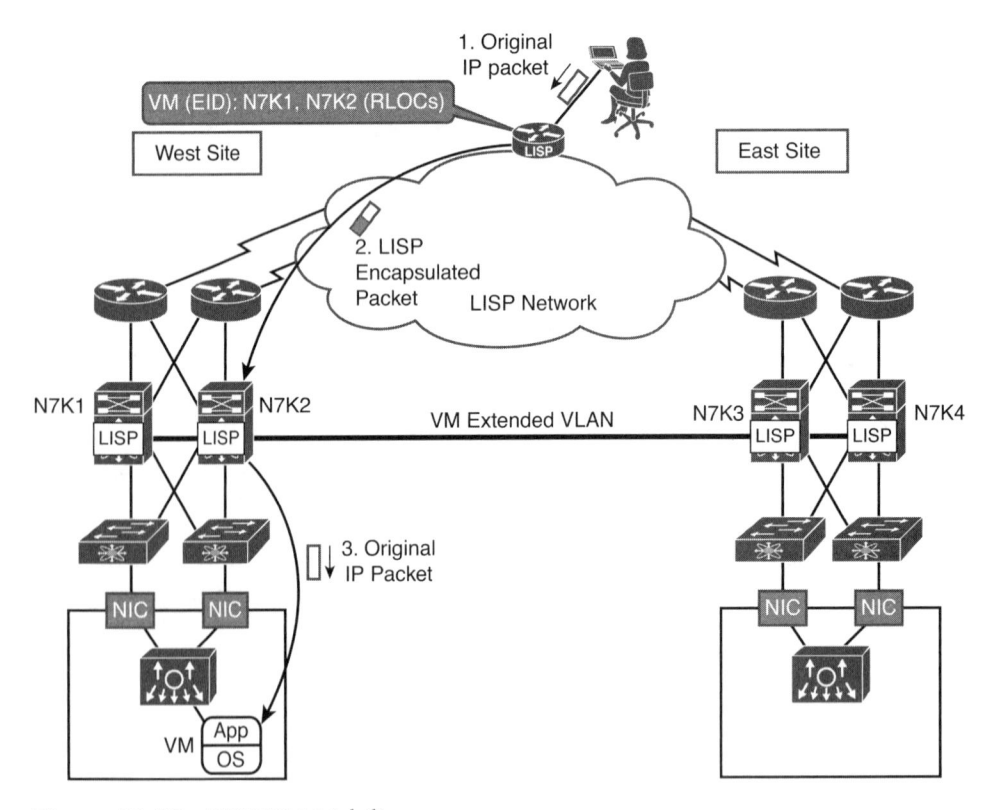

Figure 16-22 *LISP VM-Mobility*

With VM-Mobility, all LISP-enabled switches from one site can detect a VM if they receive data packets from a previously defined EID IP address. For example, because they are located at the West site, N7K1 and N7K2 declare themselves to the Map-Server as RLOCs for the VM's EID.

If the VM migrates to the East site, switches N7K3 or N7K4 will supposedly start to receive traffic from the VM because one of them must be used as the VM default gateway (as members of the same FHRP group). And from this moment on, all LISP routers in the network will encapsulate frames to N7K3 and N7K4 whenever they have to send a LISP packet that must reach the VM IP address.

As a site selection method, LISP VM-mobility

- Does not require changes on host stacks, DNS service, or load balancers to provide ingress traffic optimization
- Requires LISP implementation on remote WAN routers
- Requires FHRP filtering if any method of VLAN extension is being used between the sites

LISP VM-Mobility also supports movement of VMs across different subnets, which is currently considered to address "cold" migrations in disaster recovery scenarios.

Use Case: Virtual Data Center

After a successful merging with another company (described in Chapter 15), your IT department is taking care of a true active-active data center infrastructure, with an extended server virtualization cluster for multiple application workloads.

Because you have been increasing the company's service portfolio, your sales force started to receive unusual requests several customers: They want to hire your company to host some VMs to keep critical applications operational during a data center retrofit or migration project.

After hearing the request from the customer's CIO, you ask for more details about this hosting service. He then explains that the company's security policies impose the following restrictions for out-of-premises virtual machines:

- All hosted VMs must be connected to a dedicated bridging domain.

- Its security team needs to control the access between VMs and the firewall rules from external networks.

- An IPsec tunnel through the Internet must be established between the customer network and a firewall directly connected to the VMs.

- Some VMs with web applications must be accessible for Internet users.

After pondering for a moment, you decide to accommodate the customer request, mainly because he has been employing your services because you were a one-person consulting firm.

Rounding up your core IT team, you explain to them that the customer is really asking for a *Virtual Data Center (vDC)* structure. Immediately you challenge them to present solutions for this project, with a single condition: No additional hardware should be deployed because this is a temporary project.

After a series of brainstorming sessions, the team unanimously selected the solution portrayed in Figure 16-23.

In the solution, both data centers will be used to deploy the customer virtual machines, which are represented in the figure as VM-Web3, VM-App3, and VM-DB3. These VMs will be connected to the company's Nexus 1000V, which is currently extended between both company sites. Creating a VXLAN (30000) for this endeavor, it is possible to save a VLAN ID on the OTV extension between both of your data center sites.

An active-standby pair of ASA 1000Vs are instantiated for the customer, with their inside interface on VXLAN 30000 and their outside interface on a VLAN located at an Internet-reachable DMZ. The design also positions a dedicated pair of active-standby VSGs to provide VM-to-VM access control.

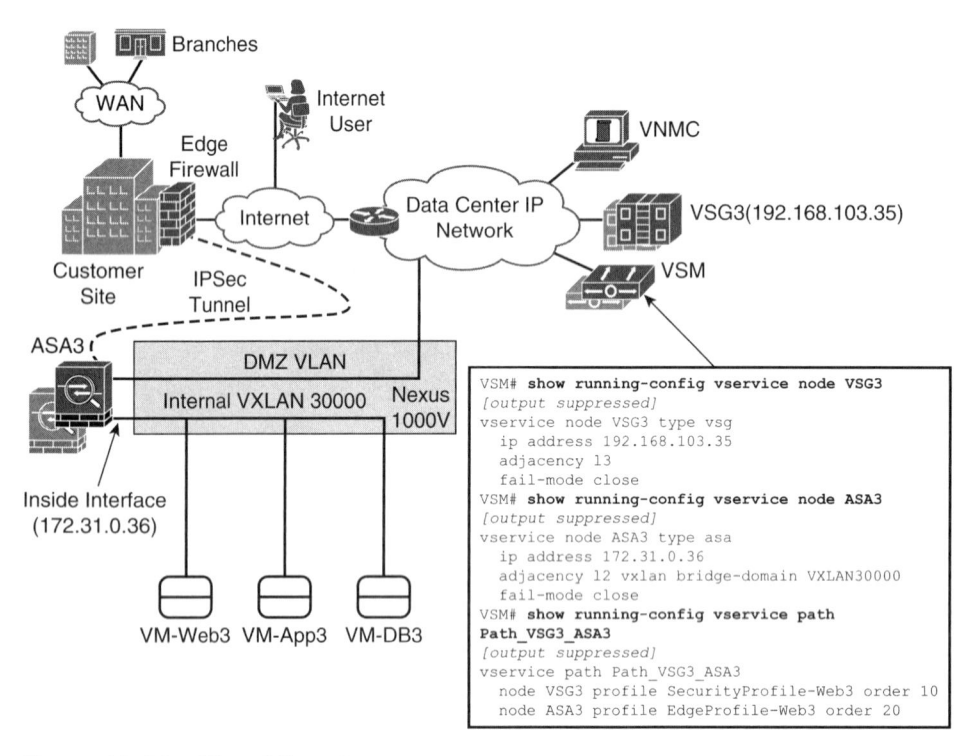

Figure 16-23 *Virtual Data Center*

Your company's VNMC will be used configure NAT, IPsec, and application inspection on ASA, and to manage firewall rules on both virtual security appliances. To logically separate the customer VMs from your environment, a new VNMC organization (root/Tenant2/vDC3) will also be created, and its management is exclusively assigned to this customer.

To deploy both virtual network services on the same port profile, a *service chain path* is configured on Nexus 1000 using the configuration detailed in Figure 16-23.

Tip To deploy a vPath Layer 3 method for VSG, it is necessary to associate a port profile with the Layer 3 virtual service capability (using the **capability l3-vservice** command) to a vmkernel interface.

Example 16-20 further explains how Nexus 1000V provides vPath redirection for both virtual nodes (VSG3 and ASA3, in that order) on a single port profile.

Example 16-20 *Service Chaining Port Profile Configuration*

```
VSM# show running-config port-profile N1KV-WEB-vDC3
[output suppressed]
port-profile type vethernet N1KV-WEB-vDC3
  vmware port-group
  switchport mode access
! This VM is connected to the internal VXLAN
  switchport access bridge-domain VXLAN30000
! It belongs to the customer organization
  org root/Tenant2/vDC3
! ... and uses both virtual firewalls
  vservice path Path_VSG3_ASA3
  no shutdown
  state enabled
```

After the VMs are successfully deployed, and you sense how this small project has greatly motivated your IT team, you begin to question yourself about more business ventures for your company.

It seems that the sky is the limit indeed....

Summary

In this chapter, you learned the following:

- Virtual network services further decrease the gap between virtual and physical network functionalities.

- vPath is a Nexus 1000V traffic redirection architecture that integrates virtual network services with transparency and scalability.

- Cisco Virtual Security Gateway (VSG) is a vPath-based virtual compute firewall that controls traffic between virtual machines.

- Cisco ASA 1000V is a vPath-based virtual edge firewall that leverages Adaptive Security Appliance (ASA) features to secure VMs from external networks. These features also include NAT, IPsec, static routing, and application inspection.

- Virtual Wide Area Application Services (vWAAS) uses vPath to intercept VM traffic and employ acceleration algorithms to increase application performance over WAN links.

- Cisco CSR 1000V brings IOS features (such as routing protocols, MPLS, IPsec, and many others) to server virtualization environments.

- Three site-selection techniques that can optimize client routing to migrating VMs: Route Health Injection (RHI), Global Server Load Balancing (GSLB), and Location/ID Separation Protocol (LISP).

Figure 16-24 illustrates the abstraction provided by virtual network services.

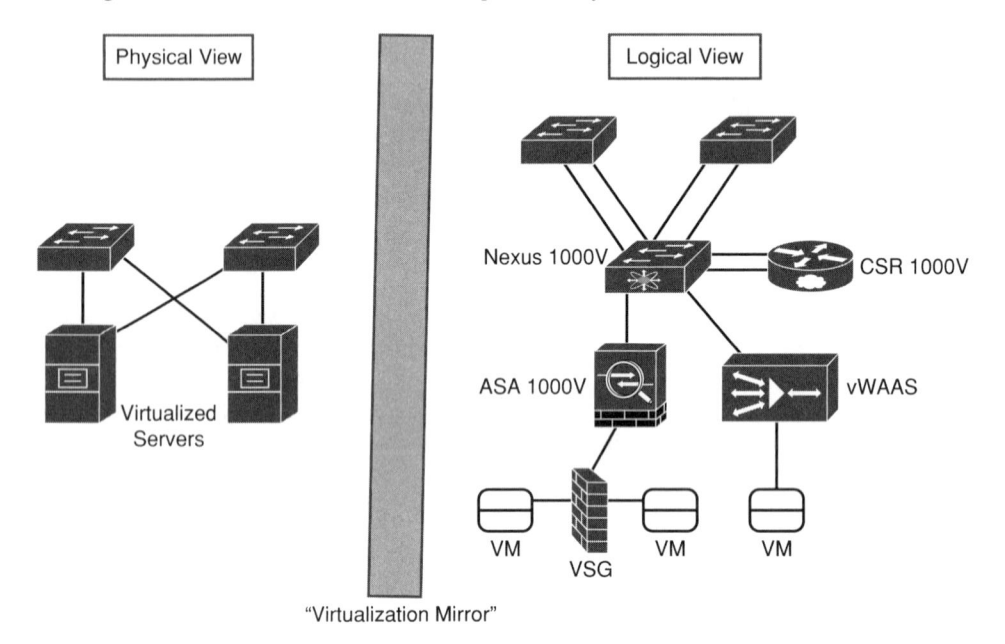

Figure 16-24 *Through the Virtualization Mirror*

Further Reading

Bhaiji, Yusuf. *Network Security Technologies and Solutions*. Cisco Press, 2008.

Seils, Zach. Christner, Joel. Jin, Nancy. *Deploying Cisco Wide Area Application Services (2nd Edition)*. Cisco Press, 2010.

Securing Virtual Applications with Cisco and Imperva, www.cisco.com/en/US/prod/collateral/switches/ps9441/ps9902/white_paper_c96-726705.pdf

Data Center Application Services, www.cisco.com/go/ace

Location/ID Separation Protocol, http://tools.ietf.org/html/rfc6830

Chapter 17

The Virtual Data Center and Cloud Computing

"'In the end?' Nothing ends, Adrian. Nothing ever ends." (Alan Moore, Watchmen*)*

In this last chapter, we examine two outcomes from data center end-to-end virtualization: virtual data centers and cloud computing. The chapter also explores how these new IT models are reshaping data center architectural designs and technologies. It contains the following topics:

- Virtual Data Centers
- Automation and Standardization
- Cloud Computing
- Networking in the Clouds

IT departments have been traditionally perceived as *cost centers* within their organizations, adding expenses but only indirectly bringing profit. Due to the ongoing challenge of maintaining a complex interdependent structure, the perception of IT as an *internal service provider* fades as users cannot have get access to a resource as fast as business objectives require.

Data center virtualization technologies have greatly helped to reverse this impression, mainly because the provisioning of a virtual computing resource (server, storage, and network) is generally effortless when compared to physical deployments. Virtualization, after all, paves the road to the *utility computing* concept, fulfilling the promises of fast and easy delivery of IT resources.

Nevertheless, this is not an easy path. During their slow technology absorption process, the majority of organizations were caught off guard, with *cloud computing* offers from nontraditional service providers such as Amazon. Its fast-provisioning and "pay-as-you-use" cost model attracted the attention of corporate users, and suddenly, every CIO had a competitor some mere clicks away.

As a result, cloud computing has been declared as the great promise for IT to bring speed and simplicity to their users, and even competitive advantages for their organizations. But what is cloud computing? And more importantly: How do you get there?

This chapter will address the trajectory between an end-to-end virtualized data center and cloud computing. Additionally, it will offer some insights about the influence of this IT delivery model in networking technologies.

The Virtual Data Center

In the previous chapters of this book, you were introduced to the individual advantages from a series of data center infrastructure virtualization technologies. Ranging from resource segmentation to the deployment of virtual network services, these techniques solved problems and overcame limitations in their specific areas of action.

Nonetheless, a key question deserves to be addressed at this point: What can be achieved with the deployment of multiple data center virtualization technologies? Is it possible to get a benefit that is greater than the sum of the advantages brought by virtual servers, virtual networks, and virtual storage?

The current state of data center evolution elicits a resounding "yes" to these questions. As emulations, virtualization technologies can be logically provisioned and configured with minimal physical interaction. In fact, an *end-to-end virtualized data center* leverages remote management and "install-and-walk-away" deployments.

Looking back at the techniques explored in this book, it is also possible to infer generic benefits for each type from the virtualization taxonomy. For example:

- **Pooling technologies:** Allow management consolidation of multiple separate resources and, consequently, simplify operations.

- **Abstraction technologies:** Create virtual structures that surpass common limitations of a technology. They also simplify operations through the abstraction of identifiers and the maintenance of existing procedures.

- **Partitioning technologies:** Spawn logical elements that can be distributed to different environments or users.

Interestingly enough, some virtualization partitioning technologies can also be understood as consumable resources. Therefore, nothing impedes an IT department from acting as an internal service provider, offering the following virtual elements to other areas of the organization:

- Virtual Local Area Networks (VLAN) and Virtual eXtensible Local Area Networks (VXLAN)

- Virtual Routing and Forwarding (VRF) and virtual service routers (such as the CSR 1000V)
- Server load balancer virtual contexts
- Firewall virtual contexts
- Virtual device contexts (VDC)
- Virtual logical unit numbers (vLUN)
- Storage array partitions
- Virtual file systems
- Virtual storage-area networks (VSAN)
- Unified Computing System service profiles
- Virtual machines (VM)
- Virtual network access connections such as the ones provided by the Nexus 1000V and VM-FEX
- Virtual network services such as Virtual Security Gateway, ASA 1000V, and virtual WAAS

With variable scalability, these logical resources can be uniquely provided to a single consumer over the same virtualized infrastructure.

As briefly discussed in Chapter 16, "Moving Targets," multiple virtual technologies can comprise a *virtual Data Center (vDC)*. This entity can be defined as a set of virtual elements that are capable of supporting the computing resources of a consumer, including servers, storage, networking, and applications. Therefore, it can be said that a vDC represents a logical partition of a virtualized data center infrastructure serving the needs of a tenant.

Virtual Data Centers can have different formats, all depending on the tenant requirements and the creativity of the infrastructure support teams. As an illustration, Figure 17-1 depicts four vDC examples with varying complexity and functionalities.

In Figure 17-1, *vDC1* portrays the simplest structure, comprised of a single virtual machine (VM). This virtual machine could be, for example, a hosted web server serving a sub-organization that cannot handle its support. Using some shared resources from the physical data center (such as the firewall and a VLAN), the vDC consumer can control the application and operating system on this VM. Optionally, he can also require special functionalities from the server virtualization infrastructure, such as high availability or fault tolerance.

vDC2 exhibits the slightly more elaborate *virtual application (vApp)* environment, which is comprised of a classic web-application-database tier group. In this setup, the consumer also utilizes a shared VLAN from the data center infrastructure to provide access to intranet clients.

788 Data Center Virtualization Fundamentals

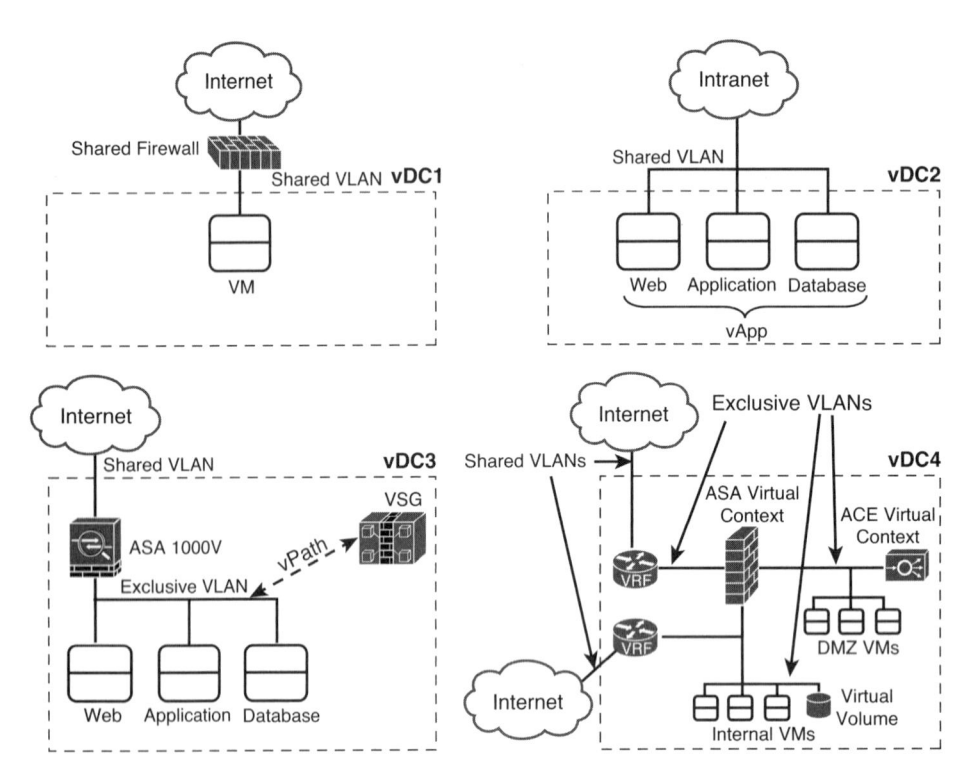

Figure 17-1 *Virtual Data Centers*

vDC3 is yet another variation, where two additional virtual networking services are required: an edge firewall (such as an ASA 1000V) to protect the VMs from Internet attacks and a compute firewall (such as a Cisco Virtual Security Gateway [VSG]) to securely control the traffic between the VMs. In this case, vDC3 shares a VLAN with the data center infrastructure and employs an exclusive VLAN for the VM's network traffic. Although this option is not depicted in Figure 17-1, both ASA 1000V and VSG virtual appliances can be deployed in active-standby pairs in vDC3.

Tip Typically, these shared VLANs are called *provider VLANs* while vDC-exclusive VLANs are called *tenant VLANs*.

Finally, *vDC4* has elements beyond the realm of server virtualization. It is comprised of the following:

- Two VRFs
- An ASA 5500 virtual context to provide security for traffic between three security zones (Internet, demilitarized zone [DMZ], and intranet)

- An Application Control Engine (ACE) virtual context to load-balance traffic to the DMZ servers

- Two provider VLANs (Internet and intranet)

- Three tenant VLANs (one for each ASA security zone)

- A virtual volume such as a LUN accessible through Internet SCSI (iSCSI)

Figure 17-1 is only depicting the active elements in vDC4. All its components can also have different levels of availability (for example, pairs of VRFs deploying Hot Standby Router Protocol [HSRP], and active-standby pairs of ASA and ACE virtual contexts).

These vDC models (and many others) can be offered to internal or external consumers. Essentially, they demonstrate how end-to-end virtualized data centers can become a very important asset for enterprise and service providers alike.

Automation and Standardization

As discussed in previous chapters, the deployment and support of a data center involve a series of processes that must be effectively executed. If these processes are not well defined, the prospect of supporting physical *and* virtual data centers can further burden these responsibilities and even increase operational complexity.

In several facilities, two initiatives are considered evolutionary steps for data center modernization beyond virtualization: automation and standardization.

Data center automation comprises a set of technologies that can streamline repetitive operational tasks to execute them as a batch in a process workflow. The objective of automation projects is to provide faster provisioning through the **orchestration** of these procedures.

The value of automation can be easily recognized if one considers the operations related with the activation of a server pool of devices (POD). Figure 17-2 illustrates how automation can be applied to such a scenario.

Figure 17-2 depicts all the involved elements that should be configured or provisioned: switches, Fabric Extenders, storage arrays, physical rack-mountable servers, and a VM manager (such as VMware vCenter). The figure also exhibits a software element called *orchestrator*, which is basically a workflow management solution that provides automation for operational processes such as resource provisioning.

Assuming that all 60 servers must be part of a server virtualization infrastructure under the VM manager authority, the orchestrator will

- Provide the initial configuration for the access switches and Fabric Extenders (on both access switches)

- Configure the VLANs that should be available in the POD (on aggregation and access switches)

- Configure access ports to servers (120 times!)
- Configure the uplinks on both access and aggregation switches and Inter-Switch Links (ISL) on the core SAN directors
- Configure the LUNs that should be available for these servers
- Obtain Media Access Control (MAC) addresses and Port World Wide Names (pWWN) from all 60 rack-mountable servers
- Perform zoning and LUN masking for all 60 servers
- Provide management IP addresses for all servers through Dynamic Host Configuration Protocol (DHCP)
- Configure Basic Input/Output System (BIOS) parameters and update firmware on all 60 servers (if necessary)
- Install the hypervisor and provide minimum settings for further administration through vCenter (60 times!)

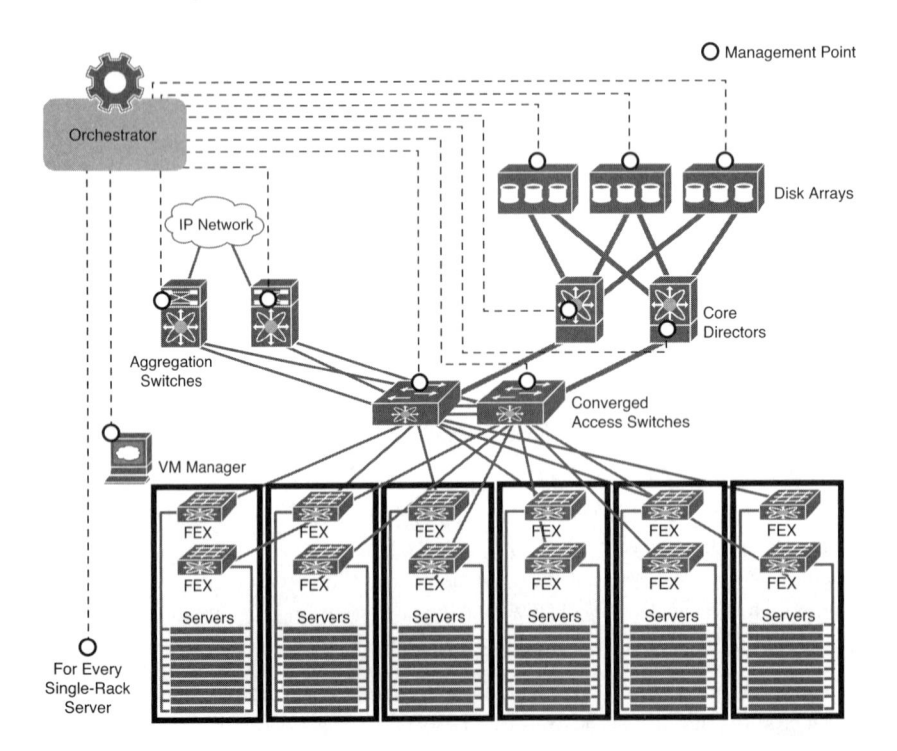

Figure 17-2 *POD Provisioning Operations*

As you can see, the number of tasks required to activate a 60-server POD can easily reach triple digits. Consequently, process automation is more effective with repetitive operations.

To interact with the POD portrayed in Figure 17-2, the orchestrator must deal with a total of 69 points of managements, including storage arrays, switches, VM manager, and servers. In general, the orchestrator must add each device to its inventory (through automatic discovery or manual registration) and afterward deploy a compatible mechanism to impose configurations on these devices. Common orchestration mechanisms include Simple Network Management Protocol (SNMP), Telnet, Secure Shell (SSH), Network Configuration Protocol (NETCONF), and Application Programming Interfaces (API).

Although the Figure 17-2 POD portrays a fair share of consolidation in the network (deploying Fabric Extenders and Fibre Channel over Ethernet), it could still benefit from an extra layer of resource pooling technologies such as Unified Computing System, Nexus 1000V, and storage array virtualization. A general rule for automation is this: The fewer management points, the better.

The orchestrators can act upon physical and virtual environments. Therefore, through VM managers, storage systems, and switches, this software tool can provision virtual Data Centers inside this POD.

Automation clearly demands a new way of thinking, where the number of manual configurations should be kept to a minimum. For example, the following operations could be deployed with that intent:

- Virtual servers can use DHCP to obtain IP addresses.

- The same *tenant* IP subnet can be used on several vDCs. Network Address Translation (NAT) can be used to hide these addresses under the same *provider* IP address.

- The use of configuration templates, such as VM templates and port profiles, is highly recommended.

In summary, automation proposes the "industrialization" of the data center. And as the fundamental principles of industry demonstrate, the efficiency of production is highly dependent on standard elements and procedures. *Excessive customization* definitely does not blend well with automation, because each new process should be painstakingly tested and thoroughly certified before being put into production.

In the context of data centers, *standardization* can be understood as a modernization initiative that intends to reduce the variety of elements and operation processes. With a smaller set of components, automation is certainly facilitated.

In a way to assist standardization projects, some technology vendors offer converged data center infrastructures that unify server, networking, storage, and virtualization infrastructure in a predefined POD design.

Some examples of converged data center infrastructures are

- **Vblock (VCE):** Encompasses Cisco UCS, Nexus switches, MDS 9000 fabric switches, EMC storage arrays, and VMware vSphere as a single product. It is primed for virtualized workloads based on VMware vSphere.

- **FlexPod (Cisco and NetApp):** A predesigned and prevalidated POD configuration that includes Cisco UCS, Nexus switches, and NetApp FAS storage components. It can be deployed with a wide range of software such as VMware vSphere, Red Hat Enterprise Linux, Microsoft Hyper-V, SAP, among others.

- **Storage Reference Architecture (VMware, Cisco, HDS):** A predesigned and pre-validated POD configuration that includes Cisco UCS, Nexus switches, MDS 9000 fabric switches, HDS Adaptable Modular Storage (AMS) 2500, and VMware vSphere infrastructure.

Although they deploy distinct designs, these infrastructures share a common objective: to provide an automation-ready replicable infrastructure that can be easily deployed with predictable performance. In a real-world comparison, these solutions offer a car rather than car parts that should be assembled by the customer.

Cisco also offers an extremely useful standardization tool in the form of the *Virtualized Multiservice Data Center (VMDC)* reference architecture. VMDC essentially provides a framework for building a fully virtualized data center with focus on integration of networking, computing, security, load balancing, and system management.

VMDC is based on releases that incrementally include new technologies at each version (for example, VMDC 2.2 introduced multimedia quality of service [QoS] support and Virtual Private LAN Service [VPLS] for Data Center Interconnect [DCI], while VMDC 3.0 introduced FabricPath). This reference architecture uses the concept of *network containers*, which are replicable standard network topologies that contain VLANs, Switch Virtual Interfaces (SVI), VRFs, firewalls, and server load balancers, among other network entities. These containers are intended to be used as network structures for more sophisticated virtual Data Centers (such as vDC4 from Figure 17-1).

Cisco *Network Services Manager (NSM)* can further scale the provisioning of network containers. Interacting with devices such as ASR 1000, Nexus switches, Catalyst 6500, and UCS Fabric Interconnect, NSM enables the standard deployment of network resources for vDC tenants.

Figure 17-3 illustrates how NSM can help scale the creation of vDCs.

In Figure 17-3, NSM acts as a network orchestrator for the physical network topology shown on the right side. Therefore, when receiving three network container requests from a higher-level orchestrator, NSM can quickly provision three topologies from a configured network container template.

More than agility, both automation and standardization initiatives provide a predictable and modular data center architecture, from both physical and virtual perspectives.

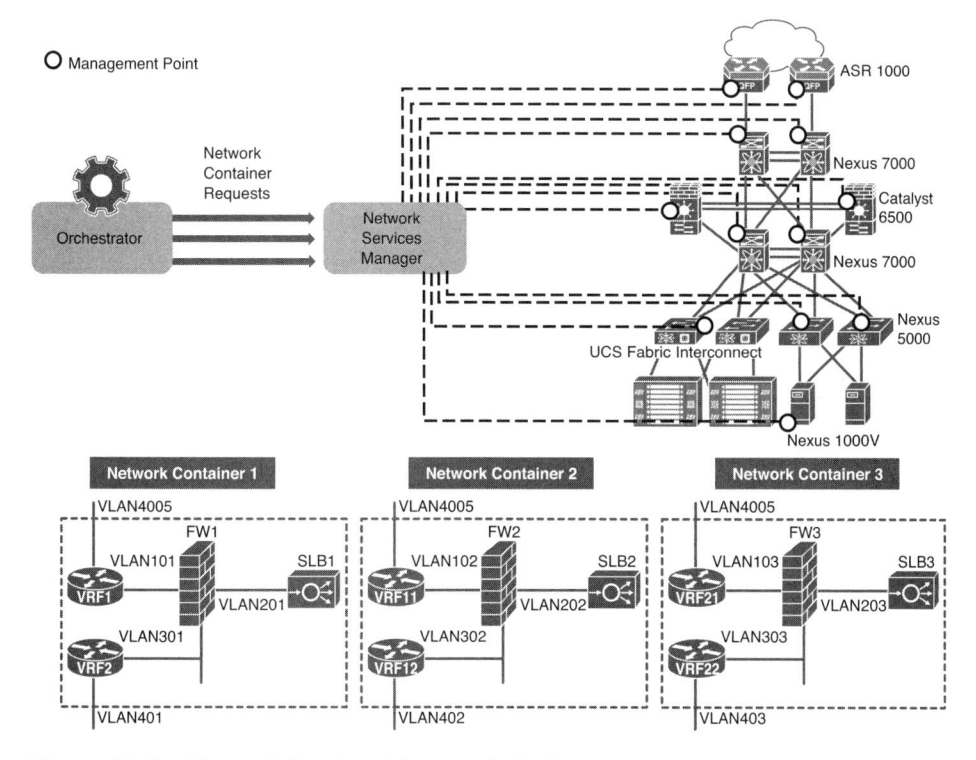

Figure 17-3 *Network Services Manager in Action*

What Is Cloud Computing?

Regarding data centers, *cloud* is probably the only word that is more overused than *virtualization*. At the time of this writing, it is extremely rare to find a technology vendor that has not jumped on the cloud computing bandwagon. And although this subject has dominated the interest of the entire IT community for some time, too much marketing **smoke** has also been puffed, unfortunately causing more confusion than results.

Contrary to many of these advertising messages, cloud computing is not a technology, but an *IT delivery model*. Its main purpose is to transform computing resources into a utility just like electricity or water, which can be easily accessible and charged according to its use.

Cloud computing implementations provide an extra layer of abstraction (another one!) that hides the complexity of IT implementations and support from its consumers. Actually, the term *cloud* borrows from the traditional graphical symbol that is used to conceal complexity in drawings.

In this book, I have used the cloud icon whenever I wanted you not to worry about what was deployed beneath it, such as network topologies. Hence, if you extend this "pay no attention to that man behind the curtain" state of mind to *any* computing resource, you will be closer to what cloud computing really means.

Although the concept of utility computing dates back to the mainframe era, it was first widely deployed by Amazon in 2006. In an effort to better use its data center resources between the highly seasonal peaks of utilization (Christmas being its bigger spike), the company launched the Amazon Web Service (AWS): a cloud computing service that offered (virtual) servers to external customers. AWS used a billing system based on the size of these computing resources and their period of effective use.

Soon, other companies, such as Rackspace and Terremark, started offering similar services, and a new market was born. With the 2008 global economic downturn, the cloud computing model started to attract even more attention as a way to improve agility and raise rationalization for IT and its main location, the data center. And that interest cross-pollinated multiple solutions that promised clouds for everyone.

Amidst this highly creative turmoil, efforts were also being made to correctly define and categorize cloud computing implementations. Officially launched in 2008, the National Institute of Standards and Technology (NIST) cloud computing program produced standards containing reference architectures, taxonomy, and many other definitions.

Even though these standards were created to accelerate the adoption of cloud computing in the U.S. federal government, they constitute a crowning achievement in the theoretical study of this subject. For example, NIST Special Publication 800-145 ("The NIST Definition of Cloud Computing") states the following:

> "Cloud computing is a model for enabling ubiquitous, convenient, on-demand network access to a shared pool of configurable computing resources (e.g., networks, servers, storage, applications, and services) that can be rapidly provisioned and released with minimal management effort or service provider interaction."

The same standard defines five essential characteristics that should comprise cloud computing implementations:

- **On-demand self-service:** A consumer can provision computing resources without human interaction with the cloud provider.
- **Broad network access:** Resources are accessible over a network through standard protocols and multiple client platforms, ranging from workstations to mobile phones.
- **Resource pooling:** The provider cloud resources are pooled to deploy a multitenant model, dynamically assigning physical and virtual resources according to the consumer demand.
- **Rapid elasticity:** Computing resources can be quickly scaled up or down according to the total consumer demand. However, from the consumer's perspective, these resources will appear unlimited.
- **Measured service:** A metering capability should be used to monitor, control, and report to the consumer the utilization of computing resources, such as storage, processing, bandwidth, and so on.

These characteristics strongly hint how virtualization technologies are crucial to the implementation of cloud environments. Primarily, these techniques represent the mechanisms that enable pooling of physical resources in the provider data center, abstraction to accelerate changes, and the resource partitions that could be offered to each tenant environment.

A cloud computing environment can potentially offer any IT resource, from virtual desktops to an entire Enterprise Resource Planning system. Nevertheless, the most common cloud offerings can be summarized in the following service models:

- **Infrastructure as a Service (IaaS):** Where consumers can provision processing, storage, networks, and other fundamental computing resources to run any operating system or application software. These services are usually targeted at IT departments.

- **Platform as a Service (PaaS):** Where consumers can deploy applications using programming languages, libraries, services, and tools (or "infrastructure software") supported by the provider. Common users are application developers, who do not want to manage the underlying infrastructure (network, servers, operating systems, storage), but require control over the deployed applications and their configuration settings.

- **Software as a Service (SaaS):** Where consumers only want to access a preprovisioned application, not requiring any control level over the underlying cloud infrastructure or the majority of application configuration settings.

Figure 17-4 illustrates the distinctions among these service models.

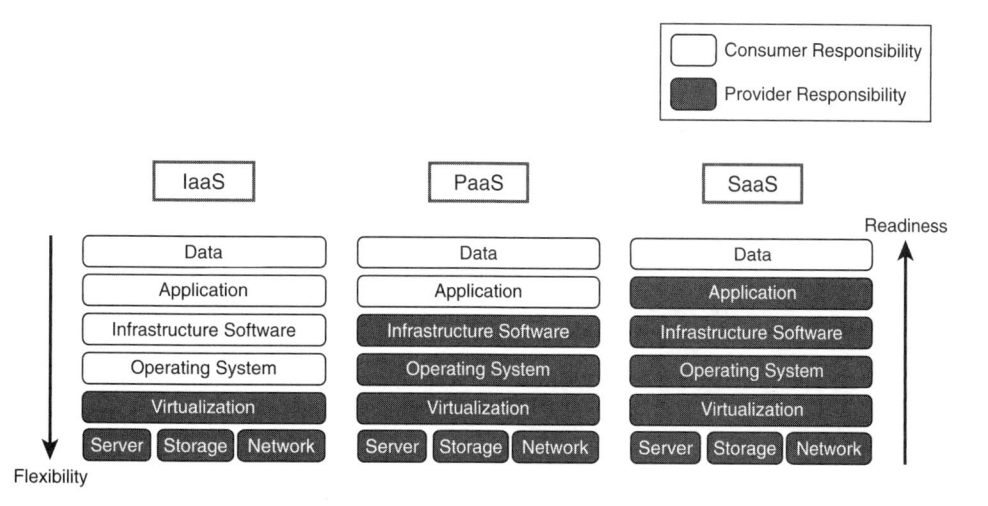

Figure 17-4 *Cloud Service Models*

The acclaim of cloud computing can also be associated to its reaffirmation of the IT department as an *internal service provider*. As a result, cloud deployments can also be classified according to the level of restriction their users are submitted to:

- **Private cloud:** Used exclusively by a single organization and managed by the organization itself, a third party, or a combination of the two.

- **Public cloud:** Provisioned for open use by the general public.

- **Hybrid cloud:** A composition of two or more distinct cloud infrastructures (private or public) bound together to enable data and application portability.

Although public clouds were created first, security concerns have kick-started private cloud projects in enterprise organizations. At the time of this writing, hybrid clouds are considered a balanced alternative that allows organizations to leverage advantages from both private and public models.

Figure 17-5 illustrates all cloud deployment models and also introduces the concept of *cloud bursting* from hybrid clouds.

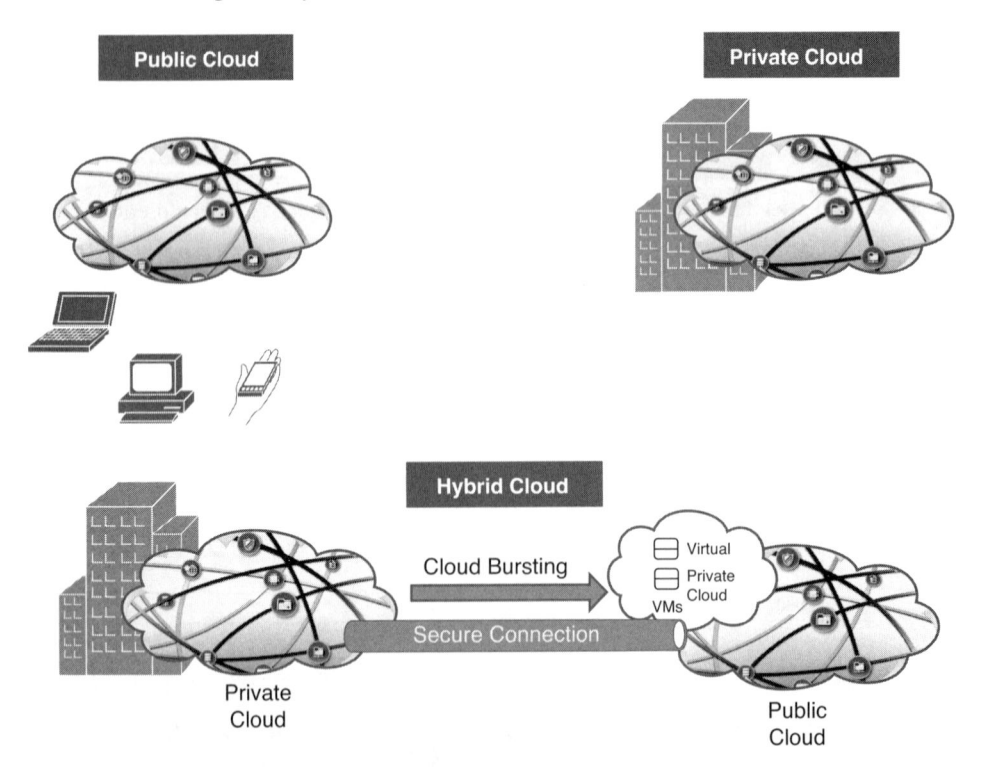

Figure 17-5 *Cloud Deployment Models*

Cloud bursting occurs when an IT department uses resources from a public cloud to fulfill a short-term requirement, such as an application peak. In addition, cloud bursting can be used for disaster avoidance objectives or even disaster recovery, depending on the application requirements.

In general, a hybrid cloud demands the following:

- A **secure connection** between the private and public cloud. It can be deployed through proprietary encrypted tunnels or standard IPsec Virtual Private Networks (VPN) created on virtual appliances such as the CSR 1000V or ASA 1000V.

- A **Virtual Private Cloud (VPC)**, which is an isolated section of the public cloud that closely resembles the private cloud.

- **Common management** to control the resources from both cloud computing environments (private and virtual private cloud).

One of the most innovative hybrid cloud solutions is the *Cisco Nexus 1000V InterCloud*, a software product that allows Layer 2 connectivity between private and public clouds through an encrypted connection. In essence, the Nexus 1000V InterCloud architecture does the following:

- Integrates with VMware vCenter and Amazon Web Services

- Manages hybrid cloud operations such as workload migrations through Cisco Virtual Network Management Center (VNMC)

- Allows the deployment of virtual networking services, such as ASA 1000V, VSG, vWAAS, and CSR 1000V

Cloud Implementation Example

Invariably, discussions about cloud computing tend to become a bit **nebulous** after some time (after all, it is difficult to maintain a foot in the ground while our head is in the clouds).

To avoid this situation in this book, I propose a high-level analysis of a real-world cloud implementation. Figure 17-6 depicts the architecture of a private cloud deployed through the Cisco Intelligent Automation for Cloud (CIAC) solution.

As Figure 17-6 demonstrates, a cloud deployment includes virtualization and automation solutions under the same architecture. Their integration hides from the consumer the cloud infrastructure complexity and provides the essential characteristics discussed in the earlier section "What Is Cloud Computing?": *on-demand self-service, broad network access, resource pooling, rapid elasticity*, and *measured service*.

Comparing a cloud implementation to a personal computer, the *cloud portal* would correspond with an application because it directly interacts with user. In the figure, its function is performed by the Cisco Cloud Portal (CCP) solution, which provides service catalogs, wizards for guided "shopping," interactive forms, approval workflows, status updates, metering, and billing.

Whenever a cloud resource such as a VM, vApp, or vDC is requested, CCP consequently generates requests for the orchestration system.

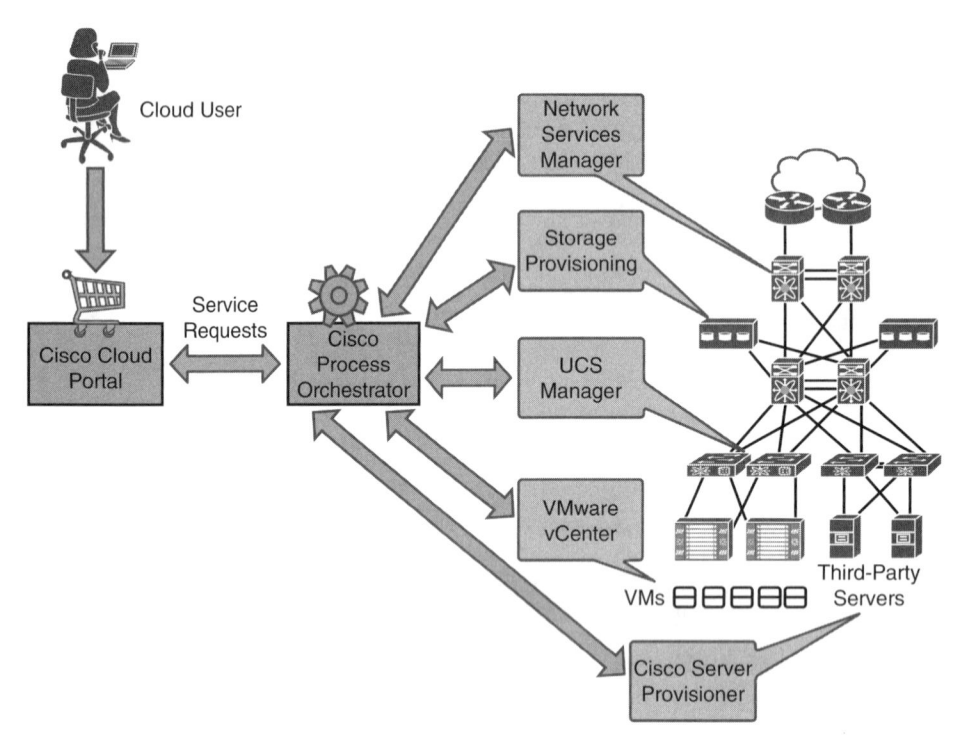

Figure 17-6 *Private Cloud Implementation*

Using the same comparison, the *orchestration system* would embody the operating system because it must coordinate hardware resources to honor user requests. In Figure 17-6, Cisco Process Orchestrator (CPO) represents the heart of this system, executing sophisticated process workflows that allow the provisioning of requested resources.

CPO can interact with several other orchestration and element management tools such as NSM, UCSM, VMware vCenter, and Cisco Server Provisioner (CSP). Additionally, CPO also integrates with storage provisioning solutions from EMC and NetApp to deploy on-demand storage resources.

Finally, in the same allegory, the infrastructure properly represents the computer hardware. The private cloud physical resources are fulfilled through a virtualized and automation-ready data center infrastructure such as the one represented in Figure 17-6.

> **Tip** Refer to Appendix A, "Cisco Data Center Portfolio," for more details about CIAC and other Cisco solutions discussed in this chapter.

Journey to the Cloud

Cisco and many other IT vendors believe that the adoption of the cloud computing model, in corporate and service provider data centers, should be a gradual progression based on defined evolutionary steps.

To further elaborate this statement, Figure 17-7 portrays a suggested development process to data centers that would like to deploy cloud computing.

Consolidation → Virtualization → Standardization → Automation → Cloud → Inter-Cloud

Figure 17-7 *Journey to the Cloud*

In the "journey to the cloud" presented in Figure 17-7, each new phase builds on the results achieved in the last phase. More precisely, each of these stages is defined as follows:

- **Consolidation:** Centralizes computing elements under the same control domain, with silo bursting, and reduction of management points.

- **Virtualization:** Uses consolidated resources to bring higher asset utilization, deployment flexibility, dynamic scalability, and resource pooling.

- **Standardization:** Achieves operational predictability through the reduction of different (physical and virtual) elements, designs, and procedures.

- **Automation:** Minimizes manual processes to enable operational efficiency and an on-demand data center infrastructure.

- **Cloud:** Provides utility computing built over an infrastructure that is automated, standardized, virtualized, and consolidated.

- **Inter-cloud:** Securely controls the distribution of cloud resources between public and private clouds.

Essentially, these phases give a general direction for data center architects who desire to direct their infrastructure toward cloud computing.

As discussed in Chapter 1, "Virtualization History and Definitions," each data center should have its own development linked to the business objectives of the organization it serves. Therefore, the speed of a model's adoption can vary widely according to the organization, industry, or region of the data center.

Again, comparing a data center to a city, the majority of cloud implementations that I have observed in corporate organizations are usually deployed in a separate "neighborhood." With that arrangement, data center architects can accelerate the cloud journey in controlled areas while maintaining other traditional environments at a gentler pace of development.

Of course, it will take a historical perspective to determine whether we have already entered the "Data Center 4.0" era.

Networking in the Clouds

Cloud computing has been changing the traditional way of deploying infrastructure in data centers. Its core principles have influenced deep modifications in every area to facilitate real-world implementations.

Arguably, networking is the technology area that is most subjected to this discussion at the time of this writing. Undoubtedly, cloud computing imposes some characteristics, such as programmability and traffic flexibility, that might not be available in traditional data center networks. Moreover, networks for cloud environments require special attention because they must serve connected resources with "gremlin-like" replication capabilities, potentially threatening their scalability (such as the number of VLANs and MAC address table sizes) and availability.

Therefore, in the next sections, I briefly examine some of the technologies and architectures that are dominating the discussions of data center networking and its adequation for cloud computing implementations.

Software-Defined Networks

According to the Open Networking Foundation (ONF), a *Software-Defined Network* (SDN) proposes a new approach to networking, where the network control layer is decoupled from the forwarding mechanisms. Through this arrangement, an SDN intends to simplify network operations and increase their programmability for applications such as automation tools.

Figure 17-8 further illustrates the SDN concept.

> **Note** Although the SDN-related references presented in the "Further Reading" section, later in this chapter, do not make a distinction between management and control planes, I depicted them in Figure 17-8 to maintain coherency with the concepts discussed in Chapter 1.

In SDNs, network intelligence is logically centralized in software-based *SDN controllers*, which abstract the underlying network infrastructure from programming applications. Hence, for administrators and such software, the network is composed of a single network device. Naturally, because of its critical role, an SDN controller should always include a redundancy method.

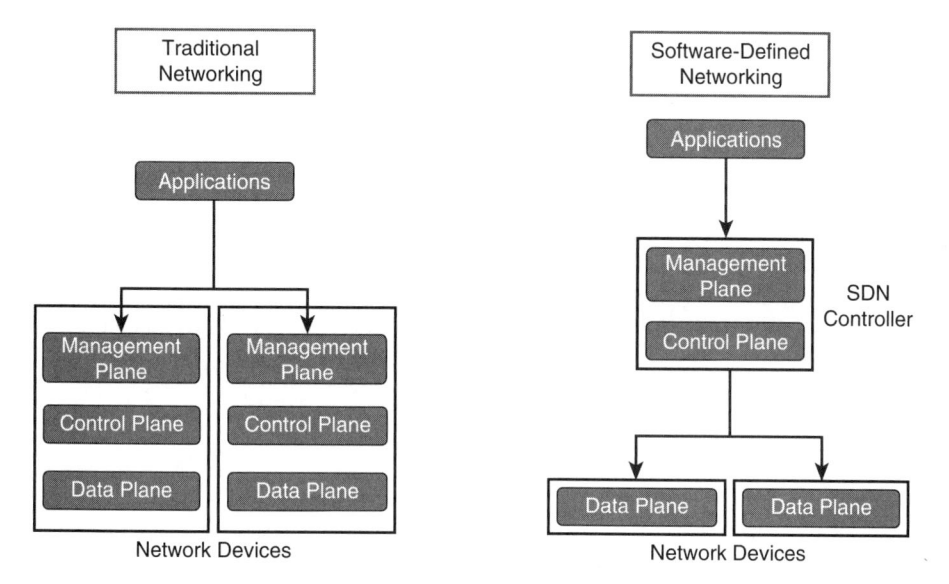

Figure 17-8 *Software-Defined Network*

As I discussed in the earlier section "Automation and Standardization," the management point consolidation proposed by SDN indeed contributes to the automation readiness of a data center infrastructure. In truth, its concept is already applied to solutions such as Nexus 1000V, where the network control and the forwarding layers are deployed in different network elements (Virtual Supervisor Module and Virtual Ethernet Module, respectively). SDN also shares some of the management consolidation objectives that are achieved with NSM.

Notwithstanding, with the intention to spread the adoption of SDN among multiple vendors, ONF has also proposed *OpenFlow* as a standard communication protocol between SDN controllers and network devices (both physical and virtual). OpenFlow is essentially based on flow table updates that contain parameters such as source MAC address, destination MAC address, source IP address, destination IP address, and action (drop, forwarding to a certain port), among others.

Tip Note that OpenFlow is not a requirement for the deployment of an SDN, according to its definition.

OpenStack

OpenStack is a community initiative launched in 2010 (by Rackspace and NASA) to build open source software for public and private clouds. It basically consists of a series of projects focused on the common components of a cloud infrastructure.

The OpenStack networking project (named Quantum at the time of this writing) intends to provide "network connectivity as a service" between devices managed by other OpenStack services. The project enables cloud automation through a pluggable and scalable API that can coordinate the offering of network elements such as virtual networks (VLANs), virtual ports, and IP subnets (IPv4 or IPv6). Other network services such as intrusion detection systems (IDS), server load balancing, firewalls, and Virtual Private Networks are also in the scope of this project.

Tip To avoid any confusion, observe that OpenStack does not require SDN OpenFlow-based networks. It can actually be used to automate all types of networks.

Other OpenStack service projects include the following:

- **OpenStack Compute (project Nova):** Provisions and manages large sets of virtual machines, including server resources (CPU, memory, disk, interfaces), image management (store, import, share images), VM management (run, reboot, suspend), Role-Based Access Control (RBAC), allocation of pooled resources, and dashboard.

- **OpenStack Storage:** Offers object (project Swift) and block storage (project Cinder) for use with servers and applications, including a distributed scale-out object and file system and block snapshot capabilities.

- **OpenStack dashboard (project Horizon):** Presents a graphical interface to access, provision, and automate OpenStack-based resources. Its design facilitates integration with third-party products and services (billing, monitoring, and so on).

- **OpenStack shared services:** Spans compute, storage, and networking projects and includes identity (project Keystone) and image management (project Glance) for VMware, Microsoft Hyper-V, KVM, and Open Virtualization Format (OVF).

In 2012, Cisco released its own version of OpenStack known as Cisco OpenStack Edition (COE), providing Quantum plug-ins for solutions such as UCS and Nexus switches.

Network Overlays

As discussed in Chapter 8, "A Tale of Two Data Centers," network overlay can be defined as a logical network created over an existing networking infrastructure. In the virtualization taxonomy described in Chapter 1, an overlay can be classified as an abstraction-based virtualization technique type with a structural subtype.

In such technologies, virtual network planes can be created independently from the original network, as Figure 17-9 exhibits.

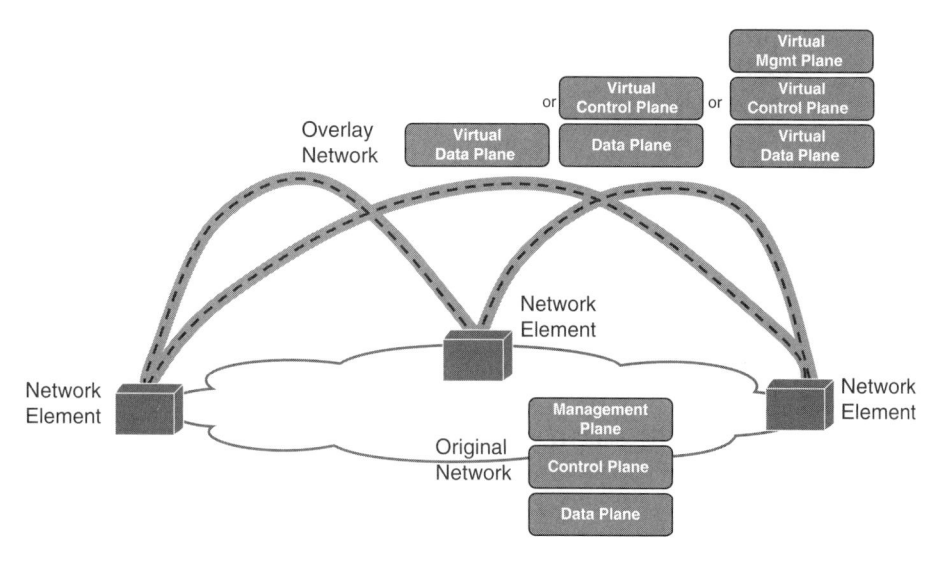

Figure 17-9 *Network Overlay*

Overlays are very common in networking, being exemplified by encapsulation-based protocols such as LAN Emulation (LANE) over ATM, generic routing encapsulation (GRE), IPsec, Virtual Private LAN Service (VPLS), Overlay Transport Virtualization (OTV), and Location/ID Separation Protocol (LISP). Generically speaking, overlays can be deployed by any network element (physical or virtual) such as routers, switches, or specialized network appliances.

In recent years, this concept has gained new traction with the popularization of hypervisor-based virtual networking. For example, a VXLAN can be seen as an overlay that offers virtual networks independence over forwarding decisions from the physical network.

In this author's opinion, the decision to deploy an overlay network, especially in data center environments, is a decision that must not be taken lightly. After all, an overlay still uses resources from the underlying network infrastructure and can easily run into the following problems:

- Maximum transfer unit (MTU) incompatibilities
- Equal Cost Multipath (ECMP) issues such as link polarization (for flow-based load-balancing algorithms) or TCP retransmissions (caused by out-of-order packets)
- Traffic contention caused by excessive oversubscription
- Scalability issues with multidestination (broadcast, multicast, and flooding) traffic handling

Therefore, an elevated level of coordination and integration between both networks (physical and the overlay) is highly recommended to enable integrated troubleshooting and proper capacity planning.

Cisco Open Network Environment

Cisco Open Network Environment (ONE) embodies the company multiproduct strategy to achieve pervasive integration between network and applications. Intrinsically, it is a portfolio of technologies and open standards that brings programmatic control and application awareness to physical and virtual hypervisor-based networks.

In essence, Cisco ONE includes

- **Cisco One Platform Kit (onePK) for developers:** Defines a comprehensive set of platform APIs that allow applications to directly control Cisco switches and routers with multiple network operating systems such as IOS and NX-OS.

- **Cisco ONE Controller framework:** Introduces the Cisco SDN controller that can support protocols such as OpenFlow, onePK, and several open APIs.

- **Overlay network technologies:** Based on Nexus 1000V, these technologies allow virtual machines to directly control their network services with a harmonic collaboration from the physical network.

As a direct alignment with Cisco ONE, Nexus 1000V can support multiple hypervisors and provide a common network layer for all virtualized workloads. Besides bringing NX-OS features to these environments, Nexus 1000V also integrates with OpenStack and Open APIs for automated, policy-based provisioning applications and can employ a VXLAN-VLAN gateway for full integration between virtual and physical networks.

Figure 17-10 summarizes the objectives of Cisco ONE.

Cisco ONE provides a non-disruptive path to open standards and network programmability, bridging multiple implementation options into an integrated hybrid solution.

More details about this strategy can be found in the "Further Reading" section.

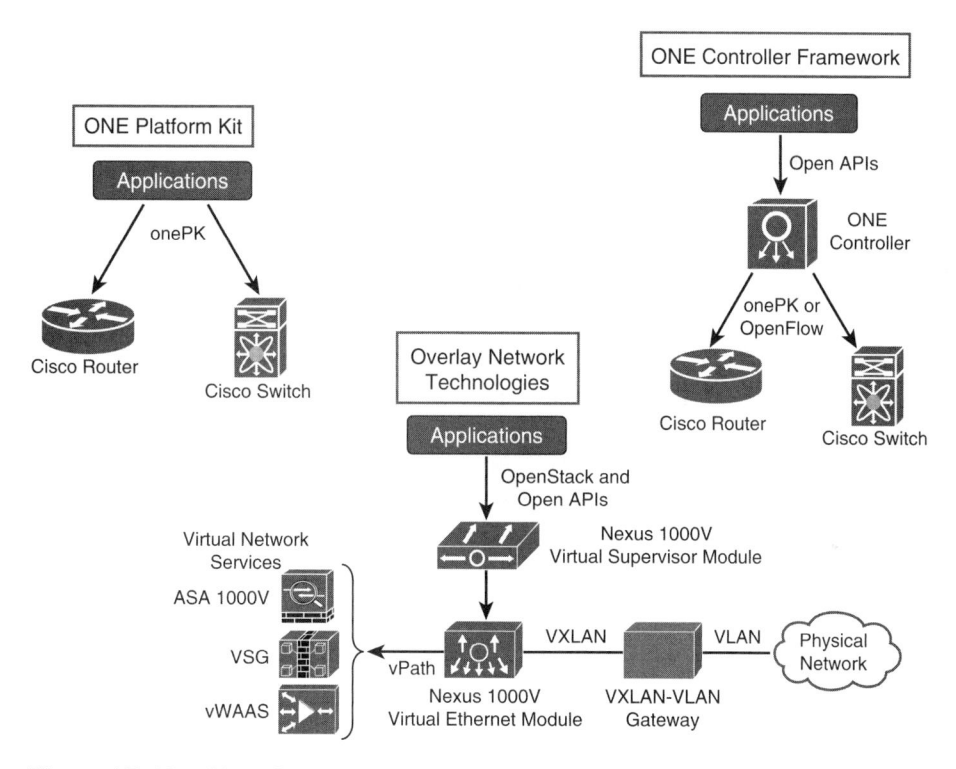

Figure 17-10 *Cisco ONE*

Before We Go...

As we approach the end of the book, it is a great idea to look back a bit and behold how far data centers have come with the help of virtualization technologies. Although they were created to offer simple emulations of individual devices, their flexibility also opened up opportunities such as the abstraction of the entire data center and the optimization of operation processes.

Inexorably, these technologies allowed steps that were unthinkable a mere decade ago, and many have transcended their original concept to become a *simulacrum* (a copy without an original).

And as you can verify in this book, great ideas are usually supported by exciting new perspectives of existing technology. Virtualization gave us a chance to rethink computing resources, maintaining their original principles and objectives but also surpassing challenges that for some time were considered insurmountable.

I believe that in some decades, other generations of IT professionals will look back to the current period in the same way that we currently that we view the nineteenth century *industry revolution*: a complete reevaluation of methods and machines that have transitioned entire industries.

Data Center city will certainly continue to serve its population, but with an efficiency and dynamism we cannot yet conceive.

Figure 17-11 *Data Center City*

Summary

In this chapter, you learned the following:

- An end-to-end virtualized data center enables flexibility, stability, resource optimization, and operational efficiency.

- A virtual Data Center (vDC) comprises a set of virtual elements that are capable of supporting the computing resources of a consumer, including servers, storage, networking, and applications.

- A virtualized data center can further evolve through standardization and automation initiatives.

- Cloud computing is an IT delivery model that presents the following essential characteristics: on-demand self-service, broad network access, resource pooling, rapid elasticity, and measured service.

- Cloud implementations can offer different service models (Infrastructure as a Service, Platform as a Service, and Software as a Service) and follow a distinct deployment model (public, private, or hybrid cloud).

- Cloud computing builds over consolidation, virtualization, standardization, and automation initiatives in data center infrastructures.

- Concepts such as Software-Defined Networks, OpenStack, and network overlays have been dominating the interest of cloud architects in recent years.

- The Cisco Open Network Environment (ONE) portfolio was created to provide a hybrid and non-disruptive approach for data center architects and network engineers that intend to deploy network programmability based on open standards.

Further Reading

Josyula, Venkata, Orr, Malcolm, Page, Greg. *Cloud Computing: Automating the Virtualized Data Center.* Cisco Press, 2012.

Vblock Systems, www.cisco.com/en/US/netsol/ns1138/index.html

DesignZone for FlexPod, www.cisco.com/en/US/solutions/ns340/ns414/ns742/ns743/ns1050/landing_flexpod.html

Storage Reference Architecture, www.cisco.com/web/partners/pr67/hitachi/index.html#~tab-1

NIST Definition of Cloud Computing, http://csrc.nist.gov/publications/nistpubs/800-145/SP800-145.pdf

Rhoton, John. *Cloud Computing Explained: Implementation Handbook for Enterprises.* Recursive Press, 2009.

Nexus 1000V InterCloud, www.cisco.com/go/intercloud

Open Networking Foundation, www.opennetworking.org

OpenStack website, www.openstack.org

OpenStack at Cisco, www.cisco.com/go/openstack

Cisco Open Network Environment: Network Programmability and Virtual Network Overlays, www.cisco.com/en/US/prod/collateral/iosswrel/content/white_paper_c11-707978.html

Appendix A

Cisco Data Center Portfolio

Started in the early 2000s, the Cisco Data Center portfolio enlists multiple products that together form a feature-rich integrated architecture. For that reason, their development has been conducted in a way to increase productivity and agility in customer environments, as well as to diminish the level of guessing and interoperability issues.

The objective of this appendix is to provide a brief description of each solution from this portfolio. And such an account will include, whenever possible, their format options, scalability numbers, and performance.

Because the portfolio is in a constant state of evolution, this appendix will offer a *snapshot* of its products at the time of this writing. In fact, you can really imagine it as a "family portrait," which is a little bit different depending on the year it is taken.

For the sake of good order, I will present each product alphabetically and exclude solutions that can integrate with it but are not formally considered part of the Data Center portfolio (for example, CSR1000V, ASR 1000, and Virtual WAAS).

For more details about each solution from this portfolio, refer to the "Further Reading" section, later in this chapter, or the Cisco online product documentation.

Cisco Application Control Engine

Cisco Application Control Engine (ACE) products provide Layer 4–7 services to data center environments, such as traffic load balancing, server offload, application optimization, and site selection.

Figure A-1 depicts the Cisco ACE products.

Figure A-1 *Application Control Engine Products*

Cisco ACE Application Delivery Controllers (ADC) come in two formats: service module for Catalyst 6500 (*ACE module*) and appliance (ACE 4710).

The latest version of the ACE module, which is ACE30, connects to a Catalyst 6500 data plane through its shared bus and switch fabric, whereas the ACE 4710 has four 10/100/1000BASE-T interfaces for traffic handling. Both solutions have one console port (for the first configuration) and can be managed afterward through a configured IP interface.

Note Both ADCs deploy management and forwarding in IP version 6.

ACE30 supports up to 250 virtual contexts, whereas ACE 4710 can implement a maximum of 20 virtual contexts. Both models support up to 4093 VLANs.

Table A-1 summarizes the performance values of both ACE form factors.

Table A-1 *ACE Performance Comparison*

	Throughput (Gbps)	Concurrent Connections	Connections per Second (L4/L7)	SSL TPS[1]	Compression (Gbps)
ACE30	16	4 million	500,000/200,000	30,000	6
ACE 4710	4	1 million	120,000/40,000	7500	2

[1] Transactions per second

The *ACE GSS 4400 Series Global Site Selector* (or simply ACE GSS) provides data center load balancing and disaster recovery through its integration with the Domain Name System (DNS) of a network. With this arrangement, ACE GSS can provide intelligent DNS responses, which are dependent on site availability and measured load.

The ACE GSS 4492R appliance has two interfaces to receive forwarded DNS queries, send health probes (ICMP, TCP, HTTP, SNMP, or a combination of them), and maintain cluster intercommunication. Up to 16 ACE GSS appliances can form a geographically distributed cluster, sharing the same availability and load information. Each ACE GSS 4492R can offer 30,000 DNS responses per second.

Cisco Adaptive Security Appliances 5585-X

Released in 2005, *Cisco Adaptive Security Appliances (ASA)* offer security, regulatory compliance, and risk management for corporate and service provider networks. And as security perimeters have changed within modern data centers, Cisco ASA has evolved accordingly.

Cisco ASA 5585-X Adaptive Security Appliance constitutes the physical device that was designed to provide scalable security for data center environments. ASA 5585-X supplies scalable firewall performance, context-aware firewall capabilities for multitenant environments (with up to 250 virtual contexts), interface modularity (up to twelve 10/100/1000 and eight 10 Gigabit Ethernet), and intrusion prevention system (IPS) capabilities with extensive threat coverage.

Figure A-2 depicts the ASA 5585-X modular chassis.

Figure A-2 *ASA 5585-X Chassis*

All ASA 5585-X models share the same two RU chassis. Their difference lies in the inserted modules, which can add firewall, IPS, or Virtual Private Network (VPN) capabilities and performance depending on their combination.

Table A-2 summarizes the performance for each ASA 5585-X model.

Table A-2 *ASA 5585-X Models Performance Comparison*

	Firewall Throughput (Gbps)	Concurrent Connections	Connections per Second	IPsec Throughput (Gbps)	IPsec VPN Peers
ASA 5585-X with SSP-10	4	1 million	50,000	1	5000
ASA 5585-X with SSP-20	10	2 million	125,000	2	10,000
ASA 5585-X with SSP-40	20	4 million	200,000	3	10,000
ASA 5585-X with SSP-60	40	10 million	350,000	5	10,000

Although all ASA 5585-X models can natively deploy high availability (active-active or active-standby), version 9.0 of the ASA software introduced *ASA clustering*, where up to eight appliances can work together as a single device. In this scenario, all appliances share the same security rules and can scale the aggregated firewall throughput to up to 320 Gbps.

Cisco ASA 5585-X supports 1024 VLANs and is fully compliant with IP version 6, offering hybrid solutions such as NAT 64 (with DNS 64).

Cisco ASA 1000V Cloud Firewall

Cisco ASA 1000V is a stateful virtual firewall solution that was designed to secure the tenant edge of private and public cloud environments.

Transparently integrated with Cisco Nexus 1000V, ASA 1000V inherits its code and perimeter security functions from Cisco ASA 5500 Adaptive Security Appliances and complements the security services provided by the Cisco Virtual Security Gateway (VSG). Therefore, through Cisco Nexus 1000V's vPath "service chaining," the same traffic flow can be analyzed by both ASA 1000V and VSG.

In summary, Cisco ASA 1000V Cloud Firewall offers the following features for virtual data centers:

- Default gateway and static routing
- Network Address Translation (NAT)
- Dynamic Host Control Protocol (DHCP)
- Stateful ASA failover between two instances
- Virtual eXtensible Local Area Network (VXLAN) gateway, sending traffic to and from a VXLAN to a traditional VLAN.

- IPsec Virtual Private Networks with physical environments and private clouds.

Cisco Virtual Network Management Center (VNMC) can both manage ASA 1000V and VSG. As an ASA 5500 physical appliance, ASA 1000V can also be managed through Cisco Adaptive Security Device Manager (ASDM).

ASA 1000V Cloud Firewall is available in the Open Virtualization Format (OVF) virtual appliance to simplify deployment. An ASA 1000V instance inherits all the flexibility of a standard virtual machine, such as cloning, high availability, and online migration.

Table A-3 portrays the performance values of a single ASA 1000V instance.

Table A-3 *ASA 1000V Performance*

Feature	Maximum Limit
Concurrent sessions	200,000
Connections per second	10,000
VPN throughput	200 Mbps
VPN tunnels	750

These values were tested on a VMware ESX 4.1 host running on an Intel Xeon Processor X5550 at 2.67 GHz with dual quad core. One vCPU, 1.5 GBP vRAM, and 2.5 GB vHD are allocated to the ASA 1000V instance.

Cisco Catalyst 6500 Series Switches

The Cisco Catalyst 6500 switches are arguably the most known and deployed Cisco products. Since its launch in the late 1990s, it has become the staple platform in corporate and service provider networks through its remarkable modular evolutionary architecture.

Figure A-3 illustrates the available Catalyst 6500 chassis at the time of this writing.

The chassis displayed in Figure A-3 are as follows:

- Catalyst 6503-E (three slots)
- Catalyst 6504-E (four slots)
- Catalyst 6506-E (six slots)
- Catalyst 6509-E (nine slots)
- Catalyst 6509-V-E (nine vertical slots)
- Catalyst 6513-E (13 slots)

Each Catalyst 6500-E can deploy one or two (redundant) *supervisor engine modules*, which are responsible for the data, control, and management planes in the switch. All

Figure A-3 *Catalyst 6500 Chassis*

supervisor modules support up to 4090 VLANs, a shared bus of 32 Gbps to all chassis slots, and dedicated switch fabric connections to them as well.

At the time of this writing, there are six supervisor engines available for the 6500 chassis, whose main characteristics are depicted in Table A-4.

Note Table A-4 and other tables in this chapter include forwarding performance expressed in millions of packets per second (Mpps).

Table A-4 *Catalyst 6500 Supervisor Engines*

Supervisor Engine	Max Throughput per Slot (Gbps)	Forwarding Performance L2/IPv4/IPv6 (Mpps)[1]	MAC Address Entries	Routes (IPv4/IPv6)	VRFs	Uplink Interfaces
SUP720-3B[2]	40	400/400/200	64,000	256,000/128,000	1024	Two GE
SUP720-3BXL[2]	40	400/400/200	64,000	1 million/500,000	1024	Two GE
SUP720-10G-3C	40	450/450/225	96,000	256,000/128,000[3]	1024	Three GE and two 10GE

Supervisor Engine	Max Throughput per Slot (Gbps)	Forwarding Performance L2/IPv4/IPv6 (Mpps)[1]	MAC Address Entries	Routes (IPv4/IPv6)	VRFs	Uplink Interfaces
SUP720-10G-3CXL	40	450/450/225	96,000	1 million/500,000[3]	1024	Three GE and two 10GE
SUP2T-10G	80	720/720/390	131,072	256,000/128,000	8192	Three GE and two 10GE
SUP2T-10G-XL	80	720/720/390	131,072	1 million/500,000[3]	8192	Three GE and two 10GE

[1]Considering that all I/O modules are using Distributed Forwarding Cards (DFC).
[2]This module does not support Virtual Switching System (VSS).
[3]This number of routes requires "XL" I/O modules.

The Catalyst 6500 switches comprise a multitude of Ethernet, WAN, and service modules (such as the aforementioned ACE30 module). As an illustration of this variety, Table A-5 portrays the available Ethernet modules and their main characteristics (at the time of this writing).

Table A-5 *Catalyst 6500 Ethernet Modules*

Module	Interfaces	Throughput (Gbps)
WS-X6148-FE-SFP	48-port Fast Ethernet (SFP)	32 (shared bus)
WS-X6148A-GE-TX	48-port 10/100/1000BASE-T	32 (shared bus)
WS-6148E-GE-45AT	48-port 10/100/1000BASE-T with Power over Ethernet	32 (shared bus)
WS-X6704-10GE	4-port 10 Gigabit Ethernet (XENPAK)	40 (switch fabric)
WS-X6708-10G-3C[1]	8-port 10 Gigabit Ethernet (X2)	40 (switch fabric)
WS-X6708-10G-3CXL[1]	8-port 10 Gigabit Ethernet (X2)	40 (switch fabric)
WS-X6716-10G-3C[1]	16-port 10 Gigabit Ethernet (X2)	40 (switch fabric)
WS-X6716-10G-3CXL[1]	16-port 10 Gigabit Ethernet (X2)	40 (switch fabric)
WS-X6716-10T-3C[1]	16-port 10GBASE-T	40 (switch fabric)
WS-X6716-10T-3CXL[1]	16-port 10GBASE-T	40 (switch fabric)
WS-X6724-SFP	24-port Gigabit Ethernet (SFP)	20 (switch fabric)
WS-X6748-GE-TX	48-port 10/100/1000BASE-T	40 (switch fabric)

Module	Interfaces	Throughput (Gbps)
WS-X6748-SFP	48-port Gigabit Ethernet (SFP)	40 (switch fabric)
WS-X6816-10G-2T[2]	16-port 10 Gigabit Ethernet (X2)	40 (switch fabric)
WS-X6816-10G-2TXL[2]	16-port 10 Gigabit Ethernet (X2)	40 (switch fabric)
WS-X6816-10T-2T[2]	16-port 10GBASE-T	40 (switch fabric)
WS-X6816-10T-2TXL[2]	16-port 10GBASE-T	40 (switch fabric)
WS-X6824-SFP-2T[2]	24-port Gigabit Ethernet (SFP)	20 (switch fabric)
WS-X6824-SFP-2TXL[2]	24-port Gigabit Ethernet (SFP)	40 (switch fabric)
WS-X6848-SFP-2T[2]	48-port Gigabit Ethernet (SFP)	40 (switch fabric)
WS-X6848-SFP-2TXL[2]	48-port Gigabit Ethernet (SFP)	40 (switch fabric)
WS-X6848-TX-2T[2]	48-port 10/100/1000BASE-T	40 (switch fabric)
WS-X6848-TX-2TXL[2]	48-port 10/100/1000BASE-T	40 (switch fabric)
WS-X6904-40G-2T[2]	4-port 40G(CFP)/4 x 10 Gigabit Ethernet (SFP+)	80 (switch fabric)
WS-X6904-40G-2TXL[2]	4-port 40G(CFP)/4 x 10 Gigabit Ethernet (SFP+)	80 (switch fabric)
WS-X6908-10G-2T[2]	8-port 10 Gigabit Ethernet (X2)	80 (switch fabric)
WS-X6908-10G-2TXL[2]	8-port 10 Gigabit Ethernet (X2)	80 (switch fabric)

[1] Not supported with SUP2T-10G or SUP2T-10G-XL

[2] Only supported with SUP2T-10G and SUP2T-10G-XL

Since the launch of Cisco Nexus data center switches, Catalyst 6500 has performed a complementary position in data center networks, such as:

- Service chassis for modules such as ACE30
- Internet edge router
- Data Center Interconnect chassis for Multiprotocol Label Switching (MPLS) technologies such as EoMPLS and Virtual Private LAN Service (VPLS).
- End-of-Row or Mid-of-Row access switch for legacy Gigabit Ethernet servers.

Cisco Cloud Portal

An outcome from the acquisition of newScale, *Cisco Cloud Portal (CCP)* is a web-based software solution that provides customization of service catalogs and life cycle management for physical, virtual, and cloud environments. Deploying an end-user self-service portal, CCP enforces access control, approvals, policy-based control, and end-to-end provisioning of IT resources.

With CCP, an organization can deploy a private (or hybrid) cloud portal to improve agility and reducing operational costs. This solution also increases visibility into IT consumption to help ensure more accurate capacity planning and resource billing.

The following components are part of Cisco Cloud Portal:

- **Cisco Portal Manager:** A single pane-of-glass view for users that consolidates data from multiple sources into a highly customizable and flexible self-service portal interface.
- **Cisco Service Catalog:** Creates a menu of services to users with controlled access to standardized IT resources.
- **Cisco Request Center:** Provides request and life cycle management for all services defined in the Cisco Service Catalog.
- **Cisco Service Connector:** A standards-based module used in the integration of CCP with other systems, such as VMware vCenter and Microsoft System Center.

Cisco Cloud Portal is also available within some Cisco Intelligent Automation solutions.

Cisco Intelligent Automation Solutions

With the acquisition of Tidal in 2009, Cisco has assembled an enviable IT automation framework that purposely integrates with ease to its Data Center portfolio.

Cisco Intelligent Automation Solutions automate manual data center tasks across servers, networks, applications, and virtual machine infrastructures to increase their efficiency, predictability, visibility, and control.

These solutions essentially provide orchestration of infrastructure and applications, which enables

- End-user self-service
- Provisioning simplification
- Dynamic reactions to trigger events
- Automation of IT processes using best practices to comply with policy and auditability

Automation Software Components

Generically speaking, each Cisco Intelligent Automation Solution uses a different set of components to reach its objective. In this section, I will present these components.

Cisco Process Orchestrator (CPO) can be understood as the core of all Cisco Intelligent Automation Solutions. CPO is basically designed to deliver orchestration to processes in complex IT environments. With an intuitive flow-based graphical interface, CPO integrates events and alert management data with best practices for operational support processes.

To deploy its predefined processes, CPO has adapters that provide control over multiple resources such as

- Cisco Server Provisioner (CSP)
- UCS Manager
- VMware vCenter
- Network Service Manager (NSM)
- And many others

Additionally, CPO allows interaction with the governance, monitoring, ticketing, and configuration management database (CMDB) of a company.

Cisco Server Provisioner (CSP) automates and simplifies server provisioning in dynamic physical environments (which is also known as "bare metal" provisioning). CSP permits the rapid deployment of new systems, repurposing of unused servers, and cloning of a system state.

CSP natively supports provisioning operating systems such as RHEL, CentOS, Fedora, Windows Server 2008 R2, Windows 7, Windows 2003, Windows XP, VMware ESXi, Debina, Ubuntu, and SUSE.

Network Services Manager (NSM) provides automation, orchestration, and control for the networking infrastructure in cloud environments. NSM allows network resources (such as Virtual Routing and Forwarding [VRF], VLANs, virtual contexts, and so on) to be combined into abstracted models that can be instantiated with speed and control.

NSM is based on the creation of *network containers*, which are defined as end-to-end replicable network topologies. Within a network container, NSM encompasses IP subnet pools, VLANs, Switch Virtual Interfaces (SVI), VRFs, routing protocols, firewall policies, Internet access, VPN access, server load balancers, Network Address Translation (NAT), among other network entities. Used as templates, these network containers can be deployed to create standardized network environments for different requirements and service-level agreements (SLA).

NSM itself is comprised of two different elements:

- **NSM Engine:** Automates the provisioning of end-to-end network services and dynamically generates the configuration instructions that control the devices and services in a multitenant environment.
- **NSM Controller:** Interacts with the network devices and services in real time to determine their exact service characteristics.

Whereas NSM uses a web-based interface for resource and configuration management, it also offers a "northbound" API to various orchestration tools such as VMware vCloud Director and other applications from BMC, IBM, and HP.

NSM closely follows the *Cisco Virtualized Multitenant Data Center (VMDC)* architecture, supporting myriad networking devices such as ASR 1000, Nexus 1000V, Nexus 5000, Nexus 7000, Catalyst 6500, and UCS Fabric Interconnect.

Cisco Tidal Enterprise Scheduler (TES) is an automation platform for heterogeneous enterprise workloads, batch job scheduling, and application integration. Cisco TES can easily run scheduled batches and event-based business processes. In addition, TES provides a single view and point of control over the jobs it manages.

TES manages process integration through the use of agents running over different operating systems such as Windows, UNIX, Linux, z/OS, zLinux, OS/400, NonStop, and OVMS. It also offers agentless adapters through scripts applied through SSH.

As a result, TES provides automation of enterprise applications such as

- **ERP:** Amisys, BAAN, JD Edwards, Lawson, Oracle, PeopleSoft, SAP.
- **Data Integration and Business Intelligence:** Actuate, BusinessObjects, Cognos, DataStage, Informatica PowerCenter, SAP BW, SAS.
- **Database and Big Data:** Hadoop, JDBC, Microsoft, Netezza, Oracle.
- **SOA:** JMS, JMX, Web Services.
- **File and Storage:** FTP, SFTP, FTPS, NetBackup, Tivoli Storage Manager.
- **Cloud:** Amazon (EC2 and S3 services).
- **Management Frameworks:** HP Operations Center, Microsoft SCOM.
- **Event and Alert Output:** File, email, database, SNMP.
- **Server Virtualization and Provisioning:** VMware.

Cisco Intelligent Automation for Cloud Solution

Cisco Intelligent Automation for Cloud (CIAC) is a complete software solution that enables companies to build their own private or hybrid cloud. In essence, CIAC includes the integration of Cisco Cloud Portal, Cisco Process Orchestrator, Cisco Server Provisioner, and Cisco Network Services Manager.

After CIAC is working in a data center infrastructure, authenticated end users can access the Cisco Cloud Portal to request one of the services defined in the catalog. Examples of these services are

- Provisioning of a new Unified Computing System (UCS) blade
- Creation of a new virtual machine

- Storage array logical unit number (LUN) provisioning
- "Bare metal" provisioning (through Cisco Server Provisioner)

If approved, these requests are forwarded to Cisco Process Orchestrator, which in turn will execute predefined processes over the infrastructure elements to fulfill what it is being asked.

Cisco Intelligent Automation for Cloud is also available in a *Starter Edition bundle*, whose objective is to initiate simple cloud environments. This specific bundle automates the provisioning of virtual machines (managed on a single VMware vCenter) and blades on a single UCS domain.

> **Note** CIAC Starter Edition only includes Cloud Portal and Cisco Process Orchestrator.

Cisco Intelligent Automation for SAP

Cisco Intelligent Automation for SAP simplifies the execution of complex best practice scripts in SAP landscapes. For example, Cisco Intelligent Automation for SAP can

- Automate SAP incident response, task management, and corrective actions
- Orchestrate predefined operational processes
- Expedite automation through preconfigured SAP content

Based on Cisco Process Orchestrator, this solution contains Tidal previous expertise in more than 200 automated flows, 100 incident analyses, and 50 flows for System Refresh and System Copy.

Although Cisco currently develops this automation solution, it is offered through the SAP global price list.

Cisco MDS 9000 Series Multilayer Switches

Released in 2002, the Cisco MDS 9000 family is comprised of fabric and director-class Fibre Channel switches. These devices are capable of deploying highly available and scalable storage-area networks (SAN) for the most demanding data center environments.

Figure A-4 portrays the available Cisco MDS 9000 switches (at the time of this writing).

Cisco MDS 9124 is a 1-RU switch that supports up to 16 virtual storage-area networks (VSAN) and has 24 Fibre Channel autonegotiable ports that are capable of speeds of 1, 2, and 4 Gbps. Both *Cisco MDS Fibre Channel Blade Switch for IBM BladeCenter* (20 ports, where 14 are for internal blade server connectivity and six are for external connections) and *Cisco MDS Fibre Channel Blade Switch for HP c-Class BladeSystem* (24 ports, where 16 are for internal blade server connectivity and eight are for external connections) share similar characteristics with MDS 9124.

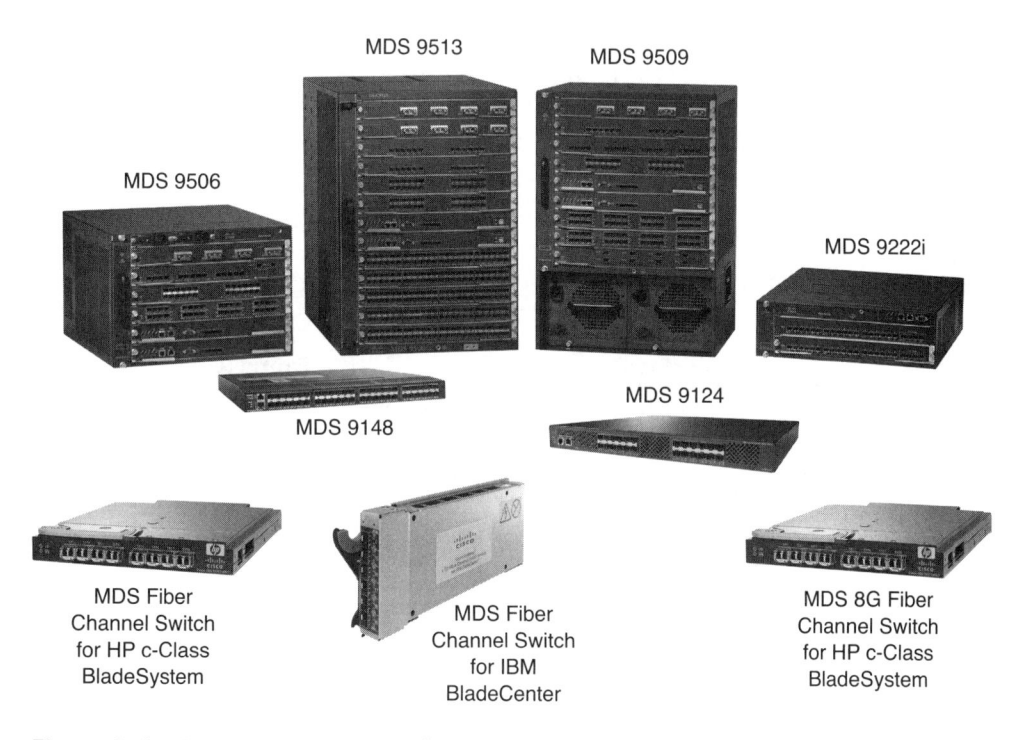

Figure A-4 *Cisco MDS 9000 Switches*

Also occupying one RU, *Cisco MDS 9148* supports up to 32 VSANs and possesses 48 Fibre Channel autonegotiable interfaces of 1, 2, 4, and 8 Gbps. Likewise, the *Cisco MDS 8G Fibre Channel Switch for HP c-Class BladeSystem* is based on MDS 9148 hardware. However, it deploys 24 ports, where 16 are for internal blade server connectivity and eight are for external connections.

Cisco MDS 9222i is a modular switch that has 18 fixed 1/2/4 Fibre Channel ports and four Gigabit Ethernet interfaces, which can deploy Internet Small Computer System Interface (iSCSI) and Fibre Channel over IP (FCIP). One available slot allows the insertion of an additional I/O module.

Cisco MDS 9500 is a series of Cisco director-class switches that are defined by components that are completely redundant to achieve 99.999 percent availability.

There are three chassis in this family:

- **MDS 9506** (six slots)
- **MDS 9509** (nine slots)
- **MDS 9513** (13 slots)

To maintain their required reliability, each chassis must have two *supervisor modules*, which are responsible for the switch control and management plane.

On MDS 9500 directors, data traffic between I/O modules traverses dual redundant crossbar switch fabrics that can be located on the supervisor modules (MDS 9506 and 9509) or in online removable modules (MDS 9513). For that reason, MDS 9513 can achieve 256 Gbps of traffic between I/O modules, while other chassis can deploy up to 96 Gbps of traffic between I/O modules.

Table A-6 shows the currently available I/O modules for MDS 9200 and 9500 chassis.

Table A-6 *MDS 9000 I/O Modules*

Module	Interfaces	Throughput to Switch Fabric (Gbps)
DS-X9248-48K9[1]	4 ports Fibre Channel 1/2/4/8 Gbps and 44 ports Fibre Channel 1/2/4 Gbps	48
DS-X9224-96K9	24-port Fibre Channel 1/2/4/8 Gbps	96
DS-X9248-96K9	48-port Fibre Channel 1/2/4/8 Gbps	96
DS-X9232-256K9[2]	32-port Fibre Channel 1/2/4/8/10 Gbps	256
DS-X9248-256K9[2]	48-port Fibre Channel 1/2/4/8/10 Gbps	256
DS-X9304-18K9[1]	18 ports Fibre Channel 1/2/4 Gbps and 4 ports Gigabit Ethernet (SFP)	48
DS-X9316-SSNK9[1]	16-port Gigabit Ethernet (SFP)	16
DS-X9704[1]	4-port Fibre Channel 10 Gbps	40
DS-X9708-K9	8-port 10 Gigabit Ethernet (FCoE)	80

[1]Also supported on MDS 9222i.

[2]These modules deploy 256 Gbps in MDS 9513 with switch fabric modules. However, they are able do deploy local switching (traffic between any two ports of the module does not have to traverse the switch fabric) on any MDS 9500 chassis.

As you can see from Table I-6, some MDS 9200 and 9500 I/O modules deploy oversubscription to the switch fabric. The employment of such cost-effective modules depends on the characteristics of a SAN design, which is intrinsically oversubscribed when one storage port is accessed by multiple servers.

Notwithstanding, oversubscribed modules can dedicate crossbar bandwidth to a storage array ports or Inter-Switch Links (ISL). This allocation is dynamic because free throughput can be used by the other ports.

Note Although MDS 9222i and 9500 switches support more VSANs per switch, the Cisco-validated limit for a physical fabric is 80 VSANs.

Cisco Prime Network Analysis Module

Cisco Network Analysis Module (NAM) software permits higher visibility into network traffic with an application level of detail. Applied to data centers, this knowledge greatly facilitates resource optimization, performance troubleshooting, and application response time monitoring.

Essentially, Cisco NAM builds a traffic database through mirrored traffic (Switched Port ANalyzer [SPAN], Remote Switched Port ANalyzer [RSPAN], or Encapsulated Remote Switched Port ANalyzer [ERSPAN]), VLAN Access Control List (VACL) captures, NetFlow collection, and specialized agents. With such database, the NAM web-based graphical interface provides interactive reports, granular monitoring, application performance analysis, detailed traffic analytics, historical analysis, packet captures, and flow- and packet-based traffic monitoring.

Cisco NAM is available in different formats including physical appliances (NAM 2300), the Catalyst 6500 module (NAM-3), the Nexus 7000 module (NAM-NX1), the ISR G2 module (NAM), the virtual blade for Nexus 1010 and 1100, and the virtual appliance (vNAM) for hypervisors such as VMware ESXi, Microsoft Hyper-V, and KVM.

When integrated with Cisco Nexus 1000V, Cisco NAM provides high visibility over virtual switching traffic, such as vMotion and inter-VM communication.

Cisco Nexus Data Center Switches

According to the *Oxford English Dictionary*, Second Edition, the word *nexus* means

1. A connection or series of connections linking two or more things.
2. A central or focal point.

In 2008, Cisco appropriately used this term to name its new family of data center switches. And since then, these devices have established their leadership in corporate and service provider data centers.

Deploying the same modular network operating system (NX-OS), the various families of data center switches brought to data centers innovations such as

- Unified Fabric with Data Center Bridging (DCB) and Fibre Channel over Ethernet (FCoE)
- Fabric Extenders
- Virtual device contexts (VDC)
- Virtual PortChannels (vPC)
- Layer 2 multipathing with FabricPath
- Intelligent virtual switching
- Algo Boost technology for ultra-low-latency applications

Cisco Nexus 1000V Series Switches

Cisco Nexus 1000V is a Layer 2 Distributed Virtual Switch for server virtualization and cloud environments. This "software switch" basically controls virtual machine connectivity exactly as a "hardware switch" provides Ethernet switching for physical servers.

As an NX-OS-based switch, Nexus 1000V brings multiple access, security, and extensibility features to multi-hypervisor environments. Such similarity allows the great majority of customer processes and tools (such as the command-line interface [CLI], Simple Network Management Protocol [SNMP], NetFlow, and ERSPAN) to be applied to both physical and virtual networking infrastructures.

Two basic components form Cisco Nexus 1000V:

- **Virtual Ethernet Module (VEM):** Runs as part of the hypervisor, replacing its native connectivity model. It deploys the data plane component of Nexus 1000V, performing Layer 2 switching, among other NX-OS advanced features (such as PortChannels, quality of service, private VLANs, and access control lists [ACL]).

- **Virtual Supervisor Module (VSM):** Coordinates multiple virtual Ethernet modules, providing the control and management plane for Nexus 1000V. Dynamically linked with virtual environment managers (such as VMware vCenter), VSM allows the creation of *port profiles* that will be exported to these managers as standard connectivity policies (to be executed by the VEM). It supports management traffic through IP version 4 and 6.

Note At the time of this writing, an active-standby VSM pair can control up to 64 VEMs and supports up to 2048 VLANs.

Additionally, Cisco Nexus 1000V provides features that are designed to optimize virtual networking, such as *VXLAN* and *Virtual Services Data Path (vPath)*.

Cisco Nexus 1000V is available in two versions: *Essential Edition* (which is free, charging only for support) and *Advanced Edition* (which includes security features such as DHCP Snooping, IP Source Guard, Dynamic ARP Inspections, Cisco TrustSec Security Groups support, and Cisco Virtual Security Gateway).

Nexus 1010 and 1100 Virtual Services Appliances

Based on the Cisco UCS C-series rack-mountable servers and leveraging NX-OS software, the *Cisco Nexus 1010 and 1100 Virtual Services Appliances* permit the installation and management of *Virtual Service Blades (VSB)*.

Each VSB can contain one of the following applications:

- Nexus 1000V Virtual Supervisor Module (VSM)
- Virtual Security Gateway (VSG)
- Network Analysis Module (NAM)
- Data Center Network Manager (DCNM)

Note Active-standby availability for a pair of VSMs is deployed with their installation over two distinct Nexus virtual services appliances.

Both Nexus 1010 and 1100 appliances offer dedicated hardware for these services, providing independence from the server virtualization infrastructure. It also deploys a setup initialization script that is very similar to a standard Cisco switch.

In summary, these devices can be found in the following models (and number of supported VSBs):

- Cisco Nexus 1010 (up to six VSBs)
- Cisco Nexus 1010-X (up to ten VSBs)
- Cisco Nexus 1110-S (up to six VSBs)
- Cisco Nexus 1110-X (up to ten VSBs)

Cisco Nexus 2000 Series Fabric Extenders

Simultaneously decreasing cabling and consolidating management of data center networking devices, the *Cisco Nexus 2000 Series of Fabric Extenders* behave as remote linecards for a parent Cisco Nexus switch.

Because of its simplicity, Nexus 2000 switches can also be deployed within server cabinets (similarly to Top-of-Rack switches) with a small space and power footprint (from 80 to 350W in one RU).

Figure A-5 portrays the current broad variety of Nexus 2000 devices, available at the time of this writing.

Table A-7 portrays the main characteristics of these models.

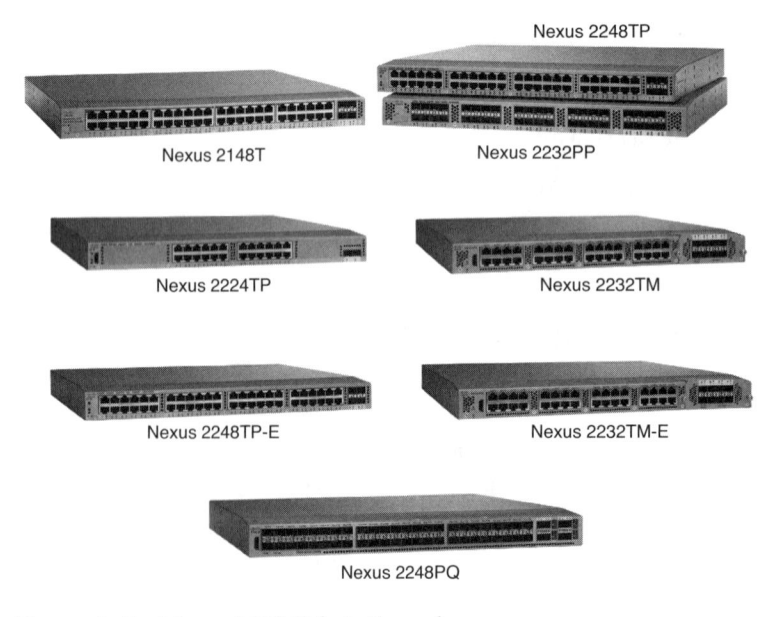

Figure A-5 *Nexus 2000 Fabric Extenders*

Table A-7 *Nexus 2000 Models*

Model	Host Interfaces	Fabric Interfaces	Performance
Nexus 2148T[1]	Forty-eight 1000BASE-T	Four 10 Gigabit Ethernet (SFP+)	176 Gbps or 131 Mpps
Nexus 2224TP	Twenty-four 100/1000BASE-T	Two 10 Gigabit Ethernet (SFP+)	88 Gbps or 65 Mpps
Nexus 2248TP	Forty-eight 100/1000BASE-T	Four 10 Gigabit Ethernet (SFP+)	176 Gbps or 131 Mpps
Nexus 2248TP-E	Forty-eight 100/1000BASE-T	Four 10 Gigabit Ethernet (SFP+)	176 Gbps of 131 Mpps
Nexus 2232PP	Thirty-two 1/10 Gigabit Ethernet (SFP/SFP+)	Eight 10 Gigabit Ethernet (SFP+)	560 Gbps or 595 Mpps
Nexus 2232TM	Thirty-two 1/10GBASE-T	Eight 10 Gigabit Ethernet (SFP+)	560 Gbps or 595 Mpps
Nexus 2232TM-E[1]	Thirty-two 1/10GBASE-T	Eight 10 Gigabit Ethernet (SFP+)	560 Gbps or 595 Mpps
Nexus 2248PQ[1]	Forty-eight 1/10 Gigabit Ethernet (SFP/SFP+)	Four 40 Gigabit Ethernet (QSFP+)[2]	960 Gbps or 952 Mpps

[1] Not supported on Nexus 7000 at the time of this writing.

[2] This model can also support sixteen 10 Gigabit Ethernet fabric interfaces using breakout cables.

Both Nexus 2248-TP-E and Nexus 2232-TM-E differ from their respective "non-E" models mainly through bigger shared buffers, which benefit applications such as large-volume databases, distributed storage, and video editing.

Besides twinax copper cables and standard 10 Gigabit Ethernet transceivers, some Nexus 2000 models also deploy cost-effective *Fabric Extender Transceivers (FET)* that can reach up to 100 meters of fiber to connect to the parent switch.

The Cisco family of Fabric Extenders is further extended with the *Cisco Nexus B22 Blade Fabric Extenders* for HP BladeSystem c3000 and c7000 enclosures (B22HP), Fujitsu PRIMERGY BX400 and BX9000 enclosure (B22F), and Dell PowerEdge M1000e. All models have 16 host interfaces (10GBASE-KR) for internal blade server connectivity and eight 10 Gigabit Ethernet SFP+ fabric interfaces.

Cisco Nexus 3000 Series Switches

The *Cisco Nexus 3000 switches* were originally designed to provide ultra-low-latency switching to High Frequency Trade (HFT) and High Performance Computing (HPC) environments. With a small footprint of one RU and a distinctive "switch-on-a-chip" architecture, these NX-OS devices are capable of providing wire-rate Layer 2 and 3 switching.

Figure A-6 shows the available Nexus 3000 models, at the time of this writing.

Figure A-6 *Nexus 3000 Models*

Meanwhile, Table A-8 describes their main characteristics.

Table A-8 *Nexus 3000 Models*

Model	Interfaces	Performance (L2 and L3)
Nexus 3016	Sixteen 40 Gigabit Ethernet (QSFP+), where each port can operate also as four independent 10 Gigabit Ethernet (breakout cable)	1.2 Tbps and 950 Mpps

Model	Interfaces	Performance (L2 and L3)
Nexus 3048[1]	Forty-eight 10/100/1000BASE-T ports and four 10 Gigabit Ethernet (SFP+)	176 Gbps and 132 Mpps
Nexus 3064-X	Forty-eight 100/1000/10 Gigabit Ethernet (SFP+) and four 40 Gigabit Ethernet (QSFP+), where each port can operate also as four 10 Gigabit Ethernet (breakout cable)	1.2 Tbps and 950 Mpps
Nexus 3064-T	Forty-eight 100/1000/10GBASE-T and 4 x 40 Gigabit Ethernet (QSFP+), where each port can operate also as four 10 Gigabit Ethernet (breakout cable)	1.2 Tbps and 950 Mpps
Nexus 3548	Forty-eight 10 Gigabit Ethernet (SFP+)	960 Gbps and 720 Mpps

[1] Nexus 3548 currently supports IPv6 for management traffic only. Refer to the Cisco documentation for updated information.

Cisco Nexus 3016, 3048, 3064-T, and 3064-X support up to 4000 VLANs, 1000 VRFs, 128,000 MAC addresses entries, 16,000 IPv4 routes, and 8000 IPv6 routes.

Cisco Nexus 3548 introduces the groundbreaking technology *Algorithm Boost (Algo-Boost)* that enables a switching latency of less than 200 nanoseconds for all types of traffic (unicast and multicast, Layer 2 or layer 3). The switch supports 512 VLANs, 200 VRFs, and depending on its mode of operation:

- From 8000 to 64,000 MAC addresses entries
- From 4096 to 16,384 IPv4 routes

All Nexus 3000 platforms deploy innovative NX-OS features such as virtual PortChannels (vPC), Embedded Event Manager (EEM), 64-way Equal-Cost Multipath (ECMP) for Layer 3 "fat tree" designs, Etheranalyzer (NX-OS built-in packet analyzer), and Precision Time Protocol (IEEE 1588).

Cisco Nexus 4000 Series Switches

The *Cisco Nexus 4001I Switch Module for IBM BladeCenter* extends NX-OS features and advantages for customers that deploy these blade server chassis.

Note Although some Cisco documents might refer to this switch as Nexus 4005I, both part numbers refer to the same device.

This Layer 2 switch deploys Data Center Bridging (DCB) standards to adequately forward Fibre Channel over Ethernet (FCoE) frames to an upstream FCoE Forwarder (FCF). In fact, Nexus 4001I is the first Cisco switch to deploy FCoE Initialization Protocol (*FIP*) *snooping*, which follows the security recommendations of standard FC-BB-5.

Figure A-7 depicts the device.

Figure A-7 *Nexus 4001I*

Cisco Nexus 4001I has 14 fixed 1/10 Gigabit Ethernet (10GBASE-KR) interfaces to provide connectivity to the blade servers and six fixed 10 Gigabit Ethernet (SFP+) uplinks to connect to upstream switches. The switch has a 400-Gbps switching capacity, a forwarding rate of 300 Mpps, and supports up to 8192 MAC addresses entries in 512 VLANs.

Cisco Nexus 5000 and 5500 Series Switches

The *Cisco Nexus 5000 and 5500 switches* are arguably the most flexible platforms within the Cisco Data Center switching portfolio.

Figure A-8 portrays all existent Nexus 5000 and 5500 models at the time of this writing.

Nexus 5010 and *Nexus 5020* were the first switches on the market to deploy Fibre Channel over Ethernet and Fabric Extenders.

Nexus 5500 switches brought further innovations in data center networks such as FabricPath, VM-FEX, and *Unified Ports*, which are interfaces that can provide Ethernet (1/10 Gbps with FCoE) or Fibre Channel (8/4/2/1 Gbps) according to the inserted transceiver.

Tip Unified Ports enable flexibility and an easier migration from Fibre Channel to FCoE networks.

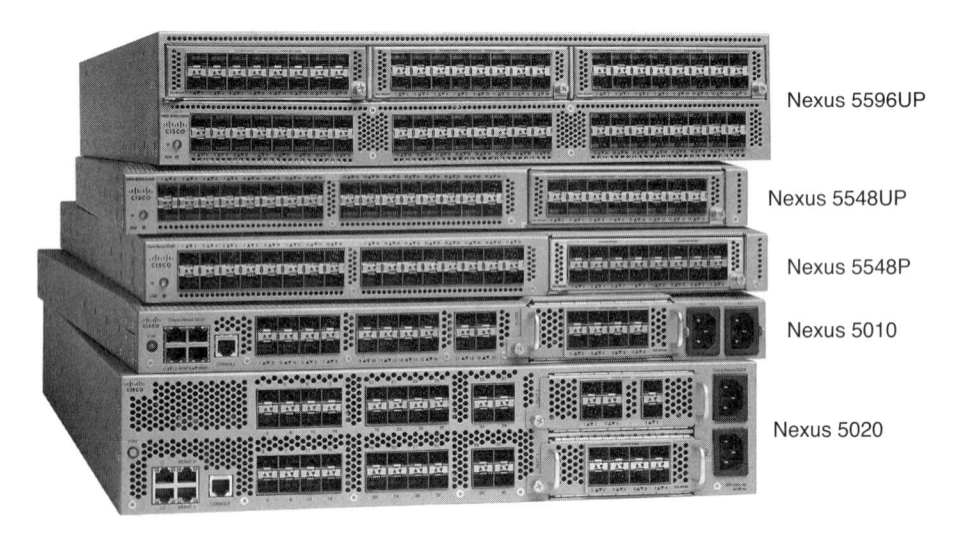

Figure A-8 *Nexus 5000 Models*

Table A-9 describes the main characteristics of the Cisco Nexus 5000 and 5500 models.

Table A-9 *Nexus 5000 and 5500 Characteristics*

Model	Fixed Interfaces	Expansion Slots	Performance (Layer 2)
Nexus 5010	Twenty 10 Gigabit Ethernet/FCoE (SFP+)	1	520 Gbps or 386.9 Mpps
Nexus 5020	Forty 10 Gigabit Ethernet/FCoE (SFP+)	2	1040 Gbps or 773.8 Mpps
Nexus 5548P	Thirty-two 10 Gigabit Ethernet/FCoE (SFP+)	1	960 Gbps or 714.24 Mpps
Nexus 5548UP	Thirty-two Unified Ports	1	960 Gbps or 714.24 Mpps
Nexus 5596UP	Forty-eight Unified Ports	3	1920 Gbps or 1428 Mpps
Nexus 5596T	Thirty-two 1000BASE-T/10GBASE-T and sixteen Unified Ports	3	1920 Gbps or 1428 Mpps

The expansion modules for Nexus 5010 and 5020 are

- Six 10 Gigabit Ethernet (SFP+)
- Four 10 Gigabit Ethernet (SFP+) and 4 Fibre Channel 1/2/4 Gbps (SFP)

- Eight Fibre Channel 1/2/4 Gbps (SFP)
- Six Fibre Channel 1/2/4/8 Gbps (SFP)

Meanwhile, the slots on the Nexus 5500 chassis allow the connection of the following expansion modules:

- Sixteen 1/10 Gigabit Ethernet and FCoE (SFP+)
- Eight 1/10 Gigabit Ethernet and FCoE (SFP+) and eight 8/4/2/1 Gbps Fibre Channel ports
- Sixteen Unified Ports
- Sixteen 10GBASE-T ports (5596T only)
- Layer 3 with 160 Gbps and 240 Mpps, and 1000 VRFs (only 5596UP and 5596T)

Additionally, Nexus 5548P and 5548UP support a Layer 3 daughter card that does not consume an expansion slot with the same performance and VRF scalability.

Nexus 5010 and 5020 support 507 VLANs, 16,000 MAC address entries, and 12 Fabric Extenders, while the Nexus 5500 switches support 4000 VLANs, 32,000 MAC addresses entries, and 24 FEX in Layer 2 mode (16 in Layer 3).

Note All Nexus 5000 and 5500 switches support up to 32 VSANs.

Cisco Nexus 6000 Series Switches

The *Cisco Nexus 6000 Data Center switches* are the latest additions to the Nexus family of data center switches. At the time of this writing, the series comprises two models: Nexus 6001 and 6004.

Deploying Layer 2 and Layer 3 switching in line rate, Nexus 6001 offers forty-eight fixed 10 Gigabit Ethernet SFP+ ports and four 40 Gigabit Ethernet QSFP+ ports. In this in-rack switch, each 40 Gigabit Ethernet port can be optionally transformed into four independent 10 Gigabit Ethernet ports (which are accessible through breakout cables).

With similar features, Nexus 6004 has forty-eight 40 Gigabit Ethernet ports (QSFP+) and four expansion slots that individually can accommodate another twelve 40 Gigabit Ethernet ports. A single Nexus 6004 can implement up to 96 40 Gigabit Ethernet ports or 384 10 Gigabit Ethernet ports (using QSFP breakout cables)

Figure A-9 portrays both Nexus 6000 models.

Nexus 60001

Nexus 6004

Figure A-9 *Nexus 6000 Models*

Both switches support 4000 VLANs, 256,000 MAC address entries, 7.68 Tbps of throughput, 4000 VRFs, 32,000 IPv4 routes, 8000 IPv6 routes, 32 VSANs, and 24 Fabric Extenders.

Cisco Nexus 7000 Series Switches

The *Cisco Nexus 7000 Series switches* are high-density Ethernet switches that can achieve up to 17.6 Tbps of switching capacity and a forwarding rate of 11.5 billions of packets per second (Bpps).

Four Nexus 7000 chassis are available at the time of this writing:

- **Nexus 7004 (7 RU):** Two slots for supervisor modules and two for I/O modules.
- **Nexus 7009 (14 RU):** Two slots for supervisor modules, seven slots for I/O modules, and four slots for switch fabric modules.
- **Nexus 7010 (21 RU):** Two slots for supervisor modules, eight slots for I/O modules (vertical), and five slots for switch fabric modules.
- **Nexus 7018 (25 RU):** Two slots for supervisors, 16 slots for I/O, and five slots for switch fabric modules.

These chassis are displayed in Figure A-10.

In Nexus 7000 switches, the supervisor modules are responsible for their control and management plane. Table I-10 describes the main characteristics of such modules and their support on each chassis.

Figure A-10 *Nexus 7000 Chassis*

Table A-10 *Nexus 7000 Supervisor Module Characteristics and Chassis Support*

Model	VDCs	Fabric Extenders	Nexus 7004	Nexus 7009	Nexus 7010	Nexus 7018
Supervisor1	4	32	No	Yes	Yes	Yes
Supervisor2	4+1 (admin) with CPU shares	32	Yes	Yes	Yes	Yes
Supervisor2 Enhanced	8+1 (admin) with CPU shares	48	Yes	Yes	Yes	Yes

Except on the Nexus 7004, traffic between I/O modules traverses *switch fabric modules*. Generically speaking, there are two available types of switch fabrics:

- **Switch Fabric-1:** Supports up to 46 Gbps (Nexus 7010 and 7018).
- **Switch Fabric-2:** Supports up to 110 Gbps (Nexus 7009, 7010, and 7018).

> **Note** The I/O slots on the Nexus 7004 share a 440-Gbps direct connection between each other.

A relatively "young" switch series, Nexus 7000 already has an enviable variety of I/O modules. Table A-11 summarizes the characteristics of its available I/O modules.

Table A-11 *Nexus 7000 I/O Modules*

Module	Interfaces	Throughput to Switch Fabrics (Gbps)	Forwarding Rate L2/IPv4/IPv6 (Mpps)
N7K-F132XP-15[1]	Thirty-two 1/10 Gigabit Ethernet (SFP/SFP+)	230	480
N7K-F248XP-25	Forty-eight 1/10 Gigabit Ethernet (SFP/SFP+)	480	720/720/720
N7K-F248XP-25E	Forty-eight 1/10 Gigabit Ethernet (SFP/SFP+)	480	720/720/720
N7K-F248XT-25E	Forty-eight 1000BASE-T/10GBASE-T	480	720/720/720
N7K-M108X2-12L	Eight 10 Gigabit Ethernet (X2)	80	120/120/60
N7K-M132XP-12[2]	Thirty-two 10 Gigabit Ethernet (SFP+)	80	60/60/30
N7K-M148GS-11[2]	Forty-eight Gigabit Ethernet (SFP)	48	60/60/30
N7K-M148GT-11[2]	Forty-eight 10/100/1000BASE-T	48	60/60/30
N7K-M132XP-12L	Thirty-two 10 Gigabit Ethernet (SFP+)	80	60/60/30
N7K-M148GS-11L	Forty-eight Gigabit Ethernet (SFP)	80	60/60/30
N7K-M148GT-11L	Forty-eight 10/100/1000BASE-T	48	60/60/30
N7K-M202CF-22L	Two 100 Gigabit Ethernet (CFP)	200	120/120/60
N7K-M206FQ-23L	Six 40 Gigabit Ethernet (QSFP+)	240	120/120/60
N7K-M224XP-23L	Twenty-four 10 Gigabit Ethernet (SFP+)	240	120/120/60

[1] Layer 2 only

[2] Not supported on Nexus 7004

A Nexus 7000 switch can support up to 16,000 VLANs and 1000 VRFs distributed over its virtual device contexts. Each Nexus 7000 I/O module can support different MAC address entries:

- **F1-series:** Up to 256,000.
- **F2-series:** Up to 196,608.
- **M1- and M2-series:** 128,000.

All M1 and M2 modules with the letter "L" at the end of their part number can work in *XL-mode*, meaning that they can support up to 1 million IPv4 routes (or 350,000 IPv6 routes). Other M1-series modules support up to 128,000 IPv4 routes (or 64,000 IPv6 routes), and F2-series modules support 32,768 IPv4 routes (or 16,384 IPv6 routes).

Note Although FCoE-enabled Nexus 7000 switches support more VSANs per switch, the Cisco-verified limit for a physical fabric is 80 VSANs.

Cisco Unified Computing System

By design, *Cisco Unified Computing System (UCS)* consolidates high-performance Intel-based servers, high-speed networking, storage access, and server virtualization into an integrated infrastructure.

With fewer points of managements than similar server solutions, UCS drastically reduces the amount of time dedicated to physical server provisioning and enables "bare metal" installations to achieve a similar performance level of server virtualization environments.

Figure A-11 portrays the main components of Cisco Unified Computing System.

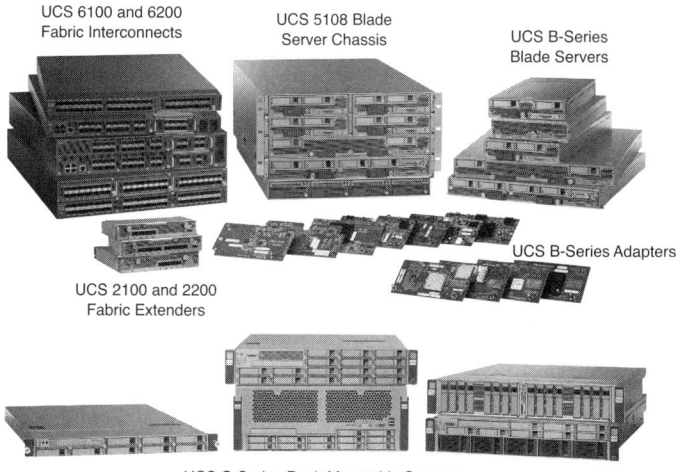

Figure A-11 *UCS Components*

Cisco 6100 and 6200 Series Fabric Interconnects

Cisco UCS Fabric Interconnects provide network connectivity and management capabilities for a Unified Computing System domain. Based on the Nexus 5000 and 5500 hardware, UCS 6100 and 6200 offer line-rate, low-latency, Ethernet, Fibre Channel, and FCoE connectivity for UCS B-series and C-series servers.

Table A-12 represents the available models of Fabric Interconnect and their main characteristics.

Table A-12 *UCS Fabric Interconnects Characteristics*

Model	Fixed Interfaces	Slots	Performance (Gbps/Mpps)	MAC Address Entries
UCS 6120XP	Twenty 10 GE/FCoE (SFP+)	1	520/386.9	16,000
UCS 6140XP	Forty 10 GE/FCoE (SFP+)	2	1040/773.8	16,000
UCS 6248UP	Thirty-two Unified Ports	1	960/714.24	32,000
UCS 6296UP	Forty-eight Unified Ports	3	1920/1428.48	32,000

The expansion modules for UCS 6100 Fabric Interconnects are

- Six 10 Gigabit Ethernet (SFP+) interfaces
- Four 10 Gigabit Ethernet (SFP+) and 4 Fibre Channel 1/2/4 Gbps (SFP) interfaces
- Eight Fibre Channel 1/2/4 Gbps (SFP) interfaces
- Six Fibre Channel 1/2/4/8 Gbps (SFP) interfaces

Meanwhile, the only expansion module for UCS 6200 has sixteen Unified Ports.

> **Note** All UCS Fabric Interconnects support up to 1024 VLANs and 32 VSANs.

Cisco UCS 5100 Series Blade Server Chassis

The *Cisco UCS 5108 Blade server chassis* enables the accommodation of up to eight blade servers into six RU. It supports one or two I/O modules for Fabric Interconnect connection and management.

UCS 5108 supports autodiscovery by UCS Manager, and its passive midplane allows up to 80 Gbps of traffic for each half-width blade server slot.

Cisco UCS 2100 and 2200 Series Fabric Extenders

Contributing to UCS's consolidation of management points, UCS 2100 and 2200 are Fabric Extenders that provide unified connectivity for all servers installed on a UCS 5100 chassis.

Table A-13 describes the main characteristics of the Fabric Extenders that can be used on Unified Computing Systems.

Table A-13 *Fabric Extenders for Unified Computing System*

Model	Fabric Interfaces	Host Interfaces
UCS 2104XP	Four 10 Gigabit Ethernet/FCoE (SFP+)	Eight (one 10 GE/FCoE per half-width slot)
UCS 2204XP	Four 10 Gigabit Ethernet/FCoE (SFP+)	Sixteen (two 10 GE/FCoE per half-width slot)
UCS 2208XP	Eight 10 Gigabit Ethernet/FCoE (SFP+)	Thirty-two (one 10 GE/FCoE per half-width slot)
Nexus 2232PP[1]	Eight 10 Gigabit Ethernet/FCoE (SFP+)	Thirty-two 10 GE/FCoE (SFP+)

[1] For UCS C-series rack-mountable servers (noninstallable in UCS 5108 chassis)

Cisco UCS B-Series Blade Servers

Cisco UCS B-series Blade Servers are Intel Xeon servers that can be accommodated into UCS 5100 chassis to integrate a UCS domain.

Since 2009, Cisco has released a great variety of B-series blade server models, as shown in Table A-14.

Table A-14 *UCS B-Series Server Models*

Model	Half- or Full-Width	CPU	Internal Hard Drives	Number of Mezzanine Cards	Memory DIMMs/ Maximum Memory
B200-M1	Half	2 (Xeon 5500)	2	1	12/96 GB
B230-M1	Half	2 (Xeon 6500 or 7500)	2	1	32/256 GB
B250-M1	Full	2 (Xeon 5500)	2	2	48/384 GB
B440-M1	Full	4 (Xeon 7500)	4	2	32/512 GB
B200-M2	Half	2 (Xeon 5600)	2	1	12/192 GB
B230-M2	Half	2 (Xeon E7-2800)	2	1	32/512 GB

Model	Half- or Full-Width	CPU	Internal Hard Drives	Number of Mezzanine Cards	Memory DIMMs/ Maximum Memory
B250-M2	Full	2 (Xeon 5600)	2	2	48/384 GB
B440-M2	Full	4 (Xeon E7-4800)	4	2	32/1 TB
B200-M3	Half	2 (Xeon E5-2600)	2	1	24/768 GB
B22-M3	Half	2 (Xeon E5-2400)	2	1	12/192 GB
B420-M2	Full	4 (Xeon E5-4600)	4	2	48/1.5 TB

Cisco UCS C-Series Rack Servers

Cisco UCS C-series Rack Servers are rack-mountable devices that can be part of a UCS domain or work as standalone servers. More specifically, UCS C-series servers can also address workloads that might depend on a higher number of PCIe adapters or internal storage resources.

Also based on Intel Xeon architecture, the variety of UCS C-series models is comparable to UCS B-series servers.

Table A-15 shows the released UCS C-series models.

Table A-15 *UCS C-Series Server Models*

Model	RU[1]	Number of Processors	Internal Hard Drives	PCIe Slots	Memory DIMMs/ Maximum Memory
C200-M1	1	2 (Xeon 5500)	4	2	12/96 GB
C210-M1	2	2 (Xeon 5500)	16	5	12/96 GB
C250-M1	2	2 (Xeon 5500)	8	5	48/384 GB
C460-M1	4	4 (Xeon 7500)	12	10	64/1 TB
C200-M2	1	2 (Xeon 5600)	4	2	12/192 GB
C210-M2	2	2 (Xeon 5600)	16	5	12/192 GB
C250-M2	2	2 (Xeon 5600)	8	5	48/384 GB
C260-M2	2	2 (Xeon E5-2800)	16	7	64/1 TB

Model	RU[1]	Number of Processors	Internal Hard Drives	PCIe Slots	Memory DIMMs/ Maximum Memory
C460-M2	4	4 (Xeon E7-4800 or E7-8800)	12	10	64/2 TB
C22-M3	1	2 (Xeon E5-2400)	8	2	12/192 GB
C24-M3	2	2 (Xeon E5-2400)	24	5	12/192 GB
C220-M3	1	2 (Xeon E5-2600)	8	2	16/512 GB
C240-M3	2	2 (Xeon E5-2600)	24	5	24/768 GB
C420-M3	2	4 (Xeon E5-4600)	16	7	48/1.5 TB

[1]Rack units

Cisco UCS Virtual Interface Cards

Besides commercializing and supporting adapters from other vendors (such as Intel, Emulex, QLogic, and Broadcom), Cisco has also designed its own line of UCS adapters.

Cisco virtual interface cards (VIC) can greatly facilitate "bare metal" and virtualization environments through the creation of virtual interfaces (network interface cards [NIC] or host bus adapters [HBA]) whose presence are identified by the server operating system as standard PCIe interfaces.

With such abstraction and high performance, Cisco VICs provide I/O management centralization, policy coherency, consistent network visibility, and practically any required server NIC and HBA configuration.

In addition, Cisco VICs can deploy dynamic vNIC interfaces for virtual machines (VM-FEX) and hypervisor bypass (pass-through switching) to optimize performance in server virtualization environments.

Table A-16 summarizes the distinct characteristics of Cisco virtual interface cards.

Table A-16 *Cisco UCS Virtual Interface Card Characteristics*

Model	Form Factor	Virtual Interfaces	Throughput (Gbps)	IOPs	Compatibility
M81KR	Mezzanine	128	20	600,000	B-series (M1 and M2)
P81E	PCIe	128	20	500,000	C-series
VIC 1225	PCIe	256	20	900,000	C-series (M2[2] and M3)
VIC 1240	Modular LOM	256	40–80[1]	900,000	B-series (M3 only)

Model	Form Factor	Virtual Interfaces	Throughput (Gbps)	IOPs	Compatibility
VIC 1280	Mezzanine	256	80	900,000	B-series (M2[3] and M3)

[1] With the use of a Port Expander Card in the optional mezzanine slot.

[2] C260-M2 and C460-M2.

[3] B200-M2, B230-M2, and B440-M2.

Note Eight virtual interfaces are reserved for internal use. Other factors, such as operating system, can limit this number further.

Although Cisco UCS VICs can deploy Single Root I/O Virtualization (SR-IOV), the creation of virtual interfaces in any VIC does not depend on the operating system support for SR-IOV. Furthermore, all VICs support Fabric Failover for their created virtual network interface cards (vNIC).

Unified Management Solutions

Cisco Unified Management solutions provide simplified management across converged data center and cloud computing infrastructures. Their graphical user interfaces (GUI) and wizards greatly facilitate the execution of complex and recurrent tasks in these environments.

Without exception, all Unified Management solutions deploy Role-Based Access Control (RBAC) to correctly restrict system resources to properly authorized administrators. This characteristic permits a less error-prone administration and an adequate distribution of tasks among operational teams.

Moreover, these solutions assume the role of "central command centers," having superior visibility over events, alarms, and performance status of distributed devices.

Cisco Application Network Manager

Cisco Application Network Manager (ANM) software offers consolidated management of Layer 4–7 network services. Essentially, Cisco ANM provides a unified interface for provisioning, operations, and monitoring of Cisco Application Control Engine (ACE) devices and ACE GSS.

Note Cisco ANM also supports operations management and monitoring for Cisco Content Services Switch (CSS), Content Switching Module (CSM), and Content Switching Module with SSL (CSM-S).

Cisco ANM is a key tool for virtual data centers that require network services such as server load balance and application optimization. Besides being available as a virtual appliance, ANM also integrates with VMware vSphere clusters through a vCenter plug-in. This software connection enables Layer 4–7 services provisioning and visibility to both ACE and vCenter administrators.

Cisco ANM is accessible through HTTP, HTTPS, and mobile apps for Apple iPhones and Android-based smartphones. A web services API offers a programmable interface for system developers to further extend Cisco ANM integration to other applications.

A single instance of Cisco ANM is designed to support up to

- 50 ACE physical devices (module or appliance)
- 40 other server load balancers from Cisco such as Content Services Switch (CSS), Content Switching Module (CSM), or Content Switching Module with SSL (CSM-S)
- Three clusters of ACE GSS

Cisco Prime Data Center Network Manager

Cisco Prime Data Center Network Manager (DCNM) provides a single pane of glass to Cisco Data Center Unified Fabric, which is comprised of Nexus and MDS 9000 switches.

> **Note** Cisco DCNM also manages Catalyst 6500 switches, and UCS 6100 and 6200 Fabric Interconnects.

Its graphical interface automates provisioning and proactively monitors LAN and SAN elements simultaneously, and its RBAC capabilities help further separate configuration of LAN and SAN networks on converged switches. Cisco DCNM authenticates administration through the following protocols: TACACS+, RADIUS, and LDAP.

Distinct LAN and SAN Java clients provide advanced monitoring and provisioning capabilities, while a web dashboard offers health and performance monitoring of a data center fabric. This dashboard allows network and storage administrators to quickly troubleshoot health and performance across the entire range of Cisco NX-OS devices.

Additionally, Cisco DCNM also deploys the following features:

- Automated discovery and topology views
- Event management and forwarding
- Web templates
- Performance and capacity planning
- Virtual machine path analysis for LAN and SAN

- Standard and customized reports
- Configuration and change management
- Device image management
- Web services APIs

This management solution can be deployed in Windows and Linux, or as a virtual service blade on Nexus 1010 or 1100. More Cisco DCNM servers can be added to a cluster to follow the growth of a network.

Cisco UCS Manager and UCS Central

Cisco UCS Manager (UCSM) provides a single point of management for a UCS domain defined by a pair of UCS Fabric Interconnects. Broadly speaking, Cisco UCSM uses service profiles, policies, pools, and templates to bring simplicity, uniformity, and speed to environments of up to 160 (blade or rack-mountable) servers. Residing on the Fabric Interconnects, UCSM can configure and manage the following elements of UCS (including firmware and settings):

- Fabric Interconnects
- I/O modules
- Servers
- Adapters

On the other hand, *Cisco UCS Central* allows the management of several UCS domains, enforcing resource pools and policies globally to be deployed locally.

In summary, Cisco UCS Central deploys the following features:

- CLI or GUI access
- Centralized inventory
- Centralized, policy-based firmware management
- Global ID pooling to eliminate identifier conflicts
- Global administrative policies
- XML API for integration with third-party management tools
- Domain grouping and subgrouping

UCS Central is available as a virtual appliance, and it is typically deployed in an active-standby configuration.

Virtual Network Management Center

Cisco Virtual Network Management Center (VNMC) provides centralized policy management for multiple Cisco network virtual devices. Cisco VNMC supports greater scalability, standardization, and consistent execution of policies across Cisco Nexus 1000V, Cisco ASA 1000V Cloud Firewall, and Cisco Virtual Security Gateway.

Through template-driven policies, Cisco VNMC enhances collaboration across security and server teams while maintaining administrative separation between them through RBAC (and using LDAP authentication).

Among other tasks, Cisco VNMC permits

- Configuration of edge firewalls
- Creation and application of edge security profiles that contain ACL policies (ingress and egress), connection timeout, NAT policies, TCP intercept, and so on
- Establishment of site-to-site IPsec VPNs

VNMC is accessible through a web GUI and is available through Open Virtualization Format (OVF) virtual appliance and ISO image.

Virtual Security Gateway

Cisco Virtual Security Gateway (VSG) is a virtual appliance that provides trusted access to secure server virtualization and cloud networks. Cisco VSG ensures that security zones are controlled within server virtualization clusters without losing the flexibility and scalability of such environments.

Intrinsically linked to Cisco Nexus 1000V, Cisco VSG uses vPath technology to offload subsequent traffic to the virtual switch, after the first packet of the communication is analyzed.

In summary, Cisco VSG provides the following features:

- Trusted access
- Dynamic operation
- Non-disruptive administration
- VXLAN awareness
- vPath service chaining to multiple virtual network services

VSG is available as an OVF virtual appliance or ISO file, which can be deployed as a virtual service blade on Cisco Nexus 1010 and 1100. At the time of this writing, a single VSG instance can support up to 256,000 concurrent connections and control up to 10,000 new connections per second.

Virtualization Techniques Mapping

Because the Cisco Data Center portfolio forms a fully integrated architecture, each product must deploy different features to perform distinct roles in a virtualized data center infrastructure.

To represent this framework at the time of this writing, Table A-17 summarizes the distribution of the virtualization techniques studied in this book over the Cisco Data Center products.

In the table, the symbol "![Cisco Systems]" represents that this product deploys the feature or is directly involved with its concept.

Further Reading

Unified Data Center Products: www.cisco.com/en/US/netsol/ns340/ns394/ns224/products.html

Data Center Application Services: www.cisco.com/go/ace

Cisco ASA 1000V Cloud Firewall: www.cisco.com/go/asa1000v

Cisco ASA 5500 Series Adaptive Security Appliances: www.cisco.com/go/asa

Cisco Catalyst 6500 Series Switches: www.cisco.com/go/6500

Cisco Cloud Portal: www.cisco.com/go/cloudportal

Storage Networking: www.cisco.com/go/mds

Network Analysis Module (NAM) Products: www.cisco.com/go/nam

Cisco Network Manager Services: www.cisco.com/go/nsm

Cisco Nexus 1000V Series Switches: www.cisco.com/go/nexus1000V

Cisco Nexus 1010 Virtual Services Appliance: www.cisco.com/go/nexus1010

Cisco Nexus 2000 Series Fabric Extenders: www.cisco.com/go/nexus2000

Cisco Nexus 3000 Series Switches: www.cisco.com/go/nexus3000

Cisco Nexus 4000 Series Switches: www.cisco.com/go/nexus4000

Cisco Nexus 5000 Series Switches: www.cisco.com/go/nexus5000

Cisco Nexus 6000 Series Switches: www.cisco.com/go/nexus6000

Cisco Nexus 7000 Series Switches: www.cisco.com/go/nexus7000

Unified Computing System: www.cisco.com/go/ucs

Unified Management Solutions: www.cisco.com/go/unifiedmanagement

Cisco Virtual Security Gateway for Nexus 1000V Series: www.cisco.com/go/vsg

Table A-17 *Virtualization Technologies in the Cisco Data Center Portfolio*

	VLAN	VRF	Context	VDC	FEX	vPC	EoMPLS	VPLS	OTV	VSAN	FCIP	IVR	NPV	FCoE	Service Profile	Virtual Switching	VM-FEX	Virtual Network Services
ACE	✓		✓															
ACE GSS																		
ASA 1000V	✓																	✓
ASA 5585-X	✓		✓															
Catalyst 6500	✓	✓					✓	✓										
Cisco Cloud Portal																		
Intelligent Automation Solutions																		
MDS 9000										✓	✓	✓	✓	✓				
Nexus 1000V	✓					✓										✓		✓
Nexus 1110	✓																	
Nexus 2000	✓				✓													
Nexus 3000	✓					✓												
Nexus 4000	✓																	
Nexus 5000	✓	✓			✓	✓				✓			✓	✓			✓	
Nexus 6000	✓	✓			✓	✓				✓			✓	✓			✓	
Nexus 7000	✓	✓		✓	✓	✓			✓	✓	✓	✓	✓	✓				
UCS	✓														✓		✓	
Unified Management Solutions																		
VSG	✓																	✓

Appendix B

IOS, NX-OS, and Application Control Software Command-Line Interface Basics

Cisco IOS Software is without a doubt the world's most deployed network operating system. With its pervasive presence in small office routers, wireless access points, campus switches, backbone routers, and many other Cisco devices, IOS has created a fully formed culture among network professionals. For that reason, the principles underlying the IOS command-line interface (CLI) are considered essential to the learning process of networking technologies.

Cisco NX-OS is the natural evolution of network operating systems for modern data center requirements (such as high availability, scalability, efficiency, and flexibility). Originated from SAN-OS, NX-OS is currently found on switches from both Cisco Nexus and MDS 9000 families.

Cisco Application Control Software (ACSW) has offered a similar development for Cisco Application Control Engine (ACE) load balancers. With advanced features, such as virtualization and extensibility, ACSW has established important foundations for the Cisco Data Center portfolio as a whole.

Both NX-OS and ACSW leverage IOS CLI interaction principles to accelerate learning and provide smooth deployments. Therefore, this appendix will introduce the basics of the IOS CLI and explore the main features of NX-OS and ACSW interfaces.

IOS Command-Line Interface Basics

There are several different ways to access the command-line interface of an IOS device. They are as follows:

- **Console interface:** Where a personal computer (equipped with a terminal emulation program) locally connects to an RS-232 serial interface on the device. The default settings of this connection are the traditional values of 9600 baud, 8 data bits, no parity, 1 stop bit, and no flow control.

- **Auxiliary interface:** Rarely used nowadays, this additional device port can be used in a serial modem connection.

- **Telnet:** A virtual terminal connection protocol that transports a bidirectional interactive text-oriented session between a client and a server. It uses TCP port 23 and was originally defined in RFC 15 (published in 1969). Telnet is popular enough to be used as a verb in IT conversations, and because of that, most computer operating systems deploy an embedded Telnet client.

- **Secure Shell (SSH):** A client-server application that also provides text-oriented interaction between two hosts, but within a secure channel that deploys authentication and cryptography. It uses TCP port 22 and was originally defined in RFCs 4250 to 4253 (published in 2006).

Generally speaking, the console connection is the only method available on an IOS device when it is turned on for the first time. The remaining methods require additional configurations, such as interface parameters or IP addresses.

Command Modes

The IOS CLI deploys distinct *modes* that can be recognized by an exclusive prompt. The main IOS command modes are

- **User EXEC:** This is the default mode for a CLI session. It accesses a more restrictive subset of commands when compared to other modes. This mode can perform basic tests and display system information, and can be identified through the **Router>** prompt (assuming that your IOS device is called "Router").

- **Privileged EXEC:** This offers access to all commands of a router and, for that reason, should be protected with a password to prevent unauthorized changes. You can recognize this mode with the **Router#** prompt.

- **Global Configuration:** This mode effectively configures parameters that will be applied to the IOS device as a whole. Its corresponding prompt is **Router(config)#**.

- **Subordinate Configuration:** This is used to configure parameters on an IOS element such as an interface (whose prompt is **Router(config-if)#**), routing protocol (which uses the **Router(config-router)#** prompt), among others.

Each command mode possesses commands that allow you to switch to other modes. Figure B-1 portrays such commands and illustrates exactly how they can be used in your navigation through the IOS command codes.

> **Note** Although some users might compare the IOS command modes to a file directory tree, I would not recommend that you go too far in such a comparison. As IOS implements actual directories for file management; I think it is better to not to link both concepts.

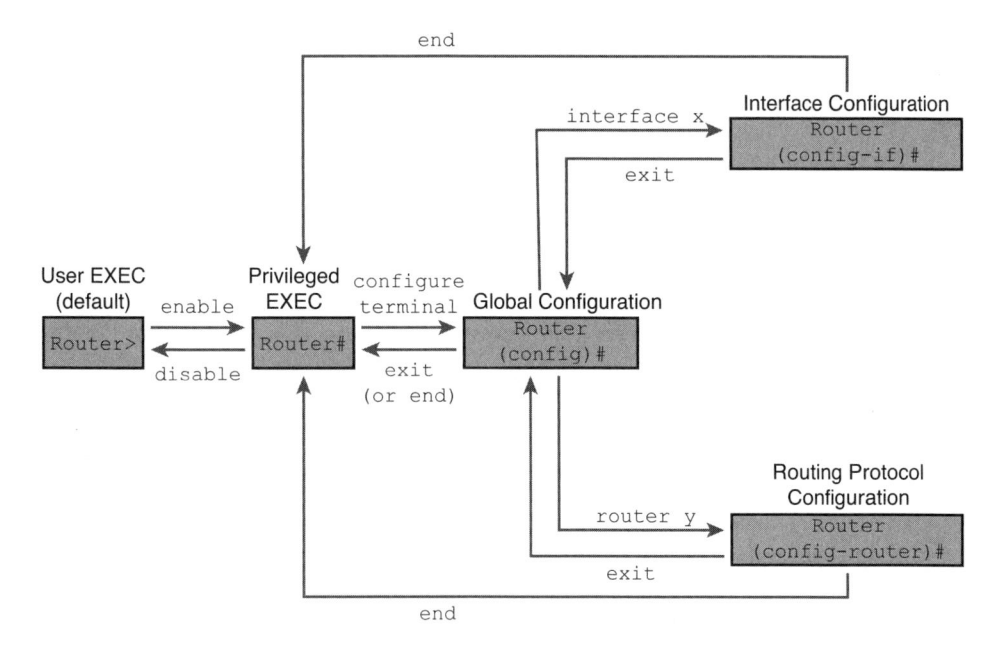

Figure B-1 *Changing Command IOS Modes*

Example B-1 illustrates these definitions through an IOS session of a user that is moving between command modes.

Example B-1 *Sample IOS User Session*

```
! Arriving at the User EXEC mode and going to privileged mode
Catalyst6500> enable
! An enable password was previously configured
Password:
! In the privileged mode you can go to the global configuration mode
Catalyst6500# configure terminal
Enter configuration commands, one per line. End with CNTL/Z.
! Here you can configure parameters for the whole device or access a
specific element such as GigabitEthernet interface 1 from slot 6
Catalyst6500(config)# interface GigabitEthernet 6/1
! Going back to the global configuration mode
Catalyst6500(config-if)# exit
! Entering RIP configuration
Catalyst6500(config)# router rip
! Going back to priviledged mode
Catalyst6500(config-router)# end
! And to user EXEC mode
```

```
Catalyst6500# disable
Catalyst6500>
```

Whenever an IOS device is turned on for the first time (or without a startup configuration file), it offers to the user an interactive setup script that can be used to establish basic connectivity. For example, this script can request

- Device name
- Enable passwords (encrypted and clear text)
- Virtual terminal passwords
- Simple Network Management Protocol (SNMP) configuration (such as communities)
- Management interface configuration (IP address, subnet mask)

Depending on your preference, you can simply skip the script or execute it later through the **setup** command in privileged mode.

Getting Context-Sensitive Help

As explained in the last section, different commands can be executed in each IOS command mode. If you are a little unsure about these commands or their syntax, I present your new best friend: the question mark (?), or simply the *help character*.

Whenever you type such a character, the IOS CLI provides you with a context-sensitive list of available commands that takes into account everything you have previously entered, as illustrated in Example B-2.

Tip In IOS, an output that surpasses the defined number of lines on a terminal screen demands that you press Enter (to show one more line of the output) or press the spacebar (to display an entirely new terminal screen). You can identify this situation with the message "--More--" and at any time you can interrupt the output by pressing the Ctrl+C key combination.

Example B-2 *Using the Help Character*

```
! Viewing the available commands in user EXEC mode (with a brief description)
Catalyst6500>?
Exec commands:
  access-enable    Create a temporary Access-List entry
  access-profile   Apply user-profile to interface
  clear            Reset functions
  connect          Open a terminal connection
  disable          Turn off privileged commands
```

```
  disconnect        Disconnect an existing network connection
  enable            Turn on privileged commands
  exit              Exit from the EXEC
  help              Description of the interactive help system
  lock              Lock the terminal
  login             Log in as a particular user
  logout            Exit from the EXEC
  mrinfo            Request neighbor and version information from a multicast
                    router
  mstat             Show statistics after multiple multicast traceroutes
  mtrace            Trace reverse multicast path from destination to source
  name-connection   Name an existing network connection
  pad               Open a X.29 PAD connection
  ping              Send echo messages
  ppp               Start IETF Point-to-Point Protocol (PPP)
  resume            Resume an active network connection
 --More--
! I have typed space here
  session           session to a module
  show              Show running system information
  slip              Start Serial-line IP (SLIP)
  ssh               Open a secure shell client connection
  systat            Display information about terminal lines
  telnet            Open a telnet connection
  terminal          Set terminal line parameters
  traceroute        Trace route to destination
  tunnel            Open a tunnel connection
  where             List active connections
  x3                Set X.3 parameters on PAD
! Entering privileged EXEC mode...
Catalyst6500> enable
Password:
! ...and asking for help
Catalyst6500# ?
! It is noticeable that the list of commands available in privileged
EXEC mode is much bigger than the user EXEC.
Exec commands:
  access-enable     Create a temporary Access-List entry
  access-profile    Apply user-profile to interface
  access-template   Create a temporary Access-List entry
  alps              ALPS exec commands
  archive           manage archive files
  attach            Connect to a module's console
  calendar          Manage the hardware calendar
  cd                Change current directory
```

```
  clear           Reset functions
  clock           Manage the system clock
  cns             CNS subsystem
  configure       Enter configuration mode
  connect         Open a terminal connection
  copy            Copy from one file to another
  debug           Debugging functions (see also 'undebug')
  delete          Delete a file
  diagnostic      Diagnostic commands
  dir             List files on a filesystem
  disable         Turn off privileged commands
  disconnect      Disconnect an existing network connection
  dot1x           Dot1x Exec Commands
--More--
! I have typed Control+C here. Now, let's enter the configuration mode.
Catalyst6500# configure terminal
Enter configuration commands, one per line. End with CNTL/Z.
Catalyst6500(config)# ?
! Now, you can visualize the available configuration commands
Configure commands:
  aaa                      Authentication, Authorization and Accounting.
  access-list              Add an access list entry
  aclmerge                 aclmerge hidden keyword
  alias                    Create command alias
  alps                     Configure Airline Protocol Support
  analysis                 Specify vlans and tie them to analysis modules
  anomaly-detector         Specify vlans and tie them to anomaly-detector
                           modules
  anomaly-guard            Specify vlans and tie them to anomaly-guard
                           modules
  arp                      Set a static ARP entry
[output suppressed]
! Entering interface configuration mode
Catalyst6500(config)# interface GigabitEthernet 6/1
! Checking the list of available interface configuration commands
Catalyst6500(config-if)# ?
Interface configuration commands:
  arp                Set arp type (arpa, probe, snap) or timeout
  backup             Modify backup parameters
  bandwidth          Set bandwidth informational parameter
  bgp-policy         Apply policy propogated by bgp community string
  bridge-group       Transparent bridging interface parameters
  carrier-delay      Specify delay for interface transitions
  cdp                CDP interface subcommands
  channel-group      Etherchannel/port bundling configuration
```

```
  channel-protocol        Select the channel protocol (LACP, PAgP)
[output suppressed]
```

As you can see in Example B-2, typing a question mark at the beginning of the line displays a list of available commands (along with a brief description of what each command comprises). Nevertheless, the help character can also be used to explore command syntax, as Example B-3 shows.

Example B-3 *Discovering Command Syntax*

```
! Identifying which interface configuration commands start with "i"
Catalyst6500(config-if)# i?
ip   isis   iso-igrp
! Displaying the list of commands that can be entered after the word "ip"
Catalyst6500(config-if)# ip ?
Interface IP configuration subcommands:
  access-group   Specify access control for packets
  address        Set the IP address of an interface
  arp            Configure ARP features
  dhcp           DHCP
  rsvp           RSVP interface commands
  rtp            RTP parameters
  vrf            VPN Routing/Forwarding parameters on the interface

! Discovering the IOS accepted format for IP address...
Catalyst6500(config-if)# ip address ?
  A.B.C.D   IP address
! ... and the subnet mask
Catalyst6500(config-if)# ip address 10.1.1.1 ?
! Configuring interface GigabitEthernet 6/1 with an IP address
Catalyst6500(config-if)# ip address 10.1.1.1 255.255.255.0
Catalyst6500(config-if)#
```

As shown in Example B-3, the type of help output depends on the exact placement of question mark in the command line. This example mirrors how IOS users usually explore the syntax of a command and also demonstrates how the IOS CLI facilitates user interaction.

Tip To undo the action of a command, you can use the word **no** before the entered command. For example, **no ip address** removes the IP address interface configuration from Example B-3.

Abbreviating Commands and Using Shortcuts

IOS also provides several improvements to speed user interaction. For example, a user does not need to type the entire command to have it recognized by IOS. In fact, IOS only requires the minimum amount of characters that unambiguously define a command.

To clarify the last statement, Example B-4 depicts yet another IOS CLI user session.

Example B-4 *Abbreviating Commands*

```
! In privileged EXEC mode there are two commands that start with "con"
Catalyst6500# con?
configure  connect
! Typing "conf", IOS recognizes that you want to execute command
"configure" since it is the only command that starts with these
characters
Catalyst6500# conf ?
  memory             Configure from NV memory
  network            Configure from a TFTP network host
  overwrite-network  Overwrite NV memory from TFTP network host
  terminal           Configure from the terminal
  <cr>

! Typing "conf t", IOS recognizes that you want to execute the
"configure terminal" command
Catalyst6500# conf t
Enter configuration commands, one per line.  End with CNTL/Z.
Catalyst6500(config)#
```

Additionally, IOS acknowledges special keys and combinations that allow faster deployment of commands. The following list compiles some of these "shortcuts":

- **Tab:** Completes the command or advances to the last similar character (if there is still ambiguity).
- **Ctrl+Z:** Executes the contents of a line in any configuration mode and exits to the privileged EXEC mode.
- **Ctrl+A:** Moves the cursor to the start of the line.
- **Ctrl+E:** Moves the cursor to the end of the line.
- **Left arrow:** Moves the cursor to the left.
- **Right arrow:** Moves the cursor to the right.

- **Backspace:** Erases the character to the left of the cursor.
- **Up arrow:** Displays previously entered commands in reverse chronological order.
- **Down arrow:** Displays previously entered commands in chronological order.

Although there are many other shortcuts, each IOS user commonly assembles a *toolkit* that contains his preferred shortcuts. Because the previous list is my basic toolkit, you are welcome to refer to Cisco documentation to build your own (and brag about it in water-cooler chats).

Additionally, IOS offers the **do** command to avoid constant switching between the configuration and privileged EXEC modes. In summary, it signals to IOS that you are about to type an EXEC mode command while you are still in the configuration mode.

Example B-5 illustrates the use of the **do** command.

Example B-5 *Accessing Privileged EXEC Commands in Configuration Mode*

```
Catalyst6500# configure terminal
Enter configuration commands, one per line.  End with CNTL/Z.
! Configuring multiple interfaces simultaneously
Catalyst6500(config)# interface range Gi6/1 - 2
! Unsuccessfully trying to access display interface status in global configuration
mode
Catalyst6500(config-if-range)# show interface Gi6/1
                              ^
% Invalid input detected at '^' marker.
! Successfully executing the same command
Catalyst6500(config-if-range)# do show interface Gi6/1
GigabitEthernet6/1 is up, line protocol is up (connected)
  Hardware is C6k 1000Mb 802.3, address is 0011.21b9.9d68 (bia 0011.21b9.9d68)
[output suppressed]
```

Managing Configuration Files

When managing an IOS device, you need to be aware of two configuration files: *running config* and *startup config*.

The running config file contains all the commands that are currently applied to the IOS device. To visualize this configuration file, you can use the **show running-config** command (or an abbreviated **sh run**) in privileged EXEC mode.

Example B-6 demonstrates a short excerpt of the running config file on a Catalyst 6500 switch.

Example B-6 *Displaying Running Configuration File*

```
Catalyst6500# show running-config
Building configuration...

Current configuration : 25741 bytes
!
! Last configuration change at 10:54:51 BRA Sat Nov 3 2012
!
version 12.2
service timestamps debug uptime
service timestamps log uptime
no service password-encryption
service counters max age 10
!
hostname Catalyst6500
!
boot system sup-bootflash:s72033-pk9sv-mz.122-18.SXD6.bin
boot system flash disk0:s72033-ipservices_wan-mz.122-33.SXH2a.bin
logging console informational
no logging monitor
enable secret [suppressed]
enable password cisco
 [output suppressed]
```

The **show running-config** command also has subcommands that can select specific parts of the running config file, as shown in Example B-7.

Example B-7 *Displaying Parts of the Running Configuration File*

```
! Discovering the available subcommands for the show running-config command
Catalyst6500# show running-config ?
  brief       configuration without certificate data
  full        full configuration
  interface   Show interface configuration
  map-class   Show map class information
  module      Show module configuration
  vlan        Show L2 VLAN information
  |           Output modifiers
  <cr>
! Displaying the running configuration of a specific interface
Catalyst6500# show running-config interface vlan 390
Building configuration...
```

Appendix B: IOS, NX-OS, and Application Control Software Command-Line Interface Basics 857

```
Current configuration : 80 bytes
!
interface Vlan390
 ip address 10.97.39.231 255.255.255.0
 ip nat outside
end
```

The *vertical bar* (|) is another option that displays parts of the running config file (or any other IOS command output).

Example B-8 illustrates how this special character allows content filtering of large outputs based on a given string.

Example B-8 *Using the Vertical Bar Character for Output Filtering*

```
! Discovering what options are available with the vertical bar character
Catalyst6500# show running-config | ?
  begin    Begin with the line that matches
  exclude  Exclude lines that match
  include  Include lines that match
! Displaying all the lines from the running-config file that contains the string
"enable"
Catalyst6500# show running-config | include enable
enable secret [suppressed]
enable password cisco
Catalyst6500#
```

On the other hand, the startup config file represents the configuration that should be loaded whenever an IOS device is reinitiated. As a result, if you want to maintain the settings you have just made across reboots, it is recommended that you save your configuration in the device's *nonvolatile RAM (NVRAM)*.

In IOS, there are two commands that can be used to save the running config file: **write memory** (which belongs to previous IOS generations) and **copy running-config startup-config**. I will explore the latter command because it is a more flexible tool for file management.

Example B-9 shows the saving of a running configuration to the NVRAM and an exploration of other **copy** command options.

Example B-9 *Saving Running Configuration and Exploring Copy Options*

```
! Saving the running-config file to the NVRAM
Catalyst6500# copy running-config startup-config
Building configuration...
! Displaying the source options for the copy command
```

```
Catalyst6500# copy ?
  /erase            Erase destination file system.
  /noverify         Don't verify image signature before reload.
  /verify           Verify image signature before reload.
  bootflash:        Copy from bootflash: file system
  const_nvram:      Copy from const_nvram: file system
  disk0:            Copy from disk0: file system
  disk1:            Copy from disk1: file system
  ftp:              Copy from ftp: file system
  null:             Copy from null: file system
  nvram:            Copy from nvram: file system
  rcp:              Copy from rcp: file system
  running-config    Copy from current system configuration
  scp:              Copy from scp: file system
  startup-config    Copy from startup configuration
  sup-bootflash:    Copy from sup-bootflash: file system
  sup-microcode:    Copy from sup-microcode: file system
  system:           Copy from system: file system
  tftp:             Copy from tftp: file system
! Diplaying the destination options for the running-config file
Catalyst6500# copy running-config ?
  bootflash:        Copy to bootflash: file system
  const_nvram:      Copy to const_nvram: file system
  disk0:            Copy to disk0: file system
  disk1:            Copy to disk1: file system
  ftp:              Copy to ftp: file system
  null:             Copy to null: file system
  nvram:            Copy to nvram: file system
  rcp:              Copy to rcp: file system
  running-config    Update (merge with) current system configuration
  scp:              Copy to scp: file system
  startup-config    Copy to startup configuration
  sup-bootflash:    Copy to sup-bootflash: file system
  sup-image:        Copy to sup-image: file system
  system:           Copy to system: file system
  tftp:             Copy to tftp: file system
```

As a result, the **copy** command also permits the running config file to be transferred to a remote server (through FTP, SCP, or TFTP) or to a PCMCIA card.

Using Debug Commands

Debug commands are extremely useful when you want to analyze a behavior or troubleshoot problems in your network device. If desired, these commands are capable to provide packet-level information of selected IOS services.

Whenever you want to receive debug information about a specific part of an IOS subsystem, all you need to do is type its corresponding **debug** command. And if you are using a Telnet or SSH session, you must also enable remote monitoring through the **terminal monitor** command.

To disable the **debug** command, you must type its *doppelganger* **undebug** command or simply **undebug all** (which disables every single **debug** command).

Example B-10 shows an execution of a **debug** command and its removal.

Example B-10 *Debugging and Undebugging*

```
! Enabling Address Resolution Protocol (ARP) debugging
Catalyst6500# debug arp
ARP packet debugging is on
! Enabling monitoring through a remote session
Catalyst6500# terminal monitor
6d03h: IP ARP: rcvd req src 10.97.37.180 0050.569a.0032, dst 10.97.37.181 Vlan370
6d03h: IP ARP: rcvd req src 10.97.37.58 0011.21ff.862d, dst 10.97.37.106 Vlan370
6d03h: IP ARP: rcvd req src 10.97.37.142 0050.569a.0077, dst 10.97.37.100 Vlan370
6d03h: IP ARP: rcvd req src 10.97.37.100 0050.569a.0022, dst 10.97.37.142 Vlan370
! Disabling ARP debugging
Catalyst6500# undebug arp
ARP packet debugging is off
! Disabling all active debugging
Catalyst6500# undebug all
All possible debugging has been turned off
```

Tip Typing **undebug all** before any debug activation can be quite handy if the debug output is very "intense." In this case, you can quickly access this command through the up-arrow key.

NX-OS Command-Line Interface

From a CLI standpoint, NX-OS is *very* similar to IOS, including abbreviations and shortcuts. With this conscious design decision, Cisco has leveraged years of IOS CLI user experience to this data center network operating system.

Through IOS user feedback, Cisco has also included several interaction improvements to the NX-OS CLI. These enhancements will be the subject of the following sections.

NX-OS Access

The CLI access methods to an NX-OS device differs a little from IOS devices. For example:

- Before an NX-OS user can execute any command, he **must** be authenticated through a login name and password.
- The NX-OS setup script demands the creation of a password for a predefined user (*admin*) who has full entitlement over the device configuration.
- Telnet is not enabled in the setup script by default, leaving SSH as the standard remote CLI access method.
- NX-OS does not have a User EXEC command mode. An authenticated NX-OS user will always start its session in the privileged EXEC mode.

Example B-11 portrays some of these characteristics in a sample NX-OS CLI user session.

Example B-11 *NX-OS Access*

```
! Accessing a NX-OS switch through and SSH client and authenticating the admin user
User Access Verification
Nexus5000 login: admin
Password:
Cisco Nexus Operating System (NX-OS) Software
TAC support: http://www.cisco.com/tac
Copyright (c) 2002-2012, Cisco Systems, Inc. All rights reserved.
The copyrights to certain works contained in this software are
owned by other third parties and used and distributed under
license. Certain components of this software are licensed under
the GNU General Public License (GPL) version 2.0 or the GNU
Lesser General Public License (LGPL) Version 2.1. A copy of each
such license is available at
http://www.opensource.org/licenses/gpl-2.0.php and
http://www.opensource.org/licenses/lgpl-2.1.php
! User default command mode is privileged EXEC
Nexus5000# show user-account
user:admin
        this user account has no expiry date
        roles:network-admin
```

In Example B-11, you can observe that NX-OS has a different default posture concerning security when compared to IOS (which is a clear sign of our times).

NX-OS Modularity

NX-OS is a modular network operating system. For that reason, its kernel supports several categories of system modules that are generically represented in Figure B-2.

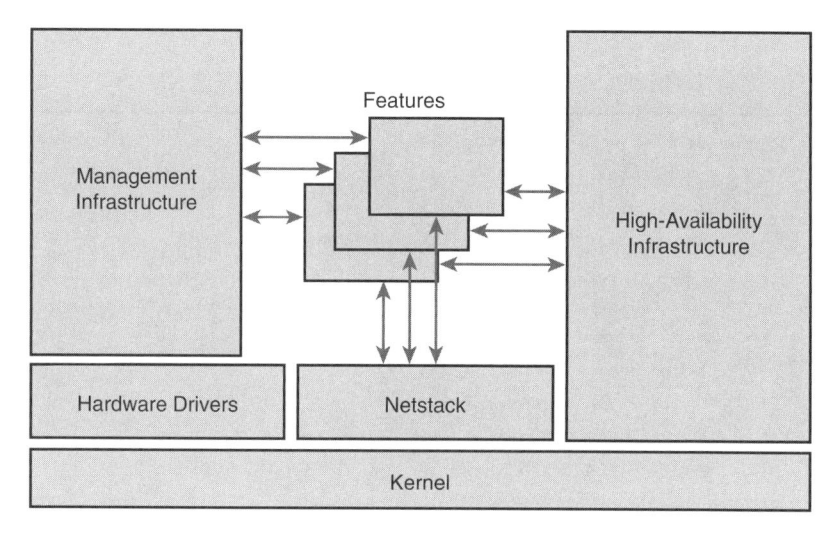

Figure B-2 *NX-OS Modular Architecture*

As shown in Figure B-2, the *NX-OS kernel* provides the basis of the entire network operating system. This fundamental module is based on Linux version 2.6, which is widely deployed because of its balance of advanced features, maturity, and stability.

Other NX-OS modules run over its kernel, such as

- **Hardware-dependent modules:** Varies from platform to platform and provides hardware abstraction for the kernel.

- **Netstack:** Provides shared networking capabilities including Layer 2, 3, and 4 properties.

- **Features:** Modules that support specific services such as routing protocols, Fibre Channel over Ethernet, and so on.

- **High-availability infrastructure:** Offers monitoring and state information for feature modules.

- **Management infrastructure:** Deploys the NX-OS interaction with external systems through SNMP, XML, and our object of study, the CLI.

Using this modular architecture, NX-OS can securely manage each feature module. And for that reason, an NX-OS user must initialize nondefault services with the **feature** command.

Example B-12 shows the NX-OS features that can be activated on a Nexus 5000 switch. This example also portrays the activation of a specific feature (TACACS+).

Example B-12 *Discovering Available Features Modules and Activating TACACS+*

```
Nexus5000(config)# feature ?
  bgp                    Enable/Disable Border Gateway Protocol (BGP)
  dhcp                   Enable/Disable DHCP Snooping
  eigrp                  Enable/Disable Enhanced Interior Gateway Routing
                         Protocol (EIGRP)
  fabric-binding         Enable/Disable Fabric Binding
  fc-port-security       Enable/Disable FC port-security
  fcoe                   Enable/Disable FCoE/FC feature
  fcoe-npv               Enable/Disable FCoE NPV feature
  fcsp                   Enable/Disable FC-SP
  fex                    Enable/Disable FEX
  flexlink               Enable/Disable Flexlink
  fport-channel-trunk    Enable/Disable Trunking F Ports and channels
  hsrp                   Enable/Disable Hot Standby Router Protocol (HSRP)
  http-server            Enable/Disable http-server
  interface-vlan         Enable/Disable interface vlan
  lacp                   Enable/Disable LACP
  msdp                   Enable/Disable Multicast Source Discovery Protocol
                         (MSDP)
  npiv                   Enable/Disable Nx port Id Virtualization (NPIV)
  npv                    Enable/Disable FC N_port Virtualizer
  ntp                    Enable/Disable NTP
  ospf                   Enable/Disable Open Shortest Path First Protocol (OSPF)
  ospfv3                 Enable/Disable Open Shortest Path First Version 3
                         Protocol (OSPFv3)
  pim                    Enable/Disable Protocol Independent Multicast (PIM)
  port-security          Enable/Disable port-security
  port-track             Enable/Disable port track feature
  private-vlan           Enable/Disable private-vlan
  privilege              Enable/Disable IOS type privilege level support
  ptp                    Enable/Disable PTP
  rip                    Enable/Disable Routing Information Protocol (RIP)
  ssh                    Enable/Disable ssh
  tacacs+                Enable/Disable tacacs+
  telnet                 Enable/Disable telnet
  udld                   Enable/Disable UDLD
```

```
    vpc                      Enable/Disable VPC (Virtual Port Channel)
    vrrp                     Enable/Disable Virtual Router Redundancy Protocol (VRRP)
    vtp                      Enable/Disable Vlan Trunking Protocol (VTP)
! Activating the TACACS+ feature module
Nexus5000(config)# feature tacacs+
```

Such system granularity also means that licenses are required to activate some features. In NX-OS, a license is activated through the **install license** command. If a proper feature license is not installed, the feature will be activated for a grace period of 120 days.

NX-OS and Running Configuration Files

Although it uses the very same **show running-config** command as IOS, NX-OS offers added flexibility to display a device's running configuration, as illustrated in Example B-13.

Example B-13 *Discovering show running-config Options*

```
Nexus5000# show running-config ?
  <CR>
  >                    Redirect it to a file
  >>                   Redirect it to a file in append mode
  aaa                  Display aaa configuration
  acllog               Show running config for acllog
  aclmgr               Show running config for aclmgr
  adjmgr               Display adjmgr information
  all                  Current operating configuration with defaults
  arp                  Display arp information
  assoc                Original ID to Translated ID Association
  callhome             Display callhome configuration
  cdp                  Display cdp configuration
  cert-enroll          Display certificates configuration
  cfs                  Display cfs configurations
  diagnostic           Display diagnostic information
  diff                 Show the difference between running and startup
                       configuration
  exclude              Exclude running configuration of specified features
  exclude-provision    Hide config for offline pre-provisioned interfaces
  expand-port-profile  Expand port profile
  fcoe_mgr             Display fcoe_mgr configuration
  fex                  Show running config of fex
  icmpv6               Display icmpv6 information
  igmp                 Display igmp information
```

include-switch-profile	Show running and switch-profile configuration
interface	Interface configuration
ip	Display ip information
ipqos	Show running config for ipqosmgr
ipv6	Display ipv6 information
l3vm	Display l3vm information
license	Display licensing configuration
lldp	Display lldp configuration
monitor	Configure Ethernet SPAN sessions
ntp	Show NTP information
port-profile	Display port-profile configuration
proxy	Show running-config for hardware proxy
radius	Display radius configuration
routing	Display routing information
rpm	Display Route Policy Manager (RPM) information
security	Display security configuration
snmp	Display snmp configuration
spanning-tree	Show spanning tree information
switch-profile	Show switch-profile information
track	Show track running configuration
vdc-all	Display config from all VDC
vlan	Vlan commands
vrf	Display VRF information
vshd	Show running config for vshd
wwnm	Display WWN Manager running configuration
zone	Display zone server running configuration
|	Pipe command output to filter

Comparing Examples B-7 and B-13, you can see that NX-OS offers a larger variety of **show running-config** outputs. For example, you can visualize the difference between running config and startup config files before saving the former to NVRAM. Additionally, the **all** option can reveal the default configurations for a feature.

Both improvements are shown in Example B-14.

Example B-14 *Comparing Configuration Files and Displaying Running Configuration Defaults*

```
! Displaying the differences between running-config and startup-config
Nexus5000# show running-config diff
*** Startup-config
--- Running-config
***************
! Defines the range of lines where the difference occurs in the startup-config file
```

```
*** 5,14 ****
! Defines the range of lines where the difference occurs in the running-config file
--- 4,14 ----

  version 5.2(1)N1(1)
  feature fcoe
  hostname Nexus5000
  feature telnet
! And here is the additional command in the running configuration
+ feature tacacs+
  feature lldp
  feature fex
  role feature-group name FC-Features
    feature fcns
    feature fcsp
! Visualizing only the TACACS+ running configuration
Nexus5000# show running-config tacacs+

!Command: show running-config tacacs+
!Time: [suppressed]

version 5.2(1)N1(1)
feature tacacs+

! Visualizing only the TACACS+ running configuration including default commands
Nexus5000# show running-config tacacs+ all

!Command: show running-config tacacs+ all
!Time: [suppressed]

version 5.2(1)N1(1)
feature tacacs+

no ip tacacs source-interface
tacacs-server test username test password test idle-time 0
tacacs-server timeout 5
tacacs-server deadtime 0
```

Tip You must use the **copy running-config startup-config** command to save the running configuration file to NVRAM (the **write memory** command is not available on NX-OS).

Whenever you disable a feature, NX-OS gets rid of all traces of its configuration in the running config file, as shown in Example B-15.

Example B-15 *Disabling a Feature*

```
! Disabling the TACACS+ feature
Nexus5000(config)# no feature tacacs+
Nexus5000(config)# exit
! As a result, the running configuration file does not have any TACACS+ command
Nexus5000# show running-config | include tacacs
Nexus5000#
```

NX-OS Command-Line Interface Optimizations

Cisco has included productivity enhancements in NX-OS to further the experience of its CLI users. For example:

- NX-OS does not require the **do** command to access an EXEC command in configuration mode.

- Command outputs can be further filtered with the **grep**, **wc** (word count), and other options.

- It is not necessary to include the **range** option to simultaneously configure multiple interfaces. The interface range can also be defined in ascending or descending order.

- When configuring subnet masks for IP, you can choose between two formats: **/xx** or **xxx.xxx.xxx.xxx**.

- VLAN ranges can also be configured in ascending or descending order.

- The **show interface** command displays the reason for failure (for example, transceiver not present).

Configuration Version Management, Batches, and Scripts

The NX-OS CLI deploys mechanisms that enable a higher control and efficiency on configuration changes, such as:

- Configuration checkpoints
- Configuration sessions
- Scheduled scripts

Configuration checkpoints are snapshots of the running config file that can be reactivated if necessary. These checkpoints can be extremely useful when a new change is being tested and an immediate return to a "stable" configuration state is necessary if a problem occurs.

These configuration snapshots are created with the **checkpoint** command, and their repurposing depends on the execution of a **rollback** command.

Example B-16 illustrates the creation and rollback to a configuration checkpoint in a Nexus 7000 switch.

Example B-16   *Checkpoint Creation and Rollback*

```
! Creating configuration checkpoint
Nexus7000# checkpoint OPEN
................................Done
! Disabling feature Telnet
Nexus7000# configure terminal
Enter configuration commands, one per line.  End with CNTL/Z.
Nexus7000(config)# no feature telnet
Nexus7000(config)# exit
! Verifying that the running configuration file does not contain any telnet command
Nexus7000# show running-config | include telnet
! Reactivating configuration defined with the checkpoint
Nexus7000# rollback running-config checkpoint OPEN
Note: Applying config parallelly may fail Rollback verification
Collecting Running-Config
#Generating Rollback Patch
Executing Rollback Patch
Generating Running-config for verification
Generating Patch for verification
Verification is Sucessful.

Rollback completed successfully.
! Due to the rollback, Telnet is active again
Nexus7000# show running-config | include telnet
feature telnet
```

NX-OS also allows several configuration commands to be executed in sequence as a batch in a *configuration session*. After such a session is created, its sequence of configuration commands can be executed with a single **commit** operation (which can be quite useful in tight change windows).

Example B-17 illustrates the creation of a configuration session that deploys a simple IP access list into ten interfaces on a Nexus 5000 switch.

Note At the time of this writing, NX-OS can only use these sessions for access list configurations.

Example B-17 *Configuration Session*

```
! Creating configuration session
Nexus5000# configure session BLOCK
Config Session started, Session ID is 1
Enter configuration commands, one per line.  End with CNTL/Z.
! Including commands that define the ordered batch
Nexus5000(config-s)# ip access-list PROTOCOLS
Nexus5000(config-s-acl)# permit tcp any any eq ftp
Nexus5000(config-s-acl)# permit tcp any any eq ftp-data
Nexus5000(config-s-acl)# permit tcp any any eq www
Nexus5000(config-s-acl)# exit
Nexus5000(config-s)# interface ethernet 1/10-20
Nexus5000(config-s-if-range)# ip access-group PROTOCOLS in
Nexus5000(config-s-if-range)# ip access-group PROTOCOLS out
Nexus5000(config-s-if-range)# end
! Verifying the configuration session contents and order
Nexus5000# show configuration session

config session BLOCK
0001   ip access-list PROTOCOLS
0002   permit tcp any any eq ftp
0003   permit tcp any any eq ftp-data
0004   permit tcp any any eq www
0005   ip access-group PROTOCOLS in
0006   ip access-group PROTOCOLS out

Number of active configuration sessions = 1
! Executing the batch
Nexus5000# configure session BLOCK
Config Session started, Session ID is 1
Enter configuration commands, one per line.  End with CNTL/Z.
Nexus5000(config-s)# commit
Verification successful...
Proceeding to apply configuration. This might take a while depending on amount of
configuration in buffer.
Please avoid other configuration changes during this time.
Commit Successful
! Checking to see if the configuration was correctly executed
Nexus5000# show running-config interface ethernet 1/10
[output suppressed]
```

```
interface Ethernet1/10
  ip access-group PROTOCOLS in
  ip access-group PROTOCOLS out
```

On selected platforms, NX-OS permits the planned execution command scripts through the *scheduler feature*. This service enables the creation and scheduled execution of jobs, which can contain EXEC and configuration commands.

As an illustration, Example B-18 deals with a very simple job that is scheduled to zero all interface statistics every day at 11:59 p.m.

Example B-18 *Scheduled Clearing of Interfaces Counters*

```
! Creating a job that clears all the interface counters on the switch
Nexus7000(config)# scheduler job name CLEAR-INTERFACE-STATISTICS
Nexus7000(config-job)# clear counters interface all
Nexus7000(config-job)# exit
! Creating the schedule for the job
Nexus7000(config)# scheduler schedule name ALMOST-MIDNIGHT
Nexus7000(config-schedule)# job name CLEAR-INTERFACE-STATISTICS
Nexus7000(config-schedule)# time daily 23:59
Nexus7000(config-schedule)# end
! Verifying the job characteristics
Nexus7000# show scheduler schedule
Schedule Name       : ALMOST-MIDNIGHT
-----------------------------
User Name           : admin
Schedule Type       : Run every day at 23 Hrs 59 Mins
Last Execution Time : Yet to be executed
-----------------------------------------------
     Job Name            Last Execution Status
-----------------------------------------------
    CLEAR-INTERFACE-STATISTICS            -NA-
==============================================================================
```

The scheduler feature can also be used for more meaningful tasks, such as:

- Quality of service policy changes
- Data backup
- Configuration saving

Application Control Software Command-Line Interface

The ACSW CLI sits between IOS and NX-OS both chronologically and in terms of CLI enhancements. Hence, while it shares the same shortcuts and tricks as IOS, it also has some of the security requirements that are native to NX-OS.

Similarly to NX-OS, ACSW does not have a user EXEC mode either, because an authenticated user is sent directly into the device privileged mode. Also, both of them have default users called *admin* that have total control over the device and whose password must be created during the initial setup.

Tip By default, ACSW is accessible through a console or internal chassis session (depending on the hardware you are deploying). Telnet, SSH, and other protocols are allowed (per context) through the use of management policy maps.

To better assist load-balancing configuration tasks, ACSW allows the use of the help character over the user-created objects (such as access lists, contexts, class maps, interfaces, parameter maps, policy maps, health probes, real servers, scripts, and sticky groups). The Tab key can also complete the object or command name or advance to the last similar character (if the ambiguity remains).

Example B-19 demonstrates these characteristics in a sample ACSW user session.

Example B-19 *ACSW CLI Object Handling*

```
! Displaying all the user-created ACE contexts through the help character
ACE4700/Admin# changeto ?
  ACE-EXCESS
  ACE-SITE-A
  ACE-SITE-B
  Admin
! Entering ACE context ACE-SITE-A
ACE4700/Admin# changeto ACE-SITE-A
ACE4700/ACE-SITE-A# configure terminal
Enter configuration commands, one per line.  End with CNTL/Z.
! Displaying all the user-created ACE contexts through the help character
ACE4700/ACE-SITE-A(config)# rserver ?
  <WORD>    Enter the name of the host rserver object (Max Size - 64)
  host      Specifies the current rserver as host server (default)
  redirect  Specifies the current rserver as redirect rserver
  SERVER01
  SERVER02
! Typing Tab after the "S"
```

Appendix B: IOS, NX-OS, and Application Control Software Command-Line Interface Basics

```
ACE4700/ACE-SITE-A(config)# rserver S
SERVER01   SERVER02
ACE4700/ACE-SITE-A(config)# rserver SERVER0
```

As IOS, Cisco Application Control Software does not permit the direct execution of EXEC commands in configuration mode. Consequently in this mode, the **do** command must be included before the EXEC commands, as shown in Example B-20.

Example B-20 *Commands in ACSW Configuration Mode*

```
! Entering configuration mode
ACE4700/ACE-SITE-A# configure terminal
Enter configuration commands, one per line.  End with CNTL/Z.
! Trying an EXEC command...
ACE4700/ACE-SITE-A(config)# show running-config
                                ^
% invalid command detected at '^' marker.
! And actually executing it
ACE4700/ACE-SITE-A(config)# do show running-config
Generating configuration....

access-list ANYONE line 8 extended permit tcp any any

probe http GET-INDEX
  expect status 200 200

rserver host SERVER01
  ip address 192.168.20.2
  probe GET-INDEX
  inservice
rserver host SERVER02
  ip address 192.168.20.3
  probe GET-INDEX
  inservice
[output suppressed]
```

Index

NUMERICS

100GBASE-SR4, 32
10BASE5 (Thicknet), 27
10GBASE2 (Thinnet), 27
10 Gigabit Ethernet, 497
40GBASE-SR4, 32

A

AAA (authentication, authorization, and accounting), 171
abstraction, cloud computing, 786
acceleration, applications, 58, 129, 763-771
accelerators, 111
ACCEPT message, 427
access
   broad network, 794
   core-aggregation-access, 36
   core-distribution-access, 34
   firmware policies, 633
   layers, 35
   lists, 164
        See also ACLs

load balancers, 114
MAC (Media Access Control), 51
NUMA (Non-Uniform Memory Access), 566
ports, 390
promiscuous access interfaces, 81
RBAC (Role-Based Access Control), 171
rules (Cisco ASA 1000V), 761
servers
   models, 287-291
   Unified Fabric designs, 536-542
storage, 391-399
   block-based, 392-397
   files, 397-398
   interfaces, 495
   mainframe, 396-397
   records, 398-399
switches, 38
UCS Manager, 590
unified access servers
   deployment, 509-523
   designs, 542-545
virtual contexts (ACE) management, 171-176

access

access-aggregation connections, 38
access control lists. *See* ACLs
accounts, user configuration, 175
ACE (Appliance Control Engine), 185
   connections, 141-144
   virtual contexts
      configuration, 163-171
      controlling management access, 171-176
      fault tolerance, 177-178
      integrating, 156-161
      multitenant data centers, 179-181
      resource allocation, 145-156
      sharing VLANs, 177
ACE (Application Control Engine), 109
   application networking services, 111
   classification, 110
   load balancers, 111-134
   physical connections, 141-145
   virtual contexts, 139-178
ACLs (access control lists), 380
   attributes, 752
   security policies, creating, 745
   virtual networks, 692
activation
   physical servers, 581
   servers, provisioning, 583-585
active-active greenfield data centers, 382-384
Active Directory. *See* AD
active nodes, 325
active-standby dual-homed topologies, 309
AD (Active Directory), 398
Adaptable Modular Storage. *See* AMS
adapters

firmware policies, 634
network convergence, 509
Adaptive Security Appliances. *See* ASAs
Adaptive Security Device Manager. *See* ASDM
addresses
   FCIDs (Fibre Channel Identifiers), 429
   Fibre Channel, 413-415
   IP (Internet Protocol)
      assigning, 59
      Layer 4/Layer 7 switches, 120
      management, 610
      virtualization clusters, 668
      VSG (Virtual Security Gateway), 752
   LBAs (Logical Block Addresses), 394
   load balancer translation, 124-127
   LUNs (logical unit numbers), 393
   MAC (Media Access Control), 51, 581
      BPDU frames, 65
      FabricPath, 331
      flooding, 340
      FPMA (Fabric-Provided MAC Address), 508
      learned in MPLS, 346
      OTV (Overlay Transport Virtualization), 355
      service profiles, 587
      sharing resources, 85
      SPMA (Server-Provided MAC Address), 508
      tables, 691
   NAT (Network Address Translation), 466
   overlapping, 87-89
   pWWN (port world wide name), 465

appliances 875

remapping, 17
URLs (Uniform Resource Locators), 116
VIP (virtual IP), 116
Address Resolution Protocol. *See* **ARP**
adjacency, OTV (Overlay Transport Virtualization), 370
adjacent pairs, 28
Admin tab (UCS Manager), 591
Advanced Encryption Standard (AES), 133
Advanced VPLS. *See* **A-VPLS**
advantages, 21
   ACE virtual contexts, 110
   Fabric Extenders, 288
   load-balancer deployments, 114
   network services, 736
   service profiles, 582
   virtualization, 454, 494
   VLANs/VRF, 45
   VM-FEX (Virtual Machine Fabric Extender), 657
   vPCs (virtual PortChannels), 231
   VSANs (virtual storage-area networks), 409
AEDs (authoritative edge devices), 365
AES (Advanced Encryption Standard), 133, 328
aggregation
   failures, 38
   layers, 36
   links, 234-240
   MC-LAG (Multi-Chassis Link Aggregation Group), 351
   virtual networking, 684-688
algorithms
   acceleration, 763
   slow-start, 116
allocation

   interfaces, 190
   memory, 210
   resources, 17
      VDCs (virtual device contexts), 202-211
      virtual contexts (ACE), 145-156
      VLANs (virtual LANs), 206
      VRF (Virtual Routing and Forwarding), 101-103
   virtual context creation, 145
Amazon Web Service. *See* **AWS**
American National Standards Institute. *See* **ANSI**
American National Standards Institute and Telecommunications Industry Association (ANSI/TIA), 29
AMS (Adaptable Modular Storage), 792
analysis, traffic, 58
ANM (Application Network Manager), 147
ANSI (American National Standards Institute), 410
ANSI/TIA (American National Standards Institute and Telecommunications Industry Association), 29
ANSI/TIA-942 standards, 40-41, 287
answer files, 585
Any Configuration option, 595
Any Transport over MPLS. *See* **AToM**
API (application programming interface), 661
APIC (Asynchronous Inter-Process Communication), 662
appliances
   ACE (Appliance Control Engine) connections, 141-144
   ASAs (Adaptive Security

Appliances), 179
Cisco ASA 1000v, 754-762
network services, 738
See also networks; services
VSG (Virtual Security Gateway), 742-763
Application Control Engine. *See* **ACE**
application control software, 142
Application Network Manager. *See* **ANM**
application programming interface. *See* **API**
applications, 19
acceleration, 129, 763-771
batch processing, 321
delivery controllers, 765
environment independence, 138-139
load balancers, 127-130
networking services, 111
resilience, 37
scaling, 113
virtual LUNs, 405
application-specific integrated circuits. *See* **ASICs**
applying load balancers, 111-134
AppNav, 765
arbitrated loops, 412
architecture
Cisco ASA 1000v, 755
Cisco Nexus 1000v, 661-663
control planes, 742
data centers, 5-7
Fabric Extender, 292
layers, 35-36
NX-OS, 189
See also NX-OS switches
SCSI (Small Computer Systems Interface), 395
servers, 560-562
services. *See* services

SSA (Serial Storage Architecture), 396
Storage Reference Architecture, 792
virtualization, extending, 185
VMDC (Virtualized Multiservice Data Center), 792
WAAS (Wide Area Application Services), 764
areas, 20, 21
operational, 5-7
security, 47
technologies, 18-21
ACE virtual contexts, 110
Fabric Extenders, 288
service profiles, 582
virtualization, 454, 494
VM-FEX (Virtual Machine Fabric Extender), 657
vPCs (virtual PortChannels), 231
VSANs (virtual storage-area networks), 409
VLANs/VRF, 45
ARP (Address Resolution Protocol), 49, 701
arrays
clusters, 403
disk, 389-390
zones, 439
ASAs (Adaptive Security Appliances), 179, 735, 737, 754-762
ASDM (Adaptive Security Device Manager), 754
ASICs (application-specific integrated circuits), 103
assignment
HBAs (host bus adapters), 595
interfaces to Fibre Channel, 413
IP addresses, 59
servers, 606-607

UUID (Universally Unique Identifier), 594
values, default path cost for switches, 64
VLAN (virtual local-area network) interfaces, 52
association
   service profiles to servers, 612-619
   VRF (Virtual Routing and Forwarding), 90
asymmetric connection management, 122
Asynchronous Inter-Process Communication (AIPC), 662
asynchronous replication, 402
ATA Packet Interface (ATAPI), 397
ATAPI (ATA Packet Interface), 397
Atlas Team, 9
AToM (Any Transport over MPLS), 333
attachments, interfaces, 343
attenuation, 29
attributes
   ACLs (access control lists), 752
   VMs (virtual machines), 751
authentication
   offloading servers, 130
   UCS Manager, 589
authentication, authorization, and accounting. *See* AAA
authoritative edge devices. *See* AEDs
automation
   cloud computing, 789-792
   provisioning, 581
autostate (VLANs), 60
auxiliary memory, 8, 388
availability, 25
   distributed data centers, 321
   geoclusters, 323
   networks, 37
   servers, 559
avoidance, loops, 326, 330
   Cisco Nexus 1000v switches, 685
   OTV (Overlay Transport Virtualization), 365-373
A-VPLS (Advanced VPLS), 350
AWS (Amazon Web Service), 794

B

backbone cabling, 41
backup interfaces, 495
bandwidth
   ETS (Enhanced Transmission Selection), 500
   load balancer performance, 135
basic input/output system. *See* BIOS
batch processing applications, 321
BDs (bridge domains), 208
behavior
   broadcast frames, 61
   disabling, 164
   hubs, 48
   paths, 47
   private VLAN ports, 79
   server responses, 118
   switches, 48
   virtual contexts (ACE), 150
   VLAN (virtual local-area network) switches, 50
Bell, Alexander Graham, 28
benefits, 25
   of networks, 42-44
   of virtualization, 2
best practices
   deployment, 36
   predictors, selecting, 117
BF (Build Fabric) frame, 423
BGP (Border Gateway Protocol), 87, 334

BI (Business Intelligence), 3
binding
    labels, 337
    MPLS (Multiprotocol Label Switching) connections, 353
    VNMC (Virtual Network Manager Center), 760
biological taxonomy, 21
    See also taxonomies
BIOS (basic input/output system), 581
    configuration, 627-633
    firmware policies, 635
    server domains, 585
    updating, 636
    x86 architecture, 563
blade servers, 488, 540-542
blade switches, 474
block-based access, 392-397
Blocked state (STP), 70
blocks, 391
    aggregation, 36
    BPDUs (bridge protocol data units), 684
    LBAs (Logical Block Addresses), 394
    SMB (Server Message Block), 398
Boggs, Dave, 26
booting
    configuration, 225
    order, servers, 604-605
BOOTP (Bootstrap Protocol), 51
Bootstrap Protocol. *See* BOOTP
Border Gateway Protocol. *See* BGP
Boucher, Larry, 392
BPDUs (bridge protocol data units), 65, 233
    blocks, 684
    Fabric Extender, 300
    Layer 2 extensions, 329
bridge domains. *See* BDs

Bridge-group Virtual Interfaces. *See* BVIs
bridge protocol data units. *See* BPDUs
bridges
    DCB (Data Center Bridging), 497-503
    Ethernets, 47
    IDs, 63
    root, 62
    virtual contexts (ACE) design, 158-160
Broadcast Alias service, 421
broadcasts
    ARP (Address Resolution Protocol), 49
    domain extensions, 325
    Ethernet loops, 62
    gatekeepers, 365
    vPCs (virtual PortChannels), 243
broad network access, 794
buffers
    buffer-to-buffer credits calculation, 418, 419
    PAUSE frames, 499
Build Fabric (BF) frame, 423
building blocks, Fibre Channel, 416
buses
    Ethernets, 47
    SCSI (Small Computer Systems Interface), 393
    shared, 392
    x86
        architecture, 563
        server expansion, 569-571
Business Intelligence. *See* BI
Bus&Tag communication, 396
BVIs (Bridge-group Virtual Interfaces), 145, 158

C

cables, 493
    See also connections
    backbone cabling, 41
    coaxial (Ethernet protocol), 27-28
    convergence, 495-497
    DCB (Data Center Bridging), 497-503
    direct-attach twinaxial (Ethernet protocol), 32-33
    FCoE (Fibre Channel over Ethernet), 504-509
    horizontal, 289
    intra-rack cabling, 40
    optical fiber (Ethernet protocol), 29-32
    optimization, 44
    trends, 34
    twisted-pair, 28-29, 34
caches, 129, 390
    memory, 9
    WCCP (Web Cache Control Protocol), 765
calculations
    sequence numbers, 133
    sliding windows, 133
Canonical Format Indicator. *See* CFI
carrier sense multiple access collision detect. *See* CSMA/CD
Catalyst 3750 switches, 240
Catalyst 6500 switches
    ACE module connections, 144
    virtual contexts (ACE), 135
    Virtual Switch System, 240
categories, ANSI/TIA-568 twisted-pair, 30
CCP (Cisco Cloud Portal), 797
CDBs (command descriptor blocks), 393
CDP (Cisco Discovery Protocol), 601
CE (customer edge) devices, 338

CEE (Converged Enhanced Ethernet), 497
central processing units. *See* CPUs
CEOs (chief executive officers), 6
Certification no. 10349, 227
certifications, governance, 583
CFI (Canonical Format Indicator), 53
CFOs (chief financial officers), 6
CFS (Cisco Fabric Services), 243, 466
changeto command, 147
channels
    Fibre Channel, 410
        See also Fibre Channel
    I/O (input/output), 388
chassis management circuit. *See* CMC
checking status of NPV (N_Port Virtualization), 477
checksums, 133
chief executive officers (CEOs), 6
chief financial officers (CFOs), 6
chief information officers (CIOs), 2, 6
chief security officers (CSOs), 6
chipsets, x86 architecture, 563
CIAC (Cisco Intelligent Automation for Cloud), 797
CIFS (Common Internet File System), 398, 763
CIMC (Cisco Integrated Management Controller), 588
    firmware policies, 633
    versions, 634
CIOs (chief information officers), 2, 6
CISC (Complex Instruction Set Computing), 561
Cisco ASA 1000V switches, 754-762
    access rules, 761
    configuration, 757

installation, 755-757
security policy configuration, 761
traffic, sending to, 758
VNMC (Virtual Network Manager Center) registration, 756
Cisco Cloud Portal (CCP), 797
Cisco Discovery Protocol. *See* CDP
Cisco Fabric Services. *See* CFS
Cisco Integrated Management Controller. *See* CIMC
Cisco Intelligent Automation for Cloud (CIAC), 797
Cisco Nexus 1000v switches
　architecture, 661-663
　communication modes, 663-664
　deployment, 666-683
　loop avoidance, 685
　online migrations, 693-697
　port profiles, 664-666
Cisco Open Network Environment. *See* ONE
Cisco Process Orchestrator (CPO), 798
Cisco Server Provisioner (CSP), 798
cladding, 29
classes
　maps
　　Layer 7, 167
　　VIP (virtual IP), 169
　resources, 150, 155
　of service (Fibre Channel), 420
classification
　ACE (Application Control Engine), 110
　Ethernet ports, 72
　Fabric Extenders, 288
　Layer 2 extensions, 320
　network services, 736
　service profiles, 582
　VDCs (virtual device contexts), 183

virtualization, 14-21, 454, 494
VLANs (virtual local-area networks), 45
VM-FEX (Virtual Machine Fabric Extender), 657
vPCs (virtual PortChannels), 231
VRF (Virtual Routing and Forwarding), 45
VSANs (virtual storage-area networks), 409
CLI (command-line interface) 20, 142
　MPC (Modular Policy CLI), 162
　prompts, 198
　VDCs (virtual device contexts), 192
client-by-client configuration, 129
clients, 111
clock generators, x86 architecture, 563
cloning, 638-639
cloud computing, 785-786
　automation, 789-792
　deployment, 799-800
　implementation, 797-798
　networks, 800, 802-804
　ONE (Cisco Open Network Environment), 804
　OpenStack, 801-802
　overview of, 793-797
　SDNs (Software-Defined Networks), 800-801
　standardization, 789-792
　virtual data centers, 786-789
Cloud Services Routers. *See* CSRs
clusters
　arrays, 403
　interfaces, 700
　IP (Internet Protocol) addresses, 668
　security policies, 737
　servers, 324
　virtualization, 737

CMC (chassis management circuit), 588
CMS (Conversational Monitor System), 10
CNAs (converged network adapters), 585
CNMs (congestion notification messages), 503
coarse wavelength-division multiplexing (CWDM), 328
coaxial cables (Ethernet protocol), 27-28
COBIT (Control Objectives for Information and Related Technologies), 583
code, SCSI commands, 393
cold-standby sites, 322
collisions
　domains, 48
　VLANs (virtual local-area networks), 377-379
command descriptor blocks. *See* CDBs
command-line interfaces. *See* CLIs
commands
　changeto, 147
　fex associate, 297
　Format Unit, 393
　Inquiry, 393
　lacp, 237
　mpls ip, 335
　Nexus 7000, 61
　Read, 393
　Read Capacity, 393
　reload vdc, 215
　SCSI (Small Computer Systems Interface), 393
　Send Diagnostic, 393
　show interface, 459
　switchmode fex-fabric, 297
　Test Unit Ready, 393
　vlan all, 55
　vrf member interface, 91
　Write, 393
Common Internet File System (CIFS), 398
Common Spanning Tree. *See* CST
communication
　errors, 48
　Ethernets, 58
　modes (Cisco Nexus 1000v switches), 663-664
　UDP (User Datagram Protocol), 120
Complex Instruction Set Computing. *See* CISC
components
　of disk arrays, 389
　FCIP (Fibre Channel over IP), 455
compression
　HTTP (Hypertext Transfer Protocol), 130, 134
　offloading servers, 130
　PLZ (Persistent Lempel-Ziv), 764
computer rooms (ANSI/TIA-942 standards), 40
concurrent connections, 135
confidentiality, 326
configuration
　BIOS (basic input/output system), 581, 585, 627-633
　boot, 225, 604
　BVIs (Bridge-group Virtual Interfaces), 158
　Cisco ASA 1000V, 757
　client-by-client, 129
　complexity, 137
　CSRs (Cloud Services Routers), 773
　DHCP (Dynamic Host Configuration Protocol), 51
　domains, 175
　EEM (Event Embedded Manager), 349

EIGRP (Enhanced Interior Gateway Routing Protocol), 96
EoMPLS (Ethernet over MPLS), 338
Ethernet 10/10, 197-198
EvPC (Enhanced virtual PortChannel), 315
Fabric Interconnect, 588
FabricPath, 272
FCIP (Fibre Channel over IP), 457-460
Flex-Attach, 487
F-Trunks, 480
interfaces
   out-of-band management switches, 143
   production switches, 142
IPMI (Intelligent Platform Management Interface), 609
LACP (Link Aggregation Control Protocol), 237
load balancers
   policies, 132
   servers, 115
MPLS (Multiprotocol Label Switching), 335
MST (Multiple Spanning Tree), 201
multihop FCoE (Fibre Channel over Ethernet), 523-535
nondisruptive reconfiguration of fabric, 423
NPIV (N_Port ID Virtualization), 476-482
operational policies, 608
OSPF (Open Shortest Path First), 94
OTV (Overlay Transport Virtualization), 359-364
PortChannels, 303, 306
   Layer 3, 236
   STP (Spanning Tree Protocol), 236
port profiles, 664
predictors, 116
private VLANs, 80-82
probes, 164-167
promiscuous access interfaces, 81
Q-in-Q tunnel interfaces, 378
RAID (Redundant Array of Independent Disks), 399-401
security policies (Cisco ASA 1000V), 761
server farms, 166
SPAN sessions, 205-206
SVIs (Switch Virtual Interfaces), 59
Switch1, 196-197
trunk interfaces, 55
unified access servers
   single-context switches, 510-518
   storage VDCs, 519-523
users
   accounts, 175
   login, 176
VDCs (virtual device contexts), 190-202
VFC (Virtual Fibre Channel), PortChannels, 528-531
vHBAs (virtual HBAs), 596
virtual contexts (ACE), 140, 163-171
virtual networking, 658-661
VLANs (virtual local-area networks), 85, 209
vNICs (virtual NICs), 599
vPath
   Nexus 1000v switches, 748, 758
   WAAS (Wide Area Application Services), 766
vPCs (virtual PortChannels), 247-254
VRF (Virtual Routing and Forwarding), 90-91, 99, 199
VSG (Virtual Security Gateway) fire-

consolidation 883

walls, 746
VSS (Virtual Switch System), 241
vSwitch (Virtual Switch), 673
VXLANs (Virtual eXtensible Local Area Networks), 703
vZones (virtual zones), 754

congestion
    control, 134
    QCN (Quantized Congestion Notification), 503

congestion notification messages. *See* CNMs

connected data centers, internal routing in, 380-382

connections, 18
    access-aggregation, 38
    ACEs (Application Control Engines), 141-145
    concurrent, 135
    cross-connections, 41
    dedicated, 392
    desktops, 34
    devices, 32
    EOBC (Ethernet Out-of-Band Channel), 144
    EoR (End-of-Row) designs, 289-291
    external, virtual networking, 684-688
    Fabric Extenders, 296-299
    hosts, 35
    internal routing, Layer 2 extensions, 380-382
    interswitch, 234
    IP (Internet Protocol), 200
        See also IP
    Layer 2 interfaces, 343
    least-connections predictors, 116
    limitations, 118
    management, 122-124
    migration, 289
    MPLS (Multiprotocol Label Switching), 353
    multiple (STP), 233
    multisite interconnections (FabricPath), 331
    N7K switches, 524
    Nexus 1000V switches, 741
    NIC (network interface card) teaming, 239
    NPV (N_Port Virtualization), 476
        See also NPV
    offloading servers, 130
    optical, Ethernet extensions over, 327-332
    optimization,
    peer keepalive links, 248
    physical, 495
    ports
        switches, 69
        VDCs (virtual device contexts), 192
    pseudowires, 343
    servers, 34
    state communications, 325
    TCP (Transmission Control Protocol), 120
    termination, 133
    Top-of-Rack (ToR) designs, 289-291
    UDP (User Datagram Protocol), 120
    vCons (virtual network interface connections), 602
    vPath, 768

connections per second (cps), 135

connectors
    RJ-45, 29
    twinax cables, 32

consolidation, 42
    management, 44
    SANs (storage area networks), 447-450

switches, 187
VM-FEX (Virtual Machine Fabric Extender), 705

content, security, 58

contention
   cloud computing, 803
   PFC (priority-based flow control), 498

Content Services Switch. *See* CSS

Content Switching Module. *See* CSM

contexts, virtual (ACEs), 109
   See also ACEs

control architecture (Cisco ASA 1000v), 755

controllers, 390
   application delivery, 765
   CIMC (Cisco Integrated Management Controller), 588
   fabric, 421
   FCoE (Fibre Channel over Ethernet), 505
   memory (x86 architecture), 562
   SDNs (Software-Defined Networks), 800

control planes, 20
   architecture, 742
   FabricPath, 269-272

Control Program (CP), 10

control units. *See* CUs

converged access models, 542

converged aggregation models, 543

Converged Enhanced Ethernet. *See* CEE

converged network adapters. *See* CNAs

convergence
   I/O (input/output), 495-497
   network adapters, 509
   RSTP (Rapid Spanning Tree Protocol), 72
   speed, 232
   STP (Spanning Tree Protocol), 66

Conversational Monitor System (CMS), 10

core-aggregation-access, 36

core-distribution-access, 34

cores, 29, 564

costs, default path cost for switches, 64

counters, sequences, 415

CP (Control Program), 10

CPO (Cisco Process Orchestrator), 798

cps (connections per second), 135

CPUs (central processing units), 4, 388
   utilization, 203
   virtual memory, 9
   x86 architecture, 562
   x86 servers, 564-566

CRC (cyclic redundancy check), 417

Create Host Firmware Package wizard, 634

Create Service Profile (expert) wizard, 594, 626, 637

creating. *See* formatting

credits, buffer-to-buffer, 418-419

CRM (Customer Relationship Management), 3

cross-connections, 41

cross-switch
   aggregation techniques, 342
   PortChannels, 240-241

crosstalk interference, 28

CSM (Content Switching Module), 139

CSMA/CD (carrier sense multiple access collision detect), 26

CSOs (chief security officers), 6

CSP (Cisco Server Provisioner), 798

CSRs (Cloud Services Routers), 735
   1000V connectivity parameters, 771

configuration, 773
CSS (Content Services Switch), 139
CST (Common Spanning Tree), 75
CUs (control units), 396
customer edge. *See* CE
Customer Relationship Management. *See* CRM
CWDM (coarse wavelength-division multiplexing), 328
cyclic redundancy check. *See* CRC

D

database management system (DBMS), 398
Data Center Bridging. *See* DCB
Data Center Bridging eXchange protocol. *See* DCBX protocol
Data Center Ethernet. *See* DCE
Data Center Interconnect. *See* DCI
data centers
 architecture, 5-7
 blade servers, 488
 convergence, 495-497
 definitions, 2-7
 evolution of, 3-5
 internal routing (Layer 2 extensions), 380-382
 limitations of, 5
 load balancers, proliferation in, 135-139
 merging, 731-733
 mixed access (Fabric Extender), 315-317
 multitenant, virtual contexts (ACE), 179-181
 optimization, 231
 origins of virtualization, 8-13
 segmentation, 103-104
 storage devices, 387-391

VDCs (virtual device contexts), 225-227
 virtual, 781-783, 785-789
  See also cloud computing
 virtual contexts (ACE), integrating, 156-161
data confidentiality, 326
Data Encryption Standard (DES), 133
data paths, 738-740
 See also vPath
data planes, 20, 266-269
data rates (Ethernet standards), 33
Data Redundancy Elimination (DRE), 764
Data Warehouses. *See* DWs
DBMS (database management system), 398
DCB (Data Center Bridging), 493, 497-503
 DCBX (Data Center Bridging eXchange) protocol, 501-503
 ETS (Enhanced Transmission Selection), 500-501
 PFC (priority-based flow control), 498-499
 QCN (Quantized Congestion Notification), 503
DCBX (Data Center Bridging eXchange) protocol, 501-503, 518
DCE (Data Center Ethernet), 497
DCE (Distributed Computing Environment), 594
DCI (Data Center Interconnect), 324
 STP (Spanning Tree Protocol), 326
 switches, 328
DCNM-SAN topologies, 531
DDR (Double Data Rate), 567
DEC (Digital Equipment Company), 26
DEC, Intel, Xerox (DIX), 26

dedicated connections, 392
dedicated processors (x86 architecture), 563
default domains, 175
default gateways, 11
default HA policies, 217
default path cost for switches, 64
default VDC resource allocation, 212
definitions
    data centers, 2-7
    dynamic vNIC connection policies, 708
    Fibre Channel, 410-420
    network services, 599-608, 735-738
    service profiles, 595-598
    storage, 8
    taxonomies, 14
    vHBAs (virtual HBAs), 596
    virtualization, 1, 8, 12
    VLANs (virtual local-area networks), 49-56
    vPCs (virtual PortChannels), 242-248
    VRF (Virtual Routing and Forwarding), 90-91
    VSANs (virtual storage-area networks), 430-447
delivery controllers, applications, 765
demilitarized zones. *See* DMZs
dense wavelength-division multiplexing (DWDM), 328
deployment
    Cisco Nexus 1000v switches, 666-683
    clients, 111
    cloud computing, 796, 799-800
    DNS load balancers, 112
    ISL (Inter-Switch-Link), 56
    redundant VPLS (Virtual Private LAN Service), 348
    routing, 58
    services, 111
    switches (STP versions), 62
    topologies, 36
    UCS (Unified Computing System), 578
    unified access servers, 509-523
    VLANs (virtual local-area networks), 52
    VM-FEX (Virtual Machine Fabric Extender), 706-720
    vSphere (VMware), 709-710
    VXLANs (Virtual eXtensible Local Area Networks), 699
    WWNs (World Wide Names), 486-488
Deploy OVF Template vCenter wizard, 745
DES (Data Encryption Standard), 133
DeSanti, Claudio, 509
design, 26
    See also configuration
    EoR (End-of-Row), 39, 44
    OTV (Overlay Transport Virtualization), 373-377
    partitioning, 47
    reverse proxies, 128-130
    router-on-a-stick, 55, 58
    STP (Spanning Tree Protocol), 232
    three-layer campus, 34
    ToR. *See* ToR (Top-of-Rack) designs
    ToR (Top-of-Rack), 39, 44
    Unified Fabrics, 535-545
    virtual contexts (ACE)
        bridges, 158-160
        one-armed, 160-161
        routers, 156-158
    VLANs (virtual local-area networks), 120
Designated Ports Selection phase, 68

desktop connections, 34
detection
　loops, 193
　volume, 440
devices
　See also hardware
　ASDM (Adaptive Security Device Manager), 754
　connections, 32
　edge, 357
　groups, 47
　load balancer concepts, 115-120
　PODs (pool of devices), 281-284
　server farms for websites, 168
　storage, 4, 18, 387-391
　　See also storage
DF (Don't Fragment) bit sets, 356
DHCP (Dynamic Host Configuration Protocol), 51, 585, 762
DIA (Domain ID Identifier) frames, 423
different security zones. *See* DMZs
Digital Equipment Company (DEC), 26
DIMMs (Dual In-Line Memory Modules), 568
direct-attach twinaxial cables, 32-33
Direct Server Return, 123-124
Disabled state (STP), 70
disabling
　behaviors, 164
　legacy extension, 371
disaster recovery plans, 321
discovery (Fabric Extenders), 297
disk arrays, 389-390, 439
disk enclosures, 390
dissimulation, 12
Distributed Computing Environment. *See* DCE

distributed data centers, 319, 321
　See also data centers
　1970s-1980s, 321-322
　1990s-mid-2000s, 322-324
　mid-2000s to present, 324
Distributed Virtual Switch. *See* DVS
distribution
　core-distribution-access, 34
　layers, 35
　power, 7
DIX (DEC, Intel, Xerox), 26
DL (Don't Learn), 268
DMZs (demilitarized zones), 136, 225-226, 737
DNS (Domain Name System), 111
Domain ID Identifier (DIA) frames, 423
Domain Name System. *See* DNS
domains
　BDs (bridge domains), 208
　broadcast extensions, 325
　collisions, 48
　creating, 175
　failures, 47
　ID distribution, 438
　infrastructure, 585, 594
　servers, 584-595
　UCS (Unified Computing System), 586
　vPCs (virtual PortChannels), 248
Don't Fragment (DF) bit sets, 356
Don't Learn. *See* DL
Double Data Rate. *See* DDR
DRAM (dynamic RAM), 566
DRE (Data Redundancy Elimination), 764
dual-homed fabric extenders, 537
dual-homed topologies (Fabric Extender), 309-315
Dual In-Line Memory Modules. *See*

888 Dual In-Line Memory Modules

DIMMs
Dual NAT, 125-126
DVS (Distributed Virtual Switch), 661
DWDM (dense wavelength-division multiplexing), 328, 455
DWs (Data Warehouses), 3
Dynamic Host Configuration Protocol. *See* DHCP
dynamic interfaces, provisioning, 664-666
dynamic RAM. *See* DRAM
Dynamic Resource Scheduling, 669
dynamic vNICs, enabling, 707-709

E

ECC (Error Correction Code), 569
ECMP (Equal Cost Multipath), 803
e-commerce, 3
EDA (Equipment Distribution Area), 41
edge devices, 357, 754-762
edge-ports, 72
Edit Virtual Machine Settings option, 690
EEM (Event Embedded Manager), 225, 349
efficiency, 25
EFP (Exchange Fabric Parameters) phase, 423
Egress Tunnel Router (ETR), 779
EIA (Electronic Industries Alliance), 287
EID (Endpoint Identifier), 779
EIGRP (Enhanced Interior Gateway Routing Protocol), 87, 96
EISL (Enhanced Inter-Switch Link), 434
elasticity, 794
electromagnetic interfaces. *See* EMIs

Electronic Industries Alliance (EIA), 287
elements
   FCoE (Fibre Channel over Ethernet), 505-506
   HDDs (hard disk drives), 389
   load balancer configuration, 115
ELP (Exchange Link Parameters) phase, 423
ELS (Extended Link Service) frames, 422
email filters, 129
EMIs (electromagnetic interfaces), 28
emulation, 12, 15, 21
   ACE virtual contexts, 110
   Fabric Extenders, 288
   LAN Emulation (LANE), 803
   network services, 736
   service profiles, 582
   virtualization, 454, 494
   VLANs/VRF, 45
   VM-FEX (Virtual Machine Fabric Extender), 657
   VMs (virtual machines), 659
   vPCs (virtual PortChannels), 231
   VSANs (virtual storage-area networks), 409
enabling
   acceleration, 769
   LACP processes, 237
   NPV (N_Port Virtualization), 533
   vNICs (virtual NICs), 707-709
Encapsulated Remote Switch Port Analyzer. *See* ERSPAN
encapsulation
   frames, 739
   GRE (generic routing encapsulation), 352-354
   ISL (Inter-Switch-Link), 56
   OTV (Overlay Transport Virtualization), 356

Q-in-Q, 378
enclosures, disk, 390
encryption
    HTTPS (Secure HTTP), 130
    offloading servers, 130
    standards, 133
End-Host mode, 592
end of frame (EOF), 417
End-of-Row (EoR) designs. *See* EoR designs
Endpoint Identifier (EID), 779
end-to-end congestion notification, 503
end-to-end SSL (Secure Sockets Layer), 132
Enhanced Interior Gateway Routing Protocol. *See* EIGRP
Enhanced Inter-Switch Link. *See* EISL
Enhanced Quad Small Form Factor Pluggable (QSFP+), 32
Enhanced Small Form Factor Pluggable (SFP+), 32
Enhanced Transmission Selection. *See* ETS
Enhanced virtual PortChannel (EvPC), 314
ENode, 505
Enterprise Resource Planning. *See* ERP
Enterprise System Connection (ESCON), 396
entrance rooms (ANSI/TIA-942 standards), 40
environment independence, applications, 138-139
EOBC (Ethernet Out-of-Band Channel), 144
EOF (end of frame), 417
EoMPLS (Ethernet over MPLS), 319, 333, 338-342
EoR (End-of-Row) designs, 39, 44, 289-291

EPP (Exchange Peer Parameter) frame, 423
Equal Cost Multipath (ECMP), 803
Equipment Distribution Area (EDA), 41
Equipment tab (UCS Manager), 591
ERP (Enterprise Resource Planning), 3
Error Correction Code. *See* ECC
errors, communication, 48
ERSPAN (Encapsulated Remote Switch Port Analyzer), 203
ESCON (Enterprise System Connection), 396
ESC (Exchange Switch Capabilities) phase, 423
estimation, memory, 211
Etheranalyzer sessions, 225
EtherChannel, 43
Ethernet 10/10 configuration, 197-198
Ethernet Adapter Policy option, 601
Ethernet Out-of-Band Channel. *See* EOBC
Ethernet over MPLS. *See* EoMPLS
Ethernets
    10 Gigabit, 497
    bridges, 47
    broadcast loops, 62
    CEE (Converged Enhanced Ethernet), 497
    communication, 58
    extensions
        IP (Internet Protocol), 352-377
        over optical connections, 327-332
    FCoE (Fibre Channel over Ethernet), 504-509
    frames, forwarding, 267
    interfaces, 591
        LACP modes, 237

890 Ethernets

VSM (Virtual Supervisor Module), 662
Layer 2. See Layer 2
MAC (Media Access Control), 505
port classification, 72
protocols, 25-26
    coaxial cables, 27-28
    direct-attach twinaxial cables, 32-33
    media, 27
    optical fiber, 29-32
    overview of, 26-34
    timelines, 33-34
    twisted-pair cables, 28-29
segments, 47
switches, 48, 184
    See also VDCs
VEM (Virtual Ethernet Module), 739, 740
ETR (Egress Tunnel Router), 779
ETS (Enhanced Transmission Selection), 500-501
Event Embedded Manager. See EEM
evolution
    of data centers, 3-5
    of hardware (x86 servers), 562-572
    of networks, 25, 281-284
    of servers, 559-560
EvPC (Enhanced virtual PortChannel), 314
Exchange Fabric Parameters (EFP) phase, 423
Exchange Link Parameters (ELP) phase, 423
Exchange Peer Parameter (EPP) frame, 423
exchanges (Fibre Channel), 415-417
Exchange Switch Capabilities (ESC) phase, 423
EXEC prompt, 147

expansion busses (x86 servers), 569-571
exporting plug-ins, 712
Extended Link Service (ELS) frames, 422
extending virtualization, 184-186
extensibility, 26
Extensible Markup Language. See XML
extensions
    broadcast domains, 325
    Ethernet over optical connections, 327-332
    FCoE (Fibre Channel over Ethernet), 545
    full-mesh, 329
    Layer 2, 319
        FabricPath, 330-332
        internal routing, 380-382
        IP (Internet Protocol), 352-377
        MPLS (Multiprotocol Label Switching), 332-351
        OTV (Overlay Transport Virtualization), 354-377
        overview of, 324-327
        solutions, 382-384
        VLAN (virtual local-area network) identifiers, 377-379
        vPCs (virtual PortChannels), 328-330
        VPLS (Virtual Private LAN Service), 342-351
    networks, 44
external connections, 684-688
external security zones, 225

F

fabric, 412
    Fibre Channel, 420-429

initialization, 422-424
Unified Fabrics design, 535-545
United Fabric, 495
Fabric Controller service, 421
Fabric Extender. *See* **FEX**
Fabric Failover, 600
Fabric Interconnect, 587-588
Fabric Interface (FIF), 292
Fabric Login, 437, 476
failures
   See FabricPath
   control planes, 269-272
   data planes, 266-269
   Layer 2 extensions, 330-332
   multipathing with, 43
   STP (Spanning Tree Protocol), 272-276, 330
Fabric-Provided MAC Address. *See* **FPMA**
Fabric Shortest Path First. *See* **FSPF**
failover (Fabric Failover), 600
failures
   See also troubleshooting
   aggregation, 38
   domains, 47
   impact of, 34
   links
      RSTP (Rapid Spanning Tree Protocol), 74
      STP (Spanning Tree Protocol), 71
      vPCs (virtual PortChannels), 245
   static pinning, 302
   VDCs (virtual device contexts), 216-217
farms, servers, 115
   configuration, 166
   round-robin predictors, 116
Fast Ethernet, 26

fast reroute, 340
fault isolation, 187, 331
fault tolerance
   increasing, 240
   virtual contexts (ACE), 177-178
FCF (FCoE Forwarder), 505, 510
FCIDs (Fibre Channel Identifiers), 413, 420, 429, 508
FCIP (Fibre Channel over IP), 453-464
   high-availability, 460-462
   SAN extension with TE, 462
FC-LS (Fibre Channel Link Services), 422, 476
FCoE (Fibre Channel over Ethernet), 186, 493, 504-509
   blade servers, 540-542
   elements, 505-506
   multihop configuration, 523-535
   NPIV (N_Port ID Virtualization), 532-535
   SAN extensions, 545
   unified access server configuration, 515
   vPCs (virtual PortChannels), 538-540
FCoE Initialization Protocol. *See* **FIP**
FCoE_LEP (FCoE Link End-Point), 506
FCoE Link End-Point. *See* **FCoE_LEP**
FEC (Forwarding Equivalence Class), 333
Federal Information Processing Standards (FIPS), 227
FEX (Fabric Extender), 287, 512
   See FEX
   connections, 296-299
   interfaces, 299-301
   mixed access data centers, 315-317
   options, 295-296
   overview of, 291-303
   redundancy, 301-303

server access models, 287-291
status verification, 298, 313
topologies, 291, 305-315
    dual-homed, 309-315
    straight-through, 305-308

fex associate command, 297

FHRPs (first-hop redundancy protocols), 380-382, 460, 775
    vPCs (virtual PortChannels), 259-265

FIB (Forwarding Information Base), 87, 92, 190, 334

Fiber Connectivity (FICON), 396

fiber optics, 327
    See also optical connections

Fibre Channel, 396, **410**
    addresses, 413-415
    classes of service, 420
    defining, 410-420
    fabric processes, 420-429
    FCoE (Fibre Channel over Ethernet), 505
    flow control, 417-419
    frames, 415-417
    layers, 411-412
    logins, 427-428
    RSCN (Registered State Change Notification), 426
    services, 421
    switches, 506
    topologies, 412-413
    zones, 429

Fibre Channel Adapter Policy option, 597

Fibre Channel Identifiers. *See* FCIDs

Fibre Channel Link Services (FC-LS), 422

Fibre Channel over Ethernet. *See* FCoE

Fibre Channel over IP. *See* FCIP

FICON (Fiber Connectivity), 396

fields, VNTag, 293

FIF (Fabric Interface), 292

files
    answer, 585
    OVF (Open Virtualization Format), 743
    storage, 391, 397-398
        See also storage

file systems, 406-407
    See also NFS

File Transfer Protocol. *See* FTP

filters
    email, 129
    reachability, 381
    VSG (Virtual Security Gateway), 742-753

Finite State Machine. *See* FSM

FIP (FCoE Initialization Protocol), 505, 507-509

FIPS (Federal Information Processing Standards), 227

firewalls, 111, 737
    Cisco ASA 1000v, 754-762
    load balancers, 127-128
    VSG (Virtual Security Gateway) configuration, 746

Firewall Service Module. *See* FWSM

FireWire, 396

firmware policies, UCS (Unified Computing System), 633-637

first-hop redundancy protocols. *See* FHRPs

flash memory, 390

Flex-Attach, configuration, 487

flexibility, 25, 281

FlexPod, 792

FLOGI (Fabric Login), 427, 437, 476, 506
    frames, 421
    verification, 513

flooding, 325
- MAC (Media Access Control) addresses, 340

flow control
- Fibre Channel, 417-419
- PFC (priority-based flow control), 498-499

formatting
- *See also* configuration
- FCIDs (Fibre Channel Identifiers), 414
- frames
  - *FCoE (Fibre Channel over Ethernet), 504*
  - *VXLANs (Virtual eXtensible Local Area Networks), 698*
- OVF (Open Virtualization Format), 743
- security policies, 745-747
- VFC (Virtual Fibre Channel) interfaces, 525
- VSANs (virtual storage-area networks), 432-434

Format Unit command, 393

forwarding
- frames
  - *Ethernet, 267*
  - *OTV (Overlay Transport Virtualization), 354*
- vPCs (virtual PortChannels), 243
- VRF (Virtual Routing and Forwarding), 45, 89-91, 199
  - *See also* VRF

Forwarding Equivalence Class. *See* FEC

Forwarding Information Base. *See* FIB

Forwarding state (STP), 70

Forwarding Tag (Ftag), 269

FPMA (Fabric-Provided MAC Address), 508

frames
- encapsulation, 739
- Ethernet, 48, 61, 267
- FCoE (Fibre Channel over Ethernet), 504
- Fibre Channel, 415-417
- OTV (Overlay Transport Virtualization), 354
- parsing, 421
- PAUSE, 499
- PFC (priority-based flow control), 498
- Q-in-Q, 378
- SDP (Satellite Discovery Protocol), 296-297
- UNPAUSE, 499
- vPCs (virtual PortChannels), 243
- VXLANs (Virtual eXtensible Local Area Networks), 698

FSM (Finite State Machine), 625

FSPF (Fabric Shortest Path First) protocol, 424-426, 442-444

Ftag (Forwarding Tag), 269

FTP (File Transfer Protocol), 167, 750

F-Trunks, 480

full-mesh extensions, 329

FWSM (Firewall Service Module), 179, 185

G

gatekeepers, broadcasts, 365

Gateway Load Balancing Protocol. *See* GLBP

gateways
- default, 11
- NAS (Network Attached Storage), 397
- VSG (Virtual Security Gateway), 742-753

generic routing encapsulation. *See* GRE
geoclusters, 322-323, 406
   broadcast domain extensions, 325
GET operations, 116-117
Gigabit Ethernet, 26
   See also Ethernet
   characteristics, 32
   FCIP (Fibre Channel over IP), 456
GLBP (Gateway Load Balancing Protocol), 12, 380
Globally Unique Identifier. *See* GUID
global resources, 225
Global Server Load Balance. *See* GSLB
governance, certifications, 583
GRE (generic routing encapsulation), 352-354, 803
greenfield data centers, 382-384
groups
   devices, 47
   hierarchies, 14
   ports, 195, 659
growth, attributes of, 25
GSLB (Global Server Load Balance), 775, 777-778
GUID (Globally Unique Identifier), 594

H

HA (high-availability)
   FCIP (Fibre Channel over IP), 460-462
   policies, 216, 767
hard disk drives. *See* HDDs
hardware, 19
   load balancers, 113
   verification, 190
   x86 servers, 562-572

hashing predictors, 116
HBAs (host bus adapters), 393, 509, 585
   assigning, 595
   vHBAs (virtual HBAs). *See* vHBAs
HDA (Horizontal Distribution Area), 40
HDDs (hard disk drives), 388-389
headers (FabricPath), 268
heartbeat communication, 324-325
hello messages, 38
Hello protocol, 424
hierarchies, groups, 14
HIF (Host Interface), 292, 591
high-availability. *See* HA
High Performance mode, 723-730
history of distributed data centers, 321
   1970s-1980s, 321-322
   1990s-mid-2000s, 322-324
   mid-2000s to present, 324
horizontal cabling, 289
Horizontal Distribution Area (HDA), 40
host bus adapters. *See* HBAs
Host Interface (HIF), 292, 591
hosts, 18
   connections, 35
   DHCP (Dynamic Host Configuration Protocol), 51
   partitioning, 47
   software packages, 633
   VSM (Virtual Supervisor Module), 662
Hot Standby Router Protocol. *See* HSRP
hot-standby sites, 322, 324
HSRP (Hot Standby Router Protocol), 11-12, 17, 380, 460, 762
HTTP (Hypertext Transfer Protocol),

116, 167
compression, 130, 134
HTTPS (Secure HTTP), 130
hub-and-spoke topologies, 329
hubs
   behavior, 48
   Ethernets, 47
hybrid clouds, 796
Hypertext Transfer Protocol. *See* HTTP

I

IaaS (Infrastructure as a Service), 795
IBM mainframe virtualization, 10
   See also mainframes
ICMP (Internet Control Message Protocol), 116, 163
IDC (International Data Corporation), 2
IDE (Integrated Drive Electronics), 397
identifiers, VLANs (virtual local-area networks), 377-379, 659
IDs, bridges, 63
IEC (International Electrotechnical Commission), 29
IEEE (Institute of Electrical and Electronics Engineers), 26
   802.1D, 62
   802.1Q, 54
   XXXX802.1Qaz. *See* ETS
   XXXX802.1Qbb. *See* PFC
   802.1w, 72
   1394 (FireWire), 396
IETF (Internet Engineering Task Force), 12, 130
imaging, 585
implementation
   cloud computing, 797-798
   partitioning, 187-188
   VM-FEX (Virtual Machine Fabric Extender), 706
importing plug-ins, 711
INCITS (International Committee for Information Technology Standards), 392
industrializing server provisioning, 637-653
inflection point positions, 119
information security, 735
infrastructure
   domains, 585, 594
   IVR (Inter-VSAN Routing), 465-467
   layers, 189
   UCS (Unified Computing System), 586
   VM-FEX (Virtual Machine Fabric Extender), 705
Infrastructure as a Service. *See* IaaS
Ingress Tunnel Router (ITR), 779
inheritance, port profiles, 665
initializing fabric, 421-424
initiating SSLs (Secure Sockets Layers), 132
input/output. *See* I/O
Inquiry command, 393
installation
   access switches, 289
   Cisco ASA 1000v, 755-757
   operating systems, 620-623
   VEM (Virtual Ethernet Module), 671
   VSG (Virtual Security Gateway), 743-745
   VSM (Virtual Supervisor Module), 671
instances (STP), 74-78
Institute of Electrical and Electronics Engineers. *See* IEEE
Integrated Drive Electronics (IDE), 397

integration
    networks, 660
    UCS VMware Integration wizard, 711-716
    virtual contexts (ACE), 156-161
Intel, 26
Intelligent Platform Management Interface. *See* IPMI
interconnections, 18
Interface Manager, 189
interfaces
    allocation, 190
    API (application programming interface), 661
    ATAPI (ATA Packet Interface), 397
    attachments, 343
    backup, 495
    BVIs (Bridge-group Virtual Interfaces), 145, 158
    CLIs (command-line interfaces), 20, 142
    clusters, 700
    DCI (Data Center Interconnect), 329
    dynamic, provisioning, 664-666
    EMIs (electromagnetic interfaces), 28
    Ethernet, 591
        10/10 configuration, 197-198
        LACP modes, 237
    Fabric Extender, 299-301
    FabricPath, 273
    FCoE (Fibre Channel over Ethernet), 186
    Fibre Channel, 413
    FIF (Fabric Interface), 292
    Gigabit Ethernet, 456
    HIF (Host Interface), 292
    internal, 357
    IPMI (Intelligent Platform Management Interface), 609
    join, 357
    Layer 2 connections, 343
    LIF (Logical Interface), 292
    loops, verifying status of, 192
    maps, 771
    migration, 687
    MPC (Modular Policy CLI), 162
    MTUs (maximum transmission units), 338
    multiple, 54
    NPV (N_Port Virtualization), 480
    out-of-band management switches, 143
    overlay, 358, 369
    PFC (priority-based flow control), 498
    policy maps, 162
    private VLANs, 79
    production switch configuration, 142
    promiscuous access, 81
    public/private, 495
    Q-in-Q configuration, 378
    redundancy, 37, 301-303
    SCSI (Small Computer Systems Interface), 392-396, 410
    servers, 591
    SVIs (Switch Virtual Interfaces), 58, 145, 669, 792
    switches
        port IDs, 65
        RSTP (Rapid Spanning Tree Protocol), 72
    trunk configuration, 55
    uplinks, 591
    vCons (virtual network interface connections), 602
    VFC (Virtual Fibre Channel), 512, 525
    VIF (Virtual Interface), 292

virtual

   placement, 602-603

   verification, 690

VLANs (virtual local-area networks), 52

VNMC (Virtual Network Manager Center), 743

VSG (Virtual Security Gateway), 744

VSM (Virtual Supervisor Module), 662, 682

interference, troubleshooting, 28

Intermediate System-to-Intermediate System. *See* IS-IS

internal interfaces, 357

internal routing (Layer 2 extensions), 380-382

internal security zones, 225

Internal Spanning Tree. *See* IST

International Committee for Information Technology Standards (INCITS), 392

International Data Corporation (IDC), 2

International Electrotechnical Commission (IEC), 29

International Organization for Standardization (ISO), 29

Internet boom (1990s), 5

Internet Control Message Protocol. *See* ICMP

Internet Engineering Task Force. *See* IETF

Internet Protocol. *See* IP

Internet SCSI. *See* iSCSI

Internet service providers. *See* ISPs

interoperability between MST/STP switches, 78

interswitch connections, 234

Inter-Switch-Link. *See* ISL

Inter-VSAN Routing. *See* IVR

intra-rack cabling, 40

intrusion prevention services. *See* IPS

I/O (input/output), 388, 493

   channel architecture, 396

   convergence, 495-497

   HDDs (hard disk drives), 388

IP (Internet Protocol), 26, 46

   addresses

      assigning, 59

      Layer 4/Layer 7 switches, 120

      management, 610

      virtualization clusters, 668

      VSG (Virtual Security Gateway), 752

   connections, testing, 200

   FCIP (Fibre Channel over IP), 453-464

   Layer 2 extensions, 352-377

   readdressing, 325

   routing, 87

   subnets, VLAN association to, 56-58

IPMI (Intelligent Platform Management Interface), 609

IPS (intrusion prevention services), 111, 225

IPSec (IP Security), 774

iSCSI (Internet SCSI), 396, 495

   vNICs (virtual NICs), 604

IS-IS (Intermediate System-to-Intermediate System), 87

   FabricPath, 330

ISL (Inter-Switch-Link), 56

   isolation, 424

   NPV (N_Port Virtualization), comparing to, 475

islands, SANs (storage area networks), 430-432

ISO (International Organization for Standardization), 29

isolation

   fault, 331

ISL (Inter-Switch-Link), 424
Layer 2 extensions, 326
private VLANs, 78-83
traffic, 47
ISPs (Internet service providers), 35
IST (Internal Spanning Tree), 77
ITR (Ingress Tunnel Router), 779
IVR (Inter-VSAN Routing), 453, 464-473
   infrastructure, 465-467
   transit VSANs (virtual storage-area networks), 472
   zones, 467-472

J

Java DataBase Connectivity. See JDBC
JBODs (Just a Bunch of Disks), 389
JDBC (Java DataBase Connectivity), 398
join interfaces, 357
Just a Bunch of Disks. See JBODs

K

keepalive links
   connections, 248
   peers, 245
Kerberos, 398
kernels, 189
KVM tool, 620

L

Label Distribution Protocol. See LDP
label edge routers. See LERs
Label Forwarding Information Base. See LFIB
labels
   binding, 337, 353
   MPLS (Multiprotocol Label Switching), 47, 332
label switch routers. See LSRs
LACP (Link Aggregation Control Protocol), 237, 686
LAN Emulation (LANE), 803
LANs (local-area networks), 11, 49
   SAN management separation, 546-555
   VXLANs (Virtual eXtensible Local Area Networks), 697-705
LAN tab (UCS Manager), 591
Layer 2
   distributed data centers. See distributed data centers
   extensions, 319
      FabricPath, 330-332
      internal routing, 380-382
      IP (Internet Protocol), 352-377
      MPLS (Multiprotocol Label Switching), 332-351
      OTV (Overlay Transport Virtualization), 354-377
      overview of, 324-327
      solutions, 382-384
      VLAN (virtual local-area network) identifiers, 377-379
      vPCs (virtual PortChannels), 328-330
      VPLS (Virtual Private LAN Service), 342-351
   interface connections, 343
   multipathing
      with FabricPath, 43
      vPCs (virtual PortChannels), 265-280
   VDCs (virtual device contexts), 190
Layer 3
   PortChannel configuration, 236

routing tables, 88
VDCs (virtual device contexts), 190
VLANs (virtual local-area networks), 58-61

Layer 4
connection management, 122
load-balancing policy maps, 168
switches, 120-121

Layer 7
class maps, 167
connection management, 122
load-balancing policy maps, 169
switches, 113, 120-121

layers
access, 35, 542-545
aggregation, 36
distribution, 35
FCoE (Fibre Channel over Ethernet), 505
Fibre Channel, 411-412
infrastructure, 189
networks, 35
parameters, 112
physical, 27
    coaxial cables, 27
    optical fiber, 29
    standards, 29
server access (Unified Fabric designs), 536-542
SSL (Secure Sockets Layer), 130-133
TLS (Transport Layer Security), 130

LBAs (Logical Block Addresses), 394
LDP (Label Distribution Protocol), 334
Learning state (STP), 70
least-connections predictors, 116
least-loaded predictors, 117
legacy extension disabling, 371
length, transfer, 394

LERs (label edge routers), 333
LFIB (Label Forwarding Information Base), 334
libraries
tape, 390-391
VTL (virtual tape library), 403

LID (Local ID), 268
LIF (Logical Interface), 292
light propagation, 31
limitations
of connections, 118
of data centers, 5
of monitor sessions (VDCs), 204
of scalability, 17
weights, 118

linecards
sharing, 191
VDCs (virtual device contexts), 195

Link Aggregation Control Protocol. *See* LACP
Link Layer Discovery Protocol. *See* LLDP
links
aggregation, 234-240
failures
    RSTP (Rapid Spanning Tree Protocol), 74
    STP (Spanning Tree Protocol), 71
    vPCs (virtual PortChannels), 245
STP (Spanning Tree Protocol), 232-234
Virtual Link, 506
virtual networking, 684-688
VSL (virtual switch link), 241

link-state records. *See* LSRs
link-state updates. *See* LSUs
Linneaus, Carl, 21
Linux, 9

LISP (Location ID/Separation Protocol), 775, 779-781, 803
Listening state (STP), 70
lists, access, 164
   See also ACLs
LLDP (Link Layer Discovery Protocol), 502
load balancers
   address translation, 124-127
   applications, 127-130
   applying, 111-134
   concepts, 115-120
   firewalls, 127-128
   offloading servers, 130-134
   performance, 135-136
   policies
      configuration, 132
      maps, 168
   proliferation in data centers, 135-139
   resources, 693
   reverse proxies, 128-130
   scalability, 135
   security policies, 136-137
   SSL offloads, 132
   suboptimal traffic, 137
   transparent mode, 126-127
   virtual contexts (ACE), 164
load balancing, 43, 58, 225
local-area networks. *See* LANs
Local Disk option, 604
Local ID. *See* LID
localization, traffic, 382
Location ID/Separation Protocol. *See* LISP
Logical Block Addresses. *See* LBAs
Logical Interface (LIF), 292
logical partitioning, 42-43
logical topologies, 213

logical unit numbers. *See* LUNs
logical units. *See* LUs
Logical Volume Manager. *See* LVM
login
   FIP (FCoE Initialization Protocol), 507
   FLOGI (Fabric Login). *See* FLOGI
   user configuration, 176
logins
   Fibre Channel, 427-428
   VLAN commands, testing, 86
Login Server service, 421
Long Distance vMotion, 693
longevity of Ethernets, 26
loop-free U topologies, 38
loops
   arbitrated, 412
   avoidance, 326, 330
   broadcasts (Ethernets), 62
   Cisco Nexus 1000v switches, 685
   detection, 193
   interfaces, verifying status of, 192
   OTV (Overlay Transport Virtualization), 365-373
   STP (Spanning Tree Protocol), 37, 70
loss, frames, 498
LSRs (label switch routers), 333
LSRs (link-state records), 424
LSUs (link-state updates), 424
LUNs (logical unit numbers), 393, 399
   masking, 585
   SCSI storage volumes, 439
   virtualization, 404-406
LUs (logical units), 393
LVM (Logical Volume Manager), 392

M

MAC (Media Access Control), 51
　addresses, 581
　　BPDU frames, 65
　　FabricPath, 331
　　flooding, 340
　　FPMA (Fabric-Provided MAC Address), 508
　　learned in MPLS, 346
　　OTV (Overlay Transport Virtualization), 355
　　service profiles, 587
　　sharing resources, 85
　　SPMA (Server-Provided MAC Address), 508
　　tables, 691
　Ethernet, 505
　pinning, 686
　security, 601
magnetic tapes, 391
Main Distribution Area (MDA), 40
mainframes, 560-561
　storage access, 396-397
　virtualization, 10
　zSeries, 397
main memory, 8
maintenance policies, 606
Manage Hosts vCenter wizard, 606
management
　ASDM (Adaptive Security Device Manager), 754
　CIMC (Cisco Integrated Management Controller), 588
　Cisco ASA 1000v, 755
　Cisco Nexus 1000v architecture, 661
　CMC (chassis management circuit), 588
　connections, 122-124
　consolidation, 44
　EEM (Event Embedded Manager), 225
　Fabric Extenders, 291
　firmware packages, 633
　interfaces, 495
　IP (Internet Protocol) addresses, 610
　IPMI (Intelligent Platform Management Interface), 609
　LUNs (logical unit numbers), 404
　planes, 20
　SNMP (Simple Network Management Protocol), 20, 85
　traffic
　　allowing to virtual contexts (ACE), 162-163
　　NPV (N_Port Virtualization), 482-486
　UCS (Unified Computing System), 578, 588
　VDCs (virtual device contexts), 185, 214-224
　　operations, 214-216
　　out-of-band, 217-222
　　process failures, 216-217
　　RBAC (Role-Based Access Control), 222-224
　virtual contexts (ACE), 163, 171-176
　VRF (Virtual Routing and Forwarding), 98-101
　VSG (Virtual Security Gateway), 751
　VSM (Network Services Manager), 792
Management Server service, 422
Manage Plug-ins option, 711
Map-Resolver (MR), 779
maps
　classes
　　Layer 7, 167
　　VIP (virtual IP), 169
　interfaces, 771
　policies, 162

    load balancers, 168
    multimatch, 169
    QoS (quality of service), 225
    vCons (virtual network interface connections), 602
Map-Server (MS), 779
masking LUNs (logical unit numbers), 585
Massive Parallel Processing. *See* **MPP**
maximum transmission units. *See* **MTUs**
MBps (megabytes per second), 568
MC-LAG (Multi-Chassis Link Aggregation Group), 351
MDA (Main Distribution Area), 40
MDS (Multilayer Data Switch), 410, 424, 456
MDS-CORE routing tables, 442
measurements
    inflection points, 119
    services, 794
media
    Ethernet protocol, 27
    Gigabit Ethernet, 32
Media Access Control. *See* **MAC**
megabytes per second. *See* **MBps**
memory
    allocation, 210
    caches, 9
    estimation, 211
    flash, 390
    modules, 568
    NUMA (Non-Uniform Memory Access), 566
    ranges, 210
    VDCs (virtual device contexts), 203
    virtual, 8-9
    x86
        architecture, 562
        servers, 566-569

merging data centers, 731-733
Message and Translation System (MTS), 662
messages
    ACCEPT, 427
    CNMs (congestion notification messages), 503
    hello, 38
    SMB (Server Message Block), 398
metadata, 391
Metcalfe, Robert, 26
Microsoft Windows, 9
migration
    Cisco Nexus 1000v switches, 693-697
    connections, 289
    OTV (Overlay Transport Virtualization), 366
    physical interfaces, 687
    servers, 325
    UCS Manager, 625
    virtual LUNs, 406
    VM-FEX (Virtual Machine Fabric Extender), 720-722
    VM-Nomad, 770
    VMs (virtual machines) to VM-FEX (Virtual Machine Fabric Extender), 716-720
    VSM (Virtual Supervisor Module) interfaces, 682
mirroring RAM (random-access memory), 569
misconceptions about VLANs (virtual local-area networks), 56-61
mismatches, native VLANs, 84
mixed access data centers (Fabric Extender), 315-317
MMF (multimode fiber), 29, 396
mobile devices, 168
    See also devices
models

converged access, 542
converged aggregation, 543
OSI (Open Systems Interconnection), 411
point-to-point server access, 537
server access, 287-291
VSG (Virtual Security Gateway) management, 751

modes
ON, 238
address translation, 124
communication (Cisco Nexus 1000v switches), 663-664
End-Host, 592
High Performance, 723-730
transparent, 126-127

modification
See also configuration
resource allocation, 156
service profile associations, 614

modularization, software, 5

Modular Policy CLI. *See* **MPC**

modules
hardware, verification, 190
memory, 568
VEM (Virtual Ethernet Module), 661, 739-740
VSM (Virtual Supervisor Module), 661

monitoring
performance, 111
policies, 611
sessions, 203

Moore's Law, 564

motherboards (x86 architecture), 564

MPC (Modular Policy CLI), 162

MPLS (Multiprotocol Label Switching), 47
connections, 353

EoMPLS (Ethernet over MPLS), 338-342
Layer 2 extensions, 332-351
over GRE (generic routing encapsulation), 352-354
overview of, 333-338

mpls ip command, 335

MPP (Massive Parallel Processing), 566

MR (Map-Resolver), 779

MS (Map-Server), 779

MSFC (Multilayer Switching Feature Card), 145

MST (Multiple Spanning Tree), 76-77, 187
configuration, 201
verification, 202

MTS (Message and Translation System), 662

MTU option, 601, 803

MTUs (maximum transmission units), 338, 460, 504, 740

Multi-Chassis Link Aggregation Group (MC-LAG), 351

multihoming, 326, 328, 365-373

multihop FCoE (Fibre Channel over Ethernet) configuration, 523-535

Multilayer Data Switch. *See* **MDS**

Multilayer Switching Feature Card. *See* **MSFC**

multimatch policy maps, 169

multimode fiber (MMF), 29, 396

multipathing
with FabricPath, 43
vPCs (virtual PortChannels), 265-280

multiple connections, STP (Spanning Tree Protocol), 233

multiple data centers, 319
See also data centers

multiple interfaces, 54

Multiple Spanning Tree. *See* **MST**

multiple VLANs, 59
Multiprotocol Label Switching. *See* MPLS
multisite interconnections (FabricPath), 331
multitenant data centers, virtual contexts (ACE), 179-181

N

N7K switches, 94, 190, 519
    connections, 524
    private VLANs, 82
NAA (network address authority), 414
names
    VDCs (virtual device contexts), 198
    VMs (virtual machines), 752
    WWNs (World Wide Names), 581
NAS (Network Attached Storage), 397
NAT (Network Address Translation), 124, 466, 762
    Dual NAT, 125-126
    Server NAT, 124-125
National Institute of Standards and Technology (NIST), 794
native VLANs, 84
neighborhood information (OSPF), 95
nesting, 199-202
NetApp, 403
NetBIOS, 398
network address authority. *See* NAA
Network Address Translation. *See* NAT
Network Attached Storage. *See* NAS
Network Control Policy option, 601
Network File System (NFS), 398
network interface cards. *See* NICs
networks

adapters, convergence, 509
availability, 37
cloud computing, 800
connections (ACE 4710), 141
convergence, 495-497
design, 289-291
    See also design
Ethernets. *See* Ethernets
evolution, 25
extensions, 44
integration, 660
LANs (local-area networks), 11, 49
load balancers, 111-134
logical partitioning, 42-43
MPLS (Multiprotocol Label Switching), 335
ONE (Cisco Open Network Environment), 804
OpenStack, 801-802
overlapping, 87
overlays, 802-804
partitioning, 47
PODs (pool of devices), 281-284
SDNs (Software-Defined Networks), 800-801
segmentation, 103-104
services, 735
    applications, 111
    data paths, 738-740
    definitions, 735-738
    profiles, 599-608
    vPath-enabled, 740-771
    VSG (Virtual Security Gateway), 742-753
simplification, 43
SNMP (Simple Network Management Protocol), 20, 85
topologies, 34-41
    layers, 35-

physical layouts, 39-40
virtualization, 8, 42-44
virtual networking, 658-661
    NX-OS features, 688-693
    VM-FEX (Virtual Machine Fabric Extender), 705-707, 720-722
    VXLANs (Virtual eXtensible Local Area Networks), 697-705
    VLANs (virtual local-area networks), 45
    VPNs (Virtual Private Networks), 47
    WANs (wide-area networks), 4

Network Services Manager. *See* **NSM**

new cps (connections per second), 135

Nexus 1000v switches
    See also switches
    application acceleration, 763-771
    connections, 741
    frame encapsulation, 739
    virtual networking topology, 741
    vPath configuration, 748, 758

Nexus 7000 switches, 92
    See also switches
    commands, 61
    OTV (Overlay Transport Virtualization), 354-377
    port groups, 195

NFS (Network File System), 398, 495, 763

NICs (network interface cards), 54, 509
    physical NIC teaming, 660
    teaming, 238
    virtual NICs. *See* vNICs

NIST (National Institute of Standards and Technology), 794

nodes, 322

    See also servers
    status, 751
    virtual service, 740

nondisruptive reconfiguration of fabric, 423

Non-Uniform Memory Access. *See* **NUMA**

no resource allocation, 17

notification
    CNMs (congestion notification messages), 503
    QCN (Quantized Congestion Notification), 503

NPIV (N_Port ID Virtualization), 476
    configuration, 476-482
    FCoE (Fibre Channel over Ethernet), 532-535

N_Port ID Virtualization (NPIV), 476

N_Port Virtualization. *See* **NPV**

NPV (N_Port Virtualization), 453, 473-490
    blade servers, 488
    port WWN virtualization deployment, 486-488
    traffic management, 482-486

NT LAN Manager. *See* **NTLM**

NTLM (NT LAN Manager), 398

NUMA (Non-Uniform Memory Access), 566

NX-OS switches, 63, 188
    virtual networking, 688-693
    VSANs (virtual storage-area networks), 432

O

ODBC (Open DataBase Connectivity), 398

offloading servers, load balancers, 130-134

on-demand self-service, 794

ONE (Cisco Open Network Environment), 804
one-armed design, virtual contexts (ACE), 160-161
ONF (Open Networking Foundation), 800
online migrations
    Cisco Nexus 1000v switches, 693-697
    VM-FEX (Virtual Machine Fabric Extender), 720-722
ON mode, 238
ONS 1500, 328
    See also DWDM
OOO (out-of-order), 148, 268
Open DataBase Connectivity. *See* ODBC
OpenFlow, 801
Open Networking Foundation (ONF), 800
Open Shortest Path First. *See* OSPF
Open Software Foundation (OSF), 594
OpenStack, 801-802
Open Systems Interconnection. *See* OSI
Open Virtualization Appliance. *See* OVA
Open Virtualization Format. *See* OVF
operating systems, 19
    converged network adapters, 509
    installation, 620-623
    NX-OS. *See* NX-OS switches
    server domains, 585
    sharing, 10
operational areas, 5-7
operational policies (service profiles), 608-612
operations, VDC (virtual device context) management, 214-216
optical connections, Ethernet extensions over, 327-332

optical fiber, 29-32, 34
optimization
    cables, 44
    data centers, 231
    responses, 130
    STP (Spanning Tree Protocol), 72-73
    vWAAS (Virtual Wide Area Application Services),
options
    Any Configuration, 595
    Edit Virtual Machine Settings, 690
    Ethernet Adapter Policy, 601
    Fabric Extenders, 295-296
    Fibre Channel Adapter Policy, 597
    Local Disk, 604
    Manage Plug-ins, 711
    MTU, 601
    Network Control Policy, 601
    Persistent Binding, 597
    Pin Group, 597, 601
    Protection Configuration, 596
    QoS Policy, 597, 601
    vHBAs (virtual HBAs), 604
    Virtual Media, 604
    vNICs (virtual NICs), 604
Organizational Unique Identifier. *See* OUI
origins of virtualization, 8-13
OSF (Open Software Foundation), 594
OSI (Open Systems Interconnection), 411
OSPF (Open Shortest Path First), 87, 94, 95, 334
OTV (Overlay Transport Virtualization), 319, 352, 354-377, 359-364, 803
OUI (Organizational Unique Identifier), 414
out-of-band management

interface configuration, 143
VDCs (virtual device contexts), 217-222
out-of-order (OOO), 148, 268
OVA (Open Virtualization Appliance), 671
overlapping
　addresses, 87-89
　FPMAs (Fabric-Provided MAC Addresses), 509
overlays
　interfaces, 358, 369
　networks, 802-804
Overlay Transport Virtualization. See OTV
oversubscription ratios, 37
OVF (Open Virtualization Format), 743, 755

P

PaaS (Platform as a Service), 795
packets
　ATAPI (ATA Packet Interface), 397
　MPLS (Multiprotocol Label Switching), 332
Palo Alto Research Center (PARC), 26
parallel expansion busses, 570
parameters
　ASA 1000v OVF, 755
　layers, 112
　VSM (Virtual Supervisor Module), installation, 671
PARC (Palo Alto Research Center), 26
parent switches
　See also switches
　connections, 296-299
　Fabric Extenders, 310
parity, 569

parsing frames, 421
partitioning
　implementation, 187-188
　networks, 42-43, 47
　VDCs (virtual device contexts), 185
PAT (Port Address Translation), 124
paths. See vPath
　behavior, 47
　default path cost for switches, 64
　network services, 738-740
patterns, traffic, 245
PAUSE frames, 499
Payment Card Industry (PCI), 227
PBR (policy-based routing), 127, 765
PCI (Payment Card Industry), 227
PCP (Priority Code Point), 53
Pearlman, Radia, 62
PE (provider edge) devices, 338
peers, keepalive links, 245, 248
Peer-to-Peer Remote Copy (PPRC), 403
Pelissier, Joe, 509
Penultimate Hop Popping. See PHP
performance
　High Performance mode, 723-730
　load balancers, 111, 135-136
　monitoring, 111
peripherals, 4
permissions, access, 391
Persistent Binding option, 597
Persistent Lempel-Ziv (PLZ) compression, 764
Per VLAN Spanning Tree. See PVST
Per VLAN Spanning Tree Plus. See PVST+
PFC (priority-based flow control), 498-499
PHP (Penultimate Hop Popping), 334
physical connections, 495
　ACE (Application Control Engine), 141-145

physical formats (x86 servers), 571-572
physical interfaces, migration, 687
physical layers, 27
    coaxial cables, 27
    optical fiber, 29
    standards, 29
physical layouts, networks, 39-40
physical NIC teaming, 660
physical servers
    See also servers
    activation, 581
    migration (UCS Manager), 625
    provisioning, 581
physical-to-logical storage, 8
Pick-up Truck Access Method (PTAM), 322
PING, 166
Pin Group option, 597, 601
pinning
    MAC (Media Access Control), 686
    static, 301
placement of virtual interfaces, 602-603
planes, 20, 98-101
plans, disaster recovery, 321
Platform as a Service. *See* PaaS
PLOGI (Port Login), 427
plug-ins
    exporting, 712
    importing, 711
    XML (Extensible Markup Language), 742
PLZ (Persistent Lempel-Ziv) compression, 764
PODs (pool of devices), 281-284, 328, 790
point-to-point
    ports, 72, 412
    server access models, 537

policies
    BIOS (basic input/output system) configuration, 627-633
    firmware (UCS), 633-637
    HA (high-availability), 216
    load balancers
        configuration, 132
        maps, 168
    maintenance, 606
    maps, 162
    MPC (Modular Policy CLI), 162
    multimatch, 169
    operational (service profiles), 608-612
    security, 737
        Cisco ASA 1000V, 761
        formatting, 745-747
        load balancers, 136-137
    services, 170
    UCS (Unified Computing System), 626-633
    verification, 752
    vPath, 739
policy-based routing. *See* PBR
pooling, 16, 405, 639-640
    cloud computing, 786
    resources, 794
    servers, 649-653
    virtualization, 116
pool of devices. *See* PODs
Port Address Translation. *See* PAT
PortChannels, 141, 203
    Cisco Nexus 1000v switches, 687
    configuration, 303, 306
    cross-switch, 240-241
    FCIP (Fibre Channel over IP), 462
    FSPF (Fabric Shortest Path First) protocol, 426
    Layer 3 configuration, 236

load-balancing methods, 225
MDS-B, configuration on, 436
STP (Spanning Tree Protocol) configuration, 236
straight-through topologies, 306
VFC (Virtual Fibre Channel) configuration, 528-531
vpc-hm (Virtual PortChannel Host-Mode), 686
vPCs (virtual PortChannels), 231, 241-265
    See also vPCs (virtual PortChannels)
Port Login (PLOGI), 427
ports
  access, 390
  connections (VDCs), 192
  Designated Ports Selection phase, 68
  Ethernets, 26, 72
  groups, 659
  IDs, 65
  Nexus 7000 switches, 195
  NPV (N_Port Virtualization), 453, 473-490
  point-to-point, 412
  private VLANs, 79
  profiles
    Cisco Nexus 1000v switches, 664-666
    vMotion, 682
    VSG data interfaces, 744
  promiscuous ports, 81
  redirection, 126
  roles, 73
  Root Port Selection phase, 68
  Smart Port Macros, 664
  states, 70-72
  switch connections, 69
  translation, 124
  types (Fibre Channel), 412-413

WWNs (World Wide Names), 486-488
port world wide name (pWWN) addresses, 465
power
  control policies, 611
  distribution, 7
  supply redundancy, 390
PPRC (Peer-to-Peer Remote Copy), 403
predictability, 25, 281
predictors, 116, 167
preprovisioning (Fabric Extender), 311
primary storage, 8, 388
printers, 4
prioritization, 37
priority-based flow control. *See* PFC
Priority Code Point. *See* PCP
private clouds, 796
private interfaces, 495
private VLANs, 78-83
PRLI (Process Login), 427
probes, 116, 136, 164-167
processes
  failures (VDCs), 216-217
  sharing, 189
Process Login (PRLI), 427
production switches, 142
profiles
  FCIP (Fibre Channel over IP), 460
  ports
    Cisco Nexus 1000v switches, 664-666
    vMotion, 682
    VSG data interfaces, 744
  services, 581
    associating to servers, 612-619
    boot order, 604-605

profiles

building, 588-623
identifying, 594
industrializing server provisioning, 637-653
installing operating systems, 620-623
maintenance policies, 606
network definitions, 599-608
operational policies, 608-612
policies, 626-633
seasonal workloads, 653-654
server assignment, 606-607
storage definitions, 595-598
templates, 640-649
UCS (Unified Computing System), 586-588
virtual interface placement, 602-603
vNICs (virtual NICs), 707-709

promiscuous access interfaces, 81

prompts
  CLI (command-line interface), 198
  EXEC, 147

propagation, light, 31
properties, security, 659
proprietary protocols, 392
protected space, 188
Protection Configuration option, 596
protocols
  ARP (Address Resolution Protocol), 49, 701
  BGP (Border Gateway Protocol), 87, 334
  BOOTP (Bootstrap Protocol), 51
  CDP (Cisco Discovery Protocol), 601
  DCBX (Data Center Bridging eXchange), 501-503, 518
  DHCP (Dynamic Host Configuration Protocol), 51, 585, 762
  EIGRP (Enhanced Interior Gateway Routing Protocol), 87
  Ethernet, 25-26
    coaxial cables, 27-28
    direct-attach twinaxial cables, 32-33
    media, 27
    optical fiber, 29-32
    overview of, 26-34
    timelines, 33-34
    twisted-pair cables, 28-29
  FHRPs (first-hop redundancy protocols), 380-382, 460, 775
  FHRPs (first-hop routing protocols), 259-265
  FIP (FCoE Initialization Protocol), 505, 507-509
  FSPF (Fabric Shortest Path First), 424-426
  FTP (File Transfer Protocol), 167, 750
  GLBP (Gateway Load Balancing Protocol), 12, 380
  Hello, 424
  HSRP (Hot Standby Router Protocol), 11-12, 17, 380, 460, 762
  HTTP (Hypertext Transfer Protocol), 130, 134, 167
  ICMP (Internet Control Message Protocol), 116, 163
  IP (Internet Protocol), 26, 46
    FCIP (Fibre Channel over IP), 453-464
    Layer 2 extensions, 352-377
    readdressing, 325
    routing, 87
  ISL (Inter-Switch-Link), 56
  LACP (Link Aggregation Control Protocol), 237, 686

LDP (Label Distribution Protocol), 334
LISP (Location ID/Separation Protocol), 775, 779-781, 803
LLDP (Link Layer Discovery Protocol), 502
proprietary, 392
RIP (Routing Information Protocol) routing, 92-98
RSTP (Rapid Spanning Tree Protocol), 72
RTSP (Real-Time Streaming Protocol), 167
SDP (Satellite Discovery Protocol), 296
SIP (Session Initiation Protocol), 167
SNMP (Simple Network Management Protocol), 20, 85, 117
SRP (Satellite Registration Protocol), 296, 298
standard, 392
STP (SATA Tunneling Protocol), 397
STP (Spanning Tree Protocol), 37
   convergence, 66
   DCI (Data Center Interconnect), 326
   design, 232
   Fabric Extender interfaces, 299-301
   FabricPath, 272-276, 330
   instances, 74-78
   link utilization, 232-234
   optimization, 72-73
   port states, 70-72
   scalability, 326
   status verification, 274
   switches, 63
   VDCs (virtual device contexts), 192

   VLANs (virtual local-area networks), 61-78
   vPCs (virtual PortChannels), 254-259
TCP (Transmission Control Protocol), 120
   offloading servers, 130, 133-134
   port redirection, 126
   timeouts, 123
TCP/IP (Transmission Control Protocol/Internet Protocol), 11
TFTP (Trivial File Transfer Protocol), 750
UDP (User Datagram Protocol), 120
   port redirection, 126
   virtual contexts (ACE), 164
ULP (upper-layer protocol), 412
VRRP (Virtual Router Redundancy Protocol), 12, 380, 460
WCCP (Web Cache Control Protocol), 765
provider edge. *See* PE
provisioning
   automation, 581
   dynamic interfaces, 664-666
   PODs (pool of devices), 790
   servers, 581
      activation, 583-585
      industrializing, 637-653
pseudowires, 343
PTAM (Pick-up Truck Access Method), 322
public clouds, 796
public interfaces, 495
PVST (Per VLAN Spanning Tree), 74
PVST+ (Per VLAN Spanning Tree Plus), 74
pWWN (port world wide name) addresses, 465

Q

QCN (Quantized Congestion Notification), 503
Q-in-Q frame encapsulation, 378
QoS (quality of service), 340
    maps, 225
    Policy option, 597, 601
    service profiles, 587
QSFP+ (Enhanced Quad Small Form Factor Pluggable), 32
quality of service. *See* QoS
Quantized Congestion Notification. *See* QCN

R

racks, 657
Rackspace, 794
rack units. *See* RUs
RADIUS (Remote Authentication Dial-In User Service), 167
RAID (Redundant Array of Independent Disks), 399-401, 596
RAM (random-access memory), 390, 566, 569
ranges, memory, 210
rapid elasticity, 794
Rapid PVST+ (Rapid Per VLAN Spanning Tree Plus), 74
Rapid Spanning Tree Protocol. *See* RSTP
RAS (Reliability, Availability, and Serviceability), 608
rate limiter (RL), 503
ratios, oversubscription, 37
RBAC (Role-Based Access Control), 171
    UCS (Unified Computing System), 586
    VDCs (virtual device contexts), 222-224
RCF (Reconfigure Fabric) frame, 423
RDIMMs (Registered DIMMs), 569
RDIs (request domain identifiers), 423
reachability, filtering, 381
Read Capacity command, 393
Read command, 393
readdressing, IP (Internet Protocol), 325
real server configuration, 164-167
Real-Time Streaming Protocol. *See* RTSP
Receive Side Scaling (RSS), 725
Reconfigure Fabric (RCF) frame, 423
records
    LSRs (link-state records), 424
    storage access, 398-399
recovery, disaster recovery plans, 321
Recovery Point Objective (RPO), 321
Recovery Time Objective (RTO), 321
redirection
    ports, 126
    vPath, 739
Reduced Instruction Set Computing. *See* RISC servers
redundancy
    CRC (cyclic redundancy check), 417
    DRE (Data Redundancy Elimination), 764
    Fabric Extender interfaces, 301-303
    FHRPs (first-hop redundancy protocols), 380-382, 460, 775
    interfaces, 37
    power supplies, 390
    storage virtualization, 402
    VPLS (Virtual Private LAN Service), 348
    VRRP (Virtual Router Redundancy Protocol), 460

VSG (Virtual Security Gateway), 744
Redundant Array of Independent Disks. *See* RAID
reflection, 29
Registered DIMMs. *See* RDIMMs
Registered State Change Notification. *See* RSCN
registration
    VNMC (Virtual Network Manager Center), 756
    VSM (Virtual Supervisor Module), 744
reliability
    attributes of, 25
    of servers, 559
Reliability, Availability, and Serviceability (RAS), 608
reload vdc command, 215
remapping addresses, 17
Remote Authentication Dial-In User Service. *See* RADIUS
Remote Shell. *See* RSH
removable mass storage media, 388
replication, asynchronous/synchronous, 402
repositioning servers, 130
request domain identifiers (RDIs), 423
Request for Comments. *See* RFCs
requests
    ARP (Address Resolution Protocol), 49
    GET operations, 117
requirements, 26
    NPV (N_Port Virtualization) connections, 476
reserved IDs (VLANs), 84-85
resilience, applications, 37
resistors, 28
Resource Manager, 190
resources
    allocation, 17

VLANs (virtual LANs), 206
VRF (Virtual Routing and Forwarding), 101-103
    classes, 155
    Fibre Channel, 417
    load balancers, 693
    pooling, 794
    sharing, 85
    VDCs (virtual device contexts), 202-211
        global, 225
        templates, 211-213
    virtual context (ACE) allocation, 145-156
responses
    ARP (Address Resolution Protocol), 49
    optimization, 130
    server behavior, 118
restarting fabrics, 424
results, LACP (Link Aggregation Control Protocol), 237
revisions, files, 391
RFCs (Request for Comments), 12
RHI (Route Health Injection), 775-777
RIB (Routing Information Base), 87, 92, 334
RIP (Routing Information Protocol)
RISC (Reduced Instruction Set Computing) servers, 561
risks, Layer 2 extensions, 325
RJ-45 connectors, 29
RL (rate limiter), 503
RLOC (Routing Locator), 779
Role-Based Access Control. *See* RBAC
roles
    ports, 73
    VDCs (virtual device contexts), 223

914 roles

virtual contexts (ACE), 172-174
vPC (virtual PortChannel) verification, 251
root bridges, 62
Root Port Selection phase, 68
Root Selection phase, 67
round-robin predictors, 116
round-trip time. *See* RTT
Route Health Injection. *See* RHI
router-on-a-stick design, 55, 58
routers
    HSRP (Hot Standby Router Protocol), 11-12
    virtual context (ACE) design, 156-158
routes
    static, 87
    types, memory ranges, 210
routing, 771-775
    deployment, 58
    frames, 421
    GRE (generic routing encapsulation), 352-354
    internal, Layer 2 extensions, 380-382
    IVR (Inter-VSAN Routing), 453, 464-473
    layers, 36
    MC-LAG (Multi-Chassis Link Aggregation Group), 351
    overview of, 87
    PBR (Policy-Based Routing), 765
    protocols, 92-98
    tables
        Layer 3 switches, 88
        MDS-CORE, 442
    VRF (Virtual Routing and Forwarding), 45, 89-91, 199
        See also VRF
Routing Information Base. *See* RIB
Routing Information Protocol. *See* RIP
Routing Locator (RLOC), 779
RPO (Recovery Point Objective), 321
RSCN (Registered State Change Notification), 426, 464
RSH (Remote Shell), 750
RSS (Receive Side Scaling), 725
RSTP (Rapid Spanning Tree Protocol), 72
RTO (Recovery Time Objective), 321
RTSP (Real-Time Streaming Protocol), 167
RTT (round-trip time), 763
rules, access (Cisco ASA 1000V), 761
RUs (rack units), 572

S

SaaS (Software as a Service), 795
SAM (SCSI Architectural Model), 395
Samba, 398
SANs (storage area networks), 392, 409
    consolidation, 447-450
    extensions
        FCoE (Fibre Channel over Ethernet), 545
        with TE, 462
    FCIP (Fibre Channel over IP), 453-464
    Fibre Channel, 410-420
    islands, 430-432
    IVR (Inter-VSAN Routing), 464-473
    LAN management separation, 546-555
    NPV (N_Port Virtualization), 473-490
    virtualization, 407-408, 453
SAN tab (UCS Manager), 591

SAS (Serial Attached SCSI), 395
SATA (Serial Advanced Technology Attachment), 397
SATA Tunneling Protocol. *See* STP
Satellite Discovery Protocol. *See* SDP
Satellite Registration Protocol. *See* SRP
SBCCS (Single-Byte Command Code Set), 397, 410, 456
scalability, 15, 21, 25
    ACE virtual contexts, 110
    cloud computing, 803
    Fabric Extenders, 288
    load balancers, 111, 135
    network services, 736
    private VLANs, 80
    service profiles, 582
    STP (Spanning Tree Protocol), 326
    virtualization, 17, 454, 494
    VLANs/VRF, 45
    VM-FEX (Virtual Machine Fabric Extender), 657
    vPCs (virtual PortChannels), 231
scaling applications, 113
SCM (Supply Chain Management), 3
scope
    VLAN (virtual local-area network) configuration, 85
    VRF (Virtual Routing and Forwarding), 99
    VSANs (virtual storage-area networks), 445-447
SCR (State Change Registration) frame, 427
scripting, 584
scrub policy, 611
SCSI (Small Computer Systems Interface), 392-396, 410
SCSI Architectural Model. *See* SAM
SDNs (Software-Defined Networks), 800-801

SDP (Satellite Discovery Protocol), 296
SDR (Single Data Rate), 567
seasonal workloads, 653-654
secondary storage, 8, 388
secret identities, 453
Secure HTTP. *See* HTTPS
Secure Shell. *See* SSH
Secure Sockets Layer. *See* SSL
security, 111
    areas, 47
    ASAs (Adaptive Security Appliances), 179
    ASDM (Adaptive Security Device Manager), 754
    content, 58
    information, 735
    IPSec (IP Security), 774
    load balancers, 136-137
    MAC (Media Access Control), 601
    policies, 737
        Cisco ASA 1000V configuration, 761
        formatting, 745-747
        verification, 752
    properties, 659
    segmentation, 187
    TLS (Transport Layer Security), 130
    VSG (Virtual Security Gateway), 742-753
    web, 129
    zones, 225
segmentation, 133
    data centers, 103-104
    Ethernets, 47
    out-of-order (OOO), 148
    security, 187
    VXLANs (Virtual eXtensible Local Area Networks), 699
segregation, private VLANs, 78-83

selection
  Designated Ports Selection phase, 68
  predictors, best practices, 117
  Root Port Selection phase, 68
  Root Selection phase, 67
  sites, 775-641
Selective Acknowledgment Options (RFC 2018), 763
Send Diagnostic command, 393
sending traffic to Cisco ASA 1000V, 758
sequences
  Fibre Channel, 415-417
  number calculations, 133
Serial Advanced Technology Attachment (SATA), 397
Serial Attached SCSI. *See* SAS
Serial Storage Architecture. *See* SSA
Server Message Block. *See* SMB
Server NAT, 124-125
Server-Provided MAC Address. *See* SPMA
servers, 19, 111
  access (Unified Fabric designs), 536-542
  architectures, 560-562
  assignment, 606-607
  blade, 488
  boot order, 604-605
  clusters, 324
  connections, 34
  DHCP (Dynamic Host Configuration Protocol), 585
  Direct Server Return, 123-124
  domains, 584-595
  evolution, 559-560
  farms, 115
    configuration, 166
    round-robin predictors, 116
  interfaces, 591
  load balancers. *See* load balancers
    configuration, 115
    offloading, 130-134
  mainframes, 560-561
  migration, 325, 625
  models, access, 287-291
  NIC (network interface card) teaming, 239
  pooling, 649-653
  provisioning, 581
    activation, 583-585
    automation, 581
    industrializing, 637-653
  real, configuration, 164-167
  responses, 118
  reverse proxies, 128-130
  RISC (Reduced Instruction Set Computing), 561
  service profiles, associating to, 612-619
  traditional formats, 571
  troubleshooting, 737
  unified access, deployment, 509-523
  virtualization, 775-781
  x86, 562
    hardware evolution, 562-572
    memory, 566-569
    time of market, 581
    UCS (Unified Computing System), 578-579
    virtualization, 572-578
Servers tab (UCS Manager), 591, 593
serviceability, 559
service-level agreements. *See* SLAs
services
  cloud computing, 795
  Fibre Channel, 420-421
  measurements, 794

networks, 735
    applications, 111
    data paths, 738-740
        See also vPath
    definitions, 735-738
    vPath-enabled, 740-771
    VSG (Virtual Security Gateway), 742-753
OpenStack, 802
policies, 170
profiles, 581
    associating to servers, 612-619
    boot order, 604-605
    building, 588-623
    identifying, 594
    industrializing server provisioning, 637-653
    installing operating systems, 620-623
    maintenance policies, 606
    network definitions, 599-608
    operational policies, 608-612
    policies, 626-633
    seasonal workloads, 653-654
    server assignment, 606-607
    storage definitions, 595-598
    templates, 640-649
    UCS (Unified Computing System), 586-588
    virtual interface placement, 602-603
    vNICs (virtual NICs), 707-709
proxy servers, 129
virtual service nodes, 740, 751
VSM (Network Services Manager), 792

Session Initiation Protocol. See **SIP**

sessions

CSR 1000v, 772
Etheranalyzer, 225
monitoring, 203
SPAN, 205-206
SSH (Secure Shell), 747
sets, zones, **430**
SFF (Small Form Factor) committee, 397
SFP+ (Enhanced Small Form Factor Pluggable), 32
shaping, traffic, **660**
sharing
    buses, 392
    linecards, 191
    operating systems, 10
    ports, 73
    processes, 189
    resources, 85
    segments, 69
    subnets, 59
    VLANs, 177
shielded twisted-pair (STP), 29
show interface command, 459
Shugart Associates, 392
SIMMs (Single In-Line Memory Modules), 568
Simple Network Management Protocol. See **SNMP**
simplification, 26, 43
simulation, 12
Single-Byte Command Code Set (SBCCS), 397
single-context switches, 510-518
Single Data Rate. See **SDR**
Single In-Line Memory Modules. See **SIMMs**
single-mode fiber (SMF), 29, 396
single-root I/O virtualization (SR-IOV), 706
SIP (Session Initiation Protocol), 167

sites, 358
    selections, 775-641
    VLANs, 358
sizes, blocks, 391
SLAs (service-level agreements), 3
sliding windows, calculations, 133
slow-start algorithms, 116
Small Computer Systems Interface. *See* SCSI
Small Form Factor (SFF) committee, 397
Smart Port Macros, 664
SMB (Server Message Block), 398
SMF (single-mode fiber), 29, 396
SMP (Symmetric Multi Processing), 566
SnapMirror, 403
SNMP (Simple Network Management Protocol), 20, 85, 117
sockets, 564
SOF (start of frame), 417, 434
Software as a Service. *See* SaaS
Software-Defined Networks. *See* SDNs
software modularization, 5
solid-state drives. *See* SSDs
space, buffers (PAUSE frames), 499
Spanning Tree Protocol. *See* STP
SPAN sessions, 205-206
speed, convergence, 232
SPMA (Server-Provided MAC Address), 508
SQL (Structured Query Language), 398
SRAM (static RAM), 566
SRDF (Symmetrix Remote Data Facility), 403
SR-IOV (single-root I/O virtualization), 706
SRP (Satellite Registration Protocol), 296, 298

SSA (Serial Storage Architecture), 396
SSDs (solid-state drives), 389
SSH (Secure Shell), 163
    to active VSM, 674
    VSG (Virtual Security Gateway), 747
SSL (Secure Sockets Layer), 130-133
StackWise, 241
standardization of cloud computing, 789-792
standard protocols, 392
standards
    See also IEEE
    AES (Advanced Encryption Standard), 328
    ANSI/TIA-942, 40-41, 287
    encryption, 133
    Ethernet, 29, 33
    Fibre Channel, 410
    NIST (National Institute of Standards and Technology), 794
    physical layers, 29
standby nodes, 325
start of frame (SOF), 417, 434
star topologies, 41
State Change Registration (SCR) frame, 427
stateless computing, 587, 625-626
states, ports, 70-72
static pinning, 301
static RAM. *See* SRAM
static routes, 87
static vNICs, creating, 599
status
    Fabric Extender verification, 298, 313
    IPSec (IP Security), 774
    NPV (N_Port Virtualization), 477
    STP (Spanning Tree Protocol) verification, 274

VCs (virtual circuits), 339
virtual service nodes, 751
vPCs (virtual PortChannels), 253
VPLS (Virtual Private LAN Service), 343-346
stickiness tables, 116
storage, 387
    access, 391-399
        block-based, 392-397
        files, 397-398
        interfaces, 495
        mainframe, 396-397
        records, 398-399
    AMS (Adaptable Modular Storage), 792
    data center devices, 387-391
    definitions, 8, 595-598
    devices, 4, 18
    disk arrays, 389-390
    HDDs (hard disk drives), 388-389
    libraries, 390-391
    memory. *See* memory
    physical-to-logical, 8
    tape drives, 390-391
    VDC (virtual device context) configuration, 519-523
    virtualization, 399-408
storage area networks. *See* **SANs**
Storage Reference Architecture, 792
STP (SATA Tunneling Protocol), 397
STP (shielded twisted-pair), 29
STP (Spanning Tree Protocol), 37
    convergence, 66
    DCI (Data Center Interconnect), 326
    design, 232
    Fabric Extender interfaces, 299-301
    FabricPath, 272-276, 330
    instances, 74-78
    link utilization, 232-234

    optimization, 72-73
    PortChannel configuration, 236
    ports, states, 70-72
    scalability, 326
    status verification, 274
    switches, 63
    VDCs (virtual device contexts), 192
    VLANs (virtual local-area networks), 61-78
    vPCs (virtual PortChannels), 254-259
straight-through topologies (Fabric Extender), 305-308
stress tests, virtual contexts (ACE), 150
Structured Query Language. *See* **SQL**
structures
    metadata, 391
    virtualization, 17
subareas, 20
    ACE virtual contexts, 110
    Fabric Extenders, 288
    service profiles, 582
    technologies, 15
    virtualization, 454, 494
    VLANs/VRF, 45
    VM-FEX (Virtual Machine Fabric Extender), 657
    vPCs (virtual PortChannels), 231
    VSANs (virtual storage-area networks), 409
subnets, VLAN association to IP (Internet Protocol), 56-58
suboptimal traffic, 137
subtypes, 15, 21
    ACE virtual contexts, 110
    Fabric Extenders, 288
    network services, 736
    service profiles, 582
    virtualization, 454, 494
    VLANs/VRF, 45

VM-FEX (Virtual Machine Fabric Extender), 657
vPCs (virtual PortChannels), 231
VSANs (virtual storage-area networks), 409

Supply Chain Management. *See* **SCM**

SVIs (Switch Virtual Interfaces), 58, 145, 669, 792

SW_ILS (Switch Internal Link Service), 425

Switch1
configuration, 196-197
tasks, 198
VDCs (virtual device contexts), 194

switches
access, 38
aggregation, 36
behavior, 48
blade, 474
broadcast frames, 61
Cisco Nexus 1000v
  architecture, 661-663
  communication modes, 663-664
  deployment, 666-683
  loop avoidance, 685
  online migrations, 693-697
  port profiles, 664-666
consolidation, 187
CSS (Content Services Switch), 139
DCI (Data Center Interconnect), 328
default path cost for, 64
DVS (Distributed Virtual Switch), 661
Ethernets, 48
Fabric Extenders, 296-299, 310
fabric initialization, 422
Fibre Channel, 506
interfaces

port IDs, 65
RSTP (Rapid Spanning Tree Protocol), 72
Layer 3, 58, 88
Layer 4, 120-121
Layer 7, 113, 120-121
MDS (Multilayer Data Switch), 410, 424, 456
MPLS (Multiprotocol Label Switching), 47
MST (Multiple Spanning Tree), 76-77
N7K, 519, 524
Nexus 1000v
  application acceleration, 763-771
  vPath configuration, 748, 758
Nexus 7000, 92
  OTV (Overlay Transport Virtualization), 354-377
  port groups, 195
NX-OS, 63, 188
out-of-band management, 143
port connections, 69
production, 142
STP (Spanning Tree Protocol), 63, 233
triangular topologies, 233
VDCs (virtual device contexts), 183-184, 214
  See also VDCs
VLANs (virtual local-area networks), 50
VPLS (Virtual Private LAN Service), 343-346
VSL (virtual switch link), 241
VSS (Virtual Switch System), 241
vSwitch (Virtual Switch), 559-661

Switch Internal Link Service. *See* **SW_ILS**

switchmode fex-fabric command, 297
Switch Virtual Interfaces. *See* SVIs
symmetric connection management, 122
Symmetric Multi Processing. *See* SMP
Symmetrix Remote Data Facility (SRDF), 403
synchronous replication, 402
System Manager, 189

T

tables
    MAC (Media Access Control) addresses, 691
    MDS-CORE routing, 442
    routing, 87-88
    stickiness, 116
Tag Protocol Identifier. *See* TPI
tags
    Bus&Tag communication, 396
    IEEE 802.1Q, 54
tape drives, 390-391, 403
targets, SCSI (Small Computer Systems Interface), 392
tasks
    server provisioning, 583
    Switch1, 198
taxonomies
    defining, 14
    virtualization, 15-17, 21
TCNs (Topology Change Notifications), 331
TCP (Transmission Control Protocol), 120
    offloading servers, 130, 133-134
    port redirection, 126
    timeouts, 123

TCP Flow Optimization (TFO), 763
TCP/IP (Transmission Control Protocol/Internet Protocol), 11
TE (Traffic Engineering), 333, 340
    SAN extension with, 462
    VSANs (virtual storage-area networks), 443
teaming NICs (network interface cards), 238
technologies
    areas, 15, 18-20, 21
        ACE *virtual contexts*, 110
        Fabric Extenders, 288
        service profiles, 582
        virtualization, 454, 494
        VM-FEX (Virtual Machine Fabric Extender), 657
        vPCs (virtual PortChannels), 231
        VSANs (virtual storage-area networks), 409
    classifying, 14-21
    network services, 736
    VLANs/VRF, 45
    wireless, 27
Telecommunications Industry Association (TIA), 287
Telnet, 163
templates
    OVF (Open Virtualization Format), 743
    resources (VDCs), 211-213
    service profiles, 640-649
terminals, 4
termination
    connections, 133
    SSL (Secure Sockets Layer), 132
terminators, 28
tertiary storage, 388
testing

IP (Internet Protocol) connections, 200
logins (VLAN commands), 86
predictors, 117
stress tests, virtual contexts (ACE), 150
Test Unit Ready command, 393
TFO (TCP Flow Optimization), 763
TFTP (Trivial File Transfer Protocol), 750
Thicknet (10BASE5), 27
Thinnet (10GBASE2), 27
thin-provisioning, 405
three-layer campus design, 34
three-way handshakes, 133
TIA (Telecommunications Industry Association), 287
timelines
    Ethernet protocol, 33-34
    virtualization, 12-13
timeouts, TCP (Transmission Control Protocol), 123
timers, 51
time-sharing mechanisms, 10
Time-to-Live. *See* TTL
TLS (Transport Layer Security), 130
tools
    KVM, 620
    MPC (Modular Policy CLI), 162
    performance monitors, 111
    Web Stress Tool, 151
Top-of-Rack (ToR) designs, 39, 289-291
topologies, 25
    DCNM-SAN, 531
    deployment, 36
    Fabric Extender, 291, 305-315
        dual-homed, 309-315
        straight-through, 305-308
    FCIP (Fibre Channel over IP), 457
    Fibre Channel, 412-413
    hub-and-spoke, 329
    IVR (Inter-VSAN Routing), 466
    logical, 213
    networks, 34-41
        layers, 35
        physical layouts, 39-40
    Nexus 1000v virtual networking, 741
    NPV (N_Port Virtualization), 476
    OTV (Overlay Transport Virtualization), 359
    SCSI (Small Computer Systems Interface), 392
    segmentation, 104
    star, 41
    triangular switch, 233
    UCS (Unified Computing System), 592
    virtual networking, 668
    VPLS (Virtual Private LAN Service), 343
Topology Change Notifications. *See* TCNs
ToR (Top-of-Rack) designs, 39, 44
TPI (Tag Protocol Identifier), 53
traditional formats, servers, 571
traffic
    analysis, 58
    Cisco ASA 1000V, sending to, 758
    direction, 35
    Direct Server Return, 123-124
    FHRPs (first-hop redundancy protocols), 380
    isolation, 47, 78-83
    load balancing, 43
    localization, 382
    management
        allowing to virtual contexts (ACE), 162-163

NPV (N_Port Virtualization), 482-486
patterns, 245
PortChannel configuration, 238
routing, 87
shaping, 660
suboptimal, 137
Telnet, 163
VSG (Virtual Security Gateway), sending to, 747
Traffic Engineering. *See* TE
transfer length, 394
transitions, STP (Spanning Tree Protocol), 70
transit VSANs (virtual storage-area networks), 472
translation, addresses, 124-127
Transmission Control Protocol/Internet Protocol. *See* TCP/IP
transparency, 12
transparent mode, 126-127
Transport Layer Security. *See* TLS
trends, cables, 34
triangular switch topologies, 233
Trivial File Transfer Protocol. *See* TFTP
tromboning, 326, 384, 775
troubleshooting
  interference, 28
  server virtualization, 737
  STP (Spanning Tree Protocol), 37
trunks
  ISL (Inter-Switch-Link), 56
  private VLANs, 81
  VLANs (virtual local-area networks), 52-56
  VSANs (virtual storage-area networks), 434-438
TTL (Time-to-Live), 61, 269
tunnels

FCIP (Fibre Channel over IP), 455, 461
GRE (generic routing encapsulation), 352
IPSec (IP Security), 774
Q-in-Q configuration, 378
STP (SATA Tunneling Protocol), 397
VRRP (Virtual Router Redundancy Protocol), 461
twisted-pair cables, 28-29, 34
types, 15, 21
  of ACE virtual contexts, 110
  of Ethernet ports, 72
  of Fabric Extenders, 288
  of network services, 736
  of optical fiber cabling, 29
  of ports (Fibre Channel), 412-413
  of predictors, 116
  of routes, 210
  of service profiles, 582
  of twinax cables, 32
  of twisted-pair cables, 28
  of virtualization, 15, 454, 494
  of VLANs/VRF, 45
  of VM-FEXs (Virtual Machine Fabric Extenders), 657
  of vPCs (virtual PortChannels), 231
  of VSANs (virtual storage-area networks), 409

U

UCS (Unified Computing System), 581
firmware policies, 633-637
policies, 626-633
service profiles, 586-588
topologies, 592
VM (virtual machine) locations, 722
vNICs (virtual NICs), 707-709

924 UCS (Unified Computing System)

vPCs (virtual PortChannels), 686
x86 servers, 578-579
UCS Manager, 588
    access, 590
    migration, 625
UCS VMware Integration wizard, 711-716
UDIMMs (Unregistered DIMMs), 568-569
UDP (User Datagram Protocol), 120
    port redirection, 126
    virtual contexts (ACE), 164
ULP (upper-layer protocol), 412
unallocated VDCs, 191
    See also VDCs
unicast responses, 49
unified access servers
    deployment, 509-523
    single-context switch configuration, 510-518
    storage VDC configuration, 519-523
Unified Computing System. *See* UCS
Unified Fabric, 495, 535-545
Uniform Resource Locators. *See* URLs
Universally Unique Identifier. *See* UUID
University of Manchester, 9
UNPAUSE frames, 499
Unregistered DIMMs. *See* UDIMMs
unshielded twisted-pair (UTP), 29
updating
    BIOS firmware, 636
    LSUs (link-state updates), 424
    virtual networking, 672
uplinks, 35, 591
upper-layer protocol. *See* ULP
URLs (Uniform Resource Locators), 116
User Datagram Protocol. *See* UDP

users
    account configuration, 175
    login configuration, 176
utilization
    CPUs (central processing units), 203
    STP (Spanning Tree Protocol), 232-234
UTP (unshielded twisted-pair), 29
UUID (Universally Unique Identifier), 594

V

values, default path cost for switches, 64
Vblock, 792
vCons (virtual network interface connections), 602
VCs (virtual circuits), 338-339, 343
vDCs (virtual data centers), 745, 781-783, 785-789, 788
    See also cloud computing
VDCs (virtual device contexts), 183-184, 378
    configuration, 190-202
    data center zones, 225-227
    management, 190, 214-224
        operations, 214-216
        out-of-band, 217-222
        process failures, 216-217
        RBAC (Role-Based Access Control), 222-224
    names, 198
    overview of, 188-190
    resources
        allocation, 202-211
        global, 225
        templates, 211-213
    storage configuration, 519-523
    uses of, 187-188

virtualization, extending, 184-186
VEM (Virtual Ethernet Module), 661, 671, 739-740
VE_Port (Virtual E_Port), 506
verification
  context creation, 147
  Fabric Extender status, 298
  FLOGI (Fabric Login), 513
  hardware, 190
  MST (Multiple Spanning Tree), 202
  policies, 752
  PortChannels (Cisco Nexus 1000v switches), 687
  roles, 251
  stateless computing, 625-626
  status (Fabric Extender), 313
  STP (Spanning Tree Protocol) status, 274
  VDC (virtual device context)
    names, 198
    resource allocation, 212
  virtual interfaces, 690
  VNMC (Virtual Network Manager Center) bindings, 761
  VSG (Virtual Security Gateway), 750
versions of CIMC (Cisco Integrated Management Controller), 634
VFC (Virtual Fibre Channel), 504
  interfaces, 512, 525
  PortChannel configuration, 528-531
VFI (Virtual Forwarding Instance), 342
VF_Port (Virtual F_Port), 506
vHBAs (virtual HBAs), 596, 604
VIF (Virtual Interface), 292
VIP (virtual IP), 116, 122
  class maps, 169
  nodes, 324
virtual circuits. *See* **VCs**
virtual contexts (ACE), 109, 139-178

  ACE (Application Control Engine) classification, 110
  application networking services, 111
  configuration, 163-171
  fault tolerance, 177-178
  integrating, 156-161
  load balancers, 111-134
  management, controlling access, 171-176
  multitenant data centers, 179-181
  resource allocation, 145-156
  VLANs, sharing, 177
Virtual Data Center. *See* **vDC**
virtual data planes, 352
virtual device contexts. *See* **VDCs**
Virtual E_Port. *See* **VE_Port**
Virtual Ethernet Module. *See* **VEM**
Virtual eXtensible Local Area Networks. *See* **VXLANs**
Virtual Fibre Channel. *See* **VFC**
Virtual Forwarding Instance. *See* **VFI**
Virtual F_Port. *See* **VF_Port**
virtual HBAs. *See* **vHBAs**
Virtual Interface (VIF), 292
virtual interfaces
  placement, 602-603
  verification, 690
virtual IP. *See* **VIP**
virtualization
  ACE (Application Control Engine) classification, 110
  benefits of networks, 42-44
  classification, 14-21, 454, 494
  clusters, 737
  defining, 12
  definitions, 1, 8
  extending, 184-186
  FCIP (Fibre Channel over IP), 453-464
  file systems, 406-407

IP (Internet Protocol) addresses, 668
LUNs (logical unit numbers), 404-406
mainframe, 10
nesting, 199-202
network services. *See* networks; services
NPV (N_Port Virtualization), 453, 473-490
origins of, 8-13
pooling, 116
routing, 771-775
SANs (storage area networks), 407-408, 453
scalability, 17
servers, 775-781
storage, 399-408
STP instances, 75
taxonomies, 15-17, 21
timelines, 12-13
troubleshooting, 737
UCS (Unified Computing System), 587
VLANs. *See* VLANs
VRF. *See* VRF
x86 servers, 572-578

Virtualized Multiservice Data Center. *See* **VMDC**

Virtual Link, 506

virtual local-area networks. *See* VLANs

virtual logical unit numbers. *See* vLUNs

Virtual Machine Fabric Extender. *See* **VM-FEX**

virtual machines. *See* VMs

Virtual Media option, 604

virtual memory, 8-9

virtual networking, 658-661
  external connections, 684-688
  NX-OS features, 688-693

topologies, 668
updating, 672
VM-FEX (Virtual Machine Fabric Extender), 705-707
  High Performance mode, 723-730
  migrations, 720-722
VXLANs (Virtual eXtensible Local Area Networks), 697-705

virtual network interface connections. *See* vCons

Virtual Network Link (VN-Link), 293

Virtual Network Manager Center. *See* **VNMC**

Virtual Network Tag (VNTag), 293

virtual NICs. *See* vNICs

Virtual N_Port. *See* **VN_Port**

Virtual PortChannel (vPC), 43

Virtual PortChannel Host-Mode (vPC-HM), 686

virtual PortChannel Plus. *See* vPC+

virtual PortChannels. *See* vPCs

Virtual Private Clouds. *See* **VPCs**

Virtual Private LAN Service. *See* **VPLS**

Virtual Private Networks. *See* **VPNs**

Virtual Router Redundancy Protocol. *See* **VRRP**

Virtual Routing and Forwarding. *See* **VRF**

Virtual Security Gateway. *See* **VSG**

virtual service nodes, 740, 751

virtual storage-area networks. *See* VSANs

Virtual Supervisor Module. *See* **VSM**

Virtual Switch. *See* **vSwitch**

virtual switch link. *See* VSL

Virtual Switch System. *See* **VSS**

virtual tape library. *See* VTL

Virtual Wide Area Application Services. *See* **vWAAS**

vlan all command, 55
VLAN ID (VLAN Identifier), 54
VLAN Identifier. *See* VLAN ID
VLANs (virtual local-area networks), 45
    classification, 45
    cloud computing, 786
    configuration, 209
    defining, 49-56
    identifiers, 659
    Layer 2 extensions, 377-379
    Layer 3, 58-61
    misconceptions about, 56-61
    native, 84
    overview of, 83-87
    private VLANs, 78-83
    reserved IDs, 84-85
    scope configuration, 85
    site VLANs, 358
    STP (Spanning Tree Protocol), 61-78
    trunks, 52-56
    VDCs (virtual device contexts), 203
    virtual context creation, 145
    virtual contexts (ACE), 177
vLUNs (virtual logical unit numbers), 787
VMDC (Virtualized Multiservice Data Center), 792
VM-FEX (Virtual Machine Fabric Extender), 589, 657, 705-707
    classification, 657
    deployment, 707-720
    High Performance mode, 723-730
    online migrations, 720-722
    VM (virtual machine) migration, 716-720
    vSphere (VMware) deployment, 709-710
VM-Mobility, 779
VM-Nomad, 770

vMotion, 660
    Long Distance, 693
    port profiles, 682
VMs (virtual machines), 8, 574-578
    attributes, 751
    characteristics, 690
    cloud computing, 787
    emulation, 659
    IP (Internet Protocol) addresses on VSG, 752
    names, 752
    VM-FEX (Virtual Machine Fabric Extender) migration, 716-720
VM tab (UCS Manager), 591
VMware, 573-574
    UCS VMware Integration wizard, 711-716
    vSphere, deploying VM-FEX, 709-710
    vSwitch (Virtual Switch), 659
vNICs (virtual NICs), 599, 706, 771
    iSCSI (Internet SCSI), 604
    options, 604
    UCS (Unified Computing System), 707-709
VN-Link (Virtual Network Link), 293
VNMC (Virtual Network Manager Center), 742-743
    bindings, 760
    Cisco ASA 1000V registration, 756
    security policies, creating, 745-747
VN_Port (Virtual N_Port), 506
VNTag (Virtual Network Tag), 293
volume detection, 440
vPath, 738-740
    connections, 768
    network services, 740-771
    Nexus 1000v switches, 748
    WAAS (Wide Area Application Services), 766

vPC+ (virtual PortChannel Plus), 276-280
vPC-HM (Virtual PortChannel Host-Mode), 686
vPCs (virtual PortChannels), 43, 231, 241-265, 466
  classification, 231
  configuration, 247-254
  defining, 242-247
  domains, defining, 248
  FCoE (Fibre Channel over Ethernet), 538-540
  first-hop routing protocols, 259-265
  Layer 2
    extensions, 328-330
    multipathing, 265-280
  link failures, 245
  role verification, 251
  status, 253
  STP (Spanning Tree Protocol), 254-259
  UCS (Unified Computing System), 686
VPCs (Virtual Private Clouds), 797
VPLS (Virtual Private LAN Service), 319, 333, 342-351, 803
VPNs (Virtual Private Networks), 47, 333
VRF (Virtual Routing and Forwarding), 45, 89
  classification, 45
  cloud computing, 787
  configuration, 90-91, 199
  Layer 2 extensions, 333
  management planes, 98-101
  resource allocation control, 101-103
  routing protocols, 92-98
  scope configuration, 99
  VDCs (virtual device contexts), 203
  VRF-awareness, 100-101
vrf member interface command, 91

VRRP (Virtual Router Redundancy Protocol), 12, 380, 460
VSANs (virtual storage-area networks), 409
  defining, 430-447
  formatting, 432-434
  FSPF (Fabric Shortest Path First) protocol, 442-444
  IVR (Inter-VSAN Routing), 464-473
  scoping, 445-447
  transit, 472
  trunking, 434-438
  zones, 439-442
VSG (Virtual Security Gateway), 735, 737, 742-753
  firewall configuration, 746
  installation, 743-745
  management model, 751
VSL (virtual switch link), 241
VSM (Network Services Manager), 792
VSM (Virtual Supervisor Module), 661
  installation, 671
  interfaces, 662
  migration, 682
  registration, 744
vSphere (VMware), 621
VSS (Virtual Switch System), 241, 329, 350
vSwitch (Virtual Switch), 659
  configuration, 673
  overview of, 660-661
VTL (virtual tape library), 403
vWAAS (Virtual Wide Area Application Services), 735, 737
  connectivity parameters, 765
  optimized connections, 767
VXLANs (Virtual eXtensible Local Area Networks), 697-705, 786
vZones (virtual zones), 751, 754

W

WAAS (Wide Area Application Services), 764, 766
WANs (wide-area networks), 4, 87, 763
warm-standby sites, 322
wavelength-division multiplexing. *See* WDM
WCCP (Web Cache Control Protocol), 765
WDM (wavelength-division multiplexing), 327-328
Web Cache Control Protocol. *See* WCCP
web security, 129
websites
   load balancers, 111
   server farms for, 168
Web Stress Tool, 151
weight limitations, 118
Wide Area Application Services. *See* WAAS
wide-area networks. *See* WANs
Windows (Microsoft), 9
Windows Scaling (RFC 1323), 763
wireless technologies, 27
wizards
   Create Host Firmware Package, 634
   Create Service Profile (expert), 594, 626, 637
   Deploy OVF Template vCenter, 745
   Manage Hosts vCenter, 606
   UCS VMware Integration, 711-716
World Wide Names. *See* WWNs
Write command, 393
WWNs (World Wide Names), 414, 421, 486-488, 581

X

x86 servers, 562
   CPU evolution, 564-566
expansion busses, 569-571
   hardware evolution, 562-572
   memory, 566-569
   physical formats, 571-572
   time of market, 581
   UCS (Unified Computing System), 578-579
   virtualization, 572-578
Xerox, 26
XML (Extensible Markup Language) plug-ins, 742
xTR, 779

Z

ZDA (Zone Distribution Area), 41
Zone Distribution Area (ZDA), 41
zones
   DMZs. *See* DMZs
   Fibre Channel, 429
   IVR (Inter-VSAN Routing), 467-472
   VDCs (virtual device contexts), 225-227
   virtual
   VSANs (virtual storage-area networks), 439-442
Zone Server service, 429
zSeries mainframes, 397, 561

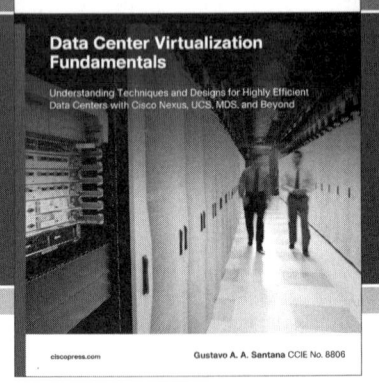

FREE Online Edition

Safari Books Online

Your purchase of **Data Center Virtualization Fundamentals** includes access to a free online edition for 45 days through the **Safari Books Online** subscription service. Nearly every Cisco Press book is available online through **Safari Books Online**, along with thousands of books and videos from publishers such as Addison-Wesley Professional, Exam Cram, IBM Press, O'Reilly Media, Prentice Hall, Que, Sams, and VMware Press.

Safari Books Online is a digital library providing searchable, on-demand access to thousands of technology, digital media, and professional development books and videos from leading publishers. With one monthly or yearly subscription price, you get unlimited access to learning tools and information on topics including mobile app and software development, tips and tricks on using your favorite gadgets, networking, project management, graphic design, and much more.

Activate your FREE Online Edition at informit.com/safarifree

STEP 1: Enter the coupon code: GVRFXBI.

STEP 2: New Safari users, complete the brief registration form. Safari subscribers, just log in.

If you have difficulty registering on Safari or accessing the online edition, please e-mail customer-service@safaribooksonline.com